T5-ARF-665

The Canadian Guide to Working and Living Overseas

Third Edition

Jean-Marc Hachey

DATE DUE

Ap. 27/01

Return Material Promptly

PUBLISHER
Intercultural Systems / Systèmes interculturels (ISSI)
P.O. Box 588, Station B, Ottawa, Ontario   K1P 5P7   CANADA
Tel.: (613) 238-6169   Fax: (613) 238-5274
E-mail: feedback@WorkingOverseas.com
Web site: http://www.WorkingOverseas.com

DISTRIBUTOR
University of Toronto Press (UTP)
5201 Dufferin Street, North York, Ontario   M3H 5T8   CANADA
Tel.: 24 hrs. 1-800-267-0105   Fax: 1-800-221-9985
E-mail: utpbooks@utpress.utoronto.ca
Order via web site: http://www.WorkingOverseas.com

BRESCIA COLLEGE
LIBRARY
68403

The Canadian Guide to Working and Living Overseas
Third Edition, March 1998
Second Edition, Second Printing, January 1997
Second Edition, First Printing, February 1995
First Edition, Second Printing, October 1993
First Edition, First Printing, June 1992

Printed in Canada by Imprimerie Transcontinental

Copyright © 1998, 1997, 1995, 1993, 1992
by Intercultural Systems / Systèmes interculturels (ISSI), Jean-Marc Hachey

All rights reserved. No part of this publication may be reproduced or transmitted in any form or by any means, electronic or mechanical, including photocopy, recording, or any information storage and retrieval system now known or to be invented, without permission in writing from the publisher, except by a reviewer who wishes to quote brief passages in connection with a review for inclusion in a magazine, web site, newspaper, or broadcast.

Canadian Cataloguing in Publication Data

Hachey, Jean-Marc, 1957-

  The Canadian guide to working and living overseas

3rd ed.
Includes bibliographical references and index.
ISBN 0-9696001-2-7

1. Job hunting--Canada. 2. Canadians--Employment--
Foreign countries. 3. Employment in foreign countries.
4. Economic development projects--Directories.
5. International agencies--Directories. I. Title.

HF5549.5.E45H33 1997   650.14   C97-900899-9

Deposited with the National Library of Canada

PUBLISHER
Intercultural Systems / Systèmes interculturels (ISSI)
P.O. Box 588, Station B, Ottawa, Ontario K1P 5P7 CANADA
Tel.: (613) 238-6169   Fax: (613) 238-5274
E-mail: feedback@WorkingOverseas.com
Web site: http://www.WorkingOverseas.com

ORDER FROM THE DISTRIBUTOR:
University of Toronto Press (UTP)
5201 Dufferin Street, North York, Ontario M3H 5T8 CANADA
Tel.: 24 hrs. 1-800-267-0105   Fax: 1-800-221-9985
E-mail: utpbooks@utpress.utoronto.ca

Canada:	$44.95 + $5.98 S&H + $3.57 GST = $54.50
United States:	US$34 + US$6 S&H = US$40
Other countries:	US$34 + US$22 S&H = US$56

Order via Web site: http://www.WorkingOverseas.com

For faster delivery, call 24 hours, fax or e-mail your credit card order. Include credit card number, expiry date, printed cardholder's name, phone number, and mailing address. Please allow 1 to 3 weeks for delivery in Canada. By courier, add $10.
Orders by individuals must be prepaid. Make cheque payable to "UTP."
Orders by institutions must be prepaid or accompanied by an authorized purchase order.
Payments from outside Canada must be in Canadian or US funds. Cheques/money orders to be drawn on Canadian or US banks.
Student discount: Order three or more copies with your friends and save 20% off the book price, plus save on shipping. Credit card phone orders only and you must ask for operator 223.

DEDICATION

This book is dedicated to an idea, to an organization, and to the Earth.

The Idea

To the nurturing of global understanding. The issues facing humanity are increasingly global. Poverty in both the South and North, human rights' violations, environmental destruction and the corresponding extinction of species are all interconnected. Our crosscultural experiences can help broaden our perspective, raise awareness of the world's interdependence, and thus enable us to chart a safer route for humanity and all the other species which inhabit the Earth.

The Organization

To all the people who make up CANADIAN CROSSROADS INTERNATIONAL / CARREFOUR CANADIEN INTERNATIONAL (CCI). Since 1958, Crossroads has made a remarkable contribution by increasing crosscultural understanding and training globally- and community-minded leaders in Canada and the South.

Planet Earth

To our home, the Earth. You can help reduce the devastating impact that humans have on the Earth's environment. Forty per cent of all energy used in North America is directly consumed by individuals, and cars contribute significantly to that figure. A major source of greenhouse gases, and a serious threat to our environment, car exhaust causes most local air pollution. Help the planet by cutting back on car trips. Consider giving up car ownership altogether, only renting a car when needed. Use public transport. Live close to your place of work. Walk. Bicycle. You'll not only help the Earth but also make more friends in your neighbourhood!

CONTENTS AT A GLANCE

THE CANADIAN GUIDE TO WORKING AND LIVING OVERSEAS (Third Edition)

How to Use This Book xxvii

PART ONE: Your International IQ
1. The Effective Overseas Employee 3
2. Myths & Realities 23
3. Living Overseas 29
4. What Canadians Overseas Say 53
5. Learning a Foreign Language 69
6. Women Working & Living Overseas 75
7. The Canadian Identity in the International Workplace 87
8. Re-Entry 109

PART TWO: Acquiring International Experience
9. Starting Your International Career 129
10. Short-term Programs Overseas 133
11. Hosting Programs 163
12. Crosscultural Travel 171
13. Global Education Centres 183
14. Study Abroad 201
15. Awards & Grants 215
16. International Studies in Canada & Abroad 237
17. International Internships 351

PART THREE: Finding that International Job
18. Your Career Path 375
19. The Hiring Process 379
20. The Job Search 385
21. The Internet Job Search 399
22. Resources for the International Job Search 429
23. Phone Research Techniques 443
24. International Résumés 455
25. Covering Letters 483
26. Interviewing for an International Job 495

PART FOUR: What Jobs Are Out There?
27. Jobs by Regions of the World 509
28. Jobs in International Development 561
29. Teaching Abroad 569
30. Freelancing Abroad 595
31. Job Hunting When You Return to Canada 603

PART FIVE: International Career Contacts
32. The Private Sector 611
33. Services for International Businesses & Entrepreneurs 693
34. Careers in Government 713
35. Nongovernmental Organizations 763
36. United Nations 835
37. Environmental & Agricultural Research Centres 857
38. International Organizations 867
39. Canadian Diplomats Abroad 887
40. Foreign Diplomats in Canada 903

INDEXES
Bibliographies (919); ID Numbers (933); Cities in Canada with International Contacts (941); Countries & Regions of the World (945); Job Categories (953); Organizations (957)

PUBLISHER: Intercultural Systems / Systèmes interculturels (ISSI)
DISTRIBUTOR: University of Toronto Press (UTP), (800) 267-0105

Table of Contents

Contents at a Glance i
Table of Contents iii
Introduction xix
  Who is this Book For? (xix); What's in this Book? (xix); Updates Until the Year 2001 on our
  Web Site (xx); Why a Book on International Careers? (xx); Why Encourage People to Work
  Overseas? (xxi)
Acknowledgements xxiii
How to Use This Book xxvii
  Profiles of Organizations (xxvii); Organizations by chapter (xxvii); Organization Address,
  Phone, and Fax (xxvii); Web Sites and E-mail Addresses (xxviii); Size of Organization
  (xxviii); Type of Organization (xxviii); Job Categories (xxviii); Description (xxviii);
  Resources (xxix); Bibliographies by Subject (xxix); Books (xxx); Resource Organizations
  (xxx); Resource Web Sites (xxx); ID Numbers and Updates on our Web Site (xxxi)

PART ONE
Your International IQ

CHAPTER 1
The Effective Overseas Employee   3

Why Do People Go Overseas? 3
What is Your International IQ? 4
Important Characteristics for Overseas Workers 5
General Traits 6
  Enjoyment of Change (7); Sense of Adventure (7); Desire for Challenge (7); Open Mind
  (7); Patience (8); Curiosity (8)
Adaptation and Coping Skills 8
  Emotional Stability and Ability to Deal with Stress (8); Culture Shock (9); Observation and
  Adjustment Skills (9); Flexibility (9); Humour (10); Self-knowledge (10)
Intercultural Communication Skills 11
  Tolerance (11); Sensitivity (11); Listening and Observing (12); Nonverbal Communication
  Skills (12); Second Language Speaking Skills (12);
Overseas Work Effectiveness Traits and Skills 13
  Independence and Self-discipline (13); Training Experience (13); Resourcefulness (13);
  Versatility (14); Persistence (14); Organizational and People Skills (14); Leadership (14);
  Energy (15); Project Planning Skills (15); Writing Skills (15); Verbal Communication Skills
  (15); Loyalty and Tenacity (15); Tact (16); Philosophical Commitment to Field of Work (16)
Key Traits of an Effective Overseas Employee 16
  Interpersonal Skills (16); Assertiveness and Sense of Identity (17); Realistic Pre-departure
  Expectations (17)
A Last Word 17
Resources: Crosscultural Skills 17

CHAPTER 2
Myths & Realities   **23**

Are You Ready for Life Overseas? 23
Myths about Living Overseas 24
Myths about Working Overseas 26
A Last Word 27

CHAPTER 3
Living Overseas   **29**

Researching Your Host Country 29
   Briefings (29); Brief Yourself (30); Meet a Host National (30); Keep in Touch (31)
Culture Shock 31
   Culture Shock or Culture Fatigue-What is it? (32)
Stages of Culture Fatigue 32
   The Honeymoon Stage (33); The Anxiety Stage (34); The Rejection or Regression Stage
   (34); The Adjustment Stage (35); How Long Does Culture Fatigue Last? (35); How to Deal
   with Culture Fatigue (35); Useful Skills for Daily Life Overseas (36)
Special Concerns for Families 36
   Male Employee and Spouse (37); Female Employee and Spouse (38); The Single Person
   Overseas (38); Lesbians, Gays and Bisexuals (38); Women Overseas (39); Children Abroad
   (39); Too Much Free Time (40)
The Westerner Overseas 41
   The Expatriate Ghetto (41); The Person in the Mirror... (41); Lifestyle and Worklife (41)
Security and Political Concerns 42
   Household Intruders (42); Street Crime (42); Political Violence (43)
Personal Matters 43
   Driving in your New Country (43); Car Accidents (44); Health Concerns (44); Finances,
   Currency Exchange, Budgeting (44); Domestics (44); Food (45)
A Last Word 45
Resources 45
   Health Overseas (45); Children & Families Overseas (47); Educating Your Children (49);
   Moving Abroad (49); Taxes & Investment (51)

CHAPTER 4
What Canadians Overseas Say   **53**

Benefits of Overseas Life 53
Working in a Foreign Country 55
Preparation and Culture Shock 59
Spouse, Family and Social Relations 61
Women Overseas, Women in Development 63
Day-to-Day Living Overseas 64
Resources: Personal Stories Overseas 66

CHAPTER 5
Learning a Foreign Language   **69**

Canadians' Second Language Advantage 69
Learning the Local Language 70
A Basic Rule about Learning Languages: Practice Makes Perfect .. 71
Four Can't-Miss Rules for Learning a New Language 71
   Begin Immediately (71); Be Humble (71); Immerse Yourself (71); Listen Carefully (72)
Other Practical Tips 72

While Overseas (72); Before You Leave (72)

Learning a Foreign Language in Canada 73
A Last Word 73
Resources 73

CHAPTER 6
Women Working & Living Overseas   **75**

Women as Managers 75
What Makes a Good Employer? 77
The Best Employers 78
Academic Credentials and Skills 79
Networking 79
Your Social Life 79
What to Wear 80
Health in Brief 81
Safety Tips 82
A Last Word 82
Resources 83

CHAPTER 7
The Canadian Identity in the International Workplace   **87**

How are We Perceived Abroad? 88
Our General Attitude Towards Work 88
    Goal-Oriented and Hard Working (88); Law-Abiding (89); Separate Work and Personal Lives
    (90); Polite but Not Necessarily Friendly (91); Lacking in General Cultural Knowledge (92)
Business Protocol 93
    The First Contact (93); Getting Down to Business (93); Giving and Receiving Hospitality
    (94); Egalitarian Relationships (95); Respect for Space (95); Blind Individualism (96)
Communicating 97
    Formal Communication and Belief in the Written Word (97); Clear and Assertive
    Communication Style (98)
Conducting Business 98
    Time Is Money (98); Assessing the Facts (99); Making Decisions (99); Getting Results
    (100)
What We Need to Improve On 100
    Be Culturally Sensitive (100); Have Realistic Goals (101); Think Long-term (101)
A Last Word 101
Resources: Crosscultural Business Skills 102

CHAPTER 8
Re-Entry   **109**

Things to Expect as Part of Re-Entry Shock 110
Re-Entry Shock Versus Culture Shock 111
The Phases of Re-Entry 112
Phase I: Euphoria or the Tourist High 112
Phase II: Shock! 113
    You Don't Expect Change on Your Home Turf (113); You Have Changed (113); No One is
    Interested in Hearing about Your Life Abroad (114); Life in Canada Changed While You
    Were Abroad (114); You are Critical of Canadian Society (115); You Miss Your Overseas
    Friends and Life Style (115); You Feel Vulnerable, Powerless (116); Summary: Why Re-
    Entry Shock Happens (116)

How to Ease Re-Entry Shock 116
    Practical And Easy Tips (117); Reflect on Your Experience Abroad (117); Start Building a
    Community (117)
Phase III: Adjustment 118
    What's Good About the Re-entry Experience? (119); Suggestions for the Long Term (119)
Individual Circumstances 120
    Unaccompanied Travellers (120); Employees (120); Accompanying Spouses (121);
    Children (122); Teenagers (122); Families (123); High-Risk Situations (124)
A Last Word 125
    About the Author (125)
Resources 125

PART TWO
Acquiring International Experience

CHAPTER 9
Starting Your International Career   129

Starting Young 130
High School and University Students 130
Career Changers 131
Internships 131
Volunteering 132
A Last Word 132

CHAPTER 10
Short-term Programs Overseas   133

Short-Term Programs for Long-Term Gain 133
What Kinds of Programs are There? 134
    Youth Exchanges (134); Internships (134); Professional Exchanges (135); Teaching Abroad
    (135); Work and Learn (135); Independent Work and Travel (135)
Applying to Programs 136
How to Make Your Overseas Volunteer Experience More Professional 136
What to Expect from the Organization 136
A Last Word 137
Resources 137
Profiles of Short-Term Programs Overseas **142**

CHAPTER 11
Hosting Programs   163

Types of Programs 163
Rewards of Hosting 164
Challenges of Hosting 164
A Last Word 165
Resources 166
Profiles of Hosting Programs **167**

CHAPTER 12
Crosscultural Travel   171

Describing Your Travel Experience 172

How to Be a Successful "Crosscultural Traveller" 172
Other Ways to Make Contact with Local People 173
Safety Tips 174
Rest Days 175
Travel and Human Rights 175
Expanding Your Experience 175
Re-Entry Concerns 175
A Last Word 176
Resources 177

CHAPTER 13
Global Education Centres   183

How Can They Help You? 183
Volunteer Opportunities 184
Other Sources of Information 184
A Last Word 185
Resources 186
    International IQ Periodicals (186); Book, Film & Video Distributors (187); Global Education
    (189); Tools for Teachers (193)
Profiles of Global Education Centres **195**

CHAPTER 14
Study Abroad   201

Who Can Study Overseas? 202
What Kinds of Programs are Available? 203
    Undergraduate Study Abroad: Academic Year or Semester Abroad (203); Graduate Study
    Abroad (203); Summer and Short-term Programs for International Students (203)
Limitations and Options 204
Preparation 205
A Last Word 206
Resources 207
Selected Opportunities **212**

CHAPTER 15
Awards & Grants   215

A Last Word 216
Resources 217
Profiles of Awards & Grants **219**

CHAPTER 16
International Studies in Canada & Abroad   237

Why International Studies? 237
International Studies in Canada 238
What Skills Will You Develop? 238
Choosing the Right Program 238
    Undergraduate Versus Graduate Degree (240); College Versus University Programs (240)
What Should You Do Besides Study? 240
Job Prospects After Graduation 241

How to Keep Your First Job 242
A Last Word 242
Resources 242
Profiles of International Studies in Canada & Abroad **245**
Index to International Studies 245
Profiles of International Studies in Canada 254
International Studies Abroad 340

CHAPTER 17
International Internships   **351**

What is an Internship? 351
Types of International Internships 352
    A Note on Canadian Internships (352)
Why Intern? 353
Finding the Right One 353
Researching the Internship 354
Creating Your Own Internship while at University 355
Negotiating Salary and Benefits 356
A Last Word 357
Resources 357
Profiles of International Internships **359**

PART THREE
Finding that International Job

CHAPTER 18
Your Career Path   **375**

Long-Term Skill Building 375
Mix Between Overseas and Canadian Experience 376
Public, Private or Nonprofit Sector? 377
Choosing Your International Work Setting 378

CHAPTER 19
The Hiring Process   **379**

Sample Lead Times in Finding a Job 380
Who Makes the Hiring Decision? 381
    Personnel Department (381); International Division (382); Large International Firm, Government Department or Institution (382); Small International Firm or Nongovernmental Organization (382)
The Ideal Selection Process 382
The Contract 383
A Last Word 384

CHAPTER 20
The Job Search   **385**

Creative Job Search Skills 385
    Knowledge of the Hiring Process (385); Confidence (385); Determination (386); Entrepreneurial Instinct (386); Verbal Communication Skills (386)

The Three Job Search Phases 386
    The Three Phases of an International Job Search (387)
Self-Evaluation 387
    Selling your Skills (387); Describing your Skills Internationally (388); Focusing on your
    Primary Skill (388); Phrases to Help you Describe your Best Skills (388)
The Research Phase 389
    Job Advertisements (389); Networking, Making Contacts (390); Networking Contacts (391);
    Contact Organizations (392); Targeting Your Research: Discovering Where the Jobs Are
    (392)
A Last Word 393
Resources 395
    General Job Search: All (395); General Job Search: Students (396)

CHAPTER 21
The Internet Job Search   399

Why is the Internet Important to Your Job Search? 400
Reality Bytes: Can You Find a Job on the Internet? 401
Components of the Internet 401
    The World Wide Web (WWW) (402); Electronic Mail (403); Newsgroups (404); Telnet
    (404); File Transfer Protocol (FTP) (404); Chat Groups (405); Gopher (405)
Resources 405
    New to the Internet? (405); Books about the Internet (406)
Searching on the Internet 407
    Keywords for Conducting Internet Job Searches (407); Sample Keyword Combinations (408)
Search Tips 408
Resources: Search Engines 409
A Dozen Ways the Internet Can Help You in Your Job Search 411
    Gain International Experience (411); Build Crosscultural Links with the Internet (412);
    Network with Professionals in Your Field (412); Maintain Contact with Your Existing
    Network (412); Contact Employers (413); Demonstrate Your Talents (413); Counselling
    Services (413); Job Banks (413); Résumé Posting (414); Mailing Lists (414); Newsgroups
    (414); Researching Companies and Organizations (415)
Resources 415
    Books on the Internet Job Search (415); Directories on the Web (416); International Job
    Hunting Services on the Internet (417)
Country Information on the Internet 423
    Country-Specific Research *Without* the Internet (424)
Resources: Country Information on the Internet 424
A Last Word 427

CHAPTER 22
Resources for the International Job Search   429

Resources 429
    International Job Search (429); Employment Agencies (432); Job Search Directories (433);
    Other Careers (437); Health Careers (438); Language Careers (441); Tourism Industry
    Careers (442)

CHAPTER 23
Phone Research Techniques   443

Getting Organized With the Card System 444
Employer Card Follow-Up System 444

Keeping track of people with the employer card system (444); Keeping track of employer terminology with the card system (445); Keeping track of follow-up information with the card system (445)

Time and Cost of a Phone Campaign 446
Self-Confidence on the Telephone 446
Dealing With People on the Phone 447
Inquiring about the Opportunity 449
Sample inquiry questions (449); "Who else is hiring?" questions (449); Word of mouth (450)
Dealing With Negative Answers 450
Follow-Up Phone Calls 451
Summary of Creative Phone Techniques 452
Why Phone (452); Phone Manners (452); Phone Techniques (453)

CHAPTER 24
International Résumés   455

Will a Creative Résumé Get You an Interview? 455
The Creative International Résumé 456
The Parts of a Creative Résumé 456
Career Objective (456); Personal Traits and Professional Skills (457); Work History (457); Personal Data (457)
What is the First Step? 457
Stating Your Career Objective 457
The "DOs" of a Career Objective 458
Geographic Setting (458); Field of Work (458); Level of Entry (458); Other Qualifiers (459)
The "DON'Ts" of a Career Objective 459
Your Personal Traits and Professional Skills 460
The "DOs" of Listing Your Skills and Traits 460
Which Résumé Format Applies to You? 462
Chronological Format (462); Functional Format (462); Combination Format (462)
Writing Your Work History 463
A Note to Career Changers (463); What Format is Best for Your Job Descriptions? (464); What to Include in Your Work Experience (464)
Educational Experience 465
Professional Certification (466); Memberships (466)
Personal Data 466
Age (466); Marital Status and Dependents (466); Spouse's Occupation (467); Availability (467); Languages (467); Nationality and National Origin (467); Foreign Travel (468); Contact Information (468)
The "Do Not Mentions" 468
Other Optional Components 469
The Writing Style 469
Format for the Creative Résumé 470
How to Create Effective E-mail and Scannable Résumés 471
Tips on How to Write An E-mail Résumé (471); Scannable Résumés and the Importance of Keywords (472); Keywords for Electronic and Scannable Résumés (473); Examples of Keywords for Electronic Résumés: (473); Web Site and Multimedia Résumés (473)
Putting Your Best Foot Forward 473
The Final Product 474
Application Forms 474
Summary of a Creative Résumé 474
Two Creative Résumés That Work 475
The Entry-level Résumé (475); The Senior-level Résumé (475)

CHAPTER 25
Covering Letters 483

Letter of Inquiry (483); Letter of Application (483)
Call Your Future Employer First 484
Writing a Creative Covering Letter 484
The Introduction (484); The Body of the Letter (485); The Closing Paragraph (486)
Follow-Up Letters 486
Letters of Continued Interest (487); Follow-up Letters After an Interview (487)
Formatting Notes 488
A Last Word 488
Letter of Application 489
Letter of Inquiry 490
Letter of Continued Interest 491
Follow-Up Letter After Interview 492
Letter of Application for Internship 493

CHAPTER 26
Interviewing for an International Job 495

A Reminder to be Cautious (496); Who Will Interview You? (496); How Long Will the
Interview Last? (496)
Different Interview Styles 496
The Structured Interview (496); The Informal Interview (497)
What an Overseas Employer is Looking For 497
Preparing for Interview Questions 498
Two Very Important Sets of Skills 498
Organizational Skills (498); Interpersonal Skills (499)
Tactics for Answering Questions 499
Questions an Interviewer May Ask 500
General Interview Questions (500); Knowledge about the Employer (500); Overseas
Working Conditions (500); Overseas Living Conditions (500)
Open-Ended Enquiries 501
Situational Questions 501
Examples of Situational Questions (502)
Things to do Before the Interview 502
Things to do During the Interview 503
Things to Avoid During the Interview 504
Things to do After the Interview 504
A Last Word 505

PART FOUR
What Jobs Are Out There?

CHAPTER 27
Jobs by Regions of the World 509

Be Bold (510); Being Canadian (510); Where to Work (511); Professions in Demand (511);
Strategies (512); Visas (513); Language and Culture (514)
A Last Word 514
Resources 515
Country-specific Guides (515); Global Guides (515)

Africa 518
The United States **518**
   Where the Jobs Are (518); Other Job Opportunities (519); NAFTA (519); The Green Card
   and Other Types of Visas (521); Job Search Strategies (522); Students (522); Lifestyle (523)
Personal Stories 523
Resources: United States 524
Mexico & Latin America **527**
Mexico 527
   The Mexican Economy and NAFTA (527); Visas (528); Business Opportunities (528);
   Strategies for Businesspeople and Entrepreneurs (529); Culture (530); Jobs for
   Professionals and Casuals (531)
Latin America 531
   Chile (532); Argentina (532); Colombia (532)
Personal Stories 532
Resources: Mexico & Latin America 534
Western Europe **536**
The European Union 536
   Visas and The European Union (537); What Professional Jobs are Available? (537);
   Strategies (538); Students and Backpackers (538)
Personal Stories 539
Resources: Western Europe 540
Eastern Europe & the former Soviet Union **542**
   The Job Market (543); Strategies (544); Russia and the Commonwealth of Independent
   States (CIS) (545)
Personal Stories 546
Resources: Russia and Eastern Europe 547
The Middle East **548**
   The Persian Gulf (549); Israel (550)
Resources: The Middle East 550
Asia Pacific **551**
   China (553); Hong Kong (553); Japan (553); Australia and New Zealand (554)
Personal Stories 554
Resources: Asia Pacific 556

CHAPTER 28
Jobs in International Development   **561**

Types of Overseas Postings 561
   The Consulting Visit (561); The Business Visit (561); The International Posting (562);
   Long-term Volunteer Placement with an NGO (562); Cooperant Placements with an NGO
   (562)
Administrative Jobs in International Development 562
   In-Country Program Coordinator (562); Project Director (563); Diplomatic Staff (563);
   Junior Professional Officer (JPO) (563); Overseas Volunteer (564); Community
   Development Worker (564); Office Manager, Accountant (564); Logistician (565); Support
   Staff (565); Project or Program Officer (in Canada) (565)
Other Fields of International Development 565
Resources 566

CHAPTER 29
Teaching Abroad   **569**

Why Teach Abroad? 569
Facing Myths and Realities 570
What Are the Qualities of an Experienced International Teacher? 570

What Returning Teachers Say 571
Who Can Teach Overseas? 572
What Types of Teaching Positions Are out There? 572
Teaching as a Volunteer in the South (572); Teaching at an International School in the South (573); Other Private Schools in the South (573); Teaching in an Industrialized Country (573); Private Tutoring as a Business Overseas (574); Teacher Exchanges (574); Provincial (574); University Teaching in the South (575)
Different Strategies for Different Levels of Experience 575
Recent Graduates, No Teaching or International Experience (575); Experienced Teachers with No International Teaching Experience (575); Two or More Years Overseas Teaching Experience (575)
The Hiring Process 576
How Long Will it Take? (576); What Time of Year Should I Start? (576); Who Makes the Hiring Decisions? (576); The First Step: Focus Your Job Search (576); Where to Research (577); Personal Contacts and Networks (577); Direct Inquiries (577); Advertisements (577); Recruiting Fairs and Agencies (578); While Living Abroad (578); While Travelling Abroad (578); The British School System (578)
The Covering Letter 579
The Résumé for Teaching Overseas 579
The Interview 581
The Contract 581
Working Conditions (582); Contracts (582)
Getting Ready 582
Learning the Language (582); Don't Burn your Bridges (583)
Words of Wisdom for When You Arrive 583
Teaching English Overseas 584
The General Market (584); Who Can Teach? (585); How Much does it Pay? (585); Qualities of a Good English Teacher (585); Training to Become an English Teacher (586); Canadian Universities with Teaching ESL Programs (586); Other Ways to Gain English Teaching Experience in Canada (586); Become a Teacher to Land Another Type of Job (586); Teaching Materials to Take (587)
A Last Word 587
Resources 587
Teaching Abroad (587); Teacher Recruitment Agencies (591)

CHAPTER 30
Freelancing Abroad 595

What Can You Do Abroad? 595
Personal Stories 596
Before You Get There 597
Getting Started and Getting Motivated 597
Where to Make Contacts? 598
Be Clear in Your Job Objective 599
How Much Can You Earn as a Self-Employed Professional? 599
Taxes and Labour Laws 600
A Last Word 600
Resources 600

CHAPTER 31
Job Hunting When You Return to Canada 603

Re-Entry Adjustments 603
Returning Home, a Stronger You 604

The Importance of Understanding Your Skills 604
Why Canadian Employers Avoid International Employees 605
Employers' Assumptions 605
Your Solutions 605
How to Explain Your International Experience to Canadian Employers 605
International Skills You Should Emphasize to Canadian Employers 607
    Interpersonal Skills (607); Professional Work Skills (607)
Skills on Which You May Have Fallen Behind 607
    Skills Related to Administration (607); Skills Related to Technology (607)
A Last Word 608

PART FIVE
International Career Contacts

CHAPTER 32
The Private Sector   611

Size of Firms 611
Sectors 612
Qualifications 612
How to Begin 612
Resources 613
Profiles of Private Firms **613**

CHAPTER 33
Services for International Businesses & Entrepreneurs   693

Why Go International? 693
Keys to Success 694
Getting Started 694
Resources 695
Profiles of International Business Services **700**
Federal Government Services 701
Provincial Government Services 708
Canadian Trade Associations 709
Foreign Trade Councils 711

CHAPTER 34
Careers in Government   713

Resources 714
The Public Service Commission (PSC) **715**
Types of Federal Government Employment 715
Criteria and Procedures for Employment 716
Post-Secondary Recruitment (PSR) 717
Student Employment in an International Division 717
    Federal Student Work Experience Program (FSWEP) (717)
Specific Programs of the PSC 718
A Last Word on the Public Service Commission 718
Department of Foreign Affairs and International Trade (DFAIT) **719**
Types of Employment with DFAIT 719

Life in the Foreign Service 721
The Foreign Service Recruitment Campaign 722
    The Application Process (722); The Foreign Service Exam (722); The Screening Phase
    (723); The Selection Phase (723)
Consulting with Foreign Affairs 724
Student Opportunities with Foreign Affairs 724
A Last Word on the Foreign Service 725
Resources 725
Canadian International Development Agency (CIDA) **727**
CIDA Programs and Structure 728
What is it Like to Work at CIDA? 729
Types of CIDA Employment 730
Consulting with CIDA 730
    Finance and Contracting Management Division, CIDA (730)
Other Consulting with CIDA 732
    Consulting and Audit Canada (CAC), International Services Directorate (732)
Professional Networking Association 732
    Canadian Association of International Development Consultants (CAIDC) (732)
Business Opportunities at CIDA 732
    Industrial Cooperation Program (INC), CIDA (732); Renaissance Eastern Europe Program
    (REE), CIDA (733)
CIDA Cooperants 733
    Contracting Management Division, CIDA (733)
Permanent or Term Positions at CIDA 733
    Personnel and Administration Branch, CIDA (733); Public Service Commission (PSC) (733)
CIDA's Strategy for Youth 734
    CIDA Public Inquiries (734); Federal Government Youth Info Line (734)
CIDA Services 735
A Last Word on CIDA 735
Resources 736
Profiles of Government Organizations **738**

CHAPTER 35
Nongovernmental Organizations   763

Brief History of NGOs 763
Who Funds NGOs? 764
NGO Work Overseas 764
Applying for a Job 765
Jobs Overseas 766
Volunteering in Canada 766
Words of Advice 766
Your Experience 767
Resources 768
Profiles of Nongovernmental Organizations **771**

CHAPTER 36
United Nations   835

Structure and Purposes 836
Recruitment 837
Qualifications 837

Entry Level Programs 838
Internships and Awards 839
Professional Opportunities 839
    Peacekeeping/Relief (840);   Consulting (840);   Technical Assistance (841);   Transla-
    tion/Interpretation (841)
Resources 841
Profiles of UN Agencies **843**

CHAPTER 37
Environmental & Agricultural Research Centres   857

Opportunities in the South 857
The Consultative Group on International Agricultural Research (CGIAR) 858
Types of Positions Available 859
Recruiting Procedures 859
What to Expect from CGIAR Employment 860
Other Considerations 860
Profiles of Environmental & Agricultural Research Centres **861**

CHAPTER 38
International Organizations   867

Types of International Organizations 867
    International NGOs (867);   Multilateral Institutions (868);   International Professional
    Associations (868); International "Think Tanks" (868)
Job Hunting Tips 868
Resources 869
Profiles of International Organizations **870**

CHAPTER 39
Canadian Diplomats Abroad   887

Services to Individuals 887
Services to Canadian Businesses 888
Foreign Aid 888
Communications and Culture 888
Other Functions 888
Canadian Diplomatic Terminology 889
A Last Word 889
Resources 890
Canadian Diplomatic Missions Abroad **890**
Canadian Representation in International Organizations 901

CHAPTER 40
Foreign Diplomats in Canada   903

A Word on Terminology 903
How Missions are Classified 904
Resources 904
Foreign Diplomatic Missions in Canada **904**

Indexes

Bibliography 919
ID Numbers 933
Cities in Canada with International Contacts 941
Countries & Regions of the World 945
Job Categories 953
Organizations 957

How This Book was Researched 970
Contents at a Glance 972

Introduction

So you want to work overseas. You're not alone! Estimates of Canadians currently working overseas vary from 50,000 to 100,000, so we know the jobs are out there. But how do you find them? In this book, we discuss ways to crack the international job market, to make the system work to your advantage. With careful planning and investigation, an international career is waiting for you!

Who is this Book For?

This guide is written for all types of international job seekers, from the entry-level to the seasoned professional, from university students and recent graduates to senior consultants, entrepreneurs, teachers, academics, guidance counsellors, managers, civil servants, and world travellers. It is for those making long-term career plans to work overseas and for those ready to make a career change now. This book is also for anyone interested in understanding the individual circumstances of those moving abroad; spouses, children, teen-agers, women, gays and lesbians, singles, and managers conducting international work in Canada and abroad.

This third edition is an indispensable desk companion—a comprehensive directory of Canada's international activities and an authoritative guide to working and living overseas.

What's in this Book?

Everything you need to know about working and living overseas. This book offers successful strategies and practical information to guide you through the necessary steps of your international job search, from start to finish. There are detailed, insightful chapters dealing with living overseas, including moving and taxes, culture shock, crosscultural communications, personal stories, and the Canadian identity overseas. There is a *completely revised chapter* dealing with hard to come by information on re-entry shock. (See Chapter 8, Re-Entry.) The job search chapters are there to explain how finding a job overseas is different from looking for work in Canada. International résumés, interviews, and job search techniques are but some of the chapter headings. A concise, *new chapter* on the Internet job search will show you how this medium has become indispensable in today's world. It is rich in international job resources and innovative ideas. (See Chapter 21, The Internet Job Search.)

At almost a half a million words, the third edition has 24 per cent more information than the second edition. (Thanks in part to a more efficient font, the page count is almost the same.)

The guide has *2,550* career building resources, *1,868* organizations and *682* bibliographic resources organized in *58* topical bibliographies. There are *1,670* web sites to help with every aspect of your international career. The profiles cover organizations with international activities in the business, government, nongovernmental, and academic sectors. Profiles have full address information and most cover size, areas of specialization, regions of operation, and qualifications required. The book provides comprehensive descriptions of international studies programs in Canada and abroad, information on grants, short-term programs overseas, and *new extensive information* on international internships (see Chapter 17, International Internships). And lastly, the 682 resource listings, comprised of books, web sites, and organizations to help you in your job search, are conveniently organized to follow each topical discussion.

Updates Until the Year 2001 on our Web Site

The 1998 third edition will be regularly updated on *www.WorkingOverseas.com,* our web site, until December, 2001. You will notice that every profile and resource listing has a unique ID number, for example: [ID:5683] is for Bombardier Inc. We expect that some of you will use this number as a quick pointer when doing your job research with this book. (For example, you may note to yourself, "Call ID:5683 page 624 re application procedures.") Most importantly however, we use these ID numbers on our web site to help you quickly search for any corresponding updated information, such as an address change. We are relying on reader feedback to help us keep information current, so visit us at *www.WorkingOverseas.com* if you have any information you want us to share or research. And while there, keep an eye out for new and related services.

Why a Book on International Careers?

The fact is, an international job search is different from a Canadian job search. During my international career, I was often approached by friends for advice on finding overseas jobs. With no idea of where or how to start and being unaware of the extent of Canada's international activities, they had invariably become discouraged. Few had any understanding of the International IQ skills that employers look for. Hence the need for a "road map" on international careers. Let this guide be your atlas!

Why Encourage People to Work Overseas?

For many, global concerns are the motivation for working abroad. How can we learn to co-exist in the global village if we don't understand each other first? If Canadians are to make "globalization" work, we must become skilled in the art of crosscultural communication. We need to preserve and build on our hard-won international reputation for sensitivity, fairness, and generosity. Professional and technical expertise alone are not enough—we must harness understanding, tolerance, and foresight to deal with problems of global survival, such as poverty, war, and ecological destruction. And we must do this in a way that includes the full participation of local peoples. This is the essence of international work.

International work is rewarding—and attainable. We hope this book will help you achieve your goals.

Acknowledgements

The Canadian Guide to Working and Living Overseas owes its success to the enthusiastic support of the many individuals and institutions who purchase our guide. It is heart-warming to hear that many of you refer to our guide as "the bible" on Canada's international work and activities. To all of you, "thanks for your support!" I'm sure you'll appreciate this latest edition.

The third edition of *The Canadian Guide to Working and Living Overseas* could not have been written without the assistance of the numerous organizations who responded to our questionnaire and provided countless suggestions for improvement. Many thanks for your participation.

ISSI must give sincere thanks to the 26 staff who were diligent and dedicated in putting together this third edition.

The ISSI research staff were organized, professional, and reliable. They researched the profiles and updated the chapter introductions. First mention must go to Leah Nord for ably completing a massive amount of research for the seven chapters related to academia, short-term programs overseas, hosting programs, and NGOs. Leah excelled on every front: efficiency, professional demeanour, organizational abilities, interpersonal contact with organisations, and most appreciated, her supportive nature. Thanks Leah. Shawn MacWha's attention to detail helped us get a good start researching the chapters on the private and government sectors. Lisa Woodward did top-notch research work on the complicated task of updating the bibliographic resources. We very much appreciated Eileen Stuart for her insistence on excellence, her follow-up communication style, and helpful disposition when researching the chapters Careers in Government and Services for International Business & Entrepreneurs. Donna Chiarelli did a great job on research and new writing for the chapter International Internships. We appreciated Jasjit Sangha for applying her academic skills and good humour to successfully completing the last five chapters touching on the international community. Thanks to the part-time researchers who also made significant contributions in areas too numerous to mention: André Dumont, Joanne Ledger, James Moran, Sarah Qualman, Anita Seiz, David Strawczynski, and Peter Woollam.

Reid Cooper and Terry Cottam both deserve special appreciation for their work and skills. As the layout team on this and the previous edition, they both have a steadfast attachment to maintaining accuracy and clarity in layout and wording. They possess good humour while working under pressure. And, they are both dedicated to the ideals presented in this book. Reid Cooper also had numerous research roles for which he so willingly volunteered at every occasion. Among his many areas of knowledge, we especially drew on his expertise in world geography and on the use of the Internet. Reid must also be given much credit for the major portion of The Private Sector chapter. Terry Cottam is ISSI's longest-term employee, having made significant contributions to each edition of this guide. He possesses a unique combination of skills. He has a brilliant mind for helping us all choose the exact word, he is a patient computer coach, and is instrumental in the design and maintenance of our databases and standards' manual. Paul Gross is our indispensable database consultant. His expertise branches out into numerous areas such as programming, problem solving, the Internet, and good customer support to mention but a few. Many thanks Paul, Terry, and Reid.

We had the help of some top-notch writers and editors. Dawna Gallagher was our much appreciated lead editor, with start-up assistance from Jane Butler. Jennifer Latham took over as editor in the final stage of production, with Helen Smith as the copy editor. Madeleine Low edited the French text. Many thanks to our editors for their flexibility and willingness to meet our production schedules. We are very proud of the new chapter, The Internet Job Search, written by Sonal Pathak with the initial draft researched by Shawn MacWha and further input from Reid Cooper. Sonal worked diligently to finalize the work, producing a chapter rich in international job resources and innovative ideas. We are equally proud of the completely revised chapter, Re-Entry, filled with hard to-come by information on re-entry shock. This chapter is an adaptation of Betty-Ann Smith's forthcoming article on re-entry, written with the assistance of her daughter, Jennifer. Elizabeth Smith has adapted it for this book. Thanks again to Sabrina Quraeshi for her professional cover design, updated from the previous editions.

The success of this edition builds on the fine work of numerous researchers from the first and second editions. Many thanks to them. Some of the excellent writing work still appearing from previous editions was updated. The original writers are: Elizabeth Smith wrote the first drafts of Living Overseas; Dianne Lepa wrote Women Working and Living Overseas; Denise Beaulieu wrote The Canadian Identity in the International Workplace; Peggy Berkowitz wrote two chapters, Jobs by Regions of the World and Freelancing Abroad.

Thanks to family and friends who helped finance the final six months of this project. Their contributions are based on friendship as well as a commitment to the ideals presented in this book.

Many thanks also to the numerous people who provided expert advice and support: Denise Beaulieu, Peggy Berkowitz, Richard Berthelsen, Louis Boudreau, David Berman, Dave Carpenter, Jacynth Desmarais, Philippe Eddie, Chris Frey, Carla Graebner, Gary Greenman, Paul Gross, Pierre and Maureen Hachey, Liz Huff, Muriel Jordan, Ken King, Denise Kupferschmid, Lorne Kupferschmid, Peter LaBelle, Mark LaPrairie, Diane Lepa, Ian McKelvie,

Sanjiv Mehta, Danuszia Mordasiewicz, Dorothy Morrison, Stephen Nairne, Eric Pelletier, Harry and Ann Qualman, Stephane Rioux, Tony Rogge, Mike Rudiak, Matthew Stepchuk, Michael Simpson, Sandra Steinhause, Jennifer Tiller, and Gerry Toomey.

My warm appreciation to my whole family from Bathurst, Fredericton, and Norman Wells for their continuing good company, love, and support. (Hi Mom!)

And lastly, to my supportive partner, Richard, who provided me with good advice at crucial moments in the production of this guide as well as ensuring we had a very happy partnership and home life together.

Jean-Marc Hachey
Ottawa, Canada

How to Use this Book

This book organizes contact information as either a "profile" of a contact organization, or as a "resource." An organization is profiled if it helps you gain experience or can offer you an international job. A resource, on the other hand, is either a book, a web site, or an organization which helps your job hunt or provides you with crosscultural information.

PROFILES OF ORGANIZATIONS

There are 1,868 profiles of organizations listed under 17 separate categories. The profiles offer up-to-date contact information and details on organization sizes, types, objectives, activities, and recruitment procedures. Whenever possible, profiles include a web site address and e-mail contact. Profiles are listed at the end of the appropriate chapters.

The two main groups of profiles are found in Part Two: Acquiring International Experience, and Part Five: International Career Contacts.

ORGANIZATIONS BY CHAPTER

Acquiring International Experience
10. Short-term Programs Overseas 142
11. Hosting Programs 167
13. Global Education Centres 195
14. Study Abroad 212
15. Awards & Grants 219
16. International Studies in Canada 245
16. International Studies Abroad 254
17. International Internships 359

International Career Contacts
32. Private Sector 613
33. International Business Services 700
34. Government 738
35. Nongovernmental Organizations 771
36. United Nations 843
37. Environmental & Agricultural
    Research Centres 861
38. International Organizations 870
39. Canadian Diplomats Abroad 890
40. Foreign Diplomats in Canada 904

Organization Address, Phone, and Fax

Always contact an organization by telephone or fax to confirm their correct mailing address, department, and title of the contact person. The World Wide Web is a convenient resource for much of this information—for example, the Yahoo web site (www.yahoo.com) can point you to sites with updates on such information as new area codes and telephone directories. However, for exact contact names and other information, the telephone is still often faster than the Web. Long distance charges are increasingly competitive with mail rates (especially when faxing), often at 15 cents per minute during business hours within Canada and 22 cents per minute to the USA, and, from as low as 60 cents to $1.20 per minute overseas. You can dial direct to most countries—

outside Canada and the US, dial 011 followed by the number. Overseas country codes are shown in parentheses, followed by the area code, also in parentheses.

Web Sites and E-mail Addresses

These are listed after the postal address and phone and fax numbers. Remember that you can always recognize an e-mail address by the "@" sign. Sometimes, additional web sites will be mentioned in the text describing the organization. (See also Resource Web Sites below.)

Size of Organization

Where applicable, organizations are categorized as SMALL, MID-SIZED, or LARGE, according to the size of their international budget. For example, NGOs with budgets in excess of $2,000,000 are designated as LARGE. Similar distinctions apply to private firms.

Type of Organization

The organization type is written in upper-case letters, immediately following the size of the organization (if listed). It identifies broad areas of activity and expertise. For example, NGOs have such types as RELIEF AND DEVELOPMENT AGENCY, while private firms have such types as CONSULTING FIRM, or ARCHITECTURAL AND PLANNING FIRM.

Job Categories

Job categories are listed alphabetically in lower-case letters for the private sector, government, NGO, and international organization profiles. They provide a useful reference guide to an organization's principal activities and skill requirements. Consult the Job Index at the end of this book. Note that this index is to be used as a guide only. Some unique job categories have not been indexed.

Description

Profiles in Part Two: Acquiring International Experience are designed to familiarize the reader with the wide variety of international study opportunities available in Canada and abroad as well as the short-term (generally unpaid) opportunities overseas. International study profiles list the degrees conferred, contact information, and brief descriptions of the nature and structure of programs. Profiles documenting short-term opportunities overseas detail eligibility requirements, duration, program objectives, and financial information.

Profiles in Part Five: International Career Contacts generally follow a standard sequence. First, an organization's principal activities and areas of expertise are outlined, followed by information on the substance and location of recent international projects. This is followed by a description of the qualifications and skills sought by prospective employers, and an indication of whether or not an organization maintains a data bank for résumés and if the organization offers internship possibilities. Often, job hunting features of an organization's web site are noted at the end of the profile.

Profiles are generally in English. As a rule, however, where an organization's only language of operation is French, profiles are written in French.

RESOURCES

There are 682 separate resources listed alphabetically in 58 bibliographies at the ends of chapters. For ease of reference, many resources are repeated in different chapters, for a total of 1,338 entries. For detailed information, consult the Bibliography Index at the end of this book.

BIBLIOGRAPHIES BY SUBJECT

Living Overseas
Crosscultural Skills ... 17
Health Overseas ... 45
Children & Families Overseas ... 47
Educating Your Children ... 49
Moving Abroad ... 49
Taxes & Investment ... 51
Personal Stories Overseas ... 66
Learning a Foreign Language ... 73
Women Working & Living Overseas ... 83
Crosscultural Business Skills ... 102
Re-Entry ... 125
International Business ... 695

Acquiring Experience
Short-term Programs Overseas ... 142
Hosting Programs ... 166
Crosscultural Travel ... 177
International IQ Periodicals ... 186
Book, Film & Video Distributors ... 187
Global Education ... 189
Tools for Teachers ... 193
International Internships ... 357

Academic Studies
Learning a Foreign Language ... 72
International IQ Periodicals ... 186
Study Abroad ... 207
Awards & Grants ... 217
International Studies
   in Canada and Abroad ... 242

The Job Search
General Job Search: All ... 395
General Job Search: Students ... 396
Books on the Internet Job Search ... 415
International Job Hunting
   Services on the Internet ... 417
Country Information on the Internet ... 424
International Job Search ... 429
Employment Agencies ... 432
Job Search Directories ... 433

Internet Job Search
New to the Internet? ... 405
Books About the Internet ... 406
Search Engines ... 409
Books on the Internet Job Search ... 415
Directories on the Web ... 416
International Job Hunting
   Services on the Internet ... 417
Country Information on the Internet ... 424

Country Information
Country Information on the Internet ... 424
Global Guide Books ... 515
United States of America ... 524
Mexico & Latin America ... 534
Western Europe ... 540
Russia & Eastern Europe ... 547
Middle East ... 550
Asia Pacific ... 556

International Career Contacts
Women Working & Living Overseas ... 83
Short-term Programs Overseas ... 137
International Internships ... 357
International Job Search ... 429
Other Careers ... 437
Health Careers ... 438
Language Careers ... 441
Tourism Industry Careers ... 442
Jobs in International Development ... 566
Teaching Abroad ... 587
Teacher Recruitment Agencies ... 591
Freelancing Abroad ... 600
International Business ... 695
Government ... 714
Foreign Affairs ... 725
CIDA ... 736
Nongovernmental Organizations ... 768
United Nations ... 841
International Organizations ... 869
Canadian Diplomats Abroad ... 890
Foreign Diplomats in Canada ... 904

This year we are including three types of resources to assist you in your job search. Books remain an indispensable source of information and these have been updated to include recent publications. This new edition also now includes web sites as resources. (See Resource Web Sites below.) Lastly, we have listed organizations as resources when they provide a service to job hunters, but no actual job.

Books 📖

In the Resources sections, book titles are in **bold** with a "📖" after it, followed by year or frequency of publication, author or editor in *italics* (if specified), then publisher. After the symbol "➤" we list the distributor's address, followed by a brief description of the book. (If the publisher and distributor are the same, only the distributor is specified.) All books listed are recommended for your research. Most have been reviewed.

Canadian mail-order distributors are listed when possible. Some books are easily found in bookstores. Many others are specialty publications which stores can order for you or which you can order directly to save time. A large research library is the best place to consult expensive, frequently updated reference volumes. And don't forget, the majority of books can now be ordered by consulting the distributor's web site.

Call, fax, write, e-mail, or visit the distributor's web site to confirm current prices, availability, and distributors' addresses. Prepayment is usually required. Prices listed are an approximate guide only; they do not include postage, GST, or provincial taxes. US distributors seldom accept cheques drawn on Canadian banks. Payment to distributors outside Canada must be by international or postal money orders in US funds or appropriate currency. The most convenient method is to order with a credit card by phone, fax, e-mail or web site. We have listed specific credit cards accepted by the distributor.

Resource Organizations

Organizations that offer services to job seekers and do not themselves offer direct employment are listed as resources. Included in this category are international employment agencies, teacher recruitment agencies, and organizations offering information or services of interest to people wanting to work and live overseas.

When listed in the Resources sections, names of organizations are in **bold** (with no symbol after it), followed by the organization's contact address and a description of services offered.

Resource Web Sites 💻

Web sites in Resources sections are listed by title in **bold** with a "💻"—a little computer—after it, followed by the web address and a description of the site's contents. When a resource can be either purchased as a book or accessed on the Web, both the book and computer symbols are shown. In the case where a resource is not specifically available on the Web, but can be ordered on the Web, the distributor's web address is listed at the end of the description.

The majority of addresses on the Web now begin http://www..., therefore we have not printed http:// except for clarity where addresses begin with something other than www. The prefix http:// isn't actually part of the address; it just tells a computer to use hypertext protocol to connect to a web site. Most browsers now allow you to omit the http:// prefix when entering addresses.

Web resources are diverse in what they offer. Many of the sites we selected post job or study opportunities and internship information. Other sites give you the current information you will need about the regions or countries that you are targeting. The Web offers a growing number of online versions of journals and other print material. We have also suggested sites that can contribute to your international and crosscultural knowledge.

Because the Web is still a quickly evolving medium, new web sites pop up almost every day, and many web sites change their location. For strategies for finding web sites as well as a more detailed discussion of the Web, see Chapter 21, The Internet Job Search. To find out about changes to this book or inform us of new, interesting web sites you've discovered, please visit our web site at www.WorkingOverseas.com.

ID NUMBERS AND UPDATES ON OUR WEB SITE

You will notice that every resource listing and organization profile has a unique ID number, for example: [ID:5683] is for Bombardier Inc. We expect that some of you will use this number as a quick pointer when doing your job research with this book. (For example, you may note to yourself, "Call ID:5683 page 624 re application procedures.") Most importantly however, we use these ID numbers on our web site to help you quickly search for any corresponding updated information, such as an address change.

We are relying on reader feedback to help us keep the contact and resource information current, so visit us at *www.WorkingOverseas.com* if you have any information you want us to share or research. Please use the ID number to identify the organization profile or resource when contacting us by phone, e-mail, or via our web site. (See inside front cover for publisher's contact information.) And while visiting our web site, keep an eye out for new and related services. The 1998 third edition will be regularly updated on our site until December of the year 2001.

PART ONE

Your International IQ

1. The Effective Overseas Employee 3
2. Myths & Realities 23
3. Living Overseas 29
4. What Canadians Overseas Say 53
5. Learning a Foreign Language 69
6. Women Working & Living Overseas 75
7. The Canadian Identity in
   the International Workplace 87
8. Re-Entry 109

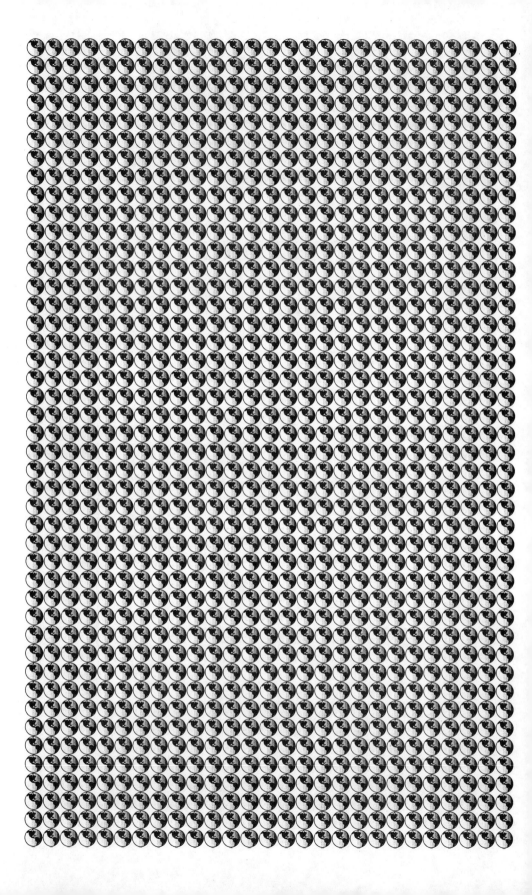

Chapter 1

The Effective
Overseas
Employee

WHY DO PEOPLE GO OVERSEAS?

It's Monday morning and you are at your desk, staring out at the bleak, cold February landscape. Imagine instead that you are gazing at palm trees and ocean surf, being fanned by tropical breezes. Many of you want to escape to warmer, friendlier climates and explore new cultures and lifestyles. While working overseas is not as simple as our February fantasy suggests, it *is* possible with the right strategy.

The reasons for working overseas are endless—from a love of new foods, the desire to travel, explore new cultures and learn new ways of living, to an interest in making new friends, improving your language skills, widening your professional experience and heightening your understanding of the world. Overseas work often requires you to take on more responsibility than you have been used to. The scope of your professional skills may be tested: you could develop a whole new perspective on your field. Certainly you'll have to develop some new skills, particularly in the area of crosscultural communication.

For those of you with families, living overseas can be a wonderful adventure. The slower pace allows for more quality time together, and for many children, immersion in another culture can be one of the most profound experiences of their early lives. (Of course, your family must be involved in the decision to move overseas, and understand where you are going and what to expect when you get there.)

One of the best reasons for working overseas is to gain a heightened sense of what it means to be Canadian. Most returning workers find they have a greater appreciation for Canada and for the things they share with other

3

Canadians. They also develop pragmatism, initiative, and the confidence to take on further challenges.

Overseas work can be a truly enriching experience. While you can't escape the hardships and challenges of adjusting to a new environment, most people find they gain immensely from the experience.

At this point in your plans for working overseas, you may be trying to determine whether you are suited to this kind of work, both in a personal and a professional sense. This chapter will help you begin your assessment.

WHAT IS YOUR INTERNATIONAL IQ?

An international employer's assessment of candidates for overseas work generally has two components:

* The *professional* component.
* The *"International IQ"* component, which measures your level of international and intercultural awareness.

Much of this book is concerned with helping you acquire the international knowledge and skills necessary to develop what we call your "International IQ." Building your International IQ will substantially increase your chances of finding an overseas job, even when you don't have overseas work experience.

Why is previous overseas experience so often a critical factor in getting that first international posting? Because employers want effective employees who know how to get the job done in a culture other than their own. In an overseas work situation, it is not enough to know the technical aspects of your work. You must understand the people, their country and their culture. You must see how cultural factors fit into the task at hand. Once you understand the "whats" and "whys" of a new culture, you'll have a greater chance of succeeding in that context.

It is possible to acquire this type of cultural and international knowledge without actually working overseas. Your International IQ is made up of your awareness and ability in four areas:

1. Political, economic and geographic knowledge
2. Knowledge about the international aspects of your field
3. Crosscultural knowledge and skills
4. Personal coping and adapting skills

While many of these skills can be acquired over time, this book helps you get a jump start on qualifying for the international job market. The following provides more detail on the above four areas.

Political, economic and geographic knowledge: If you can converse intelligently about international news and world events, you are probably sufficiently aware of world politics and economics. You also need a firm grasp of world geography and knowledge of the world's major ethnic groups and their distributions. And of course, you need detailed knowledge about the country in which you hope to work.

To increase your knowledge, you might consider the following: listening regularly to international news broadcasts, keeping a good, up-to-date world atlas close at hand, subscribing to one or two international magazines or newspapers, joining a multicultural group in your community, vacationing in offbeat places, enrolling in courses on the politics or history of regions in which you are interested.

Knowledge about the international aspects of your field: You have a good knowledge of the international aspects of your area of expertise if you know which organizations work internationally in your field, what jobs exist, and what aspects of your work have an international application. This information is extremely important in your job search and in managing your career path. Knowing how your specialization is practised in an international setting allows you to focus your education, your job research, your networking contacts and your discussions with peers on landing the right overseas job for you.

To start, a few phone calls to international organizations in your line of work will reap rewards. A bit of research will tell you what trade magazines you should be reading. Join an international trade association. Learn when international conferences take place. Talk to people in your field who work or have worked overseas. Find out which skills and what types of experience they think are important.

Crosscultural knowledge and skills: You have sufficient crosscultural knowledge and skill if you know what it takes to be effective in another culture. A good approach, once you know what country you want to work in, is to find out about that country's belief systems, modes of behaviour and attitudes.

An effective overseas employee needs a lot more than specialized technical knowledge. You should have a sound knowledge of the local culture and be able to apply it in your workplace. As well, the ability to speak the country's main language will be a great asset to you. You can generally acquire these skills in Canada by seeking out people from other cultures, becoming active in crosscultural groups, and learning a second or third language.

Personal coping and adapting skills: You can improve your personal coping and adapting skills which, in turn, will help you deal with culture shock. People who enjoy working and living overseas are adaptable and tend to embrace challenge. You will face changes in culture, friends, work and climate. Therefore, having a sense of adventure, as well as humour, curiosity, and a great deal of patience, is invaluable.

To prepare yourself, you can do volunteer work or participate in organizations that put you in contact with other cultures. If you have never visited a country where the culture is radically different from your own, you should try to do so before embarking on an international career.

IMPORTANT CHARACTERISTICS FOR OVERSEAS WORKERS

The remainder of this chapter details the skills and personal traits of a successful international worker. This sort of information is not always easy to describe in a résumé. The time to demonstrate these particular skills and traits, therefore, is during your interview.

IMPORTANT CHARACTERISTICS FOR OVERSEAS WORKERS
General Traits Enjoy change, have a sense of adventure, desire for challenge, open mind, patience, curiosity
Adaptation and Coping Skills Emotional stability and ability to deal with stress, understanding of culture shock, observation and adaptation skills, flexibility, humour, self-knowledge
Intercultural Communication Skills Tolerance, sensitivity, listening and observing skills, nonverbal communication skills, knowledge of a second language
Overseas Work Effectiveness Traits and Skills Independence and self-discipline, training experience, resourcefulness, versatility, persistence, organizational and people skills, leadership, energy, project planning skills, writing skills, verbal communication skills, loyalty and tenacity, tact, philosophical commitment to field of work
Key Traits of an Effective Overseas Employee Interpersonal skills, assertiveness and sense of identity, realistic pre-departure expectations

This list will help you assess your suitability for overseas work and assist you in preparing to live in a foreign environment.

Self-knowledge is power in today's job market. When you understand your skills and job objectives, when you have a professional self-assessment of your crosscultural work skills, you can be much more effective and focused in your international job search.

A word of caution: this list is by no means exhaustive. The importance of each skill or trait will vary with different work environments and countries of posting. If you have no previous overseas experience, it will be difficult to measure yourself against this list, as you probably have strengths you are not yet aware of. And if you don't currently have these skills, don't forget your ability to adapt and acquire new skills.

The preceding table, *Important Characteristics for Overseas Workers*, divides these skills and traits into blocks of information. This classification system will help you compile your own skills inventory and then convey these qualities to prospective employers.

GENERAL TRAITS

The following skills and traits can usually be found in successful overseas employees and their families.

Enjoyment of Change

Change will permeate your life in an overseas career. You should, therefore, ask yourself: do I adapt well to new situations? If you get upset when you find your toothpaste on the wrong shelf, chances are overseas life is not for you. You must adapt to new customs ("I now love drinking tea in the afternoon!") and give up old ones ("I can live without coffee!").

Change is an important part of an interesting life, and while it may be frightening for even the most daring people, you must learn to embrace and enjoy it. Make "when in Rome, do as the Romans do" your rule of thumb.

Sense of Adventure

Moving overseas involves navigating uncharted waters. You don't know what living arrangements you will have, what friends you will make, or how far you will have to travel for gas. Every aspect of overseas life holds unknowns. Indeed, for some of you, the proportion of unknowns may seem comparable to the explorers discovering the new world.

Having a sense of adventure is important if you are to enjoy overseas life. Expatriates revel in stories about their escapades—both pleasant and unpleasant. Many overseas employers look for a sense of adventure in applicants. In discussions and interviews with potential employers, *don't* exaggerate your taste for adventure, but *do* present yourself as someone who looks forward to tackling unknowns.

Desire for Challenge

Everyone who moves overseas encounters challenges in their work life and their personal life. Whether you are shopping for tomatoes, having the car repaired, or struggling to meet a production deadline, every activity is a challenge. An informed decision to work overseas demonstrates that you are willing to take on such challenges and able to adapt to new situations. Employers are looking for someone like you!

Open Mind

North Americans tend to look for only one solution to a problem. Once we find it, we package it and try to franchise it across the country. Much is standardized and meticulously measured. In an overseas environment, it is important not to try to apply North American solutions to the problems you encounter. You must keep your mind open to new approaches and, equally important, be able to recognize local solutions which work and need not be changed.

The CANADIAN INTERNATIONAL DEVELOPMENT AGENCY'S (CIDA) briefing material offers a good example of open-mindedness: when his boat broke down, a young man travelling down the Amazon discovered a special use for green bananas. He had heard locals talking about their sealant quality, and although he had questioned the idea at the time, his willingness to try it out got him out of a tight spot.

An open mind is a basic ingredient to success and survival in an overseas environment.

Patience

You need patience for virtually every aspect of overseas life. As a stranger to a new land, you must listen and learn. Don't jump to conclusions. Remember the old African saying that the stranger who does not suffer from alienation falls short of his calling as a stranger. You should expect to feel out of place in your new surroundings. However, overcoming your impatience and learning to follow the pace of life will ease your sense of alienation. Proceed slowly, especially in your first few months abroad.

Curiosity

Your spirit of curiosity will help you uncover much about a new culture, new land, plants, animals, customs and people. No matter what the circumstance, those who enjoy living overseas are curious about their surroundings. Think of the possibilities! You are delayed in a Middle Eastern airport—what better place to study differences in traditional dress? A trip to the hospital in an African city may offer you a chance to talk with an orderly about her village. You've been waiting outside a bureaucrat's office for an hour, enough time to witness an argument between two market women across the street. And now they are making up... Curiosity can help you appreciate, understand, and learn from virtually any situation. Don't leave home without it!

ADAPTATION AND COPING SKILLS

Culture shock is the term used to describe the difficult process of adapting to a new culture. (See Chapter 3, Living Overseas.) Adaptation skills are synonymous here with coping skills, which enable you to deal with the unfamiliar aspects of your new environment and with your overall sense of alienation.

Emotional Stability and Ability to Deal with Stress

Evidence of emotional stability is critical to an employer's assessment of a candidate's suitability for overseas work. The trouble and expense of dealing long distance with emotionally overwrought individuals make employers especially wary. Fragile personalities and those who lack a realistic self-image are particularly unsuitable. This is not to say that many successful overseas employees are not somewhat eccentric!

Think about how you have coped with stressful situations in the past. If you haven't had previous overseas work experience, international employers will look for other concrete examples of your ability to cope under stress. Surviving a two-week trek through the wilderness, studying Spanish in Mexico, taking on particularly challenging social work, or enduring a long and disruptive labour strike—all of these are indicators to a recruitment officer that you can deal with the pressures of a new environment. Situations in which you were socially isolated are also good examples: travelling by yourself for two months; living in a northern community; working alone as a forest fire warden, etc.

Employers are especially wary of applicants trying to avoid problems at home. If you imagine that an overseas post will help you escape an unhappy relationship or a drug problem, for example, your chances of succeeding overseas are slight. Remember, to survive overseas your main motivation must be the experience itself, not a personal situation. Drug dependency is a particularly bad reason for working overseas. While drugs are readily available in most countries, addiction and the consequences of being caught with illegal drugs make them something to be avoided. Literature on cultural adaptation is full of warnings about applying for overseas postings for the wrong reasons.

Another aspect of emotional stability is the effect of leaving loved ones behind in Canada. For example, if you are planning to leave your family at home, or if you rely on a small circle of friends, and you have little experience being separated from these support networks, adapting to overseas life may be very difficult. Recruiters are looking for people who are flexible and adapt quickly to new situations.

Culture Shock

Any serious overseas job hunter knows about culture shock. Recognizing the symptoms and dealing with the problem will help you adapt and cope overseas. Many an international career has been cut short by a severe case of culture shock. In recent times, however, excellent resources have been produced to help prospective overseas workers understand and prepare for it. This awareness may be crucial to your self-preservation and professional survival, and may help you assist others through their crises. (For a more detailed description of culture shock and a bibliographical list of resources, please see Chapter 3, Living Overseas.)

Observation and Adjustment Skills

Learn to stand back, observe, and adjust your behaviour accordingly. If you don't, life overseas will be very difficult, if not impossible.

The successful international employee can observe, react sensitively, if not appropriately, to new situations, and come to understand how local customs influence behaviour. People in many West African countries believe that "a stranger is like a child," and afford strangers and children a similar degree of tolerance. Indeed, until you learn appropriate social behaviour in your new environment, you *are* like a child. Tolerance for your mistakes won't last forever, however, and some Oriental cultures, for example, have little tolerance for social faux pas.

Flexibility

An important skill in cultural adaptation is the ability, when necessary, to change the way you do something. You will have to abandon many of your North American "tried and true" methods, find new ones, and roll with the punches. Leave your big ego at home.

Why is flexibility so important overseas? First, a correct assessment of a situation on Monday may be incorrect on Thursday. Second, being rigid in a new society will hurt your chances of getting things done. You must learn to bend. The traditions and practices of the local culture are much stronger than your ability to persuade. Don't ask them to "do it my way"—rather, try to learn their approach before dismissing it. Third, flexibility will help you enjoy yourself in your new environment. Learning to play soccer where there is no ice hockey or accepting the friendship of an older couple when all your friends at home are from your age group: these are examples of the value of flexibility. Fourth, being flexible will enable you to quickly switch back to North American behaviour patterns when dealing with head office, meeting Canadian delegations, or returning to Canada.

Humour

A good sense of humour is absolutely invaluable. Your ability to laugh and remain cheerful under pressure is of prime importance to recruitment officers, who know that humour can help employees adapt to even the most difficult circumstances. The ability to see the lighter side of things will make the difference between enduring and enjoying the whole adaptation process.

Self-knowledge

When you move to a new country, everything from shampoo to politics is different. The way you greet people, the way they respond, your new position as an outsider—all of these things will force you to change, to make adjustments, to adapt to your new life. When so many demands are being made on you to change, it is important to know yourself.

You need to know what aspects of your personality will help you in your overseas environment and what aspects will not. Realistically, however, you might not even appreciate certain traits until they surface in your new environment. Canadians travelling abroad for the first time are often surprised by their need for space and time alone. We may not recognize our need for solitude until we are deprived of it, which is particularly likely to happen if you are working in the South, where most cultures do not recognize this Western trait. Prepare yourself—you may find it difficult to cope with people continually entering your home without being invited or even knocking.

Knowing yourself will also help you distinguish your need to be flexible from your need to establish limits. While you must be willing to adapt, you must also be able to say no to social customs you simply cannot accept. For example, you can recognize and appreciate the importance of superstition and black magic in a society without participating in rituals you find offensive or frightening. Or, if you are a female travelling by train and you are assigned to an all-male sleeping compartment, you need not accept the situation out of fear of causing trouble or offending someone. Remember, you *do* have limits. You owe it to yourself to act accordingly.

Figure out what you can live with and what you can live without. People's quirks make them unique, so if coffee in the morning is crucial or you feel like you'll die without country and western music, take care of these needs. In summary, being able to cope in a new society depends as much on understanding yourself as it does on your openness and flexibility. Indeed, your hosts will appreciate and admire your individuality. Nothing can be gained by pretending to be something you're not.

INTERCULTURAL COMMUNICATION SKILLS

Of all the skills required for overseas work, intercultural communication skills are the least understood by prospective employees. Indeed, they are very difficult to grasp and even more difficult to demonstrate that you possess.

Our links with other cultures are growing stronger and more permanent. In an increasingly interdependent world, more and more emphasis is being placed on intercultural communication skills, which allow you to transmit your knowledge to people of other cultures, and, in return, share in the wealth of information they can give you.

Don't assume crosscultural communication is limited to language proficiency. Effective communication includes nonverbal skills, such as understanding body language and demeanour. Mastering life skills in your new environment depends on your ability to communicate across cultural barriers.

The following traits and skills are invaluable in developing good intercultural communication skills.

Tolerance

Tolerance in a foreign environment is critical to your ability to communicate. Try to get beyond your North American reaction to the new culture to understand why people behave as they do. For example, to dismiss foreign societies as inefficient because their productivity appears low by Canadian standards is to pass judgement in haste. You may discover that a group of workers is actually more cost-effective than you thought, once you understand that labour in the South is cheaper and spread among more people than it is in Canada, where labour and capital are more expensive.

Tolerance is crucial when you live in a society you don't fully understand. If someone is late for an appointment, assume there is a cultural reason. If someone invites you to supper and is then surprised when you show up, assume the situation has a cultural origin. Being tolerant means you can accept frustrating situations. Henceforth, prepare to go one step further: study the cultural background or traditions of the behaviour at hand.

Sensitivity

When you exercise tolerance in a new cultural setting, you become more aware of the makeup of this new society. Be sensitive in your dealings with others. Remember you are there to help, and to do that, you may have to put others before yourself. Practise sensitivity toward people in your new workplace. Try to see a situation from all sides. For example, do not assume that "they are ignoring me" or "they are mocking me by being late." A better approach, especially at the beginning, is to ask "why have they reacted this way?" or "what is the reason for this behaviour?"

We've all been annoyed by bureaucratic foul-ups, where the rules are supposedly "set in stone." A Canadian woman recently had some of her money seized at an African border. She knew that the maximum amount she could take out of the country had recently been increased from $40 to $100. She was within the new limit, but the customs officer, who was probably unaware of the recent change in regulations, insisted she was not. Fortunately, she was travelling with a friend who understood the subtleties of negotiating with African officials. As the official seized her money, the woman was about to fly into a rage when her friend took control and quietly asked the official if he could check to see if there had been any recent changes to the regulations. The official asked someone in the office and returned to confirm that the rules had indeed been changed. Though they had been in effect for months, the friend allowed the customs officer to save face, to believe he had cleared up the problem. (For more information on the role of women in developing countries see Chapter 6, Women Working & Living Overseas.)

Like your readiness to listen and observe, your sensitivity will enable you to understand the cultural puzzle around you and help you adapt to your new environment.

Listening and Observing

Many books have been written about living in specific countries in the South. While some can be helpful, your own listening and observing skills will determine how much you learn about your new environment. It takes a keen eye and a sense of curiosity to make these skills work for you. Observe people, then ask tactful questions of your hosts and other expatriates. Just remember: listening and observing more carefully than you've ever done before are the keys to good intercultural communication skills.

Nonverbal Communication Skills

If you've never lived outside Canada, you may be unaware of the diversity of nonverbal communication styles throughout the world. Confronted by the strange mannerisms of other cultures, we begin to see how much in our own culture is communicated nonverbally. Body language and facial expression can be as important as what is said.

In certain Arab countries, for example, you will be considered very rude if you pass an object with your left hand, as this is the one used to handle toilet paper. Other nonverbal communication forms extend from burping after a meal to indicate satisfaction, to practically ignoring visiting friends as a sign that the friendship has gone beyond the boundaries of formality. Manner of dress is another example of nonverbal communication. In some instances, it is considered the height of rudeness for a man not to wear a tie. Awareness of these subtleties is a key to success overseas.

Second Language Speaking Skills

A working knowledge of the local language is often crucial to effective intercultural communication. Even knowing a few phrases will help—if only by showing that you have made an effort. (For more detailed information see Chapter 5, Learning a Foreign Language.)

OVERSEAS WORK EFFECTIVENESS TRAITS AND SKILLS

Whether you are applying for an administrative position, a technical or research job, a teaching job, or a job in the field, most employers want to see evidence of particular work skills. This chapter discusses skills that are vital to typical overseas assignments but less crucial to North American workplaces. As part of your job hunting strategy, let employers know you understand these skills. Outline them in your résumé and discuss them in interviews.

Work environments overseas vary widely. You may be working in an office tower in downtown Rio de Janeiro, trekking the dirt roads of India in a land rover, or treating patients in a rural African community with no electricity. Your placement may be in the urban slums of Jakarta or in the cosmopolitan atmosphere of Hong Kong. Your primary contacts may be with the rural village market women in the Andes, the nomad herdsmen of the Sahara, senior government bureaucrats in Rwanda, or fellow Canadians in a CIDA office in San José.

Each of these overseas postings requires different combinations of skills. Some general skills are listed below. Please note that their relative importance varies from job to job.

Independence and Self-discipline

An overseas posting may be far removed from head office supervision. In many cases, you work totally on your own or with just one level of supervision. You will probably have a great deal of discretionary decision making power, the flip-side of which is responsibility. To thrive in these conditions, you must be independent and self-disciplined. Employers look for people who can, in effect, be their own bosses.

Training Experience

The raison d'être for most expatriate jobs is to aid in the transfer of expertise to local workers. You may have successfully implemented a program; don't commit the common, albeit unforgivable, oversight of neglecting to train local people to take over when you leave. A project's long-term success depends on the effective training of people in your host country. Since more and more employers are recognizing this, it is useful to highlight in your résumé any training experience you possess.

Resourcefulness

You are unlikely to have the kinds of support networks you enjoy in North America. The photocopier repairperson is not around the corner—if you even have access to a machine. You may not have reliable telephone service. There will likely be no temporary employment agencies. Just ordering a supply of paper and envelopes may require you to fill out an astounding number of forms.

You will have to find your own solutions, build your own contacts, and solve problems without guidance and often without benefit of previous experience. Resourcefulness involves both coping in an unfamiliar environment and improvising new combinations of solutions. A resourceful problem-solver is someone who is imaginative, determined and flexible. International recruiters look for resourceful employees.

Versatility

Many international jobs require that you work alone, without the aid of any specialists. You have an advantage if you are versatile and possess a range of skills. In many situations in the South, where you are in charge of an office, you should be proficient in some or all of the following: report writing, negotiation, personnel management, supervision of employees, training of employees, office management, computer skills, accounting, budgeting, procurement of supplies, inventory control, shipping and handling imported supplies, telex and radio skills, car repair, carpentry, and gardening. This might seem like an odd collection of skills, but if you speak to anyone who has worked in the South, they will tell you that versatility is of the utmost importance. While few people possess all of these skills, employers prefer to send versatile employees to difficult environments.

Persistence

In a culture you don't understand, it's easy to believe there's no solution to a problem. Don't be tempted to give up and become cynical, however. You may be exhausted from chasing an elusive form from an elusive government department. You may have waited four months for delivery of an important cement shipment only to be informed that the rail link to the cement factory has been shut down for repairs. Your landlord may have once again failed to fix the plumbing. Instead of throwing up your hands in frustration and defeat, be persistent! Your future employer will want to know how you react to such common aggravating situations. Enthusiasm and persistence are necessary parts of the makeup of a successful overseas employee. Be sure to discuss with your potential employer situations where you exhibited persistence.

Organizational and People Skills

These two important skill sets are discussed in Chapter 26, Interviewing for an International Job.

Leadership

As the person in charge of a project, you will be required to provide leadership. Some common leadership tasks are motivating a group, assigning duties, following up on work in progress, avoiding and solving conflict, building consensus around an objective, giving rewards and providing feedback. Impress upon a recruiter that you possess leadership skills. Outline your past accomplishments and give examples of instances where you took the lead.

Management styles can change as you cross cultural boundaries. In some places, locals may interpret your use of the North American participatory approach as a sign that you are a weak manager. A more authoritarian approach may be appropriate. Discipline and motivational methods also vary widely. In certain African countries, trying to motivate an employee by offering a promotion and salary increase can sometimes backfire: the promotion could be associated with extending the employee's family responsibilities to more people in his or her extended family, which might not be appreciated. In this situation, a different form of motivation would have to be used. Your skills in sizing up a situation will have a lot to do with your ability to provide leadership in the workplace.

Energy

An employer will be looking for energy to complement your resourcefulness. Let the recruiter know you won't allow fatigue or cynicism to get to you in a situation where it may be very hot, noisy, frustrating, or demanding. If you're going to be a successful overseas worker, you need energy. Describe your success at meeting deadlines and overcoming constraints. Talk about your need for challenge, how you don't give up until the job is done.

Project Planning Skills

As most international work is based on head office approval, some understanding of how to develop each phase of a project cycle is crucial: from writing a proposal and understanding the basic elements (objectives, background, methods and means, budget, timetable) to following through on the project (accounting, personnel management) to the formal evaluation. Speak of projects in terms of phases—research phase, start-up phase, operational phase, and evaluation phase.

Writing Skills

Many overseas jobs demand good writing skills, as extensive report writing is often required to keep head office informed. As a general rule, there is a correlation between the size of the company and the amount of report writing required. Smaller organizations tend to put more emphasis on the operational side of their work.

Verbal Communication Skills

As a representative of your institution abroad, you will meet many people and even be called upon to speak publicly. You are likely to find that the people you deal with overseas put greater emphasis on verbal skills. Many societies in the South cultivate the art of conversation; Westerners are often at a disadvantage in this respect. Your hosts will expect you to be polite and articulate. Don't let your verbal communication skills slide!

Loyalty and Tenacity

Overseas employers demand greater loyalty than is normally required in a Canadian job. Your terms of employment will place restrictions on your behaviour, both at work and in a social milieu. You will be expected to socialize with co-workers and their families. You will also have to respect local customs and observe local laws.

As many employers take on the responsibility of providing for your housing and your childrens' schooling, this opens the door to a much wider range of grievances against your employer. Despite their commitment to making your life overseas as pleasant as possible, there are bound to be disappointments. You will have to face these and continue your loyalty to your employer.

One of the most common reasons for failure at working abroad has nothing to do with job performance, but with a loss of trust and support from headquarters. Communications must be kept open and fluid, or your superiors could become suspicious. In this respect, there is a certain career risk to going overseas, because it is harder to show results. You could lose credibility at home if you can't explain what you are accomplishing overseas. Time zone differences, lack of telephone service and widely differing expectations can contribute to tensions between personnel at head office and abroad. Let potential employers know you understand this reality and are prepared to deal with it.

Tact

In your new work environment, you may encounter greater formality in day-to-day operations. Try always to observe local customs and avoid thoughtless, potentially offensive remarks. For example, never forget that money in the less affluent South is scarce. Don't make flippant comments to officials in your host country, or to everyday workmates. Be tactful at all times!

Philosophical Commitment to Field of Work

In North America, making money is a major concern for many people. In international work, however—especially with the UNITED NATIONS, the NGO community, and in government sponsored programs—be careful about asserting the making of money as your goal. Most international employers are looking for employees who are committed to a broader cause. International careerists often have a deep sense of mission. They believe they are making a contribution to humankind. International employers may be looking for these qualities, especially if you are young and just starting your career (the UN is a good example). Do not, however, overstate your case. Employers are not looking for zealots or international "do-gooders." A brief discussion of your commitment will suffice. Reserve your longer discussion for describing your organizational and people skills.

KEY TRAITS OF AN EFFECTIVE OVERSEAS EMPLOYEE

Many descriptions of good overseas candidates exist. The following profile was adapted from Frank Hawes' and Dan Kealey's 1979 study, *Canadians in Development,* produced for CIDA. It offers an employer's wish list for the successful overseas employee.

Interpersonal Skills

"Interpersonal skills" refers to the ability to communicate and get along well with others. The effective individual overseas is open to and interested in other people and their ideas. You are cooperative, friendly, respectful of others, and an attentive listener; in short, you are capable of building relationships through interpersonal trust. You will be aware of, and take into account, cultural factors overseas. You will strive to be calm in stressful conditions. And you will continue to communicate well with your family (if applicable) in this new, challenging environment.

Assertiveness and Sense of Identity

The successful overseas employee has a strong sense of self. You can express yourself confidently, with due regard for others. You are well-spoken and direct in your dealings with others. You will be unafraid of taking initiative, and risks when necessary.

Realistic Pre-departure Expectations

Prior to departure, you may have doubts and concerns about your overseas assignment, but overall you expect success in your assignment. You are realistic about constraints yet optimistic about rewards.

A LAST WORD

An open mind, a taste for adventure, an interest in other cultures, a strong self-concept, and a sense of humour—all are essential ingredients for the successful overseas worker. Of course, these traits complement the particular professional skills you bring to your assignment.

Landing that international job means you are about to experience drastic changes in your day-to-day life. Accept the changes, meet the challenges—and above all, enjoy yourself!

RESOURCES

Crosscultural Skills

These books are for anyone living overseas, including the accompanying spouse, the businessperson, the community development worker, and the government official. If you are new to the international job market, these books will help you understand the subtleties of crosscultural communication and allow you to build a knowledge base that would otherwise take years to acquire. Most of these books are very practical and non-academic.

While we may not like to admit it, Canadians have many cultural traits similar to Americans. Helpful books describing American cultural traits are listed after the section on the United States of America in Chapter 27, Jobs by Regions of the World. These books make very good reading for Canadians.

Also consult the Resources sections in the following chapters: for the more practical aspects of living overseas see Chapter 3, Living Overseas and Chapter 12, Crosscultural Travel; for material which is helpful to all, but focuses on crosscultural business skills, see Chapter 7, The Canadian Identity in the International Workplace; to improve your International IQ, see Chapter 13, Global Education Centres; and for country-specific advice on social and business customs see Chapter 27, Jobs by Regions of the World.

The Adventure of Working Abroad: Hero Tales from the Global Frontier 📖
1995, *Joyce Osland,* Jossey-Bass Publishers, 269 pages ➤ Intercultural and Community Development Resources (ICDR), P.O. Box 32108, Millwoods Station, Edmonton, Alberta T6K 4C2; $35; VISA, Amex; (800) 378-3199, fax (403) 462-1925, icdr@compusmart.ab.ca ▪ Through the personal stories of Americans working overseas, this book provides a pragmatic framework for understanding and mastering the predictable challenges of each stage in the expatriate journey. Visit the distributor's web site at www.compusmart.ab.ca/icdr. [ID:1795]

American Cultural Patterns: A Cross-Cultural Perspective 📖
1991, *Edward C. Stewart, Milton J. Bennett,* Intercultural Press, 208 pages ➤ Intercultural and Community Development Resources (ICDR), P.O. Box 32108, Millwoods Station, Edmonton, Alberta T6K 4C2; $25; VISA, Amex; (800) 378-3199, fax (403) 462-1925, icdr@compusmart.ab.ca ▪ Used extensively in international studies, and as a handbook in crosscultural training. Addresses practical crosscultural issues; distinguishes between "assumptions" and "values." Contrasts the analytical thinking and language of Americans with other cultures. Divides culture into patterns of activity, social relations, and perceptions of the world and oneself. Visit the distributor's web site at www.compusmart.ab.ca/icdr. [ID:1335]

The Art of Crossing Cultures 📖
1990, *Craig Storti,* Intercultural Press, 136 pages ➤ Intercultural and Community Development Resources (ICDR), P.O. Box 32108, Millwoods Station, Edmonton, Alberta T6K 4C2; $24; VISA, Amex; (800) 378-3199, fax (403) 462-1925, icdr@compusmart.ab.ca ▪ This bestseller offers a compelling analysis of cultural differences, using ideas from some of the world's greatest writers. Visit the distributor's web site at www.compusmart.ab.ca/icdr. [ID:1025]

Barnga 📖
1990, *Sivasailam Thiagarajan, Barbara Steinwachs,* Intercultural Press ➤ Intercultural and Community Development Resources (ICDR), P.O. Box 32108, Millwoods Station, Edmonton, Alberta T6K 4C2; $32; VISA, Amex; (800) 378-3199, fax (403) 462-1925, icdr@compusmart.ab.ca ▪ This game simulates the effects of cultural differences on human interaction. Requires a minimum of nine participants. For more information, visit www.compusmart.ab.ca/icdr, the distributor's web site. [ID:2399]

Centre for Intercultural Learning
Canadian Foreign Service Institute, 15 Bisson Street, Hull, Québec J8Y 5M2; (800) 852-9211, fax (819) 997-5409, monique.marion@bisson01.x400.gc.ca ▪ The Centre for Intercultural Learning assists Canadian professionals from NGOs, universities, private industry, and government to develop the crosscultural competencies essential for their success overseas. Services and products include pre-departure and project-related programs, on-arrival orientations, in-country programming, re-entry programs, country anthologies, and intercultural training. Their web site is under construction. [ID:2642]

Communication Between Cultures 📖
1991, *Larry A. Samovar, Richard E. Porter,* Wadsworth, 311 pages ➤ Intercultural and Community Development Resources (ICDR), P.O. Box 32108, Millwoods Station, Edmonton, Alberta T6K 4C2; $44; VISA, Amex; (800) 378-3199, fax (403) 462-1925, icdr@compusmart.ab.ca ▪ A book dealing with the basic elements of communication and culture. Provides concrete strategies for improving crosscultural communication. Visit distributor's web site at www.compusmart.ab.ca/icdr. [ID:1690]

The Cross-Cultural Adaptability Inventory 📖
1993, *Colleen Kelley, Judith Meyers,* NCS Assessments ➤ MHS Inc., 65 Overlea Blvd., Suite 210, Toronto, Ontario M4H 1P1; $49.99; VISA, MC; (800) 268-6011, fax (416) 424-1736 ▪ To help people preparing to go abroad, returning from abroad, or interacting with other cultures. May also be used as a tool to assess a person's cultural adaptability. Visit www.mhs.com, the distributor's web site. [ID:1359]

Cross-Cultural Dialogues 📖
1994, *Craig Storti,* Intercultural Press, 150 pages ➤ Intercultural and Community Development Resources (ICDR), P.O. Box 32108, Millwoods Station, Edmonton, Alberta T6K 4C2; $22; VISA,

Amex; (800) 378-3199, fax (403) 462-1925, icdr@compusmart.ab.ca ▪ A collection of brief conversations between the author, an American, and people from different cultures. Highlights the subtle differences that exist between cultures. Useful as an educational tool. Visit the distributor's web site at www.compusmart.ab.ca/icdr. [ID:1381]

Culture Clash: Managing in a Multicultural World 📖
1995, *H. Ned Seelye, Alan Seelye-James,* NTC Contemporary Publishing Co., 217 pages ➤ Intercultural and Community Development Resources (ICDR), P.O. Box 32108, Millwoods Station, Edmonton, Alberta T6K 4C2; $39; VISA, Amex; (800) 378-3199, fax (403) 462-1925, icdr@compusmart.ab.ca ▪ Analyzes 40 incidents of cultural misunderstanding that occurred in the US and 30 other countries, and illustrates how such misunderstandings can be remedied. Visit the distributor's web site at www.compusmart.ab.ca/icdr. [ID:2384]

Culture Shock! A Parent's Guide 📖
1993, *Robin Pascoe,* Times Books International, 269 pages ➤ Raincoast Books, 8680 Cambie Street, Vancouver, B.C. V6P 6M9; $17.50; VISA, MC; (800) 663-5714, fax (800) 565-3770 ▪ Based upon the author's own experience as well as consultations with child psychologists, this book deals with issues of parenting abroad. [ID:1309]

Culture Shock! Canada 📖
1993, *Pang Guek Cheng, Robert Barlas,* Times Books International ➤ Raincoast Books, 8680 Cambie Street, Vancouver, B.C. V6P 6M9; $17.50; VISA, MC; (800) 663-5714, fax (800) 565-3770 ▪ Unique guide to the culture, customs and etiquette of Canada. Excellent resource, required reading for those going abroad who may have to explain Canada and its customs. One in a series of similar guides to countries all over the world. [ID:1218]

Culture Shock! Series 📖
Occasional, *E. Webster,* Graphic Arts Center Publishing Co. ➤ Raincoast Books, 8680 Cambie Street, Vancouver, B.C. V6P 6M9; $17.50 each; VISA, MC; (800) 663-5714, fax (800) 565-3770 ▪ Guides to the customs and etiquette of various cultures. Titles for several countries in Asia, Europe, and North America. [ID:1382]

Culturgrams: The Nations Around Us 📖
1998, David M. Kennedy Center for International Studies, Two vols., 620 pages ➤ Kennedy Center Publications, Brigham Young University, 280 HRCB, Provo, UT 84602, USA; US$80; credit cards; (800) 528-6279, fax (801) 378-7075 ▪ Four-page summaries of the basic features of 164 cultures throughout the world. They cover customs, manners, lifestyles and other specialized information for those with interest but little time. Well worth the money! Free catalogue. Visit their web site, www.encarta.com. [ID:1085]

Developing Intercultural Awareness: A Cross-Cultural Training Handbook 📖
1994, *L. Robert Kohls, John M. Knight,* Intercultural Press, 158 pages ➤ Intercultural and Community Development Resources (ICDR), P.O. Box 32108, Millwoods Station, Edmonton, Alberta T6K 4C2; $24; VISA, Amex; (800) 378-3199, fax (403) 462-1925, icdr@compusmart.ab.ca ▪ This book features outline designs of one- and two-day cultural awareness workshops, and training materials that include simulation games, case studies, and exercises on values and icebreaking. Designed for intercultural educators and trainers, and useful to anyone wishing to expand his or her general training or teaching repertoire. Visit the distributor's web site at www.compusmart.ab.ca/icdr. [ID:1380]

Do's and Taboos Around the World 📖
1993, *Roger E. Axtell,* 208 pages ➤ John Wiley & Sons, 22 Worchester Drive, Rexdale, Ontario M9W 1L1; $14.95; credit cards; (800) 567-4797, fax (800) 565-6802 ▪ In a lively blend of tips, facts and cautionary tales, this fascinating guide tells travellers how to dress, exchange gifts, deal with unusual food, pronounce names and interpret body language in 96 countries. Visit the distributor's web site at www.wiley.com/products/worldwide/canada. [ID:1021]

Gestures: the Do's and Taboos of Body Language Around the World 📖
1991, *Roger E. Axtell,* John Wiley & Sons, 227 pages ➤ Intercultural and Community Development Resources (ICDR), P.O. Box 32108, Millwoods Station, Edmonton, Alberta T6K 4C2; $21; VISA, Amex; (800) 378-3199, fax (403) 462-1925, icdr@compusmart.ab.ca ▪ An interesting and useful examination of gestures and body language around the world. Cross-referenced by country, this listing covers all major geographic and cultural regions. Visit www.compusmart.ab.ca/icdr, the distributor's web site. [ID:1001]

Graveyard For Dreamers: One Woman's Odyssey in Africa 📖
1994, *Joan Baxter,* Potter's Field Press, 224 pages ➤ Nimbus Publishing, P.O. Box 9301, Stn. A, Halifax, Nova Scotia B3K 5N5; $16.95; cheque or VISA; (800) 646-2879, fax (800) 455-3652 ▪ A well-written, personal, and colourful account of living, traveling, and reporting on coups and customs in seven West African countries by a journalist from Nova Scotia. Particularly insightful are Ms. Baxter's sharing of her adaptation process and what it is like to be a white woman in rural and urban West Africa. [ID:2622]

Intercultural Communication: A Reader 📖
1993, *Larry A. Samovar, Richard E. Porter,* Wadsworth, 443 pages ➤ Intercultural and Community Development Resources (ICDR), P.O. Box 32108, Millwoods Station, Edmonton, Alberta T6K 4C2; $51; VISA, Amex; (800) 378-3199, fax (403) 462-1925, icdr@compusmart.ab.ca ▪ A good introduction to the intercultural field. Lays out the basic concepts, focusing on cultures and identity groups, cultural contexts, verbal and nonverbal interaction, the communication process, and ethical considerations. Now in its seventh edition! Visit www.compusmart.ab.ca/icdr, the distributor's web site. [ID:1332]

International Journal of Intercultural Relations 📖
Quarterly ➤ Customer Support Department, Elsevir Science Ltd., Regional Sales Office, P.O. Box 945, New York, NY 10159-0945, USA; US$100/year library fee or US$50/year; credit cards; (888) 437-4636, fax (212) 633-3680, usinfo@elsevir.com ▪ Scholarly quarterly, concerned with promoting intercultural interaction. Contains provocative articles on the theory and practice of crosscultural relations, along with book reviews. Visit the publisher's web site at www.elsevir.nl/. [ID:1248]

On Being Foreign: Culture Shock in Short Fiction, an International Anthology 📖
1986, *Tom Lewis, Robert Jungman,* Intercultural Press, 308 pages ➤ Intercultural and Community Development Resources (ICDR), P.O. Box 32108, Millwoods Station, Edmonton, Alberta T6K 4C2; $25; VISA, Amex; (800) 378-3199, fax (403) 462-1925, icdr@compusmart.ab.ca ▪ Twenty short stories selected from mainstream world literature lead you through the six stages of crosscultural adjustment. May be used as a reader in undergraduate programs and as a text in advanced ESL, world literature courses or intercultural studies. Will appeal to the recreational reader! Visit the distributor's website at www.compusmart.ab.ca/icdr. [ID:1385]

Survival Kit for Overseas Living 📖
1996, *L. Robert Kohls,* Intercultural Press, 181 pages ➤ Intercultural and Community Development Resources (ICDR), P.O. Box 32108, Millwoods Station, Edmonton, Alberta T6K 4C2; $17; VISA, Amex; (800) 378-3199, fax (403) 462-1925, icdr@compusmart.ab.ca ▪ An introduction to overseas living, with emphasis on the cultural problems likely to be encountered by first-time overseas workers. Although written for Americans, this is an invaluable practical guide for all. Visit the distributor's web site at www.compusmart.ab.ca/icdr. [ID:1177]

Transcultural Odysseys: The Evolving Global Consciousness 📖
1997, *Germaine W. Shames,* Intercultural Press, 176 pages ➤ Intercultural and Community Development Resources (ICDR), P.O. Box 32108, Millwoods Station, Edmonton, Alberta T6K 4C2; $27; VISA, Amex; (800) 378-3199, fax (403) 462-1925, icdr@compusmart.ab.ca ▪ Using the stories of individuals and families crossing cultures, Shames deals with such intercultural issues as culture shock and adjustment, identity, communication and language learning, wellness and safety, and re-entry. Visit the distributor's web site at www.compusmart.ab.ca/icdr. [ID:2446]

The Whole World Guide to Culture Learning 📖
1994, *J. Daniel Hess,* Intercultural Press, 280 pages ➤ Intercultural and Community Development Resources (ICDR), P.O. Box 32108, Millwoods Station, Edmonton, Alberta T6K 4C2; $32; VISA, Amex; (800) 378-3199, fax (403) 462-1925, icdr@compusmart.ab.ca ▪ A guide for sojourners learning about other cultures. Visit distributor's site at www.compusmart.ab.ca/icdr. [ID:1399]

Women on the Move: A Christian Perspective on Cross-Cultural Adaptation 📖
1989, *Gretchen Janssen,* Intercultural Press, 160 pages ➤ Intercultural and Community Development Resources (ICDR), P.O. Box 32108, Millwoods Station, Edmonton, Alberta T6K 4C2; $22; VISA, Amex; (800) 378-3199, fax (403) 462-1925, icdr@compusmart.ab.ca ▪ A guide for those with religious convictions who face the stress of a new environment. Suggests that one's own beliefs can help in successful adaptation. From the experiences of a woman who travelled with her husband from the US to Europe. Visit distributor's site at www.compusmart.ab.ca/icdr. [ID:1034]

The Yin and Tang of American Values 📖
1998, *Eun Y. Kim,* Kodansha International, 208 pages ➤ Fitzhenry and Whiteside Ltd., 195 Allstate Parkway, Markham, Ontario L3R 4T8; $31; VISA, MC; (800) 387-9776, fax (800) 260-9777, godwit@fitzhenry.ca ▪ A critique of American values from an Asian perspective. Insight into American behaviour and how Americans are perceived by the rest of the world, particularly Asia. Visit the distributor's web site at www.fitzhenry.ca. [ID:2429]

Chapter 2

Myths &
Realities

This chapter looks carefully at the cold realities of overseas life. If you find these points discouraging, do not despair. There are overwhelming benefits to working and living overseas as well. Moreover, most of us who have already worked overseas had no forewarning of these "realities," but we nonetheless endured, adapted to and enjoyed overseas life. If you are new to the international arena, just keep in the forefront of your mind your ability to adapt. Then you'll have a good chance of overcoming the pitfalls listed in this chapter.

ARE YOU READY FOR LIFE OVERSEAS?

Reality overseas may not always measure up to expectations. This is a fact of life that applies to any new endeavour.

The idea of a job in Geneva may sound inviting, but only if it's right for you. Be careful not to base your idea of working abroad on glamour. While living overseas may seem like a full-time touring opportunity, the realities of daily living and working must be taken into consideration before you even begin your job search, let alone sign that contract and get on the plane!

Thus, before taking the plunge and perhaps making a costly mistake in your career and personal life, here are some questions you should answer before deciding to look for work overseas:

- Are you prepared for major adjustments in your home and work life?
- Are you prepared to be separated from your family, loved ones, and friends?
- Are you prepared to live in another country where you may not understand the language?
- Are you prepared to give up all the services and facilities you take for granted here in Canada—medical, legal, financial?

- Are you willing to try new foods? Perhaps do without television? Your daily newspaper? Even a telephone?
- Are you prepared to live with new security considerations, possible political instability, crime, corruption, and major class differences?
- Are you prepared to live in a different climate with perhaps hot, humid temperatures or torrential rainfall?
- Are you prepared for living in a culture very different from your own, with customs and attitudes you have never encountered before?
- Are you prepared to be patient in a way you probably never had to be here at home?
- Are you prepared to frequently misunderstand and be misunderstood?
- Are you prepared to put in storage or divest yourself of most of your belongings for a period of one year or more?
- Are you prepared to accept alternate schooling arrangements for your children?
- Are you capable of dealing with the tremendous contrast of poverty and wealth existing side by side in the South?
- Are you capable of adapting to different situations, even unpleasant ones?

Answering carefully the above questions should give you some idea of your suitability for an overseas career.

MYTHS ABOUT LIVING OVERSEAS

There are many misconceptions about living overseas. Often, if we talk to friends or acquaintances with overseas experience, they only mention the good (or bad) things about their lives. Or, on the other hand, we sometimes only hear what we *want* to hear. Consider some of the following points which most international workers will corroborate.

"International living is exciting and exotic."

It can be, but it can also be boring. After eating a few local dishes and attending a few cultural events, the novelty of a new culture can wear off. Many expatriates complain about the lack of recreation, movies, television, radio and, especially, long-time friends and family. Part of being prepared for overseas work is being creative with your leisure time and learning to appreciate the subtleties of your host country's culture, not just its overt cultural manifestations of song, dance and food.

"Living overseas will allow me a life of leisure."

It is true that many expatriates have domestic help, but life overseas can be hectic. It takes a lot of work to supervise a cook, maid, gardener and guard. Everything from shopping to cooking to cleaning takes more time because of the lack of modern conveniences and our lack of familiarity with the culture. Inadequate public transportation may make travel more difficult, and, thus, time-consuming. Social events may be more numerous. And if you are working, you will probably also be working harder and longer.

"International work involves a lot of socializing with very interesting people from around the world."

Canadians are considered laid-back and informal by international standards. The flip side of this is Canadians find that most other nationalities are a bit formal, protocol plays a larger role in social life, and class consciousness is usually more important. Another aspect of making friends overseas is that they may not fit your age or work bracket, as there is generally a smaller circle of people to choose from and it may be difficult to build close friendships with local people because of cultural differences. Your friends may well be other Canadians or other expatriates. Since there will be fewer people to befriend, friendships will likely be broader than in Canada with less regard for age or work background. This may differ from your expectations.

"International work involves a lot of travel with time to visit and explore new cultures."

Rarely do international jobs require lots of travel once you arrive at your posting. Even if your job does require travel, you usually have little time to explore during business travel. The most rewarding, however, tends to be the regional travel you do during vacation time. That is, if home sickness doesn't force you back home for a whirlwind tour to visit your relatives.

"Living overseas is dangerous and involves substantial health risks."

Foreigners (especially Canadians) are very, very rarely the targets of political terrorism. The greatest threat in the South is a car accident. Theft may be prevalent, but is not often accompanied by violence. Learning to take precautions and refusing to be socially paralyzed by the threat of theft is often required for successful adaptation in developing countries. As for most illness, using common sense hygiene overcomes most health risks.

"My employer will solve all my housing problems and guarantee my safety."

Your employer can solve some of your problems, but don't expect him or her to solve all of them. You have to make do with your own initiatives and sometimes just learn to live with your predicaments.

"The work I find frustrating in Canada will be more interesting overseas."

Whatever the view from the office window, work is work. The frustrations of an international working environment are usually even greater than you find in Canada.

"I can escape my problems by moving overseas."

Are you having marriage, emotional or drug problems? Attempting to start anew by heading for an overseas assignment usually does not work. For example, it is generally known that strong marriages become stronger overseas and weak marriages often fall apart. There is easier access to drugs and more occasions to drink in a foreign community than at home. Personal problems tend to worsen when you have no familiar support systems to rely on. The stress of life in a new culture will put strains on even the best relationships and the hardiest of personalities.

"International development work is very rewarding and I will make a difference in the country I work in."

If you are going overseas full of zeal to impart your knowledge to improve the lives of the poor, you will be disappointed. The process of economic development is a slow one. It can take decades before you see changes in the lives of whole communities. Moreover, with the eyes of a foreigner, you may be hard put to recognize important changes in a culture which is not your own. The practice of giving assistance to countries in the South is an imprecise science and development projects can and do fail!

MYTHS ABOUT WORKING OVERSEAS

There are many misconceptions about how to find international work. The international field is a whole new ball game compared to the domestic job market. The misconceptions which abound are partly due to the mystique surrounding the whole international scene. The following may clear up some of these.

"International jobs pay extremely well and I will be able to save much of my salary."

Few people go overseas to become rich. Even if the salary is higher than at home (and often it isn't), the hidden costs of moving, travelling, living overseas and re-entry to Canada all add up. The only people who seem to manage to save money overseas are single people working in hardship posts where there is no place for them to spend their money. No matter how good the salary sounds, you can usually expect to spend more than you planned. You'll spend more on travel during holiday periods. You'll probably not recoup the full cost of furnishings, cars, etc., when it comes time to leave your overseas posting. And there are many hidden costs involved in setting up a household when you return to Canada. Be prepared to come back richer in experience but not necessarily better off financially.

"I need international work experience to find an overseas job."

Not necessarily, but it certainly helps. With or without experience, however, what you really need is an International IQ (a concept discussed throughout this book). Luck is, of course, a factor. Persistence is vital.

"There are very few international jobs. Only the most qualified professionals get them."

An estimated 50,000 to 100,000 Canadians are working overseas. Most international recruiters will tell you how difficult it is to find qualified individuals who are willing to give up their personal lives in Canada. International recruiters are always looking for people who have good technical skills as well as an International IQ. With this combination, the opportunities abound, not just for university-educated people, but for tradespeople as well.

"All I need to do is to show employers that I am willing to sacrifice myself to help the poor of the world."

Sorry, international work is no longer a place for do-gooders, as it may have been in the 1960s. If you want to contribute to improving the world, develop a skill and build your International IQ.

"I need to study something 'international' to find international work."

International studies in no way guarantee a start in an international career. You have to develop yourself and experience a lot more before an employer will consider you. International studies are invaluable, however, when they are used to complement an already-existing skill and experience base.

"It is easier to find an international job while living or travelling overseas."

Not usually. You probably won't find a salaried position that actually pays a good wage in this way. Remember that most countries place severe restrictions on employment of non-nationals and local pay scales tend to be far less than what you would be paid if you signed an international contract. You may be able to find work while travelling overseas if you are looking for grassroots volunteer experience and you are willing to ignore local employment laws. An innovative person with a good skill base can often find volunteer overseas employment on the spot.

"I need connections to break into the international job market."

No, what you need is a networking and job search plan. Then, you must stick to it tenaciously and work hard at finding an international job. Of course, connections help!

"Large multinational corporations are good places to find overseas work."

Rarely, and if a job is available, corporations usually transfer recruits from within their firm.

"The job search process is the same for a Canadian job as it is for an overseas job."

Not at all. You have to be able to uncover the jobs and describe your skills in terms of international work. Read this book to see how each step of the process is different.

A LAST WORD

You should look at both the positive and the negative aspects of living overseas. There is no question that the possibilities for a glamorous, exciting, exotic experience are very real. You will be living in a new cultural environment, possibly learning to speak a new language; you'll be eating foods you never knew existed; you'll have greater opportunities to travel than you ever had before; you may have domestic help to free you from the more tedious daily tasks. You will likely be more appreciated, and enjoy greater recognition than you did at home.

But on the other hand, you'll be isolated from family in Canada. You'll have to deal with new, sometimes stressful, situations on a day-to-day basis. Everything will be different, from the food available in the stores to the absence of the daily newspaper. You may experience a lack of privacy. You will likely encounter some health hazards unknown in Canada.

Two things are of paramount importance in your self-assessment before you begin to look for overseas employment. First, you should have a solid grasp of who you are. Second, give a lot of consideration to your ability to adapt. Think about living abroad carefully.

Chapter 3

Living Overseas

People choose to live overseas for a variety of reasons. Some go to improve the quality of their lives, others go to leave the rat race behind. Whatever the reason, you've just accepted an overseas posting: your contract is signed, your passport updated and you've done some research on your host country. In short, you're counting the days till you leave Canada—until you're face to face with the challenges of your new environment. But do you really know how you'll react to the unfamiliarity of another language, the different work ethics of your new colleagues, the frequent shortages of electricity, water and telephone service? You can only hazard a guess. Everyone reacts differently to new experiences.

This chapter outlines a few common scenarios and draws upon the cross-cultural experiences of others. If you have never lived overseas, this chapter will help you understand the intercultural experience being sought by international employers. It must be stressed however, that conditions vary from continent to continent, village to village. Remember, in taking an overseas posting, you are not only adjusting to a new country, but uprooting yourself from your own culture and identity.

For those of you who don't have the benefit of a formal briefing before departure, or are just reading this chapter to build up your International IQ, we strongly advise you to increase your knowledge by consulting the numerous resources suggested at the end of this chapter.

RESEARCHING YOUR HOST COUNTRY

Briefings

Briefings are invaluable to newcomers and it's usually assumed that a country briefing will be provided by your new employer. However, these are sometimes

29

crossed off an agenda because of time constraints. Staff veterans often overlook the importance of psychological preparation of new recruits.

A briefing can be drawn from in-house expertise or from alternative sources, and usually summarizes the socio-economic conditions of a country, its politics, history, living conditions, culture and customs. Returning Canadians are sometimes invited to discuss and share their views of a particular region.

For those of you whose overseas positions are partially or fully funded by the CANADIAN INTERNATIONAL DEVELOPMENT AGENCY (CIDA), you are eligible to attend a briefing session on your country of posting. For information contact:

Centre for Intercultural Learning
Canadian Foreign Service Institute
15 Bisson Street, Hull, Québec   J8Y 5M2
Tel: (800) 852-9211 or (819) 997-5681; Fax: (819) 997-5409

Alternatively, NGOs, such as WORLD UNIVERSITY SERVICES OF CANADA (WUSC), CANADIAN CROSSROADS INTERNATIONAL and CUSO, may be able to include you in their briefing sessions. The nearest university or college may have reference material on the country you will be posted to. (Excellent country information can be found in the Resource section under "Country Information on the Internet" in Chapter 21, The Internet Job Search.)

If you're going as a family, attempt to have everyone attend. As a single person, you may invite a family member or friend to help discover the country that will be your new home. A Crossroads volunteer wrote: "I took my mother and we both found it an educational experience. She began to view Zimbabwe as a civilized and more familiar place than a dot on the map." Having the company of another person also helps lessen the feeling of being the odd one out in a room full of families and couples. Feel free to ask questions, no matter how silly they may seem. That's the purpose of a briefing.

Brief Yourself

During the period between being offered the position and departure, consume as much information about your new country as possible. Good reference sources are libraries, video suppliers, development organizations. The CANADIAN BROADCASTING CORPORATION may be able to provide transcripts of radio programs about Country "X", or the NATIONAL FILM BOARD may have videos you can borrow or purchase for a nominal fee. Try to preview aspects of your new country through restaurant dining, craft shops, or the ethnic music section of a record store.

Meet a Host National

Make a few friends, or at least acquaintances, from the country where you'll be working. The foreign students' association and the registrar's office at a university or college is a good starting point. Failing that, call that country's embassy for more information. Many Canadian agencies will also arrange crosscultural postings. For example, CANADIAN CROSSROADS INTERNATIONAL and CANADA WORLD YOUTH both have programs of selecting representatives of certain countries for short-term visits to Canada. Ethnic communities are another source, as expatriates of the country you're going to can provide information you won't find in fact sheets and tourist guides. (Excellent suggestions on building such contacts using the Internet can be found in Chapter 21, The Internet Job Search.)

Keep in Touch

Involve your family and friends as much as possible. Remember, an adventure for you could be a sorrowful parting for them. No matter how hackneyed it sounds, remind them that they will see you again on home leaves and at the end of your contract. And encourage them to visit.

There are other ways to keep in touch while you are overseas. The Internet is making instantaneous communication possible from even the most remote locations. (See Chapter 21, The Internet Job Search.) Did you know mail could be forwarded temporarily to a Canadian consulate, or an American Express office in the capital of the country to which you are posted? And certainly, most countries now have excellent telephone linkages with Canada allowing you to call or fax.

CULTURE SHOCK

You've probably heard the term "culture shock," but you might not think it will happen to you. In fact, everyone goes through a painful process of adapting to a new culture, and your reaction can range from mild irritation to extreme trauma. Canadian Jim Shannon had a good dose of it when he arrived in Zimbabwe. The following is an excerpt from an article by him in the Ottawa Citizen:

"I was teaching and living in a rural school in Zimbabwe and it was one of the most interesting and stimulating times of my life. Learning to live without a car, telephone, television or movies was a broadening experience. Some would call it cultural deprivation. I call it the opportunity to savour the delights of a new culture and at the same time, stand back and take a good look at 'things Canadian.'

"To say that I came to prefer the lifestyle of an expatriate teacher in the African bush would be, perhaps, simplistic. After all, being without power for 24 hours after you've done your weekly grocery shopping trip—by the slowest bus imaginable to the nearest town 60 kilometres away—is no joke. And having to negotiate several days in advance to hitch a ride to Harare on the back of a school lorry can be frustrating...

"There's also the isolation. And the lack of privacy. And the intense heat. And the hopelessly overcrowded and under-equipped classrooms... And the underlying racial tension.

"I cannot say I adapted right away. But I'm glad I adjusted to the culture shock I experienced when I got off the plane one stiflingly hot night, hungry, tired and angry because the Kenyan airline on which I was travelling was 10 hours late. The long bumpy ride in the back of a truck through the pitch black night to the school in the bush did not help...

"Yet I found life there to be more 'hands on,' more real and simpler than what I had left behind in Canada. I came to appreciate the warmth of the local people, to learn to 'make do.' Evenings also became social events... talking well into the night..."

Look at culture shock as a rite of passage. When you enter a new culture, the cues and clues you normally rely on are gone. It's like having the rug pulled out from under you! In India, you'll have to get used to the fact that nodding your head doesn't necessarily mean "yes." In Muslim countries you must never receive anything in your left hand. As a woman, you can't drive or travel alone in some Middle Eastern countries. You may walk into a shop and not recognize a single product on the shelves, let alone the lettering on the packages. The lack of privacy will take getting used to. You'll be crushed and pushed in markets and buses, your children will resent having their hair stroked for the umpteenth time, and you may be asked highly personal questions. All in all, you may become so depressed you'll want to return home!

Culture Shock or Culture Fatigue—What is it?

Overseas employees must learn to deal with the stress brought on by changes in:

* home
* friends
* job
* cultural environment

Culture shock is a term used to describe the stress brought on by all these changes. It can involve any of the following areas of life: manners, customs, beliefs, ceremonies and rituals, social institutions, myths and legends, values, morals, ideals, accepted ways of behaviour, ideas and thought patterns, laws, language, and arts and artifacts. The differences threaten your own belief systems and habits. The term "culture shock" has a negative connotation for some, and for this reason experts believe "culture fatigue" is a more apt term to describe a person's response to the process of cultural adjustment. Others refer to the reaction to sudden immersion in a radically different environment as "cultural disorientation" or "change shock." What you're really doing is taking apart your own frame of reference in order to understand another culture. Because your own frame of reference has become inappropriate, naturally you feel confused, disoriented, frustrated and anxious. And unlike other health disorders, you can't get an inoculation for this one!

Like every expatriate worker, we're sure you'll devise imaginative ways to cope. Culture shock is actually a positive, necessary part of the cultural adjustment process.

STAGES OF CULTURE FATIGUE

Sociologists, anthropologists and psychologists have divided the culture shock or fatigue phenomenon into stages. They say the intensity of culture fatigue varies; it's cumulative and sometimes difficult to understand.

Experts speak of four stages: the honeymoon stage, anxiety stage, rejection or regression stage, and the adjustment stage.

The Honeymoon Stage

You're finally overseas after much preparation and anticipation. You just can't wait to see, feel, taste, experience *everything!* People seem friendly (not pushy), laid back (not inefficient), they enjoy the simple things. This is the world through the honeymooners' eyes. You have great expectations and a positive outlook. This period may last from a week or two to a month, but inevitably the let-down comes.

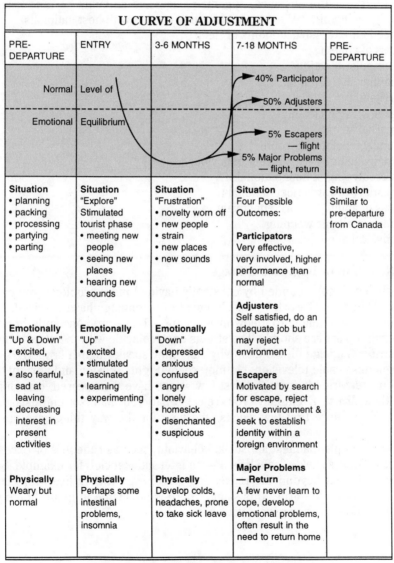

U CURVE OF ADJUSTMENT				
PRE-DEPARTURE	ENTRY	3-6 MONTHS	7-18 MONTHS	PRE-DEPARTURE
Normal Emotional	Level of Equilibrium		40% Participator 50% Adjusters 5% Escapers — flight 5% Major Problems — flight, return	
Situation • planning • packing • processing • partying • parting	**Situation** "Explore" Stimulated tourist phase • meeting new people • seeing new places • hearing new sounds	**Situation** "Frustration" • novelty worn off • new people • strain • new places • new sounds	**Situation** Four Possible Outcomes: **Participators** Very effective, very involved, higher performance than normal **Adjusters** Self satisfied, do an adequate job but may reject environment	**Situation** Similar to pre-departure from Canada
Emotionally "Up & Down" • excited, enthused • also fearful, sad at leaving • decreasing interest in present activities	**Emotionally** "Up" • excited • stimulated • fascinated • learning • experimenting	**Emotionally** "Down" • depressed • anxious • confused • angry • lonely • homesick • disenchanted • suspicious	**Escapers** Motivated by search for escape, reject home environment & seek to establish identity within a foreign environment	
Physically Weary but normal	**Physically** Perhaps some intestinal problems, insomnia	**Physically** Develop colds, headaches, prone to take sick leave	**Major Problems — Return** A few never learn to cope, develop emotional problems, often result in the need to return home	

Originally conceived by Clyde Sargeant, with subsequent revision by Daniel Kealey.

The Anxiety Stage

The need to build a new social structure to replace the one you've left behind takes precedence. You react to small difficulties as if they were major catastrophes. You may seek out compatriots to reinforce your "we-they" attitude.

At this crisis stage you may suffer varying degrees of some of the following symptoms:

* homesickness
* boredom
* withdrawal (for instance, spending excessive amounts of time reading; only seeing other Westerners; avoiding contact with host nationals)
* need for excessive amounts of sleep
* loss of appetite
* compulsive eating
* compulsive drinking
* irritability
* exaggerated cleanliness
* marital stress
* family tension and conflict
* chauvinistic or patronizing behaviour
* stereotyping of host nationals
* hostility towards host nationals
* loss of ability to work effectively
* uncontrollable weeping
* physical ailments

The Rejection or Regression Stage

Your anxiety is compounded by constantly having to face problems you cannot define. Things don't work—your shipment of belongings hasn't arrived. Local help has proven unable to follow instructions. Things are constantly breaking down and repairs are shoddy. The streets don't coincide with the maps. You are still having language difficulties (why can't they speak English properly?). The children miss cable television. Nothing seems right. Tension and anxiety build up. Your new friends from the first few weeks have disappeared, carrying on with their lives. Eventually you reject what you had so enthusiastically embraced in those first few weeks, and long for the way things are done at home.

Some people manifest antisocial behaviour, such as rudeness or excessive drinking. Others seek a "safe haven"—an international club for example. Some people never get beyond the regression stage, even if they live overseas for years. Others leave during this stage. There is no shame in going home with the satisfaction that you gave it your best.

The Adjustment Stage

Gradually, you recover. You begin to feel less isolated in your surroundings. Gone is the feeling of hopelessness. You're able to greet someone in the local language, hail a taxi, haggle with the merchants. Before they were cheating you, now they're merely trying to earn a living.

You experience a measure of biculturalism, of acceptance of the differences between two societies. No one expects you to totally assimilate or to approve of harmful practices such as bribery or the exploitation of women. Instead, you find a middle ground you're comfortable with.

How Long Does Culture Fatigue Last?

It has been observed that there are actually two low points, which stretch out according to the length of your assignment. This also depends on your resilience. But once your first low is over, remember that you'll have another, and it may be more severe. Keep in mind however, that the ultimate usually happens—you reach glorious stage four, and adjust!

How to Deal with Culture Fatigue

Experts say half the battle with culture fatigue is knowing what's happening to you. When you find yourself being judgemental, simply try to accept the differences in values and behaviours in your host culture. Here are a few pointers for coping with culture shock:

- **Participation:** Instead of sitting around your apartment or house reflecting on your sorry state, go out and socialize with the locals. Try to learn all about your new country.
- **Tolerance:** Undoubtedly, many things will appear strange to you in the beginning. So stop over-examining the local people's behaviour and habits. You'll drive yourself bonkers.
- **Language:** It always helps to understand, if not speak, the language. Who cares if your grammar and pronunciation are muddled? Your efforts will be appreciated by the local people and you'll feel less like an outsider. (See Chapter 5, Learning a Foreign Language.)
- **Find a sympathetic host national:** Other expatriates are helpful, but they're usually in the same boat as you are. A host national can provide a good sounding board. And what could be better for your overall experience than having a friend who knows your new country inside out?
- **Gather information:** Never lose your curiosity. It will give you insight into why people behave as they do. An interest in the history, geography, politics, religion and cultural norms will help you appreciate and adjust to your new environment.
- **Take a break:** Treat yourself to a day off, bake an apple pie, take a long hot bath. Do something just for yourself, something that is typically Canadian. Find a hobby that allows you to escape or take regular time off to indulge in your own culture.
- **Maintain contact with family and friends back home:** Writing home about your experiences and problems can help you deal with them. Be

cautious however, about alarming your relatives about situations they cannot understand or act on. Some people have learned to wrestle with culture shock by keeping a diary of their thoughts and feelings.

• **Be imaginative in finding solutions:** One returning overseas employee recalls West African village life:

"When we moved to Ghana, we discovered that the front door was only closed at night before going to bed. To do otherwise was inhospitable to visitors and the whole community. We finally got around this problem by advising our neighbours that we occasionally had to shut our door to pray. This turned out to be an acceptable excuse when we needed some down time."

Some of the above research on culture shock was excerpted with permission from the excellent book by Robert L. Kohls, *Survival Kit for Overseas Living*, 1984, Intercultural Press. For a detailed annotation see the Resources section at the end of this chapter.

Useful Skills for Daily Life Overseas

Some people adapt to new cultures better than others. Crosscultural experts agree that certain skills play a key role in cultural integration. Besides the skills for coping with culture shock—tolerance, open-mindedness, empathy, flexibility, adaptability, curiosity and self-reliance—there are some other useful skills that will help you survive daily life overseas:

• **Sense of humour:** The ability to laugh, particularly at yourself, is your best weapon against despair.

• **Low goal or task orientation:** North Americans abroad, or their superiors back home, often set tasks that are unrealistic. An unattainable goal can contribute to failure and frustration. From studies of Americans living overseas, results show that those who are less goal-oriented or task-driven are more likely to be relaxed and effective in their work, and derive more enjoyment from their experiences.

• **Coping with failure:** If failure is unfamiliar to you, be aware that it is almost certain you will fail at something overseas. Your dinner party may be a disaster because the food in your refrigerator has gone bad due to a power outage. Your dinner guests may have to dine on tinned sardines by candlelight. Try to look on the bright side and adapt to the fact that this will likely happen again.

SPECIAL CONCERNS FOR FAMILIES

Your family should be involved in your decision to move overseas. If it isn't a joint decision, you can expect trouble! Life overseas can add stress to family life and contribute to divorce and the breakdown of the family unit. On the other hand, members of a family can become more reliant on each other for companionship and strength.

Male Employee and Spouse

The dissatisfaction of a non-working spouse is cited as the main reason for failure and early returns from overseas assignments. Think about it! The working husband has the structure of a job and the camaraderie of colleagues to rely on. Children have the routine of school. Chances are the female, non-working spouse has given up her career, friends, family and social activities for the stay-at-home life overseas. Her interactions may be largely confined to dealing with domestic help or locals catering to other household needs. She may have to face her frustrations alone while her working husband sits in his office commiserating with colleagues in English.

From past experiences, here are some of the difficulties faced by non-working wives:

* **Lack of Preparation:** Many wives arrive not knowing what to expect. Reactions may vary from surprise and excitement to bewilderment and anxiety.

* **Culture Fatigue:** Levels of frustration can be quite high in certain conditions—dealing with domestic help who do not speak English, undependable power and water supply, a telephone that never works, and trying to understand the local goods and services available.

* **Language Problems:** The employed partner may work in English and have little need for competency in the local language, but the stay-at-home spouse will certainly need language lessons. Unfortunately, many organizations offer language training only to employees, with spouses left to their own devices.

* **Loneliness:** It's common to feel loneliness and depression after you've left family and friends behind. Someone once said, "When you've lived abroad and suffered deep loneliness, you become your own best friend." Sometimes loneliness is compounded by the isolation of being the stay-at-home spouse.

* **Loss of Identity:** One of the hardest things about moving abroad as the dependent wife of a working husband is the loss of identity and individuality. You are viewed merely as a wife, not someone with her own interests and talents.

* **Boredom:** Although it may sound like bliss to have hired help doing much of the housework and childcare, having too much time on your hands can be a real problem, particularly after a hectic life in Canada of juggling job, housework and family. Sometimes the boredom is compounded by local restrictions which prevent foreign dependants from competing with locals in the job market.

* **The Absentee Husband—Lack of Support:** The man may work long hours, thereby increasing the woman's sense of isolation. A vicious circle can develop where the working spouse feels guilty over his non-working partner's emotional state, and spends even less time at home.

Female Employee and Spouse

This kind of couple is no longer a rarity in international employment situations. The problem for non-working male spouses is that they cannot resolve their loneliness by joining a women's social group or informal network. Furthermore, other working male acquaintances will be inaccessible during the day. As a stay-at-home male spouse, you may feel resentment and may even object to your wife's elevated professional status. Domestic responsibilities such as grocery shopping and childcare can lead to unfavourable reactions and misunderstanding on the part of local men and women, and possibly even your own compatriots. On the other hand, you may find yourself inundated with requests to repair things, or act as a chauffeur or gofer.

A sampling of data from Zimbabwe shows a fairly high number of male spouses accompanying wives employed by the DEPARTMENT OF FOREIGN AFFAIRS AND INTERNATIONAL TRADE. Six men, who had left positions ranging from senior administrative and professional posts to small business owners, had to adjust to the role of male stay-at-homes. They reported that it took three to six months to adjust to their new roles. Some had high expectations of doing work similar to what they had left behind, but were thwarted by local employment regulations. Others found moderate satisfaction in doing odd jobs. Remarked one male spouse, "I now realize I was crazy to think I could land here and pick up from where I'd left off back home." They all found dealing with household staff and repair people to be frustrating.

The Single Person Overseas

Singles face many of the same problems as married couples. The loneliness, however, can be more painful. You may already feel that the world is biased in favour of couples and families. In traditional societies, where marriage and the number of children you have determine social status, you may be made to feel incomplete if you are a childless woman "of a certain age," meaning over 21! It is a good idea to bring photos of your parents, siblings, cousins just to prove that you "belong" to a family. Expect your photos to be pored over for family resemblance. A West African triumphantly remarked to one Canadian about a photograph of a family member, "you look like two tomatoes!", his variation of the "peas in the pod" expression.

Sentimental belongings help maintain your sense of identity and continuity. You should bring along reading and writing material, sports equipment or a musical instrument to help you pass the time and remind you of home.

Your social life will be what you make it. Flexibility and working at socializing are important. As a single you will be freer to mix and travel.

Lesbians, Gays and Bisexuals

Many expatriate gays thrive in the overseas environment, creating their own social support network to make it easier to adapt. Homosexuals can almost always find a distinct gay subculture overseas. Initially, however, you may have no support structure for being open with friends, and meeting others in the Lesbian, Gay and Bisexual (LGB) community. It's no surprise that for the women and men who have gone through the process of coming out, working overseas can seem like a return to the closet. You will have to gauge whether to come out to your fellow workers.

Homosexuals around the globe are invisible in mainstream society. You may not be able to locate bars, community centres or gay and lesbian associations at your destination, particularly if you are in a rural area. But it is fair to say that in almost every city in the world there is a specific place to meet other gays and lesbians. As a foreigner, you may be relatively free of social customs that inhibit local gays. But exercise caution, because in most countries the law is not on your side. Canada is one of only a handful of countries beginning to prohibit discrimination on the basis of sexual orientation, whereas open and often violent discrimination is still the norm globally.

You can prepare yourself for the prevalent social attitudes wherever you're going. Before departure, talk to returned cooperants, dig through international gay guides, make contact with international LGB organizations. Many NGOs actively support lesbian, gay and bisexual rights, as well as human rights in general. A few of the larger NGOs, such as CUSO and CANADIAN CROSSROADS INTERNATIONAL have their own internal gay support groups.

Government departments such as CIDA, FOREIGN AFFAIRS, and CITIZENSHIP AND IMMIGRATION CANADA have quietly adopted practices that accommodate the family life of lesbian and gay staff working and travelling overseas. Being open about your sexual orientation is no longer deemed a national security risk, nor is it a major impediment to promotion. It is increasingly accepted, at least as a "private" lifestyle, when living overseas.

Women Overseas

A separate chapter discusses the issues facing women (see Chapter 6, Women Working & Living Overseas). If you are the spouse of a working partner, you may want to consider part-time work. (For more information see Chapter 30, Freelancing Abroad.)

Children Abroad

As a parent it is hard to predict how your child will react to living in a strange country with different customs and language. Some children have a delayed reaction to separation from family and friends, while others are too young to appreciate the geographic move or to articulate their feelings. Parents have found looking at photographs and writing letters to friends and family members left behind can be therapeutic for their children.

When contemplating moving overseas, the single most important issue facing families with children between the ages of 6 and 16 is education. Local school systems abroad are often so different from the Canadian education system that re-integration can be very difficult. The most common solution for expatriate families living abroad is to enrol students into the worldwide English-language network of international schools. This system uses the Canadian and US model of education, and allows children to move from country to country (including back to Canada) without leaving the regular grade system. The French government also promotes a similar worldwide system.

If no adequate schooling exists, some Canadians families place their children in boarding schools, either in Canada or in capital cities abroad. But this is less common for Canadians than, say, British families. In some cases, if the housebound spouse feels able, he or she may tutor the children using widely-available correspondence course material. If your overseas employer has more than eight school-age children in a remote area, it may become feasible to hire a full-time Canadian teacher.

As mentioned previously, a spouse's or family's happiness will affect the success of the overseas employee in his or her assignment. So it follows that children require special consideration. They should be part of the whole decision making process. School-aged children must participate in discussions about the kind of school they will attend, or the form their education will take. Young children can be assigned such tasks as choosing toys and mementoes to pack and selecting clothes. Older children and teenagers should take part in selecting information from libraries, etc., and arranging travel routes or holiday destinations.

As stated, it's difficult to predict a child's reaction to moving. Factors such as personality, stage of development, and previous experiences with moving will have an impact. But research has shown that children of anxious parents have a harder time adjusting; therefore, try to downplay your own anxiety. There are many positive aspects to family life abroad. Apart from a tighter emotional bond, children learn tolerance and respect for other cultures.

Mindful of the fact that children must return to North American living, experts suggest children maintain their share of household duties. So don't assign all chores to the domestic help, should you have that option.

Too Much Free Time

Chances are there will be many occasions when you have too much free time on your hands. How do you and your family pass the time in a country without cable television or video rental outlets? Here are some tips that other expatriates have found useful.

- **Shape up:** Develop an exercise routine alone or with others.
- **Exercise the mind or learn a new skill:** Pursue your interests through a local college or by correspondence, or find a tutor. The US INFORMATION SERVICE and the BRITISH COUNCIL provide good English library services in most foreign cites.
- **Quality family time:** Finally, you have the chance to spend more time with the family.
- **Volunteer:** The Canadian mission, local NGOs, or other expatriates may provide a list of ideas of useful volunteer work you can do.
- **Travel:** Tour your host country and neighbouring ones to learn about their history, culture and language. There's nothing like the thrill of discovering new terrain.

THE WESTERNER OVERSEAS

The Expatriate Ghetto

There is a hazard of becoming too attached to the expatriate ghetto in your overseas posting. It has been said that sharing complaints is a way of forming a community, and nowhere is this more true than when expatriates get together. They can quickly become a community of complainers. Somehow, being together triggers the impulse to criticize "these people," or "this place" and encourages the us-against-them response. If you find yourself falling into this pattern, perhaps you should review why you are really there.

To rectify this problem, or avoid it completely, make a conscious decision to choose friends who are inspired by the challenges and intrigue of the local culture. Avoid expatriates who are always complaining. The choice is yours.

The Person in the Mirror...

You may discover aspects of yourself that aren't admirable. One researcher noted that Americans, on the whole, are offended by the practice of bribery and the habit of spitting in some countries. On the other hand, certain aspects of our behaviour, such as holding hands in public, direct eye contact and our straightforward way of "getting down to business" can be offensive to foreigners. As a Canadian abroad, think of yourself as an ambassador for your country. Try to be accepting and open-minded. Think twice before indulging in North American habits which could be distasteful to others. There's nothing worse than leaving a lasting negative impression.

Lifestyle and Worklife

It's difficult to divide your lifestyle and your worklife overseas. Here in Canada, we find it convenient to separate our professional life from our personal life. We often look upon international travel as an incentive, reward, or vacation in relation to our jobs. International jobs, however, generate lifestyles in which one's job and personal life merge into a unique form of worklife. A teacher posted at a rural boarding school in Kenya, for example, can hardly leave his or her job behind in the evening or on the weekend; a doctor working in a clinic in Thailand will always be identified as "the doctor", even while out for an evening stroll. Let's face it, in many overseas environments, you are indeed a "visible minority." You'll be identified in terms of your work to a much greater extent than in Canada—and your spouse and children will be similarly identified. This fact has both positive and negative ramifications. It's a matter of how you adjust to your new environment.

As an international worker, you will likely have more responsibility than you would have in a similar job back home. This can be a real challenge, offering you the chance to use your creativity along with your interpersonal skills. There will probably be fewer rules and regulations, less head office red tape to deal with.

On the other hand, you may encounter barriers to getting things done that you never dreamed of. Many Southern countries have incredibly inefficient, bureaucratic systems rife with corruption. Different customs, currency fluctuations, broken promises—all will tax even the easiest-going overseas worker.

Still, most international workers are motivated by a certain degree of restlessness, the desire for something different, a need to change a stale work environment, a commitment to a cause or an idea. They are career risk-takers, concerned more with new challenges than with how much money they will make or how many conventional creature comforts they can acquire. They are usually seeking a particular lifestyle rather than a particular job or career. However, a careful, professional self-assessment will enhance your chances of having a satisfying overseas experience, and will serve you well in developing long-term career strategies.

SECURITY AND POLITICAL CONCERNS

Before leaving Canada, you should explore the issue of crime in your new country, so you'll be prepared and not unduly alarmed. There are three categories of crime that affect foreigners:

- Household Intruders
- Street Incidents
- Political Violence

This topic should be covered in your briefing session; if it isn't, then you should raise it. Foreigners are vulnerable to crime because foreign nationality is often equated with wealth. But situations vary from country to country. Apart from registering at the nearest Canadian Consulate or High Commission, here are some other precautions you can take.

Household Intruders

Normal precautions should be taken, as well as additional ones relevant to the country you are in. This again varies with an urban or rural location. In the South, many homes are surrounded by high walls and have ornate protective grilling on doors and windows. Homeowners may also employ a guard or have watchdogs. Although regulations regarding weapon ownership may be lenient, it is unwise to possess a gun. Instead, favour burglar bars, alarms, or other electronic devices for your home and vehicle. Don't forget to insure your belongings when you arrive. You must understand that you are now a potential target for theft. Because of the lack of foreign currency for importing Western goods such as televisions, blank cassettes, even clothing and food, your possessions are desirable commodities. However, don't let paranoia cripple you to the point that you view every local face as a potential robber. As in Canada, the criminal element is only a small sector of society. After taking the necessary precautions, it is futile to expend further energy on the situation.

Street Crime

This form of crime is on the increase worldwide. Advice here is simple—don't wander alone in areas you are unfamiliar with. Don't provide temptation by displaying excessive jewelry, cameras or large handbags. If driving alone, ensure that all passenger doors are locked, including the trunk. In the event that you are robbed on the street, never tackle the robber single-handedly or put up strenuous resistance. He or she may be armed. You're better off to shout "thief" and try to attract a crowd to intercept on your behalf.

It goes without saying that you should never ship irreplaceable or costly items. Theft, minor and major, is commonplace in poor countries.

I can recall the case of one Canadian missionary who was repeatedly robbed by his house staff in Zaire. When confronted with their crime, they asserted that white people were like hens. Their possessions were like a hen's eggs: if you took them away, they simply replaced them! However, the thefts stopped after the priest explained the fallacy of their thinking and threatened to use part of their workers' salaries to replace missing items.

Political Violence

Political violence is an issue for many, though it is difficult to predict where or how it will strike you. If you believe you could become a target, your concern should be raised with the consular officer at the Canadian mission. Other precautions you could adopt should the situation arise:

* Vary your route and schedule to and from work.
* Travel with car windows closed; use air conditioning if necessary.
* Avoid demonstrations and street scenes and observe such rules as curfews. Keep abreast of news and possible evacuations.
* If there are demonstrations, either accompany your children to school or better still, stay home.

In countries where access to foreign currency or luxury goods are restricted, you may find yourself befriended by opportunists or wheeler-dealers pursuing imported items. Let common sense prevail. Helping someone is fine, but where foreign currency is restricted, never get involved in any money dealings! Often there are stiff penalties for both supplier and receiver.

Most of you will enjoy trouble-free assignments as far as these sorts of problems are concerned, but, hackneyed as it may sound, "forewarned is forearmed!"

PERSONAL MATTERS

Driving in your New Country

Don't forget to pick up an international driver's licence from the CANADIAN AUTOMOBILE ASSOCIATION (CAA) before leaving Canada. At some point your host country may require you to obtain a local licence. Make such inquiries at the time of your arrival. Be sure to learn the local rules of the road. Apart from possibly having to adjust to driving on the other side of the road, you will have to decipher and memorize foreign road signs to determine whether an ox or your car has the right of way, etc. As a pedestrian, observe street rules and keep well away from traffic by walking on sidewalks or as far to the side of the road as possible, particularly in rural areas. Don't assume drivers will go out of their way to avoid you! Cyclists should take similar precautions and bring such protective gear as helmets, bike pumps, lights, reflectors, and repair kits.

Car Accidents

Traffic accidents are a major cause of death in the South due to faulty vehicles, bad driving habits, and poor roads. Drunken driving is another hazard, as regulations are often less stringent than in Canada.

Health Concerns

Always carry adequate medical insurance. Costs for treatment can be astronomical, even in the South. Make sure your insurance covers medical emergency evacuation. We know of one case where the cost of air evacuation from an African country to Belgium was $74,000! When faced with a life-threatening emergency, you don't want the added worry of such expenses.

Several months before departure, contact HEALTH CANADA for specific information about your country of destination. Vaccinations and other precautions should be taken against tropical diseases. A mitigating factor in many illnesses is stress, which lowers your body's resistance. Treat every infection and illness seriously. Don't let an illness run too long in the hopes that it will go away.

The issue of AIDS cannot be ignored, particularly in the South, where medical standards are often inadequate or nonexistent. Forget about high risk groups: everyone is at risk. Sexual contact aside, what if you were involved in a car accident and needed blood? Without being an alarmist, you should adopt the defensive measure of packing an AIDS kit, which most organizations and companies will provide.

Finances, Currency Exchange, Budgeting

Try to settle your financial matters before leaving Canada. Appoint a Power of Attorney to look after any financial matters arising during your absence. Although you may end up in a cash-only society, you should have at least one credit card with you, kept in an imaginative and safe place.

Should you obtain nonresident status with REVENUE CANADA, you may wish to consider depositing your money in banks in such places as the Cayman Islands, the Channel Islands, Bermuda, etc., to avoid having a non-resident tax administered against your savings. The chartered Canadian banks are well-versed in these matters.

Where the black market is active, the host government normally demands that you keep an accurate record of all financial transactions during your stay. As stated earlier, avoid all dealing!

Your household expenses will probably be far less than in Canada. However, you may incur other expenses, such as customs clearing fees, money for your staff's unexpected needs, etc. The cost of fuel is also extremely high in some countries. You should keep an emergency fund handy in case of hospitalization or evacuation.

Domestics

A domestic worker is a perk for many Canadians. Apart from providing employment to the local labour market, it may seem like a perfect step up. But having someone in your home seven or eight hours a day, or living on your property, can be a loss of privacy which takes getting used to. Many expatriates experience frustration in the training and monitoring of household help.

Check with local sources to determine the wage scales, work hours, expected duties, bonuses, holidays, etc. Some countries have unions for domestic workers and may provide information, references and monitor complaints for both parties.

Food

Be both experimental and cautious. Keep in mind that your digestive system isn't accustomed to the new foods. And don't forget to pack your favourite foodstuffs, no matter how mundane. You've no idea how good macaroni and cheese can taste when you have a craving for "Canadian" food or you're simply feeling homesick.

A LAST WORD

Not all of us are cut out for overseas living. If you find you're unable to cope with the situation and have to come home, look upon it as a learning experience, not a failure. After all, there are many different ways to make a contribution to society.

But chances are you'll thrive in your new environment. An exciting experience awaits you!

RESOURCES

Books can't solve all your relocation problems, but they can warn you of situations you might encounter. There are Resources sections for Health Overseas, Children & Families Overseas, Educating Your Children, Moving Abroad, and Taxes & Investment. The listed books on these topics have been chosen for their practical advice.

Also consult the Resources sections in the following chapters for books which explain about the skills required for adapting and succeeding overseas: for books on culture shock, adaptation, and crosscultural communications see the section on Crosscultural Skills in Chapter 1, The Effective Overseas Employee; for practical travel advice see Chapter 12, Crosscultural Travel; to improve your International IQ see this section in Chapter 13, Global Education Centres; for country-specific advice on social and business customs see Chapter 27, Jobs by Regions of the World.

Health Overseas

Canadian living conditions do not prepare you for the health conditions of many developing countries. Fortunately, most health problems in tropical areas can be avoided if you are well-equipped and have the required knowledge. Having one or two of these books is a must for long-term travel or when moving to a developing country. Don't forget to contact your local travel health clinic several months prior to your departure and keep in mind that health risks vary greatly from country to country.

For information on locations and services related to international health, see the CANADIAN SOCIETY FOR INTERNATIONAL HEALTH in Chapter 35, Nongovernmental Organizations. If you are interested in working in international health see the Resources section for Health Careers in Chapter 22, Resources for the International Job Search.

Don't Drink the Water: The Complete
Traveller's Guide to Staying Healthy in Warm Climates 📖
1994, Canadian Public Health Association & Canadian Society for International Health, 110 pages ➤ Canadian Public Health Association, Suite 400, 1565 Carling Ave., Ottawa, Ontario K1Z 8R1; $14.95; VISA, MC; (613) 725-3769, fax (613) 725-9826, hrc/cds@cpha.ca ▪ Describes common health problems and provides advice on staying healthy in warm climates. Includes details on immunizations, malaria risk, acclimatization and traveller's diarrhea. Explains how travellers to hot climates can avoid becoming ill by taking simple precautions. Excellent. Visit the publisher's web site at www.cpha.ca. [ID:1107]

Get Ready! Hints for a Healthy Short-Term Assignment Overseas 📖
1995, 45 pages ➤ CUSO, Suite 400, 2255 Carling Ave., Ottawa, Ontario K2B 1A6; $5; (613) 829-7445, fax (613) 829-7996 ▪ This information booklet is a great resource when travelling overseas for short periods. Provides a list of public health centres located in major centres which specialize in travel and tropical diseases. Outlines basic preventive measures to take in preparation for, during, and following an overseas assignment. Brief and to the point. Excellent. [ID:1363]

Going Abroad: The Bathroom Survival Guide 📖
1997, *Eva Newman* ➤ Marlor Press, 4304 Brigadoon Drive, St. Paul, MN 55126, USA; US$12.95; (800) 669-4908, fax (612) 490-1182, marlor@minnet ▪ A charming and humourous look at how to handle the world's varied conveniences! [ID:2679]

Health Advice for Living Overseas 📖
1994, 130 pages ➤ CUSO, Suite 400, 2255 Carling Ave., Ottawa, Ontario K2B 1A6; $15; (613) 829-7445, fax (613) 829-7996 ▪ Written for Canadians planning to live or work in a developing country for six months or more. Provides complete up-to-date health information for preparing to, and living, overseas. Available in French under the title, *Vivre en santé à l'étranger.* [ID:1699]

Health Information for Canadian Travellers 📖
Updated regularly ➤ Canadian Society for International Health, 1 Nicholas Street, Suite 1105, Ottawa, Ontario K1N 7B7; free; (613) 241-5785, fax (613) 241-3845, csih@fox.nstn.ca ▪ Pamphlet provides health advice for travellers to warm climates and developing countries. Provides a comprehensive listing of Canadian health centres geared to Canadian travellers. Useful. Visit the distributor's web site at www.hwc.ca:8080/csih/. [ID:1504]

A Healthy Stay in Canada 📖
1994, 40 pages ➤ CUSO, Suite 400, 2255 Carling Ave., Ottawa, Ontario K2B 1A6; $5; (613) 829-7445, fax (613) 829-7996 ▪ Provides health information and advice for international students and professionals visiting Canada for six months or less. The focus is on loneliness, adaptation, stress, emergency health care, winter health issues and integrating new ideas and learning upon your return to the home country. Available in French under the title, *Un sejour en santé.* [ID:1702]

International Travel and Health 📖
Annual, World Health Organization, 106 pages ➤ Canadian Public Health Association, Suite 400, 1565 Carling Ave., Ottawa, Ontario K1Z 8R1; $21.42; VISA, MC; (613) 725-3769, fax (613) 725-9826, hrc/cds@cpha.ca ▪ Travel and health guide geared to health professionals: physicians, administrators, and others who regularly give health advice to travellers. Summarizes vaccination requirements of individual countries and main areas where malaria and other parasitic transmissions occur. Not recommended for laypersons. Visit www.cpha.ca, the distributor's web site. [ID:1563]

The International Travel Health Guide 📖
Annual, *Stuart Rose* ➤ Travel Medicine Inc., Suite 312, 351 Pleasant Street, Northampton, MA 01060, USA; US$25.90; credit cards; (413) 584-0381, fax (413) 584-6656 ▪ Written by a well-travelled physician. Contains everything you need to know, from tips on food and drink safety to AIDS information. Up-to-date maps of chloroquine-resistant malaria zones, yellow fever endemic zones, Africa's meningitis belt, etc. [ID:1254]

Staying Healthy While Living in Canada 📖
1994, 102 pages ➤ CUSO, Suite 400, 2255 Carling Ave., Ottawa, Ontario K2B 1A6; $15; (613) 829-7445, fax (613) 829-7996 ▪ Provides health information and advice for students coming to Canada from developing countries to study or work for six months or more. Addresses such issues as accessing the Canadian health care system, depression, stress, winter health issues and Canadian culture as it affects physical and mental well-being. Available in French under the title, *Visa-santé pour le Canada*. [ID:1701]

Traveler's Medical Alert Series (Mexico and China) 📖
1991, *William W. Forgey* ➤ ICS Books Inc., 1370 East 86th Place, Merrillville, IN 46410, USA; $9.95 each; VISA, MC; (219) 769-0585, fax (800) 336-8334 ▪ Designed to help travellers protect themselves from illness and disease while travelling. Endemic diseases are described in detail. List of travel advisories issued by the US Department of State. Visit the publisher's web site at www.icsbooks.com. [ID:1293]

Travelers' Self-Care Manual: A Self-Help Guide
to Emergency Medical Treatment for the Traveler 📖
1990, *William W. Forgey* ➤ ICS Books Inc., 1370 East 86th Place, Merrillville, IN 46410, USA; $6.99; VISA, MC; (219) 769-0585, fax (800) 336-8334 ▪ A first aid manual specifically designed for international travellers. Diagnose, treat or know when to seek help when faced with a variety of medical problems. Visit the publisher's web site at www.icsbooks.com. [ID:1285]

Where There is No Doctor: A Village Health Care Handbook: Revised Edition 📖
1992, *David Werner, Carol Thuman, Jane Maxwell,* Hesperian Foundation, 632 pages ➤ Intercultural and Community Development Resources (ICDR), P.O. Box 32108, Millwoods Station, Edmonton, Alberta T6K 4C2; $25; VISA, Amex; (800) 378-3199, fax (403) 462-1925, icdr@compusmart.ab.ca ▪ An absolute must for anyone working or travelling to a semi-isolated or isolated location, or for anyone connected with village-level healthcare in developing countries. Detailed, well-written, easy to use. Covers every type of ailment imaginable. Purchase as gift to leave behind when travelling. Available in other languages. Visit the distributor's web site at www.compusmart.ab.ca/icdr. [ID:1159]

Children & Families Overseas

These books will help you help your children adapt to your new home overseas. Remember that, generally, children will have the anxieties of their parents, so if you are up-beat and enjoy your move to a new culture, so will they. Getting them involved in the logistics of your move will make them feel they have an important role in the changes you will all face. This list of resources also includes books on adoption and crosscultural marriage.

The Art of Coming Home 📖
1997, *Craig Storti,* Intercultural Press, 216 pages ➤ Intercultural and Community Development Resources (ICDR), P.O. Box 32108, Millwoods Station, Edmonton, Alberta T6K 4C2; $26; VISA, Amex; (800) 378-3199, fax (403) 462-1925, icdr@compusmart.ab.ca ▪ Most people returning from an overseas sojourn find re-entry more difficult than adjustment to a foreign culture. This book provides information, analyses and suggestions to transform the re-entry experience from a struggle to an art. The re-entry of spouses, younger children, and teenagers is examined. Special attention is given to high school exchange students, Peace Corps volunteers, military personnel and their families, and missionaries and their children. Visit the distributor's web site at www.compusmart.ab.ca/icdr. [ID:2375]

A Canadian Guide to International Adoptions ⌨

1992, *John Bowen* ➤ Self-Counsel Press, 1481 Charlotte Road, North Vancouver, B.C. V7J 1H1; $11.95; VISA, MC; (604) 986-3366, fax (604) 986-3947, sales@self-counsel.com ▪ A guide for couples preparing to adopt a child from abroad. All aspects of international adoption are explored and explained. The book gives practical advice on how to deal with the paperwork, expenses, and difficulties that may be encountered. Visit distributor's site at www.self-counsel.com. [ID:1624]

Culture Shock! A Parent's Guide ⌨

1993, *Robin Pascoe,* Times Books International, 269 pages ➤ Raincoast Books, 8680 Cambie Street, Vancouver, B.C. V6P 6M9; $17.50; VISA, MC; (800) 663-5714, fax (800) 565-3770 ▪ Based upon the authors' own experience as well as consultations with child psychologists, this book deals with issues of parenting abroad. [ID:1309]

Culture Shock!: Successful Living Abroad, A Wife's Guide ⌨

1992, *Robin Pascoe,* Graphic Arts Center Publishing Co. ➤ Raincoast Books, 8680 Cambie Street, Vancouver, B.C. V6P 6M9; $17.50; VISA, MC; (800) 663-5714, fax (800) 565-3770 ▪ Written by a Canadian, the book is easy to read, and provides useful advice for the wife going overseas for the first time, especially if her husband is with Foreign Affairs or an international agency. Chapters on maids, entertaining and home leave may be off-putting, but after you've lived in her shoes, they may seem pertinent. Has a useful chapter on getting a job or freelancing overseas. [ID:1307]

Intercultural Marriage: Promises and Pitfalls ⌨

1997, *Dugan Romano,* Intercultural Press, 166 pages ➤ Intercultural and Community Development Resources (ICDR), P.O. Box 32108, Millwoods Station, Edmonton, Alberta T6K 4C2; $22; VISA, Amex; (800) 378-3199, fax (403) 462-1925, icdr@compusmart.ab.ca ▪ Examines the motives of those who marry across cultures. Identifies 18 cultural "trouble spots" such as food, finances, sex, politics, male-female roles, class, religion, raising children. Also discusses factors of success and issues in considering an intercultural marriage. Visit www.compusmart.ab.ca/icdr, the distributor's web site. [ID:1321]

A Journey of One's Own: Uncommon Advice for the Independent Woman Traveler ⌨

1996, *Thalia Zepatos,* 349 pages ➤ The Eighth Mountain Press, 624 SE 29th Ave., Portland, OR 97214, USA; US$16.95; cheques only; (503) 233-3936, fax (503) 233-0774 ▪ Expert advice is combined with tales of crosscultural encounters. A wide array of women travellers provide advice to help you with matters such as sexual harassment, staying healthy, avoiding theft, managing a long trip, and travelling safely - solo, with a partner, or with a child. [ID:1787]

Moving Your Family Overseas ⌨

1992, *Rosalind Kalb, Penelope Welch,* Intercultural Press, 135 pages ➤ Intercultural and Community Development Resources (ICDR), P.O. Box 32108, Millwoods Station, Edmonton, Alberta T6K 4C2; $22; VISA, Amex; (800) 378-3199, fax (403) 462-1925, icdr@compusmart.ab.ca ▪ Designed for the entire family. Brings the insights of a psychologist to the challenge of moving abroad. Topics include informing the children, making a look-see trip, keeping the family functioning when one spouse travels, and reverse culture shock upon returning home. Visit the distributor's web site at www.compusmart.ab.ca/icdr. [ID:1320]

Travel with Children ⌨

1996, *Maureen Wheeler,* Lonely Planet ➤ Raincoast Books, 8680 Cambie Street, Vancouver, B.C. V6P 6M9; $16.95; VISA, MC; (800) 663-5714, fax (800) 565-3770 ▪ The only guide to Third World travel with kids. An excellent resource. By seasoned travellers, who cover both logistics and cultural interchange. [ID:1284]

Where in the World Are You Going? ⌨

1996, *Judith M. Blohm,* 64 pages ➤ Intercultural and Community Development Resources (ICDR), P.O. Box 32108, Millwoods Station, Edmonton, Alberta T6K 4C2; $14; VISA, Amex; (800) 378-3199, fax (403) 462-1925, icdr@compusmart.ab.ca ▪ An entertaining activity book for children, ages five to ten, which will make any overseas move more manageable. Encourages readers to express their excitement, fears, questions and hopes about the move, and leads them through activities which will help them say goodbye to their old home and embrace the new one. Visit the distributor's web site at www.compusmart.ab.ca/icdr. [ID:2392]

Women's Guide to Overseas Living 📖
1992, *Nancy J. Piet-Pelon, Barbara Hornby,* Intercultural Press, 210 pages ➤ Intercultural and Community Development Resources (ICDR), P.O. Box 32108, Millwoods Station, Edmonton, Alberta T6K 4C2; $23; VISA, Amex; (800) 378-3199, fax (403) 462-1925, icdr@compusmart.ab.ca ■ Examines issues critical to women (and their families) who relocate abroad. Sound advice on how to cope effectively, culture shock, stress and loneliness, managing households, children, health. Visit the distributor's web site at www.compusmart.ab.ca/icdr. [ID:1322]

Educating Your Children

Need to find a school? These books will help you get started.

Canadian University Distance Education Directory 📖
Annual, Canadian Association for University Continuing Education, 154 pages ➤ AUCC Publications Office, Suite 600, 350 Albert Street, Ottawa, Ontario K1R 1B1; $26; (613) 563-1236, fax (613) 563-9745 ■ Bilingual listing of universities offering distance education courses in Canada. Useful for those wishing to study with a Canadian university while abroad. [ID:1366]

Fact Sheets 📖 🖥
Annual, US Department of State ➤ Office of Overseas Schools (A/OS), Overseas Schools Advisory Council, SA-29, Room 245, US Department of State, Washington, DC 20522-2902, USA; free; (703) 875-7800, fax (703) 875-7979, overseas.schools@dos.us_state.gov ■ Excellent descriptions of American-sponsored elementary and secondary schools overseas, including enrolment, facilities, and finances. Useful for educational job seekers or prospective users of the schools. Fact sheets distributed by country. Visit the web site www.state.gov/www/about_state/schools/ and print them for free. [ID:1225]

The ISS Directory of Overseas Schools 📖
1997, International Schools Service, 533 pages ➤ Impact Publications, 9104 North Manassas Drive, Manassas Park, VA 20111-2366, USA; US$34.95; credit cards; (703) 361-7300, fax (703) 335-9486 ■ The guide educators, corporate officials, expatriate families, and teachers seeking employment abroad rely on for accurate and up-to-date information on American-style elementary and secondary schools overseas. Visit distributor's site at www.impactpublications.com. [ID:1167]

Overseas American-Sponsored Elementary and
Secondary Schools Assisted by the US Department of State 📖 🖥
Annual, US Department of State ➤ Office of Overseas Schools (A/OS), Overseas Schools Advisory Council, SA-29, Room 245, US Department of State, Washington, DC 20522-2902, USA; free; (703) 875-7800, fax (703) 875-7979, overseas.schools@dos.us_state.gov ■ Each entry gives the name and title of the school's chief administrator, address, grade levels taught and enrolment figures. Also available in its entirety on the web at www.state.gov/www/about_state/schools/. [ID:1224]

Schools Abroad of Interest to Americans 📖
1998, 590 pages ➤ Porter Sargent Publishers Inc., Suite 1400, 11 Beacon Street, Boston, MA 02108, USA; US$48; cheques; (617) 523-1670, fax (617) 523-1021 ■ List of 800 elementary and secondary schools in 130 countries, of interest to young Americans and others seeking pre-college programs abroad. [ID:1233]

Moving Abroad

These books will help you with the logistics, as well as researching the cost, of living overseas.

Canada Year Book 📖 🖥
1997, Statistics Canada, 517 pages ➤ Renouf Books, 129 Algoma Rd., Ottawa, Ontario K1B 2W8; $54.95, CD-ROM $74.95; credit cards; (613) 745-2665, fax (613) 745-7660 ■ This book is published every two years by Statistics Canada and serves as a vital reference resource. It provides an up-to-

date picture of the social, economic, and cultural life of Canada. It's a great book to bring as a gift or as a handy reference for all the questions your overseas friends will ask you when you travel overseas. Visit the publisher's web site at www.renoufbooks.com. [ID:2775]

Craighead's International Business Travel and Relocation Guide to 78 Countries: 1996-97 📖
Annual, 4,699 pages, 3 vols. ➤ Gale Research Inc., 835 Penobscot Bldg., 645 Griswold Street, Detroit, MI 48226-4094, USA; US$575; credit cards; (800) 877-4253 ext. 1330, fax (800) 414-5043; Available in large libraries ■ Indispensable guide for anyone who needs information on the business practices, economies, customs, communication, tours, attractions and highlights of 78 countries worldwide. Provides details of local customs, arrival procedures, money matters, health services, and sources of additional information for those relocating overseas. Chapters on individual countries, extensive background information for personnel officers and employees going abroad. Covers recruiting guidelines for overseas personnel and information sources. [ID:1144]

Escape from America 💻
www.escapeartist.com/core/core2.shtml ■ If you are itching to leave the US, then this site is for you. This site stems from the book version, which provides resources for people wanting to move to "safe havens" such as New Zealand, Australia, Belize, and Costa Rica. There are also lots of other international links on this site of interests to expatriates. [ID:2774]

FGI's Global Relocation Services
FGI's Global Relocation Services, 10 Commerce Valley Dr. East, Suite 200, Thornhill, Ontario L3T 7N7; (905) 886-2137, fax (905) 886-4337, csimmond@fgiworld.com ■ This is a Canadian-owned relocation services company. FGI provides support services for Canadian expatriates and their families in over 100 countries worldwide. They can help you with immigration and Visa work, predeparture selection, crosscultural training, and repatriation services. [ID:2778]

Guide to Living Abroad 📖
Annual, *Louise M. Guido,* 150 pages ➤ Living Abroad Publishing, 199 Nassau Street, Princeton, NJ 08540, USA; US$30; Amex; (609) 924-9302, fax (609) 924-7844 ■ Published in 10 volumes, each containing practical general information of interest to expatriates, such as health, buying a house, immigration matters, personal security, and education. The guides also have a section on regional travel. Visit the distributor's web site at www.livingabroad.com. [ID:1432]

How to Emigrate 📖
1994, *Roger Jones,* 176 pages ➤ How To Books Ltd., 3 Newtec Place, Magdalen Road, Oxford, OX4 1RE, UK; £9.99; credit cards; (44) (1752) 202-301, fax (44) (1865) 202-331 ■ Essential information and advice on weighing your prospects, choosing the right location, coping with immigration, the actual move, housing, employment and settling in successfully to your new life overseas. [ID:1677]

International Retail Price Comparisons (Post Indexes) 📖
Monthly ➤ Indexes Section, Prices Division, Statistics Canada, 13th Floor, Jean Talon Bldg., Ottawa, Ontario K1A OT6; free; (613) 951-0121, fax (613) 951-2848 ■ Post indexes are an excellent way of calculating the approximate cost of living overseas. Compiled monthly for hundreds of cities abroad, the indexes are designed for Canadian civil servants and military personnel (since the federal government compensates employees for housing and fuel costs, these are not included in the indexes). Price comparisons are given for such family expenditures as food consumed in the house, meals in restaurants, household maintenance and supplies, domestic help, clothing, transportation, health and personal care, reading and recreation. Although the cost of a subscription to these indexes is high –$275/year for monthly updates on 1-10 cities, you can obtain free information over the phone for one city. [ID:2555]

Moving Abroad 📖
1992, *Virginia McKay* ➤ VLM Enterprises, P.O. Box 7236, Wilmington, DE 19803, USA; US$14.95; cheque or money order; (302) 984-1144 ■ A comprehensive and practical guide to moving abroad and living anywhere in the world. Deals with every aspect of departure preparations and adapting to life abroad. While the orientation is American, much of the information is general and practical and would be useful to anyone moving overseas. [ID:1267]

Vehicle Exports 💻
www.mapsupport.com ▪ Mission and Project Support is a Montréal firm helping expatriates with world-wide vehicle exports. Their site also includes information about motoring overseas. [ID:2719]

Working Abroad: The Daily Telegraph Guide to Living and Working Overseas 📖
1995, *Godfrey Golzen*, Kogan Page Ltd. ➤ Gage Distribution Company, 164 Commander Blvd., Agincourt, Ontario M1S 3C7; $23.95; credit cards; (416) 293-8464, fax (416) 293-0846 ▪ Oriented to UK nationals, this book provides surveys of working and living conditions in over 40 countries. It offers many practical ideas for what to do after you have secured employment abroad, such as renting your home, educating your children, etc. Useful information on various countries includes local economies, taxes, personal finances, living and working conditions. [ID:1199]

Taxes & Investment

Financial planning is always on everyone's mind when moving overseas. It can be difficult to find experts in these areas, especially when it comes to tax planning. Always ask for references and do some research before engaging in a contract with a financial advisor.

Canadians Resident Abroad 📖
1995, *Garry R. Duncan, Elizabeth Peck,* 128 pages ➤ Carswell Publishing, One Corporate Plaza, 2075 Kennedy Road, Scarborough, Ontario M1T 3V4; $24.95; credit cards; (800) 387-5164, fax (416) 298-5094, cra@inforamp.net ▪ A comprehensive sourcebook of information on the tax consequences of leaving Canada, taxation as a non-resident and returning home. Visit www.cdnsresabroad.com. [ID:2474]

Crossborder Tax and Transactions 💻
www.crossborder.com ▪ An informative site for people doing business or investing internationally, specifically between Canada and the US. The site is maintained by an international tax lawyer and provides updated Canadian and US trade laws. [ID:2757]

The Expatriate Group Inc.
The Expatriate Group Inc., Suite 280, 926 - 6th Ave. S.W., Calgary, Alberta T2P 0N7; (403) 232-8561, fax (403) 294-1222, expatriate@expat.ca ▪ The Expatriate Group Inc. offers services to expatriate Canadians on tax and financial planning. Quarterly updates, financial planning modules, and newsletters are mailed or e-mailed to over 800 clients in 50 different countries. The Expatriate Group's areas of expertise include: non-residency issues, taxation advice and tax return preparation, tax-haven banking, currency exchange, lifestyle orientation, unbiased financial planning and investments, offshore trusts, wills and estate planning, insurance advice, returning to Canada, and snowbird advice for living in the US and Mexico. Staff are bilingual in English and French. Visit their web site www.expat.ca. [ID:2765]

UPDATE 📖
3-4/year, *Elizabeth Peck* ➤ Canadians Resident Abroad, Inc., 305 Lakeshore Road E., Oakville, Ontario L6J 1J3; free; (905) 842-0080, fax (905) 842-9814 ▪ Newsletter on tax and financial advice for Canadians living overseas. Topical question and answer section. Sponsored as a marketing vehicle for the Canadian International Group of Mutual Funds. Excellent source for hard-to-find financial information. Visit the distributor's web site at www.cdnsresabroad.com. [ID:1573]

Chapter 4

What Canadians Overseas Say

In writing this book we talked to, or surveyed, dozens of men and women with overseas experience. The following is a sampling of what they told us about their experiences. (CUSO also generously provided cooperant quotes.) While there's no way of foretelling what you will encounter abroad, we hope you'll find their comments helpful, interesting and entertaining. The quotes are grouped under the following subheadings: Benefits of Overseas Life, Working in a Foreign Country, Preparation and Culture Shock, Spouse or Family and Social Relations, Day-to-Day Living Overseas.

BENEFITS OF OVERSEAS LIFE

An overseas job provides variety and job satisfaction that you don't get in a large corporation at home in Canada, according to a Canadian accountant who volunteered for CUSO in Zimbabwe.

"In a big organization, an accountant is usually stuck in one department, but here I'm dealing with the whole works. There is a lot of satisfaction in teaching accounting skills here because the people take so much interest in learning."

Unexpected and unique experiences make your stay overseas worthwhile, says one CANADIAN CROSSROADS INTERNATIONAL volunteer in Africa.

"In haste to get back to the camp before dark, the driver decided to take a shortcut down a steep ravine. The result—we got stuck in a gully and broke a window. We spent the night in the middle of the park, cold and hungry, with lions and elephants circling our van. To top it all off, it was my birthday. It was exciting and fun. A good way to turn 30."

It can be easier overseas to move among social classes. A CUSO cooperant in Africa reflects on the wide cross-section of people she met.

"Hitching from Accra to New Tafo several months ago, I found myself the sole passenger with the Secretary to the Ambassador of Liberia. For the next two hours I was chauffeured in style—enjoying fine music, air-conditioning and political small talk as we discussed the much-debated election of Samuel Doe. I alighted, much to my chagrin, at the Bunso junction—about 20 kilometres from New Tafo—only to be picked up a few minutes later by a rattling, windowless Datsun, already well-packed with four passengers and all their gear. For the next two hours (we suffered mechanical problems en route) I bounced along, assuring the driver I could survive the heat, while trying to convince the young man next to me that my husband was in Canada looking after our children."

It can take time and patience to make friends abroad. One Canadian private sector consultant—a woman—has the following suggestions for getting to know local colleagues.

"Mingle with local staff. Participate in staff weddings and funerals, when invited and when appropriate. Also try the odd Canadian custom. I had a shower for a young bride-to-be and it was a success and enjoyable to do. The stories of wives at that afternoon shower were fascinating and revealed a lot about local customary marriage and how donors' ideas of 'women-in-development' will be years in realizing."

Many of the people you meet working overseas will leave a lasting impression, says one UN employee stationed in Africa.

"Since starting on my JPO (Junior Professional Officer) contract, I can truly say that I have been fortunate to work with some of the most impressive people I have ever met—long-time UN career diplomats who have made a lifetime impression on me, even when I worked with them for a short period of time... You will be surprised how much you can learn by watching these people work for a few days—listening attentively to words chosen to communicate ideas, observing ways decisions are made, and seeing dedication and humility combine to make great ideas work."

Doing what you enjoy, and getting paid for it is an added treat. One CANADIAN INTERNATIONAL DEVELOPMENT AGENCY (CIDA) project officer couldn't believe her good fortune when an overseas position combined both.

"I experience the lows of the snail's pace decision-making and endless paperwork. Nevertheless, there are equal numbers of high times when I can scarcely believe I am actually receiving a good salary for experience, insights and thrills, when I would gladly pay for the pleasure."

Canadians normally learn as much about themselves as they do about the other culture while living overseas, explains a volunteer in Ghana with CANADIAN CROSSROADS INTERNATIONAL.

"One of the big surprises of being overseas was figuring out for the first time what it meant to be Canadian. It was only when I confronted the local as well

as other expatriate cultures that I began to assess what it means to be Canadian.

"I think Canadians like to spend time alone. This was something I had not realized and it was something most Africans could not understand.

"Also, Canadians generally forget to be respectful of people in authority or older people. In Canada we believe every new person we meet must 'earn' our respect, while in most cultures respect for certain groups is automatic."

A period overseas provides many people with the chance to develop skills they may not have realized they possessed had they remained at home, says one returned Crossroads volunteer.

"One of the things I realized after my overseas volunteer experience was that I am much more independent and willing to take on new tasks. Overseas life taught me to be creative and much more open to looking at new solutions to challenges. I am more innovative, tolerant, patient and appreciative of the little things in life."

Living abroad helps you appreciate life in Canada and recognize real priorities for a productive and contented life, says one Crossroads volunteer, after returning from a short work-term in Africa.

"After having learned to eat the same foods twice a day, every day, for four months, I realized that people don't require 10 different items for each meal. In Canada, we have such a warped notion about what constitutes adequate nutrition. We do not need a wide array of 30,000 food items in our supermarkets. People all over the world live happy, productive, and healthy lives with very basic foodstuffs. I will never again complain or worry about the future if I have access to bread, milk, rice, fish and one or two vegetables."

WORKING IN A FOREIGN COUNTRY

Management styles vary throughout the world. That's one of the first things you will notice when you work overseas, according to one UNITED NATIONS employee based in a regional office in Africa.

"The most important thing to remember is that it does not function like a Canadian office. The management style is top-down and unparticipatory, stemming in part from its isolation from North American management theory... For another, shortages in office supplies such as paper for photocopying or typewriter ribbons, and local staff who suffer from low levels of training, make office efficiency a fraction of what it is in Canada."

You will have to adapt to the workplace conditions you find. A CANADIAN CROSS-ROADS INTERNATIONAL volunteer taught in Ghana despite major problems.

"The school often runs out of money so we close it down for one or two weeks and contract out the students' labour. We dug out a fish pond for a good profit three months ago. Then we made cement blocks and built walls for a local person. We are currently thinking of building a pig barn for someone. While these projects have their practical applications and make the students proud of

their school, it really throws a cog into our efforts to give the students an ongoing, logically planned education."

Basic resources that you take for granted in Canada are not available in many parts of the world, says a CUSO volunteer working as a teacher at a paramedic school in Sierra Leone.

"The job came with some difficulties and frustrations. The school runs out of paper, pens and chalk regularly. The hospital is functioning on practically nothing. This makes it difficult to teach simple lessons, for example—taking a temperature without a thermometer. Maintaining hygienic procedures is almost impossible with no running water. At the end of the dry season one bucket of water must do a 33-bed paediatric ward for a day. With time one forgets all the shortcomings and adapts and makes use of what little resources one has."

Be prepared to wait, and wait, and wait to get things done, according to a manager with a large Canadian engineering firm working in West Africa.

"The typical office day for a management expatriate in the private sector is from about 7:30 a.m. to 7 p.m. You must work long hours to compensate for time lost during the day on items not related to your actual job. Things like personnel problems, equipment problems, long waits for meetings, and long and unnecessary meetings. You get your actual work done before 9 a.m. and after 4 p.m."

At times it's just easier to adopt the local sense of time, says a CANADIAN CROSSROADS INTERNATIONAL volunteer.

"I try to slow to the Indonesian pace. If I'm in a hurry, when I stop the breeze does too, and I really sweat. It's so hot, you have to take it easy like everyone else. The daily routine is up before dawn (which is at 5:45 a.m. and lasts five minutes) to take advantage of the cool morning. Then quit for the day at 2 p.m. and have the big meal, then a nap, during the hottest time. Most stores close and fewer people are about. Then at 5 p.m. stores reopen until nine. Many people go to bed this early."

Many Canadians overseas take their job too seriously and miss out on other aspects of their stay, says one CUSO volunteer in Sierra Leone.

"I am still learning to draw the line with regard to my work. I think that most cooperants are extremely serious about their work, and, if not careful, Canadians often 'burn out' by forgetting that work is just one part of life and they are here not only to perform professional duties but to learn about people, places and much more."

Getting things done at work takes time because local staff have many more constraints than North American employees, says one CIDA project officer based in Southeast Asia.

"The pace overseas is generally slower. Don't expect instant service and clockwork precision when each and every step taken to make things happen is dogged by time lags—phones that work fitfully, transport in poor condition, power shortages, badly-paid workers moonlighting to make ends meet, limited

numbers of highly-skilled people with demands far exceeding their capacities to respond, family and friendship obligations that affect so-called work responsibilities because there is no all-embracing social assistance system to take your place... In fact, it is amazing that so much gets done under such conditions."

Many Westerners overseas try to carry out all the work themselves for the sake of efficiency. In the long run that's a mistake, says a CUSO volunteer in Nigeria.

"Development workers often have personal ambitions. Over time they can develop 'realistic' attitudes (about local people) which can be patronizing, culturally aggressive, and cynical... At my workplace this (attitude) is sometimes translated into excessive reliance on expatriate skills and judgement, and very little consultation with people who were to 'benefit' from all this good work."

A CIDA project officer in the Philippines stresses respectful human relationships at work above 'efficiency' in an office abroad.

"Office work overseas can be deceptively like office work at home. The competent and efficient secretaries further that impression. However, human and social relationships nearly always make that impression false. Greater sensitivity is generally called for overseas.

"You must make your priority human dignity and respect. Loss of face by colleagues and those one supervises is to be avoided whenever possible. When a conflict cannot be responsibly side-stepped, it should be dealt with privately... There is no such thing as brutal honesty. Skills of mediation, compromise and quiet authority are respected."

A boss is a boss is a boss. No matter where you go in the world, your boss will make or break your job according to one Junior Professional Officer with the UNITED NATIONS who is based in Africa:

"The experience you have in the UN could depend on the office you have been assigned to and, to an extent, the boss you have been sent to work with. And like any other workplace, your boss can turn the job of your dreams into the job of your lifetime, or into a daily nightmare."

You must learn to accept the work pace and habits overseas if you want to adapt, says the regional director for Nigeria and Ghana of a large Canadian engineering firm.

"The major differences in work habits are the lack of urgency to get anything done and the lackadaisical approach to quality of work. These two items are enough to drive you crazy if you do not adapt mentally to the situation... You can try to change this but it is a long, slow process and you must recognize this.

"Try to get a local interface between workers and expatriate management. As long as you stay you will never be as good as a local administrator for certain tasks. Recognize the administrator's limitations and try to upgrade him or her."

Many Canadians find local staff efficient, professional and underpaid, according to a Canadian working for the UNITED NATIONS HIGH COMMISSION ON REFUGEES in Africa:

"Prior to leaving I had heard horror stories about working in developing countries. Things like 'The work values of locals are different from our own work values' and 'It's difficult to get work done the way we would like to get work done.'

"I didn't experience that. The local staff we worked with were fantastic, very professional, very good at what they did. And I felt terrible sometimes because here I was getting an incredible salary while they were earning peanuts. And they knew more than me and they worked just as hard. It's something I had a really difficult time dealing with."

Be prepared for a learning experience, says one UN employee.

"As an international civil servant so much can throw your work off. You've got elections, government and organizational bureaucracy, office politics, cyclones and screw-ups. Patience, and lots of it, is what you need, as well as lower expectations... You can't avoid mistakes, especially when you first arrive. You are very vulnerable emotionally, socially and professionally. Therefore, make your mistakes and learn from them."

Learn from your environment, suggests one Junior Professional Officer with the UNITED NATIONS in Africa:

"An international bureaucracy is a great training ground for life... Life here is too often built on an exchange of smiles and daggers. Working in a different and difficult cultural milieu in two foreign languages, and getting things done, is no small piece of cheese either."

Host nationals may expect Westerners to boost the economy by employing local people.

"Every time we park the car we hire a watchman, even if it is only for ten minutes. This tends to be a customary practice and many small boys depend on it for a living. Shopping excursions always include one or two hired helpers to tell us where to buy the things we want (it isn't easy to find things in the maze of the market), and to carry cartons. Washing clothes takes a full day, and if you are working there is no time for it... the same goes for cooking. It may sound very imperialistic and I must confess to a certain degree of guilt. Nonetheless, it is the only way of getting things done, and it puts money in peoples' pockets which they otherwise would not receive."

Overseas business deals take more time and patience to firm up, according to a Canadian environmental consultant who has worked throughout the world.

"Doing business overseas is much more difficult and can be frustrating if a person is not extremely patient. People overseas often promise a lot but seldom deliver... Be prepared to entertain a lot. If a client is with you for over a year with no results, politely dump them."

PREPARATION AND CULTURE SHOCK

Make every effort to speak to other Canadians who have lived in the country where you will be stationed, suggests one manager working for a Canadian consulting company in Africa.

"Before you leave Canada, make every effort to speak to another family— husband, wife, kids—who have lived in the country. Prepare for this interview well, list all your questions, concerns, fears, no matter how silly they may seem. Preferably, speak to someone not in your own organization, to avoid any bias. And if you are in the private sector DO NOT speak to a diplomat. They have no concept of what real life is like in these countries. They live in an isolated environment protected by special concessions made for the diplomatic corps."

Give some thought to the possessions you take overseas, advises one CUSO volunteer in Malaysia.

"After dragging luggage around on my way here, paying excess baggage and storage charges, I'm convinced that volunteers should be encouraged to bring nothing which cannot be carried in a small backpack. Much of what I brought with me proved to be either useless, unsuitable, or could be bought cheaper or of a more suitable design or materials. The exception might be cotton underwear. That small backpack would easily hold a year's supply, your photo album, a change of clothing, and a few small, typically Canadian gifts for special friends you make."

Once you arrive, absorb as much information as you can about your host country, says one CUSO co-operant.

"When you get to your country, read the newspaper. Read the whole newspaper—the ads, the classified, letters to the editor, obituaries. You'll quickly find out what is important and start getting a sense of where people are at."

Don't expect everything to be covered in official orientations, says a CUSO volunteer in Africa.

"The separation of black and white and underlying hostility towards white ex-pats... was completely ignored in an official orientation. I am only now beginning to see the joyful side of (the local) culture, by spending much more time with the local people... I have certainly been made aware of latent racist tendencies in myself which would never have surfaced in Canada. This has also heightened my awareness of outspoken racism in others."

All overseas workers and volunteers experience culture shock. This CUSO volunteer in Malaysia had a clear case shortly after she arrived.

"Personally, I found life in Malaysia difficult to adjust to. My senses were offended, by the smells of open sewers, exhaust fumes, garlic prawn paste, smelly toilets, by the sound of traffic, Michael Jackson singing 'Beat It,' the oft- heard male greeting 'Hello miss, want to sleep with me?' and by the sights of garbage-strewn streets, open sewers, mouldy buildings and poor imitations of western shopping centres.

"The traffic rules, or rather lack of them, left me wondering why I had left Canada to be run down by a bus or taxi driver. The physical aspects simply compounded the emotional problems caused by loneliness, lack of privacy, and my inability to deal with racial and sexual discrimination and harassment."

Some countries give new meaning to the word "bureaucracy," as a CANADIAN CROSSROADS INTERNATIONAL volunteer in Ghana explains.

"Upon arrival I was granted a 14-day visa, which had to be renewed with the government in order to get a resident visa. The problem is, the passport office referred my request to the Ministry of Culture and Sports to see if they had any information on my organization. No reason was given for this procedure. This ministry has since been split into two separate ministries and no one knows which one has the letter, who is responsible to answer it, who the letter was addressed to, or even where the new offices are located. The Passport Office now refuses to act on the matter until they get an answer and they say it is my responsibility to track it down."

Many Canadians are surprised at their own clichéd ideas of other cultures, as a CUSO volunteer in Malaysia discovered.

"I suppose, like most North Americans, I had the stereotypical view of the East as an ancient land of exotic mystery. This has in some ways turned out to be true, but in many ways Malaysia has surprised me with its modernity. The old and new meet head-on. Open-air markets compete with air-conditioned shopping malls. Rickshaws and bicycles share the road with Mercedes, Mazdas, Fords. Haute cuisine mixes with hamburgers and hot dogs. If someone tells you that 'everything' is available here, believe them."

Manners vary from country to country. One CUSO co-operant in Southeast Asia explains how these differences can contribute to culture shock.

"There are times when the famous politeness and refinement of character will grate on your nerves, seeming like cowardice, hypocrisy, ignorance or any combination thereof, and you will gnash your teeth in a fury of impotent rage. There will be times while teaching when you hear your voice being mimicked aloud by someone in the next room and you want to stalk out of the class and throttle the damn fool... There will be times when your patience will be paper thin as you stagger through, for the umpteenth dozen time, the gauntlet of 20 questions regarding your social, sexual, marital, dining habits... I've found it's usually better to ignore, if possible, what you find negative in the foreign culture and concentrate on what you find positive."

Often you find that coming home is more of a culture shock than going away. A Canadian CUSO volunteer returning from Papua New Guinea recounts his experience.

"I became angry with Canada and Canadians—both for being different from PNG, and for not being different enough. Waste, consumerism, blatant public sex disgusted me. On the other hand, I had somehow persuaded myself that in Canada, things ran on time and efficiently. When they didn't I was annoyed out of all proportion.

"Relatives have since told us that we looked like two scared rabbits for about a month. We hadn't realized how un-Canadian our behaviour had become, and we needed to watch others carefully for cues. I almost lost a job because the interviewer thought I didn't want it. I was actually very interested but my body language was all wrong."

SPOUSE, FAMILY AND SOCIAL RELATIONS

Life overseas can be tough for a non-working spouse overseas. The spouse of a CIDA employee in Harare, Zimbabwe had the following advice for adjustment.

"Have realistic expectations. You probably will not find paid employment and if you do, it may be considerably lower-paying than in Canada. Why not focus on meaningful volunteer work which could lead to a new or continued career in Canada? Get involved in something in the local community, preferably an activity in your field of interest. It's by talking to people that you hear of opportunities.

"Imagine that you won't find a job and plan for that situation. Think of doing correspondence courses. Arrange to do research in your field. Create your own job. For example, if you have a counselling degree, why not advertise among the other foreign missions and start your own practice out of your house or apartment."

A woman who was a UNITED NATIONS employee in Africa suggests that men who accompany their partners abroad must be prepared for pressures.

"When we went to Zaire together it wasn't because he got a job, it was because I got a job. I was really proud of my husband because he's quite a novelty. But it was very difficult for him. He is a translator, with a master's degree in translation and he is quite skilled at what he does. But there was no work. He tried to get contracts here and there but it wasn't very consistent... And he felt societal pressures.

"He's got to work, he's a man. I think it does put a lot of pressure on a marriage if the spouse is unhappy and wants to work and makes you feel like he is doing you a big favour by being there."

Life can be tough for the spouses of private company employees who work overseas, according to the manager of a Canadian consulting firm.

"In management the long hours affect your home life. Your wife must be happy or your life will be hell and you will have to leave. So, even if the company does not provide for it, spend some of the money you are making to ensure your family is comfortable, safe and occupied. Most problems come from bored spouses."

Sometimes Westerners with good intentions land in dangerous situations through naivete, as this CANADIAN CROSSROADS INTERNATIONAL volunteer in Ghana discovered the hard way.

"One day at the market I befriended three kids and decided to treat them to some bubble gum. I sent one to buy 20 or so pieces of gum. Once the three boys realized the gum was for them, about 100 kids swarmed the car.

"The car started to rock from the pushing of 100 pairs of hands stretched out to the car windows. They were all begging, pushing, pleading for gum. Those closest to the car began to scream from the crushing weight. The pushing finally subsided, but the most persistent 50 or so stayed on and would not leave us alone no matter how I spoke to them. The taxi driver finally saw the situation I had so naively placed myself in and drove the car to another spot."

Living and working overseas has its down side, says a Canadian working for the UNITED NATIONS in Africa.

"The requirements of living like a gypsy and moving every two or three years prevents you from putting down roots and confines your peer group to a bunch of maladapted diplomats.

"Your position as a rich foreigner makes it very difficult to integrate into the local community and instead privileges you as a member of an isolated ruling class. Some people may enjoy the instant respect you get and the easy life with chauffeurs and servants. Others who grew up with North American egalitarian values may be disgusted by the whole thing."

Your social life may be quite different from your Canadian one, according to two CUSO co-operants in Sierra Leone.

"As we live on a Seventh Day Adventist compound, we are fairly isolated and our lifestyle is conservative. We have both purchased our own Honda 70's to make the 10-mile trip to the nearest town once a week, to shop and get a beer."

In some cultures you may feel like nationals want to know everything about you, as one CUSO volunteer in Indonesia discovered.

"You may well find people here frightfully honest by Western standards, depending on the subject matter. There will be no hesitation in discussing the three kilos you recently lost or gained and you will find yourself answering very personal questions from people who seek to understand how it is that you are so different."

Life in an African village can be full of social activities says a CUSO volunteer in The Gambia.

"I'll barely have finished supper before visitors start arriving. Every evening, beginning at 7 p.m., I have anywhere from six to 20 visitors. First it is young boys, then a couple of girls, finally a few young men and women. It can be pretty loud and lively at times. Conversation between the villagers and me is usually pretty limited but there's lots of laughter. At 9 o'clock I politely explain that I want to write in my book and they all get up, shake my hand, and leave."

The impact of a high crime rate and poverty affected one UN employee's ability to meet people in a large urban centre in Africa.

"(The high rate of crime) was difficult because it caused me to be mistrustful of people immediately. I made one local friend, a woman who is very independent, works in an office, makes a good salary, and was definitely not interested in me because I was white and come from a developed country

and had money. But other than this person we were not able to make any local friends because people were not interested in us."

Many people experience loneliness and feelings of isolation during their stay overseas. One CUSO volunteer in Africa describes her experience.

"I felt socially isolated and found this quite discouraging. I had perhaps unrealistic expectations of friendships with Sierra Leonians, especially women. I wonder how much of this is due to barriers I've erected myself, how much to the fact that my cultural and background experiences are so different from those of the people I've met?"

Learning a local language can help to break down some of the barriers between people, says a CUSO volunteer in the Solomon Islands of the South Pacific.

"A gradual introduction into the world of dances and night life have polished my Pidgin, though it may have tarnished my reputation... I'd like to reiterate what was wisely repeated to us a number of times at orientation. Different language is the biggest barrier between two people. Shared language is the sweet bridge over it."

WOMEN OVERSEAS, WOMEN IN DEVELOPMENT

A woman working overseas does not have the same experiences as a man, explains a consultant who works throughout Africa.

"The most surprising treat of working overseas as a woman consultant was the pure pleasure of being able to focus my attention completely on my work, relieved of my at-home roles of wife and mother. The most difficult aspect of working overseas as a woman and a consultant is the loneliness. When the work day was over, I was often trapped in my hotel, too restrained by cultural taboos and lack of familiarity with the locale to venture far alone."

Sometimes cultural rules that apply to local women will be waived for North American women, explains a private consultant working in Africa.

"As a North American woman, I was able to work effectively with men in Moslem countries as I was not expected to conform to the cultural practices of local women. As a middle-aged woman, I commanded more respect from both women and men than younger female consultants would have."

But many Canadian women are unprepared for the advances of men or harassment in other cultural settings, as a CUSO cooperant in Malaysia explains.

"Every day I rode to language class in a minibus in which people were packed like sardines. In fact, some of the braver souls swung on the door as the bus skidded around 90-degree corners for 20 to 30 minutes. This was traumatic because it marked the beginning of another day of being stared at. Language classes were tolerable by comparison to the rest of the day.

"The worst part of the day was the walk through the shopping complex in which the language school was located—the male school drop-outs, aged 16 to

20, leered and made comments. After one particularly trying day, when a person followed me into the language school, I decided I would stay for only six months. This was a compromise between leaving immediately and staying for two years."

A private sector development consultant argues that women play such a large role they should not be ignored in the planning and execution of development projects.

"Don't forget that women constitute 50 per cent of the population, and include women in all projects from the start to end."

Sometimes the host of issues facing women in the South may seem overwhelming to North American women, says one CUSO health educator at a women's centre in Peru.

"Our health team has focused on women's reproductive health, treating items such as birth control, maternal death, cervical cancer and problems with illegal abortions. I feel we are striving for so many social justices: the right for a woman not to be beaten by her husband, the right to decent medical services, the right for women and men to have honest information about birth control and access to all methods available, the right to organize against discrimination and racism in health services and the right to fair and affordable healthcare."

In the name of North American 'efficiency' many disadvantaged groups, including women, don't get as involved as they should, according to a CUSO volunteer in Nigeria.

"In my own work the need to get things done often overrode the needs and aspirations of the disabled and the poor. Disabled people often work more slowly than able-bodied people, so it was easier to hire strong, young men. The poorest are often the least knowledgeable and lack hope. It was easier to work with those who understood English, had some education, and had hope that translated into ambition. Women had family responsibilities that made them less reliable in their attendance, especially widows who had less extended family support. They also tend to be less educated, speak less English, be less physically strong and complain less about drudgery. It was easier to educate the men and keep the women working."

DAY-TO-DAY LIVING OVERSEAS

One Crossroader shares his reluctance to try the Indonesian method for everything.

"The WCs have no toilet paper. A shock for Westerners, but people use their hands and water or a washcloth and then wash up. They would regard our way as unhygienic, but most of us are grateful to use the familiar western commode. We regrettably are passing up on another cultural experience—squatting over a ceramic basin set in the tile floor."

We take many products for granted that are used and reused in other parts of the world, says one CANADIAN CROSSROADS INTERNATIONAL volunteer in Africa.

"Ghanaians are starved for books and papers. We bring all of our papers to the life-guard at the beach. From there it seems paper reading parties materialize, with everyone reading and sharing the material. It is amazing to see 10 people all huddled under a palm hut on the beach, reading and reading, not a word being said. There is so little reading material in this country and with such a high literacy rate everyone is starved for something new or current to read. This makes me realize how much we take even daily newspapers for granted in Canada."

You may be offered odd foods while working and living in another country—as one Crossroads volunteer living in South America writes to friends:

"Now that I have eaten the local delicacy—roast guinea pig—a total of three times, I feel I am ready for almost anything. It's quite good, once you get over the shock."

Commuting can become, well, something of a nightmare as this Crossroads volunteer describes.

"Traffic has brought city problems to a village society. Indonesians believe that the other guy sees you and will give way... Scooter riders have to swerve around a clumsy Westerner, when usually they just turn a bit and whip by, braking only at the last minute.

"Traffic is an instinctive organism here, none of our slow, linear logic. People tailgate, honk, blink, yell and gesture to say 'watch out, I'm coming, don't pass, OK you can pass now' or 'I'm just glad I'm still alive.' Streamlined Mercedes buses with gutted exhausts belch by swarms of tiny motorcycles with gutted exhausts, as a steady flow of vehicles avoids imminent collision. There is no enforcement of safeguards or pollution controls. Even the helmet law is quite casual. People put their helmets on unstrapped to get through policed intersections."

Prepare for the climate to be quite different from the four seasons you know in Canada. One CUSO volunteer in Malaysia comments on the conditions.

"No one told us about the rain before we came to Sarawak. This seemed strange because Sarawak is wetter than the Sahara is dry... In Sarawak it is always raining, has always rained and will always rain... And it isn't just how it rained but when it rained... Oh sure, the monsoons are now over... but life is always wet (even on Sundays)... In the happy reminiscences of a selective memory this will all be forgotten. Is this why they never told us about the rain?"

A tropical climate can bring additional visitors to your home, says one CUSO co-operant to Indonesia.

"While much of nature lives outside the walls of my home, the inside is nonetheless resplendent with things that fly, crawl, hop, run, swim and grow... The lizards which crawl about the walls and ceilings are likely to provide the greatest amusements to newcomers to Indonesia. These guys eat their weight in insects and should not be the objects of fear and loathing.

"Every once in a while a tree frog, either the large green variety or its smaller brown cousin, manages to get in and goes nuts, bouncing off the walls in a crazed attempt to get out of my restful abode...

"Insects are the mainstay of my menagerie. While mosquitoes are constantly soliciting blood donations, it is the ants who literally threaten the foundations of my existence. There are many different kinds, the dishwashers, the musclemen, the carpenters...

"Another occasional visitor is the cockroach. These like to live in dark places and during occasional fits of frenzy and passion, take to the sky. Like everything else here, they only come in a large size."

RESOURCES

Personal Stories Overseas

This is a mixed bag of stories about living overseas, some humorous, some serious. This list of references will be of interest to anyone seeking stories and insights of how others have thrived, or survived, living overseas.

The Adventure of Working Abroad: Hero Tales from the Global Frontier 📖
1995, *Joyce Osland,* Jossey-Bass Publishers, 269 pages ➤ Intercultural and Community Development Resources (ICDR), P.O. Box 32108, Millwoods Station, Edmonton, Alberta T6K 4C2; $35; VISA, Amex; (800) 378-3199, fax (403) 462-1925, icdr@compusmart.ab.ca ▪ Through the personal stories of Americans working overseas, this book provides a pragmatic framework for understanding and mastering the predictable challenges of each stage in the expatriate journey. Visit the distributor's web site at www.compusmart.ab.ca/icdr. [ID:1795]

Graveyard For Dreamers: One Woman's Odyssey in Africa 📖
1994, *Joan Baxter,* Potter's Field Press, 224 pages ➤ Nimbus Publishing, P.O. Box 9301, Stn. A, Halifax, Nova Scotia B3K 5N5; $16.95; cheque or VISA; (800) 646-2879, fax (800) 455-3652 ▪ A well-written, personal, and colourful account of living, traveling, and reporting on coups and customs in seven West African countries by a journalist from Nova Scotia. Particularly insightful is Ms. Baxter's sharing of her adaptation process and what it is like to be a white woman in rural and urban West Africa. [ID:2622]

I Should Have Stayed at Home: The Worst Trips of the Great Writers 📖
1994, *Roger Rapoport, Marguerita Castanera,* Book Passage Press/RDR Books, 256 pages ➤ Book Passage, 51 Tamal Vista Blvd., Corte Madera, CA 94925, USA; US$13.95; credit cards; (800) 999-7909, fax (415) 924-3838, messages@bookpassage.com ▪ A compilation of the travel misadventures of many well-known travel writers, this is a poignant and humorous collection of experiences we might encounter on our own travels. Royalties from the book are being donated to Oxfam America. Visit the publisher's web site at www.bookpassage.com. [ID:1584]

No Fixed Address 📖
1993, *Hansel Fraser* ➤ University of Toronto Press, 5201 Dufferin Street, North York, Ontario M3H 5T8; $24.95; VISA, MC; (800) 565-9523, fax (416) 667-7832, utpbooks@utpress.utoronto.ca ▪ Details a Foreign Service officer's job, including life in the foreign service, lessons in foreign service living, the selection process, and organization of the Foreign Affairs headquarters. Visit the distributor's web site at www.utpress.utoronto.ca. [ID:1344]

On Being Foreign: Culture Shock in Short Fiction, an International Anthology 📖
1986, *Tom Lewis, Robert Jungman,* Intercultural Press, 308 pages ➤ Intercultural and Community Development Resources (ICDR), P.O. Box 32108, Millwoods Station, Edmonton, Alberta T6K 4C2; $25; VISA, Amex; (800) 378-3199, fax (403) 462-1925, icdr@compusmart.ab.ca ▪ Twenty short stories selected from mainstream world literature lead you through the six stages of crosscultural adjustment. May be used as a reader in undergraduate programs and as a text in advanced ESL,

world literature courses or intercultural studies. Will appeal to the recreational reader! Visit the distributor's website at www.compusmart.ab.ca/icdr. [ID:1385]

Once Again At Forty 📖
1995, *Jim Shannon,* 134 pages ➤ General Store Publishing House Inc., 1 Main Street, Burnstown, Ontario K0J 1G0; $16.95; credit cards; (800) 465-6072, fax (613) 432-7184 ■ An entertaining, inspiring account of 10 years of work and travel undertaken by the author after he quit a successful, 20-year college teaching career. If you are contemplating a change but still wondering if you can or should do it, this book could persuade you. [ID:1658]

Outpost: The Traveller's Journal 📖
Quarterly ➤ Outpost Productions, 490 Adelaide Street W., Suite 303, Toronto, Ontario M5V 1T2; $12/year; (416) 703-5394, fax (416) 504-3628, outpost@echo-on.net ■ A top notch, sophisticated travel magazine geared to the adventure traveller. Culturally sensitive and adventurous, with a broad outlook. A very good magazine! Visit the publisher's web site at www.outpostmagazine.com. [ID:2708]

A Rich Broth: Memoirs of a Canadian Diplomat 📖
1993, *David Chalmer Reese,* 231 pages ➤ Carleton University Press, 1400 CTTC, Carleton University, 1125 Colonel By Drive, Ottawa, Ontario K1S 5B6; $13.95; VISA, MC; (613) 520-3740, fax (613) 520-2893 ■ A witty autobiography based on a 38-year career in the Canadian foreign service. Visit the publisher's web site at www.carleton.ca/cupress. [ID:1342]

Roosters at Two A.M. 📖
1996, 140 pages ➤ Canadian Crossroads International, 31 Madison Avenue, Toronto, Ontario M5R 2S2; $10; cash or cheque; (416) 967-0801, fax (416) 967-9078, crossroads@web.net ■ A collection of journal excerpts from overseas volunteers. [ID:2533]

Travel That Can Change Your Life: How to Create a Transformative Experience 📖
1997, *Jeffrey A. Kottler,* 180 pages ➤ Jossey-Bass Publishers, 350 Sandsome Street, San Francisco, CA 94104, USA; US$20; credit cards; (800) 956-7739, fax (800) 605-2665 ■ Travel experiences provide ideal opportunities for personal change, testing your notion of who you are and how the world works. This book offers a wealth of practical and imaginative suggestions that will change the way you approach travel. Visit the publisher's web site at www.josseybass.com. [ID:2468]

Travels with a Laptop: Canadian Journalists Head South 📖
1994, 327 pages ➤ North-South Institute, Suite 200, 55 Murray Street, Ottawa, Ontario K1N 5M3; $15; VISA, MC; (613) 241-3535, fax (613) 241-7435, nsi@nsi-ins.ca ■ A collection of stories by 55 journalists who have worked in Asia, Africa and Latin America. An intimate, and often humorous picture of life in the South. Visit the distributor's web site at www.nsi-ins.ca. [ID:1660]

Waiting for Li Ming 📖
1993, *Alan Cumyn,* 274 pages ➤ Goose Lane Editions, 469 King Street, Fredericton, N.B. E3B 1E5; $16.95; VISA, MC; (506) 450-4251, fax (506) 459-4991 ■ Story of a young Canadian man's crosscultural experience in China, and the problems he has adjusting to life when he returns to Canada. [ID:1341]

Chapter 5

Learning a Foreign Language

It should come as no surprise that a good working knowledge of a foreign language is often a prerequisite to landing an overseas job. In fact, the ability to speak a second, third and even fourth language is so important to your international career that it deserves special attention. You can't function effectively in a situation where you are unable to communicate directly with taxi drivers, store clerks, office staff, and perhaps most important of all, your clients. While you needn't engage in complicated debates about world affairs or local politics, you will need to ask simple questions, give instructions, order a meal in a restaurant, introduce yourself or have a friendly conversation.

You'll be of more value to your employer—and gain more from the experience yourself—if you can help bridge the gap between Canada and your host country. This requires, among other things, facility with the local language.

Employment advantages are not the only reason for learning a new language, however. Your effort to speak the local tongue sends out an important message to your hosts. It tells them you have come, not to impose North American customs and standards on them, but to learn about their culture and meet them on their own terms. When you take this approach, you open yourself up to a world of new ideas and attitudes. Certainly your work overseas is important, but so is your chance for enjoyment and personal growth.

CANADIANS' SECOND LANGUAGE ADVANTAGE

Canadians are particularly fortunate to have the opportunity to learn two important international languages: English and French. The federal government's policy of official bilingualism has strongly influenced Canada's international reputation. After almost three decades of promoting acquisition of

69

one of our official languages as a second language, many Canadians are now functionally bilingual.

As for other languages, Canadians interested in the South tend to focus on Latin America and parts of the Caribbean, where Spanish predominates. As a result, the third most common language used by Canadians abroad is Spanish. In recent times, however, concern for the Pacific Basin has resulted in an increased demand for Asian languages. In other parts of the world, where finding work often hinges on your ability to provide much needed skills to locals, familiarity with less common languages such as Swahili, Arabic, Hungarian or Portuguese can be a real asset.

Even when the languages you are familiar with are not specifically required in a posting, the fact you know them will still impress employers. It suggests you have an aptitude for languages and are open to learning new ones. However, unless you are a translator or interpreter, knowing other languages will not guarantee you an overseas job; your international career must be grounded in technical or professional expertise. Foreign language proficiency is just one of many secondary elements in your total skills inventory, albeit an important one. Such proficiency makes you harder to replace, and thus provides you with greater job security.

LEARNING THE LOCAL LANGUAGE

If you are going to a country where French or English is commonly used (such as Cameroon, Côte d'Ivoire, India, Malaysia, the Netherlands, Nigeria, Togo or the United Kingdom), you can probably get by without learning the local language. In countries where very little English or French is spoken (as in Indonesia, Chile, or Mozambique), you will be in trouble if you can't speak the local language. When you can't communicate with the people around you, you are likely to become frustrated and suffer from feelings of isolation.

Learning a foreign language is not a simple task, and for some people it may seem impossible. However, most of us do, in fact, have the capacity to learn another language. And there's no better place to do this than where the language is spoken.

With a little humility on your part, everyone in your new country is a potential teacher. Whether you're a teacher, engineer, nurse or economist, you will have to set aside your status as the educated foreigner and ask locals to help you say "I need a haircut," or "Do you have this shoe in a larger size?" People will appreciate your efforts and want to help you. As you open yourself up to learning a new language, you'll find your effectiveness on the job is enhanced, you'll feel more at home in your new community, and the local people will begin to accept you.

Let's face it, though. Along with all the other demands of cultural adjustment, the stress of learning a new language may be more than some of us can bear. Fear of failure can impair our ability to learn and be more damaging than our inability to speak the new language. If you fall into this category, and decide not to learn the local language, concentrate on becoming involved in the local culture in other ways.

Your experience will be richer, however, if you can greet your hosts in their own tongue and speak at least a few common phrases. So go ahead and try, and don't underestimate the value of your efforts. They demonstrate that you recognize and respect your new country's culture. With that in mind, why not set yourself the goal of learning a few new words or phrases every day?

A BASIC RULE ABOUT LEARNING LANGUAGES: PRACTICE MAKES PERFECT

Have you wondered why, after a minimum of five years' classroom instruction in French, very few anglophone high school graduates can speak French? Well, the one fundamental truth about learning languages is that formal classroom instruction is not enough.

Learning a second language is not unlike learning your first language. As children, we add new words to our vocabularies as we need them and in this way are able to absorb them. When we come to learn a second language, we quickly find we learn best by carrying out our daily routines and responsibilities in the new language. Don't forget the tired, old truism, "necessity is the mother of invention" has yet to be proven wrong! Exchanging greetings, buying food in the market—start with the basics. As you improve, you'll feel more comfortable with the people and culture around you. You'll quickly be immersed in the local scene by going to restaurants, shopping, attending social events, and talking to people on the street. By the same token, if you don't practice every day, you'll find it almost impossible to pick up the new language.

Full summer immersion courses now help Canadians function in their second language in less than three months. Motivation is necessary, of course, but the key is practice, practice, and more practice.

FOUR CAN'T-MISS RULES FOR LEARNING A NEW LANGUAGE

Begin Immediately

When you reach your post, start learning the new language right away. Experience shows that if you put it off, you probably won't get around to it.

Be Humble

Your phrasing will be rudimentary at first, but no matter how awkward you feel, keep at it. Learn to laugh and accept help from others. People will be delighted with your efforts.

Immerse Yourself

Take every opportunity to speak the language. You cannot learn a second language by memorizing it, so don't spend too much time on books and formal classroom instruction. Concentrate on human interaction. Socialize in your new language. Better yet, why not try living your new life in the new language? Whatever you do, remember that practice is the key, whether you're bartering at the market, participating in local events, or negotiating with bureaucrats.

Listen Carefully

In the beginning you'll understand little of what you hear, but do not tune it out. Study facial expressions and gestures and listen for familiar words. Gradually your comprehension will grow. You might not catch every word, but you'll soon understand the overall ideas.

OTHER PRACTICAL TIPS

While Overseas

Always carry a notebook with you, to record new words and phrases and helpful information. Begin with common phrases, such as greetings, and add a few new words every day. Label every item in your new house in the new language. Put lists of common phrases on your bulletin board or fridge (if you have one!).

Find yourself a tutor. Trying to learn another language without an instructor is like trying to learn to swim without water.

Contact the CANADIAN EMBASSY or HIGH COMMISSION, the US PEACE CORPS or other large foreign institutions in your overseas country. They may offer orientation programs which include language training; they may also be able to assist you with materials and tutors.

Face it—you're not likely to write a great novel in your new language, so just concentrate on being able to carry on a good conversation. And don't become overly stressed about learning the language. Slow down, enjoy yourself, and explore your new world!

Before You Leave

Search out the appropriate ethnic communities in your area and participate as much as possible in their events and activities. The more exposure you get to the new language and culture before you leave, the better.

Tape programs in your new language and play them back repeatedly. At first, the dialogue will seem impossibly fast, but you can stop, rewind and listen again. You'll be amazed at what you pick up the second or third time around!

Try to arrange at least 20-30 hours of language lessons before you leave home. Listen to language tapes while you drive, on walks, or making dinner.

Read children's books in the new language. The pictures, story lines and simple words will help you learn the basics.

If you have the time, and are able, find a job in your new language environment. Working in a local Japanese or Latin American restaurant, for example, is a great idea. Better yet, try to arrange a job in a restaurant in Québec or France (or Spain, Mexico, or Japan). Or best of all, volunteer with, say, a French NGO in francophone West Africa.

An excellent method for learning French or English is to take a one-year university program in one or the other language. Many large Canadian universities allow you to write your exams in either official language. This means an anglophone who wants to become more fluent in French could move to Québec City, take classes in French, and still write their essays and exams in English. Other possibilities include taking conversational French classes, attending a French college at an anglophone university, or as mentioned earlier, taking an immersion program.

LEARNING A FOREIGN LANGUAGE IN CANADA

There are numerous public and private schools in Canada which specialize in language training. Consult the *Yellow Pages* under "Schools – Language" for detailed listings, or call your local college or university. If you want information on where to learn French in Canada or abroad, contact CANADIAN PARENTS FOR FRENCH listed in the Resource section below.

A LAST WORD

How you go about learning a foreign language depends on you, and on your destination overseas. If you are just beginning to develop long-term career strategies, your agenda will differ substantially from that of an experienced engineer heading out on his or her third international posting. One thing is certain, the more languages you are familiar with, the better you will fare in the international arena. Remember, once in your overseas posting, take advantage of every opportunity to learn about the new culture. Understanding the local language will help you in this process.

RESOURCES

While many books on this subject are theoretical, the following have been chosen for those wishing to learn another language on their own. For related resources consult the section on Language Careers in Chapter 22, Resources for the International Job Search and Chapter 29, Teaching Abroad.

Breakthrough Series: Self-Guided Language Courses ▦
1997, *Brian Hill,* 256 pages + cassette ➤ NTC Contemporary Publishing Co., 4255 West Touhy Ave., Lincolnwood, IL 60646, USA; US$59.95; credit cards; (800) 323-4900, fax (800) 998-3103 ▪ Effective method of language learning, featuring native speakers on cassette; French, German, Spanish and Italian. [ID:2416]

Canadian Parents for French
Canadian Parents for French, 176 Gloucester Street, Suite 310, Ottawa, Ontario K2P 0A6; (613) 235-1481, fax (613) 230-5940, cpf@cpf.ca ▪ This national organization provides excellent information on French second language programs available in Canada and overseas. Focus is on programs for young Canadians, but they can provide information on adult programs as well. [ID:2714]

Foreign Language Learning Resources ▣
www.call.gov ▪ Foreign language learning resources and links are collected here for language teachers and learners. The site allows you to choose one of over 60 languages, and with each language there is a set of links to various foreign language publications, radio programs, and sites of general interest. [ID:2577]

French Fun: The Real Spoken Language of Québec ▦
1993, *Steve Timmins,* 168 pages ➤ John Wiley & Sons, 22 Worchester Drive, Rexdale, Ontario M9W 1L1; $24; credit cards; (800) 567-4797, fax (800) 565-6802 ▪ This book is packed with pronunciation tips and daily expressions that distinguish French as it is spoken on the streets of Montreal, Chicoutimi, and Rivière-du-loup. [ID:1781]

How to be a More Successful Language Learner 📖
1994, *Joan Rubin, Irene Thompson,* Heinle & Heinle ➤ Nelson Canada, 1120 Birchmount Road, Scarborough, Ontario M1K 5G4; $39.95; credit cards; (800) 268-2222, fax (800) 430-4445 ▪ Covers all the issues related to learning languages. [ID:1211]

International Language Schools 📖 💻
EF International Language Schools, Suite 405, 60 Bloor Street West, Toronto, Ontario M4W 3B8; free; VISA; (800) 387-1463, fax (416) 927-8664, ilscan@ef.com ▪ This program offers language courses abroad, in France, Spain, Ecuador, Italy, and Germany, for students and adults of all ability levels. Information is available on their web site, www.ef.com. [ID:2560]

Japanese For Professionals 📖
1998, *Association for Japanese Language Learning,* Kodansha International, 288 pages ➤ Fitzhenry and Whiteside Ltd., 195 Allstate Parkway, Markham, Ontario L3R 4T8; $33.95; VISA, MC; (800) 387-9776, fax (800) 260-9777, godwit@fitzhenry.ca ▪ A comprehensive course for people who need to use Japanese in business. Visit the distributor's web site at www.fitzhenry.ca. [ID:2430]

The Language 3 Initiative 💻
http://mickey.la.psu.edu/lang3/welcome.html ▪ The Language 3 Initiative is based at Penn State University. Its web site provides links to hundreds of foreign language resources and even more language pages. It also has intercultural e-mail classroom connections and MOO sites (which are internet-accessible, text-mediated virtual environments well suited for distance learning) in several languages. [ID:2564]

Language Resource Center, American University 💻
www.american.edu/academic.depts/cas/lfs/newlrchome.html ▪ This web site is the home page of American University's Language Resource Center. "WWW Links for Language Students and Teachers" will lead you to a series of links to foreign language news groups, language resources and international mailing lists. [ID:2561]

NTC's Grammar Series 📖
1997, 192 pages ➤ NTC Contemporary Publishing Co., 4255 West Touhy Ave., Lincolnwood, IL 60646, USA; US$7.95 each; credit cards; (800) 323-4900, fax (800) 998-3103 ▪ Pocket-sized, user-friendly handbooks that take the fear out of learning those dreaded rules of grammar; French, German, Spanish and Italian. [ID:2417]

Teach Yourself Series 📖
1997, 320 pages + cassette ➤ NTC Contemporary Publishing Co., 4255 West Touhy Ave., Lincolnwood, IL 60646, USA; US$15.95 - $29.95 each; credit cards; (800) 323-4900, fax (800) 998-3103 ▪ Complete courses for beginners: Brazilian Portuguese (no cassette), Greek, Norwegian, Turkish, Ukrainian, Dutch, Latin (no cassette), Slovene (no cassette), and Vietnamese. [ID:2418]

Total Physical Response 💻
www.tpr-world.com ▪ Total Physical Response (TPR), created by Dr. James J. Asher, is a stress-free approach to acquiring another language. TPR's web site offers details about the organization, comments from around the world, an online bookstore, and ordering information. [ID:2612]

TravLang's Foreign Language for Travelers 💻
www.travlang.com/languages/ ▪ This a fun and playful web site, designed to expose you to 50 different languages. For each language, the site provides the alphabet with sounds. For those seeking more in-depth language training, you can download Travlang's various translating dictionaries. The site also provides general language tips and travel information. [ID:2607]

The Whole World Guide to Language Learning 📖
1990, *Terry Marshall,* Intercultural Press, 176 pages ➤ Intercultural and Community Development Resources (ICDR), P.O. Box 32108, Millwoods Station, Edmonton, Alberta T6K 4C2; $22; VISA, Amex; (800) 378-3199, fax (403) 462-1925, icdr@compusmart.ab.ca ▪ Practical book on do-it-yourself immersion language learning. Program is undertaken at the learner's own speed and incorporates maximum involvement with the local community. Visit the distributor's web site at www.compusmart.ab.ca/icdr. [ID:1032]

Chapter 6

Women Working & Living Overseas

Professional opportunities for women in the field of international affairs have never been better. With fewer formal and informal barriers, women are receiving recognition internationally as decision-makers, managers, and policy-makers. No longer is a woman overseas simply viewed as "the wife of."

This chapter is written for the professional woman already established in her international career and for the woman just beginning. It will explore the benefits and disadvantages facing women managers, examine the best employers for women, and specify academic credentials and skills required in today's work environment. This chapter will provide tips on how to work effectively in an overseas environment while keeping yourself healthy and safe.

WOMEN AS MANAGERS

Professional women face many challenges in the overseas job market. Although women have made considerable inroads in international development, and currently assume positions of authority in governmental, nongovernmental, and international organizations, their actual numbers, especially in the private sector, remain quite low. An expatriate woman manager is still viewed as an exception rather than the norm.

A recent study found that North American companies are hesitant, if not completely reluctant, to send professional women overseas. One of the primary reasons stated was their belief that women are not well received or respected by foreign hosts.

While it is true that in some countries professional women abroad are treated differently than their male counterparts, crosscultural experts say that foreign prejudice is exaggerated. It is often more in the minds of North Americans than the reality of women working overseas. *Expatriate women are viewed as foreigners*, and repressive standards which control local women are often not applicable—although there are some exceptions, as in Saudi Arabia.

Women have proven themselves to be extremely competent overseas. In fact, a 1990 CANADIAN INTERNATIONAL DEVELOPMENT AGENCY (CIDA) study shows women rated higher than men on many of the skills and attitudes associated with overseas effectiveness. Major differences include: 1) Women are generally less concerned about status and advancement, while men place great value on upward mobility 2) Prior to departure, women express a greater desire for contact with the local culture, and while overseas, they are more involved in the culture 3) Women place more value on and devote more time to learning the local language and 4) Women express more liberal attitudes towards development and are seen by peers as more caring of others.

In some cultures you will be given immediate respect because you are a woman, the assumption being that if your employer sent a woman in a "man's" place, you must be the best. This is true, to some degree. The women who preceded you had to be the best of the best, just to get there!

In addition, because there are so few professional women overseas, the ones who are there tend to be highly visible. This can be an advantage if you are in sales, marketing, business negotiations, or if you are simply trying to get your foot in the door. Chances are you will be better remembered than your male counterpart.

It cannot be ignored that females working abroad have difficulties with foreign colleagues and clients. To ease cultural tensions, women managers are often required to renounce some of their authority. An international development officer in charge of aid programs in Bangladesh realized soon after being posted there that she would have to relinquish much of her command in meetings and negotiations. The male government officials and male villagers refused to take instructions from a woman. They dealt instead with her male subordinates.

One woman manager deals with this problem by strategizing with her male North American colleagues prior to any meeting with foreign clients. In order for her to appear as non-threatening as possible, they divide up the agenda so all members seem equal. This exercise helps the foreign client feel more at ease and, in addition, sensitizes her male North American colleagues to the problem. Criticism from them could be disastrous as the foreign client might be waiting for any excuse to discredit her.

How successful a woman is overseas can therefore depend a great deal on how much support she is provided by her home organization. Foreign colleagues and clients might at first be confused about her status and role. Will she do the same job as her male predecessor? What is her level of authority? If her position is backed by her organization, she will have the necessary authority to properly carry out her responsibilities. If, on the other hand, her company limits her professional opportunities by restricting, for example, the scope of her job or the extent of her travel, or by criticizing her openly, she will lose credibility.

Despite some of the difficulties faced by women managers, an overseas posting provides most with opportunities they would not normally have in

Canada. Many state that they are given greater responsibility in their work, receive better work experience and are promoted faster.

WHAT MAKES A GOOD EMPLOYER?

There are private companies, government and international organizations that are better employers for women than others. Tema Frank explores this concept in her book, *Canada's Best Employers For Women* and outlines four elements that make an organization a good place for women to work. Her four elements apply equally well in an overseas context:

1. *Organizations that are good employers for women provide opportunities for advancement and career development. These firms have stopped making career-limiting assumptions, such as women do not want to return to work after childbirth and women are unwilling to travel in their jobs.*

   Many firms believe women do not want to travel in their jobs. As a result, firms often overlook women for an international posting or short-term overseas assignment. A recent study of MBA graduates in the United States, however, showed little difference between male and female preference for international work.

   No matter what industry or sector you are employed in, you should let your employer know you are interested in overseas work. Many women who are successful in their international careers have initiated the idea and encouraged their employers to send them overseas.

2. *A firm that is flexible in meeting the needs of its employees. This can include alternative working arrangements, such as flex hours, or simply time off when required.*

   Women require flexibility in their working lives, as many have primary family and household responsibilities. This is applicable both in Canada and overseas.

3. *Firms that support women in their childcare and eldercare responsibilities. As these responsibilities fall mainly on women, policies and practices that support employees' personal, as well as professional lives, are crucial.*

   An overseas posting can provide the advantage of affordable household help. Nannies for childcare and maids to clean and cook remove much of the burden that Canadian women bear.

4. *A good firm has a friendly, tolerant working environment. This includes employers with sexual or personal harassment policies and firms that will stand behind an employee if there is a problem.*

   For women, the problem of sexual harassment in the international work-place is pervasive. If you are faced with sexual harassment, like many problems you will encounter overseas, a certain level of tolerance is required. Unlike the West, many of the countries you will work in do not have policies to protect women. If, however, the harassment becomes threatening, follow your home organization's complaint procedure and know ahead of time where to go for support.

THE BEST EMPLOYERS

Economics, information technology, law, business, engineering and science are all growth areas in which women are increasingly finding international employment. The technology industry has created an information explosion, opening up a plethora of jobs around the world for programmers, software designers and other highly computer-literate individuals.

Financial service firms such as banks and insurance companies have branch offices or subsidiary operations abroad and send many women overseas. These organizations generally have policies and practices to provide equal opportunity for women. Free trade and globalization have also been boons to the fields of advertising, publishing, market research, and sales. In addition, human resource development with emphasis on crosscultural training is a high growth area, and one favoured by women.

Many women are attracted to the international consulting field because it offers a flexible working environment. Contracts are short-term with international travel usually lasting less than a month at a time. Much of the Canada-based consulting work can be done out of the home. The number of women involved in consulting work has increased dramatically in the last few years.

Government and other international organizations are offering women the chance to advance in their international careers through equal opportunity employment policies. In addition, affirmative action policies are in place in many organizations. The UNITED NATIONS, for example, is attempting to reach an equal gender representation for professional and high-level positions. To date, women account for approximately 35 per cent of staff in the professional category. CIDA is also aiming for increased representation and distribution of women in its workforce. Currently, women account for 41 per cent of the agency's total professional staff at headquarters and 32 per cent of the professionals on field postings.

There still, however, exists a difference between men and women in earning and promotion practices. For example, women make up only 17 per cent of the executive category at CIDA and 15 per cent in the high-level categories at the UNITED NATIONS.

Many organizations with gender and development policy concerns look for employees who, along with an area of expertise, are sensitive to gender issues. The WORLD BANK, for example, has just recently released a policy paper designed to enhance women's participation and economic development and will be interested in individuals with expertise on gender issues.

The UNITED NATIONS has a number of agencies with active women in development programs. In addition, the UN has a number of women's organizations which report on social and economic issues affecting women. They include the following:

- INSTRAW (INTERNATIONAL RESEARCH AND TRAINING INSTITUTE FOR THE ADVANCEMENT OF WOMEN). Main projects include credit, data on the informal sector, statistics, environment, financial and institutional arrangements for women.

- UNIFEM (UNITED NATIONS DEVELOPMENT FUND FOR WOMEN). Main programs include development projects addressing women's issues, especially water, sanitation and agriculture projects. (For more information, see Chapter 36, United Nations.)

ACADEMIC CREDENTIALS AND SKILLS

To advance in your international career, you must have the necessary academic credentials and skills. According to Nancy Adler, in her book *Competitive Frontiers*, a survey of expatriate women managers revealed that almost all held graduate degrees (MBAs being the most common), had extensive international interests and experience, and spoke, on average, two or three languages.

Without appropriate academic credentials, it is very difficult to progress in your career. In the past, women went overseas as nurses/healthcare workers, teachers or administrators and, several postings later, had advanced into positions managing field programs. Today this way of getting ahead is much less common.

NETWORKING

Networking is a means of gaining important business information. Informal networking most commonly takes place after work, over a few drinks, or during business socializing. Formal networking takes place in business seminars or conferences.

This traditional type of "old boys" network can be closed to women due to responsibilities at home or simply because of their gender. As a woman, foreigner or not, there is a good chance your overseas male colleagues will exclude you from their network.

Women have developed their own type of networking in which information is shared, issues common to women are discussed, and careers supported. It normally occurs through professional organizations and local women's groups, or during sports, arts, cultural or children's events.

Studies have shown, however, that for women to advance in their careers, they must network with *both* men and women.

Mentoring is another way to gain support in your career and social development. Having an alliance with a role model can provide greater job mobility and recognition and assist you in breaking into both male and female networks.

YOUR SOCIAL LIFE

An overseas posting is a great opportunity to meet a wide variety of people. Within the expatriate community, friends are made quickly because, like yourself, everyone is there for a short period of time and is receptive to meeting new people. If you are open to and accepting of the local culture, you will be embraced by your hosts. The unfortunate side of many overseas friendships is that they are often temporary. People come and go and you often lose contact with people you were once close to.

It is important to understand the social etiquette of the local culture in which you are living. In some countries social protocol calls for segregation of women and men, and in others it is forbidden to consume alcohol in public or eat with your left hand. Depending on the country and your host, rules can sometimes be bent, but often they are unavoidable. If you are in such a situation, don't fight it. It is important to respect the local customs.

You will find that more of your free time is given to business entertainment. Remember, business entertaining abroad is like business entertaining at home in the sense that you cannot truly relax or let your guard down. You should avoid giving too much personal information about yourself, even if you are urged to do so. What you might consider very normal, such as having a boyfriend or drinking alcohol, is often shocking to people in other cultures.

In social situations, professional women are often assumed to be dependant spouses. This is to be expected, however, as many Western women overseas *are* wives of working male expatriates.

You might suffer resentment from local women envious of your freedom to travel without your husband's or father's permission, or to pursue a professional career. North American women are viewed as overly independent in the South. You may also be resented out of fear that you will impose your Western feminism.

For single women, an overseas posting can be a lot of fun and a time to meet many interesting people. Within the diplomatic circle, however, there tends to be a focus on couples and families, and being a single woman can be socially awkward. Special effort to socialize within this circle is required. Some local cultures will look upon you with pity if you are unmarried. They will perceive you as a woman who is working because you cannot attract a marriage partner. Some single women on overseas assignments invent husbands or fiancés to avoid comments about their single status.

Expect less freedom and privacy on an overseas posting. Complete strangers may accost you with personal questions or may ridicule you as you walk by. You will be stared at, or even pinched, on the street. "I can't go anywhere without getting bothered" is the lament of one expatriate woman living in West Africa. Experienced women travellers state that it is important not to be paralyzed by this attention. A Canadian woman had this response for the forward men of the Ivory Coast who frequently asked, "When are you going to go to bed with me?" Her comic reply, "The day it rains frogs!" defused the situation through laughter.

WHAT TO WEAR

Many countries in the South put great emphasis on appearance, especially for women. No matter how polite you are, if your dress offends, chances are you will be ignored or mistreated. It is therefore very important to dress according to the culture and weather conditions of your host country. If you are working in the Middle East, it is wise to avoid body-hugging clothes, T-shirts and shorts. Some Muslim countries, like Saudi Arabia, have such strict dress codes that failure to comply can result in deportation. A brochure at a hotel in Saudi Arabia advises that "Women shall wear long dresses with long sleeves. Men shall not wear open shirts, tight trousers or chains."

Another reason to minimize your sexuality with regard to dress and conduct is because people in foreign countries invariably carry stereotypes and misconceptions of Westerners, particularly women. This is often fuelled by pornography. You may find yourself being observed to see if you fit the stereotypes. It is in your best interest to dress conservatively!

Buy good quality clothes that are easy to care for. Do not take clothes that require dry-cleaning. Your best choice in hot climates is cotton, silk or linen blends. Synthetic fabrics may not wrinkle but they retain heat. Cotton underwear and bras are essential in the tropics. For shorter trips, take silk/cotton combination blouses that can be washed in hotel sinks and hung to dry. A small travel iron can be useful. Many women swear by long, wide cotton skirts which are cool, comfortable and easy to pee in!

HEALTH IN BRIEF

Health concerns and considerations in developing countries are not specifically gender-based. Although immunizations, vaccines and thorough medical examinations should be part of anyone's pre-departure preparations, women must be aware that there may be no diagnostic facilities and a limited range of treatment options available overseas. In the areas of reproductive technology, diagnosis of breast cancer and endometriosis, treatment of recurrent vaginal infections, alternative birth control methods and complications arising out of pregnancy, there may be few facilities for testing and treatment.

Medical care abroad is often at odds with Canadian standards. For this reason, seek out country-specific information before leaving Canada. Contact organizations and clinics that specialize in tropical medicine and request current material on the status of healthcare in the countries where you will be travelling. If you require medical treatments in the South, be very selective and ensure the hygienic standards are acceptable.

Consult your family physician before departing. Your doctor should be informed of your travels, in the event you require ongoing medication or immediate access to your health records.

If you require medication, it is wise to buy it in Canada before you leave or have it sent to you. Prescription drugs are available over the counter in developing countries at greatly reduced prices, but pharmaceutical standards for drugs vary from country to country. In addition, your doctor can explain side-effects and recommend precise dosages. Self-diagnosis can create further problems; for example, yeast infections can be caused by taking high doses of antibiotics.

Prepare a customized health kit according to your destination. It needn't be elaborate, but should include feminine hygiene products, such as tampons, which may be hard to purchase or outrageously expensive overseas. Treatments for yeast and urinary track infections are essential, as many women are prone to infection while in the tropics. If you use over-the-counter medications for colds and flu, pack these as well. Take a good supply of contraceptives with you. Many countries in the South now manufacture their own but the quality of condoms and birth control pills can be substandard.

Many countries you will travel to have high incidences of HIV, the virus which leads to AIDS. It is important to protect yourself from infection by ensuring that only new needles are used when you require an injection, and that you practise safe sex, which includes use of condoms. (For more information on health-related issues, see Resources at the end of Chapter 3, Living Overseas.)

SAFETY TIPS

The following are a few tips to bear in mind while travelling overseas.

* Be alert. Remember, you are in a foreign country and do not fully understand the culture. You must remain vigilant.
* Avoid walking alone. When you don't have an alternative, walk purposefully and use well-travelled streets.
* Avoid walking the streets after dark. In some places it is unsafe, even in a group.
* Avoid isolated areas such as beaches. Don't go to bars alone.
* Don't wear jewellery on the street. Even an inexpensive watch should be kept in your pocket.
* Ensure your valuables are safely stored. Carry them only when necessary and use a money belt.
* Ensure hotel windows and doors are secure. For extra protection, put a stopper in window or sliding door.
* Don't invite strangers into your hotel room.
* Use an established taxi company, especially if you are riding alone. Don't be afraid to turn down a taxi driver if you do not feel comfortable.
* Keep your car doors locked and windows up when driving in crowded streets. In some countries, thieves will reach into an open car window and grab your purse, necklace or earrings.
* Depending on the country of posting, your single status may imply that you are an easy mark. It is not uncommon for single women to invent a spouse or fiancé. Some single women find wearing a wedding ring overseas cuts down on harassment.
* Most importantly, use your *common sense*. Exercise all the safety precautions you use at home with *added prudence*.

If you are harassed, be assertive, say "no" or "leave me alone." Don't be afraid to ask for help. To remove yourself from dangerous situations, go into a store or office building. If need be, shout or yell. If you are mugged, hand over your possessions. They are not worth your life.

A LAST WORD

There are tremendous professional and personal rewards for women working in international development. Professionally, you will be given greater responsibilities and put on the "fast track" in your career. Personally, you will gain a unique, and humbling, insight into other cultures.

It is important to remember when working overseas, you can be accepted and succeed as a professional simply by showing competence and professionalism. In the often male-dominated societies of the South, it is important to respect the positions of local men and women in their culture, including their notions of feminism. Remember, many men aren't used to working with women, especially a woman boss!

A women manager from TELECOM worked out her approach long ago. She plays both sides. She lets businessmen in any culture know that she expects to be treated like anyone else there on business, but she also creates a comfort level by abiding by their customs whenever possible. For example, at an evening reception in India, she noticed that women were moving to one side and congregating there, while the men were moving to another side to talk business. She spent an appropriate amount of time networking with the men and then moved over to the women. In this way she acknowledged the barriers that exist, and showed her respect for the way they do things, but also demonstrated that she had broken through them enough to get her business done.

RESOURCES

Most international job search books have chapters on the special concerns of women living and working in crosscultural environments. Our short list deals with books specifically focused on the issues facing women working and living overseas. For references more broadly related to women working and living overseas, see also the Resources following the section on Children & Families Overseas in Chapter 3, Living Overseas.

Adventures in Good Company 📖
1994, 430 pages ➤ The Eighth Mountain Press, 624 SE 29th Ave., Portland, OR 97214, USA; US$16.95; cheques only; (503) 233-3936, fax (503) 233-0774 ▪ A comprehensive guide to tours and outdoor trips tailored specifically to women. Profiles more than 100 firms worldwide which offer related services. [ID:1487]

Asia for Women on Business 📖
1995, *Tracey Wilen, Patricia Wilen,* Stone Bridge Press, 256 pages ➤ Weatherhill, 41 Monroe Turnpike, Trumbull, CT 06611, USA; US$15; credit cards; (800) 437-7840, fax (800) 557-5601, weath1212@aol.com ▪ This practical handbook bolsters the visiting woman's authority and effectiveness in the "Four Tigers": Hong Kong, Taiwan, Singapore and South Korea. Visit the distributor's web site at www.weatherhill.com. [ID:2407]

Canada's Best Employers for Women 📖
1994, *Tema Frank,* 257 pages ➤ Frank Communications, Suite 200, 253 College Street, Toronto, Ontario M5T 1R5; (416) 591-7191, fax (416) 591-7202 ▪ A readable book which lists the names and addresses of the best employers for women in Canada and explains what makes them the best. Also provides lists of organizations with mentoring programs, on-site day care centres, flexible benefits packages, other services of interest to women employees, and more. [ID:1710]

CanAsian Businesswomen's Network
CanAsian Businesswomen's Network, c/o Asia Pacific Foundation of Canada, Suite 666, 999 Canada Place, Vancouver, B.C. V6C 3E1; (604) 684-5986, fax (604) 681-1370, cabninfo@apfc.apfnet.org ▪ The CanAsian Businesswomen's Network assists companies led by women to increase their trade between Canada and Southeast Asia. In Canada, firms must be ready for import or export, Canadian-owned, and have a woman in a key executive or decision-making position. The network provides resources, contacts, business briefings, crosscultural readiness information, workshops and special events to members and associates. Visit the Asia Pacific Foundation web site, at www.apfnet.org, for more information. [ID:2614]

Competitive Frontiers: Women Managers in a Global Economy 📖
1994, *Nancy J. Adler, Dafna Izraeli,* 414 pages ➤ Blackwell Publishers, P.O. Box 20, Williston, VT 05495, USA; US$36.95; credit cards; (800) 488-2665, fax (802) 864-7626 ▪ This book examines the

changing nature of world business and its impact on women managers. Visit the publisher's web site at www.blackwellpublishers.co.uk. [ID:1619]

Culture Shock!: Successful Living Abroad, A Wife's Guide 📖
1992, *Robin Pascoe,* Graphic Arts Center Publishing Co. ➤ Raincoast Books, 8680 Cambie Street, Vancouver, B.C. V6P 6M9; $17.50; VISA, MC; (800) 663-5714, fax (800) 565-3770 ■ Written by a Canadian, the book is easy to read, and provides useful advice for the wife going overseas for the first time, especially if her husband is with Foreign Affairs or an international agency. Chapters on maids, entertaining and home leave may be off-putting, but after you've lived in her shoes, they may seem pertinent. Has a useful chapter on getting a job or freelancing overseas. [ID:1307]

Do's and Taboos Around the World for Women in International Business 📖
1997, *Roger E. Axtell,* 304 pages ➤ John Wiley & Sons, 22 Worchester Drive, Rexdale, Ontario M9W 1L1; $16.95; credit cards; (800) 567-4797, fax (800) 565-6802 ■ Draws on experiences of 100 women to offer advice on body language, health concerns, dress, balancing family life with work abroad, and more. Visit distributor's site at www.wiley.com/products/worldwide/canada. [ID:2426]

Doing Business with Japanese Men: A Woman's Handbook 📖
1993, *Christalyn Brannen, Tracey Wilen,* Stone Bridge Press, 176 pages ➤ Weatherhill, 41 Monroe Turnpike, Trumbull, CT 06611, USA; US$9.95; credit cards; (800) 437-7840, fax (800) 557-5601, weath1212@aol.com ■ The only book aimed at Western businesswomen meeting Japanese clients and confronting Japan's tradition of male dominance. Uses real-life anecdotes to help women establish their authority and work effectively with Japanese men. Visit the distributor's web site at www.weatherhill.com. [ID:1405]

Graveyard For Dreamers: One Woman's Odyssey in Africa 📖
1994, *Joan Baxter,* Potter's Field Press, 224 pages ➤ Nimbus Publishing, P.O. Box 9301, Stn. A, Halifax, Nova Scotia B3K 5N5; $16.95; cheque or VISA; (800) 646-2879, fax (800) 455-3652 ■ A well-written, personal, and colourful account of living, traveling, and reporting on coups and customs in seven West African countries by a journalist from Nova Scotia. Particularly insightful is Ms. Baxter's sharing of her adaptation process and what it is like to be a white woman in rural and urban West Africa. [ID:2622]

The International Businesswoman of the 1990s 📖
1990, *Marlene L. Rossman,* Praeger Publishers ➤ Greenwood Publishing Group, P.O. Box 5007, 88 Post Road W., Westport, CT 06881, USA; US$19.95; credit cards; (800) 225-5800, fax (203) 222-1502 ■ A practical guide for women pursuing careers in international business. Describes career opportunities and addresses the issues women face, including breaking down barriers in the international business world. Includes case studies. Visit web site www.greenwood.com for distributor. [ID:1180]

International Centre for Research on Women 🖥
www.icrw.org/ ■ The International Centre for research on Women's web site offers publications as well as a comprehensive set of development links. [ID:2451]

Internships in Foreign and Defense Policy: a Complete Guide for Women (& Men) 📖
1990, *Women in International Security,* 103 pages ➤ Seven Locks Press, P.O. Box 68, Arlington, VA 22210, USA; US$10.95; credit cards; (800) 354-5348, fax (714) 545-1572, sevenlocks@aol.com ■ An internship early in your career can help open doors to a successful career. This book is designed to help women (and men) pursue the many opportunities for internships in the area of international security. [ID:1245]

A Journey of One's Own: Uncommon Advice for the Independent Woman Traveler 📖
1996, *Thalia Zepatos,* 349 pages ➤ The Eighth Mountain Press, 624 SE 29th Ave., Portland, OR 97214, USA; US$16.95; cheques only; (503) 233-3936, fax (503) 233-0774 ■ Expert advice is combined with tales of crosscultural encounters. A wide array of women travellers provide advice to help you with matters such as sexual harassment, staying healthy, avoiding theft, managing a long trip, and safely travelling solo, with a partner, or with a child. [ID:1787]

Women in Management Worldwide 📖
1994, *Nancy J. Adler, Dafna Izraeli,* M.E. Sharpe Inc., 304 pages ➤ Coutts Library Services, P.O.Box 1000, 6900 Kinsmen Court, Niagara Falls, Ontario L2E 7E7; US$26.95; credit cards; (905) 356-6382, fax (905) 356-5064 ▪ The role of women in management is changing rapidly. This book describes female managers in economically developing and developed economies, in centrally planned and market economies, and in occidental and oriental cultural traditions. [ID:1621]

Women on the Move: A Christian Perspective on Cross-Cultural Adaptation 📖
1989, *Gretchen Janssen,* Intercultural Press, 160 pages ➤ Intercultural and Community Development Resources (ICDR), P.O. Box 32108, Millwoods Station, Edmonton, Alberta T6K 4C2; $22; VISA, Amex; (800) 378-3199, fax (403) 462-1925, icdr@compusmart.ab.ca ▪ A guide for those with religious convictions who face the stress of a new environment. Suggests that one's own beliefs can help in successful adaptation. From the experiences of a woman who travelled with her husband from the US to Europe. Visit distributor's site at www.compusmart.ab.ca/icdr. [ID:1034]

Women's Guide to Overseas Living 📖
1992, *Nancy J. Piet-Pelon, Barbara Hornby,* Intercultural Press, 210 pages ➤ Intercultural and Community Development Resources (ICDR), P.O. Box 32108, Millwoods Station, Edmonton, Alberta T6K 4C2; $23; VISA, Amex; (800) 378-3199, fax (403) 462-1925, icdr@compusmart.ab.ca ▪ Examines issues critical to women (and their families) who relocate abroad. Sound advice on how to cope effectively, culture shock, stress and loneliness, managing households, children, health. Visit the distributor's web site at www.compusmart.ab.ca/icdr. [ID:1322]

Chapter 7

The Canadian Identity in the International Workplace

Imagine arriving at the New Delhi office of a senior Indian executive for an appointment and finding him surrounded by relatives. Or, weeks after completing what seemed to be very successful verbal negotiations with a Malaysian businesswoman, you still have not received a contract. Or, consider the West African businessman caught by surprise when you actually show up on his doorstep in response to his dinner invitation. Each of these situations points to a clash between your Canadian culture-bound attitudes about business relations and the attitudes of those from other countries.

From culture to culture there exists a wide range of attitudes about appropriate business practices. To succeed in a crosscultural work environment, we must be aware of our own culturally-based business practices and acknowledge that each of us brings our own cultural baggage along on overseas assignments. The more aware we are, the more successful our overseas assignments will be. How do we as Canadians think in the workplace? How do our practices fit with those of other cultures? Any seasoned international employee will tell you this knowledge is crucial to success in the international realm.

"It is essential to understand the cultural dimensions of the environment in which you want to work. I have found it useful to explain to my Moroccan business associates some Canadian cultural characteristics, in particular those of Canadian business people. They then have a better understanding of where I am coming from and why I react in certain ways. It takes time, but I find it helpful."

This chapter deals with the most common culturally-influenced behaviours of Canadians in business situations. We include quotes from senior international consultants who reveal how these behavioural traits clash in the vastly different business cultures of other countries.

87

Generalizing about Canada's cultural business practices is difficult as we are a country with a complex "cultural mosaic" and an increasingly rich ethnic diversity. While recognizing our cultural diversity, we do acknowledge that there are some dominant cultural practices in Canada. It is therefore the premise of this chapter that whether you are a Jewish Montréaler or an outport Newfoundlander, your work habits and attitudes towards business protocol will likely bear some similarity. We will attempt to describe these similarities and explore their relevance to a crosscultural/overseas employment framework.

HOW ARE WE PERCEIVED ABROAD?

Canadians have forged a good reputation in the international workplace. We are seen as non-threatening and known as generous aid-givers throughout the South. We are recognized worldwide as international peacekeepers who promote a standard of fairness. The fact that we have neither invaded, nor attempted to colonize, other countries is an important factor in how we are perceived internationally.

Thanks to our multicultural heritage, we are known to have an affinity with other ethnically diverse nations. We tend to be a little more conservative than our American or European counterparts. We are often seen as self-deprecating, which contrasts with the boastfulness attributed to Americans.

The Canadians who preceded you to your foreign destination have probably helped improve the reception you will receive when you step off the plane. We hope this chapter will help you maintain, and indeed improve upon, Canada's already solid international image.

OUR GENERAL ATTITUDE TOWARDS WORK

The following is an attempt to analyze the Canadian work ethic. Quotes from international consultants will help situate the various elements in a crosscultural work context.

Goal-Oriented and Hard Working

Canadians tend to be goal-oriented and to place high value on achievement, both in our professional and personal lives. This is evident in our respect for hard work and commitment to a given task. We believe hard work will bring reward, and if financial recognition is not immediately forthcoming, we are nonetheless worthy of respect.

We tend to value organizational skills and a goal-oriented, orderly work style. We greatly value timeliness, efficiency, and progress. Even in leisure time many of us pursue a hobby or personal interest with similar concentration, setting goals and aiming for a certain level of competence.

"I once read in a magazine that a bird-watchers' association was organizing a weekend trip, during which a contest would be held. The prize would go to the person with the highest number of bird sightings! Even while we enjoy nature, we feel the need for concrete achievement."

We value upward mobility, self-improvement and professional success attained through discipline, hard work, and playing by the rules. We tend to be action-oriented, "doers" rather than "thinkers," so concerned are we with tangible evidence of work having been performed. Canadians are so committed to this pursuit of concrete results that recent surveys show a large number of us feel we neglect our personal lives for our careers. Even in social situations conversation revolves around what we do for a living, and our social status is, to a large extent, determined by the positions we hold.

"I, as a Canadian, have worked hard all my life—literally day in and day out. I am now married to a Pakistani and living in an extended family in Pakistan. Almost all disagreements stem from my work habits, as I am still work-driven and do not allow myself time to enjoy my life and my family. We Canadians are like robots when it comes to relaxing and enjoying what life offers."

As a consequence, Canadians overseas tend not to put enough energy into developing personal relationships with business colleagues, which in many cultures precedes results. In fact, we are sometimes perceived as "pushy" in our determination to complete our tasks. By not establishing trust with our overseas partners through personal relationships, many Canadians have also proven ineffectual in their work.

"In talking with my Indian counterpart about key elements for a briefing to Canadian contractors on establishing partnerships in India, my counterpart emphasized the following: 'businesspeople in Canada must recognize that they are task-oriented while we Indians are relationship-oriented. Canadians need to first relax their task orientation in order to build the trust that is the foundation of a good working relationship in India. The task will follow in its own good time.'

"When I first started doing business in Morocco, I was impatient with my partner because he wanted me to spend more time socializing with his family than discussing our joint venture. I came to realize, however, that in his view, getting to know me and having me get to know him, and his family, was a precondition to doing business. After I accepted this, things moved along just fine!"

Law-Abiding

Canadians' ethical and moral values tend to be conservative and, as peace lovers, we are, in general, a law-abiding nation. We draw a rather hard line between "right" and "wrong" and are not easily swayed from our judgements. This makes it difficult for Canadians to accept different sets of values in other countries. For instance, hiring a close relative is a common and even desirable practice in many countries, but is regarded as a serious impropriety by many Canadians.

"As a participant on a committee reviewing applications to bring exchange students from an Asian country to Canada, we were concerned that our Asian counterparts were recommending a work colleague. Our high moral ground seemed clear until someone pointed out that two of our own committee members were related, and one of us had just arranged to have a relative's tree

nursery business take a foreign student. We realized that we looked upon our own initiatives as generous and appropriate while regarding with suspicion similar decisions made by the overseas selection committee!"

Corruption in the businessplace is considered a part of normal business operations in many countries. Bribes often account for a third of the value of a contract and fall directly into civil servants' pockets. When you work in the South, sooner or later you will face the dilemma of giving into it or not. Canadian businesspeople are uncomfortable with some foreign business practices and will often walk away from a deal rather than pay a bribe. Businesspeople from other countries consider us naive. There are many platitudes and excuses offered for corruption, but no matter how it is presented, or who is involved, we agree with the following experts: corruption is wrong.

"It is possible to live and do business in the South without getting involved in corruption. Not condoning or becoming involved does not make us naive. There are always ways around it. It may come as a surprise that in an institutional culture where corruption seems pervasive, most people find it just as distasteful as you or I, but have learned to work around it.

"By paying your first bribe, you can get caught in a spiral of corruption from which it is difficult to escape. I once paid a bribe to the downtown traffic cops though I had been stopped for dubious reasons. Since I was late for a meeting, I decided to slip the officer a few bills rather than take the time to argue. From that day on, I had to pay a bribe each time I crossed the city business district. The only way out was to call their bluff and insist on being arrested. After that I was no longer bothered, and have learned an important lesson on bribery."

Separate Work and Personal Lives

As Canadians, we make a clear distinction between our professional and personal lives. We carefully protect our privacy and keep our work life separate from our home life. Interruptions at work by friends or family members are generally frowned upon. It is also common to disapprove of a colleague who uses office time to deal with family matters. In other cultures the interaction between personal and professional life flows far more naturally. Canadians posted in countries where such behaviour is the cultural norm have identified this lack of separation as a major source of stress, mostly because they use a lot of energy trying to maintain their own barriers.

"I volunteered to help develop a business plan for a dynamic Somali immigrant to Canada who had started up a professional-looking community newspaper. Despite the long volunteer hours he put in, and the obvious benefits of his work to the Somali community, I felt uncomfortable when I realized he was using his volunteer work to help start up his own graphic design business. Everyone benefited from this young man's initiative, so why the mistrust? It really struck me how much Canadians mistrust cross-overs from work, volunteer activities, and family, not to mention religion or politics. Canadians segment everything. Integrated spheres of activity are suspect."

"I had a very close African friend who was also a senior government official. Whenever I visited him at his house, it seemed like he was holding court, as there were always people waiting to see him. When I asked how he could put up with his personal life being so disrupted, he stated that he gathered more support for his programs at home than at his office, but most importantly, this was expected from an official at his level."

We also avoid doing business with friends or relatives for fear of ruining our personal relationships or creating conflicts of interest.

"As a project manager on an African assignment, I was very wary of engaging local professionals who were close friends of my local sub-consultant. It was explained to me, however, that in West Africa this was not only acceptable but preferable, as it ensures loyalty. While Canadians derive loyalty from a pay package, Africans' loyalties are based on tribal or cultural traditions, or on social obligations. This is practical given the limited pool of resources in Africa and the fact that most educated Africans have studied together at the higher education levels.

"As a Canadian I am sometimes shocked at the number of relatives and friends of one ethnic group or "tribe" being brought into the government. Appointments within the government often pay for favours, a currency in its own right. This is the world's most common form of barter and the essence of protecting one's position and family—and in many cases, the only way of getting ahead."

Entwining professional and personal lives however, can have detrimental effects in the workplace.

"A World Bank project in which I work is collapsing. After a year and a half of researching the reasons behind the project's failure we have just begun to understand. The local project director brought the project to a standstill because of a family feud between the wife of his superior and the wife of the Chief Minister. The Bank plans to close the multimillion dollar project, which was designed to aid the rural poor."

Polite but Not Necessarily Friendly

Canadians are seen as reserved and rather serious. We are often perceived by foreigners as cold and not particularly outgoing, polite but not necessarily friendly. Moreover, Canadians are generally considered humourless, unable to tell a good story or a joke. In the South, humour and tactful frankness not only help in closing business deals, but often keep them going.

"I was involved in a very lucrative project in Asia that became unravelled when a Canadian firm sent in a group of humourless professionals to manage the project after the deal was signed. No further contracts were forthcoming, as all of the goodwill gained during negotiations was lost by the unfriendly implementation team."

Lacking in General Cultural Knowledge

North Americans are known as culturally ignorant for our common inability to discuss art, literature, politics, and history. Unlike other countries where interest in these topics is widespread and encouraged, our work ethic, and in the case of Canadians, fear of treading on controversial ground, often prevent us from enjoying art and appreciating knowledge for its own sake.

"I remember being amazed in France by the level of knowledge of plumbers and other tradesmen. They were far better at discussing politics and literature than I, despite my master's degree. Our education simply does not put enough emphasis on general cultural knowledge."

Our omnipresent concern with work leaves other parts of our lives under-developed. Conversation is a rare art in our society. For many of us, our most meaningful exchange of ideas occurs at work. By avoiding discussion of such imprecise subjects as the arts, we deprive ourselves of growth into new fields of knowledge.

"When I first arrived in India I was overwhelmed by the diversity of this culture whose history spanned more than 5,000 years! When I admitted this to my host, he was both sympathetic and delighted to introduce me to his particular religion and region. He talked at length about Sikhism, his extended family in his home state of Punjab, and about the religious and political conflicts in that region. After our work-day was over, he spent hours showing me the historical monuments in and around Delhi."

Canadians tend to avoid discussion of controversial subjects. We prevent embarrassing encounters by making politics, philosophy, and spirituality taboo when socializing with co-workers. Some of us think it is inappropriate or irrelevant to discuss such things with colleagues, while others feel simply that we have nothing to contribute. We tend to be suspicious of co-workers who display expertise or even simple interest in areas unrelated to the work at hand. Moreover, Canadians are not very inquisitive in conversation, perhaps because they prefer to be in control, making statements rather than asking questions.

"Very early in my overseas career, I was confronted by a senior African official who, halfway through a three-hour dinner, berated me for being so unresponsive to conversation. He was right. I was trying so hard not to get into any controversial issues. In a gentle way, he explained that the most rewarding aspect of an overseas career was learning about other cultures. Being overly guarded in crosscultural oral interchanges was keeping me from understanding the new culture."

We generally drop a conversational item if we discover that our friends have strongly differing views from our own. We don't want to point out significant value differences for fear of creating a breach in our relationship.

"What a thrill it was to be in France and to have tremendous arguments at dinner parties over communism, capitalism, and the Pope, knowing full well

that we would all still be close friends when the evening was over. I couldn't help wondering why we can't be like that in Canada."

By taking an interest in local arts and music in their overseas work, Canadians not only develop a greater appreciation of the culture, but gain respect from their hosts and a better understanding of the business environment.

"The best piece of advice I received, and fortunately it came early in my first assignment in Africa, was that if you really want to understand the dynamics of the place, find out a little about the local music, theatre, art, media, and history. In addition to situating my business activities in a useful way, the interest I expressed was rewarded by a number of rich personal relationships."

BUSINESS PROTOCOL

In the business environment we adhere to entrenched norms. The following section examines how we as Canadians conduct our daily business activities and how these activities contrast with those of other countries.

The First Contact

In a business setting, Canadians use the handshake as their primary form of greeting. It is not uncommon among French Canadians to precede business between well-established contacts by exchanging hugs and kissing each other on both cheeks. In general, however, a reserved demeanour and a strong handshake accompanied by direct eye contact is the norm.

"Many cultures are different from Canada with regard to eye contact. Canadians tend to look people in the eyes a lot. In many cultures, women do not look men in the eyes, as this can be taken as a sign of sexual interest. Old people are shown deference in most cultures, and this can include not looking them in the eyes and, in some cases, not touching them.

"In Pakistan, the practice between male friends is to hug and immediately afterwards hold hands. This is a wonderful way to break barriers, far better than the crushing handshake!

"When I began working in Tanzania, I was initially bemused by the time-consuming practice of shaking hands and exchanging pleasantries with everyone in the room before and after a meeting. It was only after returning to Canada that I realized how much I missed this formality and how important it had become to me. Having your presence and individuality continuously acknowledged is rare in our Canadian culture."

Getting Down to Business

Because of the lines we draw between our professional and private lives, we tend to get down to business quickly, leaving little time to socialize or get acquainted with new colleagues. In many cultures, socializing with business associates is an opportunity for people to get to know their partners on a personal basis, thereby building trust, the essential ingredient in mutually satisfactory arrangements.

"I had to sit through interminable meetings in African villages, most con-sisting of long periods in which participants inquired about each other's health and my family's history. In the beginning I thought we were getting nowhere, until I realized this practice was helpful in building consensus and trust among group members."

We Canadians delude ourselves into thinking that time spent establishing interpersonal relationships will detract from our professional performance. It is said that when Canadian projects fail, it has less to do with lack of technical expertise than with breakdowns in communication and failure of Canadian counterparts to take the time to familiarize themselves with the culture.

Establishing a good interpersonal relationship can lead to successful long-term work partnerships and friendships.

"When I worked in Eastern Africa I quickly adapted to the ritual of sharing tea and biscuits with my host, regardless of the time of day. This was a time that was never rushed, when pleasantries were exchanged. In my early years in Kenya and Malawi, I learned to attach much importance to these rituals. Now, years later, many of the officials with whom I drank tea and chatted prior to 'getting down to business' are senior members of the public service. They are not only colleagues, but friends who have helped me overcome obstacles and provided me with assistance when I returned to work in their countries on other projects.

"You might be surprised to learn that in places like Africa your business partners see the work relationship as long-term, a potential friendship."

Giving and Receiving Hospitality

Canadians are accustomed to putting their professional lives ahead of their personal lives in business situations. We tend not to spend time inquiring about our colleagues' families or home environments. When faced with out-of-town business guests, we are hospitable to the extent that we ensure they are comfortable and have all the resources necessary to perform their given mission.

Canadians working abroad, however, are frequently treated with tremen-dous hospitality. Hosts take extraordinary amounts of time to welcome us and show us around. So when foreigners visit us in Canada, we have great difficulty reciprocating. Our jobs and compartmentalized lives make it extremely hard to take days or entire weeks to show visitors around, and we have no relatives willing to do the job for us. We feel unable to live up to the standards of our foreign hosts.

"I remember when our first exchange teacher arrived from Kenya. It was a very busy time of year, with many pressures on my staff and myself. I recall making a very conscious effort to allow plenty of time to greet our Kenyan associate, inquire about his trip, his family, the colleagues I knew at his home institution in Kenya, the political situation in Kenya, etc. I know that some of my Canadian staff felt I took too much time, under the circumstances, to welcome our visitor. However, I had learned from working in Kenya that

putting his needs and concerns aside to tend to what I considered the more pressing details of his program, would only impede his progress later on. To this day, I recall the stress of trying to balance our institutional and cultural perspectives on time and priorities with those of our exchange teachers from Africa."

Egalitarian Relationships

Canadian society is not so rigidly stratified as some other societies. We enjoy a high degree of social mobility and it is common for us to mix with people of different social classes and gender. Because of this, Canadians are often seen to be disrespectful of local power structures, and overseas hosts sometimes find this aspect of our behaviour embarrassing. Indeed, our overseas hosts and business colleagues are often bemused or offended by the lack of distinction we make between subordinates, peers, and superiors. We appear to treat everyone equally, even when their status differs from ours.

"When we were in East Africa we had a 'maid.' As salaries were so low and people needed jobs, it seemed like a good idea. We wanted her to eat with us at the table, but while we were very comfortable with this idea, she was not. No amount of discussion could persuade her otherwise."

Unlike countries where the class system is more firmly entrenched, we value personal experience and expertise over family origins. Belief in the concept of equality is an integral part of the Canadian identity. In crosscultural situations, both work-related and social, we tend to be insensitive to or even offended by overtly hierarchical structures. Canadian organizations are "flatter" and function with less hierarchy. Thus, subordinates have easier access to senior levels of management.

Canadians tend to question authority. We require that our superiors "earn" our respect, while in most other societies, authority is granted by status and rarely challenged.

"Canadians respect youth and not age. This is the inverse in most of the world. Abroad, it is better to have grey hair and be older, as you are accorded prestige and seen as wise. Many other cultures have great difficulty understanding our obsession with youthfulness."

Respect for Space

Canada is the second-largest country in the world and has a disproportionately small population. It is therefore hardly surprising that Canadians place a high value on large homes and ample working space. The need to maintain sufficient physical distance from colleagues is an important aspect of our business protocol. It is a factor while we are talking with others, in meetings and in our individual work-places. We neither expect, nor welcome, violations to our territory.

"I didn't realize how important our personal space or 'bubble' is to us until I started to work in China. For whatever reasons, the Chinese don't throw up as wide a psychic screen around themselves as we Canadians do. In crowds and

even in normal work situations, I initially found myself reacting against what I perceived as violations of my personal space."

The typical Canadian office reflects this need for personal space and is designed to provide individual privacy for its occupants and reduce unintentional contact. In fact, we place such importance on space that the size of our office reflects our status within the company. Some advice for the confused foreigner: if you can't tell who the boss is by the way we talk to each other, you can find her or him in the large corner office with the window!

As mentioned, our need for personal space is further reflected in how closely we stand to each other. Canadians tend to stand about one metre apart while conversing. In many other cultures people stand much closer together; we find this disconcerting.

"I remember one evening in Nigeria where, at a cocktail party, I ended up in a corner surrounded by Nigerians all standing very close to me. I felt so uncomfortable. It was only later that I realized my discomfort stemmed from the clash of the Nigerian custom of standing very close to the person they are speaking with and the Canadian custom of keeping your distance."

Canadians also place a high priority on privacy and a controlled environment free of extraneous noise.

"During a field mission to Tanzania, I asked my local partner for a quiet place to write. There were a few empty offices around, so I thought it would be easy to accommodate me. To my dismay, I was given a space next to the reception area, the busiest of all spots, with heavy office traffic, and noise and smells from the street. When I asked for the quiet office at the end of the hall, I discovered I had been given the most desirable place of all. He said the other office was not a good place to work as I would not be able to see other people."

Blind Individualism

In business situations we focus on the task at hand and pay little attention to the context. Because we are individualistic, we tend to be impatient with group efforts, preferring to work on our own toward concrete goals. This sometimes involves cutting through red tape to improve efficiency. Superiors from other cultures may be offended by our neglect of the consultative process. It is not uncommon for Canadians to be unaware of what their colleagues are doing, even when they are members of the same team.

"On a recent consultation in South Asia, I was monitoring an institutional cooperation project. The ministry of labour and planning, in partnership with Canadians working on the project, were to be involved in deciding which experts were needed to run training programs. The ministry and the Canadians were to jointly decide, on a case-by-case basis, whether the qualified local resource people could be hired at considerably less cost, or whether it was necessary to select Canadians for the job.

"The Canadian partners established a pattern of seeking the ministry's approval only after they had selected the personnel they felt were suitable for the job. Predictably, they were always Canadians. The Canadian staff were trying

to prove they could get the job done and keep the project 'on target.' They thought they were being helpful by relieving the overloaded ministry of time-consuming work reviewing applications and selecting resource people. While ministry officials were initially too polite to object to decisions made without their consultation, they became increasingly upset. They felt project resources were being wasted on Canadians when they should have been directed to local personnel. They began refusing to cooperate on other aspects of the project. The arrival of the monitor brought this issue to light. Finally the partners met to work out an acceptable approach, and the consultative process described in the management plan was resurrected."

COMMUNICATING

Canadians trust the written word and expect straight answers to questions. But while this may be comfortable for us, it is not the norm in many cultures. The next section explores the ways in which Canadians communicate and how our communication style is interpreted in the international arena.

Formal Communication and Belief in the Written Word

The way we compartmentalize our lives creates a need for formal communication systems. We tend not to be effective at verbal communication, except in structured settings such as meetings. Therefore, while many cultures place a higher value on verbal business agreements, Canadians trust the written word. To us, signing a contract is the beginning of a business liaison. This is clearly different from other cultures, where the contract is viewed merely as an outcome of an already-established relationship.

"When I began working in China, the Canadians I was with expressed frustration at the inordinate amount of time spent eating and touring prior to getting down to business and signing formal partnership agreements. However, for the Chinese to reach this point in the business relationship meant that the deal was already complete. They had accepted the Canadian partners and for them the rest was pure mechanics."

While we use formal methods of communication, such as memos, structured meetings, minutes of meetings, and letters, we tend to view verbal exchanges as not only inefficient, but unreliable. With our respect for the "documented" word, we can feel left out of the action in some overseas work environments. While our local colleagues are doing business through the grapevine and assuming we are abreast of recent developments, we are sitting in the dark, waiting for the memos to come through!

"In many instances, both written and verbal communication is inadequate. It is accepted that trust is strongest in the extended family and between old classmates from university. Otherwise, anything goes. The written word is the South's way of trying to get everything on top of the table but there is usually a lot more going on beneath."

Clear and Assertive Communication Style

Canadians strive for and respect a direct communication style. We look for straight answers to our questions and tend to discuss issues in a blunt way. This bluntness can be hurtful to someone coming from a culture where saving face is crucial. By ignoring the subtleties of human communication we miss nonverbal messages, which can be an integral part of the picture. Therefore, we must be careful not to be so honest as to humiliate others whose cultural communication styles differ from our own.

It is important to understand that every culture employs certain means of communication which are further refined by individual organizations within that culture. A good reading of your environment can dramatically increase your chances of communicating effectively with others. For instance, once you know that Southeast Asians dread offending others by expressing opposition directly and will therefore say "yes" when they mean "no," you can adjust your behaviour in the workplace to be less confrontational, more subtle.

"As a foreigner meeting high-ranking officials, I was cautioned against asking any questions for fear they would be unable to answer and would become embarrassed. Asking questions in that context is considered impolite and disrespectful. At first I was shocked and wondered how anyone up and down the ladder communicated. Now I realize that hierarchy and respect for one's 'superiors' is the glue that holds things together and without it, anarchy threatens."

CONDUCTING BUSINESS

The way we arrange our schedules, make decisions, and achieve results all affects how we interact with our foreign colleagues. The following section examines how we as Canadians structure our business lives.

Time Is Money

For most Canadians, "time is money." We value punctuality and regard it as an expression of respect towards others. We hate to waste our own and other peoples' valuable time. We conceive of time as a precious resource to be used, divided and assigned to particular projects and activities. Accordingly, our days are carefully sliced up into periods, each reflecting time allocated to a particular activity. We prefer to approach each task separately and to move on to the next only when the first is complete. Dealing with unplanned events creates stress.

"For a while I felt really lost in this environment. Meetings never started on time. We would have a meeting and agree on steps to be taken and several days later, I would realize that nothing had been done. Priorities had changed and the duration of the project had lengthened without my being informed. I was really frustrated.

"On a research project in Ecuador, I had carefully planned structured interviews of 250 farmers to correspond to my financial and time resources. I forgot to consider the questions the farmers would have for me, not to mention

the drinks to be consumed in celebration of the friendship between Canada and Ecuador!"

Assessing the Facts

Our favourite approach to problem-solving is the step-by-step, linear model: we identify the facts and where they originate from, thereby constructing a cause-and-effect chain for gathering, sharing and analysing information. In this process, intuition is not valued at all and emphasis is on hard facts. Canadians have little tolerance for ambiguity and will eliminate it rather than attempt to understand it.

Canadians approach business opportunities in the same cautious manner, ensuring they have all the facts before making a decision. As mentioned, we are known as conservative people who avoid unnecessary risks.

"In my 20 years of business travel, one comment I have received over and over is 'We really respect Canada and Canadians but why are they so conservative and unwilling to take risks? A little assertiveness would also help.'"

Making Decisions

In Canada, we value managers who take immediate, decisive action after a problem-solving exercise. We admire those who can make decisions quickly and take responsibility for the consequences. We like to see action, work in progress, and evidence that things are moving.

"Forget all your Canadian approaches to decision making, as they are rarely used in the South. In China, for example, managers were taught for 40 years not to make decisions. This is changing, but basic managerial skills are still severely lacking and responsibility for making decisions is often passed onwards and upwards."

Increasingly however, Canadian business, institutions, and management training schools are promoting decision making processes that involve both the manager and staff. This approach does not come easily to the individualistic Canadian, but it is now considered good policy to consult the people who will be affected by a decision. Based on the idea that employees know best what their needs are, supervisors are offering support to employees and allowing them to search for solutions, rather than providing ready-made answers.

This approach can also be disconcerting to non-Western societies, where employees are used to a more hierarchical process. For someone accustomed to taking orders, a supervisor's belief that an employee is equipped to solve her or his own problem might suggest incompetence on the part of the supervisor. A boss is supposed to be all-knowing!

"I spent my first few months in Zaire trying to involve my staff in all levels of decision making. They ignored me. I decided I had to become more autocratic. I was more decisive, made most decisions unilaterally, and requested more service from staff. I had the office boy bring me coffee rather than serving myself, and always used the driver instead of driving myself. Things greatly

improved. My staff liked my autocratic behaviour and in their eyes, I was assuming my responsibilities as a boss."

Getting Results

Ours is a rational attitude aimed at eliminating problems. Once a decision is made, we want it carried out immediately. Delay generates anxiety. Because we tend to design courses of action which focus on results, little attention is paid to the process.

"While conducting a training course on international negotiations in Colombia, we sometimes felt we were forcing conclusions on our students. They preferred a much longer period of exploration than we had anticipated.

"In many countries the process is more important than the product. For example, when checking in at the airport in Karachi, one goes through an intricate series of steps from checking, double-checking and triple-checking paper tags tied to hand luggage. The process is so full of holes it would be easy to slip an illicit bag on board. But the process gives 15 policemen something to do and allows them to be seen by the elite. And it gives a sense of security to the passengers, even if it is false. It is the process that matters the most."

WHAT WE NEED TO IMPROVE ON

Our interview research shows Canadians need to improve in certain key areas if they are to be comfortable, and therefore successful, in crosscultural work situations. Some useful suggestions follow.

Be Culturally Sensitive

Canada is made up of people from a wide range of cultures, but our daily lives take place in fairly homogenous communities. Even if we live in large cities, our lives are compartmentalized and present little opportunity for contact with people from other cultural backgrounds. Our limited exposure to crosscultural situations differs dramatically from regions such as Asia or West Africa, where a variety of cultures and languages interact on a daily basis.

Learning to successfully integrate into a new cultural environment means using a combination of hard facts and intuition, the latter being quite a challenge for the logically-minded Canadian. We must remember, however, that beneath apparent chaos, there is always order, and this order is understandable in culturally-specific terms. You are thus confronted with a dual learning challenge: the organizational and the societal. It is crucial you carry out your responsibilities while respecting the values of those you encounter in your crosscultural experience.

"While managing an overseas project, my counterpart informed me that his professional staff would not work with one of my Canadian staff. They believed he showed disrespect for them by co-habiting with his cook. In their view, he was also bringing disrespect upon the project and his position within the local organization. Canadians abroad must be discreet and considerate of local cultural norms. Being from another culture is not an excuse to offend."

Have Realistic Goals

In planning, we often assume we have complete control over our time and environment. We do not anticipate our work being disrupted. Planning is oriented towards quantifiable results and objective, rather than intuitive, consideration of all the options. This rigid approach can create frustration on a crosscultural posting where unexpected factors can be brought into play at any time. You must be knowledgeable about your new environment to plan your work realistically.

It is important to bear in mind potential logistical constraints when planning your work in the South. Can you imagine the impact that a shortage of fuel, the rainy season, or sudden inflation can have on a project? Even a lack of paper and pens at the local office supply store has been known to frustrate implementation of a project. What was a realistic expectation in your Canadian work environment could be totally unrealistic in a crosscultural context.

"We sent a Canadian teacher to train a counterpart in computer applications at an East African polytechnic. We shipped the computers six months in advance, figuring this would allow plenty of time for the equipment to arrive, clear customs and be installed in the polytechnic's new computer lab. The computers arrived two weeks before the teacher had to return to Canada after his four-month placement! He and his counterpart miraculously made do with old equipment, and they managed to scrounge one new computer, so that at least the counterpart could be trained on the new software. They were unable to train the teachers under these circumstances. The African counterpart ran the program very successfully after our Canadian teacher returned home. However, we learned plenty from the folly of being inflexible, and applied it to subsequent phases of the project."

Think Long-term

Canadian society is oriented towards the future. Our government reflects this in its long-term strategic planning, but even at an individual level we attempt to conduct our professional and personal lives in a strategic way. We like having one activity lead to the next in a logical manner, with our future well-being in mind.

Unfortunately, projects conducted in the South sometimes lack this long-term comprehensive focus. This is often the result of the short time Canadians spend in a particular country, in combination with poor technology transfer to our overseas counterparts. Without long-term, comprehensive development strategy, there is little continuity from one project to another.

It is important for Canadians to reverse this trend and promote long-term sustainable growth in the South.

A LAST WORD

Many of the world's cultures are thousands of years old and steeped in history and traditions. Our tendency to focus on facts and results often leads us to ignore the subtleties of these cultures and to misunderstand their business practices. We highly recommend you learn as much as you can about the corporate culture of the organization you will be working with, as well as the shared beliefs and values of the country you are going to. Often the context of a decision or particular project is an all-embracing environment, not limited to the walls of the office. By exhibiting a genuine interest in the local culture, listening to and questioning what is around you, participating in social events, and visiting public places, you will be prepared with knowledge and insight when decisions have to be made or courses of action proposed.

"In my many years of working abroad, I have seen Canadians cut them- selves off from enriching experiences by hiding behind the protective label of the 'foreign expert.' We cannot be experts in everything—if you consult in several different regions in the world, you must be prepared to open yourself up to learning about the culture in which you are working. To do this, I think Canadians have to admit they don't 'know it all,' they have to ask more questions—questions that are both sincere and diplomatic—and then they have to listen to the answers. My work in more than a dozen countries in the developing world has introduced me to people who were thoroughly delighted and proud to teach me about their culture whenever I expressed an interest. Much of my learning, therefore, has come about through my ability to take a risk—to admit my shortcomings, to listen, and to appreciate that a window on yet another world has been opened."

RESOURCES

Crosscultural Business Skills

Being knowledgeable about how people of other nationalities react to North Americans is as important as knowing how we, as Canadians, react to peoples of different nationalities. No matter what country you travel to, it's important for your business to have a head start on understanding "what the people are like."

Judging by the number of international business books on the market, you might think the art of doing business internationally is difficult to master. You will find, however, that the skills of crosscultural communication are portable, whether applied to business, diplomacy, or friendship. Moreover, once you learn to do business with the Japanese, you can easily apply your knowledge to doing business with Indonesians or Brazilians. Many of the following resources pertain to international business negotiations, but don't back away from this material if you are not a businessperson; all international employees need crosscultural negotiation skills.

While we may not like to admit it, Canadians have many cultural traits similar to Americans. Helpful books describing American cultural traits are listed after the section on the United States of America in Chapter 27, Jobs by Regions of the World. These books make very good reading for Canadians. Also consult the Resources sections in the following chapters: for general crosscultural skills see Chapter 1, The Effective Overseas Employee; for the more practical aspects of living overseas see Chapter 3, Living Overseas and Chapter 12, Crosscultural Travel; to improve your International IQ, see

Chapter 13, Global Education Centres; for country-specific advice on social and business customs see Chapter 27, Jobs by Regions of the World; and for books on the practice of international business (such as how to import and export) see Chapter 33, Services for International Businesses & Entrepreneurs.

Bargaining Across Borders: How to Negotiate
Business Successfully Anywhere in the World 📖
1995, *Dean Allen Foster,* McGraw-Hill Ryerson Ltd., 337 pages ➤ Intercultural and Community Development Resources (ICDR), P.O. Box 32108, Millwoods Station, Edmonton, Alberta T6K 4C2; $24; VISA, Amex; (800) 378-3199, fax (403) 462-1925, icdr@compusmart.ab.ca ▪ How do you convey respect in Japan? Can women negotiate contracts in Morocco? This book prepares you for the real-life situations you will face in international deal-making. Visit the distributor's web site at www.compusmart.ab.ca/icdr. [ID:2377]

Canada Year Book 📖
1997, Statistics Canada, 517 pages ➤ Renouf Books, 129 Algoma Rd., Ottawa, Ontario K1B 2W8; $54.95, CD-ROM $74.95; credit cards; (613) 745-2665, fax (613) 745-7660 ▪ This book is published every two years by Statistics Canada and serves as a vital reference resource. It provides an up-to-date picture of the social, economic, and cultural life of Canada. It's a great book to bring as a gift or as a handy reference for all the questions your overseas friends will ask you when you travel overseas. Visit the publisher's web site at www.renoufbooks.com. [ID:2775]

Centre for Intercultural Learning
Canadian Foreign Service Institute, 15 Bisson Street, Hull, Québec J8Y 5M2; (800) 852-9211, fax (819) 997-5409, monique.marion@bisson01.x400.gc.ca ▪ The Centre for Intercultural Learning assists Canadian professionals from NGOs, universities, private industry, and government to develop the crosscultural competencies essential for their success overseas. Services and products include pre-departure and project-related programs, on-arrival orientations, in-country programming, re-entry programs, country anthologies, and intercultural training. Their web site is under construction. [ID:2642]

Communicating With Customers Around the World:
A Practical Guide to Effective Cross-Cultural Business Communication 📖
1994, *K.C. Chan-Herur,* 136 pages ➤ AuMonde International Publishing Co., P.O. Box 471705, San Francisco, CA 94147-1705, USA; US$12.95; credit cards; (415) 281-8470, fax (415) 771-7731 ▪ Provides valuable insights into the nuances of business communication in over 30 countries, and offers practical tips for effective communication with international clients. A good source of information for anyone whose work entails frequent interaction with clients from different cultures. You can order this and other titles online at www.amazon.com. [ID:1579]

Competitive Frontiers: Women Managers in a Global Economy 📖
1994, *Nancy J. Adler, Dafna Izraeli,* 414 pages ➤ Blackwell Publishers, P.O. Box 20, Williston, VT 05495, USA; US$36.95; credit cards; (800) 488-2665, fax (802) 864-7626 ▪ This book examines the changing nature of world business and its impact on women managers. Visit the publisher's web site at www.blackwellpublishers.co.uk. [ID:1619]

Comportement Organisationnel 📖
1994, *Nancy J. Adler,* 352 pages ➤ Les Éditions Reynald Goulet Inc., 40 rue Mireault, Repentigny, Québec J6A 1M1; $28,95; VISA, MC; (514) 654-2626, fax (514) 654-5433 ▪ L'ouvrage traite des différences de cultures, propose une approche interculturelle pour la solution des problèmes et présente une série de problèmes propres à la direction des cadres internationaux. Traduction du livre *International Dimensions of Organizational Behavior.* [ID:1598]

Craighead's International Business Travel
and Relocation Guide to 78 Countries: 1996-97 📖
Annual, 4,699 pages, 3 vols. ➤ Gale Research Inc., 835 Penobscot Bldg., 645 Griswold Street, Detroit, MI 48226-4094, USA; US$575; credit cards; (800) 877-4253 ext. 1330, fax (800) 414-5043; Available in large libraries ▪ An indispensable guide for anyone who needs information on the

business practices, economies, customs, communication, tours, attractions and highlights of 78 countries worldwide. Provides details of local customs, arrival procedures, money matters, health services, and sources of additional information for those relocating overseas. Chapters on individual countries, extensive background information for personnel officers and employees going abroad, and recruiting guidelines for overseas personnel and information sources. [ID:1144]

Cross-Cultural Effectiveness 🕮
1990, *Daniel Kealey,* 68 pages ➤ Public Inquiries, Canadian International Development Agency, 200 Promenade du Portage, Hull, Québec K1A 0G4; free; (800) 230-6349, fax (819) 953-6088, info@acdi-cida.gc.ca ▪ Report of three-year study involving 1,400 people engaged in Canadian development programs in 16 countries. Aimed at measuring the effectiveness of technical advisors in transferring much-needed skills. Well written, in English and French. [ID:1101]

The Cultural Dimension of International Business 🕮
1994, *Gary P. Ferraro,* Prentice Hall Canada, 154 pages ➤ Intercultural and Community Development Resources (ICDR), P.O. Box 32108, Millwoods Station, Edmonton, Alberta T6K 4C2; $34; VISA, Amex; (800) 378-3199, fax (403) 462-1925, icdr@compusmart.ab.ca ▪ Shows readers how to make international business both more effective and more humane, using the theory and insights of cultural anthropology. Examines general concepts of culture, verbal and non-verbal communication patterns, contrasting value systems and culture-specific information. Visit the distributor's web site at www.compusmart.ab.ca/icdr. [ID:1388]

Culture Shock! Canada 🕮
1993, *Pang Guek Cheng, Robert Barlas,* Times Books International ➤ Raincoast Books, 8680 Cambie Street, Vancouver, B.C. V6P 6M9; $17.50; VISA, MC; (800) 663-5714, fax (800) 565-3770 ▪ Unique guide to the culture, customs and etiquette of Canada. Excellent resource, required reading for those going abroad who may have to explain Canada and its customs. One in a series of similar guides to countries all over the world. [ID:1218]

Cultures and Organizations: Software of the Mind 🕮
1991, *Geert Hofstede,* McGraw-Hill Ryerson Ltd., 292 pages ➤ Intercultural and Community Development Resources (ICDR), P.O. Box 32108, Millwoods Station, Edmonton, Alberta T6K 4C2; $56; VISA, Amex; (800) 378-3199, fax (403) 462-1925, icdr@compusmart.ab.ca ▪ Explains our world of confrontation with the premise that we all carry different mental programs, based on patterns of thinking, feeling and acting, learned through a lifetime. Shows how effective intercultural cooperation can be achieved, under what circumstances, and at what cost. Visit the distributor's web site at www.compusmart.ab.ca/icdr. [ID:1337]

Culturgrams: The Nations Around Us 🕮
1998, David M. Kennedy Center for International Studies, Two vols., 620 pages ➤ Kennedy Center Publications, Brigham Young University, 280 HRCB, Provo, UT 84602, USA; US$80; credit cards; (800) 528-6279, fax (801) 378-7075 ▪ Four-page summaries of the basic features of 164 cultures throughout the world. They cover customs, manners, lifestyles and other specialized information for those with interest but little time. Well worth the money! Free catalogue. Visit www.encarta.com. [ID:1085]

Developing Global Organizations: Strategies for Human Resource Professionals 🕮
1993, *Robert T. Moran, P. Harris, William G. Stripp,* Gulf Publishing, 318 pages ➤ Intercultural and Community Development Resources (ICDR), P.O. Box 32108, Millwoods Station, Edmonton, Alberta T6K 4C2; $47; VISA, Amex; (800) 378-3199, fax (403) 462-1925, icdr@compusmart.ab.ca ▪ Crosscultural training and education strategies aimed at developing global organizations and managers to conduct business in world markets. Visit the distributor's web site at www.compusmart.ab.ca/icdr. [ID:2381]

Do's and Taboos Around the World for Women in International Business 🕮
1997, *Roger E. Axtell,* 304 pages ➤ John Wiley & Sons, 22 Worchester Drive, Rexdale, Ontario M9W 1L1; $16.95; credit cards; (800) 567-4797, fax (800) 565-6802 ▪ Draws on experiences of 100

women to offer advice on body language, health concerns, dress, balancing family life with work abroad, and more. Visit distributor's site at www.wiley.com/products/worldwide/canada. [ID:2426]

Do's and Taboos of Hosting International Visitors 📖
1990, *Roger E. Axtell*, 236 pages ➤ John Wiley & Sons, 22 Worchester Drive, Rexdale, Ontario M9W 1L1; $17.95; credit cards; (800) 567-4797, fax (800) 565-6802 ▪ At a time when many businesspeople are hosting international visitors, this book acts as a guide to everything from entertaining and business protocol to the role of interpreters and corporate gift-giving. It lists, by country, tips on specific aspects of hosting and offers other valuable resources and references. Visit the distributor's web site at www.wiley.com/products/worldwide/canada. [ID:1011]

Do's and Taboos of International Trade: A Small Business Primer 📖
1994, *Roger E. Axtell*, 336 pages ➤ John Wiley & Sons, 22 Worchester Drive, Rexdale, Ontario M9W 1L1; $17.95; credit cards; (800) 567-4797, fax (800) 565-6802 ▪ A useful guide that shows small businesses how to increase sales by tapping into the international market. This book looks at how and where to get started, dealing with language barriers, habits and customs of other nationalities, financing and pricing per export, and much more. Visit the distributor's web site at www.wiley.com/products/worldwide/canada. [ID:1005]

Doing Business Internationally: The Guide to Cross-Cultural Success 📖
1995, *Terence Brake, Danielle Walker,* Irwin Professional Publishing, 256 pages ➤ Intercultural and Community Development Resources (ICDR), P.O. Box 32108, Millwoods Station, Edmonton, Alberta T6K 4C2; $35; VISA, Amex; (800) 378-3199, fax (403) 462-1925, icdr@compusmart.ab.ca ▪ Provides executives and managers with the basic knowledge and skills they'll need to compete in today's gigantic, multicultural marketplace. Starting with an overview of six cultural regions: Africa, Asia, Latin America, Europe, the Middle East, and North America, the authors build a framework for organizing crosscultural experiences and identifying and working with key cultural differences. Visit the distributor's web site at www.compusmart.ab.ca/icdr. [ID:2378]

Doing Business Internationally: The Workbook to Cross-Cultural Success 📖
1995, *Terence Brake, Danielle Walker,* Princeton Training Press, 232 pages ➤ Intercultural and Community Development Resources (ICDR), P.O. Box 32108, Millwoods Station, Edmonton, Alberta T6K 4C2; $68; VISA, Amex; (800) 378-3199, fax (403) 462-1925, icdr@compusmart.ab.ca ▪ This participant workbook leads you through the process analyzing global trends, recognizing cultural differences, identifying communication barriers and adapting key business skills to maximize effectiveness when working across cultures. Visit the distributor's web site at www.compusmart.ab.ca/icdr. [ID:2379]

Doing Business Internationally: The Cross-Cultural Challenges Resource Book 📖
1995, *Training Management Corporation,* Princeton Training Press, 450 pages ➤ Intercultural and Community Development Resources (ICDR), P.O. Box 32108, Millwoods Station, Edmonton, Alberta T6K 4C2; $60; VISA, Amex; (800) 378-3199, fax (403) 462-1925, icdr@compusmart.ab.ca ▪ Covers the cultural customs and business protocols of scores of countries around the world. Topics covered include social tips, customary business practices, dinning out, and public behaviour. It points out to the do's and don'ts for the successful business traveller. [ID:1357]

Dynamics of Successful International Business Negotiations 📖
1991, *Robert T. Moran, William G. Stripp,* Gulf Publishing, 264 pages ➤ Intercultural and Community Development Resources (ICDR), P.O. Box 32108, Millwoods Station, Edmonton, Alberta T6K 4C2; $39; VISA, Amex; (800) 378-3199, fax (403) 462-1925, icdr@compusmart.ab.ca ▪ A valuable tool for dealing with people from diverse cultural backgrounds. Discusses a range of cultural issues and examines negotiating styles from Europe, Africa, Asia, and Latin America. Visit the distributor's web site at www.compusmart.ab.ca/icdr. [ID:1350]

Ecotonos 📖
1993, *Dianne Hofner-Saphiere, Nipporica Associates,* Intercultural Press ➤ Intercultural and Community Development Resources (ICDR), P.O. Box 32108, Millwoods Station, Edmonton, Alberta T6K 4C2; $210; VISA, Amex; (800) 378-3199, fax (403) 462-1925, icdr@compusmart.ab.ca ▪ An excellent tool for engaging groups in problem-solving and decision making where power

106 CHAPTER 7 *The Canadian Guide to Working and Living Overseas*

issues, cultural assumptions, and expectations are stumbling blocks. Used successfully in the US and Japan in business, education, crosscultural counselling, and community development. For 12 to 50 participants. Visit the distributor's web site at www.compusmart.ab.ca/icdr. [ID:2400]

Globalwork: Bridging Distance, Culture and Time 📖
1994, *Mary O'Hara-Devereaux, Robert Johansen,* Jossey-Bass Publishers, 439 pages ➤ Prentice Hall Canada, 539 Collier MacMillan Drive, Cambridge, Ontario N1R 5W9; $35.50; credit cards; (800) 567-3800, fax (800) 563-9196 ▪ Identifies the skills managers need to succeed in today's global workplace, and offers practical strategies for working in an environment where international agreements are rapidly reshaping the global business milieu. Visit the publisher's web site at www.phcanada.com. [ID:1580]

Intercultural Interviewing: The Key to Effective Hiring in a Multicultural Workforce 📖
1992, *Christine Turkewych, Helen Guerreiro-Klinowski* ➤ International Briefing Associates, 116 Promenade du Portage, Hull, Québec J8X 2K1; $49.95; cheque or money order; (819) 776-9985, fax (819) 776-9776 ▪ This guide will help managers overcome communication barriers while conducting crosscultural job interviews in Canada and abroad. Clear, concise, insightful. [ID:1358]

International Business Case Studies for the Multicultural Marketplace 📖
1994, *Robert T. Moran, David Braaten, John Walsh,* Gulf Publishing ➤ McGraw-Hill Ryerson Ltd., 300 Water Street, Whitby, Ontario L1N 9B6; $42.95; credit cards; (800) 565-5758, fax (800) 463-5885 ▪ Real-life examples of the strategies and tactics used by some of the world's most successful international businesses and organizations to get ahead in the global marketplace. Visit the distributor's web site at www.mcgrawhill.ca. [ID:1695]

The International Businesswoman of the 1990s 📖
1990, *Marlene L. Rossman,* Praeger Publishers ➤ Greenwood Publishing Group, P.O. Box 5007, 88 Post Road W., Westport, CT 06881, USA; US$19.95; credit cards; (800) 225-5800, fax (203) 222-1502 ▪ A practical guide for women pursuing careers in international business. Describes career opportunities and addresses the issues women face, including breaking down barriers in the international business world. Includes case studies. Visit the distributor's web site at www.greenwood.com. [ID:1180]

International Dimensions of Organizational Behaviour 📖
1990, *Nancy J. Adler,* Wadsworth ➤ Nelson Canada, 1120 Birchmount Road, Scarborough, Ontario M1K 5G4; $39.95; credit cards; (800) 268-2222, fax (800) 430-4445 ▪ Intended to help executives, managers and students understand the implications of culture in the workplace. [ID:1631]

Kiss, Bow or Shake Hands: How to Do Business in Sixty Countries 📖
1994, *Terri Morrison, George A. Borden, Wayne A. Conaway,* Bob Adams, 440 pages ➤ Intercultural and Community Development Resources (ICDR), P.O. Box 32108, Millwoods Station, Edmonton, Alberta T6K 4C2; $25; VISA, Amex; (800) 378-3199, fax (403) 462-1925, icdr@compusmart.ab.ca ▪ Provides current data on foreign business and social practices. Visit the distributor's web site at www.compusmart.ab.ca/icdr. [ID:2383]

A Manager's Guide to Globalization: Six Keys to Success in a Changing World 📖
1993, *Stephen H. Rhinesmith,* Irwin Professional Publishing, 221 pages ➤ Intercultural and Community Development Resources (ICDR), P.O. Box 32108, Millwoods Station, Edmonton, Alberta T6K 4C2; $42; VISA, Amex; (800) 378-3199, fax (403) 462-1925, icdr@compusmart.ab.ca ▪ Drawing from research on business, comparative management, psychology, sociology, anthropology, philosophy, and intercultural relations, this book analyzes six key factors to management success in a constantly changing international market: managing competitiveness, complexity, organizational adaptability, uncertainty, multicultural teams, and personal and organizational learning. Visit the distributor's web site at www.compusmart.ab.ca/icdr. [ID:1391]

Managing Cultural Differences 📖
1992, *P. Harris, Robert T. Moran,* Gulf Publishing, 418 pages ➤ Intercultural and Community Development Resources (ICDR), P.O. Box 32108, Millwoods Station, Edmonton, Alberta T6K 4C2;

$58; VISA, Amex; (800) 378-3199, fax (403) 462-1925, icdr@compusmart.ab.ca ▪ Analyzes the impact of culture on managers in their roles as communicators, negotiators, and organizational leaders. Visit the distributor's web site at www.compusmart.ab.ca/icdr. [ID:1182]

Mindsets: The Role of Culture and Perception in International Relations 📖
1988, *Glen Fisher,* Intercultural Press, 200 pages ➤ Intercultural and Community Development Resources (ICDR), P.O. Box 32108, Millwoods Station, Edmonton, Alberta T6K 4C2; $23; VISA, Amex; (800) 378-3199, fax (403) 462-1925, icdr@compusmart.ab.ca ▪ Examines the impact of cultural "programming" on international affairs, how a society's reasoning affects their assumptions and values. Such "mindsets" represent a collective world view that governs how decisions are made. They influence international relations, how development assistance is implemented, and business conducted. Visit www.compusmart.ab.ca/icdr for distributor. [ID:1327]

Riding the Waves of Culture: Understanding Diversity in Global Business 📖
1996, *Fons Trompenaars,* Irwin Professional Publishing, 330 pages ➤ Intercultural and Community Development Resources (ICDR), P.O. Box 32108, Millwoods Station, Edmonton, Alberta T6K 4C2; $51; VISA, Amex; (800) 378-3199, fax (403) 462-1925, icdr@compusmart.ab.ca ▪ Reveals how the values and beliefs of various global cultures' typically impact on business interactions and influence business behaviour. Visit distributor's web site at www.compusmart.ab.ca/icdr. [ID:2376]

Survival Kit for Overseas Living 📖
1996, *L. Robert Kohls,* Intercultural Press, 181 pages ➤ Intercultural and Community Development Resources (ICDR), P.O. Box 32108, Millwoods Station, Edmonton, Alberta T6K 4C2; $17; VISA, Amex; (800) 378-3199, fax (403) 462-1925, icdr@compusmart.ab.ca ▪ An introduction to overseas living, with emphasis on the cultural problems likely to be encountered by first-time overseas workers. Although written for Americans, this is an invaluable practical guide for all. Visit the distributor's web site at www.compusmart.ab.ca/icdr. [ID:1177]

Transcultural Leadership: Empowering the Diverse Workforce 📖
1993, *George Simmons, Carmen Vazquez, Phillip Harris,* Gulf Publishing, 206 pages ➤ McGraw-Hill Ryerson Ltd., 300 Water Street, Whitby, Ontario L1N 9B6; $42; credit cards; (800) 565-5758, fax (800) 463-5885 ▪ A book dealing with the emerging global reality of culturally diverse people in the workplace. Visit the distributor's web site at www.mcgrawhill.ca. [ID:1692]

When Cultures Collide: Managing Successfully Across Cultures 📖
1996, *Richard D. Lewis,* Intercultural Press, 336 pages ➤ Intercultural and Community Development Resources (ICDR), P.O. Box 32108, Millwoods Station, Edmonton, Alberta T6K 4C2; $40; VISA, Amex; (800) 378-3199, fax (403) 462-1925, icdr@compusmart.ab.ca ▪ This book examines the psycho-social-cultural values and underpinnings of people's behaviours in fifteen countries, and offers advice on how to minimize friction between each group. Visit the distributor's web site at www.compusmart.ab.ca/icdr. [ID:2372]

Women in Management Worldwide 📖
1994, *Nancy J. Adler, Dafna Izraeli,* M.E. Sharpe Inc., 304 pages ➤ Coutts Library Services, P.O.Box 1000, 6900 Kinsmen Court, Niagara Falls, Ontario L2E 7E7; US$26.95; credit cards; (905) 356-6382, fax (905) 356-5064 ▪ The role of women in management is changing rapidly. This book describes female managers in economically developing and developed economies, in centrally planned and market economies, and in occidental and oriental cultural traditions. [ID:1621]

Chapter 8

Re-Entry

Phew! At last you're home—cozy, safe, predictable, surrounded by familiar faces. You've anticipated your homecoming with a mixture of feelings, from elation to regret. Your incredible journey—across the miles and within yourself—is over. Or is it?

You're about to enter the final, and perhaps most difficult, phase of your overseas experience. This is the *re-entry stage*, and its impact on you is at least as profound as the cultural adaptation stage.

Here are some returnees' thoughts on this period.

"You've enjoyed your homecoming, you're starting a new job, resuming your studies or setting up housekeeping. You're surprised at how easily you're settling in, then all of a sudden you're overtaken by an acute sense of malaise, of 'otherness,' of 'what on earth am I doing here?' You scoffed at the idea of reverse culture shock, but now you just don't feel right and you can't seem to shake it. You're suffering from re-entry shock!"

One young French Canadian women described the experience of returning to Canada from Africa as coming back to *l'anonyme*.

"Abroad, I had a strong sense of myself. My skin colour was different, my language was different, and I was the centre of attention even when I was buying groceries at the local market. Now I'm back in Canada, busily carrying out my responsibilities. My fabulous tan has faded; my T-shirt from Senegal is hidden under layers of winter clothing; no one seems interested in the three amazing years I spent in a tropical paradise. No one knows (or apparently cares) how much I've changed, how much I've seen, how much I've grown!"

Another traveller returning from six months in Mali and Burkina Faso felt contempt for his fellow Canadians.

109

"To my surprise, the first thing I noticed when I arrived in Ottawa was how pale and unappealing all these white people looked. Canadians seemed so undignified—they dressed sloppily, slouched, spoke too loudly. Overseas, I had grown accustomed to certain rituals around mealtimes. I was dismayed to find my family still watching TV while they ate, or eating alone, sometimes straight out of the fridge! At work, my fellow employees ate while they talked on the phone, while they walked, or even while they ran. I felt like an outsider observing a society with no culture."

In many ways, coming home can be more painful than leaving. The "weirdness" of home, its different pace and social pressures—and people's disinterest in your mind-altering experience—can make you feel like a stranger. This chapter gives an overview of the phases of re-entry and makes suggestions on how you can cope with anxieties, problems and frustrations caused by *re-entry shock.*

THINGS TO EXPECT AS PART OF RE-ENTRY SHOCK

If you are in the re-entry stage, you are probably dealing with feelings of frustration and rejection and a sense of being out of step with the people around you. Here is a list of symptoms you may experience on your return:

• **Feeling Let Down**: You have a peculiar sense of disappointment very much at odds with the joy you expected to feel when you got home. A young woman who worked for an NGO in China for several years describes her reaction. Keep in mind that hers is not a solitary experience—most returnees feel the same way!

"My thoughts about being back in Canada ranged from how great it would be to see my family and friends, to 'At last! A decent cup of coffee.' I looked forward to returning to a democratic society, to having a say in the things that affect me—as an individual, as a woman, as a consumer. Well, all that was mine when I returned—and I drank a lot of coffee in these great new coffee bars—but that old song kept playing in my head: 'Is that all there is? Is that all there is?'"

• **You Feel Disconnected from your Community**: You don't fit in anymore. You feel like you changed while everything at home stayed the same, or maybe everything at home changed while you were away. You miss the community you just left. Sometimes you're almost overwhelmed with nostalgia. You feel abnormal.

• **Your Relationships with Family and Friends are Strained**: No-one seems interested in your overseas experience. Some people didn't even notice you were gone! People around you seem boring and narrow-minded. It's hard to hide your disappointment. You withdraw from your friends and family, and not surprisingly, you feel isolated.

• **Your Emotional State is in Flux**: You feel disoriented. You sleep a lot but your dreams are disturbed. You feel out of control, even aggressive. You're angry one minute, sad the next. You try to deny the importance of your experience abroad. You're restless, forgetful, petulant. Your unpredictability begins to take its toll on your family and friends.

- **Your Life Skills are Gone**: You look the wrong way when you cross the street. You leave your gloves at home in the middle of winter. You buy powdered milk, like you did in Mozambique, because the array of milk choices at the corner store is overwhelming. The things you do without thinking are often inappropriate. You feel overwhelmed by the tasks of everyday life.

- **Your Health Deteriorates**: You catch a lot of colds and other viruses, you get headaches, your appetite fluctuates. You're irritable, lethargic, even depressed.

For more accounts of returnees' experiences with re-entry shock, see "Individual Circumstances" toward the end of this chapter. In the meantime, let's look a little closer at re-entry.

RE-ENTRY SHOCK VERSUS CULTURE SHOCK

For many of you, re-entry shock is very different from the culture shock you experienced abroad. Far from home, you were motivated to adapt because you were an outsider, and even at the worst of times, you knew you would go home one day. Now that you're back, you feel you ought to fit in, you know the territory, you shouldn't need to adjust. But being home doesn't feel right, and since for some of us returning home is forever, the stakes are much higher.

Re-adapting to your home culture can follow a similar pattern to the "U-Curve of Cultural Adaptation" described in Chapter 3, Living Overseas. Like adaptation, re-entry has three stages: euphoria ("the tourist high"), shock, and adjustment. There are differences, however.

- First, the shock of re-entry can set in faster and be more intense than culture shock.

- Every person adapts differently.

- The phases of re-entry do not follow a standard pattern and may blend into one another. You may experience symptoms of a stage you thought you'd finished long ago.

- Overseas adaptation, according to the experts, takes about one-third of the duration of your stay. When you come back to Canada, however, your stay could be forever. Many people find it takes the repetition of a season to make them feel comfortable in Canada.

In the words of one freelance writer who returned to Canada after a six-year absence:

"It was six months since I'd returned. I had lived abroad two other times and therefore hadn't given re-entry shock much thought this time around. When the first wave of depression hit me, I was taken completely off guard—I was angry, overly sensitive, and short with my co-workers, who seemed to go

merrily about their little lives. They seemed faster than me, more efficient, technically able—and a little boring.

"Eventually I had to admit that my sense of disconnectedness, and even hostility, was caused by reverse culture shock. I also had to concede that I was struggling to adjust to the time and effort required to look after myself—to do laundry, ironing, dishes. We had two maids in our house overseas! I'd gone from a four-bedroom house with attached guest house, swimming pool, and hired help to a two-bedroom apartment with noisy radiators. Overseas, my skills were highly valued; now I faced unemployment. It took more than 18 months for the most obvious symptoms of re-entry shock to disappear."

In the next few sections of this chapter, you'll find descriptions of a variety of reactions to the re-entry process. If you don't recognize your own experiences, however, don't worry! Just about any reaction is normal and none of them last forever. Remember that adaptation is a process, not a single event.

Now, let's take a closer look at the three phases of re-entry shock, and what you can expect, why it happens and what to do to ease the process.

THE PHASES OF RE-ENTRY

The re-entry process is a phase of your overseas experience—and is itself divided into three phases: Euphoria ("the tourist high"), Shock and Adjustment.

PHASE I: EUPHORIA OR THE TOURIST HIGH

Most returnees experience the "tourist high." During this phase you feel very optimistic and tend to focus on the positive, such as reuniting with loved ones, returning to a familiar culture, and for some, Tim Horton Donuts! This euphoria helps sustain you through any initial problems. You avoid difficult situations and convince yourself that everything is wonderful. You downplay or ignore that which unsettles you. You don't allow yourself to miss your life overseas.

You may actually achieve a lot during this phase, as you are quite focused and highly motivated. You accomplish immediate tasks easily, partly because you have lots of energy, enthusiasm, and the odd surge of adrenaline. Others may find you a bit high-strung or even overbearing.

In this first phase, you're generally glad to be home. You've missed your family, the seasons, your old neighbourhood, and people are happy to see you back. Here's how one lawyer felt when he returned to Canada after taking part in South Africa's transition to democracy.

"I really felt like a distinguished visitor, almost a hero. People were very interested in the dramatic changes that had occurred in South Africa, and in my role in them. Dinner parties were organized to celebrate my return. I was even asked to make a presentation at a Canadian Bar Association event, and was interviewed on the local university radio station. I had a period of a month or two of really being in demand, of feeling like a celebrity, and then it tapered off. Soon people just wanted to talk about the last movie I'd seen rather

than the last few years I'd lived. Well, it was kind of tough just being 'Mr. One-of-us' again!"

The euphoria phase of re-entry is cathartic. You've been anticipating your homecoming for months, and as your overseas adventure concludes, you reflect on it, comparing your original expectations with the outcome. Often it has turned out much better than you expected, and you may be revelling in this feeling!

PHASE II: SHOCK!

You've changed, your friends, family and co-workers have changed, indeed all of Canada has changed, and you have no choice but to adjust. This realization puts you into shock.

Re-entry shock makes us feel we don't belong in the place that is supposed to be our home; it makes us wonder where we do belong.

There are a lot of factors at play in the *shock* phase of re-entry. We've attempted to define them, as follows, to help clarify the process.

You Don't Expect Change on Your Home Turf

Because it is unexpected, re-entry shock, sometimes called reverse culture shock, catches many travellers and international workers by surprise. As mentioned, the process of readjusting to home bears some similarity to that of adjusting to a foreign culture—it's just that you feel like you shouldn't have to adjust!

One way of summing up the experience of re-entry shock is that *home culture seems foreign.* Truly, as hard as this may be to fathom, the shock of re-entry is in part due to the feeling that home isn't home any more. The more immersed you were in the culture overseas, the more adjusting you'll have to do when you leave.

It is helpful to think of culture as being all of the things you take for granted in everyday life—that's everything from which way to look when you cross the street, to the importance of religion in daily decision making. Being Canadian, you assume you belong to Canadian culture, but when you adapt to life overseas, you actually *change* your culture. Upon arriving home, you find that you no longer take for granted the same things other Canadians do. The stress of re-entry shock (and culture shock) is largely due to this fact. If you cannot take anything for granted, you cannot relax.

You Have Changed

Your experiences and adventures overseas have changed forever how you perceive the world. You adjusted to a new lifestyle, made different friends, did business in different ways, prepared and ate different food, and perhaps even functioned in a different language. Now you're home and people expect you to carry on as you did before. But as you try to settle into your old routines—or even new ones—you become acutely aware of changes in your outlook, and even in your sense of self. You must acknowledge these changes, and allow for them. Some are for the better, and will be worth preserving. And there are changes you will have to make to survive in Canada.

Virtually every returnee feels like an outsider, like he or she is observing life rather than participating in it. Here's how one traveller describes it:

"I found my perceptions had changed, I'd adjusted to a new lifestyle, with its different set of joys and stresses, and of course I'd learned to say a few words in several different languages. Yet others around me—and even I—expected that when I returned I would carry on as I had before I left. As if I was the same old me—but I felt nothing like the me who'd left Canada all that time ago."

No One is Interested in Hearing about Your Life Abroad

Whereas the people you return to may appear not to have changed, there are bound to be discernible differences, as everyday life *does* carry on without you. Children grow up, old people die, neighbours move. Governments change, the economy ebbs and flows. Your relationships with people close to you are affected by the very fact of your absence. You may not have met certain of their expectations, such as caring for elderly parents. Friendships may have suffered, either from lack of contact or because someone else filled your place. You come back expecting to slip into the seat you thought they were saving for you.

But they haven't saved you a place, and worse, they don't seem to care where you've been. As ridiculous as it seems, they don't want to hear about your experiences. They'd rather talk about last night's game or who's getting a promotion. Even close family and friends may show only passing interest in your travels and may have difficulty relating to the new you.

Routine existence goes on at home while you pack a lifetime of experiences into each day overseas. Or so it seems...

Even an international traveller who'd written on the subject of re-entry was taken aback by her friend's behaviour. While anticipating limited interest among the general populace, she believed *her* set of friends, many of them writers and international travellers, would want to see her photos of Africa at a reunion dinner. "Oh, maybe after dinner," one friend said. "Bring them into the office," said another, to her utter astonishment.

Life in Canada Changed While You Were Abroad

Your return to Canadian culture will require you to adjust to a variety of things, from the pace of life, attitudes, consumer habits, language, and food, to the sense of personal space and even the climate.

Where considerable changes took place while you were away—in your town, the economy, technology, your family, or in other ways—you can count on being confused, especially if these are unexpected changes.

Sometimes it's the small changes that throw you off. For instance, one man returned to Ontario after several years to find a multitude of long-distance telephone companies offering their services. After three years in Africa with no phone at all, he was bewildered by the choices.

"I was going crazy, signing up with one company for a few weeks, then switching when a seemingly better deal came along. Finally it struck me that I was doing most of my long-distance communicating by e-mail—and I stopped fretting about trying to find the best deal. It took a while after I got back to understand what my needs really were—and to stop being flustered by the heap of choices!"

You Are Critical Of Canadian Society

Now that you've stopped taking it for granted, you can see the flaws in Canadian society in a way you couldn't before. It's far more difficult to forgive your own culture's flaws than to accept another's, because you feel partly responsible for them.

"I was staggered by the materialism in our society. I found it hard to read-just, even though I'd only been in Russia for six months. Now, a year later, I'm still trying to maintain a "live with less" attitude—but it's a real challenge."

You find yourself being critical of others. Their lifestyles seem self-indulgent, decadent, and irresponsible. They seem callous, self-involved and unfriendly... You're lonely. It seems you'll never reconnect with your old friends, or make new ones... You're bored. You've done all the things you'd planned to do. Nothing interests you. You're fed up with moving and everything associated with it....

Some international workers find the very things that make Canada a good place to live also make it seem confining, even stifling—the regulations, social conventions, seemingly endless, petty requirements of everyday life.

Here's one returning father's comment on leisure activities.

"When I was a hockey coach in the States, I'd just get the kids together and we'd play hockey. Here there are thick books of rules, pages of regulations, and endless requirements to be addressed first—what a pain!"

You may worry that you'll never like Canada again, that it's no longer your real home. You may quit trying to get along here. When people are friendly to you, you may respond with indifference. You condemn Canadian mediocrity. You rack your brains for ways to get back to the country you left, or just to get out of Canada. In short, you resist adaptation.

You Miss Your Overseas Friends and Life Style

Your life abroad seems like a fantasy now. There was always something new and exciting and being a visitor kept you removed from the more mundane aspects of life overseas. While you were away, your letters home made you a local celebrity. Now that you're back, however, you're just like everyone else. And your standard of living may have dropped substantially.

People in Canada seem uninteresting, uninspired. You miss the exciting discussions you had with your new friends overseas. You find Canadian preoccupations small-minded and boring.

You may have romanticized North American efficiency while you were away. Now the smallest line-up or delay infuriates you. And you can never get through to anyone on the telephone! The tyranny of voice mail is a common complaint, even among Canadians accustomed to it. It's particularly aggravating when you've been somewhere with minimal or no telephone service!

"The phone system in Zimbabwe drove me crazy—not just because of the many technical problems, but because people wouldn't answer telephones, or if they did, they wouldn't pass on messages. The telephone was at the root of several of my missed deadlines. Now that I'm back in Canada, however, I resent the incredibly efficient phone service. It prevents any chance of spontaneity—invariably, you're expected to call ahead and announce your intentions! And several days in advance, if you please!"

You Feel Vulnerable, Powerless

You may feel overwhelmed by your seeming inability to find a job, or by a general sense of personal failure.

"I didn't have a job, our belongings hadn't been unpacked because we hadn't yet found suitable accommodation, and we were living with relatives. All of us were sick of living out of suitcases and not being able to find anything. There was no more household help to call on, our savings were being eroded, and everyone in the family was suffering from adjustment problems I couldn't solve."

Dwindling finances often contribute to this sense of powerlessness. The cost of living may be much higher in Canada or the lifestyle you'd grown accustomed to might be beyond your budget. Resettlement expenses can make re-entry financially draining—you have to pay for everything, from new winter coats to a new car.

Much has been said about returning to your home and your old life, but you may, in fact, be returning to very *different* personal or professional circumstances. You may be coming back to a different job or to live in a different part of Canada. You may have developed a long-term personal relationship while you were abroad, or a relationship at home may have ended. You may have to relocate soon after you return, or you may not even have a home to return to.

Summary: Why Re-Entry Shock Happens

You may be surprised to learn you are experiencing some of the symptoms of the *grieving process*. Specifically, you are suffering from the anxiety associated with separation and loss. For very good reasons:

* Change is difficult
* You have left a significant part of yourself behind
* There are no guarantees you will ever go back

HOW TO EASE RE-ENTRY SHOCK

We would like to have called this section "Cures for Re-entry Shock"—but there are none! So, expect re-entry shock. No matter how seasoned a world traveller you are, you're unlikely to get through the re-entry process unscathed. When you live so far from home, in such a different culture, and for such a long time, home begins to seem less and less real. Many people idealize Canada and Canadian society, and are horrified by the real thing. So come back with your eyes open: you've changed, home has changed, the country has changed. Be prepared to adapt.

Practical And Easy Tips

- **Enjoy Phase One, the "Tourist High"**: Take a break when you first get back, before you return to work or start looking for a job. Plan a "welcome home" party.
- **Get Organized**: Make lists of specific tasks you need to accomplish and keep track of your priorities, emotional as well as practical. Don't make snap decisions, however tempted you are to settle things quickly. You'll need to make some decisions, but keep in mind long-term consequences.
- **Take Good Care of Yourself**: You may be particularly susceptible to illness, so a healthy lifestyle is crucial. Recognize that this is an extremely stressful time, both physically and emotionally. If you experience unusual symptoms, make sure your doctor knows *where* you were posted overseas, particularly if it was a tropical area. Canadian doctors may not automatically check for malaria or bilharzia.
- **Take Breaks**: Schedule some down time, forget about the outside world, and do something you enjoy.
- **Treat Yourself to Something You Enjoyed Overseas**: Food is the best example. Plan to cook some of your favourite dishes once you get home. Make sure you bring the right spices with you.
- **Maintain Your Sense of Humour**: Remember how important this aspect of cultural adaptation was overseas? The same applies here—maybe twice over!

Reflect on Your Experience Abroad

- Choose which parts of the experience you value and which you will let go.
- Keep in mind that you have adapted before.
- Use the adaptation skills you learned overseas.
- Try to see Canadian people and events within the Canadian context.

Start Building a Community

- **Five Simple Ideas to Get You Started:** First, work on building your confidence. Second, join in, get involved. Third, search out and get to know other returnees. Fourth, look for others (not just returnees) who share common ground (e.g. other job seekers, new immigrants to Canada). And fifth, stay in touch with your overseas friends.
- **Re-kindle Old Friendships:** Prepare yourself for your friends' indifference, and try to be understanding. Some will seem unable, or worse,

unwilling, to discuss your overseas experiences. This can be particularly galling for international development or aid workers, who've devoted themselves to humanitarian causes and lived in desperate conditions among the world's most desperate peoples. Effective communication skills will help ease the transition and make the difference between a bad case of re-entry shock and a relatively mild one. If you can express yourself clearly and in a way that doesn't offend, your friends will benefit from the insights you share with them, and you will benefit from their support. The following points are worth keeping in mind.

* **Decide which parts of your experience you're going to talk about:** Try to distinguish what is important to your audience—whether it's your grandmother or the local Kiwanis Club—and what detracts from successfully making your point.

* **Choose your audience carefully, and be respectful of them:** Make sure your audience is interested before you launch into a long story about life overseas. Be mindful of their attention span. Listen to their questions. Know when to change the subject. Be especially careful about who hears you express your frustrations about Canada. Other returnees will be sympathetic, but even they have limited tolerance for complaining.

* **Think before you speak:** Try to be inclusive. Don't start every sentence with "When I was in Harare/Paris/Bangalore," or people will feel excluded. Try to make your comments relevant to the situation at hand.

* **Don't get too attached to your celebrity status:** Remember, most people are only interested in the five-minute version of your trip, and even that won't last.

* **Show interest in others:** Don't assume that what you've been doing is more interesting or exciting than what they've been doing. Ask questions. Be a good listener.

PHASE III: ADJUSTMENT

This is where the "U Curve of Adjustment" (see Chapter 3, Living Overseas) begins to swing upward. During this period, you start to fit in.

* **You Actually Like it Here in Canada**: Go on, admit it. You respect the people around you. You participate in everyday life, in work, in your community. You're not angry anymore. You feel competent and effective. Some days you even have fun.

* **You Develop Routines**: You remember garbage day. You watch regular television programs and enjoy them.

* **You Begin to Appreciate the Canadian Perspective**: You are able to talk about your experiences abroad in a way that your friends and family can understand.

* **Your Sense of Humour is Revived**: You begin to talk about your experiences of re-entry—poking some fun at yourself as you regain perspective.

- **Your Life Has Continuity**: You begin to see the long-term value of your experiences abroad. You find ways to use the skills you gained overseas in your everyday life in Canada.
- **Your Health Improves**: You sleep better, you don't get as many colds, and you have more energy. You can focus on the people and things around you.

Adaptation is hard work, but it's a natural process, a human survival skill. Think about it—if human beings weren't good at adapting, we wouldn't live in such a complex, technologically advanced world. And you wouldn't have gone overseas in the first place!

What's Good About the Re-entry Experience?

Re-entry is not an entirely negative experience. Through your struggle, you will uncover and develop a number of skills and insights.

- Not only did you have the privilege of learning about a new culture overseas, but you also gained a fresh perspective on your own culture.
- You are more adaptable and open to new ideas. You have developed greater sensitivity in inter-personal communications, especially as they relate to the traumas of crossing cultures.
- You appreciate value structures other than your own.
- You emerge a stronger, more resourceful person, with deeper insights into the human condition.

Suggestions for the Long Term

You have learned a great deal from your overseas experience *and* from going through the re-entry process. You can apply this knowledge in very useful ways:

- **Set Goals**: Figure out which aspects of your overseas experience are relevant in Canada and how you can integrate them into your work or home life. Set a course of action now, before you fall into hard-to-break habits. Here's a lesson from a teacher who has worked in many different countries:

    "From Finland to Japan, I keep coming across the same saying: 'Every ending is a new beginning.' You've probably heard it before, but it may be particularly meaningful for you now, while you're unfettered by old habits and inflexible patterns. This is your chance to do some of the things you've been meaning to do all your life!"

- **Give Back**: You have useful information to impart. Why not offer a slide show about your overseas community to a local group—Scouts, Rotarians, your neighbours? Are there particular skills you could pass on? Who needs your help? Could you offer your support to more recent returnees still in the grips of re-entry shock? Do you have something to offer new Canadians?

INDIVIDUAL CIRCUMSTANCES

Everyone has different things to manage depending on their age, personality, professional circumstances, personal and family circumstances, and every other variable that defines an individual. This part of the chapter outlines experiences common to specific groups.

Unaccompanied Travellers

If you went overseas alone, you probably had a more intense experience than you would have if you'd gone with other people. You may have been involved in projects that were humanitarian or idealistic in their goals. You may have worked in circumstances that other Canadians might consider dangerous, or been expected to work under poorer conditions and for longer hours than your colleagues with immediate family obligations. Such experiences can be very exciting, very rewarding, but also very isolating. You may now be continents away from others who shared your experience, who know what it was like, and who may be struggling with similar re-entry problems. If you travelled or worked with a group of other unaccompanied travellers, the relationships you formed were likely very close, but not necessarily permanent. Such relationships depend more on your common purpose than on your interest in each other as individuals.

Unaccompanied travellers with personal as well as professional expectations of their overseas assignments may have difficulty coming to terms with them. There is a double pressure to succeed: you feel you should have advanced your career or fulfilled certain obligations, but you also feel you should have developed your personal life.

You may, in fact, be returning to Canada with a new partner, in which case you will feel responsible for their adaptation to Canadian life while you deal with your own re-entry. The pressure of a new relationship, in a new environment, combined with the weight of your own expectations and those of your family and friends, may seem more than you can bear.

Whatever your circumstances, the key is to find a balance between your obligations to family, friends, and community and your need for support and independence. Spending time with others who have had similar experiences is very helpful, therefore. You may already have such contacts in Canada, but if you're stuck, there are resources available to help you.

You may find the Resources section at the end of this chapter, and Part Five of this book, International Career Contacts, helpful as starting points.

Employees

Whether you have a job or a job search waiting for you, you will have to re-adapt to the Canadian workforce. This can be frustrating, but it can also be an excellent opportunity to restructure your life, set short-term tasks and long-term goals, and take stock of your career.

Remember, though, that returning to jobs with comparatively little influence or autonomy can be hard on your self-esteem. On top of that, not everyone is interested in, or sees the value of, international experience. Don't be surprised if your employer or prospective employer dismisses your overseas career development.

Your best allies will be curiosity and the ability to translate your experiences into meaningful discussions with prospective employers, co-workers or clients. If you are looking for a job, be thorough. Do your research and re-learn the ropes, if necessary. At the same time, be open–minded. Do a thorough investigation of your field and the social and political factors affecting it. What are employers in your field looking for? Assume they need help to appreciate the relevance of your overseas experience. Present it in a non-threatening, inclusive manner. Once you start work, you will have to learn the politics and hierarchies of your workplace. You may have to work in environments that you thought you'd escaped forever!

Above all, be sensitive and attentive to other people. They can be sources of information and good advice, sometimes without realizing it. One Canadian returnee describes a meeting where the colleague to his right turned to him and said, "If you mention Sarajevo or Beirut one more time, I'm going to break your nose." Once he'd recovered from the rudeness of her outburst, the returnee was grateful: if she hadn't said something, he might have alienated the whole group. He stopped dropping names of foreign cities and immediately found his colleagues more receptive to his ideas.

(See Chapter 31, Job Hunting When You Return to Canada for more detailed suggestions about managing professional re-entry.)

Accompanying Spouses

As an accompanying spouse, you probably had more exposure to the culture of your overseas home than your employed partner did, and you probably had to work harder to adapt. You went overseas in support of your spouse's career and had no employment structure to rely on when you arrived. If you worked while you were abroad, it may have been for a local organization. Or perhaps you joined or developed a local network. Your cultural experiences were likely richer and more enduring because of this.

You are now faced with similar circumstances at home. You are under the same pressure as your spouse to rejoin the community and re-establish your occupation (in the workforce or at home), but you may still lack control over your life. You may be the only member of the family without a built-in community to return to. You may have to spend more time at home than your spouse and children, who have work and school to occupy their days. If you are a homemaker accustomed to a comfortable life abroad, you may find the drop in your standard of living difficult. Your family's financial situation may require you to work outside the home. You may blame your spouse for your unhappiness and feel resentful that your life has been disrupted for the sake of someone else's job.

Your best strategy is to develop some structure in your life. Find something outside the home that you can do independently, or offer your services to an organization in need. At first, any kind of activity will help, whether it's working out at the local Y or going to the art gallery. Eventually, though, you will want to find ways to integrate your overseas experience into your Canadian life.

One accompanying spouse reports that she never experienced the "tourist high" stage of re-entry, mainly because it was immediately apparent that she had lost touch with her old network. One friend told her, "I'd love to get together in a couple of months, after I've finished my PhD thesis." How could she tell them she needed company right away? Things improved for her, however, when she contacted an international organization and volunteered to help with pre-departure briefings for overseas employees.

The section entitled "Employees," above, will likely be useful to you, as will the Resources section at the end of this chapter. Chapter 31, Job Hunting When You Return to Canada, and Part Five, International Career Contacts, at the end of this book, will also be helpful.

Children

Young children tend to have the least difficulty during re-entry because their senses of security and identity are so closely linked to their families.

They do, however, notice and respond to the anxiety of their parents and older siblings. They may revert to behaviour they have outgrown, such as bed-wetting, thumb-sucking or fear of the dark. They may be particularly fussy, clingy, temperamental or prone to tears. Fortunately, these symptoms are normal and temporary, and will decrease as you establish routines. Young children adapt quickly.

It may be a good idea to visit your children's school before they begin, and to advise their teachers that they have been away from Canadian schools for the last while. On buying the right clothes—sometimes it's good to "check out what the other kids are wearing" before re-outfitting your kids. And the revived popularity of second-hand clothes takes some of the pressure off the budget.

Remember, too, that returning to Canada often means returning to extended family networks, which can be a source of pleasure for both children and family. When one little girl learned they would soon return to Canada, she told her parents she wanted to live next door to her grandmother. She planned to build a ladder over the fence and into Grandma's yard, so she could visit whenever she wanted.

Teenagers

As a young adult between the ages of 12 and 18, you perhaps stand to gain the most from living overseas. You're very flexible, able to adapt to almost anything, and you're probably a very good problem-solver. *But*—teenagers also tend to have the hardest time during re-entry. As you are already coping with an adaptation process—of trying to define yourself and establish some independence from your family—an international move can be an added and very unwelcome pressure at this stage in your life.

Here are a few tips on what to expect:

- Your old friends have changed and so have you.
- All the social rules are different.

- You're a celebrity for a day, then people lose interest in you.
- School work is different.
- You are forced to spend time with your family.
- You blame your parents for everything.
- You are lethargic and bored.
- You're rebellious, have a harder time obeying rules.

You probably feel alone, like no one else is going through what you're going through. In fact, there are lots of people in similar situations. Try to find someone around your age who has made an international move. It's a huge relief to talk to someone who knows how you feel. Find out from your parents whether any of their co-workers are returnees with kids your age. Ask around at school, too—the guidance counsellor might know someone.

Here are some suggestions put together by a group of Canadian returnees between the ages of 12 and 18:

"Be yourself. Get out of the house. Go for walks, get fresh air. Relax. Think, read, meditate, listen to music. Take a bubble bath. Get a part-time job. Go shopping. Observe others—their actions, dress and interactions. Accept them for what they are. Try to meet people. Go back to the place you came from for a visit, if you can. Keep your opinions to yourself. Be outgoing, friendly. Don't judge people before you get to know them. Don't be racist, sexist, etc. Don't put Canada down. Go to concerts. Be sociable. Be cooperative at home. Don't compromise your values just to be accepted. Organize or go to parties. Try to meet someone before school starts. Join sports teams, bands and clubs. And finally, keep a sense of humour."

Families

One family of returnees (let's call them the Smiths) tell a story about choosing a telephone for their new house. They all got excited by the pamphlet Dad picked up from the Bell Phone Centre on the way home from work. Mom, a freelance consultant, felt she needed a phone in her study. Jason, 16, wanted his own number and voice message service so his parents couldn't listen to his messages. He also really "needed" an extension in his room. Dad pointed out that it would be useful to have at least one handset in the hallway. Mom told Jason he could choose either his own handset or his own number, and he could forget about the voice message service. Dad mentioned that most of the handsets on display were ugly and suggested a rotary dial phone would be more attractive in the hallway. Jason said there was no way he was having a rotary dial phone because "they're totally useless." At this point, Emma, who was nine, burst into tears and said the only thing she had ever wanted in her whole life was a phone in the shape of a coke bottle... Two days later, they got one modern handset with no special features and plugged it into the jack in the kitchen. End of story!

The challenge for families is to find ways to convert torture into quality time. Everyone's nerves are frayed, you've seen more than enough of each other, and you all wish you had friends to complain to. On any given day, Mom is on cloud nine because she got a job offer, Dad is frustrated because the dog has to stay in quarantine for another three weeks, and older brother is threatening to stow away on a plane back to Nairobi. Everyone seems to be working against each other.

Don't allow things to get worse by pretending there's no problem. There will be lots of conflict. Parents should be prepared for their children to be angry about having to move. There will be tension about money. Everyone will feel impatient, frustrated and rebellious, and for good reason. You all need to talk about how you feel and to understand how everyone else feels.

Spend quality time together, and make sure you choose activities everyone can enjoy. You may need to be creative. For example, if you decide to go on an outing, some of you can ride bicycles, others may skateboard, and still others can rollerblade. Try to find common goals or projects that allow each person some self-expression.

Use each other for support. Complain about Canada. Appreciate that your family may be the only ones who will listen to this stuff.

High-Risk Situations

Re-entry is very stressful. Combined with other pressures, it may become impossible to manage without support. If you experienced particularly dangerous or threatening circumstances while you were abroad, such as natural disasters, accidents, robberies, personal assaults or terrorist attacks, your symptoms of shock and stress may be delayed until you return home. You may benefit from professional counselling. One Canadian woman who was physically assaulted during an assignment in Africa coped very well until she returned to Canada, where she found herself afraid to leave her apartment. Short-term counselling proved very helpful to her for managing the combined stresses of the assault and her re-entry into Canadian life.

Major life changes, such as the illness or death of someone close to you, the end of a long-term relationship, or the loss of work, can also cause excessive stress when combined with an international move. Similarly, if you have been forced to come home early for any reason, re-entry can be particularly difficult. One Canadian family cut short their posting to care for a terminally-ill parent, who died soon after their return. Three months later, the young son was still having difficulty adjusting to school, and feeling very angry. The mother and father were depressed. This family would have been good candidates for short-term counselling intervention.

We have described a few scenarios that can lead to excessively high levels of stress. Needless to say, there are countless more. As a rule, symptoms generally last a few weeks and should not be overly debilitating. However, if your symptoms continue for more than a few weeks, or if you are having difficulty managing the re-entry process, do not hesitate to contact a professional counsellor.

If you seek counselling, try to find a professional familiar with re-entry and adaptation issues. The Resources section at the end of this chapter provides a preliminary list of contacts who will be able to refer you to someone in your area.

A LAST WORD

Where in the world do I belong? Everyone who has lived or worked overseas has asked this question. We face an unusual challenge in trying to create a sense of home and community without the benefits of a stable location or even a common language. It is frighteningly easy to lose all sense of home.

We must find alternative ways to develop roots. We can create continuity in our lives through objects we carry with us from place to place, through activities we can enjoy anywhere in the world, and through rituals meaningful to us in any context. We must find ways to maintain friendships with people all over the world who we may not see for long periods of time. Most of all, we need to allow ourselves time to settle between moves.

Remind yourself that technology is advancing and the community of international travellers is expanding. Remember also that human beings have adapted to change throughout history. Ultimately, the events you experience, the cultures you encounter, and the people you meet are a rich reward for the effort of adaptation.

About the Author

This chapter is an adaptation of Betty-Ann Smith's forthcoming article on re-entry, written with the assistance of her daughter, Jennifer. Elizabeth Smith has adapted it for *The Canadian Guide to Working and Living Overseas*.

Betty-Ann Smith (MSW) is an Ottawa-based counsellor specializing in psychological and emotional aspects of adjustment to international mobility. She has 15 years' experience conducting seminars for business, government, and nongovernmental organizations. She and her family have lived in Europe and the Middle East as well as in several Canadian cities. (For contact information, see the listing for *Re-Entry Counselling Services* in the Resources section below.)

RESOURCES

The field of re-entry studies is a new one and not many books are specifically devoted to it. However, you can find the subject briefly discussed in most books on culture shock. See the Resources sections in Chapter 1, The Effective Overseas Employee; Chapter 3, Living Overseas; and Chapter 7, The Canadian Identity in the International Workplace.

The Art of Coming Home 📖

1997, *Craig Storti,* Intercultural Press, 216 pages ➤ Intercultural and Community Development Resources (ICDR), P.O. Box 32108, Millwoods Station, Edmonton, Alberta T6K 4C2; $26; VISA, Amex; (800) 378-3199, fax (403) 462-1925, icdr@compusmart.ab.ca ■ Most people returning from an overseas sojourn find re-entry more difficult than adjustment to a foreign culture. This book provides information, analyses and suggestions to transform the re-entry experience from a struggle to an art. The re-entry of spouses, younger children, and teenagers is examined. Special attention is given to high school exchange students, Peace Corps volunteers, military personnel and their families, and missionaries and their children. Visit the distributor's web site at www.compusmart.ab.ca/icdr. [ID:2375]

Centre for Intercultural Learning

Canadian Foreign Service Institute, 15 Bisson Street, Hull, Québec J8Y 5M2; (800) 852-9211, fax (819) 997-5409, monique.marion@bisson01.x400.gc.ca ▪ The Centre for Intercultural Learning assists Canadian professionals from NGOs, universities, private industry, and government to develop the crosscultural competencies essential for their success overseas. Services and products include pre-departure and project-related programs, on-arrival orientations, in-country programming, re-entry programs, country anthologies, and intercultural training. Their web site is under construction. [ID:2642]

Graybridge International Consulting Inc.

Graybridge International Consulting Inc., 76 Hôtel-de-Ville, Hull, Québec J8X 2E2; (819) 776-2262, fax (819) 776-6491, success@graybridge.ca ▪ Graybridge International Consulting Inc. offers a wide range of workshops and seminars on re-entry for Canadians who have lived and worked overseas. Programs are also available for foreign nationals who have spent extended periods of time in Canada prior to their repatriation. (For more information see Graybridge's profile in Chapter 32, The Private Sector.) [ID:2713]

People Development Ltd.

People Development Ltd., 2050 Gottingen Street, Halifax, N.S. B3K 3A9; (902) 425-6800, fax (902) 423-7214, pdltd@fox.nstn.ca ▪ People Development re-entry programs include elements of crosscultural adaption, but the primary focus is on how to "come home and be home." Many returnees go through a period of "grieving." These programs focus on how to adjust and move beyond the grieving process by establishing support systems, creating self-care systems, developing objectives to establish equilibrium, and accepting losses and emotions. The program methodology is rooted in the principles of adult education. The experiences of both the program facilitators and the returnees involved are used to their fullest as resouces for the participant group. [ID:2712]

Re-Entry Counselling Services

Re-Entry Counselling Services ▪ We have selected the following counselling resources because of their familiarity with re-entry issues. Re-entry counselling is offered to individuals, couples, and families and is usually short-term and solution focused. ▪ Betty-Ann Smith, Family Therapy Associates, 231 McLeod Street, Ottawa, Ontario, K2P 0Z8; (613) 563-4400 fax (613) 730-0241. ▪ FGI, Suite 200, 10 Commerce Drive East, Thornhill, Ontario, L3T 7N7; (905) 886-2157, fax (905) 886-4337. (See their profile in the "Moving Abroad" resource section of Chapter 2, Living Overseas.) ▪ Allan Greenwood, 1685 136th Street, White Rock, BC V4A 4E3; (604) 535-1647, allang123@aol.com. [ID:2776]

SJM Consulting

SJM Consulting, 2678 West Broadway, Suite 302, Vancouver, B.C. V6K 2G3; (604) 732-0399, fax (604) 732-0398, mcleans@cce.ubs.ca ▪ SJM Consulting provides workshops/seminars for all phases of international assignments. Re-entry workshops can be held for one or for a group of people. Participants can contribute to the design of their own workshops. Specific areas covered include reflection on the overseas experience to consolidate learning, strategies for adjustment to personal and professional aspects of returning home, and transfer of skills acquired overseas into the Canadian context. [ID:2715]

Transcultural Odysseys: The Evolving Global Consciousness 📖

1997, *Germaine W. Shames*, Intercultural Press, 176 pages ➤ Intercultural and Community Development Resources (ICDR), P.O. Box 32108, Millwoods Station, Edmonton, Alberta T6K 4C2; $27; VISA, Amex; (800) 378-3199, fax (403) 462-1925, icdr@compusmart.ab.ca ▪ Using the stories of individuals and families crossing cultures, Shames deals with such intercultural issues as culture shock and adjustment, identity, communication and language learning, wellness and safety, and re-entry. Visit the distributor's web site at www.compusmart.ab.ca/icdr. [ID:2446]

PART TWO

Acquiring International Experience

9. Starting Your International Career 129
10. Short-term Programs Overseas 133
11. Hosting Programs 163
12. Crosscultural Travel 171
13. Global Education Centres 183
14. Study Abroad 201
15. Awards & Grants 215
16. International Studies
    in Canada & Abroad 237
17. International Internships 351

Chapter 9

Starting Your International Career

Gaining international career experience—building your International IQ—is a long-term endeavour. No one experience in itself will get you that international job. Rather, it is the cumulative effect of your many efforts that makes your international IQ credible and saleable to employers.

This chapter introduces you to a range of long-term strategies for developing both international awareness and career planning. Subsequent chapters offer more information and greater detail.

In this guide, Part Two, Acquiring International Experience, is divided into academic and non-academic chapters. Non-academic chapters provide information on how to gain international experience outside of the university setting. These include: Chapter 10, Short-term Programs Overseas; Chapter 11, Hosting Programs; Chapter 12, Crosscultural Travel; and Chapter 13, Global Education Centres. Important information for planning your international career within a university setting can be found in the following locations: Chapter 14, Study Abroad; Chapter 15, Awards & Grants; Chapter 16, International Studies in Canada & Abroad; and Chapter 17, International Internships.

Gaining international work experience is always a "catch-22" situation. You need experience to get that first job, but how do you get experience if you haven't worked in the field before? You should view your first job as a stepping-stone. Often, it provides on-the-job training yet may pay less than you desire. You may be required to do mundane work, perhaps even in harsh, remote conditions. As you gain experience, however, you will be rewarded with more responsibility, better pay, and easier living conditions.

STARTING YOUNG

An International IQ is best started in adolescence, or even earlier. If children are encouraged to explore and appreciate new cultures, learn languages, and develop a sense of adventure and curiosity about the world beyond their own borders, they will be well on their way to developing their International IQ. It is our responsibility as adults to raise children with a worldly outlook, who are tolerant of people of different cultural backgrounds and who have a healthy curiosity about the many peoples of the world.

How do you encourage an international outlook in children? Children learn best by direct exposure, so travelling with your children and immersing them in different cultures will broaden their outlook, particularly when they are old enough to appreciate the contrasts. If you are travelling without your children, involve them in preparations for your trip. Give them a world map to chart your route, find books for them on the places you plan to visit. Once away, send them postcards describing foods, animals, toys, buildings, religions, etc. Suggest to your school board that it provide global education courses. Go to ethnic restaurants. Encourage your children's curiosity in children from other cultures.

Above all, remember that children can detect their parents' anxieties. If a parent is interested in the challenges and rewards of crosscultural interaction, this is likely to rub off on the children.

HIGH SCHOOL AND UNIVERSITY STUDENTS

For the high school and university student, the most important thing you can do is work hard in school. Read magazines and listen to international news coverage. There are excellent programs which allow you to spend one of your high school years living with a family in a foreign country (see Chapter 10, Short-term Programs Overseas). For university students, there is a plethora of international study programs at Canadian universities (see Chapter 16, International Studies in Canada & Abroad) and an enormous number of opportunities for internships (see Chapter 17, International Internships). As learning a second language is essential for many international careers, it is important to start early (see Chapter 5, Learning a Foreign Language). There are also a host of exchange programs for young people which provide international experience (see Chapter 10, Short-term Programs Overseas).

Join international clubs and make friends with people from other cultures living in Canada. Socialize with them, taste their food, exchange views on the world. The closer you are to graduating from university, the more important it is to match your international education with crosscultural work experience. Become a leader-organizer in international groups, travel to international conferences, volunteer for professional internship positions. Start reading books on crosscultural business skills: being able to articulate and discuss your crosscultural work environment to others will be a crucial part of your international career.

Finally, don't be overwhelmed by the vast amount of information and range of approaches suggested in this book. Genuine curiosity and good humour are often the greatest motivators for a career of meeting and dealing with people from other cultures.

CAREER CHANGERS

If you are currently employed but wish to change careers, there are still many ways to increase your International IQ. Your challenge with international employers is to reshape the knowledge and experience you have of the Canadian workplace and translate it into the crosscultural environment. How can you do this when you haven't been overseas?

The possibilities are endless, and described in detail throughout this book. As a first step, work at becoming an expert on the international aspects of your field of work. Look for opportunities to meet people with international responsibilities whose work is similar to yours. Read books on doing business abroad. Attend seminars on international subjects relevant to you. Organize a group or conference around an international theme, or volunteer your services at international conferences in your area. Subscribe to international journals. Join the international branch of the CHAMBER OF COMMERCE. Start a local chapter of a national organization involved in international affairs. Become a member of a trade organization which has an international branch. Call the mayor's office to see what international visitors, delegates or trade missions are coming to your area and volunteer your talents. Research your community's links to international trade. Talk to your local trade development council for information on its international efforts. Become familiar with intercultural groups and join intercultural commissions and studies at provincial and municipal levels. Participate in ethnic events. Join refugee and immigrant support groups. Become a volunteer on short-term programs overseas.

Remember, it is never too late to learn the pleasures of international work, travel, and friendship.

INTERNSHIPS

The newest trend to emerge in the late 1990s is the increasing number of internship opportunities. Internships are usually short-term professional positions, ranging in length from two months to one year. While internship positions offer little or no salary, they can provide invaluable training and professional experience, and they are plentiful. Over 30 per cent of the nongovernmental organizations and private firms profiled in this book stated that they would consider internship positions. (For more ideas, check out Chapter 10, Short-term Programs Overseas; Chapter 32, The Private Sector; Chapter 34, Careers in Government; and Chapter 35, Nongovernmental Organizations.) Many international organizations have formal internships, and the federal government's International Internship Programs offer an astonishing 4,000 internships. (See the profile listed under Canadian Government International Internships Program in Chapter 17, International Internships.)

VOLUNTEERING

Many people start their international careers by volunteering for international organizations. Several organizations offer professional volunteer positions in Canada as well as abroad. But as with any job, you must earn your volunteer position. If you live in a small town, you can begin your international volunteer work by starting a local committee of any one of the numerous NGOs with a structure for volunteers. Remember, money is not the most important factor; acquiring work experience is.

The best way to learn about an organization is to make yourself useful. Rather than announcing that you're looking for work (guaranteed to put some people off!), look for opportunities to volunteer in your area of expertise. A good volunteer is one who does not expect to be waited on. Most organizations find it difficult to manage volunteers, so it may be up to you to manage yourself. And it is your responsibility to overcome the frustrations and institutional roadblocks you encounter.

Don't be concerned with targeting a precise area in which to volunteer. Take a long-term view by making yourself useful and getting involved anywhere you're needed in the international field. A generalist approach will help you acquire many essential skills and introduce you to the broader international community.

A LAST WORD

International work is a fascinating way to live your life and see the world. Whether you decide to live abroad for a short or a long time, the insights you acquire—the wonders of other cultures, people, food and geography—will forever fill your thoughts and bring a deeper appreciation for life, wherever you live. Good luck with your international career, and happy journey!

Chapter 10

Short-term Programs Overseas

This chapter contains important information not only for those who want to enhance their chances of landing a job overseas, but also for individuals who are simply seeking personal growth through cultural travel.

SHORT-TERM PROGRAMS FOR LONG-TERM GAIN

Participating in short-term placements and internships overseas is often the only way to begin an international career. Although these programs generally combine hard work with minimal financial compensation in the short-term, they can be a source of long-term gain, providing relevant job experience or a "foot-in-the-door" with a Canadian organization engaged in international activities. Your willingness to participate in short-term programs will demonstrate to future employers your commitment and initiative.

Short-term placements overseas offer brief and invaluable experience. Challenging your skills, they allow you to demonstrate your strengths. Giving up the comfort and security of your home for unfamiliar languages, cultures, climates and accommodations can, after all, require courage, enterprise and adaptability. And as an opportunity to experience overseas work on a temporary basis, a placement can help you decide if an international career is for you!

Many people feel that working abroad should involve work in a field directly related to their studies. Though study-related work has obvious benefits, it is important to recognize that any kind of work abroad adds to one's maturity, ability to adapt and function effectively outside of Canada, and international career profile. As one placement officer put it, *"Working as a waiter in a pub in London or as a lifeguard in Sydney can impress a potential employer offering a career position."*

WHAT KINDS OF PROGRAMS ARE THERE?

A wide variety of short-term programs are available, but not all will be appropriate for you. Although the majority of short-term programs are less than a year in duration and are geared to individuals with little or no previous experience, some programs are more career-oriented and last up to two years. Qualifications vary. While some programs are open as to who may participate, others have age, nationality, and educational restrictions. Respect the restrictions rather than manipulate your skills and background into a specific category. For example, it is best only to apply for missionary work if you are committed to its doctrine. Remuneration for most short-term placements is generally low, but gains in crosscultural knowledge can be invaluable.

The 73 short-term programs overseas profiled in this chapter are divided into the following six categories: Youth Exchanges, Internships, Professional Exchanges, Teaching Abroad, Work and Learn, and Independent Work and Travel.

Youth Exchanges

There are a number of popular international exchange programs open to youth. These programs, which operate in a variety of industrialized and developing countries, are usually geared to young people between 15 and 30 years of age, or a target age group within this range. Some are true exchanges, meaning that for every person or group sent overseas, a person or group comes to Canada, while others operate differently. Be sure to understand the terms of the exchange and its time frame as some are designed for the summer and others for the school year.

A number of group exchanges are coordinated by Provincial Boards of Education and nonprofit organizations with limited funds. Group fundraising is common in many of these programs. While the organizations cover the costs of administering the program, participants are required to cover a large portion of the cost and are expected to help with fundraising efforts before or after the trip.

Keep in mind that youth exchanges are not study-abroad programs which offer students academic credit. For such programs see Chapter 14, Study Abroad, and Chapter 16, International Studies in Canada & Abroad.

Internships

This section covers opportunities for recent graduates or youth interested in gaining international work experience in their fields. Unlike the internships listed in Chapter 17, International Internships, the opportunities listed in this chapter are offered by Canadian-based organizations. These programs allow young Canadians to live and work in another country, gain valuable skills, and make international contacts which will benefit their future careers, whether in Canada or abroad.

Federal and provincial governments run a number of internship programs. The latest and biggest boon are the international internship programs offered by the federal government. The programs, which are administered by six government departments, will provide approximately 4,000 international internships over two years. This is an enormous number in comparison to the size of the Canadian job market. Many of these internships have an international component and are invaluable for young people wanting to "go international." For information on these international internships see the Canadian Government International Internships profile in Chapter 17, International Internships.

Some internships involve cost to the intern. When salaries are paid, they are usually only sufficient to cover living and travel expenses and in some cases interns are provided with room and board in exchange for volunteer service. Again, the idea of short-term experience for long-term gain applies to internships and the experience and exposure you can get from internships is second to none.

Professional Exchanges

The professional exchanges listed in this chapter are offered through nongovernmental organizations. Professional exchanges are geared to the participant's area of expertise, and usually require at least a few years of relevant experience. They vary in length, but usually last one year. Salaries often only cover travel expenses and a stipend for living, but the professional rewards usually surpass monetary compensation. These exchanges offer first-hand experience with other cultures and lasting personal and business contacts.

Teaching Abroad

Teaching abroad is an excellent way to see and experience a new area of the world. Your daily interaction with students will give you unparalleled exposure and insight into your host countries. The length of programs varies, but a commitment of at least one year is usually required. Usually travel expenses are covered and a stipend is provided. Requirements vary. Although some programs require a teaching certificate or university degree, many require no prior experience. For more information see also Chapter 29, Teaching Abroad.

Work and Learn

These programs are seldom professional work opportunities. They usually, but not always, offer an opportunity to volunteer with a community work project or development organization. Most offer a combination of work, scheduled events and free time. These projects can be useful opportunities for studying a foreign language or immersing yourself in another culture. Lodgings are usually provided, but not travel expenses. Salaries are sometimes offered.

Independent Work and Travel

Several countries issue working holiday visas to youth for a period ranging from six months to two years. Working holiday programs are designed to allow youths to extend the length of their overseas holiday by engaging in short-term casual employment. Finding employment is usually the responsibility of the visa holder.

APPLYING TO PROGRAMS

Many short-term programs don't require much international experience or any professional skills. Instead, they depend upon mature, committed and enthusiastic individuals who can work well in groups and in situations which require hard work and initiative.

Having leadership and organization skills, and demonstrating a history of involvement in other projects or organizations is beneficial, but don't panic if your résumé shows little volunteer experience. Many programs are designed for inexperienced participants. Some organizations look for commitment to their ideals and aims and it's a good idea to discuss with them how your participation will help further their goals. Your involvement may, for example, increase your own community's awareness of global issues.

Begin your search for short-term overseas programs well in advance of your intended departure date. Application dates vary widely and it is important to leave yourself enough time for applying and preparing for departure. With some organizations you can expect to wait 18 months prior to departure, and most require at least six to eight months.

If you are turned down by the selection committee, don't be afraid to appeal. Participants often cancel at the last minute, giving rejected applicants a second opportunity to be considered. It is important to maintain contact with the selection committee and to show continued enthusiasm for the programs you are interested in. If all else fails, reapply the following year.

HOW TO MAKE YOUR OVERSEAS VOLUNTEER EXPERIENCE MORE PROFESSIONAL

Altruistic impulses, often the motivation for volunteer work, can also help your career. Volunteering for a project, even a project unrelated to your career field, may enhance your chance of securing overseas work at a later date. Whatever volunteer work you do, show initiative, work hard and put yourself in positions of responsibility. These traits will not go unnoticed. For example, help your program leader with administrative work and look for similar opportunities with organizations in your host country. You could also extend your visit by volunteering with an organization and living with a host family or by creating your own internship with a local organization. Don't forget to ask supervisors and managers for letters of recommendation. It's much harder to contact them after the program has ended and you have returned to Canada.

It goes without saying that it is important to expand your international experience by travelling around your host country. It's worthwhile to discover new areas and see the country from outside the formal structure of your work program. The well-travelled individual gains a greater sensitivity to other people, and is more comfortable and effective in crosscultural work situations.

WHAT TO EXPECT FROM THE ORGANIZATION

Most short-term overseas programs are not heavily structured and many organizations will not give you a lot of guidance. You will be expected to be independent and cope on your own. Being in an unfamiliar place and trying to get access to basic services overseas can sometimes be a daunting experience, to say the least. You will probably surprise yourself with your own tenacity, enterprise and ability to survive. Be prepared to be challenged, be patient, and make sure you read Chapter 3, Living Overseas.

A LAST WORD

There are a number of points to consider when comparing short-term overseas programs. The first considerations are cost, availability of a work or activity schedule, travel arrangements, health insurance, and orientation program or materials. You should then consider the location of the program and the political stability of the region. On a more philosophical level, consider the purpose of the program and whether or not you are comfortable with the ideals and objectives of the organization. Lastly, look at the track record of the program or organization. Ask the organization to put you in touch with former participants. They will be an invaluable source of information and can give you advice on how to apply, and what to expect.

RESOURCES

This list covers a wide range of short-term opportunities overseas, mostly focusing on summer and young adult programs. Programs usually require little skill, but demand hard work, enthusiasm, and initiative. Summer or short-term programs are important for anyone wishing to build experience towards future, paid international employment. Remember, learn about crosscultural communication and focus on intercultural understanding.

Refer also to the Resources sections in Chapter 12, Crosscultural Travel; Chapter 14, Study Abroad; Chapter 16, International Studies in Canada & Abroad; Chapter 17, International Internships.

The Au Pair & Nanny's Guide to Working Abroad 📖
1993, *Susan Griffith, Sharon Legg,* Vacation Work, 432 pages ➤ Capricorn Business Services, Inc., 28 Clear Lake Ave., West Hill, Ontario M1C 4L6; $27.95; credit cards; (416) 282-3331, fax (416) 282-0015 ▪ Information on preparing for and finding a childcare job in another country. Includes a directory of over 200 agencies, and offers specific advice on topics such as regulations, health and insurance for Australia, countries in Europe and North America. [ID:1417]

Directory of Summer Jobs Abroad 📖
Annual, *David Woodworth,* Vacation Work ➤ Capricorn Business Services, Inc., 28 Clear Lake Ave., West Hill, Ontario M1C 4L6; $23.95; credit cards; (416) 282-3331, fax (416) 282-0015 ▪ Details more than 30,000 jobs – ranging from couriers and hotel workers to teachers – in over 45 countries worldwide. Each entry lists contact person, duration of employment contract, number of openings, pay rates, how and when to apply, duties, qualifications, plus visa and work permit regulations. British publication, but great value for Canadian and American readers. [ID:1207]

Directory of Summer Jobs in Britain 📖
Annual, *Susan Griffith,* Vacation Work ➤ Capricorn Business Services, Inc., 28 Clear Lake Ave., West Hill, Ontario M1C 4L6; $23.95; credit cards; (416) 282-3331, fax (416) 282-0015 ▪ Lists over 30,000 jobs in Scotland, Wales, England, and the Channel Islands. Includes openings for hotel and resort workers, office help, farm labourers, carpenters, chambermaids and lorry drivers, plus tips on applications, visas, work permits. [ID:1155]

Directory of Volunteer Opportunities 📖

1992, *Kerry Mahoney,* University of Waterloo, 90 pages ➤ Career Resource Centre, Volunteer Directory, Room 1115, Needles Hall, University of Waterloo, Waterloo, Ontario N2L 3G1; $10; cash or cheque; (519) 888-4047 ext. 3001, fax (519) 746-1309 ■ Easy to read, this 90-page manual lists 122 well-researched, full- and part-time volunteer opportunities in North America and overseas. [ID:1268]

The Directory of Work & Study in Developing Countries 📖

1997, *David Leppard,* Vacation Work ➤ Capricorn Business Services, Inc., 28 Clear Lake Ave., West Hill, Ontario M1C 4L6; $23.95; credit cards; (416) 282-3331, fax (416) 282-0015 ■ British reference guide to short- and long-term work, volunteer and educational opportunities in the developing world. Listings in each of the three sections are organized by region. [ID:1158]

Doing Voluntary Work Abroad 📖

1997, *Mark Hempshell,* 160 pages ➤ How To Books Ltd., 3 Newtec Place, Magdalen Road, Oxford, OX4 1RE, UK; £9.99; credit cards; (44) (1752) 202-301, fax (44) (1865) 202-331 ■ Doing voluntary work abroad offers you a great chance to combine foreign travel and valuable work experience, while helping others and learning about a different way of life. This book provides information on the qualifications, skills, and experience you may need, finding the work opportunities, and more. [ID:1682]

Employment in France for Students 📖

1991 ➤ Cultural Services of the French Embassy, 464 Wilbrod Street, Ottawa, Ontario K1N 6M8; free; (613) 238-5711, fax (613) 238-5713 ■ Brochure of work regulations and opportunities for students in France. Includes additional references. [ID:1418]

Exchange Opportunities for Canadians 📖

Biennial, 53 pages ➤ Citizens' Participation and Multiculturalism Branch, Canadian Heritage, Canadian Studies and Special Projects Directorate, Room 62, 7th floor, 15 Eddy Street, Hull, Ontario K1A 0M5; free; (819) 994-1544, fax (819) 994-1314 ■ Bilingual directory with brief, concise listings that give purpose, description and deadline for application for each program. A valuable reference. [ID:1347]

The Exchange Student Survival Kit 📖

1993, Intercultural Press, 122 pages ➤ Intercultural and Community Development Resources (ICDR), P.O. Box 32108, Millwoods Station, Edmonton, Alberta T6K 4C2; $20; VISA, Amex; (800) 378-3199, fax (403) 462-1925, icdr@compusmart.ab.ca ■ Helps students better understand the exchange experience and adjust to a new culture. Based on years of research and professional involvement with AFS Intercultural Programs. Uses examples based on the experiences of exchange students from various cultures. A useful resource for native English speakers. Visit the distributor's web site at www.compusmart.ab.ca/icdr. [ID:1324]

Golden Opportunities: A Volunteer Guide for Americans Over 50 📖

1994, *Andrew Carroll,* Peterson's Guides ➤ Nelson Canada, 1120 Birchmount Road, Scarborough, Ontario M1K 5G4; $20.95; credit cards; (800) 268-2222, fax (800) 430-4445 ■ Detailed information for older adults who want to offer their services abroad. The book also mentions special opportunities for doctors and health care professionals, and recommends resources. [ID:1448]

Host Family Survival Kit: A Guide for American Host Families 📖

1985, *Nancy King, Ken Huff,* Intercultural Press, 168 pages ➤ Intercultural and Community Development Resources (ICDR), P.O. Box 32108, Millwoods Station, Edmonton, Alberta T6K 4C2; $17; VISA, Amex; (800) 378-3199, fax (403) 462-1925, icdr@compusmart.ab.ca ■ A guide to understanding the exchange experience, being an effective host family, and making the most of the hosting experience. Also has a guide to evaluating sponsoring organizations and their programs. Visit the distributor's web site at www.compusmart.ab.ca/icdr. [ID:1314]

How to Become an Au Pair 📖

1994, *Mark Hempshell,* 144 pages ➤ How To Books Ltd., 3 Newtec Place, Magdalen Road, Oxford, OX4 1RE, UK; £8.99; credit cards; (44) (1752) 202-301, fax (44) (1865) 202-331 ■ There are thousands of vacancies for au pair work and other domestic employment, waiting to be filled each year, and the work often provides the chance to travel and live abroad in exotic locations. This book explains the work involved, the personal qualities required, where to find the vacancies and more. [ID:1676]

International Centre, Queen's University ▣
www.quic.queensu.ca ▪ This extensive site offers many services to help you find overseas placements, whether volunteer, pleasure or academic. From health insurance upon departure to culture shock upon re-entry, Queen's can help you plan your international adventure. Its Resource Library section is particularly useful. This is a great spot to look if you are in the initial stages of looking for an international placement. [ID:2432]

The International Directory of Voluntary Work ▢
1997, *David Woodworth,* Vacation Work, 272 pages ➤ Capricorn Business Services, Inc., 28 Clear Lake Ave., West Hill, Ontario M1C 4L6; $23.95; credit cards; (416) 282-3331, fax (416) 282-0015 ▪ British guide, details over 600 organizations. Includes a brief section on long-term voluntary positions as well as short- and long-term residential volunteer work around the world. [ID:1152]

International Workcamp Directory ▢
Annual, 128 pages ➤ International Workcamps, Volunteer for Peace (VFP), 43 Tiffany Rd., Belmont, VT 05730, USA; US$15; VISA, MC; (802) 259-2759, fax (802) 259-2922, vfp@vfp.org ▪ Published every April, the directory contains over 900 program announcements for two- and three-week programs, mostly during summer and fall. These include work, travel and study opportunities in 70 countries around the world. Volunteers pay $175 to register with VFP. This covers full cost of room and board for the duration of the program. Ninety per cent of workcamp volunteers register between mid-April and mid-May. Write or call any time for a free copy of their newsletter. Visit the distributor's web site at www.vfp.org. [ID:1269]

International Youth and Young Workers Exchange Programs ▣
www.dfait-maeci.gc.ca/english/culture/youthex.html ▪ This site, maintained by the Department of Foreign Affairs and International Trade (Canada) offers information on a number of government-sponsored programs for international employment and study. Many of the bilateral exchange and working holiday programs profiled in this chapter are listed on the site. There are also a number of thematic programs designed to help individuals with specific interests find employment overseas. This is a very good site, although many of the programs listed are not online and must be contacted through conventional means. [ID:2505]

Internships in Foreign and Defense Policy: a Complete Guide for Women (& Men) ▢
1990, *Women in International Security,* 103 pages ➤ Seven Locks Press, P.O. Box 68, Arlington, VA 22210, USA; US$10.95; credit cards; (800) 354-5348, fax (714) 545-1572, sevenlocks@aol.com ▪ An internship early in your career can help open doors to a successful career. This book is designed to help women (and men) pursue the many opportunities for internships in the area of international security. [ID:1245]

Invest Yourself: The Catalogue of Volunteer Opportunities ▢
1994, *Susan Angus,* 233 pages ➤ Commission on Voluntary Service and Action, P.O. Box 117-37X, New York, NY 10009, USA; $US8; credit cards; (800) 356-9315, fax (800) 242-0036 ▪ Comprehensive listings of full-time volunteer positions offered through North American nonprofit organizations. Placements are located in North America and overseas and range from a few weeks, to a summer, to a few years. International opportunities are not listed separately, but are indexed. Usually updated yearly. Visit www.upperaccess.com. [ID:1046]

Jobs Abroad: Opportunities Overseas ▢
Annual, 50 pages ➤ Christian Service Centre, Holloway Street W., Lower Gornal, Dudley, West Midlands DY3 2DZ, UK; £3.50; cheque or money order; (44) (1902) 882-836, fax (44) (1902) 881-099 ▪ Booklet lists over 3,000 job vacancies outside Britain of interest to Christians, most of them for two-year postings with UK-based mission agencies. Cost includes an annual supplement. [ID:1044]

Kibbutz Volunteer 📖
1996, *John Bedford,* Vacation Work, 176 pages ➤ Capricorn Business Services, Inc., 28 Clear Lake Ave., West Hill, Ontario M1C 4L6; $21.95; credit cards; (416) 282-3331, fax (416) 282-0015 ▪ Gives full details on over 200 kibbutzim, and describes the special atmosphere of kibbutz life. Includes information on other short-term work opportunities in Israel and advice on living in Israel, to help the reader experience the country as an insider. [ID:1431]

Médecins Sans Frontières/Doctors Without Borders (MSF)
Médecins Sans Frontières/Doctors Without Borders (MSF), Suite 5B, 355 Adelaide Street, Toronto, Ontario M5V 1S2; (416) 586-9820, fax (416) 586-9821, msfcan@passport.ca ▪ The international MSF sends over 2,000 volunteers per year to work in over 70 countries. The Canadian arm of MSF also sends many professionals overseas, including doctors, paramedical personnel, and nurses. Their web site, www.msf.org, includes information on how to volunteer. (See their profile in Chapter 35, Nongovernmental Organizations.) [ID:2571]

Overseas Jobs Express 🖳
www.overseasjobs.com ▪ This wonderful site lists over 1,500 new international jobs each month. Searches can be conducted by keyword, category, or region and the search engine is very user-friendly. There is also a free résumé posting service. A number of career counselling resources, an online "bookshop" specializing in international employment, and a travel advisory section are also available. This site includes 700 links to job banks in over 40 countries. You can go directly to Brazil and look for a job there without ever leaving your home. This is the best site for international employment opportunities. [ID:2541]

Overseas Summer Jobs 📖
Annual, 256 pages ➤ Peterson's Guides, P.O. Box 2123, Princeton, NJ 08543-2123, USA; US$16.95; cheque or money order; (800) 338-3282, fax (609) 243-9150 ▪ Listings of more than 30,000 summer jobs worldwide, with complete job and application information. Visit the publisher's web site at www.petersons.com. [ID:2499]

Peace Corps and More: 120 Ways to Work, Study and Travel in the Third World 📖
1997, *Medea Benjamin,* 127 pages ➤ Seven Locks Press, P.O. Box 68, Arlington, VA 22210, USA; US$8.95; credit cards; (800) 354-5348, fax (714) 545-1572, sevenlocks@aol.com ▪ This unique guide offers an impressive variety of work, study and travel options in developing countries, from building houses and doing basic repairs to protecting human rights. In addition to providing a selective listing of 120 organizations, the book includes invaluable tips on financing trips, securing low travel fares, and staying safe and healthy. [ID:1247]

Spending a Year Abroad 📖
1994, *Nick Vandome* ➤ How To Books Ltd., 3 Newtec Place, Magdalen Road, Oxford, OX4 1RE, UK; £8.99; credit cards; (44) (1752) 202-301, fax (44) (1865) 202-331 ▪ A year abroad is now a popular option for thousands of graduates, students, and people taking a mid-life break. This book helps with the decision-making process and sets out the numerous options available, from working on a kibbutz, to teaching English as a foreign language, to adapting to life at home on your return. [ID:1683]

Student Travels Magazine 📖
Semiannual ➤ Publications Dept., Council on International Educational Exchange, 205 East 42nd Street, New York, NY 10017, USA; free; VISA, MC; (212) 822-2600, fax (212) 822-2699 ▪ Student magazine with information on how to travel, study, work or volunteer abroad. [ID:2405]

Summer Jobs Search 🖳
www.summerjobs.com/index.html ▪ This is a relatively small database with limited counselling and other job-related services. However, it is unique in that it provides a listing of short-term and summer employment opportunities throughout the world. From high-tech jobs in India to babysitting in London, this may be the place to find a summer adventure. Very easy to use. [ID:2515]

Summer Jobs USA 📖
Annual, Peterson's Guides ➤ Capricorn Business Services, Inc., 28 Clear Lake Ave., West Hill, Ontario M1C 4L6; $26.95; credit cards; (416) 282-3331, fax (416) 282-0015 ▪ Lists 20,000 job vacancies in the US, from arts and crafts instructors, to nurses, wranglers and washers-up! Includes advice on visa and other requirements for non-US citizens, plus employer comments on the advantages of particular jobs. [ID:1591]

Transitions Abroad: The Magazine of Overseas Opportunities 📖
Bimonthly, *Clay Hubb* ➤ Department TRA, Transitions Publishing, P.O. Box 3000, Denville, NJ 07834, USA; $29.95/year; VISA, MC; (413) 256-3414, fax (413) 256-0373, trabroad@aol.com ▪ An excellent periodical. Required reading for students and globe trotters planning to travel, study or work abroad. Promotes learning through direct involvement in the daily lives of peoples of host countries. Describes publications, information sources, organizations, and programs offering study opportunities, entry-level jobs, and living arrangements abroad. Visit the distributor's web site at www.transabroad.com. [ID:1253]

United Nations Volunteers 💻
www.unv.org ▪ This program offers mid-career professionals the opportunity to volunteer overseas in a humanitarian effort. Currently, over 2,000 people from more than 100 countries are volunteering in developing countries as specialists and field workers. This site can help start you on the way to becoming a volunteer for the United Nations. [ID:2482]

What In The World Is Going On? A Guide For Canadians
Wishing to Work, Volunteer, or Study in Other Countries 📖
1996, *Jennifer Humphries, Sienna Filleul,* 253 pages ➤ Canadian Bureau for International Education (CBIE), Suite 1100, 220 Laurier Ave W., Ottawa, Ontario K1P 5Z9; $14; VISA, Amex; (613) 237-4820, fax (613) 237-1073 ▪ Offers a bird's eye view of volunteer and study opportunities abroad. Good coverage of short- to medium-term volunteer positions. Also lists study abroad opportunities and international grants available to Canadian students. Available in French under the title, *Le tour du monde en 1001 projets.* [ID:1090]

Work Abroad: The Complete Guide to Finding a Job Overseas 📖
1997, *Clay Hubb,* Transitions Abroad, 224 pages ➤ Department TRA, Transitions Publishing, P.O. Box 3000, Denville, NJ 07834, USA; $15.95; VISA, MC; (413) 256-3414, fax (413) 256-0373, trabroad@aol.com ▪ Comprehensive guide to all aspects of international work, including work permits, short-term jobs, teaching English, volunteer opportunities, planning an international career, starting your own business, and more. Visit www.transabroad.com, the publisher's web site. [ID:2558]

Work Your Way Around The World 📖
Annual ➤ Peterson's Guides, P.O. Box 2123, Princeton, NJ 08543-2123, USA; US$17.95; cheque or money order; (800) 338-3282, fax (609) 243-9150 ▪ An excellent resource describing numerous ways the enterprising traveller can find work anywhere in the world, travel free by working for passage, and survive when money runs out. Appropriate for the non-career-minded, the book lists jobs by country, describing everything from orange picking to sheep shearing, with direct quotes from people who have actually done the jobs. Well-written and inspiring. Visit the publisher's web site at www.petersons.com. [ID:1154]

A World of Options: Guide to International Education Exchange,
Community Services, and Travel for Persons with Disabilities 📖
1997, *Susan Sygall,* 600 pages ➤ Mobility International USA, P.O. Box 3551, Eugene, OR 97403, USA; US$30; (541) 343-1284, fax (541) 343-6812 ▪ A descriptive resource covering hundreds of opportunities for the disabled in international educational exchange programs, work camps, and volunteer positions. Includes first-person accounts of travel and learning experiences. Visit the distributor's web site at www.miusa.org. [ID:1205]

WorldWorks 💻
www.vcn.ba.ca/idera/ww.htm ▪ WorldWorks is the Resource Centre for Overseas Opportunities profiled in this chapter. Most of their services are available via internet. Their web site provides

information on starting your search and contacting programs and organizations. They also include a list of over 300 organizations in their database, and another specifically for youth opportunities. An excellent place for anyone interested in travelling overseas to gain valuable information. [ID:2425]

A Year Between 📖
1994 ➤ Central Bureau for Educational Visits and Exchanges, Seymour Mews House, Seymour Mews, London, W1H 9PE, UK; VISA, MC, Eurocard; (44) (171) 486-5101, fax (44) (171) 935-5741 ▪ This British guide describes work placement schemes from six months to one year. Also outlines adventure organizations, sponsorships, and travel opportunities. [ID:1217]

Youth Link 1997-1998 📖 🖳
Annual, 199 pages ➤ Public Inquiries Centre, Human Resources Development Canada, 140 Promenade du Portage, Phase 4 Level 0, Hull, Québec K1A 0J9; free; (613) 994-6313, fax (819) 953-7260 ▪ A resource booklet for Canadian youth looking for work and study opportunities in Canada or abroad. Lists 200 Government of Canada youth programs, services and resources. Although most are not international, this is a great reference for government addresses and phone numbers as well as application details for government travel programs. If you're between the ages of 15 and 30, go for it! Visit the web site at www.youth.gc.ca. [ID:1797]

Youth Resource Network of Canada's International Job Opportunities Page 🖳
www.youth.gc.ca/jobopps/intern-e.shtml ▪ This resource site is part of the Canadian government's Youth Employment Strategy. The site offers information on training and education, self-employment, and news releases. It also provides notices of employment opportunities for youth who want to work overseas. [ID:2521]

Profiles Of
Short-Term Programs Overseas

There are a total of 73 Short-term Programs Overseas (SPO) listed in this chapter. These programs have been divided into six categories. There are 22 Youth Exchanges; 11 Internships; five Professional Exchanges; nine Teaching Abroad Programs; 21 Work and Learn Programs; and six Independent Work and Travel Programs.

Forty-one programs operate between Canada and a broad range of countries. Of the remaining 33 programs, four are situated in the Asia Pacific region; two are within Canada; two are in the Caribbean; 20 are in Europe; three are in Latin America; one is in the Middle East, and one is in the USA.

Participating in a short-term overseas program is an important step in expanding your global horizons and building ties across cultures. For many, it is also the initial step required for launching an international career. Good luck and have fun on your short-term program overseas!

AFS Interculture Canada (AFS)
Suite 505, 1231 St. Catherine Street W., Montréal, Québec H3G 1P5;
(800) 361-7248, fax (514) 843-9119, info-canada@afs.org, www.afs.org

YOUTH EXCHANGE ▪ AFS Interculture Canada's core programs immerse Canadians from 15 to 18 years of age in a foreign cultural and linguistic environment. Students can choose a year, a semester or a summer term in one of more than 30 countries. AFS also provides placements in Canada for some 250 foreign students from 36 countries, to attend high school and live with volunteer families. Participants must be in good health and mature enough to handle the challenges of adapting to a new way of life. AFS also offers adult programs for participants over 18. The programs currently offered are Dialogue Across The Americas, Internship, Young Workers, Teaching and Discovery and International Community Service. (For more information on AFS see Chapter 11, Hosting Programs and Chapter 35, Nongovernmental Organizations.) [ID:5000]

Aga Khan Foundation Canada (AKF):
Fellowship in International Development Management
Fellowship in International Development Management, Suite 1820, 350 Albert Street,
Constitution Square, Ottawa, Ontario K1R 1A4; (613) 237-2532, fax (613) 567-2532

INTERNSHIP ▪ Opportunity for 15 to 20 Canadians to travel to South Asia for an eight-month (September to April) management and work internship with an Asian nongovernmental organization. Applicants should have at least an undergraduate degree and be committed to a career in international development. Return fare and a living allowance is provided. Participants are expected to contribute $1,500. This program includes a four-week intensive preparation course at the University of Ottawa in the summer preceding departure. It includes development theory, management principles, and language training. During the program, participants undertake a practical research project in conjunction with their host nongovernmental organization. [ID:5001]

Agence Québec / Wallonie-Bruxelles pour la jeunesse
Bureau 301, 1441, boul. René-Lévesque ouest,
Montréal, Québec H3G 1T7; (514) 873-4355, fax (514) 873-1538, aqwbj@cam.org

PROFESSIONAL EXCHANGE ▪ L'Agence Québec/Wallonie-Bruxelles pour la jeunesse permet annuellement à près de 350 jeunes Québécois âgés de 18 à 30 ans de vivre une expérience d'immersion, de prospection, de coopération ou de travail-formation en Communauté française de Belgique. Les meilleurs projets individuels ou de groupe sont retenus par les membres d'un jury indépendant et les stages se déroulent généralement sur une période de 14 jours. Des frais d'inscription individuels généralement de 475 $ donnent droit, dans la plupart des cas, au financement d'un billet d'avion et à une indemnité de séjour. Le but des programmes est de faciliter l'accès à la plate-forme internationale francophone et de mettre en place des réseaux durables entre partenaires dynamiques de tous les secteurs. [ID:5003]

Alberta Education: Alberta Teacher Exchange Programs
Alberta Teacher Exchange Programs, National and International
Education Building, 7th Floor, East Tower, 11160 Jasper Ave., Edmonton, Alberta
T5K 0L2; (403) 427-2035, fax (403) 422-3014, cbexte@edc.gov.ab.ca, http://ednet.edc.gov.ab.ca/nie

TEACHING ABROAD ▪ Alberta Education offers several national and international exchange programs to Alberta's teachers. Approximately 20 teachers each year are sent to the UK, the US, and Germany to study German as a second language. These programs are usually for a period of one year, from August to July. The Calendar Year Exchanges which begin in January and end in December send approximately 25 teachers to various parts of Australia. Interprovincial exchanges with other Canadian provinces are also possible through the School Year Exchanges program.

Teachers selected for the exchange programs must hold a Permanent Professional Alberta Teaching Certificate and have a minimum of five years of successful, full-time teaching experience. Applicants are selected on the basis of aptitude, experience, and contributions to the profession. Successful candidates must be good ambassadors for both Alberta and Canada. [ID:5004]

Amigos de las Americas
5618 Star Lane, Houston, TX, 77057, USA; (713) 782-5290,
fax (713) 782-9267, info@amgioslink.org, www.amigoslink.org

WORK AND LEARN ▪ Amigos de las Americas provides summer volunteer service in Latin
America. This service is designed for (but not limited to) high school and college students.
Short-term assignments in Mexico, the Dominican Republic, Costa Rica, Honduras, Ecuador,
Paraguay and Brazil focus on improving public health. Participants inoculate patients against
communicable diseases, teach community sanitation, build wells and latrines, teach dental
hygiene, distribute toothbrushes, and vaccinate dogs against rabies. Volunteers live with
families in remote rural villages and urban barrios. Training is provided. Participation costs
about US$3,000 plus domestic airfare. Successful applicants are 16 years or older, have one
year of Spanish or Portuguese, and must show particular interest in Latin America or service
work. Visit the Amigos de las Americas web site for program information and applications.
[ID:5005]

Archaeological Institute of America (AIA)
656 Beacon Street, Boston, MA, 02215-2010, USA; (617) 353-9361,
fax (617) 353-6550, aia@bu.edu, www.saws.brynmawr.edu/aia/html

WORK AND LEARN ▪ AIA publishes the Archaeological Fieldwork Opportunities Bulletin,
which lists volunteer positions available at archaeological excavations and field schools in
various countries around the world. The bulletin has a valuable resource list which includes
contact names and other key information. Some positions require experienced workers, but
most accept beginners. Applicants should be in good health and adaptable to local food and
conditions. The bulletin can be ordered from Kendall/Hunt Publishing Company: (800) 228-
0810 or (319) 589-1000. [ID:5006]

ASSE International Student Exchange Programs:
ASSE College Abroad Program
Coordinator, ASSE College Abroad Program, Suite 204,
7, De La Commerce Street W., Montréal, Québec H2Y 2C5; (800) 361-3214, fax (514) 281-1525

YOUTH EXCHANGE ▪ ASSE offers qualified students, aged 15 to 18, from Western Europe,
North America, Australia, New Zealand, Japan and Thailand, the opportunity to spend a high
school year abroad with a host family in another one of these countries. Applicants must
have a B average over the previous two years. ASSE also offers a six-week summer
homestay program in Europe during June and July, as well as a four-week language program
with instruction and other activities in France, Germany, and Spain. Program costs range
from US$2,000-$2,600 for the summer program, to US$4,600-$6,500 for the school year
program. A limited number of school year program scholarships are available.

ASSE also has a College Abroad Program designed for recent high school graduates.
Single or multi-semester programs are located at educational institutions throughout North
America, Europe, Australia, New Zealand, and Japan. Courses are available in community
colleges, CEGEPs, and universities. Candidates choose the country and program from
which to start their training. Accommodation ranges from dormitory to family living.
Applicants are screened for character and proficiency in the English language. [ID:5007]

Association for International Practical Training (AIPT):
Career Development Exchange Program
Coordinator, Career Development Exchange Program, Suite 250, 10400 Little Patuxent Parkway,
Columbia, MD, 21044-3510, USA; (410) 997-2200, fax (410) 997-3924, cd@aipt.org, www.aipt.org

INTERNSHIP ▪ The Career Development Exchange Program was established in 1982 to
facilitate on-the-job practical training exchanges in countries such as Finland, France,
Germany, Ireland, Switzerland, and the UK. The program is open to high school, vocational
school and college graduates in a variety of fields such as hospitality, public relations,

archaeology and wine-making. Candidates should have completed their education or have at least one year of work experience in their chosen field. The application fee covers health insurance, formal training and workshop opportunities. One hundred and fifty to 200 applications are accepted each year. [ID:6391]

Association Québec-France
Maison Fornel, 9, place Royale, Québec, Québec G1K 4G2; (418) 643-1616, fax (418) 643-3053

WORK AND LEARN ▪ Ce programme d'échanges offre, pour les étudiants résidents du Québec qui ont entre 18 et 30 ans et parlent couramment le français, l'opportunité de travailler dans une municipalité française durant l'été ou d'obtenir des permis de travail d'une durée de trois mois s'ils ont une offre de travail écrite. Un autre programme d'une durée de 8 à 10 jours pour participer aux vendanges est aussi proposé aux personnes ayant entre 18 et 35 ans. [ID:5008]

Australia Working Holiday Program
Australia High Commission, 50 O'Connor Street,
Ottawa, Ontario K1P 6L2; (613) 236-0841, fax (613) 236-4376, www.immi.gov.au

INDEPENDENT WORK AND TRAVEL ▪ The Australia Working Holiday Program offers Canadians aged 18 to 25 years of age opportunities to work in Australia for a period of up to 12 months. A maximum of three months work per employer is permitted. Participants are fully responsible for finding work and must pay their own expenses. A working holiday visa is required, at a cost of $170. Applications are processed at the High Commission in Ottawa, as well as the Australian Consulate in Vancouver. [ID:5009]

AYUSA International
7th Floor, 1 Post Street, San Francisco, CA, 94104, USA;
(800) 727-4540, fax (415) 986-4620, elechnera@ayusa.org, www.ayusa.org

YOUTH EXCHANGE ▪ AYUSA International's Study Abroad Department offers programs for high school students, ages 15 to 18, to participate in an academic year, semester or summer homestay abroad. Students live with host families and attend local schools. Some programs require two years of high school language coursework. Cost to participants ranges from US$1,900 to US$6,000, including international airfare and insurance. Scholarships are available and announced throughout the year. (For more information see Chapter 11, Hosting Programs.) [ID:6690]

Boston University: Internship Programs
Internship Coordinator, Office of International Programs, 5th Floor, 232 Bay State Road, Boston,
MA, 02215, USA; (617) 353-9888, fax (617) 353-5402, abroad@bu.edu, www.web.bu.edu/abroad

INTERNSHIP ▪ Boston University offers a broad range of overseas programs. Global internships are offered in Beijing, London, Madrid, Moscow, Paris, Sydney, and Washington, DC. Each internship combines coursework with eight to 12 weeks of working experience in one of the following areas: Advertising and Public Relations, the Arts, Business and Economics, Health and Human Services, Hospitality Administration, Politics, pre-Law, and the Media including Journalism, Broadcasting, and Film. Language and liberal arts programs are offered in Dresden, Grenoble, Haifa, Madrid, Niamey, Oxford, Padova, and Quito. Students may also study archaeology in Belize and tropical ecology in Ecuador. Costs range from US$8,800 to US$14,700 per semester. Programs are available in the fall, spring and summer. Program information, application instructions, and forms are available on their web site. [ID:5015]

British Columbia Centre Teacher Exchange Office
2870 Seaview Road, Victoria, B.C. V8N 1L1; (250) 472-1106, fax (250) 472-1107

TEACHING ABROAD ▪ Exchange opportunities are available with Australia, New Zealand, the UK, Germany, France, Switzerland, and the Canadian provinces except Québec. Exchanges are generally for one school year. Teachers pay living, travel, and any documentation costs. Participants should have at least five years of teaching experience and a permanent teaching certificate, be prepared to exchange accommodations, and have the consent of their school principal and school board. Teachers taking part in European exchanges must have a working knowledge of the host country's language and be able to satisfy specific requirements of the host countries. Successful applicants are committed to learning, through experience, about education and culture in other countries. [ID:6880]

Canada Netherlands Student Exchange Programs
24 Goulding Crescent, Kanata, Ontario K2K 2N9;
(613) 599-7607, fax (613) 599-9397, rosemieke@cyberus.ca, www.uitwisseling.nl

INDEPENDENT WORK AND TRAVEL ▪ Opportunity for students or recent graduates between the ages of 18 and 30 to work in the Netherlands for a period of up to one year. Placement assistance in agriculture and horticulture is offered to students with work experience in these fields. Participants not working in these fields must arrange their own employment and accommodation. Cost to participants includes a $125 registration fee. [ID:5018]

Canada World Youth (CWY)
2330 Notre Dame West, Montréal, Québec H3J 1N4;
(514) 931-3526, fax (514) 939-2621, cwy-jcm@cwy-jcm.org, www.cwy-jcm.org

YOUTH EXCHANGE ▪ Large and well-respected exchange programs offering youth a cultural exchange experience for four to seven months, depending on the program. There are four key areas of programming for young people. The Youth Exchange Programs are Canada World Youth's longest running programs for young people between the ages of 17 and 20. They are six- to seven-month exchanges in which participants spend half their time living and working as volunteers in a host community in Canada, and the other half in Africa, Asia, Latin America or the Caribbean. The Central and Eastern Europe Programs follow a similar structure, and are adapted to the realities of these regions.

The Work Partner Programs provide youth from 18 to 29 years of age with an opportunity to participate in international cooperation and development through volunteer work placements overseas, in partnership with host-country organizations. Although it does not have a Canadian phase, the volunteers undertake public awareness activities before and after their programs.

The Customized Programs meet the needs of specific clientele or partners, or are designed around a specific theme. They respect the underlying philosophy of Canada World Youth's educational programming while customizing the structure, components and form to fit the specific project.

The Joint Initiatives Programs are responsive in nature. Canada World Youth assists other organizations to carry out their programs by offering them the service or expertise they need. [ID:5017]

Canadian Association of University Teachers of German (CAUTG): Student Summer Work Program
Coordinator, Student Summer Work Program, Department of
Germanic and Slavic Studies, Brock University, St. Catherines, Ontario
L2S 3A1; (905) 688-5550 ext. 3311 or 3312, fax (905) 688-2789, dmacrae@spartan.ac.brocku.ca

WORK AND LEARN ▪ Each year CAUTG sends about 75 Canadian university students to paid summer job positions in Germany, primarily in the tourism industry. The exchange, administered through university German departments, comprises eight weeks of work, followed by approximately three weeks of travel. Students with a working knowledge of German (at least two years or equivalent) may apply. Although jobs will not be matched to career or study plans, this is an excellent opportunity to learn about German language and culture first-hand. Travel is handled by CAUTG, and jobs and accommodation are the responsibility of employment services (ZAU) in Germany. Participants must pay for their return flight but subsidies are usually available.

The deadline for applications is November 30 for the following summer. Applicants should be flexible, possess good language skills, and have a sense of adventure. [ID:5019]

Canadian Baptist Ministries (CBM): Canadian Baptist Volunteers
Canadian Baptist Volunteers, 7185 Millcreek Drive, Mississauga, Ontario
L5N 5R4; (905) 821-3533 ext. 157, fax (905) 826-3441, cbvol@cbmin.org, www.cbmin.org

WORK AND LEARN ▪ Canadian Baptist Volunteers, a department of Canadian Baptist Ministries (CBM), offers individuals the opportunity to broaden their international experience while making significant contributions to their host countries. Volunteers aged 18 and over are placed for periods of two weeks to two years. Projects are identified by CBM and its Relief and Development Department, The Sharing Way. Volunteers must be recommended by their local church, which usually provides financial support. Visit their web site for articles from those who have served as volunteers and for links to the *Finger Tip* database to learn of current needs and how to apply. [ID:5020]

Canadian Crossroads International /
Carrefour Canadien International (CCI)
Crossroads Placement Programs, 31 Madison Ave., Toronto, Ontario M5R 2S2;
(416) 967-0801, fax (416) 967-9078, cci@web.net, www.crossroads-carrefour.ca

WORK AND LEARN ▪ Crossroads offers two main programs. The Individual Placement Program sends volunteers over 19 years of age with little or no prior overseas living experience to developing countries for four months to work on a variety of development projects. CCI provides a training program, meals, and accommodation, but no salary. Participants are expected to assist in fundraising before departure and in educational activities when they return.

The Group Placement Program is aimed at individuals 19 years of age or older who speak French and are interested in going overseas in small groups of five to seven people. Groups work on projects in French West African countries and live with host families.

Successful applicants have keen interests in crosscultural learning, are open-minded, flexible and resourceful, and are in good health. Application deadlines are August 1 for the Individual Placement Program and October 15 for the Group Placement Program. Their web site is currently under construction. (For more information on CCI see Chapter 11, Hosting Programs and Chapter 35, Nongovermental Organizations.) [ID:5021]

Canadian Federation of Students:
Student Work Abroad Programme (SWAP)
Coordinator, Student Work Abroad Programme (SWAP), Suite 500, 243 College Street,
Toronto, Ontario M5T 2Y1; (416) 977-3703, fax (416) 977-4796, www.travelcuts.com

YOUTH EXCHANGE ▪ By far Canada's largest international exchange program, with nearly 2,000 participants annually, SWAP arranges work permits for Canadian students (and youth who are non-students in some cases) interested in short-term work opportunities while travelling abroad. The minimum age for participation is 18, and maximum age limit varies by country. SWAP offers programs in the following countries: Australia, New Zealand, Britain, France, Ireland, the Netherlands, Germany, South Africa, Japan, Jamaica, and the US. Services also vary by country, but all offer a welcome orientation and ongoing advice and assistance regarding employment and accommodation. Participants are responsible for conducting their own job search. The SWAP hosting organizations assist participants by providing employer contacts and information regarding résumés and job strategies. Historically, job success rates have been excellent. Program fees range from $200 to $450, excluding airfares.

SWAP is an excellent, affordable way for young people to gain experience by working with another culture. It also provides participants with a great deal of flexibility to travel at their leisure. Brochures and further information are available at local student association offices, campus placement/career centres and any of the 43 travel offices of Travel Cuts/Voyages Campus across Canada. [ID:5024]

Canadian Federation of Students:
Volunteer Abroad/Bénévoles à l'étrange
Coordinator, Volunteer Abroad/Bénévoles à l'étrange, 5th Floor, 243 College Street, Toronto, Ontario M5T 2Y1; (416) 977-3703, fax (416) 977-4796, vap.bae@travelcuts.com, www.travelcuts.com

YOUTH EXCHANGE ▪ Volunteer Abroad/Bénévoles à l'étranger allows Canadians to see the world and become involved in international and global issues. Set in a "workcamp," up to 20 volunteers from around the world give two to four weeks of their time to a variety of environ-mental, archaeological or community service projects. Projects include working on an archeo-logical dig at a Spanish castle, travelling with developmentally-challenged adults in the US or teaching English to Polish youth. Participants must be at least 18 years of age. A $170 fee (1997) covers administrative costs and the development of camps in Canada. Most camps require a working knowledge of English, and in some cases a second language. Volunteer Abroad looks for people with a generous spirit and an interest in working with others. Please note that fees may change. [ID:5025]

Canadian Foundation for World Development (CFWD)
2441 Bayview Ave., Willowdale, Ontario M2L 1A5; (416) 445-4740, fax (416) 441-4025

PROFESSIONAL EXCHANGE ▪ The Canadian Foundation for World Development (CFWD) recruits skilled Canadian volunteers to assist in community development projects designed to increase local self-sufficiency in developing countries. These commitments range from two weeks to one year. Depending on the project, it provides a range of surplus equipment, from dental and medical equipment, to construction material and agricultural supplies. Since its inception in 1977, CFWD has sent $1 billion worth of surplus equipment overseas and has fitted 1.5 million people with recycled prescription eyeglasses.

Volunteers are assigned where their skills are appropriate. CFWD recruits carpenters, welders, medical doctors, nurses, agronomists, and forestry specialists, to name only a few. Over 8,000 volunteers have participated in the program to date. Volunteers are generally responsible for their own costs through group fund-raising and donations, but basic accom-modation is often provided. [ID:5026]

Canadian Government International Internships
International Internship Programs, Human Resources Development Canada, Phase IV, 4th Floor, Place du Portage, Hull, Québec K1A 0J9; (800) 935-5555, fax (613) 941-5992, http://youth.hrdc-drhc.gc.ca

INTERNSHIP ▪ For a detailed description of this great program, see the Canadian Government International Internships profile in Chapter 17, International Internships. [ID:6884]

Canadian Polish Congress:
Education and Training Programs for Poland (ETPP)
Director, Education and Training Programs for Poland (ETPP), 2nd Floor, 77 Elizabeth Street, Toronto, Ontario M5G 1P4; (416) 971-6464, fax (416) 971-6812, etpphal@popd.netcruiser

TEACHING ABROAD ▪ Education and Training Programs for Poland (ETPP) is a non-profit organization in Toronto which recruits, screens, and selects volunteers to teach English in

Poland. It works closely with the federal and municipal governments, government agencies, community organizations, boards of education, high schools and primary schools in Poland. Teaching ESL and training teachers are ETPP main areas of expertise. However, the program is expanding to include internships in general administration and in the banking industry.

Volunteers need to posses a bachelor's degree and experience in teaching English as a second language, as well as the ability to adapt well to a different culture. Volunteers are required to commit to a minimum of six months of living abroad. [ID:7066]

Canadian Society for International Health (CSIH): International Health Exchange Program
International Health Exchange Program, Suite 1105, 1 Nicholas Street, Ottawa, Ontario K1N 7B7; (613) 241-5785, fax (613) 241-3845, csih@fox.nstn.ca, www.csih.org

PROFESSIONAL EXCHANGE ▪ The Canadian Society for International Health (CSIH), on behalf of the Pan American Health Organization (PAHO), promotes PAHO's Training Program on International Health. The program promotes leadership in public health by enabling participants to develop a broader vision of international and regional health trends, and a more profound understanding of technical cooperation in this field. Participants are engaged in the work of PAHO for a period of 11 months. Minimum requirements include: a graduate degree in public health or in the social sciences related to health; two years experience directing programs or projects in education or in health research; and a working knowledge of Spanish. Participants receive a non-taxable subsistence stipend of US$2,194 per month. Applications by Canadians or Canadian residents must be forwarded to CSIH by July 15. (For more information on CSIH see Chapter 35, Nongovernmental Organizations, and, for information on PAHO see Chapter 38, International Organizations.) [ID:5027]

Canadian Teachers' Federation (CTF): Project Overseas
Director of International Programs, 110 Argyle Ave., Ottawa, Ontario K2P 1B4; (613) 232-1505, fax (613) 232-1886, rbark@ctf-fce.ca, www.ctf-fce.ca

TEACHING ABROAD ▪ Project Overseas is an opportunity for Canadian elementary and secondary school teachers with at least five years teaching experience in Canada to volunteer for short-term teaching work in developing countries. Applicants should be in excellent health, flexible and demonstrate mature judgement. Academic or administrative specialization is an asset. Placements last up to two months and are arranged throughout the year. Travel and living expenses are paid, but no salary is offered. Applicants must possess an appropriate teachers' certificate and belong to a provincial or territorial teachers' organization which is a member of CTF. [ID:5028]

Carrefour de solidarité internationale (CSI)
555, rue Short, Sherbrooke, Québec J1H 2E6; (819) 566-8595, fax (819) 566-8076, csi-sher@login.net

YOUTH EXCHANGE ▪ Le Carrefour de solidarité internationale (CSI) offre un programme de stages outre-mer au Mali, en Haiti, au Pérou, au Nicaragua ou en République domini-caine, pour les jeunes de 18 à 29 ans de l'Estrie. Ces stages comprennent une phase de préparation-formation, un séjour à l'étranger et des activités de sensibilisation au retour. [ID:5029]

Chantiers jeunesse
C.P. 1000, succursale M, Montréal, Québec H1V 3R2; (514) 252-3015, fax (514) 251-8719, chantier@microtec.net

WORK AND LEARN ▪ Chantiers jeunesse, un organisme sans but lucratif a pour principal objectif de soutenir le développement de l'autonomie chez les jeunes adultes. Le programme Chantier jeunesse est destiné aux 16 à 25 ans et aux organismes à but non lucratif du Québec. Les chantiers se déroulent au Québec autour de projets utiles à la communauté (construction, rénovation, présentation du patrimoine, travail communautaire) pour des périodes de trois à dix semaines. Le programme des échanges internationaux permet aux jeunes de 16 à 25 ans du Québec de vivre l'expérience d'un chantier pendant environ trois semaines dans un pays européen ou aux États-Unis. Dix-huit pays, dont la France, la Belgique et plusieurs pays de l'Europe de l'Est, sont offerts. [ID:5030]

Children's International Summer Villages (CISV)
5 Dunvegan Road, Ottawa, Ontario K1K 3E7; (613) 749-9680, fax (613) 749-9680

YOUTH EXCHANGE ▪ Children's International Summer Villages (CISV) Canada promotes global peace education. The organization has 10 chapters across Canada in Victoria, Vancouver, Calgary, Saskatoon, London, Waterloo, Toronto, Ottawa, St. Grégoire, and Fredericton.

In addition to its Canadian activities, CISV offers four main overseas programs to youth aged 11 to 19. Through International Villages (age 11), Interchanges (ages 12/13, 13/14, and 14/15), Summer Camps (ages 13, 14 or 15), and Seminar Camps (ages 18 and 19), delegations from a number of countries around the world meet for a period of approximately three or four weeks in a host country. In some cases delegations stay in their home country. The programs are designed to promote crosscultural awareness and understanding. Participants spend four weeks with a host family overseas, and in turn host their billet the following year for a period of four weeks. There are some group activities. Cost to participants varies by local chapter and program.

Opportunities are available for youth aged 16 and 17 to work as junior counsellors, and individuals over 21 years of age to become program leaders. Leaders and counsellors are provided with valuable leadership and emergency first-aid training. Those interested in learning more about CISV should contact their local chapter, or contact the Secretary of CISV Canada at the number listed above. (For more information on CISV see Chapter 11, Hosting Programs.) [ID:5031]

Cultural Homestay International (CHI)
P.O. Box 904, Chase, B.C. V0E 1M0;
(800) 463-1061, fax (250) 679-5361, cbellchi@mail.netshop.net, www.chinet.org

WORK AND LEARN ▪ Cultural Homestay International places high school graduates in French, German, Finnish, Swedish, and Spanish homes as au pairs. Participants work from six months to one year. Costs are about $2,900. This covers return airfare, insurance, and the services of a CHI representative in the host country. Minimum qualifications include a basic working knowledge of the language of the host country, a high school diploma and babysitting experience. [ID:5032]

Earthwatch
P.O. Box 9104, 680 Mount Auburn Street, Watertown, MA, 02272, USA;
(617) 926-8200, fax (617) 926-8532, info@earthwatch.org, www.earthwatch.org

WORK AND LEARN ▪ Earthwatch offers a unique opportunity to join ongoing scientific research projects in Canada, the US and all over the world. Participants are volunteers on expedition sites, and assist scholars and scientists in field research. Projects of one- to three-weeks are coordinated in small groups. Participants must pay travel and living costs, ranging from US$595-$2,3595, which includes all expenses except airfare to the site. As Earthwatch is a nonprofit organization, these costs, along with annual membership fees of US$35, directly support research efforts. Earthwatch currently has over 100,000 supporters. Volunteers gain hands-on experience in over 15 fields of study, including archaeology, ornithology, marine mammology, ecology and public health. Successful applicants are 16-80 years old, open-minded, curious to learn about other cultures, and in good physical condition. (For more information on Earthwatch see Chapter 38, International Organizations.) [ID:5035]

El Refuerzo
5615, rue Woodbury, Montréal, Québec H3T 1S6; (514) 733-1781, fax (514) 735-8511

YOUTH EXCHANGE ▪ Nous organisons chaque été un project de coopération dans la region de Canete (Pérou; 150 km au sud de Lima). Il est offert à des étudiantes de niveau collégial et universitaire de n'importe quel domaine. Là-bas, nous assistons au Centre de formation pour la femme péruvienne, «Condoray,» qui travaille depuis 33 ans dans le développement communautaire. Les projets que nous réalisons sont : rénovation matérielle des dispensaires, écoles, etc.; cours de nutrition et couture aux paysannes; collations nutritives et programme "Niño a niño"; assistance médicale. Les personnes interessées doivent faire demande au courant des mois de septembre à novembre. La sélection se fait au début de décembre. Six mois de préparation sont requis avant le départ (qui a lieu normalement vers juin- juillet) durant lesquels les participants doivent approfondir la langue espagnole. «El Refuerzo» fonctionne avec des volontaires à temps partiel et recherche des stagiaires capables de travailler en groupe, flexibles et possédant de l'initiative. [ID:6402]

Elderhostel Canada
4 Cataraqui Street, Kingston, Ontario K7K 1Z7;
(613) 530-2222, fax (613) 530-2096, ecmail@elderhostel.org, www.elderhostel.org

WORK AND LEARN ▪ Elderhostel Canada's travel/study programs for people in their retirement years are developed cooperatively with a variety of organizations and host institutions in Canada and around the world. These programs combine the best of both an academic experience and a popular study tour. Participants learn about, analyze, experience, discuss, and enjoy the places and people of the countries they visit. To receive Elderhostel Canada Catalogues free of charge, please contact the National office listed above. In the US, Elderhostel Inc. publishes an extensive international catalogue which can be ordered by writing to Elderhostel Inc., 75 Federal Street, Boston MA, 02110-1941, or by visiting the Elderhostel web site. [ID:5037]

Expérience-Jeunesse International:
Programme d'Échanges de Jeunes Travailleurs Canada-Suisse
Coordinator, Canada-Switzerland Young Trainee Exchange Program, 12, rue Laval, Alymer, Québec
J9H 1C5; (819) 684-9212, fax (819) 684-5630, j.larochelle@experience.qc.ca, www.experience.qc.ca

YOUTH EXCHANGE ▪ Le programme d'échanges de jeunes travailleurs entre le Canada et la Suisse est destiné aux Canadiens qui désirent parfaire en Suisse leurs connaissances linguistiques et acquérir des compétences professionnelles reliées à leur domaine d'études. Quelque soit ce dernier, un stage d'une durée de quatre à dix-huit mois leur est accessible par le biais de ce programme officiel entre le Canada et la Suisse. Pour participer à ce programme, les candidats doivent avoir la citoyenneté canadienne, détenir un diplôme d'un institut de technologie ou d'une institution d'enseignement équivalente, désirer faire un stage directement relié à leurs études, être agés de 18 à 30 ans et posséder une connaissance suffisante du français, de l'allemand ou de l'italien.

Le canadidat doit lui-même faire les démarches pour rechercher en Suisse un débouché de stage possible. Expérience-Jeunesse International (EJI) fournit cependant une aide dans ces démarches. EJI peut fournir des listes d'employeurs potentiels, une critique du curriculum vitae et une assistance dans l'obtention du permis de travail. Les participants doivent organiser eux-même leur voyage et assumer leurs frais de déplacement. Certains frais d'insription sont aussi demandés. [ID:6385]

Department of Foreign Affairs and International Trade (DFAIT): Canada-Sweden Working Holiday Program

Canada-Sweden Working Holiday Program, Lester B. Pearson Bldg.,
125 Sussex Drive, Ottawa, Ontario K1A 0G2; (613) 992-6142, fax (613) 992-5965, www.dfait-maeci.gc.ca

INDEPENDENT WORK AND TRAVEL ▪ The Canada-Sweden Working Holiday Program offers the opportunity for Canadian youth aged 18 to 30 to gain overseas experience by living and working in Sweden. Students who have made an arrangement to work or receive training with an organization in Sweden may obtain a working holiday visa free of charge from the Embassy of Sweden. Training may last up to three months, or, in a professional applicant's case, up to 12 months. (For information on their international internships see the Canadian Government International Internships profile in Chapter 17, International Internships.) [ID:5039]

Department of Foreign Affairs and International Trade (DFAIT): International Youth Exchange

International Youth Exchange Programs, Lester B. Pearson Bldg., 125 Sussex Dr.,
Ottawa, Ontario K1A 0G2; (613) 992-6142, fax (613) 992-5965, www.dfait-maeci.gc.ca

YOUTH EXCHANGE ▪ The Department of Foreign Affairs and International Trade (DFAIT) administers approximately 60 international youth exchange programs in more than 20 countries. These are for Canadians aged 18-30, with a postsecondary education who want a career-related work experience in industry, commerce, tourism, agriculture, services, science or technology. Programs are designed to expand and enhance professional skills during a period of training in a foreign country. Positions are paid but travel and accommodation are the responsibility of the participant. Programs tend to be very competitive, so although not required, it is recommended that interested individuals contact a firm or organization in their selected country ahead of time. Language skills and some Canadian work experience are important for successful application. Certain programs are targeted for certain fields. For specific information check through some of the resources listed at the end of this chapter. (For information on their international internships see the Canadian Government International Internships profile in Chapter 17, International Internships.) [ID:5040]

Friends of World Teaching

Director, P.O. Box 1049, San Diego, CA, 92112-1049, USA;
(619) 224-2365, fax (619) 224-5363, fowt@wordnet.att.net, www.fowt.com

TEACHING ABROAD ▪ Friends of World Teaching is affiliated with more than 1,000 English-language schools and colleges in 100 countries worldwide. The organization offers teaching and administrative opportunities to American and Canadian educators. Positions exist in most subject areas and at most levels, from kindergarten to university, and are filled throughout the year. Qualifications are similar to those in North America and foreign language knowledge is usually not required. Salaries vary from country to country, and, in most cases, are adequate for overseas living. [ID:5041]

German Embassy: The Canada-Germany Young Worker's Exchange Program

Coordinator, The Canada-Germany Young Worker's Exchange Program,
1 Waverley Street, Ottawa, Ontario K2P 0T8; (613) 232-1101, fax (613) 594-9330,
100566.2620@compuserve.com, www.docuweb.ca/Germany

INDEPENDENT WORK AND TRAVEL ▪ The Canada-Germany Young Worker's Exchange Program is designed for candidates 18 to 30 years of age who have graduated in disciplines related to industry, science and technology or commerce. Applicants must also have one year of work experience directly related to their academic degree or diploma and a working knowledge of German. Applications meeting the eligibility requirements are sent to the German government, which begins a job search based on the applicant's qualifications. Applicants may not enter the country until they have found employment and are in possession of a work permit and/or visa. Exchanges may last up to 18 months. [ID:6378]

Global Change Game
Volunteer.Coordinator, P.O. Box 1632, Winnipeg, Manitoba R3C 2Z6;
(204) 783-2675, fax (204) 783-2680, gcg@solutions.net, www.mbnet.mb.ca/lucas/gcg/

WORK AND LEARN ▪ The Global Change Game is an international development education program which visits high schools, universities and community groups across Canada teaching about world issues in a fun and innovative way. Each year, 8-12 volunteers travel with our team for periods of 6-12 weeks. All costs are covered. To apply, you must be a high school graduate over 18 years old, and a non-smoker. You also must have some knowledge of environmental and development issues, and the curiosity to learn more. You don't have to be an expert, but you must be able to discuss complicated issues in clear and simple language, and be good at creative-problem solving and thinking quickly and logically. [ID:7074]

Great Britain Working Holidaymaker Scheme
Program Officer, British High Commission,
80 Elgin Street, Ottawa, Ontario K1P 5Y8; (613) 237-2008, fax (613) 232-2533

INDEPENDENT WORK AND TRAVEL ▪ The Great Britain Working Holidaymaker Scheme provides opportunities for youth aged 17 to 27 to take a vacation in the UK while undertaking occasional work for a period of up to two years. Participants pay for all expenses, including the cost of the Working Holidaymaker entry clearance of $79.20 (price is subject to change). Commonwealth citizens who have close connections with the UK through birth, marriage or ancestry may be eligible for admission without any restriction on the length of their stay or freedom to take employment. [ID:5042]

HOPE International Development Agency
214 - 6th Street, New Westminster, B.C. V3L 3A2;
(604) 525-5481, fax (604) 525-3471, hope@web.net, www.idirect.ca/~hope

WORK AND LEARN ▪ HOPE offers a development education program for Canadians interested in international development. A group of 15 to 20 people spend five months, part-time, preparing in Canada, followed by one month working in a developing country at the community level. (For more information on HOPE see Chapter 35, Nongovernmental Organizations.) [ID:5043]

International Agricultural Exchange Association
Suite 105, 7710 5th Street S.E., Calgary, Alberta T2H 2L9; (403) 255-7799, fax (403) 255-6024

WORK AND LEARN ▪ The International Agricultural Exchange is an opportunity for Canadians aged 18 to 30 to travel and gain first-hand agricultural work experience in Europe, the UK, Japan, Australia, and New Zealand. This unique program is open to agricultural students or individuals with practical farming experience. The exchange ranges in length from four to 13 months and costs between $2,500 and $8,000 depending on the length of the trip. This amount covers travel costs, orientation seminars, and accommodation with a host family. Participants receive an allowance each month and are given vacation time. [ID:5045]

International Association for the Exchange of Students for Technical Experience (IAESTE) / Association for International Practical Training (AIPT)
Coordinator, Student Exchanges/IAESTE Program, Suite 250, 10400 Little Patuxent Parkway, Columbia, MD, 21044-3510, USA; (410) 997-2200, fax (410) 992-3924, se@aipt.org, www.aipt.org

INTERNSHIP ▪ Candidates for the Student Exchanges Program can apply for training in the field of their choice, from hospitality to law. Applicants must be enrolled full-time in a vocational, undergraduate, or graduate school and must have prearranged training assignments overseas.

The Student Exchange Program also serves as the American affiliate of IAESTE, which arranges exchanges between over 60 member countries, for students of engineering, math, agriculture, and the sciences. The duration of the program ranges from 1 to 12 months and salaries vary according to host employers. Two hundred to 400 applications are accepted each year. [ID:6774]

International Association for the Exchange of Students for Technical Experience (IAESTE): International Student Exchange
International Student Exchange, P.O. Box 1473,
Kingston, Ontario K7L 5C7; (613) 549-2243, fax (613) 545-6869

YOUTH EXCHANGE ▪ IAESTE is an international exchange program providing on-the-job training experience for students in their own fields of study. It includes 62 member countries in five continents. During the past 40 years, over 5,000 students from 64 Canadian institutions have benefited from the program.

Students of engineering, science, and related technologies can apply each fall for an 8-12 week placement the following summer. Some longer placements may be available. A modest salary covers living costs, but generally does not cover travel. Applicants must be full-time students and have completed at least two years of postsecondary study, preferably with some practical experience. Costs include a registration fee which is partially refunded if a placement is not found. [ID:5047]

International Rural Exchange (IRE)
Box 111, Elgin, Manitoba R0K 0T0; (204) 769-2448, fax (204) 769-2177

INTERNSHIP ▪ International Rural Exchange (IRE) programs are designed to give young adults the opportunity to learn about the agriculture, horticulture and customs of other countries while working and living with host families in those countries. IRE matches qualifications and interests with a suitable farm or horticultural operation, and gives participants an orientation seminar when they arrive in the host country. IRE also provides supervision at the training facility. A monthly allowance is paid, and room and board are provided. Participating countries include the Scandinavian countries, countries of Western Europe, Australia, and the US. IRE operates both incoming and outgoing programs. [ID:5048]

Japan Exchange and Teaching Programme (JET)
Information and Cultural Section, Embassy of Japan, 255 Sussex Drive, Ottawa, Ontario
K1N 9E6; (613) 241-7613, fax (613) 241-4261, infocul@embjapan.can.org, www.embjapan.can.org

TEACHING ABROAD ▪ The Japan Exchange and Teaching (JET) Programme promotes international understanding of Japan through foreign language education and international exchange activities. One-year placements are available to assist in teaching English in the public school system. Applicants must be Canadian citizens, have a university degree, show strong interest in both Japan and teaching, and have excellent English language skills. They should also be well-rounded in terms of work, study, and volunteer experience. Placements are also available with local governments in the area of international relations for applicants with strong Japanese language skills. Please contact the Embassy of Japan or your local consulate in September to obtain an application. Applications must be made to the Embassy of Japan by mid-November for placements beginning the following July. [ID:5050]

Japan Working Holiday Program
Program Officer, Japan Embassy, 255 Sussex Drive,
Ottawa, Ontario K1N 9E6; (613) 241-8541, fax (613) 241-7415, www.embjapan.can.org

INDEPENDENT WORK AND TRAVEL ▪ The Japan Working Holiday is an opportunity for Canadian citizens aged 18 to 30 to work for an initial period of up to six months, and a possible extension of an additional six months. The working holiday visa is designed for youth who intend primarily to holiday in Japan for a specific period, and who may take on casual employment during their stay.

Participants cover all costs. General information is located on their web site, however, for specifics, interested applicants must contact the Japan Embassy or one of the consulates which are located in Toronto, Vancouver, Montréal, and Edmonton. [ID:5051]

Junior Professional Officer Program (JPO)
Human Resources Division, Personnel and Administration Branch,
Canadian International Development Agency (CIDA), 200 Promenade du Portage,
Hull, Québec K1A 0G4; (819) 997-5456, fax (819) 953-6382, http://w3.acdi-cida.gc.ca

INTERNSHIP ▪ The Junior Professional Officer Program (JPO) is a program administered under the auspices of the United Nations. Its primary objectives are to provide experience in managing a development program, support the UN through JPO services, place Canadians in the UN, and repatriate knowledge gained from assignments. General duties of a JPO include the administration and coordination of projects and liaison between local authorities, regional offices, and headquarters.

Through the Canadian International Development Agency (CIDA), Canada sponsors several JPOs annually in the following UN Agencies: United Nations Development Program (UNDP), United Nations International Children's Fund (UNICEF), United Nations High Commissioner for Refugees (UNHCR), and the World Food Program (WFP).

Candidates should be under the age of 30, and possess a completed master's degree in a relevant discipline. Knowledge of a third language is an asset and work experience (paid or voluntary) is becoming increasingly important as placements become more competitive.

Information about the JPO program and application forms are available on CIDA's web site. [ID:6885]

Latin America Mission (LAM)
Unit 14, 3075 Ridgeway Drive, Mississauga,
Ontario L5L 5M6; (905) 569-0001, fax (905) 569-6990, lam@idirect.com

YOUTH EXCHANGE ▪ Participants are expected to share their Christian faith through development and evangelism projects. Intensive Spanish language classes and the study of Mexican life, culture, and history are an integral part of the program. A $700 fee covers room and board. Participants are responsible for travel expenses. [ID:5053]

Manitoba Education and Training:
Manitoba - Federal Republic of Germany Student Exchange
Coordinator, Manitoba - Federal Republic of Germany Student Exchange,
Program Implementation Branch, West Wing 130, 1970 Ness Ave., Winnipeg, Manitoba R3J 0Y9;
(204) 945-7967, fax (204) 945-1254, rbaren@minet.gov.mb.ca, www.uwinnipeg.ca/~german/mtg/html

YOUTH EXCHANGE ▪ Opportunity for Grade 11 Manitoba (and Saskatchewan) students with a minimum of two years of German language classes to attend school and live with a family in Germany for three months, from April to June. Students are accompanied to Germany by two chaperons who ensure that students are picked up at the airport by their host families. Students are responsible for return airfare to Germany (approximately

$1,200), as well as spending money (approximately $700 to $800). Successful candidates are open-minded, flexible, adaptable, have good academic standing, are interested in new cultures and able to cope well with challenging situations. A second stream was introduced in 1996 for social studies students. This exchange is shorter in duration and students are not required to have studied German. [ID:5054]

Medical Group Missions (Canada) Inc.
Suite 301, 15 John Street N., Hamilton, Ontario L8R 1H1;
(905) 524-3544, fax (905) 524-5400, vwhz69a@prodigy.com, www.mmiusa.org

PROFESSIONAL EXCHANGE ▪ Medical Group Missions (Canada) Inc. provides the chance to participate in short-term (two-week) projects in developing countries. Healthcare professionals and volunteers assist patients. Medical and dental surgery as well as medications and eyeglasses are provided. Participants' donations cover travel and living expenses. Applications are processed on a first-come-first-served basis and project size is determined by project directors and the number of physicians or dentists registered. [ID:5038]

Montréal Israel Experience Centre
Kibbutz Aliyah Desk, Israel Experience Centre, 5151 Côte St. Catherine,
Montréal, Québec H3W 1M6; (514) 345-6449, fax (514) 345-6418, miec@total.net

WORK AND LEARN ▪ The Kibbutz Aliyah Desk offers you a wonderful inexpensive way to experience Israel. Work on a kibbutz for a minimum of two months in exchange for full room and board and tours throughout the country. Programs take place all year round and are open to 18 - 28 year olds. It is also possible to study Hebrew. Successful applicants are generally sociable, in good health and possess a strong work ethic. Costs include a US$110 registration fee and insurance. Kibbutz program centres are also located in Toronto, Ottawa, Vancouver, and Winnipeg. [ID:5049]

NACEL Canada
Suite 208, 8925 - 82 Ave., Edmonton, Alberta T6C 0Z2;
(800) 661-6223, fax (403) 465-7583, can@nacel.org, www.nacel.org

YOUTH EXCHANGE ▪ NACEL Canada offers a variety of opportunities for students aged 13 to 18 to travel abroad. The majority of NACEL's programs are language-based and involve a family homestay element. NACEL offers summer programs in France, Québec, Spain, Mexico, Ireland, and Australia. Students aged 15 to 18 may choose to spend a semester or school year in France, Québec, Spain, Mexico or Australia. NACEL Canada also offers an au pair program in France for individuals between the ages of 18 and 27. As well, through the school system, NACEL's Discovery Tours offer teachers and students the opportunity to travel and experience the world. Visit the NACEL web site for further details. (For more information see Chapter 11, Hosting Programs.) [ID:6810]

Office Franco-Québecois pour la Jeunesse
Directrice de programme, 1441, boul. René-Lévesque ouest, Bureau 301,
Montréal, Québec H3G 1T7; (800) 465-4255, fax (514) 873-0067, ofqj@cam.org, www.ofqj.qc.ca

INTERNSHIP ▪ L'Office Franco-Québécois pour la Jeunesse (OFQJ) est un outil d'éducation et de formation au service des jeunes Français et Québécois. L'OFQJ vise au renforcement de l'identité francophone des deux sociétés et de ce fait, encourage les initiatives des jeunes québécois de 18 à 35 ans ayant trait à la formation professionnelle, à la recherche et à la diffusion d'expertise. Les projets doivent s'inscrire dans l'une des priorités de l'OFQJ, soit le commerce, la communication, la culture, le droit international, l'environnement, l'intégration-insertion, le management, les sciences et technologie ou le tourisme.

Pour participer à un stage, on doit avoir entre 18 et 35 ans, être soit étudiant, travailleur ou professionnel, habiter au Québec depuis au moins un an et être motivé et dynamique. Les coûts d'inscription, lorsqu'un projet est sélectionné, sont de 350 $.

Les candidats doivent préparer une soumission de stage contenant les objectifs, la forme et la durée du séjour, un budget et une confirmation d'un partenaire ou employeur en France. Environ 1000 participants sont retenus. Le site Web de l'OFQJ contient plusieurs renseignements pertinents. [ID:5057]

Ontario Foundation for Educator Exchanges
Fairmeadow Centre, 17 Fairmeadow Ave. N.,
York, Ontario M2P 1W6; (416) 222-5107, fax (416) 222-2387

TEACHING ABROAD ▪ Ontario teachers with five or more years of successful teaching experience may apply for a one year exchange of position and accommodation with a counterpart in Australia, New Zealand, the UK, France, Germany, Spain, Switzerland, the Netherlands, the US or other Canadian provinces. Application fees are $50, plus an additional $300 if a successful match is arranged. Applications are available in September and the deadline for submissions is November 30. Applicants must have the endorsement and approval of their principal and school board. [ID:5058]

Organization for Cooperation in Overseas Development (OCOD)
Suite 307, 1 Wesley Ave., Winnipeg, Manitoba R3C 4C6;
(204) 946-0600, fax (204) 956-5939, ocod@ocod.mb.ca, www.mbnet.mb.ca/~ocod

TEACHING ABROAD ▪ Organization for Cooperation in Overseas Development (OCOD) sends Canadian teachers with successful teaching experience in their subject areas to deliver education training programs in Eastern Caribbean countries. The intent of the program is to upgrade local instructors' teaching skills and train local trainers. Service is on a voluntary basis, but OCOD provides return travel costs, hotel accommodations, and a modest meal allowance. Successful applicants must be flexible, adapt easily to local conditions and be able to modify programs as necessary. OCOD also has a Youth Volunteer Program that is open to any graduate of a postsecondary institution between the ages of 18 and 30. As youth volunteer positions become available they are posted on the OCOD web site. [ID:5059]

Saskatoon Board of Education: German Exchange
German Exchange Coordinator, 405 Third Ave. S., Saskatoon, Sask.
S7K 1M7; (306) 683-8352, fax (306) 683-8207, freund.margaret@sbe.saskatoon.sk.ca

YOUTH EXCHANGE ▪ This exchange program is designed to enhance language skills and cultural understanding between students from Saskatoon and Germany. Students spend three months in the host country, living with host families and attending school. Canadian applicants must be Canadian citizens or landed immigrants and attend a Saskatoon public school. Exchange students must have sufficient academic standing to allow for three months away from their home schools. Canadian students must have three semesters of German language training to qualify. Costs to students include airfare, spending money, medical insurance, plus associated hosting costs. Successful participants must have an average of 75 per cent in all subjects at the time of application and be recommended by their school, based on an evaluation of academic competence, maturity, and sociability. [ID:5061]

Shastri-Indo-Canadian Institute:
Shastri Foundation Summer Programme
Coordinator, Shastri Foundation Summer Programme, University of Calgary,
Education Tower 1402, 2500 University Drive N.W., Calgary, Alberta T2N 1N4;
(403) 220-7467, fax (403) 289-0100, sici@acs.ucalgary.ca, www.ucalgary.ca/~sici

INTERNSHIP ▪ The Shastri Foundation Summer program is an opportunity for full-time students registered in degree-granting Canadian Institutions of higher education to participate in a nine-week credit course in India. The program focuses on four development themes: Development and the Environment, Social and Economic Reform, Private-sector

Development, and Gender and Development. Program costs, including domestic and international travel and living expenses, are borne mainly by the institute with its funding from the Canadian International Development Agency. However, participants are required to contribute $2,500 to the programme. Participants are selected on the basis of academic background, personal suitability and commitment to India or development studies in Canada. Contact the institute in September for an application form. For detailed information, visit the Shastri-Indo-Canadian Institute's web site. [ID:5062]

University of Toronto, Faculty of Law:
International Human Rights Internship Programme (IHRP)
Coordinator, International Human Rights Internship Programme (IHRP), 78 Queen's Park Crescent, Toronto, Ontario M5S 2C5; (416) 978-4908, fax (416) 978-7899, www.law.utoronto.ca

INTERNSHIP ▪ The International Human Rights Law Internship Programme (IHRP) seeks opportunities for practical involvement by law students or recent law graduates in the international, regional and domestic protection of human rights. Approximately 12 students each year are placed in legal positions in countries from Hong Kong to South Africa, with such organizations as the World Health Organization, the International Labour Organization, and the European Court of Human Rights. Individual internship projects vary, and are developed by faculty members or students working with faculty members.

Participation is limited to University of Toronto Faculty of Law students and recent graduates. Interns are selected on the basis of legal qualifications, language where relevant, and ability to work with others in challenging situations. [ID:5065]

Union des producteurs agricoles: Agricultural Exchange
555 Roland-Therrien Blvd., Longueuil, Québec J4H 3Y9; (514) 679-0530, fax (514) 679-2375

YOUTH EXCHANGE ▪ Union des producteurs agricoles offers Québec residents an opportunity to experience life on a farm in France. Participants must be between 18-30, have agricultural training or experience, and be fluent in French or English. Participants can stay in France for three or six months and receive room and board as well as a small living allowance in exchange for work. Fees, including return airfare, are about $500. [ID:5064]

Up With People
Admissions, 1 International Court, Broomfield, CO, 80021, USA;
(800) 596-7353, fax (303) 438-7301, uwp-admissions@upwithpeople.org, www.upwithpeople.org

YOUTH EXCHANGE ▪ Up With People is the international learning program that provides personal and professional growth through the unique combination of international travel, performing arts and community service.

There are five international casts on tour each year; each cast has 100 to 150 students ages 17 to 27, representing an average of 25 nationalities. Each cast is guaranteed a two-continent tour and visits over 75 cities. In every city, students stay with a host family, perform a professional musical show, and do community service. This unique program offers students the chance to gain professional skills and to become more aware of the people and the world they are a part of. Successful applicants are between 17 and 25, open-minded, with a desire to learn and a desire for adventure. They are also internationally-oriented and have an interest in international travel, the performing arts, and community service. See the Up With People web site for more information. [ID:5066]

Veterans Affairs Canada: Vimy Tourist Guides Program
Coordinator, Vimy Tourist Guides Program, Veterans Services, P.O. Box 7700, Charlottetown, P.E.I.
C1A 8M9; (902) 566-8392, fax (902) 566-8781, hlhupe@hures.vac-acc.gc.ca, www.vac-acc.gc.ca

WORK AND LEARN ▪ This unique program is open to bilingual, Canadian, postsecondary students. Students who apply are expected to have a knowledge and interest in the history of the battle of Vimy Ridge in France as well as some tour guide or interpreter experience.

Positions are for 12 weeks and involve giving guided tours, in English and French, of the Vimy Ridge battlefield. Rate of pay is set at Cdn$9.62 per hour for guides, and Cdn$10.27 per hour for chief guides. A daily allowance of $24 is paid to students to compensate for the higher cost of living in France. Students must express a willingness to work in France and assume the costs of their accommodation, meals, and healthcare. Applications must be received by November 12 for work the following tourist season. [ID:5067]

The VIEW Foundation

13 Hazelton Ave., Toronto, Ontario L1S 3B4; (800) 387-1387, fax (416) 964-3416, view@octonline.com

WORK AND LEARN ▪ The VIEW Foundation is a Canadian nonprofit organization providing challenging and dynamic opportunities for international volunteers to support community and environmental projects around the world through direct participation.

Since 1994, over 300 volunteers have participated in VIEW projects in over 20 projects. Volunteers of all ages learn intercultural dynamics, language and practical skills by living overseas and contributing to projects. The VIEW Foundation presently has projects in Costa Rica and Antarctica. The ratios on project sites are nine adults to one leader, and 13 students to two leaders.

Successful applicants are individuals between the ages of 15 and 75, who are physically fit and want to contribute to a volunteer project. There are no special language requirements, but applicants must display a strong desire to participate in environmental education. Costs to participants vary by project. [ID:6374]

Visions in Action

2710 Ontario Road N.W., Washington, DC, 20009, USA; (202) 625-7403, fax (202) 625-2353, visions@igc.org, www.igc.org/visions

WORK AND LEARN ▪ Visions in Action coordinates volunteer placements in Mexico, Burkina Faso, Uganda, Zimbabwe, Tanzania, and South Africa. Visions matches volunteers with expatriate and indigenous nonprofit organizations overseas. Volunteers work in various fields, including community development, health, human rights, journalism, youth, gender and the environment for six months or one year. Volunteers must raise their own funds, between US$5,000 and US$6,000 per year. Candidates must be at least 20 years of age. University graduates are preferred. Successful applicants are dynamic, outgoing and demonstrate initiative. [ID:5069]

Volunteers for Peace

43 Tiffany Road, Belmont, VT, 05730, USA; (802) 259-2759, fax (802) 259-2922, vfp@vfp.org, www.vfp.org

YOUTH EXCHANGE ▪ Volunteers for Peace offers approximately 500 volunteer positions annually, with a view to promoting goodwill through people-to-people exchanges and community service. Volunteers cooperate with locals on host community projects in the areas of archaeology, social sciences, natural resources, construction, agriculture, and the environment. Positions are available in 70 countries worldwide. Most programs are from May to September, with a few in winter and spring. Room and board are provided, but travel expenses are not paid. [ID:5567]

World Language Program

language@WEBPAL.org, www.WEBPAL.org/language/

PROFESSIONAL EXCHANGE ▪ The World Language Program (WLP) is a project of the International Association of Educators for World Peace and the UNKOMMON Foundation, a Canadian nonprofit corporation. WLP is a volunteer program with representatives in over 30 countries. Currently, there are several hundred volunteers working with WLP and the program is rapidly expanding. For information on WLP, or to apply as a volunteer, visit their web site. [ID:7047]

World Learning
P.O. Box 676, Brattleboro, VT, 05302-0676, USA; (802) 257-7751,
fax (802) 258-3248, info@worldlearning.org, www.worldlearning.org

YOUTH EXCHANGE ▪ World Learning was founded in 1932 as The Experiment in International Living, a pioneer in people-to-people exchange. It is one of the oldest nonprofit, international educational service organizations in the world, and the oldest institution of its kind in the US. For 65 years, it has sustained its founding concept—that to learn the culture of another country one must be living as a member of one of its families—but it has also pioneered new initiatives in response to a changing world. The scope and diversity of World Learning's programs have grown well beyond the institution's original homestay exchanges; however, its mission remains the same: to enable participants to develop the knowledge, skills, and attitudes needed to contribute effectively to international understanding and global development.

World Learning's School for International Training was established in 1964 in response to the Peace Corp's demand for original language training and teaching materials. Today, the school offers a bachelor's degree program in international studies, master's degree programs in intercultural management and the teaching of languages, and college semester-abroad programs in more than 40 countries. [ID:5070]

World University Service of Canada (WUSC)
P.O. Box 3000, Stn. C, 1404 Scott Street, Ottawa, Ontario
K1Y 4M8; (613) 798-7477, fax (613) 798-0990, wusc@wusc.ca, www.wusc.ca

YOUTH EXCHANGE ▪ World University Service of Canada (WUSC) sends 50 Canadian university and college students on different summer programs to developing countries for six to eight week periods each year. Participants gain an understanding of development issues in a particular country through working on various development research or field projects. Upon return to Canada, students must complete a report and are encouraged to participate in development education activities in their own communities. The summer programs are held in both French and English and bring together participants from across Canada. Participants must each fund-raise approximately $2,500 to cover a portion of the program cost. (For more information on WUSC see Chapter 35, Nongovernmental Organizations.) [ID:5071]

World Vision Canada: Operation Helping Hand
6630 Turner Valley Road, Mississauga, Ontario L5N 2S4;
(905) 821-3030, fax (905) 821-9794, helping_hand@worldvision.ca, www.worldvision.ca

WORK AND LEARN ▪ World Vision Canada is a humanitarian Christian relief and development agency, working in partnership with communities in more than 100 countries. Our short-term volunteer program entitled Operation Helping Hand, enables individuals to be integrated into some of our international development projects. The program offers individuals an opportunity to gain a deeper understanding of international development while lending a helping hand to people in need.

Programs range from one to three months in duration. Currently, there are opportunities to serve in Eastern Europe, the Middle East, Latin America and Africa. Participants are involved in a number of capacities, such as teaching conversational English, caring for HIV/AIDS children, assisting in children's summer camps and helping at national orphanages. Operation Helping Hand is open to anyone 18 years or older. Applicants must have an open mind and demonstrate a positive outlook, flexibility, and sensitivity to the customs and traditions of other cultures. Participants must make a tax deductible contribution towards accommodation and living expenses, and costs vary according to the program. In addition, volunteers are responsible for their own travel arrangements. [ID:7224]

WorldTeach, Inc.
Director of Recruiting and Admissions,
Harvard Institute for International Development, 1 Eliot Street, Cambridge, MA,
02138-5705, USA; (617) 495-5527, fax (617) 495-1599, info@worldteach.org, www.igc.org/worldteach

TEACHING ABROAD ▪ WorldTeach, a private, nonprofit organization based at the Harvard Institute for International Development, was formed in 1986 with the purpose of contributing to education in developing countries. Every year WorldTeach places approximately 250 volunteers as teachers of English as a Foreign and Second Language in countries which request assistance. Currently, WorldTeach provides college graduates with one-year contracts in Costa Rica, Ecuador, Namibia, Poland, Thailand, Lithuania and Vietnam. Six-month opportunities are available in China, Mexico and Honduras. There is also a summer program in Shanghai, China.

Participant's program fee covers the cost of international, round-trip airfare, health insurance, placement and training, and support. Applications are accepted year-round. Participants on all but the summer program must have a bachelor degree, but no previous language or teaching experience is required. Visit the WorldTeach web site for full details. [ID:5072]

WorldWorks
Suite 200, 2678 West Broadway, Vancouver, B.C. V6K 2G3;
(604) 732-1496, fax (604) 738-8400, idera@web.net, www.vcn.bc.ca/idera

WORK AND LEARN ▪ WorldWorks is a resource centre that makes it easier for people of all ages to find volunteer opportunities overseas. The centre's collection has information on hundreds of opportunities, from two-week work camps and informal drop-ins to longer two-year volunteer programs, for every pocketbook interest and skill level. WorldWorks also offers orientation workshops to help people prepare to go. As well, WorldWorks' returnee network supports people returning from overseas by allowing them to reflect on their experiences and act on them in their local communities. It is important to stress that WorldWorks does not place people overseas, but does everything possible to support positive overseas volunteer experiences. Visit the WorldWorks web site for links to web sites of volunteer-placing organizations. [ID:6370]

YMCA International Camp Counselor Program Abroad
Suite 1904, 71 West 23th Street, New York, NY, 10010, USA; (212) 727-8800 ext. 119, fax (212) 727-8814

WORK AND LEARN ▪ The International Camp Counselor Program offers four-to-eight week positions for summer camp counsellors around the world in Asia, Africa, South America, and Europe. Requirements include a high school diploma and previous experience with the YMCA. In some cases, special educational, language, or athletic skills may be required. Applicants should be between the ages of 21 and 30, be flexible, and possess organizational and leadership skills. Program fees are US$155 which covers insurance and continual support staff. Room, board, and other expenses are usually provided but travel costs are the responsibility of the participant. [ID:5074]

Youth Challenge International (YCI)
11 Soho Street, Toronto, Ontario M5T 1Z6;
(416) 971-9846, fax (416) 971-6863, info@yci.org, www.yci.org

WORK AND LEARN ▪ YCI combines community development, health work and environmental research in adventurous projects conducted by international teams of volunteers aged 18 to 25 years. YCI is looking for youth to participate in 10-week long projects in Costa Rica and Guyana. They must be excited by the idea of contributing to community development, working with youth from around the world, sharing existing skills and learning new ones. Projects run throughout the year and application deadlines are in March and October, six to eight months prior to each project. Youth participants do not require any specific skills, but rather, need an abundance of energy and enthusiasm and a desire to work hard. Attaining a fund-raising goal is a part of the in-Canada component of the YCI project, and this goal covers most expenses related to the project. YCI is also seeking volunteer project group leaders with experience in community development, youth leadership, or logistics. Visit the YCI web site or call the office for more details. [ID:6615]

Youth for Understanding Canada
690 Fountain Street N., Cambridge, Ontario N3H 4R7;
(800) 833-6243, fax (519) 653-5792, info-is@mail.yfu.org

YOUTH EXCHANGE ▪ Youth for Understanding (YFU) International Exchange is a non-profit, educational organization exchanging more than 6,000 youths a year worldwide. YFU Canada currently arranges exchanges to Australia, Belgium, Denmark, Equador, Finland, Japan, the Netherlands, New Zealand, and Venezuela for students aged 15 to 18. Students stay with families and attend high school in their host countries for either one semester of one year.

Students applying should be open-minded, flexible and willing to adapt to and show interest in a different culture. There are no language requirements. [ID:6859]

Chapter 11

Hosting Programs

It is possible to gain a unique crosscultural experience without actually making a trip abroad simply by hosting visitors from overseas. Sharing your home and lifestyle with someone from another culture offers many benefits to both the host and the guest. Most host families are surprised by how much they learn, not only about the guest's culture, but also themselves and the subtleties of Canadian culture they had never questioned in the past.

The profiles you find at the end of this chapter are by no means an exhaustive listing of Canadian hosting programs (only 12 profiles are listed). They offer examples of both short- and long-term possibilities that may be suitable to your interests. Keep in mind that hosting options often arise through informal channels, so personal initiative may be the best way to get involved.

TYPES OF PROGRAMS

There are a variety of different hosting experiences that may be appropriate for you. You may wish to take someone from another culture into your home for a period of time, ranging from four months to a year. Youth and student exchanges are examples of longer-term hosting possibilities. You can contact any one of the organizations profiled in this chapter, or call your local university or college's International Centre and English-as-a-Second-Language department to find out what opportunities they offer. Working with refugees or landed immigrants is another option. This type of host experience is certainly both very challenging and very rewarding. Your efforts will provide a strong, long-lasting friendship and relationship of trust between you and your guest.

If you are unable to commit to the length of time and amount of energy necessary for a long-term host experience, it is possible to take a brief glimpse into the lifestyle of others by hosting guests for a few days, or even one evening. A short-term encounter opens your eyes to new people and world views. Individuals from overseas will appreciate any time you spend assisting them in getting accustomed to Canadian culture. Greeting someone at the airport or helping her get settled in her new location eases the pressure of arriving in a foreign place. Helping familiarize a newcomer to Canada with the city's transportation system or the daily want-ads makes him feel welcome, confident and independent. Entertaining people in town on business for an evening provides a welcoming atmosphere and makes their stay in Canada more pleasant and memorable. If you think short-term hosting is for you, contact organizers of international conferences, local organizations with a focus on new immigrants, professors, and international student services of universities. They often look for volunteers willing to assist international arrivals and visitors.

REWARDS OF HOSTING

All crosscultural experiences have both benefits and challenges; hosting is certainly no exception. Perhaps one of the most obvious benefits is the opportunity it provides to broaden your international outlook. Hosting sensitizes you to another culture's way of life, and allows you to understand how people interpret events from their own cultural perspective. It is also an excellent start in your quest for information about what life will be like overseas.

Through the daily contact that hosts have with their international guests, they begin to understand the cultural attitudes and norms that govern each society or community. Cultural attitudes and norms exert a strong influence over the way people live, and are unique to every culture. Dress, body language, ways of expressing happiness, love, anger or disagreement, sense of humour, behaviour associated with food and alcohol, and concepts of space are key areas around which cultures differ. Living with someone from overseas offers exposure to these differences, and forces you to examine elements of Canadian culture that you may have never considered in the past. This process enables you to become more attuned and flexible to different perspectives on world issues, and more accepting of other cultures. This type of awareness is crucial to a successful experience overseas.

CHALLENGES OF HOSTING

It is important to recognize the demands that subtle cultural differences place on hosts and guests alike. Particularly in the initial stages of hosting, both parties will be uncertain about what constitutes appropriate behaviour. You will likely be faced with awkward situations with your guests because of limited communication and cultural differences. What may seem like a polite gesture to you might actually be received very negatively by someone with a different cultural perspective. Take for example Canadians' concept of space. Many Canadian families place importance on personal, private space in the home. As a result, providing children or guests with their own bedroom is highly valued. However, a guest from a more communal culture in which shared accommodation is the norm may be insulted, or feel isolated or abandoned in a private room. The guest might misinterpret this situation as a sign that he is considered an outsider by the host family. Misunderstandings such as these are inevitable, but not insurmountable.

With time, patience, an open mind and lots of discussion you can work through these challenges. Be prepared to spend many hours communicating with your guest. This is a necessary component of hosting, and will make your host experience all the more worthwhile. Keep in mind that learning to communicate with someone from another culture can be a lot of fun, a way of sharing humour and happy times. Not only will both parties learn more about the intricacies of each other's culture, but a strong, and potentially long-lasting relationship will develop.

A LAST WORD

Remember: Set realistic goals for your host experience. Don't expect to solve the world's problems during your guest's stay, and certainly don't expect to change the way your guest sees the world. Instead, think of hosting as a way to situate yourself in a complex and interdependent world. Listening to what others have to say is the first step towards a more just and equitable social order. And besides, hosting international guests is a lot of fun!

RESOURCES

Listed below are resources for those interested in hosting international visitors. They range from directories of hosting programs to information guides offering survival tips for potential hosts. Whether you are hosting someone on a brief visit for international business purposes, or taking someone in (perhaps a student) for a longer period of time, at least one of these books should be appropriate for you.

AYUSA International ▣
www.ayusa.org ▪ This is an American nonprofit high school exchange organization dedicated to promoting world peace and understanding by enabling students to study outside their own country. AYUSA's web site offers information on both inbound (hosting an international exchange student) and outbound programs (studying abroad). [ID:2420]

Do's and Taboos of Hosting International Visitors ▥
1990, *Roger E. Axtell,* 236 pages ➤ John Wiley & Sons, 22 Worchester Drive, Rexdale, Ontario M9W 1L1; $17.95; credit cards; (800) 567-4797, fax (800) 565-6802 ▪ At a time when many businesspeople are hosting international visitors, this book acts as a guide to everything from entertaining and business protocol to the role of interpreters and corporate gift-giving. It lists, by country, tips on specific aspects of hosting and offers other valuable resources and references. Visit the distributor's web site at www.wiley.com/products/worldwide/canada. [ID:1011]

The Exchange Student Survival Kit ▥
1993, Intercultural Press, 122 pages ➤ Intercultural and Community Development Resources (ICDR), P.O. Box 32108, Millwoods Station, Edmonton, Alberta T6K 4C2; $20; VISA, Amex; (800) 378-3199, fax (403) 462-1925, icdr@compusmart.ab.ca ▪ Helps students better understand the exchange experience and adjust to a new culture. Based on years of research and professional involvement with AFS Intercultural Programs. Uses examples based on the experiences of exchange students from various cultures. A useful resource for native English speakers. Visit the distributor's web site at www.compusmart.ab.ca/icdr. [ID:1324]

A Healthy Stay in Canada ▥
1994, 40 pages ➤ CUSO, Suite 400, 2255 Carling Ave., Ottawa, Ontario K2B 1A6; $5; (613) 829-7445, fax (613) 829-7996 ▪ Provides health information and advice for international students and professionals visiting Canada for six months or less. The focus is on loneliness, adaptation, stress, emergency health care, winter health issues and integrating new ideas and learning upon your return to the home country. Available in French under the title, *Un sejour en santé.* [ID:1702]

Host Family Survival Kit: A Guide for American Host Families ▥
1985, *Nancy King, Ken Huff,* Intercultural Press, 168 pages ➤ Intercultural and Community Development Resources (ICDR), P.O. Box 32108, Millwoods Station, Edmonton, Alberta T6K 4C2; $17; VISA, Amex; (800) 378-3199, fax (403) 462-1925, icdr@compusmart.ab.ca ▪ A guide to understanding the exchange experience, being an effective host family, and making the most of the hosting experience. Also has a guide to evaluating sponsoring organizations and their programs. Visit the distributor's web site at www.compusmart.ab.ca/icdr. [ID:1314]

NACEL International ▣
www.nacel.org ▪ NACEL International's web site is useful for those wishing to host and those wishing to travel. The site gives information on NACEL's Hosting Programs, hosting in general and answers some of the most common questions. Along with offering a variety of contests, this site provides links to airlines, cities, museums and travel information. [ID:2414]

Staying Healthy While Living in Canada ▥
1994, 102 pages ➤ CUSO, Suite 400, 2255 Carling Ave., Ottawa, Ontario K2B 1A6; $15; (613) 829-7445, fax (613) 829-7996 ▪ Provides health information and advice for students coming to Canada from developing countries to study or work for six months or more. Addresses such issues as

accessing the Canadian health care system, depression, stress, winter health issues and Canadian culture as it affects physical and mental well-being. Available in French under the title, *Visa-santé pour le Canada*. [ID:1701]

Profiles of Hosting Programs

The following are but 12 hosting programs. New hosting programs are difficult to research, so if you are familiar with any hosting programs not listed here, please let us know and they can be included in the next edition of the book.

AFS Interculture Canada (AFS)
Suite 505, 1231 St. Catherine Street W., Montréal, Québec H3G 1P5;
(800) 361-7248, fax (514) 843-9119, info-canada@afs.org, www.afs.org

AFS Intercultural Canada's Hosting Program welcomes any type of family—single-parent families, couples with children, couples without children. Hosting periods range from four weeks to 11 months, and AFS assumes responsibility for the welfare and safety of the participant. Orientation camps and social activities are organized by AFS volunteers. (For more information on AFS see Chapter 10, Short-term Programs Overseas and Chapter 35, Nongovernmental Organizations.) [ID:5075]

AYUSA International
7th Floor, One Post Street, San Francisco, CA, 94104, USA;
(800) 727-4540, fax (415) 986-4620, rchan@ayusa.org, www.ayusa.org

AYUSA International is a nonprofit high school exchange program dedicated to promoting peace and personal growth through international exchange.

Over 1800 international students, aged 15 to 18, stay with volunteer host families and attend local high schools in communities across North America each year. AYUSA host families and students receive orientation and support local representatives. AYUSA host families accept an international student as an additional member of their family for a semester or academic year. (For more information on AYUSA see Chapter 10, Short-term Programs Overseas.) [ID:6858]

BENDAS
Executive Director, 174 Cobourg Ave., Ottawa, Ontario K1N 8H5; (613) 789-2132, fax (613) 789-2133

BENDAS provides orientation programs for international visitors and requires hosts, generally for one evening only. Individuals living in the Ottawa area who are interested in hosting can contact the firm for more information. BENDAS also offers post-return briefings for Canadians travelling overseas. [ID:5076]

Bowers International Homestay Placement Services
1 Holswade Road, Scarborough, Ontario M1L 2G1; (416) 751-0698,
fax (416) 751-3670, rbowers@arcos.org, www.arcos.org/rbowers/homestay/index.htm

Bowers International Homestay Placement Services believes that providing an international student with a safe and comfortable place to live and learn provides a unique opportunity to learn about people from around the world. Bowers International Homestay brings students of all ages from several countries to Canada for at least a four-week period.

Canadian families must provide their host student with a private and furnished room and two meals a day. They must also include their host student in family activities on a regular basis. Honorariums for host families are provided. The most important criteria that

Bowers looks for in a host family is the desire to share their time and interests with an international student. Visit the Bowers International Homestay web site for details. [ID:6803]

Canadian Crossroads International / Carrefour Canadien International (CCI)
31 Madison Ave., Toronto, Ontario M5R 2S2; (416) 967-0801,
fax (416) 967-9078, cci@web.net, www.crossroad-carrefour.ca

Canadian Crossroads International (CCI) is a volunteer association which provides crosscultural learning experiences. Among its goals, CCI aims to educate volunteers from developing countries by providing them with opportunities to live and work in Canada and in other developing countries. To this end, Crossroads has developed two programs which involve a hosting component in Canada: The To-Canada Program, and the Africans to Québec Program.

The To-Canada Program gives volunteers from developing countries the opportunity to live and work in Canada for a three-month period. Projects are arranged to match the volunteer's skills and interests with the host agency. By living and working together, the volunteer and the host gain a better understanding of life in each other's countries. Candidates begin their 11-week internship in May or September. The Africans to Québec Program is an eight-week exchange during the fall.

Home Hosts for the To-Canada Program provide food and accommodation for anywhere from one to 11 weeks. If the cost of providing food and accommodation is donated to CCI, the host will be issued an income tax receipt. Otherwise, a small home hosting allowance will be provided. Their web site is currently under construction. (For more information see Chapter 10, Short-term Programs Overseas and Chapter 35, Nongovernmental Organizations.) [ID:5077]

Canadian Relief Fund for Chernobyl Victims in Belarus
190 Bronson Ave., Ottawa, Ontario K1R 6H4;
(613) 567-9595, fax (613) 567-9971, crfcvb@cyberus.ca, www.cybertap.com/belarus

The Canadian Relief Fund for Chernobyl Victims in Belarus was created with the aim of helping the Belarussian people cope with the fall-out of the April 1986 Chernobyl explosion. The fund is involved in a variety of medical and educational projects in Canada. Each year the Canadian Relief Fund invites several hundred children from the contaminated areas of Belarus to Canada for several weeks of life in a clean environment. Knowledge of a Slavic language is helpful, but not necessary. Families interested is hosting a child should contact the Ottawa Head Office to find out the contact organization in their region. [ID:6687]

Carrefour Canadien International (CCI)
Programme de groupe, 912, rue Sherbrooke est,
Montréal, Québec H2L 1L2; (514) 528-5363, fax (514) 528-5367

Carrefour Canadien International est un organisme pan-canadien sans but lucratif, sans affiliation religieuse ou politique, qui offre des programmes de stages de courte durée, en groupe ou de façon individuelle, dans des pays en développement d'Asie, d'Océanie, d'Amérique Latine, des Antilles et d'Afrique. De plus, Carrefour reçoit des stagiaires agés d'au moins 19 ans provenant de ces mêmes régions du monde pour une durée de 2 à 4 mois. Les participants sélectionnés effectuent un stage de perfectionnement bénévole dans leur domaine professionel respectif. Un encadrement et une compensation financière relative au transport, à la nourriture et à l'hébergement leur sont fournis. [ID:5078]

Children's International Summer Villages (CISV)
5 Dunvegan Road, Ottawa, Ontario K1K 3E7; (613) 749-9680, fax (613) 749-9680

Children's International Summer Villages (CISV) Canada promotes global peace education. The organization has 10 chapters across Canada in Victoria, Vancouver, Calgary, Saskatoon, London, Waterloo, Toronto, Ottawa, St. Grégoire, and Fredericton.

In addition to its Canadian activities, CISV offers four main overseas programs geared to youth aged 11 to 19. Through its Interchange Program, a Canadian delegation of 10 youths, aged 12 to 15 and a delegation from another country (countries vary by interchange) meet for approximately three to four weeks for two consecutive summers. Delegations engage in a variety of activities which promote crosscultural awareness and international understanding. Each Canadian participant is matched to a participant in the host country. Participants spend four weeks with the host family of their billet, and in turn host their billet the following year for the same period of time. Cost to participants varies by local chapter.

Families interested in hosting through this program must have a child participating in the interchange. For more information, contact your local CISV chapter or contact the CISV Canada secretary at the number listed above. (For more information on CISV see Chapter 10, Short-term Programs Overseas.) [ID:5079]

University of Manitoba International Centre for Students
Host Family Coordinator, 541 University Centre, University of Manitoba, Winnipeg, Manitoba R3T 2N2; (204) 474-8501, fax (204) 474-7562, isc@cc.umanitoba.ca, www.umanitoba.ca/student/ics

Like many universities, the University of Manitoba's International Centre for Students has a Host Family Program. The program assists international students when they first arrive in Winnipeg by placing them with a Canadian family for three to five days. This gives the students an opportunity to recover from "jet lag," adjust to a new country and culture, find accommodations and register at the university. Students who request a host can look forward to meeting and getting to know Canadians. Host families are not necessarily language or culture specialists, but people interested in broadening their horizons by befriending individuals from around the world. [ID:5083]

NACEL Canada
Suite 208, 8925 - 82 Ave., Edmonton, Alberta T6C 0Z2;
(403) 468-0941, fax (403) 465-7583, can@nacel.org, www.nacel.org

NACEL Canada is dedicated to coordinating quality educational experiences for both host families and exchange students. NACEL Canada is an associate of Nacel International, which has served more than 230,000 participants since 1957. Host families have the opportunity of welcoming an international exchange student into their home for a period of four weeks to one year. Students are between 13 and 18 years old, have three to six years of English study and are individually matched with their host family's interest. Successful host family applicants are of various ages and family size, but all are warm, welcoming, open-minded and interested in learning a new culture. Visit the NACEL web site for further details, applicant requests, and to have any questions answered via e-mail. (For more information on NACEL see Chapter 10, Short-term Programs Overseas.) [ID:6689]

SERVAS Canada
229 Hillcrest Ave., North York, Ontario M2N 2P5; fletcher@hookup.net

Servas (an Esperanto word meaning to serve) is an international association of hosts and travellers which provides opportunities for meaningful personal contacts between people of diverse cultures and backgrounds. Visitors are invited to take part in the home and community, and to share their concerns on social and international problems, their interest in creative activity, and mutual responsibility for their fellow beings. Participants are sincerely interested in learning about other cultures and have an adaptable personality. The visitor usually stays for two nights. An interview and reference are required. [ID:5081]

Up With People
1 International Court, Broomfield, CO, 80021, USA;
(303) 460-7100, fax (303) 438-7300, uwp-info@upwithpeople.org, www.upwithpeople.org

Up With People is the international learning program that provides personal and professional growth through the unique combination of international travel, performing arts and community service.

The five Up With People casts each have 100 to 150 participants who range in age from 17 to 27. Each cast travels for approximately one year on a tour that takes them to over 75 cities. In every city, cast members perform a professional musical show, participate in community service and stay with local families. Local families have the opportunity to open their homes to one or more students from 20 to 25 countries. A schedule of tours and more information can be found on the web site, or you can contact the Up With People marketing department for information. [ID:5084]

Chapter 12

Crosscultural Travel

You don't have to wait for a professional job or a volunteer posting to get international experience. You can increase your International IQ by travelling overseas on your own. Crosscultural travel has little in common with *tourist travel*. It does not have much to do with lounging on beaches, eating in restaurants with other tourists, shopping for souvenirs or touring the sights. Crosscultural travel can involve living with a local family or volunteering your services to an indigenous organization. It is about integrating yourself into a different culture.

Imagine herding sheep to market, 150 kilometres across mountains, with a Mongolian caravan. How about living with a Syrian family for a few weeks? Working for a few months in an Indonesian manufacturing plant, teaching software applications and living in the workers' quarters? Maybe you would like to visit Bombay's well-developed financial district and spend three weeks meeting with bankers, attending conferences, and researching the bond market and stock exchange? All these enriching crosscultural travel experiences are available to you *and* they can help in your international career.

Successful crosscultural travel experiences will help you develop a stronger International IQ. You will learn about cultural differences, crosscultural communications, culture shock, other languages, travel logistics, and world geography. You will come to know your levels of tolerance, your limitations and your strengths, and you will begin to develop your observation skills. These are precisely the skills sought by international employers. Of course, the other benefit to crosscultural travel is *fun*.

171

DESCRIBING YOUR
TRAVEL EXPERIENCE

It is important to learn to describe your travel skills in a professional way. International employers hire people who, along with their technical expertise, have the capacity to integrate into and accept local cultures. If you have travelled extensively overseas, especially in the South, you will have some of the crosscultural skills employers are looking for.

Let's look at two ways to describe your international travel skills: casually, when talking to friends, and professionally, when speaking to a prospective employer.

First, describing your travel experiences to your friends:

"I love travelling and meeting new people. Being surrounded by a foreign culture, the smells, the colours, the noise, is exciting. The food is great—I even like eating with my fingers ... It can be difficult at times, even a little scary— like the time I was pulled into the police station for no reason. I got out of it without paying a bribe ... I was sick a few times but, like everything else, people were kind to me and helped me out. I got over it ... The line-ups! I would stand for hours at the bank rubbing shoulders with the locals. It turned out to be a great way to make friends and find out about the local scene. I loved to haggle for hours with the market mamas ... Travelling is such a wonderful, life-enriching experience!"

Second, describing the same travel experiences as professional skills, to potential employers:

"I am culturally sensitive, able to communicate effectively with people from other cultures. I am aware of differences in approaches to decision making in various parts of the world. I have a good understanding of the crosscultural environment. I appreciate the importance of tact and diplomacy and understand the subtleties of crosscultural negotiations. I am able to cope under stress and thrive in conditions of uncertainty. I enjoy change and am mobile and/or willing to relocate."

HOW TO BE A SUCCESSFUL
"CROSSCULTURAL TRAVELLER"

Crosscultural travel usually means spending most of your trip in one country, or in one region of a large country. Hopping through 12 countries on a three-month vacation is not crosscultural travel. One traveller advises, "Use the three weeks or three visits rule. Stay in one place for three weeks, or return to a place where you have made good friends three or four times for short visits during your stay."

To make contact with the local culture, you need a vehicle that allows you to interact. Sitting on beaches, visiting tourist sites, or dancing in nightclubs, won't work. You need a reason to become involved for longer than one week. *Try volunteer work, professional networking, and/or living with a family.*

Volunteering your services to an organization is one of the best ways to integrate into a community. You can approach a local NGO for work, offer to give a talk about Canada to a local school, teach English at an adult learning centre, or assist at a local orphanage. Offer to give a presentation to a local professional association. Try networking with businesses operating in your area of expertise.

The possibilities are endless for both volunteer work and professional networking. The best approach is to find an organization that you are interested in and speak to the person in charge. Explain that you are travelling and will be staying in this village/town/city for the next few weeks and would like to offer your services. Call it what you want: research, interest in the culture, searching for experience, providing a service, sharing your expertise, learning the language. Don't expect accommodation or food but feel free to accept it when offered. Once you commit yourself to an organization, respect the agreement! By not following through, you not only make yourself look bad but spoil things for the foreign travellers who follow you.

If you are invited to stay in someone's home, you should participate in their family activities and show respect and interest in their daily lives. Until you become familiar with your host, a crosscultural friendship can be an emotional roller-coaster ride, so remember to sit back and observe carefully. Don't jump to any conclusions, as you probably don't understand what is going on around you. You are there to learn. Talk and ask questions. Enjoy being with your host family.

When you live with a host family, you have to give up some of the freedom you had while travelling. You can't always retire to your room and close your door, or come and go as you please. In addition, you probably won't be involved in the family's decision making processes, and will be unsure about what plans are being made. You might find yourself wondering, "Where are we going? Who are we meeting? When is supper?" An experienced crosscultural traveller will sit back, observe the drama unfolding before them, and fight the need to know "the plan." It is best just to accept what comes your way.

OTHER WAYS TO MAKE CONTACT WITH LOCAL PEOPLE

Other ways to make contact are:
- striking up conversations while waiting in long lines at banks or in post offices
- speaking with fellow passengers while travelling by bus, train or plane
- talk to people about their children, admire and play with the child
- registering at a foreign university, or just visiting and attending lectures
- taking up offers to visit other people's friends or relatives, or just visiting friends living abroad

Learning a new language is another excellent way to make new friends. Always carry a small notepad in your pocket to record new words and phrases. In addition to guidebook phrases, such as "Where are the restaurants? Where is the toilet?" you will want to learn things that link you to people. These include: daily greetings; the names for family members; "thank you;" "the food is delicious;" "this is beautiful;" "I enjoy this." Learn also to count to 10, the months of the year, and names of the most common foods. With a vocabulary of as few as 20 or 30 words, you will be able to interact with local people and your efforts will be appreciated.

Should you travel alone, with a friend, or with a partner? It is easiest to integrate into another culture if you are travelling alone. Your potential hosts will find it difficult to accommodate groups of people. Two females, or two males travelling together is the next best travel arrangement. A female and male travelling together have the hardest time integrating, especially into traditional cultures. Mixed couples are difficult for hosts to accommodate. Most cultures in the world, including our own, segregate women from men. This is relevant when you are looking for venues to meet people across cultures. Platonic, same-sex relationships are the easiest: men can meet other men, women can befriend other women. It is generally difficult for men and women from different cultures to connect professionally in the South. Romance is usually implied.

SAFETY TIPS

Developing crosscultural friendships while travelling implies a certain amount of risk. This can be minimized, however, by using your common sense and street smarts. Here are a few tips to help keep you safe:

• Avoid making friends with people who approach *you*. It is generally safer if you initiate a crosscultural friendship. People you approach are likely to be genuine, interested more in your friendship than in your pocket book.

• Never befriend someone who approaches you at a beach, bus stop, train station or airport. Be careful about making friends where there are many tourists. There are con artists everywhere you find tourists.

• Be prepared to flee the company of anyone who makes you feel physically threatened, who shows erratic behaviour, disregard or lack of compassion for others, who participates in illegal activities, or who exhibits uncontrolled behaviour. (You might also cut short friendships where the culture gap is just too great or the person is just plain boring!)

• Be careful and alert with a host family until you feel secure. You will know you are in a trusting crosscultural relationship when your host takes care of you, is considerate of your needs, inquires if you are hungry or have slept well, and protects you from making mistakes. Good crosscultural friendships offer companionship and a sense of security.

• If you are travelling to a country with a history of instability and/or violence, contact the INQUIRIES SERVICE at the DEPARTMENT OF FOREIGN AFFAIRS AND INTERNATIONAL TRADE (DFAIT) or the nearest Canadian mission, close to your departure date. They provide excellent one- or two-page travel reports concerning the political climate, high-risk areas, and other precautionary measures. (For more information see Chapter 33, Services for International Business and Entrepreneurs.)

REST DAYS

Travelling, visiting, touring, talking, sharing, absorbing, analyzing, adapting, searching, discovering, appreciating, liking and loving can be exhausting. Give yourself time to rest. Full days away from the demands of a foreign culture are necessary from time to time. They will refresh you and make you once again enthusiastic, curious, and open to new things.

TRAVEL AND HUMAN RIGHTS

You may want to consider the political ramifications of your crosscultural travels. In some instances, travelling to a country may lend support, or help finance, an oppressive government. At the time of writing, I believe Burma (Myanmar) is an example of a country you should avoid travelling to. For similar reasons, the Canadian government has closed its High Commission in Nigeria. Whatever your choice, a conscientious reflection on human rights can be a useful guide in deciding where you travel and spend your hard currency.

EXPANDING YOUR EXPERIENCE

Sending postcards home and sharing your experiences through letters will widen the crosscultural impact of your trip. Send post cards to extended family and friends, especially children, from each of your destinations. Send your family a tourist map so they can follow your route. Mail cards from all your stops to one address, so when you return home you can retrace your trip through the postcard collection. You might even send cards to a classroom in Canada, so the children can follow your travels.

Describe where you are as you write—a train station, a café overlooking a busy street. Describe what you see, eat, smell, the conversations you have. Talk about the religion, the festivals, the animals of the country. Write about the *marvels* of this new culture. Choose postcards that depict the daily life, such as markets, foods, festivals, modes of transportation.

RE-ENTRY CONCERNS

You will likely experience re-entry shock upon your return to Canada. The familiar may have become unfamiliar. Thus, instead of peace, relaxation and familiarity, your exploration may continue—you will observe your own country with a fresh perspective. You may, for the first time, understand what it means to be "Canadian!"

A LAST WORD

Crosscultural travel is a deeply rewarding experience. It takes more time, effort, patience and trust than regular tourist travel. My experience is that despite the many challenges, I was rewarded with kindness, friendship, hospitality and new insights. It is an opportunity you shouldn't miss! Enjoy!

RESOURCES

Many of these books are in travel guide series. Besides tips on travel destinations, they often provide excellent insights on the local culture.

For more information on building your crosscultural communication skills consult the following Resources sections: Chapter 1, The Effective Overseas Employee offers material focused on general crosscultural skills required by all international employees; Chapter 27, Jobs by Regions of the World lists books of particular importance to businesspeople because they provide country-specific advice on social and business customs; the resources in Chapter 3, Living Overseas discuss the more practical aspects of living overseas; Chapter 13, Global Education Centres has resources to help you improve your International IQ.

If you want to combine travel and study, consult the following: Chapter 14, Study Abroad; Chapter 15, Awards & Grants; Chapter 16, International Studies in Canada & Abroad; Chapter 17, International Internships; and Chapter 10, Short-term Programs Overseas.

Berkeley Guides 📖
Annual, Berkeley Guides ➤ Random House, 1265 Arrowood Drive, Mississauga, Ontario L4W 1B9; $26 each; credit cards; (905) 624-0672, fax (905) 624-6217 ▪ Budget guides with off-beat and adventurous travel ideas. Written for travellers between 18 and 35. Titles now available: Central America, Eastern Europe, Europe, France, Germany, Great Britain and Ireland, Italy, and Mexico. [ID:1486]

Adventures in Good Company 📖
1994, 430 pages ➤ The Eighth Mountain Press, 624 SE 29th Ave., Portland, OR 97214, USA; US$16.95; cheques only; (503) 233-3936, fax (503) 233-0774 ▪ A comprehensive guide to tours and outdoor trips tailored specifically to women. Profiles more than 100 firms worldwide which offer related services. [ID:1487]

Airlines of the World 💻
w4.itn.net/airlines ▪ Dedicated to online information and reservations for air travel. It enables you to plug into over 500 airlines worldwide and it provides deals only offered online. You can even make travel arrangements over the Internet, including car reservations and a database of over 30,000 hotels. [ID:2745]

All Hotels on the Web 💻
www.all-hotels.com ▪ Planning to scout out your new job in Venezuela? With this site you can search through lists of the world's finest hotels and connect directly to their home pages. Many will even allow you to make online registrations. This is a well-designed, easy-to-use site. [ID:2578]

The Alternative Travel Directory 1996 📖
Annual, *Transitions Abroad,* 400 pages ➤ Department TRA, Transitions Publishing, P.O. Box 3000, Denville, NJ 07834, USA; $19.95; VISA, MC; (413) 256-3414, fax (413) 256-0373, trabroad@aol.com ▪ The definitive annual guide to the "best of the best" resources on working, studying, and travelling abroad. Includes hundreds of annotated listings. A rich resource for navigating the international arena. Visit the distributor's web site at www.transabroad.com. [ID:1758]

Bon Voyage But... 📖
1997, 60 pages ➤ InfoCentre, Department of Foreign Affairs and International Trade (DFAIT), 125 Sussex Dr., Ottawa, Ontario K1A 0G2; free; (800) 267-8376, fax (613) 996-9709 ▪ The standard government travel booklet. Information on insurance, travel expectations, health, security, travel do's and don'ts. Issued to anyone who obtains a Canadian passport. It's free; have a look! [ID:1137]

Book Passage Catalogues 📖
Semiannual ➤ Book Passage, 51 Tamal Vista Blvd., Corte Madera, CA 94925, USA; free; credit cards; (800) 999-7909, fax (415) 924-3838, messages@bookpassage.com ▪ Mail-order travel book and map service. Wide selection of language tapes. Order by regions: Northern Europe, Southern Europe, Mexico, Latin America and the Caribbean, and East Asia and the South Pacific. Visit the distributor's web site at www.bookpassage.com. [ID:1083]

Canadian Passport Office 💻
www.dfait-maeci.gc.ca/passport/passport.htm ▪ Provides useful information needed for both novice to seasoned travellers. There are details on how to obtain a passport, office locations, and what to do in case of a lost or stolen passport. [ID:2746]

The CIA World Factbook 💻
www.odci.gov/cia/publications/nsolo/wfb-all.htm ▪ This is one of the most authoritative sources available on international geography. Information on current political, economic, and social conditions is provided as well as a discussion of the country's physical geography and resources. Very comprehensive, but the juicy stuff may have been left out! [ID:2580]

Directory of Low Cost Vacations with a Difference 📖
1992, *J. Crawford* ➤ Pilot Books, P.O. Box 2102, Greenport, NY 11944, USA; US$5.95; credit cards; (516) 477-1094, fax (516) 477-0978 ▪ Extensive listings of about 300 free and low-cost alternative vacation opportunities worldwide. Emphasis is on personal contacts in foreign countries. Visit the distributor's web site at www.pilotbooks.com. [ID:1231]

Ecotours and Nature Getaways:
A Guide to Environmental Vacations Around the World 📖
1993, *Alice M. Geffen, Carole Berglie,* Crown Publications ➤ Random House, 1265 Arrowood Drive, Mississauga, Ontario L4W 1B9; $26.99; credit cards; (905) 624-0672, fax (905) 624-6217 ▪ A comprehensive guide that offers ecology-conscious travellers ideas for tours to the unspoiled and biologically diverse areas of the world. Identifies the top tour operators and provides details on the trips they offer, from cost and duration to mode of travel. Includes information on touring with children. [ID:1340]

Europrail International 💻
www.odyssey.on.ca/~europrail ▪ This is North America's leading source for European rail passes such as Eurail Pass, Eurail Flexipass, Eurail Saver Pass, the Eurail Youth Pass, and individual country passes. Also included are country and city maps and interactive rail route maps to help plan your trip properly. [ID:2747]

Fielding's: The World's Most Dangerous Places 📖 💻
1997, *Pelton, Robert Young, Aral, Coskun, Dulles, Wink,* 960 pages ➤ Fielding WorldWide Inc., 308 South Catalina Ave., Redondo Beach, CA 90277, USA; US$21.95; credit cards; (310) 372-4474, fax (310) 376-8064 ▪ A fascinating travel guide to the world's most dangerous regions, such as Bosnia, Chechnya, and Rwanda. Apart from narrative, the guide provides information on tourist offices, health services, rescue, environmental organizations, statistics, maps, and tables. To learn more, visit their web site at www.fieldingtravel.com. [ID:2762]

Department of Foreign Affairs and International Trade (DFAIT) 💻
www.dfait-maeci.gc.ca/ ▪ This excellent homepage for DFAIT provides a vast amount of information on the international system, from travel advisories to international trade. It has links to DFAIT departments, services, country profiles, foreign embassies and missions in Canada, and Canadian government activities abroad. [ID:2565]

Going Abroad: The Bathroom Survival Guide 📖
1997, *Eva Newman* ➤ Marlor Press, 4304 Brigadoon Drive, St. Paul, MN 55126, USA; US$12.95; (800) 669-4908, fax (612) 490-1182, marlor@minnet ▪ A charming and humourous look at how to handle the world's varied conveniences! [ID:2679]

Hostelling International 📖
Hostelling International, Suite 400, 205 Catherine Street, Ottawa, Ontario K2P 1C3; (613) 237-7884, fax (613) 237-7868 ▪ Hostelling International - Canada is a network of 80 hostels from coast to coast offering budget accommodation for travellers of all ages. Reservations can be made by calling the hostel direct. Membership is required and can be purchased at any Hostelling International - Canada office and at most hostels. Provides access to 5,000 hostels in 70 countries worldwide. [ID:1639]

How to Be An Importer and Pay for Your World Travel 📖
1993, *Mary Green, Stanley Gilmar,* 160 pages ➤ Ten Speed Press, P.O. Box 7123, Berkeley, CA 94707, USA; US$11.95; credit cards; (510) 845-8414, fax (510) 559-1629, order@tenspeed.com ▪ This book covers all the major aspects of importing, including what to buy, developing markets, working in a foreign culture, and customs procedures and clearances. [ID:1459]

How to Travel Around the World 📖
1995, *Nick Vandome,* 224 pages ➤ How To Books Ltd., 3 Newtec Place, Magdalen Road, Oxford, OX4 1RE, UK; £8.99; credit cards; (44) (1752) 202-301, fax (44) (1865) 202-331 ▪ How to plan your itinerary, earning as you go, and more. [ID:2444]

A Journey of One's Own: Uncommon Advice for the Independent Woman Traveler 📖
1996, *Thalia Zepatos,* 349 pages ➤ The Eighth Mountain Press, 624 SE 29th Ave., Portland, OR 97214, USA; US$16.95; cheques only; (503) 233-3936, fax (503) 233-0774 ▪ Expert advice is combined with tales of crosscultural encounters. A wide array of women travellers provide advice to help you with matters such as sexual harassment, staying healthy, avoiding theft, managing a long trip, and travelling safely—solo, with a partner, or with a child. [ID:1787]

Latin America Traveller 🖥
www.goodnet.com/~crowpub ▪ Offers information for those travelling to Latin America. The site also has a directory of Spanish language schools in the region as well as links to general sites related to travel and culture in Latin America. [ID:2769]

Let's Go Guides 📖
Annual, St. Martin's Press ➤ McClelland & Stewart, 380 Esna Park Drive, Markham, Ontario L3R 1H5; $14-$30; credit cards; (800) 399-6858, fax (800) 363-2665 ▪ These all-purpose guides include most areas of Europe, Northern Africa, and Mexico. [ID:1480]

Lonely Planet 🖥
www.lonelyplanet.com ▪ While this is a commercial site dedicated to selling guide books, there is a considerable amount of free information. Country profiles, photographs, and travel tips as well as information on travel health and safety are all accessible from this site. [ID:2582]

Lonely Planet Travel Survival Kits 📖
Annual, Lonely Planet ➤ Raincoast Books, 8680 Cambie Street, Vancouver, B.C. V6P 6M9; $22.95-$35.50; VISA, MC; (800) 663-5714, fax (800) 565-3770 ▪ Highly recommended all-purpose guide for adventurous travellers; extensive range of titles focusing on countries, regions, cities. [ID:1478]

On a Shoestring Guides 📖
Annual, Lonely Planet ➤ Raincoast Books, 8680 Cambie Street, Vancouver, B.C. V6P 6M9; $25-$42; VISA, MC; (800) 663-5714, fax (800) 565-3770 ▪ Low-budget guides of considerable reputation. Titles on most countries of the world. [ID:1484]

Once Again At Forty 📖
1995, *Jim Shannon,* 134 pages ➤ General Store Publishing House Inc., 1 Main Street, Burnstown, Ontario K0J 1G0; $16.95; credit cards; (800) 465-6072, fax (613) 432-7184 ▪ An entertaining, inspiring account of 10 years of work and travel undertaken by the author after he quit a successful, 20-year college teaching career. If you are contemplating a change but still wondering if you can or should do it, this book could persuade you. [ID:1658]

Outpost: The Traveller's Journal 📖
Quarterly ➤ Outpost Productions, 490 Adelaide Street W., Suite 303, Toronto, Ontario M5V 1T2; $12/year; (416) 703-5394, fax (416) 504-3628, outpost@echo-on.net ▪ A top notch, sophisticated travel magazine geared to the adventure traveller. Culturally sensitive, adventurous, with a broad outlook. A very good magazine! Visit publisher's web site at www.outpostmagazine.com. [ID:2708]

Rough Guides 📖
Annual, Rough Guides ➤ Penguin Books Canada Ltd., Suite 300, 10 Alcorn Ave., Toronto, Ontario M4V 3B2; $19.99-$24.99; VISA, MC; (416) 925-2249, fax (416) 925-0068 ▪ For independent budget travellers, these guides are written with a political awareness and a social and cultural sensitivity that makes them unique. Currently close to 40 titles. [ID:1451]

Round-the-World Travel Guide 💻
www.travel-library.com ▪ This site provides travel information with emphasis on personal travelogues. It also offers useful advice on matters such as accommodation, transportation, and healthy travelling. [ID:2737]

Tourism Offices Worldwide Directory 💻
www.towd.com ▪ A useful site if you are searching for pre-departure tourist information for a specific country. It lists contact information for 750 tourism-related offices worldwide. [ID:2736]

Transitions Abroad: The Magazine of Overseas Opportunities 📖
Bimonthly, *Clay Hubb* ➤ Department TRA, Transitions Publishing, P.O. Box 3000, Denville, NJ 07834, USA; $29.95/year; VISA, MC; (413) 256-3414, fax (413) 256-0373, trabroad@aol.com ▪ An excellent periodical. Required reading for students and globe trotters planning to travel, study or work abroad. Promotes learning through direct involvement in the daily lives of peoples of host countries. Describes publications, information sources, organizations, and programs offering study opportunities, entry-level jobs, and living arrangements abroad. Visit the distributor's web site at www.transabroad.com. [ID:1253]

Travel Cuts
Travel Cuts, 187 College Street, Toronto, Ontario M5T 1P7; (416) 979-2406, fax (416) 979-8167 ▪ Owned and operated by the Canadian Federation of Students (CFS), and with 40 offices in Canada and one in the UK, Travel Cuts serves the travel needs of over 250,000 students each year. Offers student class airfares to domestic and international destinations, and comprehensive "Bon Voyage" travel insurance. Also offers working holidays through its Student Work Abroad Program (SWAP), and volunteer opportunities through its Volunteer Abroad program. Their International Student Identity Card (ISIC), offers discounts and student rates in 70 countries worldwide. For details see their web site at www.travelcuts.com. [ID:1704]

Travel Finder 💻
www.travel-finder.com ▪ Specialized search engine designed to help you find web sites about specific countries. Categories you can search by include: activity, travel category, and type of traveller. Contains 8,000 sites in its database; you can add your favourite travel-related site. [ID:2583]

Travel That Can Change Your Life: How to Create a Transformative Experience 📖
1997, *Jeffrey A. Kottler*, 180 pages ➤ Jossey-Bass Publishers, 350 Sansome Street, San Francisco, CA 94104, USA; US$20; credit cards; (800) 956-7739, fax (800) 605-2665 ▪ Travel experiences provide ideal opportunities for personal change, testing your notion of who you are and how the world works. This book offers a wealth of practical and imaginative suggestions that will change the way you approach travel. Visit the publisher's web site at www.josseybass.com. [ID:2468]

Travel Tips for the 90's 📖
1989, *Dan Weiss, Phyllis Wachel Weiss*, 160 pages ➤ ICS Books Inc., 1370 East 86th Place, Merrillville, IN 46410, USA; $16.50; VISA, MC; (219) 769-0585, fax (800) 336-8334 ▪ A guide full of tips on how to avoid the common annoyances and pitfalls of international travel, including money exchange, health, culture shock, and a "different" set of social do's and don'ts. Visit the publisher's web site at www.icsbooks.com. [ID:1286]

Travel with Children 📖
1996, *Maureen Wheeler,* Lonely Planet ➤ Raincoast Books, 8680 Cambie Street, Vancouver, B.C. V6P 6M9; $16.95; VISA, MC; (800) 663-5714, fax (800) 565-3770 ▪ The only guide to Third World travel with kids. An excellent resource. Written by seasoned travellers, who cover both logistics and cultural interchange. [ID:1284]

The Traveller's Reading Guide 📖
1993, *Maggy Simony,* Facts on File Publications, 528 pages ➤ Fitzhenry and Whiteside Ltd., 195 Allstate Parkway, Markham, Ontario L3R 4T8; $26.95; VISA, MC; (800) 387-9776, fax (800) 260-9777, godwit@fitzhenry.ca ▪ This classic compilation offers thousands of new travel reading suggestions, each entry provides the book's author, title, publisher, year of publication, a concise description of the book, and suggestions for further reading. Visit the distributor's web site at www.fitzhenry.ca. [ID:1490]

"The Treasures and Pleasures... Best of the Best" Series 📖
1998 ➤ Impact Publications, 9104 North Manassas Drive, Manassas Park, VA 20111-2366, USA; US$14.95 each; credit cards; (703) 361-7300, fax (703) 335-9486 ▪ A travel series exploring the major regions and exotic countries of the world. Includes information on the fascinating worlds of artisans, craftspeople, shopkeepers, as well as on fine hotels, restaurants and sightseeing. Country and region-specific guides include the Caribbean, China, Hong Kong, Indonesia, Italy, France, Singapore, Thailand, and more. Visit www.impactpublications.com. [ID:1774]

Vacation Study Abroad 📖
Annual, *Sara Steen* ➤ Publication Service, Institute of International Education, P.O. Box 371, Annapolis Junction, MD 20701-0371, USA; US$36.95; VISA, MC; (800) 445-0443, fax (301) 206-9789 ▪ Details summer study programs by region and country, and short-term programs available year-round to US students. Covers costs and application procedures, academic programs, and living arrangements. [ID:1168]

The Web Magazine 📖 🖥
Monthly, *Burton Fox* ➤ Web Magazine Subscription Services, P.O. Box 56944, Boulder, CO 80322-6944, USA; US$30/year; (303) 604-1465, fax (303) 604-7644, webhelp@neodata.com ▪ This magazine features reviews of both cultural and technological developments in the World Wide Web. Each month, hundreds of Web site reviews give the reader an idea of what's hot on the Net. A travel section lists several helpful sites. Visit www.webmagazine.com/webmag/html, the publisher's web site, or e-mail webhelp@neodata.com. [ID:2527]

Web Sites All Countries: Martindale's "The Reference Desk" 🖥
www-sci.lib.uci.edu/HSG/RefHealth.html ▪ An extensive dictionary of links including over 200 official country web sites, world reports on weather, transport, and culture, lists of international organizations, new internet and software developments, travel advisories, language and translation dictionaries, international newspapers, international health and law, and much more. [ID:2768]

The Whole World Guide to Culture Learning 📖
1994, *J. Daniel Hess,* Intercultural Press, 280 pages ➤ Intercultural and Community Development Resources (ICDR), P.O. Box 32108, Millwoods Station, Edmonton, Alberta T6K 4C2; $32; VISA, Amex; (800) 378-3199, fax (403) 462-1925, icdr@compusmart.ab.ca ▪ A guide for sojourners learning about other cultures. Visit distributor's web site, www.compusmart.ab.ca/icdr. [ID:1399]

Work Your Way Around The World 📖
Annual ➤ Peterson's Guides, P.O. Box 2123, Princeton, NJ 08543-2123, USA; US$17.95; cheque or money order; (800) 338-3282, fax (609) 243-9150 ▪ An excellent resource describing numerous ways the enterprising traveller can find work anywhere in the world, travel free by working for passage, and survive when money runs out. Appropriate for the non-career-minded, the book lists jobs by country, describing everything from orange picking to sheep shearing, with direct quotes from people who have actually done the jobs. Well-written and inspiring. Visit the publisher's web site at www.petersons.com. [ID:1154]

World of Maps Catalogue 📖 🖥
Semiannual ➤ World of Maps, 118 Holland Ave., Ottawa, Ontario K1Y 0X6; VISA, MC; (613) 724-6776, fax (613) 724-7776, dgreen@worldof maps.com ▪ The World of Maps is a Canadian retail and mail-order business selling maps and travel publications to customers around the world. Inventory of thousands of maps of all kinds. Quality travel guides. The store has a home on the World Wide Web at www.worldofmaps.com, with an online catalogue to help you select the most appropriate map or travel book. Print catalogue also available by mail. [ID:1711]

**A World of Options: Guide to International Education Exchange,
Community Services, and Travel for Persons with Disabilities** 📖
1997, *Susan Sygall,* 600 pages ➤ Mobility International USA, P.O. Box 3551, Eugene, OR 97403, USA; US$30; (541) 343-1284, fax (541) 343-6812 ▪ A descriptive resource covering hundreds of opportunities for the disabled in international educational exchange programs, work camps, and volunteer positions. Includes first-person accounts of travel and learning experiences. Visit the distributor's web site at www.miusa.org. [ID:1205]

A Year Between 📖
1994 ➤ Central Bureau for Educational Visits and Exchanges, Seymour Mews House, Seymour Mews, London, W1H 9PE, UK; VISA, MC, Eurocard; (44) (171) 486-5101, fax (44) (171) 935-5741 ▪ This British guide describes work placement schemes from six months to one year. Also outlines adventure organizations, sponsorships, and travel opportunities. [ID:1217]

Chapter 13

Global Education Centres

This chapter describes the main activities of public resource groups called Global Education Centres (formerly know as Learner Centres).

The chapter lists 24 Global Education Centres located in over 20 communities across Canada. They provide Canadians with information on global issues, mainly with respect to North-South relations and international development. The term "Global Education" has replaced "Development Education" in response to a conceptual shift away from the problems of developing countries, towards an understanding of the political and economic linkages between North and South.

Global Education Centres are financed through local fundraising, membership dues and grants. Over the past few years, CANADIAN INTERNATIONAL DEVELOPMENT AGENCY (CIDA) funding to Global Education Centres has been cut, forcing some to reduce their services or even to close. Each Global Education Centre is different, ranging from large organizations with international reputations such as the LONDON CROSS-CULTURAL LEARNER CENTRE, to smaller centres. Generally, Global Education Centres have the following characteristics, and can help you in your job search.

HOW CAN THEY HELP YOU?

First, Global Education Centres are often the focal point for all international activities in their communities. Peace groups, cultural groups and international conferences are usually advertised through Global Education Centres. Importantly, local jobs and volunteer positions related to international activities are also advertised through Global Education Centres.

Second, they often stage special events designed around international development themes such as craft sales, film festivals, guest speakers, school visits, workshops and development education courses. Thus, they are an excellent place to begin searching for networking contacts. Staff and members are usually returned overseas volunteers or have some connection to the international community.

Third, they usually have a resource library with specialized and alternative popular information on international development issues that is not readily available in the mainstream media. As such, they're a great source for anyone interested in heightening their awareness of international issues. Staff will help you find information of interest to you.

VOLUNTEER OPPORTUNITIES

Global Education Centres are always looking for volunteers interested in global issues. Volunteering with a centre is an excellent way to demonstrate your commitment to the field of international development, and it is also a lot of fun. Many of the activities you'll be engaged in will give you the opportunity to meet people with interests similar to yours. It will also increase your exposure to people from other cultures, as you get the chance to mingle with the international speakers sponsored by your centre.

A valuable way to make use of your global education is to write an article for a magazine or a newspaper on one aspect of an international subject. This can go a long way towards "polishing" your résumé and establishing yourself as an authority in your field. For career-starters, researching your article will provide you with invaluable opportunities to network with people in your newly-chosen international field. (For more information on how volunteering can benefit your career see Chapter 9, Starting Your International Career.)

OTHER SOURCES OF INFORMATION

Most libraries, especially large university research libraries, have excellent information on North-South issues. Three important libraries specifically geared to international development and located in the Ottawa region are the CIDA library, the INTERNATIONAL DEVELOPMENT RESEARCH CENTRE (IDRC), and the POST BRIEFING CENTRE library at the DEPARTMENT OF FOREIGN AFFAIRS AND INTERNATIONAL TRADE (DFAIT). Access to these Ottawa libraries is sometimes restricted unless you can demonstrate an actual research interest. Therefore, be specific about your topic, and call ahead. (For profiles and addresses see Chapter 34, Careers in Government.)

There is an assortment of other globally-oriented public resource centres across Canada that offer excellent services. For example, there are the PUBLIC INTEREST RESEARCH GROUPS (PIRGs) based on many campuses in Ontario (where they are usually called OPIRGs), Nova Scotia, B.C. and Québec (QPIRGs or GRIP in French). They can help you improve your International IQ through their resource libraries, and provide volunteer opportunities in social and environmental issues. They offer the chance for informal networking with faculties on campus.

A LAST WORD

Global education, development education, and your International IQ are all concepts that can all be bundled together. As someone who is trying to become internationally oriented, you are really talking about educating yourself on how humans from around the world organize themselves into different cultures, and how these cultures interact.

This book contains many more resources, but the following are specifically geared to self-guided education.

Index to Resources in this Chapter

International IQ Periodicals 186
Book, Film & Video Distributors 187
Global Education 189
Tools for Teachers 193

RESOURCES

International IQ Periodicals

The following is a list of resources to help you improve your International IQ. While there's no shortage of good material available, we think this list includes a few of the best sources of information and news about the world around us, and represents a diversity of perspectives.

If you live in a major city, you can find many of the following resources at a university or public library. Your local global education centre will probably have some of these titles on hand. If they don't, they'll be able to recommend good substitutes. For those of you who live in a smaller centre or rural area, we've included distributors' addresses and phone numbers so you can contact them directly. If you're not sure what you're looking for and want to check out a magazine or journal before subscribing, get hold of a few back issues. These are usually cheaper and available by the issue.

Developing an International IQ is an important part of your international job search strategy. If you haven't already begun this process, start yesterday!

For more information on building your crosscultural communication skills while abroad consult the following Resources sections: Chapter 1, The Effective Overseas Employee offers material focused on general crosscultural skills required by all international employees; Chapter 27, Jobs by Regions of the World lists books which provide country-specific advice on social and business customs; Chapter 3, Living Overseas has resources which discuss the more practical aspects of living overseas.

The Economist 📖
Weekly ➤ The Economist, P.O. Box 58524, Boulder, CO 80322, USA; $175.55/yr; credit cards; (800) 456-6086, fax (800) 604-7455 ▪ The best magazine for keeping up-to-date on the economic and political situations in both developed and developing countries, as well as for classified ads for senior management jobs. Visit their web site at www.economist.com. [ID:1635]

Far Eastern Economic Review 📖
Weekly ➤ Subscription Department, Far Eastern Economic Review, P.O. Box 160, General Post Office, Hong Kong, CHINA; $6.75 per issue or $215 per year; credit cards; (852) 2508 4300, fax (852) 2503 1526, subscription@feer.com ▪ This news weekly focuses on the business, politics and economics of the Asia Pacific region. You can subscribe for six months or a year. [ID:1650]

Financial Times 📖
Daily ➤ Financial Times, 4th Floor, 14 East 60th Street, New York, NY 10022, USA; (800) 628-0007, fax (212) 308-2397; Available at international newsstands ▪ A world-renowned daily paper which provides excellent international coverage. [ID:1654]

Le Monde 📖
Daily ➤ Le Monde, 1 Place Hubert-Beauvre-Méry, Ivry-sur-Seine, 94852, FRANCE; $2.25/issue; (33) (1) 40-65-25-25, fax (33) (1) 49-60-34-90 ▪ A world-renowned French language daily with superb international coverage. [ID:1656]

Manchester Guardian Weekly 📖
Weekly, Guardian Publications Ltd. ➤ Manchester Guardian Weekly, P.O. Box 2515, Champlain, New York, NY 12919-2515, USA; US$2.50 per issue; VISA, MC; (514) 630-1106, fax (514) 697-3490, gwsubsna@time.ca ▪ A weekly newspaper with excellent coverage of international events and issues, with international job postings. Visit www.time.ca. [ID:1655]

New York Times 📖
Daily ➤ New York Times Co., 229 West 43rd Street, New York, NY 10036, USA; US$3.60/week; credit cards; (800) 631-2500, fax (201) 342-2539; Available at international newsstands ▪ A daily newspaper with excellent international coverage. You can subscribe online at www.nytimes.com. [ID:1653]

South Magazine 📖
Monthly, South Magazine ➤ Gordon & Gotch, Unit 11, 110 Jardin Drive, Toronto, Ontario L4K 4R4; $76.40/year; VISA; (800) 438-5005, fax (905) 669-3654 ▪ Business-oriented magazine concerned with issues affecting the Third World. Good source of expert, in-depth analyses of economic and political trends. [ID:1249]

Wall Street Journal 📖
Daily ➤ Wall Street Journal, Suite 200, 2 Summit Park Drive, Independence, OH 44131, USA; $135/13 weeks; credit cards; (800) 975-9750, fax (212) 597-5600 ▪ A daily newspaper with a focus on business and financial news. Excellent international business coverage. Note also its sister publication, the *Asian Wall Street Journal*. Visit www.dowjones.com. [ID:1652]

World Press Review 📖
Monthly ➤ World Press Review, P.O. Box 228, Shrub Oak, NY 10588-0228, USA; US$30.97/year; (212) 889-5155 ▪ A monthly magazine which reprints articles and excerpts from respected newspapers and magazines outside the US, translating as necessary. It assembles under one cover a diverse sampling of world opinion on current events around the globe. Published by the Stanley Foundation as "a nonprofit educational service to foster the international exchange of information." Visit the magazine's web site at www.worldpress.org. [ID:2793]

Book, Film & Video Distributors

There are many sources of information to help you in your international career. These are the ones which are very specialized, offer the most choices, or provide information for your global education.

Africa on Film and Videotape: A Guide to
Audio-Visual Resources Available in Canada 📖
1990 ➤ IDERA Films, Suite 200, 2678 West Broadway, Vancouver, B.C. V6K 2G3; free or small donation; credit cards; (604) 738-8815, fax (604) 738-8400 ▪ Excellent catalogue of films on Africa. IDERA Films is one of the best sources for development films in Canada. Visit the distributor's web site at www.vcn.bc.ca/idera. [ID:1161]

Apex Press Catalogue 📖
Annual ➤ Council on International and Public Affairs, Apex Press, Suite 3C, 777 United Nations Plaza, New York, NY 10017, USA; VISA, MC; (914) 271-6500, fax (914) 271-2039 ▪ Specialized distributor of books on human rights, grassroots and sustainable development, peace and security, third world politics, social change, and international education. [ID:1521]

CIDA: International Development Photo Library (IDPL) 📖
Communications Branch, Canadian International Development Agency (CIDA), Communications Branch, 200 Promenade du Portage, Hull, Québec K1A 0G4; (613) 997-5006, fax (613) 953-6087 ▪ IDPL is a resource of over 80,000 slides depicting life in the South, international development, and Canada's role in it. Staff will provide photo editing/research services to the public for a nominal fee. Requests take five to 10 working days to complete. [ID:2644]

Crossing Cultures Through Film 📖
1993, *Ellen Summerfield,* Intercultural Press, 197 pages ➤ Intercultural and Community Development Resources (ICDR), P.O. Box 32108, Millwoods Station, Edmonton, Alberta T6K 4C2; $24; VISA, Amex; (800) 378-3199, fax (403) 462-1925, icdr@compusmart.ab.ca ▪ Examines the rich resource of film and video. Analyzes over 70 classic films and suggests how educators can use them most effectively. Discusses teaching and research, availability and sourcing. Emphasizes the

unique role of film in treating controversial topics, and in helping students understand and unlearn stereotypes. Visit the distributor's web site at www.compusmart.ab.ca/icdr. [ID:1397]

Impact Publications Catalogue ⌨
Annual ➤ Impact Publications, 9104 North Manassas Drive, Manassas Park, VA 20111-2366, USA; free; credit cards; (703) 361-7300, fax (703) 335-9486 ■ The single best mail-order source of career books in North America, including international career books. Also available online at www.impactpublications.com. [ID:1713]

Insight: International Development Film and Video Catalogue ⌨
1993, 189 pages ➤ Canada Government PublishingOttawa, Ontario K1A 0S9; free; VISA, MC; (819) 956-4800, fax (819) 994-1498, publishing@ccg-gcc.ca ■ Excellent catalogue of films and videos on international development. Organized by subject area. Films can be obtained by calling your regional NFB Film and Video Library. Call 800 Directory Assistance for the toll-free number nearest you. Visit the publisher's web site at http://publications.pwgsc.gc.ca. [ID:1105]

Intercultural and Community Development Resources (ICDR) Catalogue ⌨
Updated regularly ➤ Intercultural and Community Development Resources (ICDR), P.O. Box 32108, Millwoods Station, Edmonton, Alberta T6K 4C2; VISA, Amex; (800) 378-3199, fax (403) 462-1925, icdr@compusmart.ab.ca ■ Canadian distributor for Intercultural Press and other fine crosscultural resources. Visit their web site www.compusmart.ab.ca/icdr. (See the Intercultural Press Catalogue profile below.) [ID:2706]

Intercultural Press Catalogue ⌨
Semiannual, Intercultural Press ➤ Intercultural and Community Development Resources (ICDR), P.O. Box 32108, Millwoods Station, Edmonton, Alberta T6K 4C2; VISA, Amex; (800) 378-3199, fax (403) 462-1925, icdr@compusmart.ab.ca ■ Easily the best source of crosscultural books in the world. Highly recommended. Includes many titles on crosscultural training, international business, diversity, overseas living, and community development. The Canadian distributor of this US publisher and distributor is Intercultural and Community Development Resources (ICDR), web site www.compusmart.ab.ca/icdr, (see their profile above). [ID:1712]

Kumarian Press Catalogue ⌨
Quarterly, 45 pages ➤ Kumarian Press, Inc., 14 Oakwood Avenue, West Hartford, CT 06119, USA; free; VISA, MC; (860) 233-5895, fax (860) 233-6072, kpbooks@aol.com ■ Book publisher with concentration on international development. Visit the publisher's web site at www.kpbooks.com. [ID:1045]

Lynne Rienner Catalogue ⌨
Lynne Rienner Publishers, Suite 314, 1800 30th Street, Boulder, CO 80301, USA; VISA, MC; (303) 444-6684, fax (303) 444-0824 ■ An excellent source for academic books and videos on international political topics. Visit their web site at www.rienner.com. [ID:2705]

Renouf Catalogue ⌨
Quarterly ➤ Renouf Publishing Co. Ltd., Unit 1, 5369 Canotek Road, Ottawa, Ontario K1J 9J3; free; credit cards; (613) 745-2665, fax (613) 745-7660 ■ Mail-order book distributor specializing in publications by the United Nations, governments of Canada, USA, and the European Community, international organizations and private business. Renouf stores are located in Ottawa and Toronto. [ID:1714]

Westview Press Catalogue ⌨
Annual ➤ Westview Press, 5500 Central Ave., Boulder, CO 80301-2877, USA; free; (800) 456-1995, fax (303) 449-3356 ■ Comprehensive listing of the latest academic publications in the areas of development and regional studies. [ID:1503]

Wiley Publishers and Distributors Catalogue ⌨
1997 ➤ John Wiley & Sons, 22 Worchester Drive, Rexdale, Ontario M9W 1L1; free; credit cards; (800) 567-4797, fax (800) 565-6802 ■ North America's largest professional book distributor and

publisher. Wide selection of business books, many pertaining to international subjects. Visit their web site at www.wiley.com/products/worldwide/canada. [ID:1715]

Global Education

Global education teaches us about global issues and usually focuses on North-South relations. Issues such as poverty, human rights, social justice, sustainable development, and the inequities of the global economic system are concerns of global education literature.

The wide range of material listed here will help you begin building your International IQ. These books and web sites have been chosen to help you broaden your perspective and knowledge of the world. Many references attempt to sensitize North Americans to different world views. Some cover a wide range of topics, while others focus on specific issues. If you are planning to work overseas, it is important to be attuned to these issues prior to your departure. This eclectic list of resources is really just the tip of the iceberg.

Also consult the Resources sections in the following chapters: for general crosscultural skills see Chapter 1, The Effective Overseas Employee; for the more practical aspects of living overseas see Chapter 3, Living Overseas and Chapter 12, Crosscultural Travel; for material which is helpful to all, but focuses on crosscultural business skills, see Chapter 7, The Canadian Identity in the International Workplace; for country-specific advice on social and business customs see Chapter 27, Jobs by Regions of the World.

Barnga 📖
1990, *Sivasailam Thiagarajan, Barbara Steinwachs,* Intercultural Press ➤ Intercultural and Community Development Resources (ICDR), P.O. Box 32108, Millwoods Station, Edmonton, Alberta T6K 4C2; $32; VISA, Amex; (800) 378-3199, fax (403) 462-1925, icdr@compusmart.ab.ca ■ This game simulates the effects of cultural differences on human interaction. Requires a minimum of nine participants. Visit the distributor's web site at www.compusmart.ab.ca/icdr. [ID:2399]

Basics and Tools - A Collection of Popular Education Resources and Activities 📖
1988 ➤ CUSO, Suite 400, 2255 Carling Ave., Ottawa, Ontario K2B 1A6; $10; (613) 829-7445, fax (613) 829-7996 ■ Handbook provides basic models and principals of experiential adult learning as well as a compilation of popular exercises, role plays, simulation games, and activities for development education. Includes an annotated list of recommended resources. [ID:2413]

Canadian Development Report 1997-98 📖
Annual, North-South Institute ➤ Renouf Publishing Co. Ltd., Unit 1, 5369 Canotek Road, Ottawa, Ontario K1J 9J3; $30; credit cards; (613) 745-2665, fax (613) 745-7660 ■ This second volume in an annual series explores the extent and impact of Canadian corporate involvement in developing countries, and examines how the forces propelling globalization are consistent with the advancement of social programs, democratic development, and human rights. The previous volume explores the evolving dynamics of Canada's relationships with the developing world through a series of essays on Canadian policy and action. [ID:2556]

Canadian Human Rights Commission 🖥
www.chrc.ca/ ■ This site is dedicated to ensuring the universal rights and dignity of all persons. Resources include the text of the Canadian Human Rights Act and links to other sources of information on human rights. [ID:2567]

Connexions Online 🖥
www.connexions.org ■ Features information on resources and organizations (mostly Canadian) fostering democratization, economic justice, environmental responsibility, civil liberties, and the creation and preservation of community. Connexions is a nonprofit organization working to

connect individuals and groups devoted to social change with each other and the general public. The site includes directory of organizations, events and actions calendar, and more. [ID:1117]

Cultural Survival 📖
www.cs.org ▪ Cultural Survival's primary focus is indigenous peoples and ethnic groups worldwide (and links to a number of web resources in this area), but it also provides links to sites and organizations dealing with environment, gender, and regional development issues. [ID:2454]

Cultural Survival Quarterly 📖
Quarterly ➤ Cultural Survival Inc., 96 Mount Auburn Street, Cambridge, MA 02138, USA; US$5/issue; VISA; (617) 441-5400, fax (617) 441-5417, csinc@cs.org ▪ Since 1972 Cultural Survival has helped indigenous peoples and ethnic minorities deal as equals with Western society. Features articles on indigenous peoples worldwide. Visit the distributor's web site at www.cs.org. [ID:1649]

Developing Ideas 📖
Bimonthly ➤ International Institute for Sustainable Development (IISD), 6th Floor, 161 Portage Ave. East, Winnipeg, Manitoba R3B 0Y4; $35; (204) 958-7700, fax (204) 958-7710, reception@iisdpost.iisd.ca ▪ This journal provides a snapshot of the most influential ideas shaping the international sustainable development dialogue. Available by annual subscription, e-mail or in print. Visit the publisher's web site at http://iisd1.iisd.ca/. [ID:2504]

Development Dictionary: A Guide to Knowledge as Power 📖
1992, *Wolfgang Sachs,* Zed Books, 352 pages ➤ Council on International and Public Affairs, Apex Press, Suite 3C, 777 United Nations Plaza, New York, NY 10017, USA; US$25; VISA, MC; (914) 271-6500, fax (914) 271-2039 ▪ The world's most eminent development critics review the key concepts of international development in the last 50 years. Includes a guide to relevant literature. [ID:2401]

Development is... An Introductory Study Kit on Development 📖
1987 ➤ CUSO, Suite 400, 2255 Carling Ave., Ottawa, Ontario K2B 1A6; $15; (613) 829-7445, fax (613) 829-7996 ▪ This popular education resource is a series of four two-hour sessions which challenge and expand people's understanding of development through role plays, problem-solving activities, case studies and readings. Participants develop plans for future educational work and action. [ID:2412]

Development: Journal of the Society for International Development 📖
Quarterly ➤ Sage Publications, 6 Bonhill Street, London, EC2A 4PU, UK; Introductory price £20/year, £25/year; credit cards; (44) (171) 374-0645, fax (44) (171) 374-8741, subscription@sagepub.co.uk ▪ Presents the current debates in development from a wide range of perspectives. Each issue covers two main themes, plus book reviews, interviews and announcements. Visit www.sagepub.co.uk/journals/details/j0152.html, the distributor's web site. [ID:1651]

Fundraising for Social Change 📖
1996, *Kim Klein,* 320 pages ➤ Chardon Press, P.O. Box 11607, Berkeley, CA 94712, USA; US$25; VISA, MC; (510) 704-8714, fax (510) 649-7913, chardn@aol.com ▪ The nuts-and-bolts strategies all nonprofit groups need to understand to raise money. Learn how to motivate your board of directors, use direct mail techniques and plan and implement major gift campaigns, endowments and planned giving programs, and more. Visit the distributor's web site at www.chardonpress.com. [ID:1110]

Health, Population and Reproductive Health Resources 🖳
www.jhpiego.jhu.edu/RELATED/RELATED.HTM#Health ▪ Johns Hopkins University has compiled a list of links to organizations involved in this area of development. [ID:2453]

How We Work for Peace 📖
1988, *Christine Perringer,* 446 pages ➤ Peace Research Institute, 25 Dundana Ave., Dundas, Ontario L9H 4E5; $15; (905) 628-2356, fax (905) 628-1830, newcombe-prid@hwcn.org ▪ Readable, offers ideas, advice and motivation. Somewhat dated, but still essential reading for peace activists

or anyone wishing to get involved in the peace movement. Excellent material on working in groups, reaching the unconverted, peace activities and campaigns. [ID:1229]

IISD Products Catalogue 📖
Annual ➤ International Institute for Sustainable Development (IISD), 6th Floor, 161 Portage Ave. East, Winnipeg, Manitoba R3B 0Y4; free; (204) 958-7700, fax (204) 958-7710, reception@iisdpost.iisd.ca ▪ This not-for-profit Canadian corporation produces a range of publications and products on the theme of sustainable development. Visit the distributor's web site at http://iisd1.iisd.ca/. [ID:2503]

IISDnet 💻
http://iisd1.iisd.ca ▪ Have a look at this site by the International Institute for Sustainable Development, linking with other leading institutions to deliver the latest information on sustainable development: research, new trends, global activity, contacts, and a list of products available for bringing sustainable development from concept to practice. [ID:2502]

International Centre for Research on Women 💻
www.icrw.org/ ▪ The International Centre for research on Women's web site offers publications as well as a comprehensive set of development links. [ID:2451]

International Development Research Centre (IDRC) 💻
www.idrc.ca ▪ The IDRC helps communities in the developing world find solutions to social, cultural and environmental problems. This site contains a library of related literature, reviews of current research programs, and a resource desk. (See their profile in Chapter 35, Nongovernmental Organizations.) [ID:2568]

International Human Rights Resources 💻
www.law.csuohio.edu/lawlibrary/int_resources.html ▪ A list of links to organizations and online databases with a focus on human rights. [ID:2452]

Multi-sector Directory of BC Global Organizations and Resources 📖 💻
1998, *BCCIC,* 152 pages ➤ BC Council for International Cooperation (BCCIC), 930 Mason Street, Vancouver, B.C. V8T 1A2, Canada; $15; no credit cards; (250) 360-1405, fax (250) 360-2295 ▪ Created by a nongovernmental organization, this directory contains over 140 listings of global organizations, information on resources concerning international issues, and global education. Visit the publisher's web site at www.bccic.bc.ca/bccicweb/. [ID:2795]

The New Internationalist 📖 💻
Monthly ➤ Subscription Office, New Internationalist, Unit 17, 35 Riviera Drive, Markham, Ontario L3R 8N4; $38.50/year; credit cards; (905) 946-0407, fax (905) 946-0410 ▪ This magazine has been used for years by development education groups as a primer on global social justice issues. Each issue covers one broad theme, in a popularized style. Good reading for an alternative perspective. Back issues are available online at www.newint.org/. [ID:1212]

Oxfam Country Profiles 📖
1996, OXFAM UK, 64 pages each ➤ Fernwood Books Ltd., P.O. Box 9409, Stn. A, Halifax, N.S. B3K 5S3; $7.95-$9.95; VISA; (902) 422-3302, fax (902) 422-3179 ▪ This series focuses on the lives of ordinary people and the major development issues that affect them. Over 70 country profiles available. [ID:2483]

The Oxfam Handbook of Development and Relief 📖
1995, OXFAM UK, 1200 pages ➤ Fernwood Books Ltd., P.O. Box 9409, Stn. A, Halifax, N.S. B3K 5S3; $39; VISA; (902) 422-3302, fax (902) 422-3179 ▪ This three-volume set is a valuable reference tool for development practitioners, planners, students, and teachers of development. [ID:2479]

The Oxfam Poverty Report 📖
1995, *Kevin Watkins,* OXFAM UK, 240 pages ➤ Fernwood Books Ltd., P.O. Box 9409, Stn. A, Halifax, N.S. B3K 5S3; $15.95; VISA; (902) 422-3302, fax (902) 422-3179 ▪ Identifies the structural forces which deny people their basic social and economic rights, using case studies from Africa,

Latin America, and Asia. Outlines policy and institutional reforms needed to reduce poverty. [ID:2480]

Resources for Development and Relief: 1996 Oxfam Catalogue 📖
1996, Oxfam Canada, 39 pages ➤ Fernwood Books Ltd., P.O. Box 9409, Stn. A, Halifax, N.S. B3K 5S3; free; VISA; (902) 422-3302, fax (902) 422-3179 ▪ This excellent catalogue includes books, journals, videos, research papers and training manuals on a wide variety of topics, including: Trade, Aid and Debt, Understanding Global Issues, Health, Gender, Agriculture and Environment, Conflict and Development, and more. [ID:2428]

Review 📖 💻
3/year ➤ North-South Institute, Suite 200, 55 Murray Street, Ottawa, Ontario K1N 5M3; free; VISA, MC; (613) 241-3535, fax (613) 241-7435, nsi@nsi-ins.ca ▪ The North-South Institute's newsletter features research updates, reviews of recent publications, and other news items on international development and Canada's foreign policy. Available electronically at www.nsi-ins.ca. [ID:2557]

Third World Guide 📖
Annual, Third World Institute ➤ Subscription Office, New Internationalist, Unit 17, 35 Riviera Drive, Markham, Ontario L3R 8N4; $49.95; credit cards; (905) 946-0407, fax (905) 946-0410 ▪ The seventh edition of this excellent publication offers a survey of the world's countries from the point of view of journalists, researchers and academics from the Third World. An alternative to established sources of information, the book contains 630 pages of information on development, with 55 maps, 780 diagrams and 6,800 easy-to-use references. Visit the distributor's web site at www.newint.org/. [ID:1586]

Third World Quarterly: Journal of Emerging Areas 📖
Quarterly ➤ CARFAX Publishing Co., P.O. Box 25, Abingdon, Oxfordshire, OX14 3UE, UK; US$82; VISA, MC, Amex, Eurocard; (44) (1235) 401-000, fax (44) (1235) 401-550 ▪ Setting the agenda since the 1970s, *Third World Quarterly* is considered one of the most influential journals covering the emerging areas of the world. Provides original, interdisciplinary analysis of political, economic and social issues. [ID:1648]

Third World Resurgence 📖
Monthly, *Evelyne Hong* ➤ Third World Network, 228 Macalister Road, Penang, 10400, MALAYSIA ▪ A magazine devoted to providing a Southern perspective on issues facing the Third World. This magazine has earned high praise among many in the NGO community. It covers the environment, basic needs, politics, current affairs, and culture. Write to get a subscription. [ID:1657]

Virtual Library on International Development 💻
w3.acdi-cida.gc.ca/virtual.nsf ▪ Published by the Canadian International Development Agency (CIDA), this site is an excellent collection of links to international development resources on the Internet. Organized by theme, organization, region and country, report and publication. A constantly-updated new links section. [ID:2450]

The World 1995/1996: A Third World Guide 📖
1995, *Third World Institute*, OXFAM UK, 640 pages ➤ Fernwood Books Ltd., P.O. Box 9409, Stn. A, Halifax, N.S. B3K 5S3; $39.95; VISA; (902) 422-3302, fax (902) 422-3179 ▪ A reference book of facts, figures and opinions, which presents a global picture from the Third World's point of view. Organized by country as well as theme. Also available on CD-ROM. [ID:2481]

World Development 📖
Monthly ➤ Customer Support Department, Elsevier Science Ltd., Regional Sales Office, P.O. Box 945, New York, NY 10159-0945, USA; US$191; credit cards; (888) 437-4636, fax (212) 633-3680, usinfo@elsevir.com; Available in large libraries ▪ Multidisciplinary journal publishing research and review articles on the social, economic and political consequences of development. Focuses on reforms and cooperative efforts to eliminate disease, poverty and illiteracy. Visit the distributor's web site at www.elsevir.nl/. [ID:1708]

The World in Your Kitchen 📖
1994 ➤ Subscription Office, New Internationalist, Unit 17, 35 Riviera Drive, Markham, Ontario
L3R 8N4; $13.95; credit cards; (905) 946-0407, fax (905) 946-0410 ■ This book is listed because of
our belief that vegetarian diets are far less draining of the world's resources than non-vegetarian
ones. Many global education programs recognize the value of vegetarianism. Visit
www.newint.org/.
[ID:1585]

Tools for Teachers

The magnitude of current global problems calls for promotion of international
awareness among the young. Increasingly, teachers at the primary and
secondary school levels are incorporating global education into the classroom.
The following list of resources will be useful for anyone wishing to educate
youth about international issues, particularly within the classroom.

Cross-Cultural Dialogues 📖
1994, *Craig Storti,* Intercultural Press, 150 pages ➤ Intercultural and Community Development
Resources (ICDR), P.O. Box 32108, Millwoods Station, Edmonton, Alberta T6K 4C2; $22; VISA,
Amex; (800) 378-3199, fax (403) 462-1925, icdr@compusmart.ab.ca ■ A collection of brief
conversations between the author, an American, and people from different cultures. Highlights
the subtle differences that exist between cultures. Useful as an educational tool. Visit the
distributor's web site at www.compusmart.ab.ca/icdr. [ID:1381]

Developing Global Development Perspectives in Home Economics Education 📖
1992, *Linda Peterat, Gale Smith,* 62 pages ➤ Canadian Home Economics Association, Suite 901,
151 Slater Street, Ottawa, Ontario K1P 5H3; $10; cheque or money order; (613) 238-8817, fax
(613) 238-8972 ■ Introduces teachers to the theoretical and practical aspects of global education.
A handy reference book. Visit the distributor's web site at www.chea.ca. [ID:1609]

Developing Intercultural Awareness: A Cross-Cultural Training Handbook 📖
1994, *L. Robert Kohls, John M. Knight,* Intercultural Press, 158 pages ➤ Intercultural and
Community Development Resources (ICDR), P.O. Box 32108, Millwoods Station, Edmonton,
Alberta T6K 4C2; $24; VISA, Amex; (800) 378-3199, fax (403) 462-1925, icdr@compusmart.ab.ca ■
This book features outline designs of one- and two-day cultural awareness workshops, and
training materials that include simulation games, case studies, and exercises on values and ice-
breaking. Designed for intercultural educators and trainers, and useful to anyone wishing to
expand his or her general training or teaching repertoire. Visit the distributor's web site at
www.compusmart.ab.ca/icdr. [ID:1380]

Development Alternatives: Communities of the South
in Action—A Teacher's Guide for World Issues Courses 📖
1993 ➤ Is Five Press, 400 Mount Pleasant Road, Toronto, Ontario M4J 3L9; $69.95; cheque or
money order; (416) 480-2408, fax (416) 480-2546 ■ A series of case studies designed to supplement world issues, environmental and social science courses from Grade 11 to OAC. Topics
include rainforest management, women in development, children and nutrition, tourism and land
use, recycling and composting, and rural development. [ID:1616]

Global Change Game 📖
1997 ➤ Global Change Game, P.O. Box 1632, Winnipeg, Manitoba R3C 2Z6; (204) 783-2675, fax
(204) 783-2680, gcg@solutions.net ■ The Global Change Game is an international development
education program which visits highschool, university, and community groups across Canada
teaching about world issues in a fun and innovative way. It is a three-hour workshop, played on a
hand-painted world map the size of a basketball court, in which players deal with challenges such
as hunger, war, biodiversity, refugees, and deforestation. If you are interested in having the Global
Change Game come to your school, please contact the address above. [ID:2680]

Global Winners: 74 Activities for Inside and Outside the Classroom 📖
1994, *Jan Drum, Steve Hughes, George Otero,* Intercultural Press, 229 pages ➤ Intercultural and Community Development Resources (ICDR), P.O. Box 32108, Millwoods Station, Edmonton, Alberta T6K 4C2; $24; VISA, Amex; (800) 378-3199, fax (403) 462-1925, icdr@compusmart.ab.ca ▪ A guide to strategies for global education with role plays, simulations and other hands-on exercises. Aimed at K-to-12 educators, but also useful for college and adult education. Examines other countries and cultures, stresses our global interdependence, and discusses competitive versus cooperative outlooks. Visit the distributor's web site at www.compusmart.ab.ca/icdr. [ID:1398]

Green Teacher Magazine 📖
Bimonthly, 48 pages ➤ Green Teacher, 95 Robert Street, Toronto, Ontario M5S 2K5; $6/ issue, $25/ year; cash or cheque; (416) 960-1244, fax (416) 925-3475 ▪ A Canadian magazine, with contributions from regional editors across the country, on global education ideas and developments. Visit the distributor's web site at www.web.ca/~greentea. [ID:1611]

Introducing the World: A Guide to Developing
International and Global Awareness Programs 📖
1985, Redford McCandless Institute, 174 pages ➤ Publications Secretary, Canadian Institute of International Affairs, 15 King's College Circle, Toronto, Ontario M5S 2V9; $20; VISA, MC; (800) 668-2442, fax (416) 979-8575 ▪ Designed as a high school curriculum supplement to interest students in the world and Canada's place in world affairs. Some of the program activities include: inter-school conferences on world affairs, leadership development workshops, research, publications, seminars, and simulation games. [ID:1041]

It's Only Right: A Practical Guide for Learning
About the Convention on the Rights of the Child 📖
1993, *Susan Fountain* ➤ UNICEF Ontario, 443 Mount Pleasant Road, Toronto, Ontario M4S 2L8; $15; credit cards; (416) 482-4444, fax (416) 482-8035, unicef@secretary.ca ▪ Guide for secondary schools and youth groups. The activities in this user-friendly guide (complete with reproducible materials) follow a learning cycle of exploring, responding and taking action. This process underlines the responsibilities young people have to recognize, respect and protect, not only their own rights, but the rights of others, all over the world. [ID:1614]

Learning Across Cultures 📖
1994, *Gary Althen,* 200 pages ➤ National Association for Foreign Student Affairs, P.O. Box 1020, Sewickley, PA 15143, USA; US$19; VISA, MC; (800) 836-4994, fax (412) 741-0609 ▪ A vital overview of the application of the concepts and practices of intercultural communication to inter national educational exchange. Includes recent developments in intercultural relations, counselling student sojourners, the dynamics of adapting to a new cultural environment, managing culture in the ESL classroom, and more. Visit the publisher's web site at www.nafsa.org. [ID:1687]

Monarch ESL Catalogue 📖
Annual ➤ Monarch Books of Canada Ltd., 5000 Dufferin Street, Downsview, Ontario M3H 5T5; free; VISA, MC; (416) 663-8231, fax (416) 736-1702 ▪ A catalogue of educational titles listed under such headings as Grammar, TOEFL Preparation, Basic Text, Conversation and Phonics. This is a useful planning tool for teachers before planning to go overseas. [ID:1578]

The New Internationalist 📖 🖥
Monthly ➤ Subscription Office, New Internationalist, Unit 17, 35 Riviera Drive, Markham, Ontario L3R 8N4; $38.50/year; credit cards; (905) 946-0407, fax (905) 946-0410 ▪ This magazine has been used for years by development education groups as a primer on global social justice issues. Each issue covers one broad theme, in a popularized style. Good reading for an alternative perspective. Back issues are available online at www.newint.org/. [ID:1212]

On Being Foreign: Culture Shock in Short Fiction, an International Anthology 📖
1986, *Tom Lewis, Robert Jungman,* Intercultural Press, 308 pages ➤ Intercultural and Community Development Resources (ICDR), P.O. Box 32108, Millwoods Station, Edmonton, Alberta T6K 4C2; $25; VISA, Amex; (800) 378-3199, fax (403) 462-1925, icdr@compusmart.ab.ca ▪ Twenty short

stories selected from mainstream world literature lead you through the six stages of crosscultural adjustment. May be used as a reader in undergraduate programs and as a text in advanced ESL, world literature courses or intercultural studies. Will appeal to the recreational reader! Visit the distributor's website at www.compusmart.ab.ca/icdr. [ID:1385]

Pacific Rim Profiles 📖
1997, 12 pages each ➤ Asia Pacific Foundation, Suite 666, 999 Canada Place, Vancouver, B.C. V6C 3E1; $9.50 each or $99.50 for set; VISA, MC; (604) 684-5986, fax (604) 681-1370 ▪ A series of booklets on 14 Pacific Rim countries plus APEC. A teaching resource for senior high school and college levels. Includes historical background, government and economy, international trade profiles, information on student life, current affairs, crosscultural information, and more. Visit the distributor's web site at www.apfc.ca. [ID:2404]

Profiles of Global Education Centres

The chapter lists 24 Global Education Centres located in over 20 communities across Canada.

Arusha Centre
233 - 10th Street N.W., Calgary, Alberta T2N 1V5; (403) 270-3200, fax (403) 270-8832

The Arusha Centre is a collectively-run, member-supported organization that provides resources and programming on local and global social justice issues. Throughout most of their 25-year history, the centre's work has been dedicated to public understanding of issues of global development. The past five years have seen a shift to more local issues, including an anti-racist program for teachers, students, community organizations, institutions and the public. Work also addresses the local and global economy and has included workshops on de-mystifying debt and deficit issues, and women and economic justice.
    Arusha's lending library has a wide selection of print and audiovisual materials on social justice and international development issues. Volunteers play an integral role in Arusha's daily activities, programming, committee work and fundraising. [ID:5086]

Camrose International Institute (CII)
Room 3, 4908-50 Street, Camrose, Alberta T4V 1R1; (403) 672-8780, fax (403) 672-4331

Camrose International Institute's (CII) mission is "to encourage and support equitable, ecologically sound human development in Canada and the Developing World and to make links between the people of Canada and the Developing World through partnership, education and development programs." CII works towards these goals through a variety of activities. Its Development Education Program teaches about developing countries and global issues, raises funds for community self-help projects in developing countries, and promotes creation of alternative solutions to world problems. [ID:5087]

Carrefour de solidarité internationale (CSI)
555, rue Short, Sherbrooke, Québec J1H 2E6; (819) 566-8595, fax (819) 566-8076, csi-sher@login.net

Carrefour de solidarité internationale (CSI) est un centre régional de ressources en développement international mis sur pied pour le soutien de projets de développement. Cet organisme d'éducation et de formation maintien quatre programmes complémentaires dont des projets de développement pour soutenir des ONG, des stages à l'étranger et des programmes d'animation et de communication. [ID:5088]

Centre de solidarité internationale
C.P. 278, bureau 206, 520, Sacré-Coeur, Alma, Québec G8B 5V8; (418) 668-5211, fax (418) 668-5638

Le Centre de solidarité internationale Alma repose sur l'interdépendance entre les peuples du Nord et du Sud et la recherche d'un meilleur développement qui doit se réaliser dans un climat de justice et de liberté. Il regroupe des bénévoles qui s'engagent dans des actions telles les tournées régionales et les conférences, ceci en vue de favoriser une meilleure compréhension et amener à faire évoluer les mentalités. [ID:5092]

Centre for International Alternatives
10020 Whyte Ave., Edmonton, Alberta T6E 1Z3; (403) 439-8744, fax (403) 413-0698, edtnlctr@web.net

The Centre for International Alternatives works toward building a more just and equitable world through its global education programs. These include: a resource centre with over 350 international development audiovisual materials; a labour-worker program, which connects Canadians to other workers in the global labour market and builds solidarity among them; and their communities program, which assists groups promoting international awareness. The centre publishes a bimonthly newsletter entitled Connections and is also involved in outreach programming with teachers and students in an effort to integrate global justice issues into the school curriculum. [ID:5094]

Comité régional d'éducation pour le développement international de Lanaudière (CREDIL)
200, de Salaberry, Joliette, Québec J6E 4G1; (514) 756-0011, fax (514) 759-8749, credil@pandore.qc.ca

Le Comité régional d'éducation pour le développement international de Lanaudière (CREDIL) a pour objectifs l'éducation au développement international dans la région de Lanaudière, la solidarité avec des organisations populaires et l'initiation et le support d'engagements concrets en appui aux efforts de justice dans le monde. Pour ce faire, il entretient des liens directs avec l'Afrique australe et sahélienne, le Moyen-Orient et l'Amérique latine et accueille des nouveaux arrivants. [ID:5095]

Cooper Institute
81 Prince Street, Charlottetown, P.E.I. C1A 4R3; (902) 894-4573, fax (902) 368-7180

Cooper Institute works with various social change organizations located on Prince Edward Island (PEI). The institute facilitates the exchange of information, experience, analysis, and action plans between PEI groups and similar organizations in the South, especially in the Caribbean, Central America, and Africa. [ID:5097]

Global Awareness Project of Northwestern Ontario (GAP)
285 Bay Street, Thunder Bay, Ontario P7B 1R7; (807) 345-0914, fax (807) 345-0372, gap@web.net

The Global Awareness Project (GAP) is a community-based global education centre whose mission is to encourage people to participate in social justice actions that work towards global equity. To this end, it publishes a newsletter 10 times per year and has a resource centre accessible to the public. GAP also conducts community education programs such as seminars and workshops. [ID:5100]

Global Community Centre
89-91 King Street N., Waterloo, Ontario N2J 2X3; (519) 746-4090, fax (519) 746-4096, gccwat@web.net

The Global Community Centre offers development education to communities in the Waterloo region through its resource centre and through workshops, presentations, and guest speakers addressing international, national and local social justice issues. [ID:5101]

Global Village (Nanaimo)
International Development Education Association
Suite 101, 259 Pine Street, Nanaimo, B.C. V9R 2B7;
(604) 753-3322, fax (250) 390-3363, stewart@island.net

Global Village delivers a program of development education to local schools and the general public in the mid-Vancouver Island region. Global Village operates a resource centre, publishes the newspaper *Horizons* five times per year, and provides alternative trading for 40 Southern cooperatives through craft sales. It also sponsors public meetings and discussions and facilitates visits by guest speakers from the South. [ID:5102]

Guelph International Resource Centre (GIRC)
Suite 1, 123 Woolwich Street, Guelph, Ontario N1H 3V1; (519) 822-3110, fax (519) 822-7089

The Guelph International Resource Centre (GIRC) promotes a just and sustainable future by assisting the community in developing awareness and actions around global issues. In addition to its resource library and publication of a quarterly newsletter, GIRC holds special events and sponsors guest speakers. The centre is also home to the *Speed River Current*, a community newspaper, and a car co-op. GIRC has several volunteers who assist with the centre in various capacities. [ID:5103]

International Development Education Resource Association (IDERA)
Suite 400, 1037 West Broadway, Vancouver, B.C. V6H 1E3;
(604) 732-1496, fax (604) 738-8400, idera@web.net, www.vcn.bc.ca/idera

International Development Education Resource Association (IDERA) is committed to fostering a better understanding among Canadians of global development issues, with an emphasis on peace, social justice and human dignity, and to translating such awareness into active debate and action. The organization's current educational programming involves film, video, library resources and affiliated experts focusing on global economics, the environment and media literacy as it relates to development issues. IDERA also engages in a limited number of projects which are identified through formal and informal linkages with the NGO community and in cooperation with the British Columbia Council of International Cooperation (BCCIC). IDERA welcomes volunteers to its Canadian educational programming activities. [ID:5105]

London Cross Cultural Learner Centre (LCCLC)
717 Dundas Street E., London, Ontario N5W 2Z5; (519) 432-1133, fax (519) 660-6168, cclc@esc.net

The global education program of the London Cross Cultural Learner Centre (LCCLC) reaches out to the London and area community to increase awareness of global issues and to provide opportunities for involvement. LCCLC provides events and workshops to the general public throughout the year. It also offers programs for students at every level, from elementary to postsecondary. A multi-media resource centre with materials on development and global issues is open to the public.

LCCLC also publishes a monthly newsletter and calendar of events which allows other community organizations to publicize their own events. Many of these groups use LCCLC facilities for their meetings. Fact sheets and bibliographies are produced occasionally. Volunteers are important in every area of LCCLC programming. [ID:5109]

Marquis Project
711 Rosser Ave., Brandon, Manitoba R7A 0K8; (204) 727-5675, fax (204) 727-5683, marquis@docker.com

Marquis operates a resource centre and development education program, which places emphasis on the environment and rural development. It focuses its efforts on a target group of schools and rural Manitoba communities. In addition to providing speakers, teacher inservices, and classroom presentations, Marquis organizes conferences and workshops on a variety of issues. It produces four newsletters annually, along with various other publications. Marquis also runs a multicultural crafts outlet on its premises. Volunteers participate by staffing sales tables, organizing the resource centre, hosting events, etc. [ID:5117]

OPIRG-Carleton
326 Unicentre, Carleton University, 1125 Colonel By Drive, Ottawa, Ontario K1S 5B6;
(613) 520-2757, fax (613) 520-3989, opirg@carleton.ca, www.web.net/opirg/description

OPIRG-Carleton (Ontario Public Interest Research Group at Carleton University) works on a variety of human rights, social justice and environment issues. Their resource centre has extensive sections on international issues, food, human rights and peace. Working groups, which are the hub of the centre's educational programming, are organized by theme: i.e. Southeast Asia, Multilateral Agreement on Investment, and the impacts of Dams and Reservoirs. Visit their web site for more information and links to other PIRGs across Canada. [ID:6323]

OXFAM-Canada
Suite 300, 294 Albert Street, Ottawa, Ontario K1P 6E6;
(613) 237-5236, fax (613) 237-0524, enquire@oxfam.ca, www.oxfam.ca

OXFAM-Canada is a non-profit international development agency that works with partner organizations to develop self-reliant and sustainable communities. Domestically, OXFAM works through regional offices across Canada to raise public awareness of international development issues and build support for their work.

Program themes are Food and Health Security, Democratic Rights, Women, and Youth. OXFAM produces pamphlets, videos, posters, and a quarterly newsletter, *The Campaigner*. Bridgehead Inc. is OXFAM's ethical trading organization.

OXFAM has a national web site with regional and international links, providing information about the organization's mission, history, and OXFAM International. [ID:6351]

Peace and Environment Resource Centre
P.O. Box 4075, Stn "E", Ottawa, Ontario K1S 5B1; (613) 230-4590,
fax (613) 230-3608, perc@web.net OR perc@flora.org, www.perc.flora.org

The Peace and Environment Resource Centre offers a resource library with materials in the form of books, magazines and vertical files on global social justice issues. It also produces a monthly newspaper, a radio show, talks, and workshops. The centre is volunteer-driven and works closely with local grassroots groups seeking social change. Open part-time, the Peace and Environment Resource Centre is located at 174 First Ave., Ottawa. [ID:6352]

RESULTS Canada
Suite 503, 49th Ave. S.W., Calgary, Alberta T2S 1G4; (403) 287-7212,
fax (403) 287-7212, littlec@cadvision.com, www.ualberta.ca/~ckunle/results/

RESULTS Canada (Responsibility for Ending Starvation Utilizing Legislation, Trimtabs and Support) is an international aid policy advocacy group with a decentralized structure and offices across Canada and abroad. Participants learn to communicate their knowledge powerfully and effectively; they write letters and make direct appeals to their elected representatives, government officials and to the media to ensure the political system is accountable and responsible for ending hunger and poverty. Resource materials include videos, tapes, documents and action sheets; there is a monthly mailout of media updates. Visit their web page where there is more information and links. [ID:6350]

St. John's OXFAM Committee
P.O. Box 18000, St. John's, Nfld. A1C 6C2; (709) 753-2202, fax (709) 753-4110

St. John's OXFAM Committee operates a resource library which provides books, videos, and other materials with a global focus to the people of Newfoundland and Labrador. It carries out educational activities, such as lectures, workshops, and conferences, and brings international guests together with their local counterparts to address issues of global concern— gender, health, labour, etc. It also offers its facilities and meeting space to community groups concerned with social justice. [ID:5115]

Unisphere Global Resource Centre
101 - 6th Street S.E., Medicine Hat, Alberta T1A 1G7; (403) 529-2656,
fax (403) 529-0540, unispher@tst-medhat.com, www.combdyn.com/~med-hat/unisphere/

Unisphere is a nonprofit volunteer organization, focusing on international development and social justice concerns. Unisphere maintains a resource centre, lending videos, magazines, books, and educational kits to its members. Unisphere publishes a monthly newsletter, *Our Backyard*, and produces a weekly cable show *Unisphere Presents*. Unisphere works in cooperation with like-minded nonprofit agencies to provide displays, speakers, workshops, educational resources and special events programming. [ID:5119]

Village International Sudbury (VIS)
Global Education Centre, Centre d'éducation globale,
495 Notre Dame, Sudbury, Ontario P3C 5K9; (705) 671-2648, fax (705) 674-6311

Village International Sudbury (VIS) is a nonprofit, bilingual, community-based global education centre whose mission is to promote awareness and action on global development issues. VIS also promotes fair trade by providing a marketplace for goods produced by artisans from around the world. Its services to the public include a resource library, publication of the newsletter *Global Village Sudbury*, and organization of special events. [ID:5122]

World Citizens Centre
1011 - 4th Ave. S., Lethbridge, Alberta T1J 0P7; (403) 328-5725,
fax (403) 328-5733, worldcitizen@upanet.uleth.ca, http://upanet.uleth.ca/~worldcitizen

The World Citizens Centre maintains an excellent library of resources on global, environmental, and anti-racist education themes. The library is open to public in the Lethbridge area; membership in the organization permits users to borrow resources. The Tapestry Project, an antiracist teacher education project, works with school boards, teachers, and other interested parties to provide workshops and education aimed at institutional change. Other programs include an International Film Festival and International Dinner.

The World Citizens Centre is a member agency of Lethbridge Lifelong Learning Association and receives partial financial assistance through the Alberta Human Rights, Citizenship and Multiculturalism Branch. [ID:5123]

World Inter-Action Mondiale (WIAM)
180 Argyle, Ottawa, Ontario K2P 1B7; (613) 238-4659, fax (613) 564-4428, wia@web.net

World Inter-Action Mondiale (WIAM) is founded on the belief that solutions to global development rest with community-level action and awareness. WIAM works with local individuals and organizations to promote progressive educational and cultural events, with a view to fostering links between local and world communities. World Inter-Action Mondiale offers a number of programs and services. In addition to maintaining an extensive resource library and publishing a bimonthly newsletter, WIAM coordinates the One World Film Festival—an annual alternative film event focusing on development, human rights, and environmental issues—and organizes workshops on a variety of related issues. WIAM is also active in radio programming and community support. [ID:5124]

Worldwise International Resource Centre
125 Welland Ave., St. Catharines, Ontario L2R 2N5; (905) 641-2525, fax (905) 682-4314

Worldwise International Resource Centre is a community-based global education resource centre, dedicated to fostering awareness among Canadians of global issues and the interdependence of all peoples. The centre promotes understanding of the relationships between Canadians and the peoples of Central and South America, Asia, Africa, and the Caribbean. Worldwise has an extensive resource library and, in concert with international, national and local community groups, organizes a variety of special events. The centre also publishes a quarterly newsletter. Worldwise is one of the 14 global education centres of Ontario, and a member of the Ontario Council for International Cooperation. [ID:5125]

Chapter 14

Study Abroad

No matter what your career path, studying abroad can benefit you. Quite simply, it will enrich your life in a number of ways. As an overseas student, you will gain important insights into international issues and acquire new skills and sensibilities. The whole experience will improve your International IQ, giving you a necessary edge in an increasingly internationalized world.

Students returning from overseas study will be the first to tell you that learning is not restricted to the classroom. Living day-to-day in a foreign environment gives you a deeper understanding of life outside Canada and forces you to examine your own cultural values as you become sensitive to those of your host country. Studying abroad allows you to come away with a better understanding of the people and politics of the country you are studying in. This will impress a potential employer and prove to her that you are willing to live overseas and are able to adapt to new surroundings.

Studying abroad also gives you the chance to learn a new language or brush up on your existing language skills. In fact, for those embarking on an international career, proficiency in a second, and often third, language is usually mandatory. Stories abound about people losing out on the perfect job opportunity because they weren't able to speak a second language like Spanish, French or Japanese. Even if the language you are proficient in is not the one required by an overseas employer, it demonstrates that you are capable of learning another language. Learn a second language is a recurring piece of advice given by Canadian businesses with international operations to job seekers.

WHO CAN STUDY OVERSEAS?

For years, the opportunity to travel and enjoy overseas education was restricted to the wealthy. In the last twenty years however, international educational traffic has risen exponentially, thanks to the relative ease of international travel, a growing appreciation for the practical value of international education, and a huge increase in international study programs. These days, almost any student, in any given subject area, with interests in any region of the world, can find an appropriate study program. Because of the number and variation of study programs out there, researching the program that best serves your interests and objectives is important.

If you make a commitment to study abroad, seek out the situation that is right for you, and face it with a spirit of adventure and independence. The benefits you will derive from an international education will be enormous and will pay big dividends in your future international career.

Let's look at two people who chose to study abroad.

• Ted is dedicated to improving the international environment. A master's student in Ottawa, he has a particular interest in governments and organizations in the European community which stress environmental issues. Feeling that his Ottawa program lacked a hands-on element, he looked into spending a year studying in Europe. His decision to live in Scotland and study at the UNIVERSITY OF EDINBURGH has had a lasting effect on his life, personally and professionally, giving him an invaluable preparation for his international career. He has now travelled throughout the United Kingdom, as well as Europe and Russia. Because of his determination to study abroad, Ted has gained a good understanding of issues and cultures in the European community, especially as they relate to the environment. He has made friends and contacts and has already been back to attend student conferences.

• Fiona wanted to improve her French and take a break after a demanding year in her graduate program in Alberta. She applied for one of many short-term language study programs through EUROCENTRES. Although the program was relatively expensive, all the arrangements and details were taken care of as part of the package. Fiona enrolled in three weeks of intensive language instruction and lived with a family in Amboise, located in the scenic Loire Valley, who provided accommodation and meals. Above all, the program provided a wonderful opportunity to live in a French milieu and practice the language every day. Although three weeks was not a long enough period to become fluent, Fiona's French improved considerably. Equally important, she met students from around the world and travelled in France and Britain after she completed her course. Apart from the linguistic and cultural benefits, she found that studying abroad and travelling on her own gave her a strong sense of independence and made her more self-reliant and confident.

WHAT KINDS OF PROGRAMS ARE AVAILABLE?

Educational programs vary in length, price, academic rigor, course type, student mix, etc. In general, there are three categories of overseas educational programs.

Undergraduate Study Abroad: Academic Year or Semester Abroad

Most Canadian universities and colleges have already established exchange programs or formal exchange agreements that allow students to accumulate academic credits overseas. It is often possible to spend an entire year abroad, though sometimes these programs are restricted to specific countries and particular universities. Opportunities vary widely from university to university.

Contact your university international centre to explore the options available to you. You should also investigate study abroad programs in your field of study offered by other Canadian universities, as several universities accept students from other schools, and credits are usually transferable. Some foreign universities offer programs designed specifically for visiting students. These are usually in the arts and humanities, and emphasize language training. It may be more difficult to acquire academic credit at your university for this type of study abroad, but credit or not, this is a great way to learn a language and immerse yourself in another culture.

Graduate Study Abroad

Overseas universities openly welcome non-nationals who already possess undergraduate degrees. There is an advantage here because many more scholarships and bursaries are open to graduate than undergraduate students. A number of resources listed at the end of this chapter, and elsewhere in this section, will provide further information on foreign universities and scholarship programs. Another source of information is professors in the faculty of your chosen field of study. Seek them out: many professors will have studied or taught abroad themselves. Keep in mind that every university has its own guidelines and procedures for accepting international students.

Even if you are enrolled in a Canadian university for your graduate degree, opportunities to study abroad are numerous. Programs vary in length, formality and structure. Again, your university's international centre and the faculty within your department are the best places to make inquiries.

Summer and Short-term Programs for International Students

This is a popular route for those who may not wish to pursue a complete university degree or academic credit, and for students who prefer not to interrupt their academic year. Entrance requirements are usually more lenient and short-term cultural programs and intensive language courses can be squeezed into the summer or combined with holidays. However, the classes are usually comprised of North Americans like yourself and hence, they may not be as beneficial from a crosscultural point of view. For information on such programs, see the resources at the end of this section. Embassies and High Commissions located here in Canada are another source of information.

LIMITATIONS AND OPTIONS

For the most part, enrolling in a formal exchange program at a Canadian university is fairly easy; applicants should be in good academic standing and be able to demonstrate the relevance of a particular program in their area of study. Acquiring credit for these programs is usually part of the deal, so this isn't an issue. However, regardless of the reality, some Canadian universities perceive academic standards in some countries, particularly in the South, as less rigorous than those in Canada. This may create problems in having the courses you take recognized for full academic credit when you return to Canada. If getting academic credit for your program overseas is a priority, then it is probably a good idea to discuss these sorts of issues with the appropriate administrators before you embark upon your overseas learning experience. In some cases it is possible to arrange for academic credit in advance of your departure, often by enrolling in a special topics or self-directed reading course offered through your department. If your department doesn't offer these types of courses, ask around to find out which departments or professors are inclined to support a similar arrangement. Perhaps you'll be able to work something out and have the courses you take overseas applied to your degree program.

Even if you are forced to forgo academic credit, your study abroad experience can still be worthwhile, especially if you are planning an international career. And you don't always have to be enrolled at a Canadian university to qualify for these programs.

Another significant barrier to studying overseas is financing. Unless you are studying in Japan, scholarships and bursaries are difficult to come by, and are often reserved for nationals. Getting assistance in Canada can also be tricky. It will take an extra effort to have the CANADA STUDENT LOAN PROGRAM cough up the additional money for studies overseas. (For suggestions on how to secure funding and financial support see Chapter 15, Awards & Grants.) Language can also be a barrier, not only for studying, but also for living in your host country. If your program doesn't include language training, language lessons, for at least the basics beforehand, is a good idea.

Be sure to choose your living arrangements carefully. You want to ensure that you don't surround yourself solely with Canadians and other English-speakers. One of the best ways to maximize your study abroad experience is by living with a host family. You will get insight into the culture and improve your language skills considerably. If you decide to live with a host family, you should try and make sure that you are compatible with the family before moving in, and also have backup options in case things don't work out.

An academic contact in the country you're planning to visit is also an asset. Find out which professors at your university are engaged in overseas projects or research and ask them to link you up with a college or friend in the country in which you are heading. A helpful and friendly voice in an otherwise confusing and daunting environment, especially at first, will be most welcome.

Apart from considering how much time you're willing to devote to an international study program, you should also look at the viability of a particular program. Determine whether the institution has adequate resources and facilities. What is the status of the library and how are the laboratories equipped? Does it have computer facilities? If you are planning to live on campus, the conditions of the living quarters and who and how many share accommodations are important questions to ask. You might also want to consider the social aspects of university life: are there any athletic or social clubs? Does the university provide counseling services to foreign students? All of these elements are important factors in a successful overseas educational experience and should be taken into account throughout the planning process.

PREPARATION

Taking the time to select an overseas study program is important. If you decide on a short-term summer study program, it usually won't entail a lot of complicated planning or take a lot of preparation. But if you are planning a long-term academic exchange or year abroad, you will have to start thinking ahead, at least nine to 12 months prior to the date of your intended departure. Most applications must be submitted by early January. Scholarship programs also usually require completed applications, accompanied by letters of reference, by January or February. If you are applying to graduate studies, you may have to write relevant subject exams, and probably a *Graduate Records Exam* (GRE), in the summer or fall.

The *International Student Identity Card* is available from the VIA RAIL and TRAVEL CUTS offices, which are found in most large Canadian cities. This card offers internationally-recognized proof of student status and is available to full-time students from the age of 12 and up. To get the card you will have to provide proof of your student status along with a passport size photo and your student card. For under $20, the card is well worth the price; you can receive discounts for lodging, restaurants, museum admissions and even transportation.

For many destinations, you will also require various immunization shots. Receiving these shots can take several weeks, so don't leave them until the last minute. Contact your provincial health department, or HEALTH CANADA, to find out about requirements for particular countries. And also be sure to arrange for medical and other insurance coverage.

Lastly, don't arrive in ignorance. Read up on the history, culture and current political-economic climate of the country you will be visiting. It's also a good idea to read up on culture shock and its effects.

A LAST WORD

The most important thing to remember in planning a study abroad program is to match your needs and interests with the program you choose. Consider what length of time you are willing to spend studying abroad, how rigorous a program you want, whether you want to receive academic credit at your home university, and how much money you have at your disposal.

You also have to realize that certain trade-offs may be involved. You may have to forego academic credit in exchange for the cultural benefits you will receive. A long-term program may interrupt your program of study at your Canadian university, and will require a long separation from family and friends. Short-term programs, while unlikely to interrupt your study program and living pattern, may only allow you to scratch the surface of a foreign culture and only rarely provides enough time to learn another language. If you also want time to travel, your study time will likely be further limited. Similarly, while living with a host family might take some adjusting to at first, it will enrich your overseas experience immeasurably.

In general, you should study in a country or a region of the world which you find interesting or would like to get to know better. And, as always, consider how the experience is going to help you along your chosen path—a career in the international arena.

RESOURCES

Many of these books focus on American study abroad programs which are usually open to Canadians. The programs range from leisurely, vacation-oriented study to serious, degree-oriented academic study. Whatever your field, make sure you broaden your experience by getting involved in the local culture.

To help you further, consult Chapter 10, Short-term Programs Overseas; Chapter 15, Awards & Grants; Chapter 16, International Studies in Canada & Abroad; and Chapter 17, International Internships.

Also consult the Resources sections in the following chapters: for general crosscultural skills see Chapter 1, The Effective Overseas Employee; for the more practical aspects of living overseas see Chapter 3, Living Overseas and Chapter 12, Crosscultural Travel; for material which is helpful to all, but focuses on crosscultural business skills, see Chapter 7, The Canadian Identity in the International Workplace; for country-specific advice on social and business customs see Chapter 27, Jobs by Regions of the World; and for books on the practice of international business (such as how to import and export) see Chapter 33, Services for International Businesses & Entrepreneurs.

Academic Year Abroad 📖
Annual, *Sara Steen* ➤ Publication Service, Institute of International Education, P.O. Box 371, Annapolis Junction, MD 20701-0371, USA; US$42.95; VISA, MC; (800) 445-0443, fax (301) 206-9789 ▪ Detailed information on all study-abroad programs (graduate and undergraduate) sponsored by US universities and colleges during the regular academic year. Contains good annotated bibliography by regions of the world. [ID:1169]

University of Alberta International Centre 💻
www.intlcent.ualberta.ca ▪ The University of Alberta International Centre offers a number of resources for undergraduate university students wishing to study abroad. While some of the services offered at this site are exclusively for the students of the University of Alberta, much of the information is available to the general public. The site provides international news, advice for exchange students, and links to several international programs. If you are considering studying abroad, this site is worth a look. [ID:2423]

The Alternative Travel Directory 1996 📖
Annual, *Transitions Abroad,* 400 pages ➤ Department TRA, Transitions Publishing, P.O. Box 3000, Denville, NJ 07834, USA; $19.95; VISA, MC; (413) 256-3414, fax (413) 256-0373, trabroad@aol.com ▪ The definitive annual guide to the "best of the best" resources on working, studying, and travelling abroad. Includes hundreds of annotated listings. A rich resource for navigating the international arena. Visit the distributor's web site at www.transabroad.com. [ID:1758]

Canadian Bureau for International Education 💻
www.cbie.ca ▪ CBIE is an organization of 110 colleges and universities which promotes international understanding through active exchange of people and ideas. A number of schools, organizations and companies also participate in CBIE's programs. The organization focuses on international exchanges at the university level, and provides information and advice for Canadian students travelling abroad and foreign students in Canada. [ID:2473]

Canadian University Distance Education Directory 📖
Annual, Canadian Association for University Continuing Education, 154 pages ➤ AUCC Publications Office, Suite 600, 350 Albert Street, Ottawa, Ontario K1R 1B1; $26; (613) 563-1236, fax (613) 563-9745 ▪ Bilingual listing of universities offering distance education courses in Canada. Useful for those wishing to study with a Canadian university while abroad. [ID:1366]

Commonwealth Universities Yearbook 📖
Annual, Association of Commonwealth Universities ➤ UBC Press, University of British Columbia, 6344 Memorial Rd., Vancouver, B.C. V6T 1Z2; $289; VISA, MC; (604) 822-3259, fax (800) 668-0821, orders@ubcpress.ubc.ca; available in large libraries ▪ The most comprehensive guide to courses, staff, organizations and special interests of over 400 Commonwealth universities worldwide. Four volumes. [ID:1079]

Cours de français langue étrangère et stages pour professeurs.
Répertoire des centres de formation en France. 📖
1994-95, Ministère des Affaires Étrangères Sous-Direction de la politique linguistique et éducative, 153 pages ➤ Service Culturel, Ambassade de France, 464 rue Wilbrod, Ottawa, Ontario K1N 6M8; gratuit; (613) 238-5713, fax (613) 238-7884 ▪ Cette brochure propose un répertoire des cours de français langue étrangère destinés aux étudiants et des stages pédagogiques pour professeurs organisés en France. [ID:1067]

Culture Shock: All You Need to Know about Studying Overseas 📖
1996, *Robert Barlas, Guek-Cheng Pang,* Graphic Arts Center Publishing Co., 156 pages ➤ Raincoast Books, 8680 Cambie Street, Vancouver, B.C. V6P 6M9; $17.50; VISA, MC; (800) 663-5714, fax (800) 565-3770 ▪ This book is for students who want to attend institutions of higher learning outside their home country. Its wealth of information will put students in a better position to make informed decisions about where to study and how to take that first step. Also examines the initial problems of adjustment that are bound to arise when away from home. [ID:2717]

The Directory of Work & Study in Developing Countries 📖
1997, *David Leppard,* Vacation Work ➤ Capricorn Business Services, Inc., 28 Clear Lake Ave., West Hill, Ontario M1C 4L6; $23.95; credit cards; (416) 282-3331, fax (416) 282-0015 ▪ British reference guide to short- and long-term work, volunteer and educational opportunities in the developing world. Listings in each of the three sections are organized by region. [ID:1158]

Employment in France for Students 📖
1991 ➤ Cultural Services of the French Embassy, 464 Wilbrod Street, Ottawa, Ontario K1N 6M8; free; (613) 238-5711, fax (613) 238-5713 ▪ Brochure of work regulations and opportunities for students in France. Includes additional references. [ID:1418]

The Exchange Student Survival Kit 📖
1993, Intercultural Press, 122 pages ➤ Intercultural and Community Development Resources (ICDR), P.O. Box 32108, Millwoods Station, Edmonton, Alberta T6K 4C2; $20; VISA, Amex; (800) 378-3199, fax (403) 462-1925, icdr@compusmart.ab.ca ▪ Helps students better understand the exchange experience and adjust to a new culture. Based on years of research and professional involvement with AFS Intercultural Programs. Uses examples based on the experiences of exchange students from various cultures. A useful resource for native English speakers. Visit the distributor's web site at www.compusmart.ab.ca/icdr. [ID:1324]

Foreign Government Awards Program 💻
www.iccs-ciec.ca ▪ An excellent resource for students planning graduate studies abroad. Outlines the awards, applications and qualification requirements of foreign government awards in nine countries of Europe and South America. [ID:1029]

Guide to Living, Studying, and Working in the People's Republic of China and Hong Kong 📖
Annual, *Jane Parker, Janet Rodgers* ➤ Yale-China Association, 442 Temple Street, Box 208223, New Haven, CT 06520, USA; US$5; cheque or money order; (203) 432-0880, fax (203) 432-7246, ycassoc@minerva.cis.yale.edu ▪ Contains information on language programs, tuition, travel, living conditions and up-to-date information on procedures for obtaining teaching positions and other jobs. [ID:1274]

The Handbook of Foreign Student Advising 📖
1995, *Gary Althen,* Intercultural Press, 296 pages ➤ Intercultural and Community Development Resources (ICDR), P.O. Box 32108, Millwoods Station, Edmonton, Alberta T6K 4C2; $28; VISA, Amex; (800) 378-3199, fax (403) 462-1925, icdr@compusmart.ab.ca ▪ A systematic examination of virtually every phase of foreign student advising. Reviews the basic process, discusses problem areas, recommends new strategies, and identifies resources needed. Analyzes the place of the foreign student and advisor in the academic environment. Visit the distributor's web site at www.compusmart.ab.ca/icdr. [ID:1329]

How to Study Abroad 📖
1996, *Teresa Tinsley,* 128 pages ➤ How To Books Ltd., 3 Newtec Place, Magdalen Road, Oxford, OX4 1RE, UK; £8.99; credit cards; (44) (1752) 202-301, fax (44) (1865) 202-331 ▪ A wealth of fascinating advice and reference information. This book covers what to study (everything from short study visits to postgraduate opportunities), entrance requirements, when and how to apply, grants and scholarships, helpful agencies and contacts, and more. [ID:1679]

I Am Going to France: 1994-1995 📖
Annual, Centre National des Oeuvres Universitaires et Scolaires ➤ Cultural Services of the French Embassy, 464 Wilbrod Street, Ottawa, Ontario K1N 6M8; free; (613) 238-5711, fax (613) 238-5713 ▪ A handbook intended for students wishing to study in France. Provides a wealth of information on French higher education, accommodation, and settling for foreign students. Contains a brief presentation on France from geographical, economic, technological and cultural points of view, and a description of the practical organization of daily life in France. Also available in French under the title, *Je vais en France.* [ID:1640]

International Directory of Canadian Studies 📖
1997, *Didier Cencig, Christian Pouyez* ➤ International Council for Canadian Studies, Suite 800, 325 Dalhousie Street, Ottawa, Ontario K1N 7G2; $30; VISA, MC; (613) 789-7834, fax (613) 789-7830 ▪ Listing of centres around the world who offer Canadian Studies programs. Visit the distributor's web site at www.iccs-ciec.ca. [ID:1186]

International Handbook of Universities 📖
1993 ➤ Stockton Press, 345 Park Avenue South, New York, NY 10010-1707, USA; US$245; credit cards; (800) 221-2123, fax (212) 689-9711; Available in large libraries ▪ A comprehensive and authoritative source of in-depth information on all graduate degree-granting universities worldwide. Excellent for initial research on where to study abroad. Visit the distributor's web site at www.grovestocktn.com. [ID:1642]

International Youth and Young Workers Exchange Programs 💻
www.dfait-maeci.gc.ca/english/culture/youthex.html ▪ This site, maintained by the Department of Foreign Affairs and International Trade (Canada) offers information on a number of government-sponsored programs for international employment and study. Many of the bilateral exchange and working holiday programs profiled in this chapter are listed on the site. There are also a number of thematic programs designed to help individuals with specific interests find

employment overseas. This is a very good site, although many of the programs listed are not online and must be contacted through conventional means. [ID:2505]

Learning Across Cultures 📖
1994, *Gary Althen,* 200 pages ➤ National Association for Foreign Student Affairs, P.O. Box 1020, Sewickley, PA 15143, USA; US$19; VISA, MC; (800) 836-4994, fax (412) 741-0609 ▪ A vital overview of the application of the concepts and practices of intercultural communication to international educational exchange. Includes recent developments in intercultural relations, counselling student sojourners, and the dynamics of adapting to a new cultural environment, managing culture in the ESL classroom. Visit the publisher's web site at www.nafsa.org. [ID:1687]

Learning Adventures Around the World 📖
Annual, 960 pages ➤ Peterson's Guides, P.O. Box 2123, Princeton, NJ 08543-2123, USA; US$24.95; cheque or money order; (800) 338-3282, fax (609) 243-9150 ▪ A vast array of opportunities for travel and learning, with details on each program's focus, costs, location, housing and more. Visit the publisher's web site at www.petersons.com. [ID:2497]

NAFSA's Guide to Education Abroad for Advisors and Administrators 📖
1997, *William Hoffa, John Pearson, Marvin Slind,* 494 pages ➤ National Association for Foreign Student Affairs, P.O. Box 1020, Sewickley, PA 15143, USA; US$45; VISA, MC; (800) 836-4994, fax (412) 741-0609 ▪ An indispensable reference for education abroad offices. Gives an overview of the education abroad office, as well as tips on advising principals, diversity in education abroad, health issues, and pre-departure and re-entry programming. The final section covers planning, budgeting, and implementation of programs, as well as work abroad. Includes case histories, a bibliography, and a program evaluation guide. Visit www.nafsa.org. [ID:1605]

Online Study Abroad Directory 🖥️
www.istc.umn.edu/osad/ ▪ This site, a service of the International Study and Travel Centre at the University of Minnesota–Twin Cities, is the site for study abroad information. It allows you to search for programmes using any criteria, supplying a profile and e-mail address for each program you are interested in. Lists the most affordable programs in the "Rock Bottom Study Abroad" sub-field. Also has a large database for scholarships. [ID:2683]

Peterson's Guides 📖 🖥️
Annual, Peterson's Guides ➤ Nelson Canada, 1120 Birchmount Road, Scarborough, Ontario M1K 5G4; credit cards; (800) 268-2222, fax (800) 430-4445 ▪ An annual series of books which provides exhaustive coverage of the institutions and subject areas of undergraduate and graduate academic programs in Canada and the US. Contains information on entrance and degree requirements, expenses, financial aid and programs of study. Series includes: Graduate Programs in the Humanities, Arts, and Social Sciences; Biological and Agricultural Sciences; Physical Sciences and Mathematics; Engineering and Applied Sciences; Business, Education, Health, and Law. As well, there are *Peterson's Guide to Four-Year Programs* and *Peterson's Guide to Two-Year Programs,* both of which provide a detailed look at undergraduate academic institutions. Visit their web site at http://www.petersons.com/ for prices and contents of each guide. [ID:1543]

Sports Scholarships and College Athletic Programs in the USA 📖
1996, Peterson's Guides ➤ Capricorn Business Services, Inc., 28 Clear Lake Ave., West Hill, Ontario M1C 4L6; $41.95; credit cards; (416) 282-3331, fax (416) 282-0015 ▪ A college-by-college guide to sports scholarships and collegiate sports programs. Intended for men and women who want to use their athletic abilities either to pay their college bills or improve their chances of admission to a US college. [ID:1593]

Student Travels Magazine 📖
Semiannual ➤ Publications Dept., Council on International Educational Exchange, 205 East 42nd Street, New York, NY 10017, USA; free; VISA, MC; (212) 822-2600, fax (212) 822-2699 ▪ Student magazine with information on how to travel, study, work or volunteer abroad. [ID:2405]

Students Abroad, Strangers At Home: Education for a Global Society 📖
1992, *Norman L. Kauffmann, Judith N. Martin, Henry D. Weaver,* Intercultural Press, 208 pages ➤ Intercultural and Community Development Resources (ICDR), P.O. Box 32108, Millwoods Station, Edmonton, Alberta T6K 4C2; $27; VISA, Amex; (800) 378-3199, fax (403) 462-1925, icdr@compusmart.ab.ca ▪ A guide to designing study-abroad programs that work. Aimed at educators wishing to re-evaluate their study-abroad college programs. Examines the experience from the students' viewpoint. Offers a framework to evaluate programs, increase their effectiveness and integrate them into the curriculum. Visit the distributor's web site at www.compusmart.ab.ca/icdr. [ID:1023]

Study Abroad 📖
Annual, UNESCO, 1008 pages ➤ Renouf Publishing Co. Ltd., Unit 1, 5369 Canotek Road, Ottawa, Ontario K1J 9J3; $41.95 for book or CD-ROM, $54 for both; credit cards; (613) 745-2665, fax (613) 745-7660 ▪ A listing of more than 2,500 international study programs around the world, and a sourcebook for financial assistance offered by governments, international organizations, universities and foundations in over 100 countries. [ID:1239]

Study Abroad 📖
44 pages ➤ Publications Dept., Council on International Educational Exchange, 205 East 42nd Street, New York, NY 10017, USA; free; VISA, MC; (212) 822-2600, fax (212) 822-2699 ▪ This brochure describes the CIEE's programs at international universities. Opportunities span the globe with detailed course, elegibility, cost information, and with personal accounts offered for each university. [ID:2681]

Study Abroad 1997/1998 Council Study Centres 📖
44 pages ➤ Publications Dept., Council on International Educational Exchange, 205 East 42nd Street, New York, NY 10017, USA; free; VISA, MC; (212) 822-2600, fax (212) 822-2699 ▪ This brochure describes each of the CIEE's Study Centres. Centres are located in Europe, Asia, Oceania, Africa, the Caribbean, and Latin America. A plethora of courses and internships are offered at each location. [ID:2682]

Studying Abroad / Learning Abroad 📖
1997, *J. Daniel Hess,* Intercultural Press, 159 pages ➤ Intercultural and Community Development Resources (ICDR), P.O. Box 32108, Millwoods Station, Edmonton, Alberta T6K 4C2; $20; VISA, Amex; (800) 378-3199, fax (403) 462-1925, icdr@compusmart.ab.ca ▪ A student-friendly framework for sorting through the dynamics of studying abroad as well as a thorough review of the cultural learning process. Visit the distributor's web site at www.compusmart.ab.ca/icdr. [ID:2447]

Transitions Abroad: The Magazine of Overseas Opportunities 📖
Bimonthly, *Clay Hubb* ➤ Department TRA, Transitions Publishing, P.O. Box 3000, Denville, NJ 07834, USA; $29.95/year; VISA, MC; (413) 256-3414, fax (413) 256-0373, trabroad@aol.com ▪ An excellent periodical. Required reading for students and globe trotters planning to travel, study or work abroad. Promotes learning through direct involvement in the daily lives of peoples of host countries. Describes publications, information sources, organizations, and programs offering study opportunities, entry-level jobs, and living arrangements abroad. Visit the distributor's web site at www.transabroad.com. [ID:1253]

Update 📖
Bimonthly ➤ Publications Dept., Council on International Educational Exchange, 205 East 42nd Street, New York, NY 10017, USA; free; VISA, MC; (212) 822-2600, fax (212) 822-2699 ▪ A resource dealing with international education. Covers work, study, and travel abroad for US students. [ID:1552]

Vacation Study Abroad 📖
Annual, *Sara Steen* ➤ Publication Service, Institute of International Education, P.O. Box 371, Annapolis Junction, MD 20701-0371, USA; US$36.95; VISA, MC; (800) 445-0443, fax (301) 206-9789 ▪ Details summer study programs by region and country, and short-term programs available year-round to US students. Covers costs and application procedures, academic programs, and living arrangements. [ID:1168]

What In The World Is Going On? A Guide For Canadians
Wishing to Work, Volunteer, or Study in Other Countries 📖
1996, *Jennifer Humphries, Sienna Filleul,* 253 pages ➤ Canadian Bureau for International Education (CBIE), Suite 1100, 220 Laurier Ave W., Ottawa, Ontario K1P 5Z9; $14; VISA, Amex; (613) 237-4820, fax (613) 237-1073 ▪ Offers a bird's eye view of volunteer and study opportunities abroad. Good coverage of short- to medium-term volunteer positions. Also lists study abroad opportunities and international grants available to Canadian students. Available in French under the title, *Le tour du monde en 1001 projets.* [ID:1090]

World of Learning 1997 📖
1997, Europa Publications., 2,000 pages ➤ Gale Research Inc., 835 Penobscot Bldg., 645 Griswold Street, Detroit, MI 48226-4094, USA; US$445; credit cards; (800) 877-4253 ext. 1330, fax (800) 414-5043; Available in large libraries ▪ An excellent source for initial research on where to study abroad. This comprehensive, up-to-date international directory of educational, cultural and scientific institutions provides the names, addresses and details on more than 26,000 academies and learned societies, universities, colleges and other institutions of higher education. Also provides details on more than 400 international organizations. Visit the distributor's web site at www.gale.com. [ID:1146]

A World of Options: Guide to International Education Exchange,
Community Services, and Travel for Persons with Disabilities 📖
1997, *Susan Sygall,* 600 pages ➤ Mobility International USA, P.O. Box 3551, Eugene, OR 97403, USA; US$30; (541) 343-1284, fax (541) 343-6812 ▪ A descriptive resource covering hundreds of opportunities for the disabled in international educational exchange programs, work camps, and volunteer positions. Includes first-person accounts of travel and learning experiences. Visit the distributor's web site at www.miusa.org. [ID:1205]

Selected Opportunities

The following is a description of 7 selected opportunities for studying abroad. Chosen from universities across Canada and representing a variety of academic fields, these opportunities send students all over the world.

UNIVERSITY OF ALBERTA
The Tokyo Institute of Technology -
University of Alberta Science and Engineer Exchange
Coordinator, The Tokyo Institute of Technology - University of Alberta
Science and Engineering Exchange, International Centre, 172 HUB International,
Edmonton, Alberta T6G 2E2; (403) 492-2692, fax (403) 492-1134, www.intlcent.ualberta.ca

The Tokyo Institute of Technology - University of Alberta Student Exchange allows science and engineering graduate students at the University of Alberta to spend a full academic year studying in Japan. A central feature of the exchange is academic and social integration of participants into life at the university. A select number of courses are offered in English so a knowledge of Japanese is not necessary. The Tokyo Institute of Technology had played a major role in fostering the development of science and technology in Japan, and has a policy of educating the whole person by emphasizing both technical and liberal arts subjects.

Once accepted as an exchange student tuition and fees are paid at the University of Alberta. The equivalent costs incurred in Japan are waived by the Institute of Technology. Students are responsible for their accommodation and meals, return airfare, books, supplies, and other miscellaneous expenses. Exchange students are eligible for Canada and Alberta

Student Loans. Students that remain registered at the University of Alberta for the duration of the exchange are also eligible for University of Alberta scholarships and awards. [ID:6887]

BROCK UNIVERSITY
Intermediate Italian
Program Director, Department of French, Italian, and Spanish, Brock University,
St. Catharines, Ontario L2S 3A1; (905) 688-5550 ext. 3308, fax (905) 688-2789, www.brocku.ca

This six-week program in Florence and Rome reviews grammar and emphasizes complex structures, composition, and oral practice. Preference is given to students with at least an introductory knowledge of Italian, but special consent from the instructor is also available. The program costs $3,300 and includes airfare from Toronto. [ID:5127]

CONCORDIA UNIVERSITY
Guadalajara Watershed Program
Centre for International Academic Cooperation, Concordia University,
7141 Sherbrook Street W., Montréal, Québec H4B 1R6; (514) 848-4988,
fax (514) 848-2888, francis@vax2.concordia.ca, www.concordia.ca

As part of the Human Resources Development Program for North American Mobility in Higher Education, Concordia University, in conjunction with the University of Guelph, the University of Wisconsin-Madison, the University of Illinois and the University of Guadalajara, offers the Guadalajara Watershed Program, a program in Geography and Environmental Sciences. Offered to graduate students, and some highly-qualified under-graduate students, the program provides the opportunity of doing fieldwork in watershed management. The program begins with course work at Concordia University, which includes a placement in an outside agency, and then provides several months of field study at the University of Guadalajara. [ID:7100]

DALHOUSIE UNIVERSITY
Intensive Russian Language Program
Coordinator, Russian Studies Program, Department of Russian Studies, Dalhousie University,
Halifax, N.S. B3H 3J5; (902) 494-3473, fax (902) 494-1997, www.dal.ca/russwww/russwww.html

This intensive interdisciplinary Russian Studies Program, the first of its kind in Canada, allows students to undertake Russian language studies at St. Petersburg University in Russia during the Spring Term (end of January to the end of May). Students are encouraged to attend the Intensive Fall Term Study Program at Dalhousie University beforehand. Students must have a minimum of two years to four semesters of Russian, or the equivalent, with a standing of B or better. The cost of the program (which includes round-trip airfare, tuition and accommodation) is approximately $4,000. [ID:6886]

UNIVERSITY OF MANITOBA
Doing Business in Brazil Summer Program
Coordinator, International Exchange Programs, Faculty of Management,
University of Manitoba, 268 Drake Centre, Winnipeg, Manitoba R3T 2N2; (204) 474-6752,
fax (204) 474-7529, www.umanitoba.ca/management.services/interex/interex.html

The Doing Business in Brazil Summer Program is open to undergraduate and graduate students in the Faculty of Management at the University of Manitoba. This three week program is housed at the Fundaçáo Getulio Vargas Escola de Administraçáo de Empresas de Sáo Paulo, Brazil. This is one of many exchanges offered by the Faculty of Management, and serves as an opportunity to experience another culture, become aware of global issues and broaden personal perspectives. Courses include lectures on the political and social condition in Brazil, financing and banking, corporate taxes and capital flows and cultural environment.

The program includes weekly visits to Brazilian companies in various industries. The cost of the program, excluding airfare, is approximately US$700. [ID:7042]

SIMON FRASER UNIVERSITY
Southeast Asia Field School
Coordinator, Southeast Asia Field School, International and Exchange Centre,
MBC 1200, Simon Fraser University, Burnaby, B.C. V5A 1S6; (604) 291-4232,
fax (604) 291-5880, sfu-international@sfu.ca, www.reg.sfu.ca/iess/iess/html

The Department of Sociology and Anthropology at Simon Fraser University hosts the Southeast Asia Field School during the Spring semester (January to April). After one week of mandatory orientation at Simon Fraser, participants spend six weeks at Chiang Mai University, located on the outskirts of Chiang Mai city in northern Thailand. This is followed by six weeks of travel throughout northeastern, central and southern Thailand. The program examines current issues in Southeast Asian development, mainland Southeast Asian society, and Ecological Anthropology. The prerequisite for participation in the school is a good academic standing at a postsecondary institution; an introductory course in Anthropology is recommended. The program cost of approximately $5,000 covers accommodation, tuition and both international and domestic travel. Simon Fraser University also organizes other field schools in the Asian Pacific Region, including Bali, China, Fiji, and Java. [ID:7067]

UNIVERSITY OF WATERLOO
Institute of Peace and Conflict Studies Internship Program
Internship Program for Students of Peace and Conflict Studies, Conrad Grebel College, Waterloo,
Ontario N2L 3G6; (519) 885-0220, fax (519) 885-0014, ipacs2@watserv1.uwaterloo.ca, www.uwaterloo.ca

The Institute of Peace and Conflict Studies, located within Conrad Grebel College at the University of Waterloo, sends approximately 12 students overseas annually. Students must have completed at least two PAC courses. The internship is offered in all three semesters, and covers a four-month period. A stipend of up to $1,500 is available to approved candidates, and additional support comes from the hosting agencies overseas. There is no set fee for the program. However, if the entire cost is not covered through program funding, then the remainder is the student's responsibility. The program covers all regions of the world. Visit the University of Waterloo's web site for program information and course descriptions offered at the institute. [ID:5044]

Chapter 15

Awards & Grants

Going overseas to study can be an expensive proposition. To offset these costs, however, you can apply for awards, scholarships and grants. Finding the appropriate awards will involve much background research, careful planning, lots of follow-up, and a great deal of patience. This chapter lists 69 awards and grants to help you get started on finding funds for that exciting year of study abroad. But there are many other places to look, as well.

Start your research at a university, college, or public library. Libraries have a number of general guides which provide details on awards, and staff can help you find the right ones. Because the guides in libraries are often out of date, however, it is crucial that you follow up your initial research by directly contacting the institution that administers or disburses a particular award. Make sure all your information is up to date and you are aware of deadlines.

Some awards have a higher public profile than others. While these tend to be the ones of significant value, they also tend to be awarded on a very general, nationwide or even worldwide basis. As a result, they not only attract the most applicants, but have very rigid selection criteria and procedures, as well as inflexible deadlines. Consider looking for less prominent awards in your area of interest, and don't end your search at the library. Almost every university and college calendar lists internal awards which are scholarships available to students attending that university. There are literally hundreds of these awards at each school, and many of them are available for overseas study. Be sure also to check out the resources at your university's international centre. And it is generally worthwhile to ask your graduate association, your department, or your professors about awards and grants of which they may be aware.

When you find one, note the restrictions before you apply. Some awards are available only to candidates nominated by faculty, professional associations, or employers.

Many federal, provincial, and territorial government departments have specialized award programs. In addition, the Canadian government provides considerable amounts of money to universities and colleges for research. About 80 per cent of all federal research funds are channeled through three granting councils: The MEDICAL RESEARCH COUNCIL (MRC), the SOCIAL SCIENCES AND HUMANITIES RESEARCH COUNCIL (SSHRC), and the NATURAL SCIENCES AND ENGINEERING RESEARCH COUNCIL (NSERC). All of these councils have a variety of awards programs available for overseas study. Some of these are attached to specific research areas; but in many cases, the councils have general funds available for which you must submit a proposal for a specific project. An excellent way to find out what these councils have to offer is to check out their web sites. (For specific web site addresses see the profiles in this chapter.)

The CANADA STUDENT LOANS PROGRAM also supports overseas study. These funds are only available if the candidate can demonstrate that the particular program is relevant to their academic objectives and that a comparable program is not available in Canada. Provincial loans generally cannot be used outside the province from which they originate. However, your postsecondary institution may offer courses overseas in conjunction with other institutions, in which case you could be eligible for loans. Contact your university awards officer to find out which ones you are eligible for and how they apply to your program.

Before you go overseas, contact the embassy of the country in which you intend to study. Embassies sometimes administer programs, and they have information on organizations and institutions in that country which offer awards to foreign students. You can also contact professional associations, national foundations, international organizations and private corporations that offer specialized awards for overseas study. A surprising number of employers offer scholarships to their employees' children, so be sure to find what is available at your parents' places of work.

A LAST WORD

It is crucial that you start your search early. The deadline for many applications is six months to one year before the award is granted. We speak from experience when we say that there is nothing worse than finding a scholarship for which you fit all the criteria, only to discover that the deadline has passed. When filling out applications for awards, scholarships and grants, start the process well in advance of the deadline. This cannot be stressed enough: many applications require extensive documentation, carefully-written project proposals, letters of reference, résumés, and in some cases, short essays. These requirements put demands on your time, as well as the time of others. Don't underestimate how long it will take to properly complete an application.

RESOURCES

Researching awards and grants can be a slow, painstaking process. This list of books will help you find a program tailored to your particular international interest.

For more help consult Chapter 10, Short-term Programs Overseas; Chapter 14, Study Abroad; Chapter 16, International Studies in Canada & Abroad; and Chapter 17, International Internships.

After Latin American Studies: A Guide to Graduate Study, Fellowships, Internships, and Employment for Latin Americanists ⌨
1995, *Shirley A. Kregar,* 142 pages ➤ Center for Latin American Studies, 4E04 Forbes Quad, University of Pittsburgh, Pittsburgh, PA 15260, USA; $10; MC, Amex; (412) 648-7392, fax (412) 648-2199, clas+@cpitt.edu ■ Provides information on graduate study, research and internships. For graduate as well as undergraduate students, opportunities in the private sector, and career opportunities in the US government and in international organizations. An essential resource for anyone with career or scholarly interests in the region. Visit the distributor's web site at www.edu/~clas. [ID:1118]

Association of Universities and Colleges of Canada ▬
www.aucc.ca ■ AUCC operates several programs to help increase cooperation between Canadian and foreign universities. This site provides information on a number of international programs as well as academic exchanges, scholarships, and institutional links. There are also databases containing information on the international exchange agreements of various universities. [ID:2477]

The Awards Almanac ⌨
1996, *George W. Schmidt,* St. James Press, 899 pages ➤ Gale Research Inc., 835 Penobscot Bldg., 645 Griswold Street, Detroit, MI 48226-4094, USA; US$105; credit cards; (800) 877-4253 ext. 1330, fax (800) 414-5043 ■ Comprehensive information on grants, awards, scholarships, fellowships, and research funding in all disciplines. Profiling over 2,500 awards offered to citizens of any nation, the book is an invaluable tool for anyone pursuing advanced education or career development. Visit the distributor's web site at www.gale.com. [ID:1538]

Awards for First Degree Study at Commonwealth Universities ⌨
Biennial, Association of Commonwealth Universities, 88 pages ➤ UBC Press, University of British Columbia, 6344 Memorial Rd., Vancouver, B.C. V6T 1Z2; $19.95; VISA, MC; (604) 822-3259, fax (800) 668-0821, orders@ubcpress.ubc.ca ■ A guide to almost 150 scholarships, bursaries, grants, and loans for Commonwealth students wishing to study for a first degree at a university in another Commonwealth country. Many of the awards are for students from developing countries, and a substantial number are open to students of any nationality. [ID:1075]

Awards for Postgraduate Study at Commonwealth Universities ⌨
Biennial, Association of Commonwealth Universities, 428 pages ➤ UBC Press, University of British Columbia, 6344 Memorial Rd., Vancouver, B.C. V6T 1Z2; $49.95; VISA, MC; (604) 822-3259, fax (800) 668-0821, orders@ubcpress.ubc.ca ■ Information on 1,050 awards available to Commonwealth graduate scholars outside their own countries. Includes nearly 600 awards open to students of any nationality and nearly 200 tenable at non-university institutions. [ID:1668]

Awards for University Administrators and Librarians ⌨
Biennial, Association of Commonwealth Universities, 40 pages ➤ UBC Press, University of British Columbia, 6344 Memorial Rd., Vancouver, B.C. V6T 1Z2; £10.50; VISA, MC; (604) 822-3259, fax (800) 668-0821, orders@ubcpress.ubc.ca ■ Describes 43 sources of financial aid in both Commonwealth and non-Commonwealth countries. Lists awards tenable in one Commonwealth country by staff from another, awards for movement between Commonwealth and other countries, and other important information. [ID:1565]

Awards for University Teachers and Research Workers 📖
Biennial, Association of Commonwealth Universities, 364 pages ➤ UBC Press, University of British Columbia, 6344 Memorial Rd., Vancouver, B.C. V6T 1Z2; $49.95; VISA, MC; (604) 822-3259, fax (800) 668-0821, orders@ubcpress.ubc.ca ▪ Contains 730 award schemes, primarily within the Commonwealth. Includes information on some non-university institutions, organizations providing appointments, services, and consultancy opportunities, and organizations providing other forms of assistance. [ID:1566]

Canada-US Fulbright Program 🖳
www.usis-canada.usia.gov/fulbrigh.htm ▪ This web site provides information on the scholarships and fellowships offered to Canadian and American faculty and graduate students under the Canada-US Fulbright progam. [ID:2733]

Canadian Awards Program 📖
Annual, Association of Universities and Colleges of Canada (AUCC), 15 pages ➤ AUCC Publications Office, Suite 600, 350 Albert Street, Ottawa, Ontario K1R 1B1; free; (613) 563-1236, fax (613) 563-9745 ▪ Contains information on scholarships administered by the Association of Universities and Colleges of Canada for both undergraduate and graduate students. The booklet also lists scholarships offered by organizations for their employees' dependents. [ID:2495]

Canadian Directory to Foundations and Grants 📖
Annual ➤ Canadian Centre for Philanthropy, Suite 200, 1329 Bay Street, Toronto, Ontario M5R 2C4; $250; VISA, MC; (416) 515-0764, fax (416) 515-0773, ccp@ccp.ca; Available in large libraries ▪ Lists grants offered by various foundations and institutions for study, research, and travel. Visit the publisher's web site at www.ccp.ca. [ID:1091]

Commonwealth Universities Yearbook 📖
Annual Association of Commonwealth Universities ➤ UBC Press, University of British Columbia, 6344 Memorial Rd., Vancouver, B.C. V6T 1Z2; $289; VISA, MC; (604) 822-3259, fax (800) 668-0821, orders@ubcpress.ubc.ca; available in large libraries ▪ The most comprehensive guide to courses, staff, organizations and special interests of over 400 Commonwealth universities worldwide. Four volumes. [ID:1079]

Federal and Provincial Support to Post-Secondary Education in Canada 📖
Annual, 30 pages ➤ Public Inquiries Centre, Human Resources Development Canada, 140 Promenade du Portage, Phase 4 Level 0, Hull, Québec K1A 0J9; free; (613) 994-6313, fax (819) 953-7260 ▪ A quick summary of federal and provincial funding programs. Includes a bibliography of selected documents on postsecondary education. [ID:1244]

Fellowships in International Affairs:
A Guide to Opportunities in the United States and Abroad 📖
1994, *Women in International Security* ➤ Lynne Rienner Publishers, Suite 314, 1800 30th Street, Boulder, CO 80301, USA; US$17.95; VISA, MC; (303) 444-6684, fax (303) 444-0824 ▪ A handy reference guide that takes the guesswork out of finding and applying for research support. Clarifies qualifications, deadlines, and conditions for each grant or fellowship listed. Organized alphabetically by granting institution, the entries are also indexed by geographic focus, academic and career qualifications, and grant name. Visit distributor's web site, www.rienner.com. [ID:1454]

Financial Aid for Research & Creative Activities Abroad: 1996-98 📖
1996, *Gael Ann Schlachter, R. David Weber* ➤ Reference Service Press, Suite 4, 5000 Windplay Drive, El Dorado Hills, CA 95762, USA; US$45; VISA, MC; (916) 594-0743, fax (916) 939-9626, fiindaid@aol.com ▪ Lists over 1,300 funding opportunities open to undergraduate students, graduate students, postdoctorates, professionals, and other individuals looking for funding to support research, lectureships, exchange programs, work assignments, conference attendance, professional development, or creative projects abroad. The listings cover every major subject area, are tenable in practically every country and region of the world, and are sponsored by more than 500 private and public agencies. Visit distributor's web site at www.rspfunding.com. [ID:1634]

Foreign Government Awards Program 🖳
www.iccs-ciec.ca ▪ An excellent resource for students planning graduate studies abroad. Outlines the awards, applications and qualification requirements of foreign government awards in nine countries of Europe and South America. [ID:1029]

Natural Science and Engineering Research
Council of Canada (NSERC) – International Relations 🖳
www.nserc.ca ▪ This site gives full details on NSERC's international programs, research projects, bilateral agreements and fellowships. It provides links to other Canadian organizations and programs in all fields which provide international exchanges and awards, as well as to the Community of Science's Funding Opportunities database. [ID:2424]

Online Study Abroad Directory 🖳
www.istc.umn.edu/osad/ ▪ This site, a service of the International Study and Travel Centre at the University of Minnesota–Twin Cities, is the site for study abroad information. It allows you to search for programmes using any criteria, supplying a profile and e-mail address for each program you are interested in. Lists the most affordable programs in the "Rock Bottom Study Abroad" sub-field. Also has a large database for scholarships. [ID:2683]

Sports Scholarships and College Athletic Programs in the USA 📖
1996, Peterson's Guides ➤ Capricorn Business Services, Inc., 28 Clear Lake Ave., West Hill, Ontario M1C 4L6; $41.95; credit cards; (416) 282-3331, fax (416) 282-0015 ▪ A college-by-college guide to sports scholarships and collegiate sports programs. Intended for men and women who want to use their athletic abilities either to pay their college bills or improve their chances of admission to a US college. [ID:1593]

Study Abroad 📖
Annual, UNESCO, 1008 pages ➤ Renouf Publishing Co. Ltd., Unit 1, 5369 Canotek Road, Ottawa, Ontario K1J 9J3; $41.95 for book or CD-ROM, $54 for both; credit cards; (613) 745-2665, fax (613) 745-7660 ▪ A listing of more than 2,500 international study programs around the world, and a sourcebook for financial assistance offered by governments, international organizations, universities and foundations in over 100 countries. [ID:1239]

What In The World Is Going On? A Guide For Canadians
Wishing to Work, Volunteer, or Study in Other Countries 📖
1996, *Jennifer Humphries, Sienna Filleul,* 253 pages ➤ Canadian Bureau for International Education (CBIE), Suite 1100, 220 Laurier Ave W., Ottawa, Ontario K1P 5Z9; $14; VISA, Amex; (613) 237-4820, fax (613) 237-1073 ▪ Offers a bird's eye view of volunteer and study opportunities abroad. Good coverage of short- to medium-term volunteer positions. Also lists study abroad opportunities and international grants available to Canadian students. Available in French under the title, *Le tour du monde en 1001 projets.* [ID:1090]

Profiles of Awards & Grants

The following lists 69 awards and grants for international studies. To help you read through them quickly, profiles are classified by primary category. The number of profiles in each primary category are: All Levels 13, Doctoral 10, Graduate 27, Professional 9, Undergraduate 4.

Asia Pacific Foundation of Canada (APFC)
Asean Travel Grant Coordinator, Suite 666, 999 Canada Place,
Vancouver, B.C. V6C 3E1; (604) 684-5986, fax (604) 681-1370, www.apfc.ca

GRADUATE & DOCTORAL ▪ The mandate of the Asia Pacific Foundation of Canada (APFC) is the establishment of links between Canada and the Association of Southeast Asian Nations (ASEAN). The Graduate Student Travel Grant Fund has been created and funded by the Canadian International Development Agency (CIDA) in an effort to increase Canadians' knowledge and understanding of the ASEAN region. Annual travel grants of $5,000 are awarded to 15 students to fund study-related field research. Eligible applicants must be full-time master's or doctoral/post-doctoral candidates, whose focus of research is Southeast Asia. Deadline for applications is January 8. (For more information on the APFC see Chapter 35, Nongovernmental Organizations.) [ID:7073]

Association of Universities and Colleges of Canada (AUCC)
Coordinator, Emergency Preparedness Canada Research Fellowship, Suite 600,
350 Albert Street, Ottawa, Ontario K1R 1B1; (613) 563-1236, fax (613) 563-9745, www.aucc.ca

GRADUATE ▪ The Emergency Preparedness Canada Research Fellowship is awarded to one student in the field of Disaster and Emergency Studies each year. Preference is given to students who plan to pursue doctoral work, and who focus on the one of the following areas: urban and regional planning, economics, risk analysis and management, systems science, sociology, business administration and health administration. The fellowship is valued at $10,000, and may be tenable at a university overseas. Deadline for applications is February 1. Visit the AUCC web site for details and application forms. [ID:6394]

Association of International Education, Japan (AIEJ)
Exchange and Follow-up Division, Programs and Activities Department,
4-5-29 Komaba, Meguro-ku, Tokyo 153, JAPAN; (81) (3) 5454-5214, fax (81) (3) 5454-5234

ALL LEVELS ▪ The Association of International Education, Japan (AIEJ) was founded in 1957 as a nonprofit organization affiliated to the Japanese Ministry of Education, Science, Sports and Culture. The Peace and Friendship Scholarships provide student exchanges between Japanese and international university students. The program was created to promote mutual understanding and friendship between Japan and other countries. The scholarships are available for the qualified students accepted by Japanese universities or graduate schools. Application should be made to the Japanese host university, as AIEJ does not correspond with students or overseas universities directly. Applicants should contact their home university for more information,. [ID:6937]

Association of Universities and Colleges of Canada (AUCC)
Coordinator, The Forum - Department of National Defence
and Security Scholarships and Internships, Suite 600, 350 Albert Street,
Ottawa, Ontario K1R 1B1; (613) 563-3961 ext. 305, fax (613) 563-9745, www.aucc.ca

GRADUATE AND DOCTORAL ▪ The Department of National Defence offers several scholarships and internships, which are administered by the Association of Universities and Colleges of Canada. Successful applicants of all awards are involved in strategic studies, namely the political, international, historical, social, military, industrial and economic dimensions of current and future Canadian national security problems. There are four master's scholarships valued at $12,000 each and eight doctorate scholarships valued at $16,000 each, and study must be undertaken in Canada. Six one-year internships worth $16,000 each are also awarded annually, and are undertaken at a Canadian nongovernmental organization or private firm. Deadline for all applications is February 1. Visit the AUCC web site for details and application forms. [ID:6364]

Association of Universities and Colleges of Canada (AUCC)
Coordinator, Canada-Taiwan Scholarship Program, Suite 600,
350 Albert Street, Ottawa, Ontario K1R 1B1; (613) 563-1236, fax (613) 563-9745, www.aucc.ca

ALL LEVELS ▪ The Association of Universities and Colleges of Canada (AUCC), in cooperation with the Taipei Economic and Cultural Office in Canada and the Department of Human Resources Development, award ten scholarships annually to students wishing to pursue Mandarin language training. Applicants must be presently enrolled as a full-time student at a Canadian university, or have graduated within the past three years. Return airfare, a monthly allowance and health insurance are included. The period of study is six to twelve months at the Mandarin Training Centre of the National Taiwan Normal University. The application deadline is March 31. Visit the AUCC web site for details and application forms. [ID:6362]

Association of Universities and Colleges of Canada (AUCC)
Coordinator, Going Global - Science and Technology with European Partners, Suite 600,
350 Albert Street, Ottawa, Ontario K1R 1B1; (613) 563-1236 ext. 321, fax (613) 563-9745, www.aucc.ca

PROFESSIONAL ▪ The Going Global - Science and Technology with European Partners (STEP) program enables Canadian university researchers and professors to explore, establish, or consolidate projects with partners in Europe. The project is funded by the Department of Foreign Affairs and International Trade and covers travel costs to a maximum of $5,000 per project. Canadian university-based researchers and professors in the fields of pure and applied sciences, engineering, and related disciplines are eligible to apply. Deadlines are in the spring and fall of each year. [ID:6630]

Association of Universities and Colleges of Canada (AUCC)
Coordinator, Frank Knox Memorial Fellowship Program, Suite 600,
350 Albert Street, Ottawa, Ontario K1R 1B1; (613) 563-3961 ext. 305, fax (613) 563-9745, www.aucc.ca

GRADUATE ▪ The Frank Knox Memorial Fellowship is awarded to one graduate student annually, to enable them to pursue a year of studies at Harvard University. The program is open to graduate students in the fields of arts and sciences, business administration, design, education, law, public administration, medicine, and public health. Students presently studying in the US will not be considered unless they are recent graduates applying to the MBA program. Applicants must have graduated from an AUCC-affiliated university. The fellowship is valued at US$14,500, plus tuition and student health insurance. Deadline for application is February 1. Visit the AUCC web site for details and application forms. [ID:6365]

University of British Columbia
Faculty of Graduate Studies, 6371 Crescent Road, Vancouver, B.C.
V6T 1Z2; (604) 822-4564, fax (604) 822-8108, grad-award@mercury.ubc.ca

GRADUATE ▪ The Mackenzie King Travelling Scholarship is awarded to graduates of a Canadian university to pursue graduate studies in the US or the UK, in International Relations or Industrial Relations. There are four scholarships of $12,500 each. Applicants can apply to the Canadian university where they have received their most recent degree. Application deadline is February 1. [ID:5181]

University of British Columbia
Faculty of Graduate Studies, 6371 Crescent Road, Vancouver, B.C.
V6T 1Z2; (604) 822-4564, fax (604) 822-8108, grad-award@mercury.ubc.ca

GRADUATE ▪ The Mackenzie King Open Scholarship is awarded to a graduate of a Canadian university to pursue master's or PhD level studies in Canada or abroad. The award is valued at $8,000. Applicants can apply at the Canadian university where they have received their most recent degrees. Application deadline is February 1. [ID:5180]

Brookings Institution
Coordinator, Foreign Policy Research Fellowship, 1775 Massachusetts Ave. N.W.,
Washington, DC, 20036-2188, USA; (202) 797-6000, fax (202) 797-6004, www.brook.edu

DOCTORAL ▪ The Brooking Institution awards a limited number of resident fellowships for policy-oriented pre-doctoral research in US foreign policy and international relations. Only candidates nominated by graduate departments can be considered for these fellowships; applications from individuals not so nominated cannot be accepted. The fellowships carry a stipend of US$15,000, payable on a 12 month basis. The institution will also provide supplementary assistance for support services, research requirements and research related travel. Current Brookings topics place a special emphasis on tools of American foreign policy, security policy and international economic issues, and focus primarily on East Asia, the Commonwealth of Independent States, Eastern Europe, Germany, the Middle East, Africa, and Latin America. See their web site for eligibility, procedures and the specifics of each fellowship. [ID:5159]

Cambridge University
Board of Graduate Studies, 4 Mill Lane, CambridgeCB2 1RZ, UK; , fax (44) (1223) 338-723

DOCTORAL ▪ In collaboration with various trusts, foundations, corporations, organizations and individuals, the Cambridge Commonwealth Trust offers a number of scholarships to Canadian students wishing to pursue doctoral studies at Cambridge University. Awards include the Canada Cambridge Commonwealth Trust, which is awarded to five Canadian students anually, and the William and Margaret Brown Cambridge Scholarship which is awarded to a Canadian doctoral student in Engineering, Natural Sciences, Physical Sciences or Political Sciences. There is also the Peagasus Cambridge Scholarship, eligible to students pursuing their Master of Law Degree, and the Tidmarsh Cambridge Scholarship, tenable at Trinity Hall, Cambridge. All applicants must be under the age of 26, must in high academic standing and must have been successful in winning a ORS award, which pays the difference between the home and overseas rate of the University Composition Fee. Application deadlines vary according to awards. (For information on the ORS Award Scheme see their profile in this chapter.) [ID:6852]

Canada Council for the Arts
Visual Arts Section, P.O. Box 1047, 350 Albert Street,
Ottawa, Ontario K1P 5V8; (800) 263-5588, fax (613) 566-4332, www.canadacouncil.ca

PROFESSIONAL ▪ The Prix de Rome recognises the work of a professional architect engaged in the field of contemporary architecture who is a Canadian citizen or permanent resident. In addition to a grant of $34,000 for subsistence, travel and working expenses, the winner has the use of an apartment studio in the Tratevere district of Rome for one year. The prix de Rome is not an academic award; rather, it is intended to enable the winner to pursue independent work in architecture and to make an original contribution to the discipline. The winner is chosen by a peer assessment committee for the Canadian Council Creation/ Production Grants. [ID:5189]

Canada Council for the Arts
Music Section, P.O. Box 1047, 350 Albert Street, Ottawa, Ontario
K1P 5V8; (800) 263-5588 ext. 4073, fax (613) 566-4409, www.canadacouncil.ca

PROFESSIONAL ▪ The Grants to Individual Musicians program offers emerging, mid-career and established professional musicians in non-classical or classical music of all world cultures opportunities to pursue their creative development. Grants to Individual Musicians cover subsistence, project and transportation costs related to a program of work lasting from a few weeks to one year, and Travel Grants award individual musicians funds in order to travel on occasions important to their career. In addition, a studio, with living accommodation, at the Cité Internationale des Arts in Paris is available at moderate cost to qualifying Canadian professional musicians. (These may include instrumentalists, singers, composers, arrangers, performers, singers, songwriters, and conductors). [ID:7034]

Canada Council for the Arts
Visual Arts Section, P.O. Box 1047, 350 Albert Street, Ottawa, Ontario
K1P 5V8; (800) 263-5588 ext. 4095, fax (613) 566-4332, www.canadacouncil.ca

PROFESSIONAL ■ Two studios, with living accommodation, at the Cité Internationale des Arts in Paris are available at moderate cost to Canadian professional visual artists (including architects, independent critics and curators, photographers and craft artists). These studios may be used to pursue creative work for a period of three months to one year. A grant of $24,000 or less, to cover subsistence and travel expenses, is provided. [ID:5187]

Canada Council for the Arts
Endowment and Prize Unit, P.O. Box 1047, 350 Albert Street, Ottawa, Ontario K1P 5V8;
(800) 263-5588 ext. 4116, fax (613) 566-4390, bruno.jean@canadacouncil.ca, www.canadacouncil.ca

PROFESSIONAL ■ A bequest from the estate of the late John B.C. Watkins, this award provides fellowships of $5,000 to professional Canadian artists in any field who are pursuing graduate studies, and who are graduates of a Canadian university, postsecondary art institution or training school. Preference is given to those who wish to carry out their postgraduate studies in Denmark, Norway, Sweden, or Iceland, but applications are accepted for study in any country other than Canada. Postgraduate schools include postsecondary institutions or training schools, whether or not these are degree-granting institutions. Fellowships are normally awarded in music, the visual arts, theatre, and media arts. [ID:5170]

Canada Student Loan Program
Contact your provincial government's student aid branch for specific address, fax, and e-mail.

ALL LEVELS ■ The Canada Student Loans Program helps postsecondary students who are unable to pursue their education without financial assistance. Students apply to their provincial or territorial government for student aid. Students who plan to study abroad can receive loans from this program only if they provide information that clearly demonstrates the applicability and viability of their intended program. [ID:5144]

Canada-US Fulbright Program
Program Officer, Suite 2015, 350 Albert Street, Ottawa, Ontario K1R 1A4;
(613) 237-5366, fax (613) 237-2029, info@fullbright.ca, www.usis-canada.usia.gov/fullbrigh.htm

GRADUATE ■ The Canada-US Fulbright Program offers research, teaching and study opportunities for Canadian and American faculty and students studying the relationship between Canada and the US. Full-time graduate students or students awaiting acceptance into such a program are eligible to apply. The award consists of US$15,000 for an academic year (nine months). The deadline for applications is September 30. [ID:5160]

Canadian Bureau for International Education (CBIE)
Coordinator, Celanese Canada Internationalist Fellowships, Suite 1100, 220 Laurier Avenue W.,
Ottawa, Ontario K1P 5Z9; (613) 237-4820, fax (613) 237-1073, rchampagne@cbie.ca, www.cbie.ca

GRADUATE ■ This program is administered by the Canadian Bureau for International Education (CBIE) on behalf of the chemical and fibre company, Celanese Canada Inc. The program offers awards to university graduates from across Canada in order that they may acquire skills that will help make Canadian firms competitive in the global economy. The program, which began in 1997, is scheduled to award 125 to 150 fellowships over five years. Each fellowship is valued at $10,000, and must be undertaken as study and/or research, possibly combined with an internship, at any institution outside of Canada. The deadline for

applications is February 15. Visit CBIE's web site for program details and application forms.
[ID:6432]

Canadian Bureau for International Education (CBIE)

Coordinator, CIDA Awards Program for Canadians, Suite 1100, 220 Laurier Avenue W.,
Ottawa, Ontario K1P 5Z9; (613) 237-4820, fax (613) 237-1073, gbeaudoin@cbie.ca, www.cbie.ca

GRADUATE & PROFESSIONAL ▪ This program is administered by the Canadian Bureau
for International Education (CBIE) on behalf of the Canadian International Development
Agency (CIDA). The awards program is designed for Canadian citizens seeking to
undertake an international development volunteer project of their own creation. Projects
must relate to CIDA's Aid Policy, and must be carried out in eligible countries. The program
is divided into Academic Awards, for master's students undertaking fieldwork, and
Professional Awards, for professionals who wish to volunteer in international development.
For both, the duration is up to twelve months and the maximum value is $15,000. Deadline
for proposals is March 31. At the time of publication this program was under review. Visit
the CBIE's web site for program details and application forms. [ID:6431]

Canadian Bureau for International Education (CBIE)

Coordinator, Nortel Globalization Challenge Program, Suite 1100, 220 Laurier Avenue W.,
Ottawa, Ontario K1P 5Z9; (613) 237-4820, fax (613) 237-1073, jhumphries@cbie.ca, www.cbie.ca

GRADUATE ▪ The Nortel Globalization Challenge Program offers awards to MBA students
with undergraduate degrees in Electrical Engineering, Computer Science, or Information
Technology and related fields. These awards are for academic exchanges with universities in
Brazil, Hong Kong, Colombia, France, Germany, Mexico, and the UK. Nortel also offers
internships to those selected; they are posted in the company's offices of the countries listed
above. Applications must be submitted to one's respective Dean of Business. Complete
information and applications forms can be downloaded from the CBIE web site. [ID:5147]

Canadian Federation of University Women (CFUW)

Fellowships Chair, Suite 600, 251 Bank Street, Ottawa, Ontario
K2P 1X3; (613) 234-2732, fax (613) 234-8221, bw725@freenet.carleton.ca

GRADUATE & DOCTORAL ▪ The Canadian Federation of University Women (CFUW) was
founded in 1919, and established its first fellowship in 1921. Since then, the CFUW has
awarded more than $800,000 to Canadian women who have obtained a first degree.
Applicants for these fellowships must be Canadian citizens, full-time students, and possess
an undergraduate degree. Study may take place in Canada or abroad. Among the fellowships
that the CFUW presently administers are the Margaret McWilliams Pre-Doctoral Fellowship
($10,000), the Dr. Marion Elder Grant Fellowship ($8,000) and the Professional Fellowship
($5,000). [ID:5135]

Canadian Institute of Ukrainian Studies

Scholarships Officer, 352 Athabasca Hall, University of Alberta,
Edmonton, Alberta T6G 2E8; (403) 492-2972, fax (403) 492-4967, cius@gpu.srv.alberta.ca

UNDERGRADUATE ▪ The Leo J. Krysa Family Foundation Undergraduate Scholarship, in
the amount of $1500 is awarded to undergraduate university students about to enter their
final year of study in pursuit of a degree with an emphasis on Ukrainian studies. This can be
through a combination of courses in Ukrainian and East European, or Canadian studies in an
Arts or Education Program. The scholarship is for study at any Canadian university.
Candidates must be Canadian citizens or landed immigrants at the time of application and be
studying at a Canadian university. The deadline for applications is May 1. [ID:5178]

Canadian Institute of Ukrainian Studies
Fellowships Officer, 352 Athabasca Hall, University of Alberta,
Edmonton, Alberta T6G 2E8; (403) 492-2972, fax (403) 492-4967, cius@gpu.srv.alberta.ca

GRADUATE ▪ The Marusia and Michael Dorosh Endowment Fund Master's Fellowship (one fellowship for $4,500) and the Helen Darcovich Memorial Endowment Fund Doctoral Fellowship (one fellowship for $8,000) are awarded in the fields of Education, History, Law, Humanities, Social Science, Women's Studies and Library Science. The awards aid students in the completion of their theses on a Ukrainian or Ukrainian Canadian topics. The fellowships are awarded only in the thesis year of the academic program for thesis work. Canadian citizens or permanent residents studying at any institution of higher learning in Canada or elsewhere are eligible. The deadline for applications is May 1. [ID:5182]

Canadian Women's Club
President, 1 Grosvenor Street, LondonW1X 0AB, UK; (44) (171) 258-6344, fax (44) (171) 258-6473

GRADUATE ▪ The Canadian Women's Club, was founded in 1932 to provide a venue where Canadian women residing in the UK could meet each other. The Canadian Centennial Scholarship Fund (CCSF), funded by the Canadian Women's Club and coordinated by the Trustees of the Canadian Centennial Scholarship Fund, is available to Canadian citizens pursuing postgraduate studies at a university or polytechnic institute in the UK. Students should already have completed at least one full term of study and intend to return to Canada upon completion of study. The value of the award is up to £2,000 and the deadline for application is March 6. [ID:5146]

Canadian-Scandinavian Foundation
CSF Secretary, c/o Office of the Director of Libraries, 3459 McTavish Street, McGill University, Montréal, Québec H3A 1Y1; (514) 398-4740, fax (514) 398-7356, moller@libi.lan.mcgill.ca

GRADUATE ▪ The Canadian-Scandinavian Foundation invites young and talented Canadians to submit applications for research and study in Denmark, Finland, Ireland, Norway or Sweden. In all cases both orientation and format of the research or study exercise should clearly state its beneficial character to Canada upon the return of the researcher or student. Research fields are open and the candidate may work as an independent professional or in academia. The special purpose grants are valued between $600 and $1,000 and are intended to help defray travel costs in connection with short-term research or study. Application deadline is January 31. [ID:5154]

Canadian-Scandinavian Foundation
CSF Secretary, c/o Office of the Director of Libraries, 3459 McTavish Street, McGill University, Montréal, Québec H3A 1Y1; (514) 398-4740, fax (514) 398-7356, moller@libi.lan.mcgill.ca

ALL LEVELS ▪ This scholarship is awarded to promising young Canadian artists. The award is intended to finance a two-month stay at the Brucebo Studio of the Gotland Museum of Fine Arts, near Visby, Sweden. It includes round-trip transportation, two months residence at Brucebo Studio and a two month food stipend. The scholarships are administered by the Canadian-Scandinavian Institute, and must be used within the period June 10 to August 20. Application deadline is January 31. [ID:5142]

Canadian-Scandinavian Foundation
CSF Secretary, c/o Office of the Director of Libraries, 3459 McTavish Street, McGill University, Montréal, Québec H3A 1Y1; (514) 398-4740, fax (514) 398-7356, moller@libi.lan.mcgill.ca

PROFESSIONAL ▪ This award, administered by the Canadian-Scandinavian Foundation on behalf of the Gotland Museum of Fine Arts in Visby, is intended to assist a practising Canadian artist in their formative phase of professional development. The Committee finances a European Travel Study Tour for the recipient. A visit to Stockholm and Gotland is prescribed as part of the journey, which takes place either in the spring or the fall. Application deadline is January 31. [ID:5202]

Centre for International Affairs

Harvard Academy for International and Area Studies Fellowships, Harvard Academy Scholars, 1737 Cambridge Street, Harvard University, Cambridge, MA, 02138, USA; (617) 495-3671, fax (617) 495-8292

DOCTORAL ▪ The Academy Scholars Program at Harvard University is open to doctoral candidates whose work has combined disciplinary excellence in the social sciences with an in-depth grounding in particular countries or regions. Selected scholars are given time, guidance, access to Harvard's facilities, and substantial financial assistance as they work for two years conducting either dissertation or postdoctoral research in their chosen fields. Stipends range between US$20,000 and $35,000, depending upon the circumstances of the individual, and are supplemented by funding for conference and research travel, and some health coverage. For further information regarding the Academy Scholars Program, please call (617) 495-2137. [ID:5164]

Centre for International Mobility (CIMO)

International Programs in Finnish Higher Education, P.O. Box 343, Hakaniemenkatu 2, FIN-00531 Helsinki, FINLAND; (358) (9) 7747-7033, fax (358) (9) 7747-7064, cimoinfo@cimo.fi, www.cimo.fi

ALL LEVELS ▪ The Centre for International Mobility (CIMO) is a specialist service organization working under the Finnish Ministry of Education. It enhances international cooperation by coordinating and implementing a range of exchange and scholarship programs. Programs are offered in almost all fields of study, from area studies, to fine arts, to business, to engineering to tourism. Programs are offered in both the university and non-university sector, and although students are encouraged to take Finnish and/or Swedish courses, the language of instruction is English. CIMO and other organizations grant many scholarships for advanced studies and research in Finland. For full scholarship and program information, visit the CIMO web site or contact the address listed above. [ID:6386]

Embassy of France

Scientific Affairs Section, 464 Wilbrod Street, Ottawa, Ontario K1N 6M8; (613) 238-1051, fax (613) 238-7884, sciefran@amba-ottawa.fr, http://ottawa.ambafrance.org/hyperlab

GRADUATE ▪ The Chateaubriand Scholarship Program for Pure and Applied Sciences, Engineering, Medicine, and Social Sciences is available to Canadian citizens currently completing a PhD or who have completed a PhD in the last three years. The scholarships are awarded by the government of France and are tenable at a French university, engineering school or private laboratory. Scholarships are available for periods of six to 12 months. with a stipend of 8,500 to 10,500 FF per month. Health insurance and the cost of travel to and from France is covered. The deadline for applications is January 31. Visit their web site for details. [ID:5150]

Embassy of Italy

Scholarships Officer, 21st Floor, 275 Slater Street, Ottawa, Ontario K1P 5H9; (613) 232-2401, fax (613) 233-1484, ambital@trytel.com

ALL LEVELS ▪ The government of Italy offers long-term and short-term scholarships to Canadian citizens wishing to pursue studies in Italy. Awards are given to graduate and undergraduate students, professionals, teachers and artists to study at Italian universities, attend specialized courses or undertake research in specific fields. Scholarships consist of a monthly living allowance of $1,000 Italian lire and medical insurance. Long-term scholarships (usually beginning in November) are awarded for study or research at a public postsecondary institution in any of the following fields: Italian language and literature, music, visual arts, performing arts, art restoration, and sciences. Short-term grants (two months in the summer) are available for language studies only. All candidates must meet the admission requirement of the institutions to which they are applying. They will also be assessed on the basis of the following criteria: curriculum studiorum and vitae; program, study, or research proposed by the candidate; letters of reference; and contact between the candidate and Italian academics and/or institutions of higher learning. Deadlines for applications are March for long-term programs and September for short-term programs (which commence the following summer). [ID:5169]

Embassy of Japan
Information and Culture Section, 255 Sussex Drive, Ottawa, Ontario K1N 9E6;
(613) 241-8541, fax (613) 241-4261, infocul@embjapan.can.org, www.embjapan.can.org

ALL LEVELS ▪ Through the Ministry of Education, Science, and Culture, the Japanese government offers Monbusho Scholarships to Canadian students who wish to study at Japanese universities as research students. Research can take place in a wide variety of disciplines including the humanities, social sciences, and the pure and applied sciences. Separate awards are available to undergraduate and graduate level candidates, all of whom must be, or intend to become, fluent in Japanese. Recipients of this scholarship will receive a monthly allowance, return airfare, university fees, and a housing allowance. For more information please write to the Information and Culture Section of the Embassy of Japan. Applications will not be accepted via fax transmission or e-mail. [ID:5173]

Embassy of the People's Republic of China
Second Secretary and Program Manager, Education Office, 80 Cobourg Street, Ottawa, Ontario
K1N 8H1; (613) 789-6312, fax (613) 789-0262, xyang@buildlink.com, www.chinaembassycanada.org

ALL LEVELS ▪ The government of the People's Republic of China offers 13 awards to Canadian scholars of Chinese studies or related fields, to study at Chinese institutions of higher learning. Applicants should be faculty members or students enrolled in Canadian universities. Preference will be given to those students who already have a postgraduate degree. Valid for four to 12 months, the award consists of a living allowance, on-campus accommodation, return airfare, tuition fees, textbooks and basic medical coverage. A written proposal is required. [ID:5151]

Embassy of the People's Republic of China
Second Secretary and Program Manager, Education Office, 80 Cobourg Street, Ottawa, Ontario
K1N 8H1; (613) 789-6312, fax (613) 789-0262, xyang@buildlink.com, www.chinaembassycanada.org

GRADUATE ▪ The Chinese Culture Research Fellowship gives financial assistance to foreign scholars studying modern China and exploring the country's long history, rich culture and profound traditions. The goal of the fellowship is to promote friendship between the people of China and the rest of the world. The awards are available to individuals who possess a minimum of three years of research experience and have a master's degree or PhD. Awards are also available to assistant and full professors studying Chinese language, culture, history, philosophy, education, economy, art history or other subjects. All applicants must have a command of the Chinese language and be under 55 years of age. Information about this program and an application may be obtained from any Chinese Embassy or Consulate. [ID:5152]

Fondation Desjardins
C.P. 7, succursale Desjardins, Montréal, Québec H5B 1B2; (514) 281-7171, fax (514) 281-2391

DOCTORAL ▪ La fondation Desjardins est une institution vouée à l'éducation, à la culture et à l'action sociale. C'est dans ce cadre qu'elle favorise le développement de l'éducation et des connaissances chez les jeunes. La Fondation Desjardins offre son programme de bourses Girardin-Vaillancourt. Au total, 150 bourses sont offertes: 60 de 1000 $ et 90 de 500 $ au niveau du baccalauréat, 13 bourses de 5 000 $ au niveau de la maîtrise et 8 bourses de 7 000

$ au niveau du doctorat. Trois subventions de recherche sont offertes au niveau du doctorat: Société et environnement (25 000 $), Gestion urbaine, un défi (15 000 $) et Coopération (7 500$). Le candidat admissible doit résider au Québec et avoir la citoyenneté canadienne. Il doit être étudiant à plein temps en vue de l'obtention d'un diplôme universitaire. Les bourses couvrent les champs d'étude suivants: projets reliés aux coopératives; informatique (gestion ou génie); économie, finance, gestion, administration; sciences naturelles, appliquées, de la santé; humanités et arts; arts de création ou d'interprétation. La date limite d'inscription est le 1er mars de chaque année. Toute bourse est renouvelable une fois par cycle. Le formulaire d'inscription peut être obtenu à l'université de son choix. [ID:5140]

Department of Foreign Affairs and International Trade (DFAIT)
Academic Relations Division, Youth and Personality
Exchanges Section (ACEE), 125 Sussex Drive, Ottawa, Ontario K1A 0G2;
(613) 996-4527, fax (613) 992-5965, www.dfait-maeci.gc.ca/english/culture/canstud.htm#pepc

ALL LEVELS ▪ The Bank of Missions Program offers exchanges between Canada and other countries with which bilateral cultural agreements have been reached. The program is intended to reward outstanding Canadians who do not meet the eligibility criteria of other existing programs. Applications from all cultural, social and academic fields are considered, and Canadian Studies abroad is emphasized. Participants receive approximately $100 per day from the host country, while the Canadian government pays for round trip economy-class airfare. Length of stay is limited to 21 days. Applicants must submit a full proposal of their project and upon return are required to complete a report. For full details, visit the web site. (For information on their international internships see the Canadian Government International Internships profile in Chapter 17, International Internships.) [ID:6681]

Griffith University
Postgraduate Scholarships Officer, Nathan, Brisbane, Queensland, 4111,
AUSTRALIA; (61) (7) 3875-6596, fax (61) (7) 3875-7994, rhd-school@or.gv.edu.au, www.gu.edu.au

GRADUATE ▪ These awards are intended to attract high-quality applicants from both Australia and overseas, and provide them with financial assistance to pursue a program of research leading to the award of a master's or PhD. The awards are tenable at Griffith University and include a living stipend of $15,637 per annum, relocation and travel allowance, sick leave, maternity and leave of absence provisions, and an extension clause. The MA scholarships are available on a two-year basis, while the PhD awards may be held for up to three years. Applications must be submitted by 31 October of the year preceding the one in which studies commence. [ID:5162]

Institut Universitaire des Hautes Études Internationales
Secretary General, C.P. 36, 132 rue de Lausanne, CH 1211, Genève 21,
SWITZERLAND; (41) (22) 731-1730, fax (41) (22) 738-4306, info@hei.unige.ch, http://heiwww.unige.ch

GRADUATE ▪ The Institut Universitaire des Hautes Études Internationales is a teaching and research establishment devoted to the scientific and interdisciplinary study of contemporary international relations. This plural approach draws upon the methods of history and political science, of law and economics. Between 15 and 20 scholarships are awarded each year on the basis of both academic performance and the financial status of applicants. Amount of support is 10,000 Swiss francs per year. Candidates for admission must address an application to the institute on forms obtained from the secretariat. The application must reach the institute by March of the preceeding academic year. [ID:5165]

Inter-American Development Bank
Scholarship Programs, Stop #W0602, 1300 New York Ave. N.W.,
Washington, DC, 20577, USA; (202) 623-1000, fax (202) 623-3096, www.iadb.org

GRADUATE ▪ Funded by the government of Japan, this scholarship is open to all IADB-borrowing member countries, and is tenable at any institutions of higher education which offer MA and PhD programs. Candidates must hold a BA, have received superior grades in any development-related discipline, been admitted to an MA or PhD program, and have at least two years of work experience, preferably in the public sector. The scholarship provides full tuition, university medical and accident insurance, subsistence, and economy class airfare. Upon completion of their studies, recipients must return and contribute to their native countries' development. [ID:5166]

International Council for Canadian Studies
Program Officer, Suite 800, 325 Dalhousie Street,
Ottawa, Ontario K1N 7G2; (613) 789-7828, fax (613) 789-7830, general@iccs-ciec.ca, www.iccs-ciec.ca

GRADUATE ▪ The Organization of American States PRA (Regular Training Program) offers fellowships to graduate students wishing to pursue study or research in Latin America and the Caribbean. Those in the fields of medical sciences and languages are not considered. Applications must be postmarked by January 23 to be considered for the following September. Consult the International Council for Canadian Studies' web site for further information and application forms. [ID:6397]

International Council for Canadian Studies
Program Officer, Suite 800, 325 Dalhousie Street,
Ottawa, Ontario K1N 7G2; (613) 789-7828, fax (613) 789-7830, general@iccs-ciec.ca, www.iccs-ciec.ca

GRADUATE & PROFESSIONAL ▪ As part of the implementation of international cultural agreements, the government of Canada and the governments of Colombia, Finland, France, Germany, Italy, Mexico, the Netherlands, and Spain, will offer a number of awards to Canadian graduate students. These awards are intended to help Canadian students further their studies or conduct research abroad at the MA, PhD and postdoctoral level, and usually cover a period of at least six months. Most countries offer awards in a wide selection of disciplines. Although all of the awards are similar, the specific cost items covered by each award are determined by the offering country. Complete details on each award are contained in the Foreign Government Awards Handbook which is available from all Graduate Studies Offices or Student Awards Offices at any university or by consulting the International Council for Canadian Studies web site. [ID:5158]

International Council for Canadian Studies
Program Officer, Suite 800, 325 Dalhousie Street,
Ottawa, Ontario K1N 7G2; (613) 789-7828, fax (613) 789-7830, general@iccs-ciec.ca, www.iccs-ciec.ca

GRADUATE ▪ The Commonwealth Scholarship Plan is available to master's and PhD students who want to study or conduct research in India, New Zealand, UK, Sri Lanka or Uganda. Scholarships are granted by the awarding country and the value of the scholarships and deadlines for applications vary. Consult the International Council for Canadian Studies' web site for further information and application forms. [ID:6398]

International Development Research Centre
Training and Awards Unit, P.O. Box 8500, 250 Albert Street,
Ottawa, Ontario K1G 3H9; (613) 236-6163, fax (613) 238-7230, cta@idrc.ca, www.idrc.ca

DOCTORAL ▪ These awards support Canadian field research in Latin America, Africa, the Middle East, and Asia. PhD candidates are eligible. Research must address one of the six core multidisciplinary themes which integrate environmental, social, and economic politics.

Core themes are: food security, equity in natural resource use, biodiversity conservation, sustainable employment, strategy and policies for a healthy society, and information and communication. The awards are valued at up to $20,000 annually. Candidates must be registered at a Canadian university and be Canadian citizens. The research portion of the program must take place in a Southern country. Applications will be accepted throughout the year, but the deadline is December 15. [ID:5206]

International Development Research Centre
Senior Program Officer, P.O. Box 8500, 250 Albert St., Ottawa, Ontario
K1G 3H9; (613) 236-6163, fax (613) 238-7230, elaferriere@idrc.ca, www.idrc.ca

PROFESSIONAL ▪ Gemini News Service is a nonprofit organization with a small staff based in London, England. It provides an exchange of news coverage between the North and the South. The International Development Research Centre sponsors an internship with Gemini News Service for a Canadian with at least three years' experience who is employed by a newspaper or news agency. The award has a value of $30,000. The candidate will participate in reporting and editorial research on a wide range of topics and will work both in London and a three- to four-month assignment in a developing country. Application deadline is May 15. [ID:5161]

International Development Research Centre
Training and Awards Unit, P.O. Box 8500, 250 Albert St.,
Ottawa, Ontario K1G 3H9; (613) 236-6163, fax (613) 238-7230, cta@idrc.ca, www.idrc.ca

GRADUATE ▪ The John G. Bene Fellowship is intended to provide assistance to Canadian graduate students to undertake research on the relationship of forest resources to the social, economic, and environmental welfare of people – especially less privileged people – in developing countries. Awards are valued at $10,000 and may be renewed for up to two additional years. Candidates must be registered at a Canadian university and be Canadian citizens. Applications will be accepted throughout the year but the deadline is February 1. [ID:5174]

The Japan Foundation
Fellowship Officer, Suite 213, 131 Bloor St. W., Toronto, Ontario
M5S 1R1; (416) 966-1600, fax (416) 966-9773, jftor@interlog.com, www.jfp.go.jp

ALL LEVELS ▪ Students who receive outstanding scores on a language test prepared by the Japan Foundation are eligible for study tours of Japan. The test is normally administered in March. For more information contact the Japan Foundation, Toronto, and request a program guide or consult your nearest Japanese Embassy or Consulate. [ID:7058]

The Japan Foundation
Fellowship Officer, Suite 213, 131 Bloor Street W., Toronto, Ontario
M5C 1R1; (416) 966-1600, fax (416) 966-9773, jftor@interlog.com, www.jpf.go.jp

DOCTORAL ▪ These dissertation fellowships provide PhD students with funding to conduct on-site research in Japan for four to 14 months. The awards are administered by the Japan Foundation (established in 1972) which introduces Japanese culture overseas and promotes cultural exchanges between Japan and other countries. An applicant's field of study must be in the humanities or social sciences and should be substantially related to Japan. The candidate must be in good health, have sufficient ability in Japanese and/or English to conduct research in Japan, and have completed all degree requirements except the dissertation prior to commencing the fellowship. The term of the fellowship, which is only tenable in Japan, must begin in the Japanese fiscal year for which the grant is made and may not be held concurrently with another grant supporting the same research in Japan. The deadline for applications is December 1, for the funding year beginning the following April 1.

For more information contact the Japan Foundation, Toronto, and request a program guide. [ID:5171]

John Simon Guggenheim Memorial Foundation
Coordinator, Guggenheim Fellowships, 90 Park Ave., New York, NY,
10016, USA; (212) 687-4470, fax (212) 697-3248, fellowships@gf.org, www.gf.org

GRADUATE ▪ The Guggenheim Foundation offers fellowships to scholars and artists to engage in research in any field of knowledge or creation in any of the arts, under the freest possible conditions. Fellowships are awarded to men and women who have already demonstrated exceptional capacity for productive scholarship or exceptional creative ability in the arts. Appointments are ordinarily made for one year, and never less than six months. The value of the grants will depend on the applicant's need and the purpose and scope of the applicant's plans. In 1997 the foundation awarded 164 fellowships in the US and Canada, for a total value of $4,890,000 (the average grant was $29,817). The deadline for applications is October 1. [ID:5163]

Lady Davis Fellowship Trust
Executive Secretary, P.O. Box 1255, Hebrew University, Givat Ram, Jerusalem91904,
ISRAEL; (972) (2) 6512306, fax (972) (2) 5663848, LDFT@vms.huji.ac.il, http://sites.huji.ac.il/LDFT/

DOCTORAL & PROFESSIONAL ▪ The Lady Davis Fellowship Trust offers fellowships to visiting professors, post-doctoral researchers, and doctoral students at the Hebrew University of Jerusalem and at the Technion, Israel Institute of Technology in Haifa.

Over the past 25 years fellowships provided by the Trust-Developing Research Network have allowed nearly 1,400 distinguished scholars to spend from three months to one year at these institutions, teaching and enjoying a young, world-class, academic environment in a fascinating country.

We offer superior scholars of any age, in any field and from any region the opportunity to participate in this unique program. Please consult our web site for further information. [ID:5177]

London School of Economics and Political Science
Scholarship Office, Houghton Street,
LondonWC2A 2AE, UK; (44) (171) 955-7163, fax (44) (171) 831 1684

GRADUATE ▪ The Robert McKenzie Canadian Scholarship is awarded to students who have completed an undergraduate degree at a Canadian university and want to pursue an MA or PhD at the London School of Economics. The scholarship is valued at $5,000 and may be held concurrently with other awards. Closing date for applications is March 31. [ID:5193]

University of Manitoba
Awards Officer, Faculty of Graduate Studies, 500 University Centre,
Winnipeg, Manitoba R3T 2N2; (204) 474-9836, fax (204) 474-7553,
ikrentz@bldeumsu.lan.umanitoba.ca, www.umanitoba.ca/gradstud/awards/html

GRADUATE ▪ The J.W. Dafoe Graduate Fellowship is designed to encourage the study of international relations at the graduate level and to promote international understanding. The fellowship has a value of $10,000 and is tenable at the University of Manitoba. The award is open to graduates of any recognized university who possess an honours BA, or its equivalent, and who intend to pursue a higher degree in the fields of international studies, political studies, economics or history. Applications should be directed to the awards officer at the Faculty of Graduate Studies. Visit their web site for information on this and other scholarships, fellowships, bursaries, and awards which students may apply for. [ID:5175]

McEuen Scholarship Foundation Inc.
Secretary, Suite 100, 60 Queen Street,
Ottawa, Ontario K1P 5Y7; (613) 237-5160, fax (613) 230-8842, ottinfo@scottaylen.com

UNDERGRADUATE ▪ The McEuen Scholarship Foundation provides scholarships to undergraduate Canadian students who wish to obtain an undergraduate degree at St. Andrews University in St. Andrews, Scotland. The scholarship is tenable for three years (ordinary degree) or four years (honours degree) and comprises full tuition and residence fees plus a book allowance. One scholarship is awarded annually to a Canadian citizen residing in Canada, who attends or is qualified to attend a university in Canada. Applicants must not be more than 21 years of age on December 31 of the year preceding the award of the scholarship. Closing date is January 31. [ID:5183]

McGill University
Coordinator, Bursaries and Scholarships, Faculty of Medicine, 3655 Drummond Street,
Montréal, Québec H3G 1Y6; (514) 398-3520, fax (514) 398-3595, danielle@medusa.medcor.mcgill.ca

UNDERGRADUATE ▪ The Osler Medical Aid Foundation, in cooperation with the McGill Centre for Tropical Diseases, provides three to four scholarships to undergraduate students currently enrolled in the Faculty of Medicine at McGill to help finance an elective in a developing country. All second year students are eligible to apply. The elective must be at least six weeks in duration. The scholarship covers travelling expenses and a living allowance for the duration of the stay, up to a maximum of $1,500. Please direct your inquiries to Danielle Lefebvre, Coordinator, Bursaries and Scholarships. [ID:5185]

Medical Research Council of Canada
Program Director, International Scientific Exchanges,
Tower B, 5th Floor, Jeanne Mance Bldg., 1600 Scott Street, Ottawa, Ontario
K1A 0W9; (613) 954-1951, fax (613) 954-1800, mrcinfocrm@hpb.hwc.ca, www.mrc.hwc.ca

PROFESSIONAL ▪ The Medical Research Council of Canada participates in seven distinct programs, which are intended to foster collaboration between scientists in Canada and those in Argentina, Brazil, China, France, Italy, and the UK. Candidates must be Canadian scientists. Recipients receive a living allowance from the host-country agency and a travel allowance from the Medical Research Council of Canada. Application deadline is October 1 for all programs. Visit their web site for further details and an application form. [ID:5168]

Medical Research Council of Canada
Fellowship Programs, Tower B, 5th Floor, Jeanne Mance Bldg.,
1600 Scott Street, Ottawa, Ontario K1A 0W9; (613) 954-1964, fax (613) 954-1800, www.mrc.hwc.ca

GRADUATE ▪ These awards are offered to candidates of academic distinction for full-time training in the health sciences, medicine, dentistry, nursing, pharmacy or veterinary medicine, and may be used for study abroad. Candidates must have completed a health professional degree or PhD degree. Candidates with a PhD degree must have three to four years of postdoctoral research experience. Holders of a professional degree receive $44,520 per annum and holders of a PhD degree receive $37,420 per annum. A yearly research and travel allowance is also provided. Deadline for applications is December 1. [ID:5149]

Natural Sciences and Engineering Research Council
Scholarships and Fellowships Section, 350 Albert Street,
Ottawa, Ontario K1A 1H5; (613) 996-3762, fax (613) 996-2589, schol@nserc.ca, www.nserc.ca

GRADUATE ▪ This award enables outstanding science students to undertake graduate studies and research leading to a PhD in Canada or abroad. Canadian citizens and permanent residents are eligible to apply for the award. Deadline for application is December 1. Visit their web site for information and application forms. [ID:5134]

Natural Sciences and Engineering
Research Council of Canada (NSERC)
Scholarships and Fellowships Division, 350 Albert Street,
Ottawa, Ontario K1A 1H5; (613) 996-2009, fax (613) 996-2589, www.aucc.ca

PROFESSIONAL ▪ The Science and Technology Agency of Japan (STA) offers fellowships to outstanding young foreign researchers in the fields of science and technology, to conduct research at Japan's national laboratories and public research corporations. Fellowships are both short-term (one to three months) and long-term (six months to two years). Fellowships include round-trip airfare, housing, an international moving allowance and a family allowance.

Applicants must have a doctoral degree in a scientific, technological, engineering, or medical field. Applicants must also have sufficient language abilities; although Japanese is preferred, English is sufficient in most cases. The Natural Science and Engineering Research Council of Canada (NSERC) is responsible for selecting Canadian nominees for these fellowships. It is recommended that applications reach NSERC at least six months before the intended starting date. [ID:6625]

Natural Sciences and Engineering
Research Council of Canada (NSERC)
Scholarship and Fellowship Division, 350 Albert Street,
Ottawa, Ontario K1A 1H5; (613) 996-2009, fax (613) 996-2589, www.aucc.ca

DOCTORAL ▪ The Japan Society for the Promotion of Sciences (JSPS) has established a Postdoctoral Fellowship for Foreign Researchers to conduct research in Japan. The program allows for collaborative research at Japanese universities and other institutions, helping visiting researchers advance their own work while stimulating the research activities of the host institution. Fellowships are awarded for a period of 12 months, and include round-trip airfare, a monthly stipend and health insurance. Allowances for moving, settling-in, language training are also provided. Approximately five fellowships per year are granted to Canadian citizens.

Applicants in the fields of humanities, social sciences, natural and engineering sciences, and medicine are considered. Applicants must hold a doctoral degree and have made prior arrangements on their research plan with a Japanese host researcher. The Natural Science and Engineering Research Council of Canada is responsible for selecting Canadian nominees for JSPS Fellowships. [ID:6626]

ORS Awards Scheme
Executive Assistant, The Secretary, CVCP, Woburn House,
20 Tavistock Square, London WC1H HQ, UK; (44) (171) 419-6111,
fax (44) (171) 383-4573, ORS_SCHEME@CVCP.ac.uk, www.cvcp.ac.uk/orsas.html

GRADUATE ▪ The Overseas Research Students Awards Scheme (ORS) was established in 1979 to provide awards for full-time graduate research students registered at an institution of higher learning in the UK. Approximately 850 awards are disbursed annually on a competitive basis and cover the difference between tuition fees for UK graduate students and fees for overseas students. ORS awards do not cover maintenance expenses. All applications for the award should be made to the academic institution where the student has been accepted. For details see the ORS web site. [ID:5186]

Rhodes Scholarship Secretariat
General Secretary for Rhodes Scholarships in Canada, Suite 4700,
Toronto Dominion Centre, Toronto, Ontario M5K 1E6; (416) 601-7500, fax (416) 868-1793

GRADUATE ▪ The Rhodes Scholarship is designed for Canadian citizens or permanent residents who are between the ages of 18 and 24, and have at least three years' university training. Qualities of both character and intellect are the most important requirements for the Rhodes Scholarships and these are what the selection committees will seek. Recipients study at the undergraduate or graduate level at the University of Oxford, UK. Eleven Canadians are accepted annually. Each scholarship is worth £7,000 plus tuition annually, for two to three years. Application deadline is October 24. [ID:5192]

Rotary Foundation Ambassadorial Scholarships
For further information contact your local Rotary Club

ALL LEVELS ▪ The Rotary Foundation Ambassadorial Scholarships were created to increase international understanding among people of different countries and cultural backgrounds. Rotary Clubs across Canada offer graduate, undergraduate, vocational, journalism and teachers of the handicapped scholarships. These awards allow candidates to complete one academic year of study or training in a country where Rotary Clubs are located. Undergraduate and graduate scholarships can be used for almost any field of study. Scholarships cover transportation costs, academic fees, some educational supplies and meals and accommodation on campus. Candidates should apply to their local Rotary Club. Deadline for applications is July 15 . [ID:5195]

Royal Society of Canada
Konrad Adenauer Research Award Committee, Suite 308, 225 Metclafe Street,
Ottawa, Ontario K2P 1P9; (613) 991-6990, fax (613) 991-6996, admin@rsc.ca, www.rsc.ca

DOCTORAL ▪ The Konrad Adenauer Research Award, established in 1988, is disbursed annually to a Canadian scholar engaged in research in the humanities and the social sciences. The award is administered by the Alexander von Humboldt Foundation in Germany, in cooperation with the Royal Society of Canada and the University of Toronto and aims to promote academic relations between Germany and Canada. An amount of up to DM$100,000 is made to a highly qualified Canadian scholar whose work has brought them international recognition and who belongs to a group of leading scholars in their area of specialization. Candidates should be nominated by their university. Dossiers must be received by the Executive Director of the Royal Society of Canada by no later then December 1. [ID:5176]

Royal Society of Canada
Sir Arthur Sims Scholarship Committee, Suite 308, 225 Metcalfe Street,
Ottawa, Ontario K2P 1P9; (613) 991-6990, fax (613) 991-6996, admin@rsc.ca, www.rsc.ca

GRADUATE ▪ In 1952 Sir Arthur Sims of London, England, established an endowment fund with the Royal Trust Company to support a Canadian student enrolled in a graduate program in Great Britain. Today, the scholarship is administered by the Royal Society of Canada. The scholarship is awarded for outstanding merit and promise in any subject of the humanities, social sciences or natural sciences. It is open to Canadian students who have completed one year of graduate study at a British institution and are continuing towards an advanced degree. The annual value of the scholarship is £700 and is normally awarded for two years, subject to satisfactory progress. Applications should be forwarded to the Sir Arthur Sims Scholarship Committee of the Royal Society of Canada before February 15.
[ID:5198]

Royal Society of Canada
NATO Fellowships Committee, Suite 308, 225 Metcalfe Street,
Ottawa, Ontario K2P 1P9; (613) 991-6990, fax (613) 991-6996, adminrsc@rsc.ca, www.rsc.ca

GRADUATE ▪ The NATO fellowships, sponsored by the Committee on the Challenges of Modern Society (CCMS), were established in 1969 with the mandate to support research that examines "how to improve, in every practical way, the exchange of views and experience among the allied countries in the task of creating a better environment for their societies." The CCMS sponsors a small fellowship program, which makes modest grants to a number of scholars each year, to encourage research linked to the committee's ongoing pilot projects. A complete list of these projects can be obtained from the fellowship contact. Some recent research titles include: "Desertification in Desert Areas," "Pollution Prevention Strategies for Sustainable Development," "Protection Against Marine Biological Fouling," "Methodologies in the Focalization," and "Evaluation and Scope of the Environmental Impact Assessment." [ID:5184]

School for International Training (SIT)
Scholarship Committee, SIT Admissions Office, Brattleboro, VT, 05301, USA;
(802) 257-7751, fax (802) 258-3500, admissions@sit.edu, www.worldlearning.org/sit.html

UNDERGRADUATE ▪ The School for International Training's (SIT) Bachelor of Arts Degree challenges its students to understand global problems and to work towards their resolution through a combination of classroom and experiential learning. SIT offers awards of up to US$3,000 to a World Issues Program applicant who has participated in an international exchange, work-abroad program, or an accredited college study-abroad program. Candidates are judged on their ability to articulate their learning experience and crosscultural maturity. Visit the SIT web site for program and admission details. [ID:5167]

Shastri Indo-Canadian Institute
Executive Director, University of Calgary, 1407 Educational Towers, Calgary, Alberta
T2N 1N4; (403) 220-7467, fax (403) 289-0100, sici@acs.ucalgary.ca, www.ucalgary.ca/~sici

ALL LEVELS ▪ These fellowships allow artists to travel to India either to further their training or expand their knowledge. The Senior Fellowships provide a training stipend, a living allowance of 12,000 rupees per month and return airfare to India. The Junior Fellowships also include a training stipend and return airfare, with a living allowance of 8,000 rupees per month. Recipients of the Junior Fellowships must demonstrate their need for training in India, and undertake study there for a minimum of four months. [ID:5196]

Shastri Indo-Canadian Institute
Executive Director, The University of Calgary, 1407 Education Towers, Calgary, Alberta
T2N 1N4; (403) 220-7467, fax (403) 289-0100, sici@acs.ucalgary.ca, www.ucalgary.ca/~sici

ALL LEVELS ▪ The Shastri Institute's Language Training Fellowship is intended to assist anyone who would like to improve their knowledge of an Indian language. The award provides financial assistance for fellows and senior scholars in the humanities and social sciences and will support research initiatives that are between three months and a year in length. Applicants must have a BA or MA and some prior training in an Indian language. [ID:5197]

Social Science Research Council
Coordinator, Program on International Peace and Security,
605 Third Ave., New York, NY, 10158, USA; (212) 377-2700, fax (212) 377-2727

DOCTORAL ▪ The Social Science Research Council will award approximately seven dissertation awards and six postdoctoral awards to support innovative and interdisciplinary research on emerging issues of international peace and security in a changing world. The program, funded by the John D. and Catherine T. MacArthur Foundation, encourages women, members of minority groups, and scholars residing outside the US to apply. Dissertation fellowships pay a stipend of US$17,500. Postdoctoral fellows will also be granted a stipend, of US$37,500. Applications should be directed to the Social Science Research Council and must be received by November 14 of the competition year. [ID:5157]

Social Sciences and Humanities Research Council of Canada

Director, P.O. Box 1610, 350 Albert Street, Ottawa, Ontario K1P 6G4;
(613) 992-0530, fax (613) 992-1787, cpe@sshrc.ca, www.sshrc.ca

---

DOCTORAL ▪ The Social Sciences and Humanities Research Council offers doctoral and PhD fellowships that can be used for overseas study. Candidates must be Canadian citizens or permanent residents. The current value of a doctoral fellowship is $15,000, and PhD fellowships are valued at $28,428 plus a $5,000 research allowance. Visit SSHRC's web site for information and applications. [ID:5199]

Chapter 16

International Studies in Canada & Abroad

WHY INTERNATIONAL STUDIES?

Much of Canada's wealth comes from our interaction with other countries. We derive 38 per cent of our Gross National Product (GNP) from the export of goods and services. International trade supports a third of all Canadian jobs, and, as the North American Free Trade Agreement (NAFTA) extends south into Latin America, projections for the future indicate that Canada will increasingly rely on international trade to sustain long-term economic growth.

As Canada moves into the 21st century there is an increasing demand for managers, policy-makers, and professionals familiar with the international community. While the need for intercultural skills and overseas experience grows, many educators refer to practical knowledge of international fields as "the new literacy."

There isn't a university or college in Canada that doesn't offer some kind of international study program, whether it's a diploma, degree, or a coordinated area of specialization. Virtually every Canadian university and college has included as part of their mandate "the internationalization of their campus and curriculum." As this chapter clearly shows, there is an abundance of expertise in international subject areas on campuses across the country, and the programs offered vary dramatically in rationale, scope, breadth, and rigor. Whether you are interested in politics, history, education, business, environmental studies, law, or rural planning, most programs integrate international perspectives into their curriculum.

INTERNATIONAL STUDIES IN CANADA

We have documented a total of 314 international study programs and international academic research centres at Canadian universities and colleges. The list of 264 international study programs is limited to diploma and degree programs which specifically state the international field on the certificate of completion. The 50 academic research centres are listed because their international focus can enhance the corresponding international study program. These centres raise the profiles of their departments and offer academic support, research opportunities, internship programs, and job possibilities to students. For those universities with substantial international activity, we have included a *university international profile* detailing their international strengths and expertise.

At the end of this chapter we have "International Studies Abroad," a list of 110 programs from a variety of disciplines where the focus of study is international. Based on the recommendations of academics and professionals, these programs are located at schools from around the world which have solid reputations and where the language of instruction is either French or English.

We hope the information in this chapter will help you find the program best suited to your career objectives.

WHAT SKILLS WILL YOU DEVELOP?

International programs increase your awareness and appreciation of other cultures and help you develop crosscultural communication skills. As a student just starting university, you have probably had little or no real exposure to the world outside of Canada. By *internationalizing* your education through the study of other languages, legal systems, cultures, politics and economies, you will become conversant with the international scene and gain insight into the global community. A university education in any of these areas demonstrates that you have developed breadth and flexibility in your thinking, analytical writing and verbal skills, the ability to take and defend a position, and so on. Therefore, your increased knowledge base, plus these skills, make you attractive to recruiters from international agencies and businesses. Of course, completing a semester or year of study abroad or an overseas internship will make you all the more appealing in today's competitive job market.

CHOOSING THE RIGHT PROGRAM

Selecting a program can be an intimidating prospect. It is a choice that will affect the rest of your life, so taking the time and effort to research your options is very important. You should start by reading the list of programs in this chapter. Almost all university libraries have recent university calendars from Canada and abroad which contain program and course descriptions, entry requirements, and special attributes. And, of course, most universities now put their course calendar on their web site as well.

Whether you are beginning a first degree or moving on to graduate work, there are a number of practical factors to consider in selecting a program:

duration, location, cost, funding available, reputation of the program, and a variety of crucial intangibles. The two most common considerations for evaluating a program are the reputation of its faculty and the selectivity of its admissions policy. A program with a tough admissions policy, a limited enrolment, and a prestigious faculty is likely one which provides graduates with excellent employment prospects.

Once you've found a program that appeals to you, set up an informational interview with a faculty representative. Prepare a list of questions and topics for discussion ahead of time, so that you get the maximum benefit from the meeting. What are the goals of the program? What courses are offered? Seek out graduates and current students as well.

Next, find out if the program has internships with international agencies, government, or nongovernmental organizations in Canada. Practical experience of this in and of itself is incomparable, and it will help you make contact with people who can help you with your employment search once you have completed your studies. The NORMAN PATERSON SCHOOL OF INTERNATIONAL AFFAIRS at CARLETON UNIVERSITY, for example, offers practical, unpaid internships with a variety of governmental agencies, embassies, and nongovernmental organizations in Ottawa. And, as part of the MBA Program at DALHOUSIE UNIVERSITY in Halifax, a Foreign Studies Mission course sends students to Europe to explore trade opportunities for Nova Scotian companies.

Another important question to ask is whether there are opportunities for overseas studies as part of the program. This component allows you to make valuable contacts abroad and gives you the chance to improve your foreign language and crosscultural skills. Such opportunities are commonplace with most international studies programs, especially business programs. (See Chapter 14, Study Abroad.) Most international business programs have an overseas option. As a requirement of the Bachelor of International Business (BIB) honours degree at CARLETON UNIVERSITY in Ottawa, students must spend one year of study at a university abroad.

Find out what percentage of students accepted into the program are foreign nationals. Obviously, the higher the number of students from other cultures and countries, the greater your opportunity for exposure to different attitudes, traditions, and belief systems. Many US schools list the percentage of foreign nationals (as well as women, members of visible minorities, etc.), but most Canadian universities, and particularly specific programs, do not. One program that strives for a truly international student body is the TRENT INTERNATIONAL PROGRAM (TIP) at TRENT UNIVERSITY in Peterborough, Ontario. In the last 10 years, the TIP program has welcomed Canadian students and students from over 110 countries. Of more than 300 students enrolled each year, at least one quarter of them are foreign students.

You should also inquire about language requirements for graduation from the program. An increasing number of undergraduate degrees have language stipulations; for graduate programs, proficiency in a second language is usually a requirement. Language training is an important consideration at any level because few employers will hire someone for an international position without a second and possibly a third language. Starting language training at the beginning of your university career will allow you time to build proficiency gradually, instead of cramming it into your last year of undergraduate, or first year of graduate, studies. Over time, this strategy is definitely more effective, and may allow you to learn a third or fourth language as well. (See Chapter 5, Learning a Foreign Language.)

Finally, find out about the rate of placement for your program graduates. How many have found work? How many of those working are in jobs related to the program? How many are working in the international realm? What sort of jobs do they have and in what sectors?

The information from this interview, plus prior research should help you decide if this is the right program for you. On the other hand, the interview may have helped clarify what sort of program you really need, and you may decide to go elsewhere or continue your search. There are a lot of options out there and the more you know, the more discerning you can be.

Undergraduate Versus Graduate Degree

With very few exceptions, undergraduate degrees are now considered a minimum in the workforce. In most fields, students must have completed graduate studies to be considered for international positions. International studies should be the focus of your MA degree, regardless of whether or not your undergraduate degree has an international focus. In today's world you almost always need an MA to be taken seriously in your international career; a graduate degree will not guarantee you an overseas job, but it will certainly increase your chances of getting an interview.

In most disciplines, a PhD often renders you as overqualified unless you plan to teach at the university level. Economics and sciences are exceptions; for example, a PhD in Economics can lead to jobs with international organizations under the umbrella of the UNITED NATIONS.

College Versus University Programs

Another important consideration is whether to attend a college or university program. Many colleges offer programs of university quality for considerably less cost. Moreover, many college credits are transferable to university, so taking your first few years at the college level and then continuing at university is a path some students follow. Many colleges also have post-graduate diplomas, especially in business-related areas, which are highly specialized and reputable. As with any international studies program, it is important to ensure the quality of the program, that the program matches your needs, and that credits are transferable to the university level.

WHAT SHOULD YOU DO BESIDES STUDY?

In this day and age, a formal education alone isn't sufficient to interest a prospective employer. In addition to the skills needed for the actual job, three other things are important: fluency in *at least* one other language, the ability to travel and move often, and experience working in stressful or unfamiliar situations. Finding an overseas job depends as much on practical experience as academic preparation.

To gain experience, develop extracurricular interests that not only complement your academic record, but also demonstrate your concern, initiative, and ability to work cooperatively. Get involved on campus: join a club with an international focus, volunteer at your international student centre, make friends with international students and get involved in their activities. Tutor someone in English. Such activities not only add to your *International IQ*, but are also personally rewarding. Help organize international conferences at your university, and, if possible, attend conferences elsewhere. Offer to volunteer or intern at research centres on campus or at nongovernmental organizations in the community. Apply for summer jobs with the international affairs sections of private companies.

Apply for scholarships to study overseas. (See Chapter 15, Awards & Grants.) Arrange a summer internship with an international organization. (See Chapter 17, International Internships.) Take a vacation or a working holiday abroad to expose yourself to other peoples and other cultures. Involve yourself in research projects which require meeting representatives of Canadian international development agencies, international nongovernmental organizations, foreign diplomats, etc. These are important initiatives to pursue in order to add a hands-on element to your academic career.

JOB PROSPECTS AFTER GRADUATION

You have just completed six years of post-secondary study. You need a job. The question is, where do graduates with an international specialization find work? A survey of firms in the private sector showed that they want to hire graduates with MAs or MBAs that include an international specialization or concentration. However, graduates from Canadian business programs rarely enter international postings immediately after graduation. According to a survey prepared by the CORPORATE HIGHER EDUCATION FORUM, only 16 per cent of the private sector's overseas positions are filled by recent university graduates. Canadian companies generally hire new graduates for entry-level positions in Canada. Only after they have proven themselves at home are they rewarded with overseas postings.

New graduates interested in careers in the private sector should approach smaller companies experiencing rapid growth phases. These organizations tend to move new employees into overseas positions more quickly. Alternatively, your job search can focus only on companies or agencies based overseas. This generally works for entry-level positions where wages are lower.

Graduates with a MA in Economics are recruited by banks, big business, and government. As mentioned, those with PhDs often find work in international agencies such as the INTERNATIONAL MONETARY FUND (IMF), the WORLD BANK, or the UN. An MA in International Relations or Political Science qualifies you for positions in government departments and some nongovernmental organizations (NGOs). Job opportunities in international law are generally rare. Canadian graduates can be recruited by the government departments of FOREIGN AFFAIRS AND INTERNATIONAL TRADE (DFAIT) and JUSTICE, as well as by a few international law firms.

HOW TO KEEP YOUR FIRST JOB

Many university graduates learn a hard lesson in their first full-time, salaried position. The most common reason for losing your first job is failure to come to grips with office politics. Natural enthusiasm and hard work only take you so far. You must focus on learning people-skills *first*. Be respectful of your supervisor's position and responsibilities. Practice tact at meetings, and find ways to recognize the accomplishments of co-workers. Master the imprecise arts of listening, and taking and giving constructive criticism. Understand the value of compromise, work to build consensus, learn to mediate, practice motivating others. In crosscultural work, as in many other fields, good people skills are at least as important as technical knowledge and personal ambition.

A LAST WORD

Growing up in rural New Brunswick, I had no role models to lessen the fear of unknown places and exotic peoples. Aside from an aunt living in Peru, I knew no one who had lived abroad. It was the university environment that allowed me to challenge my assumptions, mix with a diverse group of people, and develop my interest in working overseas. I learned that the international realm is populated by interesting people from many backgrounds. So, to my fellow small town readers I say, *go for it*! Now is the time to explore and to broaden your world view.

RESOURCES

This list of books will help you decide where to study all things international in Canada and the US. A word of caution, however: much of this study is theoretical and academic. A large part of the skill and knowledge you need to be successful overseas is practical and functional, so complement your academic studies with practical experience. And if you want to follow a course of self-study, read books describing actual development projects, international business success stories, or the personality skills required to manage overseas contracts. Tidbits of this kind of information expressed at the right time during an interview will help make up for your possible lack of overseas work experience.

To help you with your international studies consult: Chapter 10, Short-term Programs Overseas; Chapter 14, Study Abroad; Chapter 15, Awards & Grants; and Chapter 17, International Internships.

Also consult the Resources sections in the following chapters: for general crosscultural skills see Chapter 1, The Effective Overseas Employee; for the more practical aspects of living overseas see Chapter 3, Living Overseas and Chapter 12, Crosscultural Travel; for material which is helpful to all, but focuses on crosscultural business skills, see Chapter 7, The Canadian Identity in the International Workplace; for country-specific advice on social and business customs see Chapter 27, Jobs by Regions of the World; and for books on the practice of international business (such as how to import and export) see Chapter 33, Services for International Businesses & Entrepreneurs.

After Latin American Studies: A Guide to Graduate Study, Fellowships, Internships, and Employment for Latin Americanists 📖
1995, *Shirley A. Kregar*, 142 pages ➤ Center for Latin American Studies, 4E04 Forbes Quad, University of Pittsburgh, Pittsburgh, PA 15260, USA; $10; MC, Amex; (412) 648-7392, fax (412) 648-2199, clas+@cpitt.edu ■ Provides information on graduate study, research and internships. For graduate as well as undergraduate students, opportunities in the private sector, and career opportunities in the US government and in international organizations. An essential resource for anyone with career or scholarly interests in the region. Visit the distributor's web site at www.edu/~clas. [ID:1118]

Canadian Bureau for International Education 🖳
www.cbie.ca ■ CBIE is an organization of 110 colleges and universities which promotes international understanding through active exchange of people and ideas. A number of schools, organizations and companies also participate in CBIE's programs. The organization focuses on international exchanges at the university level, and provides information and advice for Canadian students travelling abroad and foreign students in Canada. [ID:2473]

The Canadian College Directory 📖
Annual, Association of Universities and Colleges of Canada (AUCC), 282 pages ➤ AUCC Publications Office, Suite 600, 350 Albert Street, Ottawa, Ontario K1R 1B1; $24.95; (613) 563-1236, fax (613) 563-9745 ■ An excellent source for information on every college in Canada. Colleges are listed by province, and each profile outlines information on general admission requirements, campus life and student services, areas of expertise and international involvement. An index of programs is included. Visit the publisher's web site, www.aucc.ca, for ordering information. [ID:2493]

Choices That Count: Co-operative Education in the Public Service of Canada 📖 🖳
Annual, 145 pages ➤ External Recruitment Programs, Public Service Commission, 18th Floor, L'Esplanade Laurier, 300 Laurier Avenue W., Ottawa, Ontario K1A 0M7; free; (613) 992-9630, fax (613) 947-5875 ■ A listing of work-study programs at Canadian postsecondary institutions. If you are registered in one of these programs, check out the possibilities of arranging co-op placements with the international branch of a government department. The web version of this publication should be available by 1998 at the Public Service Commission web site. Visit it at www.psc-cfp.gc.ca/jobs.htm. [ID:1666]

Directory of Canadian Universities 📖
Biennial, Association of Universities and Colleges of Canada (AUCC), 482 pages ➤ AUCC Publications Office, Suite 600, 350 Albert Street, Ottawa, Ontario K1R 1B1; $42; (613) 563-1236, fax (613) 563-9745 ■ A comprehensive, bilingual guide to higher education in Canada. Provides information about campuses, facilities, admission requirements, programs, degrees, financial assistance, and student life and services. National index to all university programs. [ID:1365]

Economics Departments, Institutes and Research Centres Around the World 🖳
www.er.uqam.ca/nobel/r14160/economics ■ This web site indexes 2,983 economics institutions in 132 countries. Included are economics departments, research centres as well as finance ministries, statistical offices, central banks, and other nonprofit institutions useful for economists. [ID:2731]

Global Directory of Peace Studies Programs 📖
Annual, 180 pages ➤ Consortium on Peace Research, Education, and Development (COPRED), George Mason University, Fairfax, VA 22030-4444, USA; US$25; cheque; (703) 993-2405, fax (703) 993-3070, copred@gmu.edu ■ This directory tells where in the world to get certificate, college and postgraduate degrees, in more than 350 peace-related programs. [ID:2678]

The Group of Ten ⌨

http://admin1.intlcent.ualberta.ca/GOTSEPinfo/gotsep.html ▪ This program is intended to help undergraduate university students live and study in a foreign country. Eligible students must be enrolled in one of the following: McGill University, McMaster University, Queen's University, Université Laval, Université de Montréal, University of Alberta, University of British Columbia, University of Toronto, University of Waterloo or University of Western Ontario. [ID:2472]

Guide to Business Schools 📖

1997, *Rebecca Carpenter* ➤ Nelson Canada, 1120 Birchmount Road, Scarborough, Ontario M1K 5G4; $24.95; credit cards; (800) 268-2222, fax (800) 430-4445 ▪ This book features in-depth profiles of 49 business schools with answers to such questions as: Which school is the best for finance, entrepreneurship, accounting, co-op, or general management? Which grads command the highest salaries? Which schools have the best reputations? What is campus life like? This book tells you how Canada's 31 MBA, 11 Executive MBA, 16 PhD, and 49 undergrad programs stack up. [ID:2710]

How to Study and Live in Britain 📖

1990, *Jane Woolfenden,* 221 pages ➤ How To Books Ltd., 3 Newtec Place, Magdalen Road, Oxford, OX4 1RE, UK; £8.99; credit cards; (44) (1752) 202-301, fax (44) (1865) 202-331 ▪ Provides information on schools and colleges, courses, qualifications, immigration, money, accommodation and more. [ID:1162]

International Centre, Queen's University ⌨

www.quic.queensu.ca ▪ This extensive site offers many services to help you find overseas placements, whether volunteer, pleasure or academic. From health insurance upon departure to culture shock upon re-entry, Queen's can help you plan your international adventure. Its Resource Library section is particularly useful. This is a great spot to look if you are in the initial stages of looking for an international placement. [ID:2432]

The New Internationalist 📖 ⌨

Monthly ➤ Subscription Office, New Internationalist, Unit 17, 35 Riviera Drive, Markham, Ontario L3R 8N4; $38.50/year; credit cards; (905) 946-0407, fax (905) 946-0410 ▪ This magazine has been used for years by development education groups as a primer on global social justice issues. Each issue covers one broad theme, in a popularized style. Good reading for an alternative perspective. Back issues are available online at www.newint.org. [ID:1212]

Peterson's Guides 📖 ⌨

Annual, Peterson's Guides ➤ Nelson Canada, 1120 Birchmount Road, Scarborough, Ontario M1K 5G4; credit cards; (800) 268-2222, fax (800) 430-4445 ▪ An annual series of books which provides exhaustive coverage of the institutions and subject areas of undergraduate and graduate academic programs in Canada and the US. Contains information on entrance and degree requirements, expenses, financial aid and programs of study. Series includes: Graduate Programs in the Humanities, Arts, and Social Sciences; Biological and Agricultural Sciences; Physical Sciences and Mathematics; Engineering and Applied Sciences; Business, Education, Health, and Law. As well, there are *Peterson's Guide to Four-Year Programs* and *Peterson's Guide to Two-Year Programs,* both of which provide a detailed look at undergraduate academic institutions. Visit their web site at http://www.petersons.com for details on prices and contents of each guide. [ID:1543]

University Affairs 📖

10/year, Association of Universities and Colleges of Canada (AUCC) ➤ AUCC Publications Office, Suite 600, 350 Albert Street, Ottawa, Ontario K1R 1B1; $35 year, $4 per issue; (613) 563-1236, fax (613) 563-9745 ▪ This bilingual magazine, published ten times a year, is of general interest to Canadian students and academic staff. It contains articles on a wide range of topics related to Canadian universities and colleges, and posts job openings at affiliated member institutions as well as job postings at educational institutions around the world. Visit the publisher's web site, www.aucc.ca, for ordering information. [ID:2494]

Your Guide to Canadian Colleges 📖
1994, *Kevin Paul,* 256 pages ➤ Self-Counsel Press, 1481 Charlotte Road, North Vancouver, B.C. V7J 1H1; $14.95; VISA, MC; (604) 986-3366, fax (604) 986-3947, sales@self-counsel.com ▪ A close look at 90 Canadian community colleges, with contact information for 30 more. Information on programs and courses offered, as well as facts about each college's services, location, outreach centres, and tuition. Tips on how to adapt to student life, set goals, study effectively, and stay motivated. Visit the distributor's web site at www.self-counsel.com. [ID:1623]

Profiles of International Studies in Canada & Abroad

The remainder of this chapter has three sections. First, an index of international study programs sorted by the type of program. Second, 314 profiles sorted by academic institution (47 universities and 23 colleges). These profiles document 264 international studies programs available in Canada as well as 50 related international academic research centres. Keep in mind that universities usually offer numerous international courses, but we have only listed programs that meet the following criteria:

• certificate, diploma, and degree programs that are exclusively international in their orientation and are noted as such on official transcripts;

• established international programs (concentration or specialization) supervised and coordinated by faculty;

• doctoral programs with a designated international focus.

Universities with significant international focus have a "university international profile" at the beginning of their listing. And third, the last section of this chapter, International Studies Abroad, documents 110 programs from around the world.

Index to International Studies

This index to Canadian international studies and academic research centres is in alphabetical order by type of study program. Of the 314 international studies programs and international academic research centres profiled, the breakdown is as follows: Area Studies, 92; Development Studies, 37; Intercultural Studies, 12; International Business, 61; International Education, 10; International Health, 2; International Law, 8; International Sciences, 2; International Studies (such as international affairs/relations), 48; Peace/Conflict Studies, 12; and University International Profiles, 30.

AREA STUDIES

UNIVERSITY OF ALBERTA
Consortium for Middle Eastern and African Studies (CMEAS) (BA & BA (honours): special interest in Middle East & African Studies)
Department of East Asian Studies (BA (major) IN EAST ASIAN STUDIES)

UNIVERSITY OF BRITISH COLUMBIA
Centre for Asian Legal Studies (RESEARCH CENTRE)
Department of Asian Studies (BA, MA & PhD IN ASIAN STUDIES)
Department of Germanic Studies (BA, BA (honours), MA & PhD IN GERMANIC STUDIES)
Department of Hispanic Studies (BA, BA (honours), MA & PhD IN HISPANIC STUDIES)
Institute of Asian Research (RESEARCH CENTRE)
Modern European Studies Program (BA IN MODERN EUROPEAN STUDIES)

BROCK UNIVERSITY
Department of Germanic Studies (BA & BA (honours) IN GERMANIC STUDIES)

UNIVERSITY OF CALGARY
Faculty of General Studies (BA & BSc: minor in African, East Asian, South Asian, Latin American or Central and East European Studies)
Italian Department (BA: minor in Italian Studies)

CAMOSUN COLLEGE
Pacific Rim Studies Program (DIPLOMA IN PACIFIC RIM STUDIES: general or business option)

CAPILANO COLLEGE
Asia Pacific Management Co-operative Program (DIPLOMA IN ASIA PACIFIC MANAGEMENT)

CARLETON UNIVERSITY
Centre for Research on Canadian-Russian Relations (RESEARCH CENTRE)
East-West Project (RESEARCH CENTRE)
Institute of Central/East European and Russian-Area Studies (RESEARCH CENTRE)
Institute of Central/East European and Russian-Area Studies (BA (honours) & MA IN CENTRAL/EAST EUROPEAN AND RUSSIAN AREA STUDIES)
Institute of Interdisciplinary Studies (BA (honours) IN DIRECTED INTER-DISCIPLINARY STUDIES: concentration in Aboriginal Studies, African Studies, Asian Studies, Latin American Studies, Caribbean Studies, Environmental Studies or Third World Studies)

Research Unit on Southern European Literature and Culture (RESEARCH CENTRE)

CONCORDIA UNIVERSITY
Department of History (BA IN SOUTHERN ASIAN STUDIES)

DALHOUSIE UNIVERSITY
Department of Russian (BA & BA (honours) IN RUSSIAN STUDIES)

UNIVERSITY OF GUELPH
Scottish Studies Program (MA & PhD IN SCOTTISH STUDIES)
Waterloo-Laurier-Guelph Centre for East European and Russian Studies (RESEARCH CENTRE)

LANGARA COLLEGE
Latin American Studies Program (DIPLOMA PROGRAM IN LATIN AMERICAN STUDIES)
Pacific Rim Studies Program (DIPLOMA IN PACIFIC RIM STUDIES)

UNIVERSITÉ LAVAL
Centre d'études nordiques (CENTRE DE RECHERCHE)
Centre international de recherche en aménagement linguistique (CIRAL) (CENTRE DE RECHERCHE)
Études africaines (BA: mineure ou certificat en études africaines)
Études Russes ou Slaves (CERTIFICAT OU MINEURE D'ÉTUDES RUSSES ou BACCALAURÉAT INDIVIDUALISÉ EN ÉTUDES RUSSES ET SLAVES)

UNIVERSITY OF MANITOBA
Asian Studies Centre (BA: minor in Asian Studies)
Central and Eastern European Studies Program (BA: major in Central and Eastern European Studies)
Department of Religion (BA IN RELIGION: concentration in Judaic Studies)
Latin American Studies Program (BA: minor in Latin American Studies)

MCGILL UNIVERSITY
Centre for East Asian Research (RESEARCH CENTRE)
Department of German Studies (BA, MA & PhD IN GERMANIC STUDIES)
Department of Russian and Slavic Studies (BA, BA (honours), MA & PhD IN SLAVIC STUDIES)
East Asian Studies Program (BA (honours & joint honours): major in East Asian Studies)
Institute of Islamic Studies (MA & PhD IN ISLAMIC STUDIES)
Latin American and Caribbean Studies Program (BA (major & honours) IN LATIN-AMERICAN AND CARIBBEAN STUDIES)
Middle East Studies Program (BA (honours, joint honours, major & joint major) IN MIDDLE EAST STUDIES)
North American Studies Program (BA IN NORTH AMERICAN STUDIES)

MCMASTER UNIVERSITY
Japanese Studies Program (BA (honours) IN JAPANESE STUDIES)

UNIVERSITÉ DE MONTRÉAL
Centre d'études de l'Asie de l'Est (CENTRE DE RECHERCHE)
Études arabes (MINEUR EN ÉTUDES ARABES (1er cycle))
Études est-asiatiques (CERTIFICAT ou DIPLÔME EN ÉTUDES EST-ASIATIQUES)
Études italiennes (MINEUR EN ÉTUDES ITALIENNES)
Études latino-américaines (CERTIFICAT EN ÉTUDES LATINO-AMÉRICAINES)
Études russes (CERTIFICAT EN ÉTUDES RUSSES)
Groupe de recherche sur l'Amérique Latine (GRAL) (GROUPE DE RECHERCHE)

MOUNT ALLISON UNIVERSITY
American Studies Program (BA & BA (honours) IN AMERICAN STUDIES)
Japanese Language Program (BA: minor in Japanese Studies)

UNIVERSITY OF NEW BRUNSWICK
Russian Studies Program (BA IN RUSSIAN STUDIES)

UNIVERSITÉ DU QUÉBEC À CHICOUTIMI
Études régionales et développement régional (MA EN ÉTUDES RÉGIONALES et PhD EN DÉVELOPPEMENT RÉGIONAL)

QUEEN'S UNIVERSITY
Centre for Canada-Asia Business Relations (RESEARCH CENTRE)
Commonwealth Studies Program (BA (honours) IN COMMONWEALTH STUDIES)
Department of German Languages and Literature (BA, MA & PhD IN GERMANIC LANGUAGE AND LITERATURE)
Jewish Studies Program (BA IN JEWISH STUDIES)

UNIVERSITY OF REGINA
Asian Pacific Management Institute (RESEARCH CENTRE)

SIMON FRASER UNIVERSITY
Department of Spanish and Latin American Studies (BA & MA IN LATIN AMERICAN STUDIES)
Faculty of Arts (CERTIFICATE IN CHINESE STUDIES)

ST. FRANCIS XAVIER UNIVERSITY
Department of Celtic Studies (BA IN CELTIC STUDIES)

ST. MARY'S UNIVERSITY
Asian Studies Program (BA IN ASIAN STUDIES)

UNIVERSITY OF TORONTO
African Studies Program (BA (minor, major & specialization) IN AFRICAN STUDIES)
American Studies Program (BA: concentration in American Studies)

Centre for Russian and East European Studies (MA IN RUSSIAN AND EAST EUROPEAN STUDIES)
Centre for South Asian Studies (BA & MA IN SOUTH ASIAN STUDIES)
Department of East Asian Studies (BA (minor, major & specialization), MA, MPhil & PhD IN EAST ASIAN STUDIES)
Department of Italian Studies (BA, BA (honours), MA & PhD IN ITALIAN STUDIES)
Department of Middle East and Islamic Studies (BA, MA & PhD IN MIDDLE EAST AND ISLAMIC STUDIES)
Department of Near and Middle Eastern Civilizations (BA, MA & PhD IN NEAR EASTERN STUDIES)
Department of Slavic Languages and Literature (BA IN CROATIAN AND SERBIAN STUDIES; BA IN CZECH AND SLOVAK STUDIES; BA IN POLISH STUDIES; BA & BA (honours) IN RUSSIAN OR UKRAINIAN)
Department of Spanish and Portuguese (BA (minor & major) IN IBERO-AMERICAN STUDIES)
Jewish Studies Program (BA & BA (honours) IN JEWISH STUDIES)
Department of Modern Languages and Literature (BA & BA (honours) IN HISPANIC STUDIES)
German Studies (BA & BA (honours) IN GERMAN STUDIES)

VANIER COLLEGE
Jewish Studies Program (DIPLOMA IN JEWISH STUDIES)
Slavic Studies Program (DIPLOMA IN SLAVIC STUDIES)

UNIVERSITY OF VICTORIA
Centre for Asia-Pacific Initiatives (CAPI) (RESEARCH CENTRE)
Department of Hispanic and Italian Studies (BA: minor in Italian Studies)
Department of Pacific and Asian Studies (BA IN PACIFIC STUDIES)

UNIVERSITY OF WATERLOO
Department of German (BA & BA (honours) IN GERMANIC STUDIES)
Department of German and Slavic Languages and Literature (BA: option in Russian and East European Studies)

UNIVERSITY OF WINDSOR
Asian Studies Program (BA (honours) IN ASIAN STUDIES)
Japanese Studies (CERTIFICATE IN JAPANESE STUDIES)
Latin American Studies Committee (CERTIFICATE IN LATIN AMERICAN AND CARIBBEAN STUDIES)

YORK UNIVERSITY
African Studies Program (BA IN AFRICAN STUDIES)
Centre for Jewish Studies (RESEARCH CENTRE)
Centre for Research on Latin America and the Caribbean (CERLAC) (GRADUATE DIPLOMA IN

LATIN AMERICAN
AND CARIBBEAN STUDIES)
East Asian Studies Program (BA (honours)
IN EAST ASIAN STUDIES)
Jewish Studies Program
(BA IN JEWISH STUDIES)
Joint Centre for Asia Pacific Studies
(RESEARCH CENTRE)
Latin American and Caribbean Studies Program
(BA (honours) IN LATIN AMERICAN AND
CARIBBEAN STUDIES)

DEVELOPMENT STUDIES

AUGUSTANA UNIVERSITY COLLEGE
Prairies/Mexico Rural Development Exchange
(DIPLOMA IN INTERDISCIPLINARY
STUDIES)

UNIVERSITY OF BRITISH COLUMBIA
School of Community and Regional Planning
(MA, MSc & PhD IN PLANNING: concen-
tration in International
Development Planning)

UNIVERSITY OF CALGARY
Division of International Development (DID)
(RESEARCH CENTRE)
Faculty of General Studies (BA & BA (honours)
IN DEVELOPMENT STUDIES)
Faculty of Social Work (MSW:
International concentration)

UNIVERSITY COLLEGE OF CAPE BRETON
School of Community Studies (BACS IN
COMMUNITY STUDIES: option in
Comparative Development Studies)

CARLETON UNIVERSITY
Development Administration Program (MA IN
PUBLIC ADMINISTRATION: specialization
in Development Administration)
Research Resource Division for Refugees
(RRDR) (RESEARCH CENTRE)

DALHOUSIE UNIVERSITY
College of Arts and Science
(BA IN INTERNATIONAL
DEVELOPMENT STUDIES)
International and Regional Development Studies
Program (MA IN DEVELOPMENT
ECONOMICS)
International Development Studies (BA, BA
(honours), & MA IN INTERNATIONAL
DEVELOPMENT STUDIES: specialization
in African Studies)

UNIVERSITY OF GUELPH
Collaborative International Development Studies
(BA, MA & MSc IN INTERNATIONAL
DEVELOPMENT STUDIES)
Collaborative Program in International
Development Studies (BA & MA IN
POLITICAL STUDIES: focus on Interna-
tional Development)

International Agricultural Program (BSc
IN AGRICULTURE: program in International
Agriculture)
University School of Rural Planning and Development
(MSc IN INTERNATIONAL RURAL PLANNING
AND DEVELOPMENT)

UNIVERSITÉ LAVAL
Agriculture et alimentation (CERTIFICAT, BScA, BSc,
DIPLÔME DE DEUXIÈME CYCLE, MSc, PhD)

MCGILL UNIVERSITY
Centre for Developing Area Studies (RESEARCH
CENTRE)
International Development Studies (BA: minor in
International Development Studies)
School of Architecture (MArch IN MINIMUM COST
HOUSING IN DEVELOPING COUNTRIES)

UNIVERSITÉ DE MONTRÉAL
Gestion urbaine pour les pays en développement
(DIPLÔME D'ÉTUDES SUPÉRIEURES
SPÉCIALISÉES EN GESTION URBAINE POUR
LES PAYS EN DÉVELOPPEMENT)

UNIVERSITY OF NEW BRUNSWICK
International Development Studies Program (BA
(honours) IN INTERNATIONAL DEVELOPMENT
STUDIES; BA: major in Third World Studies)

NIPISSING UNIVERSITY
Faculty of Arts and Sciences (BA (honours) IN
GEOGRAPHY: specialization in Community
Economic Development or International
Development)

UNIVERSITY OF OTTAWA
International Water Engineering Centre (RESEARCH
CENTRE)

UNIVERSITÉ D'OTTAWA
Sociologie du développement (MA EN SOCIOLOGIE:
spécialisation en sociologie du développement)

UNIVERSITÉ DU QUÉBEC À RIMOUSKI
Développement régional (MA et PhD EN
DÉVELOPPEMENT RÉGIONAL)

QUEEN'S UNIVERSITY
Development Studies Medial (BA (honours) IN
DEVELOPMENT STUDIES)

CÉGEP DE RIVIÈRE-DU-LOUP
Direction du développement interculturel (DDI)
(BUREAU DE LIAISONS INTERNATIONALES)
Programme Coopérant Volontaire (ATTESTATION
D'ÉTUDES COLLÉGIALES EN COOPÉRATION
INTERCULTURELLE)

UNIVERSITÉ DE SHERBROOKE
Gestion et développement des coopératives (MA EN
GESTION ET DÉVELOPPEMENT DES
COOPÉRATIVES)

ST. MARY'S UNIVERSITY
International Development Studies Program (BA, BA
(honours) & MA IN INTERNATIONAL
DEVELOPMENT STUDIES)

UNIVERSITY OF TORONTO
Co-operative Program in International Development Studies (IDS) (BA & BSc: specialization in International Development Studies)
Department of Political Science (BA, MA & PhD IN POLITICAL SCIENCE: specialization in Development Studies, Comparative Politics or International Relations)

TRENT UNIVERSITY
Comparative Development Studies Program (CDS) (BA (general, honours & joint major) IN COMPARATIVE DEVELOPMENT STUDIES)

WILFRID LAURIER UNIVERSITY
Development & International Studies Program (BA IN THIRD WORLD STUDIES)

UNIVERSITY OF WINNIPEG
International Development Studies (BA IN INTERNATIONAL DEVELOPMENT STUDIES)

YORK UNIVERSITY
Centre for Refugee Studies (GENERAL CERTIFICATE & GRADUATE DIPLOMA IN REFUGEE AND MIGRATION STUDIES)
Faculty of Environmental Studies (BES (honours), MES & PhD: concentration in Global Development)

INTERCULTURAL STUDIES

ACADIA UNIVERSITY
Fred C. Manning School of Business Administration (BBA: major in French, Spanish or German)

UNIVERSITY OF ALBERTA
International and Intercultural Education Programs (BEd IN INTERCULTURAL EDUCATION; MEd IN INTERNATIONAL/INTERCULTURAL EDUCATION)
Research Institute for Comparative Literature and Cross-Cultural Studies (RESEARCH CENTRE)

CAPILANO COLLEGE
Ethnic and Cultural Relations Program (CERTIFICATE IN ETHNIC AND CROSS-CULTURAL RELATIONS)

UNIVERSITÉ DE MONTRÉAL
Centre d'études ethniques de l'Université de Montréal (CENTRE DE RECHERCHE)
Groupe de recherche ethnicité et société (GROUPE DE RECHERCHE)
Intervention en milieu multiethnique (CERTIFICAT D' INTERVENTION EN MILIEU MULTIETHNIQUE)

UNIVERSITÉ DU QUÉBEC À CHICOUTIMI
Chaire d'enseignement et de recherche inter-ethniques et interculturels (CERII) (CENTRE DE RECHERCHE)

SIMON FRASER UNIVERSITY
David Lam Centre for International Communication (NON-CREDIT PROGRAM IN EAST ASIAN LANGUAGES)
Department of Sociology and Anthropology (POST BACCALAUREATE DIPLOMA IN ETHNIC AND INTERCULTURAL RELATIONS)

TRENT UNIVERSITY
Cultural Studies Program (BA & BA (honours) IN CULTURAL STUDIES)

UNIVERSITÉ DU QUÉBEC À MONTRÉAL
Immigration et relations interethniques, Module de sociologie (CERTIFICAT EN IMMIGRATION ET RELATIONS INTERETHNIQUES)

UNIVERSITY OF WINDSOR
Department of Classical and Modern Languages, Literatures and Civilizations (BA IN MULTICULTURAL STUDIES)

INTERNATIONAL BUSINESS

UNIVERSITY OF ALBERTA
Centre for International Business Studies (RESEARCH CENTRE)
Faculty of Business (MBA: specialization in International Business)
Undergraduate Business Program (BComm IN INTERNATIONAL BUSINESS: specialization in Chinese Studies, Japanese Studies, German Studies or Spanish American Studies)

BISHOP'S UNIVERSITY
Division of Business Administration (BBA: concentration in International Business)

COLLÈGE BOIS-DE-BOULOGNE
Commerce international (DIPLÔME D'ÉTUDES COLLÉGIALES EN TECHNIQUES ADMINISTRATIVES option commerce international)

BRITISH COLUMBIA INSTITUTE OF TECHNOLOGY
International Trade and Transportation Program (DIPLOMA IN INTERNATIONAL TRADE AND TRANSPORTATION)

UNIVERSITY OF BRITISH COLUMBIA
Faculty of Commerce and Business Administration (BComm: option in International Business)

BROCK UNIVERSITY
Faculty of Business (BBA: concentration in International Business)

CARLETON UNIVERSITY
Centre for the Study of Business/Government/NGO Relations (RESEARCH CENTRE)
Centre for the Study of Training, Investment and Economic Restructuring (CSTIER) (RESEARCH CENTRE)
International Business Study Group (IBSG) (RESEARCH CENTRE)

School of Business (BACHELOR OF
INTERNATIONAL BUSINESS (BIB))

CONCORDIA UNIVERSITY
Centre for International Business
(RESEARCH CENTRE)
Faculty of Commerce and Administration
(BComm & BAdm: minor in
International Business)
MBA Program (MBA: concentration
in International Business)

**CONFEDERATION COLLEGE OF
APPLIED ARTS AND TECHNOLOGY**
Faculty of Business (DIPLOMA IN INTER-
NATIONAL BUSINESS AND INTERNA-
TIONAL BUSINESS MANAGEMENT)

DALHOUSIE UNIVERSITY
Centre of International Business Studies (CIBS)
(RESEARCH CENTRE)
School of Business (MBA: concentration
in International Business)

**ÉCOLE DES HAUTES
ÉTUDES COMMERCIALES (HEC)**
Centre d'études en administration internationale
(CENTRE DE RECHERCHE)
Commerce international (CERTIFICAT EN
COMMERCE INTERNATIONAL)
Gestion internationale (BAA: spécialisation
en gestion internationale)
Gestion internationale (MSc & MBA: option
en gestion internationale)

**ÉCOLE NATIONALE
D'ADMINISTRATION PUBLIQUE**
Maîtrise en administration publique (MAP avec
concentration en management international)
Programme de diplôme d'études supérieures
spécialisées en administration internationale
(DESS EN ADMINISTRATION
INTERNATIONALE)

GEORGE BROWN COLLEGE
International Trade Program (DIPLOMA IN
INTERNATIONAL TRADE)

**HUMBER COLLEGE OF
APPLIED ARTS AND TECHNOLOGY**
International Marketing Program (DIPLOMA
IN INTERNATIONAL MARKETING:
specialization in Asia Pacific, Europe
or Latin America)

LANGARA COLLEGE
Department of Business Administration
(DIPLOMA IN INTERNATIONAL
BUSINESS)

UNIVERSITÉ LAVAL
Gestion internationale des entreprises
(MBA—gestion internationale)

UNIVERSITY OF LETHBRIDGE
Faculty of Management (BMgt: major in
International Management)

UNIVERSITY OF MANITOBA
The Centre for International Business Studies (CIBS)
(RESEARCH CENTRE)

MCGILL UNIVERSITY
Centre for International Management Studies
(RESEARCH CENTRE)
Faculty of Management (MBA: concentration
in International Business)

MCMASTER UNIVERSITY
Michael G. DeGroote School of Business (MBA:
concentration in
International Business)

MEMORIAL UNIVERSITY
Centre for International Business Studies (RESEARCH
CENTRE)

UNIVERSITÉ DE MONCTON
Centre de commercialisation internationale (CCI)
(CENTRE DE RECHERCHE)
Commerce international (BA: concentration commerce
international)

UNIVERSITY OF NEW BRUNSWICK
Centre for International Business Studies (RESEARCH
CENTRE)
Faculty of Administration (BBA & MBA: concentration
in International Business)
Faculty of Business (MBA: concentration
in International Business)

**UNIVERSITY OF
NORTHERN BRITISH COLUMBIA**
Business Program (BComm: specialization
in International Business or Marketing)

UNIVERSITY OF OTTAWA
Faculty of Administration
(INTERNATIONAL MBA)
Faculty of Administration (BComm:
option in International Management)

QUEEN'S UNIVERSITY
School of Business (BComm:
concentration in International Business)

UNIVERSITY OF SASKATCHEWAN
Centre for International Business Studies (RESEARCH
CENTRE)

SHERIDAN COLLEGE
Post-Graduate International Business Program (POST-
GRADUATE DIPLOMA
IN INTERNATIONAL BUSINESS)

SIMON FRASER UNIVERSITY
Faculty of Business Administration (BBA:
concentration in International Business)

SIR SANDFORD FLEMING COLLEGE
International Education Office (DIPLOMA
IN INTERNATIONAL TRADE)

ST. MARY'S UNIVERSITY
The Frank H. Sobey Faculty of Commerce (MBA:
concentration in International Development
Management)

The Frank H. Sobey Faculty of Commerce
(BComm: specialization in Global
Business Management)

UNIVERSITÉ DU QUÉBEC À MONTRÉAL
Bureau de la coopération internationale du
Département des sciences administratives
(CENTRE DE RECHERCHE)
Commerce international, module
d'administration (CERTIFICAT EN
COMMERCE INTERNATIONAL)
Gestion internationale, module d'administration
(BAA: concentration en gestion interna-
tionale)
Programme de M.B.A.-Recherche (MBA avec
spécialisation en gestion internationale)

UNIVERSITY OF VICTORIA
Faculty of Business (MBA: option
in International Business)
School of Business (BComm: concentration
in International Business Management)

UNIVERSITY OF WATERLOO
Department of Economics (BA: applied
studies cooperative specialization
in International Trade)

UNIVERSITY OF WESTERN ONTARIO
Centre for International Business Studies
(RESEARCH CENTRE)
Richard Ivey School of Business (HBA & MBA:
specialization in International Business)

UNIVERSITY OF WINDSOR
Faculty of Business Administration (BComm &
MBA IN INTERNATIONAL BUSINESS)

YORK UNIVERSITY
Schulich School of Business
(INTERNATIONAL MBA)

INTERNATIONAL EDUCATION

**COLLÈGE DE TECHNOLOGIE
AGRICOLE D'ALFRED**
Agriculture et développement international
(DIPLÔME COLLÉGIAL EN AGRI-
CULTURE ET DÉVELOPPEMENT
INTERNATIONAL)

CÉGEP ANDRÉ LAURENDEAU
Baccalauréat International (DIPLÔME
D'ÉTUDES COLLÉGIALES EN SCIENCES
DE LA NATURE et EN SCIENCES
HUMAINES)

UNIVERSITY OF CALGARY
Graduate Division of Educational Research
(MA, MEd & PhD IN EDUCATIONAL
POLICY: specialization in Comparative
Education)

COLLÈGE ÉDOUARD-MONTPETIT
Baccalauréat international (DIPLÔME
D'ÉTUDES COLLÉGIALES - B.I.)

**INSTITUT DE TECHNOLOGIE
AGRO-ALIMENTAIRE DE
SAINTE-HYACINTHE (ITA)**
Techniques agro-alimentaires (DIPLÔME D'ÉTUDES
COLLÉGIALES EN TECHNIQUES AGRO-
ALIMENTAIRES)

UNIVERSITÉ DE MONTRÉAL
Éducation comparée et internationale (DIPLÔME
D'ÉTUDES SUPÉRIEURES SPÉCIALISÉES EN
ÉDUCATION COMPARÉE ET
INTERNATIONALE)

**ONTARIO INSTITUTE
FOR STUDIES IN EDUCATION**
The Comparative, International and Development
Education Centre (MA, MEd, EdD & PhD:
specialization in Comparative, International or
Development Education)

UNIVERSITY OF PRINCE EDWARD ISLAND
Centre for International Education
(RESEARCH CENTRE)
Faculty of Education (BEd: specialization
in International Education)

UNIVERSITY OF REGINA
Centre for International Teacher Education
(RESEARCH CENTRE)

INTERNATIONAL HEALTH

UNIVERSITY OF ALBERTA
Centre for the Cross-Cultural Study of Health and
Healing (RESEARCH CENTRE)

QUEEN'S UNIVERSITY
International Centre for the Advancement of
Community-Based Rehabilitation (ICACBR)
(RESEARCH CENTRE)

INTERNATIONAL LAW

UNIVERSITY OF BRITISH COLUMBIA
International Centre for Criminal Law
Reform and Criminal Justice Policy
(RESEARCH CENTRE)

MCGILL UNIVERSITY
Institute and Centre of Air and Space Law (RESEARCH
CENTRE)
Institute of Comparative Law (ICL) (LLM:
concentrations in International Business Law,
Human Rights or Cultural Diversity)

UNIVERSITY OF OTTAWA
Graduate Studies in Law (LLM & LLD: concentration in
International Law)
Human Rights Research and Education Centre
(RESEARCH CENTRE)

QUEEN'S UNIVERSITY
Faculty of Law (LLM: concentration
in International Legal Studies)

UNIVERSITY OF REGINA
School of Human Justice (BA AND CERTIFICATE IN
HUMAN JUSTICE)

YORK UNIVERSITY
Osgoode Hall Law School (LLB: concentration in International and Comparative Law or Immigration and Refugee Law)

INTERNATIONAL SCIENCES

UNIVERSITY OF BRITISH COLUMBIA
Department of Agricultural Economics (BSc (Agr) & MSc: specialization in International Trade and Resource Management)

UNIVERSITY OF WINNIPEG
Environmental Studies/Urban Studies Program (BA & BSc IN ENVIRONMENTAL AND URBAN STUDIES)

INTERNATIONAL STUDIES

ACADIA UNIVERSITY
International Relations Program (BA & MA IN POLITICAL SCIENCE: specialization in International Relations)

UNIVERSITY OF ALBERTA
Department of Political Science (PhD IN POLITICAL SCIENCE: concentration in International Relations)

UNIVERSITY OF BRITISH COLUMBIA
Centre for Human Settlements (RESEARCH CENTRE)
Institute of International Relations (RESEARCH CENTRE)
Sustainable Development Research Institute (SDRI) (RESEARCH CENTRE)

BROCK UNIVERSITY
Department of Politics (BA & MA IN POLITICS: concentration in International Relations)
International Studies Program (CERTIFICATE AND CONCENTRATION IN INTERNATIONAL STUDIES)

UNIVERSITY COLLEGE OF CAPE BRETON
Centre for International Studies (RESEARCH CENTRE)

CARLETON UNIVERSITY
Centre for International Research and Training (CIRT) (RESEARCH CENTRE)
Department of Economics (PhD IN ECONO-MICS: specialization in International Economics or Development Economics)
Institute of Political Economy (MA IN POLITICAL ECONOMY)
Norman Paterson School of International Affairs (MA IN INTERNATIONAL AFFAIRS; MA IN INTERNATIONAL AFFAIRS/LLB)

CHAMPLAIN LENNOXVILLE
International Studies Program (CERTIFICATE IN INTERNATIONAL STUDIES)

DALHOUSIE UNIVERSITY
Department of Political Science (BA (honours), MA & PhD IN POLITICAL SCIENCE: specialization in International Politics, Foreign Policy or International Development)

UNIVERSITY OF GUELPH
Don Snowden Program for Development Communication (RESEARCH CENTRE)

LAKEHEAD UNIVERSITY
Department of Political Science (BA & BA (honours) IN POLITICAL SCIENCE: minor in International Politics)

UNIVERSITÉ LAVAL
Institut québécois des hautes études internationales (CENTRE DE RECHERCHE)
Journalisme international (DIPLÔME DE 2e CYCLE EN JOURNALISME INTERNATIONAL)
Relations internationales (MA EN RELATIONS INTERNATIONALES)

LESTER B. PEARSON
COLLEGE OF THE PACIFIC
International Baccalureate Program (International Baccalureate)

UNIVERSITY OF MANITOBA
Centre for Defence and Security Studies (RESEARCH CENTRE)

MCGILL UNIVERSITY
Department of Political Science (MA & PhD IN POLITICAL SCIENCE: specialization in International Politics)
McGill Centre for Society, Technology and Development—STANDD (RESEARCH CENTRE)

MCMASTER UNIVERSITY
Department of Political Science (MA & PhD IN POLITICAL SCIENCE: concentration in International Relations or Comparative Politics)
International Studies, Department of Economics (PhD IN ECONOMICS: specialization in International Economics)

MEMORIAL UNIVERSITY
Canadian Centre for International Fisheries Training and Development (RESEARCH CENTRE)

UNIVERSITÉ DE MONTRÉAL
Centre de recherche sur les transports (CENTRE DE RECHERCHE)
Centre international de criminologie comparée (CENTRE DE RECHERCHE)
Sciences économiques (MSc (ÉCONOMIQUE): options économie du développement ou économie et finances internationales)

UNIVERSITY OF
NORTHERN BRITISH COLUMBIA
International Studies (BA & MA IN INTERNATIONAL STUDIES)

UNIVERSITY OF OTTAWA
Department of Economics (PhD IN
INTERNATIONAL ECONOMICS)
Faculty of Administration (MA IN
INTERNATIONAL AFFAIRS
ADMINISTRATION)

UNIVERSITÉ DU QUÉBEC À RIMOUSKI
Maîtrise en gestion de projet (MGP ou MSc EN
GESTION DE PROJECT)
Maîtrise en gestion des ressources maritimes
(MSc EN GESTION DES RESSOURCES
MARITIMES)

QUEEN'S UNIVERSITY
Centre for International Relations
(RESEARCH CENTRE)
Department of Political Studies (MA & PhD
IN POLITICAL STUDIES: concentration in
International Politics or Politics of Devel-
opment)

**SASKATCHEWAN INDIAN
FEDERATED COLLEGE**
Centre for International Indigenous Studies
and Development (CERTIFICATE IN
INTERNATIONAL INDIGENOUS
MANAGEMENT)

UNIVERSITY OF SASKATCHEWAN
International Studies Program (BA (honours)
IN INTERNATIONAL STUDIES)

UNIVERSITY OF TORONTO
International Relations Programme (BA (major
& specialist) IN INTERNATIONAL
RELATIONS)

TRENT UNIVERSITY
Trent International Program (BA (honours):
special interest in International Studies)

VANIER COLLEGE
International Studies Program (CERTIFICATE
IN INTERNATIONAL STUDIES)

UNIVERSITY OF WATERLOO
International Studies Program (BA: option
in International Studies)

UNIVERSITY OF WESTERN ONTARIO
Graduate Program in Journalism
(MA (journalism): focus in
International Journalism)

UNIVERSITY OF WINDSOR
International Relations Program (BA (honours)
IN INTERNATIONAL RELATIONS; MA
IN POLITICAL SCIENCE: specialization
in International Relations)

UNIVERSITY OF WINNIPEG
Department of Political Science (BA (honours)
IN POLITICAL SCIENCE: concentration
in International Relations)

YORK UNIVERSITY
Centre for Research in Earth and Space Science
(CRESS) (RESEARCH CENTRE)
Department of Political Science (BA (honours),
MA & PhD IN POLITICAL SCIENCE:
concentration in International Relations)

International Studies Program (BA (honours) IN
INTERNATIONAL STUDIES)

PEACE/CONFLICT STUDIES

LANGARA COLLEGE
Peace and Conflict Studies Program (DIPLOMA IN
PEACE AND CONFLICT STUDIES)

MCMASTER UNIVERSITY
Centre for Peace Studies
(BA: minor in Peace Studies)

UNIVERSITY OF NEW BRUNSWICK
Centre for Conflict Studies
(RESEARCH CENTRE)

ROYAL MILITARY COLLEGE OF CANADA
Faculty of Arts (MA IN WAR STUDIES)

UNIVERSITY OF TORONTO
Peace and Conflict Studies Program (BA IN PEACE
AND CONFLICT STUDIES)

UNIVERSITÉ DU QUÉBEC À MONTRÉAL
Centre d'études des politiques
étrangères et de sécurité (CEPES)
(CENTRE DE RECHERCHE)
Chaire Téléglobe Raoul-Dandurand en études
stratégiques et diplomatiques
(CENTRE DE RECHERCHE)
Groupe de recherche sur l'industrie militaire
(GROUPE DE RECHERCHE)

UNIVERSITY OF VICTORIA
Institute for Dispute Resolution
(RESEARCH CENTRE)

UNIVERSITY OF WATERLOO
Peace and Conflict Studies Program (PACS) (BA
(honours): minor in Peace and Conflict Studies;
DIPLOMA IN PEACE
AND CONFLICT STUDIES)

UNIVERSITY OF WINNIPEG
Conflict Resolution Studies Program (BA IN
CONFLICT RESOLUTION STUDIES)

YORK UNIVERSITY
Centre for International and Security Studies
(GRADUATE DIPLOMA IN
STRATEGIC STUDIES)

Profiles of International Studies in Canada

The following 314 profiles are listed in alphabetical order by university or college name. (For example, the University of Alberta is sorted under "A," the University of Toronto is under "T" and so on.) After being sorted by name, the profiles are then sorted by program name. Universities with a significant international focus have a "university international profile" at the beginning of their listing.

ACADIA UNIVERSITY—INTERNATIONAL PROFILE
ACADIA UNIVERSITY
Acadia University, P.O. Box 1269, Wolfville, N.S.
B0P 1X0; (902) 542-2201, fax (902) 585-1084, www.acadiau.ca

International programs and research centres in this chapter: 2
Number of students: 3,600 **Percentage of international students:** 8%

    International offices: Acadia University's International Centre and full-time International Student Advisor provide support and services to international students, including a buddy and orientation program.
    Language programs: BA, BA (honours) in Spanish. [ID:6631]

ACADIA UNIVERSITY—INTERCULTURAL STUDIES
Fred C. Manning School of Business Administration
Director, School of Business Administration, Acadia University,
Wolfville, N.S. B0P 1X0; (902) 585-1216, fax (902) 585-1057, grieve@ace.acadia.ca, www.acadiau.ca

BBA: major in French, Spanish or German ▪ The Fred C. Manning School of Business Administration promotes internationalization by encouraging students in the BBA program to undertake a year of study at a university overseas or in the US. Students can also earn a Bachelor of Business Administration with Language, combining their business with either French, German, or Spanish. For information on applying to Acadia University, visit their web site. [ID:5207]

ACADIA UNIVERSITY—INTERNATIONAL STUDIES
International Relations Program
International Relations Program, Department of Political Science, Acadia University, Wolfville, N.S.
B0P 1X0; (902) 585-2201 ext. 1780, fax (902) 585-1070, grieve@ace.acadia.ca, www.acadiau.ca

BA & MA IN POLITICAL SCIENCE: specialization in International Relations ▪ Acadia University's Political Science Department offers an honours degree program with a specialization in International Relations, focusing on Human Rights, Development Studies and East-West Relations. The program is open to political science majors. Also offered are MA degrees in the above fields as well as in International Political Economy. Visit the department web site for course descriptions, information on financial assistance, faculty members, and e-mail links. [ID:5208]

UNIVERSITY OF ALBERTA
1A University Campus N.W., Edmonton, Alberta
T6G 2E1; (403) 492-3111, fax (403) 492-1134, www.ualberta.ca

International programs and research centres in this chapter: 9
Number of students: 29,000 **Percentage of international students:** 4%

International focus: The University of Alberta is known for high student achievement, teaching excellence, and outstanding research. Among the five largest universities in Canada, the University of Alberta houses the second largest library in the country. With more than 80 formal linkages to institutions in over 20 countries, foreign students from 85 countries are drawn to study at the University of Alberta.

International offices: The University of Alberta's International Centre, one of the most extensive facilities of its kind in Canada, helps foreign and Canadian students pursue international education. The centre works with students by offering programs which facilitate direct access to international education and by fostering an international dimension on campus. Alberta International provides support to the central administration in international relations, acts as University liaison with both national and international external agencies, facilitates international project work, and offers advice and assistance to international policy development on campus.

Language programs within Area Studies described in this chapter: Department of East Asian Studies; Consortium for Middle Eastern and African Studies (CMEAS). **Other language programs:** BA, BA (honours), MA, PhD in German; BA, BA (honours), MSc and PhD in Linguistics; BA (honours) in Romance Languages; BA (honours) in Scandinavian Languages. [ID:6632]

Department of East Asian Studies
Chairperson, Department of East Asian Studies, Faculty of Arts, University of Alberta, Edmonton,
Alberta T2G 2E1; (403) 492-2836, fax (403) 492-7440, crossctr@gpu.srv.ualberta.ca, www.ualberta.ca

BA (major) IN EAST ASIAN STUDIES ▪ This program allows students to major in East Asian Studies while completing the requirements of a BA. The program is designed to provide a broad, interdisciplinary understanding of East Asia, considerable insight into one or two disciplines, and a solid grounding in an East Asian language. Students are required to complete core courses and choose from a number of selected electives in the fields of history, anthropology, philosophy, religion, political science, literature, and economics. [ID:5319]

Consortium for Middle Eastern and African Studies (CMEAS)
Department of History and Classics, Faculty of Arts,
University of Alberta, 2-28 Tory Bldg., Edmonton, Alberta T6G 2H4;
(403) 492-6695, fax (403) 492-9125, amcdoug@gpu.srv.ualberta.ca, www.ualberta.ca/~cmeas/

BA & BA (honours): special interest in Middle East & African Studies ▪ Consortium for Middle Eastern and African Studies (CMEAS) is a forum for university students devoted to the discussion of contemporary issues facing the Middle East and Africa. As part of this discussion the CMES hosts community and student activities such as films and lectures. Students can major or minor in a chosen discipline and also be recognized for their specialized knowledge of Middle Eastern and African studies. The primary focus of CMEAS is on the regions and disciplines which relate to Arabic-speaking, Islamic peoples. However, the consortium's diverse faculty and student base allow for topics of the Middle East and Africa which are neither Arab nor Islamic. Course materials are drawn from anthropology, classics, literature, history, religious studies, Arabic and French. [ID:6840]

UNIVERSITY OF ALBERTA—INTERCULTURAL STUDIES
International and Intercultural Education Programs
Coordinator, International and Intercultural Education Programs, Department of Educational
Policy Studies, University of Alberta, 7-104 Education Bldg. N., Edmonton, Alberta T6G 2G5;
(403) 492-7625, fax (436) 492-2024, s.h.toh@ualberta.ca, www.ualberta.ca/cied/default.htm

BEd IN INTERCULTURAL EDUCATION; MEd IN INTERNATIONAL/INTERCULTUAL
EDUCATION ▪ The Intercultural Education Program seeks to provide knowledge, skills,
and values in pre-service education. This program is valuable and relevant for prospective
teachers wishing to work in intercultural contexts. The Intercultural Education focus area or
minor in the BEd program is designed to meet the increasing need for qualified teachers in
culturally diverse schools or communities outside Canada, and in First Nations school
systems and other federal territory schools. [ID:5321]

UNIVERSITY OF ALBERTA—INTERCULTURAL STUDIES
Research Institute for Comparative
Literature and Cross-Cultural Studies
Director, Research Institute for Comparative Literature and Cross-Cultural Studies,
University of Alberta, Edmonton, Alberta T6G 2E6; (403) 492-4776,
fax (403) 492-5662, stotosy@gpu.srv.ualberta.ca, www.ualberta.ca/arts/ricl/html

RESEARCH CENTRE ▪ The purpose of the Research Institute for Comparative Literature is
to foster individual and team interdisciplinary research in comparative literature and culture.
This work is done in collaboration with scholars from the University of Alberta, other Canadian universities, and foreign universities. The institute is involved with a variety of programs and publications. Depending on funding, postgraduate and postdoctoral positions are
offered by the Institute. [ID:6841]

UNIVERSITY OF ALBERTA—INTERNATIONAL BUSINESS
Undergraduate Business Program
Assistant Dean, Faculty of Business, University of Alberta, Edmonton, Alberta TG6 2R6;
(403) 492-5773, fax (403) 492-5863, ugradbus@gpu.srv.ualberta.ca, www.bus.ualberta.ca

BComm IN INTERNATIONAL BUSINESS: specialization in Chinese Studies, Japanese
Studies, German Studies or Spanish American Studies ▪ The Faculty of Business' Undergraduate Program provides specialized degree programs for students interested in International Business: a BComm in Chinese Studies, Japan Studies, German Studies and Spanish
American Studies. In addition, students can take an International Business major as part of a
regular BComm degree. All of these programs require language study during the four-year
program. The specialized degrees require courses in history, economics, culture and political science in addition to the International Business courses. The faculty also encourages
students to attend one of their international student exchange programs during their third or
fourth year. Course credit is given for work completed on our official exchange. The
BComm is a quota program and admission is based on one year of pre-professional studies
and a competitive academic standing. The Faculty of Business has also established a Centre
for International Business Studies whose objective is to prepare students for the challenges
and opportunities of a globally competitive environment, and to ensure that Alberta's business community has access to the best available information and expertise in international
business. [ID:5322]

UNIVERSITY OF ALBERTA—INTERNATIONAL BUSINESS
Faculty of Business
MBA Program Officer, Faculty of Business, University of Alberta, Room 2-30 Business Building,
Edmonton, Alberta T6G 2R6; (403) 492-3946, fax (403) 492-7825, www.bus.ualberta.ca/MBA/

MBA: specialization in International Business ■ The MBA with a specialization in International Business at the University of Alberta trains managers to excel in today's global economy. It is designed to give students experience in addressing the challenges and identifying the opportunities of the global market. After taking the core managerial skills courses, students are required to take 12 credits in international business and undertake a project covering an international topic. There are several international exchanges offered at foreign universities. [ID:7217]

UNIVERSITY OF ALBERTA—INTERNATIONAL BUSINESS
Centre for International Business Studies
Associate Director, Centre for International Business Studies, Faculty of Business,
University of Alberta, Room 2-20, Faculty Of Business Bldg., Edmonton, Alberta T6G 2R6;
(403) 492-2235, fax (403) 492-5037, fccentres@gpu.srv.ualberta.ca, www.bus.ualberta.ca

RESEARCH CENTRE ■ The Centre for International Business Studies was established in 1989. Its mission is to prepare students for a globally competitive environment and to provide corresponding information to the business community. The centre works closely with the Faculty of Business to develop exchange links, administer the faculty's study-abroad program and facilitate international majors. In addition, the centre supports research on international business, publishes a Series on Competitiveness, and hosts conferences, seminars and public lectures. [ID:5323]

UNIVERSITY OF ALBERTA—INTERNATIONAL HEALTH
Centre for the Cross-Cultural Study of Health and Healing
Director, Centre for the Cross-Cultural Study of Health and Healing,
Department of Anthropology, University of Alberta, Edmonton, Alberta T6G 2E1;
(403) 492-0135, fax (403) 492-5273, crossctr@gpu.srv.ualberta.ca, www.ualberta.ca

RESEARCH CENTRE ■ The Centre for the Cross-Cultural Study of Health and Healing is a nonprofit organization established in 1984 at the University of Alberta to study multicultural health issues. It is comprised of a multidisciplinary team of academics, healthcare professionals, graduate students, and members of the community. The centre's focus is to document different healing practices throughout the world, investigate how pluralistic societies in various parts of the world deal with the relationship among traditional, alternative, and modern medicine, and to promote multicultural healthcare in Canada. [ID:6839]

UNIVERSITY OF ALBERTA—INTERNATIONAL STUDIES
Department of Political Science
Graduate Coordinator, Department of Political Science,
University of Alberta, Room 10-16, Tory Bldg., Edmonton, Alberta T6G 2H4;
(403) 492-4771, fax (403) 492-2586, marilyn.calvert@ualberta.ca, www.ualberta.ca/~polisci/index.html

PhD IN POLITICAL SCIENCE: concentration in International Relations ■ The Department of Political Science provides doctoral candidates with the opportunity to concentrate in a number of areas including international politics and comparative politics. The department has 22 full-time academic staff who strive to provide students with an informal yet intellectually challenging environment which encourages student/instructor contact. Currently there are 25 PhD students enrolled in the program. Visit their web site for program and admission details. [ID:5324]

COLLÈGE DE TECHNOLOGIE AGRICOLE D'ALFRED—INTERNATIONAL EDUCATION
Agriculture et développement international
31, rue St- Paul, Alfred, Ontario K0B 1A0; (613) 679-2218, fax (613) 679-2449

DIPLÔME COLLÉGIAL EN AGRICULTURE ET DÉVELOPPEMENT INTERNATIONAL ▪ Le Collège d'Alfred offre, en collaboration avec l'Haute École Provinciale du Hainaut Occidental à Ath en Belgique, un programme en agriculture et développement international. Ce programme vise à former, sur une durée minimale de deux ans et demi, des techniciens hautement qualifiés en agriculture tropicale et en développement international. Il est complété par deux stages. [ID:5232]

CÉGEP ANDRÉ LAURENDEAU—INTERNATIONAL EDUCATION
Baccalauréat International
1111, rue Lapierre, LaSalle, Québec H8N 2J4;
(514) 364-3320, fax (514) 364-7130, courrier@claurendeau.qc.ca, www.claurendeau.qc.ca

DIPLÔME D'ÉTUDES COLLÉGIALES EN SCIENCES DE LA NATURE et EN SCIENCES HUMAINES ▪ Reconnu dans les universités de plus de 80 pays, le Baccalauréat International est une formation pré-universitaire supérieure, sanctionnée par l'Office du Baccalauréat International situé à Genève. Offert en sciences de la nature et en sciences humaines, ce programme d'une durée de deux ans fournit aux étudiantes et étudiants une formation enrichie facilitant l'accès à des études universitaires au Québec et à l'étranger. [ID:6806]

AUGUSTANA UNIVERSITY COLLEGE—DEVELOPMENT STUDIES
Prairies/Mexico Rural Development Exchange
Director, Prairies/Mexico Rural Development Exchange,
Augustana Community College, 4901 - 46th Ave., Camrose, Alberta 1K9;
(403) 679-1574, fax (403) 679-1129, hveng@corelli.augustana.ab.ca, www.augustana.ab.ca

DIPLOMA IN INTERDISCIPLINARY STUDIES ▪ The Prairies/Mexico Rural Development Exchange is a two-semester work/study program on how to create and maintain sustainable rural communities. One semester is spent in Alberta and the other in Mexico. Students are at least of second-year standing or have mature student status. Throughout the program they are paired with Mexican counterparts from the University of Morelos, Cuernavaca, and live with a rural host family or campesinos. Students work in the villages and learn participatory action research. [ID:6728]

BISHOP'S UNIVERSITY—INTERNATIONAL BUSINESS
Division of Business Administration
Director of Liaison, Division of Business Administration,
Bishop's Unversity, P.O. Box 5000, Stn. Lennoxville, Sherbrooke, Québec
J1M 1Z7; (819) 822-9681, fax (819) 822-9720, jbowey@ubishops.ca, www.ubishops.ca

BBA: concentration in International Business ▪ The BBA program prepares students for positions of responsibility in business and covers the fundamentals in all business areas. In addition to the core course requirements students select a concentration, one of which is International Business. This concentration seeks to develop in students a broad vision of the world and its structures and familiarize them with new strategies and management practices. Language training is recommended, and a study-abroad program for at least one semester is required. [ID:6437]

COLLÈGE BOIS-DE-BOULOGNE—INTERNATIONAL BUSINESS
Commerce international
10555, ave. de Bois-de-Boulogne, Montréal, Québec
H4N 1L4; (514) 332-3000, fax (514) 332-0527, http://collegebdeb.qc.ca

DIPLÔME D'ÉTUDES COLLÉGIALES EN TECHNIQUES ADMINISTRATIVES option commerce international ▪ La formation Commerce international du programme Techniques administratives tente de répondre aux besoins de plusieurs entreprises qui font de l'exportation ou qui songent à étendre leur marché. Élaborée en étroite collaboration avec l'Association des transitaires et courtiers en douanes du Québec et avec l'aide de nombreux intervenants de l'import-export, cette formation permet au diplômé de se familiariser avec le marketing, le droit commercial, le transit, la douane et les paiements internationaux, de même qu'avec toutes les procédures reliées aux échanges de marchandises entre divers pays du monde. Des cours de géographie, d'anglais langue seconde, de langues modernes et un stage au Québec ou à l'étranger complètent la formation. [ID:6807]

BRITISH COLUMBIA INSTITUTE OF TECHNOLOGY—INTERNATIONAL BUSINESS
International Trade and Transportation Program
Admissions, 3700 Willingdon Ave., Burnaby, B.C.
V5G 3H2; (604) 434-1610, fax (604) 436-0810, www.bcit.bc.ca

DIPLOMA IN INTERNATIONAL TRADE AND TRANSPORTATION ▪ The International Trade and Transportation Program offers students a broad training in the fundamentals of business and their application to trade and transport. It is a two-year program which stresses the importance of successful market analysis, effective entry strategies, knowledge of transportation alternatives, and logistic planning in international business. Career opportunities for graduates occur in marketing, finance, and management with firms such as trading houses, importers and exporters, customs brokers, freight forwarders, and transport providers. [ID:6605]

UNIVERSITY OF BRITISH COLUMBIA—INTERNATIONAL PROFILE
UNIVERSITY OF BRITISH COLUMBIA
2329 West Mall, Vancouver, B.C. V6T 1Z1; (604) 822-2211, fax (604) 822-9888, www.ubc.ca

International programs and research centres in this chapter: 13
Number of students: 33,300 Percentage of international students: 7%

International focus: The University of British Columbia (UBC) is known for its beautiful campus set in the multicultural city of Vancouver. UBC is one of Canada's top research universities with a tradition of excellence in teaching and learning. UBC is committed to focused international cooperation as a strategic element in its pursuit of excellence. UBC strives to enhance the international and intercultural competencies of faculty and students through research, study, cooperative work abroad, and through the establishment of linkages with foreign universities and organizations.

International offices: The University of British Columbia's International Liaison Office fulfils its mandate by providing central support to the university; its International Students Services provide support and assistance to international and exchange students, including social, cultural, and recreational programs.

Language programs within Area Studies described in this chapter: Department of Germanic Studies; Department of Asian Studies; Modern European Studies Program; Department of Hispanic Studies. **Other language programs:** BA, BA (honours), MA, PhD in Linguistics; BA in Modern Languages. [ID:6635]

UNIVERSITY OF BRITISH COLUMBIA—AREA STUDIES
Modern European Studies Program
Coordinator, Modern European Studies Program, Germanic Studies, University of British Columbia,
Vancouver, B.C. V6T 1Z1; (604) 822-6403, fax (604) 822-9344, mornin@unixg.ubc.ca, www.ubc.ca

BA IN MODERN EUROPEAN STUDIES ▪ Modern European Studies is an interdepartmental undergraduate program of the Faculty of Arts. The program offers students the opportunity to combine European languages, history, art, music, literature, philosophy, geography, sociology, anthropology, politics and economics in a broadly-based concentration that will extend and deepen their understanding of European issues. The program will be particularly valuable for students planning to enter such careers as teaching, journalism, business and the foreign service. Through its Education Abroad Program, UBC has active student exchange agreements with a number of European universities (in Belgium, Denmark, France, Germany, the Netherlands, Sweden, and the UK). It is expected that additional agreements with European universities in other countries will be signed in the coming years. Students are encouraged to participate in such exchanges for the enhancement of their Modern European Studies Programs. Graduate work in the European Studies area can be pursued at a number of universities in North America and Europe. Financial aid for study-abroad falls under the same criteria as financial aid for study at UBC and is disbursed on the basis of academic achievement. UBC will be opening a new Graduate Institute of European Studies in September 1998. [ID:5328]

UNIVERSITY OF BRITISH COLUMBIA—AREA STUDIES
Department of Asian Studies
Chairperson, Department of Asian Studies, Asian Centre,
University of British Columbia, 1871 West Mall, Vancouver, B.C.
V6T 1W5; (604) 822-5728, fax (604) 822-8937, astudies@unixg.ubc.ca, www.ubc.ca

BA, MA & PhD IN ASIAN STUDIES ▪ The Department of Asian Studies offers language study from beginner to advanced levels in Chinese, Japanese, Korean, Indonesian, Hindi, Punjabi, Sanskrit, and Urdu. A wide range of undergraduate and graduate courses, seminars and tutorials are offered on the literature and civilizations of East, South, and Southeast Asia. Undergraduate students may pursue a BA with a major in Chinese, Japanese, or South Asian languages, an honours program in Chinese or Japanese, or a major in Asian Studies with specializations in either East, South, or Southeast Asia. At the graduate level, programs are offered in Chinese, Japanese, and South Asian languages in fields such as literature, linguistics, religion, philosophy, and history. Degree programs may also be arranged between Asian Studies and other departments. A limited number of teaching assistantships are available for eight-month appointments and are awarded through the department. [ID:5325]

UNIVERSITY OF BRITISH COLUMBIA—AREA STUDIES
Department of Germanic Studies
Chairperson, Department of Germanic Studies, University of British Columbia,
Vancouver, B.C. V6T 1Z1; (604) 822-6403, fax (604) 822-9344, german@unixg.ubc.ca, www.ubc.ca

BA, BA (honours), MA & PhD IN GERMANIC STUDIES ▪ The University of British Columbia offers courses in German language, literature, and literature in translation. There are exchange agreements which allow students to complete one year of study at selected German universities. [ID:6440]

UNIVERSITY OF BRITISH COLUMBIA—AREA STUDIES
Department of Hispanic Studies
Chairperson, Department of Hispanic Studies, 2329 West Mall, Vancouver, B.C.
V6T 1Z1; (604) 822-2268, fax (604) 822-5387, ehowarth@unixg.ubc.ca, www.ubc.ca

BA, BA (honours), MA & PhD IN HISPANIC STUDIES ▪ The University of British Columbia offers undergraduate, graduate, and doctoral programs in Spanish studies. Courses are interdisciplinary and include history, language, culture, literature, and women's studies. [ID:6441]

UNIVERSITY OF BRITISH COLUMBIA—AREA STUDIES
Centre for Asian Legal Studies
Director, Centre for Asian Legal Studies, Faculty of Law,
University of British Columbia, Curtis Bldg., 1822 East Mall, Vancouver, B.C.
V6T 1Z1; (604) 822-4780, fax (604) 822-8108, cals@law.ubc.ca, www.ubc.ca

RESEARCH CENTRE ▪ The Centre for Asian Legal Studies was established to provide a forum for the exchange of ideas and information on Asian legal systems and law. The centre also encourages dynamic and creative approaches to Canada-Asia legal issues with the aim of promoting Pacific Rim cooperation. The centre offers course work that may be taken in sequence, by upper division and graduate law students. [ID:5326]

UNIVERSITY OF BRITISH COLUMBIA—AREA STUDIES
Institute of Asian Research
Manager of Administration and Programs, Institute of Asian Research,
University of British Columbia, Room 251, C.K. Choi Bldg., 1885 West Mall,
Vancouver, B.C. V6T 1Z2; (604) 822-2746, fax (604) 822-5207, capri@unixg.ubc.ca, www.ubc.ca

RESEARCH CENTRE ▪ The Institute for Asian Research was established in 1978 to sponsor and coordinate research activities concerning Asia and the Pacific. In 1992 the Institute was restructured to include five area research centres: the Centres for Chinese, Japanese, Korean, South Asian, and Southeast Asian Research. It was also given an expanded mandate to conduct interdisciplinary, issue-oriented research on Asia Pacific affairs; organize workshops, conferences, and seminars on Asia; be the focal point on campus for worldwide networking through publications, data and knowledge-based development; and promote interest in the Asia Pacific region through art exhibits, films, cultural performances, and other outreach programs. [ID:5327]

UNIVERSITY OF BRITISH COLUMBIA—DEVELOPMENT STUDIES
School of Community and Regional Planning
Director, School of Community and Regional Planning,
University of British Columbia, Vancouver, B.C. V6T 1Z2; (604) 822-4422,
fax (604) 822-3787, wrees@unixg.uba.ca, www.interchg.ubc.ca/plan/scarp.html

MA, MSc & PhD IN PLANNING: concentration in International Development Planning ▪ The mission of the School of Community and Regional Planning (SCARP) is to advance the transition to sustainability through excellence in integrated policy and planning research, professional education and community service. SCARP emphasizes an interdisciplinary approach by admitting a class with diverse backgrounds, encouraging students to complete courses in a variety of departments, and joint teaching and research. The school's Centre for Human Settlements offers research opportunities in international development planning, and fellowships for candidates interested in doing research or completing part of their studies overseas. [ID:5329]

UNIVERSITY OF BRITISH COLUMBIA—INTERNATIONAL BUSINESS
Faculty of Commerce and Business Administration
Director of Undergraduate Programs, University of British Columbia, Faculty of Commerce and
Business Adminstration, Room 103, 403-2053 Main Mall, Vancouver, B.C. V6T 1Z2; (604) 822-8333,
fax (604) 822-0655, bcom@commerce.ubc.ca, www.commerce.ubc.ca/ugrad/Welcome.html

BComm: option in International Business ▪ The International Business Option prepares
students for careers in international business by combining studies in Commerce with
courses in language and culture. Over the course of this four-year program participants will
study in the Faculty of Commerce and the Faculty of Arts in order to develop expertise in a
particular area of the world as well as deepen their understanding of international business
practices. Students are encouraged to develop language skills and experience different
cultures through exchange opportunities in 23 countries worldwide. [ID:5330]

UNIVERSITY OF BRITISH COLUMBIA—INTERNATIONAL LAW
International Centre for
Criminal Law Reform and Criminal Justice Policy
Executive Director, International Centre for Criminal Law Reform and Criminal Justice Policy,
Faculty of Law, University of British Columbia, 1822 East Mall, Vancouver, B.C. V6T 1Z1;
(604) 822-9875, fax (604) 822-9317, prefont@law.ubc.ca, www.law.ubc.ca/centres/iccir/

RESEARCH CENTRE ▪ The Faculty of Law's International Centre at the University of
British Columbia contributes to national and international policy development and law
reform as well as providing implementation assistance. As part of the network of Institutes
contributing to the United Nations Crime Prevention and Criminal Justice Program, the
centre's objectives are the promotion of democratic principles, the rule of law, respect of
human rights in criminal law, and the administration of criminal justice. The centre focuses
its activities on technical cooperation, research training, and advisory services. It is
currently involved in projects in China, Southeast Asia, and Latin America. [ID:5331]

UNIVERSITY OF BRITISH COLUMBIA—INTERNATIONAL SCIENCES
Department of Agricultural Economics
Chairperson, Department of Agricultural Economics, University of British Columbia, Room 303,
Angus Bldg., 2053 Main Mall, Vancouver, B.C. V6T 1Z2; (604) 822-5685, fax (604) 822-2184, www.ubc.ca

BSc (Agr) & MSc: specialization in International Trade and Resource Management ▪ The
Department of Agricultural Economics at UBC offers undergraduate programs in Agri-
cultural Economics and Agribusiness, and participates in an interdisciplinary program in
Forest Economics. All of the department's faculty are engaged in overseas work, focused
primarily in Asia, but also in Europe. The department has an active exchange program with
universities in Indonesia, Poland, the Philippines, Malaysia, the US and the Netherlands.
Exchanges with other universities in Asia, Europe, and South America are also possible.
[ID:6438]

UNIVERSITY OF BRITISH COLUMBIA—INTERNATIONAL STUDIES
Centre for Human Settlements
Director, Centre for Human Settlements,
University of British Columbia, 4th Floor, 2206 East Mall, Vancouver, B.C.
V6T 1Z3; (604) 822-5254, fax (604) 822-6164, chevans@unixg.ubc.ca, www.interchg.ubc.ca/chs

RESEARCH CENTRE ▪ The UBC Centre for Human Settlements is a multi-disciplinary
research arm of the School of Community and Regional Planning. The centre's research
focuses on human settlements, which are, simply put, where people live, work and seek a
good quality of life. CHS links Canadians with international development initiatives and
integrates research, education, training, and professional development focused on urban and

rural settlements. Students are encouraged to use the centre's resources and take advantage of the benefits of the programs offered. [ID:5332]

UNIVERSITY OF BRITISH COLUMBIA—INTERNATIONAL STUDIES
Institute of International Relations
Director, Institute of International Relations, University of British Columbia, C456 - 1866 Main Mall, Vancouver, B.C. V6T 1Z1; (604) 822-5480, fax (604) 822-5540, instir@unixg.ubc.ca, www.iir.ubc.ca

RESEARCH CENTRE ■ The mandate of the Institute of International Relations is to facilitate interdisciplinary work on a broad range of international relations issues among faculty and students of the University of British Columbia and other institutions in Canada and abroad. The institute promotes individual and group research at the graduate, postdoctoral and faculty levels, sponsors conferences, seminars and lectures, and hosts postdoctoral fellows and visiting scholars. [ID:5333]

UNIVERSITY OF BRITISH COLUMBIA—INTERNATIONAL STUDIES
Sustainable Development Research Institute (SDRI)
Director, Sustainable Development Research Institute (SDRI),
University of British Columbia, B5, 2202 Main Mall, Vancouver, B.C.
V6T 1Z4; (604) 822-8198, fax (604) 822-9191, sdri@sdri.ubc.ca, www.sdri.ubc.ca

RESEARCH CENTRE ■ Established in 1991 to conduct multidisciplinary research on the links between the environment, the economy and social equity, the Sustainable Development Research Institute (SDRI) encourages collaboration among UBC faculty and other provincial institutes. The institute also works to foster connections between government, non-governmental organizations, and the private sector, regionally and internationally. While SDRI is not a teaching institute, interested undergraduate and graduate students should contact the office for information on related programs and courses. [ID:5334]

BROCK UNIVERSITY—INTERNATIONAL PROFILE
BROCK UNIVERSITY
500 Glenridge Ave., St. Catherines, Ontario L2S 3A1;
(905) 688-5550, fax (905) 688-2789, jkaethle@sparten.ac.brocku.ca, www.brocku.ca

International programs and research centres in this chapter: 4
Number of students: 10,800 **Percentage of international students:** 2%

International focus: Brock University promotes internationalization in several ways. It welcomes international students, administers 19 exchange programs on 5 continents, emphasizes foreign language acquisition, and has TESL (Teaching English as a Second Language) programs. Brock's international projects involve Thailand, China, and Argentina.

International offices: Brock University's Associate Vice-President Academic is responsible for international liaison activities and the development of institutional linkages. The Office of International Services helps international students adjust to life in Canada by administering student exchange programs, providing a work and study abroad resource centre, and promoting development education.

Language programs within Area Studies described in this chapter: Department of Germanic Studies. **Other language programs:** BA in Italian; BA, BA (honours) in Spanish. [ID:6636]

BROCK UNIVERSITY—AREA STUDIES
Department of Germanic Studies
Chairperson, Department of Germanic Studies,
Brock University, 500 Glenridge Ave., St. Catharines, Ontario L2S 3A1;
(905) 688-5550 ext. 3312, fax (905) 688-2789, blittle@spartan.ac.brocku.ca, www.brocku.ca

BA & BA (honours) IN GERMANIC STUDIES ▪ Brock University offers courses in Russian language, literature, and history. In conjunction with Trent and McMaster Universities, Brock's Department of Germanic Studies offers a Study Program in Freiburg, Germany. The program is one year in duration and is open to students after their second year. [ID:6444]

BROCK UNIVERSITY—INTERNATIONAL BUSINESS
Faculty of Business
Dean, Faculty of Business, Brock University, 500 Glenridge Ave.,
St. Catharines, Ontario L2S 3A1; (905) 688-5550 ext. 4006, fax (905) 984-4188,
lewelsh@spartan.brocku.ca, http://peregrine.bus.brocku.ca

BBA: concentration in International Business ▪ To fulfil the requirements of the International Business concentration, students of the Faculty of Business can choose international courses from finance, marketing, management and economics. As well, intermediate language courses count as fourth-year electives in the program. Opportunities abroad include exchange programs to the UK, the US, and Japan. [ID:5210]

BROCK UNIVERSITY—INTERNATIONAL STUDIES
International Studies Program
Dean of Humanities, International Studies Program,
Brock University, 500 Glenridge Ave., St. Catharines, Ontario L2S 3A1;
(905) 688-5550 ext. 3425, fax (905) 688-2789, jsivell@spartan.ac.brocku.ca, www.brocku.ca

CERTIFICATE AND CONCENTRATION IN INTERNATIONAL STUDIES ▪ The International Studies Program at Brock University is an interdisciplinary program offering a concentration (pursued concurrently with a degree) and a certificate (for part-time students). There are two foundation courses, a language requirement and a wide range of elective options. Students are encouraged to study abroad as part of the program. Visit Brock University's web site for the International Studies web page. [ID:6449]

BROCK UNIVERSITY—INTERNATIONAL STUDIES
Department of Politics
Chairperson, Department of Politics,
Brock University, 500 Glenridge Ave., St. Catharines, Ontario L2S 3A1;
(905) 688-5550 ext. 3476, fax (905) 988-9388, bsmart@spartan.ac.BrockU.ca, www.brocku.ca/politics/

BA & MA IN POLITICS: concentration in International Relations ▪ The Politics Department at Brock University offers undergraduate and graduate degrees in politics and the opportunity to specialize in International Relations. All students must complete requirements in political theory and research methods. Students may combine their degrees with the broader concentration in International Studies. Brock has formed exchange programs with universities in Britain, Western Europe, Japan, Korea, Thailand, Australia, and Latin America. [ID:5211]

UNIVERSITY OF CALGARY—INTERNATIONAL PROFILE
UNIVERSITY OF CALGARY
2500 UNIVERSITY DRIVE N.W., Calgary, Alberta T2N 1N4; (403) 220-5110, www.calgaryu.ca

International programs and research centres in this chapter: 6
Number of students: 22,000 **Percentage of international students:** 3.7%

International focus: The University of Calgary is recognized nationally and internationally as a leading research university, with research funding exceeding $64 million in 1996. The University of Calgary, with 16 faculties and 60 teaching departments, most with an international component in their programs, is committed to internationalization in its research, teaching and student recruitment policies. International exchanges with universities throughout the world have resulted in a dynamic and global environment. The Canadian International Development Agency named the University of Calgary as a Centre of Excellence in International Development.

International offices: The University of Calgary's International Centre houses the divisions of International Development, International Business and International Relations. In addition, there is an office of International Marketing and Recruitment housed in the Division of Student Affairs. All these offices are involved in encouraging internationalization on campus. Advisors in the International Student Centre provide advice and support for both international students and Canadians going abroad, as well as organizing a number of programs which provide an opportunity for interaction between international and Canadian students.

Language programs within Area Studies described in this chapter: Faculty of General Studies; BA: minor in Italian Studies. **Other language programs:** BA, BA (honours) in German; BA, BA (honours), MA in Linguistics; BA, BA (honours) in Russian.
[ID:7232]

UNIVERSITY OF CALGARY—AREA STUDIES
Italian Department
Chairperson, Department of French, Italian and Spanish,
University of Calgary, 2500 University Drive N.W., Calgary, Alberta T2N 1N4;
(403) 220-5300, fax (403) 284-3634, www.ucalgary.ca/uofc/faculties/hum/fis/fis.htm

BA: minor in Italian Studies ▪ The minor in Italian Studies provides students with a comfortable command of the language and considerable knowledge of Italian culture. Students may elect to do a minor in Italian Studies by taking five full courses in the field. Courses may also be taken in the Departments of Greek, Latin, History, Ancient History, Art and Music. The minor can be completed in four years, and is ideally suited for combination with other disciplines in joint or double programs. The Italian government offers a few scholarships to Canadian students every year. [ID:6451]

UNIVERSITY OF CALGARY—AREA STUDIES
Faculty of General Studies
Dean, Faculty of General Studies, University of Calgary, 2500 University Drive N.W.,
Calgary, Alberta T2N 1N4; (403) 220-5885, fax (403) 282-6716, www.ucalgary.ca

BA & BSc: minor in African, East Asian, South Asian, Latin American or Central and East European Studies ▪ All of the interdisciplinary minor programs may be usefully combined with major programs in the Faculty of General Studies, Humanities, Science, and Social Sciences. The minor programs offer students an opportunity to do concentrated work in an area which crosses the boundaries of traditional disciplines. Each program incorporates a required or recommended interdisciplinary course, along with a selection of courses from the relevant specialized disciplines. With the help of faculty advisors, students plan their minor program. [ID:5335]

UNIVERSITY OF CALGARY—DEVELOPMENT STUDIES
Faculty of General Studies
Dean, Faculty of General Studies, University of Calgary, 2500 University Drive N.W., Calgary,
Alberta T2N 1N4; (403) 220-5885, fax (403) 282-6716, www.ucalgary.ca/UofC/faculties/NST

BA & BA (honours) IN DEVELOPMENT STUDIES ▪ The degree programs in Development
Studies are interdisciplinary and provide students with a broad understanding of the nature
of, and problems connected with, international development. Students will learn about
development issues from a variety of perspectives. They will also acquire information on
government and local, national or international agencies that deal with such development
issues as health, poverty, the environment and sustainable tourism. Second language
competency is highly recommended. A five-year degree in Development Studies: Co-
operative Education Program is also offered and includes 20 months of supervised work
experience in various private and government agencies. The program offers students a
variety of study-abroad and exchange program opportunities. [ID:5336]

UNIVERSITY OF CALGARY—DEVELOPMENT STUDIES
Faculty of Social Work
Student Services, Faculty of Social Work, 2500 University Drive N.W., Calgary, Alberta T2N 1N4;
(403) 220-5942, fax (403) 282-7269, socialwk@acs.ucalgary.ca, www.ucalgary.ca/UofC/faculties/SW/

MSW: International concentration ▪ The Faculty of Social Work offers a concentration in
International Social Work as part of its Community Organization, Management, and Social
Policy (COMP) specialization. Its focus is on knowledge and skills associated with
development, administration, and service delivery to: 1) populations dependent on
international agencies for basic needs (e.g. refugees, disaster victims); and 2) communities
and groups subject to international social and economic programs (e.g. the homeless,
marginalized, socially excluded, and oppressed peoples). International field placements are
arranged on an individualized basis with limited available financial assistance. The COMP
specialization admits approximately 25 students each year, 10 of whom are admitted to the
international concentration. [ID:6452]

UNIVERSITY OF CALGARY—DEVELOPMENT STUDIES
Division of International Development (DID)
Director, Division of International Development (DID), International Centre,
University of Calgary, 2500 University Drive N.W., Calgary, Alberta T2N 1N4;
(403) 220-8215, fax (403) 289-0171, cabraham@acs.ucalgary.ca, www.ucalgary.ca/international

RESEARCH CENTRE ▪ The University of Calgary's Division of International Development
(DID) is committed to forging partnerships within the developing world to improve the
quality of life for the poor and disadvantaged. DID is the leader of a network of Canadian and
international partners which excel in knowledge-building and dissemination, and the
practice of participatory development in order to enhance quality of life in civil society. DID
provides human resource development and technical assistance to many projects in Asia and
Latin America. Students, staff, and faculty members integrate their overseas experience into
their courses and curricula. [ID:5337]

UNIVERSITY OF CALGARY—INTERNATIONAL EDUCATION
Graduate Division of Educational Research
Chairperson, Graduate Divison of Educational Research,
University of Calgary, 2500 University Drive N.W., Calgary, Alberta T2N 1N4;
(403) 220-5675, fax (403) 282-3005, 18501@ucdasvm1.admin.ucalgary.ca, www.ucalgary.ca

MA, MEd & PhD IN EDUCATIONAL POLICY: specialization in Comparative Education ▪
The Department of Educational Policy and Administrative Studies offers programs on inter-

national and global education, with a focus on Asia and Japan. As the degree title suggests, the department maintains a strong orientation toward policy issues. [ID:5339]

CAMOSUN COLLEGE—AREA STUDIES
Pacific Rim Studies Program
Pacific Rim Studies Program, Camosun College, 3100 Foul Bay Road, Victoria, B.C.
V8P 5J2; (250) 370-3376, fax (250) 370-3417, masayuki@camosun.bc.ca, www.camosun.bc.ca

DIPLOMA IN PACIFIC RIM STUDIES: general or business option ▪ Camosun College's Pacific Rim Studies Program provides students with the education and training needed for an understanding and appreciation of the Asia Pacific region. Given the increased emphasis on the relationship of the Asia Pacific region to Canada and specifically to British Columbia, this program will meet a critical knowledge demand. The program offers both a general and a business option and encourages students to develop a proficiency in a related language. [ID:5212]

UNIVERSITY COLLEGE OF CAPE BRETON—DEVELOPMENT STUDIES
School of Community Studies
Administrative Secretary, School of Community Studies, University College of Cape Breton, P.O. Box 5300, Sydney, N.S. B1P 6L2; (902) 563-1386, fax (902) 563-1247, www.uccb.ns.ca

BACS IN COMMUNITY STUDIES: option in Comparative Development Studies ▪ The BACS degree is an innovative liberal arts degree which differs from traditional programs in several ways. First of all, it is career-oriented and students may select courses from both the degree and diploma programs. Students are also required to take three courses in Problem-centred Studies (P.C.S.) which are designed to give practical insights into communication, problem-solving and team work skills. The BACS program also allows students to merge theory with practice by incorporating two work placements into their degree program. Work placements can involve local and international development agencies; Canadian Crossroads International reserves a small number of places for those in the program. In the Comparative Development Studies option, students take courses in Comparative Development, Environmental and Development Planning, Organizations for Development, and Program and Project Management. [ID:5317]

UNIVERSITY COLLEGE OF CAPE BRETON—INTERNATIONAL STUDIES
Centre for International Studies
Director, Centre for International Studies, University College of Cape Breton, P.O. Box 5300, Stn. A, Sydney, N.S. B1P 6L2; (902) 563-1286, fax (902) 562-0119, tennyson@uccb.ns.ca, www.uccb.ns.ca

RESEARCH CENTRE ▪ The Centre for International Studies is the UCCB's international office and is responsible for international linkages, including recruitment of international students and exchange programs. The centre also helps to locate international placements for students enrolled in cooperative programs, carries out development education programming in the local community, and coordinates the BA in Comparative Development Studies at UCCB. The members of the centre carry out research projects, both individually and collectively, on international issues and engage in extensive consulting work as well as managing international development projects on behalf of the university. [ID:5318]

CAPILANO COLLEGE—AREA STUDIES
Asia Pacific Management Co-operative Program
Coordinator, Asia Pacific Management Co-operative Program,
Capilano College, 2055 Purcell Way N., North Vancouver, B.C. V7J 3H5;
(604) 984-4981, fax (604) 984-4992, dmorriso@capcollege.bc.ca, www.capcollege.bc.ca/apmcp

DIPLOMA IN ASIA PACIFIC MANAGEMENT ▪ For ten years, this award-winning post-graduate diploma program has offered training to Canadians considering international careers. It is a joint venture in educational programming, bringing together Canadian employers with management trainees to form a unique blend of experiential and academic training. The program's emphasis is on Canada's relationship with Pacific Rim countries and our potential economic growth through trade, business, applied technology, and development projects. Students follow an integrated program which includes the historical, economic, political, cultural, and business dynamics of the region. The program requires students to develop proficiency in one of five Asian languages and to complete a 12-month co-op work placement in an Asian country or with an internationally focused Canadian organization. Students then join the Alumni Network active in Canada and 14 Asian countries. [ID:5213]

CAPILANO COLLEGE—INTERCULTURAL STUDIES
Ethnic and Cultural Relations Program
Chairperson, Ethnic and Cross-Cultural Relations Program,
Capilano College, 2055 Purcell Way N., Vancouver, B.C. V7J 3H5;
(604) 984-4953, fax (604) 983-7520, www.capcollege.bc.ca

CERTIFICATE IN ETHNIC AND CROSS-CULTURAL RELATIONS ▪ The Ethnic and Cross-Cultural Relations Program is a two-term multidisciplinary program. It studies ethnic relations in the context of the multicultural and polyethnic nature of Canadian society as well as from an international perspective. The program includes course work in a variety of disciplines and encourages students to gain proficiency in at least one other language. [ID:5214]

CARLETON UNIVERSITY—INTERNATIONAL PROFILE
CARLETON UNIVERSITY
1125 Colonel By Drive, Ottawa, Ontario K1S 5B6; (613) 520-7400, www.carleton.ca

International programs and research centres in this chapter: 16
Number of students: 18,200 **Percentage of international students:** 4.5%

International focus: Carleton University is a contemporary, enterprising institution situated in Canada's capital. Specialized research is carried out in more than four organized research centres with some 18,200 students from the Ottawa area, across Canada, and more than 100 countries worldwide. Carleton's location in Canada's capital has shaped its philosophy and character in special ways, making it a truly national and international institution. In pursuit of academic excellence, Carleton has played a national and international role in contributing to the quality of public discourse in Canada and to the advancement of our country's national role. Carleton has an international reputation for their programs in public policy, business management, national affairs, political science, and high technology. The university is in the forefront of developing new partnerships and new programs; new directions in teaching and research will engage its graduates to lead in meeting the challenges of globalization.

International offices: Carleton International is the university's focal point for relations with international universities and state agencies and promotes internationalization on campus and in the Ottawa community. In building community on campus, the International Student Centre encourages and facilitates the interaction of international and Canadian students. Carleton also has an International Student Service operated by Counseling and Student Life Services.

Language programs within Area Studies described in this chapter: Institute of Central/East European and Russian-Area Studies. **Other language programs:** BA, BA (honours), MA in German; BA, BA (honours) in Italian; BA, BA (honours), MA in Linguistics. [ID:6640]

CARLETON UNIVERSITY—AREA STUDIES
Institute of Central/East European and Russian-Area Studies
Administrator, Institute of Central/East European and Russian-Area Studies,
Carleton University, Room 3A59, Paterson Hall, 1125 Colonel By Drive, Ottawa, Ontario
K1S 5B6; (613) 520-2888, fax (613) 520-7501, ceras@carleton.ca, www.carleton.ca/ceras/

BA (honours) & MA IN CENTRAL/EAST EUROPEAN AND RUSSIAN AREA STUDIES ▪ The institute offers two degree programs in Central/East European and Russian-Area Studies, the BA (honours) and the MA. The MA program, the first and largest of its kind in Canada, is an interdisciplinary program with an emphasis on the social sciences and history. It draws upon courses from 10 disciplines. The program is designed for students wishing to acquire specialized knowledge of the region, including proficiency in the use of Russian as a research tool. After completion of the MA program, many graduates go on to professional careers in business or government. The program also provides excellent training for students who aspire to a doctoral degree in one of the various disciplines of the program, either at Carleton or at other universities. [ID:5215]

CARLETON UNIVERSITY—AREA STUDIES
Institute of Interdisciplinary Studies
Director, Institute of Interdisciplinary Studies,
Carleton University, Room 2216, Dunton Tower, 1125 Colonel By Drive,
Ottawa, Ontario K1S 5B6; (613) 520-2368, fax (613) 520-3985, iis@carleton.ca, www.carleton.ca

BA (honours) IN DIRECTED INTERDISCIPLINARY STUDIES: concentration in Aboriginal Studies, African Studies, Asian Studies, Latin American Studies, Caribbean Studies, Environmental Studies or Third World Studies ▪ Directed Interdisciplinary Studies is a program based upon student-generated plans of study. Many students have developed plans of study based upon area studies, such as Asian Studies, Latin American Studies, and African Studies as well as programs in International Development. Each plan of study includes courses reflecting the breadth of a liberal education and student-selected courses relating to the particular theme. Admission to DIS requires submission of a proposal form as well as acceptance to the degree programs of the university at large. [ID:5217]

CARLETON UNIVERSITY—AREA STUDIES
Centre for Research on Canadian-Russian Relations
Director, Centre for Research on Canadian-Russian Relations,
History Department, Carleton University, 1125 Colonel By Drive, Ottawa, Ontario
K1S 5B6; (613) 520-2600 ext. 6653, fax (613) 520-4439, larry_black@carleton.ca, www.carleton.ca

RESEARCH CENTRE ▪ The Centre for Research on Canadian-Russian Relations (CRCR) is an organized research unit located in the History Department, Faculty of Arts and Social Sciences. It provides the means for students to study Canadian-Russian relations—historical, economic, cultural, and political. It holds unique collections of archival documents and secondary literature, as well as a wide variety of research projects supported by governments, NGOs and foundation funds. Students are employed on many projects, and CRCR subsidizes Canadians and Russians who wish to travel for research. [ID:6480]

CARLETON UNIVERSITY—AREA STUDIES
East-West Project
Director, East-West Project, Institute of Central/East European and Russian Area Studies,
Carleton University, 1125 Colonel By Drive, Ottawa, Ontario K1S 5B7;
(613) 520-2600 ext. 8480, fax (613) 520-7501, www.carleton.ca/ceras/

RESEARCH CENTRE ▪ The East-West Project was established in 1972 to provide academic expertise on relations between the centrally-planned economies of the communist East and the advanced industrialized economies of the capitalist West. For 20 years, through publications and related activities, the project met its goals of public education and training of young Canadians in this important dimension of international affairs. In recent years, the project has had to adapt to momentous changes and the focus of its activities has accordingly shifted to questions of post-communist social, political, and economic transformation in the countries of the former East Bloc. There are six associated faculty, one part-time administrator, and several part-time student research assistants. The project provides opportunities for students to gain experience in contract research, project administration, and general administrative skills. [ID:6483]

CARLETON UNIVERSITY—AREA STUDIES
Institute of Central/East European and Russian-Area Studies
Director, Institute of Central/East European and Russian-Area Studies, Carleton University, 1125 Colonel By Drive, Ottawa, Ontario K1S 5B6; (613) 520-2888, fax (613) 520-7501, www.carleton.ca/ceras/

RESEARCH CENTRE ▪ The Institute of Central/East European and Russian-Area Studies assists students who seek specialized knowledge in the area of Russian and Central/East European studies, including proficiency in the use of Russian as a research tool. The institute also offers an interdisciplinary program emphasizing the social sciences, history, and international affairs. [ID:5216]

CARLETON UNIVERSITY—AREA STUDIES
Research Unit on Southern European Literature and Culture
Director, Research Unit on Southern European Literature and Culture, School of Language, Literatures and Comparative Literary Studies, Carleton University, 1125 Colonel By Drive, Ottawa, Ontario K1S 5B7; (613) 520-2177, fax (613) 520-2564, www.carleton.cf

RESEARCH CENTRE ▪ The Research Unit on Southern European Literature and Culture (RUSELC) encourages discussions of a theoretical and/or critical nature which reconsider the cultural legacy of countries such as France, Greece, Italy, Spain, and those in the Mediterranean basin. Research is approached in light of current events and current sociocultural climates. RUSELC sponsors seminars, lectures, colloquia, and publications in cooperation with other research groups in Canada and abroad. Students are welcome to participate in RUSELC activities. [ID:6482]

CARLETON UNIVERSITY—DEVELOPMENT STUDIES
Development Administration Program
Coordinator, Development Administration Program,
School of Public Administration, Carleton University, 1125 Colonel By Drive, Ottawa, Ontario K1S 5B6; (613) 520-2547, fax (613) 520-2551, public_administration@carleton.ca, www.carleton.ca/spa

MA IN PUBLIC ADMINISTRATION: specialization in Development Administration ▪ The MA Program in Development Administration provides mid-career professionals working in development with an opportunity to strengthen their technical and analytical skills. Areas of study include decision-making, organizational theory, micro/macroeconomics, accounting and finance, and quantitative methods. It also enables them to broaden their internationally-comparative knowledge of particular policy fields. Past participants have come from 50 developing countries as well as from Canada. In addition to academic background, the program looks for significant work experience and leadership qualities in their applicants. [ID:5218]

CARLETON UNIVERSITY—DEVELOPMENT STUDIES
Research Resource Division for Refugees (RRDR)
Director, Research Resource Division for Refugees (RRDR),
Department of Sociology/Anthropology, Carleton University, 1125 Colonel By Drive, Ottawa, Ontario
K1S 5B6; (613) 520-2717, fax (613) 520-3676, gneuwirt@ccs.carleton.ca, www.carleton.ca

RESEARCH CENTRE ▪ The Research Resource Division for Refugees (RRDR) is both an archival resource and an active research unit for settlement issues concerning refugees. Archival resources include reports and newsletters by national and international governmental and nongovernmental organizations. RRDR publishes a quarterly newsletter called INSCAN (International Settlement Canada) and is actively involved in the International Refugee Documentation Network. Graduate students interested in refugee problems can pursue a PhD in political science or sociology/anthropology. Candidates will spend a year at the Refugee Studies Centre at Oxford. [ID:5219]

CARLETON UNIVERSITY—INTERNATIONAL BUSINESS
School of Business
Supervisor, Bachelor of International Business Program,
Carleton University, 1125 Colonel By Drive, Ottawa, Ontario K1S 5B6;
(613) 520-2388, fax (613) 520-4427, bib@business.carleton.ca, www.business.carleton.ca

BACHELOR OF INTERNATIONAL BUSINESS (BIB) ▪ The Bachelor of International Business (BIB) is a four-year honours undergraduate degree. It offers specialized programs uniquely targeted at students wishing to pursue intensive language and business studies. What makes BIB unique is the combination of elements: not only do students complete core courses in business fundamentals and specialized courses in international business, but they undertake studies in an additional language. As well, BIB students must complete a year of study abroad. [ID:5220]

CARLETON UNIVERSITY—INTERNATIONAL BUSINESS
Centre for the Study of Business/Government/NGO Relations
Centre for the Study of Business/Government/NGO Relations, School of Business,
Carleton University, 1125 Colonel By Drive, Ottawa, Ontario K1S 5B6; (613) 520-2600 ext. 2375,
fax (613) 520-2532, Ian_Lee@carleton.ca, http://gsro.carleton.ca/ors/oru/s52.html

RESEARCH CENTRE ▪ Dedicated to the study of relations among business, government and nongovernmental organizations in Canada and abroad, the centre's research program focuses on both process and policy issues. Research includes a study of advocacy relationships among corporate government relations offices, trade associations, peak associations and third-party government relations consulting firms; a comparative analysis of NGOs in Canadian social movements; business and NGO influence on federal government policy; environmental NGOs; and the evolving role of business-government-NGO partnerships in the development and delivery of public policy. [ID:5222]

CARLETON UNIVERSITY—INTERNATIONAL BUSINESS
Centre for the Study of Training,
Investment and Economic Restructuring (CSTIER)
Director, Centre for the Study of Training, Investment and Economic Restructuring (CSTIER),
Carleton University, 1125 Colonel By Dr., Ottawa, Ontario K1S 5B6; (613) 520-2600 ext. 8241,
fax (613) 520-3561, tjackson@ccs.carleton.ca, www.carleton.ca/cstier

RESEARCH CENTRE ▪ CSTIER is a multidisciplinary research centre affiliated with the Faculty of Public Affairs and Management at Carleton University. The centre promotes innovative approaches to community and workplace change. The centre networks within the university community and establishes linkages between other centres engaged in research and education on small enterprise, regional investment, local development, sustainable agriculture, gender and development, and literacy and adult training. CSTIER is currently developing student field placements in Asia, Africa, Eastern Europe and the Americas. [ID:5223]

CARLETON UNIVERSITY—INTERNATIONAL BUSINESS
International Business Study Group (IBSG)
International Business Study Group (IBSG), School of Business, Carleton University,
1125 Colonel By Drive, Ottawa, Ontario K1S 5B6; (613) 520-2600 ext. 2382,
fax (613) 520-2532, IBSG@business.carleton.ca, http://gsro.carleton.ca/ors/oru/s55.html

RESEARCH CENTRE ▪ The International Business Study Group (IBSG) was established in 1984 to conduct, coordinate and disseminate the results of research in international business. The group's activities revolve around a conceptual framework that stresses research on the global competitiveness of the business firm within the bounds of good corporate citizenship; focuses on the management of international enterprise; studies both the problems of Canadian firms abroad and foreign firms in Canada; and recognizes the importance of Canada-US economic relations, while also considering Canada's need to diversify its international trade and investment relationships. [ID:5225]

CARLETON UNIVERSITY—INTERNATIONAL STUDIES
Institute of Political Economy
Director, Institute of Political Economy, Carleton University, Room A818, Loeb Bldg.,
1125 Colonel By Drive, Ottawa, Ontario K1S 5B6; (613) 520-7414, fax (613) 520-2154, www.carleton.ca

MA IN POLITICAL ECONOMY ▪ This interdisciplinary MA in Political Economy is the only program of its kind in Canada. It is designed to provide students from a wide range of disciplines with a solid grounding in political economy, while allowing them to develop their own research interests. Students pursue an assortment of topics, such as international development, gender, labour studies, and political economy with an international, Canadian, or comparative focus. Visit the university's web site for faculty and program information. [ID:5227]

CARLETON UNIVERSITY—INTERNATIONAL STUDIES
Norman Paterson School of International Affairs
Administrator, Norman Paterson School of International Affairs,
Carleton University, Paterson Hall 2A, 1125 Colonel By Dr., Ottawa, Ontario K1S 5B6;
(613) 520-6655, fax (613) 520-2889, international_affairs@carleton.ca, www.carleton.ca/npsia/

MA IN INTERNATIONAL AFFAIRS; MA IN INTERNATIONAL AFFAIRS/LLB ▪ The Norman Paterson School of International Affairs offers an interdisciplinary MA degree in International Affairs in three streams of study: Conflict Analysis, Development Studies and International Political Economy. Within each stream, students may choose a concentration, of which five are available: a Canadian concentration, Environment, International Management, North American Free Trade Agreement (NAFTA) or Trade Policy. The MA in International Affairs is a degree by course work and dissertation (research essay or thesis), and normally requires one to two years to complete. A joint program leading to an MA in International Affairs and LLB is available through Carleton's School of International Affairs and the Faculty of Law at the University of Ottawa. A limited number of teaching and research assistantships are offered to high-ranking students in the incoming class each year. [ID:5228]

Department of Economics
Chairperson, Department of Economics,
Carleton University, Room C877, Loeb Bldg, 1125 Colonel By Drive, Ottawa, Ontario
K1S 5B6; (613) 520-3744, fax (613) 520-3906, chair economics@ccs.carleton.ca, www.carleton.ca

PhD IN ECONOMICS: specialization in International Economics or Development Economics ▪ Carleton University and the University of Ottawa offer a joint PhD program in Economics. A student can choose from six fields of specialization; three of these, Development Economics, International Trade, and Environmental Economics are of particular interest to students of international development. The program, offered in English, has a diverse student body representing many different countries. Students admitted into the program are eligible for financial awards, teaching assistantships, and scholarships. [ID:5226]

Centre for International Research and Training (CIRT)
Director, Centre for International Research and Training (CIRT), Norman Paterson
School for International Affairs, Carleton University, 1125 Colonel By Drive, Ottawa, Ontario
K1S 5B6; (613) 520-2600, fax (613) 520-2889, international_affairs@carleton.ca, www.carleton.ca

RESEARCH CENTRE ▪ The Centre for International Research and Training (CIRT) provides a range of research, training and consulting services to government, business, and other organizations on various aspects of international affairs. The centre is composed of experts drawn from the Carleton faculty. CIRT's activities include a negotiating skills training course for officials of the Department of Foreign Affairs and International Trade (DFAIT), a course for developing country trade representatives, a faculty retraining program for an African university, a foreign policy executive training course for a Central American country, and international security seminars for the Department of National Defence. [ID:5229]

International Studies Program
Coordinator, International Studies Program, Champlain Regional College,
Lennoxville, Québec J1M 2A1; (819) 564-3666, fax (819) 564-5171, www.lennox.chaplaincollege.qc.ca

CERTIFICATE IN INTERNATIONAL STUDIES ▪ There are two components of International Studies at Champlain Lennoxville. Students can participate in a variety of extra-curricular activities, including Amnesty International, WUSC (World University Service of Canada), the Refugee Sponsorship Committee, and an ongoing series of speakers, films, and radio programs on international issues. There is also a work/study program in Peru and several development projects currently underway in Guyana.

In addition to these extra-curricular activities, students undertake formal course work towards their certificate. Courses offered include African Literature, World Religions, A Human Rights Perspective, Weapons of War/Tools of Peace, Chinese Philosophy, and Comparative Political Systems. With this foundation, students may go on to university and specialize in International Studies if they wish. [ID:6808]

CONCORDIA UNIVERSITY
1455 de Maisonneuve Blvd. W., Montréal, Québec
H3G 1M8; (514) 848-2424, fax (514) 848-2814, www.concordia.ca

International programs and research centres in this chapter: 4
Number of students: 25,000 Percentage of international students: 4%

International focus: Concordia University was the first Canadian university to establish a PhD program with a university in China. The university is currently involved in CIDA-funded engineering projects in China and Jordan, education projects in South Africa and Zimbabwe, commerce projects in West Indies and Tunisia, and geography projects in Mexico and the US. Concordia's international focus is on the Asia-Pacific Rim and NAFTA partners, but the university has student exchanges and mobility programs with many other countries.

International offices: Concordia University has a Centre for International Cooperation which facilitates, coordinates, and monitors international academic activities. It is also very active in international project development and faculty and student exchanges. The university also has an International Students' Office.

Language programs within Area Studies described in this chapter: Department of History;. **Other language programs:** BA, BA (honours) in German; BA, BA (honours) in Italian; BA, BA (honours) in Linguistics; BA, BA (honours) in Spanish. [ID:6639]

CONCORDIA UNIVERSITY—AREA STUDIES
Department of History
Chairperson, Department of History, Concordia University, 1455 de Maisonneuve Blvd. W.,
Montréal, Québec H3G 1M8; (514) 848-2435, fax (514) 848-4538, www.concordia.ca

BA IN SOUTHERN ASIAN STUDIES ▪ This is an interdisciplinary program designed to provide undergraduate students with an understanding of the customs, social and political organization, ideas, historical experiences and present-day conditions of India, Pakistan, Bangladesh, and their neighbours. There are major and minor programs, with core courses in religion, history and political science. There are also electives in cinema, economics, education, linguistics, sociology and anthropology, English, and geography. [ID:6487]

CONCORDIA UNIVERSITY—INTERNATIONAL BUSINESS
Faculty of Commerce and Administration
Admissions, Sir George Williams Campus,
Concordia University, Room GM-201-13, Montréal, Québec H3G 1M8;
(514) 848-2721, fax (514) 848-2822, bcomm@vax2.concordia.ca, www.concordia.ca

BComm & BAdm: minor in International Business ▪ The Faculty of Commerce and Business Administration of Concordia University is a recently accredited Faculty by the American Assembly of Collegiate Schools of Business (AACSB) International Association for Management Education. The faculty offers two four-year undergraduate degree programs: the Bachelor of Commerce (BComm) and the Bachelor of Administration (BAdmin). The BComm is a structured program involving education in all aspects of business with emphasis on one particular area, such as accounting, finance, marketing, or international business. The BAdmin is a program providing students with a fundamental grounding in administration and offers them the opportunity to pursue a wide range of interests such as Political Science or languages. Both programs offer the opportunity to minor in international business, which introduces students to the cultural, social, political, economic, legal, and financial environments governing the world economy. The Faculty has currently over 4,000 students registered in its undergraduate programs. [ID:5234]

CONCORDIA UNIVERSITY—INTERNATIONAL BUSINESS
MBA Program
Director, MBA Program, Concordia University, Suite 710,
1550 de Maisonneuve Blvd. W., Montréal, Québec H3G 1M8;
(514) 848-2727, fax (514) 848-2816, profmba@vax2.concordia.ca, www.concordia.ca

MBA: concentration in International Business ▪ The MBA Program is a 63-credit graduate-level experience intended to provide a broad interdisciplinary understanding of business theory and its practical applications. It is designed to educate individuals with a wide variety of undergraduate and work backgrounds to become professional managers. Students in the program have the opportunity to participate in one of several international exchanges, including ones to the US, France, Sweden, and the UK. [ID:5235]

CONCORDIA UNIVERSITY—INTERNATIONAL BUSINESS
Centre for International Business
Centre for International Business, 1455 de Maisonneuve Blvd. W., Montréal, Québec
H3G 1M8; (514) 848-7598, fax (514) 848-4152, exchange@vax2.concordia.ca, www.concordia.ca

RESEARCH CENTRE ▪ The mission of the Centre for International Business is to foster a leadership position in academic activities pertaining to international business. The centre will facilitate the globalization of its teaching and research activities. Its comparative advantage lies in the bilingual and multicultural environment in which it operates. The Centre for International Business is involved in an International Business Program, an International Exchange Program, Development Projects, and Distance Education Projects. For more information, visit their web site. [ID:6790]

CONFEDERATION COLLEGE OF APPLIED ARTS AND TECHNOLOGY—INTERNATIONAL BUSINESS
Faculty of Business
Office of the Registrar, Business Division, Confederation College of
Applied Arts and Technology, P.O. Box 398, Thunder Bay, Ontario P7C 4W1;
(807) 473-3809, fax (807) 623-4512, schroede@confederationc.on.ca, www.confederationc.on.ca

DIPLOMA IN INTERNATIONAL BUSINESS AND INTERNATIONAL BUSINESS MANAGEMENT ▪ The Faculty of Business at Confederation College offers a diploma in International Business (two years) and a diploma in International Business Management (three years). The two-year program provides an understanding of global events, technical trade skills, language studies and an optional international study experience. The third year emphasizes decision-making and students operate an international consulting business in the final semester. Student exchanges, international degree articulation agreements and post-diploma internships are available to qualifying students. Enrolment includes many foreign students. Visit the Confederation College web site for admission requirements, program descriptions and student services information. [ID:6597]

DALHOUSIE UNIVERSITY—INTERNATIONAL PROFILE
DALHOUSIE UNIVERSITY
1236 Henry Street, Halifax, N.S. B3H 3J5; (902) 494-2211, fax (904) 494-1472, www.dal.ca

International programs and research centres in this chapter: 7
Number of students: 13,100 Percentage of international students: 4%

International focus: Dalhousie University has developed and operated several international projects with partner institutions in Southeast Asia, the Caribbean and Cuba, China, and the Baltic States. Projects involve various departments and academic units, but disciplines particularly active internationally include those concentrating on the environment, management, health, oceans and marine sciences. The university has established many student exchange programs and now has over 35 linkages with international institutions. As well, Dalhousie is an active member in the Commonwealth Universities Study Abroad Consortium.

International offices: Lester Pearson International is the official unit at Dalhousie University responsible for providing leadership in the internationalization of the university. Dalhousie also has an International Student Centre.

Language programs within Area Studies described in this chapter: Department of Russian. **Other language programs:** BA, BA (honours), MA in German; BA, BA (honours) in Spanish. [ID:6641]

DALHOUSIE UNIVERSITY—AREA STUDIES
Department of Russian
Chairperson, Department of Russian, Dalhousie University,
1236 Henry Street, Halifax, N.S. B3H 3J5; (902) 494-3473, fax (902) 494-1997, www.dal.ca

BA & BA (honours) IN RUSSIAN STUDIES ▪ The Russian Studies Program at Dalhousie University offers courses in Russian language, literature, history and culture. The department also offers an Intensive Russian Program (the first of its kind in Canada), an interdisciplinary course of instruction which allows students to undertake intensive study of the Russian language in Canada and at the St. Petersburg University in Russia. Students may enroll in a third-year intensive fall preparatory session at Dalhousie prior to going to Russia. [ID:6490]

DALHOUSIE UNIVERSITY—DEVELOPMENT STUDIES
College of Arts and Science
Registrar's Office, College of Arts and Science, University of King's College, Dalhousie University,
Halifax, N.S. B3H 2A1; (902) 422-1271, fax (902) 423-3357, edmissions@ukings.ns.ca, www.ukings.ns.ca

BA IN INTERNATIONAL DEVELOPMENT STUDIES ▪ The BA in International Development Studies is offered through the College of Arts and Sciences in conjunction with Dalhousie and Saint Mary's University. The program enables students to work within an interdisciplinary framework and draw upon the international development experience of over 20 overseas linkage programs. A number of scholarships and assistantships are available. Visit their web site for general program information. [ID:5346]

DALHOUSIE UNIVERSITY—DEVELOPMENT STUDIES
International Development Studies
Coordinator, International Development Studies, Dalhousie University, 1444 Seymour Street,
Halifax, N.S. B3H 3J5; (902) 494-3814, fax (902) 494-2105, mmackinn@adm.dal.ca, www.dal.ca

BA, BA (honours), & MA IN INTERNATIONAL DEVELOPMENT STUDIES: specialization in African Studies ▪ This program provides undergraduate students with core classes in International Development Studies. Students build their own program and can choose from a wide range of electives that focus on international themes such as: gender and development, political economy, environment, economics, and the social aspects of development. The undergraduate program also offers an honours degree, and a master's degree in development studies as of September 1997. [ID:5237]

DALHOUSIE UNIVERSITY—DEVELOPMENT STUDIES
International and Regional Development Studies Program
MDE Coordinator, International and Regional Development Studies Program,
Department of Economics, Dalhousie University, 6214 University Ave., Halifax, N.S.
B3H 1X1; (902) 494-2026, fax (902) 494-6917, economic@ac.dal.ca, www.dal.ca

MA IN DEVELOPMENT ECONOMICS ▪ The Department of Economics offers this interdisciplinary program of graduate study and field work in the Economics of Development, with a choice of emphasis on either Canadian Development Studies or International Development Studies. The program is designed primarily for students and young professionals pursuing, or intending to embark upon, careers in government, nongovernmental organizations or private corporations. The program's small enrolment ensures effective tutorial and group work. Applicants are advised to apply well before the start of the academic year in September. Since it was embarked on in 1984, students from across Canada and 43 nations have joined this program. Fields of specialization include disaster relief and development, trade and regional development, ocean studies and community health, the environment and development. This program works closely with other schools and departments of the university and sister institutions. [ID:5238]

DALHOUSIE UNIVERSITY—INTERNATIONAL BUSINESS
School of Business
Director, School of Business, Dalhousie University, 6152 Coburg Rd.,
Halifax, N.S. B3H 1Z5; (902) 494-7080, fax (902) 494-1107, www.dal.ca

MBA: concentration in International Business ▪ The Dalhousie MBA program prepares managers for the rapidly-changing business environment of the 1990s. To complement their own resources the School of Business draws upon the expertise of the Centre for International Business Studies. The International Business concentration offers students a wide range of courses, including a Foreign Business Program that prepares them for positions within the private sector. [ID:5239]

DALHOUSIE UNIVERSITY—INTERNATIONAL BUSINESS
Centre of International Business Studies (CIBS)
Director, Centre of International Business Studies (CIBS), Dalhousie University,
6152 Coburg Road, Halifax, N.S. B3H 1Z5; (902) 494-6553, fax (902) 494-1483, www.dal.ca

RESEARCH CENTRE ▪ The Centre for International Business Studies (CIBS) at Dalhousie was established in 1975 and currently receives its primary funding from the Department of Foreign Affairs and International Trade. The mission of the CIBS is to foster teaching and research in international business and to provide outreach services to enhance Canada's competitiveness in the global economy. The centre manages a range of activities aimed at training MBA and BComm students in international business by offering fellowships, internships, exchanges, and missions to foreign countries as well as providing outreach services to the local business community. [ID:5240]

DALHOUSIE UNIVERSITY—INTERNATIONAL STUDIES
Department of Political Science
Coordinator of Graduate Programs, Dalhousie University, Halifax, N.S.
B3H 4H6; (902) 494-6631, fax (902) 494-3825, robert.finbow@dal.ca, www.dal.ca

BA (honours), MA & PhD IN POLITICAL SCIENCE: specialization in International Politics, Foreign Policy or International Development ▪ The Department of Political Science offers a wide variety of courses and graduate seminars in international and comparative politics and is complemented by the interdisciplinary work of the Centre for Foreign Policy Studies. Students can choose courses that focus on the Americas, Africa, Asia, and the United Nations. [ID:5241]

ÉCOLE DES HAUTES ÉTUDES COMMERCIALES (HEC)—INTERNATIONAL PROFILE
ÉCOLE DES HAUTES ÉTUDES COMMERCIALES (HEC)
3000, chemin de la Côte Ste-Catherine,
Montréal, Québec H3T 2A7; (514) 340-6000, fax (514) 340-6888, www.hec.ca

Nombre de programmes et de centres de recherche internationaux : 4
Nombre d'étudiants étrangers : 16% du total des étudiants à temps plein

Expertise internationale : Première école de gestion au Canada, fondée en 1907, HEC-Montréal se classe aujourd'hui au rang des grandes écoles de gestion de calibre international. Elle acceuille des étudiants étrangers et provenance d'une soixantaine de pays dans le cadre, principalement, de ses programmes de baccalauréat et de maîtrise en administration des affaires (BAA et MBA), de maîtrise ès science de la gestion (M.Sc.) et de doctorat en administration (PhD). Grâce au programme d'échanges internationaux «Passeport pour le monde», les étudiants de l'École peuvent faire une partie de leurs études dans l'une des 55 grandes écoles ou universités étrangères partenaires, dans une vingtaine de pays.

Bureaux internationaux : Le Service aux étudiants HEC administre le programme d'échanges internationaux «Passeport pour le monde» et est responsable de l'accueil des étudiants étrangers. Composée d'étudiants, l'Association HEChange aide les étudiants étrangers à s'intégrer à leur nouveau milieu de vie et ceux qui participent au programme d'échange à préparer leur voyage. [ID:7069]

ÉCOLE DES HAUTES ÉTUDES COMMERCIALES (HEC)—INTERNATIONAL BUSINESS
Centre d'études en administration internationale
5255, ave. Decelles, Montréal, Québec H3T 1V6; (514) 340-6182, fax (514) 340-6177, www.hec.ca

CENTRE DE RECHERCHE ▪ Le Centre d'études en administration internationale de l'École des hautes études commerciales a pour mission de promouvoir la recherche et l'enseignement dans le domaine de la gestion internationale ainsi que le développement et la réalisation de projets de collaboration internationale. [ID:5491]

ÉCOLE DES HAUTES ÉTUDES COMMERCIALES (HEC)—INTERNATIONAL BUSINESS
Commerce international
Centre d'études en administration internationale, 3000, chemin de la Côte Ste-Catherine, Montréal, Québec H3T 2A7; (514) 340-6188, fax (514) 340-6177, cetai@hec.ca, http://cetai.hec.ca

CERTIFICAT EN COMMERCE INTERNATIONAL ▪ Le certificat en commerce international a pour objectif de former des gestionnaires capables de fournir un apport efficace aux entreprises exportatrices ou à toute autre organisation s'occupant de commerce international. Le cours est axé sur la pratique de la gestion. [ID:5244]

ÉCOLE DES HAUTES ÉTUDES COMMERCIALES (HEC)—INTERNATIONAL BUSINESS
Gestion internationale
Centre d'études en administration internationale, 3000 chemin de la Côte Ste-Catherine, Montréal, Québec H3T 2A7; (514) 340-6468, fax (514) 340-6469, www.hec.ca

MSc & MBA: option en gestion internationale ▪ La spécialisation offerte en gestion internationale a pour objectif de préparer les étudiants à l'analyse des problèmes de gestion en contexte international que ce soit dans le domaine des entreprises privées, des organismes publics ou parapublics. [ID:5245]

ÉCOLE DES HAUTES ÉTUDES COMMERCIALES (HEC)—INTERNATIONAL BUSINESS
Gestion internationale
Centre d'études en administration internationale, 3000, chemin de la Côte Ste-Catherine, Montréal, Québec H3T 2A7; (514) 340-6185, fax (514) 340-6177, cetai@hec.ca, http://cetai.hec.ca

BAA: spécialisation en gestion internationale ▪ Le BAA avec spécialisation en gestion internationale a pour objectif de former des administrateurs familiers à l'environnement international et équipés d'outils efficaces pour leurs opérations avec l'étranger. Les étudiants devront maîtriser une langue et participer au programme d'échanges internationaux. [ID:5243]

ÉCOLE NATIONALE D'ADMINISTRATION PUBLIQUE—INTERNATIONAL BUSINESS
Maîtrise en administration publique
945, rue Wolfe, Sainte-Foy, Québec G1V 3J9;
(418) 657-2485, fax (418) 657-2533, www.uquebec.ca/enap/

MAP avec concentration en management international ▪ La maîtrise en administration publique, concentration en management international, offerte par l'ENAP assure une formation professionnelle théorique et pratique aux gestionnaires qui oeuvrent dans le domaine international, que ce soit dans le secteur public, privé ou associatif. Il vise à former des gestionnaires capables de saisir la nature et l'évolution de l'environnement international afin de pouvoir répondre aux besoins actuels et futurs de ce secteur. Le site web comporte un annuaire électronique contenant tous les renseignements nécessaires aux candidats potentiels incluant la description des cours et des programmes, les conditions d'admission et les frais à prévoir. [ID:5303]

ÉCOLE NATIONALE D'ADMINISTRATION PUBLIQUE (ENAP)—INTERNATIONAL BUSINESS
Programme de diplôme d'études supérieures spécialisées en administration internationale
945, rue Wolfe, Sainte-Foy, Québec G1V 3J9;
(418) 657-2485, fax (418) 657-2533, www.uquebec.ca/enap/

DESS EN ADMINISTRATION INTERNATIONALE ▪ Le diplôme d'études supérieures spécialisées en administration internationale proposé par l'ENAP assure une formation professionnelle théorique et pratique aux gestionnaires oeuvrant dans le domaine international (secteur public, privé ou associatif). Il vise également à former des gestionnaires capables de saisir la nature et l'évolution de l'environnement international pour répondre aux besoins de ce secteur. Ce programme s'adresse aux titulaires d'un premier diplôme universitaire et qui ont quatre années d'expérience de travail. Le site web comporte un annuaire électronique contenant tous les renseignements nécessaires aux candidats potentiels incluant la description des cours et des programmes, les conditions d'admission et les frais à prévoir. [ID:5299]

COLLÈGE ÉDOUARD-MONTPETIT—INTERNATIONAL EDUCATION
Baccalauréat international
Service des programmes, Collège Édouard-Montpetit, 945, chemin Chambly,
Longueuil, Québec J4H 3M6; (514) 679-2630 ext. 406, fax (514) 679-7487, www.collegeem.qc.ca

DIPLÔME D'ÉTUDES COLLÉGIALES - BI ▪ Les programmes du baccalauréat international mènent au D.E.C. en sciences de la nature et en sciences humaines et préparent aux examens du baccalauréat international. Ils offrent une solide formation générale et s'adressent à des étudiants motivés et talentueux, qui bénéficieront d'un encadrement particulier dans des groupes homogènes. Des conditions particulières d'admission ainsi que des frais supplémentaires s'appliquent. Le site web du collège donne plus de détails concernant l'admission, les particularités du programme, et les débouchés universitaires. [ID:6820]

GEORGE BROWN COLLEGE—INTERNATIONAL BUSINESS
International Trade Program
Director, International Trade Program, P.O. Box 1015, Stn. B, Toronto, Ontario
M5T 2T9; (416) 415-2134, fax (416) 415-2600, info@gbrownc.on.ca, www.gbrownc.on.ca

DIPLOMA IN INTERNATIONAL TRADE ▪ This highly specialized and unique program gives its students the solid foundation needed to succeed in the international market. Areas of study include banking, finance, communications, market culture, business, and strategic planning. Each semester of study includes a work placement related to the students' career goals. Applicants must have a university degree or a college diploma and two years of professional experience. [ID:6595]

UNIVERSITY OF GUELPH—INTERNATIONAL PROFILE
UNIVERSITY OF GUELPH
Suite 158, 50 Stone Road E., Guelph, Ontario N1G 2W1; (519) 824-4120, www.uoguelph.ca

International programs and research centres in this chapter: 7
Number of students: 14,000 Percentage of international students: 3.2%

International focus: The University of Guelph is renowned for its successful agriculture and rural development projects in Africa, Asia, and Latin America. It is also known for its reception of international students and fellows, its applied research overseas, its network of over 70 partnerships around the world, and its 35 exchange programs.

International offices: The University of Guelph's Centre for International Programs (CIP) promotes internationalization of the university through the support and administration of research, international linkages, study abroad programs, and training initiatives. The Centre for International Programs (CIP) and the International Student Advisor's Office provide support to international students by helping them meet their living and learning needs while attending the university.

Language programs within Area Studies described in this chapter: Waterloo-Laurier-Guelph Centre for East European and Russian Studies. **Other language programs:** BA, BA (honours) in German; BA in Italian; BA, BA (honours) in Spanish. [ID:6642]

UNIVERSITY OF GUELPH—AREA STUDIES
Scottish Studies Program
Scottish Studies Program, Department of History, University of Guelph,
50 Stone Road East, Guelph, Ontario N1G 2W1; (519) 824-4120 ext. 3209,
fax (519) 766-4384, scottish@arts.uoguelph.ca, www.uoguelph.ca/history/scotstudy.html

MA & PhD IN SCOTTISH STUDIES ■ The program offers MA & PhD degrees in Scottish Studies within individual departments, primarily History and English. Students must meet the minimum requirements of the department to which they apply. The MA is usually completed in two years, the PhD in five years. PhD students usually do research in Scotland and internal scholarships are available to assist with expenses. The program generally has 10-12 students, with about 10 per cent being foreign students. [ID:6493]

UNIVERSITY OF GUELPH—AREA STUDIES
Waterloo-Laurier-Guelph Centre for East European and Russian Studies
Director, Waterloo-Laurier-Guelph Centre for East European and Russian Studies,
Department of Political Science, University of Guelph, Guelph, Ontario N1G 2W1;
(519) 824-4120 ext. 3469, fax (519) 837-9561, feidlin@polnet.css.uoguelph.ca, www.uoguelph.ca

RESEARCH CENTRE ■ The Waterloo-Laurier-Guelph Centre for East European and Russian Studies (CREES) was founded in 1988 and is a cooperative venture of the three universities. The current objectives of CREES are to encourage and facilitate research, training, teaching, publishing, information exchanges, language training, international exchanges, international development, business promotion and business consulting with reference to Russia and Eastern Europe. CREES membership extends beyond those who study Russia and Eastern Europe, and includes faculty, technical staff and students from a wide variety of applied and theoretical disciplines who are interested in applying their knowledge and skills to this part of the world. [ID:6573]

UNIVERSITY OF GUELPH—DEVELOPMENT STUDIES
International Agricultural Program
Coordinator, International Agricultural Program, Office of the Dean,
Ontario Agricultural College, University of Guelph, Guelph, Ontario N1G 2W1;
(519) 824-4120 ext. 2285, fax (519) 824-0813, jenkinso@oac.uoguelph.ca, www.uoguelph.ca

BSc IN AGRICULTURE: program in International Agriculture ▪ The International Agricultural Program is a series of courses available to undergraduate students. The program also includes a two-week field study course to Jamaica or Mexico. [ID:5342]

UNIVERSITY OF GUELPH—DEVELOPMENT STUDIES
Collaborative Program in International Development Studies
Coordinator, Collaborative Program in International Development Studies,
Department of Political Studies, University of Guelph, Guelph, Ontario N1G 2W1;
(519) 824-4120 ext. 6503, fax (519) 837-9561, mancuso@ccs.uoguelph.ca, www.uoguelph.ca

BA & MA IN POLITICAL STUDIES: focus on International Development ▪ Both the BA and MA programs in the Department of Political Studies involve interdisciplinary work with the Departments of Geography, Sociology, Economics and others, under the umbrella of the Collaborative Program in International Development Studies. Within the Department of Political Science there are strong research interests in Latin America, Africa, China, and India. There are also thematic concentrations available in The Americas, Development Theory, Development Administration and Policy, and Third World Ideologies. Financial aid is available to students of the program through a combination of scholarships, fellowships and teaching assistantships. [ID:5341]

UNIVERSITY OF GUELPH—DEVELOPMENT STUDIES
Collaborative International Development Studies
Graduate Coordinator, Collaborative International Development Studies, College of Social
Science, University of Guelph, Guelph, Ontario N1G 2W1; (519) 824-4120 ext. 8966 (graduate),
2140 (undergraduate), fax (519) 766-4797, cids@ccs.uoguelph.ca / cidsundh, www.uoguelph.ca

BA, MA & MSc IN INTERNATIONAL DEVELOPMENT STUDIES ▪ The BA and MA/MSc programs in Collaborative International Development Studies (CIDS) at University of Guelph are integrated social science programs which emphasize innovative theoretical and research approaches. The programs include course work and research. The graduate degree may be entered from any department at the university which offers MA or MSc degrees; application is made jointly to the department and the collaborative international program. The undergraduate degree is a self-contained specialization with the BA program. Details, including the graduate handbook, are available from the above web site. [ID:5340]

UNIVERSITY OF GUELPH—DEVELOPMENT STUDIES
University School of Rural Planning and Development
Graduate Officer, University School of Rural Planning and Development,
University of Guelph, Guelph, Ontario N1G 2W1; (519) 824-4120 ext. 3637,
fax (519) 767-1692, hcumming@rpd.uoguelph.ca, www.uoguelph.ca/GraduateStudies/rpd/Orpd.html

MSc IN INTERNATIONAL RURAL PLANNING AND DEVELOPMENT ▪ The University School of Rural Planning and Development has a four-part mission of teaching, research, training and outreach. The program provides students with the opportunity to pursue graduate study, research and professional development in either Canadian or international (developing areas) contexts.

The objective of the program is to ensure that students have the knowledge and skill to conduct interdisciplinary research and, in a professional capacity, guide the process of change in the rural planning and development context. They offer training and research in the context of the PhD, MSc, and Graduate Diploma. Visit their web site for program descriptions and faculty details. [ID:5344]

UNIVERSITY OF GUELPH—INTERNATIONAL STUDIES
Don Snowden Program for Development Communication
Director, Don Snowden Program for Development Communication, Department of
Rural Extensions, University of Guelph, Guelph, Ontario N1G 2W1; (519) 824-4120
ext. 3811, fax (519) 836-9941, drichard@uguelph.ca, http://tdg.uoguelph.ca/~drichard/snowden

RESEARCH CENTRE ▪ The purpose of the Don Snowden Program for Development Communication is to promote, through training, research and advisory activities, communication for community development, and the mobilization of human resources in developing regions of Canada and in developing countries.

The program supports and is affiliated with a number of initiatives including participatory video activities, the use of small format video as an instrument of social change, and the Internet as it applies to rural and developing regions of Canada and the Third World. International projects have been carried out in partnership with universities, nongovernmental organizations, and governments in Brazil, Cameroon, Chile, Egypt, Mexico, Nepal, Pakistan, Philippines, Thailand, Zanzibar, Zambia, and Zimbabwe. The program actively supports the Devmedia Internet Listserve and the associated Devmedia links at tdg.uoguelph.ca/~drichard/devmedia. [ID:5267]

HUMBER COLLEGE OF APPLIED ARTS AND TECHNOLOGY—INTERNATIONAL BUSINESS
International Marketing Program
Director, International Marketing Program, 205 Humber College Blvd.,
Etobicoke, Ontario M9W 5L7; (416) 675-5000, fax (416) 252-8842, www.humberc.on.ca

DIPLOMA IN INTERNATIONAL MARKETING: specialization in Asia Pacific, Europe or Latin America ▪ The International Marketing Program at Humber College is designed for university or college diploma graduates as well as those with a minimum of five years' related work experience. It is intended for those entering a career in international operations and for those wishing to update and expand their skills in international marketing. The program provides the option of concentrating on one of three profiles: Asia/Pacific, Europe, or Latin America. Program courses focus on International Marketing, International Trade and Distribution as well as International Banking and Finance. As well, students take a language and culture course related to their region of study. [ID:6599]

INSTITUT DE TECHNOLOGIE AGRO-ALIMENTAIRE
DE SAINTE-HYACINTHE (ITA)—INTERNATIONAL EDUCATION
Techniques agro-alimentaires
3230, rue Sicotte, C.P. 70, Sainte-Hyacinthe, Québec J2S 7B3; (514) 778-6504,
fax (514) 778-6536, YvonG.Blanchard@agr.gouv.qc.ca, site web en construction

DIPLÔME D'ÉTUDES COLLÉGIALES EN TECHNIQUES AGRO-ALIMENTAIRES ▪ Relevant du Ministère de l'Agriculture, des Pêcheries et de l'Alimentation du Québec, l'Institut de technologie agro-alimentaire (ITA) se spécialise dans les domaines de la production, de la transformation et de la conservation des aliments et facilite la mise en place d'équipement et de documentation sur les sources d'énergies renouvelables. En tant qu'établissement d'enseignement, il dispense des programmes de formation de niveau collégial touchant à ces domaines (gestion et exploitation de l'entreprise agricole, productions animales, horticulture, technologie du génie rural ou de la transformation des aliments).

L'expertise du personnel de l'ITA est largement reconnue dans le domaine agroalimentaire. L'ITA exécute ou a exécuté des projets dans les pays suivants: Burkina Faso, Niger, République du Congo, Sénégal, Algérie, Tunisie, Brésil, Mexique, Chine, Vietnam et Pologne. L'ITA compte sur un effectif de près de 200 employés pour assurer la formation initiale et continue. Une équipe multidisciplinaire composée d'agronomes, d'ingénieurs, de biologistes, de chimistes et de gestionnaires dispense la formation à ses 700 élèves. Les étudiants profitent, de plus, de l'expérience des stagiaires internationaux accueillis par l'ITA. L'ITA forme son personnel enseignant en psychopédagogie. [ID:6063]

LAKEHEAD UNIVERSITY—INTERNATIONAL STUDIES
Department of Political Science
Chairperson, Department of Political Science, Lakehead University,
955 Oliver Road, Thunder Bay, Ontario P7B 5E1; (807) 343-8307,
fax (807) 346-7831, pradip.sarbadhikari@lakehead.ca, www.lakeheadu.ca

BA & BA (honours) IN POLITICAL SCIENCE: minor in International Politics ▪ The Department of Political Science at Lakehead University offers a minor in international politics. Students are required to take an introduction to political science and a world politics course. Students may also select courses in US politics, Modern European politics, Third World politics, international economic relations, and international law and development. [ID:6421]

LANGARA COLLEGE—AREA STUDIES
Latin American Studies Program
Coordinator, Latin American Studies Program, Langara College., 100 West 49th Ave.,
Vancouver, B.C. V5Y 2Z6; (604) 323-5339, fax (604) 323-5555, kgilley@langara.ba.ca, www.langara.bc.ca

DIPLOMA PROGRAM IN LATIN AMERICAN STUDIES ▪ The Diploma Program in Latin American Studies is a two-year interdisciplinary program which provides students with a broad introduction to Latin America and a basis from which to pursue further study. The program offers students the opportunity to consider the environmental, developmental, and institutional foundations of Latin America from an interdisciplinary perspective. Courses are offered in the following fields: geography, political studies, sociology, and economics. Students enrolled in the program are encouraged to develop a proficiency in Spanish. [ID:5400]

LANGARA COLLEGE—AREA STUDIES
Pacific Rim Studies Program
Coordinator, Pacific Rim Studies Program, Langara College,
100 West 49th Ave., Vancouver, B.C. V5Y 2Z6; (604) 323-5262,
fax (604) 323-5555, jplaczek@langara.ba.ca, www.langara.bc.ca

DIPLOMA IN PACIFIC RIM STUDIES ▪ The mandate of the Pacific Rim Studies program at Langara College is to sensitize Canadian students to the cultures and peoples of the Asia Pacific region, to prepare them to work and live as citizens of our local and global community. The program assists students to develop skills and competencies necessary for successful university study in the third and fourth year. Overseas study options are available to program students. [ID:6624]

LANGARA COLLEGE—INTERNATIONAL BUSINESS
Department of Business Administration
Admissions, Office of the Registrar, Department of Business Administration, Langara College,
100 West 49th Ave., Vancouver, B.C. V5Y 2Z6; (604) 323-5221, fax (604) 323-5555, www.langara.bc.ca

DIPLOMA IN INTERNATIONAL BUSINESS ▪ The International Business Program at Langara College is a practical, interdisciplinary, career-oriented program, leading to a diploma in business while offering a number of university transfer courses. The program provides knowledge of the history, culture, economics and business practice of the world's major trading countries. Students also have the opportunity to participate in an internship option, which includes a four-, six- or twelve-month work period. [ID:6607]

LANGARA COLLEGE—PEACE/CONFLICT STUDIES
Peace and Conflict Studies Program
Coordinator, Peace and Conflict Studies Program,
Langara College, 100 West 49th Ave., Vancouver, B.C. V5Y 2Z6;
(604) 323-5360, fax (604) 323-5555, mgoldie@langara.bc.ca, ww2.langara.bc.ca

DIPLOMA IN PEACE AND CONFLICT STUDIES ▪ The Peace and Conflict Studies (PACS) program at Langara College focuses on the problem and resolution of human conflict. PACS takes an interdisciplinary approach to analyzing conflict, drawing on perspectives from the physical and social sciences, history, and philosophy. Peace and Conflict Studies is one of the fastest growing fields in North America and helps prepare students for a future in politics and diplomacy, international relief and development, community and social services, public administration, law or education. [ID:6609]

UNIVERSITÉ LAVAL—INTERNATIONAL PROFILE
UNIVERSITÉ LAVAL
Québec, Québec G1K 7P4; (418) 656-2131, fax (418) 656-2336, www.ulaval.ca

Nombre de programmes et centres de recherche internationaux : 9
Nombre d'étudiants étrangers : 5% d'une population étudiante de 32 000

Expertise internationale : L'Université Laval a signé 215 ententes avec des établissements d'enseignement supérieur de plusieurs pays permettant aux étudiants de toutes les facultés d'effectuer un séjour d'études à l'étranger et d'effectuer des stages dans les entreprises associées à ces établissements. Les domaines de l'agriculture, de la foresterie, de la santé, de la géographie, des sciences de l'éducation, des sciences sociales, du génie, des sciences de l'administration et bien d'autres offrent une ouverture internationale à leurs étudiants. L'Université Laval gère aussi de nombreux projets de développement en Afrique, en Amérique latine et en Asie, auxquels les étudiants peuvent participer.

Bureaux internationaux : Le Bureau de la coopération internationale fait la promotion des activités internationales, appuie les membres de l'Université à cet égard, coordonne les actions internationales et il sert aussi d'agent de liaison avec les orgranismes extérieurs. Le Bureau d'acceuil des étudiants étrangers organise des activités d'animation et d'acceuil, répond aux demandes des étudiants étrangers et aide les facultés et les départements dans leurs actions d'encadrement des étudiants étrangers. [ID:6786]

UNIVERSITÉ LAVAL—AREA STUDIES
Études russes et slaves
Département de langues et linguistiques, Québec, Québec
G1K 7P4; (418) 656-2131 ext. 3322, fax (418) 656-2622, www.ulaval.ca

CERTIFICAT OU MINEURE D'ÉTUDES RUSSES ou BACCALAURÉAT INDIVIDUALISÉ EN ÉTUDES RUSSES ET SLAVES ▪ Le programme de mineure ou certificat d'études russes de l'Université Laval prépare des spécialistes dans les domaines de la langue, de la littérature, de l'histoire, de la géographie, de la politique, du cinéma et du théâtre russe. En plus les étudiants peuvent faire leur baccalauréat individualisé en études russes et slaves. L'Université permet aussi aux étudiants de continuer leur apprentissage aux 2e et 3e cycles. L'Université Laval est la seule au pays ayant des rapports polydimensionnels et actifs avec l'Université d'État des sciences humaines de Russie, leader dans le champs des sciences sociales à Moscou. L'accord-cadre et le programme d'échanges entre les deux universités permettent aux étudiants de l'Université Laval d'être exemptés - totalement ou en partie - des frais de scolarité et de résidence de l'Université des sciences humaines, de travailler à cette université en donnant des cours, ainsi que de participer dans divers projets de recherche sous les auspices du Centre interuniversitaire "Moscou-Québec," et de collaborer à la rédaction d'articles pour des journaux de Moscou ayant des liens avec l'Université des sciences humaines. [ID:5308]

UNIVERSITÉ LAVAL—AREA STUDIES
Études africaines
Département de sociologie, Québec, Québec
G1K 7P4; (418) 656-2227, fax (418) 656-7390, www.ulaval.ca

BA: mineure ou certificat en études africaines ▪ Le programme en études africaines permet aux étudiants d'acquérir, grâce aux cours dispensés, une vue précise sur le développement et la situation de l'Afrique dans le système politique international et favorise une étude appropriée des systèmes socioculturels des peuples africains. [ID:5307]

UNIVERSITÉ LAVAL—AREA STUDIES
Centre d'études nordiques
Québec, Québec G1K 7P4; (418) 656-3340, fax (418) 656-2978, cen@cen.ulaval.ca, www.ulaval.ca

CENTRE DE RECHERCHE ▪ Les activités de recherche du Centre d'études nordiques (CEN) concernent l'étude des écosystèmes continentaux des régions froides subarctiques et arctiques. Le Quaternaire, le pergélisol, l'écologie végétale, l'écologie de populations animales, la limnologie et les processus littoraux sont étudiés. Des collaborations de recherche existent avec certains pays notamment les États-Unis, la France, la Russie, la Chine et le Japon. [ID:5309]

UNIVERSITÉ LAVAL—AREA STUDIES
Centre international de recherche
en aménagement linguistique (CIRAL)
Faculté des Lettres, Pavillon Charles de Koninck, Québec, Québec G1K 7P4;
(418) 656-3232, fax (418) 656-7244, ciral@ciral.ulaval.ca, www.ciral.ulaval.ca

CENTRE DE RECHERCHE ▪ Le CIRAL poursuit deux objectifs : décrire le français en usage au Québec et étudier la langue comme objet social. Les recherches touchent la phonétique, l'analyse du discours, la lexicologie, la terminologie et l'informatique linguistique. Dans tous les cas, la perspective de l'application des résultats de la recherche est encouragée. Le Centre abrite un centre de documentation, de nombreux corpus tant oraux qu'écrits et des banques de données sur le français. Le CIRAL compte 15 chercheurs réguliers qui encadrent plusieurs étudiants gradués et stagiaires. Le Centre accueille notamment plusieurs étudiants étrangers intéressés à poursuivre des recherches sur l'aménagement linguistique ou l'application des politiques linguistiques dans les pays de la francophonie tout particulièrement. [ID:6693]

UNIVERSITÉ LAVAL—DEVELOPMENT STUDIES
Agriculture et alimentation
Faculté des sciences de l'agriculture et de l'alimentation, Québec, Québec
G1K 7P4; (418) 656-3145, fax (418) 656-7806, fsaa@fsaa.ulaval.ca, www.ulaval.ca

CERTIFICAT, BScA, BSc, DIPLÔME DE DEUXIÈME CYCLE, MSc, PhD ▪ La Faculté des sciences de l'agriculture et de l'alimentation (FSAA) offre une gamme complète d'enseignements allant du premier au troisième cycle dans les domaines tels l'agroéconomie, la bioagronomie, le génie rural et agroalimentaire, les sciences et la technologie des aliments ou encore la biologie végétale, la zootechnie et la nutrition. Ces programmes ainsi que les équipes de recherche de la faculté sont décrits sur son site web.

La FSAA participe à de nombreux projets internationaux de recherche et à des ententes institutionnelles. Des opportunités de recherche à l'étranger existent aussi pour les étudiants. Dans certains programmes de la FSAA, le pourcentage d'étudiants étrangers peut atteindre 30%. En tout, la faculté compte environ 2000 étudiants. [ID:5311]

UNIVERSITÉ LAVAL—INTERNATIONAL BUSINESS
Gestion internationale des entreprises
Département de finance et assurance, Québec, Québec G1K 7P4;
(418) 656-2584, fax (418) 656-2624, www.fsa.ulaval.ca=80/formation/maîtrise/index.html

MBA—gestion internationale ▪ Le cheminement MBA - Gestion internationale a pour objectif de former des cadres et des dirigeants capables d'évoluer dans un monde international en pleine mutation où les concepts de globalisation, de compétitivité et de flexibilité doivent faire partie de la réflexion stratégique. Les étudiants désireux de suivre ce programme devront faire preuve de connaissances de base en administration et avoir une bonne connaissance de trois langues. [ID:5313]

UNIVERSITÉ LAVAL—INTERNATIONAL STUDIES
Institut québécois des hautes études internationales
Bureau 5460, Pavillon de Koninck, Québec, Québec G1K 7P4;
(418) 656-7771, fax (418) 656-3634, hei@hei.ulaval.ca, www.ulaval.ca/iqhei

CENTRE DE RECHERCHE ▪ L'Institut québecois des hautes études internationales, créé en juin 1994 comme point de ralliement de l'activité internationale à l'Université Laval, a un champ d'action organisé autour de trois axes: relations internationales, développement international et affaires internationales. L'Institut poursuit des activités en enseignement supérieur et en recherche ainsi qu'en publication et en animation. L'Institut a pour objectif d'étudier l'évolution de l'environnement international du Canada et du Québec ainsi que son influence sur les différents secteurs de notre société. L'Institut touche aux questions tant politiques, juridiques ou économiques que de défense ou de sécurité afin de développer une expertise canadienne et québecoise de haut niveau en études internationales. [ID:5316]

UNIVERSITÉ LAVAL—INTERNATIONAL STUDIES
Journalisme international
Institut québécois des hautes études internationales, Bureau 5460, Pavillon de Koninck,
Québec, Québec G1K 7P4; (418) 656-7771, fax (418) 656-3634, hei@hei.ulaval.ca, www.ulaval.ca/iqhei

DIPLÔME DE 2e CYCLE EN JOURNALISME INTERNATIONAL ▪ Le programme de diplôme en journalisme international s'adresse aux journalistes et futurs journalistes intéressés par l'actualité internationale. Le programme permet à l'étudiant de mieux connaître les circuits par lesquels transite l'information internationale et de mieux comprendre les enjeux internationaux de façon à les présenter de manière adéquate. Au terme des études, l'étudiant devrait avoir acquis, par un assemblage approprié de cours et de stages, une méthode de lecture de la matière internationale qui lui permette de sélectionner rapidement les informations importantes et de créer des liens entre elles. Des cours du programme de maîtrise en relations internationales sont inclus dans les cours optionels. [ID:6691]

UNIVERSITÉ LAVAL—INTERNATIONAL STUDIES
Relations internationales
Institut québécois des hautes études internationales, Bureau 5460, Pavillon de Koninck,
Québec, Québec G1K 7P4; (418) 656-3813, fax (418) 656-3634, mri@ulaval.ca, www.ulaval.ca/iqhei

MA EN RELATIONS INTERNATIONALES ▪ La maîtrise en relations internationales a pour objectif de former des professionnels qui sauront non seulement appréhender les problèmes économiques, juridiques et politiques auxquels doivent faire face États et entreprises dans leurs activités internationales, mais aussi concevoir les stratégies nécessaires pour les résoudre. Au terme de leur scolarité, les étudiants doivent effectuer un stage de trois mois ou plus. Ce programme est offert à tous les diplômés venant d'universités québécoises, canadiennes et étrangères. [ID:5314]

LESTER B. PEARSON COLLEGE OF THE PACIFIC—INTERNATIONAL STUDIES
International Baccalaureate Program
Canadian Student Selection Office, United World Colleges,
R.R.1, Victoria, B.C. V9B 5T7; (250) 391-2411, fax (250) 391-2412,
admin@pearson-college.uwc.ca, www.pearson-college.uwc.ca/pearson

International Baccalaureate ▪ Pearson College is part of the United World Colleges (UWC) project which, through education, seeks to promote a greater understanding between peoples of the world; students from many countries and cultures are brought together to study and to serve the community. UCW provides the International Baccalaureate program for member colleges.

Students are selected in open competition and full scholarships are provided for the one hundred places available each year. The widest possible range of nationalities, races, religions, and political allegiances are represented. Qualifications include being between 16 and 17 years of age with eleven years of school completed and having first class standing in over half the subjects studied in the past few years. Applicants must also demonstrate enthusiasm for the idea of understanding between people of widely different cultures.

A limited number of scholarships are reserved for Canadian students to enrol at other UWCs located in Venezuela, Hong Kong, India, Norway, Singapore, Swaziland, Italy, the UK, and New Mexico. [ID:7076]

UNIVERSITY OF LETHBRIDGE—INTERNATIONAL BUSINESS
Faculty of Management
Undergraduate Admissions, Faculty of Management, University of Lethbridge,
Room E-480, Student Programs Office, 4410 University Drive, Lethbridge, Alberta
T1K 3M4; (403) 329-2768, fax (403) 329-2253, stosc@gw.uleth.ca, www.uleth.ca/man/min

BMgt: major in International Management ▪ The International Management major provides a focus on finance, strategy and policy, trade, and laws in the international marketplace. Students must also gain speaking, reading and writing competency in another language, and an in-depth understanding of the related culture. There are 900 students in the Faculty of Management, with admission to the major coming in the second, third, or fourth year of study. Students possessing a business diploma may also be admitted. Visit their web site for program and faculty information as well as application forms. [ID:5347]

UNIVERSITY OF MANITOBA—INTERNATIONAL PROFILE
UNIVERSITY OF MANITOBA
66 Chancellors Circle, Winnipeg, Manitoba R3T 2N2;
(204) 474-8501, fax (204) 474-7562, www.umanitoba.ca

International programs and research centres in this chapter: 6
Number of students: 22,000 **Percentage of international students:** 3%

International offices: The mission of the International Centre for Students is to support international students at the University of Manitoba and foster awareness and involvement of Canadians in the international community. The centre is responsible for international student exchange programs and the operation of a work/study abroad resource centre.

Language programs within Area Studies described in this chapter: Latin American Studies Program; Asian Studies Centre; Central and Eastern European Studies Program. **Other language programs:** BA, BA (honours), MA in German; BA, BA (honours) in Italian; BA, BA (honours), MA in Icelandic; BA, BA (honours) minor in Polish;

BA, BA (honours), MA in Russian; BA, BA (honours) in Spanish; BA, BA (honours), MA in Ukrainian. [ID:6645]

UNIVERSITY OF MANITOBA—AREA STUDIES
Asian Studies Centre
Director, Asian Studies Centre, University of Manitoba, Winnipeg, Manitoba R3T 2N2; (204) 474-9516, fax (204) 474-7601, hueckst@cc.umanitoba.ca, www.umanitoba.ca/faculties/arts/asian_studies

BA: minor in Asian Studies ▪ The Asian Studies Centre was created in 1990 and coordinates Asia-related teaching and research by faculty members in a variety of departments and faculties. The centre offers instruction in the following Asian languages: Japanese (three levels), Hindi/Urdu (three levels), Mandarin (three levels) and Sanskrit (two levels). Students in the BA program are eligible to declare a major or a minor in Asian Studies, while graduate students from other departments are invited to make use of the centre's resources and its faculty's expertise. [ID:5348]

UNIVERSITY OF MANITOBA—AREA STUDIES
Latin American Studies Program
Coordinator, Latin American Studies Program, Anthropology Department,
University of Manitoba, 443 Fletcher Building, Winnipeg, Manitoba R3T 2N2;
(204) 474-6330, fax (204) 474-7600, chodkie@cc.umanitoba.ca, www.umanitoba.ca

BA: minor in Latin American Studies ▪ The interdisciplinary Latin American Studies Program (minor) permits students to gain a deeper understanding of the subject area and to take an optimum number of courses in Latin American affairs. A minor in Latin American Studies consists of at least three full courses, or the equivalent, from a minimum of two different departments. Summer study in Mexico is an option. [ID:5351]

UNIVERSITY OF MANITOBA—AREA STUDIES
Central and Eastern European Studies Program
Coordinator, Central and Eastern European Studies Program, St. John's College, University of Manitoba, Winnipeg, Manitoba R3T 2N2; (204) 474-8101, fax (204) 474-7610, www.umanitoba.ca

BA: major in Central and Eastern European Studies ▪ With an emphasis on the countries of the Commonwealth of Independent States (CIS), the Central and Eastern European Studies Program involves a core of five courses drawn from the Departments of Economics, History, Political Studies, Geography, and Slavic Studies. Students must fulfil a language requirement in Russian, Ukrainian, or Polish and are encouraged to attend a series of seminars on related areas of interest. The program also offers opportunities for study abroad and some financial assistance in the form of scholarships for excellence in Slavic languanges. [ID:5349]

UNIVERSITY OF MANITOBA—AREA STUDIES
Department of Religion
Department of Religion, University of Manitoba, Winnipeg, Manitoba R3T 2N2;
(204) 474-9516, fax (204) 474-7601, eastern@bldgarts.lan1.umanitoba.ca, www.umanitoba.ca

BA IN RELIGION: concentration in Judaic Studies ▪ This interdisciplinary program enables students to concentrate in Judaic and Near Eastern studies. The concentration is based in the Department of Religion, consists of approximately five full courses, and encourages the study of Hebrew. [ID:5350]

UNIVERSITY OF MANITOBA—INTERNATIONAL BUSINESS

The Centre for International Business Studies (CIBS)

Assistant Director, Centre for International Business Studies (CIBS), University of
Manitoba, 465 Drake Centre, 181 Freedman Crescent, Winnipeg, Manitoba R3T 5V4;
(204) 474-9730, fax (204) 474-7545, marova_bowman@umanitoba.ca, www.umanitoba.ca

RESEARCH CENTRE ■ In cooperation with the Office of the Exchange Programs Director,
The Centre for International Business Studies (CIBS) promotes interest in international
business by inviting international guest speakers, providing language training programs,
working with the International Association for Students of Economics and Commerce
(AIESEC), and assisting internationally-minded students explore their options on campus.
Exchange opportunities exist in the US, Europe, Asia, and Latin America. The centre also
provides links to and programs for local small business. [ID:5353]

UNIVERSITY OF MANITOBA—INTERNATIONAL STUDIES

Centre for Defence and Security Studies

Director, Centre for Defence and Security Studies, University College,
University of Manitoba, Winnipeg, Manitoba R3T 2N2; (204) 474-6472,
fax (204) 474-7645, cdssum@cc.umanitoba.ca, www.umanitoba.ca/centres/defence

RESEARCH CENTRE ■ Established in 1985, the Centre for Defence and Security Studies
(CDSS) undertakes research into all aspects of international security. Its main areas of focus
are defence industrial analysis, European security, and new challenges to security. The centre publishes occasional papers, conducts long- and short-term research projects, teaches
graduate and undergraduate courses and sponsors students' conferences. CDSS has links to
other centres and institutes in Canada and around the world, which enable it to pursue an
interdisciplinary approach to questions of international security. CDSS also recruits a number of associate fellows, graduate fellows and external/visiting fellows. [ID:6495]

MCGILL UNIVERSITY—INTERNATIONAL PROFILE

MCGILL UNIVERSITY

University Relations, 845 Sherbrooke Street W.,
Montréal, Québec H3A 2T5; (514) 398-8305, fax (514) 398-7364, www.mcgill.ca

International programs and research centres in this chapter: 17
Number of students: 30,500 **Percentage of international students:** 11.5%

International focus: McGill University is a pioneer in Canadian higher education and
has grown into a major university with an enviable reputation in scholarly achievement and
worldwide scientific investigation and discovery. Long recognized as one of the most international universities in North America, McGill attracts some of the brightest students and
scholars from over 140 countries. McGill's international outreach extends well beyond the
cosmopolitan nature of its student body. McGill's faculty is equally diverse in origin and is
drawn from the best schools around the world. In the last fifteen years McGill professors
from a myriad of disciplines have been involved in more than 120 international development
projects. Moreover, McGill has collaborative agreements with more than eighty institutions
in other countries. Bilateral international student exchange agreements are in place with
more than fifty partner institutions, while through the consortium of Québec universities
(CREPUQ), students have access to approximately 500 more. Although some programs are
more extensively focused on international themes than others, it is very difficult to find an
area of study or research at McGill which does not incorporate some international dimension.

International offices: The International Student Advisor at McGill is responsible for
providing programs to promote the growth and development of international students. To
this end, the university provides a buddy system program for international students to

facilitate their adaption to McGill and Montréal. The Office of International Research (OIR) coordinates international agreements and projects, working with McGill faculty members to enhance their international research activity. Student exchange programs are administered by the Office of Student Exchanges and Study Abroad.

Language programs within Area Studies described in this chapter: Department of German Studies; East Asian Studies Program; Institute of Islamic Studies; Middle East Studies Program; Department of Russian and Slavic Studies. **Other language programs:** Lingustics: BA, BA (honours), MA & PhD. [ID:6646]

MCGILL UNIVERSITY—AREA STUDIES
North American Studies Program
Chairperson, North American Studies Program, McGill University, 845 Sherbrooke Street W., Montréal, Québec H3A 2T5; (514) 398-3861, fax (514) 398-8365, www.mcgill.ca

BA IN NORTH AMERICAN STUDIES ▪ The North American Studies Program at McGill University is an interdisciplinary major that consists of 54 credits in Canadian and American history, literature, politics, economics, and electives. The first classes (18 required credits) are at the introductory level, and the remainder, at least six credits from each of the departments, are advanced. Students may also choose to substitute designated offerings in the Latin American area. All must attend a final North American Studies seminar. Currently, there are approximately 100 undergraduate students in the program. [ID:5252]

MCGILL UNIVERSITY—AREA STUDIES
East Asian Studies Program
Coordinator, East Asian Studies Program, McGill University, Room 200, 3434 McTavish Street, Montréal, Québec H3A 1X9; (514) 398-6742, fax (514) 398-1882, eastasia@peterson.lan.mcgill.ca, www.arts.mcgill.ca/programs/eas

BA (honours & joint honours): major in East Asian Studies ▪ The Department of East Asian Studies offers instruction in the languages and cultures of East Asia. As well as offering a different perspective on the human condition, it provides excellent preparation for a future professional career in international business management, education, law, journalism and communication, in addition to the necessary training for advanced study at the graduate level. Check their web site for detailed information. [ID:5247]

MCGILL UNIVERSITY—AREA STUDIES
Latin American and Caribbean Studies Program
Advisor, Latin American and Caribbean Studies Program, Department of Hispanic Studies, McGill University, 680 Bronfman Bldg., Montréal, Québec H3A 1G5; (514) 398-6683, fax (514) 398-8239, claras@leacock.lan.mcgill.ca, www.mcgill.ca

BA (major & honours) IN LATIN AMERICAN AND CARIBBEAN STUDIES ▪ Established in 1971, the interdisciplinary Latin American and Caribbean Studies Program aims to provide undergraduate students with a comprehensive understanding of this geographic region. This program also provides language and research skills that are necessary for advanced scholarship. As part of McGill's Faculty of Arts and drawing upon the academic resources of the university as a whole, the program offers a broad array of courses dealing with the people, culture, history, literature, politics, economy, and geography of Latin America and the Caribbean. Cooperative research and exchange agreements between McGill and universities in Spain, Mexico, and Argentina also provide important opportunities for foreign study and field work. In both its educational and research functions, the Latin American and Caribbean Studies Program is committed to the free exchange of ideas and perspectives so as to foster an environment suitable for serious reflection and critical analysis. [ID:5250]

MCGILL UNIVERSITY—AREA STUDIES
Middle East Studies Program
Advisor, Middle East Studies Program, Department of Political Science, McGill University, 845 Sherbrooke Street W., Montréal, Québec H3A 2T5; (514) 398-8960, fax (514) 398-1770, www.mcgill.ca

BA (honours, joint honours, major & joint major) IN MIDDLE EAST STUDIES ▪ The Middle East Studies Program is designed for students who wish to pursue an interdisciplinary program of study focusing on the Middle East since the rise of Islam. Courses include language, history, religion and philosophy, political science, and anthropology. Students may pursue either a full major or honours program, or combine Middle East Studies with another discipline for a joint honours or combined major degree. [ID:5251]

MCGILL UNIVERSITY—AREA STUDIES
Department of German Studies
Chairperson, Department of German Studies, McGill University, 1001 Sherbrooke Street W., Montréal, Québec H3A 1G5; (514) 398-3650, fax (513) 398-8239, german@leacock.lan.mcgill.ca, www.mcgill.ca

BA, MA & PhD IN GERMANIC STUDIES ▪ At the undergraduate level, McGill University offers honours, major, joint honours, joint major and minor degrees in Germanic Studies. At the graduate level, there are MA and PhD programs offered. Courses are offered in German language, literature, history, and culture. [ID:6499]

MCGILL UNIVERSITY—AREA STUDIES
Department of Russian and Slavic Studies
Chairperson, Department of Russian and Slavic Studies, McGill University, 1001 Sherbrooke Street W., Montréal, Québec H3A 1G5; (514) 398-3639, fax (514) 398-8239, www.mcgill.ca

BA, BA (honours), MA & PhD IN SLAVIC STUDIES ▪ The Department of Russian and Slavic Studies offers courses in Russian language, literature, and translation. Students interested in Russian, Soviet, and East-Central European fields are encouraged to take courses from the Departments of Political Science, History, and Economics. [ID:6504]

MCGILL UNIVERSITY—AREA STUDIES
Institute of Islamic Studies
Director, Institute of Islamic Studies, McGill University, Room 319, 3485 McTavish Street, Montréal, Québec H3A 1Y1; (514) 398-6077, fax (514) 398-6731, islamics@leacock.lan.mcgill.ca, www.mcgill.ca

MA & PhD IN ISLAMIC STUDIES ▪ The MA and PhD Programs at the Institute of Islamic Studies are concerned with the disciplined study of Islamic civilization throughout the scope of its history and geographical spread. It gives attention to the rise of Islamic faith, to the forces which shaped the civilization, and to the changes it has undergone. The program also concerns itself with contemporary issues relating to the Islamic world and how Muslims seek to relate their heritage to the present. Graduate students have access to the research and extensive library facilities of the Institute. The program also offers courses in Arabic, Turkish, Persian, and Urdu languages at various levels. [ID:5249]

MCGILL UNIVERSITY—AREA STUDIES
Centre for East Asian Research
Director, Centre for East Asian Research, McGill University, 3434 McTavish Street, Montréal, Québec H3A 1X9; (514) 398-6741, fax (514) 398-1882, www.mcgill.ca

RESEARCH CENTRE ▪ The Centre for East Asian Studies is designed to coordinate, integrate, and facilitate funding research related to East Asia in different departments, programs, and areas at McGill University. [ID:5248]

MCGILL UNIVERSITY—DEVELOPMENT STUDIES
International Development Studies
Coordinator, International Development Studies, McGill University,
855 Sherbrooke Street W., Montréal, Québec H3A 2T7; (514) 398-4829,
fax (514) 398-4938, inmf@musicb.mcgill.ca, www.arts.mcgill.ca/programs/ids

BA: minor in International Development Studies ▪ This program provides students with a recognized concentration in International Development Studies. Core courses have been chosen from a range of disciplines to give students a broad theoretical basis in more than one discipline, while optional courses and seminars are intended to help them deepen their understanding of the development process and its cultural context. In addition to the resources and expertise provided by faculty, students in this program are encouraged to make use of the documentation centre and research generated by the Centre for Developing Area Studies. [ID:5253]

MCGILL UNIVERSITY—DEVELOPMENT STUDIES
School of Architecture
Coordinator, Minimum Cost Housing in Developing Countries Program, School of
Architecture, McGill University, Macdonald-Harrington Building, 815 Sherbrooke St. W.,
Montréal, Québec H3A 2K6; (514) 398-6700, fax (514) 398-7372, www.mcgill.ca/arch

MArch IN MINIMUM COST HOUSING IN DEVELOPING COUNTRIES ▪ The Minimum Cost Housing option, established in 1971, addresses the human settlement problems of developing countries. Its intent is neither social nor technical, but represents a professional philosophy with respect to the design of human settlements. Topics include new delivery mechanisms for mass housing, upgrading strategies, and design tools for planning large settlements. Ongoing research is presently being conducted in India and China. [ID:7107]

MCGILL UNIVERSITY—DEVELOPMENT STUDIES
Centre for Developing Area Studies
Director, Centre for Developing Area Studies, McGill University, 3715 Peel Street,
Montréal, Québec H3A 1X1; (514) 398-3507, fax (514) 398-8432, ed10@musica.mcgill.ca, www.mcgill.ca

RESEARCH CENTRE ▪ The Centre for Developing Area Studies was founded in 1963 to promote and support interdisciplinary research on international development issues. The centre contributes to the ongoing dialogue on international development by conducting workshops, organizing seminars and colloquiums, and running a resource library. Fellows and associates come from a wide variety of academic disciplines and nongovernmental organizations. Through their involvement with the centre students gain access to a larger community of students from various disciplines working on international development. [ID:5254]

MCGILL UNIVERSITY—INTERNATIONAL BUSINESS
Faculty of Management
Director of Student Recruitment, Faculty of Management, McGill University,
1001 Sherbrooke Street W., Montréal, Québec H3A 1G5; (514) 398-4066,
fax (514) 398-2499, major@management.mcgill.ca, www.management.mcgill.ca

MBA: concentration in International Business ▪ A 20-month MBA degree with an international business concentration is offered. Exchange opportunities are available with leading European, North and South American, and Asian schools. The McGill MBA program has one of Canada's highest percentages of international students; each year up to 40 per cent of the entering class comes from outside Canada. Also offered is a Bachelor of Commerce degree in International Management, in which students focus on a particular geographic region of the world. [ID:5255]

MCGILL UNIVERSITY—INTERNATIONAL BUSINESS
Centre for International Management Studies
Executive Director, Centre for International Management Studies,
McGill University, 1001 Sherbrooke Street W., Montréal, Québec H3A 1G5;
(514) 398-4004, fax (514) 398-6773, amand@management.mcgill.ca, www.management.mcgill.ca

RESEARCH CENTRE ▪ The Centre for International Management Studies acts as an umbrella for international activities within McGill's Faculty of Management. This includes a large number of student exchange programs at the undergraduate and graduate levels as well as many university linkages and long-term "train the trainer" development projects. As evidenced by the number of international students coming to the faculty and the number of McGill students studying abroad, the faculty has a strong commitment to international education. [ID:5256]

MCGILL UNIVERSITY—INTERNATIONAL LAW
Institute of Comparative Law (ICL)
Graduate Programs Coordinator, Institute of Comparative Law,
Faculty of Law, McGill University, 3661 Peel Street, Montréal, Québec H3A 1X1;
(514) 398-6646, fax (514) 398-8197, gradprog@falaw.lan.mcgill.ca, www.law.mcgill.ca

LLM: concentrations in International Business Law, Human Rights or Cultural Diversity ▪ The Institute of Comparative Law (ICL) is dedicated to the promotion of research in private, commercial, international, and public law. The ICL encourages openness to diverse legal cultures in teaching and research, while accommodating national, international and transnational studies. The institute offers a concentration in International Business Law which enables students to apply the experience of many legal systems in developing multijurisdictional "international" commercial rules. The institute also promotes the comparative study of domestic and international human rights law by allowing students to concentrate in human rights and cultural diversity. This program allows students to reflect critically upon the emergence and institutionalization of human rights norms in both domestic and international settings. [ID:5257]

MCGILL UNIVERSITY—INTERNATIONAL LAW
Institute and Centre of Air and Space Law
Director, Institute and Centre of Air and Space Law, McGill University, 3661 Peel Street, Montréal,
Québec H3A 1X1; (514) 398-5094, fax (514) 398-8197, milde_m@falaw.lan.mcgill.ca, www.iasl.mcgill.ca

RESEARCH CENTRE ▪ The Institute and Centre of Air and Space Law offers research expertise and graduate training in the field of international aviation and space application law. The centre is part of the Faculty of Law and offers a graduate certificate, LLM, and DCL. The centre also provides consulting services, organizes seminars and conferences, and publishes manuscripts and journals. Manuscripts in English or French are welcome for evaluation, with a view to publication. [ID:5258]

MCGILL UNIVERSITY—INTERNATIONAL STUDIES
Department of Political Science
Director of Graduate Studies, McGill University, 855 Sherbrooke Street West,
Montréal, Québec H3A 2T7; (514) 398-4800, fax (514) 398-1770, www.arts.mcgill.ca/programs/polisci

MA & PhD IN POLITICAL SCIENCE: specialization in International Politics ▪ The Department of Political Science's MA and PhD programs are designed to provide graduate students with appropriate breadth in their studies without sacrificing depth of knowledge in their chosen fields. The department is composed of 22 tenured or tenure-track professors who represent a wide range of intellectual traditions and methods within the discipline. Together, the faculty offers students the opportunity to concentrate in five major fields: Canadian Politics, Comparative Government and Politics in Developing Countries, International Politics, and Political Theory. Graduate students can also take advantage of the interdisciplinary research generated by the Centre for Developing Areas Studies and other research facilities on campus. Visit their web site for program information, course descriptions, and to request a graduate application. [ID:5259]

MCGILL UNIVERSITY—INTERNATIONAL STUDIES
McGill Centre for Society, Technology and Development—STANDD
Director, McGill Centre for Society, Technology and Development – STANDD, McGill University, Suite 2400, 2020 University Street, Montréal, Québec H3A 2A5; (514) 398-1807, fax (514) 398-4619, galaty@leacock.lan.mcgill.ca, www.mcgill.ca

RESEARCH CENTRE ▪ This interdisciplinary centre was founded to support and coordinate research on the interaction between society and technology in the process of development. The centre has been involved in projects in many parts of the globe, including Eastern Africa, East Asia, Latin America, the Caribbean, Oceania, and the Canadian North. Currently, the centre is primarily concerned with the implications of property rights, environmental sustainability and development in the poorer regions of the world. [ID:5260]

MCMASTER UNIVERSITY—INTERNATIONAL PROFILE
MCMASTER UNIVERSITY
1280 Main Street W., Hamilton, Ontario L8S 4L8; (905) 525-9140, www.mcmaster.ca

International programs and research centres in this chapter: 6
Number of students: 14,000 **Percentage of international students:** 2%

   International focus: At McMaster University, various departments, centres, and institutes participate in international training and research programs around the world. McMaster has spearheaded interdisciplinary research and training projects to improve coastal management in Indonesia and Maldives, community health in Uganda, drought management in Nigeria, training nurses and healthcare workers in Pakistan, and developing health-priority-based-education in Chile.
   International offices: McMaster International has become increasingly involved around the world in exchange agreements, institutional linkages and externally funded international programs concerned with collaborative research, education, human resource development, and with improving the delivery of services in such sectors as business, environmental protection, community health, engineering, technology development and transfer. The Office of International Affairs facilitates international collaboration and coordinates activities that bring McMaster closer to the University's vision of being acclaimed internationally for its research and education quality; its areas of activities include student recruitment, development projects, international programs, fundraising, and development. The International Student Advisor provides a number of services to international students.
   Language programs within Area Studies described in this chapter: Japanese Studies Program. [ID:6647]

MCMASTER UNIVERSITY—AREA STUDIES
Japanese Studies Program
Director, Japanese Studies Program, McMaster University, 1280 Main Street West, Hamilton, Ontario L8S 4L8; (905) 525-9140 ext. 23393, fax (905) 525-8161, shinohar@mcmail.cis.mcmaster.ca, www.mcmaster.ca

BA (honours) IN JAPANESE STUDIES ▪ The Japanese Studies Program at McMaster University offers a four-year combined honours in Japanese Studies and another subject. A minor in Japanese Studies is also available. Courses in Japanese language and Japanese

Studies course work are required for each. The program also offers an exchange to Seinan Gakuin. [ID:6505]

MCMASTER UNIVERSITY—INTERNATIONAL BUSINESS
Michael G. DeGroote School of Business
Graduate Admissions, DeGroote School of Business, McMaster University, Hamilton, Ontario L8S 4L8; (905) 525-9140 ext. 24433, fax (905) 521-8995, mbainfo@mcmaster.ca, www.business.mcmaster.ca

MBA: concentration in International Business ▪ The DeGroote School of Business requires both commerce and MBA students to take a course in international business. Our MBA program offers an international business stream, and most other MBA streams have courses that focus on the international/global business scene. In addition, we have international exchange programs with universities in Asia, Mexico and Europe and many others in the planning stage. Most of our faculty have academic and work contacts abroad. [ID:5261]

MCMASTER UNIVERSITY—INTERNATIONAL STUDIES
Department of Political Science
Chairperson, Department of Political Science, McMaster University, Hamilton, Ontario L8S 4M4; (905) 525-9140 ext. 24741, fax (905) 527-3071, polisci@mcmaster.ca, www.socsci.mcmaster.ca/~polisci

MA & PhD IN POLITICAL SCIENCE: concentration in International Relations or Comparative Politics ▪ The Department of Political Science offers an MA with a concentration in international relations as well as a PhD with a public policy program that includes, where appropriate, field research abroad. Visit their web site for program information. [ID:5264]

MCMASTER UNIVERSITY—INTERNATIONAL STUDIES
International Studies, Department of Economics
Chairperson, International Studies, Department of Economics, Graduate Studies Committee, McMaster University, 1280 Main Street W., Hamilton, Ontario L8S 4M4; (905) 525-9140 ext. 24731, fax (905) 521-8232, econ@mcmaster.ca, www.socsci.mcmaster.ca/~econ/

PhD IN ECONOMICS: specialization in International Economics ▪ The McMaster PhD in Economics has specializations in quantitative economics, public finance, monetary economics, and international economics. All study is undertaken at McMaster, but after course work has been completed, field work abroad may be permitted in special cases. All study is in English; a minimum TOEFL score of 580 is required for admission.

All external fellowships for graduate study in economics are tenable at McMaster and the School of Graduate Studies may provide support for students in the forms of scholarships and teaching assistantships. [ID:5263]

MCMASTER UNIVERSITY—PEACE/CONFLICT STUDIES
Centre for Peace Studies
Director, Centre for Peace Studies, McMaster University, Room B104, University Hall, Hamilton, Ontario L8S 4L8; (905) 525-9140, fax (905) 570-1167, peace@mcmaster.ca, www.mcmaster.ca/peace

BA: minor in Peace Studies ▪ The Centre for Peace Studies supports multidisciplinary study, teaching, and research in Peace and Conflict Studies. The centre's research and teaching focuses on four areas: social movements, warfare and security arrangements, religious and philosophical approaches to peace and war, and human rights. The centre offers students the opportunity to pursue their minor in Peace Studies with over 23 courses from a variety of disciplines. [ID:5265]

MEMORIAL UNIVERSITY—INTERNATIONAL PROFILE
MEMORIAL UNIVERSITY
P.O. Box 4200, Stn. C, St. John's, Nfld. A1C 5S7; (709) 737-8000, fax (709) 737-3514, www.mun.ca

International programs and research centres in this chapter: 2
Number of students: 15,900 **Percentage of international students:** 2.5%

International offices: The International Programs Office serves as the focal point for the international commitment of Memorial University. This office provides information on the university's international projects, programs, funding sources, and acts as a liaison with external organizations. The International Student Advisor's Office provides international students with a variety of support services.

Language programs: BA, BA (honours), MA, MPhil in German; BA, BA (honours), MA, MPhil in Linguistics; BA in Russian; BA in Spanish. [ID:6648]

MEMORIAL UNIVERSITY—INTERNATIONAL BUSINESS
Centre for International Business Studies
Director, Centre for International Business Studies, Memorial University, St. John's, Nfld. A1B 3X5; (709) 737-4504, fax (709) 737-7999, cibs@morgan.ucs.mun.ca, www.mun.ca/cibs

RESEARCH CENTRE ▪ The Centre for International Business Studies was established at Memorial University in 1994. The centre is mandated to provide students and faculty with the opportunity to research issues in international business and trade and to facilitate exchanges with teaching institutions throughout the world. The centre also works with local business to enhance their ability to compete internationally. [ID:6506]

MEMORIAL UNIVERSITY—INTERNATIONAL STUDIES
Canadian Centre for International Fisheries Training and Development
Director, Canadian Centre for International Fisheries
Training and Development, Memorial University, St. John's, Nfld.
A1C 5S7; (709) 737-4356, fax (709) 737-4330, adickins@morgan.ucs.mun.ca, www.mun.ca

RESEARCH CENTRE ▪ The mandate of the Canadian Centre for International Fisheries Training and Development is to develop, staff, and find funding for the fisheries and marine projects of the university and its partners in developing countries. Institutional linkages exist between Memorial and other universities overseas, and funding is available for postgraduate research on those aspects of marine science of concern to Memorial University. [ID:5266]

UNIVERSITÉ DE MONCTON—INTERNATIONAL BUSINESS
Centre de commercialisation internationale (CCI)
Faculté d'administration, Moncton, N.B. E1A 3E9;
(506) 858-4499, fax (506) 858-4416, Landryjo@umoncton.ca, www.umoncton.ca

CENTRE DE RECHERCHE ▪ La mission du CCI est d'encourager et de promouvoir le commerce international auprès des entreprises du Nouveau-Brunswick en maximisant la synergie entre les étudiants, le corps professoral et les entreprises privées. Parmi ses activités, le CCI coordonne le Programme de Partenariat Académique (PPA) qui jumelle des étudiants de MBA à des entreprises locales, avec lesquelles ils collaborent à préparer un plan de marketing pour un pays étranger. [ID:5291]

UNIVERSITÉ DE MONCTON—INTERNATIONAL BUSINESS
Commerce international
Faculté d'administration, Centre universitaire de Moncton, Moncton, N.B.
E1A 3E9; (506) 858-4499, fax (506) 858 4416, www.umoncton.ca

BA: concentration commerce international ▪ Le Centre de commercialisation internationale offre à ses étudiants des cours de marketing international, de gestion et d'économie internationale, et de langues, ainsi que d'autres cours optionnels à orientation internationale. [ID:5290]

UNIVERSITÉ DE MONTRÉAL—INTERNATIONAL PROFILE
UNIVERSITÉ DE MONTRÉAL
C.P. 6128, succursale Centre-ville, Montréal, Québec
H3C 3J7; (514) 343-6111, fax (514) 343-5976, www.umontreal.ca

Nombre de programmes et centres de recherche internationaux : 15
Nombre d'étudiants étrangers : 5.1 % d'une population étudiante de 39 000

Expertise internationale : Depuis quelques années, des professeurs-chercheurs de l'Université de Montréal ont mené 128 actions de coopération dans 30 pays. Les différents gouvernements et organismes subventionnaires y ont consacré plus de six millions de dollars. Deux nouveaux centres d'excellence créés par l'Agence canadienne de développement international (ACDI) font appel à plusieurs professeurs-chercheurs, stagiaires et étudiants de l'Université. De plus, un nouveau programme de bourses d'études supérieures à l'intention des Latino-américains vient d'être mis sur pied conjointement par l'ACDI et l'Université de Montréal. L'Université de Montréal a également signé plus de 200 ententes formelles de collaboration scientifique, d'échanges de professeurs, de chercheurs et d'étudiants avec des universités de tous les continents. Ainsi, sont en vigueur à l'heure actuelle: plus de cent ententes de coopération institutionnelle, avec des établissements de trente pays, et plus de deux cents ententes d'échanges d'étudiants, avec des établissements de neuf pays.
Bureaux internationaux : L'Université de Montréal dispose d'un Bureau de liaison internationale pour faciliter la conclusion d'ententes internationales, ainsi que d'un Bureau de la coopération internationale et des services aux étudiants pour accueillir les étudiants étrangers. [ID:6779]

UNIVERSITÉ DE MONTRÉAL—AREA STUDIES
Centre d'études de l'Asie de l'Est
C.P. 6128, succursale Centre Ville, Montréal, Québec H3C 3J7; (514) 343-5970, fax (514) 343-7716

CENTRE DE RECHERCHE ▪ Le Centre d'études de l'Asie de l'Est (CETASE) a pour mission de regrouper les professeurs et chercheurs de l'institution qui s'intéressent à l'Asie de l'Est et de mettre sur pied des programmes d'enseignement, de recherche et de documentation multidisciplinaire permettant de répondre aux besoins du milieu en ce qui touche à la connaissance des sociétés, des cultures et des relations internationales de l'Asie de l'Est: Chine, Japon, Corée et Viêt-nam. Plus de 15 professeurs oeuvrent au Cetase qui accueille plus de 100 étudiants. [ID:6698]

UNIVERSITÉ DE MONTRÉAL—AREA STUDIES
Études arabes
C.P. 6128, succursale Centre-Ville, Montréal, Québec
H3C 3J7; (514) 343-7327, fax (514) 343-6311, www.umontreal.ca

MINEUR EN ÉTUDES ARABES (1er cycle) ▪ Le programme d'études arabes permet d'aborder le monde arabe selon une approche multidisciplinaire comprenant l'anthropologie, l'histoire, la philosophie, la religion, l'économie, la géographie, la politique et la sociologie. Il donne l'occasion d'apprendre la langue arabe, de l'alphabet à l'écriture et la conversation. Le programme, ouvert à tous, dure 2 ou 3 trimestres. [ID:5294]

UNIVERSITÉ DE MONTRÉAL—AREA STUDIES
Études est-asiatiques
C.P. 6128, succursale Centre Ville, Montréal, Québec H3C 3J7; (514) 343-5970, www.umontreal.ca

CERTIFICAT ou DIPLÔME EN ÉTUDES EST-ASIATIQUES ▪ Le Centre d'études est-asiatiques offre une formation multidisciplinaire sous forme de majeure ou de mineure en études est-asiatiques. Le Centre se concentre sur la Chine, le Japon et la Corée et dispose d'une bibliothèque spécialisée de 35 000 documents. Les professeurs du Centre gèrent des projets de recherche au sein desquels participent les étudiants gradués. [ID:6708]

UNIVERSITÉ DE MONTRÉAL—AREA STUDIES
Études italiennes
Direction des programmes facultaires, C.P. 6128, succursale Centre Ville,
Montréal, Québec H3C 3J7; (514) 343-7327, fax (514) 343-6311, www.umontreal.ca

MINEUR EN ÉTUDES ITALIENNES ▪ Le programme d'Études italiennes de l'Université de Montréal est une Mineure ouverte à tous. Avec une orientation fortement interdisciplinaire, le programme s'adresse à une clientèle variée incluant de nombreux italophones ainsi que des spécialistes comme des musiciens. Un trait original et nouveau du programme est l'accent posé sur la Méditerranée. Tous les cours, de celui d'introduction à la littérature italienne à celui sur le théâtre, encadrent la production culturelle italienne dans le contexte des cultures méditerranéennes. Le cours l'Italie méditerranéenne comprend un séjour en Italie. [ID:6695]

UNIVERSITÉ DE MONTRÉAL—AREA STUDIES
Études latino-américaines
Département d'histoire, C-1000, Pavillon Lionel-Groulx,
Montréal, Québec H3C 3J7; (514) 343-7327, fax (514) 343-6311, www.umontreal.ca

CERTIFICAT EN ÉTUDES LATINO-AMÉRICAINES ▪ Le programme d'études latino-américaines offre à l'étudiant une approche pluridisciplinaire mettant en valeur les dimensions historiques, économiques, politiques, sociales et culturelles de son développement. Une place importante est réservée aux langues et littératures donnant accès à cette région. [ID:5295]

UNIVERSITÉ DE MONTRÉAL—AREA STUDIES
Études russes
C.P. 6218, succursale A, Montréal, Québec H3C 3J7;
(514) 343-7327, fax (514) 343-6311, www.umontreal.ca

CERTIFICAT EN ÉTUDES RUSSES ▪ Le programme d'études russes offre à l'étudiant une approche pluridisciplinaire mettant en valeur les dimensions historiques, économiques, politiques, sociales et culturelles de la Russie ancienne et moderne et de l'URSS. Une place importante est accordée aux langues. [ID:5296]

UNIVERSITÉ DE MONTRÉAL—AREA STUDIES
Groupe de recherche sur l'Amérique latine (GRAL)
Faculté des arts et des sciences, Département de science politique,
C.P. 6128, succursale Centre Ville, Montréal, Québec H3C 3J7;
(514) 343-5723, fax (514) 343-2360, GRAL@ere.umontreal.ca, www.umontreal.ca

GROUPE DE RECHERCHE ▪ Le GRAL est un groupe de recherche multidisciplinaire impliquant la science politique, la science économique, l'anthropologie, l'histoire, la littérature, les communications et les sciences de l'éducation. Ce groupe a des activités de recherche et de publication, il organise des conférences et colloques et en maintient des liens avec plusieurs universités des États-Unis, d'Europe et d'Amérique latine. [ID:6700]

UNIVERSITÉ DE MONTRÉAL—DEVELOPMENT STUDIES
Gestion urbaine pour les pays en développement
Institut d'Urbanisme, Université de Montréal, C.P. 6128, succursale Centre Ville, Montréal, Québec H3C 3J7; (514) 343-5699, fax (514) 343-2338, urbanisme@ere.umontreal.ca, www.umontreal.ca

DIPLÔME D'ÉTUDES SUPÉRIEURES SPÉCIALISÉES EN GESTION URBAINE POUR LES PAYS EN DÉVELOPPEMENT ▪ Le programme de gestion urbaine pour les pays en développement vise à donner une formation spécialisée à des étudiants ou professionnels possédant déjà un diplôme de premier cycle et une expérience ou des connaissances sur les problématiques urbaines des pays en développement. L'étudiant du programme a la possibilité de se spécialiser dans deux domaines: la gestion des habitats urbains ou la gestion des environnements urbains. Le programme dure un an pour les étudiants inscrits à plein temps. Le programme accueille des étudiants des pays en développement et des pays développés. L'Institut d'Urbanisme est impliqué dans plusieurs programmes de recherche-formation internationaux; il offre ainsi aux étudiants la possibilité de réaliser des stages et des activités de recherche, notamment au Viêt-nam et en Amérique latine. [ID:6694]

UNIVERSITÉ DE MONTRÉAL—INTERCULTURAL STUDIES
Centre d'études ethniques de l'Université de Montréal
C.P. 6128, succursale Centre Ville, Montréal, Québec H3C 3J7;
(514) 343-7244, fax (514) 343-7078, cee@ere.umontreal.ca, www.ceetum.umontreal.ca

CENTRE DE RECHERCHE ▪ Le Centre est un foyer de recherche, de formation, d'animation et de diffusion des connaissances dans le domaine des relations ethniques. Il remplit essentiellement trois mandats: coordonner et développer les activités d'enseignement, de recherche et de rayonnement entreprises par les groupes qui le composent; coordonner et développer les relations des groupes qui le composent avec la collectivité, notamment les intervenants actifs dans le domaine; participer aux efforts de développement d'une stratégie institutionnelle d'adaptation au pluralisme à l'Université. Le Centre compte 18 membres. [ID:6699]

UNIVERSITÉ DE MONTRÉAL—INTERCULTURAL STUDIES
Groupe de recherche ethnicité et société
C.P. 6128, succursale Centre Ville, Montréal, Québec H3C 3J7;
(514) 343-6111 ext. 3803, fax (514) 343-7078, gres@ere.umontreal.ca, www.umontreal.ca

GROUPE DE RECHERCHE ▪ Le Groupe de recherche ethnicité et société (GRES) a pour objectif d'analyser la transformation des rapports sociaux ethniques tant au Québec qu'ailleurs dans le monde. Il vise également à approfondir la connaissance des enjeux découlant de ces rapports et à développer de nouveaux modèles permettant de mieux les cerner. Le GRES regroupe des chercheurs d'anthropologie, de démographie, d'histoire et de sociologie. Les quatres thèmes principaux autour desquels s'articule le programme de recherche du GRES sont : flux migratoires et insertion des immigrants et réfugiés; économie et marché du travail, État et organisations, culture et idéologie. [ID:6705]

UNIVERSITÉ DE MONTRÉAL—INTERCULTURAL STUDIES
Intervention en milieu multiethnique
Faculté de l'éducation permanente, C.P. 6128, succursale Centre Ville, Montréal, Québec H3C 3J7; (514) 343-6090, fax (514) 343-2447, info@fep.umontreal.ca, www.umontreal.ca

CERTIFICAT D'INTERVENTION EN MILIEU MULTIETHNIQUE ▪ Le Certificat d'intervention en milieu multiethnique est un programme de premier cycle universitaire de 450 heures de la Faculté de l'éducation permanente de l'Université de Montréal. Il offre une formation multidisciplinaire d'études théoriques et pratiques en intervention interculturelle. Ce programme s'adresse aux professionnels intervenant dans le réseau des affaires sociales, de la justice ou de l'éducation ainsi qu'à toute personne oeuvrant auprès de diverses ethnies et désireuse de se doter d'instruments de travail appropriés à l'exercice de ses fonctions. Pour être admis au programme, il faut avoir 21 ans, être détenteur d'un diplôme d'études collégiales ou l'équivalent et avoir une expertise pertinente de travail. Le site web procure aussi des informations au sujet du programme et de ses conditions d'admission. [ID:6703]

UNIVERSITÉ DE MONTRÉAL—INTERNATIONAL EDUCATION
Éducation comparée et internationale
Faculté des sciences de l'éducation, C.P. 6128, succursale Centre Ville, Montréal, Québec
H3C 3J7; (514) 343-6659, fax (514) 343-2497, fserens@scedu.umontreal.ca, www.scedu.umontreal.ca

DIPLÔME D'ÉTUDES SUPÉRIEURES SPÉCIALISÉES EN ÉDUCATION COMPARÉE ET INTERNATIONALE ▪ Le programme en Éducation comparée et internationale permet à ceux qui ont déjà une première formation universitaire d'acquérir et d'approfondir, par la voie de l'éducation comparée, la dimension interculturelle et internationale des systèmes, des méthodes et des organisations en éducation. Les objectifs de ce programme sont de faire acquérir à de futurs intervenants un ensemble de connaissances visant à favoriser chez eux la décentration par rapport à leurs propres normes culturelles et par rapport aux modèles d'éducation vécus dans leur propre milieu; et à les équiper de repères éducatifs fondamentaux. [ID:5297]

UNIVERSITÉ DE MONTRÉAL—INTERNATIONAL STUDIES
Centre de recherche sur les transports
C.P. 6128, succursale Centre Ville, Montréal, Québec H3C 3J7;
(514) 343-7575, fax (514) 343-7121, crt@crt.umontreal.ca, www.crt.umontreal.ca/CRT/

CENTRE DE RECHERCHE ▪ Le Centre de recherche sur les transports (C.R.T.) est un organisme de recherche stable, reconnu sur le plan national et international. Le champ d'expertise du C.R.T. est celui des analyses et méthodes quantitatives et informatiques appliquées aux réseaux de transports urbains, régionaux, interurbains et internationaux, pour les passagers comme pour les marchandises. Il comprend également l'analyse de l'environnement et des politiques qui les affectent. Le C.R.T. se consacre plus particulièrement à la conception et au développement de modèles, de méthodes et d'instruments d'évaluation, d'analyse, de simulation et d'optimisation rendus nécessaires par la complexité des problèmes rencontrés en pratique. L'équipe du Centre est composé de 35 à 40 chercheurs, 15 à 20 professionnels et plus de 80 étudiants provenant de différentes disciplines et universités. [ID:6704]

UNIVERSITÉ DE MONTRÉAL—INTERNATIONAL STUDIES
Centre international de criminologie comparée
C.P. 6128, succursale Centre Ville, Montréal, Québec H3C 3J7; (514) 343-7065,
fax (514) 343-2269, cicc@ere.umontreal.ca, http://tornade.ere.umontreal.ca/~jezequej

CENTRE DE RECHERCHE ▪ Le Centre international de criminologie comparée (CICC) regroupe des chercheur(e)s ainsi que des étudiant(e)s de deuxième et troisième cycle dont les activités gravitent autour de trois axes principaux: 1) la prévention du crime et les opérations policières; 2) la connaissance du phénomène criminel et la prise en charge par le processus judiciaire; et 3) l'application des sanctions pénales et les alternatives à l'incarcération. À chaque année le Centre offre une bourse de 20 000 $ à des étudiants étrangers afin qu'ils puissent réaliser leur étude postdoctorale au CICC. [ID:6701]

Sciences économiques
Département de sciences économiques, C.P. 6128, succursale Centre Ville, Montréal, Québec H3C 3J7;
(514) 343-7213, fax (514) 343-7221, econo@ere.umontreal.ca, http://tornade.ere.umontreal.ca/scecon

MSc (ÉCONOMIQUE): options économie du développement ou économie et finances internationales ▪ La maîtrise spécialisée permet à l'étudiant de concentrer ses études dans un domaine d'application particulier. Ce programme comporte sept cours, un atelier ainsi que la rédaction d'un mémoire de recherche. L'étudiant peut remplir ces exigences au cours d'une période de douze mois.

L'option Économie du développement a comme objectif de former des spécialistes capables d'analyser les politiques de croissance, d'ajustement structurel et de stabilisation mises en place par les pays en développement et en transition et pouvant répondre aux besoins d'expertise émanant des organisations internationales, des États et du secteur privé. L'option Économie et finances internationales, quant à elle, a pour objectif de former des spécialistes capables d'analyser les transactions économiques et financières internationales et d'appliquer cette analyse aux besoins des gouvernements, des entreprises commerciales et des institutions financières. Le site web présente des informations plus détaillées sur le programme et sur les options. [ID:6696]

Japanese Language Program
Coordinator, Japanese Studies Program, Department of Modern Languages and Literatures,
Sackville, N.B. E0A 3C0; (506) 364-2478, fax (506) 364-2478, mll@mta.ca, www.mta.ca

BA: minor in Japanese Studies ▪ Japanese language courses were started at Mount Allison University in 1993. The program offers two levels of courses with emphasis placed on understanding grammatical elements and acquiring written and spoken communication skills. In order to enhance the understanding of the language, various aspects of Japanese culture are explained as well. Mount Allison University has an exchange program with Kwansei Gakuin University, located near the city of Kobe. [ID:6851]

American Studies Program
Director, American Studies Program, Department of History,
Mount Allison University, Sackville, N.B. E0A 3C0; (506) 364-2316,
fax (506) 364-2645, dbeatty@mta.ca, ww.aci.mta.ca/History/American_Studies/Ams.html

BA & BA (honours) IN AMERICAN STUDIES ▪ The American Studies program at Mount Allison University is an interdisiplinary program offering students the opportunity to study the history, literature, music, economy, art, and government of the US. The program enables the student to gain a panoramic view of America as a nation and civilization, studying its place in history and its impact on the world. The program's broad approach provides a base for careers in business, teaching, law, and journalism. [ID:6507]

UNIVERSITY OF NEW BRUNSWICK
University of New Brunswick, P.O. Box 4400, Stn. A,
Fredericton, N.B. E3B 5A3; (506) 453-4666, fax (506) 453-4599, www.unb.ca

International programs and research centres in this chapter: 6
Number of students: 12,000 **Percentage of international students:** 5%

International offices: International Liaison Offices are located at both the Fredericton and St. John campuses.

Language programs within Area Studies described in this chapter: Russian Studies Program. **Other language programs:** BA, BA (honours), MA in German; BA in Linguistics, BA, BA (honours), MA in Spanish. [ID:6651]

UNIVERSITY OF NEW BRUNSWICK—AREA STUDIES
Russian Studies Program
Chair, Department of German and Russian, University of New Brunswick,
P.O. Box 1400, Stn. A, Fredericton, N.B. E3B 5A3; (506) 453-4636, fax (506) 453-4659, www.unb.ca

BA IN RUSSIAN STUDIES ▪ Russian Studies are interdisciplinary major and minor programs offered jointly by the University of New Brunswick and Saint Thomas University. They provide the opportunity to combine the study of language, literature, history, and political science of Russia and geographically-related areas. [ID:6510]

UNIVERSITY OF NEW BRUNSWICK—DEVELOPMENT STUDIES
International Development Studies Program
Director, International Development Studies Program,
Department of Spanish, University of New Brunswick, P.O. 4400, Fredericton, N.B.
E3B 5A3; (506) 453-3571, fax (506) 453-4599, ids@unb.ca, www.unb.ca/web.arts.ids/dev

BA (honours) IN INTERNATIONAL DEVELOPMENT STUDIES; BA: major in Third World Studies ▪ The International Development Studies program is administered by a committee drawn from members of eight participating departments in the Faculty of Arts. This interdisciplinary program gives students the opportunity to focus on issues from several perspectives. Currently, the program participates in two study-abroad initiatives: Intersession in the West Indies and Field School in Latin America. This program is linked to the Canada-wide IDSNet. [ID:5354]

UNIVERSITY OF NEW BRUNSWICK—INTERNATIONAL BUSINESS
Faculty of Administration
Assistant Undergraduate Dean, Faculty of Administration, University of New Brunswick, P.O. Box 4400,
Fredericton, N.B. E3B 5A3; (506) 453-4869, fax (506) 453-3561, rmaher@unb.ca, www.fadmin.unb.ca

BBA & MBA: concentration in International Business ▪ The first-year undergraduate Business Administration Program offers students a concentration in International Business. Exchange programs with universities in the UK and Sweden provide the opportunity to spend terms abroad. The international concentration in the MBA Program features an international internship which places students in countries such as Mexico, Venezuela, and Poland. International students make up approximately 20 per cent of the full-time student population. [ID:5355]

UNIVERSITY OF NEW BRUNSWICK—INTERNATIONAL BUSINESS
Faculty of Business
Dean, Faculty of Business, School of Graduate Studies,
University of New Brunswick, Saint John Campus, P.O. Box 5050, Saint John, N.B.
E2L 4L5; (506) 648-5746, fax (506) 648-5574, mba@unbsj.ca, www.unbsj/academic/mba/htm

MBA: concentration in International Business ▪ The University of New Brunswick's 11-month MBA Program is intensive and innovative, designed to produce graduates ready to deal with the challenges of modern business in the global economy. Highly condensed, this program provides more content and managerial skill-building than most two-year programs. As part of the requirements, there is a 12-week international co-op work term. Visit their web site for program, admission and faculty information. [ID:6588]

UNIVERSITY OF NEW BRUNSWICK—INTERNATIONAL BUSINESS
Centre for International Business Studies
Director, Centre for International Business Studies, University of New Brunswick, P.O. Box 4400, Stn. A, Fredericton, N.B. E3B 5A3; (506) 453-4557, fax (506) 447-3081, cibs@unb.ca, www.fadmin.unb.ca/cibs

RESEARCH CENTRE ▪ The Centre for International Business Studies is dedicated to bolstering New Brunswick's international competitiveness and fostering a greater awareness of today's international economic opportunities and challenges. The centre provides a number of services, such as encouraging research of practical value to members of the business community and/or governmental agencies; providing management development and training in international business through a number of conferences, courses, seminars, and workshops; arranging for visits by leading speakers on topics of international business and entrepreneurship; maintaining a collection of resource materials; incorporating Total Quality Management (TQM) into activities and focusing on TQM as a competitive international business strategy. The centre also contributes to student education and skill by organizing international conferences, and by sponsoring international industry internships and educational exchanges. [ID:5356]

UNIVERSITY OF NEW BRUNSWICK—PEACE/CONFLICT STUDIES
Centre for Conflict Studies
Director, Centre for Conflict Studies, University of New Brunswick, P.O. Box 4400, Stn. A, Fredericton, N.B. E3B 5A3; (506) 453-4587, fax (506) 447-3175, www.unb.ca

RESEARCH CENTRE ▪ The Centre for Conflict Studies is a research institute with a mandate to conduct research, publish, and teach in the field of conflict studies. The centre focuses on modern military history with particular emphasis on low-intensity conflict. The centre maintains a specialized research library, publishes a journal, and holds conferences and workshops. UNB students working on related topics are encouraged to use the centre's resources. [ID:5357]

NIPISSING UNIVERSITY—DEVELOPMENT STUDIES
Faculty of Arts and Sciences
Office of the Registrar, P.O. Box 5002, Stn. Main, North Bay, Ontario P1B 8L7; (705) 474-3461 ext. 4515, fax (705) 495-1772, nipureg@unipissing.ca, www.unipissing.ca

BA (honours) IN GEOGRAPHY: specialization in Community Economic Development or International Development ▪ The goal of this program is to provide students with the skills necessary for a career related to geography and the economic development of developing countries. The human and physical geographies of selected parts of the developing world are thoroughly studied. Supplementary studies of the economic, political, and social aspects of Third World development are intended to prepare students with a more complete understanding of life and development problems encountered in developing countries. The program gives students a critical understanding of the international dynamic while conveying cultural sensitivities and perspectives. [ID:6513]

UNIVERSITY OF NORTHERN BRITISH COLUMBIA—INTERNATIONAL BUSINESS
Business Program
Admissions Office, Faculty of Business, University of Northern British Columbia, 3333 University Way, Prince George, B.C. V2N 4Z9; (250) 960-6305, fax (250) 960-6330, registrar-info@unbc.edu, www.unbc.edu

BComm: specialization in International Business or Marketing ▪ The Business Administration Program is a four-year program offering courses leading to the Bachelor of Commerce degree. There is the opportunity to have one or two business majors in accounting, finance, general business, international business or marketing. The objective is to prepare students to deal effectively with the increasingly complex and dynamic environment in which business and management must operate. Visit the UNBC web site for more information and to apply online. [ID:6514]

UNIVERSITY OF NORTHERN BRITISH COLUMBIA—INTERNATIONAL STUDIES
International Studies
Program Director, International Studies, University of Northern British Columbia,
P.O. Box 450. Stn. A, Prince George, B.C. V2N 4Z9; (250) 960-6644, fax (250) 960-5544, www.unba.edu

BA & MA IN INTERNATIONAL STUDIES ▪ The BA and MA programs in International Studies seek to familiarize students with the global community and prepare them for international careers. International issues are explored from a variety of contending cultural, social, economic, political, and environmental perspectives. Special emphasis is given to the Asia Pacific region, the circumpolar North, and the Americas. [ID:6516]

ONTARIO INSTITUTE FOR STUDIES IN EDUCATION—INTERNATIONAL EDUCATION
The Comparative, International and Development Education Centre
Director, The Comparative, International and Development Education Centre,
Ontario Institute for Studies in Education, 252 Bloor Street W., Toronto, Ontario
M5S 1V6; (416) 923-6641, fax (416) 926-4754, jfarrell@oise.utoronto.ca, www.oise.utoronto.ca

MA, MEd, EdD & PhD: specialization in Comparative, International or Development Education ▪ The Ontario Institute for Studies in Education (OISE) offers an integrated set of courses for those students who wish to engage in a systematic study of comparative, international and development education. Students in the program compare formal and non-formal educational programs, for children and adults, as they occur in both the South and the North, from a variety of theoretical perspectives. The common core is an interest in the study of learning as it occurs in a variety of national and cultural settings. Approximately 100 students are in the program, from all parts of the world; most do their thesis research overseas. Roughly one-third of the full-time students in the program hold OISE scholarships or assistantships. [ID:5268]

UNIVERSITY OF OTTAWA—INTERNATIONAL PROFILE
UNIVERSITY OF OTTAWA
P.O. Box 450, Stn. A, Ottawa, Ontario K1N 6N5; (613) 562-5800, www.uottawa.ca

International programs and research centres in this chapter: 8
Number of students: 26,000 **Percentage of international students:** 4.6%

International focus: The University of Ottawa has many areas of international cooperation. These include the areas of Canadian Studies, second-language training, comparative law and international trade policy, training and research in human rights and good governance, botanical alternative to synthetic pesticides, water resource management and sanitation, health administration, and public health networks.

International offices: The University of Ottawa's Bureau for International Cooperation is responsible for promoting international activities on campus and for providing administrative support to faculty and departments participating in international development projects. The Bureau's activities are concentrated in two areas: international development cooperation and academic exchange programs. The International Students' Office is responsible for advising and guiding foreign students throughout their studies at the university.

Language programs: BA in German; BA, BA (honours)in Italian; BA, BA (honours), MA & PhD Linguistics; BA specialization in Polish; BA, MA & PhD Russian; BA, BA (honours), MA Spanish; BA specialization in Ukranian. [ID:6653]

UNIVERSITY OF OTTAWA—DEVELOPMENT STUDIES
International Water Engineering Centre
Director, International Water Engineering Centre, University of Ottawa, P.O. Box 450, Stn. A, Ottawa, Ontario K1N 6N5; (613) 562-5800 ext. 6139, fax (613) 562-5173, droste@eng.uottawa.ca, www.uottawa.ca

RESEARCH CENTRE ▪ The International Water Engineering Centre offers expertise in the following areas: specific research on particular water resource problems, project consulting both in Canada and overseas, training of overseas personnel and Canadians at the postgraduate level in water resource development, and training courses tailored to meet the needs of personnel in developing countries. The centre also coordinates a specialized set of courses, in conjunction with a master's program, that are oriented toward international water resources engineering. The centre also works closely with the Institute for International Development and Co-operation in the fields of water management, planning, and the socioeconomic aspects of water resource development. [ID:5359]

UNIVERSITÉ D'OTTAWA—DEVELOPMENT STUDIES
Sociologie du développement
Département de sociologie, 550, ave. Cumberland, Ottawa, Ontario K1N 6N5; (613) 562-5720, fax (613) 562-5906, socio@ottawa.ca, www.uottawa.ca/academic/socsci/socio

MA EN SOCIOLOGIE: spécialisation en sociologie du développement ▪ Le programme de maîtrise en sociologie a pour objectifs d'assurer une formation spécialisée en sociologie, et de permettre l'intégration la plus complète possible de la recherche empirique et de la théorie. Les principaux champs de spécialisation du Département sont les relations inter-ethniques, le développement et la sociologie politique. La problématique des rapports sociaux de sexe traverse ces trois champs de spécialisation. [ID:5286]

UNIVERSITY OF OTTAWA—INTERNATIONAL BUSINESS
Faculty of Administration
Director, Faculty of Administration, P.O. Box 450, Stn. A, Ottawa, Ontario K1N 6N5; (613) 562-5731, fax (613) 562-5164, www.uottawa.ca

BComm: option in International Management ▪ The BComm's international management option is designed to promote knowledge of the way in which business is conducted internationally, while permitting students to focus on an area of their choice.

The Faculty of Administration offers several international exchange programs to its undergraduate students, including academic exchanges to Germany, Denmark, England, France, Norway, Thailand, Sweden, Mexico, the US, and the Netherlands. [ID:5287]

UNIVERSITY OF OTTAWA—INTERNATIONAL BUSINESS
Faculty of Administration
Director, International MBA Program, Faculty of Administration, Room 245, University of Ottawa, P.O. Box 450 Stn. A, Ottawa, Ontario K1N 6N5; (613) 562-5821, fax (613) 562-5167, imba@admin.uottawa.ca, www.admin.uottawa.ca

INTERNATIONAL MBA ▪ The International MBA of the University of Ottawa is a 12-month bilingual program. The IMBA covers broad international environmental issues such as trade policy, global and crosscultural management, and functional topics such as international marketing, finance, human resources, management, and accounting. In order to foster cross-cultural sensitivity, the IMBA draws a third of its student body from outside Canada, and applicants must prove competency in both English and French. Internships in an international setting in Canada or abroad are a compulsory part of the program. [ID:6929]

UNIVERSITY OF OTTAWA—INTERNATIONAL LAW

Graduate Studies in Law

Graduate Studies, Faculty of Law, University of Ottawa, P.O. Box 450, Stn. A, Ottawa, Ontario
K1N 6N5; (613) 562-5774, fax (613) 562-5124, sleblan@uottawa.ca, www.uottawa.ca/academic/droitcivil

LLM & LLD: concentration in International Law ▪ The Faculty of Law offers master's and doctoral programs which focus on international law, human rights, and family law. It also offers a master's program specializing in Women's Studies and a diploma in Legal Drafting and Legislation. See their web site for details. [ID:5288]

UNIVERSITY OF OTTAWA—INTERNATIONAL LAW

Human Rights Research and Education Centre

Director, Human Rights Research and Education Centre,
University of Ottawa, P.O. Box 450, Stn. A, Ottawa, Ontario K1N 6N5;
(613) 562-5775, fax (613) 562-5125, hrrec@human-rights.cdp.uottawa.ca, www.uottawa.ca/hrrec

RESEARCH CENTRE ▪ The Human Rights Research and Education Centre is Canada's foremost bilingual source of research, information, and strategies for education on human rights. The centre collaborates with a broad range of partners in Canada and overseas to advance the human rights content of legislative and public policy agendas. Currently, the centre has projects in Canada, Thailand, China, Vietnam, and Tanzania. [ID:5360]

UNIVERSITY OF OTTAWA—INTERNATIONAL STUDIES

Faculty of Administration

Director, Faculty of Administration, University of Ottawa, P.O. Box 450, Stn. A,
Ottawa, Ontario K1N 6N5; (613) 562-5821, fax (613) 562-5167, www.uottawa.ca

MA IN INTERNATIONAL AFFAIRS ADMINISTRATION ▪ The master's degree in International Affairs Administration emphasizes three abilities required in administration: communication, teamwork, and leadership. Internships in the public or private sector are obligatory for students majoring in international management. [ID:5289]

UNIVERSITY OF OTTAWA—INTERNATIONAL STUDIES

Department of Economics

Chairperson, Department of Economics, University of Ottawa,
P.O. Box 450, Stn. A, Ottawa, Ontario K1N 6N5; (613) 562-5753,
fax (613) 562-5999, econ@uottawa.ca, www.uottawa.ca/academic/socsci/economics

PhD IN INTERNATIONAL ECONOMICS ▪ This PhD program is administered jointly by the University of Ottawa and Carleton University. Students admitted to the program must complete core courses in Economic Theory and Econometrics, and choose two fields of specialization. Two of the fields available are International Economics and the Economics of Natural Resources and the Environment. Comprehensive exams are required and students are encouraged to pursue thesis topics in one of their declared fields. [ID:5361]

UNIVERSITY OF PRINCE EDWARD ISLAND—INTERNATIONAL EDUCATION

Faculty of Education

Dean, Faculty of Education, University of Prince Edward Island, 550 University Drive,
Charlottetown, P.E.I. C1A 4P3; (902) 566-0349, fax (902) 566-0416, gtaylor@upei.ca, www.upei.ca

BEd: specialization in International Education ▪ The BEd specialization in international education is a unique program which offers five courses for a total of 15 semester hours in the field of international education. The Faculty of Education has 15 staff members who are involved in international consultation and research. An International Job Placement Service as well as an International Student Exchange Program are offered. [ID:7060]

UNIVERSITY OF PRINCE EDWARD ISLAND—INTERNATIONAL EDUCATION
Centre for International Education
Director, Centre for International Education, 550 University Ave.,
Charlottetown, P.E.I. C1A 4P3; (902) 566-0370, fax (902) 566-0416, www.upei.ca/~cie

RESEARCH CENTRE ▪ The Centre for International Education offers information on various education and work-related opportunities in overseas settings for Canadian youth. The centre operates an international teaching service, either in person or online. It seeks international opportunities for faculty to consult and/or do research. It also acts as a resource for the International Liaison Officer and for the new Bachelor of Education program which specializes in International Education. Their web site has information on individual teaching opportunities, travel tips, country profiles, and online registration for teachers looking for work and for schools/employers looking for teachers. [ID:7059]

UNIVERSITÉ DU QUÉBEC À CHICOUTIMI—AREA STUDIES
Études régionales et développement régional
Département des sciences humaines, 555, boul. de l'Université,
Chicoutimi, Québec G7H 2B1; (418) 545-5011 ext. 5291, fax (418) 545-5012,
dbernard@uqac.uqebec.ca, www.uqac.uquebec.ca/dsh/dsh.html

MA EN ÉTUDES RÉGIONALES et PhD EN DÉVELOPPEMENT RÉGIONAL ▪ La maîtrise en études régionales a pour objectifs de former des intervenants à appréhender les réalités socio-spatiales et historiques régionales et de proposer des stratégies d'action propres à chaque conjoncture. Les candidats doivent avoir un diplôme de baccalauréat ou l'équivalent dans des disciplines aussi variées que l'anthropologie, l'économie, l'ethnologie, la géographie, l'histoire ou l'environnement.

Le doctorat en développement régional veut contribuer, dans une perspective interdisciplinaire, à un avancement des connaissances théoriques et méthodologiques, qui favorise une meilleure compréhension des phénomènes de développement régional, aux plans: 1) des dynamiques socio-historiques de structuration et de déstructuration des espaces régionaux; 2) des mouvements sociaux et des régionalismes; et 3) des processus de mise en valeur des ressources et de l'environnement.

Le site web du département décrit les objectifs, conditions d'admission et structure des programmes, les perspectives d'emploi, la recherche, et l'aide financière. [ID:5306]

UNIVERSITÉ DU QUÉBEC À CHICOUTIMI—INTERCULTURAL STUDIES
Chaire d'enseignement et de recherche inter-ethniques et interculturels (CERII)
555, boul. de l'Université, Chicoutimi, Québec G7H 2B1; (418) 545-5011 ext. 5522,
fax (418) 545-5519, cerii@uqac.uqebec.ca, www.uqac.uquebec.ca/cerii/cerii.htm

CENTRE DE RECHERCHE ▪ La Chaire est une structure de recherche, d'enseignement, d'animation et de sensibilisation sur les problématiques ethniques et interculturelles. Elle s'intéresse à l'étude des processus d'intégration et de cohabitation interethniques et interculturels au Québec, principalement dans les milieux autres que les métropoles. Elle s'intéresse également à connaître la contribution des populations issues de l'immigration au développement régional et à mettre de l'avant des stratégies pour favoriser l'intégration socio-économique de ces populations : attraction des gens d'affaires, de travailleurs spécialisés, de scientifiques et d'étudiants néo-québécois ainsi que le rapprochement entre ces différents groupes et le milieu régional du travail. En outre, la CERII a développé une expertise sur l'organisation et l'analyse de réseaux de soutien entre les Québécois issus de l'immigration et la communauté d'accueil. [ID:7021]

UNIVERSITÉ DU QUÉBEC À MONTRÉAL—INTERNATIONAL PROFILE
UNIVERSITÉ DU QUÉBEC À MONTRÉAL
C.P. 8888, succursale Centre Ville, Montréal, Québec
H3C 3P8; (514) 987-3000, fax (514) 987-3251, www.uqam.ca

Nombre de programmes et centres de recherche internationaux : 10
Nombre d'étudiants étrangers : 3.7% d'une population étudiante de 37 000

Expertise internationale: L'Université du Québec à Montréal gère des projets de coopération internationale dans toutes les régions du monde, principalement dans quatre grands secteurs: les sciences de l'environnement, les sciences de la gestion, les sciences de l'éducation et les communications. Ces recherches sont menées en collaboration avec des entreprises, des gouvernements, des organisations non gouvernementales et des réseaux scientifiques internationaux. L'Université collabore également avec des institutions de pays industrialisés dans plus de vingt-cinq projets de recherche. Au niveau de la formation, l'UQAM fournit de plus en plus des contenus internationaux dans ses programmes d'enseignement, particulièrement à l'École des sciences de la gestion, ou elle a développé les missions et projets d'études internationaux (PEI), les écoles internationales d'été et les échanges universitaires. Enfin, grâce à sa nouvelle École supérieure de mode de Montréal, l'Université contribue à la visibilité de cette industrie au niveau national et son rayonnement au niveau international.

Bureaux internationaux : Le Bureau de la coopération internationale est maintenant sous la responsabilité du Bureau de développement des partenariats au Vice-rectorat au partenariat et affaires externes. Le Service aux étudiants offre un Accueil des étudiants étrangers. [ID:6783]

UNIVERSITÉ DU QUÉBEC À MONTRÉAL—INTERCULTURAL STUDIES
Immigration et relations interethniques, Module de sociologie
C.P. 8888, succursale Centre Ville, Montréal, Québec H3C 3P8;
(514) 987-3616, fax (514) 987-4644, www.regis.uqam.ca/Programmes/4375.html

---

CERTIFICAT EN IMMIGRATION ET RELATIONS INTERETHNIQUES ▪ Le certificat en immigration et relations interethniques vise l'acquisition de connaissances théoriques sur les systèmes migratoires contemporains, sur les interactions entre société d'accueil et communautés ethniques, sur les relations interethniques et les dimensions socioculturelles, sociopolitiques et sociopsychologiques rattachées aux dynamiques d'adaptation. Il tend aussi au perfectionnement des pratiques d'intervention en milieu pluriethnique, en développant une réflexion critique sur les modèles actuels d'intervention.

Le programme s'adresse plus particulièrement aux personnes qui oeuvrent dans des milieux à caractère ethnique ou qui s'y destinent. [ID:5305]

UNIVERSITÉ DU QUÉBEC À MONTRÉAL—INTERNATIONAL BUSINESS
Bureau de la coopération internationale
du Département des sciences administratives
C.P. 6192, succursale Centre Ville, Montréal, Québec H3C 4R2;
(514) 987-4139, fax (514) 987-6625, coop@dsa.dsa.uqam.ca, www.uqam.ca

---

CENTRE DE RECHERCHE ▪ Le Bureau de la coopération internationale du DSA offre une assistance technique dans les domaines de la formation et du perfectionnement en sciences de la gestion aux pays dont l'économie est en transition. Les formations dispensées le sont au niveau MBA recherche et MBA cadres/doctorat. Les projets actifs du Bureau se situent en Roumanie, Pologne, Guinée, Viêt-nam, Équateur, République Dominicaine ainsi que dans d'autres pays en voie de développement. [ID:5304]

UNIVERSITÉ DU QUÉBEC À MONTRÉAL—INTERNATIONAL BUSINESS
Commerce international, module d'administration
C.P. 8888, succursale Centre Ville, Montréal, Québec
H3C 3P8; (514) 987-8513, fax (514) 987-4655, www.regis.uqam.ca

CERTIFICAT EN COMMERCE INTERNATIONAL ▪ Ce programme vise à donner une formation à la fois théorique et pratique dans le domaine du commerce international à une clientèle déjà en exercice ou ayant déjà une formation générale de base en gestion. Le programme veut répondre aux besoins des oganisations privées et publiques transigeant au niveau international en formant les étudiants aux activités d'exportation de produits et de services, notamment aux stratégies commerciales du Québec avec ses principaux partenaires et les grands blocs économiques, au développement de marchés internationaux, aux négociations commerciales internationales et à l'importance des facteurs socioculturels lors de ces négociations. Les détenteurs de ce certificat s'ouvrent une fenêtre internationale dans un domaine de spécialisation préferablement acquis (p. ex: analyse financière.) Donc, toute entreprise de biens ou de services engagée dans l'exportation constitue un débouché possible. De plus, l'étudiant intéressé à mettre sur pied sa propre entreprise d'import-export aura les connaissances nécessaires pour ce faire, surtout si ce certificat complète sa formation de BAA. [ID:6712]

UNIVERSITÉ DU QUÉBEC À MONTRÉAL—INTERNATIONAL BUSINESS
Gestion internationale, module d'administration
C.P. 8888, succursale Centre Ville, Montréal, Québec H3C 3P8;
(514) 987-8333, fax (514) 987-4655, rheault.francine@uqam.ca, www.uqam.ca

BAA: concentration en gestion internationale ▪ Le BAA avec concentration en gestion internationale prépare les futurs administrateurs à des rôles de types informationnels, interpersonnels et décisionnels, et ceci dans l'optique d'un modèle dynamique cherchant à favoriser l'adéquation entre le milieu intra et extra-organisationnel. Le programme a pour buts l'acquisition de connaissances, le développement d'habiletés et d'attitudes indépendantes de fonctions spécifiques, de niveaux hiérarchique et des types d'organisations. [ID:5302]

UNIVERSITÉ DU QUÉBEC À MONTRÉAL—INTERNATIONAL BUSINESS
Programme de MBA – Recherche
Secrétariat du programme de MBA – Recherche, Département des sciences administratives,
École des sciences de la gestion, C.P. 6192, succursale Centre Ville, Montréal, Québec
H3C 4R2; (514) 987-4448, fax (514) 987-3084, www.regis.uqam.ca/Programmes/3665.nSec

MBA avec spécialisation en gestion internationale ▪ La spécialisation en gestion internationale vise d'abord à développer et à renforcer chez l'étudiant une attitude positive et des habiletés d'analyse et de management au niveau international. Le second objectif consiste à familiariser l'étudiant avec les principales décisions et responsabilités d'un gestionnaire oeuvrant sur un marché étranger, et finalement à le rendre apte à développer un plan d'affaire préliminaire dans un contexte d'internationalisation des activités de l'entreprise. L'étudiant pourra alors servir de conseiller, analyste ou gestionnaire d'affaires internationales. Il est à noter que les classes sont de taille réduite favorisant l'interaction avec les professeurs et que l'ensemble des diplômés obtiennent du travail correspondant à leur champ d'études. Le site web informe sur le programme et les conditions d'admission. [ID:6713]

UNIVERSITÉ DU QUÉBEC À MONTRÉAL—PEACE/CONFLICT STUDIES
Centre d'études des politiques étrangères et de sécurité (CEPES)
Département de sciences politiques, C.P. 8888, succursale Centre Ville, Montréal,
Québec H3C 3P8; (514) 987-8929, fax (514) 987-4749, www.er.uqam.ca/nobel/cepes7

CENTRE DE RECHERCHE ▪ Le Centre d'Études des politiques étrangères et de sécurité a pour mandat d'étudier la politique et le comportement des grandes puissances, particulièrement a l'égard des organisations internationales de sécurité, telles l'OTAN, l'ONU, l'OSCE, etc. Le Centre collabore avec des chercheurs partout dans le monde et mène présentement plusieurs recherches portant sur la sécurité en Europe, en Méditéranée et en Asie. [ID:6717]

UNIVERSITÉ DU QUÉBEC À MONTRÉAL—PEACE/CONFLICT STUDIES
Chaire Téléglobe Raoul-Dandurand en études stratégiques et diplomatiques
C.P. 8888, succursale Centre Ville, Montréal, Québec H3C 3P8;
(514) 987-6781, fax (514) 987-8502, chaire.strat@uqam.ca, www.unites.uqam.ca/dandurand

CENTRE DE RECHERCHE ▪ La Chaire Téléglobe Raoul-Dandurand en études stratégiques et diplomatiques s'est définie une mission d'information, de formation, de recherche, d'expertise et de consultation afin de renforcer l'action stratégique et diplomatique des entreprises et des organisations du Québec et du Canada à l'étranger. Elle offre deux stages rémunérés à des étudiants inscrits aux études avancées en science politique à l'UQAM. [ID:6854]

UNIVERSITÉ DU QUÉBEC À MONTRÉAL—PEACE/CONFLICT STUDIES
Groupe de recherche sur l'industrie militaire
Département de science politique, C.P. 8888, succursale A, Montréal, Québec
H3C 3P8; (514) 987-6964, fax (514) 987-4749, belanger.yves@uqam.ca, www.uqam.ca

GROUPE DE RECHERCHE ▪ Depuis 1985, le groupe analyse les politiques de défense et étudie leur impact sur le développement économique au Canada et dans les autres pays occidentaux. La poursuite de plusieurs programmes d'enquête a permis au GRIM d'accumuler de l'information sur les entreprises qui composent la base industrielle de défense du Canada. Depuis 1988, le GRIM investit de façon intensive dans l'étude de la reconversion des entreprises de défense. Il se concentre sur deux cibles, soit l'analyse des marchés en cours au sein des pays occidentaux et la mise en oeuvre de la reconversion au niveau de l'entreprise. [ID:7045]

UNIVERSITÉ DU QUÉBEC À RIMOUSKI—DEVELOPMENT STUDIES
Développement régional
Programmes d'études supérieures, 300, allée des Ursulines,
Rimouski, Québec G5L 3A1; (418) 724-1630, fax (418) 724-1847, www.uqar.uquebec.ca

MA et PhD EN DÉVELOPPEMENT RÉGIONAL ▪ Le diplôme en développement régional a pour objectif de présenter les dimensions tant économiques que sociales, historiques et géographiques du développement régional, en accordant plus d'attention aux problèmes de développement des régions périphériques aussi bien des pays industrialisés que des pays du tiers-monde. [ID:5300]

UNIVERSITÉ DU QUÉBEC À RIMOUSKI—INTERNATIONAL STUDIES
Maîtrise en gestion de projet
300, allée des Ursulines, Rimouski, Québec G5L 3A1; (418) 724-1552,
fax (418) 724-1851, eco-gestion@uqar.uquebec.ca, www.uqar.uquebec.ca/decogest/m-gespro.htm

MGP ou MSc EN GESTION DE PROJECT ▪ L'objectif fondamental du programme en gestion de projets est de former des professionnels dotés d'une vision globale et articulée du domaine et aptes à gérer efficacement des projets de nature et de taille diverses depuis leur conception jusqu'à leur achèvement. Outre l'obtention d'un baccalauréat spécialisé ou l'équivalent, les exigences d'admission sont d'une expérience pratique récente d'une durée minimale de trois ans dans un environnement projet. Le programme est offert à temps complet ou à temps partiel sur le campus de Rimouski ou celui de Lévis. L'UQAR offre également un programme court de 15 crédits en gestion de projet (moins d'un an). Des ententes existent avec des universités françaises afin de permettre aux étudiants de poursuivre leur programme en Europe et il existe plusieurs programmes de coopération entre l'UQAR et l'Europe, l'Afrique et l'Amérique latine permettant de réaliser des recherches conjointes. [ID:6813]

UNIVERSITÉ DU QUÉBEC À RIMOUSKI—INTERNATIONAL STUDIES
Maîtrise en gestion des ressources maritimes
Secrétariat du programme de maîtrise en gestion des ressources maritimes,
Université du Québec à Rimouski, C.P. 3300, Rimouski, Québec G5L 3A1;
(418) 724-1544, fax (418) 724-1525, grm@uqar.uquebec.ca, www.uqar.uquebec.ca

MSc EN GESTION DES RESSOURCES MARITIMES ▪ Les programme de Maîtrise en gestion des ressources maritimes est un programme interdisciplinaire de type professionnel, fondé sur l'économie, la gestion et les sciences de la mer. Seul programme francophone au Canada orienté vers la formation de gestionnaires et d'analystes pour les organisations publiques et privées du secteur maritime, il offre trois champs d'études : la gestion des ressources halieutiques, la gestion de l'environnement maritime et la gestion du transport maritime. Les études durent de 16 à 20 mois. Jusqu'à 30 candidats sont acceptés annuellement dont plus de la moitié proviennent d'universités de la Francophonie. Le site web de l'UQAR contient toutes les informations pertinentes au programme et aux exigences d'admission. [ID:6804]

QUEEN'S UNIVERSITY—INTERNATIONAL PROFILE
QUEEN'S UNIVERSITY
99 University Ave., Kingston, Ontario K7L 3N6; (613) 545-2000, fax (613) 545-6300, www.queensu.ca

International programs and research centres in this chapter: 10
Number of students: 16,000 **Percentage of international students:** 4.8%

International focus: Queen's University has exchange agreements with over 50 universities in more than 25 countries, with current projects in the Asia-Pacific region, Central and Eastern Europe, and Francophone Africa. Queen's also has an International Study Centre at Hertsmonceux Castle in East Sussex, England, where a variety of courses are offered.

International offices: At Queen's University, the Associate Vice-President Academic/International is responsible for international academic linkages and the Associate Vice-Principal Research/International is responsible for international research projects. Queen's International Centre is responsible for international student services and the Coordinator of University Exchanges and International Study is responsible for international exchange programs.

Language programs within Area Studies described in this chapter: Jewish Studies Program. **Other language programs:** BA, BA (honours), MA, PhD in German; BA,

BA (honours) in Italian; BA (honours) Linguistics; BA, BA (honours), MA in Spanish.
[ID:6655]

QUEEN'S UNIVERSITY—AREA STUDIES
Jewish Studies Program
Director, Jewish Studies Program, Queen's Theological College, Queens University,
99 University Ave., Kingston, Ontario K7L 3N6; (613) 545-2110, fax (613) 545-6879, www.queensu.ca

BA IN JEWISH STUDIES ▪ This multidisciplinary program explores Jewish civilization in its evolution and manifold expressions in religion, Hebrew language, literature, and history from biblical times to the present. The program is designed to provide a balanced view of the different components of Judaism and its interaction with other cultures as well as the varied experiences of Jewish people. Students have the option of studying for one year at select universities in Israel. [ID:6522]

QUEEN'S UNIVERSITY—AREA STUDIES
Commonwealth Studies Program
Coordinator, Commonwealth Studies Program, Department of English, Queen's University,
99 University Ave., Kingston, Ontario K7L 3N6; (613) 545-2153, fax (613) 545-6872, www.queensu.ca

BA (honours) IN COMMONWEALTH STUDIES ▪ The Departments of History and English at Queen's University offer a special field of concentration in Commonwealth Studies. Courses are drawn from the Departments of English, History, Sociology, Anthropology, Political Science, and Geography. [ID:6793]

QUEEN'S UNIVERSITY—AREA STUDIES
Department of German Languages and Literature
Chairperson, Department of German Languages and Literature, Queen's University,
99 University Ave., Kingston, Ontario K7L 3N6; (613) 545-2075, fax (613) 545-6930, www.queensu.ca

BA, MA & PhD IN GERMANIC LANGUAGE AND LITERATURE ▪ Queen's University offers a BA, MA and PhD in Germanic Language and Literature. Courses are offered in German language, literature, drama, and German culture. The department also offers a variety of extracurricular activities. [ID:6519]

QUEEN'S UNIVERSITY—AREA STUDIES
Centre for Canada-Asia Business Relations
Director, Centre for Canada-Asia Business Relations, School of Business, Queens University, Kingston, Ontario K7L 3N6; (613) 545-6438, fax (613) 545-2321, ccabr@qsilver.queensu.ca, www.queensu.ca

RESEARCH CENTRE ▪ The mandate of the Centre for Canada-Asia Business Relations is to promote links between Asian nations and Canada, and help Canadian business develop their international competitiveness. The centre promotes and develops programs for the academic enrichment of students in all Queen's programs, funds applied research on the Asia Pacific area, and works with companies with interests in Asia. Activities on campus include regionally-focused theme weeks, a speaker series which addresses current issues affecting the business community in Asia, and the Far Horizons Competition and Conference in which students from across Canada write papers on the theme "Doing Business in a Changing Asia." The centre also offers students use of its resources for academic and career planning and offers companies research and training services. [ID:5270]

QUEEN'S UNIVERSITY—DEVELOPMENT STUDIES
Development Studies Medial
Coordinator, Development Studies Medial, Queen's University, C-400 Mackintosh-Corry Hall, Kingston, Ontario K7L 3N6; (613) 545-6250, fax (613) 545-6848, qds@qsilver.queensu.ca, www.queensu.ca

BA (honours) IN DEVELOPMENT STUDIES ▪ Development Studies at Queen's University teaches students to think critically about international issues. The role of economic and political systems, historical contexts, culture, gender relations, and physical environments are examined as agents of change. The program is offered as a medial which is combined with one other discipline to complete the requirements of the degree. Students are admitted on a competitive basis. In their final year some will be able to participate in a work-study placement program in Canada or abroad. [ID:6794]

QUEEN'S UNIVERSITY—INTERNATIONAL BUSINESS
School of Business
Undergraduate Chair, School of Business, Queen's University, Kingston, Ontario K7L 3N6; (613) 545-2301, fax (613) 545-2316, angert@qsilver.queensu.ca, www.queensu.ca

BComm: concentration in International Business ▪ The four-year undergraduate program in business is entered directly from high school. The program strives to provide a broad, liberal education with an emphasis on business and to prepare its graduates for positions of leadership in the business community. Important dimensions of the commerce program are the availability of a number of courses in international business, and the exchange agreements between the School of Business and other institutions in Belgium, Chile, Finland, France, Germany, Hong Kong, Mexico, the Netherlands, Norway, Sweden, Taiwan, and the US. The school also has summer programs in Germany, England, Japan, and Mexico and offers summer internship programs in Japan, Taiwan, and the US. [ID:5271]

QUEEN'S UNIVERSITY—INTERNATIONAL HEALTH
International Centre for the Advancement of Community-Based Rehabilitation (ICACBR)
Director, International Centre for the Advancement of Community-Based Rehabilitation (ICACBR), Lasalle Bldg., Queen's University, 146 Stuart Street, Kingston, Ontario K7L 3N6; (613) 545-6881, fax (613) 545-6882, icacbr@queensu.ca, www/meds.queensu.ca/icabr

RESEARCH CENTRE ▪ Governments, agencies and communities are seeking innovative programs to help persons with disabilities live more independently, participate more fully in the community and reduce their dependence on health and social systems. Community-based rehabilitation (CBR) is an internationally-recognized strategy that addresses these needs. CBR builds partnerships among peoples with disabilities, healthcare professionals and the community to design programs and services that are appropriate, efficient and cost-effective. ICACBR at Queen's University is a world leader in bringing CBR to communities in Canada and the rest of the world. Dedicated to teaching, research and service, the centre is a unique resource for the promotion and implementation of CBR programs. The centre is composed of multidisciplinary and multisectoral groups of professionals with extensive experience in rehabilitation, research, practice and community development, and implements projects in Eastern Europe, Asia, Latin America, and Africa. Currently, the centre, in conjunction with the School of Rehabilitation Therapy, employs 10 professionals and a number of support and administrative personnel. New opportunities depend on the mobilization of grants. Theses are also of limited (three to five years) duration. [ID:6797]

QUEEN'S UNIVERSITY—INTERNATIONAL LAW
Faculty of Law
Coordinator of Graduate Studies, Faculty of Law, Queen's University, MacDonald Hall, Kingston,
Ontario K7L 3N6; (613) 545-2220, fax (613) 545-6611, llm@qsilver.queensu.ca, www.qsilver.queensu.ca

LLM: concentration in International Legal Studies ▪ The Master of Laws Program is designed to enable students of outstanding merit to pursue advanced study and independent research in a particular area of law. Students can choose to concentrate in International Legal Studies or in a number of other areas where the faculty and library resources are particularly rich. [ID:5272]

QUEEN'S UNIVERSITY—INTERNATIONAL STUDIES
Department of Political Studies
Graduate Student Coordinator, Department of Political Studies,
Queen's University, Kingston, Ontario K7L 3N6; (613) 545-6233,
fax (613) 545-6848, scp2@qsilver.queensu.ca, www.qsilver.queensu.ca/politics.index.html

MA & PhD IN POLITICAL STUDIES: concentration in International Politics or Politics of Development ▪ The Department of Political Science seeks outstanding students for its graduate programs. Students develop the skills necessary to assume academic, research, or service positions in the leading institutions of Canada and abroad. [ID:5273]

QUEEN'S UNIVERSITY—INTERNATIONAL STUDIES
Centre for International Relations
Director, Centre for International Relations, Queen's University, Kingston, Ontario K7L 3N6;
(613) 545-2381, fax (613) 545-6885, qcir@qsilver.queens.ca, www.qsilver.queensu.ca/cir/home.html

RESEARCH CENTRE ▪ The Centre for International Relations was established in 1975 as an interdisciplinary research institution within the university. Its scope is international relations, with special emphasis on issues relevant to Canadian-American relations, general Canadian political and security interests in a changing international context, and increasingly, to the evolving security environment in Europe and the former Soviet Union. The centre offers no courses, but does encourage graduate students at the thesis-writing stage to get involved in its research programs and activities. [ID:5274]

UNIVERSITY OF REGINA—INTERNATIONAL PROFILE
UNIVERSITY OF REGINA
Suite 100, 3737 Wascana Parkway, Regina, Sask.
S4S 0A2; (306) 585-4111, fax (306) 585-4997, www.uregina.ca

International programs and research centres in this chapter: 3
Number of students: 11,000 **Percentage of international students:** 3%

International offices: The mandate of the University of Regina's International Liaison Office includes acting as a resource centre, facilitating the establishment and maintenance of international academic relations, and signing all international contracts and agreements. International Student Services offers assistance and information on student visas, workshops on cross-cultural issues, and manages study and work abroad programs.
Language programs: BA in German; BA, MA in Linguistics. [ID:6656]

UNIVERSITY OF REGINA—AREA STUDIES
Asian Pacific Management Institute
Director, University of Regina,
Regina, Sask. S4S 0A2; (306) 585-4724, fax (306) 585-4805, www.uregina.ca

RESEARCH CENTRE ▪ The Asian Pacific Management Institute develops a knowledge base of the people, cultures, resources, institutions, government policies, economies and businesses of the region. It then disseminates this knowledge to the academic, business and government communities, as well as to other interested parties. Its mandate is to promote collaboration within the university to develop interdisciplinary programs related to the Asia Pacific Region. [ID:6847]

UNIVERSITY OF REGINA—INTERNATIONAL EDUCATION
Centre for International Teacher Education
Director, Centre for International Teacher Education, University of Regina,
Regina, Sask. S4S 0A2; (306) 585-4521, fax (306) 585-4880, cite@uregina.ca, www.uregina.ca

RESEARCH CENTRE ▪ The purpose of the Centre for International Teacher Education (CITE) is to promote national and international teacher education initiatives on a short- and long-term basis. CITE promotes the development of current, researched-based teacher education programs. It also develops projects that reflect international development and cooperation, sustainable changes in teacher education programs, curriculum development, and instructional techniques.

CITE coordinates projects throughout the world, with special emphasis on teacher education, educational administration, educational policy development, gender equity, environmental education, and curriculum planning. CITE currently works closely with the Canadian International Development Agency, the Asia Pacific Foundation, and the Centre for International Languages. CITE also has close affiliations with China, Panama, Chile, India, Cameroon, Ghana, Nigeria and Bhutan. [ID:6846]

UNIVERSITY OF REGINA—INTERNATIONAL LAW
School of Human Justice
Director, School of Human Justice, University of Regina,
3737 Wascana Parkway, Regina, Sask. S4S 0A2; (306) 585-4779, fax (306) 585-4872, www.uregina.ca

BA AND CERTIFICATE IN HUMAN JUSTICE ▪ Engaged in professional education and research on justice, the School of Human Justice concentrates on criminal, legal and social justice. The basic orientation is Canadian, but courses are available in international law, peace studies and development studies. The faculty is involved in international programs through the United Nations as well as through various conferences and projects abroad. [ID:5363]

CÉGEP DE RIVIÈRE-DU-LOUP—DEVELOPMENT STUDIES
Direction du développement interculturel (DDI)
80, rue Frontenac, Rivière-du-Loup, Québec G5R 1R1;
(418) 862-6903 ext. 230, fax (418) 862-4959, www.cegep-rdl.qc.ca/inter.htm

BUREAU DE LIAISONS INTERNATIONALES ▪ La Direction du développement interculturel (DDI) a le mandat de développer et gérer des projets de partenariat avec des institutions de pays en développement. Par son travail, la DDI vise à favoriser le développement et l'autonomie d'institutions de formation ou de structures gouvernementales reliées à la formation professionnelle et technique, particulièrement par le développement et l'acquisition de matériel didactique et la formation de personnes ressources. La DDI intervient également dans les domaines de la santé et de l'entreprenariat, et collabore aux activités du Centre de formation à la coopération interculturelle (CFCI). Les pays d'inter-

vention de la DDI sont le Mali, le Burkina Faso, l'Île Maurice, le Burundi et le Bénin.
[ID:6759]

CÉGEP DE RIVIÈRE-DU-LOUP—DEVELOPMENT STUDIES
Programme Coopérant Volontaire
Centre de formation à la coopération interculturelle (CFCI), 80, rue Frontenac, Rivière-du-Loup,
Québec G5R 1R1; (418) 862-6903 ext. 404, fax (418) 867-2137, cfci@cegep-rdl.qc.ca, www.cegep-rdl.qc.ca

ATTESTATION D'ÉTUDES COLLÉGIALES EN COOPÉRATION INTERCULTURELLE ▪
Le Centre de formation à la coopération interculturelle (CFCI), corporation affiliée au Cégep
de Rivière-du-Loup offre aux personnes intéressées à travailler dans les pays en voie de
développement une formation d'appoint en coopération internationale. Le Programme
Coopérant Volontaire, qui a pour but de former des coopérants volontaires efficaces et
compétents, comporte une session de 15 semaines de cours théoriques à Rivière-du-Loup,
suivie d'un stage d'intervention, également de 15 semaines, en Afrique de l'Ouest. Les
personnes intéressées doivent parler français, être âgées de 22 à 32 ans et avoir une
formation dans les domaines tels que l'administration, l'agriculture, la foresterie, le génie,
l'informatique, la santé ou les sciences humaines. Le programme est offert deux fois par
année, soit un groupe en septembre et un autre en avril. Le nombre de participants par
groupe est limité à 20. [ID:5231]

ROYAL MILITARY COLLEGE OF CANADA—PEACE/CONFLICT STUDIES
Faculty of Arts
Admissions, Royal Military College of Canada, War Studies Committee,
Kingston, Ontario K7O 5L0; (613) 541-5010 ext. 6426, fax (613) 536-4801, www.rmc.ca

MA IN WAR STUDIES ▪ The MA Program in War Studies is open to regular and reserve
officers of the Canadian Forces and to a limited number of civilians. This inter-departmental
program gives students the opportunity to pursue studies in the theory of war, international
politics and relations, military doctrine, and the economics of defence. [ID:5275]

SASKATCHEWAN INDIAN FEDERATED COLLEGE—INTERNATIONAL STUDIES
Centre for International Indigenous Studies and Development
Director, SIFC Regina Campus, Room 118 College West,
Regina, Sask. S4S 0A2; (306) 584-8333, rhoenes@tansi.sifc.edu

CERTIFICATE IN INTERNATIONAL INDIGENOUS MANAGEMENT ▪ The Centre for
International Indigenous Studies and Development of the Saskatchewan Indian Federated
College (CIISD-SIFC) offers a one-year program to First Nations students. The main
objective of the International Indigenous Management program is to provide its graduates
with leadership skills in the areas of research, design, implementation, evaluation, and
management of community development programs in Canada and abroad. By studying how
organizations function, the program teaches students to improve their analytical skills and
obtain a broader understanding of management practices from an international Indigenous
perspective. The program, open to natives from any part of the globe, is divided into a first
semester at the Saskatchewan Indian Federated College in Regina and a second semester at
a partner institution in Mexico, Nicaragua, Costa Rica, Peru, or Chile. Basic Spanish and
English are required. The program is funded by the Canadian International Development
Agency (CIDA) and partner institutions. [ID:5277]

UNIVERSITY OF SASKATCHEWAN—INTERNATIONAL BUSINESS
Centre for International Business Studies
Director, Centre for International Business Studies, University of Saskatchewan,
College of Commerce Bldg., Saskatoon, Sask. S7N 5A7; (306) 966-4798,
fax (306) 966-5408, vicq@commerce.usask.ca, www.commerce.usask.ca

RESEARCH CENTRE ▪ The Centre for International Business Studies provides graduate
and undergraduate students with international business and cultural experiences, and assists
small and medium-sized organizations in the penetration of international markets. This is
done in cooperation with the University of Saskatchewan's College of Commerce, through
the provision of both undergraduate and graduate courses. The centre's areas of geographic
interest are the US, Japan, Malaysia, Singapore, Ukraine, and Thailand. [ID:5364]

UNIVERSITY OF SASKATCHEWAN—INTERNATIONAL STUDIES
International Studies Program
Coordinator, International Studies Program, Department of History,
College of Arts and Sciences, University of Saskatchewan, Saskatoon, Sask.
S7N 0W0; (306) 966-5796, fax (306) 966-5852, handy@sask.usask.ca, www.usask.ca

BA (honours) IN INTERNATIONAL STUDIES ▪ International Studies is an interdisciplinary
program which affords students the opportunity to choose classes from anthropology,
economics, geography, history, political studies, and sociology. By pursuing an integrative
approach across disciplines, this unique program allows students to gain a broad multidisciplinary introduction to international events, issues, and ideas as well as a strong grounding
in one or two of the participating disciplines. Students are encouraged to take advantage of
study abroad programs in Guatemala, Germany, and Ukraine. [ID:5365]

UNIVERSITÉ DE SHERBROOKE—DEVELOPMENT STUDIES
Gestion et développement des coopératives
Institut de recherche et d'enseignement pour les coopératives,
Faculté des lettres et de sciences humaines, Université de Sherbrooke,
Sherbrooke, Québec J1K 2R1; (819) 821-7220, fax (819) 821-7213, www.usherb.ca

MA EN GESTION ET DÉVELOPPEMENT DES COOPÉRATIVES ▪ Le diplôme en gestion
et développement des coopératives complète la formation de l'étudiant dans un domaine
pertinent à la pratique professionnelle en milieu coopératif. Il accueille des étudiant(e)s du
Canada, et fait aussi une large place à la clientèle étudiante de l'étranger, notamment des
pays en voie de développement. [ID:5298]

SHERIDAN COLLEGE—INTERNATIONAL BUSINESS
Post-Graduate International Business Program
Registrar's Office, 1430 Trafalgar Road, Oakville, Ontario L6H 2L1;
(905) 845-9430, fax (905) 815-4048, infosheridan@sheridanc.on.ca, www.sheridanc.on.ca

POST-GRADUATE DIPLOMA IN INTERNATIONAL BUSINESS ▪ This one-year program is
based on the belief that understanding cultural diversity and applying this knowledge to
achieve business goals is critical to the success of international business transactions. The
program provides students with the knowledge, skills, and attitudes to work collaboratively
on researching foreign markets, identifying marketing opportunities, and developing solid
business to support an international venture. Specific areas covered include: managing
cultural differences, international marketing, financing trade, getting goods to market,
Spanish, NAFTA and geopolitical differences between countries. The program also includes
an optional work term component. Applicants must have a three-year college or university
degree or at least five years of relevant business experience. [ID:6602]

SIMON FRASER UNIVERSITY
8888 Barnett Highway, Burnaby, B.C. V5A 1S6; (604) 291-3111, fax (604) 291-5880, www.sfu.ca

International programs and research centres in this chapter: 5
Number of students: 20,600 **Percentage of international students:** 3.2%

International focus: Students and recent graduates of Simon Fraser University have access to a myriad of unique experiences and opportunities by becoming involved in any of the university's many international and domestic activities, including student exchanges and field schools. The university can also offer some assistance in accessing employment and volunteer opportunities overseas.

International offices: Simon Fraser's International Exchange and Student Services provides support services to all international students as well as students going abroad.

Language programs within Area Studies described in this chapter: Department of Spanish and Latin American Studies; Faculty of Arts. **Other language programs:** BA, BA (honours) in Linguistics. [ID:6660]

Faculty of Arts
Advisor, Faculty of Arts, Office of the Dean, Simon Fraser University, Burnaby, B.C.
V5A 1S6; (604) 291-4774, fax (604) 291-4989, naomi_ludington@sfu.ca, www.sfu.ca

CERTIFICATE IN CHINESE STUDIES ▪ The Certificate in Chinese Studies offers students a series of courses related to contemporary China. In addition to socio-political core courses, the program requires an introductory course in the Chinese language, and a stay at a university in China. [ID:5279]

Department of Spanish and Latin American Studies
Chairperson, Department of Spanish and Latin American Studies,
Simon Fraser University, Burnaby, B.C. V5A 1S6; (604) 291-4774, fax (604) 291-4989, www.sfu.ca

BA & MA IN LATIN AMERICAN STUDIES ▪ The Department of Spanish and Latin American Studies encourages interdisciplinary studies in the humanities and social sciences. The department offers flexible programs designed to accommodate students' interests, including a Latin American Field Study School. Students may choose to specialize in a multidisciplinary study of Latin America or study the language and literature of Spain and Latin America. In addition to BA programs in Spanish and Latin American Studies, the department also offers a graduate program that combines flexibility and breadth with the possibility of specialization in order to accommodate students interested in both academic and professional careers. [ID:5278]

David Lam Centre for International Communication
Director, David Lam Centre for International Business Studies,
Simon Fraser University, Harbour Centre, 515 West Hastings Street,
Vancouver, B.C. V6B 5K3; (604) 291-5111, fax (604) 291-5112, www.sfu.ca

NON-CREDIT PROGRAM IN EAST ASIAN LANGUAGES ▪ The Canada Program in East Asian Languages and Cross-Cultural Communications offered by the School of Communication addresses the communication needs of career professionals, co-op students, diplomats, teachers and trainees who expect to work in East Asia or with people from East Asia. The emphasis is on verbal and non-verbal interactive competence in about 30 situations common to business and professional life. In certain cases, credit can be arranged under the supervision of the School of Communications. [ID:5280]

SIMON FRASER UNIVERSITY—INTERCULTURAL STUDIES
Department of Sociology and Anthropology
Departmental Assistant, Department of Anthropology,
Simon Fraser University, Burnaby, B.C. V5A 1S6; (604) 291-3726, fax (604) 291-5799, www.sfu.ca

POST BACCALAUREATE DIPLOMA IN ETHNIC AND INTERCULTURAL RELATIONS ▪ The objective of this program is to foster an understanding of the dynamics of cultural diversity and inter-group relations in Canada and within the global context. This program is designed to assist students to critically assess social forces that generate inequality and intolerance as well as those that form the basis of a genuinely multicultural and just society. The program is intended for human services professionals and for those who wish to develop their general educational background. [ID:5281]

SIMON FRASER UNIVERSITY—INTERNATIONAL BUSINESS
Faculty of Business Administration
Coordinator, Simon Fraser University, Room 3302, West Mall Complex,
Burnaby, B.C. V5A 1S6; (604) 291-4624, fax (604) 291-4920, www.sfu.ca

BBA: concentration in International Business ▪ The Simon Fraser BBA and MBA program are designed to allow students to concentrate in a variety of areas including International Business. Students in the International Business concentration analyze the problems of the global business community, study Canada's involvement in the GATT, FTA, and NAFTA treaties, and learn about doing business in the Pacific Rim and around the world. Students may pursue a joint degree in business administration and another field of study. Joint programs are currently being offered with the Departments of Communications, Psychology, Geography, Economics, Computer Science, Latin American Studies, and Political Science. The faculty also encourages students to take advantage of exchange opportunities with universities in Mexico, Korea, Germany, the US, the Netherlands, and Norway. [ID:5282]

SIR SANDFORD FLEMING COLLEGE—INTERNATIONAL BUSINESS
International Education Office
International Program Advisor, Sutherland Campus,
Sir Sandford Fleming College, Brealey Drive, Peterborough, Ontario K9J 7B1;
(705) 749-5530 ext. 1242/1262, fax (705) 749-5526, international@flemingc.on.ca, www.flemingc.on.ca

DIPLOMA IN INTERNATIONAL TRADE ▪ Sir Sanford Fleming College offers a wide range of language instruction and postsecondary programs to Canadian and international students. Of particular note is their International Business Exchange Program, a three year diploma program which allows students to spend one semester in Mexico and one in the US. Graduating students are eligible to work in all North American countries. [ID:5283]

ST. FRANCIS XAVIER UNIVERSITY—AREA STUDIES
Department of Celtic Studies
Department Chair, St. Francis Xavier University,
P.O. Box 5000, Stn. Main, Antigonish, N.S. B2G 2W5; (902) 867-2300, fax (902) 867-2448, www.stfx.ca

BA IN CELTIC STUDIES ▪ The Celtic Studies Program at St. Francis Xavier University focuses on the Gaelic language, history, and culture of Scotland, Nova Scotia, and Ireland. Language courses are offered, but not required. The program also offers courses in Celtic literature, history, and folklore. [ID:6525]

ST. MARY'S UNIVERSITY—INTERNATIONAL PROFILE
ST. MARY'S UNIVERSITY
923 Robie Street, Halifax, N.S. B3H 3C4; (902) 420-5400, fax (902) 420-5530, www.stmarys.ca

International programs and research centres in this chapter: 4
Number of students: 6,500 **Percentage of international students:** 8%

International focus: St. Mary's University's mission statement integrates internationalization as a major priority. In addition to international programming that includes International Development Studies, Asian Studies, and Global Business, most academic programs have an international component. The university is active in international projects in Asia, Africa, and South America. Students from over 65 countries attend the university.

International offices: The International Activities Office is responsible for international projects, exchange programs, visitors, and promotion.

Language programs within Area Studies described in this chapter: Asian Studies Program. **Other language programs:** BA in German; BA in Spanish. [ID:6658]

ST. MARY'S UNIVERSITY—AREA STUDIES
Asian Studies Program
Area Coordinator, Asian Studies Program, St. Mary's University,
923 Robie Street, Halifax, N.S. B3H 3C3; (902) 420-5768, fax (902) 420-5181, www.stmarys.ca

BA IN ASIAN STUDIES ▪ St. Mary's University is the only academic institution in Atlantic Canada to offer an interdisciplinary degree program in Asian Studies, a minor in Asian Studies and a Certificate in Chinese and Japanese Studies. Facility in an Asian language is a requirement to graduate and many exchange programs in Asia are offered. Students who have completed this program have found positions in foreign services, international trade, and academic appointments in Canada and Asia. [ID:6526]

ST. MARY'S UNIVERSITY—DEVELOPMENT STUDIES
International Development Studies Program
Secretary, International Development Studies Program, Saint Mary's University, Halifax, N.S. B3H 3C3; (902) 420-5768, fax (902) 420-5181, awright@huskyl.stmarys.ca, www.stmarys.ca/academic/arts/ids/

BA, BA (honours) & MA IN INTERNATIONAL DEVELOPMENT STUDIES ▪ International Development Studies is an interdisciplinary graduate and undergraduate program which focuses on problems of development and the strategic responses of governments as well as international, nongovernmental, and grassroots organizations. Specializations include gender issues, forms of sustainable development, planning in a global context, and community development. The program includes a thesis requirement and offers some opportunities for research and work abroad through program-initiated projects. There are approximately 30 students in the graduate program, about half of whom come from developing countries. Visit their web site for information about various requirements, courses and faculty. [ID:5276]

ST. MARY'S UNIVERSITY—INTERNATIONAL BUSINESS
The Frank H. Sobey Faculty of Commerce
Committee Coordinator, Committee on Global Business Management,
The Frank H. Sobey Faculty of Commerce, St. Mary's University, 923 Robie Street,
Halifax, N.S. B3H 3C4; (902) 420-5735, fax (902) 420-5892, www.stmarys.ca

BComm: specialization in Global Business Management ▪ St. Mary's BComm program with a specialization in global business management helps students integrate into the globalized business world. It focuses on teaching students to work together and communicate effectively with foreign companies and to manage global teamwork with synergy instead of conflict. Courses are offered in economics, management, marketing, accounting, finance, and area studies in the regions of Africa, Americas, Asia, and Europe. [ID:6527]

ST. MARY'S UNIVERSITY—INTERNATIONAL BUSINESS
The Frank H. Sobey Faculty of Commerce
MBA Program Manager, The Frank H. Sobey Faculty of Commerce, St. Mary's University,
923 Robie Street, Halifax, N.S. B3H 3C4; (902) 420-5729, fax (902) 420-5119, www.stmarys.ca

MBA: concentration in International Development Management ▪ The program recognizes the present and future importance of newly-industrialized countries such as Singapore, South Korea, and Brazil; attention is also given to countries involved in bilateral trade with Canada such as India, Nigeria, and Brazil. The cultures of these societies are vastly different from those of Canada's traditional trading partners; understanding the business and social practices in these countries is imperative if Canadian managers are to be successful. The program does not aim to make the student a global management expert or an area expert, but rather it sensitizes students to these cultures and the unique demands posed on managers in development settings. [ID:6528]

UNIVERSITY OF TORONTO—INTERNATIONAL PROFILE
UNIVERSITY OF TORONTO
27 King's College Circle, Toronto, Ontario
M5S 1A1; (416) 978-2011, fax (416) 978-8182, www.utoronto.ca

International programs and research centres in this chapter: 15
Number of students: 50,300 **Percentage of international students:** 4.3%

International focus: The University of Toronto is Canada's foremost research-intensive university. A large part of the $1 million per day of research carried out at the university involves international partners, sponsors, and/or subject matter. With approximately 6,000 faculty members and 10,000 graduate students, along with one of North America's largest academic Health sciences complexes, the University of Toronto holds international positions of prominence across the spectrum of research disciplines. Specific cultural and language programs are offered in more than 40 languages. The university has a proud array of formal research and academic partnerships with leading institutions and organizations, both public and private, across Asia, the Americas, Australia, and Europe. These represent innovative alliances across a range of sectors and substantive strength-to-strength collaborations.

International offices: The University of Toronto's Director of International Liaison and Exchange serves to support internationalization of the University of Toronto, to support student and faculty mobility, research links, and collaboration. The International Student Advisor promotes and supports international education through the provision of university services, programs, and facilities for students with intercultural interests, international students, and students looking for work or study opportunities abroad.

Language programs within Area Studies described in this chapter: Department of Slavic Languages and Literature; Jewish Studies Program; African Studies Program; Centre for Russian and East European Studies; Department of East Asian Studies; Department of Middle East and Islamic Studies; Department of Spanish and Portuguese; Department of Italian Studies; Centre for South Asian Studies; Department of Near and Middle Eastern Civilizations. **Other language programs:** BA, BA (honours), MA, PhD in German; BA, BA (honours), MA, PhD in Linguistics; BA in Modern Languages. [ID:6661]

UNIVERSITY OF TORONTO—AREA STUDIES
American Studies Program
Coordinator, American Studies Program, University of Toronto, Victoria College, 73 Queen's Park Crescent, Toronto, Ontario M5S 1K7; (416) 585-4475, fax (416) 585-4584, www.utoronto.ca

BA: concentration in American Studies ▪ The six-course major program in American Studies is made up of courses offered on American topics throughout the Faculty of Arts and

Science. Courses are available from the Departments of History, Geography, Political Science, Economics, Music, Film, and English. The American Studies concentration must be paired with another major. [ID:5371]

UNIVERSITY OF TORONTO—AREA STUDIES
African Studies Program
Director, African Studies Program, New College, University of Toronto, 300 Huron Street, Toronto, Ontario M5S 1A1; (416) 978-8288, fax (416) 978-0554, dickson.eyoh@utoronto.ca, www.utoronto.ca

BA (minor, major & specialization) IN AFRICAN STUDIES ▪ The African Studies Program is designed to give students a wide range of knowledge on the history, culture and politics of Africa. The courses demand effort on the part of the student to integrate ideas and information from several different disciplines. Courses are taught by faculty members who have administrative, teaching and research experience in various parts of Africa. Students registered in the program are encouraged to pursue a complementary focus in one of the traditional disciplines. The University of Toronto offers a wide range of bursaries and in-course scholarships for which African Studies students are eligible. [ID:5366]

UNIVERSITY OF TORONTO—AREA STUDIES
Department of East Asian Studies
Undergraduate Coordinator, Department of East Asian Studies,
University of Toronto, Room 14207, Robarts Library, 130 St. George Street, Toronto, Ontario
M5S 3H1; (416) 978-3301, fax (416) 978-5711, eas.office@utoronto.ca, www.chass.utoronto.ca/eas

BA (minor, major & specialization), MA, MPhil & PhD IN EAST ASIAN STUDIES ▪ The Department of East Asian Studies offers a wide range of courses and programs, both at the undergraduate and graduate levels, in South and East Asian Studies, especially of India, China, Korea, and Japan. The program focuses on the humanities. Students are required to develop a proficiency in a language related to their studies. [ID:5368]

UNIVERSITY OF TORONTO—AREA STUDIES
Department of Spanish and Portuguese
Undergraduate Secretary, Department of Spanish and Portuguese,
University of Toronto, Room 217, 21 Sussex Ave., Toronto, Ontario M5S 1A1; (416) 978-6412,
fax (416) 971-2061, spanport@epas.utoronto.ca,www.chass.utoronto.ca/spanish_portuguese

BA (minor & major) IN IBERO-AMERICAN STUDIES ▪ The University of Toronto offers a degree program in Ibero-American Studies. This program is interdisciplinary, mounted jointly by the Department of Spanish and Portuguese and other departments in the humanities and social sciences, and will encourage students majoring in other disciplines to study Latin American and Iberian cultures. [ID:5373]

UNIVERSITY OF TORONTO—AREA STUDIES
Department of Italian Studies
Chair, Department of Italian Studies, University of Toronto, 21 Sussex Ave.,
Toronto, Ontario M5S 1J6; (416) 978-3348, fax (416) 978-5593, www.utoronto.ca

BA, BA (honours), MA & PhD IN ITALIAN STUDIES ▪ The University of Toronto offers undergraduate and graduate degrees with specializations in Italian Studies. Offered at both the St. George and Erindale campuses, the undergraduate program includes courses in Italian language, literature, linguistics, culture, film, and Italian-Canadian studies. This program can lead to minor, major, and specialist designations for a BA degree. Undergraduates may also spend their third year in Italy and summer programs are offered in Siena. The graduate program, offered at the St. George Campus only, includes courses in

Italian language, literature, linguistics, and film and leads to an MA (one year) or PhD (six years) degree. [ID:6533]

UNIVERSITY OF TORONTO—AREA STUDIES
Department of Slavic Languages and Literature
Department Chair, Department of Slavic Languages and Literature,
University of Toronto, 21 Sussex Ave., Toronto, Ontario M5S 1A1;
(416) 978-4895, fax (416) 971-1387, slavic@utoronto.ca, www.utoronto.ca/slavic

BA IN CROATIAN AND SERBIAN STUDIES; BA IN CZECH AND SLOVAK STUDIES; BA IN POLISH STUDIES; BA & BA (honours) IN RUSSIAN OR UKRAINIAN ▪ The Department of Slavic Languages and Literatures offers undergraduate courses in Croatian, Czech, Macedonian, Polish, Serbian, Russian and Ukrainian languages and literatures, as well as in Slavic linguistics. Courses in Estonian, Finnish and Hungarian, although not Slavic languages, are also offered through the department. These courses are suitable for inclusion in a wide variety of programs of study, whether or not the student has any previous knowledge of the languages. Specialist and major concentrations are available in most of these areas. The department also offers graduate study at the MA and PhD levels. [ID:6534]

UNIVERSITY OF TORONTO—AREA STUDIES
Jewish Studies Program
Director, Jewish Studies Program, University of Toronto,
Room 314, 15 King's College Circle, Toronto, Ontario M5S 1A1;
(416) 978-5301, fax (416) 971-2027, david.novak@utoronto.ca, www.utoronto.ca/jewishstudies

BA & BA (honours) IN JEWISH STUDIES ▪ The Jewish Studies Program at the University of Toronto is a multidisciplinary program which encompasses and coordinates courses in the Departments of English, German, History, Near and Middle Eastern Civilizations, Philosophy, Sociology, and Religion. The program is unique in Canada for the breadth and depth of its curriculum and offers over sixty courses in archaeology, history, language, literature, philosophy, theology and sociology. It is one of the major Jewish Studies programs in North America. The various undergraduate programs in Jewish Studies provide useful preparation for such fields as primary and secondary school teaching, library science, the rabbinate, government, and diplomatic service as well as an ever-increasing range of positions in the Jewish communal service. [ID:6535]

UNIVERSITY OF TORONTO—AREA STUDIES
Centre for South Asian Studies
Director, Centre for South Asian Studies, University of Toronto, Room 2057, Sidney Smith Hall,
Toronto, Ontario M5S 1A1; (416) 978-4294, south.asian@utoronto.ca, www.utoronto.ca

BA & MA IN SOUTH ASIAN STUDIES ▪ The Centre for South Asian Studies, which is interdisciplinary and interdepartmental, provides the opportunity for undergraduate and graduate students to undertake both classical and modern studies of India, Nepal, Pakistan, Bangladesh, and Sri Lanka. All students are strongly advised to study at least one South Asian language. [ID:5369]

UNIVERSITY OF TORONTO—AREA STUDIES
Department of Middle East and Islamic Studies
Chairperson, University of Toronto, Robarts Library, Room 14095,
130 St George Street, Toronto, Ontario M5S 1A1; (416) 978-3306, fax (416) 978-3305, www.utoronto.ca

BA, MA & PhD IN MIDDLE EAST AND ISLAMIC STUDIES ▪ The Department of Middle East and Islamic Studies is concerned with the interdisciplinary study of the civilization and culture of the Islamic world from the advent of Islam until the present. It concentrates on language, literature, history, archeology, religion, philosophy, and art of the Middle East in both the medieval and contemporary periods. Courses are taught within the broad tradition of the humanities. The study of language is strongly recommended. [ID:5372]

UNIVERSITY OF TORONTO—AREA STUDIES
Department of Near and Middle Eastern Civilizations
Chairperson, Department of Near and Middle Eastern Civilizations,
University of Toronto, 4 Bancroft Ave., Toronto, Ontario M5S 1C1;
(416) 978-3306, fax (416) 978-3305, dagnija.gotch@utoronto.ca, www.utoronto.ca

BA, MA & PhD IN NEAR EASTERN STUDIES ▪ The Department of Near and Middle Eastern Civilizations offers both undergraduate and graduate degrees in the comprehensive study of the Near and Middle East from earliest times to present. The department is heavily involved with archaeological excavations, including work in Egypt, Jordan, Sudan, Syria and Turkey. [ID:5374]

UNIVERSITY OF TORONTO—AREA STUDIES
Centre for Russian and East European Studies
Chairperson, Centre for Russian and East European Studies, University of Toronto, 14th Floor, Robarts Library, Toronto, Ontario M5S 1A1; (416) 978-8192, fax (416) 978-3817, www.utoronto.ca

MA IN RUSSIAN AND EAST EUROPEAN STUDIES ▪ Candidates for the MA in Russian and East European Studies are accepted into the program under the general regulations of the School of Graduate Studies. At least some of the work in the program is based on the study of original texts and presupposes a reading knowledge of a language relevant to the program. The program requires a minimum of two sessions of full-time graduate study and comprises six full courses or their equivalent. Visit their web site for the graduate handbook. [ID:5367]

UNIVERSITY OF TORONTO—DEVELOPMENT STUDIES
Co-operative Program in International Development Studies (IDS)
Coordinator, Co-operative Program in International Development Studies,
University of Toronto, Scarborough Campus, 1265 Military Trail, Scarborough, Ontario M1C 1A4;
(416) 287-7113, fax (416) 287-7283, maxwell@tsunami.scar.utoronto.ca, www.scar.utoronto/~ids

BA & BSc: specialization in International Development Studies ▪ The Co-operative Program in International Development Studies (IDS) is a five-year undergraduate program which combines academic study in the environmental and socio-economic sciences with practical work experience in Latin America, Africa and Asia. The program consists of 20 courses of study focusing on environmental, economic, social and political change in the developing world, as well as management of natural resources. IDS students also study the history, culture and language of the area where they will be carrying out their work placement. During their fourth year, IDS students work as development interns in the South with a Canadian or Southern development agency. Placement costs are covered by scholarships and in some cases, by Canadian NGO employers who provide a monthly living allowance. While in the field, students begin a major research paper based on their placement experience. In their fifth year they return to the University of Toronto to complete their course credits and research paper. The IDS program admits 10 students each year into a total student body of approximately 60. Visit the IDS web site for program details and admission procedures. [ID:5375]

UNIVERSITY OF TORONTO—DEVELOPMENT STUDIES
Department of Political Science
Graduate Administrator, University of Toronto, Room 3026, 100 St. George Street, Toronto, Ontario
M5S 1A1; (416) 978-7170, fax (416) 978-5566, poliscm@artsci.utotoronto.ca, www.utoronto.ca

BA, MA & PhD IN POLITICAL SCIENCE: specialization in Development Studies, Comparative Politics or International Relations ▪ The Department of Political Science offers BA, MA, and PhD programs in the major areas of the discipline. Degree programs include a specialized MA program in development studies, environmental studies, and international relations. About 35 per cent of students registered in the doctoral program and about 15 per cent of those registered in the MA program come from outside Canada. Funding opportunities include the University of Toronto Connaught and Open Fellowships, providing $11,100 and $3,600 respectively. Visit their web site for course and scholarship information. [ID:5376]

UNIVERSITY OF TORONTO—INTERNATIONAL STUDIES
International Relations Programme
Coordinator, International Relations Programme, Trinity College,
University of Toronto, 6 Hoskin Ave., Toronto, Ontario M5S 1H8;
(416) 978-8248, fax (416) 971-2087, irpro@chass.utoronto.ca, www.trinity.utoronto.ca

BA (major & specialist) IN INTERNATIONAL RELATIONS ▪ The International Relations Programme, established in 1976, is one of the most comprehensive and best-known undergraduate degree programs of its kind in Canada. The aim of the program is to provide students with an understanding of the evolution and structure of the modern international system, the conduct of foreign policy, and the variety of approaches to the study of international relations. The program offers a structured, multidisciplinary education combining the insights and methods of the academic disciplines of history, political science, and economics. [ID:5379]

UNIVERSITY OF TORONTO—PEACE/CONFLICT STUDIES
Peace and Conflict Studies Program
Peace and Conflict Studies Program, University College, University of Toronto,
15 King's College Circle, Toronto, Ontario M5S 3H7; (416) 978-8148, fax (416) 978-8416,
pcs.programme@utoronto.ca, www.library.utoronto.ca/www/pcs/pcs.htm

BA IN PEACE AND CONFLICT STUDIES ▪ This undergraduate program provides 60 selected students an opportunity to gain wide-ranging understanding of the causes and nature of violence and peace. It moves beyond the traditional study of international relations by examining the causes of violent strife, both among and within countries. Topics include war, revolution, insurgency, and ethnic clashes. The program emphasizes practical knowledge, the interdisciplinary nature of peace and conflict studies, and the importance of bringing leading-edge research directly into the classroom. The program operates within the University College, part of the University of Toronto. [ID:5378]

TRENT UNIVERSITY—INTERNATIONAL PROFILE
TRENT UNIVERSITY
P.O. Box 4800, Stn. Main, Peterborough, Ontario
K9J 7B8; (705) 748-1011, fax (705) 748-1246, www.trentu.ca

International programs and research centres in this chapter: 5
Number of students: 5,100 Percentage of international students: 2%

International focus: Trent University is active in international research, education, and student mobility initiatives, primarily in Latin America, Europe, and Asia. The university is well known for its focus on both environmental sciences and indigenous studies. At present, Trent is the lead institution in a CIDA-funded five year project for sustainable environmental rehabilitation of watersheds in Mexico and Ecuador. Trent has additional expertise in areas including, but not restricted to, international development policy, socio-economic change, natural resource management, Latin-American archeology, and international political economy.

International offices: The Trent International Program houses both international liaison and international student advisory services. The International Liaison Office acts as the catalyst for international activity within the university, coordinates international development activity, negotiates international linkages, and is responsible for liaison between the university and external agencies. The International Student Advisory Office provides orientation and reception services as well as crosscultural support to international students.

Language programs within Area Studies described in this chapter: Department of Modern Languages and Literature; German Studies. [ID:6662]

TRENT UNIVERSITY—AREA STUDIES
Department of Modern Languages and Literature
Director, Section of Hispanic Studies, Trent University, P.O. Box 4800. Stn. Main,
Peterborough, Ontario K9J 7B8; (705) 748-1394, fax (705) 748-1630, spanish@trentu.ca, www.trentu.ca

BA & BA (honours) IN HISPANIC STUDIES ▪ The Section of Hispanic Studies of Trent University offers a year-abroad program in Mexico, hosted by Univerisad del Valle de Mexico at its campuses in Queretaro and San Miguel de Allende. The program is open to full-time Trent students entering their second or third year who are developing a major in Hispanic Studies. Courses are offered in the areas of language, civilization, and literature with full accreditation toward the Trent degree. Classes run from September to April with a four-week Christmas vacation. [ID:6539]

TRENT UNIVERSITY—AREA STUDIES
German Studies
Department Chair, Trent University, P.O. Box 4800, Stn. Main,
Peterborough, Ontario K9J 7B8; (705) 748-1423, fax (705) 748-1630, www.trentu.ca

BA & BA (honours) IN GERMAN STUDIES ▪ German Studies at Trent University offers courses in German language, history, literature, and culture. In conjunction with Brock University and McMaster University, Trent offers an eleven-month Year Abroad Program in Freiburg, Germany. A Canadian professor helps students integrate into the German university. A work permit is also part of the program. To apply, students must have completed their first year. [ID:6538]

TRENT UNIVERSITY—DEVELOPMENT STUDIES
Comparative Development Studies Program (CDS)
Chairperson, Comparative Development Studies Program (CDS),
Champlain College, Trent University, Peterborough, Ontario K9L 1Z7;
(705) 748-1398, fax (705) 748-1624, jhillman@trentu.ca, www.trentu..ca/cds

BA (general, honours & joint major) IN COMPARATIVE DEVELOPMENT STUDIES ▪ The Comparative Development Studies Program (CDS) is an interdisciplinary program with a broad mandate. It encompasses the emergence and consolidation of a global market economy and its effects on various regions of the world. Students normally complete an honours BA, often in conjunction with another department or program. Opportunities to experience the challenge of development first-hand are offered through programs in Ecuador, Thailand, and Ghana. They provide a comprehensive analysis of the history, culture and economy of their respective regions, and require an extensive field placement with a development agency. Visit Trent's web site for more details. [ID:5284]

TRENT UNIVERSITY—INTERCULTURAL STUDIES
Cultural Studies Program
Program Chair, Cultural Studies, Trent University, Peterborough, Ontario
K9J 7B8; (705) 748-1771, fax (705) 748-1826, cultstudies@trentu.ca, http://ivory.trentu.ca/www/cu

BA & BA (honours) IN CULTURAL STUDIES ▪ Cultural Studies at Trent University, now in its second decade, is the first program in North America to make the interdisciplinary study of modern culture the foundation of an undergraduate degree. Among many similar programs that have developed worldwide, it is unique in including the arts in its plan of education. As well as offering important courses in social and cultural study, media, and popular culture, the program offers specific sites in music, theatre, film, the visual arts, and literary studies. It is an ideal of the program to facilitate dialogue among different viewpoints and practices which the artists, theorists, and activists contest culture and give shape and substance to themselves and their work. In this way, the program provides a versatile, liberal education to individuals who go on to contribute to the social life of Canada through teaching, scholarship, the arts, journalism, the media, public relations, or the forming of public policy. [ID:6537]

TRENT UNIVERSITY—INTERNATIONAL STUDIES
Trent International Program
Trent International Program, Trent University,
Peterborough, Ontario K9J 7B8; (705) 748-1300, fax (705) 748-1626, tip@trentu.ca, www.trentu.ca

BA (honours): special interest in International Studies ▪ This program is available as an interdisciplinary degree for students who wish to focus on international relations. It combines globally-oriented studies in three or more disciplines which include anthropology, comparative development, cultural studies, economics, environmental and resource studies, history, modern languages, political studies, sociology and women's studies. Students spend one year of their studies in another country. [ID:5285]

VANIER COLLEGE—AREA STUDIES
Jewish Studies Program
Director, Jewish Studies Program, Vanier College, 821 Sainte-Croix Ave.,
Saint-Laurent, Québec H4L 3X9; (514) 744-7500, fax (514) 744-7952, www.vaniercollege.qc.ca

DIPLOMA IN JEWISH STUDIES ▪ The Jewish Studies Program at Vanier College is open to any student who wishes to study Jewish life and culture, Judaism and Israel as it relates to their own consciousness and sensibilities. Jewish Studies courses are interdisciplinary and drawn from the disciplines of history, psychology, literature, religion, philosophy, language, political science, and popular culture. [ID:6612]

VANIER COLLEGE—AREA STUDIES
Slavic Studies Program
Director, Slavic Studies Program, Vanier College, 821 Sainte-Croix Ave.,
Saint-Laurent, Québec H4L 3X9; (514) 744-7500, fax (514) 744-7952, www.vaniercollege.qc.ca

DIPLOMA IN SLAVIC STUDIES ▪ The Slavic Studies Program is designed to introduce students to the vast and varied region of Central/Eastern Europe and the former Soviet Union. Courses are offered in history, literature, and Russian language. The program enables students to pursue careers in journalism, politics, business, government service, languages and the arts. [ID:6613]

VANIER COLLEGE—INTERNATIONAL STUDIES
International Studies Program
Director, International Studies Program, Vanier College, 821 Sainte-Croix Ave.,
Saint-Laurent, Québec H4L 3X9; (514) 744-7500, fax (514) 744-7952, www.vaniercollege.qc.ca

CERTIFICATE IN INTERNATIONAL STUDIES ▪ The International Studies Program at Vanier College recognizes that, as the world's nations and peoples become increasingly interdependent, knowledge of various cultural issues and an awareness of international issues are crucial for today's students. A variety of courses, taught in English, are offered including the humanities, physical education, anthropology, economics, geography, history, religious studies, sociology, modern languages and methodology. [ID:6614]

UNIVERSITY OF VICTORIA—INTERNATIONAL PROFILE
UNIVERSITY OF VICTORIA
P.O. Box 1700, Victoria, B.C. V8W 2Y2; (250) 721-7211, fax (250) 721-7212, www.uvic.ca

International programs and research centres in this chapter: 6
Number of students: 15,865 **Percentage of international students:** 3.6%

International focus: The University of Victoria has over 80 active academic cooperation agreements providing faculty and student exchanges as well as other collaborative initiatives. The majority of linkages are in the Asia-Pacific region, but with a growing presence in Europe, Australia, and Latin America.

International offices: The University of Victoria's International Office coordinates the university's international activities, including exchange agreements, development and research projects, off-shore program delivery and internationalization of curricula. The Advisor of International Students, located in the Student and Ancillary Services Division, provides advice to students interested in exchange opportunities at partner universities abroad.

Language programs within Area Studies described in this chapter: Department of Hispanic and Italian Studies; Department of Pacific and Asian Studies;. **Other language programs:** BA in German; BA, BA (honours) BSc, MA, PhD in Linguistics; BA in Russian.
[ID:6663]

UNIVERSITY OF VICTORIA—AREA STUDIES
Department of Hispanic and Italian Studies
Chairperson, Department of Hispanic and Italian Studies, University of Victoria, P.O. Box 3045,
Victoria, B.C. V8W 3P4; (250) 721-7413, fax (250) 721-6608, spanit@uvvm.uvic.ca, www.uvic.ca

BA: minor in Italian Studies ▪ The University of Victoria offers a minor in Italian Studies. There are a variety of courses in history, fine arts, literature, and language. [ID:6567]

UNIVERSITY OF VICTORIA—AREA STUDIES
Department of Pacific and Asian Studies
Chairperson, Department of Pacific and Asian Studies, University of Victoria,
P.O. Box 3045, Victoria, B.C. V8W 3P4; (250) 721-7480, fax (250) 721-7219, www.uvic.ca

BA IN PACIFIC STUDIES ▪ The Pacific Studies Major Program provides students with an overview of the entire Asia Pacific region while allowing them to concentrate on one of three possible areas: China, Japan, or Southeast Asia/Oceania. The China and Japan concentrations require three years of language training in Chinese or Japanese, while the Southeast Asia-Oceania concentration requires two years of Indonesian. The program focuses on the history, culture, and social structures of the various Asia Pacific areas. Scholarships may be awarded to outstanding students. Exchange programs are in effect with universities in Shanghai, China, and Kyoto, Japan. [ID:5380]

UNIVERSITY OF VICTORIA—AREA STUDIES
Centre for Asia-Pacific Initiatives (CAPI)
Director, Centre for Asia-Pacific Initiatives (CAPI), University of Victoria, P.O. Box 1700,
Victoria, B.C. V8W 2Y2; (250) 721-7020, fax (250) 721-3107, capisec@uvvm.uvic.ca, www.capi.uvic.ca

RESEARCH CENTRE ▪ The aim of the Centre for Asia Pacific Initiatives (CAPI) is to
encourage, conduct and support the University of Victoria's Asia Pacific public policy
research and related initiatives, and to encourage development of the university's Asia
Pacific programs and resources. The centre has a director, three chairpersons and a number
of associates with common research interests. The faculty focuses on law and economic
development, economic relations with China and Japan, and Asia Pacific legal relations.
Linkages are established with other centres on campus for purposes of collaborative
research, as well as with individuals and institutions across Canada and in the Asia Pacific.
In addition to research activities undertaken by CAPI, a wider role is taken on campus to
disseminate information through conferences, workshops, symposiums, and publications.
The centre is not a teaching unit. CAPI's web site provides full information about the centre
and its activities. [ID:5381]

UNIVERSITY OF VICTORIA—INTERNATIONAL BUSINESS
School of Business
International Programs Coordinator, School of Business, University of Victoria, P.O. Box 1700, Victoria,
B.C. V8W 2Y2; (250) 721-6407, fax (250) 721-6067, ktoor@business.uvic.ca,www.business.uvic.ca

BComm: concentration in International Business Management ▪ The International Business
Management Program has adopted a mandate to focus on the Asia Pacific region. A variety
of international business courses are offered which provide students with a solid grounding
in the issues related to the international marketplace. An international exchange program
has been established with over 20 universities throughout Europe and Southeast and North
Asia. Students live, study, and complete cooperative work terms abroad, ideally spending up
to one year overseas. Students in the International Business Program are required to complete a minimum of one year of language study. [ID:5382]

UNIVERSITY OF VICTORIA—INTERNATIONAL BUSINESS
Faculty of Business
MBA Admissions, P.O. Box 1700, Victoria, B.C.
V8W 2Y2; (250) 721-6058, fax (250) 721-7066, www.business.uvic.ca/mba/

MBA: option in International Business ▪ The MBA international business program option is
21 months long. The first nine months are spent at the University of Victoria, followed by a
six week business practice in Malaysia and a three month work term overseas. There are
also two four-month exchange terms in either France, Mexico, Thailand, Taiwan, Indonesia,
or Singapore. About 40 full-time MBA students are accepted each year from over 200
applications. The program starts each year at the beginning of August. [ID:6568]

UNIVERSITY OF VICTORIA—PEACE/CONFLICT STUDIES
Institute for Dispute Resolution
Director, Institute for Dispute Resolution, University of Victoria, P.O. Box 2400, Victoria, B.C.
V8W 3H7; (250) 721-8777, fax (250) 721-6607, uvicidr@uvic.ca, http://dispute.resolution.uvic.ca/

RESEARCH CENTRE ▪ The Institute for Dispute Resolution is an interdisciplinary centre
focused on dispute resolution education and research, including resource and environmental
management, crosscultural conflict, aboriginal justice, and conflict in education systems.
Program focus is on public policy issues at local, national and global levels, including justice
reform, good governance, and sustainable development. Research has resulted in over 200
publications. Courses in a new interdisciplinary academic program begin in the summer of
1998. [ID:6569]

UNIVERSITY OF WATERLOO—INTERNATIONAL PROFILE
UNIVERSITY OF WATERLOO
200 University Ave. W., Waterloo, Ontario N2L 3G1;
(519) 885-1211, fax (519) 746-3051, www.uwaterloo.ca

International programs and research centres in this chapter: 5
Number of students: 26,000 **Percentage of international students:** 2.6%

International focus: The University of Waterloo is committed to international studies through overseas programs in a number of departments, through research associations with overseas universities, and through personal commitments and associations of many faculty members. Several schools and institutes on campus have an international mandate; the university has international connections which include collaborative and educational research projects in many countries.

International offices: The University of Waterloo's International Liaison Office has services and programs geared especially to the needs of international students. The university also has an International Student Advisor and an International Student Office.

Language programs within Area Studies described in this chapter: Department of German and Slavic Languages and Literature; Latin American Studies Program. **Other language programs:** BA minor in Croatian; MA & PhD in German; BA minor in Italian; BA, BA (honours) in Spanish; BA, BA (honours) in Russian. [ID:6664]

UNIVERSITY OF WATERLOO—AREA STUDIES
Department of German and Slavic Languages and Literature
Chairperson, Department of German and Slavic Languages and Literature,
University of Waterloo, Room 215, Modern Languages Bldg., Waterloo, Ontario
N2L 3G1; (519) 888-4567 ext. 3118, fax (519) 746-5243, www.uwaterloo.ca

BA: option in Russian and East European Studies ■ In cooperation with the Waterloo-Laurier-Guelph Centre for East European and Russian Studies, the University of Waterloo offers undergraduate students an interdisciplinary program in Russian and Eastern European Studies. This program, available as an option or an independent diploma package, integrates the study of history, politics, geography, economics and culture with language and literature in a coherent, interdisciplinary area studies package. There are also travel possibilities and fully accredited study-abroad opportunities offered by several participating departments. [ID:5383]

UNIVERSITY OF WATERLOO—AREA STUDIES
Department of German
Chairperson, Department of German, University of Waterloo, 200 University Ave. W.,
Waterloo, Ontario N2L 3G1; (519) 885-2260 ext. 2260, fax (519) 746-5243,
mbechtol@watarts.uwaterloo.ca, http://arts.uwaterloo.ca/GERM/german.html

BA & BA (honours) IN GERMANIC STUDIES ■ The University of Waterloo offers a variety of courses leading to the BA and BA (honours) in Germanic Studies. The Department of German also offers the Waterloo-Mannheim exchange which is the oldest exchange program of its kind in Canada. This is an academic exchange open to students from both universities for one or two semesters. Approximately 10 students from each university participate annually. [ID:6570]

UNIVERSITY OF WATERLOO—INTERNATIONAL BUSINESS
Department of Economics
Director, International Trade Specialization, University of Waterloo,
Faculty of Arts, HH 146, Waterloo, Ontario N2L 3G1; (519) 888-4567,
fax (519) 725-0530, rkumar@watarts.uwaterloo.ca, www.arts.uwaterloo.ca

BA: applied studies cooperative specialization in International Trade ▪ As part of the Applied Studies Co-op Program through the Faculty of Arts students must complete 12 courses. This includes required courses, electives, and two languages. Most students spend an eight-month specialized work-term abroad in their senior year. Graduates have worked in Europe and Asia. [ID:5386]

UNIVERSITY OF WATERLOO—INTERNATIONAL STUDIES
International Studies Program
Director, International Studies Program, Department of History, HH 109,
University of Waterloo, Waterloo, Ontario N2L 3G1; (519) 885-1211 ext. 5138,
fax (519) 746-2658, ghayes@watarts.uwaterloo.ca, www.uwaterloo.ca

BA: option in International Studies ▪ The University of Waterloo has a well-established commitment to international studies through its overseas study programs, a variety of research associations with overseas universities, and the expertise of its faculty. The International Studies Option is available to any student registered in any four-year general or honours program in any faculty. This option aims to improve students' understanding of the growing interconnectedness of the international community, and lead them to an under-standing of the world's diverse communities. Check the University of Waterloo's web site for the International Studies Program homepage. [ID:5387]

UNIVERSITY OF WATERLOO—PEACE/CONFLICT STUDIES
Peace and Conflict Studies Program (PACS)
Director, Peace and Conflict Studies Program (PACS),
Conrad Grebel College, University of Waterloo, Waterloo, Ontario
N2L 3G6; (519) 885-0220 ext. 236, fax (519) 885-0014, ipacs2@watserv1.uwaterloo.ca, www.uwaterloo.ca

BA (honours): minor in Peace and Conflict Studies; DIPLOMA IN PEACE AND CONFLICT STUDIES ▪ Nine departments at the University of Waterloo cooperate to enable students to examine the problems of human conflict and the ways in which such conflict is construc-tively and non-violently resolved. Issues range from war, peace, and disarmament to family conflicts, mediation and Third World development. PACS students participating in intern-ships and field studies in Canada and abroad are eligible for a stipend of up to $1,500 to cover recognized costs. Visit the University of Waterloo's web site for program information and course descriptions. [ID:5388]

UNIVERSITY OF WESTERN ONTARIO—INTERNATIONAL PROFILE
UNIVERSITY OF WESTERN ONTARIO
1151 Richmond Road, London, Ontario N6A 3K7; (519) 679-2111, www.uwo.ca

International programs and research centres in this chapter: 3
Number of students: 26,000 **Percentage of international students:** 3%

International focus: The University of Western Ontario and its affiliated colleges maintain over 200 collaborations and student exchange programs with institutions of higher education around the world. These programs involve faculty and students of arts, science, social science, communications and open learning, and applied health science as well as those in professional faculties such as Business Administration, Engineering Sciences, Medi-cine, and Dentistry.

International offices: The University of Western Ontario has an Office of International-al Research, International Student Office, and an Office of International Exchange/Student Affairs. Together, these offices are responsible for academics and student development.

Language programs: BA, BA (honours) in German; BA, BA (honours) in Russian; BA, BA (honours) in Spanish. [ID:6665]

UNIVERSITY OF WESTERN ONTARIO—INTERNATIONAL BUSINESS
Richard Ivey School of Business
Admissions Director, Richard Ivey School of Business, University of Western Ontario,
London, Ontario N6A 3K7; (519) 661-3212, fax (519) 661-3431, admiss@ivey.uwo.ca, www.ivey.uwo.ca

HBA & MBA: specialization in International Business ▪ The Richard Ivey Business School aims to be recognized throughout the world for developing decisive business leaders who are strategic in their orientation, entrepreneurial in how they think and act, and global in their outlook. By helping students to develop their business leadership skills, we contribute to the success of our Canadian and international customers in today's highly competitive global markets. International academic exchanges, LLB/MBA Programs, an Executive MBA Program and Executive Education courses are also available. Their web site provides information on application procedures, courses offered, and career services. [ID:5389]

UNIVERSITY OF WESTERN ONTARIO—INTERNATIONAL BUSINESS
Centre for International Business Studies
Director, Centre for International Business Studies,
Richard Ivey School of Business, University of Western Ontario, London, Ontario
N6A 3K7; (519) 661-3308, fax (519) 661-3959, jweston@ivey.uwo.ca, www.ivey.uwo.ca

RESEARCH CENTRE ▪ The Centre for International Business Studies supports the University of Western Ontario's Business School's academic programs and promotes development of knowledgeable and effective managers for today's global business environment. The centre initiates and coordinates specific projects and programs, hosts guest speakers and lecturers, organizes special events, and assists in the development of exchange programs. Two part-time persons are employed at the centre. [ID:5390]

UNIVERSITY OF WESTERN ONTARIO—INTERNATIONAL STUDIES
Graduate Program in Journalism
Office of the Dean, Faculty of Communication and Open Learning, University of Western Ontario,
London, Ontario N6C 1H1; (519) 661-3542, fax (519) 661-3506, www.fcol.uwo.ca

MA (journalism): focus in International Journalism ▪ The Graduate Program in Journalism enrols about 40 students annually in its one-year, two-term MA program. This is a nonthesis master's degree. Applicants are expected to have an honours degree from a Canadian university or the equivalent from a foreign university. International students from Europe and Africa have participated in the program and for the past five years the school has been twinned with the Graduate Journalism program at the University of Nairobi. The program also sponsors, in collaboration with the Department of Information and Communications at Laval University, an annual conference during which Canadian journalists and journalists representing the South explore issues related to the media and development. [ID:5392]

WILFRID LAURIER UNIVERSITY—DEVELOPMENT STUDIES
Development & International Studies Program
Coordinator, Development & International Studies Program,
Wilfrid Laurier University, 75 University Ave. W., Waterloo, Ontario N2L 3C5;
(519) 884-1970 ext. 3406, fax (519) 884-8854, jpeters@mach1.wlu.ca, www.wlu.ca

BA IN THIRD WORLD STUDIES ▪ The International Development Studies Program deals with issues from the historical origins of development and underdevelopment, to global change, to the experience of marginalized peoples, and the international efforts to offer alternative policy prescriptions. Students may choose one of five streams: political and economic development, environment and development, belief systems, First Nations, or ethnic studies. Students can choose from various courses, directed studies, fieldwork opportunities, and upper level seminars. [ID:5402]

UNIVERSITY OF WINDSOR—INTERNATIONAL PROFILE
UNIVERSITY OF WINDSOR
401 Sunset Ave., Windsor, Ontario N9B 3P4; (519) 253-3000, www.uwindsor.ca

International programs and research centres in this chapter: 6
Number of students: 13,700 **Percentage of international students:** 5%

International offices: The University of Windsor's Liaison and Applicant Services Office provides information and applications to potential undergraduate and graduate students. The university also has an International Student Advisor and an International Student Centre which is home to cultural clubs and provides support services to students.
Language programs within Area Studies described in this chapter: Latin American Studies Committee; Japanese Studies; Asian Studies Program;. **Other language programs:** BA, BA (honours) in German; BA, BA (honours), MA Italian; BA Russian; BA, BA (honours) in Spanish. [ID:6667]

UNIVERSITY OF WINDSOR—AREA STUDIES
Japanese Studies
Japanese Studies, Liaison and Applicant Office, University of Windsor, 401 Sunset Ave., Windsor, Ontario N9B 3P4; (519) 973-7014 ext. 3919, fax (519) 971-3653, liaison@uwindor.ca, www.uwindsor.ca

CERTIFICATE IN JAPANESE STUDIES ▪ The certificate in Japanese Studies combines courses from several departments in a comprehensive program of study intended to provide students with an in-depth understanding of Japan. Visit the "Information for Prospective Students" heading under Liaison Services on the University of Windsor web site for details. [ID:5394]

UNIVERSITY OF WINDSOR—AREA STUDIES
Latin American Studies Committee
Latin American Studies Committee, Liaison and Applicant Services, University of Windsor, 401 Sunset Ave., Windsor, Ontario N9B 3P4; (519) 973-7014 ext. 3919, fax (519) 971-3653, www.uwindsor.ca

CERTIFICATE IN LATIN AMERICAN AND CARIBBEAN STUDIES ▪ The Certificate in Latin American and Caribbean Studies combines courses from several different departments. This is a comprehensive program intended to provide students with an understanding of history and current events in Latin America and the Caribbean. Students are encouraged to take summer courses offered by Canadian and American universities in Latin America and the Caribbean. Visit the "Information for Prospective Students" heading under Liaison Services on the University of Windsor web site for details. [ID:5395]

UNIVERSITY OF WINDSOR—AREA STUDIES
Asian Studies Program
Asian Studies Program, Liaison and Applicant Services, University of Windsor, 401 Sunset Ave.,
Windsor, Ontario N9B 3P4; (519) 973-7014, fax (519) 971-3653, liaison@uwindsor.ca, www.uwindsor.ca

BA (honours) IN ASIAN STUDIES ▪ Through an interdisciplinary study of language, literature, religion, culture and the humanities, the Asian Studies Program produces graduates with an understanding and appreciation of the peoples, cultures and lands of Asia and their contemporary socio-economic and geo-political development. Combined honours programs between Asian Studies and other departments can be arranged in consultation with the Coordinator of the Asian Studies Program. Visit the "Information for Prospective Students" heading under Liaison Services on the University of Windsor web site for details. [ID:5393]

UNIVERSITY OF WINDSOR—INTERCULTURAL STUDIES
Department of Classical and
Modern Languages, Literatures and Civilizations
Program Coordinator, Multicultural Studies, Department of Classical
and Modern Languages, Literatures and Civilizations, University of Windsor,
401 Sunset Ave., Windsor, Ontario N9B 3P4; (519) 253-3000 ext. 2884, fax (519) 973-7050,
cmllc@uwindsor.ca, www.uwindsor.ca/faculty/arts/classical.and.modern.languages

BA IN MULTICULTURAL STUDIES ▪ University of Windsor's innovative and unique humanities-based Multicultural Studies Program has gained international recognition as a comprehensive socio-educational philosophy-practice program that enhances both human values and material advancement. The program brings together Canadian and foreign students in research, study, and appreciation of our roots and common goals. [ID:6578]

UNIVERSITY OF WINDSOR—INTERNATIONAL BUSINESS
Faculty of Business Administration
Faculty of Business Administration, Liaison and Applicant Services,
University of Windsor, 401 Sunset Ave., Windsor, Ontario N9B 3P4;
(519) 253-3000, fax (519) 973-7073, liaison@uwindsor.ca, www.uwindsor.ca

BComm & MBA IN INTERNATIONAL BUSINESS ▪ The Faculty of Business Administration's programs feature small classes, internationally diverse faculty and high-quality lectures. The programs are dynamic, responsive to changes in the workplace, and strategy-driven. They focus on entrepeneurship, international business and labour issues. Programs include a BComm (co-op optional available), BComm for university graduates, MBA (co-op option available) and a joint MBA/LLB. Visit the "Information for Prospective Students" heading under Liaison Services on the University of Windsor web site for details. [ID:6710]

UNIVERSITY OF WINDSOR—INTERNATIONAL STUDIES
International Relations Program
International Relations Program, Liaison and Applicant Services, University of Windsor, 401 Sunset Ave.,
Windsor, Ontario N9B 3P4; (519) 973-7014, fax (519) 973-7032, liaison@uwindsor.ca, www.uwindsor.ca

BA (honours) IN INTERNATIONAL RELATIONS; MA IN POLITICAL SCIENCE: specialization in International Relations ▪ The International Relations Program links social science courses from three departments to provide students with a broad understanding of the dynamics of global society and prepare them for a wide variety of international careers. The program focuses on the major international challenges of our time and gives students the necessary historical perspective and analytical skills to respond positively to these challenges. Visit the "Information for Prospective Students" heading under Liaison Services on the University of Windsor web site for details. [ID:5396]

UNIVERSITY OF WINNIPEG—INTERNATIONAL PROFILE
UNIVERSITY OF WINNIPEG
515 Portage Ave., Winnipeg, Manitoba R3B 2E9; (204) 786-7811, fax (204) 779-3443, www.uwinnipeg.ca

International programs and research centres in this chapter: 4
Number of students: 7,000 Percentage of international students: 7%

    International offices: The University of Winnipeg's International Recruitment Officer coordinates recruitment of and services for international students. The International Student Centre provides various resources as well as a place where students can meet and discuss issues of interest. The International Student Advisor advises students on academic matters. [ID:6668]

UNIVERSITY OF WINNIPEG—DEVELOPMENT STUDIES
International Development Studies
Coordinator, International Development Studies, Menno Simons College,
University of Winnipeg, 380 Spence Street, Winnipeg, Manitoba R3B 2E9;
(204) 786-9895, fax (204) 783-3699, buckland@uwinnipeg.ca, www.uwinnipeg.ca/~msc

BA IN INTERNATIONAL DEVELOPMENT STUDIES ■ International Development Studies (IDS) is an interdisciplinary program offered by Menno Simons College and the University of Winnipeg. IDS seeks to understand the forces that marginalize communities and nations through processes of exploitation and dependence. Moreover, IDS is concerned with the transformation of these communities and nations towards interdependent self-reliance. The program analyses the forces of underdevelopment and development at a variety of levels, focusing on the southern regions (Africa, Asia, and Latin America) and marginalized communities in Canada. Students can design their own program, drawing on courses from both the College and the University. Visit their web site for program details. [ID:5397]

UNIVERSITY OF WINNIPEG—INTERNATIONAL SCIENCES
Environmental Studies/Urban Studies Program
Environmental Studies/Urban Studies Program, University Admissions Office, University of Winnipeg,
515 Portage Ave., Winnipeg, Manitoba R3B 2E9; (204) 786-9225, fax (204) 774-4134,
andrew.lockery@uwinnipeg.ca, www.uwinnipeg.ca/academic/as/envirostd/index.htm

BA & BSc IN ENVIRONMENTAL AND URBAN STUDIES ■ The Environmental Studies/Urban Studies Program at the University of Winnipeg has been developed with the assistance of private sector, environmental consultants, relevant government departments, Crown corporations and previous graduates. All of the degree programs stress contemporary issues. The university has specialized in areas where it has considerable expertise, which includes urbanization and sustainability in developing countries. [ID:6580]

UNIVERSITY OF WINNIPEG—INTERNATIONAL STUDIES
Department of Political Science
Chairperson, Department of Political Science, University of Winnipeg,
515 Portage Ave., Winnipeg, Manitoba R3B 2E9; (204) 786-9306, fax (204) 774-4134,
poli-sci@uwinnipeg.ca, www.uwinnipeg.ca/academic/as/polsci/polsci.html

BA (honours) IN POLITICAL SCIENCE: concentration in International Relations ■ The Department of Political Science offers 12 courses, to be taken over several years, in the areas of international relations, organization and law. The courses are scattered over the different levels of both the BA (general) and the BA (honours) programs. There are no language requirements. [ID:5398]

UNIVERSITY OF WINNIPEG—PEACE/CONFLICT STUDIES
Conflict Resolution Studies Program
Coordinator, Conflict Resolution Studies Program, Menno Simons College,
University of Winnipeg, 3rd Floor, 380 Spence Street, Winnipeg, Manitoba R3B 2E9;
(204) 786-9463, fax (204) 783-3699, bernie.wiebe@uwinnipeg.ca, www.uwinnipeg.ca/~msc

BA IN CONFLICT RESOLUTION STUDIES ▪ The Conflict Resolution Studies Program emphasizes the need to understand the parameters of the transition from conflict to violence,
and encourages appreciation for appropriate dispute responses. It is a three- year BA degree
program, with opportunities for special laboratory training and practicum experience. There
is a good mix of Canadian and foreign CRS majors. [ID:5399]

YORK UNIVERSITY—INTERNATIONAL PROFILE
YORK UNIVERSITY
4700 Keele Street, North York, Ontario M3J 1P3; (416) 736-2100, fax (416) 736-5700, www.yorku.ca

International programs and research centres in this chapter: 15
Number of students: 40,000 Percentage of international students: 4%

International focus: The international focus of York University is international business. York's international areas of expertise are also international development, international
political economy, international public policy, and environmental studies. York University is
known internationally for its Osgoode Hall Law School, Schulich School of Business, Faculty
of Environmental Studies, Faculty of Fine Arts, Faculty of Education, Political Economy,
History, Centre for Research on Latin American and the Caribbean, Joint Centre for Asia
Pacific Studies, and Centre for International and Security Studies.

International offices: York International assists the university community in the identification and development of international research, scholarly opportunities and linkages; it
encourages and promotes the participation of the York community in international education, including research and study abroad opportunities. At the university's International
Students' Advisor Office, students may obtain information on academic exchanges while
international students receive assistance on both academic and non-academic concerns.

Language programs within Area Studies described in this chapter: Jewish
Studies Program; Latin American and Caribbean Studies Program; East Asian Studies Pro-
gram; Centre for Research on Latin America and the Caribbean (CERLAC); African Studies
Program. **Other language programs:** BA, BA (honours), Certificate of proficiency in
German; BA, BA (honours), Certificate of proficiency in Italian; Certificate of proficiency in
Japanese; BA (honours) in Modern Languages and Linguistics; BA, Certificate of proficiency
in Russian; BA, BA (honours) in Spanish. [ID:6669]

YORK UNIVERSITY—AREA STUDIES
African Studies Program
Coordinator, African Studies Program, Founder's College, Room 220, York University, 4700 Keele
Street, North York, Ontario M3J 1P3; (416) 736-5148 ext. 66905, fax (416) 736-5732, www.yorku.ca

BA IN AFRICAN STUDIES ▪ The purpose of the African Studies Program is to enable
students to pursue studies on Africa through a series of courses chosen from a variety of
disciplines. The diverse thematic concerns, combined with the program's concern for the
material and cultural well-being of the people of Africa, constitute an exciting, interdisciplinary enquiry into Africa's historic and contemporary role in world affairs. Students who
wish to major in African Studies must register in the honours double major program in the
Faculty of Arts. [ID:5404]

YORK UNIVERSITY—AREA STUDIES
Jewish Studies Program
Coordinator, Jewish Studies Program, York University, Vanier 260, 4700 Keele Street,
North York, Ontario M3J 1P3; (416) 736-5823, fax (416) 736-5823, www.yorku.ca/research/cjs

BA IN JEWISH STUDIES ▪ The BA in Jewish Studies at York University is offered through
the Centre of Jewish Studies. Faculty research interests range from ancient Israel to contemporary Jewry, but the modern thrust and interdisciplinary nature of the centre make it dis-
tinctive. Courses are offered in textual studies, history, language, literature, and the social
sciences. [ID:6587]

YORK UNIVERSITY—AREA STUDIES
East Asian Studies Program
Administrative Assistant, East Asian Studies Program, York University,
Room 202B, Founders College, 4700 Keele Street, North York, Ontario M3J 1P3;
(416) 736-5148 ext. 33058, fax (416) 736-5732, easp@yorku.ca, www.yorku.ca/dept/easp

BA (honours) IN EAST ASIAN STUDIES ▪ The East Asian Studies Program offers a varied
approach to the study of China and Japan. Degree programs have been designed to present
the broadest range of choices to suit students' academic interests and career aspirations.
Although the program's focus is modern, all students are required to complete course work
in pre-modern topics. Language training in either Chinese or Japanese is required for all
degrees except the honours minor. The centre also encourages students to avoid undue
concentration on China or Japan. Visit their web site for information on degree requirements, course descriptions and schedules, the East Asian Studies Students' Association and
the Jerome Ch'en East Asian Studies Reading Room, and on alumni and faculty. [ID:5406]

YORK UNIVERSITY—AREA STUDIES
Latin American and Caribbean Studies Program
Coordinator, Latin American and Caribbean Studies Program,
York University, 314 Founder's College, North York, Ontario M3J 1P3;
(416) 736-5148 ext. 66939, fax (416) 736-5732, pidahosa@yorku.ca, www.yorku.ca

BA (honours) IN LATIN AMERICAN AND CARIBBEAN STUDIES ▪ The Program in Latin
American and Caribbean Studies is an interdisciplinary honours program (double major)
combining courses in anthropology, economics, history, humanities, political studies, social
science, sociology, and Spanish. Students must satisfy a language requirement. The program
also has an exchange agreement with the University of the West Indies. [ID:5407]

YORK UNIVERSITY—AREA STUDIES
Centre for Research on
Latin America and the Caribbean (CERLAC)
Director, Centre for Research on Latin America and the Caribbean (CERLAC),
York University, 240 York Lanes, 4700 Keele Street,, North York, Ontario M3J 1P3;
(416) 736-5237, fax (416) 736-5737, cerlac@yorku.ca, www.yorku.ca

GRADUATE DIPLOMA IN LATIN AMERICAN AND CARIBBEAN STUDIES ▪ The Centre
for Research on Latin America and the Caribbean (CERLAC) is an interdisciplinary research
unit concerned with the economic development, political and social organization, and cultural contributions of Latin America and the Caribbean. The centre works to build academic
links between these regions and Canada; to inform researchers, policy advisors, and the
public on matters concerning the regions; and to assist in the development of research and
teaching institutions that directly benefit the people of the regions. CERLAC offers a
graduate diploma program to any student currently enrolled in a York University graduate
degree program. Diploma requirements are: concurrent completion of an MA or PhD at
York University; a speaking ability in a language needed for research in Latin America or the

Caribbean (other than English); experience in Latin America and the Caribbean; two research papers, one of which can be the candidate's thesis or dissertation, which address problems or issues related to the area; and an examination designed to test breadth of knowledge about Latin America and the Caribbean. [ID:5405]

YORK UNIVERSITY—AREA STUDIES
Centre for Jewish Studies
Director, Centre for Jewish Studies, York University, Vanier 260, 4700 Keele Street, North York, Ontario M3J 1P3; (416) 736-5823, fax (416) 736-5823, michaelb@yorku.ca, www.yorku.ca/research/cjs

RESEARCH CENTRE ▪ The Centre for Jewish Studies is an interdisciplinary research and teaching unit at York University. It has exchange programs with Hebrew University, Rostov University, Saratov State University, and Glasgow University. Through the centre, scholarships are available to York University students for study in Israel. [ID:6583]

YORK UNIVERSITY—AREA STUDIES
Joint Centre for Asia Pacific Studies
DIrector, Joint Centre for Asia Pacific Studies, York University, Suite 270, York Lanes, 4700 Keele Street, North York, Ontario M3J 1P3; (416) 736-5784, fax (416) 736-5688, jcaps@yorku.ca, www.yorku.ca

RESEARCH CENTRE ▪ The University of Toronto - York University Joint Centre for Asia Pacific Studies is the largest university-based research centre in Canada focusing on the Asia Pacific. The centre's objectives are to advance academic study of the Asia Pacific region by encouraging research and publication, supporting faculty and staff appointments, assisting language training, developing library materials, and fostering exchange with Asian institutions. The centre's activities include the ASEAN-ISIS Cooperation Program, the Asian Business Studies Program, the Canada Hong Kong Resource Centre, and several other security projects. The centre also publishes books, monographs, research reports and conference proceedings in addition to organizing seminars and workshops. [ID:6584]

YORK UNIVERSITY—DEVELOPMENT STUDIES
Centre for Refugee Studies
Director, Centre for Refugee Studies, York University, Suite 322, York Lanes, 4700 Keele Street, North York, Ontario M3J 1P3; (416) 736-5663, fax (416) 736-5837, www.yorku.ca

GENERAL CERTIFICATE & GRADUATE DIPLOMA IN REFUGEE AND MIGRATION STUDIES ▪ The General Certificate or Graduate Diploma in Refugee Studies is awarded through various faculties to students enrolled in undergraduate or graduate programs who, in addition to completing all degree requirements, also complete courses and a thesis or dissertation with focus on refugee and migration issues. Students wishing to study for the General Certificate or the Graduate Diploma must already be enrolled in an undergraduate or graduate program at York University. [ID:5409]

YORK UNIVERSITY—DEVELOPMENT STUDIES
Faculty of Environmental Studies
Coordinator, External Relations, Faculty of Environmental Studies, York University, 4700 Keele Street, North York, Ontario M3J 1P3; (416) 736-5252, fax (416) 736-5679, fesinfo@yorku.ca, www.yorku.ca/faculty/fes

BES (honours), MES & PhD: concentration in Global Development ▪ The Faculty of Environmental Studies offers three interdisciplinary, flexible and individualized programs leading to a bachelor's (BES), master's (MES) or doctoral (PhD) degree in Environmental Studies. The faculty's broad definition of environment encompasses the social, built, and organizational, as well as natural environments. Faculty members and students have participated in many international projects, both as members of interdisciplinary teams and as individuals. Several large-scale projects are or have been funded by the Canadian International Development Agency (CIDA), the International Development Research Centre (IDRC) and similar organizations in Africa, Asia, Latin America, and the Caribbean. Students interested in global development at the undergraduate level study under the theme area "Global Development, Peace and Justice," while students at the graduate level develop an area of concentration reflecting their particular interdisciplinary focus. York University's web site offers specific information on each degree program, requirements, length of study, faculty member profiles, publications, and areas of concentration. [ID:5408]

YORK UNIVERSITY—INTERNATIONAL BUSINESS
Schulich School of Business
Director, Schulich School of Business, York University, 4700 Keele Street, North York, Ontario M3J 1P3; (416) 736-5942, fax (416) 650-3552, intl@bus.yorku.ca, www.bus.yorku.ca/program/imba

INTERNATIONAL MBA ▪ Established in 1989, York's International MBA educates and trains Canadians and visa students to be effective international managers. This full-time, 24-month program consists of: a strong core curriculum in management; focused international courses; second language training; and specialized study of a major international region, as well as a country from that region. During the second year, all students participate in a four-month work internship overseas. Most students also study at a business school overseas for another four-month period. [ID:5410]

YORK UNIVERSITY—INTERNATIONAL LAW
Osgoode Hall Law School
Student Services, York University, 4700 Keele Street,
North York, Ontario M3J 1P3; (416) 736-5040, fax (416) 736-5736, www.yorku.ca

LLB: concentration in International and Comparative Law or Immigration and Refugee Law ▪ The undergraduate law program at Osgoode Hall Law School offers students a concentration in international and comparative law and an advanced intensive program, including a clinical placement, in immigration and refugee law. Students at Osgoode can benefit from a variety of international exchange agreements between York University and law schools in Sweden, China, France, Japan, and Italy. [ID:5411]

YORK UNIVERSITY—INTERNATIONAL STUDIES
Department of Political Science
Chairperson, Department of Political Science, York University, Room S672, Ross Bldg., 4700 Keele Street, North York, Ontario M3J 1P3; (416) 736-5265, fax (416) 736-5686, www.yorku.ca/dept/polisc/

BA (honours), MA & PhD IN POLITICAL SCIENCE: concentration in International Relations ▪ The international relations concentration at York University is divided into four main areas: foreign policy analysis, strategic studies, international political economy, and international organizations and public law. Each of the four areas represents a variety of courses and research opportunities supported by faculty and individual professors' expertise. The program emphasizes both theories of international relations and the substance of international practice. [ID:5412]

YORK UNIVERSITY—INTERNATIONAL STUDIES
International Studies Program
Coordinator, International Studies Program, Glendon College,
York University, Room 160, York Hall, 2275 Bayview Ave.,
Toronto, Ontario M4N 3M6; (416) 487-6704, fax (416) 487-6851, ilst@glendon.yorku.ca, www.yorku.ca

BA (honours) IN INTERNATIONAL STUDIES ▪ The International Studies Program at Glendon College, the bilingual campus of York University, enables students to develop a sophisticated and systematic understanding of the problems, paradoxes, and potentialities of international society. Glendon College offers a variety of courses in history, economics, sociology, Hispanic studies, and political science which are taught in both English and French. Students enrolled in International Studies must learn a third language. Each year the program accepts 100 students who have the option of participating in an array of activities sponsored by the International Studies Students' Association. [ID:5413]

YORK UNIVERSITY—INTERNATIONAL STUDIES
Centre for Research in Earth and Space Science (CRESS)
Director, Centre for Research in Earth and Space Science (CRESS),
York University, 4700 Keele Street, North York, Ontario M3J 1P3;
(416) 736-5247, fax (416) 736-5626, www.yorku.ca/faculty/grads/gradhome.ca

RESEARCH CENTRE ▪ The Centre for Research in Earth and Space Science (CRESS) has operated since 1965. Based within the Faculty of Science, this research unit has an associated graduate program (MSc and PhD). Its mission is to support research by scientists with interests in near-Earth space, atmospheric science, planetary science, astronomy and astro physics, remote sensing of the Earth's surface, and atmosphere and earth sciences including geodynamics. Active research projects are funded by, among others, the Canadian Space Agency, NASA, and the Institute for Space and Terrestrial Science. Personnel includes 40 professors, 20 non-faculty members, and 30 graduate students. [ID:5415]

YORK UNIVERSITY—PEACE/CONFLICT STUDIES
Centre for International and Security Studies
Deputy Director, Centre for International and Security Studies,
York University, 3rd Floor, York Lanes, 4700 Keele Street, North York,
Ontario M3J 1P3; (416) 736-5156, fax (416) 736-5752, yciss@yorku.ca, www.yorku.ca/ciss

GRADUATE DIPLOMA IN STRATEGIC STUDIES ▪ This diploma program, the first of its kind in Canada, provides York MA and PhD students with the opportunity to specialize in Strategic Studies, and to have this specialization noted on their transcripts. The diploma is awarded concurrently with the degrees for which the student is registered. Students must compose a major research paper, thesis, or dissertation, supervised by a member of the Faculty of Graduate Studies affiliated with the Centre for International and Security Studies, on a topic approved by the director of the diploma program. Visit their web site for information on the centre's activities. [ID:5416]

International Studies Abroad

The following list of 110 international studies programs from around the world is intended as a guide to assist you in your selection of an overseas university. Based on the recommendations of academics and professionals, the list comprises eight areas of study. These areas are Intercultural Studies, International Business, International Studies/Affairs, Development Studies, International Law, Peace/Conflict Studies, International Education, and International Health.

We focus on schools with good reputations, where the language of instruction is either English or French, and include a variety of programs from many world regions. Forty of the universities are based in Western Europe, 34 are based in the USA, while the remaining 36 are located in Africa, Asia, the Caribbean, the Middle East, and the Pacific region. Degrees or courses from abroad may not always be recognised by Canadian universities (particularly from the South), however, we've included them to encourage you to gain invaluable crosscultural experience.

This list provides a solid point of departure for your investigation into the exciting world of International Studies overseas. (For other information see Chapter 14, Study Abroad.)

Development Studies

AUSTRALIAN NATIONAL UNIVERSITY
National Centre for Development Studies

MA IN ECONOMIC DEVELOPMENT, ENVIRON-MENTAL MANAGEMENT AND DEVELOPMENT & DEVELOPMENT ADMINISTRATION ▪ Australian Development Studies Network, Australian National University, P.O. Box 4, Canberra A.C.T. 2601, AUSTRALIA; (61) (6) 249 2466, fax (61) (6) 257 2886, development.network@ncds.anu.edu.au, www.anu.edu.au [ID:7134]

CORNELL UNIVERSITY
Mario Einaudi Center
for International Studies

MASTERS OF PROFESSIONAL STUDIES (MPS) IN INTERNATIONAL DEVELOPMENT ▪ Director, Mario Einaudi Center for International Studies, Cornell University, 170 Iris Hall, Ithaca, NY, 14853-7601, USA; (607) 255-6370, fax (607) 254-5000, helpdesk@cornell.edu, www.cornell.edu [ID:5461]

UNIVERSITY OF EAST ANGLIA
School of Development Studies

MA IN DEVELOPMENT STUDIES ▪ Manager of Post Graduate Programs, University of East Anglia, Norwich NR4 7TJ, UK; (44) (1603) 592-331, fax (44) (1603) 451-999, s.simpson@uea.ac.uk [ID:5431]

UNIVERSITY OF GUYANA
Institute of Development Studies

POSTGRADUATE DIPLOMA IN DEVELOPMENT STUDIES ▪ Department Chair, Department of Political Science and Law, Faculty of Social Sciences, University of Guyana. P.O. Box 101110, Georgetown, GUYANA; (592) (22) 5500, fax (592) (22) 2122 [ID:5449]

INSTITUTE OF SOCIAL STUDIES
Institute of Social Studies

MA, MPhil & PhD IN DEVELOPMENT STUDIES ▪ External Relations Officer, Institute of Social Studies, P.O. Box 90733, 2509 LS, The Hague, NETHER-LANDS; (31) (70) 351-0100, fax (31) (70) 354-9851, promotions@niss.nl, www.iss.nl [ID:5472]

INTERNATIONAL INSTITUTE
FOR POPULATION SCIENCES
Department of Development Studies

MSc IN POPULATION SCIENCES: concentration in Development Studies ▪ Director, International Institute for Population Sciences, Govandi Station Road, Deonar, Bombay, Maharashtra, 400088, INDIA; (91) (22) 556-3254, fax (91) (22) 556-3257 [ID:5443]

INTERNATIONAL
UNIVERSITY OF JAPAN
Research Institute for Asian Development

MA IN ASIAN DEVELOPMENT STUDIES ▪ Director, Office of Research Institutes, International University of Japan, Yamato-machi, Minami Uonuma-gun, Niigata 949-72, JAPAN; (81) (257) 79-1111, fax 81 (257) 79-4444, admis@iuj.ac.jp, www.iuj.ac.jp/research [ID:7129]

KOBE UNIVERSITY
Graduate School of
International Cooperation Studies

MA IN INTERNATIONAL COOPERATION STUDIES: concentration in Development Affairs ▪ Department of International Cooperation Policy Studies, Kobe University, 1-1 Rokkodai-cho, Nada-ku, Kobe-shi, Hyogo, 657, JAPAN; (81) (78) 881-1212 ext. 6512, fax (81) (78) 861-6718, kokusomu@rose.roddadai.kobe-u.ac.jp, www2.kobe-u.ac.jp [ID:7133]

LONDON SCHOOL OF
ECONOMICS AND POLITICAL SCIENCE
Development Studies Institute

MSc IN DEVELOPMENT STUDIES ▪ Director, Development Studies Institute, London School of Economics, Houghton Street, LondonWC2A 2AE, UK; (44) (171) 995-6844, fax (44) (171) 995-7425, graduate-school@lse.ac.uk, www.lse.ac.uk [ID:5425]

UNIVERSITY OF LONDON
School of Oriental and African Studies

BA, LLB & MA IN DEVELOPMENT STUDIES ▪ Registrar, University of London, Thornhaugh St., Russell Sq., LondonWC1 H 0XG, UK; (44) (171) 637 2388, fax (44) (171) 464 4211, registrar@soas.ac.uk, www.soas.ac.uk/ [ID:7130]

MASSEY UNIVERSITY
Institute of Development Studies

MA IN DEVELOPMENT STUDIES ▪ Director, Institute of Development Studies, Massey University, Private Bag 11222, Palmerston North, NEW ZEALAND; (64) (6) 356-9099, fax (64) (6) 350-5603, IDS@massey.ac.nz, www.massey.ac.nz [ID:5456]

MOSCOW STATE UNIVERSITY
Institute of Asian and African Studies

BA & MA IN PHILOLOGY; BA & MA IN HISTORY AND SOCIO-ECONOMICS ▪ Head, International Education Department, Moscow State University, 119899 Moscow, RUSSIA; (7) (095) 939-3510, fax (7) (095) 938-0165, admission@rector.msu.ru, www.rector.msu.su [ID:7131]

UNIVERSITY OF NAIROBI
Institute for Development Studies

MA IN DEVELOPMENT STUDIES ▪ Director, Institute for Development Studies, P.O. Box 31097, University of Nairobi, Nairobi, KENYA; (254) (2) 334-244 [ID:5439]

NATIONAL
UNIVERSITY OF SINGAPORE
Southeast Asian Studies Program

MA IN EAST ASIAN DEVELOPMENT STUDIES ▪ Director, Southeast Asian Studies Program, National University of Singapore, Block AS5, Level 4, 10 Kent Ridge Cres., 119260, SINGAPORE; (65) 779 1037, fax (65) 779 3409, seasec@nus.edu.sg, www.nus.sg/nusinfo [ID:7135]

SCHOOL OF
INTERNATIONAL TRAINING
School for International Training

BA IN WORLD ISSUES ▪ Admissions Office, World Issues Program, School of International Training, P.O. Box 676, Kipling Road, Battleboro, VT, 05302-0676, USA; (800) 451-4465, fax (802) 258-3500, admission.sit@worldlearning.org, www.worldlearning.org/sit/html [ID:5428]

UNIVERSITY OF SUSSEX
Department of Development Studies

MPhil & DPhil IN DEVELOPMENT STUDIES ▪ Postgraduate Admission, Sussex House, University of Sussex, Falmer, Brighton, BN1 9RH, UK; (44) (1273) 678-412, fax (44) (1273) 678-545, pg.admissions@sussex.ac.uk, www.sussex.ac.uk [ID:5481]

YOKOHAMA NATIONAL UNIVERSITY
Graduate School of
International Development Studies

PhD IN DEVELOPMENT AND MANAGEMENT; PhD IN DEVELOPMENT PUBLIC POLICY ▪ Graduate School Section, Faculty of Business Administration, Yokohama National University, 156 Tokiwadai, Hodogaya-ku, Yokohama-shi, Kanagawa, 240, JAPAN; (81) (45) 335-1451, fax (81) (45) 341-2582, www.ynu.ac.jp/ynu/ynu-e.html [ID:7132]

UNIVERSITY OF ZAMBIA
African Development Studies Program

MSc IN AFRICAN DEVELOPMENT STUDIES ▪ Director, African Development Studies Program, University of Zambia, P.O. Box 32379, Great East Road, Lusaka, ZAMBIA; (260) (1) 229-377, fax (260) (1) 253-952, www.zamnet.zm/unza/unza.html [ID:5441]

Intercultural Studies

ANTIOCH COLLEGE
The McGregor School

MA IN INTERCULTURAL STUDIES ▪ Admissions Officer, Antioch University, 800 Livermore Street, Yellow Springs, OH, 45387, USA; (513) 767-7331, fax (513) 767-1891, admissions@antioch-college.edu www.antioch-college.edu [ID:5459]

HARVARD UNIVERSITY
JFK School of Government

MA IN PUBLIC ADMINISTRATION: concentration in International Affairs ▪ Dean, JFK School of Government, Harvard University, 79 JFK Street, Cambridge, MA, 02138, USA; (617) 495-1100, fax (617) 496-1165, ksg admissions@harvard.edu, www.harvard.edu [ID:5462]

INTERNATIONAL
UNIVERSITY OF JAPAN
Institute of Middle Eastern Studies

MA IN CULTURAL STUDIES: concentration in Middle East Studies ▪ Office of Research Institutes, International University of Japan, Yamato-machi, Minami, Uonuma-gun, Niigata 949-72, JAPAN; (81) (257) 79-1111, fax 81 (257) 79-4441, admis@iuj.ac.jp, www.iuj.ac.jp [ID:7146]

KOBE UNIVERSITY
Faculty of Cross Cultural Studies

MA IN CROSS CULTURAL STUDIES ▪ Director, Faculty of Cross Cultural Studies, Kobe University, Rokkodai, Nada-ku, Kobe-shi657, JAPAN; (81) (78) 881 1212, fax (81) (78) 861 6718, office@cs.cla.kobe-u.ac.jp, www2.kobe-u.ac.jp [ID:7147]

LESLEY COLLEGE
GRADUATE SCHOOL
Intercultural Relations Program

MA IN INTERCULTURAL RELATIONS ▪ Office of Graduate Admission, Lesley College Graduate School, 29 Everett Street, Cambridge, MA, 02138-2790, USA; (617) 349-8369, fax (617) 349-8526, communic@mail.lesley.edu, www.lesley.edu [ID:5463]

UNIVERSITY OF MALAYA
Department of Malay
Socio-Cultural Studies

BA MALAY STUDIES ▪ Registrar, University of Malaya, 50603 Kuala Lumpur, MALAYSIA; (60) (3) 759-5468, fax (60) (3) 756-5466, www.cc.um.edu.my [ID:7128]

SCHOOL FOR
INTERNATIONAL TRAINING
School for International Training

MA IN INTERCULTURAL ADMINISTRATION ▪ Admissions Counsellor, School for International Training, P.O. Box 676, Kipling Road, Brattleboro, VT, 05302, USA; (802) 258-3173, fax (802) 258-3500, admission.sit@worldlearning.org, www.worldlearning.org/sit/html [ID:5466]

UNIVERSITY OF STRATHCLYDE
Centre for the Study of Public Policy

BA IN PUBLIC POLICY STUDIES ▪ Director, Centre for the Study of Public Policy, University of Strathclyde, Glasgow, Scotland, G11XH, UK; (44) (141) 548-3217, fax (44) (141) 552-4711, webperson@stracth.ac.uk, www.strath.ac.uk/departments/cspp [ID:7148]

THE SWEDISH INSTITUTE
Swedish and Cultural Studies

MA IN CULTURAL STUDIES: concentration in Swedish culture ▪ Director, Swedish Cultural Studies, The Swedish Institute, Hamngatan/kungsstradgarden, P.O. Box 7434, S-103 91 Stockholm, SWEDEN; (46) (8) 789 2000, fax (46) (8) 789 7248, webmaster@si.se, www.si.se [ID:7149]

International Business

UNIVERSITÉ D'AIX-MARSEILLE III
Faculté d'Économie Appliquée

CERTIFICATE OF APTITUDE IN BUSINESS ADMINISTRATION ▪ Director of Studies, Faculté d'Économie Appliquée, Université D'Aix-Marseille III, 3, ave. Robert Scuman, 13628 Aix-en-Provence, FRANCE; (33) (4) 42 28 0808, fax (33) (4) 42 28 0800, iae@romarin.univ-aix.fr, www.u-3mrs.fr/ulll [ID:7125]

ATENEO DE MANILA UNIVERSITY
Graduate School of Business

MBA: concentration in International Business ▪ Director of Admissions, Graduate School of Business, Ateneo de Manila University, P.O. Box 154, Manila 1009, PHILIPPINES; (63) (2) 924-4601, agsb@pusit.admu.edu.ph, www.admu.edu.ph [ID:7123]

BOND UNIVERSITY
Faculty of Humanities and Social Sciences

BA IN INTERNATIONAL BUSINESS ▪ Registrar, Bond University, Gold Coast, Queensland, 4229, AUSTRALIA; (61) (7) 5595 1024, fax (61) (7) 5595 1015, information@bond.edu.au, www.bond.edu.au [ID:5454]

UNIVERSITY OF DENVER
Graduate School
of International Studies

MA IN INTERNATIONAL MANAGEMENT ▪ Director of Administration and Student Affairs, University of Denver, Denver, CO, 80208, USA; (303) 871-2544, fax (303) 871 2456, gsisdm@du.edu, www.du.edu/gsis [ID:5470]

ERASMUS UNIVERSITY ROTTERDAM
Faculty of Business Administration

EXECUTIVE MBA; MA IN BUSINESS INFORMATICS (MBI) ▪ Dean, Faculty of Business Administration, Erasmus Universiteit Rotterdam, Burgemeester Oudlaan 50, P.O. Box 1738, 3000 DR Rotterdam, NETHERLANDS; (31) (10) 4081111, fax (31) (10) 4520204, m.wolven@fac.fbk.eur.nl, www.eur.nl/homeeng.htm [ID:7119]

HELSINKI SCHOOL OF ECONOMICS
AND BUSINESS ADMINISTRATION
Faculty of International Business

INTERNATIONAL MBA ▪ Head of Administration, Helsinki School of Economics and Business Administration, Runeberginkatu 14-16, 00100 Helsinki, FINLAND; (358) (9) 43131, fax (358) (9) 43138707, webmaster@hkkk.fi, www.hkkk.fi/ [ID:7121]

INTERNATIONAL INSTITUTE
FOR MANAGEMENT DEVELOPMENT
International Institute for
Management Development (IMD)

MBA IN INTERNATIONAL MANAGEMENT ▪ MBA Office, International Institute for Management Development, P.O. Box 915, Chemin de Bellerive 23, CH-1001, Lausanne, SWITZERLAND; (41) (21) 618-0298, fax (41) (21) 618-0707, mbainfo@imd.ch, www.imd.ch [ID:5423]

INTERNATIONAL
UNIVERSITY OF JAPAN
Intensive International Executive Program

CERTIFICATES OF COMMUNICATION, TRANSCULTURAL & MANAGEMENT TRAINING ▪ Director, Intensive International Executive Program, International University of Japan, Yamato-machi, Minami Uonuma-gun, Niigata949-72, JAPAN; (81) (257) 79-1111, fax 81 (257) 79-4444, admis@iuj.ac.jp, www.iuj.ac.jp [ID:7126]

UNIVERSITY OF LIEGE
Faculty of Business Administration

MBA: concentration in international business ▪ Dean, Place du 20-Août, 4000 Liege, Belgium; 32) (4) 66-21-11, fax (32) (4) 66-57-00, www.ulg.ac.be/homepage_en.html [ID:7118]

LIMBURG BUSINESS SCHOOL
Faculty of Business Economics

MBA & MA IN INTERNATIONAL MARKETING ▪ Administrative Director, Faculty of Business Economics, Limburg Business School, Universitaire Campus, 3590 Diepenbeek, BELGIUM; (32) (11) 26-81-11, fax (32) (11) 24-23-87, www.lgu.ac.uk/bs/limburg.htm [ID:7117]

MOSCOW STATE INSTITUTE OF INTERNATIONAL RELATIONS
Faculty of International Business Management and Administration

INTERNATIONAL MBA ▪ Dean, International Student Education, Moscow State Institute of International Relations, 76 Vernadsky Prospect, 117454 Moscow, RUSSIA; (7) (095) 434-9174, fax (7) (095) 434-9061, www.wmin.ac.uk/dal/moscow.htm [ID:7124]

NATIONAL UNIVERSITY OF SINGAPORE
Centre for Business Research and Development

BComm IN INTERNATIONAL BUSINESS ▪ Director, Centre for Business Research and Development, National University of Singapore, 10 Kent Ridge Crescent, 0511, SINGAPORE; (65) 775-6666, fax (65) 778-5281, www.nus.edu.sg [ID:5446]

NEW YORK UNIVERSITY
Stern School of Business

MBA: concentration in International Business ▪ Director, Stern School of Business, New York University, 70 Washington Square S., New York, NY, 10003, USA; (212) 998-1212, fax (212) 988-4100, sternmba@stern.nyu.edu, www.stern.nyu.edu [ID:5464]

NIJENRODE UNIVERSITY, THE NETHERLANDS BUSINESS SCHOOL
Faculty of International Business

INTERNATIONAL MBA ▪ IMBA Office, Nijenrode University, The Netherlands Business School, Straatweg 25, 3621 BG Breukelen, NETHERLANDS; (31) (346) 291211, fax (31) (346) 291300, imba@nijenrode.nl, www.nijenrode.nl/degree/imba [ID:7120]

UNIVERSITY OF PENNSYLVANIA
Wharton School of Business

MBA: concentration in International Business ▪ Graduate Division, University of Pennsylvania, Room 102, Vance Hall, 3733 Spruce Street, Philadelphia, PA, 19104-6361, USA; (215) 898-6183, fax (215) 898-0120, mba.admissions@wharton.upenn.edu, www.upenn.edu [ID:5434]

SAINT MARY'S COLLEGE
Graduate School of Business

MBA IN INTERNATIONAL BUSINESS ▪ Director of Admissions, P.O. Box 4240, Saint Mary's College of California, Moraga, CA, 94575, USA; (510) 376-4500, fax (510) 376-6521, smcmba@galileo.stmarys-ca.edu, www.stmarys-ca.edu [ID:5465]

SCHILLER INTERNATIONAL UNIVERSITY
Schiller International University

BComm: concentration in International Business ▪ Admissions Officer, Schiller International University, Bergstrasse 106, Heidelberg6900, GERMANY; (49) (6221) 49-159, fax (49) (6221) 40-2703, SIUmuriel@aol.com, www.schiller.edu/hd.html [ID:5474]

STOCKHOLM SCHOOL OF ECONOMICS
Institute of International Business

MSc IN INTERNATIONAL ECONOMY AND BUSINESS ▪ Director of Administration, Stockholm School of Economics, P.O. Box 6501, 113 83 Stockholm, SWEDEN; (46) (8) 736-90-00, fax (46) (8) 31-81-86, iibkw@hhs.se, www.hhs.se/iib [ID:7122]

THUNDERBIRD, AMERICAN GRADUATE SCHOOL OF INTERNATIONAL MANAGEMENT
American Graduate School of International Management

MA IN INTERNATIONAL MANAGEMENT (MIM) ▪ Dean of Admissions, Thunderbird, American Graduate School of International Management, 15249 North 59th Ave., Glendale, AZ, 85306, USA; (602) 978-7210, fax (602) 439-5432, t-bird@t-bird.edu, www.t-bird.edu [ID:5417]

UNIVERSITY OF WITWATERSRAND
Graduate School of Public and Development Management

MA IN BUSINESS ADMINISTRATION ▪ Chairperson, Graduate School of Public and Development Management, University of Witwatersrand, Private Bag 3, WITS 2050,, Johannesburg, REPUBLIC OF SOUTH AFRICA; (27) (11) 488-5700, fax (27) (11) 643-2729, mpatron@zeus.mgmt.wits.ac.za, www.wits.ac.za [ID:5440]

International Education

UNIVERSITY OF CALIFORNIA AT LOS ANGELES
Graduate School of Education and Information Studies

MA, PhD IN COMPARATIVE AND INTERNATIONAL EDUCATION ▪ Department Head, Graduate School of Education and Information Studies, University of California at Los Angeles, c/o Mail Services, Box 951 361, Los Angeles, CA, 90095-1361, USA; (310) 825-8326, fax (310) 825-2833, www.ucla.edu [ID:7207]

UNIVERSITY OF DURHAM
Department of Education

DOCTOR OF EDUCATION (EdD): concentration in International Education ▪ Chief Clerk's Office, University of Durham, Old Shire Hall, Durham DH1 3HP, UK; (44) (191) 374 2000, fax (44) (191) 374 3506, international.office@durham.ac.uk, www.dur.ac.uk [ID:7136]

UNIVERSITY OF STRATHCLYDE
Faculty of Education

BA IN EDUCATION: concentration in International Education ▪ Dean, Faculty of Education, University of Strathclyde, McCance Bldg., 16 Richmond St., Glasgow, Scotland, G1 1XW, UK; (44) (141) 552-4400, fax (44) (141) 552-0775, webperson@strath.ac.uk, www.strath.ac.uk [ID:7137]

UMEA UNIVERSITY
Department of Educational Measurement

PhD IN INTERNATIONAL EDUCATION ▪ Department Head, Department of Educational Measurement, UMEA University,, Besoksadress Universitetsomradet, Petrus Laestadiusvag, 901 87 Umea, SWEDEN; (46) (90) 786 5000, fax (46) (90) 786 5488, umea.universitet@adm.umu.se, www.umu.se [ID:7138]

UNIVERSITY OF VAASA
Centre for Continuing Education

DIPLOMA OF COOPERATION IN HIGHER EDUCATION AND TRAINING ▪ Course Administrator, Centre for Continuing Education, University of Vassa, Raastuvankatu 31, P.O. Box 297, 65101 Vaasa, FINLAND; (358) (6) 324 8111, fax (358) (6) 324 8488, he@uwasa.fi, www.u.wasa.fi/taky [ID:7139]

International Health

BOSTON UNIVERSITY
School of Public Health

MSc IN PUBLIC HEALTH ▪ Department Chairman, School of Public Health, Boston University, Room A-310, 80 East Concord St., Boston, Massachusetts, 02118-2394, USA; (617) 638-5234, fax (617) 638-4476, cih@bu.edu, http://web.bu.edu [ID:7142]

UNIVERSITY OF CALIFORNIA AT LOS ANGELES
School of Public Health

MA & PhD IN PUBLIC HEALTH ▪ Director, School of Public Health, University of California at Los Angeles, c/o Mail Services, Box 951 361, Los Angeles, CA, 90095-1361, USA; (310) 825-4321, fax (310) 825-2833, www.ucla.edu [ID:7208]

ERASMUS UNIVERSITY ROTTERDAM
The Netherlands Institute for Health Sciences

MSc IN EPIDEMIOLOGY, CLINICAL EPIDEMIOLOGY, HEALTH SERVICE RESEARCH, MEDICAL INFORMATICS, AND PUBLIC HEALTH ▪ Director, The Netherlands Institute for Health Sciences, Erasmus University Rotterdam, P.O. Box 1738, 3000 DR, Rotterdam, NETHERLANDS; (31) (10) 408-1111, fax (31) (10) 452-0204, m.wolven@fac.fbk.eur.nl, www.eur.nl/homeeng.htm [ID:7206]

THE HEBREW UNIVERSITY OF JERUSALEM
School of Public Health and Community Medicine

MSc IN PUBLIC HEALTH AND COMMUNITY MEDICINE ▪ Office of Academic Affairs, Canadian Friends of the Hebrew University of Jerusalem, Suite 5024, 3080 Younge Street, Toronto, Ontario M4N 3N1; (416) 485-8000, fax (416) 485-8565, mlitvack@cfhu.org, www.cfhu.org [ID:7140]

JOHNS HOPKINS UNIVERSITY
School of Hygiene and Public Health

MSc IN PUBLIC HEALTH ▪ Admissions Office, School of Hygiene and Public Health, The Johns Hopkins University, 615 North Wolfe Street, Baltimore, Maryland, 21205, USA; (410) 955-3543, webadmin@jhsph.edu, www.jhu.edu [ID:7144]

UNIVERSITY OF LIVERPOOL
Liverpool School of Tropical Medicine

MA IN TROPICAL MEDICINE; MA IN COMMUNITY HEALTH ▪ Director, Liverpool School of Tropical Medicine, University of Liverpool, Pembroke Place, LiverpoolL3 5QA, UK; (44) (151) 708 9393, fax (44) (151) 708 8733, www.liv.ac.uk/lstm/lstm.html [ID:7143]

UNIVERSITY OF LONDON
The London School of
Hygiene and Tropical Medicine

MSc: concentrations in Epidemiology and Population Health, Infectious and Tropical Diseases, and Public Health and Policy ▪ Department Head, The London School of Hygiene and Tropical Medicine, University of London, Keppel St., LondonWC1E 7HT, UK; (44) (171) 636 8636, fax (44) (171) 436 5389, www.lshtm.ac.uk [ID:7145]

UNIVERSITY OF MALAYA
Faculty of Medicine

MSc IN PUBLIC HEALTH ▪ Dean, Faculty of Medicine, University of Malaya, Pantai Valley, 59100 Kuala Lumpur, MALAYSIA; (60) (3) 756-0022, fax (60) (3) 755-2975, www.cc.um.edu.my [ID:7141]

International Law

UNIVERSITY OF
CALIFORNIA, BERKELEY
Boalt Hall School of Law

LLM IN INTERNATIONAL LAW ▪ Dean, Boalt Hall School of Law, University of California, Berkeley, CA, 97420, USA; (510) 642-6000, fax (510) 643-8245, webmanager@www.law.berkely.edu, www.law.berkeley.edu [ID:7160]

UNIVERSITY OF CAMBRIDGE
Lauterpacht Research
Centre for International Law

LLM IN INTERNATIONAL LAW ▪ Director, Lauterpacht Research Centre for International Law, Lauterpacht Residence, University of Cambridge, 5 Cranmer Road, CambridgeCB3 9BL, UK; (44) (1223) 335 358, fax (44) (1223) 300 406, gh10008@hermes.cam.ac.uk, www.law.cam.ac.uk [ID:7161]

COLUMBIA UNIVERSITY
IN THE CITY OF NEW YORK
Columbia University School of Law

LLM IN INTERNATIONAL LAW ▪ Dean of Admissions, Columbia University in the City of New York, 435 West 116 St., New York, NY, 10027, USA; (212) 854-2674, fax (212) 854-7946, webmaster@columbia.edu, www.columbia.edu/cu/law [ID:7159]

UNIVERSITY OF ESSEX
Human Rights Centre

MA IN THE THEORY AND PRACTICE OF HUMAN RIGHTS; LLM IN INTERNATIONAL HUMAN RIGHTS LAW ▪ Director, Human Rights Centre, University of Essex, Wivenhoe Park, ColchesterCO4 3SQ, UK; (44) (1206) 872-587, fax (44) (1206) 873-428, law@essex.ac.uk, www.sx.ac.uk/law [ID:5476]

UNIVERSITY OF EXETER
Department of Law

LLM IN INTERNATIONAL PUBLIC AND REGULATORY LAW ▪ Departmental Secretary, Department of Law, University of Exeter, Amory Building, Rennes Drive, ExeterEX4 4RJ, UK; (44) (1392) 263-380, fax (44) (1392) 263-381, N.L.Symons@ex.ac.uk, www.exeter.ac.uk [ID:5477]

INTERNATIONAL
INSTITUTE OF HUMAN RIGHTS
International Institute of Human Rights

CERTIFICATE OF TRAINING IN THE PROGRAM IN HUMAN RIGHTS ▪ General Secretary, International Institute of Human Rights, 2, allée Zaepfel, F-67000 Strasbourg, FRANCE; (33) (3) 88-45-84-45, fax (33) (3) 88-45-84-50, iidhiihr@mail.srv.fr [ID:5473]

UNIVERSITY OF NOTTINGHAM
International Law Program

LLM IN PUBLIC INTERNATIONAL LAW; LLM IN INTERNATIONAL COMMERCIAL LAW; LLM IN INTERNATIONAL LAW AND ARMED CONFLICT ▪ Director, Department of Law, University of Nottingham, University Park, NottinghamNG7 2RD, UK; (44) (1602) 515-700, fax (44) (1602) 515-696, law@nottingham.ac.uk, www.nott.ac.uk [ID:5479]

UNIVERSITY OF SAN DIEGO
Institute on International
and Comparative Law

LLM IN INTERNATIONAL LAW & COMPARATIVE LAW ▪ Graduate Programs, School of Law, University of San Diego,, 5998 Alcalá Park, San Diego, CA, 92110-2492, USA; (619) 260-4600, fax (619) 260-2218, llminfo@acusd.edu, www.acusds.edu [ID:5435]

UNIVERSITY OF SYDNEY
Faculty of Law

LLM IN INTERNATIONAL LAW ▪ Director, Faculty of Law, University of Sydney, 173 Phillip Street, Sydney, NSW, 2000, AUSTRALIA; (61) (2) 9351 0351, fax (61) (2) 9351 0200, stuserv@law.usyd.edu.au, www.law.usyd.edu.au [ID:7162]

UNIVERSITY COLLEGE OF WALES
Department of Law

POSTGRADUATE DIPLOMA IN INTERNATIONAL LAW AND RELATIONS ▪ Postgraduate Admissions, University College of Wales, Hugh Owen Building, Penglais, Aberystwyth, CeredigionSY23 3DY, UK; (44) (1970) 622-712, fax (44) (1970) 622-729,

csh@uk.ac.aberystwyth, www.aber.ac.uk/~law
[ID:5475]

International Studies/Affairs

AMERICAN UNIVERSITY
School of International Service

MA IN INTERNATIONAL AFFAIRS ▪ Dean, School of International Service, American University, 4400 Massachusetts Ave. N.W., Washington, DC, 20016-6014, USA; (202) 885-1600, fax (202) 885-2494, afa@american.edu, www.american.edu [ID:5418]

AUSTRALIAN NATIONAL UNIVERSITY
Department of International Relations

MA & PhD IN INTERNATIONAL RELATIONS ▪ Director of Studies, Australian National University, Canberra0200, AUSTRALIA; (61) (6) 249 2167, fax (61) (6) 279 8010, main@anu.edu.ac, www.anu.edu.au [ID:7166]

BILKENT UNIVERSITY
International Relations Department

MA IN INTERNATIONAL RELATIONS ▪ Departmental Head, International Relations Department, Bilkent University, Maltepe06572, TURKEY; (90) (4) 266-4000, fax (90) (4) 266-4127, gradinfo@bilkent.edu.training, www.bilkent.edu.tr [ID:5452]

BRANDEIS UNIVERSITY
The Lemberg Program in International Economics and Finance

MA IN INTERNATIONAL ECONOMICS AND FINANCE ▪ Admissions Officer, Brandeis University, P.O. Box 9110, Waltham, MA, 02257-9110, USA; (617) 736-2250, fax (617) 736-2263, admissions@Lemberg.brandeis.edu, www.brandeis.edu [ID:5460]

UNIVERSITY OF CALIFORNIA AT LOS ANGELES
International Affairs Program

MA IN INTERNATIONAL STUDIES ▪ Departmental Chair, International Affairs Program, c/o Mail Services, Box 951361, Los Angeles, CA, 90095-1361, USA; (310) 825-4321, fax (310) 825-2833, www.ucla.edu [ID:5468]

UNIVERSITY OF CALIFORNIA SAN DIEGO
Graduate School of International Relations and Pacific Studies

MA IN PACIFIC INTERNATIONAL AFFAIRS ▪ Dean of Student Affairs, University of California San Diego, La Jolla, CA, 92093-0520, USA; (619) 534-5914, fax (619) 534-3939, kwaller@ucsd.edu, www.ucds.edu [ID:5430]

CENTRAL EUROPEAN UNIVERSITY, BUDAPEST
Department of International Relations

MA & PhD IN INTERNATIONAL RELATIONS AND EUROPEAN STUDIES ▪ Department Coordinator, Department of International Relations, Central European University, Nador U., 9-1051 Budpest, HUNGARY; (36) (1) 327-3000, fax (36) (1) 327-3001, www.ceu.hu/ires/iresdir.html [ID:7163]

UNIVERSITY OF CHICAGO
Committee on International Relations

MA IN INTERNATIONAL STUDIES ▪ Preceptor, University of Chicago, 5828 South University Ave., Chicago, IL, 60637, USA; (773) 702-8073, fax (773) 702-1689, cir1@cicero.spc.uchicago.edu, www.uchicago.edu [ID:5469]

COLUMBIA UNIVERSITY
School of International and Public Affairs

MA IN INTERNATIONAL AFFAIRS ▪ Office of Admissions, Columbia University, Suite 408 IAB, 420 West 118th Street, New York, NY, 10027, USA; (212) 854-6216, fax (212) 854-3010, lm259@columbia.edu, www.columbia.edu [ID:5419]

GEORGE WASHINGTON UNIVERSITY
Elliot School of International Relations

MA IN INTERNATIONAL RELATIONS ▪ Office of Graduate Admissions, George Washington University, 101 Stuart Hall, 2013 G Street N.W., Washington, DC, 20052, USA; (202) 994-7050, fax (202) 994-9537, esiagrad@gwis2.circ.gwu.edu, www.gwu.edu [ID:5420]

GEORGETOWN UNIVERSITY
Edmund A. Walsh
School of Foreign Service

MSc IN FOREIGN SERVICE ▪ Director of MSFS Admissions, P.O. Box 571028, Georgetown University, Washington, DC, 20057-1028, USA; (202) 687-5763, fax (202) 687-5116, www.georgetown.edu [ID:5421]

GRADUATE INSTITUTE OF INTERNATIONAL STUDIES
Graduate Institute of International Studies

DES, PhD & LICENCE IN INTERNATIONAL RELATIONS ▪ General Secretary, Graduate Institute of International Studies, P.O. Box 36, CH-1211, Geneva 21, SWITZERLAND; (41) (22) 731-1730, fax (41) (22) 738-4306, info@hei.unige.ch, http://heiwww.unige.ch [ID:5422]

GRIFFITH UNIVERSITY
International Studies Program

BA IN INTERNATIONAL STUDIES ▪ Director, International Studies Program, Griffith University, Nathan, Brisbane, Queensland, 4111, AUSTRALIA; (61) (7) 3875-7200, fax (61) (7) 3875-5280, ugais@ais.gu.edu.au, www.gu.edu.au [ID:5455]

THE HEBREW
UNIVERSITY OF JERUSALEM
Rothberg School for Overseas Students

MA IN INTERNATIONAL RELATIONS ▪ Office of Academic Affairs, Canadian Friends of the Hebrew University of Jerusalem, Suite 5024, 3080 Yonge Street, Toronto, Ontario M4N 3N1; (416) 485-8000, fax (416) 485-8565, mlitvack@cfhu.org, www.cfhu.org [ID:5453]

INTERNATIONAL
UNIVERSITY OF JAPAN
Graduate School of International Relations

MA IN INTERNATIONAL RELATIONS ▪ Coordinator, Graduate School of International Relations, International University of Japan, Yamato-machi, Minamiuonuma-gun, Niigata-ken, 949-72, JAPAN; (81) (257) 79-1200, fax (81) (257) 79-1187, admis@iuj.ac.jp, www.iuj.ac.jp [ID:5444]

JAWAHARLAL NEHRU UNIVERSITY
Centre for International Politics,
Organizations and Disarmament

MA IN INTERNATIONAL RELATIONS ▪ Director, Centre for International Politics, Organizations and Disarmament, Jawaharlal Nehru University, New Mehrauli Road, New Delhi110067, INDIA; (91) (11) 667-676, www.nyu.edu/jnu [ID:5445]

JOHNS HOPKINS UNIVERSITY
Paul H. Nitze School of
Advanced International Studies

MA & PhD IN INTERNATIONAL RELATIONS ▪ Dean of Admissions, The Johns Hopkins University, 1740 Massachusetts Ave. N.W., Washington, DC, 20036, USA; (202) 663-5600, fax (202) 663-5615, admissions@mail.jhuwash.jhu.edu, www.jhu.edu [ID:5424]

UNIVERSITY OF LEEDS
Institute for International Studies

MA IN INTERNATIONAL STUDIES ▪ Postgraduate Admissions Secretary, c/o Director, Institute for International Studies, University of Leeds, Leeds LS2 9JT, UK; (44) (113) 233-6843, fax (44) (113) 233-6784, l.j.tams@leeds.ac.uk, www.leeds.ac.uk [ID:5478]

LONDON SCHOOL OF ECONOMICS
AND POLITICAL SCIENCE
Suntory and Toyota International Centre
for Economic and Related Disciplines

MA IN INTERNATIONAL RELATIONS ▪ Graduate Admissions, London School of Economics and Political Science, P.O. Box 13420, Houghton Street, LondonWCZA 2AR, UK; (44) (171) 955 6699, fax (44) (171) 242 2357, graduate school@lse.ac.uk, www.lse.ac.uk [ID:7168]

MONTEREY INSTITUTE OF
INTERNATIONAL STUDIES
Monterey Institute of International Studies

MA IN INTERNATIONAL POLICY STUDIES; MBA IN INTERNATIONAL MANAGEMENT ▪ Admissions Office, Monterey Institute of International Studies, 425 Van Buren Street, Monterey, CA, 93940, USA; (408) 647-4100, fax (408) 647-4199, admit@miis.edu, www.miis.edu [ID:5426]

UNIVERSITY OF OXFORD
Faculty of Social Studies

MPhil IN INTERNATIONAL RELATIONS ▪ University Offices, University of Oxford, Wellington Square, OxfordOX1 2JD, UK; (44) (1865) 270-0060, fax (44) (1865) 270-708, graduateadmissions@admin.ox.ac.uk, www.ox.ac.uk [ID:5432]

UNIVERSITY OF THE PHILIPPINES
International Relations Program

MA IN INTERNATIONAL RELATIONS ▪ Dean, College of Social Sciences and Philosphy, University of the Philippines, Quezon City 1101Diliman, PHILIPPINES; (63) (2) 982-471, fax (63) (2) 961-572, www.upd.edu.ph/~kssp [ID:5448]

PRINCETON UNIVERSITY
Woodrow Wilson School
of Public and International Affairs

MA IN PUBLIC ADMINISTRATION & INTERNATIONAL AFFAIRS ▪ Admissions Officer, Princeton University, Robertson Hall, Princeton, NJ, 08544-1013, USA; (609) 258-4836, fax (609) 258-2095, admiss@wws.princeton.edu, www.princeton.edu [ID:5427]

QUAID-I-AZAM UNIVERSITY
Department of International Relations

MA IN INTERNATIONAL RELATIONS ▪ Registrar, P.O. Box 1090, Quaid-I-Azam University of Islamabad, Islamabad, PAKISTAN; (92) (51) 824-801 [ID:5447]

UNIVERSITY OF READING
Graduate School of
European and International Studies

MA IN INTERNATIONAL STUDIES ▪ Admissions Officer, Department of Politics, University of Reading, Whiteknights, P.O. Box 218, ReadingRG6 6AA, UK; (44) (118) 931-8378, fax (44) (118) 975-5442, c.bluth@reading.ac.uk, www.reading.ac.uk [ID:5480]

UNIVERSITY OF SOUTHERN CALIFORNIA
School of International Relations

MA & PhD IN INTERNATIONAL AFFAIRS ▪ Graduate Admissions, University of Southern California, Los Angeles, CA, 90089-0913, USA; (213) 740-1111, gradapp@afs2000a.usc.edu, www.usc.edu [ID:5471]

UNIVERSITY OF SYDNEY
School of Asia Pacific Studies

GRADUATE DIPLOMA & GRADUATE CERTIFICATE IN INTERNATIONAL STUDIES ▪ Postgraduate Advisor, University of Sydney, Merewether Building, H04, SydneyNSW 2006, AUSTRALIA; (61) (2) 9351 3086, fax (61) (2) 9351 4433, info@io.usyd.edu.au, www.usyd.edu.au [ID:5457]

TUFTS UNIVERSITY
Fletcher School of Law and Diplomacy

MA & PhD IN LAW AND DIPLOMACY ▪ Director of Admissions, Tufts University, Medford, MA, 02155, USA; (617) 627-3700 ext. 2410, fax (617) 627-3712, admissions@staff.fletcher.tufts.edu, www.tufts.edu [ID:5467]

VICTORIA UNIVERSITY OF WELLINGTON
Department of Politics

MA IN INTERNATIONAL RELATIONS ▪ Admissions, Department of Politics, P.O. Box 600, Victoria University, Wellington, NEW ZEALAND; (64) (4) 471-5351, fax (64) (4) 496-5414, Graduate-students@vuw.ac.nz, www.vuw.ac.nz [ID:5458]

UNIVERSITY COLLEGE OF WALES, ABERYSTWYTH
Department of International Politics

MA IN INTERNATIONAL POLITICS, STRATEGIC STUDIES, INTERNATIONAL RELATIONS & INTERNATIONAL HISTORY ▪ Director, Department of International Politics, University College of Wales, Penglais, Aberystwyth, Wales, SY23 3DA, UK; (44) (1970) 622 691, fax (44) (1970) 622 709, inpwww@aber.ac.uk, www.aber.ac.uk/~inpwww [ID:7167]

WOODROW WILSON INTERNATIONAL CENTER FOR SCHOLARS
Division of International Studies

MA IN INTERNATIONAL STUDIES ▪ Director, Division of International Studies, Woodrow Wilson International Center for Scholars, 1000 Jefferson Drive S.W., Washington, DC, 20560, USA; (202) 357-2968, fax (202) 357-4439, http://wwics.si.edu [ID:7164]

UNIVERSITY OF ZIMBABWE
Social Studies Program in International Relations

MSc IN INTERNATIONAL RELATIONS ▪ Coordinator, Social Studies Program in International Relations, P.O. Box MP 167, University of Zimbabwe, Mount Pleasant, ZIMBABWE; (263) (4) 303-211, fax (263) (4) 732-828, www.zimweb.com/Education.html [ID:5442]

Peace/Conflict Studies

UNIVERSITY OF BRADFORD
Department of Peace Studies

MA, POST GRADUATE DIPLOMA IN PEACE STUDIES ▪ Director, Department of Peace Studies, University of Bradford, West YorkshireBD1 1DP, UK; (44) (1274) 385235, fax (44) (1274) 385240, p.f.rogers@bradford.ac.uk, www.brad.ac.uk/acad/peace/home.html [ID:7209]

FINLAND FUTURES RESEARCH CENTRE
World Future Studies Federation

DIPLOMA IN WORLD FUTURE STUDIES ▪ Head, World Future Studies Federation, P.O. Box 110, Finland Futures Research Institute, FIN-20521, Turku, FINLAND; (358) 21-638-3529, fax (358) (2) 12330-755, malask@utu.fi, www.tukkk.fi/tutu/general.htm [ID:7195]

UNIVERSITY OF HAWAII
Spark M. Matsunaga Institute for Peace

MA IN PEACE STUDIES ▪ Director, Spark M. Matsunaga Institute for Peace, University of Hawaii, 2424 Maile Way, Porteus Hall 717, Honolulu Hawaii, USA; (808) 956-7427, fax (808) 956-5708, uhip@uhunix.uhcc.hawaii.edu, www2.hawaii.edu/mip [ID:7210]

INTERNATIONAL ASSOCIATION OF EDUCATORS FOR WORLD PEACE
Graduate and Postgraduate Program in International Relations and International Affairs

VARIOUS MASTER & DOCTORAL DEGREES AVAILABLE IN CONJUNCTION WITH INTERNATIONAL UNIVERSITIES ▪ Head, International Association of Educators for World Peace, 6 rue Moncrabeau, B-5000 Namur, BELGIUM; (32) (81) 220676, www.hck.hr/iaewp/iaewp.htm [ID:7225]

UNIVERSITY OF KENT AT CANTERBURY
Graduate School of Political Science and International Relations

MA IN INTERNATIONAL CONFLICT ANALYSIS ▪ Director, The Graduate Office, The Registry, University of Kent, CanterburyCT2 7NZ, UK; (44) (1227) 764000 ext. 7561, fax (44) (1227) 452196, graduate-office@ukc.ac.uk,
http://snipe.ukc.ac.uk/international/ [ID:7196]

LANCASTER UNIVERSITY
Department of Politics and International Relations

MA IN CONFLICT RESOLUTION, DEFENCE & SECURITY STUDIES, DIPLOMACY, & PEACE STUDIES ▪ Director, Department of Politics and International Relations, Cartmel College, Lancaster University, LancasterLA1 4YF, UK; (44) (1524) 594190, fax (44) (1524) 594238, pgadmissions@lancaster.ac.uk, www.lancs.ac.uk [ID:7202]

THE UNITED NATIONS UNIVERSITY
Regional Training Seminar

CERTIFICATE FOR CONFLICT RESOLUTION AND NEGOTIATION ▪ Head, Regional Training Seminar, The United Nations University, Toho Seimei Building, 15-1 Shibuya 2-chome, Shibuya-ku, Tokyo, 150, JAPAN; (81) (3) 3499-2811, fax (81) (3) 3499-2828, www.unu.edu [ID:7203]

WAYNE STATE UNIVERSITY
College of Urban, Labour, and Metropolitan Affairs

MA IN DISPUTE RESOLUTION ▪ Interim Director, College of Urban, Labour, and Metropolitan Affairs, Wayne State University, 3198 Faculty/Administration Building, Detroit, MI, 48202, USA; (313) 577-5071, fax (313) 577-8269, agraham@cms.cc.wayne.edu, www.wayne.edu [ID:7211]

Chapter 17

International Internships

Internships are one of the quickest routes into the international job market. Why? Because they help you over one of your biggest obstacles—lack of international work experience. Even with years of schooling and language training, you may find doors closed and few opportunities available. For this reason, interning is an increasingly popular and effective way to focus your international career, gain practical training, and build a network of contacts for your future job search.

This chapter focuses on internships with international organizations. At the end of the chapter, you will find profiles of 42 international organizations engaged in research and policy development, with which internships can be arranged. Also included are three Canadian-sponsored international internship programs. You'll find many other Canadian-based internship programs profiled throughout the book.

WHAT IS AN INTERNSHIP?

There is no simple answer to this question. Generally speaking, it refers to the exchange of work for knowledge and in this way is similar to an apprenticeship. A good internship allows you to work on a specific project of interest to you and builds on your academic specialization or previous work experience. You may not receive a "real" salary as an intern, but typically the sponsoring organization will invest some time and money in structuring your internship and making it a beneficial training experience for you. Being new to the field and to the organization, your work will likely be monitored by a supervisor or mentor. The underlying principle of an internship is to provide both knowledge and practical experience.

351

TYPES OF INTERNATIONAL INTERNSHIPS

There are many different types of international internships. Some conform to an established structure while others are tailored to meet the needs of the individuals and organizations involved. Internships range in duration from a month or two, to a year. Often, they are available for an academic semester or summer term. They may vary in terms of financial support available and the degree of independence accorded interns.

The international organizations that offer internships are diverse and numerous. They generally look for highly skilled and motivated people to work in research, advocacy, communications, or public policy. In many cases, internships are designed for students or recent graduates. For example, of the 42 internships profiled in this chapter, 28 are aimed at undergraduate students or those with bachelor's degrees, while 14 are restricted to graduate students.

Here are some examples of typical international internships:

- An honours political science student, focusing on Human Rights and Development Studies, successfully applies to The Department of Foreign Affairs and International Trade (DFAIT) International Youth Internship Program to work with a human rights organization overseas. The internship includes a few weeks preparing in Canada, 5-6 months working with the organizations overseas, and a follow-up session in Canada upon return.

- An I.M.B.A. student with export trade and business planning skills receives a modest stipend and travel costs for a summer internship with a Mississauga firm studying the feasibility of exporting to Latin America.

- A recent law graduate works with the United Nations Commission on International Trade Law (UNCITRAL) in Vienna on legal policy related to the illicit drug trade.

- An urban planning student, funded by his academic institution, spends eight months in Nairobi developing a social housing project with the UN Centre for Human Settlements (Habitat).

- An inexperienced journalist gets quality reporting jobs while interning with a national news magazine in New York for six months.

- The International Development Research Centre (IDRC) provides $28,000 for a biology intern who uses the funds to study theories and issues of alternative medicine for one year in Ottawa.

- An Ottawa-based student, enrolled in Central/East European and Russian-Area Studies, arranges a 2-day per week internship during the winter school term with the Russian Embassy.

A Note on Canadian Internships

In the past, internships were not as common in Canada as they were in the United States and Europe. However, with fewer job opportunities for recent graduates, internships in Canada are now much more common. Of all the organizations profiled in this book, between 25 and 30 per cent offer internship opportunities. The majority of these opportunities are found in the areas of pharmacy, travel and hospitality, and energy and communications. Both formal and informal internships are available. (For more ideas see Chapter 10, Short-term Programs Overseas; Chapter 32, The Private Sector; Chapter 34; Careers in Government; and Chapter 35, Nongovernmental Organizations.)

The latest and biggest boon are the international internship programs offered by the federal government. The programs provide close to 4,000 international internships over two years (a whopping number for the size of the Canadian market) and are administered by six government departments. Many of these internships have an international component and are invaluable for young people wanting to "go international." (For details, see the profiles listed in the Canadian Government International Internships section in this chapter.)

WHY INTERN?

You probably won't hear of people embarking on international internships to make loads of fast cash. But internships do pay off. Why? Because they provide invaluable international work and life *experience*. Surprisingly, the skills you gain as an intern are often greater than those you would gain with the same organization in an entry-level position. Often, your sponsoring organization will take the time to train you, precisely because you are unpaid. Internships also provide more challenges. Usually they are project-based and offer responsibilities that are broader in scope than those required for the day-to-day operations of an organization. If you are lucky enough to be assigned to an internship overseas, you will acquire essential crosscultural living and working experience. So, while an internship may not appear financially attractive in the short term, it usually pays off!

If you prove your reliability and competence as an intern, you are likely to be first in line for a job with that organization. Some estimates of interns who find employment with their sponsoring agencies are as high as 60 per cent. Employers state that they "appreciate the initiative and diligence of interns. Interns tend to work hard and show a keen interest in learning about the business." Yet internships that do not lead directly to employment can still be extremely valuable. The diverse array of professional contacts you make as an intern will help tremendously with your job search. Contacts can give you the inside scoop on jobs in your field, and if your work has been valued, your supervisor can provide you with a strong recommendation. The old saying, "having a foot-in-the-door" certainly applies to internships.

FINDING THE RIGHT ONE

While many internships are available, not all will correspond to your needs and interests. You will have to do some preliminary research to locate the one that's right for you. The first step in evaluating any internship is to consider whether the experience will be worth the time and effort required. To do this, it is important to take into account the international aspects of the internship. If the position involves an overseas assignment and you have little or no overseas experience, you should be less concerned about matching other aspects of the work assignment to your needs. In this situation, you should also be less concerned that an assignment is unstructured. The crosscultural living and working experience you gain will make it worthwhile!

If on the other hand, you already have previous international living experience, you might want to consider a Canadian-based international internship, such as working for an NGO or the international branch of a large corporation or government department. Gaining international experience at home can be equally valuable and just as essential to your résumé as your international experience abroad.

For most internships, but particularly for Canadian-based ones, it is best to work out in advance the substance of the internship assignment, the terms of participation, and the organization's expectations. Pay close attention to the organization's description of an intern's duties. This will help you determine whether your own needs will be met. Most internships involve some combination of administrative work and substantive projects, and you will want to know in advance that the balance between the two will enable you to meet your personal learning needs. If possible, contact former interns and arrange information interviews in person or over the telephone. Once these steps have been taken, you will be in a much better position to determine whether a position suits you. Be selective! Find the internship that best matches your skills and aspirations.

RESEARCHING THE INTERNSHIP

Once you've decided the type of internship you want, you can focus your research. In what field of work are you interested? With what type of organization do you want to intern? (NGO, multinational corporation, international agency, etc.) In what city, country or region of the world would you like to work?

Have your CV ready before you begin contacting organizations. You will need both printed and electronic versions. You will also need a good covering letter, and in some cases, a written proposal for your internship.

Begin your research well in advance of your availability. Six to eight months lead-time is a safe bet. For example, for a summer internship, start your research in early fall and begin making direct contact with organizations by December.

For a formal internship program like the ones described in this chapter, contact the internship coordinator to request an application form. Be sure to note any eligibility requirements that might disqualify you from applying, such as age restrictions, field of study, or others.

If you are making cold calls to create your own internship make sure you have a phone strategy ready. You would generally ask to speak with someone in your area of expertise to discuss the possibility of setting up an internship for you. For example, "Hi. I would like to speak to a manager in your international finance department." After reaching the person you requested, begin your inquiry. Include a brief profile of yourself and your internship plan. "Hello my name is Joan Landry. I am an MBA student with a specialization in international finance. I have a strong interest in selling mutual funds portfolios of market stocks from the South. I am looking for a three-month work internship starting next April. Who should I speak with to discuss the possibility of arranging this?" You may also use this approach when writing to someone on the Internet.

Your first phone call or e-mail to an organization is a good time to request information. When you are preparing a cover letter or statement of interest, the more you know about an organization the better. Browsing an organization's web site is another quick and easy way to gather this type of information. Or you can use the Internet to research companies in such places as Bangkok, Karachi, or Abidjan. (See Chapter 21, The Internet Job Search, for more information.) Getting into a good internship program can be a competitive process and you will have better results if you can show what you will bring to an organization. In your application, therefore, it is important to high-light experiences and qualities that demonstrate how well your interests and skills suit the needs of the organization.

Finally, follow up your application with a telephone call to ensure that all your materials were received and given serious consideration.

CREATING YOUR OWN INTERNSHIP WHILE AT UNIVERSITY

It is important to understand that while many organizations have formal internship programs, just as many or more do not. This doesn't mean they won't take an intern—rather, it may mean they will take one on an ad hoc basis if the person can contribute something valuable to the organization. From an organization's perspective, a proposal from an enthusiastic applicant offering services at no cost is alluring.

There are many ways to create your own internship. Here are a few approaches:

• It is worth noting that many of the sponsoring organizations of the Canadian government's international internship programs allow interns to go out and make their own arrangements. These programs generally cover up to $12,000 of your costs for a six- to eight-month internship. You will be particularly desirable to an organization if, in addition to volunteering your services, you are already receiving a basic salary at no cost to them.

• Tailor your university course load and research to match the work of an organization you are targeting for an internship or summer job. Perhaps your goal is to work at home or overseas on environmental issues in developing industrial nations. At the beginning of the school year, choose to write a research paper on CIDA's environmental policy in Asia. Supplement your library research by speaking directly to the CIDA project officer in Hull, Québec. Even if you live in Halifax, make long-distance calls. If possible, arrange a meeting and fly to Ottawa on a discount fare. Have the officer arrange appointments with other CIDA environmental and policy officers. Arrange a meeting with an embassy official of a country that interests you. Call on the officers at Foreign Affairs. Ask them to show you around. Inquire about their research interests and possibilities for summer jobs or internships.

• At the beginning of the school year, ask your professors about upcoming conferences in this field. Go to the conference prepared. For example, study the list of presenters and their topics. Arrange to do an essay on a related topic. Produce your own business cards to hand out at the conference. Once at the meeting, make contacts. Network! Connect with participants whose professional interests are similar to yours. Afterwards, follow up. Another good way to make contacts toward creating your own internship is to volunteer as a conference coordinator. Needless to say, you're guaranteed to meet a lot of people!

• University research centres, especially those specialized in business or area studies, can also provide leads to organizations interested in hosting interns.

Don't let long-distance telephone charges or the time it takes to write an e-mail message stand in your way. If you live in Moncton, New Brunswick and want to work for Foreign Affairs in Ottawa, these small efforts will go a long way toward establishing the foundations of a wonderful international career.

NEGOTIATING SALARY AND BENEFITS

An internship requires a substantial investment. Not only will it involve a great deal of your time and energy, but the costs of travel and your living expenses for the duration of the assignment will not be insignificant. So, while you may not be able to negotiate a salary, it is important to know that many "unpaid" interns do manage to negotiate some benefits.

You can broach the subject by asking if there is a possibility of being paid an "honorarium." This term describes a salary which covers only very basic living costs. It can be as low as $25 per day to cover transportation and food, or $350 per week to also include accommodation.

If you travel abroad for the internship, most organizations will agree to pay for accommodation. If they don't do this, ask to be billeted with an employee's family. Many organizations will also either cover airfare or agree to a departure payment equivalent to airfare. It is also important to discuss health coverage, and if necessary, make alternative arrangements.

You may be able to get funding for your internship from a sponsoring institution, such as your school's faculty of graduate studies, or your academic department. With some scholarships or awards, a portion can be used for research undertaken during an internship. If you are submitting a proposal for a scholarship, factor the cost of an internship into your budget.

The cost of an internship may seem prohibitive, especially if you are just finishing a degree and have large student debts. However, if you compare the cost of one term at university with the benefits of an opportunity abroad, you will see that your internship is really a short-term expense for long-term investment.

A LAST WORD

International internships can provide exciting professional experiences and are an excellent means of launching your international career. So remember to take your internship seriously. Think of it as a "real job" with real importance for the organization. The value you place on your internship will translate into value placed on your skills by your sponsoring organization, and could lead to an offer of paid employment.

RESOURCES

Here are more books to help you find that first job and get you started on your international career. Remember that 25 to 30 per cent of the organizations in this book have indicated that they provide formal and ad hoc internships within their organizations, so contacting them directly is a good start. You should also consult the numerous Resources sections in this guide related to job searching and volunteering.

After Latin American Studies: A Guide to Graduate Study,
Fellowships, Internships, and Employment for Latin Americanists 📖
1995, *Shirley A. Kregar,* 142 pages ➤ Center for Latin American Studies, 4E04 Forbes Quad, University of Pittsburgh, Pittsburgh, PA 15260, USA; $10; MC, Amex; (412) 648-7392, fax (412) 648-2199, clas+@cpitt.edu ■ Provides information on graduate study, research and internships. For graduate as well as undergraduate students, opportunities in the private sector, and career opportunities in the US government and in international organizations. An essential resource for anyone with career or scholarly interests in the region. Visit the distributor's web site at www.edu/~clas. [ID:1118]

Choices That Count: Co-operative Education in the Public Service of Canada 📖 💻
Annual, 145 pages ➤ External Recruitment Programs, Public Service Commission, 18th Floor, L'Esplanade Laurier, 300 Laurier Avenue W., Ottawa, Ontario K1A 0M7; free; (613) 992-9630, fax (613) 947-5875 ■ A listing of work-study programs at Canadian postsecondary institutions. If you are registered in one of these programs, check out the possibilities of arranging co-op placements with the international branch of a government department. The web version of this publication should be available by 1998 at www.psc-cfp.gc.ca/jobs.htm, the Public Service Commission web site. [ID:1666]

Directory of International Internships: A World of Opportunities 📖
1997, *Charles Gliozzo, Vernicka Tyson, Adela Pena, Bob Dye,* 170 pages ➤ Attn: International Placement, Michigan State University, Career Development and Placement Services, 113 Student Services Bldg., East Lansing, MI 48824, USA; US$25; cheque or money order; (517) 355-9510 ext. 371, fax (517) 353-2597 ■ Describes a variety of experiential educational opportunities offered through educational institutions, governments, and private organizations; for academic credit, for pay, or simply for experience. Indexed by subject and country. Visit www.msu.edu/csp. [ID:1425]

International Directory for Youth Internships 📖
1993, *M. Culligan, C. Morehouse,* 58 pages ➤ Council on International and Public Affairs, Apex Press, Suite 3C, 777 United Nations Plaza, New York, NY 10017, USA; $7.50; VISA, MC; (914) 271-6500, fax (914) 271-2039 ■ Booklet includes list of about 40 intern positions related to UN secretariat and other international programs sponsored by nongovernmental organizations. All academic levels represented, but many positions require graduate or postgraduate status. [ID:1071]

International Youth and Young Workers Exchange Programs 💻
www.dfait-maeci.gc.ca/english/culture/youthex.html ■ This site, maintained by the Department of Foreign Affairs and International Trade (Canada) offers information on a number of government-sponsored programs for international employment and study. Many of the bilateral exchange and working holiday programs profiled in this chapter are listed on the site. There are also a

number of thematic programs designed to help individuals with specific interests find employment overseas. This is a very good site, although many of the programs listed are not online and must be contacted through conventional means. [ID:2505]

Internships 📖
Annual, Peterson's Guides, 517 pages ➤ Capricorn Business Services, Inc., 28 Clear Lake Ave., West Hill, Ontario M1C 4L6; $45.95; credit cards; (416) 282-3331, fax (416) 282-0015 ▪ Over 30,000 listings plus a number of informed essays on internships. Lists categories such as law and criminal justice, government and public administration, and newspapers and journalism. A useful book with chapters on US internships for foreign applicants and international internships for Americans. [ID:1043]

Internships & Careers in International Affairs 📖
1992, *James Muldoon* ➤ Model UN & Youth Dept., United Nations Association of the USA, 801 Second Ave., New York, NY 10017-4706, USA; US$10; cheque or money order; (212) 697-3232, fax (212) 682-9185, unhq@unausa.org ▪ Aimed at postsecondary students wishing to pursue careers in international affairs. The booklet concentrates on three areas: the US government, the UN, and nongovernmental organizations. Visit the distributor's web site at www.unausa.org. [ID:1040]

Internships 1997: The Hotlist for Job Hunters 📖
1997, *Sara D. Gilbert,* 418 pages ➤ Simon & Shuster Macmillan Co., 1633 Broadway Ave., New York, NY 10019-6785, USA; US$19.95; credit cards; (800) 428-5331, fax (212) 654-4762 ▪ An up-to-the-minute guide to over 25,000 internship opportunities in the U.S. [ID:1804]

Internships in Foreign and Defense Policy: a Complete Guide for Women (& Men) 📖
1990, *Women in International Security,* 103 pages ➤ Seven Locks Press, P.O. Box 68, Arlington, VA 22210, USA; US$10.95; credit cards; (800) 354-5348, fax (714) 545-1572, sevenlocks@aol.com ▪ An internship early in your career can help open doors to a successful career. This book is designed to help women (and men) pursue the many opportunities for internships in the area of international security. [ID:1245]

Study Abroad 1997/1998 Council Study Centres 📖
44 pages ➤ Publications Dept., Council on International Educational Exchange, 205 East 42nd Street, New York, NY 10017, USA; free; VISA, MC; (212) 822-2600, fax (212) 822-2699 ▪ This brochure describes each of the CIEE's Study Centres. Centres are located in Europe, Asia, Oceania, Africa, the Caribbean, and Latin America. A plethora of courses and internships are offered at each location. [ID:2682]

United Nations Volunteers 💻
www.unv.org ▪ This program offers mid-career professionals the opportunity to volunteer overseas in a humanitarian effort. Currently, over 2,000 people from more than 100 countries are volun-teering in developing countries as specialists and field workers. This site can help start you on the way to becoming a volunteer for the United Nations. [ID:2482]

Youth Resource Network of Canada's International Job Opportunities Page 💻
www.youth.gc.ca/jobopps/intern-e.shtml ▪ This resource site is part of the Canadian government's Youth Employment Strategy. The site offers information on news releases, training and education, and self-employment. It also provides notices of employment opportunities for youth who want to work overseas. [ID:2521]

Profiles of International Internships

This chapter profiles the formal internship programs of 42 international organizations engaged in research and policy, and also includes three Canadian internship programs with a strong international component. Most of the internships take place at the headquarters of the organizations profiled. About half of these are located in the United States, 12 are based in Europe, and eight are located in developing countries. Profiles include information on objectives, fields of assignment, duration, number of internships, required qualifications and financial considerations.

Keep in mind that many organizations listed elsewhere in this book accept interns on an ad hoc basis, so if the organization you are interested in is not listed here, contact it anyway. Many Canadian organizations listed in the government, private sector, and NGO chapters also have internship possibilities. Most are identified as such in the profile descriptions which follow.

AIESEC - International Student Exchange Organization
Coordinator, International Traineeship Exchange Program, Suite 208, 8 King Street E., Toronto, Ontario, M5C 1B5, CANADA; (416) 368-1001, fax (416) 368-4490, aiesec@ca.aiesec.org, www.ca.aiesec.org

AIESEC is an international, student-run exchange organization which caters to students of all disciplines. The International Traineeship Exchange Program (ITEP) offers globally-minded undergraduate and graduate students the opportunity to manage and participate in a cultural experience in one of 87 countries. Students are placed in paid positions related to management, economics, or computer science. An administration fee, travel costs, insurance, and living expenses are the responsibility of the participant. Placements range from eight to 78 weeks. The logistics of the exchange including housing, reception, and cultural integration are arranged and supported by AIESEC. Approximately 5,000 students worldwide, including over 110 Canadians, participate annually. Participants are involved with AIESEC chapters at their university and serve as ambassadors for both Canada and AIESEC. [ID:5046]

Amnesty International (AI)
322 Eighth Ave, New York, NY, 10001, USA;
(212) 807-8400, fax (212) 627-1451, admin-us@aiusa.org, www.amnesty.org

Amnesty International's internship program gives interns a chance to become actively involved in its human rights work. Assignments are available in a diverse array of fields, including: casework/country action, capital punishment, law, refugees, religious affiliations, information services, direct mail, finance and administration, women's programs, advertising and marketing, membership, communications, media, special projects, liaison, and computer systems.

Each of the nine US offices of Amnesty International offers internships throughout the year. Approximately 15 internships are offered which vary both in duration and compensation. Positions are open to undergraduate and graduate students as well as to those not currently enrolled but holding a university degree. Application forms are available upon request from the New York office. (For more information on Amnesty International see Chapter 38, International Organizations.) [ID:5543]

Ashoka Innovators for the Public
Suite 1920, 1700 North Moore Street, Arlington, Virginia, 22209, USA;
(703) 527-8300, fax (703) 527-8383, Ashoka@tmn.com, www.ashoka.org

ASHOKA Innovators for the Public is a nonprofit organization that seeks out and helps fund public service entrepreneurs in developing countries who are launching innovative solutions to special problems. ASHOKA offers three main types of internships at its headquarters in Virginia. On an annual basis, one to two development interns assist the director with program tasks dealing with ASHOKA funding, including researching and composing status reports on fellow activities and progress for current funders, and assisting in the preparation of grant proposals. One or two global fellowship interns collaborate with program directors on tasks including development and maintenance of global fellowship information networks on a broad range of development and human rights issues. Finally, four regional desk interns assist the regional divisions with program management tasks related to ASHOKA fellows and country representatives.

Internships are available to students of junior, senior or graduate standing, and are offered year-round. College credit can often be obtained with part-time internships. A small monthly stipend of $50 for daily transportation costs is provided, but all other costs are borne by the interns. Applicants must submit a detailed résumé, cover letter and a three-page writing sample. [ID:6745]

Asian Vegetable and Research Centre (AVRDC)
Director, ICP, P.O. Box 42, Shanhua741, TAIWAN;
(886) (6) 5837801 ext. 500, fax (886) (6) 5830009, sundar@netra.AVRDC.org.TW, www.avrdc.org.tw

The Asian Vegetable and Research Centre (AVRDC) provides a limited number of internships, with a view to allowing graduate and undergraduate students of agricultural colleges and universities to gain practical experience under the supervision of scientists. Research areas include plant breeding, soil science, and crop management. Other related areas, such as the dissemination of research and publications, are also included in the centre's activities. [ID:5544]

Association to Unite the Democracies
1506 Pennsylvania Avenue S.E., Washington, DC, 20003, USA;
(202) 544-5150, fax (202) 544-3742, AtUnite@aol.com, http://msx4.pha.jhu.edu/aud.html

Association to Unite the Democracies is a small, nonprofit educational organization which advocates the development of a federal union of the world's free democracies to promote freedom of liberty, create international stability, and aid in the development of peace, prosperity, and democracy throughout the world.

AUD internships are available year-round to students of any educational level or major. Preference is given to students with a background in international affairs. Duration of internship varies according to the student's needs. Interested applicants should send a résumé and cover letter to the above address. [ID:6746]

Canadian Government International Internships
International Internship Programs, Human Resources Development Canada,
Phase IV, 4th Floor, Place du Portage, Hull, Québec, K1A 0J9, CANADA;
(800) 935-5555, fax (613) 941-5992, http://youth.hrdc-drhc.gc.ca

The resources that follow are a fantastic way to gain international experience in your field. In 1997, the Canadian government announced a two-year program that would provide support for 4,000 international internships in a wide range of fields, including communications, international development, international trade, and the environment. Indications are that this program will be extended beyond 1999. The program gives young college or university graduates the opportunity to gain work experience in the private, nongovernmental, and nonprofit sectors for a period of up to a year. Placements may include both a domestic and an international component. Participants are normally under 30 years of age, and have college or university degrees. However, the Human Resources Development Canada program listed below (Youth International) has no minimal educational requirements. Although it is not official policy, in practice, some restrictions such as age are not always strictly applied.

The internships are administered by the following six government departments: the DEPARTMENT OF FOREIGN AFFAIRS AND INTERNATIONAL TRADE (DFAIT), the CANADIAN INTERNATIONAL DEVELOPMENT AGENCY (CIDA), ENVIRONMENT CANADA, INDUSTRY CANADA, HUMAN RESOURCES AND DEVELOPMENT CANADA (HRDC), and CANADIAN HERITAGE. The programs are described below. Application procedures for each program vary. For example, for those administered by CIDA and DFAIT, candidates must apply directly to the partner organizations these departments have chosen. For others, including those administered by Canadian Heritage and Industry Canada, candidates can apply using the National Graduate Register (NGR), a central résumé database on the Internet available for employer searches. If you are a postsecondary candidate or are within three years of having graduated, simply visit the web site at http://ngr.schoolnet.ca, and enter your résumé directly online. In many instances, we have heard of interns setting up their own internship with a company and arranging for a government-sponsored partner to fund them. There is no doubt that these internships are an invaluable opportunity to get your international career started—take advantage of them!

The DEPARTMENT OF FOREIGN AFFAIRS AND INTERNATIONAL TRADE (DFAIT) Youth International Internship Program provides career-related, internationally-focused work experience that furthers the objectives of Canada's foreign policy, specifically the promotion of prosperity and employment, the promotion of peace and global security, and the projection of Canadian values and culture abroad. 401 internships will be awarded in 1998-99. For more information, contact DFAIT by phone at (800) 559-2888, or consult their web site at www.dfait-maeci.gc.ca.

The CANADIAN INTERNATIONAL DEVELOPMENT AGENCY (CIDA) Youth Internship Program offers recent graduates the opportunity to gain first work experience in an international development setting. Internships fall under at least one of CIDA's six programming priorities: basic human needs; women in development; infrastructure service; human rights, democratic development and good governance; private sector development; and environment. Approximately 400 internships are expected to be awarded in 1998-99. For more information and application procedures, contact the Government of Canada Youth Info Line at (800) 935-5555, or consult CIDA's web site at www.acdi-cida.gc.ca.

ENVIRONMENT CANADA'S International Environmental Youth Corps (IEYC), delivered by the Canadian Council for Human Resources in the Environment Industry (CCHREI), provides opportunities for young Canadians to undertake an international internship with a Canadian company in the environmental industry sector. Approximately 140 internships are expected to be awarded in 1998-99. For more information, and to solicit an application package, consult Environment Canada's web site at www.ec.gc.ca, or the web site of the CCHREI at www.chatsubo.com/CCHREI. You may also phone the CCHREI at (800) 962-9562.

INDUSTRY CANADA'S Horizons Plus will match young qualified graduates seeking careers as export managers with export-ready small- and medium-size enterprises (SMEs) and potential exporter SMEs across Canada. In each year of the program, 113 interns will be placed in Canadian SMEs requiring assistance to become exporters, and 180 interns will be placed in Canadian SMEs who are already exporting but wish to expand into new markets. Candidates are encouraged to apply using the National Graduate Register (NGR). Information on the program may be obtained by phone at 1-888-467-4046, or by Internet at http://horizonsplus.com. Interested applicants can also call the Government of Canada Youth Info Line at (800) 935-5555, or consult Industry Canada's web site at the following web address: http://strategis.ic.gc.ca/youth.

HUMAN RESOURCES DEVELOPMENT CANADA'S (HRDC) Youth International seeks to provide out-of-school youth that are unemployed or under-employed with an internationally-focused work experience with Canadian and foreign businesses and organizations (including nonprofit, employer, professional and labour organizations); public health or educational institutions; and/or municipal governments and band/tribal councils. Project activities will reflect the needs of local communities. Note that for this particular program there is no minimum educational requirement. The only prerequisite is that the candidate is under 30, out of school, and under- or unemployed. Approximately 1,500 youth will be assisted over the two-year period. For more information, you can either contact your local Human Resource Centre of Canada (HRCC), consult HRDC's web site at http://youth.hrdc-drhc.gc.ca, or phone the Government of Canada's Youth Info Line at (800) 935-5555.

CANADIAN HERITAGE'S Young Canada Works Internationally focuses on international tourism, the dissemination of Canadian cultural products and second-language training materials/methods and promotional tools associated with these products and areas of expertise. 67 interns are expected to be hired over the two-year period. Candidates may apply through the National Graduate Register (NGR). For more information, applicants can call the Government of Canada Youth Info Line at (800) 935-5555. [ID:6953]

Center for the Study of Conflict
Director, 5846 Bellona Ave, Baltimore, MD, 21212, USA; (410) 323-7656

The Center for the Study of Conflict is an independent, politically non-aligned corporation that performs scientific research to find general, creative and peaceful approaches to resolving social conflicts. The centre's principle to seek ways to prevent violence, is applied to a range of conflict situations, from interpersonal to international.

The center provides internships to those interested in conflict resolution, nonviolence, and peacemaking. Interns are generally involved in library research, editing and office work, and are given ample opportunity to explore their own interests. No stipend is provided. Applicants should send their résumé, the names and addresses of two references (one academic and one job-related), a one-page writing sample and a statement of interest. [ID:6748]

Cooperative Housing Foundation (CHF)
Suite 420, 8300 Colesville Road, Silver Spring, MD, 20910, USA; (301) 587-4700, fax (301) 587-2626, west@chfhq.com, www.friends-partners.org/oldfriends/ccsi/csusa/socwlfr/coophous.html

The Cooperative Housing Foundation is a private, nonprofit organization that helps families throughout the world build better housing and communities. CHF provides technical and financial assistance to over eighty developing countries that have requested assistance in creating and updating local housing and community services.

CHF seeks a limited number of interns to assist senior staff members in a broad range of activities, including research, maintenance and updating of an extensive research and audio-video library, video and graphics production, computer programming and systems design, fundraising, and intern staff management. Internships vary in scope and duration, but the organization is particularly interested in people with academic or practical experience in housing and community development issues, and a sensitivity to the needs and interests of developing countries. Compensation is negotiable, but those wishing to volunteer or accept a nominal wage are preferred. [ID:6751]

The European Union
Internship Coordinator, Delegation of the European Commission, Third Floor, 2300 M Street, Washington, DC, 20037, USA; (202) 862-9500, fax (202) 429-1766, www.eurunion.org

The Delegation of the European Commission offers internship positions at its offices in Washington, DC, Brussels, and Luxembourg. Internships are intended to provide students and recent graduates with the opportunity to acquire considerable knowledge of the European Union, its institutions, activities, law, and statistics. The delegations in Washington that accept interns include Public Inquiries, the Economic/Financial Section, the Agriculture Section, the Environmental/Energy Section, and the European Magazine. The Commission Internship and The ESC (Economic and Social Committee) Internships are offered in Brussels and at the European Parliament in Luxembourg. Internships are usually offered on a volunteer basis and a working knowledge of French is useful, but not essential. Deadlines vary according to position. Visit the European Union web site for specific information and application forms. [ID:6798]

Family Health International (FHI)
P.O. Box 13950, Research Triangle Park,
Durham, NC, 27709, USA; (919) 544-7040, fax (919) 544-7261, www.fhi.org

Family Health International (FHI) conducts research and analysis on issues related to the development and distribution of contraceptive technologies, and around issues of contraceptive safety and reproductive health. Its summer internship program is committed to providing a limited number of interns with an opportunity to better understand the international dimension of research and technical assistance programs.

Interns work during the summer months and are provided with a small stipend of $200 per week to defray expenses. The program is open to university students studying in a field relevant to FHI. Along with a résumé and a letter of recommendation from their advisor, interested applicants should send a letter which specifies the internship which interests them and explaining how it fits in with their career goals. (For more information on FHI see Chapter 38, International Organizations.) [ID:6757]

Global Information Network
Suite 1206, 275 Seventh Ave., New York, NY,
10001, USA; (212) 647-0123, fax (212) 627-6137, ipsgin@igc.org

The Global Information Network is the distributor of newswire services from developing countries. The network also generates stories on a wide range of topics, from politics to culture. Students who are interested in news writing and international affairs and who are highly motivated are welcome to apply. Internships generally involve copy editing, news writing and many other newsroom tasks. English- and Spanish-speaking candidates are preferred. Internships range in duration and are unpaid. [ID:6752]

Human Rights Watch
Everett Public Service Summer Internships, 485 Fifth Ave.,
New York, NY, 10017, USA; (212) 972-8400 ext. 264, fax (212) 972-0905, hrwnyc@hrw.org, www.hrw.org

Human Rights Watch is devoted to promoting worldwide attention to international human rights issues. In conjunction with the Everett Public Service Internship Program, HRW offers four summer internships to one of its regional divisions (Africa, Americas, Asia, Middle East or Europe), to one of its thematic projects (arms, children's rights, or women's rights), or to one of its special programs (business and human rights, drugs and human rights, prisons or free expression). Interns work closely with the research staff, under the direction of the regional or project director or HRW counsel.

Internships last from eight to 10 weeks at a minimum of 30 hours per week. A small stipend of $180 per week for undergraduate and graduate students is provided to offset expenses. There is no formal application process, but a résumé, writing sample, letter of recommendation and statement of interest indicating the HRW division you wish to work with should be forwarded to the office by March 31st.

It is also possible to arrange ad hoc internships with HRW during the academic year, but different conditions apply. (For more information about Human Rights Watch see Chapter 38, International Organizations.) [ID:6755]

INet for Women
P.O. Box 6178, McLean, VA, 22106, USA; (703) 893-8541, fax (703) 893-8541

INet for Women is an international trade and business organization offering internships in four areas: information systems development and integration, public relations and advertising, marketing and international relations, and membership administration and events planning.

Candidates should have a background in business or economics, excellent organizational skills and the ability to speak foreign languages. Assignments last between six weeks and six months and are unpaid, although reduced rent is available for international interns. INet also offers placement assistance upon completion of the internship. [ID:5547]

Inter-American Development Bank (IADB)
Junior Professional Program, Employment Programs Section, 1300 New York Ave. N.W., Washington, DC, 20577, USA; (202) 623-1000, fax (202) 623-3096, www.iadb.org

The Inter-American Development Bank's (IADB) Junior Professional Program is a starting point for careers at the bank. Assignments are available in the bank's traditional areas of economics, finance, business management, public administration, health, computer science, engineering or law, or in emerging areas such as trade, labour, modernization of the state, governance, the environment, and women in development.

The number of internships available varies annually according to budgetary allocations. The duration of the program is 18 months, beginning with two six-month assignments in different departments. Junior Professionals are treated as full-fledged staff members with specific responsibilities. Participants are generally hired as regular staff members during the course of their program.

To be considered, candidates must be citizens of a member country of the bank, have at least a master's degree and be under the age of 32 (candidates applying from within the bank can be under 35). Applicants should also have at least one year of professional level experience.

The bank also offers an unpaid internship program for those who wish to gain practical experience and do research in the operational and administrative activities of the bank. IADB will accept up to 15 interns at any given time for a minimum of three months. Interns must be at least 21 years of age and enrolled in full-time studies at the time of the internship. (For more information about IADB see Chapter 36, United Nations.) [ID:5548]

International Atomic Energy Agency
P.O. Box 100, Wagramerstrasse 5, A-1400 Vienna, AUSTRIA; (43) (1) 2060, fax (43) (1) 20607, iaeo@iaea1.iaea.or.at, www.iaea.or.at/

The International Atomic Energy Agency provides a limited number of internships to students specializing in areas relevant to the agency's programs. Internships are flexible in scope and range in duration from one month to one year. All costs must be borne by the intern for the duration of the internship. Interested applicants must complete the agency's personal history form and attach a detailed résumé. Applicants must have an excellent knowledge of spoken English and be able to write in English. (For more information on the International Atomic Energy Agency see Chapter 36, United Nations.) [ID:6743]

International Development Research Centre (IDRC)
P.O. Box 8500, Ottawa, Ontario, K1G 3H9, CANADA; (613) 236-6163, fax (613) 563-2476, info@idrc.ca, www.idrc.ca

IDRC offers three types of internships in its effort to support scientific research in Africa, Asia, Latin America, and the Caribbean as it relates to social, economic, and environmental problems.

Centre internships involve a program of work and research dealing with any of IDRC's six core programming areas: food security, biodiversity conservation, sustainable employment, equity in natural resource use, strategies and policies for healthy societies, and information and communication. Internships range in duration from four months to one year, and are remunerated at a rate of between $25,000 and $28,000. Travel and research expenses up to a maximum of $4,000 may also be provided. While candidates should have at least some training at the master's level, they need not be affiliated with an institution. Application forms are available from the IDRC Training and Awards Unit, Special Initiatives Program, Corporate Services Branch.

Gender and Sustainable Development Internships aim to enhance gender research capacity and gender equity, and involve work on two major themes: innovative projects that address major gaps in Agenda 21 and indicate areas where IDRC might play a leadership role in knowledge creation on gender and sustainable development; and those that build on previous IDRC investments in gender research and represent areas where Canada has a comparative advantage. Internships can be either four months or one year in duration, and compensation varies depending on the experience and qualifications of the intern. Candidates must have completed their master's degree or be working towards a doctorate degree. Proposals can be submitted year-round.

IDRC also awards two journalism internships each year. The Gemini Internship involves an eight-month period of work with Gemini News Service in London, England followed by a three- to four-month field assignment in a developing country. Candidates must possess strong oral and written English skills. The Periscoop Internship involves work with L'Agence Periscoop Multimedia in Montpellier, France and includes assignments in Africa. Strong oral and written French skills are required. Both internships are one year in duration, and are compensated up to $30,000. Candidates require a minimum of three years professional work experience in the media. [ID:6747]

International Fund for Agricultural Development (IFAD)
1889 F Street N.W., Washington, DC, 20006, USA;
(202) 331-8670, fax (202) 331-9191, ifad@ifad.org, www.unicc.org/ifad/home.html

The International Fund for Agricultural Development (IFAD) exposes interns to a wide range of development issues, including small-scale rural development, agricultural extension projects, sustainability, gender concerns, project development, and financing. Interns assist in a number of activities such as attending relevant meetings and Congressional hearings on US foreign aid policy and reviewing publications on international development.

Applicants must be able to commit a minimum of 20 hours per week during the school year and full-time hours during the summer. Candidates should be upper-level undergraduates or graduate students and have excellent analytical and writing abilities. [ID:5549]

International Labour Organization (ILO)
Personnel Planning and Career Development Branch, 4, route des Morillons,
1211 Geneva 22, SWITZERLAND; (41) (22) 7997250, fax (41) (22) 7998576, www.ilo.org/

The International Labour Organization (ILO) arranges ad hoc internships for undergraduate and postgraduate students specializing in fields related to the work of the ILO. Internships are intended to promote a better understanding among participants of international labour issues and insights into the work of the ILO.

Internships are non-remunerated and interns must bear all costs involved, such as travel and accommodation. There is no brochure available nor is there a formal application form. Applicants should send a letter of application indicating the required duration of the internship (minimum one month) as well as the exact starting date, together with a detailed résumé. Applications should be sent at least three months in advance to allow sufficient processing time. (For more information on ILO see Chapter 36, United Nations.) [ID:5550]

International Monetary Fund (IMF)
Summer Internship Program, Recruitment Division, 700 19th Street N.W.,
Washington, DC, 20431, USA; (202) 623-8243, fax (202) 623-7333, recruit@imf.org, www.imf.org

The International Monetary Fund (IMF) offers a Summer Internship Program to provide interns with a first-hand opportunity to familiarize themselves with the operations of the IMF. Opportunities are in the fields of monetary economics, public finance, international trade and finance, and econometrics.

Each summer approximately 40 internships, normally lasting 10 to 13 weeks, are offered. Candidates should be in the latter stages of their doctoral programs. Those with outstanding backgrounds in economics will be considered. Interns receive a stipend of nearly US$3,000 per month and round-trip airfare to Washington, DC. Applicants should submit a completed IMF employment application or résumé and include a list of economics courses taken and grades obtained at the university level. (For more information on IMF see Chapter 36, United Nations.) [ID:5551]

International Telecommunications Satellite Organization (INTELSAT)
Summer Intern Program, Human Resources Division, Box 24 INT,
3400 International Drive, N.W., Washington, DC, 20008-3098, USA;
(202) 944-7243, fax (202) 944-7661, www.intelsat.int/hrd/jobs/interns.htm

The International Telecommunications Satellite Organization (INTELSAT) owns and operates the world's most extensive global communications satellite system. The Summer Intern Program is designed to provide an opportunity for students to obtain practical work experience in an international, high technology environment. The program supports approximately 25 summer interns for a 12-week period between late May and late August.

Interns are expected to work 40 hours per week and are paid a net stipend of $10.00 per hour. The program is open to students currently enrolled in their final year of undergraduate study or any level of graduate study. Strong preference is given to international students studying in the US. Information and application procedures for the program are available on INTELSAT's web site. (For more information on INTELSAT see Chapter 38, International Organizations.) [ID:6760]

Junior Professional Officer Program (JPO)
Human Resources Division, Personnel and Administration Branch,
Canadian International Development Agency (CIDA), 200 Promenade du Portage,
Hull, Québec, K1A 0G4, CANADA; (800) 230-6349, fax (819) 953-6088, http://w3.acdi-cida.gc.ca

The Junior Professional Officer Program (JPO) is administered under the auspices of the United Nations. Its primary objectives are to provide experience in managing a development program, support the UN through JPO services, place Canadians in the UN, and use knowledge gained from assignments. General duties of a JPO include the administration and coordination of projects and liaison between local authorities, regional offices, and headquarters.

Through the Canadian International Development Agency (CIDA), Canada sponsors several JPOs annually in the following UN agencies: United Nations Development Program (UNDP), United Nations International Children's Fund (UNICEF), United Nations High Commissioner for Refugees (UNHCR), and the World Food Program (WFP).

Candidates should generally be under the age of 30 and possess a completed master's degree in a relevant discipline. Knowledge of three languages and prior work experience (paid or voluntary) is becoming increasingly important as placements become more competitive.

CIDA also funds a similar program called the Associates Professional Officer program (APO), which places two or three participants each year with the Food and Agricultural Organization (FAO). (For more information see Chapter 35, United Nations.)

Information about the JPO program and application forms are available on CIDA's web site. [ID:5552]

The Population Institute
107 2nd Street N.E., Washington, DC, 20002, USA;
(202) 544-3300, fax (202) 544-0068, www.populationinstitute.org/

The Population Institute's Future Leaders of the World Program provides students interested in international affairs the opportunity to work on the issue of population growth for a period of six months. Four to six internships are offered each year. One to three interns work in the area of public policy, providing information to legislators and key staff. One intern is hired every six months to work as a media coordinator preparing press lists, liaising with media, writing, reporting, proofreading, and editing. During the spring, two to three interns are hired as field coordinators to plan and implement trips around the nation for speakers of the institute. In the fall session, interns manage special programs, such as the Global Media Awards or World Population Awareness Week.

Interns earn US$1,000 per month plus benefits. Applicants must be able to demonstrate leadership qualities, international experiences and perspectives, a good academic record, and strong oral and writing skills. Applicants must have completed at least two years of college or university and be between the ages of 21 and 25. To apply, send résumé, cover letter, three recommendations (two from academic sources), and an official transcript. [ID:5554]

Radio Free Europe/Radio Liberty
Intern Program Manager, 1201 Connecticut Ave. N.W.,
Washington, DC, 20036, USA; (202) 457-6949, fax (202) 457-6913, www.rferl.org/index.html

The Radio Free Europe/Radio Liberty intern program introduces graduate students of journalism, political science or international relations to the distinct environment of news reporting in Central Europe and the successor states of the Soviet Union. Two types of internships are available. The first entails work for two weeks in Washington for the News and Current Affairs (NCA) department, followed by six to eight weeks in Prague, where interns produce broadcast-ready news copy in English to hourly deadlines. The second type is located exclusively in Prague, where interns train with staff in studio operations, and depending on the level of interest and experience in radio production, learn to prepare and produce live, live-to-tape or digital audio radio programs.

Interns are provided with round-trip airfare, a daily stipend and modest living quarters. Applicants are normally graduate students of journalism, communications, political science or international relations who have demonstrated competence in their particular fields. Applicants are asked to submit a completed application form, two letters of recommendation, samples of broadcast or published material, and a résumé and cover letter indicating interest and summarizing qualifications. [ID:5555]

United Nations Centre for Human Settlements (Habitat)
P.O. Box 30030, Nairobi, KENYA; (254) (2) 621234, fax (254) (2) 624266/7, www.undp.org/un/habitat/

The UN Centre for Human Settlements (Habitat) coordinates activities within the UN system principally related to housing, building, and planning. Internships are available on an ad hoc basis for students specializing in fields of study relevant to the organization.

Internships range in duration and are unpaid. Applicants should be currently enrolled in at least the latter stages of their undergraduate degree and must be sponsored by their academic institutions. The centre has a formal application form for interested students. (For more information on Habitat see Chapter 36, United Nations.) [ID:6762]

United Nations Children's Fund (UNICEF)
Training and Staff Development, UNICEF Internship Programme,
3 United Nations Plaza, New York, NY, 10017, USA; (212) 303-7915, fax (212) 303-7984, www.unicef.org/

The UN Children's Fund (UNICEF) combines humanitarian and development objectives to help developing countries protect their children and maximize their development efforts. Internships are offered at the graduate or postgraduate level in fields related to international or social development, child survival or development, or management.

Internships are unpaid and responsibility for travel and living expenses must be borne by the applicant or sponsoring institution. Applications are accepted on an ongoing basis and internships are available during three periods: January to May, June to August, and September to December. (For more information on UNICEF see Chapter 36, United Nations.) [ID:5558]

United Nations Commission on International Trade Law (UNCITRAL)
P.O. Box 500, Vienna International Centre, A-1400 Vienna, AUSTRIA;
(43) (1) 21345-4060, fax (43) (1) 21345-5813, uncitral@unov.un.or.at, www.un.or.at/uncitral

The UN Commission on International Trade Law (UNCITRAL) occasionally accepts interns with law degrees to take on ongoing projects of the International Trade Law Branch of the Office of Legal Affairs, which is the substantive secretariat of UNCITRAL.

Internships are unpaid and are a minimum of three months in length. Interns must be sponsored by an organization, university, or governmental agency to qualify. Interested applicants can request a detailed application form from the commission. (For more information on UNCITRAL see Chapter 36, United Nations.) [ID:6764]

United Nations Economic and Social
Commission for Asia and the Pacific (ESCAP)
United Nations Building, Rajadamnern Ave., Bangkok10200, THAILAND;
(66) (2) 288-1234, fax (66) (2) 288-1000, yoo.unescap@un.org, www.un.org/Depts/escap

The UN Economic and Social Commission for Asia and the Pacific (ESCAP) offers an ad hoc internship program designed to meet the research interests of students in a diverse range of areas relevant to the commission, including development research and policy analysis, international trade and economic cooperation, industry and technology, environment and natural resources, rural and urban development, transport, communication and tourism, and others.

Internships range in duration and all costs are the responsibility of interns. Candidates must be sponsored by their academic institution to qualify. Interested applicants should submit a completed application form and attach an outline of their preferred research or work to be undertaken during the internship. (For more information on ESCAP see Chapter 36, United Nations.) [ID:6763]

United Nations Economic Commission for Europe (ECE)
Palais des Nations, CH-1211 Geneva 10, SWITZERLAND;
(41) (22) 9171234, fax (41) (22) 9170123, www.unece.org/Welcome.html

The UN Economic Commission for Europe (ECE) offers an ad hoc internship program designed to promote a better understanding of the work of the ECE in the area of East-West economic cooperation. ECE accepts graduate students or those with specialized professional experience in fields relevant to the ECE, including agriculture, chemicals, coal, energy, environment, electric power, gas, housing, building and planning, inland transport, economic plans, programs and perspectives, standardization, statistics, steel, timber, trade, and water problems.

Internships do not normally exceed three months in duration and all costs associated with the internship must be borne by interns. In addition, interns must be sponsored by their academic institution, government, or Permanent Mission to the United Nations in Geneva. To apply, submit a detailed résumé and a statement of interest to the ECE. (For more information on the ECE see Chapter 36, United Nations.) [ID:6754]

United Nations Economic Commission for Latin America and the Caribbean
P.O. Box 179-D, United Nations Building,
Santiago, CHILE; (56) (2) 2085061, fax (56) (2) 2081946, www.eclac.cl

The UN Economic Commission for Latin America and the Caribbean accepts interns from around the world whose interests and academic backgrounds are consistent with the organization's mission and objectives. Internships are generally restricted to students enrolled in an academic program and are not remunerated. Interns must also cover the costs of travel and accommodation. Interested applicants should forward a complete résumé specifying courses taken, along with a letter from their university or academic institutions sponsoring their request for an internship. (For more information on the UN Economic Commission for Latin America and the Caribbean see Chapter 36, United Nations.) [ID:6742]

United Nations Educational, Scientific and Cultural Organization (UNESCO)
Staff Training Section, Bureau of Personnel, 1 rue Miollis,
75732 Paris CEDEX 15, FRANCE; (33) (1) 4568-1000, fax (33) (1) 4567-1690, www.unesco.org

The United Nations Educational, Scientific and Cultural Organization (UNESCO) offers interns the opportunity to develop a better understanding of UNESCO while working in an international setting. Approximately 40 internships, lasting an average of two months, are offered in the area of international development. Candidates must be enrolled in post-graduate studies in a relevant field and be able to cover all their expenses; no stipend is available. (For more information on the UNESCO see Chapter 36, United Nations.) [ID:5560]

United Nations Environment Programme Regional Office for North America (UNEP/RONA)
Internship Coordinator, Room DC2-0803, United Nations, New York, NY,
10017, USA; (212) 963-8093, fax (212) 963-7341, uneprona@un.org, www.unep.org

UNEP Regional Office for North America (UNEP/RONA) offers three-month internship programs during the periods mid-January to mid-March, mid-April to mid-June and early September to mid-December to candidates enrolled in master's degree programs in graduate schools at the time of the application and also during the internship. Depending on the particular areas of expertise, postings may be arranged at regional offices.

Applications are available from UNEP/RONA at the above address. (For more information on the UN Environment Programme see Chapter 36, United Nations.) [ID:5561]

United Nations Headquarters Internship Programme
Internship Coordinator, Office of Human Resources Management,, Room S-2570,
United Nations, New York, NY, 10017, USA; (212) 963-4437, fax (212) 963-3683, www.un.org/

The United Nations Headquarters Internship Programme is designed to promote among the participants a better understanding of major problems confronting the world and to provide insight into how the United Nations attempts to find solutions to these problems. Internships are available in a variety of fields, including: development planning and analysis, international relations, international law, economics, political affairs, population studies, translation and terminology, transnational corporations, and women's studies.

Internships are offered in three two-month program periods throughout the year: mid-January to mid-March, early June to early August, and mid-September to mid-November. Applications must be submitted six months prior to the proposed commencement date. Candidates must be enrolled in graduate school and under age 30 to qualify. Interns are not paid; costs of travel and accommodation must be borne by the interns or their sponsoring institutions. (For more information on the UN see Chapter 36, United Nations.) [ID:5562]

United Nations Industrial Development Organization (UNIDO)
Director, Personnel Services, P.O. Box 300, Room D1662,
Vienna International Centre, Wagramerstrasse 5, A-1400 Vienna, AUSTRIA;
(43) (1) 26026/4146 or 4147, fax (43) (1) 269 26 69, org_web@www.UNIDO.org, www.UNIDO.org

The United Nations Industrial Development Organization's (UNIDO) Internship Programme accepts a limited number of unpaid interns who wish to obtain practical experience with UNIDO or to do research on items of direct relevance to UNIDO's program of work. Internships are available in such areas as public administration, legal affairs, economic development, technology transfer, and industrial planning. Internship candidates must have completed an advanced university degree or be enrolled in an advanced program. They also must be nominated by their national mission to the UN or their university. (For more information on UNIDO see Chapter 36, United Nations.) [ID:5563]

United Nations Office at Vienna (UNOV)
Ad-Hoc Internship Programme, Human Resources Management Section,
P.O. Box 500, Vienna International Centre, A-1400 Vienna, AUSTRIA;
(43) (1) 21345-3659, fax (43) (1) 21345-5886, www.un.or.at/

The United Nations Office at Vienna offers internships on an ad hoc basis in areas relevant to its activities, which include administration, crime prevention and criminal justice, space law and policy, international trade law, drug control, electronic support, statistics, communications, and finance.

Internships range in duration from three months to one year and are unpaid. Applicants must hold at least a university degree and have their applications recommended or endorsed by an educational institution, or in exceptional cases, by their respective Permanent Mission in Vienna. Application forms are available on request from UNOV, and when completed, should be accompanied by an official transcript. [ID:6765]

United Nations Population Fund (UNFPA)
Summer Internship Programme, Personnel Branch, 220 East 42nd Street,
New York, NY, 10017, USA; (212) 297-5358, fax (212) 297-4908, choo@unfpa.org, www.unfpa.org

The United Nations Population Fund (UNFPA) Summer Internship Program offers a small group of outstanding graduate students the opportunity to acquire direct exposure to UNFPA operations. It is designed to complement development-oriented studies with practical experience in various aspects of technical assistance, as interns gain an understanding of multilateral assistance in population activities.

Internships are offered primarily at New York headquarters. Candidates must have completed their first year of studies in a master's degree program or equivalent in a social science field, with a concentration in population studies. Written and spoken proficiency in English is required and fluency in French, Spanish or Arabic is an asset. Interns are not paid, and all costs must be borne by the intern or nominating institution. (For more information on UNFPA see Chapter 36, United Nations.) [ID:5564]

United Nations Research Institute for Social Development (UNRISD)
Palais des Nations, 1211- Geneva 10, 16 ave. Jean-Tremblay, 1209 Geneva,
SWITZERLAND; (41) (22) 798-8400, fax (41) (22) 740-0791, info@unrisd.org, www.unrisd.org

The United Nations Research Institute for Social Development (UNRISD) accepts interns on an ad hoc basis to work on research activities including issues related to rebuilding war-torn societies, ethnic conflict and development, gender and development policy, social change and social movements, among others.

Internships range in duration and are unpaid. Students in advanced years of their undergraduate studies or currently enrolled in graduate studies are eligible to apply, but must be sponsored by their academic institution. (For more information on UNRISD see Chapter 36, United Nations.) [ID:6766]

Visions in Action
2710 Ontario Road N.W., Washington, DC, 20009, USA;
(202) 625-7402, fax (202) 625-2353, visions@igc.org, www.igc.org/visions

Visions in Action is a small, nonprofit organization committed to social change in Africa and Latin America through grassroots volunteer efforts. The organization provides nine internships on a continuous basis at its Washington office. Assignments are available in the areas of recruitment, public relations, administration, fundraising, and international research.

Internships each require a commitment of three months or more, for 15 to 40 hours per week. Internships are unpaid but interns who decide to go overseas with the program receive an $800 credit toward the Visions in Action program fee. [ID:5566]

Women's International League for Peace and Freedom (WILPF)
P.O. Box 28, 1211 Geneva 20, SWITZERLAND;
(41) (22) 7336175, fax (41) (22) 7401063, www.cruzio.com/~wilpf

The Women's International League for Peace and Freedom (WILPF) is a grassroots, community-based international organization which aims to bring together women opposed to war, violence, exploitation, and all forms of discrimination and oppression. Internships focus on work undertaken by the UN, WILPF, and nongovernmental organizations. Interns live in Geneva and New York.

Assignments normally begin in January and last one year, with interns working in both Geneva and New York. Priority is given to women between the ages of 21 and 30. Travel expenses and housing are covered, and a small stipend is provided. Applicants must submit a detailed résumé, a 1000 to 1500 word essay giving their reasons for wanting to participate in the program, and two recommendations from non-family members. [ID:5568]

World Bank Young Professionals Program
Staff Development Division, 1818 H Street N.W.,
Washington, DC, 20433, USA; (202) 473-0312, fax (202) 522-3741, www.worldbank.org

The World Bank (also known as the International Bank for Reconstruction and Development - IBRD) Young Professionals Program offers an exciting beginning to a career in the World Bank Group. Young Professionals serve in two 12-month rotational assignments in the operations, financial, or research areas of the bank, International Finance Corporation (IFC), and the Multilateral Investment Guarantee Agency (MIGA).

Candidates must be under the age of 32, have a master's degree or equivalent in economics, finance, or a technical field in the group's operations, plus a minimum of two years of relevant work experience. The technical fields of interest to the bank group are education, public health, environment and natural resource management, social sciences, and urban planning. Approximately 30 positions are available annually, and they typically lead to permanent employment with the bank. (For more information on the World Bank see Chapter 36, United Nations.) [ID:5569]

World Bank/MIGA Summer Employment Program
Staff Development Division, Room O-4146, 1818 H Street N.W., Washington, DC,
20433, USA; (202) 473-8151, fax (202) 522-3741, sprogram@worldbank.org, www.miga.org

The World Bank/Multilateral Investment Guarantee Agency (MIGA) Summer Employment Program offers interns an opportunity to improve their skills while working in an international environment. Assignments are available in these areas of: economics, finance, human resource development, social sciences, environment, private sector development, statistics, accounting, and other related fields.

Approximately 160 interns are accepted annually. Candidates should be enrolled in a full-time graduate program and have plans to return to full-time study in the fall. Applicants with strong computer skills and knowledge of World Bank Group languages (French, Spanish, Russian, Arabic, Portuguese, or Chinese) are preferred. The bank pays a monthly salary to all interns and provides an airfare allowance. Students are responsible for their own living accommodations. Applicants should forward a detailed résumé to the above address. (For more information on the World Bank see Chapter 36, United Nations.) [ID:5570]

World Food Programme
Human Resources and Administrative Services Division, 426, Via Cristoforo,
00145 Rome, ITALY; (39) (6) 522821, fax (39) (6) 5127400 or 5133537, www.wfp.org/

The World Food Programme accepts interns in order to promote a better understanding of the United Nations and the operations of the World Food Programme. Interns are fully involved in the work of the division that selects them for an internship and carry out their assignments under the supervision of a professional staff member.

Candidates are generally under 30 years of age and must be currently enrolled in graduate school. Internships are unpaid and all related costs are the responsibility of the intern. To apply, send a detailed résumé along with a completed World Food Programme Personal History form. (For more information on the World Food Programme see Chapter 36, United Nations.) [ID:6758]

World Health Organization (WHO)
Division of Personnel (Interns), 1211 Geneva 27,
SWITZERLAND; (41) (22) 791-2111, fax (41) (22) 791-0746, www.who.ch/

The World Health Organization (WHO) offers a number of internships at its Geneva headquarters, with a view to deepening interns' knowledge and understanding of WHO's goals, principles, and activities. Assignments are confined to health-related areas.

Candidates must be engaged in a course of study related to health work and preference will be given to postgraduate students. The internships are only available in WHO headquarters in Geneva; internships last a minimum of six weeks and a maximum of three months. No financial assistance is available. (For more information on the World Health Organization see Chapter 36, United Nations.) [ID:5571]

PART THREE

Finding that International Job

18. Your Career Path 375
19. The Hiring Process 379
20. The Job Search 385
21. The Internet Job Search 399
22. Resources for the
       International Job Search 429
23. Phone Research Techniques 443
24. International Résumés 455
25. Covering Letters 483
26. Interviewing for an International Job ... 495

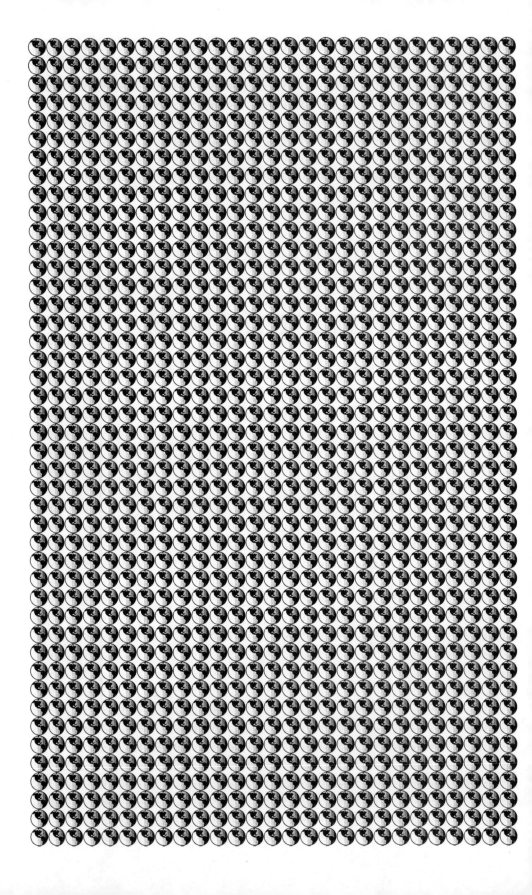

Chapter 18

Your
Career
Path

Before you can land the overseas job you want, it's important to understand the factors which affect your international career path and the types of jobs available to you.

The phrase "international career" does not necessarily mean "working abroad." An international career usually means first working in Canada, and then being posted overseas. There are many international jobs in Canada which require you to have international expertise and to interact with people from abroad, while other international, Canadian-based jobs do not put much emphasis of crosscultural communication skills.

LONG-TERM SKILL BUILDING

More than in a domestic Canadian career, you must have a long-term strategy for building your international career, block by block. International careers are built on experience in various areas. When contemplating a new international job, therefore, salary and your place in the pecking order are not as important as they would be in the domestic market. Choose jobs that lead to new careers, or are prerequisites to the job you eventually want.

An important consideration in your job strategy is to recognize how volatile the international job market is. Whether it's shifts in trade, government policy or your personal timing, you must always be willing to take advantage of changes as they occur and accept new paths in your career. You must be flexible, adaptable and resourceful. For example, in assessing new job possibilities, always consider cross-industry transfers of your skills, going from one sector to another. You may be able to do this rather easily, given the transferability of many international skills.

Remember that diversity and flexibility are the hallmarks of an international career. It is always a good idea to develop your experience in at least two broad work areas. Thus, if you are an overseas teacher, make sure you take on some extra administrative duties at your school. If you are a researcher, develop a sideline in computer skills. If you are an accountant, look up and keep abreast of the sales elements in your business. A mix of skills is often required in an overseas career: for example, business-minded people with experience in community work or engineers with some social science background. A great deal of importance is placed on the right mix of *soft* skills (intercultural understanding skills) and *hard* skills (technical, specialized knowledge).

It's also important to maintain the breadth of your international skills. Don't allow your knowledge to become outdated. If you specialized in African studies and took a few courses in Southeast Asian politics, keep your readings current on Asian affairs even if you are now a project administrator in Africa. If you are an academic-theorist-researcher, make sure you continue to dabble in administration, organization and budgeting. Remember, specialization aside, it is the generalist who will get ahead in an international environment.

There is one key factor in your long-term skill-building strategies. This is your *International IQ*. (For a more detailed of discussion of this concept, see "What is Your International IQ?" in Chapter 1, The Effective Overseas Employee.) Because international and intercultural skills are not easily acquired, having these skills gives you access to a wide range of careers in many fields. An international employer can teach you about his or her business, but it is difficult, time-consuming and highly speculative to attempt to teach you the refinements of intercultural communication. Thus, no matter what your international career path, always concentrate on developing your International IQ. It will provide you with security and flexibility in a volatile job market.

In summary, what is important in any long-term strategy is to acquire a list of accomplishments that are both specialized and general, and at the same time, continue to build your International IQ.

MIX BETWEEN OVERSEAS
AND CANADIAN EXPERIENCE

Keep the right mix in your inventory of international skills; that is, skills acquired abroad versus skills acquired in Canada.

In deciding your international career path, consideration must be given to the balance between the time you spend working overseas and the time you spend working in Canada. A useful grid for assessing your "mix" is to look at your skills inventory in terms of future needs. First, ask yourself the question, "What international skills must be developed in Canada?" Second, "What skills must be developed overseas?" And third, "What skills can be developed in either setting?" By breaking your skills inventory into these three categories, you will be better able to assess where you should be working.

Some international jobs are based in Canada and do not require intercultural awareness skills. For example, most international departments have information officers whose sole job is to guide people through the maze of international publications and sources of information. And an international currency buyer need not have overseas experience. The skills required for these international jobs must be acquired in Canada.

If you are just starting an international career, most international jobs in Canada or abroad require some overseas experience. Even if you work in Canada in an international job that doesn't require overseas experience, your credibility with colleagues in other departments will be dependent on your understanding of the overseas working environment. Thus, it is highly recommended that you have at least one intensive overseas experience (usually volunteer) early in your career. Do not postpone this crucial step. The longer you wait, the less your chances are of finding an opportunity. Married life, older children and, indeed, your ability to adapt to the rigours of some overseas environments will hinder your chance of being chosen for that all-important first overseas posting.

After four or five years of living abroad, most employees lose touch with Canadian realities and the Canadian way of doing things. While they may not notice it, men and women have a tremendous ability to adapt to new surroundings, and in a short time, lose sight of old methods of work and communication. A return to work in Canada will keep your work habits current as well as make you aware of the changing facts of Canadian life.

PUBLIC, PRIVATE OR NONPROFIT SECTOR?

The differences between overseas work in the *public, private* and *nonprofit* sectors illustrate the standard stereotypes: government jobs tend to be bureaucratic, with less room to manoeuvre, and have slower, more rigid, career paths; private firms offer more fast-track job opportunities with greater remuneration; nonprofit careers, while providing adequate salaries, have much less of the dollar-valued perks often attributed to overseas work. Nonprofit jobs are often more hands-on, less bureaucratic. Job security is relatively secure in public institutions, whereas overseas private employment can be particularly erratic and harsh. Working overseas for an NGO or as a private-sector employee certainly tends to allow for more creativity.

Overall, government jobs offer wider international experience, whereas private firms concentrate on narrow, specialized fields. In most cases, government will give you greater exposure to the varied facets of another culture, such as language training and dealing with different levels of the local government and population. However, this wider perspective is also available to employees with NGOs and some international consulting firms.

Employees in private business are not as insulated from the potential aggravations of living in a foreign culture. Whereas a Canadian government official or NGO employee will get paid whether or not he or she closes that deal, a private businessperson must live with the consequences of failure doing business overseas. The businessperson's life overseas has a lot more built-in hazards than the government official's. Another factor is the difference in support systems. A private individual must face the overseas market alone. A government official has a massive support system whereby housing, medical, and transportation concerns are taken care of by support staff and work problems are resolved by teams of experts.

A major advantage of working for a government agency (or, to a certain extent, an NGO) is the protection you have in foreign countries. Diplomatic status or close linkages to the Canadian diplomatic corps are an extra measure of security and insurance against all types of problems overseas. Whether you are suffering from foreign bureaucratic stonewalling, mulling your way through customs or have inadvertently brushed up against unknown foreign laws (or corrupt officials), having close diplomatic ties is very helpful in resolving these problems or insulating you from them in the first place.

While you may never work for the FOREIGN SERVICE in a Canadian mission abroad, knowledge of their services and operations is important. Embassies, High Commissions and Consulates are a ready source of information on local economic and political situations. The federal, and increasingly, provincial governments are putting in services to facilitate trade and business. Whatever your type of overseas employment, take the time to visit and research our Canadian foreign missions. (For more information on government services see Chapter 33, Service for International Businesses & Entrepreneurs.)

CHOOSING YOUR INTERNATIONAL WORK SETTING

Don't be too strict about your choice of countries when you are researching overseas job opportunities. International employees know you often have little choice about the country you will live in. They take advantage of the opportunities that come to them or accept the choice of their employers. Moreover, most people who have worked internationally have learned not to prejudge a country. Surprises abound. You never really know what life will be like in a particular posting until you get there.

It may be difficult to focus your international job search on a specific country. Your chances of landing a job in your country of choice may be slim. Focus instead on larger regions of the world—Asia, Latin America, Africa. You can, however, make some concrete decisions about certain geographical work settings. For some, Southern countries are too difficult; for others, the isolation of certain areas is a major issue. You can decide to work only in a rural area, or only in an urban setting, but these types of decisions must be made ahead of time.

Chapter 19

The Hiring Process

Finding a job overseas takes persistence, good qualifications, contacts and a measure of luck. You may be asked to leave "yesterday," or it may take 12 months to place you in your post once you have been offered a position. Compared to a job in Canada, the verification process and pre-departure activities for an overseas posting may be lengthy, especially if your employer is not situated in Canada.

The hiring process for overseas work follows a number of patterns, from "can you leave for Kuala Lumpur in three days?" to "we have your résumé on file from last year. Are you still available?" Don't be discouraged if you hear nothing or are told that your résumé has been placed on file. Overseas job offers are often received a long time after the résumé has been submitted. On the other hand, don't be surprised if you are asked to be packed and ready in one week! There are numerous reasons why the timing factor dominates international hiring.

One of the primary delaying factors is that overseas work is often awarded on a contract basis. To derive the maximum competitive bidding advantage, most large overseas employers spend a great deal of time and money maintaining computerized data banks of qualified candidates. Having a readily-available labour pool is an important part of being successful in the bidding process. (In Part Five of this book, International Career Contacts, the descriptions of organizations show whether they maintain résumé data banks.)

When bidding on a project, a firm will often consult their résumé data bank for qualified candidates. If you are registered with them, you may be contacted at this time for permission to submit your résumé with the proposal. Don't get your hopes up, since the decision to award a contract may take over a year. On the other hand, immediate hiring action is also common, as many of the candidates whose names were submitted with the proposal will have found other employment by the time the project is awarded.

To take full advantage of these situations, keep your résumé active in the minds of employers by making regular calls to them. Let them know you are available. Your objective when first speaking to employers is not to find out if they are hiring, but whether there is a possibility they will need your services over the coming year. If you accept an employer's standard response that they do not presently have anything to offer, you are ignoring a *basic* element of the international hiring process, and you will become discouraged needlessly.

Once the decision to hire you has been made, there are many factors which can delay your departure. Verification processes and pre-departure activities can easily add another six months to your waiting time. A strong word of caution goes out especially to those who have been tentatively offered a post. While your employer may be enthusiastic about getting you into the field as quickly as possible, there are numerous delaying factors which can impede (or prevent) your departure. Examples include: cultural orientation sessions which (may) assess your overseas aptitudes; security clearance which can take several weeks; medical exams and their approval by in-house specialists; acceptance of your credentials by the overseas country representative or the foreign government paying your salary; securing a visa (not always easily done); tedious delays as a result of long distance mailing times; and wherever government is concerned, the multi-level approval process.

There are other instances which require immediate hiring action. For example: the long-awaited decision to proceed with a new program is suddenly taken, creating an urgent need to fill several positions; a crisis situation arises overseas requiring immediate staffing; new monies are found at budget-year end (especially with government contracts) and must be allocated; an overseas employee returns to Canada before his or her contract expires (this situation occurs frequently).

The lead times required for certain overseas posts are easier to predict. For example, teachers should start applying for overseas positions a full year ahead of their planned departure date, just prior to the beginning of a new school year. For UNITED NATIONS positions, most candidates can plan on waiting at least one full year from the point of initial contact. Those who apply for positions which involve placement on a UN waiting list have been known to wait two and even three years. For business and other nongovernmental organizations, you can usually plan on a minimum four-month job search. If you are applying to institutions or firms outside Canada, the process is normally even longer.

SAMPLE LEAD TIMES IN FINDING A JOB

There are no standard lead times involved in an international job search, but it is safe to say you should buckle down and plan for a long haul. Here are the actions taken by one individual, a university graduate in her last year of a master's program.

September-January
Does library research to find addresses and writes away for information from 50 organizations. Information is received by mail over next six months until March. Starts speaking with friends and acquaintances to familiarize herself with job market.

February
Decides on job objective. Makes use of information received during letter campaign to compose covering letters and résumé. Rewrites résumé four times until it is perfect.

March-June
Starts active phone campaign (four hours a day). Contacts 60 organizations, makes 145 follow-up phone calls. Rewrites résumé twice and composes three new covering letters to fit new information received during job search.

July-August
Accepts six-week contract at minimum wage with NGO to accumulate experience. Continues active job search. Follow-up phone calls indicate three or four good leads.

August
Receives offer for permanent position with NGO in Canada. Immediate follow-up with all other possible employers to inquire if other opportunities are imminent. Another NGO offers overseas opportunity with departure in October. Accepts overseas position.

October
Departs for overseas.

This successful job search took approximately 12 months, but it could have been a lot shorter...or even longer.

WHO MAKES THE HIRING DECISION?

Contrary to what you might logically expect, the personnel department rarely makes the international hiring decision. Most hiring decisions are made by managers from the department with the job to offer. For this reason, it is a good rule to always contact the department most likely to need your services and speak to the most senior person available.

Depending on the organization, there are a number of places where you can begin your search for the person with the mandate to hire you.

Personnel Department
When contacting corporations whose main interest is not international affairs, insist on speaking to someone in your field who has international experience. Do not accept being automatically directed to the personnel department. This will most often be a waste of time. Except for organizations involved exclusively

in international affairs, the personnel department is rarely able to appreciate international qualifications.

International Division

International departments of Canadian institutions or firms are often considered separate, independent departments, existing alongside Canadian operations divisions. This structural observation is important to the job seeker as many of the personnel decisions related to international activities are considered so unique they are handled strictly by the international division, whereas the personnel office handles the Canadian domestic departments. Always start your job inquiries with the international department. If the international division is a small one, ask to speak to the director. If it is a very large department, ask to speak to the department head in charge of the area you are interested in.

Large International Firm, Government Department or Institution

If you are contacting an organization whose main purpose is international, it is best to have a two-tiered approach. First, focus on the specific department involved in your area of interest; second, contact the personnel department. Thus, a marketing director would contact the international sales division director, an engineer would call the project leader, and a person specializing in Asian studies would speak to the chief of the Asia department. All of these candidates would at the same time follow the normal procedures of the personnel department. This dual strategy is especially crucial with government and UN agencies. Unless your dossier is known in these two areas of a UN agency or government department, your chances of landing a job are slim.

Note also that most large consulting and engineering firms are often an umbrella for a myriad of smaller independent companies. Separate companies seem to be set up to manage individual projects. There is no easy method for deciphering this maze. Suffice it to say that they exist and make job searching somewhat difficult.

Small International Firm or Nongovernmental Organization

In this case you should speak directly to the chief executive officer or the president of the firm. If you are unable to speak to the chief executive officer, ask to speak to another senior member of the firm. If you are looking for a volunteer position with an NGO, do not contact the chief executive. As a volunteer you can increase your chances by registering with the personnel department and, at the same time, contacting the specific country placement officer dealing with programs of your interest.

THE IDEAL SELECTION PROCESS

Depending on the sophistication of the company doing the international hiring and the level of the position you are applying for, you can assess a company's expertise in the international field on the thoroughness of their selection process. You should be wary of a firm which skirts standard international hiring procedures. They will likely also skirt their responsibilities to an overseas employee.

Here are some of the most important points to look for during the selection process:

The job advertisement information should include a detailed job description as well as an honest description of overseas working and living conditions. Be wary of employers who paint too rosy a picture. Experienced international recruiters know that deception at this stage will lead to a high failure rate and mistrust of head office. They want candidates to deselect themselves. Ads should be "truthful to a T."

The interview process should be conducted by experienced international managers who have lived overseas. The employer should question you extensively in the following areas: your personality, your technical expertise, your career path now and upon return, your domestic or family situation, your spouse's willingness to move, your health and the health of your family, your understanding of overseas living conditions.

Orientation information on the country of posting should be provided on these essential areas: housing, social life, recreation, schooling, churches, health facilities, cost of living, local shopping conditions, local transportation, security, current political/socioeconomic situation, cultural norms and customs, language information, working conditions.

The spouse should always be interviewed and given a thorough orientation session. While some may say this is paternalistic, pressures from family life account for over half the failures in international appointments. Any firm in the international arena which fails to take the spouse into account is operating naively.

THE CONTRACT

Any employer who shrugs off its responsibility to an expatriate family is being shortsighted. It is part of the employer's responsibility to see that a family can function well abroad. Such items as proper housing and adequate schooling are essential components of contract negotiations.

Clarify beforehand all of the benefits associated with a contract. Knowing exactly what your industry's standards are will go a long way in helping you evaluate how you are being treated by your employer. For example, an NGO may only provide $2,000 in air freight allowance, whereas a private firm may cover the full cost of your move up to a maximum of $15,000. Both conform to their different industry standards. For a detailed description of CIDA's policy on remuneration and benefits for its executing agencies, see the Resource list at the end of this section.

Many Canadian organizations are too small, or perhaps just too lax, to develop standard remuneration policies. In these cases, you will have to negotiate your remuneration package from scratch.

Compared to a Canadian-based employment contract, an overseas contract may include some of the following benefits: a post adjustment to salary allowance (including protection against local inflation rates), payment in convertible currency, a severance allowance or political risks allowance, relocation time off and allowance (including a moving and set-up allowance), a return visit to Canada and visit by children to the country of placement, a schooling allowance, medical insurance including special evacuation insurance, a special housing and car allowance, Canadian warehousing costs, and sometimes even a paid visit to the country of posting by the candidate and his or her spouse in the final stages of the selection process before the appointment is made.

The following table summarizes important strategies in landing that international job contract.

UNDERSTANDING THE INTERNATIONAL HIRING PROCESS
What does it mean for you?

1. Lead times for international work are usually much longer than for other work.
2. Plan on accepting other work to put food on the table while you are looking for that international job.
3. Organize your affairs so when opportunity knocks, you can leave on short notice.
4. Do not make any irreversible decisions with regard to present conditions or personal affairs on the basis of a tentative job offer. Horror stories abound! Only a signed contract will do.
5. When contacting overseas employers, ask to speak to the managers most likely to require your services, rather than the personnel department. Concentrate on international divisions in large organizations and executive directors in small international firms. For government and UN organizations, use the dual strategy of contacting both the personnel department and department heads.
6. Contact employers not with the objective of finding out who is hiring, but to enquire "who may need my services over the next year?"
7. Don't give up: follow up regularly with past employer contacts; keep looking elsewhere (even when you have a tentative offer); keep adding related international experiences to your dossier.

A LAST WORD

Since most international job assignments involve either competitive bidding on projects or political influencing to acquire work visas, no job is guaranteed unless you have signed a contract or letter of employment. Despite whatever verbal promises or guarantees are made to you, never take irreversible action before you have a signed contract in your hand. This cannot be over-stressed. There are countless horror stories of people leaving their jobs, selling their businesses and renting out their homes only to find that the overseas assignment did not materialize!

Chapter 20

The Job
Search

Before undertaking an active job search, certain skills are required. While almost anyone can pursue an overseas job, successful candidates have a number of traits that lead them to success. In reading the following list, keep in mind that these job search skills are often the same ones required for the overseas work itself, and it is therefore to your benefit to demonstrate these skills to employers.

CREATIVE JOB SEARCH SKILLS
* Knowledge of Hiring Process
* Confidence
* Determination
* Entrepreneurial Instinct
* Verbal Communication Skills

Knowledge of the Hiring Process
People who find jobs are not necessarily those with the most job-related skills; rather, they are often the people most skilled in job search techniques. Therefore, you should practice interview and phone techniques with friends, write and rewrite your résumé to make it the best possible, and research and understand the overseas job market by consulting books or the Internet on the subject. In short, plan on becoming an effective job seeker.

Confidence
Be confident and persistent. Many recruiters and friends can sometimes discourage you in your endeavour. Finding that overseas job is not easy! It's

normal to have moments of doubt, but to be successful, you have to be relentless.

Determination

The single most vital factor in achieving success is determination. For example, we know of one candidate who visited Ottawa from Toronto five times over a four-month period and contacted over 60 organizations before landing a job. Another candidate had a job washing floors in a hospital for one year while he pursued international job openings with the UNITED NATIONS. He remained active in the international community by writing articles for development journals. Another became the co-ordinator for a crosscultural volunteer committee and vigorously searched for funds for a development project he had developed while unemployed. All of these candidates were successful and are now working in challenging jobs in Madagascar, Bangladesh, and for an NGO in Ottawa. The key to their success was determination, both long- and short-term.

Entrepreneurial Instinct

To be a successful international job hunter, you must be innovative, willing to take risks, and confident in putting yourself in the forefront of new, unknown challenges.

Many international job seekers have positioned themselves overseas in low-level jobs with the express purpose of making contacts in the industry in which they want to work. An English teacher took a low-paying job teaching English to businessmen in Hong Kong with the goal of becoming an executive assistant to a VP with business affairs in Canada. A tour guide made contacts during his excursions in Asia which helped him establish a craft import company in Ottawa. The key to success is to aggressively pursue a larger goal while working at a job you know you won't have forever. Make contacts, join clubs, research, and find out all there is to know about the environment you wish to work in. This includes not only the specific field, but also the business climate, the people, the language and politics of your targeted host country or culture.

Verbal Communication Skills

In undertaking a job search, you should have excellent communication skills. Whether speaking on the phone or in an interview, you should have a clear idea of what you want to say. You must be able to speak convincingly and enthusiastically about your skills and character traits. It is especially crucial to convey to employers what makes you valuable to them. For those of you with uncertainty about your ability to communicate effectively, rest assured that this can be learned. You will improve as your job search progresses.

THE THREE JOB SEARCH PHASES

You must approach the international job market with more acumen than if you were searching for a typical domestic job. You need a plan for each phase. Your first task will be self-evaluation. As discussed throughout this book, the key to the creative job search is being able to identify and label your skills for employers. Your second task will be to target your efforts efficiently by researching your field to uncover potential employers. The third task involves direct contact with employers, from telephoning and cruising the World Wide Web to e-mailing and face-to-face interviews.

The Three Phases of an International Job Search

1. SELF-EVALUATION: What do I have to offer?
   a. Assessing your personal skills inventory
   b. Deciding on a target job type
   c. Writing your first résumé

2. RESEARCH: Where do I Look?
   a. Applying to advertisements
   b. Networking
   c. Contacting executive search firms
   d. Targeting firms or specific countries
   e. Searching the Internet (See Chapter 21, The Internet Job Search)

3. APPLYING FOR THE JOB: How do I approach the employer?
   a. Phone research techniques (See Chapter 23, Phone Research Techniques)
   b. Rewriting your résumé using the language of your future employer (See Chapter 24, International Résumés)
   c. Writing the covering letter (See Chapter 25, Covering Letters)
   d. The job interview (See Chapter 26, Interviewing for an International Job)

SELF-EVALUATION

You should already have read Part One of this book, Your International IQ. You are now preparing to find a new job overseas: making plans and organizing your affairs for that important move. You have been building up your International IQ. You know yourself. You know you have the personal traits to enjoy an international assignment and you know you have the right skills. You have, perhaps, acquired a second language, done volunteer work for a number of international organizations, travelled in a developing country for three months, and even managed to swing a conference in, say, Belize. You know that within the next year your current job contract will be finished and, therefore, you are now ready to begin a serious job search for that overseas posting. But how and where do you start?

Selling your Skills

One good method for assessing, and selling, your skills is to think of them as separate components. Compartmentalize them into blocks. In conversations with employers, stay away from detailed lists that are difficult to grasp. For example, speak about your block of business skills, your block of language skills and your block of intercultural awareness skills. These components are your selling blocks to employers. Ignore the overlap in skills, use these selling blocks anyway.

In speaking of your abilities in this manner, you'll be able to paint a broad picture of yourself. This also simplifies the analytical profiling which employers must do when hiring. And you will have the employer thinking about you the way you want him or her to!

Describing your Skills *Internationally*

Most job searchers, including students, make the mistake of portraying themselves according to their past experience. Thus, the graduate student with a specialization in Middle East economics portrays herself as a graduate student looking for work. The shipping clerk still refers to his work as a clerk even though he has five years of experience with international customs clearance. The point here is that you must sell yourself under the label of your future work and not under the labels of the past. The student presents herself as an economist with Middle East expertise, and the shipping clerk presents himself as a trade agent in international shipping. If you want respect, if you want to be treated as a professional, develop the language and attitude that demonstrate your confidence and reflect your International IQ.

Match your background to the international job. Don't rely on an employer to do the matching analysis for you. Show the recruiter exactly how your skills and experience are compatible with the job.

Focusing on your Primary Skill

Most international employees have a range of knowledge: linguistics, economics, politics, technical and administrative skills. Whatever your background, you must arrange your skills to ensure that it is the primary one which dominates in your résumé and interview, and not the complementary ones. For example, a businessperson must sell himself or herself first as business-oriented, with a complementary knowledge of economics, even though his or her education may be all economics. You don't want to be perceived as an economist dabbling in business!

Phrases to Help you Describe your Best Skills

It is often difficult to describe your qualities to employers. Here are a few starting phrases that may help you. Remember to keep your language concise and direct.

* "I have been commended on..."
* "My colleagues tell me that I have an ability to..."
* "I can attribute my successes to being able to..."
* "I have an aptitude for..."
* "My previous supervisor relied on me mainly to..."
* "I am particularly well-known for my skills in..."
* "I have positioned myself to accept responsibility in..."

- "The background aspects of my experience which are particularly relevant are..."
- "If my co-workers had to sum up my management style, they would probably say..."

(For more information on job searching check out the Resource section, International Job Hunting Services on the Internet in Chapter 21, The Internet Job Search.)

THE RESEARCH PHASE

There are five basic ways to research a job:
- Applying to advertisements in the Careers section of newspapers
- Networking with friends, acquaintances, professional contacts
- Contacting executive search and employment services firms
- Targeting your research to specific firms, specific sectors, or specific countries of interest
- Surfing the Internet for the millions of web sites on job search techniques, job banks, résumé posting, and much more

Job Advertisements

It is common knowledge that 80 per cent of jobs are not found through job advertisements but through personal networking. Responding to job ads is the easiest way to research a job, but it is also the most competitive and thus most unlikely to succeed, especially for those trying to break into the field. If you have solid international credentials, by all means, the job advertisement is a good option. Whatever your situation, no research method should be discounted. We shall mention a few tips here.

Canadian newspapers, such as the *Globe and Mail*, *La Presse* and the *Montreal Gazette*, regularly carry international job opportunities of all types and levels. Don't forget to read the financial section of newspapers for information on new foreign contracts. Other international publications carry ads for highly-specialized and senior management positions, such as the *Economist*, *L'Express*, the *Wall Street Journal*, the *Financial Times* (London), *Le Monde* (Paris), the *Washington Post* and the *New York Times*. The Sunday editions of these publications are usually the best choice. (For more information on job postings, see the Resources section in this chapter and Chapter 21, The Internet Job Search.)

Most professions in Canada have a trade magazine. They are an invaluable source of ideas on how to build your international experience. Many of them carry international job advertisements. International articles are featured in most issues and can be useful for uncovering job information. For example, if you read about a new international initiative in your industry, contact the source immediately to find out about international employment possibilities. Do not wait for formal job postings to appear.

Don't get hung up on formal, narrow job requirements when applying for international work. While Canadian jobs have many specialized requirements, the breadth of skills for international jobs is so wide that recruiting officers are often very flexible in their hiring criteria. While the job advertisement may state otherwise, always remember this fact. Knowing what to do overseas, how to work and think in other cultures—this is the key to your mobility.

Don't let the term "expert," scare you. Despite what you may have heard, becoming an expert has lost its original meaning and now stands for "has experience in."

Networking, Making Contacts

Contacts are everything. Making international networking contacts is not easy. Internationally experienced people see themselves as having unique insights into how the world works and how cultures interact. They are not only attuned to world political and economic trends, but understand the diplomatic dancing that is required to make crosscultural communication easier. Such people can be quick to dismiss the efforts of rookies trying to enter the field. Thus, you face the problem of how to network with little international experience behind you.

Here are a few pointers to help you decide on your networking style.

Approach each new aspect of your job search with curiosity. Curiosity is a trait appreciated and recognized as a legitimate vehicle for pursuing knowledge. Aggressive, pushy behaviour, on the other hand, is not appreciated, as this is often in direct conflict with Southern cultures and would interfere with your success overseas.

What differentiates curious researchers from aggressive ones is that the curious have a passion for the process of discovery, while the aggressive are motivated solely by outcome. The curious take delight in the people and situations they meet in their discovery of a new culture.

Do everything you can to meet people in your field. We know of one individual who decided he wanted to work in disaster relief management. For one year he read, researched and wrote letters to people and organizations involved in this area. The objective of his research was not to uncover job openings, but to find out what was happening in the field. In the process, this person discovered which major international organizations were involved in disaster relief and what their links were to Canadian organizations. Later, when a Canadian job opportunity came up, he was interviewed for it. As he had knowledge of the field, he was hired and sent to work on a Colombian volcano disaster relief effort.

As the above example demonstrates, networking is not necessarily direct job searching. Your networking conversations may have different purposes but all can lead to jobs. There is a strong case to be made for focusing on information-gathering when you are searching for a job. Ask specific questions about the activities of a given organization. Information-gathering thus becomes a process of elimination in who you apply to.

Involve yourself in international affairs by getting to know the organizations, departments, periodicals and conferences that relate to your field. This does not mean going to a library to do research. Rather, go out and meet people, make contacts, network. Visit trade offices, subscribe to trade journals, attend conferences. Get a "working knowledge" of your area of expertise. Volunteer for any international committee that you can. Offer to set up meetings, do research, take tickets at the door. Do anything that will allow you to make connections. With these strategies, you will get to know people and find out what is going on in the international community, and you will be even more valuable to the employer who hires you for that overseas job.

When networking, make sure that you are armed with as much crosscultural knowledge as possible. International contact persons want to know how you would solve problems overseas, how you make contacts, what your insights are on the cultural peculiarities that affect negotiations and administration, what you know about import and export regulations, and the organizations which dominate or stand out in your international field. This sort of concrete information will impress potential employers and your other contacts. Don't make the common mistake of trying to impress your networking contact by discussing macro economic development policy, world injustices or liberation movements. Speak instead of your organizing techniques, your administrative skills in a crosscultural context, your language abilities and accounting skills. Discussions of why you are successful in your field or your solid understanding of overseas environments are more impressive to employers than academic theorising on political or economic processes.

If you are currently unemployed or in the final stages of an overseas contract, the trick is to expose yourself to as many opportunities as possible. Go to international conferences, drop in to check bulletin boards in international offices regularly, volunteer to manage a project, research and write an article on your field, join and become active in the international activities of an association, learn a second or third language and make use of the contacts you develop in the process. Each of these tactics puts you in line for meeting people and making contacts.

Wherever you work in the international field, you should be forging links with other competing, or similar institutions or companies. Take the time, and every opportunity to build relationships outside your office. Never lose interest in what others are doing. This continued interest will provide you with contacts when you are again actively searching for that international job, and will help you in your present job by broadening your understanding and exposure.

Networking, as opposed to job hunting, is a long-term process. You are not actively soliciting people for jobs, but rather for their understanding of the job market. Don't ask, "Do you have a job?" but rather, "What new developments or programs are starting up?" and "How do people normally enter this field?" and, especially, "What does your organization do and how does it do it?"

Networking Contacts

- University professors in your field who have international links
- Researchers in all fields and types of organizations
- Employees of internationally-oriented organizations
- Recent immigrants who have international ties
- Foreign students from developing countries

- Business executives working internationally
- International consultants concerned with work trends
- Government employees at CIDA, Foreign Affairs and International Trade (DFAIT)
- People you meet at conferences, trade associations or while learning a second language
- Returned overseas volunteers and their contacts
- People you meet during international travel
- Colleagues or friends of anyone on this list

Contact Organizations

- All the organizations profiled or listed as resources in this book
- Federal or provincial trade or business development offices (foreign ones in Canada or Canadian ones overseas)
- Foreign embassies and consulates
- Foreign associations in Canada, foreign government trade offices etc.
- Chamber Of Commerce
- Trade associations in manufacturing, etc.
- Large municipalities, mayor's office, city twinning programs
- Convention and tourism bureaus
- University international centres (see Chapter 16, International Studies in Canada & Abroad)
- Economic development agencies

Targeting Your Research: Discovering Where the Jobs Are

This book is full of contact addresses, resources, and Internet web addresses of international employers and opportunities. Since research strategies are discussed in detail throughout our guide, we shall limit ourselves here to pointing out important sectors in the Canadian economy.

Thousands of Canadians work overseas. Many work for the numerous Canadian firms who have expanded globally during the past few decades. The types of firms who have found international markets for their products and often hire Canadians for overseas positions are involved in: the services industry, consulting, engineering, construction, oil, manufacturing, banking, finance.

An important untapped market for Canadians is American firms working overseas. Given our cultural similarity, our good international standing, plus our advantage of speaking French, Canadians are attractive to many American firms.

Other Canadians find work directly with foreign companies. These are not as easy to research but nonetheless represent a substantial, unexploited area.

Canadians also work in international development, that is, providing aid to countries in the South, either directly with the federal government or with private firms or nongovernmental organizations (NGOs).

Wherever English is in short supply, there are opportunities not only for teaching English, but for skilled employees able to operate in English as well as the local language. Japan, Hong Kong, and increasingly, Korea are examples of places where many Canadians have found employment because of their language skills.

Canada has three main centres for finding international work. By far the largest is the Montréal-Ottawa-Toronto triangle. In almost every field represented, Canadian companies and organizations working abroad have their head offices in this region. Obviously the federal government plays a major role here, as do international development organizations and private consulting firms (many concentrated in the Montréal area). In the Western provinces, many international oil jobs are based in Alberta, although the oil job market is much smaller than it used to be. In Nova Scotia, education and trade partnerships with Cuba and Western Europe exist, and more partnerships are emerging. And lastly, there is the Vancouver area, with its natural resources and smaller, emerging business links with the Pacific Rim countries. If you are not close to one of these areas, do not despair. Long distance phone calls to specifically targeted companies can be very effective and usually receive more attention than a local call. Keep in mind also that all provinces have at least some individual in an overseas job.

A LAST WORD

In today's high-tech world, the Internet is an essential part of any job search. For advice on how to successfully "surf the Net" and survive consult Chapter 21, The Internet Job Search. For names and addresses of leads that can support you in your quest see Chapter 22, Resources on the International Job Search. Before you continue however, here is a checklist of what we think is required for an international job search. Re-read the following points to see if you are ready for your international job search.

* Have you worked hard at building your International IQ?
* Are you prepared to spend time and money in an active job search campaign?
* Do you have a clear idea of the type of international job you want? Can you do that job right now? Are you willing to work your way up, pay your dues?
* Do you know people working internationally in your field? Have you spoken to at least five people who have worked overseas?
* Does your résumé highlight your international experience and awareness?
* Can you clearly explain to employers what you do well and enjoy doing? Can you explain this in the context of an overseas work assignment?
* Why would an employer hire you?
* Have you written a two-sentence and a two-paragraph description of yourself and your key qualifications to use when networking?
* Have you researched the international aspects of your field? Have you conducted research into the international job market to determine where you fit in?

- Do you have a good idea of what your skills are worth to potential employers, or if not, do you know how to find out?
- Do you possess the skills required to carry out an effective job search (letter-writing techniques, phoning techniques, résumé-writing skills, interview and communication techniques)?
- Are you knowledgeable about the international hiring process? Who to contact? Who makes the hiring decisions? How long an international job search takes?

If you answered no to many of these questions, read on. This book is here to help you.

RESOURCES
General Job Search: All

You have to start somewhere, and it has to be here: get your résumé done, figure out how to research your industry, and find that job you always wanted. Job hunting is not all misery. It's the one time in your life when you get to look seriously at your professional self, talk to people who are doing what you want to do, and learn all about who is doing what in your field of expertise. That sounds exciting! Get started. Good luck.

101 Dynamite Questions to ask at Your Interview 📖
1996, *Richard Fein,* 139 pages ➤ Impact Publications, 9104 North Manassas Drive, Manassas Park, VA 20111-2366, USA; US$14.95; credit cards; (703) 361-7300, fax (703) 335-9486 ■ Learn the importance of asking questions at job interviews. 101 questions about the job, the company, and the industry or profession are listed. Communication tips are also provided. Visit the distributor's web site at www.impactpublications.com. [ID:2419]

175 High Impact Cover Letters 📖
1996, *Richard H. Beatty,* 256 pages ➤ John Wiley & Sons, 22 Worchester Drive, Rexdale, Ontario M9W 1L1; $15.50; credit cards; (800) 567-4797, fax (800) 565-6802; Available at international news-stands ■ Contains 175 highly effective cover letter samples that can be used in a wide range of circumstances. Visit distributor's web site, www.wiley.com/products/worldwide/canada. [ID:1801]

Change Your Job, Change Your Life:
High Impact Strategies for Finding Great Jobs in the '90s 📖
1997, *Ronald Krannich,* 363 pages ➤ Impact Publications, 9104 North Manassas Drive, Manassas Park, VA 20111-2366, USA; US$17.95; credit cards; (703) 361-7300, fax (703) 335-9486 ■ Acclaimed career book. Outlines how to develop the necessary skills for success in today's job market. Eleven "how-to" chapters on job search, relocation, entrepreneurship, and implementation. Visit the distributor's web site at www.impactpublications.com. [ID:1048]

Contact Point 💻
www.contactpoint.ca/index.stm ■ Contact Point provides resources on career counselling and job services. There is also an online discussion forum for career counselling. This site is primarily for career counsellors, but the information could be useful to any job seeker. [ID:2445]

Do What You Are 📖
1995, *Paul D. Tieger, Barbara Barron-Tieger,* 350 pages ➤ Little, Brown and Company, 148 Yorkville Ave., Toronto, Ontario M5R 1C2; $22.95; (800) 387-6922, fax (416) 967-4591; Available through bookstores only ■ Discover the perfect career for you through the secrets of personality typing. Using workbook exercises, you will find lists of occupations that are popular with your type, as well as the strengths and pitfalls of each personality type. [ID:1814]

High Impact Resumes & Letters:
How to Communicate Your Qualifications to Employers 📖
1997, *Ronald Krannich, W. Banis,* 263 pages ➤ Impact Publications, 9104 North Manassas Drive, Manassas Park, VA 20111-2366, USA; US$19.95; credit cards; (703) 361-7300, fax (703) 335-9486 ■ This book sets the standard for other guides. Well-written and easy to follow, this new edition provides step-by-step guidance on understanding today's job market, developing job search skills, selecting résumé formats, writing each résumé section, producing different types of letters, and distributing résumés to employers. Shows users how to organize, write, produce, distribute, follow up, and evaluate written communication for maximum impact. Visit the distributor's web site at www.impactpublications.com. [ID:1049]

Resumes that Work: How to Sell Yourself on Paper 📖
1993, *L. Foxman,* 128 pages ➤ John Wiley & Sons, 22 Worchester Drive, Rexdale, Ontario M9W 1L1; $14.95; credit cards; (800) 567-4797, fax (800) 565-6802 ▪ Updated for the '90s job market, this book helps readers get the jobs they desire. The unique workbook format uses the latest time-tested strategies for developing attention-grabbing, professional résumés. Goals are defined, résumé-writing dos and don'ts are explained, and effective use of employment resources is discussed. Visit distributor's web site at www.wiley.com/products/worldwide/canada. [ID:1022]

The Smart Interviewer 📖
1990, *Bradford D. Smart,* 205 pages ➤ John Wiley & Sons, 22 Worchester Drive, Rexdale, Ontario M9W 1L1; $19.95; credit cards; (800) 567-4797, fax (800) 565-6802 ▪ A how-to course in selection interviewing. Presents a simple, elegant technique based on sound psychological and universal management principles. The step-by-step approach shows how to plan the interview, demonstrates the psychology behind interview questions, and explains how to interpret answers. Also discusses legal aspects of interviewing and how to prepare job descriptions and "person specifications." Visit the distributor's web site at www.wiley.com/products/worldwide/canada. [ID:1016]

Swan's How to Pick the Right People Program 📖
1989, *William S. Swan,* 304 pages ➤ John Wiley & Sons, 22 Worchester Drive, Rexdale, Ontario M9W 1L1; $19.95; credit cards; (800) 567-4797, fax (800) 565-6802 ▪ Advice on how to attract, interview and select the best employees. Visit www.wiley.com/products/worldwide/canada, the distributor's web site. [ID:1015]

The Three Boxes of Life: An Introduction to Life Work Planning 📖
1981, *Richard Bolles,* Ten Speed Press, 466 pages ➤ Publisher's Group West, 74 Rolark Drive, Scarborough, Ontario M1R 4G2; $26.75; VISA; (800) 463-3981, fax (416) 293-5756 ▪ If you want to change careers during the next three years, or you're just not satisfied with your present job, but don't know what you want to do with your professional life, this book is for you. This classic book helps you understand and assess your skills. Looks at long-term strategies for life planning. Particularly useful for those planning career changes. Highly recommended. [ID:1166]

The 1997 What Colour Is Your Parachute?
A Practical Manual for Job Hunters and Career Changers 📖
Annual, *Richard Bolles* ➤ Ten Speed Press/PGW Sales Warehouse, 2775 Matheson Blvd. E., Mississauga, Ontario L4W 4P7; $23.95; VISA; (800) 463-3981, fax (416) 293-5756 ▪ A practical manual for job hunters and career changers. The 1997 edition includes a workbook and resource guide, and a new section entitled "Job Hunting On the Internet." Topics range from the growing importance of "cyberia" as a job hunting ground, to the effective use of search engines and the importance of net etiquette. Given the other job hunting approaches discussed in this book, it is one of the best buys available. Arguably the best job search book on the market. [ID:1251]

General Job Search: Students

This list of books will be especially important if you are just graduating from university or if you have not recently looked for a job. Job search techniques have changed a lot during the past 15 years. In today's job market, greater emphasis is placed on having a solid understanding of your skill base. These books will help you focus on your skills and on using this knowledge for job hunting. If you have not already bought and spent a week studying the classic *What Colour is Your Parachute*, mentioned above, you should seriously think of doing so. Learning how to job hunt is a life-skill you'll need until you retire. Good luck, and happy careering.

Career Options: The Graduate Recruitment Annual 📖
Annual ➤ Canadian Association of Career Educators and Employers, Suite 205, 1209 King Street W., Toronto, Ontario M6K 1G2; $3.95; credit cards; (416) 535-8126, fax (416) 532-0934 ▪ Useful magazine-style publication for graduating students. Contains good information about career

planning, job hunting and employment opportunities. *Available in French as Option Carrières: L'annuaire de recrutement des diplômées et diplômé.* [ID:1063]

Choices That Count: Co-operative Education in the Public Service of Canada 📖 💻
Annual, 145 pages ➤ External Recruitment Programs, Public Service Commission, 18th Floor, L'Esplanade Laurier, 300 Laurier Avenue W., Ottawa, Ontario K1A 0M7; free; (613) 992-9630, fax (613) 947-5875 ■ A listing of work-study programs at Canadian postsecondary institutions. If you are registered in one of these programs, check out the possibilities of arranging co-op placements with the international branch of a government department. The web version of this publication should be available soon at the Public Service Commission web site, www.psc-cfp.gc.ca/jobs.htm. [ID:1666]

Employment Resources on the Internet 💻
www.cs.purdue.edu/homes/swlodin/jobs.html ■ This is an outstanding collection of links. The links can connect dozens of professional recruiters, regional career sites, university counselling services, and newspaper classified sections. Additionally, there are several useful links to other career-related sites, some of which specialize in international employment. [ID:2513]

First Job: A New Grad's Guide to Launching Your Business Career 📖
1992, *Richard Fein,* 240 pages ➤ John Wiley & Sons, 22 Worchester Drive, Rexdale, Ontario M9W 1L1; $12.95; credit cards; (800) 567-4797, fax (800) 565-6802 ■ Built around basic employment search principles applied by actual students, this book presents key elements for job search success, such as identifying your positive characteristics, developing résumés, writing cover letters, the principles of interviewing and how to use them, and a no-lose approach to negotiating your starting salary. Visit www.wiley.com/products/worldwide/canada, the distributor's web site. [ID:1014]

The Gordon Group Home Page 💻
www.owt.com/jobsinfo.jobstext.html ■ This is a useful list of North American and international careers-related sites. In addition to over 100 links, this site also has some of the best counselling services available online. The advice can help you with everything from time management during a job hunt, to increasing your networking skills. This is one of the best sites to visit when you're starting your international job hunt. [ID:2512]

The Looking for Work Series 📖
1990, 56 pages ➤ Canadian Association of Career Educators and Employers, Suite 205, 1209 King Street W., Toronto, Ontario M6K 1G2; $12.50; credit cards; (416) 535-8126, fax (416) 532-0934 ■ Series of four books entitled *Self-Assessment, The Résumé, The Job Search, The Interview.* Takes the reader through all the steps of the job hunt. Great value for recent university graduates. [ID:1518]

National Graduate Register 💻
http://ngr.schoolnet.ca ■ Industry Canada's online database connects students and recent graduates looking for work with employers looking for qualified candidates. "Virtual Career Fairs" allow you to search the database by location and type of employment. The site also maintains a "Career Development Centre" with links to many excellent resources. [ID:2611]

The Student Center 💻
www.studentcenter.com ■ This site is dedicated to helping students and recent graduates find their place in life. More of a career counselling site than a job bank, this resource helps you to understand your strengths and weaknesses in the marketplace. It also provides information on dozens of countries and links to their embassies in Washington, where you can obtain information on employment conditions. If you are shopping for a new country this may be a good site to investigate. [ID:2542]

The Top Companies to Work for in Canada 📖
1997, *Stephen Kaplin,* 352 pages ➤ John Wiley & Sons, 22 Worchester Drive, Rexdale, Ontario M9W 1L1; $22.95; credit cards; (800) 567-4797, fax (800) 565-6802 ■ Job search tool for students. Features 150 corporate profiles. Provides info on what it's like to be "on the inside" of the organization, and what's in it for students including: salary, challenge of entry-level positions, staff

retention, what makes the organization unique, training opportunities, potential for advancement, hiring strategies, and number of people hired. For more information, visit the distributor's web site at www.wiley.com/products/worldwide/canada. [ID:1784]

Youth Link 1997-1998 📖 🖥
Annual, 199 pages ➤ Public Inquiries Centre, Human Resources Development Canada, 140 Promenade du Portage, Phase 4 Level 0, Hull, Québec K1A 0J9; free; (613) 994-6313, fax (819) 953-7260 ▪ A resource booklet for Canadian youth looking for work and study opportunities in Canada or abroad. Lists 200 Government of Canada youth programs, services and resources. Although most are not international, this is a great reference for government addresses and phone numbers as well as application details for government travel programs. If you're between the ages of 15 and 30, go for it! Visit the web site at www.youth.gc.ca. [ID:1797]

Youth Resource Network of Canada's International Job Opportunities Page 🖥
www.youth.gc.ca/jobopps/intern-e.shtml ▪ This resource site is part of the Canadian government's Youth Employment Strategy. The site offers information on training and education, self-employment, and news releases. It also provides notices of employment opportunities for youth who want to work overseas. [ID:2521]

Chapter 21

The Internet Job Search

Can you imagine finding the overseas job you have always dreamed about from the comfort of your own home? This is now possible using the Internet, which is a global system of networks and computers allowing people to share information. The Internet is part of a communications network (sometimes called "cyberspace") and includes such components as the World Wide Web, and Usenet newsgroups. The recent explosion in the size and popularity of the Internet, has made it one of the most effective tools available for your international job search. Using the "Net" you can learn about various international organizations, network with colleagues in Brazil, and research the current political conditions in Kyrgyzstan. You can obtain valuable professional counselling, list your résumé with hundreds of job banks throughout the world, or search through lists of job offerings in almost every conceivable country. Previously, looking for work overseas was a slow and expensive process, but today's technology permits a rapid, efficient, and inexpensive job search conveniently conducted with your own computer.

While the popularity and accessibility of the Internet is a recent development, it has permanently affected the way in which we approach job hunting. A recent study noted that 19 per cent of Canadians now have access to the Internet on a regular basis and that figure is growing every day. The size of the Internet is now doubling at an incredible rate as Internet Service Providers become more established and more organizations come online. The Internet is fast becoming an essential tool for any job search.

This is a source of concern for many people. You may consider yourself computer illiterate and feel that the Internet is beyond you. Fortunately, this fear is unwarranted. You do not need to understand how the Internet works to use it. Millions of people drive cars without knowing how they work. It's the same for the Internet; using the Net requires only a basic knowledge of computers. In just a few hours you can develop the skills needed to avoid becoming roadkill on the information superhighway.

Index to Internet Resources in this Chapter

New to the Internet? 405
Books about the Internet 406
Search Engines 409
Books on the Internet Job Search 415
Directories on the Web 416
International Job Hunting Services on the Internet 417
Country Information on the Internet 424

WHY IS THE INTERNET IMPORTANT TO YOUR JOB SEARCH?

There are many reasons why the Internet is important to your job search. It's a global library of free information, available from your own home. Imagine how this can boost your job search! Other reasons include:

* Access to the Internet is available 24 hours a day, 365 days a year.

* The Internet is growing at a phenomenal rate and many places that are not currently online are likely to be so very soon.

* Books can be out-of-date before they hit the bookstore but many web sites are updated weekly or even daily.

* You can apply for many jobs directly over the Internet.

* The convenience of the Internet makes it an ideal tool for the international job search.

* By "surfing" the Internet you can be among the first to learn of choice international jobs, long before they reach newspaper want ads or monthly magazines.

* By submitting your résumé and cover letter electronically you can get them to a project manager in Namibia in a matter of seconds. Your application can now be on your future boss's desk weeks before someone who has sent their application by conventional mail.

* Institutions and organizations throughout the world have established web sites, allowing you to obtain first hand information from around the globe in a matter of seconds.

* Censorship is minimal on the Net. There are some exceptions, notably in Southeast Asia (in particular, Indonesia, Malaysia, and China), but few governments have made a systematic effort to regulate the Internet. Beyond physically shutting down web sites located in their countries, there is little governments can do to control the flow of information on the Internet outside their borders.

* Compared to long distance phone bills and international postage, the Internet is very inexpensive. Monthly service can cost as little as $5 and give you access to vast amounts of job-related resources. Nonprofit Internet providers are available in many Canadian cities, providing free (or

sometimes, very cheap) Net access. Called "FreeNets," or sometimes "Community Nets," these services rely on donations and volunteers to operate. Usually, you can find one in your community by looking under "FreeNet" in your phone directory.

The Internet has, in many ways, made the international job search much easier. You can send and receive overseas job information in a matter of seconds.

REALITY BYTES:
CAN YOU FIND A JOB ON THE INTERNET?

There are many advantages to using the Internet to land a job, but it's important to put your Internet job search into perspective.

Who is hiring on the Internet? Evidence suggests that current hiring via the Internet is primarily in technology-related fields. However, as use of the Internet grows, employers in non-technical fields will increase their use of the Net for hiring.

What Happens to the Traditional Job Search? Let's be realistic. The Internet has not yet replaced traditional job hunting methods. Except in the computer industry, it is unusual for someone to be hired solely by responding to an Internet job posting or by sending their résumé via e-mail without first calling ahead. Keep in mind that the Internet should be used to complement traditional job hunting approaches.

Beware the Wild Goose Chase. The Internet can be a wild goose chase if you don't know where to find the information you want. This means that you might sift through sites containing unreliable information, costing you time and money. Be aware also that time flies on the Internet, so if you are paying for Internet access by the hour, it pays to shop around for the best prices.

Outdated Postings. Just as millions of web sites are created or updated daily, many become out-of-date or abandoned. Responding to outdated job postings is another way to waste time. Therefore, it's best to either phone or e-mail the potential employer before you apply for a job. While web site job postings are often faster to access than those in the print media, your chances of being the very first to hear about an opportunity are quickly diminishing as the Internet is rapidly becoming more accessible to greater numbers of people. Competition for jobs on the Internet is global in scope, rather than regional or national.

COMPONENTS OF THE INTERNET

Let's review some basic features of the Internet, especially those you can use with the job search techniques described in this chapter. For Internet guides with more detailed information, take a look at the resources listed in this chapter after the sections entitled New to the Internet? and Books About the Internet.

The World Wide Web (WWW)

The "Web" is a collection of millions of web sites set up by companies, governments, social action groups, and individuals like you. Topics on web sites range from beer-making to nursing. Sites can be text-only or may contain elaborate graphics with video and sound. Information is written in a computer language called *HyperText Markup Language* (HTML) and can be viewed, saved, and even printed. These sites can be found by inputting the web address or by using search engines with keywords. Most web sites include links (or hyperlinks) that directly connect you to other, related sites, making searches faster.

Web Browser: A web browser is the software program you use to get to specific web sites using web addresses. *Netscape Navigator* and Microsoft's *Internet Explorer* are the two main browsers. Your browser offers you various options for viewing web sites. For example, web sites with lots of graphics often take a long time to download before you can view them. If you are tired of waiting for fancy graphics to download, you can turn off the graphics display feature in your browser. This means that only the text comes on screen (which is usually what you really want) and it downloads very quickly, saving you time. Another older alternative, is to use the text-only web browser called *Lynx*. Although some more sophisticated web sites cannot be read using *Lynx*, it is a good tool if you are going to do extensive online job hunting. You can learn more about *Lynx* on the Internet and in most Internet books.

Web Address: Also known as the URL (Universal Resource Locator), a web address functions like a street address. For example, our URL is www.WorkingOverseas.com; if you type this into a web browser it will take you to our web site. Don't confuse an e-mail address with a web address. An e-mail address has an @ symbol. For example, info@pax.com. In contrast, a web address usually has www at the beginning of the address and contains no @ symbol.

There are four components to the URL: the protocol, the domain or server, directory path, and file name. The prefix http:// is the hypertext protocol, which tells the browser that it is a web site. On many web browsers, such as *Netscape Navigator*, you don't even have to write the http:// since the web browser will do it for you. Simply input the full URL, beginning with www, into the web browser and voilà!

The domain is either the name of the server or it can be customized to be the name of the subject or organization, such as our own web site, www.WorkingOverseas.com. In this case WorkingOverseas is the domain name and .com is the domain suffix. There are six basic codes used to indicate the different domain suffixes: .com for commercial; .gov for US government; .edu for US postsecondary education institutions; .mil for the US military, .net for generic Internet providers; and .org for nonprofit organizations around the world. In countries other than the US, country codes tend to be the suffix. Canada's code, for example, is .ca while Singapore's is .sg. In late 1998, ten or more new domain names will be released.

The third and fourth component of the URL is, respectively, the directory and file name. This appears as the last component of the address and indicates where the file is located within the site. They are similar to computer files in your word processing program when you organize your documents within directories. For the web site www.youth.gc.ca/jobopps/intern-e.shtml, the directory is jobopps and the file is intern-e.shtml. URLs, directories, and file names change frequently, so if you are unable to find a site with an address, our advice is to work your way from the end of a given address until you get to the site. For example, eliminate the file name, intern-e.shtml, and type in www.youth.gc.ca/jobopps/. If that fails, eliminate the directory, jobopps/, too, and just type in www.youth.gc.ca. If you are still unable to locate a web site, your next step is to use a search engine like *Infoseek*.

Search Engines: Search engines, also known as spiders, are online services that search the Internet for requested information. They are essential in locating web sites if you do not know the exact URL. Keyword search terms must be typed into the search engine, which will look for them in individual documents. *AltaVista* and *Excite* are two well-known search engines. For more information on search engines see the section entitled Searching on the Internet, in this chapter.

Electronic Mail

Electronic mail, alias e-mail, is a way to send and receive written messages around the world almost instantaneously. This is one of the most popular and basic services provided with Internet software. You will be able to send résumés to potential employers in Bogota or e-mail a recruiter in Calgary. E-mail is also a good way to network with people in your field. You can always recognize an e-mail address because it uses the @ symbol; for example, you can e-mail the author of this book at JHachey@WorkingOverseas.com. Except in rare circumstances, e-mail is not case-sensitive: for the above e-mail address, jhachey@workingoverseas.com would work just as well.

You can also send attachments, which are documents created in your word processing program and sent through e-mail. When sending attachments, ensure that the receiver has software that is compatible with yours. Unsolicited attachments are considered poor "netiquette" (as Internet etiquette is commonly called).

Mailing lists: Mailing lists are services (not related to Canada Post) that automatically deliver messages via e-mail to those who subscribe to a mailing list. This is a convenient job hunting tool because job postings can be mailed to you. Mailing lists are an important medium of communication because subscribing allows you to contribute your opinions, ask questions, and receive answers from people in your fields of interest. On the technical side, three common types of mailing list distributors are: listserv, listproc, or majordomo. The official way to subscribe is to send an e-mail to the distributor and in the body of the text type: subscribe then the list-serve name, your first and last name—in that order. We do not provide resources for mailing lists only because their content and status is constantly changing. For a large descriptive list of mailing lists organized by categories, go to *Liszt: Mailing List Resources* at www.liszt.com/resources.html. Read more about mailing lists and their importance to job hunting in this chapter by consulting the section below, A Dozen Ways the Internet Can Help You in Your Job Search.

Newsgroups

Newsgroups are open forums for discussion or the exchange of information on specific topics. *Usenet (User's Network)* is a global system of newsgroups— you'll sometimes see references to "Usenet Newsgroups." Usenet is connected to a variety of computer networks and is usually part of any Internet service. The newsgroups available to you will depend on the Internet service provider you rely on. Different from mailing lists, newsgroup posts are usually not automatically mailed to you—although it is technically possible to have this done. Instead, you normally have to visit the newsgroups to read the posts. Some newsgroups have parallel mailing lists for those without newsgroup access.

Newsgroup users can look for a specific discussion group and read the messages posted there by other users. Except for moderated newsgroups, anyone who can read a newsgroup can post to it; posting is just sending e-mail to a specified newsgroup. As the name suggests, a moderated newsgroup (like sci.archeaology.moderated) is one which has a person authorized to control what can be posted in that specific newsgroup. Newsgroup topics range from Elvis sightings (alt.fan.elvis-presley is but one of several newsgroups devoted to the King) to human rights (soc.rights.human is just one of many examples), with plenty of room to include job resources.

There are over 10,000 newsgroups. Newsgroups are organized around what are commonly called *hierarchies.* The primary hierarchy has eight divisions: alt. (alternative); comp. (computers); misc. (miscellaneous); news. (news for Usenet users); rec. (recreation); sci. (science); soc. (social issues); and talk. (talk, for hotly debated, general interest topics). There are also divisions for many countries, such as uk. (United Kingdom) and can. (Canada). Note that newsgroups that begin with ca. are about California, not Canada, so the newsgroup ca.jobs is about jobs in California while can.jobs is about jobs in Canada. Many major cities also have their own division, such as tor. (Toronto) and ott. (Ottawa).

Telnet

Telnet is a useful application for globetrotters with e-mail accounts. Provided you have access to an Internet account that supports Telnet, it allows users to log on to a remote computer. You can connect to your server and your e-mail account in Halifax even if you are using a computer in Bangkok—without paying long distance fees. Telnet provides global access to online databases, newsgroups, and other programs. You can learn more about Telnet on the Internet and by reading books about the Internet.

File Transfer Protocol (FTP)

This is a method the Internet uses to transfer to your e-mail account files that you found on another Internet connected computer. *FTP* has many other applications; for example you can use it to download files from web sites to your personal computer. You should be very discriminating about what you download—you may also unknowingly download a computer virus!

This is only the tip of the iceberg, but this is all you need to know as a beginner.

Chat Groups

Chat Groups may not be the best way to network with employers because you are "talking" to a group of people simultaneously. This medium tends not to be used by employers, so it isn't the best tool to use when looking for employment. Chat programs vary according to the computer system your e-mail account is connected to. The most popular program is *Internet Relay Chat* (IRC).

Gopher

Gopher is an early system which predates the Web and is quickly losing popularity. Originally a text-based system, it was made popular by its series of menus containing information. While some graphics are beginning to appear in Gopher, many Gopher sites are being retired in favour of web sites, which are more user-friendly. For this reason, we have not provided many gopher-type resources.

RESOURCES
New to the Internet?

Are you someone who thinks the Net is something you wear on your head? We recommend that you take the time to learn how to use the Internet. One of the best ways to learn is to just start using it and experimenting. A plethora of web sites exist for beginners, which explain how to use the Internet and provide information on computer functions and programs. The following sites are a sampling of what you can find; some concentrate on in-depth explanations of the Internet and others are good for quick reference.

Canadian Women's Internet Association 💻
www.women.ca/internet-help.html ▪ This Canadian site was created to help women understand the Internet. It gives advice on how to use the Internet, provides searching tips, and has links to women's issues and special events sites. [ID:2670]

Internet Literacy Consultants 💻
www.matissenet/files/glossary.html ▪ This is a quick reference glossary of Internet and computer-related terms. Links to related sites are provided. [ID:2659]

John December's Internet Guide 💻
www.december.com/web/text/index.html ▪ This thorough and well-organized Internet help site offers a wide range of topics including tips on keyword searches and how to find list-serves. [ID:2657]

Newbies Anonymous: A Newcomer's Guide to the Internet 💻
www.geocities.com/TheTropics/1945/index1.htm ▪ This site provides a step-by-step program on how to manoeuvre around cyberspace. Clearly written, this site is recommended for the technically-challenged. [ID:2673]

Polaris Internet Guide ⌨

http://users.southeast.net/~habedd/polaris/index.html ▪ This Internet guide provides online tutorials on Internet use and includes an index of computer definitions. [ID:2671]

Virtual Internet Guide ⌨

www.dreamscape.com/frankvad/internet.html ▪ This guide consists of links to sites that provide Internet first aid. [ID:2672]

Books about the Internet

If the web sites listed in the New to the Internet section do not answer your questions you can always turn to the many books on the Internet that have swamped the market. Books can be less intimidating for those who are new to computer technology, are often simpler to use, and sometimes contain helpful indexes. The following books offer detailed advice on how to use the Internet and practical searching strategies—some even include Internet software and CD-ROMs!

The Complete Idiot's Guide to the Internet 📖

1995, *Peter Kent,* Simon & Shuster Macmillan Co., 412 pages ➤ Prentice Hall Canada, 539 Collier MacMillan Drive, Cambridge, Ontario N1R 5W9, Canada; $28.95; credit cards; (800) 567-3800, fax (800) 563-9196 ▪ This book discusses various Internet features and searching techniques. It comes with the software needed to establish Internet access. Visit the publisher's web site at www.phcanada.com. [ID:2522]

Internet Access Essentials 📖

1994, *Ed Tittle, Margaret Robbins,* 374 pages ➤ AP Professional, 1300 Boylston St., Chestnut Hill, MA 02167, USA; US$29.95; (800) 313-1277 ▪ A complete guide to accessing and using the entire range of Internet resources. This book also provides practical search strategies to make your time online more efficient. [ID:2523]

The Internet for Dummies 📖

1997, *John R. Levine, Carol Baroudi, Margaret Levine Young,* 462 pages ➤ IDG Books Worldwide Inc., Suite 400, 919 East Hillside Blvd., Foster City, CA 94404, USA; $26.99; credit cards; (800) 762-2974, fax (650) 293-0864 ▪ This basic how-to guide to the Internet explains such fundamentals as services provided on the Internet, getting hooked up, and navigating in cyberspace. There is also a smaller *Internet for Dummies Quick Reference Guide* for $17.99 that offers almost as much information. Visit the publisher's web site at www.dummies.com. [ID:2524]

Mastering the Internet 📖

1996, *Glee Harrah Cady, Pat McGregor,* Sybex Inc., 1152 pages ➤ Firefly Books Ltd., 3680 Victoria Park Ave., Willowdale, Ontario M2H 3K1, Canada; $55; credit cards; (416) 499-8412, fax (416)499-8313 ▪ This encyclopedic work is one of the most extensive books on Internet access and use. If you want to know everything about the Internet, this is your book. It also comes with a CD-ROM with several software programs including an HTML workshop. [ID:2525]

Teach Yourself the Internet in 24 Hours 📖

1997, *Noel Estabrook,* Simon & Shuster Macmillan Co., 300 pages ➤ Prentice Hall Canada, 539 Collier MacMillan Drive, Cambridge, Ontario N1R 5W9, Canada; $28.95; credit cards; (800) 567-3800, fax (800) 563-9196 ▪ This book for both Macintosh and PC computer users describes how to use the Internet. It is up-to-date and features easy-to-follow lessons on Internet use. Visit the publisher's web site at www.phcanada.com. [ID:2526]

The Web Magazine 📖 ⌨

Monthly, *Burton Fox* ➤ Web Magazine Subscription Services, P.O. Box 56944, Boulder, CO 80322-6944, USA; US$30/year; (303) 604-1465, fax (303) 604-7644, webhelp@neodata.com ▪ This magazine features reviews of both cultural and technological developments in the World Wide Web. Each month, hundreds of web site reviews give the reader an idea of what's hot on the Net.

A travel section lists several helpful sites. E-mail webhelp@neodata.com or visit the publisher's web site at www.webmagazine.com/webmag/html. [ID:2527]

Zen and the Art of the Internet 📖
1996, *Brendan Kehoe* ➤ Prentice Hall Canada, 539 Collier MacMillan Drive, Cambridge, Ontario N1R 5W9, Canada; $23.95; credit cards; (800) 567-3800, fax (800) 563-9196 ■ The book identifies all of the major features of the Internet and offers guidance on using them. It also discusses the latest developments in online services. Visit the publisher's web site at www.phcanada.com. [ID:2528]

SEARCHING ON THE INTERNET

Trekking through cyberspace can be an overwhelming experience. This section provides you with the tools and techniques for conducting a search on the Internet.

The best way to find a web site is by knowing the exact URL. You can try guessing the URL, but why guess when a search engine can find you the exact address? Search engines are like spiders, as their nickname suggests, that go onto the Web to retrieve information you have requested. However, search engines work best when they are combined with the right keywords and searching techniques. There are also metasearch engines that will search a number of search engines one at a time and then organize the information requested in order of relevancy. To aid your quest, we have included search engines, metasearch engines, keyword terms relevant to job hunting, and searching tips that will navigate you quickly through the Internet job search maze.

Keywords for Conducting Internet Job Searches

Keywords are the basis of any Internet search. Choosing the right keyword is a matter of common sense, imagination, and experimentation. Using general terms can result in thousands of matches, called "hits," including many topics irrelevant to your goal. For instance, typing in jobs in the *Infoseek* search engine resulted in 1,778,303 web pages mentioning job information. Most search engines scan all sites in their database for the word "jobs" regardless of the focus of the site. Amongst the thousands of sites found, many have nothing to do with job opportunities; they focus on job trends or jobless rates—anywhere in the world. On the other hand, a specific query that mixes and matches two or more keywords will produce a better response. The most obvious keyword is the specific occupation you are looking for, matched with the keyword jobs. For example, type: accounting jobs. (Watch out for variances in spellings, like "labour" and "labor.") These keywords can also be applied to metasearch engines. The list below is just a start and is by no means the ultimate list of keywords. It is up to you to come up with the best keywords tailored to your specific search.

Combining the following tested *General Job Search Keywords* with the *International Job Search Keywords* will yield a variety of positive results. And, you can make your search more specific by adding a profession and/or a country.

JOB SEARCH KEY WORDS		

GENERAL JOBS
careers
career counselling
career development
career opportunities
employment opportunities
help wanted
job banks
job directories
job hunting
job listings
job openings
job postings
job search
job vacancies
jobs
jobs offered
jobs wanted
labour
positions available
position announcements
résumé banks
résumé posting
résumé writing
résumé board
work
	INTERNATIONAL
	abroad
	By continent or region (for
	  example, "Europe" or
	  "Middle East")
	By country name (for
	  example, "Panama" or
	  "Canada")
	international
	international opportunities
	opportunities overseas
	overseas
	
	LIVING OVERSEAS
	crosscultural
	communications
	culture shock
	expatriate
		GAINING INTERNATIONAL EXPERIENCE
		Canadian global education
		internships
		international scholarships
		  travel
		volunteer abroad
		volunteer overseas
		nongovernmental
		  organizations
		youth exchange
		international professional
		  exchange
		international academic
		  exchange
		development education
		global education
		language training

Sample Keyword Combinations

Here are a few search combinations for finding international opportunities that we tested; each set of terms is separated by a semi-colon. Mix and match them or combine them with other specific information: accounting, inter-national employment; employment, international humanitarian; engineers, jobs overseas; environmental engineers, international jobs; freelance writer; finance jobs, foreign affairs, international; healthcare jobs, international; higher education, jobs; humanitarian jobs, international; journalism; medical jobs and international; non-governmental organizations; nursing jobs and international; oil industry, international employment; oil jobs, international; research positions, Asia; research positions, university; teaching English, Indonesia; teaching English, overseas; teaching jobs, Korea.

SEARCH TIPS

There are other simple tricks that can improve your searches. Here are a few you can use with most search engines:

Read the help sections offered by search engines. All search engines are not created equal. Each search engine's instructions will indicate if you can search through Usenet newsgroups, FTP, or Web documents. Also note, that the tips below are general rules and might not pertain to all search engines listed in the following resource list.

Type in the keyword. This is the most basic tip. After reading your search engine's instructions, type in a keyword(s) and click on the search button.

Check your spelling. Not knowing how to spell a company or person's name can be a big time-waster, causing the search engine to look for something you don't want.

Capitalize names and titles. You don't have to do this with all search engines, but it is still good to do if you are looking for a title or name of a person. If you are looking for the company "Job Hunters," but you type job hunters instead of Job Hunters, the search result will be much broader, listing sites with topics ranging from job hunting tips, stories about job hunters, and job counselling.

Avoid common articles and conjunctions such as the, in, etc. The search engine will drop them from the search anyway, and they could cause the search to fail.

Use commas and the word "and" to separate lists of terms. Enter Japan, Teaching Jobs or Japan and Teaching Jobs, rather than Japan Teaching Jobs. Without the comma, the engine treats the phrase as one long name and will likely produce no results. Note that some search engines use the "+" sign instead of "and."

Use quotation marks around a phrase. If you are looking for résumé postings in California, type California Résumé Postings. This tells the search engine that all of the words are directly associated.

Type in key players in your industry. Chances are that they have a web site or they are listed on one that provides links to industry sites. In addition, many company sites are worth a visit—after all, you never know when you are going to stumble onto something good, such as a list of job postings.

Go beyond the official job title. Think of skills that would be required in a potential job description and make a list of those that you possess. A nurse can say "coordinator, teacher, administrator, care provider." This entry could result in a wide range of job postings or web sites, giving you a larger selection of information to choose from.

Think creatively! Use synonyms and related concepts and don't be afraid to change search engines if you feel the one you are using isn't getting you anywhere.

RESOURCES

Search Engines

The following is a resource list of search engines with databases containing millions of web sites. Each one is organized differently so results may vary using the same keyword. It is best to try the keywords and see which one suits you best. Most search engines can be found by typing them in as you would with any other web site. Some search engines are limited, but others can lead you to a smorgasbord of web sites including country information, climate, financial news, and other online resources.

The Big 9: The Most Commonly Used Search Engines ⌨

These search engines can scan millions of URLs, covering a wide variety of topics. Each engine is organized differently and databases vary in size, so it's best to try them out and discover which ones you like. Locating search engines is easy—simply go to your browser's homepage (for example, Netscape Navigator and Microsoft's Internet Explorer), and you'll find a list of them. They can also be found, while in another search engine, by typing their URL. One disadvantage of search engines is the presence of advertisements which can slow down a search because they have to be downloaded. ▪ AltaVista, www.altavista.digital.com, the largest database, AltaVista lets you search in 25 languages and can search Usenet newgroups. ▪ Excite, www.excite.com, allows "concept" and key word searches. You can also search the most recent two weeks of Usenet newgroups. ▪ HotBot, www.hotbot.com, is easy to use, but is slower than most because of the amount of advertisements. ▪ Infoseek, www.infoseek.com, is well organized and no Boolean searching terms are required. ▪ Lycos, www.lycos.com, is one of the largest databases and it can search through the Web, and FTP. ▪ Northern Light, www.nlsearch.com, this is a relatively new search engine but it is well organized. ▪ Magellan, www.mckinley.com, Technically speaking this is a directory not a search engine. Human beings, rather than just computers, read each site and allocate them to categories, ensuring that query results are more likely to be relevant. ▪ Open Text Index, www.opentext.com, created at the University of Waterloo and a favourite of many users, allows for "power searches" and "weighted searches" with Boolean search techniques. ▪ Yahoo!, www.yahoo.com, popular because of its limited advertisements and well-organized, fast service. Like Magellan, this is really a directory, not a search engine. The Canadian Yahoo! is, www.yahoo.ca. ▪ WebCrawler, www.webcrawler.com, loved by some because it's fun to use, but disliked by some Net pros because it is part of America Online, which markets itself to non-technical people. [ID:2652]

The Big 9: The Most Commonly Used Metasearch Engines ⌨

Metasearch engines send your query to other search engines (like Excite and Infoseek). A metasearch engine organizes the results from a number of search engines it sifts through and then ranks the information according to relevance. The following is only a short list of metasearch engines available online. ▪ All-In-One-Search Page, www.albany.net/allinone, posts fields that search almost every search engine, directory, or specialized site. ▪ Ask Jeeves, www.askjeeves.com, good for people new on the Net because it lets you use basic search techniques. ▪ Dogpile, www.dogpile.com, uses 14 different search engines, but does not remove duplicate results. ▪ EZ-Find at the River, www.accesscom.net/~alexp, searches many search engines one at a time. ▪ Find-It, www.itools.com/find-it, allows you to use advanced search techniques for greater results. ▪ Mamma, www.mamma.com, only uses seven search engines but ranks information according to relevancy. ▪ MetaCrawler, www.metacrawler.com, the oldest and most popular metasearch tool, is well organized, ranks information according to relevancy. ▪ MetaFind, www.metafind.com, does not search through Usenet or FTP sites and omits descriptions about relevant information. ▪ SavvySearch, http://guaraldi.cs.colostate.edu:2001, lets you select the search engines you want it to search through, organizes the results for you, and removes any duplicate information. [ID:2784]

The Argus ClearingHouse ⌨

www.clearinghouse.net ▪ This site is good for researching subjects of interest. By viewing these lists you can link to sites in a specific field, such as education, science, or the environment. There are also a few international links. [ID:2579]

Canadian Based Information Systems ⌨

www.cs.cmu.edu ▪ This site provides an extensive alphabetical listing of commercial and government web sites. There are also links to Canadian gopher servers and the Canadian WWW Central Index (see listing in this section). [ID:2587]

Canadian Gophers ⌨

gopher://Dvinci.Usask.CA/1/.world/.CanadianGophers ▪ This meta-list of links allows you to locate Canadian gophers by province or territory. In addition, there is an alphabetical listing of several dozen educational and institutional gophers throughout the country, and a link to a list of Canadian WWW servers. This is an excellent resource for finding information within Canada. [ID:2589]

Canadian WWW Central Index ⌨

www.csr.ists.ca/w3can ▪ This index of Canadian web sites allows you to locate sites by province, city, or subject. There are thousands of indexed sites available through this list. You can also browse recent additions to the database. [ID:2588]

Directory of E-mail Discussion Groups ⌨

www.liszt.com ▪ This search engine for list-serves allows you to search over 71,000 international mailing lists using keywords. By subscribing you will receive regular information about countries, professions, or institutions. This engine also allows searches by keywords of over 18,000 newsgroups. [ID:2590]

Infinite Ink Newsgroup Search ⌨

www.jazzie.com/ii/internet/newsgroups.html ▪ This site provides links to several newsgroup search engines, plus provides a list of over 18,000 existing newsgroups. If you want to find out about a certain newsgroup, this is your spot. [ID:2594]

Internet Jumpstation ⌨

www.cen.uiuc.edu/exploring.html ▪ This site, operated by the University of Illinois, provides a fast and efficient link to all of the Internet's major search engines. From here you can connect to Alta Vista, Yahoo, WebCrawler, etc. There are also instant connections to Gopher, newsgroups, Telnet, and FTP sites. [ID:2596]

The Internet Sleuth ⌨

www.isleuth.com ▪ A new meta-search tool which allows you to search the databases of up to six different spiders using only one search request. The Internet Sleuth accesses information from Alta Vista, Excite, Lycos, Open Text, and a number of other popular engines. On this site, you can search for keywords or do directory searches of specific topics. [ID:2597]

Life on the Internet Resource Lists ⌨

www.screen.com/understand/reslists.html ▪ A basic guide to Internet search tools, this site includes several articles on how to maximize the results of a search and how to use your search engine effectively. There are also reviews of several popular search engines and a number of tutorials on how to use them. [ID:2598]

Travel Finder ⌨

www.travel-finder.com ▪ This specialized search engine is designed to help you find web sites about specific countries. Categories you can search by include: activity, travel category, and type of traveller. It contains 8,000 sites in its database and you can add your favourite travel-related site. [ID:2583]

A DOZEN WAYS THE INTERNET CAN HELP YOU IN YOUR JOB SEARCH

Gain International Experience

The Internet is not, of course, used strictly for finding employment. An abundance of information on studying abroad, international exchanges, major events, travel, and trade information can be found on the Internet. Most universities around the world, even many in the South, now have web sites to provide information on their academic programs. By looking at Canadian university web sites, you can find out which ones offer international exchanges and scholarships. For those interested in humanitarian efforts, web sites are often set up within hours after an international disaster occurs. Travel sites also exist, detailing culture, climate, and current events for almost every country in the world. Trade information is accessible on government web sites even for the smallest countries. The Internet is called the information superhighway for good reason, so exploit the routes available to you.

Build Crosscultural Links with the Internet

Internet technology has been instrumental in increasing the pace of globalization by diminishing geographical and cultural barriers between people. The Internet lets you meet people from all corners of the earth and connect with them on a more personal level. If you yearn to go to China, and only have a Hollywood image of it, then you can use the Internet to talk (or rather, type) to people who are there. Many newsgroups, mailing lists, and web sites can cater to your burning desire to know what it's like to live in the world's most populated country. Beware though: the Internet is no substitute for real human contact. And of course, only a small minority of the South can afford to access the Internet. So, if you make Internet friends in China, your crosscultural experience will be even more valuable by visiting them in real time.

Network with Professionals in your Field

"It's *who* you know, not what you know"—sound familiar? The Internet can greatly enhance your circle of acquaintances in a given field. The different mediums of communication such as mailing lists, newsgroups, and e-mail have created "Internetworking," which is the 90's version of an age-old job hunting strategy. There are currently over 20,000 mailing lists and newsgroups dedicated to specific topics. From a forum on culture in Ecuador to a listing of jobs in Denmark, discussion groups can be a tremendous source of information. With e-mail you can cultivate important relationships with any number of people who can offer you a job or refer you to someone else. But you have to be selective: not every one of the hundreds of articles posted daily on soc.culture.indian is worth reading. Learn how to use the delete key aggressively. Used properly, the Internet can be an effective tool for global networking, establishing vital, international contacts that would otherwise be difficult and expensive using traditional methods.

Maintain Contact with your Existing Network

Even in this high-tech world, friends and family remain an important source for leads on job postings. The Internet makes it easier than ever for you to keep in touch with old friends and co-workers, distant relatives, and academic mentors, and this makes it easier for them to help you find a job. Not only can old professors or high school buddies forward you leads, but your regular e-mail correspondence with them means they'll know what kind of job you're looking for. Using e-mail to network with friends means you can pass along to each other web sites or job postings you find on the Net, rather than just give a vague description of a job you've heard about. As an added bonus, if you've lost touch with friends or other contacts, you can often track down their e-mail address or phone number using the Web. And this works both ways: if you move around a lot, your contacts may find your e-mail address is the most stable, reliable way of reaching you.

Contact Employers

Accessing the Internet will make communicating with your international employer easier, regardless of country and hour. There are many ways you can use this technology to build contact with employers. At the touch of your fingertips you can e-mail an employer in Hong Kong to ask about career opportunities. You can send documents, like your résumé, electronically— saving the employer time. In a matter of seconds, you can send an informal follow-up thank you note after a helpful information interview. With the Internet and an abundance of web sites at your fingertips, research on any imaginable topic is now possible. Many countries in the South have excellent Internet capabilities, but note that many companies in the South do not use e-mail as an integral part of their communication.

Demonstrate Your Talents

Computers are here to stay and employers want to see that you are not afraid of them. You don't need to know how to build a computer out of spare parts or program in four languages. Still, most employers want employees who can use computers effectively, not as glorified nightlights. By job searching online, e-mailing your résumé, or creating a home page, you show a potential employer that you are comfortable with the world of computers. In a competitive marketplace, this may be the edge that you need. Novices should take heart. Using the Internet is really quite simple and most people can master the basics in an afternoon.

Counselling Services

If you go to the career section of any large bookstore you will find dozens of books on career planning, résumé writing, and job hunting skills. The Internet now offers many of these services online, either for free or for a fraction of the cost of a quality book. Web sites range from advice on résumé writing for the international market to general aptitude tests. Specialized information is often available for a variety of people such as women in the workforce, minorities or challenged employees. These resources can be particularly useful to persons new to the job market or those who feel out of touch with current trends. These career sites can enhance your job hunting skills and knowledge of the market by making you more competitive in what is an inherently competitive process.

Job Banks

Every week thousands of job openings are posted on the Internet. For the job hunter who wants to work in the United States, there are massive job bank listings in every state. For people wanting to work further afield, there are many job banks with sections devoted to international jobs. Sites are well organized and executing searches, based upon your desired job or location, is possible. Many transnational and nongovernmental organizations (NGOs) are finding the Internet to be an inexpensive place to advertise job openings. As the Internet grows in size and scope, many jobs will no longer be advertised in the conventional places. In the coming years we expect the number of international jobs listed on the Internet to grow. Familiarity with various Internet job banks will greatly increase your exposure to overseas opportunities.

Résumé Posting

There are hundreds of places on the Internet where you can post your e-mail résumé in hopes that a potential employer will see it. Many online job banks and career centres provide résumé databases, often free-of-charge. People are also posting their résumés on their own homepage, complete with multimedia graphics. For those in the arts or computer fields, this medium offers a new and effective way to display their talents, but for the most part, such résumés distract employers from the document's key points. Online résumé posting is convenient. This means that thousands of other job seekers will also be posting résumés, increasing the competition. Having your résumé online increases your exposure. However, few personnel managers have the time to surf the Net looking for your résumé. Simply posting your résumé is not going to get you a job. A résumé is only a résumé if it is accompanied by other job hunting tools. Showing employers your talents is still up to you!

Mailing Lists

Mailing lists automatically deliver notices to you via e-mail. They are based on any conceivable subject matter, with topics ranging from toy-making to job counselling. Mailing lists are more interactive than web sites, making two-way communication between the receiver and sender possible. They are also a convenient method to network for industry contacts and receive notices of opportunities. As with real-life networking, building relationships with people within mailing lists takes time. A constant presence will keep people in your field aware of your knowledge. Also look at mailing lists that discuss industry news because many people will want to keep current, and, occasionally job postings circulate. Beware of mailing lists that will inundate you with too much e-mail.

Newsgroups

As described earlier in this chapter, newsgroups are forums for posting information and discussion on a range of topics—and this includes newsgroups devoted to nothing but job openings or a specific profession. You can e-mail someone directly after reading their message in a newsgroup, which means you can use these groups to network with employers.

Job opportunities in country-specific newsgroups tend to be for locals rather than foreigners, but occasionally, international job competitions will be posted. Also, note that many country-specific newsgroups (for example, chile.jobs or soc.culture.china), mainly feature postings written in that country's national language(s). It's sometimes worthwhile to read newsgroups that are not primarily focused on employment, such as industry-related discussion groups. Newsgroups that discuss issues of interest to you will sometimes post employment opportunities. For instance, in an environmental science newsgroup, sci.environment, an opening for an environmental engineer was posted.

Some newsgroups, especially moderated ones, can be useful for gathering information and you'll sometimes learn about new web sites or mailing lists. An important feature of many newsgroups is the *FAQ* (Frequently Asked Questions), a post which lists common questions and answers related to a specific topic or newsgroup. FAQ topics can range from sci.environment's four-part Ozone FAQ to the alt.comp.virus "Mini-FAQ" on computer viruses. There are even FAQs about some countries. Most FAQs are re-posted to the relevant newsgroup(s) on a regular basis and are now also often available on the Web. The newsgroup news.answers consists of nothing but FAQs on a broad range of topics, which makes it easy to find a useful introduction to all sorts of fields. Newsgroups make it possible for you to ask professionals questions about their field, but read the FAQ before you post. Lastly, every newsgroup has its own tone of discussion, ranging from casual to even obnoxious, therefore we advise you to get a feel for the discussions before participating in them.

Researching Companies and Organizations

The Internet is the largest, most up-to-date virtual encyclopedia in existence. If you think that you may want to work for Joe's English School in Thailand, but are leery about the firm, you can likely find out more information on them by using the Internet. If you have an upcoming interview with Megacorp Inc. and want to know about the company's international operations or job postings, odds are that the information you need is available online. The Internet can provide information that will help you in deciding where you want to go, and what and *who* will help you to get there. Information obtained can also help to distinguish you from other applicants during the interview process. Imagine the points you would score with a personnel manager, when, during an interview for a job in Kenya, you mention the latest labour unrest situation and can identify its potential effects upon the company's interests. They will certainly take note of your international knowledge as well as your computer skills. Not surprisingly, up-to-date information is essential for success in the information age.

RESOURCES

Books on the Internet Job Search

In addition to web sites on job searching, the following books give practical advice on how to look for international and Canadian jobs online. These useful primers on how to use the Internet can be read before you begin your captivating journey into cyberspace. They also offer advice on job counselling, résumé writing, and networking on the Internet.

Adams Electronic Job Search Almanac 1997 📖

1997, *Emily Ehrenstein,* Adams Media Corporation, 292 pages ➤ Monarch Books of Canada Ltd., 5000 Dufferin Street, Downsview, Ontario M3H 5T5, Canada; $12.95; VISA, MC; (416) 663-8231, fax (416) 736-1702 ▪ This book starts with a how-to section on creating and posting electronic and multimedia résumés and proceeds to job-finding strategies on the Internet. Check out the web site at www.careercity.com. [ID:1796]

Get Wired, You're Hired 📖

1997, *Mark Swartz,* 296 pages ➤ Prentice Hall Canada, 539 Collier MacMillan Drive, Cambridge, Ontario N1R 5W9, Canada; $21.95; credit cards; (800) 567-3800, fax (800) 563-9196 ▪ This is the most thorough guide on finding jobs online in Canada. It also provides an introduction on how to use the Internet. Visit the publisher's web site at www.phcanada.com. [ID:2621]

The Guide to Internet Job Searching 📖 💻

1996, *Margaret Riley, Frances Roehm, Steve Oserman,* VGM Career Horizons, 96 pages ➤ NTC Contemporary Publishing Co., 4255 West Touhy Ave., Lincolnwood, IL 60646, USA; US$14.95; credit cards; (800) 323-4900, fax (800) 998-3103 ▪ This comprehensive book provides advice on how to create electronic résumés. It also has a list of online career development resources, and an extensive list of electronic job banks and résumé posting services. The international section has Internet contacts for dozens of countries. Unlike most Internet job services, this book is especially useful for job hunters without technical expertise. The electronic version offers links to job-related Usenet and web sites in dozens of countries. There is also a link to a site on how to find international information, which in turn links to extensive Gopher and Web meta-lists. Visit the site at www.dbm.com/jobguide. [ID:1799]

Hook Up, Get Hired! 📖

1995, *Joyce Kennedy,* 250 pages ➤ John Wiley & Sons, 22 Worchester Drive, Rexdale, Ontario M9W 1L1, Canada; $18.50; credit cards; (800) 567-4797, fax (800) 565-6802 ▪ Organized like an auto club trip ticket, this book provides extensive information about sites of interest along the information highway. A detailed appendix provides lists of books, publications and software. A well-written book which has survived all of the technical developments since 1995. Visit the publisher's web site at www.wiley.com/products/worldwide/canada. [ID:1798]

The On-Line Job Search Companion 📖

1995, *Gonyea, James C,* 267 pages ➤ McGraw-Hill Ryerson Ltd., 300 Water Street, Whitby, Ontario L1N 9B6, Canada; $21.95; credit cards; (800) 565-5758, fax (800) 463-5885 ▪ This book explains how to find a job on the Internet using online databases, newsgroups, software, and CD-ROM programs. Written by the creator of the America Online Career Center and the Internet Career Connection, it offers job couselling, résumé postings, and advice on where to find job opportunities. Visit the publisher's web site at www.mcgrawhill.ca. [ID:2651]

Directories on the Web

Web directories are the online yellow pages of the Internet. These sites can help you locate e-mail and phone numbers of individuals and companies. Depending on the directory, they can be specific to country, province, and sometimes, subject of interest. Some sites will also provide postal addresses. For similar information in book form, consult the Resources for the section on Job Search Directories in Chapter 22, Resources for the International Job Search. Here is our list of recommended directories on the Web:

Canada Post Corporation 💻

www.mailposte.ca/CPC2/menu_01.htm ▪ Created by Canada Post, this convenient directory provides Canadian postal codes, parcel rates, delivery confirmation, and postal outlet locations. [ID:2694]

Department of Foreign Affairs and International Trade (DFAIT)- Business Directories 📖
These sites were created by various departments within DFAIT. They provide information on companies doing business in specific countries, including their addresses, phone numbers, various local government addresses, and links to local companies. At the time of publication the following six sites were found: [ID:2699]
- Asia: Business Directories, www.dfait-maeci.gc.ca/res/fhap/bdasia.htm
- Canadian Business Directory, China & Hong Kong,
  www.dfait-maeci.gc.ca/english/geo/asia/company.htm
- Guyana: Business Guide, www.dfait-maeci.gc.ca/english/geo/lac/825054-e.htm
- Hong Kong: Trade and Commerce, www.dfait-maeci.gc.ca/res/english/hongtrad.htm
- Singapore: Trade and Commerce, www.dfait-maeci.gc.ca/res/english/singtrad.htm
- Sri Lanka: Trade and Commerce, www.dfait-maeci.gc.ca/res/sriltrade.htm.

Department of Foreign Affairs and International Trade (DFAIT)-Directory 📖
www.198.103.104.20/InternetPhoneDirectory ■ This is a good directory for anyone wanting to contact someone at DFAIT. The directory provides personnel, organization, and building information for various DFAIT departments. It also has a quick reference guide for Canadian representatives abroad, trade missions, and frequently called numbers. [ID:2698]

Four 11 Directory Services 📖
www.four11.com ■ This self-proclaimed "white pages" of the Internet helps you find e-mail addresses. With over ten million listings in their database, this is the largest e-mail directory online. Of course, many people are not included in the database, but it's a good place to start if you're looking for someone. It also offers more than 100 million US telephone numbers, celebrity addresses, and a number of other goodies. [ID:2592]

International Telephone Directory 📖
www.contractjobs.com/tel ■ This site features telephone and e-mail directories from around the world. Norway, Pakistan, and Slovenia are just three of the 50 countries included in this directory. [ID:2696]

ON VILLAGE Yellow Guide 📖
http://cgi2.onvillage.com ■ This is a business directory for Canada and the United States. The directory permits you to search by industry sector, name, region, and city. The site also provides phone numbers and mailing addresses. [ID:2697]

United States Postal Service 📖
www.usps.gov/ncsc ■ Similar to the Canada Post site, this will give you postal information for the United States. You can look up zip codes, location of postal outlets, and make parcel inquiries. [ID:2695]

WhoWhere 📖
www.whowhere.com ■ Using this e-mail directory, you can look up e-mail addresses, phone numbers, conventional addresses, corporate homepages, and a number of other contact points. While its database is smaller than that of www.four11.com, this site's range is considerably broader. Service is also in French. [ID:2603]

International Job Hunting Services on the Internet

The following web sites provide services such as career counselling, job banks, and résumé posting. Most of the sites listed here are internationally oriented. Considering the numerous applications of the Internet, target job searching is a viable option. Many career counsellors recommend this kind of job searching rather than processing a general résumé and sending it to a variety of employers.

For an international job search, target job searching entails knowing what type of job interests you, the names of contacts and companies involved in that industry, and the location of your job market. Fortunately, most of this information can be found online, which will make your search efficient and increases your chances of discovering the right opportunity. The majority of these sites are free and updated regularly, so take advantage of the extensive information they provide. (For more resources on this subject, consult the non-Internet Resources for the section entitled International Job Search in Chapter 22, Resources for the International Job Search.)

Asia-Net ⌨
www.asia-net.com ▪ Appropriate for people who can juggle more than one (or even two) languages. This is a job resource site for people who are fluent in English, Japanese, Chinese, or Korean and are also professionals in technical areas. [ID:2755]

Canadian Business Advertising Network ⌨
www.cban.com ▪ This network provides a résumé posting service for international job seekers. While there is no job bank, you can post your résumé according to preferred location of employment. [ID:2488]

Canadian Corporate News ⌨
www.cdn-news.com ▪ A full-text database of news releases issued by over 1,000 Canadian companies and indexed by company name, stock symbol, industry, and keywords. [ID:2725]

Career and Job Links ⌨
http://wings.buffalo.edu/student-life/sa/muslim/etc/career/html ▪ A truly extensive meta-list with links to thousands of domestic and international job hunting resources. Links extend to many employment centres as well as Usenet newsgroups, many of which are internationally-oriented. If, after reading about online career services, newsgroups, and other resources, you know where you want to go, this is a good vehicle to get you there. [ID:2544]

Career City ⌨
www.careercity.com ▪ This site offers advice on a number of valuable job hunting skills, such as writing résumés, interview strategies, and the basics of job hunting. Job postings are limited to the US with a heavy emphasis on computer-related employment. If you need information on beginning a job search, this is a good site, but for the actual search, it is of limited use. [ID:2487]

Career Mosaic ⌨
www.careermosaic.com ▪ Career Mosaic is a comprehensive resource which provides several useful online job hunting options. It includes a free résumé posting service, profiles of hundreds of companies, listings of online job fairs, and an extensive career resource centre. Of particular usefulness is the International Gateway and J.O.B.S. data which allows you to search specific countries for career-specific job openings. Type in "teacher - Malaysia" and see if there is a posting. Too simple! This is one of the best sites available. [ID:2486]

Career Path ⌨
www.careerpath.com ▪ This career search engine examines the want ads from almost 30 major newspapers in the US. Each month over 350,000 new jobs are posted by this service. The service is free and can be useful, particularly if you are looking for work in the US. However, international listings are buried within the newspaper classifieds and are sometimes hard to sort through. Specifying "international" as a key word will help overcome this problem. This site also maintains a database of employer profiles which includes links to companies. [ID:2485]

Career Resource Center ⌨
www.careers.org ▪ An excellent launch pad into cyberspace, this site contains over 10,000 links to various job-related resources. The sites are organized into geographical divisions, by province, state, and other international areas. There are also links to university career offices, job banks, government resources, and career counselling services. This is a very good place to initiate an Internet job hunt, particularly if you have an idea of what you want to do and where you want to go. [ID:2492]

Career Web 🖳
www.cweb.com ▪ This site offers an extensive international database of jobs throughout the world. Most of the jobs listed here are technical in nature, but this may change with the growth of the Internet. You may search job openings by category, country name, or keyword. In addition, there is an extensive career counselling facility with employer profiles and a résumé listing service. A very versatile site, it has links to various professional associations, career counselling services, and information on summer employment and internships. [ID:2491]

Catapult Employment Centers 🖳
www.jobweb.org/CATAPULT/jobsall.htm ▪ This site allows job searches through a number of different venues. Options include links to college career centres, newsgroups and field-specific listings. There are also links to professional headhunters, search firms and employment agencies. The jobs tend to favour the technically-minded, and international postings are poorly organized. [ID:2546]

Catapult Sites for General Job Listings by Region 🖳
www.jobweb.org/CATAPULT/jgenlst.htm ▪ This is a very useful compilation of links to 26 international job sites. Choices range from regional job sites such as Asia-Net or Eurojobs Online to more specific and unusual sites, like Calcutta Online or Prosper Wales. There is a wide variety of technical and non-technical jobs available through these links. There are also over 100 links to regional job banks in the US. [ID:2545]

Contact Point 🖳
www.contactpoint.ca/index.stm ▪ Contact Point provides resources on career counselling and job services. There is also an online discussion forum for career counselling. This site is primarily for career counsellors, but the information could be useful to any job seeker. [ID:2445]

Eastern and Central Europe Job Bank 🖳
This site proclaims itself as the first Eastern and Central European Internet Job Bank. It is created by a private firm looking to find the best people in the computer and management fields. The job bank is mainly for people who live in this part of Europe, but some postings are open to worldwide competition. [ID:2707]

Employment Opportunities for Australia 🖳
http://employment.com.au/index.html ▪ This is a job site listing opportunities "down under." The site is searchable by companies, consultants, and government positions. Also contains an international database of job listings. [ID:2770]

Employment Resources on the Internet 🖳
www.cs.purdue.edu/homes/swlodin/jobs.html ▪ This is an outstanding collection of links. The links can connect dozens of professional recruiters, regional career sites, university counselling services, and newspaper classified sections. Additionally, there are several useful links to other career-related sites, some of which specialize in international employment. [ID:2513]

ESL Job Links 🖳
www.pacificnet.net/~sperling/joblinks.html ▪ Primarily oriented to those seeking international work as English teachers, this site has a number of links to general overseas recruiting agencies and job opportunities. This site is impressive in its scope, offering links to countries throughout the world. There are also several links to American-based job centres which offer career counselling and résumé assistance services. This is a very good site, with opportunities for all job seekers, not just those interested in teaching overseas. [ID:2547]

The ESLoop 🖳
www.linguistic-funland.com/esloop ▪ The ESLoop is a collection of sites for English Language Teaching. Each site is linked to the next, so that no matter your point of departure, you will make your way around all the sites. [ID:2792]

The Gordon Group Home Page 🖳
www.owt.com/jobsinfo.jobstext.html ▪ This is a useful list of North American and international careers-related sites. In addition to over 100 links, this site also has some of the best counselling services available online. The advice can help you with everything from time management during a job hunt, to increasing your networking skills. This is one of the best sites to visit when you're starting your international job hunt. [ID:2512]

Hoovers On-Line 🖳
www.hoovers.com ▪ This company maintains detailed profiles of thousands of domestic and international companies. This resource allows you to research potential employers and connect to thousands of corporate home pages. There are no job listings at this site, but there is a tremendous amount of information available which could be useful in preparing for an interview or determining the scope of international operations of Canadian and American companies. Services are free for AOL and CompuServe patrons. For others, there is a US$9.95 fee to access the information. [ID:2581]

International Career and Employment Network 🖳
www.indiana.edu/~intlcent/icen/index/html ▪ This site, run by the International Centre of Indiana University of Bloomington, offers a variety of overseas job listings. While the site is smaller than many, job listings are often of interest to those in non-technical careers. [ID:2506]

International Employment Resources, On-line 🖳
http://bertie.usfca.edu/usf/career/international/html ▪ This list includes links to job banks in Asia, Australia, and Europe and several general resources which are global in scope. This is a good on-ramp to the information highway. [ID:2549]

International Jobs and Expat Career Opportunities 🖳
www.netmatters.co.uk/users/adiann ▪ This UK-based firm offers job placement services throughout the world. There are fees for some of their services. [ID:2530]

International Resources Group 🖳
www.panix.com/~compreal/index.html ▪ This commercial headhunting firm specializes in finding overseas contracts for a variety of professional occupations, from teaching to engineering. Services (which are not free) include job placements and career counselling. [ID:2536]

Internet Job Surfer 🖳
www.rpi.edu/dept/cdc/jobsurfer/joba.html ▪ This slightly disorganized but very useful list contains links to hundreds of commercial human resource firms throughout the world. Companies providing job databases, résumé banks, and career counselling are among those listed in alphabetical order. The drawback of this site is that the listings are arranged by corporate name rather than location. Nevertheless, there are dozens of international organizations listed here. Finding them is a matter of guesswork and common sense. [ID:2548]

The Irish Jobs Page 🖳
www.exp.ie ▪ A useful site for finding employment in Ireland, Australia, and New Zealand. Services include job postings, résumé boards, and a list of recruiting agencies. The bulk of postings are for information technology specialists, but there are employment services for people in other fields, such as engineering and teaching. [ID:2756]

Job and Career Related Sites 🖳
www.owt.com/jobsinfo/jobsinfo.htm ▪ This web site is a good stepping stone to your international career. There are links to hundreds of services, most offering career counselling and employer previews. Some links reach international recruiting services or job banks. [ID:2551]

Job Listings 🖳
www.brandeis.edu/hiatt/web_data/job_listings.html ▪ This site, maintained by Brandeis University, provides an excellent international employment section with links to resources in Western and Eastern Europe, and Asia. There are also links to international job listings by career. Special attention is given to education, journalism, environmental issues, government jobs, and high-tech jobs. Links to other useful career centres are also helpful. [ID:2550]

Job Serve ▣
www.jobserve.com ▪ This site offers job listings for those in the information technology field. Most listings are for people wanting to work in the UK, but a few other countries, such as Singapore and Saudi Arabia, are also listed. Not only do you have access to recent job notices, but you can also subscribe to a mailing list. [ID:2750]

Job Track ▣
www.jobtrack.com ▪ This is a particularly useful resource for students as the site is associated with over 500 university employment centres. Job listings are targeted at college students and recent graduates. While most of the jobs are in the US, there are some international listings. Moreover, this site contains very good counselling services and a link to Margaret Riley's excellent book, *The Guide to Internet Searching*. [ID:2514]

JobWeb ▣
www.jobweb.com ▪ This site offers a wide variety of career-related services. You can search their database for international jobs by both country and field. Many of the job profiles link directly to employers' own web sites. JobWeb's Special Interest Network also provides several interesting articles on living and working overseas as well as links to dozens of international job banks. While this site is sometimes more difficult to navigate than other job banks, there is a lot of useful information here. [ID:2537]

Master Craft ▣
www.master-craft.com ▪ This employment service offers clients access to its database containing over 11 million employers from over 100 countries. They also help you write a successful international résumé. For a US$5 fee, they will send you an application package. [ID:2538]

The Monster Board ▣
www.monster.com ▪ This is one of the most popular and useful job hunting resources on the Internet. The site provides employer profiles and a user-friendly search engine for international jobs. Simply enter the country where you want to work, your profession, and the Monster will search for available vacancies in its database. Also useful are links to newsgroups and "communities" of related careers such as the biotechnology industry or CEO search. Finally, there is an extensive section on the United States which allows job searches on a state-by-state basis. [ID:2539]

Department of National Defence (DND) ▣
www.dnd.ca ▪ From information on the latest UN peacekeeping operations to recruiting guidelines, this is the gateway to Canada's military. It also provides a statement of defence policy and information on financial management assistance. [ID:2566]

National Graduate Register ▣
http://ngr.schoolnet.ca ▪ Industry Canada's online database connects students and recent graduates looking for work with employers looking for qualified candidates. "Virtual Career Fairs" allow you to search the database by location and type of employment. The site also maintains a "Career Development Centre" with links to many excellent resources. [ID:2611]

NetJobs ▣
www.netjobs.com:8000 ▪ This Canadian-based resource provides many of the services provided by the larger US job sites. Its easy-to-use search engine allows you to look for jobs by location; there are several international listings. This site focuses on Canadian jobs. As with other quality job sites, NetJobs offers career counselling services, corporate reviews, and some useful links. [ID:2540]

Overseas Employment ▣
www.run-ti.com/employment/world/world.html ▪ This is a small but excellent series of links to job banks and employment services in several countries. The site is focused on the Asia-Pacific region but there are also links to Europe and several worldwide resources. [ID:2552]

Overseas Jobs Express ⌨
www.overseasjobs.com ▪ This wonderful site lists over 1,500 new international jobs each month. Searches can be conducted by keyword, category, or region and the search engine is very user-friendly. There is also a free résumé posting service. A number of career counselling resources, an online "bookshop" specializing in international employment, and a travel advisory section are also available. This site includes 700 links to job banks in over 40 countries. You can go directly to Brazil and look for a job there without ever leaving your home. This is the best site for international employment opportunities. [ID:2541]

Purdue International Career Center ⌨
www.ups.purdue.edu/Student/picc ▪ Maintained by Purdue University, this centre is an excellent gateway to the international Internet job search. Databases arrange job listings by country, region, or professional field. There are also links to general employment servers which often offer career counselling and résumé assistance. [ID:2553]

Russian and Eastern European Institute Employment Opportunities ⌨
www.indiana.edu/~reeiweb/indemp.html ▪ Created by Indiana University, this site is useful for people interested in working in Russia and Eastern Europe. It is particularly good for those knowledgeable in language, history, or cultures of this region. [ID:2772]

SASIS INC ⌨
www.sasis.com, sasis@cncnet.com ▪ Web site for SASIS Inc., a company which specializes in recruiting western personnel for contract positions in the Middle East, Africa and South America. Also has some general international postings. [ID:2520]

The Student Center ⌨
www.studentcenter.com ▪ This site is dedicated to helping students and recent graduates find their place in life. More of a career counselling site than a job bank, this resource helps you to understand your strengths and weaknesses in the marketplace. It also provides information on dozens of countries and links to their embassies in Washington, where you can obtain information on employment conditions. If you are shopping for a new country this may be a good site to investigate. [ID:2542]

TESOL Online (Teachers of English to Speakers of Other Languages) ⌨
www.tesol.edu ▪ TESOL's online service provides a worldwide link for those involved in teaching English to speakers of other languages. Areas covered include: professional preparation, programs, services, and products. [ID:2791]

The World Wide Web Employment Office ⌨
www.jobsweb.com ▪ A good starting point for searches of the Web, with connections to Gopher and Usenet. This site offers job boards for regions throughout the world, such as Africa, Asia, and the Middle East. Jobs may also be searched by profession. Several useful links are found at this site, including an alphabetical listing of employment agencies, résumé databases, corporate home pages, and several international links. Finally, there are useful links to corporate research facilities and lists of corporations on the Internet. There is also a résumé posting service, which costs US$10/year. [ID:2543]

WorldClass ⌨
http://web.idirect.com/~tiger ▪ The WorldClass supersite links you to over 650 of the world's best business sites in over 80 countries. From here you can obtain news of current business trends or research a potential employer. The site also offers an excellent opportunity to connect with important people in your field. [ID:2584]

Youth Resource Network of Canada's International Job Opportunities Page ⌨
www.youth.gc.ca/jobopps/intern-e.shtml ▪ This resource site is part of the Canadian government's Youth Employment Strategy. The site offers information on training and education, self-employment, and news releases. It also provides notices of employment opportunities for youth who want to work overseas. [ID:2521]

COUNTRY INFORMATION ON THE INTERNET

An online Internet search by country does not have to be limited to jobs. It can also be used to find information on such topics as culture, geography, and politics. Awareness of a country's cultural diversity and socio-economic background will enhance your job search and improve your chances of success at the interview stage. Knowing the current affairs of a country is essential for any international career seeker and the Internet can help you stay informed. Here is a list of ideas on what type of country information is available on the Internet:

Current Affairs/News: Internet online news services can help you find out about current affairs before they are posted in newsgroups, not to mention newspapers and television. The Internet has quickly become the medium of choice for instantaneously informing people about any major news event. Web sites such as CNN and Reuters provide news updated by the minute about politics, finance, weather, and international headlines. Such coverage is also more comprehensive, allowing you to follow events in countries generally ignored by the Western media.

Country Profiles: To broaden your knowledge base of a country, you can look at its profile posted on the web site of The Department of Foreign Affairs and International Trade (DFAIT) or the US State Department. They provide a general overview of the social and political climate of countries around the world. Nongovernmental groups sometimes also provide country profiles on their homepages; for example, Canadian Friends of Burma has a web site on Burma (www.web.net/~cfob). Just a note of caution—pay close attention to who is writing the country profiles and try to understand their perspective.

Government Web Sites: Many governments have web sites in which official information about their country is posted. These can be very useful for specific data on the country, such as its culture, current events, economy, geography, history, trade, and tourism. These web sites usually provide links to various government departments, major national newspapers, and related organizations.

Business Opportunities: The Internet is a gold mine of resources for the entrepreneur. Some country web sites contain government and trade association information on export/import ventures, financial markets, and contacts to various government agencies and trade programs.

Embassy Services: Most people would not think of contacting the embassy of a foreign country for anything other than traditional services such as visas or travel permits. Yet, in fact, they are responsible for providing information about their culture, trade, and investment. Their web sites also offer material similar to government homepages with links to official sites. Foreign embassy web sites are listed in Chapter 40, Foreign Diplomats in Canada.

Tourist/Travel Information: Many government and privately-sponsored web sites can help answer your inquiries about accommodations, weather, cultural events, or other general travel questions. Some of these web sites also provide information on travel conditions in politically unstable countries.

Travel-oriented newsgroups such as rec.travel.misc and rec.travel.asia can also be useful, as are many country FAQs, which typically included a travel section.

Country-Specific Research *Without* the Internet

For the adventurous who wish to get off their computers, there are, of course, many non-cyber sources for country information. You can contact embassies and organizations directly by phone, fax, or by personally visiting their offices. Consult your libraries for international and local newspapers from around the world. Don't just visit the web site, visit the country: a "job-hunting vacation" in a desired country could be fruitful by targeting potential employers before and after you arrive. (For more country-specific information and resources, see Chapter 27, Jobs by Region of the World.)

RESOURCES

Country Information on the Internet

The following are country-specific web sites. Local governments and associations that provide information on local news, climate, and culture created a few of these web sites. Other sites offer news on business, politics, and culture. (For country information in printed form, read the Resources for the section on Global Guide Books as well as all the country-specific Resources found in Chapter 27, Jobs by Regions of the World.)

Canadian International Development Agency (CIDA) 🖳
w3.acdi-cida.gc.ca/cida_ind.nsf ▪ This web site provides a list of CIDA's activities, news releases, and country profiles. The profiles are concise, listing current basic statistics about a country. Information such as the system of government, main exports, and maps are included. The site is also fully bilingual. [ID:2661]

Canadian Representatives Abroad 📖 🖳
Annual, Department of Foreign Affairs and International Trade (DFAIT), 142 pages ➤ Canada Government Publishing, Ottawa, Ontario K1A 0S9; $17.95; VISA, MC; (819) 956-4800, fax (819) 994-1498, publishing@ccg-gcc.ca ▪ A bilingual directory of Canadian diplomatic and consular missions. Available on the web at the DFAIT site, under "Embassies and Missions" at www.dfait-maeci.gc.ca/english/missions. [ID:1089]

The CIA World Factbook 🖳
www.odci.gov/cia/publications/nsolo/wfb-all.htm ▪ This is one of the most authoritative sources available on international geography. Information on current political, economic, and social conditions is provided as well as a discussion of the country's physical geography and resources. Very comprehensive, but the juicy stuff may have been left out! [ID:2580]

CNN Interactive 🖳
www.cnn.com ▪ This site, created by one of the world's largest media giants, Interactive, provides updated international headlines, including news, weather, sports, science, and health. Most of the news is related to the US and is a reflection of what you can see watching their television broadcast. [ID:2687]

Current World Leaders 📖 🖳
3/year ➤ International Academy at Santa Barbara, 5385 Hollister Avenue, Suite 5385, Santa Barbara, CA 931111-2305, USA; US$195; credit cards; (805) 683-4927, fax (805) 683-4637 ▪ Provides information on the people, politics, economics and international relations of over 190 countries. A complementary publication, *International Issues*, integrates feature stories with official reports, articles and speeches from respected authorities in the field. Their web site,

www.iasb.org/cwl, offers information on countries, territories, colonies and international organizations, and will provide a research engine specific to this subject in 1998. [ID:1184]

Department of Foreign Affairs and International Trade (DFAIT) 🖳

www.dfait-maeci.gc.ca/ ▪ This excellent homepage for DFAIT provides a vast amount of information on the international system, from travel advisories to international trade. It has links to DFAIT departments, services, country profiles, foreign embassies and missions in Canada, and Canadian government activities abroad. [ID:2565]

International Agencies and Programs 🖳

www.lrc.state.ky.us/other/internat/bmiller.htm ▪ Maintained by the state government of Kentucky, this site provides links to various international organizations as well as information on international law, culture, and foreign languages. Offers a link to the CIA World Factbook, which provides basic information on almost every country in the world. [ID:2563]

Latin America Traveller 🖳

www.goodnet.com/~crowpub ▪ Offers information for those travelling to Latin America. The site also has a directory of Spanish language schools in the region as well as links to general sites related to travel and culture in Latin America. [ID:2769]

Lonely Planet 🖳

www.lonelyplanet.com ▪ While this is a commercial site dedicated to selling guide books, there is a considerable amount of free information. Country profiles, photographs, and travel tips as well as information on travel health and safety are all accessible from this site. [ID:2582]

Reuters On-Line 🖳

www.reuters.com/news ▪ This is a news service provided by Reuters, one of the world's largest newswire agencies. This is a comprehensive site with current international headlines and news about financial markets. [ID:2650]

The Student Center 🖳

www.studentcenter.com ▪ This site is dedicated to helping students and recent graduates find their place in life. More of a career counselling site than a job bank, this resource helps you to understand your strengths and weaknesses in the marketplace. It also provides information on dozens of countries and links to their embassies in Washington, where you can obtain information on employment conditions. If you are shopping for a new country this may be a good site to investigate. [ID:2542]

Tourism Offices Worldwide Directory 🖳

www.towd.com ▪ A useful site if you are searching for pre-departure tourist information for a specific country. It lists contact information for 750 tourism-related offices worldwide. [ID:2736]

Travel Finder 🖳

www.travel-finder.com ▪ This specialized search engine is designed to help you find web sites about specific countries. Categories you can search by include: activity, travel category, and type of traveller. It contains 8,000 sites in its database and you can add your favourite travel-related site. [ID:2583]

United States State Department 🖳

www.state.gov/index.html ▪ This recommended site includes recent and detailed information on almost every country. Web sites include US press statements, regional topics, country vital statistics, US foreign policy, and information on foreign relations between countries. [ID:2662]

Web Sites All Countries: Martindale's "The Reference Desk" 🖳

www-sci.lib.uci.edu/HSG/RefHealth.html ▪ An extensive dictionary of links including over 200 official country web sites, world reports on weather, transport, and culture, lists of international organizations, new internet and software developments, travel advisories, language and translation dictionaries, international newspapers, international health and law, and much more. [ID:2768]

Web Sites on Africa and the Middle East 💻
These sites contain trade information, local news, and general country information. Sites such as Africa Online and ArabNet provide quick reference information for almost any country in these fascinating parts of the world. [ID:2666]
- Africa Online, www.africaonline.co ▪ Africa Index, www.africaindex.africainfo.no/
- ArabNet, www.arab.net ▪ Egypt, http:intercom.com/egypt ▪ Gambia, www.gambia.com
- Ghana, www.helloghana/com/info/contents.htm ▪ Israel Information Service, www.israel.org
- Jerusalem One, www.jer1.co.il ▪ Kenya, www.africa.online.co.ke
- Malawi, http://spicerack.sr.unh.edu/~llk ▪ Morocco, www.maghreb.net
- Uganda, www.africaindex.africainfo.no/africaindex1/countries/uganda.html.
- South Africa, http://africa.com ▪ Tunisia, www.tunisiaonline.com ▪ UAE, www.ecssr.ac.ae.

Web Sites on Asia/Pacific 💻
Many of these sites provide government and trade information concerning this rapidly developing region. There is country and travel information, local news, and a few site links to job opportunities. [ID:2663]
- Asia On-Line Homepage, www.asia-online.com
- Asian Development Bank, www.asiandevbank.org ▪ Australia, http://gov.info.au
- China, www.cnd.org ▪ Hong Kong Trade Development Council, www.tdc.org.hk
- India, www.indiaonline.com/index.html ▪ Japan, www.jetro.go.jp ▪ Malaysia, www.jaring.my
- New Zealand, www.gov.nz ▪ Pakistan, www.pak.gov.pk ▪ Philippines, www.philexport.org
- Singapore, www.singapore.com ▪ Thailand, www.nectec.or.th/bureaux
- Western Samoa, www.interwebinc.com/samoa

Web Sites on Eastern Europe and the Former Soviet Union 💻
These are a sample of sites providing information on this region of the world. The sites include local news, travel, export-import information, and job opportunities. [ID:2668]
- Belarus, www.friends-partners.org/friends/community/lists/belarus.htmlopt-tables-unix-english
- Bosnia-Herzegovina, www.funet.fi/pub/doc/World/Factbook93/countries.bosnia%2bherzegovina
- Bulgaria, http://pisa.rockefeller.edu:8080/Bulgaria
- Croatia, www.hr/lookup/wwwhr/politics/government ▪ Czech Republic, www.muselink.com/
- Estonia, www.ciesin.ee/estcg ▪ Latvia, www.lda.gov.lv ▪ Lithuania, http://neris.mii.lt
- Poland, http://polanianet.comleng ▪ Romania, www.embassy.org/romania.
- Russia, www.wtr.ru ▪ Serbia, www.yugoslavia.com/Library/Facts/FACTS01.htm
- Slovakia, www.slovak.com ▪ Slovenia, www.uvi.si/slo ▪ Ukraine, www.gu.kiev.ua.

Web Sites on Latin America and the Caribbean 💻
If you have always wanted to go somewhere warm, these sites can help you get there. There is information on current events, job opportunities, and news related to trade and government activities. The listings below are only a few examples of what's available on the Internet. [ID:2664]
- Argentina, www.mecon.ar/default ▪ Bahamas, www.bahamas-on-line.com
- Bolivia, www.ine.gov.bo ▪ Bermuda, www.bermudacommerce.com
- Brazilian Business Connection, www.brazilbiz.com.br/english ▪ Chile, www.prochile.cl
- Costa Rica, www.cool.co.cr/toping/bus/business.html ▪ Cuba, www.cubaweb.cu/indice.html
- Dominican Republic, www.caribbean-on-line.com/earleltd/dr/drm.html
- Ecuador, http://mia.lac.net/minture/ing ▪ Grenada, www.grenada.org
- Haiti, www.caribbeansupersite.com/haiti/index.htm
- Guatemala, www. escapeartist.com/guatemala/guatemala.htm
- Jamaica, www.exportjamaica.org ▪ Mexico, www.mexguide.net/monterrey/index-i.html
- Peru, www.peruonline.com/indice_e.htm ▪ Panama, www.presidencia.gvn.pa
- Trinidad and Tobago, www.nisc.gov.tt ▪ Venezuela, www.venezuelaonline.com/indice_e.htm

Web Sites on Western Europe 💻
The following are only a fraction of what you can find concerning Western Europe. Information includes current local news, travel and trade information, and links to job opportunities. [ID:2667]
- Austria, http://gov.austria-info.at/bmaa/content.html ▪ Belgium, www.belgium.fgov.be
- Denmark, www.um.dk ▪ Finland, www.cfce.fr ▪ France, www.premier-ministre.gov.fr

■ Germany, www.ihk.de ■ Greece, www.hri.org ■ Iceland, www.icetrade.is ■ Ireland, www.itw.ie
■ Italy, www.globescope.com/italy/stats.htm ■ Luxembourg, www.ne(o)stena.lu
■ Malta, www.magnet.mt ■ Netherlands, www.cbs.nl ■ Norway, www.ssb.no/www-open/english
■ Portugal, www.portugal.org ■ Spain, klk/www.impi.es ■ Sweden, www.swedishtrade.se
■ Switzerland, www.admin.ch ■ United Kingdom, www.open.gov.uk.

A LAST WORD

The Internet has become an indispensable medium of global communication. The Net allows you to communicate with people around the globe in minutes, if not seconds, and learn about other cultures. The technology itself makes it possible to look for employment overseas without ever leaving your home.

We have provided you with a thorough list of Internet resources covering a broad variety of topics, but it is just a small taste of what you can find in this virtual Milky Way of information. As with any medium, however, it pays to verify important information where possible—don't believe everything you read. Using this tool to get a job might sound easy, but ultimately your job search results will depend on how much time and effort you are willing to invest, on *and* off the Net. As more people use the Internet on a daily basis, employers from various professions will increasingly use it to hire new talent. Traditional methods of job searching are still essential, and the high-tech version should only be used as an added dimension—the Net supplements, not replaces, traditional job hunting. Armed with a variety of resources, techniques, and determination, the Net makes it easier for you to land the job you always wanted.

Chapter 22

Resources for the International Job Search

Resources in this chapter are *directly* related to international jobs and careers.

International job search and career resources in this chapter

International Job Search 429
Employment Agencies 432
Job Search Directories 433
Other Careers 437
Health Careers 438
Language Careers 441
Tourism Industry Careers 442

Other job search resources found elsewhere in this book

CHAPTER 20, The Job Search:
General Job Search: All 395
General Job Search: Students 396

CHAPTER 21, The Internet Job Search:
Books on the Internet Job Search 415
Directories on the Web 416
International Job Hunting
    Services on the Internet 417
Country Information on the Internet 424

RESOURCES

International Job Search

These are the best, general books on international jobs. While most of them are American, many have excellent introductory essays. Moreover, many American firms are interested in hiring bilingual Canadians. For more related information, you *must* also consult the Resources for the section on International Job Hunting Services on the Internet found in Chapter 21, The Internet Job Search. See also Chapter 27, Jobs by Regions of the World.

Careers in International Affairs 📖
1997, *Linda Powers,* Georgetown University ➤ Scholarly Book Services, 77 Mowat Avenue, Suite 403, Toronto, Ontario M6K 3E3; $27.95; VISA, MC; (800) 847-9736, fax (800) 220-9895 ■ One of the best sources of information on international careers. Contains background, addresses and

telephone numbers for 378 international organizations, including public, government, commercial banking, business, consulting, research, nonprofit and educational organizations. [ID:1150]

The Complete Guide to International Jobs and Careers 📖
1993, *Caryl Krannich, Ronald Krannich,* 306 pages ➤ Impact Publications, 9104 North Manassas Drive, Manassas Park, VA 20111-2366, USA; US$13.95; credit cards; (703) 361-7300, fax (703) 335-9486 ■ The second edition of this popular book helps job seekers better understand the what, where, and how of today's highly competitive international job markets. Exposes numerous myths and shows how to find employment with key international employers: multinationals, government agencies, nonprofit organizations, consulting firms, foundations, education and research organizations. Examines opportunities in both developed and developing countries. Includes additional resources. Visit the distributor's web site at www.impactpublications.com. [ID:1050]

The Directory of Jobs and Careers Abroad 📖
1993, *André de Vries,* Peterson's Guides, 408 pages ➤ Capricorn Business Services, Inc., 28 Clear Lake Ave., West Hill, Ontario M1C 4L6; $16.95; credit cards; (416) 282-3331, fax (416) 282-0015 ■ Best British reference book for everyone, from recent graduates to fully qualified professionals. Includes tips on finding jobs with the United Nations and other international bodies, listings of openings by career, plus noncommercial and voluntary work in developing countries. Aimed at British citizens. [ID:1153]

The Economist 📖
Weekly ➤ The Economist, P.O. Box 58524, Boulder, CO 80322, USA; $175.55/yr; credit cards; (800) 456-6086, fax (800) 604-7455 ■ The best magazine for keeping up-to-date on the economic and political situations in both developed and developing countries, as well as for classified ads for senior management jobs. Visit their web site at www.economist.com. [ID:1635]

Evaluating an Overseas Job Opportunity 📖
1992, *John Williams* ➤ Pilot Books, P.O. Box 2102, Greenport, NY 11944, USA; US$5.95; credit cards; (516) 477-1094, fax (516) 477-0978 ■ Of special interest to those who have already chosen an overseas posting, this book addresses potential problems in living arrangements, salaries and benefits and, most interestingly, how your posting abroad could affect your standing with your company at home. Visit the distributor's web site at www.pilotbooks.com. [ID:1232]

Finding Work Overseas 📖
1996, *Matthew Cunningham,* 200 pages ➤ How To Books Ltd., 3 Newtec Place, Magdalen Road, Oxford, OX4 1RE, UK; £9.99; credit cards; (44) (1752) 202-301, fax (44) (1865) 202-331 ■ How and where to contact international recruitment agencies, consultancies, and employers. [ID:2433]

Great Jobs Abroad 📖
1997, *Arthur H. Bell,* 378 pages ➤ McGraw-Hill Ryerson Ltd., 300 Water Street, Whitby, Ontario L1N 9B6; $21.95; credit cards; (800) 565-5758, fax (800) 463-5885 ■ This book offers practical techniques for finding international employment. Includes internet job listings as well as company and employer profiles. Lists local U.S. companies and foreign corporations that hire Americans for overseas work, federal job centres, and provides information on American missions overseas. Visit the publisher's web site at www.mcgrawhill.ca. [ID:1788]

Group Fischer
Group Fischer, P.O. Box 2770, Laguna Hills, CA 92654, USA; (714) 699-3380, fax (714) 699-3381, hobos1@aol.com ■ Group Fischer's database, called Manlink, is used extensively by employers around the world to locate employee candidates in engineering and construction, oil and gas, operations and maintenance, aircraft services, healthcare, mining and metals, defence, education, training, and communications. Visit the distributor's web site at www.hobos1.com. [ID:2455]

Guide to Careers in World Affairs 📖
1993, Foreign Policy Association, 432 pages ➤ Impact Publications, 9104 North Manassas Drive, Manassas Park, VA 20111-2366, USA; US$14.95; credit cards; (703) 361-7300, fax (703) 335-9486 ■ Reveals hundreds of international job opportunities. Identifies major international employers in the fields of business, consulting, finance, banking, journalism, law, translation/interpretation,

nonprofit organizations, federal and state government, and the UN. Special chapters outline internship opportunities, international graduate programs, and job hunting strategies. Entries include annotated descriptions of organizations, along with names, addresses and telephone numbers for employers. Visit the distributor's web site at www.impactpublications.com. [ID:1143]

How to Get a Job Abroad 📖
1994, *Roger Jones,* 272 pages ➤ How To Books Ltd., 3 Newtec Place, Magdalen Road, Oxford, OX4 1RE, UK; £10.99; credit cards; (44) (1752) 202-301, fax (44) (1865) 202-331 ▪ Information on medium- and long-term job opportunities and possibilities, arranged by region and country, and by profession. Includes contact names and addresses, as well as a guide to overseas recruitment agencies. Essential reading for anyone intending to work abroad. [ID:1671]

International Dimensions of Human Resource Management 📖
1993, *Peter Dowling, Randall Schuler,* Wadsworth ➤ Nelson Canada, 1120 Birchmount Road, Scarborough, Ontario M1K 5G4; $38.95; credit cards; (800) 268-2222, fax (800) 430-4445 ▪ Focuses on managing human resources in the international environment. Examines recruitment and selection of international employees, performance appraisal, training and development and international labour relations. A new edition will be published in 1998. [ID:1183]

International Employment Gazette 📖
Biweekly, *Robert L. Whitmore* ➤ International Employment Gazette, P.O. Box 1446, Greenville, SC 29602, USA; US$7/issue, US$40/3 months; credit cards; (864) 235-4444, fax (864) 235-3369 ▪ Provides information on job openings in all occupations worldwide. For an additional fee, the International Placement Network provides current overseas job openings in the subscriber's occupation and geographic location of choice. [ID:1275]

International Employment Hotline 📖
Monthly ➤ International Employment Hotline, P.O. Box 3030, Oakton, VA 22124, USA; $39/year; (703) 478-0055, fax (703) 478-0055 ▪ Published regularly since 1980, each issue offers up-to-date job listings around the world with mailing addresses and application instructions. Includes many good articles of interest to job seekers. [ID:2459]

International Employment Resources 📖
1997, *Robert L. Whitmore,* 100 pages ➤ International Employment Gazette, P.O. Box 1446, Greenville, SC 29602, USA; US$19.95; credit cards; (864) 235-4444, fax (864) 235-3369 ▪ A compilation of stories and articles from past issues of the International Employment Gazette. Contains necessary information from experts in a wide variety of fields. Provides an overview of working abroad and what to expect from overseas employment. [ID:2529]

International Employment Resources, On-line 💻
http://bertie.usfca.edu/usf/career/international/html ▪ This list includes links to job banks in Asia, Australia, and Europe and several general resources which are global in scope. This is a good on-ramp to the information highway. [ID:2549]

International Jobs 📖
1993, *Eric Kocher,* 394 pages ➤ Addison Wesley Longman Publishers, P.O. Box 580, Don Mills, Ontario M3C 2T8; $20.95; credit cards; (800) 387-8028, fax (800) 465-0536 ▪ A popular handbook of over 500 career opportunities around the world, aimed at Americans seeking jobs abroad. The book describes international careers and lists US companies operating in various parts of the world. Aims to broaden the reader's knowledge of the international employment scene. Part 1 covers career planning and job strategy; Part 2, the international job market in areas such as government, the UN, nonprofit organizations, business, banking, and teaching. Includes the former Soviet Union and Eastern Europe. [ID:1066]

The International Jobs Directory: A Guide to Over 1001 Employers 📖
1997, *Caryl Krannich, Ronald Krannich,* 348 pages ➤ Impact Publications, 9104 North Manassas Drive, Manassas Park, VA 20111-2366, USA; US$14.95; credit cards; (703) 361-7300, fax (703) 335-9486 ▪ The organizational companion to the Complete Guide to International Jobs and Careers. This directory provides critical contact information on hundreds of public and private organiza-

tions which offer international job opportunities. Provides annotated lists of: government agencies; international organizations; associations, societies, and research institutes; business firms; foreign firms operating in the US; contracting and consulting firms; private voluntary organizations (PVOs); nonprofits and foundations; and colleges and universities. Includes names, addresses, phone numbers, and descriptions of each employer. An indispensable guide to hundreds of international employers. Visit www.impactpublications.com, the distributor's web site. [ID:1051]

Jobs Worldwide 📖
1994, *David Lay, Benedict Leerburger,* 380 pages ➤ Impact Publications, 9104 North Manassas Drive, Manassas Park, VA 20111-2366, USA; US$17.95; credit cards; (703) 361-7300, fax (703) 335-9486 ▪ This rich resource outlines effective international job search strategies. Includes a country-by-country examination of employment opportunities, and critical contact information for reaching major international employers in the US and abroad. Visit the distributor's web site at www.impactpublications.com. [ID:1472]

La recherche d'un emploi dans les organisations internationales 📖
1994, *Louis Sabourin,* 143 pages ➤ Éditions Vermette Inc., 6255, Hutchison, Montréal, Québec H2V 4C7; $14.95; VISA, MC; (514) 278-3025, fax (514) 278-3030 ▪ Un guide qui présente un tableau d'ensemble des principaux organismes internationaux, qui indique leurs adresses complètes et qui propose des suggestions quant à la meilleure façon de se préparer pour obtenir un emploi. [ID:1587]

Overseas Jobs Express 💻
www.overseasjobs.com ▪ This wonderful site lists over 1,500 new international jobs each month. Searches can be conducted by keyword, category, or region and the search engine is very user-friendly. There is also a free résumé posting service. A number of career counselling resources, an online "bookshop" specializing in international employment, and a travel advisory section are also available. This site includes 700 links to job banks in over 40 countries. You can go directly to Brazil and look for a job there without ever leaving your home. This is the best site for international employment opportunities. [ID:2541]

Passport to Overseas Employment: 100,000 Job Opportunities Abroad 📖
1990, *Dale Chambers* ➤ Prentice Hall Canada, 539 Collier MacMillan Drive, Cambridge, Ontario N1R 5W9; $19.95; credit cards; (800) 567-3800, fax (800) 563-9196 ▪ Provides vital information for obtaining temporary employment abroad or launching a long-term international career. Visit the publisher's web site at www.phcanada.com. [ID:1665]

Vacancies in International Organizations 💻
www3.itu.ch/MISSIONS ▪ This Italian site provides links to the personnel departments of several international organizations. The focus is on supra-national organizations rather than NGOs. Links range from the Asian Development Bank to the World Trade Organization, and to other specialized organizations. [ID:2573]

Work Abroad: The Complete Guide to Finding a Job Overseas 📖
1997, *Clay Hubb,* Transitions Abroad, 224 pages ➤ Department TRA, Transitions Publishing, P.O. Box 3000, Denville, NJ 07834, USA; $15.95; VISA, MC; (413) 256-3414, fax (413) 256-0373, trabroad@aol.com ▪ Comprehensive guide to all aspects of international work, including work permits, short-term jobs, teaching English, volunteer opportunities, planning an international career, starting your own business, and more. Visit www.transabroad.com, the publisher's web site. [ID:2558]

Employment Agencies

Employment Conditions Abroad Ltd. (ECA)
Employment Conditions Abroad Ltd. (ECA), Anchor House, 15 Britten Street, London, SW3 3TY, UK; (44) (171) 351 5000, fax (44) (171) 351 9396 ▪ ECA is an information and advisory service for companies worldwide which employ expatriates or local nationals abroad. These services help members administer international work assignments. ECA serves a wide range of industries

including banking, pharmaceutical, drilling, software, manufacturing and engineering. ECA is not a recruitment agency for individuals seeking employment. ECA maintains a useful web site, with links to its global offices, that contains information on the products and services it offers. [ID:2422]

Group Fischer
Group Fischer, P.O. Box 2770, Laguna Hills, CA 92654, USA; (714) 699-3380, fax (714) 699-3381, hobos1@aol.com ▪ Group Fischer's database, called Manlink, is used extensively by employers around the world to locate employee candidates in engineering and construction, oil and gas, operations and maintenance, aircraft services, healthcare, mining and metals, defence, education, training, and communications. Visit the distributor's web site at www.hobos1.com. [ID:2455]

Human Resources International (HRI)
Human Resources International (HRI), Suite 705, 50 Burnhamthorpe Road W., Mississauga, Ontario L5B 3C2; (613) 232-6772, fax (613) 232-6544, rnaccarato@hrii.com ▪ Human Resources International Inc. (HRI) is a subsidiary of ADECCO S.A., a human resources placement company headquartered in Europe. HRI operates both nationally and internationally in the staffing and recruitment of highly-trained human resources professionals. HRI specializes in placing telecommunications personnel from North America, Central and South America, the Middle East, India and the Philippines. HRI recruits personnel with extensive experience in the telecommunications business. [ID:2647]

INTERCRISTO, The Christian Career Specialists
INTERCRISTO, The Christian Career Specialists, P.O. Box 33487, 19303 Fremont Ave. N., Seattle, WA 98133, USA; (800) 426-1342, fax (206) 546-7375, rlr@crista.org ▪ INTERCRISTO is a Christian nonprofit job referral ministry dedicated to helping Christians connect with Christian nonprofit organizations throughout the world. There are currently over 20,000 jobs and service opportunities listed on INTERCRISTO's computerized database. Their excellent web site includes links to other Christian ministries, as well as information on the ministry's activities and opportunities. First-hand accounts of recent placements are both friendly and encouraging. Visit the distributor's web site at www.jobleads.org. [ID:2457]

International Employment Gazette ▥
Biweekly, *Robert L. Whitmore* ➤ International Employment Gazette, P.O. Box 1446, Greenville, SC 29602, USA; US$7/issue, US$40/3 months; credit cards; (864) 235-4444, fax (864) 235-3369 ▪ Provides information on job openings in all occupations worldwide. For an additional fee, the International Placement Network provides current overseas job openings in the subscriber's occupation and geographic location of choice. [ID:1275]

Master Craft ▭
www.master-craft.com ▪ This employment service offers clients access to its database containing over 11 million employers from over 100 countries. They also help you write a successful international résumé. For a US$5 fee, they will send you an application package. [ID:2538]

Job Search Directories

Associations Canada 1997/98 ▥
Annual, Canadian Almanac and Directory ➤ Renouf Publishing Co. Ltd., Unit 1, 5369 Canotek Road, Ottawa, Ontario K1J 9J3; $249.50; credit cards; (613) 745-2665, fax (613) 745-7660 ▪ An alphabetical listing of over 18,000 Canadian organizations and 1,000 international groups covering industry, commercial and professional associations, registered charities, special interest and common interest organizations. Indexed by subject, geographic location, and budget size, this directory includes contact names, conferences, publications, acronyms, and mailing list availability. Available in libraries. [ID:1348]

Blue Book of Canadian Business ▥
Annual, *Brian Gilligan* ➤ Canadian Newspaper Services International, Suite 495, 2130 Lawrence Ave. E., Scarborough, Ontario M1R 3A6; $149.95, or $249.95 with web site facility; VISA; (888)

422-4742, fax (416) 752-8303, info@bluebook.ca ▪ Provides directory information for over 2,000 companies plus excellent, detailed profiles of leading firms. Also ranks firms according to a variety of criteria. The 1997 edition includes the option of subscribing to the Blue Book web site which provides information to keep you up to date between editions: www.bluebook.ca. [ID:1496]

Bottin International du Québec 📖
Annuelle, *Denis Turcotte* ➤ Québec dans le monde, C.P. 8503, Ste-Foy, Québec G1V 4N5; $27,95; chèque ou mandat poste; (418) 659-5540, fax (418) 659-4143 ▪ Le bottin prend en compte un millier d'intervenants internationaux québécois ou partenaires étrangers du Québec. Il énumère leur adresse postale, leur numéro de téléphone, leurs secteurs d'activités, et le pays ou les régions d'intervention. [ID:1597]

Canadian Key Business Directory 📖
1997, 3180 pages ➤ Dun and Bradstreet Canada Ltd., 5770 Hurontario Street, Mississauga, Ontario L5R 3G5; $450; credit cards; (800) 668-1168, fax (905) 568-5815; Available in large libraries ▪ This directory is the most comprehensive listing for public and private Canadian companies. To be included, companies must have a minimum of $10,000,000 in sales, 100 employees, or $1,000,000 net worth. [ID:1507]

The Consultants and Consulting Organizations Directory 📖
1997, 725 pages, 2 vols. ➤ Gale Research Inc., 835 Penobscot Bldg., 645 Griswold Street, Detroit, MI 48226-4094, USA; US$545; credit cards; (800) 877-4253 ext. 1330, fax (800) 414-5043; Available in large libraries ▪ Provides details on over 24,000 firms and individuals, from services offered to client profiles, full contact information, and more. Arranged alphabetically, under 14 general fields of consulting activity, ranging from agriculture to marketing. Visit the distributor's web site at www.gale.com. [ID:1147]

Corpus Almanac and Canadian Sourcebook 📖
Annual ➤ Southam Information and Technology Group, 1450 Don Mills Rd., Don Mills, Ontario M3B 2X7; $179; credit cards; (800) 668-2374, fax (416) 442-2219; Available in large libraries ▪ Contains a broad range of information on Canadian business and government, including associations, societies, industry and trade, government and finance. [ID:1512]

Diplomatic, Consular, and Other Representatives in Canada 📖
Annual, Department of Foreign Affairs and International Trade (DFAIT), 151 pages ➤ Canada Government PublishingOttawa, Ontario K1A 0S9; $19.95; VISA, MC; (819) 956-4800, fax (819) 994-1498, publishing@ccg-gcc.ca ▪ A bilingual directory of diplomatic missions in Ottawa and consular and other missions throughout Canada, including names and titles of staff. Visit the publisher's web site at http://publications.pwgsc.gc.ca. [ID:1088]

Directory of American Firms Operating in Foreign Countries 📖
1996 ➤ Uniworld Business Publications, 257 Central Park West, New York, NY 10024, USA; US$220; (212) 496-2448, fax (212) 769-0413; Available in large libraries ▪ Lists some 2,600 American companies with more than 19,000 subsidiaries and affiliates in 127 foreign countries. One volume lists US firms with foreign operations, two volumes list countries in which US firms operate. Individual country editions are also available; prices range from US$29-$99 each. Visit the distributor's web site at www.uniworldbp.com. [ID:1272]

The Directory of Associations 📖
Annual, 1307 pages ➤ Micromedia Ltd., 20 Victoria Street, Toronto, Ontario M5C 2N8; $270; VISA, MC; (800) 387-2689, fax (416) 362-6161; Available in large libraries ▪ Listing of 20,000 major associations in Canada. Includes addresses, contacts, branches, number of staff, membership information, publications, and association mandates. [ID:1204]

Directory of Canadian Consulting Engineers 1994-95 📖
Annual, 409 pages ➤ Association of Consulting Engineers of Canada (ACEC), Suite 616, 130 Albert Street, Ottawa, Ontario K1P 5G4; $150 or $100 for CD-Rom; VISA; (613) 236-0569, fax (613) 236-6193 ▪ This one-stop, highly efficient sourcebook has a section with names and addresses of

overseas operations of Canadian consulting firms. The introduction is in English, French, Spanish, Portuguese, Arabic, Russian and Mandarin. [ID:1076]

Directory of Executive Recruiters ⌘
Biennial, Kennedy Center Publications, 1123 pages ➤ Impact Publications, 9104 North Manassas Drive, Manassas Park, VA 20111-2366, USA; US$44.95; credit cards; (703) 361-7300, fax (703) 335-9486 ▪ Includes 3,200 offices of 1,965 firms in the US, and Mexico. Lists names, addresses, and telephone numbers for key firms with employment contacts. Also has excellent advice on job hunting and working with executive recruiters. Visit www.impactpublications.com, the distributor's web site. [ID:1057]

Directory of Foreign Firms Operating in the US ⌘
Annual ➤ Uniworld Business Publications, 257 Central Park West, New York, NY 10024, USA; US$200; (212) 496-2448, fax (212) 769-0413; Available in large libraries ▪ Similar to its counterpart, *Directory of US Firms Operating in Foreign Countries*, this is a comprehensive resource. Individual country editions are available for US$29-$99 each. Visit www.uniworldbp.com, the publisher's web site. [ID:2532]

Directory of Non-Governmental Organizations (NGOs)
Active in Sustainable Development ⌘
1997, 768 pages ➤ Organization of Economic Cooperation and Development (OECD), Suite 700, 2001 L Street N.W., Washington, DC 20036, USA; US$138; credit cards; (202) 785-6323, fax (202) 785-0350 ▪ This updated and revised directory is a comprehensive source of information on 3,900 NGOs in 26 countries in Europe. Contains NGO profiles, indexes of their activities in developing countries and Europe. Visit the publisher's web site at www.oecdwash.org. [ID:1220]

Encyclopedia of Associations: International Organizations 1997 ⌘
1997, *Linda Irvin,* 3,300 pages, 2 vols. ➤ Gale Research Inc., 835 Penobscot Bldg., 645 Griswold Street, Detroit, MI 48226-4094, USA; US$550; credit cards; (800) 877-4253 ext. 1330, fax (800) 414-5043; Available in large libraries ▪ Directory provides descriptions of 19,400 multinational for-profit and international nonprofit organizations around the world. Indexed by geographic region, name, and key word. Visit the distributor's web site at www.gale.com. [ID:1148]

The Executive Contact List: US Private and Voluntary
Organizations Registered with the Agency for International Development ⌘
Semiannual, 192 pages ➤ Bureau for Humanitarian Assistance and Response, US Agency for International Development, 1300 Pennsylvannia Avenue N.W., Washington, DC 20523, USA; free; (202) 712-4810, fax (202) 216-3237 ▪ Lists names of executive contacts for US organizations registered with the US Agency for International Development. [ID:1263]

Financial Post Survey of Predecessor and Defunct Companies ⌘
Annual, 224 pages ➤ Financial Post, 333 King Street E., Toronto, Ontario M5A 4N2; $89.95; credit cards; (416) 350-6000, fax (416) 350-6301 ▪ A cumulative comprehensive listing of all Canadian companies no longer active due to mergers, name changes, takeovers, liquidations, and charter cancellations. Dates back almost 60 years. Contains over 12,000 Canadian corporate entries. [ID:1511]

Fischer Report ⌘
Bimonthly ➤ George E. Fischer & Associates, Inc., P.O. Box 9348, Newport Beach, CA 92658, USA; US$400 first year, $US300 renewal; VISA, MC; (714) 759-3374, fax (714) 760-1792 ▪ Excellent source of information on contracts awarded in the field of international business. [ID:1149]

Hoover's Directory of World Business ⌘
1996, *Gary Hoover, Alta Campbell, Alan Chai,* 421 pages ➤ Impact Publications, 9104 North Manassas Drive, Manassas Park, VA 20111-2366, USA; US$27.95; credit cards; (703) 361-7300, fax (703) 335-9486 ▪ This directory provides detailed information on major international businesses. includes statistics, corporate profiles and contact information. Identifies the world's top 10 companies. Visit the distributor's web site at www.impactpublications.com. [ID:1762]

Hoovers On-Line 💻

www.hoovers.com ▪ This company maintains detailed profiles of thousands of domestic and international companies. This resource allows you to research potential employers and connect to thousands of corporate home pages. There are no job listings at this site, but there is a tremendous amount of information available which could be useful in preparing for an interview or determining the scope of international operations of Canadian and American companies. Services are free for AOL and CompuServe patrons. For others, there is a US$9.95 fee to access the information. [ID:2581]

The International Directory of Importers 📖

1998 ➤ International Directory of Importers, 1741 Kekamek NW, Poulsbo, Washington 98730, USA; Price varies from US$225 to $450; credit cards; (800) 818-0140, fax (360) 697-4696 ▪ This extensive directory has 150,000 listings of worldwide importers. Designed for use by exporters, manufacturers, and trading firms, this nine-volume set covers Europe, the Middle East, North America, South and Central America, Asia Pacific, and Africa. Firms are listed alphabetically under commodity headings. Area directories sell at different prices ranging from $225 to $450. [ID:1188]

Moody's International Manual 📖

Annual ➤ Moody's Investors' Service, 99 Church Street, New York, NY 10007, USA; US$3,175; credit cards; (212) 553-0300, fax (212) 553-4700; Available in large libraries ▪ Exhaustive reference source for financial and business information on approximately 10,000 major corporations, sovereigns and their municipalities, and national and supranational institutions in 105 countries. Four volumes. [ID:1208]

Multiculturalism Means Business: a Directory of Business Contacts 📖

1993, 88 pages ➤ Department of Canadian Heritage, Multiculturalism and Citizenship Canada, 15 Eddy Street, Hull, Québec K1A 0M5; free; (819) 953-0628 ▪ Designed to promote networking, this directory reflects the ethnocultural diversity of Canada. Extensive listings of bilateral business councils and ethnocultural directories are very useful for establishing contacts. Also in French. [ID:1310]

Principal International Businesses: The World Marketing Directory 📖

1997, 3358 pages ➤ Dun and Bradstreet Canada Ltd., 5770 Hurontario Street, Mississauga, Ontario L5R 3G5; $625; credit cards; (800) 668-1168, fax (905) 568-5815; Available in large libraries ▪ An invaluable tool to any businessperson, this directory presents up-to-date information on approximately 55,000 leading enterprises in 140 countries around the world. Data classified by country and products; businesses listed alphabetically. [ID:1062]

Report on Business: Canada Company Handbook 📖

1997, Globe and Mail ➤ Renouf Publishing Co. Ltd., Unit 1, 5369 Canotek Road, Ottawa, Ontario K1J 9J3; $59.95; credit cards; (613) 745-2665, fax (613) 745-7660 ▪ Provides current news, ratios, and price performance charts, and annual and quarterly information for 402 major Canadian public companies. A full page is devoted to each company. Companies are grouped by industry and arranged alphabetically within each industry. [ID:1509]

Service Contracts and Lines of Credit 📖

Semiannual, *External Business Relations, Corporate Management Branch,* 66 pages ➤ Public Inquiries, Canadian International Development Agency, 200 Promenade du Portage, Hull, Québec K1A 0G4; free; (800) 230-6349, fax (819) 953-6088, info@acdi-cida.gc.ca ▪ A listing of firms and consultants who currently have contracts with CIDA. Lists contracts according to size, project title, supplier and approximate dollar value. A must for Canadian international job seekers. [ID:1103]

Yearbook of International Organizations 📖

Annual, *Union of International Associations (Geneva)* ➤ Bowker-Saur, 121 Chanlon Road, New Providence, NJ 07974, USA; US$1170; credit cards; (800) 521-8110, fax (908) 665-6688; Available in large libraries ▪ Exhaustive, comprehensive listings of 32,000 international organizations by subject, region and organization type, including descriptions and contact information. Visit www.reedref.com. [ID:1198]

Other Careers

Awards for University Administrators and Librarians 📖
Biennial, Association of Commonwealth Universities, 40 pages ➤ UBC Press, University of British Columbia, 6344 Memorial Rd., Vancouver, B.C. V6T 1Z2; £10.50; VISA, MC; (604) 822-3259, fax (800) 668-0821, orders@ubcpress.ubc.ca ▪ Describes 43 sources of financial aid in both Commonwealth and non-Commonwealth countries. Lists awards tenable in one Commonwealth country by staff from another, awards for movement between Commonwealth and other countries, and other important information. [ID:1565]

Bowker Annual Library and Book Trade Almanac 📖
Annual ➤ Bowker-Saur, 121 Chanlon Road, New Providence, NJ 07974, USA; US$175; credit cards; (800) 521-8110, fax (908) 665-6688 ▪ This almanac has a small section on overseas library jobs, exchange programs and jobs in non-library settings for librarians. Visit the distributor's web site at www.reedref.com. [ID:1236]

Career Opportunities for American Planners in International Development 📖
1994, *Charles Boyce, Ralph Gakenheimer,* 86 pages ➤ International Division, American Planning Association, c/o The Institute of Public Administration, 55 West 44th Street, New York, NY 10016, USA; $10; credit cards; (212) 730-5480 ext. 340 or 330, fax (212) 768-9071 ▪ Aimed at the American reader, this book provides a wealth of information on educational requirements and how to get started. Planners with varying backgrounds provide their insights on opportunities with international development agencies, the US government, consulting firms and nongovernment organizations. Publishers of a monthly newsletter called *Interplan*. [ID:1638]

Careers in International Business 📖
1996, *Ed Halloran,* 227 pages ➤ Impact Publications, 9104 North Manassas Drive, Manassas Park, VA 20111-2366, USA; US$17.95; credit cards; (703) 361-7300, fax (703) 335-9486 ▪ This book looks at careers in international finance, marketing, management, logistics and sales—and outlines the path from entry-level assistant to multinational CEO. Visit www.impactpublications.com, the distributor's web site. [ID:1761]

Careers in International Law 📖
1993, *Mark W. Janis,* 240 pages ➤ Publication Orders, American Bar Association, P.O. Box 10892, Chicago, IL 60610-0892, USA; US$19.95; VISA, MC; (312) 988-5522, fax (312) 988-5568 ▪ Sixteen international lawyers practicing in public and private international law present essays based on their experiences. Their observations help create a comprehensive picture of what it's like to practice international law and show how to become an international lawyer. [ID:1458]

For the Working Artist 📖
1992, *Judith Luther,* California Institute of the Arts ➤ National Network for Artists Placement, 935 West Avenue 37, Los Angeles, CA 90056, USA; US$30; cheque or money order; (213) 222-4035, fax (213) 222-4035 ▪ A comprehensive artists' survival handbook, including sections on grants and international opportunities. [ID:1087]

Golden Opportunities: A Volunteer Guide for Americans Over 50 📖
1994, *Andrew Carroll,* Peterson's Guides ➤ Nelson Canada, 1120 Birchmount Road, Scarborough, Ontario M1K 5G4; $20.95; credit cards; (800) 268-2222, fax (800) 430-4445 ▪ Detailed information for older adults who want to offer their services abroad. The book also mentions special opportunities for doctors and health care professionals, and recommends resources. [ID:1448]

INTERCRISTO, The Christian Career Specialists
INTERCRISTO, The Christian Career Specialists, P.O. Box 33487, 19303 Fremont Ave. N., Seattle, WA 98133, USA; (800) 426-1342, fax (206) 546-7375, rlr@crista.org ▪ INTERCRISTO is a Christian nonprofit job referral ministry dedicated to helping Christians connect with Christian nonprofit

organizations throughout the world. There are currently over 20,000 jobs and service opportunities listed on INTERCRISTO's computerized database. Their excellent web site includes links to other Christian ministries, as well as information on the ministry's activities and opportunities. First-hand accounts of recent placements are both friendly and encouraging. Visit the distributor's web site at www.jobleads.org. [ID:2457]

Jobs Abroad: Opportunities Overseas 📖
Annual, 50 pages ➤ Christian Service Centre, Holloway Street W., Lower Gornal, Dudley, West Midlands DY3 2DZ, UK; £3.50; cheque or money order; (44) (1902) 882-836, fax (44) (1902) 881-099 ▪ Booklet lists over 3,000 job vacancies outside Britain of interest to Christians, most of them for two-year postings with UK-based mission agencies. Cost includes an annual supplement. [ID:1044]

Health Careers

Our web site *www.WorkingOverseas.com* has more on health careers.

Canadian Association of University Schools of Nursing (CAUSN)
Canadian Association of University Schools of Nursing (CAUSN), Suite 324, 350 Albert Street, Ottawa, Ontario K1R 1B1; (613) 563-1236 ▪ If you are a member of CAUSN, and a nursing teacher with international experience, you can register with the CAUSN Resource Directory on International Health. This new directory can be searched by potential employers for candidates to work overseas. CAUSN also has a database on their web site listing international linkages maintained by university schools of nursing in Canada. Visit their web site at www.causn.org. [ID:2685]

Canadian Nurses Association 📖
Canadian Nurses Association (CNA), 50 Driveway, Ottawa, Ontario K2P 1E2; (800) 361-8404, fax (613) 237-3520 ▪ This is an excellent place to begin looking for work abroad by requesting their information package on international nursing and health. The package includes information about the latest international development programs including a list of NGOs that need health professionals. For information on nursing in a specific country, including requirements for registration, the CNA has a list of addresses of all member countries of the International Council of Nurses. Although the CNA does not employ health professionals to work overseas, they sometimes send expert Canadian nursing consultants overseas. The Helen K. Mussallem Library at the CNA subscribes to a number of nursing journals/newsletters from other countries which may provide information about employment opportunities. Their web site, www.cna-nurses, includes information on overseas projects and nursing opportunities with details of who to contact as well as visa requirements for Canadian health professionals working in the United States. (See their profile in Chapter 35, Nongovernmental Organizations.) [ID:2469]

Canadian Red Cross
Canadian Red Cross, 1800 Alta Vista Drive, Ottawa, Ontario K1G 4J5; (613) 739-3000, fax (613) 731-1411 ▪ "The world's largest humanitarian network." The Red Cross provides humanitarian aid to victims of natural disasters and conflict. Last year they sent about 75 delegates overseas, 25 percent of whom were nurses. Red Cross healthcare professionals work in clinics, dispensaries, prisons, and hospitals. The Red Cross looks for health professionals who have solid character, adapt easily to change and have some experience in a foreign or northern setting. The Canadian Red Cross has an ongoing program to recruit prosthetic technicians and bilingual (French and English speaking) RNs. Given the working environment, it emphasizes recruiting professionals who have worked in difficult situations. Their web site, www.ifrc.org, provides information on the Red Cross/Red Crescent, listings of national societies, and access to a number of online publications. (See their profile in Chapter 35, Nongovernmental Organizations.) [ID:2686]

Canadian Society for International Health (CSIH)
Canadian Society for International Health, 1 Nicholas Street, Suite 1105, Ottawa, Ontario K1N 7B7; (613) 241-5785, fax (613) 241-3845, csih@fox.nstn.ca ▪ The CSIH network extends across Canada and around the world, linking individuals and organizations from all health sectors. The CSIH maintains the International Health Human Resources Registry, which is open to health and

health-related professionals experienced in working in developing countries, or with expertise that is applicable internationally. Add your name to the roster through the CHIS web site, www.csih.org. For recent healthcare graduates under the age of 30, the web site also has information about the International Youth Internship Program. CSIH publishes the newsletter *Synergy* as well as an online bulletin about international health, both of which can provide information about overseas job opportunities. CSIH members receive the Membership Directory which is a good networking tool for Canadians in international health. (See their profiles in Chapter 10, Short-term Programs Overseas Chapter 15, Awards and Grants; and Chapter 35, Nongovernmental Organizations.) [ID:2554]

Culture and the Clinical Encounter:
An Intercultural Sensitizer for the Health Professions 📖
1996, *Rena C. Gropper,* Intercultural Press, 184 pages ➤ Intercultural and Community Development Resources (ICDR), P.O. Box 32108, Millwoods Station, Edmonton, Alberta T6K 4C2; $28; VISA, Amex; (800) 378-3199, fax (403) 462-1925, icdr@compusmart.ab.ca ▪ Critical incidents in which communication between a health care professional and a patient breaks down due to lack of knowledge about cultural differences. The reader is challenged to choose the best of four possible explanations and to search for answers and accompanying discussions in another part of the book. Gives the reader a chance to actively participate in the learning process while gaining skills and motivation to be alert to intercultural misperceptions. Visit the distributor's web site at www.compusmart.ab.ca/icdr. [ID:2391]

Directory of US Based Agencies Involved In International Health Assistance 📖
1997 ➤ National Council for International Health, 1701 K Street N.W., Washington, DC 20006, USA; US$70; VISA, MC; (202) 833-5900, fax (202) 833-0075 ▪ Provides comprehensive information about US-based international organizations, including areas of expertise and contact persons. Lists a wide range of positions in international health fields. Visit the distributor's web site at www.ncih.org. [ID:1436]

Effective Communication in Multicultural Health Care Settings 📖
1994, *Gary Krebs, Elizabeth Kunimoto,* Sage Publications, 160 pages ➤ Intercultural and Community Development Resources (ICDR), P.O. Box 32108, Millwoods Station, Edmonton, Alberta T6K 4C2; $25; VISA, Amex; (800) 378-3199, fax (403) 462-1925, icdr@compusmart.ab.ca ▪ Illuminates the complexities of multicultural relations in healthcare and demystifies the myriad regional, ethnic, socioeconomic and cultural orientations of healthcare. Visit the distributor's web site at www.compusmart.ab.ca/icdr. [ID:2390]

Golden Opportunities: A Volunteer Guide for Americans Over 50 📖
1994, *Andrew Carroll,* Peterson's Guides ➤ Nelson Canada, 1120 Birchmount Road, Scarborough, Ontario M1K 5G4; $20.95; credit cards; (800) 268-2222, fax (800) 430-4445 ▪ Detailed information for older adults who want to offer their services abroad. The book also mentions special opportunities for doctors and health care professionals, and recommends resources. [ID:1448]

Health, Population and Reproductive Health Resources 💻
www.jhpiego.jhu.edu/RELATED/RELATED.HTM#Health ▪ Johns Hopkins University has compiled a list of links to organizations involved in this area of development. [ID:2453]

Helen Ziegler and Associates
Helen Ziegler & Associates, Suite 2403, 180 Dundas Street W., Toronto, Ontario M5G 1Z8; (416) 977-6941, fax (416) 977-6128, hza@medhunters.com ▪ In business since 1981, Helen Ziegler & Associates recruits healthcare staff for international locations, specifically Saudi Arabia and Beijing, China. Although they recruit all healthcare professionals, HZA's focus is on "hard-to-get" staff for clinical and technical positions such as MDs, management staff, nurses, medical imaging staff, respiratory therapists, etc,. They maintain a data bank for résumés and an interesting web site, www.hziegler.com, focusing on HZA's relations with Saudi Arabia and identifies international contacts in the Middle East and China. (See their profile in Chapter 33, The Private Sector.) [ID:2456]

Helping Health Workers Learn 📖
1986, *David Werner, Bill Bower,* Hesperian Foundation, 632 pages ➤ Intercultural and Community Development Resources (ICDR), P.O. Box 32108, Millwoods Station, Edmonton, Alberta T6K 4C2; $25; VISA, Amex; (800) 378-3199, fax (403) 462-1925, icdr@compusmart.ab.ca ▪ A collection of methods, aids and "triggers of the imagination," based on experience with a village-run health program in the mountains of western Mexico. Methods and experiences from at least 35 countries are discussed. Very useful for anyone involved in health training, adult education or community development work. Visit the distributor's web site at www.compusmart.ab.ca/icdr. [ID:2389]

International Federation of Red Cross and Red Crescent Network 🖥
www.ifrc.org ▪ "The world's largest humanitarian network." This site provides information about the Red Cross/Red Crescent, listings of national societies, and access to a number of online publications. [ID:2570]

Médecins Sans Frontières/Doctors Without Borders (MSF)
Médecins Sans Frontières/Doctors Without Borders (MSF), Suite 5B, 355 Adelaide Street, Toronto, Ontario M5V 1S2; (416) 586-9820, fax (416) 586-9821, msfcan@passport.ca ▪ The international MSF sends over 2,000 volunteers per year to work in over 70 countries. The Canadian arm of MSF also sends many professionals overseas, including doctors, paramedical personnel, and nurses. Their web site, www.msf.org, includes information on how to volunteer. (See their profile in Chapter 35, Nongovernmental Organizations.) [ID:2571]

MedHunters 🖥
MedHunters, Suite 2403, 180 Dundas Street W., Toronto, Ontario M5G 1Z8; (800) 664-0278, fax (416) 977-6128, jobs@medhunters.com ▪ MedHunters (MH) is the sister company of Helen Ziegler & Associates, Inc., a leading international healthcare recruitment agency. MH was founded in 1996 to provide worldwide recruitment services on the Internet for healthcare employers and professionals. MH, at the forefront of healthcare recruitment on the net, has developed unique and advanced job-matching technology. MH has also established links with many hospitals and employers in the USA, UK, New Zealand, Singapore, and other international locations. Visit their web site, www.medhunters.com, which has an electronic résumé database and internationally-oriented medical news. (See their profile in Chapter 33, The Private Sector.) [ID:2623]

OPTIONS (Project Concern International)
OPTIONS (Project Concern International), P.O. Box 85323, San Diego, CA 92186, USA; (619) 279-9690, fax (619) 694-0294, postmaster@projcon.cts.com ▪ OPTIONS is a nonprofit, non-sectarian, volunteer healthcare placement service of Project Concern International. They refer experienced healthcare professionals who wish to volunteer in hospitals, community clinics and medical facilities in critically under-serviced areas in the US and Asia, Africa, and Latin America. Placements are on a volunteer basis and range in duration from a few months to a few years. Visit www.serve.com/PCI. [ID:2460]

Trillium Human Resources Inc.
Trillium Human Resources Inc., RR 3, Ayr, Ontario N0B 1E0; (800) 335-9668, fax (519) 632-8364, thr@easynet.on.ca ▪ Trillium is a placement agency that assists registered nurses, doctors, physical/occupational therapists, and speech pathologists in professional positions throughout Canada, the US, and the UK. Applicants must be eligible to be licensed in other countries. Trillium recruits recent graduates and experienced candidates. Applicants pay no fees. Trillium's web site offers an online application that can be e-mailed to the agency. Visit their web site at www.easynet.on.ca/~thr. [ID:2624]

Where There is No Doctor: A Village Health Care Handbook: Revised Edition 📖
1992, *David Werner, Carol Thuman, Jane Maxwell,* Hesperian Foundation, 632 pages ➤ Intercultural and Community Development Resources (ICDR), P.O. Box 32108, Millwoods Station, Edmonton, Alberta T6K 4C2; $25; VISA, Amex; (800) 378-3199, fax (403) 462-1925, icdr@compusmart.ab.ca ▪ An absolute must for anyone working or travelling in a semi-isolated or isolated location, or for anyone connected with village-level healthcare in developing countries. Detailed, well-written, easy to use. Covers every type of ailment imaginable. Purchase as gift to

leave behind when travelling. Available in other languages. Visit the distributor's web site at www.compusmart.ab.ca/icdr. [ID:1159]

Language Careers

The following offers resources for linguists, translators, and interpreters. For advice on teaching English overseas, consult Chapter 29, Teaching Abroad. For related language information see also Chapter 5, Learning a Foreign Language.

Bilingual-Jobs.Com 💻
www.bilingual-jobs.com ▪ This is a job resource site for people who are fluent in English and any other major business language, for example, Japanese and German. This is a useful site for multilingual professionals with experience in fields related to technology and finance. The services are also free-of-charge. [ID:2490]

Careers for Foreign Language Aficionados and Other Multilingual Types 📖
1992, *H. Ned Seelye, Laurence Day,* VGM Career Horizons, 128 pages ➤ NTC Contemporary Publishing Co., 4255 West Touhy Ave., Lincolnwood, IL 60646, USA; US$11.95; credit cards; (800) 323-4900, fax (800) 998-3103 ▪ This catalogue of jobs for foreign-language speakers looks at domestic and overseas opportunities in embassies, trade offices, foreign language departments, multinational corporations, and banks. The authors outline mainstream and off-beat jobs for teachers, translators, tour guides, and others who want to use a foreign language on the job. [ID:1457]

Great Jobs for Foreign Language Majors 📖
1994, *Julie DeGalan, Stephen Lambert,* VGM Career Horizons, 256 pages ➤ NTC Contemporary Publishing Co., 4255 West Touhy Ave., Lincolnwood, IL 60646, USA; US$11.95; credit cards; (800) 323-4900, fax (800) 998-3103 ▪ This handy guide shows foreign language majors the many and varied career paths they can follow, and how they can prepare themselves for their first job after graduation. The authors help students assess their strengths, consider their options, and outline strategies for finding the right job. [ID:1477]

Human Languages Page 💻
www.june29.com/HLP ▪ This is a catalog of over 1,600 language-related Internet resources. These links are divided into six broad categories, with a seventh category based on language-related job announcements under way. [ID:2735]

Opportunities in Foreign Language Careers 📖
1992, *Wilga Rivers,* VGM Career Horizons, 160 pages ➤ NTC Contemporary Publishing Co., 4255 West Touhy Ave., Lincolnwood, IL 60646, USA; US$14.95; credit cards; (800) 323-4900, fax (800) 998-3103 ▪ Includes some information on US public and private sector employment abroad. This is a useful, although somewhat dated, guide to many jobs available to people who speak more than one language. Covers opportunities in foreign trade, various vocations, government positions and teaching. [ID:1120]

Special Career Opportunities for Linguists/Translators/Interpreters 📖
Annual ➤ Language Services Division, US Department of State, Room 2212, Washington, DC 20520, USA; free; (202) 647-3492, fax (202) 647-3881 ▪ Publications of the US Department of State listing career opportunities for linguists, translators and interpreters. [ID:1446]

The World on a String: How to Become a Freelance Foreign Correspondent 📖
1997, *Al Goodman, John Pollack,* Harry Holt and Company Inc., 198 pages ➤ Fitzhenry and Whiteside Ltd., 195 Allstate Parkway, Markham, Ontario L3R 4T8; $17.95; VISA, MC; (800) 387-9776, fax (800) 260-9777, godwit@fitzhenry.ca ▪ Colorful anecdotes and practical advice from successful stringers around the world highlight the trials and triumphs of freelancing abroad. This is a step-by-step manual which describes how to choose a region to work in, select the right equipment, establish vital editorial contacts at home and abroad, make ends meet while filing stories to various media, prepare for the risks of reporting from war zones, and work effectively with distant editors. Visit the distributor's web site at www.fitzhenry.ca. [ID:2711]

Tourism Industry Careers

Career Opportunities in Travel and Tourism 📖
1996, *John K. Hawks,* 309 pages ➤ Impact Publications, 9104 North Manassas Drive, Manassas Park, VA 20111-2366, USA; US$29.95; credit cards; (703) 361-7300, fax (703) 335-9486 ▪ Details requirements and rewards of 70+ jobs in travel and tourism, from travel agents to support services. Identifies key educational programs, associations, national travel employers, and travel recruiting firms. Visit the distributor's web site at www.impactpublications.com. [ID:1753]

Careers for Travel Buffs 📖
1992, *Paul Plawin,* 174 pages ➤ Impact Publications, 9104 North Manassas Drive, Manassas Park, VA 20111-2366, USA; US$14.95; credit cards; (703) 361-7300, fax (703) 335-9486 ▪ This book covers travel writers, photographers, tour guides, and cruise staff as well as other jobs in travel and tourism. Visit the distributor's web site at www.impactpublications.com. [ID:1754]

Guide to Cruise Ship Jobs 📖
1994, *George Reilly* ➤ Pilot Books, P.O. Box 2102, Greenport, NY 11944, USA; US$6.95; credit cards; (516) 477-1094, fax (516) 477-0978 ▪ The author, a Chief Purser, offers inside information on planning your job search, positions available, and the necessary qualifications. Lists major cruise lines and firms that recruit for cruise ship companies. Visit www.pilotbooks.com. [ID:1230]

Jobs for People Who Love Travel 📖
1995, *Caryl Krannich, Ronald Krannich,* 304 pages ➤ Impact Publications, 9104 North Manassas Drive, Manassas Park, VA 20111-2366, USA; US$15.95; credit cards; (703) 361-7300, fax (703) 335-9486 ▪ Surveys hundreds of jobs in business and government, including summer jobs abroad, travel industry jobs, import/export and sales opportunities, training positions, and more. Job search tips and employer contact information. Visit www.impactpublications.com. [ID:1039]

Jobs in Paradise 📖
1994, *Jeffrey Maltzman,* 337 pages ➤ Impact Publications, 9104 North Manassas Drive, Manassas Park, VA 20111-2366, USA; US$14; credit cards; (703) 361-7300, fax (703) 335-9486 ▪ A guide to cruise ship, resort, and 200,000+ dream jobs in the US, South Pacific, and Caribbean. Mountain climbing to amusement parks—contact information provided. Visit www.impactpublications.com. [ID:1752]

Tourism Training Institute
International Department, Tourism Training Institute, 1754 West Broadway, Vancouver, B.C. V6J 1Y1; (604) 736-7008, fax (604) 736-7723, tourism@tourismti.bc.ca ▪ This institute offers diploma programs for travel, airline, hospitality management, flight attendant, cruise hospitality, and business management in tourism. Graduates benefit from on-the-job work experience offered with selected programs and use their acquired skills to work internationally. Visit the institute's web site at www.axionet.com/tourism for information on courses, programs, and work-terms. [ID:2709]

Working as a Holiday Rep 📖
1996, *Steve Marks,* 128 pages ➤ How To Books Ltd., 3 Newtec Place, Magdalen Road, Oxford, OX4 1RE, UK; £9.99; credit cards; (44) (1752) 202-301, fax (44) (1865) 202-331 ▪ Discover what qualities are desirable in a holiday rep and how to apply for vacancies. [ID:2436]

Working in Ski Resorts—Europe & North America 📖
1997, *Victoria Pybus, Charles James,* Vacation Work ➤ Capricorn Business Services, Inc., 28 Clear Lake Ave., West Hill, Ontario M1C 4L6; $25.95; credit cards; (416) 282-3331, fax (416) 282-0015 ▪ Work as a ski instructor, teacher, au pair, etc. Covers 80+ resorts in Europe, and North America. [ID:1419]

Working on Cruise Ships 📖
1997, *Steve Marks,* 128 pages ➤ Capricorn Business Services, Inc., 28 Clear Lake Ave., West Hill, Ontario M1C 4L6; £9.99; credit cards; (416) 282-3331, fax (416) 282-0015 ▪ Describes jobs available and provides details on the main employers. [ID:2435]

Chapter 23

Phone Research Techniques

Aside from some basic pointers on phoning techniques, this chapter also illustrates the importance of calling potential overseas employers.

You have a list of overseas employers: consulting firms, nongovernmental organizations (NGOs), and international organizations, their addresses and phone numbers. You don't know who to contact, their job titles or departments. You are probably unfamiliar with the companies' hiring procedures, what job openings are or will be available, or which professional qualifications are being sought. You may be unsure how to find out.

Surprisingly, this information is easy to come by! The simple solution is to telephone potential employers and directly ask these questions *before you send your résumé*. Personnel officers are in the business of hiring, and are usually quite willing to answer many of your questions over the telephone. Sure, they are often portrayed as mean, horrible creatures who specialize in rejection, but this is usually not the case. Try calling the human resources department or personnel department of the company or organization you are pursuing.

The initiative you show in obtaining information on the company can kindle the employer's interest in you, and might even result in an interview. Phone research is especially important, as it allows you to insert specific new information into your covering letter and résumé.

Human contact is another reason for using the telephone as a basic tool in your job search strategy. The telephone gives you access to the people on the inside. Follow-up phone calls are also a key element in sustaining and building contacts with potential employers. They help keep your dossier alive in their minds.

GETTING ORGANIZED WITH THE CARD SYSTEM

Once you have completed the initial research stage of compiling a potential employer address list, you are ready to begin telephoning employers to gather information. The phone system proposed here is based on a follow-through planning technique facilitated by a card filing system for each employer. As you will be phoning many employers, speaking to many other people, and collecting a variety of information, the information should be assembled into an easy-to-read format. One method is to use large recipe cards (8" x 5"), organized like the one below.

This employer card system should focus information-gathering on three important areas:

- the people involved in hiring you
- key terminology used by potential employers
- follow-up information and reminders

EMPLOYER CARD FOLLOW-UP SYSTEM

NAME OF FIRM:		
DATE	Contact Persons/Title/Phone	Comments Follow-up Action
Key Words, Programs, Skills		Mailing Address of Personnel Department Date résumé sent: Date résumé acknowledged:

Keeping track of people with the employer card system

When making your contacts, it is important to note names and exact titles of everyone you reach—the secretaries, project officers, as well as recruiting officers.

Prior to being introduced to your speaker, you should request the proper spelling of his or her name and specific job title. If this is not possible, you may request this information at the end of the conversation, particularly if you have agreed to mail documents or other materials. Otherwise, call back and obtain this information from the receptionist or the person's secretary.

Treat each contact with professionalism. Make brief notes (the point may be trivial) to trigger your memory of the conversation. People are impressed and responsive to personal details about themselves and will treat your dossier with similar consideration. For example:

"Hello, Ms. Jones. This is Philippe Roy calling from Calgary. We spoke on the phone a month ago regarding my application forms. It was just before your field trip to Indonesia."

"I'm the person who spoke to you about the Nigerian development program just prior to your vacation. I trust you had a relaxing holiday."

Keeping track of employer terminology with the card system

An employer card filing system should help to familiarize you with, and keep track of, the particular language and terminology (jargon) used by each organization. You may want to use this information in your covering letter and résumé, as well as during your interview and in future phone conversations. There are two important groups of words to listen for: skill identification words and specific in-house program jargon.

For example: a recruitment officer may emphasize that an overseas post is "field-oriented, working with community-based organizations, at the grassroots level." Another example may be, "to liaise effectively with senior government officials overseas and have intercultural problem-solving skills." Deciphering these phrases, and even using them yourself, can be critical in achieving success in your job search. Take advantage of these free verbal clues offered by employers. These new words can be adopted to describe the skills you have developed in your previous and current jobs.

Specific in-house jargon could be used to describe positions, programs, departments and processes. For example, words such as: field rep, program officer, field officer, cooperant, volunteer, country representative—all could be used by different institutions to describe the same overseas position. By using the appropriate terminology with each firm, you will avoid verbal confusion and demonstrate your ability to adapt to that firm's corporate culture. This could well increase your chances of getting that job.

Keeping track of follow-up information with the card system

The card system allows you to organize follow-up phone calls to inform prospective employers of your continuing interest. The follow-up process dictates that you call or write potential employers on a regular basis, such as every two or three months. This means that you should have the organization's name, address, telephone number and the name of a contact person on record.

On ending a telephone conversation, always inquire about or suggest a suitable date for your next call, and make careful note of this date somewhere on the card. Examples of such calls:

- "Hello Ms. Thompson? This is Dean Allen speaking from Kingston. We spoke a few months ago regarding an administrative posting in Bangkok..."

- "I was just calling to reaffirm my interest in, and availability for, the posting, if funding for the project does come through."
- "I'm calling to inform you that I'll be out of the country for a month. Are there further developments regarding this project?"
- "I just wanted to mention that I'm still very much interested in keeping my dossier active with your firm. I'm currently enrolled in an upgrading course at Carleton University. Nevertheless, I'm available for full-time employment."
- "I've just updated my résumé. I wanted to call prior to putting it in the mail to re-express my interest in working with your firm."

TIME AND COST OF A PHONE CAMPAIGN

You may need to contact as many as 40 or 50 firms within your targeted field. If you make six telephone calls in a four-hour period, you are using your time efficiently. On average, it could take three telephone calls per hour to make one direct contact.

Long distance telephone charges could be expensive. But this is still a small price to pay for direct contact with the right individual. (After all, the cost of being idle can be far greater.) When a potential employer sees that you're willing to spend money pursuing a position, it helps establish your credibility as a serious job candidate.

SELF-CONFIDENCE ON THE TELEPHONE

The most important factor in acquiring self-confidence on the telephone is believing in the importance of your call. Think of it as a perfect opportunity to speak to people who can help you in your job search.

It's not an easy task to make a good impression while bothering someone on the phone. But confidence comes from practice. You might practice by calling first those companies you are least interested in.

A sure-fire confidence-building technique is to arm yourself with a two-sentence or a 20-second summary of your best points. A few prepared responses will not only give you a measure of confidence, but also add to your peace of mind as you are dialling another faceless name.

For example: What if you were asked to describe your strongest attributes over the phone? How could you quickly summarize yourself to set yourself apart from all those other job seekers?

- "I am fully bilingual. I also have a master's degree in economics, plus two years of travelling experience in West Africa. My strongest skills are in economic policy analysis, particularly in environmental impact studies."
- "As chief mechanic, I am appreciated by my current employer for my ability to control costs and plan work schedules. I have been told by my employer that one of my invaluable skills is the ability to keep productive and loyal employees."

- "Throughout my career, I have always been able to meet deadlines, and have consistently and accurately forecast work requirements when setting up new programs. This was the case when I worked for... and later at..."

For more detailed information on how to promote yourself, see Chapter 26, Interviewing for an International Job.

DEALING WITH PEOPLE ON THE PHONE

Who should you talk to? Try to speak directly with a manager in one of the international divisions. Failing that, an employment officer in one of the international divisions is also a good starting point. But keep in mind that hiring decisions are rarely made by personnel officers or the personnel department. These decisions are made by project officers and other executives.

You may have difficulty in getting past the secretary, or receptionist. He or she will likely ask such questions as: "What is this in reference to?" or "May I help you?"

Prepare yourself with a set of responses. Rather than answering, "to discuss employment possibilities," or simply, "no," a preferable response would be: "I'm looking for information on your organization's African projects, specifically in relation to agricultural studies," or "yes, could you possibly connect me with the manager of your African projects?" Chances are your call will be transferred to someone who can help you. If you are still having difficulty getting through to the right person, call the president's office, or the person at the top of the corporate hierarchy, and politely ask: "Who would I speak to about (this field)?"

Take the initiative. Be persistent in trying to make direct contact with a certain individual. Try not to leave your name and number, because you will wind up wasting valuable time sitting by the telephone waiting for a return call that could take days or never come at all.

In the course of tracking down the right person, you may be shuffled from one administrator to another. Each time you are transferred, reintroduce yourself by giving your full name, regardless of who you are speaking to, secretary or manager.

"Hello, my name is Paula Doucet. I'm calling long distance from Orillia, Ontario, and would like to speak to someone concerning your overseas junior professional officer program."

"Hello, my name is Nancy Vautour. I'm calling to inquire about overseas employment possibilities in the area of community health. Who would be best to talk to?"

"Could you direct me to someone with information on your international division in relation to urban development?"

If the objective of your call is to gather information, then it is polite to suggest: "Do you have a few moments to spare? I have several questions to ask about working overseas in your particular field."

Once you have made contact with a desired manager, you should be candid about the purpose of your call. Otherwise, you will not only waste his or her valuable time, but also weaken your professional credibility by beating around the bush. Some examples:

"Hello Mr. Devon? My name is Alain Keta. I spoke to Ms. Ricks, your Director of Human Resources. She told me that you were the best person to speak to concerning your firm's upcoming contract with CIDA in Ghana."

"Hello my name is Francine Dugas. Mr. Kyle, your name was referred to me by the consultant, John Smith, who has worked with your firm. He mentioned that you could possibly provide me with some information on the type of overseas employment I'm interested in."

If you were referred by someone, then mention the name and title of your referral. This way, you are reducing the chance of rejection by your new contact. Example:

"Hello, my name is Carl Arthur. I was speaking with Glen Allard from SCN who told me that you could direct me to someone in your firm with information on overseas employment possibilities in industrial plant management."

Always acknowledge your contact's expertise or abilities before imposing demands upon his or her time.

"Mr. Dupont has told me that you're one of the most respected people in the industry."

"Ms. Robin mentioned that you've spent many years in the business."

"Ms. Petrella told me that you're very knowledgeable in the field and understand how the system works."

From your telephone campaign, you should have accumulated a wealth of information regarding international organizations, such as: the organizations that are hiring, hiring authorities, current trends and opinions in your field. This should put you in a good position to speak comfortably and knowledgeably with recruitment and program officers. After all, recruitment and program officers are always interested in updating information about other firms in their industry. Mentioning names of other people you have spoken to could also improve your chances of landing a job. The international community is relatively small; many of the professionals know each other, or know of each other. For example:

"Mr. Bollack from WUSC has mentioned the same organization, and has recommended to me that I contact Mr. Ameh at Inter Pares. Do you know of him?"

Phrase your questions in a non-threatening manner. That is, do not pose questions that demand a commitment from the other party, or that directly show your self-interest. Save those for later. For example:

DO NOT ASK:

- "When can I expect an answer from you?"
- "What would I expect to earn in such a position?"
- "Do you have a current job opening in my field?"

INSTEAD ASK:

- "Will a decision be made by the end of the month?"
- "Do you have any idea of the salary range for someone with my experience?"
- "Are you currently accepting résumés?"

INQUIRING ABOUT THE OPPORTUNITY

Before you pick up the telephone, make a list of questions you want answered. As you become more familiar with a particular field, your knowledge and list of questions will also expand.

Sample inquiry questions

Here are some suggestions to help you develop a more specific list of questions geared to your field of work.

- "What type of jobs are there that would be suitable for someone of my skills and experience?"
- "How do people typically get hired for these types of positions?"
- "Do you have any overseas job descriptions that you could send me?"
- "What is the typical profile of someone hired in these types of positions?"
- "What types of skills and traits are required?"
- "What level of experience is required? Is Canadian work experience judged on an equal footing as overseas experience?"
- "Are there any volunteer possibilities within your Canadian international division which I could undertake to help me better understand your organization?"

"Who else is hiring?" questions

Use the contact to network with others. Here are sample questions to pose:

- "Are you aware of other organizations which offer similar entry-level positions?"
- "Thank you for the information on your firm. Are there other firms with new overseas contracts that you know about? Can you refer me to someone else? May I mention your name as having referred me?"
- "Do you know anyone who works in that department? What type of people do they recruit? What can you tell me about their hiring policies or work

philosophy? Do you have any information about their overseas programs or their major field of interest?"

- "Is there anything else you could suggest for someone with my qualifications?"

Word of mouth

Talk to as many people as possible to discover how they obtained their overseas positions. Do they know of anyone who could offer you an introduction to a firm with an international branch? What about their suggestions of possible employers and locations of work?

DEALING WITH NEGATIVE ANSWERS

Remember that recruitment officers are not interested in hiring someone who seems unsure of his or her career path, or is uncommitted to working overseas. International employment officers are known to make the occasional disparaging remark about their particular field. Their pessimism stems from the fact that their business is often a frenetic mixture of hiring followed by long periods of quiet. They sometimes even encourage newcomers to seek other employment. Whenever you encounter a negative response to your telephone questions, persist. Show the recruiter you are determined to land a position. He or she will respect your persistence.

Here are some tactics you might try in response to negative answers:

EMPLOYER: "We are not hiring."

YOUR RESPONSE:

- "Yes, I understand. Your secretary mentioned this to me. Nonetheless, would it be possible to have my résumé kept on file in case your organization needs someone on short notice? I expect to be available over the next six months."
- "If a job does open up, how would it be advertised?"
- "Is it possible to send in my résumé for inclusion in your data bank?"
- "Is there anything coming up in the foreseeable future?"

EMPLOYER: "We only hire the most qualified candidates with five years' overseas experience."

YOUR RESPONSE:

- "Yes, I'm aware that there is a lot of competition, but I think my background demonstrates that many of my skills are transferable to an overseas work environment, and I would appreciate having you look at my résumé."
- "I am aware of your organization's requirements but I believe that some of my qualifications, especially my experience in working in isolated environments, have prepared me for that type of work."

An unreceptive secretary or receptionist can compound the discomfort of making "cold" calls. Still, they can be a wealth of information. Don't be daunted by their screening techniques or their standard response of "Send us your résumé." You should persist with statements such as:

- "I was hoping to speak to someone who could give me more information prior to sending in my résumé. Is there someone I could speak to first?"
- "When would it be best to call back? I have some specific questions about your project in Zaire."
- "Would it be possible to speak to an information officer who could provide more information on your organization?"

Persistence, a little charm, and genuine politeness will go a long way in making contact with the right person. If these tactics all fail, then address any written material to the secretary's (or receptionist's) attention, even though the covering letter and résumé is directed to the boss. A follow-up phone call to confirm the spelling of a name will fix your name in the secretary's memory, and may improve the chances of having your résumé singled out for the boss's attention. These tactics should help in future follow-up calls.

Negative answers are a familiar part of the job search, even for highly-qualified candidates. Get used to "No, No, No." It's all part of getting a "YES!" In other words, don't be discouraged.

FOLLOW-UP PHONE CALLS

Most job seekers neglect to follow up with a phone call once they have made an initial contact. To ignore the follow-up stage is to ignore the basic fact that many job opportunities appear "out of the blue." They often appear with little advance notice to the recruiter, and they are usually filled within a short time. Follow-up phone calls improve your chances of being in the right place at the right time. Moreover, they allow you to build a relationship with someone in that firm who could be crucial in your obtaining an overseas posting.

When should you make a follow-up telephone call?

- Three to seven days after sending a résumé, or after an interview.
- One to three months after your last contact with an employer. (This is done whether or not potential job openings were mentioned.)
- When you have new information to add to your résumé and wish to inform a potential employer.
- Two days after you have received a negative reply following an interview. As a candidate, you have the right to feedback on why you were not offered the job. (Do not make this call while distraught. Wait until you are calm and your thoughts lucid. You may find this a difficult call, but it is extremely important to assess your approach and improve your chances next time around.)
- When you have received a job offer.

Surprisingly, this is when most people stop their job search. A mistake! Your search should move into high gear the moment you have an offer. You should phone every potential employer from whom you have had the slightest encouragement. If an employer is really interested in you, he or she may offer you a position. For example:

"Hello Mr. Smith. I'm calling to let you know that I've just received an interesting job offer from another firm. But I'm still interested in your company, and I thought it prudent to call to see if there is anything available in your department at this time."

"Since you'd mentioned that I may be considered for any openings, and since I am particularly interested in your firm's line of work, I decided to call before accepting another offer."

In a follow-up phone call always mention the circumstance of your last call. For example: "There were no postings at the time of our last conversation, but you had mentioned that some positions were possibly going to be advertised this spring." Be forthright in your questions. For example: "I'm calling to inquire about possible openings since our last conversation."

You don't want to be perceived as a nuisance, but there is nothing to lose by asking permission to call back at a later date. "May I check with you again next month? What time or date is best for you?"

Your follow-up phone calls are a strong indicator of your interest and show that you have the motivation and drive to follow through on your job search.

SUMMARY OF CREATIVE PHONE TECHNIQUES

Why Phone

- To find out what jobs are open, or will be open.
- To address your résumé to the proper person.
- To make contacts and build relationships.
- To make yourself known.
- To find out what personality traits are being sought.
- To find out what skills are essential.
- To learn the special language (jargon) of your future field.
- To facilitate writing a résumé patterned on employer expectations and needs.
- To follow up and keep your résumé active.
- To uncover other sources of overseas jobs.
- To demonstrate and improve your communication skills.
- To learn about the overseas job market in general.

Phone Manners

- Always announce yourself by name.
- Always address the person by name.
- Always mention your referral.
- Always be polite, courteous and persistent.
- Always treat everyone with the utmost respect.
- Always be direct about the nature of your call.

Phone Techniques

- Use the card system to keep track of people.
- Use the card system to note the in-house language of the field.
- Use the card system to keep track of follow-up calls.
- Have a written list of questions before phoning.
- Directly ask employers what type of candidates are sought and the exact criteria.
- Phrase your questions with diplomacy, without forcing employers to commit themselves.
- Treat everyone as an expert and acknowledge his or her expertise in your conversation.
- Approach each information-gathering exercise with enthusiasm and confidence.
- If you're unable to get past a secretary, ask your questions to him or her.
- First practice your phone techniques with employers of least interest to you.
- When calling long distance, mention this fact to the other party.
- Share your knowledge of the job market with recruitment officers.
- Persist with requests for information and in sending your résumé, despite negative feedback.
- Ask for further information on other overseas employers.
- Send a thank-you note to those who have been particularly helpful.
- Make full use of follow-up phone calls.

Chapter 24

International
Résumés

This chapter is written mostly for those who've had international exposure, but perhaps no international work experience. It will discuss the important differences between an international résumé and a Canadian-based résumé, and, how you can demonstrate, on paper, that you have the required overseas skills and professional experience to qualify for an international job.

The problem in finding a suitable international posting is the same as it is in any line of work. That is, competition is fierce. Moreover, we have also seen that international recruitment offices are particularly concerned with personality profiling. Keeping these facts in mind, your résumé should portray you as a capable and talented professional while at the same time highlight your personality in action. Thus, we develop herein a technique for writing a *creative international résumé*. This résumé style highlights your skills profile as it relates to your future international job. By focusing on your international skills, your résumé will get you that precious interview.

How to go about kindling a recruiter's interest? That is the question this chapter will answer!

WILL A CREATIVE RÉSUMÉ GET YOU AN INTERVIEW?

Imagine an over-worked recruitment officer sifting through a pile of résumés, looking for the candidate that best matches his or her organization's ideal profile. The recruitment officer's task is to find the right mix of occupational and personal skills. In an eight-hour work day, the recruiter's workload might consist of meetings, phone calls, interruptions, and scheduled appointments, along with the task of sorting through hundreds of résumés. Each candidate's résumé gets a three-minute cursory glance. The majority will be dismissed for a number of reasons: poor visual presentation, lack of experience and qualifications. The résumés that pass first reading will likely undergo a second and more detailed reading to select candidate interviews.

An ideal profile for an international careerist is usually weighted heavily on personality traits, followed by professional abilities. But a normal résumé does not allow you to highlight your personality. The limitation of the standard-style résumé is the omission of character and personality traits and facts that demonstrate your international awareness. That means a recruitment officer has the task of searching your résumé for clues to your suitability to the organization's ideal profile. Chances are many of your abilities and qualifications will be overlooked.

In a creative résumé you leave nothing to chance or misinterpretation. To catch the eye of a recruitment officer, you must begin your creative résumé with a concise summary of your professional skills and personal traits. For an international position, heavy emphasis is placed on character. You should spoon-feed the recruiter by emphasizing those qualifications he or she is seeking. For emphasis, you should adopt the language and terminology of your prospective international employer.

THE CREATIVE INTERNATIONAL RÉSUMÉ

A creative résumé for international employment requires three basic ingredients:

* Begin your résumé with a *Profile Analysis:* a statement of a career objective followed by a summary of your professional skills and personal traits.
* Write your résumé using some of the language and terminology of your future international profession.
* Include in your résumé an *International Experience* section.

Your résumé should be visually designed for speed reading. The objective is to catch the recruiter's attention on the first reading with the aim of obtaining a second, more detailed reading.

This means you should highlight your career positions in bold italics, or consistently format and underscore each section. Each position should begin with a job title (the most important summary of your work), followed by employer information, then description. Use point form as much as possible.

Your résumé should also be proofread by a professional, and printed on a laser printer.

THE PARTS OF A CREATIVE RÉSUMÉ

The body should consist of four parts: Career Objective, Personal Traits and Professional Skills, Work History, and Personal Data.

Career Objective

Inform overseas employers exactly what you can do for them. Delete any information that does not support this objective, or what your potential employer is seeking.

Personal Traits and Professional Skills

Summarize who you are and what you can do. Also focus on the skills which are important for the international posting. By adding this section, you will cut a recruiter's analysis work in half and you guarantee that your important skills are not overlooked.

Work History

Write this section in a way that substantiates your objective. Provide concrete examples of your professional skills and personal traits. It is under this heading that you must assemble an international experience section; that is, your work or volunteer experience, travel, and schooling which relate to international work.

Personal Data

Provide information about yourself, your family, health, spouse's employment, hobbies, etc.

WHAT IS THE FIRST STEP?

Before you write your career objective and summary, you should first research your desired job position and determine the ideal profile of the international candidate. Ask yourself honestly, have you got the necessary qualifications? It is important that you understand and obtain as much information as possible about the position you are seeking. You need to allocate time and resources to the task of research before writing the résumé.

Job Research means exploring your international work options. What jobs are out there? What skills are important to international employers? What about the terminology used to describe those skills? (See Chapter 23, Phone Research Techniques.)

Self-Assessment entails evaluating your skills, interests and priorities in terms of positions you are professionally qualified for. You should already have read Part One of this book, Your International IQ (Chapters 1 to 8), on assessing your overseas employment skills before continuing further into this chapter.

STATING YOUR CAREER OBJECTIVE

From an employer's perspective, your career objective is nothing more than a label used to sum up your field of work and level of expertise. This is particularly true for international employers, as they often recruit from a wide cross-section of employment categories. If you have a clearly defined career objective, you can be well assured that your résumé will be placed in the right categories of the firm's data bank. A clear objective also helps the recruitment officer focus on your most salient professional characteristics.

Your career objective should not only reflect your professional goals, but should also be credible and supportive of your documented work experience and abilities.

In the age of specialization, recruiters often demand specific job skills from candidates. You would be incorrect to assume that a general or ambiguously worded objective (such as, "I'll do anything, anywhere") will work in your favour, or open any doors. A potential employer may rule you out as a serious job candidate if he or she cannot identify your career interest and how you may fit into the agency or organization's structure.

On the other hand, if you are changing careers, your objective should focus on what you are capable of. Some of your previous career skills are transferable, but you should still demonstrate interest in the international aspects of your newly chosen field. This could be through volunteer services, travel, readings or conferences.

Your résumé should also be rewritten using language and terminology appropriate to your potential employer. If you are unsure of your career objective, you are better off to write more than one résumé, highlighting specific skills that match each objective. For example, if you are equally suited to economic research and international banking, you should really compose two separate résumés, each focusing on a different career objective. Career changers should take careful note to demonstrate to a potential international employer how his or her previous work skills are relevant to the position sought.

THE "DOs" OF A CAREER OBJECTIVE

Keep your objective under three lines; use wording that is clear and precise.

Your objective should address three points: geographic setting, field of work, and level of entry. Other qualifiers may be included according to your particular circumstances.

Geographic Setting

Many international organizations hire for both domestic and overseas positions, and their data banks are often sorted on this basis. If you are applying to an international organization, and your intention is to travel or work abroad, this intention should be revealed from the onset. You may also mention your preference with reference to continent, region, rural or urban.

Field of Work

Are you a trainer, mechanic, public health specialist, community development worker? Use the terminology of your future international employer when describing your background. If you are changing careers, you should mention your new field of interest. But don't dwell on your previous experience, unless it corresponds to your new objective.

Level of Entry

It is important, particularly if you are an administrator, to state whether you are seeking a mid-level, senior or management position. If you are just starting out, you may wish to use such phrases as entry-level position, assistant, or junior program officer. Don't slot yourself into one level if you are prepared to accept another. In other words, don't state that you are a mid-level officer willing to accept an entry-level position. It could disqualify you altogether. Simply state that you are willing to accept an entry-level position.

Other Qualifiers

This is the place to mention crucial limiting factors or qualifiers; such as whether you are willing to work as a volunteer or a salaried employee. Other qualifiers include preference for supervisory or research work, availability for short- or long-term contract work. You may also include the environment in which you wish to work, such as, "growing new project," "grassroots community-based urban organization," or "major international organization."

Remember, short is sweet! Four words will often suffice. Example: Overseas Community Development Officer.

You may use any one of a number of subtitles to summarize your career objective, and may even combine your career objective with a description of your personal and professional skills (discussed in the next section). Some possible subtitles and examples include:

CAREER OBJECTIVE
Overseas Economic Analyst specializing in field studies in rural Africa or Asia.

OBJECTIVE
Country or Regional Field Representative position involving administration of volunteers in Africa.

CAREER INTERESTS
Program administrator in urban environment in the South.

PROFESSIONAL GOAL
Entry-level position as a Logistician or Administrator in hardship post where computer skills are important.

POSITION DESIRED
Short- or long-term contract work as a senior agronomist in rural Africa.

Once you have stated your objective, the rest of your résumé should be devoted to supporting this objective.

THE "DON'Ts" OF A CAREER OBJECTIVE

Don't confuse personal and professional objectives. That is, don't state your objective as: "an opportunity to use my talents to further my five-year career plan." This may be so, but it would be more productive to concentrate on *what you could offer a prospective employer.* Rework your objective as: "to work in a international organization where I could offer my seven years of management experience in the field of financial accounting."

Avoid using flowery language, such as: "My objective is to obtain a challenging international position where my highly developed skills and outstanding knowledge in administration will be recognized."

If you are responding to an advertisement, do not duplicate the exact wording of the position being offered. This could convey the impression that parts of your résumé are fabricated or fictitious.

Avoid an overly precise objective which may also disqualify you from other job openings.

Avoid disclosing your real *long-term* career objective if it does not correspond with the position that you are seeking. The career objective in a résumé is an immediate one, not a long-term goal.

YOUR PERSONAL TRAITS AND PROFESSIONAL SKILLS

These two categories are the most important parts of a creative international résumé. They summarize who you are and what you are capable of. Without this summary, a recruitment officer would have to very carefully read your résumé (perhaps one of hundreds) and determine your professional and personal strengths to see if they match the company's ideal profile. This method leaves much to chance. The recruitment office will certainly miss or forget some aspects of your profile.

When your résumé begins with an accurate summary of your professional skills and personal traits, the recruiting officer's work is cut in half. Your chances of being able to guide analysis of your résumé along the lines that you want are almost guaranteed. This tactic is especially important for international work where personality profiling plays a greater role in candidate selection than for Canada-based employment. The process of clarifying your major skills and traits is a difficult one that can take days of work. The end result, however, will be that you understand yourself better. This knowledge will be crucial in explaining your worth to employers, on the phone and during interviews. Moreover, this self-appraisal will help you recognize strengths and weaknesses in your work, thus putting you on a better footing for performing new tasks and searching for areas for improvement.

THE "DOs" OF LISTING YOUR SKILLS AND TRAITS

Keep your list short, usually no more than six categories for each skill or trait. Focus only on your strongest attributes.

Mention only those skills applicable to the position you are applying for. In other words, promote yourself, but don't add extraneous information that has no bearing on your job objective.

Support *each* skill and trait with one or two concrete examples. If you can't support it, don't write it.

Be honest and choose your words carefully. During the interview, your credibility could be called into question if you are asked to defend each skill or accomplishment that you have listed. If you cannot provide evidence that you were "an effective communicator," or "an experienced computer trainer," or had "initiated a project" or "worked independently" as a "self-starter" or "a team leader," then it is probably not one of your strong assets, or not worth mentioning.

Listing your character traits can be a difficult exercise. You could ask yourself, "if my friends had to mention my best work-related attributes, what would they say?" It could be an eye-opening experience to ask a colleague or supervisor to evaluate and list your professional attributes. Remember, having a firm grasp of your professional attributes and strengths will greatly help you during your interviews and phone campaign.

For those of you who are changing careers, you should place the emphasis on your abilities rather than job experience. If you have had overseas volunteer experience or have travelled abroad, you could list aspects of overseas life you most enjoyed. For example, if you enjoyed working as a teacher, you might wish to add: "can communicate effectively in other cultures." Or, if you enjoyed a degree of success in accomplishing tasks under difficult economic or political conditions, you might wish to add: "able to maintain a sense of optimism under difficult socioeconomic conditions."

You could combine your professional and personal skills under a single heading, or list them separately. If you list them under a single heading you may try one of the following titles: *Major Traits, Summary of Professional Qualifications (Skills), Professional Summary, Professional Profile.*

Our preference is to separate *Personal Traits* from *Professional Skills.* These two categories have no clear delineation, and may overlap somewhat. Items may even change depending on your job objective. For example, being a "proficient communicator" is a personal trait for an administrator, but would be a professional skill for a public relations expert. Whatever the final outcome of your analysis, it will help categorize your qualities for the recruitment officer.

Personal traits tend to be "soft" skills, those you learned from your parents, from life experiences. Here is a list of examples: self-starter, high energy, adaptability, initiative, tolerance, relates well to people from all walks of life, pays attention to detail, able to focus on key result areas, pragmatic, committed, sense of humour, creative, resourceful, team-oriented, demonstrated communication skills, cheerful under pressure, strong interpersonal skills, adaptable to difficult living and working conditions, enjoys the challenge of demanding responsibilities.

Professional qualifications tend to be "hard" skills, those learned in school. The obvious ones include professional qualifications such as accounting or engineering. Others may include computer skills ("adept in using X software"), proposal and report writing skills, analytical abilities, training experience in particular fields, ability to communicate effectively with officials, ability to develop policies and procedures, and bilingual proficiency.

Don't forget to include management skills in your professional qualifications, such as project planning, negotiating, follow-up management style, leadership, grassroots organizing skills, demonstrated skill in starting new projects, able to motivate staff, able to chair meetings, skilled in recruiting, past success in conflict resolution and mediation, successful at drawing out the skills and talents of others, effective in promoting a cordial, professional atmosphere among associates, systematic and thorough in identifying and assembling project inputs.

You should also have some international skills. For example: intercultural group facilitation skills, sensitivity to people from other cultures, international development experience, theoretical understanding of environments in the South, three years experience in crosscultural environments in Canada and South America, administered programs and workshops focusing on women in development, experience in promoting Canadian volunteer international development committees, experience in crosscultural orientation of visitors from the South to Canada, facilitated orientation programs for volunteers going abroad, knowledgeable of cultural and social sensitivities associated with international work.

For those of you who need assistance assessing your skills, there is an excellent book on life and work planning entitled *The Three Boxes of Life,* by Richard N. Bolles. (For a full bibliographical reference see the Resources section of Chapter 20, The Job Search.)

WHICH RÉSUMÉ FORMAT APPLIES TO YOU?

The résumé format that you choose should emphasize your career strengths. There are three general formats: chronological, functional and combination.

Chronological Format

For those of you who are trying to break into the international field, the chronological format is the least desirable. This résumé style is best suited to veterans with extensive work experience and excellent qualifications. In other words, this format is suited only for those who can amply demonstrate a long, uninterrupted progression of job experience, as it draws attention to the dates and job positions of your entire career history. Avoid this traditional format if you are seeking a career change at an entry-level position, or if you have a spotty employment record with glaring time gaps. (However, the UNITED NATIONS, with its hierarchical organization, prefers this format.)

Functional Format

If you are looking for a career change or if you lack overseas experience, then this is the format to use. The functional style allows you to highlight your more impressive qualifications instead of attracting attention to your last or current job position. It also allows you to skim over questionable gaps in your career, either due to unemployment, travel, or whatever.

The main advantage of this style is that you can highlight your career experiences under key headings: Adult Learning Skills, Intercultural Communications Skills, Understanding of the Southern Environment, Community Development Skills, Field Experience, etc.

Combination Format

This format is a blend of both the functional and chronological, and is particularly useful if you have worked for an extended period of time for the same employer. The combination style allows you to include a description of your career skills and work history under functional headings accompanied by a short chronological outline of employers and promotions. This method stretches out your one-employer experience by highlighting and breaking down your areas of expertise.

WRITING YOUR WORK HISTORY

One of the key strategies in documenting your career experience is to describe it in terms of what you accomplished and how you accomplished it, rather than listing the positions you held and the duties you performed. The recruiter is interested in what you can do, that is, your accomplishments. Job titles and description of duties convey little information to an employer. Talk about the problems you solved, why you were promoted, what your achievements were, and what programs you initiated. Use the active voice to emphasize your experience.

The active voice, in combination with adjectives or descriptive phrases, helps to animate your accomplishments. For example, "successfully managed, independently designed and developed, implemented and trained two departments, or managed the local staff"—all serve to describe and amplify.

Employers are also interested in knowing *why* you were promoted, or *why* you are successful. These are some examples of phrases that point to the *why* of your accomplishments: "aptitude for," "proficient in the use of," "was recognized as," "became known for," "was identified as." Use this technique sparingly, however—overuse will diminish your credibility. The purpose of this technique is to focus an employer's attention on your strengths.

Avoid using fully-formed sentence style. The active voice in point form will suffice. The purpose of a résumé is to arouse interest. During the interview you will be given ample opportunity to expand on the various points outlined in your résumé. On the other hand, this does not mean that you should confine yourself to a one-page résumé. A creative résumé is usually three pages in length.

Quantify your accomplishments. Be specific: "Increased membership by 30%. Reduced turnover time by four weeks. Increased public inquiries tenfold." Examine your previous positions, and try to measure your past successes.

The scope of your responsibility should be the first item in your work description (after *Position Held, Employer Name* and *Address of Employment*). This often-used approach gives a recruitment officer a clear idea of the scope of your responsibilities. For example: "Managed a staff of 15, supervised the disbursement of $5-million for projects."

If you held several positions with a firm, mention your most recent first. Then, emphasize the progression by stating, "advanced from desk clerk to area supervisor in three months." If you suffered a demotion, then simply mention the new skills you learned. Your future employer need not know that your most recent position carried less responsibility than your previously-held one.

A Note to Career Changers

Your résumé should clearly convey the link between your past work experience and your overseas career objective. As described in the previous chapters, many jobs require certain skills or qualifications which may be applicable to an overseas assignment. Every attempt should be made to portray your past jobs in terms of the ideal profile being sought by employers.

You should edit and rework your job descriptions to highlight only those experiences that are relevant to the position you are currently seeking.

(Remember to draw attention to the international aspects of each of your experiences, character traits, adaptability to new environments, cultural sensitivity.) For example, if you previously worked for the Unemployment Insurance Commission and are seeking a position in international development, you would emphasize those skills you possess in community liaison work and project design, rather than your skills in job creation and employment counselling.

Also, reinforce your new career objective by eliminating in-house jargon from your previous employer, and use the particular language of your potential international employer.

What Format is Best for Your Job Descriptions?

Unless you have an impeccable and progressive career history, you may wish to avoid highlighting dates. Dates of employment should be on the right-hand side of the page. To further de-emphasize them, simply place job dates in brackets at the end of job description paragraphs.

Job titles should be placed at the front of each job description in either bold italics or underlined. This will help the speed-reading process. Official titles (the jargon of your previous employers) are sometimes redundant. It is often best to select a new title that more clearly describes your responsibilities to people outside of your field.

Name of employer, address of employer, description, and dates of employment are the preferred sequence. Don't include supervisors' names or phone numbers. This information should be reserved for use under *References*.

What to Include in Your Work Experience

For each employer, include the name of the firm and the city.

If your current employer is unaware that you are seeking other employment, you may wish to write "in confidence" or "personal and confidential" above your work experience. This should ensure that your employer won't be contacted without your consent.

Include any *volunteer work* that you have performed under the headings of: Positions Held, Events Organized, Awards Received and Accomplishments. Volunteer work can demonstrate that you possess leadership skills, the ability to work independently, and other attributes that are pertinent to an overseas posting. It is sometimes viewed as being on par with paid employment. If you have significant volunteer experience, by all means list it under work experience.

Don't list *summer* or *part-time* positions unless they clearly give you valuable experience for the position you are seeking, or if they focus directly on your personal initiative, stamina and drive. For example: if you are applying for a hardship post in Ethiopia, and have spent a summer working with a small group conducting geology exploration in northern Manitoba, this strongly suggests that you are able to work with others in an isolated environment. If you are just beginning your career, your summer and part-time employment should indicate a level of discipline, persistence, and an ability to work with others.

But if your summer experiences bear no relevance to your career objective, they should be listed under a separate heading. For example:

SUMMER AND PART TIME EMPLOYMENT
Warehouse worker, menswear sales clerk, gardener.

The "when" and the "where" are usually unimportant unless the position reinforces your career objective. In these circumstances you would list the jobs under your work history using the full format described in this chapter.

EDUCATIONAL EXPERIENCE

If you are a recent graduate, you may wish to list your *educational experience* after your career objective. It is most likely your strongest asset. For other job seekers, the format of your résumé (that is, functional, chronological or combination) will determine how your academic qualifications are listed. If you have relevant work experience but not an advanced or recent degree, then you are better off adding your academic credentials at the end of your résumé.

You may also list published works, theses and conferences you've attended if they are relevant to your overseas job search.

Start with your most recent degree and work backwards. If you're in the process of completing your degree, then state this clearly: "degree expected in December 1999" or "course work completed, thesis in progress." If you've taken courses leading to a degree, but didn't complete the program, then you should mark either "incomplete" or "in progress" after the degree title.

If your academic standing was "B" or higher, you may wish to include this in your résumé, particularly if it enhances a weak résumé. For example, you might wish to add, "consistent B+ average," or "maintained B+ average while working full-time."

University graduates needn't mention their high school curriculum unless they wish to highlight a particular achievement, for example: "voted student of the year"; "educated for six years in French Immersion program"; or "studied for three years in Norway." In fact, overseas education should always be highlighted, as evidence of your initiation into another culture.

Don't list all the courses you've taken or papers you've written, unless you're applying for a job as a university professor. Only list those courses which relate to the position you're applying for, under the heading of Other Courses or within job descriptions, if they add weight to the description; for example, "St. John Ambulance First Aid Course, Car Maintenance Courses, Management Development Seminars, Leadership Training."

List *academic internships, teaching assistant jobs or important research work* separately as jobs. They *are* jobs. Don't bury them in your educational listing.

List separately all *awards and scholarships* you've received, especially those earned during university. Many international employers look at these awards as initiative indicators and illustrations of important character traits. Don't neglect to mention leadership awards from service clubs and sport groups.

Professional Certification

If you're a teacher, doctor or engineer, or if you work within a profession or trade where provincial certification is required, you should provide the full details of your licensing as well as an address where your credentials can be verified. You may wish to attach photocopies of your certificates, especially to employers based overseas. Never send original certificates.

Memberships

Include only current affiliations relevant to the position you're seeking. Recent graduates should list all affiliations to demonstrate their level of participation and experience. On the other hand, if you don't belong to any association, you may wish to join one that interests you.

PERSONAL DATA

Personal data is best listed at the very end of your résumé since these details can detract from the importance of your career objective, personal and professional skills, and work history. Many of the items often excluded from résumés in Canada (age, marital status, and nationality) are often crucial to overseas recruiters. Overseas employers don't always follow the guidelines of government legislation with regard to violations of privacy or civil rights. Therefore, I strongly advise you to consider including the following personal data in your résumé: *Date of Birth, Marital Status and Dependents, Spouse's Employment, Language, Nationality, Available Date, Security Clearance.* (Contact information is discussed at the end of this section.)

Age

Age should certainly be mentioned as it's often a consideration in many overseas positions. Despite overtones of discrimination, it is a reality that must be addressed. For example, young people between the ages of 24 and 30 are often automatically considered for entry-level positions. People over 50 are rarely considered for hardship postings. Many traditional organizations such as the UNITED NATIONS and foreign governments automatically (though informally) apply age restrictions to job postings. Contrary to Canadian norms, ability can take second place to age in assessing a person's capacity to manage a department. If you're concerned about your age, you may wish to give your date of birth rather than your age. Employers have been known to disregard arithmetic calculation!

Marital Status and Dependents

The international employer is aware of the family situation; housing, education, and benefits are crucial issues that must be addressed. Being single has its advantages: it is less costly to an employer. If you're single and applying for a hardship post where families are unlikely to be sent, it's to your advantage to inform a recruiter of your single status. On the other hand, if you're married, but have worked out an arrangement with your family to work abroad, you may wish to state, "Married, willing to consider (or available for) single status posting." If you are married with no dependents, this also should be mentioned.

Children are often a crucial factor in the final hiring process; you may either wish to omit the subject of children in your résumé, or give brief mention to being "married with two school-aged dependents." Some candidates prefer to provide full details of their dependents: names, ages and schooling status. Either way, the topic of children will most certainly arise during the interview process, and the issue of placement and mobility will have to be addressed. Finding the right overseas school for high school students can be a difficult matter; this is sometimes resolved through placing them in a boarding school. University-aged children are usually considered independent.

Many employers insist on conducting interviews with the spouses of their employees; it's common knowledge that a spouse's enthusiasm (or lack of same) can impact on one's effectiveness working abroad.

Spouse's Occupation

If your spouse has intentions of seeking work overseas, you should briefly mention his or her occupation in the event that a work opportunity may arise. Many employers promote the idea of working couples, and are often helpful with overseas employment opportunities.

Availability

Availability is an important category in many instances. You may have a definite preference for certain countries, or you may wish to state, "Availability: Immediate for worldwide employment." Clearly state your availability date if you're currently employed overseas and have begun your job search six months prior to the end of your current contract.

Languages

List all the ones that you know, no matter how obscure. In many cases, knowledge of a second language is a prerequisite to working overseas. Even if the language is uncommon, second language proficiency is an indicator of your ability to learn other languages. In your résumé, you should rate your language proficiency in the areas of reading, writing, speaking and understanding as fluent, good, fair, etc. Do not use "Poor writing ability," but rather "Some writing ability."

Nationality and National Origin

If you're forwarding your résumé to an employer outside of Canada, by all means mention your nationality. If you were born abroad, but have become a Canadian or landed immigrant, you should indicate so. Many Canadian organizations look favourably upon foreign-born Canadians, or foreign country nationals, since many of these people carry dual citizenship along with an understanding of another culture. If you think your religious or ethnic background will help you adjust to a particular overseas working environment, then it would be beneficial to mention this in your résumé.

Foreign Travel

You should also include the dates and names of countries you've visited as evidence that you've been exposed to other cultures. Employers look favourably upon candidates who have shown an interest in exploring cultures other than their own. Sometimes, a long list of overseas travel (even tourist travel) can act as an acceptable replacement to overseas work experience.

Listing your *passport number* has become an increasingly standard feature in international résumés.

If you've had or have *security clearance,* mention the clearance level along with the date obtained. Other relevant information should be added in brackets (for instance, "can be upgraded to X level").

Contact Information

Your address and phone numbers should generally be positioned as the first item in your résumé. Since your résumé is often circulated overseas, you should include "Canada" in the address. To avoid confusion, abbreviations in the address should be omitted. Area codes for telephone numbers should be included. Given long lead times, include both a personal contact address (current address) and a permanent contact address. A recent survey of large nongovernmental organizations showed that at least 20 per cent of the candidates who were listed in résumé data banks couldn't be contacted because they left no forwarding addresses. Many organizations keep their promising résumés on file for a year, while other organizations have been known to retain them for as long as three years.

You may need to purchase an answering machine. Otherwise, it's imperative that you have a telephone number where you can be contacted at all hours of the day, or where messages are taken on your behalf.

THE "DO NOT MENTIONS"

You should delete all information that doesn't support your career objective, or is irrelevant to the position you're seeking.

Don't give a reason for *terminating a position* in a résumé. During the interview process avoid detailed discussions of past controversies or conflicts. When they're brought up, keep your explanations brief. Avoid lengthy justifications of your behaviour and end the topic on a positive and non-vindictive note.

Omit *salary expectations* or past salary levels in your résumé. This should be reserved for the interview.

Avoid the mention of *political or religious* affiliations. If you have extensive participation in religious or political groups, but your work experience is weak, then simply describe your role in the organization without mentioning its name. For instance, the Young Men's Evangelical Society could be described as a large nongovernmental organization. If the information is requested, mention the organization's name, but don't dwell on its religious or political aspects.

Don't over-emphasize any *military experience* you have had. It may be frowned upon. You may wish to omit it altogether.

Many international organizations require a *photo,* but don't include one unless it's requested. Send only passport photos or an equivalent.

Don't list your *hobbies* unless relevant to the job.

Don't list your *social insurance number.*

Don't list *references* with names, addresses and phone numbers. You may complete your résumé with the phrase "references available upon request," though it's taken for granted that references will be provided. A good reason for not listing the names and addresses of references is that organizations sometimes verify these references indiscriminately, regardless of job openings. It's advisable that you control the number of reference checks to ensure that only serious potential employers are calling upon your references.

References are usually previous employers or academic advisors. You should contact these people in advance as a matter of common courtesy, and as a method of controlling the kind of information given to potential employers. Your references should be informed of the fact that many international organizations base their reference questions on lengthy evaluation questionnaires; also inform them of the important aspects of the position you're seeking.

There are a number of situations where it would be advantageous to supply *reference letters along with your résumé.* If you're applying to an employer located overseas where transit time is a consideration, an accompanying reference letter could help expedite the application process. Or if you're just beginning your career after a stint of volunteer work overseas, references from overseas host employers who are difficult to reach by mail could strengthen the credibility of your dossier.

OTHER OPTIONAL COMPONENTS

Depending on the level of your qualifications, you may find it to your advantage to include a descriptive paragraph or personal statement highlighting your particular strengths and knowledge of the overseas work environment. The personal statement or descriptive paragraph is usually inserted before the personal data section of your résumé. One of its objectives is to help separate you from the mass of other applicants. A few examples of these personal statements are:

- personal management philosophy
- performance factors in overseas work
- women and development
- international development
- intercultural communications
- understanding of environments in the South

THE WRITING STYLE

Don't hire a professional to write you a slick résumé full of over-used terms, such as "seven years of progressively responsible positions." The last impression you want to convey is that you're a professional job seeker. The task of writing a detailed résumé can be quite arduous—it's also not unusual to spend two or three weeks working on the final copy. The following are important points to remember:

- *Omit* all information which doesn't support your career objective.
- *Be brief* in your job descriptions. Keep your résumé under four pages, but don't sacrifice valuable information on your expertise just to save space.
- *Be direct.* Focus on what you did and the results achieved.
- *Be clear.* Adopt the in-house terminology of your potential employer in describing your work for previous employers.
- *Be consistent.* In listing your work history, use the same format and sequence of information for each job. Use the same verb format, same dating style, same character font changes. These facilitate speed reading.
- *Use short words,* short sentences, and short paragraphs. After completing your résumé, re-read it from beginning to end with the intention of eliminating everything superfluous or imprecise.
- *Use outline format.* Avoid the use of "I." Stay away from narrative paragraphs in job descriptions.
- *Use the active voice* to begin sentences.
- *Never use an acronym* without first mentioning the full title. For example: Nongovernmental Organization (NGO), or Canadian International Development Agency (CIDA).
- Your résumé *must* be grammatically correct.
- Use the language of the position you are seeking.
- Use *management terms* when describing yourself.
- Don't hesitate to *improve* and *revise* your résumé as often as you wish during your job search.

FORMAT FOR THE CREATIVE RÉSUMÉ

Résumés should be visually appealing and organized for speed-reading. A number of formatting styles can easily promote readability. For instance:

- Try to be consistent with the arrangement of each *employer, time* and *date* block.
- Use titles and subtitles.
- Divide blocks of information with double lines.
- Use white space to separate segments.
- Underline or bold, to focus the main point in each paragraph.
- Use narrow margins to permit the insertion of more information, without making the résumé appear lengthy.
- Number the pages from page two. You may also include your name (discreetly) near the page numbering on each page.
- Have your résumé prepared on a computer and printed on a laser printer to ensure a high-quality type.
- Use only white or off-white paper, as international résumés are often photocopied and sent to other offices around the world. Never print on

both sides of a paper. If you're photocopying, make sure the quality of the paper is above standard, minimum 40 bond.

- Use a 9" x 12" business envelope. Don't staple your résumé or use a title page. However, appendices may be stapled together.
- Have your résumé proofread by a competent professional.

HOW TO CREATE EFFECTIVE E-MAIL AND SCANNABLE RÉSUMÉS

Knowing how to create an e-mail résumé is becoming an essential job hunting strategy as the popularity of online career services rise. For numerous reasons, companies are requesting that résumés be sent in this form. E-mail also provides a quick and cost-effective way of hiring from any region of the world for employers. For job hunters, this is an inexpensive way of sending your résumé to any corner of the earth. Sending an e-mail résumé is simple, but crucial technical restrictions must be respected. If you don't follow the basic rules for writing an e-mail résumé, potential employers might not be able to access your résumé. (For more on e-mail and the Internet generally, see Chapter 21, the Internet Job Search.)

Tips On How to Write An E-mail Résumé

Here are some vital tips on writing an e-mail résumé:

- Keep it short and simple.
- Save your résumé as a plain Text Only ASCII file instead of saving it as a regular word processing document (usually indicated by the term ".doc"). ASCII text automatically removes all the fancy fonts, italics, underlines, bullets and other features that you have traditionally used to make your résumé look special. You may want to remove your formatting codes and graphics before saving it in ASCII so you can use your original formatting to guide you in designing your text in ASCII. E-mailing a document that is saved as a word processing file will result in unreadable binary code. Don't forget to save an alternative copy of your résumé in word processing format so you can include fancy fonts and styles for non e-mail purposes.
- Font should be in Courier with a font size of 12. Section headings can use a slightly larger font size but nothing larger than 14.
- Keep margins flushed left at 0", right margins at 6.5" or margin settings that will give you 65 characters per line.
- Do not send attachments and binary files. Most people do not want to receive these files because they can take up space in hard drives (employers do not want 3,000 attachment files for the same position). Not all e-mail software supports attachments and binary files. They might also harbour viruses which can cause severe damage to computer systems.
- Allow for a lot of blank space between sections of the résumé. Keeping it simple means keeping it clean.
- Place asterisks (*) or plus symbols (+) around important words or section headings to highlight them; asterisks can also be used as bullets. To divide

sections use asterisks or dashes (-). To emphasize words you can also write words in upper case. Do not overdo it because upper case lettering is the electronic equivalent of shouting.

Once you have written a résumé suitable for e-mailing, you have to get the text into an e-mail message. There are four basic ways. One, open the plain text version in your word processor, select the desired text, then copy it (using the Copy command from the Edit menu in your word processor), switch to your e-mail message and paste the text (using the Paste command from the Edit menu) into your e-mail message. Two, you can "import" the plain text file into your e-mail message using a command like Insert/Text from File or File/Import if your e-mail program has such a feature. Three, if you don't work in a graphic computer environment like Windows or Apple, you can "upload" a document from your personal computer to your e-mail account using a file transfer program—your Internet provider should be able to tell you what programs their system supports and walk you through the steps. And finally, if worst comes to worst, you can type your résumé directly into your e-mail account—slow but effective. By following these guidelines you will ensure that the receiver will be able to access your résumé. E-mail résumés seem unexciting, but personnel managers understand the limits of e-mail résumés, and the technical restrictions that are out of your control will be taken into consideration. They're looking more for content, not fancy layout.

Scannable Résumés and the Importance of Keywords

Many large companies are increasingly using automated data bases (applicant tracking systems) to select new employees from a pool of candidates. A computer will read your electronic résumé before the human recipient, and if the computer cannot read it, due to complicated formatting, your résumé will be discarded. Having the right keywords is vital to your résumé's effectiveness. The computer will select those that contain the keywords describing the qualifications needed by the company. If it doesn't find the prescribed keywords in your résumé it will move onto the next candidate. Résumés can be submitted into an employer's résumé data base through a variety of ways. You can use e-mail, post mail, or fill in a blank résumé on the company web site.

Below are a few tips on how to write a résumé for most applicant tracking systems. For the most part, these guidelines do not have to be followed if you are asked to fill out a blank résumé (E-Form) on a company's web site.

- Send original résumés. If you are not e-mailing your résumé then send them by regular mail. Poor photocopies and faxed copies will degrade the text when it is scanned by the employer's scanning system.
- Use 8 1/2" x 11" paper, printed on one side only.
- Use wide margins.
- Font should be Courier, Helvetica, or Arial.
- Font size should be 10 to 14.
- Avoid tabs.
- No Graphics, italics, underlines, brackets, parentheses or any other fancy trimmings.

- No compressed lines of text.
- Résumés should not be folded.
- Avoid printing on a dot matrix to maintain clarity.
- Do not use staples. They will not go through the scanners.
- Depending on the type of system the employer uses, you may be able to include a cover letter.

Keywords for Electronic and Scannable Résumés

Below are a few tips on how to choose keywords.

- Use industry specific nouns and phrases, avoid verbs if possible.
- Use terms that are common to the industry, companies or organizations that you were involved with.
- List your educational background including universities and colleges attended, major area of study, and certificates and degrees.
- Create a keyword summary immediately after your personal information to summarize your qualifications and experience.
- Consider looking at some of the résumés posted at various online databases. You can use these as guides for your résumé.

Examples of Keywords for Electronic Résumés:

Accounts Payable, BA, Economics, Dalhousie University, Business Unit Manager, Co-operative, Coordinator, Crosscultural Communication, Demand Management, Detail Minded, Distribution Network, Education, Grant Writing, Instructor, Interpersonal Skills, Java, Multi-Modal Analysis, Multi-Tasking, National Accounts Manager, Negotiator, Oracle, Oral Communication, Problem-Solving Abilities, Project Manager, Project Officer, Proposal Writing, Public Presentations, Public Relations, Representative, Sales Associate, Sales Manager, Teacher, Troubleshooting, Written Communication.

Web Site and Multimedia Résumés

You can also feature your résumé on your own or someone elses web site. Graphics, pictures, videos, sounds, hypertext links to your publications or photographs of your work, and direct e-mail are all features that can be incorporated into a hypertext résumé. There are plenty of resources available to help you create your web résumé, including web sites and books. Be forewarned that these types of résumés are ideal for those in the multimedia field. For the rest of us, simple, text-based résumés are appropriate because most employers are not going to actively look on the Internet for your web site.

PUTTING YOUR BEST FOOT FORWARD

Writing a good résumé is an exercise which should allow you to reflect on the achievements of your professional life. Zero in on your strengths and skills. Forget modesty and take credit for your accomplishments without boasting or making unfounded claims.

Don't volunteer information that could result in your being passed over. Downplay facts which aren't easily explained or are confusing. In other words, show an employer what you're capable of, not what you have failed at.

Lastly, have pride in your accomplishments, and speak of them with confidence and assurance.

THE FINAL PRODUCT

You should have your résumé professionally evaluated for clarity, order, continuity, etc. And try to accept constructive criticism.

Your venture into the international job market will heighten your sensitivity to the nature of the marketplace. Don't hesitate to make improvements to your résumé format or add to the content of the résumé using the terminology appropriate to the international field.

APPLICATION FORMS

It's often a practice with international organizations to have candidates complete a formal application form. The UNITED NATIONS "Personal History Form" is the best-known of these forms as it is used widely by UNITED NATIONS agencies. Many of the questions are obviously repetitive, but you shouldn't succumb to the temptation of writing, "See Résumé." As these application forms are seen by many recruiters as a standard evaluation tool, don't underestimate the form's value in the selection process. Be aware that a completed application form may hold greater weight in the selection process than your résumé!

It's a common practice in Europe to analyze the handwriting of candidates, so when you are asked to write answers to certain questions, employers may be looking at both your handwriting and your writing ability. Treat open-ended questions seriously. Be concise. The grammatical clarity of your response is as important as the content. Questions that aren't applicable should be answered with "N/A" rather than left blank, which can misconstrued as a deliberate omission. Also, attach a copy of your résumé to the form.

SUMMARY OF A CREATIVE RÉSUMÉ

In a creative international résumé you have clearly stated your overseas career objective and summarized key professional and personal skills which match the qualities of a person successfully working overseas (the employer's "ideal profile"). You've used the language of your future work in your résumé and deleted information irrelevant to, or not supportive of, your objective. Your work history is organized around a few key functions which relate to your future overseas working environment. Your job descriptions highlight your responsibilities and focus on your accomplishments rather than the duties you performed.

TWO CREATIVE RÉSUMÉS THAT WORK

The Entry-level Résumé

The first résumé was used to acquire an entry-level position as a logistics officer with the UNITED NATIONS HIGH COMMISSION FOR REFUGEES. The candidate had only six months' overseas experience and had many interruptions in his professional and academic work history. Originally, he had written a traditional chronological résumé, sending out 40 copies to potential employers over a two-month period. He received no positive responses.

After spending another $700 on long distance phone calls to research the job market and to build up contacts, this job hunter compiled a very good picture of the ideal profile for his particular field. He rewrote his résumé using a combination format, re-targeted his career objective with a supporting work history, and sent out his new version to the previously-contacted 40 employers. Within two months, he received five job offers for work overseas!

Why did his second résumé work? The candidate kept his occupational objective broad, but specific enough for entry-level positions. His "major traits" indicated that he had the personality to survive and be productive in his field. The functional breakdown between "Understanding of the South" and "Business Experience" was in keeping with the combination most sought by the employer. The amount of overseas experience was "stretched" by emphasizing volunteer work in Canada along with a personal statement regarding his management philosophy. Many of his phrases and words were taken directly from conversations with his potential employers.

The Senior-level Résumé

The second résumé is representative of what a senior professional with 20 years experience might write. The candidate has just moved to Geneva with her husband.

Her résumé combines the chronological and functional résumé formats. Many of the techniques used in the junior-level résumé are applied, but because of her long experience the candidate does not have to be as creative in presenting her skills.

The challenge with a more senior résumé is to organize a wide range of job experiences into a readable and understandable format. The most important part (and the most challenging) is the summary of "Professional Skills" on page one. This page summarizes a complicated but enticing set of skills. Note how the bold "skills group headings" on the first page are reinforced by the underlined "functional job headings" on the second and third pages. The résumé is clearly set up for speed reading (potential employers can quickly get a sense of the candidate by scanning the résumé and reading only bold and underlined phrases). Concise descriptions are available one paragraph at a time.

RÉSUMÉ

MARC J. DOUCET

Current address:
45 Laurier Street
Ottawa, Ontario K1N 7Z2
CANADA
Tel: (613) 231-4215

Permanent address:
804 O'Neil Avenue
Miramichi, N.B. E2W 2L8
CANADA
Tel: (506) 333-7786

OBJECTIVE: Overseas Field Administrator

PERSONAL TRAITS: Self-starter, high energy, proven administrative abilities, communicates effectively with people from other cultures, cheerful under pressure, follow-up management style.

PROFESSIONAL SKILLS: Business Administration BA degree, MA Third World Political Economics, fully bilingual, proficient with computers, four years volunteer leadership experience in crosscultural environment, six months overseas management experience.

UNDERSTANDING OF THE SOUTH

Masters in Political Science, *Université Laval*
Specialization, Third World Economics. Consistent B+ average. Skilled in organizing and defining concepts. Gained a firm understanding of the political and economic forces which operate in developing countries. (May 1997).

Orientation Counsellor, *Canadian Crossroads International (CCI)*
Helped orient over 35 African and Canadian volunteers. Proficient in topics such as culture shock, health tips, West African and North American social customs, dealing with officials, currency problems. Acquired three years experience recruiting and interviewing candidates for Crossroads (1993-present).

Assistant to the Director, *German Volunteer Service (GVS)*, Ghana
Successfully organized four-day conference for 60 participants under conditions of severe food and transportation shortages; liaised effectively with Ghanaian ministries for increased fuel rations and food supplies; organized the importation of trucks and equipment and handled customs clearances; gave country orientation to GVS volunteers, their families and other visiting GVS staff, handled daily office problems (August-November 1993).

CCI Volunteer Administrator, *Abetiffi Vocational Training Institute*, Ghana
Taught English part-time, assisted German Volunteers in managing school, developed school accounting system, implemented student recruitment program, procured school supplies, equipment and food from government ministries for students (May-July 1993).

Travel to other developing countries
Togo, Burkina Faso, Ivory Coast, 1993; visited Nigeria for four weeks in 1990/91.

BUSINESS EXPERIENCE
Leadership and Organization Abilities

Bachelor of Business Administration, *University of New Brunswick*
B+ average. Specialization in marketing and management (1990).

Small Business Consultant, *U.N.B. School of Administration*
Assisted small and medium-sized businesses; designed and implemented marketing strategy; organized major consumer telephone survey; developed accounting and cost control systems (summer, 1989).

Manager Trainee, *General Motors of Canada, Forward Planning Department, Parts Division.* Compiled and analyzed industry data for senior management; gained strong reputation for analytical abilities; was the first to develop a reliable manpower analysis. AC Delco Supplier Rep: Successfully resolved long-standing problems with rebuilt suppliers that led to the elimination of my position. Inventory Planner: Managed $2 million parts inventory (June 1990 - January 1992).

Computer skills
Using Microsoft Excel designed and implemented a new *Survey of Enrolment and Teaching in Political Science* which was very well received by the chairpersons of the Canadian Political Science Association. Wrote master's thesis using Word 7.0. Currently employed as the Resource Person, computer laboratory, Faculty of Social Sciences. Developed an administrative workbook for lab.

Active Member, *Canadian Crossroads International*
National Finance and Fundraising Committee: involved in financial policy formulation, expense and revenue monitoring, revision of national fundraising campaigns; developed Third World project evaluation forms. Special Project Coordinator: national resource person for Care Package projects, development of local committee fundraising support material (see manuals below). Francophone Regional Representative: liaison for francophone committees; initiated and coordinated national bilingual program for all major documents (1994-present). CCI Local Committee Fundraising Coordinator, Québec City: developed several successful fundraising projects generating revenues of $25,000 per year, enabling the committee to increase the number of overseas volunteers from four to nine in three years (1993-97).

President, *U.N.B. Business Society*
Initiated many new programs and raised membership by 35 per cent (1988-89).

Member of several high school and university committees
Enjoyed organizing events and working with people (1980-94).

President of Graduation Committee and awarded Most Active Student of the Year (1984-85); Class President (1983-84); Troop Scout Leader (1982-83).

MANUALS AND PUBLICATIONS

Graphic and Advertising Manuals for Crossroaders and Local Committees,
Canadian Crossroads International (CCI) 1993 98 p.

Local Committee Finance and Fundraising Manual,
CCI: First edition, 1993, second edition 1995, 64 p.

Master's Thesis: *The Political Economy of State-Economic Relations in Ghana* Université
Laval, 1997, 168 p.

Book Review: Naomi Chazan, An Anatomy of Ghanaian Politics, *Managing Political
Recession, 1974-1987.* Boulder Colorado, Westview Press, 1995, 429 p.; published in *Etudes
Internationales,* Vol XV, No. 4, December 1996, pp. 963-965

*Parts Manual: for Projecting Business Growth, Warehousing, Equipment, and Manpower
Needs.* General Motors of Canada, Forward Planning Department, Oshawa, 1992, 114p.

SHORT COURSES

Emergency First Aid, St. John Ambulance	1990
Dealer Business Management GM of Canada	1991
Technicians Guild GM	1991

PERSONAL MANAGEMENT PHILOSOPHY

I am a "shirt-sleeve" organizer who likes to stay in contact with the people and programs I
manage. Since most administrative problems and opportunities are people-related, it is
important to have a "hands-on" understanding of the issues and personalities that surround a
project. Qualities such as follow-up, persistence, and personal contact are those which have
helped me most to maintain a consistent record of achievement in Africa as well as with the
many volunteer organizations I have worked with in Canada. People who work with me say
that I am an effective organizer because I have a good sense of humour and remain
enthusiastic even in the face of frustration.

PERSONAL DATA

DATE & PLACE OF BIRTH: November 12th, 1970; Chatham, New Brunswick
STATUS: Single, no dependents, mobile
NATIONALITY: Canadian
LANGUAGES: French & English (written French fair, otherwise fully fluent)

Robin Millar

OBJECTIVE: Senior program officer or consultant for an international organization based in Geneva.

KEY QUALITIES: Team leader, experienced and effective in introducing new
policies, adept at long-term institutional planning and program
design, visionary, competent administrator, personable, good
communicator, pragmatist, fluent in three languages.

PROFESSIONAL SKILLS

Policy:
* Policy and strategic planning at the global, regional and country level.
* Astute in distilling key components of policy and steering teams of experts towards
  solutions.
* Aware of ethical and cultural issues as they develop over time and impact on policy.
* Sensitive to public attitudes and how they affect government policy.
* Six years of community development programming.
* Able to balance pure research, applied/field research and capacity-building.

Program Management:
* Thirteen years experience in international development project management
  (Tanzania, Sudan, Canada).
* Familiar with developing and monitoring all phases of projects from needs analysis,
  program designs, implementation plans, monitoring and evaluations.
* Numerous overseas field missions in direct collaboration with local populations and
  communities.

Administration:
* Worked in the field and at headquarters, and in all facets of project administration.
* Organized international meetings, official visits, field missions, and development
  studies. Monitored the implementation of numerous programs and related projects.
* Competent organizer, effective writer, experienced trainer and supervisor of staff,
  adept in financial and office systems management.

SECTORS OF EXPERIENCE

Health, education, communications, human resources, social policy, gender and
development, institutional development.

PROFESSIONAL ASSIGNMENTS

First Secretary & Head of CIDA Operations, Tanzania, Canadian High Commission, Canadian International Development Agency (CIDA), Dar es Salaam, Tanzania (1994 - present)

- Manager: Managed CIDA's development programs in Tanzania.
- Project Planner: Responsible for reviewing the project implementation and management activities related to bilateral, institutional co-operation, and partnership program activities in Tanzania.
- Areas of Responsibility: Managed complex bilateral program consisting of four sub-programs and 20 projects; sectors included health, social policy, gender and development, and institutional development.
- Reports/Studies: Reported to headquarters on social, economic and political factors influencing program delivery: realities of hyperinflation and introduction of currency reforms and price/wage freezes; outbreak of HIV/AIDS and socioeconomic disparities.
- Coordinator/Planner: Assumed overall responsibility for multi-disciplinary teams to plan Third Phase of CIDA's bilateral program in Tanzania.
- Negotiator: Developed and negotiated, on behalf of CIDA, framework for a new bilateral technical co-operation program valued at $10 million, with Tanzanian authorities in May 1996.
- Program Evaluator/Monitor: Monitored CIDA-sponsored nongovernmental and institutional co-operation activities and analyzed new project proposals.

Sudan Bilateral Development Officer, Regional Program, Africa Branch, (CIDA) Headquarters, Ottawa/Hull, Canada (1989 - 1994)

- Strategic Planner: Participated in drafting the Regional Program Review, a five-year policy framework for CIDA's activities in Sudan.
- Program Review: Evaluated community development and educational programs. Developed project implementation framework of a vocational training project. Secured co-operation and support of senior management in Department of Employment and Immigration Canada.
- Negotiator: As Team Leader, developed Memorandum of Understanding for $10 million goods and services line of credit for Sudan.
- Project Manager: Managed day-to-day activities of three bilateral projects: Functional Literacy, Primary Health Care, and Human Resource Development.
- Advisor: Analyzed, within headquarters and in field, emergency balance-of-payment options and instruments specific to Sudan's development needs and prepared draft papers for senior management which outlined social, economic and political considerations of policy options.

Overseas Country Director (Sudan), Canadian Save the Children Fund (1985 - 1989)
* Manager: Initiated Canadian Save the Children Fund in Sudan and held responsibility for all financial and operational matters of program budgeted at $250,000. Established agency office, hired administrative and program staff, and initiated necessary management procedures. Set personnel policies: job descriptions, salary scales and office procedures.
* Negotiator: Identified and negotiated projects involving rural self-help schools, rural women's community training centres, and integrated community development. Projects involved both direct support to community groups and support to local Sudanese NGOs.
* Report/Studies: Reported to headquarters on social, economic and political factors influencing program delivery, outbreak of HIV/AIDS and socioeconomic disparities between rural and urban populations.
* Personnel Manager: Supervised one Canada-based employee, two senior-level, locally-engaged program assistants, and two administrative assistants.

Program Officer, Employment Development, Employment and Immigration Canada (EIC) (1982 - 1985)
* Project Manager: Development of community-based projects designed to alleviate unemployment, particularly for women, youth, minority groups and disabled persons.
* Monitor: Monitored financial audit for operating projects.
* Liaison: Liaised with elected Members of Parliament and community organizations. Chaired advisory boards composed of community and business leaders. Clients ranged from small voluntary ad hoc group and public sector groups to large multinational companies.
* Report/Studies: Produced reports and briefing materials detailing the socioeconomic disparities existing in the country, ongoing study of social, political and economic climate of the area, analysis of proposals including relevant research and determination of financial feasibility.

JPO Program Officer, United Nations Development Program (UNDP), Jakarta, Indonesia (1980 - 1982)
* Advisor: Drafted position papers, speeches, briefing notes and correspondence for Resident Representative.
* Monitor: Monitored UNDP-assisted community development projects.
* Coordinator: Selection committee responsible for disbursing funds for community development projects.
* Negotiator: Project for the Government of Indonesia, the Indonesian Association of Voluntary Organization (IAVO) and the UNDP which provided management training and management services for indigenous NGOs.
* Administrator: Responsible for day-to-day program management of UNDP projects.

EXPERIENCE WITH
NONGOVERNMENTAL ORGANIZATIONS

World University Service of Canada (WUSC)
Member of WUSC Board of Directors (1990 - 1994). Led a WUSC seminar on development to Costa Rica in 1989. In charge of selecting both professors and student participants for seminars in Haiti, Egypt and Thailand. Active on the University of Ottawa WUSC committee in recruiting seminar students and raising funds for refugee students.

Canadian Crossroads International
Crossroads participant in Kenya and, later, group leader in Tanzania. Board member and active volunteer for over 10 years.

Canadian Association of African Studies (CAAS)
Coordinated the successful 13th Annual Conference of the CAAS at Carleton University in 1989 with 300 participants.

EDUCATION

* MA in International Affairs, Norman Paterson School of International Affairs, Carleton University (1981)
* BA in Political Science, Carleton University (1975)

LANGUAGES	Oral	Comprehension	Written
English	Excellent	Excellent	Excellent
French	Good	Excellent	Good
Spanish	Good	Excellent	Good

PERSONAL

Nationality: Canadian citizen
Foreign Travel: Travelled extensively in Africa and Asia
Marital Status: Married with two teenage children, both attending university
Mobility: Able to travel on assignments
References: Available upon request

Home Address in Geneva	Contact Address in Geneva	Permanent Contact in Canada
68 Avenue Appia	International Labour Organization (ILO)	Attention:
1211 Geneva 27	Attention: Mr. Robert Millar	Mr. Jim Eastman
SWITZERLAND	4, route des Morillons	40 Isabella Street
Tel: (41) (22) 352-2445	1211 Geneva 22	Ottawa, Ontario K1S 8G8
	SWITZERLAND	CANADA
	Tel: (41) (22) 352-6387	Tel: +1 (613) 238-6189
	Fax: (41) (22) 352-7315	

Chapter 25

Covering
Letters

This chapter discusses the importance of follow-up letters and covering letters. These are important to the job search process because they are a visible part of your dossier as it is passed from one recruitment officer to the next.

The covering letter accompanies every résumé. It is a one-page marketing tool for drawing an employer's attention to your particular set of skills and experience. Its main purpose is to help you get that interview.

There are basically two types of covering letters:

- The letter of inquiry
- The application letter

Letter of Inquiry

This is used to inquire about possible job openings, to determine application procedures and to register your name in a recruitment data bank. A letter of inquiry is often part of the research phase of the job search. In many instances, it is part of a mass mailing and is sent well in advance of your employment target-date, because exchanges of information can take several months.

Letter of Application

Use this to respond to a specific job opening. If you are replying to an advertisement, tailor the information in your letter to either match or come close to the employer's criteria.

CALL YOUR FUTURE EMPLOYER FIRST

Telephone the company before mailing your résumé. After all, we know only too well what is done with unsolicited mail. (For a full discussion on this subject, please see Chapter 23, Phone Research Techniques.)

Here are a few reasons to call before sending your résumé and covering letter:

- To obtain the *exact name and title* of the recruitment officer for inclusion in your covering letter
- To inquire about the employer's *ideal profile* so that these important characteristics can be highlighted in your covering letter;
- To make reference to that conversation in the covering letter. This serves to demonstrate your communication skills and to remind the employer of who you are.

Calling ahead will not only demonstrate your communication and planning skills, but will also help build a relationship with a particular recruiter. If you are unable to speak to a recruitment officer, you can still create a link through the secretary. For example: "Further to my telephone conversation with your secretary, Ms. Moores, I'm forwarding my résumé and application for the civil engineering position in Islamabad, Pakistan."

WRITING A CREATIVE COVERING LETTER

You simply must have an effective covering letter. It should not only demonstrate the clarity of your thoughts, but must be a sterling reflection of your writing abilities. Do not use humour, jargon or an approach that does not reflect a serious professional attitude. Limit your use of the word "I." It is not unheard-of to spend four or five hours composing a good covering letter to achieve the payoff of an interview.

The standard format should not exceed one page in length. It is as follows:

- The *first paragraph* states the purpose of your letter.
- The *second (and possibly third)* highlights your experience (one paragraph usually focuses on overseas or international experience).
- The *last paragraph* states desired follow-up action (usually to arrange an interview date or follow-up phone call), along with a closing affirmative sentence about yourself.

The Introduction

Keep this first paragraph short. The objective is to be precise and personable. As a courtesy, briefly mention how you became aware of the position. If you were introduced to the company through an employee, mention his or her name. It could very well become a relevant networking contact for you and the recruitment officer. For example:

"Mr. Nemo, the information officer at the Canadian Council of International Co-operation (CCIC) suggested that I write to you regarding employment possibilities in overseas international education."

State the purpose of your letter in the first paragraph (that is, a letter of inquiry, an application for a specific job, or in response to a phone conversation related to a specified item). State the position you are applying for or your career objective (field, level of entry, geographic preference).

Be personable. Include something specific to arouse an employer's interest such as a reference to your previous phone conversation or a particular problem that you might be able to resolve for the company.

The Body of the Letter

Sell yourself! Reveal only your most outstanding skills and experience. Draw attention to your best qualifications with the objective of arousing the employer's interest.

Describe your work experiences from an employer's perspective, rather than your own. "I believe my grassroots overseas experience with the United Nations Development Program would allow me to make an effective contribution to your rural water program in Ghana," rather than, "I want to work overseas because I enjoy new experiences." State how you can help the employer.

Highlight your accomplishments. Be specific. Use the "active voice" when possible. Examples:

- "I developed a new program in..." or "I initiated a successful program in..."
- "My past successes demonstrate my ability to handle this kind of work."
- "My work with the Refugee Committee in Montréal and teaching secondary school in an ethnic neighbourhood in Toronto exposed me to the challenges of crosscultural communication. I have the background experience and understanding needed to teach effectively in another culture."

Mention how your past experiences relate to the international field or why you are qualified for the position. This should be a major theme in at least one of the paragraphs of your covering letter. Example:

- "As the son of a military officer in the Canadian Armed Forces, I have lived and travelled in many countries. I recently spent four months in Africa, with my parents, who are now posted in Kinshasa, Congo. These experiences, along with my master's degree in International Relations, have given me a solid understanding of social and economic conditions in the South."

Draw attention to an overall trend in your career and tie this to an important skill. You should also make reference to material in your attached résumé; for instance:

- "As my résumé shows, I seek leadership roles where motivation is the crucial factor."

Turn your weaknesses into strengths! Don't say,

- "While I have never worked overseas, my five years of work with visiting Chinese students at…"

It would be much better to simply say,

- "Five years of working with visiting Chinese students at the Winnipeg Vocational Training School has provided me with a wealth of crosscultural knowledge."

You can also list career highlights in point form rather than in paragraphs. For example:

- "The highlights of my career which qualify me for an overseas posting are:
   a) A bachelor's degree specializing in international affairs with some courses in business administration;
   b) Two years as a CUSO volunteer school administrator in Guyana;
   c) Two years project programming experience with ABC Consultants;
   d) Active volunteer participation with the Oxfam Local Committee of Kingston."

The Closing Paragraph

In the closing paragraph you should stress your interest in the employer's field of work and state that you will be in touch in the near future. You should suggest an interview in your letter of inquiry, though it would be inappropriate to mention a specific date. In the case of an advertised job-opening, there is usually a pre-arranged recruitment schedule. A closing sentence might be:

- "I look forward to hearing from you in the near future, and to discussing how my finance skills would best fit your organizational objectives."

- "I want to restate my interest in your Zimbabwe project. I look forward to discussing my possible contribution to this exciting work."

In the case of a letter of inquiry:

- "I understand that you are not currently in need of an office administrator, but I believe a short meeting would be beneficial to both of us, in light of your continuing overseas requirements."

FOLLOW-UP LETTERS

Imagine the recruiting officer who has just received the company's request to hire an overseas employee for a contract in Nigeria. The recruitment officer immediately consults the company's data bank for suitable candidates. If you had recently called the organization, the recruitment officer would likely pull your file for a quick review. It would contain: the standard company evaluation form, your résumé and covering letter, as well as one or two letters of continuing interest. One letter might mention your current short-term contract in a particular field; another might be addressed to the Nigeria project officer and discuss your particular interest in the company's upcoming contract. All letters should demonstrate enthusiasm for the organization and for overseas employment.

In many cases, recruitment officers rely on computerized data banks for candidates. An excellent method of keeping your file active is to send out periodic letters expressing continued interest.

Letters of Continued Interest

The objective is to keep your dossier active.

1. Letters should be sent every three to six months to employers who have your file on record.
2. Follow up your phone calls with a letter expressing interest or adding new information related to your conversation.
3. Document any changes to your résumé, such as new employment, new courses taken, a change of address or phone number.
4. If you decide to accept a position overseas, inform other employers in writing of your change in job status. It is important to maintain good relations and contacts. After all, you will probably be looking for another job at the end of your contract.

Follow-up Letters After an Interview

This is a crucial step that should be taken within hours of a formal interview or an information interview. There are a number of reasons this will strengthen your employment prospects.

- A "thank you for having met with me" letter will differentiate you from other candidates and may make a difference in the hiring decision. Always express enthusiasm for the position offered in light of your discussion. Example:

    "Thank you for taking the time to meet with me yesterday. I appreciated the opportunity to learn more about the Nigerian project, your management philosophy, and your aim of integrating Nigerians into the project. As my engineering background includes training experience, I am optimistic about being able to contribute to the success of your endeavours."

- The follow-up letter should contain additional information related to your interview. Example:

    "Further to our discussion yesterday, I am forwarding you an article which discusses the new program developments being implemented by... In light of our discussion, I wish to restate my enthusiasm for the position being offered."

- A follow-up letter gives you the opportunity to clarify a point or correct an error. Errors should be dealt with immediately, either by phone or letter. For example:

    "In reviewing our interview discussion of December 10 concerning desert irrigation systems, I find myself uncomfortable with a point I had made, and wish to elaborate on the subject a little further..."

FORMATTING NOTES

Never send photocopies. Letters to potential employers should be individually typed on a good typewriter or word processor. Remember, you are competing with people who have access to high-quality laser printers. *Never* handwrite a letter.

If you do not know, never assume a person's gender or title in the opening salutation. Rather than "Dear Recruitment Officer," or "Dear Superintendent," you should begin with "Dear Sir/Madam." (Your cause will be lost if you use "To whom it may concern," "Gentlemen," or "Dear friends.") Similarly, if you are replying to an advertisement in which only the name or initials are given, and you have no knowledge of gender, simply address your inquiry to "Dear J.C. Boyle." If a PhD degree is indicated, address your letter to "Dear Dr. Boyle." If an appropriate title is given, use it in the salutation; example "Dear Minister Boyle," or "Dear President Boyle." If the recruitment officer is female and she does not identify herself during a conversation as "Miss" or "Mrs.," you should use "Ms."

The *full address* is usually listed in the following order: Name, title, department, organization name, postal box, street address, floor or suite number, town or city, country, and postal code. To avoid confusion in international correspondence, never use address abbreviations (P.O., St., Dr., Ave., Ont., Alta.).

If a résumé and other items are included, complete your letter with the lists of *items enclosed* by using the abbreviation "Encl." Example:

"Encl.: Résumé, three reference letters, application form."

It is perfectly acceptable to increase your chances of employment by sending your résumé to more than one person in the same agency. You must, however, inform both parties by including the abbreviation "cc." on the last line of your letter; example, "cc. Mr. Jack Smith, Manager, International Finance."

A LAST WORD

Covering letters are crucial to your job search. They should be revised as often as necessary. They may be the key to getting someone to send you that application form, study your résumé, grant you an interview or even decide you are the person for the job. Covering letters give you the chance to "sell yourself in less than a page." Don't minimize their importance!

LETTER OF APPLICATION

15 April 1999

Ms. Sandy Welsh
Personnel Director
Plenty Canada
R.R. 3
Lanark, Ontario K0G 1K0

Dear Ms. Welsh,

Further to a recent conversation with your assistant, Ms. Debbie Wilson, I wish to apply for the position of Assistant Administrator – the Dominican Republic, as advertised in the March Job Bulletin of the Canadian Council for International Co-operation.

As the coordinator of volunteer services at the Williamson Memorial Regional Hospital, I supervised a staff of over 300 volunteers. I am also the volunteer treasurer of the Alberta Alliance for Peace, supervising the accounting of a $30,000 annual budget. My résumé points out numerous other activities which attest to my ability to organize and administer a large staff operating within a tight budget.

I have a realistic understanding of overseas living and working conditions and possess good crosscultural communication skills. Since returning three years ago from Zaire where I worked with Canada World Youth (CWY), I have been active with numerous volunteer groups in Medicine Hat, Alberta. Besides being a member of the local World University Service of Canada (WUSC) committee, I have remained especially active with CWY in the areas of volunteer recruitment and assessment. I also had the opportunity to travel extensively in Latin America for two months last year. I am fluent in Spanish.

Please note that I am available for an interview during the week of May 8th. You may also contact me during regular office hours at my business. I look forward to hearing from you and discussing how my organizational skills could make a strong contribution to the challenging post of administrative assistant in the Dominican Republic.

Yours truly,

Ms. Patty Carter
23-1334 Avenue Road
Medicine Hat, Alberta R9T 5G5

Encl.: Résumé

LETTER OF INQUIRY

15 January 1998

Dr Phil Kilpatrick
Superintendent
Seoul International School
4-1 Hwayang-dong
Sungdong-ku
Seoul 120
KOREA

Dear Dr. Kilpatrick,

I am writing you to inquire about teaching possibilities at the primary level during the 1998-99 school year. I have spoken to a number of people at the Department of Foreign Affairs and International Trade in Ottawa, who have informed me that your international school is held in high regard by the families of Canadian diplomats who reside in Seoul.

Please find attached my résumé and an open letter of recommendation from my current supervisor, Mr. Matthew Godin, Principal at St.Michael's school. I am enjoying my fourth year of teaching since graduating with honours from the University of New Brunswick in 1990. For the past two years I have been chairman of two provincial committees dealing with the introduction of new primary school teaching methods in mathematics and sciences. I have also been involved in coaching team sports, and recognize the rewards of working with children outside of the classroom.

My overseas experience includes two extensive cultural visits through Southeast Asia during the summers of 1992 and 1994 with the New Brunswick Teachers Federation. In 1994, I was group leader in charge of coordinating meetings between our group and local government officials.

Please send me an application package and any information on possible openings in the upcoming school year. I have included a self-addressed envelope and three UNESCO international reply coupons. In speaking to other teachers who have worked abroad, and in reviewing my own experiences in Southeast Asia, I am confident of my abilities to contribute to your international school and a multi-racial student body.

Sincerely yours,

Mr. Joe Eddie
13 O'Connor Street
Saint John, New Brunswick E2A 3B4
CANADA

Encl.: Résumé

LETTER OF CONTINUED INTEREST

15 April 2000

Bernard C. Perkins
Chief, CDRS
United Nations High Commissioner
for Refugees (UNHCR)
Case postale 2500
1211 Geneva 2 Dépot
SWITZERLAND

Dear Mr. Perkins,

Further to our recent phone conversation, I am including an updated copy of my résumé, along with my completed Personal History form.

As I pointed out in my recent application for a position as a Junior Professional Officer, I believe my abilities and experience in intercultural, refugee, international development and community development fields, as well as my studies in sociology, make me suitable for a position with the HCR. I also believe I possess the spirit, determination and diplomatic skills, as well as the humanitarian commitment, that are required for employees of the United Nations.

I wish to reaffirm my admiration for the work the UNHCR does in the international arena and assure you of my continuing sincere interest in joining your organization. Thank you again for considering my candidacy. I look forward to hearing from you soon.

Yours sincerely,

Jonas C. Boudreau
254 Edith Drive
Toronto, Ontario M2B 5X1
CANADA

FOLLOW-UP LETTER AFTER INTERVIEW

12 July 2000

Ms. Linda Lim
Senior Visiting Recruitment Officer
United Nations High Commissioner
for Refugees (UNHCR)
280 Albert Street, Suite 401
Ottawa, Ontario K1P 5G8

Dear Ms. Lim,

I wish to express my thanks for your interview of July 10. After this meeting, I am even more certain that UNHCR is the type of international agency for which I want to work. I believe my skills would be well-used and I could make an important contribution to the work being done by your organization.

After hearing your description of work in a refugee camp, I am convinced I possess the sound judgement, organizational and leadership skills, and intercultural understanding required of UNHCR employees in the field. This JPO opportunity would also give me valuable experience which I could later apply in my own region of Canada, where so much work with refugees has to be done.

Once again, thank you for considering me. I am excited about the prospect of joining UNHCR and look forward to hearing from you soon.

Yours sincerely,

Denise Haché
324 Rocheforte Drive
Apartment 511
Don Mills, Ontario M3C 1H5

LETTER OF APPLICATION FOR INTERNSHIP

14 July 1999

Mr. Christopher Lee
Executive Director
Citizens' Clearinghouse on Waste Management
3128 W 10th Avenue
Vancouver, B.C. V6K 2R6

Subject: Internship Position

Dear Mr. Lee:

Further to our conversation of 13 July, please find enclosed my résumé outlining my qualification for the Composting Internship position available with the Cooperative Community Composting Center Project in Mexico.

I am both a strong advocate and a practitioner of ecologically sound development. My bachelor's degree in Biology broadened my understanding of ecology and our world environment. I apply the "Three R's" of waste reduction in my everyday life, by avoiding disposable items, reusing bags and various paper products, and purchasing many things at garage sales. I also compost leaves, grass clippings and food scraps.

As an adaptable and sociable person, I interact well with others. My previous jobs have provided me with the opportunity to work with a variety of people and hold a considerable amount of responsibility. My resourcefulness and ability to work independently have helped me win the appreciation of employers and co-workers. My communication skills are also well-developed and I am fluent in English, French and Spanish.

I believe I am well-suited to this internship where cultural sensitivity, teamwork and resourcefulness are essential. In addition, my scientific background and language skills would contribute greatly to your program. I look forward to hearing from you in the near future.

Sincerely,

Sarah K. Singleton
88 Sunset Court
Calgary, Alberta T2X 1K8

(403) 284-8512

Chapter 26

Interviewing for an International Job

You want to work overseas. You've spent a lot of time preparing. You have researched hundreds of possibilities and sent your résumé and a covering letter to a multitude of organizations. You have been in contact with a number of potential employers and, finally, you've been invited to an interview for a specific job.

The interview is the most critical point in your job search. It is here that an employer assesses your suitability for overseas employment, based on their criteria. How closely do you match the employer's *ideal profile?* Do you have the qualifications? Do you and the company share similar management styles? Will you present a good company image abroad? Will you survive culture shock?

Most candidates are nervous at the prospect of an interview. They feel they have no control, they are at the mercy of a recruitment officer and an interview team. But is the process really that one-sided, skewed to the candidate's detriment? Does the employer have anything to lose? You probably have these and other questions on your mind as you contemplate the all-important interview. Let's first discuss the interview from the employer's point of view.

Imagine the recruitment officer who must select a candidate for an over-seas position. There is a great responsibility resting on his or her shoulders. The recruiter's professional expertise is on the line. People are relying on him or her to come up with the right person for the position. The firm or organization is investing time and money to interview candidates from across the country. The cost of posting an employee overseas is exorbitant: airfare, moving, settling-in allowance, cost of dependants, housing, salary, etc. The price of failure is equally high, in terms of the firm's reputation abroad and finding a replacement candidate.

495

The stakes are high on both sides. Both parties are depending on the outcome of the interview. With this in mind, a helpful strategy for overcoming your anxiety is to focus on co-operating with the selection committee. Help them with their difficult hiring decision. They will likely have an equally positive attitude towards you.

How do you go about preparing for the interview?

Prior to your interview, carry out a "profile analysis" by matching your skills to those specified in the overseas job description. You must be able to discuss your professional work history in terms of specific skills that match the overseas position. Work on your sales presentation until you've got it down pat!

A Reminder to be Cautious

Some overly enthusiastic candidates ignore the negative aspects of living and working overseas and are then faced with discussing them in their interview. *Be careful not to hear only what you want to hear.* Assess carefully all the information. A wrong decision not only results in your failure to adjust overseas, but leaves its mark on your work history.

Who Will Interview You?

An interview team often consists of a minimum of three people: a personnel officer, the overseas manager or in-Canada liaison officer, and another senior-level manager. On the other hand, you may be interviewed by only one or two people.

How Long Will the Interview Last?

The interview process begins with your first telephone call. Remember, despite the impersonal nature of the exchange, you are being assessed by the other party. The interview itself can last from one hour to a full day. The private sector often prefers a day-long series of one-on-one interviews with managers of different levels. The preferred format for government institutions and NGOs is a formal interview with a three-person selection panel, usually lasting an hour.

Second interviews are rare for overseas positions, as recruitment is usually done on a national scale. If an offer is made, you will be given time to finalize all questions and negotiate the terms of the contract.

DIFFERENT INTERVIEW STYLES

It is important to recognize and react appropriately to different interviewing styles. Some interviewers talk non-stop while others expect you to take the initiative. Then there are those interviewers who treat the interview as nothing more than an informal chat, barely discussing the job in question.

The Structured Interview

This type of interview is common for government positions. Screening is based on a candidate's education and work experience. Government interviews are often loaded with pre-written questions and you are judged in three critical areas: knowledge, ability, and personal suitability. You must obtain a minimum score of 60 per cent in each area. So if you are competing for a permanent position at CIDA, it is crucial that you study the policies and structure of CIDA as it relates to your job area.

The Statement of Qualifications sets out the basic job requirements for the federal government. You should study the text and incorporate the buzzwords into your interview. Government interviews are often conducted by a panel of three people. You should answer each question directly, without rambling, as your answers are measured and tabulated against a rating guide. The objective is to score as many points as possible. Don't indulge in elaborate details, just mention the highlights of your subject and move on. And let your interviewers know when you are expanding on a topic which might demonstrate your suitability for the job.

Remember, your interviewers will offer you little feedback on your performance, as this can be seen as prejudicial. Your best tactic is to probe; example, "would you like me to continue, or to elaborate further?"

The Informal Interview

The informal interview is the most popular interview style and the one which best lends itself to pre-interview preparation. In this setting the candidate is expected to play an active role in the interview process. This is your opportunity to present yourself in the best possible light by steering the discussion to focus on your skills.

Let the interviewer lead the interview. Despite their personal and friendly tone, remember, the interviewer is probing for facts that will enable him or her to assess your suitability for the job.

WHAT AN OVERSEAS EMPLOYER IS LOOKING FOR

Chapter 1 discussed the skills needed for living and working overseas. Employers may not directly mention them, but they will be looking for evidence that you possess certain of these attributes. You will be questioned about the following:

* Are there limiting factors such as health, family or other extenuating circumstances?
* Do you have a realistic understanding of overseas living and working conditions?
* Do you have the technical skills and social competence to work with colleagues of different nationalities?
* Will you fulfil the terms of your contract and demonstrate loyalty to the firm in the face of frustrations?

To explain these areas further:

* Expect to be probed on your personal life and family situation: willingness of your spouse to relocate, the number of school-aged children you have and their planned education, the health of family members. If an

interviewer neglects to bring up these issues, the firm's credibility is suspect.

* Major emphasis is placed on the character of the recruit. In a culturally strange environment, you are not only exposed to unforeseen hardships, but must work and live in close proximity to your colleagues. One of the recruiter's tasks is to probe for your feelings about these situations and judge your ability to survive in a different, perhaps difficult, setting.

* Team effort is an important consideration in assessing your suitability for an overseas post. How will you respond to subordinates or superiors of different nationalities? In the interview more emphasis will be placed on character evaluation than technical competence. If you have been invited to an interview, you can usually assume that your professional credentials have passed the test.

* Fulfilling the terms of a contract is extremely important. Untimely departures are costly. An employer will look for tenacity, flexibility and tolerance. For example: Will you threaten to quit if your home is without running water for three months, or if the replacement part for your air conditioner does not arrive?

PREPARING FOR INTERVIEW QUESTIONS

The key to a successful interview is preparation. It is surprising how few people prepare for interviews, given that one chance is all you get.

A good method is to run through a practice session with a friend, from the first greeting to your departure. Have your (professional) friend ask questions from your résumé, followed by suggestions for improvement. Then incorporate these improvements into another interview rehearsal with someone else.

TWO VERY IMPORTANT SETS OF SKILLS

Every employer, regardless of the position advertised, seeks people who possess organizational and interpersonal skills. These are often overlooked by candidates; yet if you can describe them well, employers can fairly easily distinguish you from other job seekers.

Organizational Skills

North American employers place great importance on efficiency, regardless of the field of work. Therefore, it is important to convey to employers that you can organize your work and manage your time. Elaborate on your work day. Do you compile a list of things to do? How do you establish priorities? Explain the process you use to accomplish your tasks. For example:

"In every job there is conflict between the things you would like to do and the time it takes to do them. That's why I keep a running list of things outstanding. By continually prioritizing jobs and assessing time available, I'm able to juggle my tasks without missing my deadlines."

Interpersonal Skills

Employers are interested in knowing how you deal with people in different situations: Do you have problems with authority figures? How would you cope with a request for information that you couldn't fulfil? How do you handle rejection? Could you continue to work with someone who had disappointed or insulted you?

Interpersonal skills are better demonstrated through statements of opinion. For example:

"In a work environment, it is crucial that everyone recognizes the seriousness of making and following commitments. I recognize that my boss's performance is assessed by his superior, as mine is assessed by him..."

"In an overseas situation, I'll be particularly attentive to the role played by different authority figures in influencing the success or failure of projects. Overseas communities seem to have a more developed local leadership structure than our highly mobile, unstructured society in Canada. I think it would be important to recognize this hierarchy by having community leaders endorse new projects."

TACTICS FOR ANSWERING QUESTIONS

The interview is one of the few times in your life when you are asked to speak about yourself, your accomplishments, skills and strengths. You may feel uncomfortable "boasting." Here are a few suggestions to help make the task easier.

One of the best tactics is to discuss your skills through a third party. For example:

- "My colleagues tell me the reasons they like working with me are..."
- "All my past employers have mentioned my enthusiasm..."
- "If my friends had to describe three important character traits I possess, they would probably say..."

Another tactic is to mention the reasons for your success, or examples of your strengths:

- "In my previous job I was particularly well-known for..."
- "I always try to understand a situation from my adversary's point of view..."
- "The reasons I have been successful in developing new programs are..."

Develop an *opening theme* when answering questions, in order to reinforce your personality profile. For example, an opening theme response to an overseas project manager's question, "what qualifications and skills do you possess that would make you effective overseas?" might be:

"Throughout my career, both with the International Red Cross and in my numerous volunteer jobs, I have seen myself as a grassroots organizer. Planning, making lists, and communicating with the other people involved are my priorities. These attributes have made me effective in my work. Other skills which have helped me in my career are..."

A response to the same question by a UN project assessment officer might be:

"I have a universal rule which allows me to identify the important facts quickly, regardless of the situation. I always approach new ideas with enthusiasm. And I encourage others by helping them clarify their ideas. This allows me to assess the situation, and also makes me more approachable. My writing and communication skills have also contributed to my effectiveness..."

QUESTIONS AN INTERVIEWER MAY ASK

Thorough preparation for an interview means that you have researched each of the following questions. Don't forget that each answer, if possible, should have an "international component."

General Interview Questions

* "Tell me about yourself."
* "What are your major strengths/weaknesses?"
* "What would your colleagues say if they had to describe your working style?"

Knowledge About the Employer

* "What do you know about this organization?"
* "Why do you want to work with us and not an NGO (or government, private firm, or as a consultant)?"

Overseas Working Conditions

* "Why do you want to work overseas?"
* "What qualifications/skills do you possess that will make you effective overseas?"
* "What working conditions do you anticipate will be different in another culture?"
* "Tell us about your previous overseas experience."

Overseas Living Conditions

* "Have you ever lived through a difficult situation? How did you cope?"
* "Have you been separated from your family or your loved ones for extended periods of time?"
* "Have you ever had to cope with loneliness?"
* "How would you occupy your spare time?"
* "How important is privacy for you? Have you ever lived in situations where you have not had a lot of privacy?"

OPEN-ENDED ENQUIRIES

Most international interviews use open-ended enquiries, such as, "tell me about yourself," or "what do you think of development?" There is no right or wrong answer. Interviewers are really probing for bits of information they might not get through specific questions. It is therefore to your advantage to use these open-ended enquiries to emphasize your most important international, administrative and interpersonal skills.

SITUATIONAL QUESTIONS

One of the most interesting and challenging tactics used by international recruitment officers is the situational question. These usually concern a predicament you might encounter overseas. Trying to come up with a *right* answer can be quite unnerving.

There usually is no clear *right* answer. The recruitment officer is looking for sound judgement and analytical ability. Your worst mistake would be to make a hasty remark without first asking questions and considering the situation carefully. If you are unable to arrive at an answer, you can still score an excellent rating by presenting a carefully thought-out, cautious approach to solving the problem. Here are a few tips to guide you in your answers.

Demonstrate your thinking process to the recruitment officer by *thinking out loud.* Outline important facts for serious consideration. An answer might go like this: "In this situation it would be important to give serious consideration to (these factors). One would have to weigh the importance of (this fact) and see if it is crucial to the assessment. It is only after considering all of these factors that I would be able to make a proper decision."

Explain how you would study a situation. For example: "This is a very delicate situation. The first thing I would do would be to study the facts, and then depending on my findings, I would have a discussion with..." Mention general principles of evaluation such as, "In these circumstances it is best to proceed cautiously, record and investigate the facts. I would refrain from forming an opinion until all the information was compiled."

You should, however, try to provide a concrete answer. State your assumptions prior to giving your assessment. For example: "If one were to assume that (this situation) were true, and that the cultural traits of the society were (these), then it's possible the best approach to this problem would be to..."

Try to prioritize the items for consideration. For example: "It is clear that the major limiting factors in this situation are... and must be considered before looking at less important factors such as..."

State your limitations, and how you would react in light of them. For example: "Since I have never travelled to Southeast Asia and am unfamiliar with the social norms, I might be more cautious and sit and wait until my guide/interpreter returned before making a firm decision."

If uncertain of the situation, make a comparison with a more familiar one. For example: "While I am unfamiliar with the ethical standards binding a United Nations employee, I know that as an NGO employee I would pay a small bribe rather than have ten volunteers spend the night sleeping at the border."

Involve the recruitment officer in your answer by probing, but don't ask more than a few questions; the object is not to demonstrate your interrogation skills, but to show that you think before acting. For example: "Would it be right to assume that..." or, "Are there any policies that would guide me in this situation?"

In some situations the best answer is that you would seek someone else's advice. For example: "If I am a new arrival in the country and am not yet aware of the social customs, I would seek out another expatriate who has had more experience with this situation."

Examples of Situational Questions

* You are a Canadian project officer of a large funding organization, doing an evaluation tour overseas. At one of the projects, you are told by several employees that the expatriate project manager is stealing funds. How would you handle this situation?

* You are a Junior Officer with the UNITED NATIONS DEVELOPMENT PROGRAMME (UNDP) posted in a large Southern city. You are at the airport to meet a visiting expert sent by the FOOD AND AGRICULTURE ORGANIZATION (FAO). The expert has lost her passport and the local airport official insists on putting her in jail despite all pleas. It is late in the evening and you have exhausted every conceivable argument. Suddenly, the official asks for a $25 bribe to free the expert. Would you pay?

* As a teacher posted at a rural African school, you discover another teacher is making sexual demands on students. How would you react?

* As an office manager, you have caught four labourers and one of your most trusted assistants stealing supplies from the warehouse. How would you handle this situation?

* As manager of a work site, one of your employees is asking for a loan and time off to visit a sick family member in another city. Would you grant the request?

* You have just been asked to accompany a very important dignitary on an official three-day visit of a provincial district. During these next three days, you must submit next year's financial requirements to head office. How would you handle this dilemma?

THINGS TO DO BEFORE THE INTERVIEW

The interview and evaluation process actually begin with your first contact with an organization.

You should carefully research the organization. Find out some of the following: the types of programs they conduct in Canada and abroad, the basic structure of the organization, their annual budget, number of employees, and their mandate. Usually this information can be found in a company's annual report. If not, speak to someone who knows something about the organization.

Telephone for a detailed job description (see Chapter 23, Phone Research Techniques). Plan your responses to standard questions based on your reading of the job description. Try to contact a manager beforehand to find out more about the job. Speak to someone who has worked in a similar position overseas. Examples of an opening conversation:

"I'm calling to find out a little more about a job for which I'm scheduled to be interviewed."

"I am doing a little research prior to my interview to ensure that I have a good understanding of what the job entails."

Try beforehand to learn something about your interviewer, such as his or her name and job title. Will it be a structured interview? How long is it likely to last? This information can probably be obtained from a secretary.

Write down at least 10 questions you would like to ask. They should pertain to the company's major projects and your possible role with the company. Avoid questions and remarks about how the company might further your career goals.

Practice reciting out loud your personal and professional qualifications and experience that match the job you seek.

Dress professionally. Males should wear a suit and tie. Women should dress conservatively. If two candidates are equal in ability (and this often happens), the final choice can rest on appearance.

Look organized and prepared. Carry a briefcase containing: pen, notepad, a typed list of references, two extra copies of your résumé and covering letter packaged in envelopes, two or more examples of your past work, such as reports or publications.

THINGS TO DO DURING THE INTERVIEW

You have probably heard the popular theory that interviewers make up their minds during the first five minutes of the interview. It is only human to pass judgement on others. Here are some helpful hints to create a good first impression.

Arrive 15 minutes early. Familiarize yourself with your surroundings, read company newsletters, the bulletin board or something of interest to mention during the interview. Double-check your appearance. Hang your coat, have your arms free when you enter the interview room.

Use a firm handshake when introducing yourself: "Hello, my name is Francis Drummond." If there is an interview team, extend your hand to each member. And, unless otherwise informed, use the titles of Mr. or Ms. and their surnames. As simple as all of this may seem, experience has shown that many candidates are unable to carry this off with confidence.

Sit with your pad and pen ready to make notes (but don't be too obvious about this). You may want to jot down contract terms, key ideas and any follow-up actions that may arise from the interview. Even if you don't make use of the pen and paper, you are signalling to the employer your preparedness.

Be conscious of your nonverbal communication such as a nervous foot tapping or excessive laughter. Sit in a relaxed manner, hands out of your pockets, back straight. Lean forward a little when listening, and back when speaking. Make eye contact with each interviewer.

Be dynamic and project enthusiasm through your voice.

Approach the overseas job interview as a meeting ground in which both parties interview each other. Try to make the recruiter's job easier by feeding him or her information about yourself in logical order.

Allow the recruitment officer to set the pace. Always ask how long the interview will last. But if two-thirds of the interview time has elapsed and you feel the interview team has not covered your important skills (some interviewers are not great at their jobs), this is the time to take the initiative. Example:

"I would like to elaborate on some relevant job experience that would allow you to better analyze my skills."

"I would like to mention a few more factors in my background that could help you assess my qualifications."

"Would you permit me to add a few words about some of my other skills?"

At the end of the interview, thank your interviewers by name while shaking their hands firmly:

"Thank you for your time and consideration. I appreciated this opportunity to learn more about your organization. You have an interesting program and I look forward to hearing from you."

And ask when you may expect an answer.

THINGS TO AVOID DURING THE INTERVIEW

* Do not dominate the conversation. The normal guide is to speak half the time.
* Don't linger on a topic for more than five to eight minutes. Your answers should be short, preferably under three minutes.
* Do not overuse humour; the interview is a serious meeting.
* Never smoke, even if permitted.
* Don't be late. If there is a remote chance that you will be, mitigate the damage by phoning ahead to apologize and explain your delay.

THINGS TO DO AFTER THE INTERVIEW

At the first opportunity, jot down what you could have done better. Use each successive interview to improve your performance for the next.

Call the company at an appointed date to inquire about their decision to hire. If the answer is negative, it is appropriate to ask why you were not considered. If you are too emotionally devastated to ask, call back a day or two later.

"I'm calling to discuss the results of my interview. I would like to ask a few questions... Since I'm interested in profiting from this experience, I was wondering if you would have time to discuss the reasons I did not get the job; how may I improve my chances? May I keep in touch regarding other job openings?"

If the answer is positive, celebrate!

A LAST WORD

Never contact a potential employer without first arranging your thoughts. Explain who you are and what you aspire to. Always describe the background that has brought you to your search for an overseas job. In most interview situations the employer is interested in your thought processes, your flow of ideas, and is not looking for right or wrong answers. Let the interview team see how you analyze information; don't just offer the results of your analysis.

Be prepared. Be confident. Relax, and go for the job you've always wanted!

PART FOUR

What Jobs Are Out There?

27. Jobs by Regions of the World 509

28. Jobs in International Development 561

29. Teaching Abroad 569

30. Freelancing Abroad 595

31. Job Hunting When
    You Return to Canada 603

Chapter 27

Jobs by Regions of the World

You have probably pointed to a world map and said, "How can I find a job in Hong Kong...London...Los Angeles? How exciting that would be!" But is it really possible to focus your job search on a specific country? This chapter will try to answer this question by looking specifically at international job opportunities in eight regions of the world where private-sector jobs for expatriates are most abundant. We have, therefore, concentrated most of our analysis on industrialized countries and emerging markets.

The regions covered are: the United States, Mexico and Latin America, Western Europe, Eastern Europe and Russia, the Middle East, and Asia Pacific. In this chapter we focus mainly on private-sector jobs and, to some extent, opportunities for self-starters and entrepreneurs. The intent is not to provide an exhaustive overview of each region, but rather to highlight current hot job markets and touch on some of the idiosyncrasies of finding work in different parts of the world. We will outline the prospects, strategies and skill require-ments for each region.

The 1990s are an excellent time to be thinking about an international career. Global trade and financial flows are expanding at unprecedented rates. Technological advances have made business communications both quicker and less costly. Alongside these developments, companies are increasingly expanding overseas, creating numerous opportunities for international jobs.

A manager with a Canadian telecommunications concern who has respon-sibility for the Middle East says, "I tell my son, who is going to university now, 'Don't focus on getting a job in North America. Broaden your horizons. The world is small. And from a résumé point of view, it's very valuable to work a couple of years offshore.' "

Be Bold

People who get overseas jobs in the private sector are not necessarily those with the best qualifications, but often they are the most determined. As you read the personal stories at the end of each section in this chapter, you'll find that the men and women who get jobs with international businesses are generally self-starters who have firm goals and make things happen. We all have various amounts of motivation. The lesson is—use all that you've got.

A Canadian lawyer in his thirties took a leave of absence from a large Toronto law firm to earn an MBA degree from the LONDON SCHOOL OF ECONOMICS. With the help of his Canadian law contacts, he was hired for the summer by a Parisian law office. But he returned to the Toronto law firm after several unsuccessful months trying to get a job in business, law or finance in Europe. He has not given up, and has this to say:

"The best advice, after having been through the whole process, is to have a dream and stick to it. The people that have been most successful in obtaining jobs overseas are single-minded people—not those who have a vague notion that they'd like to work abroad or maybe try something different. They are the people who say they know they want to work in finance in London and start early and make all the necessary applications and contacts."

Being Canadian

Being Canadian can be a tremendous advantage in international business. Even though Canada has a tiny population by world standards, it is well known as an active trader and member of the Group of Seven industrialized nations. Most importantly, Canada has an international reputation as a country that doesn't carry a great deal of ideological baggage. For that reason alone, many countries prefer to do business with Canadian firms. A partner in a large Toronto law firm that practices commercial law all over the world put it this way:

"Being Canadian means you're not German or Japanese or American, and that is a remarkable advantage. I think too few Canadian companies understand the extent to which having that Canadian passport or flying that Canadian flag will give you an enormous advantage over your American, Japanese and German competitors...

"Many international firms would welcome a Canadian application. I know dozens of lawyers, accountants and MBAs who couldn't get jobs with Canadian firms. But Americans, Germans and Japanese are doing a megatrade in these new markets and the service industries are really keen to hire Canadians."

Although being Canadian can be an asset because our country is not a dominant one, it can also prove to be a liability for the same reason. In most societies, especially in the corporate world, which schools you studied at and which companies you've worked for are of great importance. Compounding this problem is the fact that neither our universities nor our companies (with a few notable exceptions) are well-known abroad, and even these tend to be overshadowed by their larger American, European, and Japanese counterparts.

Canadian business acumen and university degrees are not inferior. In fact, in most cases they stand up extremely well to foreign scrutiny. The problem lies in convincing potential overseas employers and clients who have never heard of the Canadian company or university. If it is any consolation, this is a handicap we share with job seekers from most small countries.

In your job applications, make sure you describe the position of your university ("one of the top three schools in Canada") or company ("market leader in..."). This should be mentioned directly in your résumé or covering letter and certainly in your direct discussions with future employers. Also, consider the option to study abroad. A degree earned at a well-known institution such as the LONDON SCHOOL OF ECONOMICS or HARVARD will help pave the way for an international career. A prestigious school with an international reputation can certainly help its graduates find jobs.

Where to Work

So, you know you want a job overseas, but where in the world should you go? Many people are equally happy to find a job in Europe or Asia or Latin America. In this case, your job search should focus on regions where demand is strongest for your specific skills and experience. This can be a moving target. The country that was hot for computer programmers yesterday may be stone cold tomorrow.

A big key to success is to go where the action is, where business is booming and there are lots of opportunities. In the field of finance, for example, the action was in New York and London in the mid- to late 1980s. In the early 1990s, it moved to Eastern Europe and Japan. In 1993-94, emerging markets in the Asia Pacific and Latin America were attracting the most capital. In the next years, who knows? There may be finance jobs opening in Lebanon or India, to name just two.

Big infrastructure projects such as airports, highways and electric power projects for which Western expertise is frequently sought tend to move around the world, chasing the healthier economies. Mining and oil and gas exploration follow the latest finds in fuels and minerals, according to a variety of other country- and commodity-specific variables.

Professions in Demand

Every career, every level of expertise has an international component where Canadians are finding work abroad. From the grape picker to the financial analyst, the English teacher to the heavy-duty mechanic, all professions are represented.

If you haven't yet made a definite career choice, ask yourself whether any of the following professions interest you: engineer, geologist, computer specialist, telecommunications expert. Our research shows that these professionals have the best chance of getting a job outside Canada. If none of these avenues appeal to you, what about opportunities in finance, law, the environment, agriculture, medicine, project management, consulting, teaching English, or human resource development? These professions are similarly in demand around the globe, although the choice of countries may be somewhat narrower.

Companies that move people abroad are looking for unique packages of skills that they are unable to hire locally. The strongest combination for an international career is probably engineering with an MBA or law degree, but any double-barrelled combination is a strong ticket. (For more information on skill blocks, please see Chapter 18, Your Career Path.)

In the legal services field, try applying to large worldwide firms like BAKER & MACKENZIE or foreign firms with exchange programs like FRESH FIELDS in London. Because Canadian jurisprudence is based on common law (with the exception of Québec), it is relatively easy to qualify for work in the UK or any other Commonwealth countries.

Accounting is growing more and more international in scope, as a few large firms acquire and form partnerships with smaller firms around the world. ARTHUR ANDERSEN and COOPERS & LYBRAND are just two examples of international chartered accounting firms operating in Canada as well as dozens of other countries. Another option is to work for the financial department of a large international company, such as ROYAL DUTCH SHELL, which moves accountants to overseas posts.

Engineers working in construction will want to try one of the large Canadian firms that have a substantial share of their business overseas, such as SNC-LAVALIN or GOLDER ASSOCIATES. (For a full listing of these and other companies that hire Canadians overseas, see Chapter 32, The Private Sector.)

Whatever your expertise, there are international jobs available. Just remember that determination, persistence, and the single-minded pursuit of your international objective are crucial.

Strategies

There are four principle ways of getting a private-sector job overseas:

1. Apply to a North American company with international operations and try to get transferred abroad.
2. Go to the region where you want to work and try to get hired.
3. Base yourself in Canada and go abroad on short or long-term contracts as a consultant.
4. Start your own international business.

The first of these routes can be both the most comfortable and most secure. If you're successful in getting a transfer, the company will likely pay for the transfer of your family and household goods, and will take care of visas. The benefits often include a housing allowance, tax exemptions, and private schooling for your children.

But it's a competitive route. There is often a long queue in the organization for a transfer. (If you have the necessary working papers for a foreign jurisdiction, they may give you the jump over others.) You will also be expected to work extremely hard—the days when a company moved you overseas to put in a 35-hour week are history.

Don't be too choosy about where you will go. The human resources manager with a large international oil company says everybody wants to move to London, but she can never staff all the company's open positions in Nigeria. If you do agree to take a posting in Nigeria, which is considered difficult and dangerous, you will most likely be offered a more attractive destination the next time around.

The second route is to move overseas, possibly as a student, and look for work from there. This path is more or less successful depending on the person and region in question, and will be discussed in greater depth later in the chapter. But a few general tips: cold calls from Canada do not work, nor do a rash of CVs sent out to foreign companies—you have to go there. Some experienced overseas workers suggest you save enough for a two- or three-week exploratory trip where you meet with local officials, people in your field and Canadian trade officials. As one expert suggested, what you can learn about the market grows exponentially every day you spend there soaking up information.

The third route, to base yourself in Canada and go abroad on short or long-term contracts, is typically open only to people who have built up a considerable network of good contacts and specialized expertise. International consulting work is competitive and expensive. There is an active grapevine among international companies and organizations, and consultants must work hard at establishing a reputation for quality.

The fourth and final route has become increasingly common among young graduates, especially in Asia Pacific and Eastern Europe. It is discussed at length in the applicable regional sections.

Visas

While a Canadian passport is well-suited to an international career, having a second passport is always an asset. That's because those precious work visas— so important yet so hard to come by—are easier to get when you can claim citizenship in the country you're working in. If you have a relative from another country (no matter how distant), it is worth making inquiries with the appropriate consulate or embassy as to whether your distant roots might qualify you for citizenship or immigrant status.

Always verify visa information before heading to a foreign country. Work visas are almost always necessary to work legally at a full-time job in a foreign country. In a few countries, a work visa can be applied for locally, but more often you must have one before leaving Canada. By the same token, it is almost impossible to get a working visa without a firm job offer. If you are hired by a large, international company, the firm will take care of the bureaucratic paperwork and usually pay any expenses to do with visas. The importance of confirming visa requirements with embassies or consulates before leaving Canada cannot be stressed too strongly. Visa regulations change all the time, and the information in this book or any other book may well be out of date by the time you read it.

A few countries with high demand for skilled labour will allow you to arrive on a tourist visa, look for work, and then, when you have a firm job offer, leave the country briefly to apply for a work visa from a neighbouring country.

In addition to speaking with visa officials, it is always worth canvassing people who have lived in the regions where you want to work for other practical (and usually unofficial) advice. Countries in Asia, Latin America and Eastern Europe, where English-language teachers are in great demand, may not require work visas, or may simply turn a blind eye to infractions. The same holds true for casual jobs in the service industry in some countries.

If you plan to travel to a foreign country to explore job possibilities or business opportunities, be wary about telling immigration officials that you are looking for work. You may not have the correct visa, and might be turned away. It's usually better to say you're a tourist if you have no intention of working on this particular trip. A self-employed Canadian journalist who travels around the world writing about the banking industry for some 40 trade publications says he almost never tells officials he is going there to work.

Language and Culture

Speaking the local language is a valuable, if not crucial, skill for any type of overseas employment. In a few countries, however, including Singapore and the Netherlands, mastering the local language is not as important. While English is clearly emerging as the language of international business, almost all overseas employees have second-language skills.

Traditionally, some of the soft skills of international relations discussed elsewhere in this book have not been considered as important by the private sector. But this attitude is changing. Large international companies spend thousands of dollars training their overseas workers in crosscultural skills, which are essential to effectiveness in an overseas environment. International MBA graduates are required to take courses in crosscultural management and communications.

Clearly, an international skills set is increasingly crucial to landing international work. In some fields, such as oil exploration and computer software design, companies are looking for trained and experienced engineers for particular jobs they have to fill. But they assume you can quickly learn the "soft" skills of tolerance, patience and getting along with people of another culture. Even when these skills aren't yet considered critical for your work, it can't help but enhance your job prospects to refine them. At the very least, it will help you enjoy your posting.

A LAST WORD

The opportunities for Canadians around the world vary depending on your skills, experience and the economic conditions of the region or country you're targeting. While some professions are constantly in demand (such as medical and oil industry personnel in the Gulf States), economic and political conditions change rapidly, and so does job demand. Your best preparation is to read the most up-to-date and solid information you can get your hands on and talk to as many knowledgeable people as you can, before targeting your job search.

Much can be accomplished before you leave home, but in most cases, there is no substitute for spending a few weeks in the country of your choice on an exploratory mission. Best of luck!

RESOURCES

Country-specific Guides

These books and web sites are listed at the end of each region. (Exceptions are Global Guides listed below and Africa, which has no section since there are few conventional, private sector opportunities there.) Most of these guides were chosen because they are career guides focused on a particular country or region, or because of their practical, country-specific advice on business or day-to-day living. While travel guides are not listed here, they can often provide good advice; see Chapter 12, Crosscultural Travel.

Also consult the Resources sections in the following chapters: for general crosscultural skills see Chapter 1, The Effective Overseas Employee; for the more practical aspects of living overseas see Chapter 3, Living Overseas and Chapter 12, Crosscultural Travel; for material which is helpful to all, but focuses on crosscultural business skills, see Chapter 7, The Canadian Identity in the International Workplace; and for books on the practice of international business (such as how to import and export) see Chapter 33, Services for International Businesses & Entrepreneurs.

Global Guides

These books provide snap-shot pictures of country conditions and are excellent resources to consult before an interview, prior to a consulting visit abroad, or when you are moving abroad for a new, international posting. Large university libraries also have excellent yearbooks providing factual information on the politics, economy, geography, and culture of every country in the world. We have listed just a few here. If you are looking for web sites with country profiles, see the Resources for the section on Country Information on the Internet in Chapter 21, The Internet Job Search. If you're looking for Job Search Directories, this Resources section is in Chapter 22, Resources for the International Job Search.

Background Notes Series 📖
Annual ➤ Department of State, CA/PA, US Government Printing Office, Room 5807, Washington, DC 20520-4818, USA; $42.50/set, $1.25/copy; VISA, MC; (202) 512-1800, fax (202) 512-2250 ▪ A series of well-written, factual pamphlets produced by the US Department of State's geographical bureaus. Includes information on each country's geography, people, history, government, political conditions, economy and foreign relations. Visit www.access.gpo.gov/su_docs/, the distributor's web site. [ID:1256]

Canada Year Book 📖 💻
1997, Statistics Canada, 517 pages ➤ Renouf Books, 129 Algoma Rd., Ottawa, Ontario K1B 2W8; $54.95, CD-ROM $74.95; credit cards; (613) 745-2665, fax (613) 745-7660 ▪ This book is published every two years by Statistics Canada and serves as a vital reference resource. It provides an up-to-date picture of the social, economic, and cultural life of Canada. It's a great book to bring as a gift

or as a handy reference for all the questions your overseas friends will ask you when you travel overseas. Visit the publisher's web site at www.renoufbooks.com. [ID:2775]

The CIA World Factbook 💻

www.odci.gov/cia/publications/nsolo/wfb-all.htm ▪ This is one of the most authoritative sources available on international geography. Information on current political, economic, and social conditions is provided as well as a discussion of the country's physical geography and resources. Very comprehensive, but the juicy stuff may have been left out! [ID:2580]

Country Backgrounders 📖

1994, 8 pages each ➤ Asia Pacific Foundation, Suite 666, 999 Canada Place, Vancouver, B.C. V6C 3E1; $6.50 each or $75 for set; VISA, MC; (604) 684-5986, fax (604) 681-1370 ▪ A series of booklets on 12 Asia Pacific countries and Canada's economic relationship with each of them. Includes key facts and figures, economic and trade statistic comparisons, Canada's ranking among major trading partners, imports and exports, main sectors of opportunity for Canadian business, and more. Visit the distributor's web site at www.apfc.ca. [ID:1686]

Craighead's International Business Travel and Relocation Guide to 78 Countries: 1996-97 📖

Annual, 4,699 pages, 3 vols. ➤ Gale Research Inc., 835 Penobscot Bldg., 645 Griswold Street, Detroit, MI 48226-4094, USA; US$575; credit cards; (800) 877-4253 ext. 1330, fax (800) 414-5043; Available in large libraries ▪ An indispensable guide for anyone who needs information on the business practices, economies, customs, communication, tours, attractions and highlights of 78 countries worldwide. Provides details of local customs, arrival procedures, money matters, health services, and sources of additional information for those relocating overseas. Chapters on individual countries, extensive background information for personnel officers and employees going abroad. Covers recruiting guidelines for overseas personnel and information sources. [ID:1144]

Culture Shock! Series 📖

Occasional, *E. Webster,* Graphic Arts Center Publishing Co. ➤ Raincoast Books, 8680 Cambie Street, Vancouver, B.C. V6P 6M9; $17.50 each; VISA, MC; (800) 663-5714, fax (800) 565-3770 ▪ Guides to the customs and etiquette of various cultures. Titles for several countries in Asia, Europe, and North America. [ID:1382]

Culturgrams: The Nations Around Us 📖

1998, David M. Kennedy Center for International Studies, Two vols., 620 pages ➤ Kennedy Center Publications, Brigham Young University, 280 HRCB, Provo, UT 84602, USA; US$80; credit cards; (800) 528-6279, fax (801) 378-7075 ▪ Four-page summaries of the basic features of 164 cultures around the world. They cover customs, manners, lifestyles and other specialized information for those with interest but little time. Well worth the money! Free catalogue. Visit www.encarta.com. [ID:1085]

Current History 📖 💻

9/year ➤ Current History, 4225 Main Street, Philadelphia, PA 19127-9989, USA; US$39.75/year; VISA, MC, AMEX; (215) 482-4464, fax (215) 482-9197, curhistpub@aol.com ▪ This magazine is useful for its region by region annual summaries. Each issue focuses on one region or country, providing annual coverage on China, the former Soviet Union, the Middle East, Latin America, Africa and South and Southeast Asia. It also has a country by country "Month in Review" feature. Excellent if you're about to travel to a region and need a quick overview of its current political trends; order back issues or visit the indexed web site, www.currenthistory.com. [ID:2794]

Current World Leaders 📖 💻

3/year ➤ International Academy at Santa Barbara, 5385 Hollister Avenue, Suite 5385, Santa Barbara, CA 931111-2305, USA; US$195; credit cards; (805) 683-4927, fax (805) 683-4637 ▪ Provides information on the people, politics, economics and international relations of over 190 countries. A complementary publication, *International Issues,* integrates feature stories with official reports, articles and speeches from respected authorities in the field. Their web site, www.iasb.org/cwl, offers information on countries, territories, colonies and international organizations, and will provide a research engine specific to this subject in 1998. [ID:1184]

Directory of EC Information Sources 📖
Annual, 1250 pages ➤ Euroconfidentiel s.a., BP 29, Rixensart, B-1330, BELGIUM; £180; credit cards; (32) (2) 652 02 84, fax (32) (2) 653 01 80 ▪ A comprehensive listing of over 6,000 sources of European Community information, including trade associations, senior EC officials, law and consultancy firms, embassies and others. [ID:1313]

Do's and Taboos Around the World 📖
1993, *Roger E. Axtell*, 208 pages ➤ John Wiley & Sons, 22 Worchester Drive, Rexdale, Ontario M9W 1L1; $14.95; credit cards; (800) 567-4797, fax (800) 565-6802 ▪ In a lively blend of tips, facts and cautionary tales, this fascinating guide tells travellers how to dress, exchange gifts, deal with unusual food, pronounce names and interpret body language in 96 countries. Visit the distributor's web site at www.wiley.com/products/worldwide/canada. [ID:1021]

Guide to Export Services 📖
1997, 26 pages ➤ InfoCentre, Department of Foreign Affairs and International Trade (DFAIT), 125 Sussex Dr., Ottawa, Ontario K1A 0G2; free; (800) 267-8376, fax (613) 996-9709 ▪ InfoCentre, the public information office of DFAIT, has over 2,000 publications on the subject of international trade. A variety of country-specific booklets containing detailed economic overviews, tips on doing business, customs, and foreign exchange regulations are available. [ID:1497]

Guide to Living Abroad 📖
Annual, *Louise M. Guido,* 150 pages ➤ Living Abroad Publishing, 199 Nassau Street, Princeton, NJ 08540, USA; US$30; Amex; (609) 924-9302, fax (609) 924-7844 ▪ Published in 10 volumes, each containing practical general information of interest to expatriates, such as health, buying a house, immigration matters, personal security, and education. The guides also have a section on regional travel. Visit the distributor's web site at www.livingabroad.com. [ID:1432]

International Retail Price Comparisons (Post Indexes) 📖
Monthly ➤ Indexes Section, Prices Division, Statistics Canada, 13th Floor, Jean Talon Bldg., Ottawa, Ontario K1A OT6; free; (613) 951-0121, fax (613) 951-2848 ▪ Post indexes are an excellent way of calculating the approximate cost of living overseas. Compiled monthly for hundreds of cities abroad, the indexes are designed for Canadian civil servants and military personnel (since the federal government compensates employees for housing and fuel costs, these are not included in the indexes). Price comparisons are given for such family expenditures as food consumed in the house, meals in restaurants, household maintenance and supplies, domestic help, clothing, transportation, health and personal care, reading and recreation. Although the cost of a subscription to these indexes is high—$275/year for monthly updates on 1-10 cities—you can obtain free information over the phone for one city. [ID:2555]

Kiss, Bow or Shake Hands: How to Do Business in Sixty Countries 📖
1994, *Terri Morrison, George A. Borden, Wayne A. Conaway,* Bob Adams, 440 pages ➤ Intercultural and Community Development Resources (ICDR), P.O. Box 32108, Millwoods Station, Edmonton, Alberta T6K 4C2; $25; VISA, Amex; (800) 378-3199, fax (403) 462-1925, icdr@compusmart.ab.ca ▪ Provides current data on foreign business and social practices. Visit the distributor's web site at www.compusmart.ab.ca/icdr. [ID:2383]

Oxfam Country Profiles 📖
1996, OXFAM UK, 64 pages each ➤ Fernwood Books Ltd., P.O. Box 9409, Stn. A, Halifax, N.S. B3K 5S3; $7.95-$9.95; VISA; (902) 422-3302, fax (902) 422-3179 ▪ This series focuses on the lives of ordinary people and the major development issues that affect them. Over 70 country profiles available. [ID:2483]

Tips for Travellers Series 📖
Occasional, US Department of State ➤ Department of State, CA/PA, US Government Printing Office, Room 5807, Washington, DC 20520-4818, USA; $1 each; VISA, MC; (202) 512-1800, fax (202) 512-2250 ▪ Series includes the Middle East & North Africa, Sub-Saharan Africa, South Asia, Caribbean, Republic of China, Russia and the Newly Independent States, and Central and South America. Visit the publisher's web site at www.access.gpo.gov/su_docs/. [ID:1288]

Africa

We have not included a section on Africa in this chapter as there are few conventional private sector jobs open to expatriates. There are, however, many jobs in Africa in the field of international development. Consult the Resources for Chapter 28, Jobs in International Development and Chapter 35, Nongovernmental Organizations.

The United States
STILL THE HIGH-TECH MECCA

Without a doubt, the United States offers the most opportunities for Canadian professionals who want to work in another country. This huge market of some 250 million people is right next door, the working language is English, and the customs, training, and business culture are similar to our own.

Even before the Free Trade Agreement (FTA) was signed in 1989, Canada and the US were each other's largest trading partners. Since then, the opportunities for Canadian companies, entrepreneurs, consultants and professionals have never been better. US demand for university educated, experienced workers in the high technology field, especially the computer industry, looks insatiable at the moment.

In this chapter, international work in the US is different from that described for other countries in this book. Many Canadians who move to work in the US eventually settle and immigrate there. US jobs offered to Canadians are often full-time and permanent. This contrasts with international work in other countries, which tends to be for two- or three-year assignments.

It often seems Canadians find more to damn than to praise about the US. But keep an open mind. As similar as it is, the US is still a foreign country where you'll gain valuable experience—and we haven't even mentioned the better weather!

Where the Jobs Are

The hottest job market right now is the voracious computer industry. The FTA (replaced by the North American Free Trade Agreement, or NAFTA, in January 1994) has meant Canadians are often regarded by high-tech companies in the same light as Americans. Demand is strong for software programmers, networking specialists, systems engineers, systems analysts, systems architects, hardware designers, data processing professionals and database administrators. In late 1994, the industry had an enviable unemployment rate of just two per cent, and most of the unemployed were new graduates or older middle managers who had moved away from the technology.

The Pacific Northwest, including Oregon and Washington State, is emerging as an important region for software design. Washington, D.C. and suburbs in Virginia are strong on hardware jobs, while New York City is growing in computer systems design, especially for financial applications. California, though a more mature market, is still booming. There are literally hundreds of Windows programming jobs available in California's Silicon Valley for experienced programmers. Salaries are equal to those offered to Americans, and usually higher than what you'll get in Canada, especially when combined with the lower cost of living south of the border.

The emphasis is on experience. Like most other sectors, the computer industry wants workers with a few years' job experience under their belts. A management consulting firm in New Jersey that recruits Canadian "techies" says the minimum requirements are a college degree in math, computer science, physics or business administration and two years' experience in the industry.

Other Job Opportunities

Job demand is strongest in the most highly-specialized and highly-trained careers. If you're an experienced microbiologist, for example, you should have no trouble finding a job in the US.

Despite a recent glut of MBAs, experienced professionals in the finance and banking industries, including financial analysts, investment dealers and accountants, can often find US jobs. But the glut of MBAs does make finding your first job a tougher assignment than it was in the late 1980s. Lawyers with unique specialties should be able to tailor a career to meet US requirements. Specialized Canadian doctors are often wooed by US hospitals and clinics, and nurses can usually find work in some states, but nursing salaries tend to be lower than at home. Experienced teachers can often find work in private or public schools, but these are usually in states offering the lowest salaries.

To find out whether there is demand in the US for people in your trade or profession, check with the union or professional association in the state or city you want to move to. The careers section of the *New York Times* and other large city newspapers will give you an idea of which professions are in demand and where.

International jobs with the UNITED NATIONS in New York or the IMF and WORLD BANK in Washington are open to Canadians and are discussed in Chapter 36, United Nations, and Chapter 38, International Organizations.

The US is a huge job market and it's close by—it's likely that any job you can think of is filled by a Canadian somewhere south of the border.

NAFTA

The free trade pact has made life easier for members of some 60 professions who can now cross the Canada-US border to work for one to two years without applying for a visa. (See table below for a partial list of those professions.)

If you fall into one of the lucky professions, all you need to do is present proof of Canadian citizenship, proof of your licence or degree, the contract with your US employer, and $50, to a US official at any border crossing. (Most professionals exempted under Chapter 15, Section 2 of NAFTA already had privileged access before 1989, but the process was more cumbersome, requiring proof of special expertise and several letters of reference.) If you qualify under the exempt-professions category, your spouse and children may accompany you but they won't be permitted to work. Children are allowed to attend public school.

The trade pact also eliminates the need for a labour market test when a company moves its staff south of the border. Instead of having to prove that a certain employee from Canada is the only one who can do the job, the firm merely has to show that she is an engineer, for example, and has a work contract in hand.

LIST OF SELECT PROFESSIONS UNDER NAFTA		
GENERAL	**SCIENTIST**	**MEDICAL/ALLIED**
Accountant	Agriculturalist	Dentist
Architect	Animal Breeder	Dietician
Computer Systems Analyst	Animal Scientist	Medical Laboratory
Economist	Apiculturist	Technologist
Engineer	Astronomer	Nutritionist
Forester	Biochemist	Occupational Therapist
Graphic Designer	Biologist	Pharmacist
Hotel Manager	Chemist	Pharmacologist
Industrial Designer	Dairy Scientist	Physicist
Interior Designer	Entomologist	Plant Breeder
Land Surveyor	Epidemiologist	Poultry Scientist
Landscape Architect	Geneticist	Soil Scientist
Lawyer	Geologist	Zoologist
Librarian	Geochemist	
Management Consultant	Geophysicist	
Mathematician	Horticulturist	**TEACHER**
Physician	Meteorologist	College
Physiotherapist	Scientific Technician	Seminary
Psychologist	Social Worker	University
Range Conservationist	Silviculturist	
Recreational Therapist	Technical Publications	
Registered Nurse	Writer	
Research Assistant,	Urban Planner	
University	Vocational Counsellor	
Veterinarian		

It's worth keeping in mind that NAFTA is really about *trade* and the free movement of capital. In contrast with the provisions of the European Union, which allows its citizens to seek work anywhere in the 16 member countries, NAFTA does not guarantee the free movement of labour. For most job seekers, the rules of employment haven't changed. And a Canadian won't find it any easier to get permanent residency status in the US, post-NAFTA.

But it *is* easier for Canadian companies and investors to do business and to trade in the US since the FTA took effect in 1989. Visitors who are on business for their Canadian employers find it simpler and less bureaucratic to travel back and forth. So do people who work for a Canadian company that carries on substantial trade in the US and those investing a substantial amount in an enterprise in the US.

Canadian companies, large and small, are benefiting from the low tariffs and easier access, as well as from a low Canadian dollar (in 1995) which makes Canadian exports more attractive. A 1994 study (by Québec's Caisse de dépôt pension fund) showed Québec's exports of high value, low tariff goods expanded 90 per cent in the four years following the signing of the accord, while total Canadian exports in that sector grew 49 per cent.

Entrepreneurs and businesspeople who are considering relocating to the US will need to conduct market research and have a business plan before making a successful move.

The Green Card and Other Types of Visas

There are several other US work visas available to Canadians. The rules change, so make sure you check with the US consulate before attempting to work in the US.

The famous Green Card signals permanent residency status and is extremely difficult to come by unless you marry an American. Unlike most countries, the US offers a "fast-track" route for permanent residency to people who are deemed truly unique, but you might have to be CEO of a Fortune 500 company.

The US offers a yearly lottery for several thousand immigrant visas, or Green Cards, specifying each year which nationalities may apply. Canadians are rarely eligible because Canada is considered a "high admission" state. Canadian residents of another nationality may be eligible—call the US consulate nearest you for further details. Beware of advertisements that occasionally run in Canadian newspapers offering legal help with the US lottery. You don't need a lawyer if you are an "eligible" nationality, and Canadians cannot apply anyway.

There is also a three-year visa with a possibility of extension available to the same professionals who qualify under NAFTA, but in 1994 only 65,000 of these visas were available worldwide.

A Canadian studying at a US university may apply for a visa to work on campus during the school year. You aren't supposed to work off campus, but some students do find off-campus jobs "under the table."

There is another visa (known as the E2 or Treaty Investor Visa) for people interested in starting a small business in the US. Prospective applicants require a minimum US $500,000 capital investment in order to qualify. In other words, it's *not* awarded to individuals investing in small or marginal businesses solely to earn a living.

Finally, it is illegal to enter the US as a tourist and then look for work. Of course, many backpackers, students and other travellers do, but working for cash in the black market as an illegal immigrant is not the advised route.

Job Search Strategies

The job search process is pretty much the same in the US as in Canada. Résumé styles, phone techniques, interview styles and professional skill profiling are exactly the same. Canadians, with their similar education systems and way of life, are often considered "the same as Americans" by US employers. However, you are probably unfamiliar with the US job geography and will therefore have to do a lot of research and networking. Calling, making contacts via your profession, and a job-search holiday are good methods.

Besides a visa, two things are generally needed to work in the US: specialized training (usually including at least one university degree), and experience. But there are exceptions to every rule and Canadian students have found good jobs with US firms. (See Personal Stories.)

There are four main strategies to consider in looking for your American job. Some of these routes apply to all international job-hunting strategies and have been touched on in the introduction to this chapter. They are explored in more depth in Chapter 20, The Job Search.

One route is to apply directly to an American branch or subsidiary of a Canadian company. For instance, NORTHERN TELECOM LTD. and its research arm BELL-NORTHERN RESEARCH have skilled Canadians working at their research operations in several states.

Another strategy is to get a job with a US, international or large Canadian company in Canada and let it be known that you'd like to transfer to the US when possible. Companies that consider themselves international are most likely to transfer employees around the world. If you're interested in moving south, it makes sense to research what specific skills and experience the company needs in the US branch. Remember, it is most often you who must take the initiative. Do not expect your employer to work hard at transferring you to the US.

An increasingly successful route is to apply directly to a US employer. Obviously, this strategy works best when your sector is experiencing a boom, the way the computer industry is in the 1990s.

Some Canadian professionals are making a good living by commuting to contracts in the US from a home base in Canada. It is easiest when you're on the preferred list of professions under NAFTA (see box above). Telecommunications engineers, computer trainers with specialized areas of expertise, and systems designers are finding consulting work this way.

Students

The US is not a mecca for foreign student jobs, but every year some Canadian students manage to find work in their fields or in the service industry through ingenuity and persistence. Like everyone else, students must have a job offer before leaving for the US. There are also jobs for students available at international agencies and through various exchange programs. If you're graduating from a well-recognized computer degree program, you should consider applying directly to US firms. Co-op university programs in either computer science or engineering, which include stints working in industry, are proving a useful ticket for graduates seeking jobs in the US. (See Resources at the end of this section for more information.)

Lifestyle

Even though the US is similar to Canada, it *is* a different country. Experiences south of the border vary widely, depending on which region you live in and whether you work in a big city or small town. Except for high housing costs in many large cities and parts of California, Canadians tend to be enthusiastic about cheap housing, low taxes, rock bottom gas and food prices and the lower cost of living in general. American university education is also held in high esteem, although it's expensive. Canadians invariably praise the weather. On the other side of the scale, Canadians living there complain about the high crime rate in many parts of the US, more expensive health insurance and "too many fundamentalist religious types."

PERSONAL STORIES

• In 1993, four UNIVERSITY OF TORONTO law students finishing second year were discussing what they would do for the summer, and decided then and there to apply to American law firms for summer work. After some research and the mailing of many CVs, all four of them managed to get summer jobs in the US, and one had to choose between two offers, in California or New York City. He chose to work for a New York patent law firm, where he earned US$22,000 for the summer and was treated royally, with frequent lunches and dinners at company expense and limousine service home whenever he had to work after 9 p.m. The firm offered him a job after graduation, but agreed to wait a year while he articled in Toronto, so that he could qualify to practise law in Canada. At the age of 28, he's earning more than US$100,000 and loving the job and the city. A definite advantage: he had an engineering degree before deciding to become a patent lawyer. Patent law offices are eager to hire people with strong scientific backgrounds.

• A young financial analyst who specialized in the telecommunications industry for a large Toronto-based pension fund accepted a job offer with a small, high-tech company based in New York City that manufactured a crucial component for personal computers. He wrote an innovative business plan that managed to attract $5 million in investment and a takeover offer from the giant computer-chip maker, Intel. He was hired by Intel as marketing manager for Europe and is now working for Intel out of Oxford, England. He plans to transfer to Singapore soon. He says, "There are excellent opportunities in both financial analysis and computers in the US. The US is a mecca for computer work and it is very easy for talented engineers to get work permits. Financial analysis may be a little more difficult since there is a glut of MBAs."

• A software engineer got a job with BELL-NORTHERN RESEARCH (BNR) in Ottawa and two years later, transferred to BNR's offices in Richardson, Texas. She is enjoying her work in software analysis, design and development, as well as the lifestyle and climate. "We live in the suburbs of Dallas," she writes.

"The lifestyle is comfortable, the cost of living is low, the crime rate is about five times that of Toronto!" Her husband is not allowed to work without a degree and is attending university instead. They would like to stay a few more years and then possibly move somewhere else within the US. "Come on down y'all—Richardson Texas is the telecommunications corridor of the USA and there are lots of opportunities," she adds.

• A man in his mid-forties certified to teach a specialized computer science program, lives in Toronto with his family, but spends a lot of time south of the border, training computer systems people with US firms. "One way to get started in this field is to work for a computer manufacturer or reseller and gain valuable training, and then strike out on your own," he advises. He warns that you must be prepared for the ups and downs of entrepreneurship. "I had a pot of money, about $40,000, that I was prepared to sink into the business, and if it hadn't worked by the time I'd spent it, I would have had to get a job." He had computer sales experience to fall back on. "Your success depends on how well-known you are in the industry. If you're known and respected, then you can get to travel," he adds. He advises anyone pursuing the consulting route that it's important to live near a large airport, otherwise you'll waste too much time travelling.

RESOURCES

United States

Access North America 📖 💻
Monthly ➤ InfoCentre, Department of Foreign Affairs and International Trade (DFAIT), 125 Sussex Dr., Ottawa, Ontario K1A 0G2; (800) 267-8376, fax (613) 996-9709 ▪ A monthly newsletter of the Access North America Program. Provides news about government activities, visas, and programs and publications under the North American Free Trade Agreement (NAFTA). Published as a supplement to the *CanadExport Newsletter*. Also available on their web site under the heading "Trade" at www.dfait-maeci.gc.ca. [ID:1636]

American Cultural Patterns: A Cross-Cultural Perspective 📖
1991, *Edward C. Stewart, Milton J. Bennett,* Intercultural Press, 208 pages ➤ Intercultural and Community Development Resources (ICDR), P.O. Box 32108, Millwoods Station, Edmonton, Alberta T6K 4C2; $25; VISA, Amex; (800) 378-3199, fax (403) 462-1925, icdr@compusmart.ab.ca ▪ Used extensively in international studies, and as a handbook in crosscultural training. Addresses practical crosscultural issues; distinguishes between "assumptions" and "values." Contrasts the analytical thinking and language of Americans with other cultures. Divides culture into patterns of activity, social relations, and perceptions of the world and oneself. Visit the distributor's web site at www.compusmart.ab.ca/icdr. [ID:1335]

American Ways: A Guide for Foreigners 📖
1988, *Gary Althen,* Intercultural Press, 192 pages ➤ Intercultural and Community Development Resources (ICDR), P.O. Box 32108, Millwoods Station, Edmonton, Alberta T6K 4C2; $22; VISA, Amex; (800) 378-3199, fax (403) 462-1925, icdr@compusmart.ab.ca ▪ Designed for non-Americans who want to understand the "strange ways" of the Americans they meet. Visit the distributor's web site at www.compusmart.ab.ca/icdr. [ID:1027]

Border Crossings: American Interactions with Israelis 📖
1995, *Lucy Shahar, David Kurz,* Intercultural Press, 202 pages ➤ Intercultural and Community Development Resources (ICDR), P.O. Box 32108, Millwoods Station, Edmonton, Alberta T6K 4C2; $24; VISA, Amex; (800) 378-3199, fax (403) 462-1925, icdr@compusmart.ab.ca ▪ The first

systematic analysis of American-Israeli cultural differences in commercial, bureaucratic, professional and social settings. Visit the distributor's web site at www.compusmart.ab.ca/icdr. [ID:2396]

Career City 💻
www.careercity.com ▪ This site offers advice on a number of valuable job hunting skills, such as writing résumés, interview strategies, and the basics of job hunting. Job postings are limited to the US with a heavy emphasis on computer-related employment. If you need information on beginning a job search, this is a good site, but for the actual search, it is of limited use. [ID:2487]

A Common Core: Thais and Americans 📖
1989, *John Paul Fieg, Elizabeth Mortlock,* Intercultural Press, 120 pages ➤ Intercultural and Community Development Resources (ICDR), P.O. Box 32108, Millwoods Station, Edmonton, Alberta T6K 4C2; $18; VISA, Amex; (800) 378-3199, fax (403) 462-1925, icdr@compusmart.ab.ca ▪ Emphasizes both the commonalities and the differences between Thais and Americans, by examining attitudes towards individualism, self-reliance, saving face, competition, group harmony, and the expression of negative emotion. Visit www.compusmart.ab.ca/icdr, the distributor's web site. [ID:1024]

Crossborder Tax and Transactions 💻
www.crossborder.com ▪ An informative site for people doing business or investing internationally, specifically between Canada and the US. The site is maintained by an international tax lawyer and provides updated Canadian and US trade laws. [ID:2757]

Directory of American Firms Operating in Foreign Countries 📖
1996 ➤ Uniworld Business Publications, 257 Central Park West, New York, NY 10024, USA; US$220; (212) 496-2448, fax (212) 769-0413; Available in large libraries ▪ Lists some 2,600 American companies with more than 19,000 subsidiaries and affiliates in 127 foreign countries. One volume on US firms with foreign operations, two volumes on countries with US firms operating there. Individual country editions are also available; prices range from US$29-$99 each. Visit the distributor's web site at www.uniworldbp.com. [ID:1272]

A Fair Go for All: Australian and American Interactions 📖
1991, *George W. Renwick,* Intercultural Press, 96 pages ➤ Intercultural and Community Development Resources (ICDR), P.O. Box 32108, Millwoods Station, Edmonton, Alberta T6K 4C2; $17; VISA, Amex; (800) 378-3199, fax (403) 462-1925, icdr@compusmart.ab.ca ▪ Explores similarities and reveals points of potential conflict between Australians and Americans. Cultural trainers examine a variety of issues, and offer guidelines for managing interpersonal relations more effectively. Visit the distributor's web site at www.compusmart.ab.ca/icdr. [ID:1317]

Get the Right Visa:
To Work or Do Business in the United States or Mexico Under NAFTA 📖
1994, *Mark Ivener,* 136 pages ➤ Self-Counsel Press, 1481 Charlotte Road, North Vancouver, B.C. V7J 1H1; $11.95; VISA, MC; (604) 986-3366, fax (604) 986-3947, sales@self-counsel.com ▪ If you are expanding an existing business, starting a new venture, investing, or looking for employment, getting into the US needn't be difficult if you know what kind of visa you need. This book explains all there is to know on the subject. Visit the distributor's web site at www.self-counsel.com. [ID:1571]

How to Get a Job in America 📖
1997, *Roger Jones,* 224 pages ➤ How To Books Ltd., 3 Newtec Place, Magdalen Road, Oxford, OX4 1RE, UK; £10.99; credit cards; (44) (1752) 202-301, fax (44) (1865) 202-331 ▪ Information on the range of jobs available, the locations, pay, and conditions, and how to get hired. Also includes information on US immigration rules and regulations. Essential reading for anyone intending to work in the US. [ID:1673]

Living and Working in America 📖
1997, *Steve Mills,* 222 pages ➤ How To Books Ltd., 3 Newtec Place, Magdalen Road, Oxford, OX4 1RE, UK; £12.99; credit cards; (44) (1752) 202-301, fax (44) (1865) 202-331 ▪ A highly readable

and informative book on American rules and regulations on immigration, plus work and lifestyle prospects for expatriates. [ID:1670]

Living in the USA 📖
1996, *C. William Gay,* Intercultural Press, 219 pages ➤ Intercultural and Community Development Resources (ICDR), P.O. Box 32108, Millwoods Station, Edmonton, Alberta T6K 4C2; $23; VISA, Amex; (800) 378-3199, fax (403) 462-1925, icdr@compusmart.ab.ca ■ Practical advice that makes American lifestyles comprehensible to the foreigner. Widely used in ESL classrooms and by corporations, international organizations, governmental and nongovernmental agencies. Sprinkled with American idioms, a delight for teaching and orienting the newcomer. Visit the distributor's web site at www.compusmart.ab.ca/icdr. [ID:1316]

Management in Two Cultures: Bridging the Gap between US and Mexican Managers 📖
1995, *Eva Kras,* Intercultural Press, 126 pages ➤ Intercultural and Community Development Resources (ICDR), P.O. Box 32108, Millwoods Station, Edmonton, Alberta T6K 4C2; $23; VISA, Amex; (800) 378-3199, fax (403) 462-1925, icdr@compusmart.ab.ca ■ Pinpoints major differences in culture and management style, and examines areas of conflict including religion, education, nationalist feelings, and basic values. Offers recommendations to both US and Mexican managers on working together. Visit the distributor's web site at www.compusmart.ab.ca/icdr. [ID:1351]

Summer Jobs USA 📖
Annual, Peterson's Guides ➤ Capricorn Business Services, Inc., 28 Clear Lake Ave., West Hill, Ontario M1C 4L6; $26.95; credit cards; (416) 282-3331, fax (416) 282-0015 ■ Lists 20,000 job vacancies in the US, from arts and crafts instructors, to nurses, wranglers and washers-up! Includes advice on visa and other requirements for non-US citizens, plus employer comments on the advantages of particular jobs. [ID:1591]

Understanding Cultural Differences: Germans, French and Americans 📖
1989, *Edward T. Hall, Mildred Reed Hall,* Intercultural Press, 208 pages ➤ Intercultural and Community Development Resources (ICDR), P.O. Box 32108, Millwoods Station, Edmonton, Alberta T6K 4C2; $24; VISA, Amex; (800) 378-3199, fax (403) 462-1925, icdr@compusmart.ab.ca ■ Helps German, French, and American readers understand one another's psychology and behaviour. Provides a meaningful context in which the international businessperson can analyze other cultures. Visit the distributor's web site at www.compusmart.ab.ca/icdr. [ID:1315]

US Government National trade Data Bank 💻
www.stat-usa.gov/BEN/databases.html ■ The US government's comprehensive international trade and export promotion database includes international market research reports, export opportunities, indexes of foreign and domestic companies, how-to market guides, and reports on demographic, political, and socio-economic conditions for hundreds of countries. [ID:2616]

US Immigration Resource for Canadians 💻
www.americanlaw.com ■ A handy source of information for Canadians who want to immigrate south of the border. [ID:2767]

The Yin and Yang of American Values 📖
1998, *Eun Y. Kim,* Kodansha International, 208 pages ➤ Fitzhenry and Whiteside Ltd., 195 Allstate Parkway, Markham, Ontario L3R 4T8; $31; VISA, MC; (800) 387-9776, fax (800) 260-9777, godwit@fitzhenry.ca ■ A critique of American values from an Asian perspective. Insight into American behaviour and how Americans are perceived by the rest of the world, particularly Asia. Visit the distributor's web site at www.fitzhenry.ca. [ID:2429]

Mexico & Latin America
FOR ENTREPRENEURS & LONG-TERM INVESTORS

Latin American countries offer similar opportunities to entrepreneurs as do other emerging markets, with certain advantages for Canadians. They share the same time zones as Canada, and in many cases seem more familiar. The ratification of the North American Free Trade Agreement (NAFTA) has already spurred Canadian-Mexican trade and investment, and is likely to extend to other Latin American countries over the next few years. In the last decade, nearly every country in the region has embarked upon a dramatic political and economic transformation, creating a sense of stability and predictability. Several countries are now experiencing or seem well-positioned to enjoy a healthy growth in the foreseeable future. Canada's technological expertise, natural resources and high-end services and products match Latin America's current import needs, creating many untapped trade and investment opportunities. Direct Canadian investment in the region has soared, and was estimated at $10 billion in 1994, up from $3.4 billion two years earlier.

Here are three pieces of advice that businesspeople will hear over and over from those who have tried to make inroads into Mexico and Latin America: One, get a local partner—even big companies cannot make it on their own. Two, don't underestimate the time and patience it will take to initiate, develop and maintain a business venture. Three, expect to put up most of the financing.

So why bother? Many Canadian companies do come to the conclusion that the time and effort are not worth it. But many others expect to reap the big rewards that come from entering a new market at the right time. Mexico's middle class—read, consuming class—is already as large as Canada's in absolute numbers and in terms of spending power, and is growing rapidly.

Mexico and Latin America are not as fertile for professionals seeking overseas work. For one thing, there is a growing indigenous pool of well-educated lawyers, engineers, doctors, technicians and so forth. And second, interested individuals hired by Mexican companies will, at least in the short-term, earn considerably less than they would at home. But for those dedicated to discovering the culture and gaining work experience, there are a number of possibilities, especially for people with backgrounds in marketing, product development, and management and high-tech industries.

MEXICO

The Mexican Economy and NAFTA

The Mexican economy has undergone a radical transformation over the last decade, lifting myriad trade and investment restrictions, and initiating a widespread program of privatization. Foreign debt indicators have shown considerable improvement since the late 1980s and inflation is down dramatically (from 180 per cent in 1988). By 1994, foreign investment in Mexico had tripled to US$71 billion from $24 billion in 1988.

Investors can be easily spooked, as in the 1994 Mexican recession, the Chiapas uprising and the murder of former PRI presidential candidate Luis Donaldo Colosio. Responding to the December 1994 economic crisis, the government of Mexico imposed stringent fiscal policies and devalued the peso. As of 1997, a recovery seems to be taking place although employment opportunities do not yet reflect this.

In the longer term, most observers are bullish on Mexico as a market for Canadian business. The provisions of NAFTA have improved access to potential investors, especially in mining, construction, petrochemicals, agriculture, autos, financial services and other professional services. Government procurement markets will be open to Canadian suppliers and investment laws continue to ease.

Visas

Visa requirements have been loosened for business visitors who qualify under the temporary entry provisions of NAFTA. Visas are available from airlines and at entry points, as well as from Mexican embassies and consulates. As always, visitors should check for up-to-date visa information before making a trip.

If you are hired by a Canadian firm and posted to Mexico or elsewhere in Latin America, the procedure is quite simple and requires little paper work on your behalf. But if you arrive without a work visa, it is next to impossible to get one. That said, many employers are not fussy about dealing with the government—the black market economy is estimated by some at as much as 30 per cent of GDP.

Business Opportunities

Many Canadian companies are producing the capital goods currently needed in Mexico, such as equipment for bottling and packaging plants. This kind of equipment represents a large, one-off sale with a high value-added component—technical people and training are often part of the package. The most promising sectors for Canadian firms include:

- Agricultural equipment, chemicals, services and expertise
- High technology
- Auto parts
- Beverage industry and equipment
- Construction and engineering
- Environmental industries: impact assessment, pollution control, waste management and water resources
- Mining and mining equipment
- Petrochemicals
- Telecommunications equipment, systems and services
- Banking and financial services
- Transportation

Strategies for Businesspeople and Entrepreneurs

Mexico, although it shares a continent with Canada and the US, is a very different country, which becomes increasingly clear the longer you try to do business there. Most of the steps to making a successful business deal apply equally to other countries in Latin America.

The first step is to collect as much information as you can prior to making a visit. Fortunately, there are now plenty of resources available, from government reports and programs to specific books on Canadian-Mexican trade to seminars and private consultants who help make connections between Canadian and Mexican firms. The DEPARTMENT OF FOREIGN AFFAIRS AND INTERNATIONAL TRADE has detailed market studies for several sectors which could cover a lot of your early footwork. Many US and Mexican government agencies and trade groups can provide additional information, as can the "Trade Talks" division of the MEXICAN EMBASSY in Ottawa. (See Resources at the end of this section for more information.)

If the prospects look promising for your business, the next step is to make an exploratory visit, with a view to establishing local contacts. The Canadian government has recently opened a business centre in Mexico City that should serve as an excellent meeting point for liaising with Mexican counterparts. Some Canadians suggest setting up a hospitality suite in a hotel room for a few days to meet as many local people as possible. But don't expect to make a deal or choose a partner on your first visit.

Use any Mexican business contacts available to you through government or personal sources. As you will hear more than once, forging business relationships is extremely important and you need time and patience to do so. Fluency in Spanish, although not mandatory, is a definite asset.

Finding a Mexican partner is crucial, helping to overcome the myriad barriers impeding entry, such as cultural factors, lack of familiarity with consumer taste, government regulations or corporate concentration. Partnering can take many forms depending on whether it is a case of technology transfer, an exchange of marketing rights or sharing product development costs. Common forms of partnership include joint ventures, licensing arrangements, co-manufacturing agreements, franchising and joint production. The handbook *Canada-Mexico: Partnering for Success* (see Resources at the end of this section) offers a good introduction to the kinds of partnering arrangements available, and the preparation needed.

Poor choice of partners is one of the key reasons cited by managers for the disappointing performance of business ventures. Many business people underestimate the amount of time and resources it will take to find, let alone develop, a successful partnership. The owner of an Ottawa computer services firm which recently signed an agreement with a Mexican partner figures it took a full year of his time over three years at a total cost of $150,000 just to get to this point! (See Personal Stories.)

Once you have decided to make the plunge, you'll have to select a target market. Most Canadians select one of the three main business areas: Mexico

City, Guadalajara, or Monterrey. Increasingly, however, there are financial incentives to set up operations in less populous regions.

Entrepreneurs have another word of caution: if you need a partner with deep pockets, then Mexico is not the market for you. Most financing will have to come from your side, with the deal structured in such a way to benefit you further down the road. "There really is no money there—you have to tailor the deal accordingly," says the Ottawa businessman.

Culture

A number of books have been written advising North Americans how to do business in Mexico, and it is probably a good idea to read one or two.

Cultivate patience and be prepared for major delays. The culture of each Latin American country is unique, but they share a common attitude to time, which doesn't mesh with the stress Canadians put on scheduling and keeping appointments.

Mexicans are extremely polite, so it is important to keep asking questions and make sure you understand the nuances of the conversation—it's often said that Mexicans dislike saying no, even when that's what they mean.

Canadian businesspeople often expect to sit down and quickly finalize a deal, but Mexicans view the art of doing business differently. They expect to develop a relationship with the person they may do business with—the process can take months, if not years. Patience is paramount.

"The primary thing down there is building relationships, and the longer you're down there the greater chance there is of building a relationship," says a Spanish-speaking Canadian businessman who has made several visits. "But at the end it doesn't necessarily mean they'll become buyers, it may just mean you'll be good friends."

Mexicans, who are proud of their Aztec history and culture, take music, art and literature seriously. If you have some knowledge of Mexican culture, you'll have something to talk about at business lunches and cocktail parties. Mexican businesspeople do not like to discuss business during a meal; they wait until the meal is finished before launching into production costs and markets.

If Canadians are popular in Mexico and Latin America, then Québecers are especially so. They are often called the Latins of North America. They seem to share an affinity with Mexicans and several other Latin American cultures, partly because of a similar language, classical education and the ways they enjoy life.

Mexico's business culture is more formal than Canada's, so err on the side of formality. Women, especially, are advised to dress conservatively, but this holds true for men as well.

Finally, the Latin *machismo* cannot go unmentioned. One woman lawyer who worked in Mexico found the "constant come-ons" so annoying that she left after six months. Another woman who reports happier experiences says it is important to be professional and businesslike, to dress appropriately and to know your field.

"I sound very official and I always have agendas typed out for meetings, which I hand to my counterpart before starting. I wear expensive suits and

*expensive jewellery because they know the difference ... (In Mexico) the rich are
very rich and the poor are very poor, and if you want to play the rich man's
game you have to act accordingly."*

Jobs for Professionals and Casuals

For Canadian professionals fluent in Spanish who want to work in Mexico, your
best bet is to apply to the large Canadian or American firms that are doing
business there. NORTHERN TELECOM, BOMBARDIER, SHL SYSTEMHOUSE, and
LABATT'S are a few Canadian names investing heavily in Mexico. In many fields,
the prospects are slim because there are many well-educated Mexicans, and
professional salaries in Mexico are low, even compared with many Asian
countries.

But there is also something to be said for being on the ground, and Canadians who have found jobs in Mexico have often started this way. An
experienced salesman advises bringing enough money for a few months or
teaching English while you look for other work.

In many Latin American countries, the demand for English-language instruction is high, from exclusive schools to backstreet commercial institutes to
tutoring. Experience isn't usually necessary to land a job teaching English on the
spot. Often working papers won't be necessary. Jobs are sometimes available in
the tourist industry, albeit at low wages. It is essential for anyone interested in
working in Latin America, including students and backpackers, to appear neat
and well-groomed.

LATIN AMERICA

While Canada's commercial ties with the rest of Latin America remain modest,
they have expanded in recent years as economic and political reforms have
been consolidated, and a modicum of stability has been restored in the region.

The formation of several regional trading blocs has promoted the disman-
tling of trade barriers and has greatly enhanced prospects for intra-regional
trade. These arrangements include the Andean Pact (Venezuela, Colombia,
Bolivia, Peru, and Ecuador); the MERCOSUR group (Argentina, Brazil,
Paraguay, and Uruguay) and the Central American Common Market (Costa
Rica, El Salvador, Guatemala, Honduras, and Nicaragua).

These groupings, along with a variety of other bilateral free trade agreements in the region, have paved the way for a possible broadening of NAFTA
into a hemispheric trade zone. Several Latin American countries have already
made bids to become members of NAFTA, with Chile most likely to be granted
accession.

Argentina, Brazil, Chile, Colombia and Venezuela are currently the countries of greatest interest to the Canadian business community. The most promising sectors include forestry, mining, oil and gas, telecommunications, power
generation, machinery manufacturing, auto parts, agriculture, and environmental industries. Throughout the region, Canadian companies are benefiting
from the sweeping privatization programs, and are actively buying formerly
state-owned companies in the natural resource and communications sectors.

Canadians with Latin American roots caution that each country has a different culture. You can't assume that because you know Mexico, Colombia will come easily. Mexicans are welcoming, whereas Venezuelans are cool to foreigners, partly due to fallout from the last oil boom. Ecuador, Colombia, and Peru are very formal and "European" in their business circles.

Chile

Canada is Chile's largest foreign investor, with mining (and high quality ore deposits in particular) accounting for the lion's share of investment. At last count, Canadian mining firms had $2 billion invested in Chile alone, and it remains a hot spot for the foreseeable future. Pulp and paper, transportation, telecommunications, industrial machinery, mining equipment and service sectors all look good as well.

Moreover, Chile is expected to become the next NAFTA signatory. Chile placed fifth in the 1993 World Competitiveness Record's ranking of most competitive newly-industrialized countries, after Singapore, Hong Kong, Taiwan, and Malaysia and its trade barriers are among the lowest in the world.

Argentina

Argentina is the third-largest Latin American market, after Mexico and Brazil, and has one of the highest per capita incomes in the region. Government moves to deregulate, privatize, fight inflation and control the deficit have reaped rewards: high growth rates, an influx of capital, and a return of business confidence. Opportunities for Canadians exist in oil and gas, mining, energy transmission, environmental technologies, telecommunications, and food processing and packaging equipment sectors.

Colombia

The most promising sectors for Canadian firms are oil and gas, telecommunications, and power generation. Despite Colombia's fairly healthy economy, Canadian businesses and citizens remain wary of Colombia because of the extremely high rate of violent crime. However, a businesswoman who travels frequently to Colombia describes Bogota as a city where she feels safe. Colombia is the only Latin American country with which Canada had a trade surplus in 1992, of $98.3 million.

PERSONAL STORIES

• The owner of an Ottawa computer services company with annual sales of $8 million is just beginning a Mexican effort. It took three years and more than $150,000 in his time and professional services to get to the first stage. "I'd travelled there quite a bit," says the entrepreneur who is fluent in Spanish. "My interest was piqued at a NAFTA conference, when I became aware their economy was booming while ours was flat. Then, having looked, we found we were going into a market without competition," he says. On his first visit down, he met with representatives of 12 companies in two days, all arranged by a Mexican friend of a friend. He explained the kind of service he offered—

custom-designed software programs to help businesses meet specific needs —"and the response I got was, 'Can we place an order today?'" After two more exploratory trips, the businessman selected Guadalajara as a target market and tried several avenues to find a partner, including the Canadian Consul General's office in Guadalajara, the embassy in Mexico City, and FOREIGN AFFAIRS officials in Ottawa. But the route that worked best was placing an ad in English in the local Guadalajara newspaper, which the company did three times. The first time, after months of negotiations with the front-runner, the company backed out for lack of capital. The second time, the chosen partner also backed out when they were close to signing a deal. The third time—which was going to be the last try—the second company came forward again and went through with the deal, owing to a change in senior management. Now the deal is at the final approval stage, after which several Mexican personnel will come to Ottawa for training. Then Canadian technicians will spend as much as 10 weeks training the staff in Guadalajara. "Is it worthwhile? Yes. But if someone had said it's going to take three years and cost $150,000, I wouldn't have done it, so in a sense, maybe it's better not to know ahead of time." The company plans to "spend a fortune" on direct marketing, and ultimately hopes to have offices in Mexico City and Monterrey before moving into other Latin American countries.

• An Ottawa consultant went to Mexico to perfect his Spanish and ended up with a job working for an American company that bought and sold aluminum. He had two university degrees, one of them in international affairs, plus sales experience: he had put himself through university as a Xerox salesman. By chance he met the country manager of the firm (also a Canadian) and learned of an opening for an aluminum salesman, which he jumped at. "I did almost all my work by phone, selling aluminum from Brazil and Venezuela to Volkswagen, Nissan and the like in Mexico." Despite the phone work, developing personal bonds was important. His boss took him around to meet the buyers. "There was a degree to the relationship, too. I was never seen in the same light as my boss, who had been there 10 years." He says the job seeker who wants to work in Mexico is in a bind: the all-important working papers are easier to get if you're hired from Canada, but it's important to be there on the ground. Try both methods. "Be prepared to earn, at the onset, considerably less than you'd earn in Canada."

• A marketing consultant in telecommunications has worked on contract for Mexican and other telephone companies for five years, from a base in Guelph, Ontario. She currently spends two weeks a month in Mexico City, on contract for a Mexican version of UNITEL. With two master's degrees (one in English, the other in Business Administration), she began her career with "excellent training" in marketing at STANDARD BRANDS and an ad agency before joining NORTHERN TELECOM. When the company wanted to transfer her, she decided to strike out on her own. And she advises would-be consultants to get some hands-on business experience first. (Now she earns enough to fly her husband down to Mexico at least once a month for a long weekend—"a cost of doing business.") Though she works for Canadian, US and Hong Kong telecommunications companies, most of her work is in Latin America. "I love it—I love the language, the food, the people, everything about it. Second, when you're recommended in Latin America, people place enormous store by that so it's easier for me to get work from one country to another. I've been asked to work in China but I feel I'm building an expertise in Latin America. . . .I see a lot of opportunity because most of these economies have been closed so there is very little true marketing talent, especially in the high-tech areas." "A problem is the great machismo, whether you're male or female. I might sit across from someone who says 'you don't know my market,' even though I have knowledge from five years in Mexico. I know Inegi (Mexico's department of statistics) better than I know Stats Canada, and I can throw back information in tremendous detail." She adds that relationships are extremely important to doing business. "It's not personal relationships the way we have them in Canada, it's more having a history with a company. There's a company I have yet to do business with, but we've been exchanging business information for three years. Maybe in five years we'll do business."

• A young Canadian befriended a Mexican while on holiday, and invited him to visit Canada. Eventually, the Mexican became manager of a restaurant in a westcoast Mexican city, and the Canadian graduate went back to visit (without any working papers). After a few weeks teaching English at a language institute, his Spanish had improved enough to be offered a job as a waiter in his friend's restaurant. The restaurant manager had "an arrangement" with the local immigration official who ate at the restaurant, so there were no questions asked about the Canadian employee, who continued to work there for three months. "The other staff weren't too happy about my working there. I had to earn their respect by working harder and being paid less than any of them. Earning their respect made all the difference and after several weeks I became one of the locals."

RESOURCES
Mexico & Latin America

Access North America 📖 🖥
Monthly ➤ InfoCentre, Department of Foreign Affairs and International Trade (DFAIT), 125 Sussex Dr., Ottawa, Ontario K1A 0G2; (800) 267-8376, fax (613) 996-9709 ▪ A monthly newsletter of the Access North America Program. Provides news about government activities, visas, and programs and publications under the North American Free Trade Agreement (NAFTA). Published as a supplement to the *CanadExport Newsletter*. Also available on their web site under the heading "Trade" at www.dfait-maeci.gc.ca. [ID:1636]

After Latin American Studies: A Guide to Graduate Study, Fellowships, Internships, and Employment for Latin Americanists 📖
1995, *Shirley A. Kregar*, 142 pages ➤ Center for Latin American Studies, 4E04 Forbes Quad, University of Pittsburgh, Pittsburgh, PA 15260, USA; $10; MC, Amex; (412) 648-7392, fax (412) 648-2199, clas+@cpitt.edu ▪ Provides information on graduate study, research and internships. For graduate as well as undergraduate students, opportunities in the private sector, and career opportunities in the US government and in international organizations. An essential resource for anyone with career or scholarly interests in the region. Visit www.pitt.edu/~clas, the distributor's web site. [ID:1118]

Canada-Mexico: Partnering for Success 📖
1996, *JoAnn Townsend,* 170 pages ➤ Prospectus Publications, Suite 900, Barrister House, 180 Elgin Street, Ottawa, Ontario K2P 2K3; $20; VISA, MC; (613) 231-2727, fax (613) 237-7666 ▪ A primer for Canadian firms on doing business in Mexico. Gives an overview of the Mexican market: demographic characteristics, current economic trends and regional variations; also explains how to develop an export market in Mexico through discussion of various types of business arrangements, the regulations on operating in Mexico, and cultural tips on the Mexican business community. Visit the distributor's web site at www.prospectus.com. [ID:1361]

Chile: A Partner for the Future 📖
1996, 103 pages ➤ Prospectus Publications, Suite 900, Barrister House, 180 Elgin Street, Ottawa, Ontario K2P 2K3; $20; VISA, MC; (613) 231-2727, fax (613) 237-7666 ▪ A primer for Canadian firms on doing business in Chile. Gives an overview of the Chilean market: demographic characteristics, current economic trends and regional variations; also explains how to develop an export market in Chile through discussion of various types of business arrangements, the regulations on operating in Chile, and cultural tips on the Chilean business community. This title is also available in French. Visit the distributor's web site at www.prospectus.com. [ID:2779]

**Get the Right Visa: To Work or Do Business
in the United States or Mexico Under NAFTA** 📖
1994, *Mark Ivener,* 136 pages ➤ Self-Counsel Press, 1481 Charlotte Road, North Vancouver, B.C. V7J 1H1; $11.95; VISA, MC; (604) 986-3366, fax (604) 986-3947, sales@self-counsel.com ▪ If you are expanding an existing business, starting a new venture, investing, or looking for employment, getting into the US needn't be difficult if you know what kind of visa you need. This book explains all there is to know on the subject. Visit the distributor's web site at www.self-counsel.com. [ID:1571]

Good Neighbours: Communicating with the Mexicans 📖
1985, *John C. Condon,* Intercultural Press, 112 pages ➤ Intercultural and Community Development Resources (ICDR), P.O. Box 32108, Millwoods Station, Edmonton, Alberta T6K 4C2; $17; VISA, Amex; (800) 378-3199, fax (403) 462-1925, icdr@compusmart.ab.ca ▪ Examines how Mexicans and Americans perceive themselves and each other and how their behaviour, based on these perceptions, too often leads to crosscultural misunderstanding. Visit the distributor's web site at www.compusmart.ab.ca/icdr. [ID:1031]

IESCOnet-International Trade with Mexico 🖳
www.iesconet.com ▪ The main purpose of this site is to encourage trade with Mexico. The site describes services related to export-import businesses. It also includes information on immigration issues and currency exchange. [ID:2759]

Latin America Traveller 🖳
www.goodnet.com/~crowpub ▪ Offers information for those travelling to Latin America. The site also has a directory of Spanish language schools in the region as well as links to general sites related to travel and culture in Latin America. [ID:2769]

Latin American Weekly Reports 📖
Weekly ➤ Latin American Newsletters, 61 Old Street, London, EC1 V9HX, UK; US$895 10-week trial, US$55; credit cards; (44) (171) 251-0012, fax (44) (171) 253-8193; Available in large libraries ▪ Weekly digest of Latin American news. [ID:1709]

Management in Two Cultures: Bridging the Gap between US and Mexican Managers 📖
1995, *Eva Kras,* Intercultural Press, 126 pages ➤ Intercultural and Community Development Resources (ICDR), P.O. Box 32108, Millwoods Station, Edmonton, Alberta T6K 4C2; $23; VISA, Amex; (800) 378-3199, fax (403) 462-1925, icdr@compusmart.ab.ca ▪ Pinpoints major differences in culture and management style, and examines areas of conflict including religion, education, nationalist feelings and basic values. Offers recommendations to both US and Mexican managers on working together. Visit the distributor's web site at www.compusmart.ab.ca/icdr. [ID:1351]

SASIS INC 🖳
www.sasis.com, sasis@cncnet.com ▪ Web site for SASIS Inc., a company which specializes in recruiting western personnel for contract positions in the Middle East, Africa and South America. Also has some general international postings. [ID:2520]

Trade Office for the Mexican Embassy 🖳
www.secofi.gob.mx ▪ At this site you can obtain information on investment in Mexico, how to do business in Mexico, government laws and regulations governing business, and more. [ID:2484]

Western Europe
MAINLY FOR STUDENTS &
SELECTED PROFESSIONALS

Imagine flying into The Hague to work in an international scientific institute and setting up a new home along a canal. Or landing a job as a financial analyst in Britain and renting a flat near Hyde Park in London. Or working for UNESCO and living in the Latin quarter of Paris.

These are the real-life stories of determined individuals who have engaged in long-term planning and have taken the initiative as opportunities presented themselves. These are the stories of people who, 10 years ago, took a year off to work in Europe as grape pickers, hotel maids, and as nannies. Many Canadians with European jobs have also spent a year of study as poor students in Berlin, Lisbon or Oxford. In some instances, entry into their European job was eased by an European Community (EC) passport acquired because of European-born relatives.

THE EUROPEAN UNION

In order to understand the job market in Europe you must understand the EC. The 15 members of the powerful European Community have adopted a treaty of European Unity which commits all signatories to take up common foreign, security, and immigration policies and to share a single currency—the so-called "euro"—by the end of the century. As of January 1, 1999, exchange rates between EC members' national currencies will be fixed and the Frankfurt-based European Central Bank will determine monetary policy. The "euro" itself is not scheduled to appear until January 1, 2002. To underline these closer ties, the EC is now commonly called the European Union or EU. The term "EU" is fast replacing "EC" as the preferred name.

The EU includes Austria, Belgium, Denmark, Finland, France, Germany, Greece, Ireland, Italy, Luxembourg, the Netherlands, Portugal, Spain, Sweden and the United Kingdom. As part of its "Agenda 2000" strategy for expansion, the EU plans to extend its borders as far eastwards as Ukraine, Belarus and Moldova. Accession negotiations with Hungary, Poland, Estonia, the Czech Republic and Slovenia are scheduled to begin in 1998. Other East European countries have been invited into partnerships with the European Union to help them prepare for eventual membership. Turkey has also expressed a desire to join the EU, but some controversy surrounds its application. (Note that

Iceland, Norway and Switzerland are three West European countries who have opted not to join the EU.)

Visas and The European Union

Any EU citizen may obtain work permits for jobs in any of the member countries. The free movement of labour is already noticeable, as people are drawn to the stronger economies and seasonal work around Europe. This means a Canadian with a passport from any EU country may work in any of the member countries. With respect to professional jobs, the barriers are down in theory, but in practice it sometimes takes longer to harmonize qualifications for certain types of positions.

Many Canadians of European ancestry do not realize how easy it is to obtain an EU passport. For example, Canadians with a European-born parent often can apply for citizenship to that country. Canadians with an Irish-born grandparent are eligible to apply for Irish citizenship. "The key point is you need all the original documents, including your grandparent's birth certificate," says a Canadian who is now an Irish citizen. "Once you have all the documents, it takes about 10 or 12 months." It is well worth your while to query an Irish consulate in Canada if you think you may be eligible, because an Irish passport will give you entrée to work in any EC country.

Each member country has its own laws governing working visas for non-EU members. Most are exclusionary, but there are some exceptions. For example, under a Commonwealth program, a Canadian aged 17 to 26 may obtain a work-holiday visa to travel and work in the UK for up to two years. *Working Abroad Made Easy!* provides work and travel visa information specifically geared to Canadians (see Resources at the end of this section) but remember to check with the appropriate embassy or consulate for up-to-date regulations.

What Professional Jobs are Available?

With the development of the European Union and the monumental changes in Eastern Europe, the Continent is an exciting place to live these days. In the immediate run-up to the 1992 common market, Canadian companies made significant investments in the region. Excluding the United States, the EU is the second most favoured destination of outward direct investment, with Canadian companies having European assets in excess of $20 billion. (See Resources at the end of this section for guidance on how to contact these companies.)

Individuals with exotic backgrounds, specialized technical knowledge and "UN types" continue to find positions in Europe. Lawyers, scientists, MBAs, engineers, professors, accountants, financial analysts and computer experts are among the expatriates who are working in Europe in relatively large numbers. International agencies, including UN and NATO agencies employ significant numbers of Canadians. (For more information see Chapter 36, United Nations, and Chapter 38, International Organizations.)

It is obvious that high unemployment and a highly-skilled European workforce mean that it is not the easiest place for Canadians to find jobs, especially for those looking for jobs at the entry level or lower management level. Unlike many other parts of the world, there are few mid-level or trade jobs available on a contract basis. Most jobs are for senior managers or professionals on an assignment with an international corporation, as part of their long-term employment with them.

Strategies

Once again, the watchwords in your European job search are "Be bold!" and "Be persistent!"

Wherever you may be on the chain of career experiences, the strongest link between you and a European job is knowledge of the continent itself. Once you have acquired European experience through travel and study, additional resources that are most useful in your European job hunt are: a valid working visa, good contacts, determination, qualifications from a recognized school or firm, languages, and luck.

There are generally two main paths to a professional job in Europe: through a North American company with European operations, or directly with a European company. Long-term planning is required if working for a North American firm. The most crucial decision you make will be to choose the right firm during your job search and then work your way into the European posting. Finding work directly with a European firm entails greater risks and usually requires European contacts.

The established Western European capitals are sometimes considered saturated for those seeking professional jobs, but there are hundreds of Canadians working as professionals in London, Paris, Rome, Frankfurt, and other Western European financial capitals. What is required is some basic research. The best sources of advice are members of your profession who are working in Europe or who have recently returned from a European stint. Almost invariably, you will have to go there to get a job, though you can do a lot of legwork before you leave Canada. What was discovered in our research interviews was that the network of people you know is of critical importance— word of mouth can get you in to see the right person at the right time.

Always make sure your credentials are impeccable and well documented. European firms are often more traditional in their résumé style, favouring the formal chronological format.

Students and Backpackers

Even though Europe isn't the casual job mecca of the 1960s and '70s, there are still opportunities for the determined traveller or student.

Opportunities include seasonal work such as fruit and vegetable picking, harvesting and other agricultural work; service jobs in tourism; working as an *au pair* or other childcare duties; and teaching English.

Although you won't get rich in any of these pursuits, they offer a wonderful way to extend a summer vacation into an affordable and unforgettable year in Europe. An advantage is that you will meet Europeans, share in their customs and learn or practise their languages. (When you stay exclusively in youth hostels, you'll mainly meet other North Americans and student travellers.) A Canadian editor now in his 40s says a summer spent picking grapes in Europe changed his life. He discovered good food and wine, made life-long friends and realized he loved farming, which he now does on a part-time basis.

Young people who are determined to work in Europe should get an up-to-date copy of the best resource book in the field, *Work Your Way Around the World* by Susan Griffith. You should also consider subscribing to *Transitions Abroad*, a bimonthly magazine that offers articles on studying, travelling and working overseas. (See Resources at the end of this section.)

Studying in Europe is another invaluable experience that will serve you well later in your international career, especially if you follow a degree program. Several Canadian lawyers, professors and financial analysts have credited their European study programs as crucial in landing their first job in Europe. The EU offers a few scholarships and study visits to non-EU members, and Canadians are also eligible to apply for certain other university scholarships in European countries. (For more information, see Chapter 15, Awards and Grants and Chapter 14, Study Abroad.)

PERSONAL STORIES

• A 31-year-old with a BSc and law degree from the University of Western Ontario is working for a financial advisory firm in London, involved in the privatization process in Russia. She travels to Moscow about once a month, where she works with government officials to help train Russians to become fund managers, stockbrokers, investment analysts and to understand their own capital system. "There's a lot of travel in a finance job in London," she says, "much more international exposure than in Toronto" where she worked before. Her six months' travel in Asia was seen as important to European employers (she has had three), "but in Canada they look on it as time-out."

   She concedes that her dual citizenship (Canadian-British) was a big help in getting her a job, but insists that many others are doing it without working visas beforehand—only it's mostly Australians who talk themselves into jobs. "There's a huge difference between Canadians and Australians," she says. "Canadians see the restraints, look at all the opposition and give up. The Australians don't see it that way. The bottom line is that you can talk people into things in Britain, you can fight for it and show it can be done." She advises professionals to make as many contacts as they can—and use them!

• A Canadian accountant charted an international career by joining the Canadian subsidiary of a US oil exploration company when he graduated from university in the 1970s. Eight years later he was offered his first foreign posting. "It was a combination of persistence on my part and an opportunity that came up," he recalls. His first son was born in Trinidad and his second in Denmark. He was then posted to the Netherlands for three years, before the family decided to return to Calgary to give their children a wider sense of family and a Canadian childhood. "It was a big growth opportunity and one that I'm glad we took," he says. Since the accounting profession is becoming more global, he advises accountants to aim for jobs in international firms or with industrial companies that have foreign operations.

• A history major from Ottawa travelled in Europe for several summers and his experiences picking grapes (and savouring the results!) helped direct him to his chosen profession as a wine importer. After university, he continued to cultivate his wine tasting and sales skills and soon was hired by a major wine importer in Toronto. He moved up the company ladder, making contacts in Europe and Canada and saving money until he could follow his dream of starting his own wine import company. Now in his early 40s, he has just embarked on his own, specializing in the wines of Burgundy. (He says in Burgundy his fluency in French gives him an advantage over American wine buyers, whereas French fluency isn't so important in Bordeaux, where every wine producer has English-speaking sales representatives.) His first six months have been so successful that he wishes he had set out on his own years ago! Based in Toronto, he makes at least three trips to France every year, tasting and buying wines for sale to the Liquor Control Board of Ontario and directly to Ontario restaurants and hotels. "I've always done what I wanted to do, at least to some extent. Before, it was 10 per cent of my time and now it's 80 per cent."

RESOURCES
Western Europe

The Canada Post 📖
Monthly ➤ The Canada Post, 6 Pembridge Road, Notting Hill Gate, London, W11 3HL, UK; £15/12 issues; (44) (171) 243 4243, fax (44) (171) 243 4245 ▪ Don't lose touch! For Canadians living in London. Focus is on news and events that relate to the Canadian community in the U.K. [ID:2562]

Directory of EC Information Sources 📖
Annual, 1250 pages ➤ Euroconfidentiel s.a., BP 29, Rixensart, B-1330, BELGIUM; £180; credit cards; (32) (2) 652 02 84, fax (32) (2) 653 01 80 ▪ A comprehensive listing of over 6,000 sources of European Community information, including trade associations, senior EC officials, law and consultancy firms, embassies and others. [ID:1313]

Employment in France for Students 📖
1991 ➤ Cultural Services of the French Embassy, 464 Wilbrod Street, Ottawa, Ontario K1N 6M8; free; (613) 238-5711, fax (613) 238-5713 ▪ Brochure of work regulations and opportunities for students in France. Includes additional references. [ID:1418]

Euromanagers & Martians: The Business Cultures of Europe's Trading Nations 📖
1994, *Richard Hill,* Europublic SA/NV, 264 pages ➤ Intercultural and Community Development Resources (ICDR), P.O. Box 32108, Millwoods Station, Edmonton, Alberta T6K 4C2; $35; VISA, Amex; (800) 378-3199, fax (403) 462-1925, icdr@compusmart.ab.ca ▪ Examines the cultural norms and attitudes of managers from various European countries. Visit the distributor's web site at www.compusmart.ab.ca/icdr. [ID:2386]

Exploring the Greek Mosaic: A Guide to Intercultural Communication in Greece 📖
1996, *Benjamin J. Broome,* Intercultural Press, 192 pages ➤ Intercultural and Community Development Resources (ICDR), P.O. Box 32108, Millwoods Station, Edmonton, Alberta T6K 4C2; $25; VISA, Amex; (800) 378-3199, fax (403) 462-1925, icdr@compusmart.ab.ca ▪ Examines the cornerstones of Greek culture - community, family and religion - and their part in daily life. A frank discussion of the images Americans and Greeks have of each other. Visit the distributor's web site at www.compusmart.ab.ca/icdr. [ID:2395]

French or Foe? 📖
1995, *Polly Platt,* Intercultural Press, 256 pages ➤ Intercultural and Community Development Resources (ICDR), P.O. Box 32108, Millwoods Station, Edmonton, Alberta T6K 4C2; $28; VISA, Amex; (800) 378-3199, fax (403) 462-1925, icdr@compusmart.ab.ca ▪ Explores the cultural hurdles to understanding the French and leads you through the steps to dealing effectively with French people in business and daily life. Visit www.compusmart.ab.ca/icdr, the distributor's web site. [ID:2475]

How to Get a Job in Europe 📖
1996, *Mark Hempshell,* 208 pages ➤ How To Books Ltd., 3 Newtec Place, Magdalen Road, Oxford, OX4 1RE, UK; £9.99; credit cards; (44) (1752) 202-301, fax (44) (1865) 202-331 ▪ A step-by-step guide to finding the vacancies, applying, and adapting to the cultural and legal framework of the different European countries. An essential starting point for job hunting in Europe. [ID:1055]

How to Get a Job in France 📖
1993, *Mark Hempshell,* 208 pages ➤ How To Books Ltd., 3 Newtec Place, Magdalen Road, Oxford, OX4 1RE, UK; £9.99; credit cards; (44) (1752) 202-301, fax (44) (1865) 202-331 ▪ The first book to set out information and provide guidance on every aspect of the French employment scene in the aftermath of the Single Market (European Union of 1992). A valuable resource. [ID:1674]

How to Get a Job in Germany 📖
1994, *Christine Hall,* 144 pages ➤ How To Books Ltd., 3 Newtec Place, Magdalen Road, Oxford, OX4 1RE, UK; £9.99; credit cards; (44) (1752) 202-301, fax (44) (1865) 202-331 ▪ A step-by-step guide on getting a job in Germany, identifying vacancies, applying and being selected, settling in, and adapting to working in a German organization and social environment. [ID:1672]

How to Live and Work Series—Western Europe 📖
How To Books Ltd., approx. 150 pages each ➤ Capricorn Business Services, Inc., 28 Clear Lake Ave., West Hill, Ontario M1C 4L6; approx. $25 each; credit cards; (416) 282-3331, fax (416) 282-0015 ▪ This series offers practical advice on a country-by-country basis for those preparing to live and work in Europe. Series includes Germany, Greece, Italy, Portugal, Belgium, the Netherlands and Luxembourg, France, Scandinavia, Spain, Britain, and Switzerland. [ID:2501]

How to Study and Live in Britain 📖
1990, *Jane Woolfenden,* 221 pages ➤ How To Books Ltd., 3 Newtec Place, Magdalen Road, Oxford, OX4 1RE, UK; £8.99; credit cards; (44) (1752) 202-301, fax (44) (1865) 202-331 ▪ Provides information on schools and colleges, courses, qualifications, immigration, money, accommodation and more. [ID:1162]

The Irish Jobs Page 💻
www.exp.ie ▪ A useful site for finding employment in Ireland, Australia, and New Zealand. Services include job postings, résumé boards, and a list of recruiting agencies. The bulk of postings are for information technology specialists, but there are employment services for people in other fields, such as engineering and teaching. [ID:2756]

Job Serve 💻
www.jobserve.com ▪ This site offers job listings for those in the information technology field. Most listings are for people wanting to work in the UK, but a few other countries, such as Singapore and Saudi Arabia, are also listed. Not only do you have access to recent job notices, but you can also subscribe to a mailing list. [ID:2750]

Mind Your Manners: Managing Business Cultures in Europe 📖
1996, *John Mole,* Nicholas Brealy Publishing, 240 pages ➤ Intercultural and Community Development Resources (ICDR), P.O. Box 32108, Millwoods Station, Edmonton, Alberta T6K 4C2; $26; VISA, Amex; (800) 378-3199, fax (403) 462-1925, icdr@compusmart.ab.ca ▪ Major new edition of the best-selling practical guide for managers in the new Europe. Expanded to cover the three new members of the European Union, Austria, Finland, Sweden, and a new section on Russia. Visit the distributor's web site at www.compusmart.ab.ca/icdr. [ID:2380]

Spain is Different 📖
1992, *Helen Wattley Ames,* Intercultural Press, 130 pages ➤ Intercultural and Community Development Resources (ICDR), P.O. Box 32108, Millwoods Station, Edmonton, Alberta T6K 4C2; $19; VISA, Amex; (800) 378-3199, fax (403) 462-1925, icdr@compusmart.ab.ca ▪ Explores similarities and differences between Spaniards and Americans. Makes particular reference to contemporary history. Describes how Spain differs from its neighbours and how the country changed after joining the EU. Visit www.compusmart.ab.ca/icdr, the distributor's web site. [ID:1035]

Summer Jobs Britain 📖
Annual, 256 pages ➤ Peterson's Guides, P.O. Box 2123, Princeton, NJ 08543-2123, USA; US$16.95; cheque or money order; (800) 338-3282, fax (609) 243-9150 ▪ Information on positions and vacation traineeships in England, Scotland, Wales, and Northern Ireland. Visit the publisher's web site at www.petersons.com. [ID:2498]

Understanding Cultural Differences: Germans, French and Americans 📖
1989, *Edward T. Hall, Mildred Reed Hall,* Intercultural Press, 208 pages ➤ Intercultural and Community Development Resources (ICDR), P.O. Box 32108, Millwoods Station, Edmonton, Alberta T6K 4C2; $24; VISA, Amex; (800) 378-3199, fax (403) 462-1925, icdr@compusmart.ab.ca ▪ Helps German, French, and American readers understand one another's psychology and behaviour. Provides a meaningful context in which the international businessperson can analyze other cultures. Visit the distributor's web site at www.compusmart.ab.ca/icdr. [ID:1315]

We Europeans 📖
1995, *Richard Hill,* Europublic SA/NV, 431 pages ➤ Intercultural and Community Development Resources (ICDR), P.O. Box 32108, Millwoods Station, Edmonton, Alberta T6K 4C2; $24.95; VISA, Amex; (800) 378-3199, fax (403) 462-1925, icdr@compusmart.ab.ca ▪ A qualitative and objective assessment of the underlying characteristics of the European community. Visit the distributor's web site at www.compusmart.ab.ca/icdr. [ID:1691]

Your Own Business in Europe 📖
1996, *Mark Hempshell,* 160 pages ➤ How To Books Ltd., 3 Newtec Place, Magdalen Road, Oxford, OX4 1RE, UK; £12.99; credit cards; (44) (1752) 202-301, fax (44) (1865) 202-331 ▪ How to organize finance, getting help from official/trade organizations, manage premises, staff, and much more. [ID:2443]

Eastern Europe & the former Soviet Union
FOR LANGUAGE TEACHERS, STRONG-HEARTED INVESTORS, & THE YOUNG

The indications are that Eastern Europe and the former Soviet Union will experience massive changes during the next generation. These upheavals, while disruptive, have created many job opportunities for Westerners. The large cities in the western region of the former Soviet Union are now attracting numerous foreign job seekers. Large and small companies are trying to cash in on the void in capitalist know-how. Job seekers are cashing in on the massive demand for business expertise.

As noted in the discussion of the EU in the above section on Western Europe, more stable capitalist Eastern European countries such as Hungary, Poland, Estonia, the Czech Republic and Slovenia are all likely candidates for

EU membership in the foreseeable future. The line between Eastern and Western Europe is already starting to blur.

But the road from communism to capitalism has been difficult. Governments in these countries continue to struggle with the transition to private ownership, and as recent elections have indicated, there remains a great deal of political uncertainty in certain areas. Because of this turmoil, and the accompanying crime rate, the job search in Eastern Europe and the former Soviet Union is reserved mainly for strong-willed individuals. If you are young, a recent graduate with marketable skills, an aggressive entrepreneur, or a seasoned professional who likes to take risks, there are numerous jobs to be had.

The Job Market

Despite the lower standard of living in Eastern Europe and the former Soviet Union, there are several qualities that distinguish these regions from countries in the South and make them ripe for growth and international work: the people are highly educated, the region's advanced military technology can be reapplied to other industrial sectors, advanced information systems and institutions already exist, and they have a more or less sound infrastructure, except for outlying areas of Russia.

Since the collapse of the former Soviet Union, and the subsequent transition toward market-based economies, foreign investment has poured into the region, providing both technology and expertise, and taking advantage of a number of new business opportunities.

In 1993, Canada's exports to Eastern Europe and the former Soviet Union totalled $865 million, and imports from the region were $744 million. No reliable figures on Canadian direct investment are yet available, but there has been a significant amount invested recently in the mining and petrochemicals sectors. (Job seekers in these sectors should know that Canadian petrochemical firms are mainly based in Calgary and mining firms tend to be based in British Columbia, often with offices in Toronto and Vancouver.)

There are many job opportunities for those familiar with business management practices. A Canadian lawyer who travels for business to Moscow and Eastern Europe (as well as Asia and Latin America) has this to say:

"In the new markets, provided you have two or three months' savings, you can arrive in Beijing or Prague or Moscow or Mexico City and really, you'll be bombarded with job opportunities. It's very unpredictable. A lawyer could end up working as a general manager for a cosmetics firm in St. Petersburg. An accountant ended up working as a general director of a joint venture in the Ukraine. The idea is that you know western business and you are in high demand for that reason. It all has to do with this explosion of deals, export, trade, market development and sales. There are jobs in business accounting, franchising, secretarial support and medical services."

Among the independent states of the former Soviet Union and Eastern Europe, the countries where most foreign businesses are locating (and thus with the most to offer westerners in the way of jobs and business opportunities) are Russia, the Ukraine, the Czech Republic, Hungary, and Poland.

Strategies

Speaking the local language is often a necessity, rather than just an asset, in many East European countries. German and Russian are more widely spoken than English. One expert says that an inexperienced engineer who speaks Polish or Russian or Czech will get a job with an international concern in the appropriate country before an experienced engineer without the language. Nevertheless, many young westerners have gone to Eastern Europe speaking only English and have landed jobs in banking, marketing, and related businesses. Having relatives or contacts prior to arriving can make getting started without language skills a less daunting prospect.

In all countries, the teaching of languages, especially English, is in demand. Both the Czech Republic and Hungary have had some bad experiences with untrained English teachers, and now require either a degree or previous teaching experience. Editors, writers, translators and other language experts should also find it relatively easy to get work. Your first enquiries can be made to the appropriate embassy, which can refer you to suitable teaching agencies and school boards.

Now, almost a decade since the collapse of the Berlin Wall, the major cities are saturated with foreign residents. Housing can be both expensive and difficult to find, particularly in Prague. Major cities are filled with young, predominantly American graduates who have opened English-language newspapers, restaurants and other businesses in the tourist industry. Hungary had more than 13,000 foreign companies by 1994.

With this in mind, you may have to go further afield to improve your chances of finding work or starting up a business. English-language newspapers published in the major East European cities are a good place to go to start making contacts.

For Canadian businesses interested in investing in Eastern Europe and Canadian professionals seeking work, a good place to start is with the BUREAU FOR ASSISTANCE FOR CENTRAL AND EASTERN EUROPE at the DEPARTMENT OF FOREIGN AFFAIRS AND INTERNATIONAL TRADE. The Bureau funds projects in Eastern Europe, and accepts unsolicited proposals from businesses (you should make enquiries regarding guidelines for what is required in a project proposal). The Bureau can also provide a list of projects awarded by country, including the name of the company that is project manager, but it will not furnish contact names.

The Bureau's mandate is not to help companies make a profit, but sometimes its assistance can lead to profit-making down the road. For example, a Canadian company that received a small loan from the Bureau to advise the Polish Ministry of Health on how to restructure the country's health policy was able to bid on a WORLD BANK contract to carry out the plan. Because the Polish officials knew and liked working with the Canadians, their company won the $24 million contract.

Another federal program called RENAISSANCE EASTERN EUROPE provides funding on a matched basis up to a maximum $100,000 for straight business proposals by companies looking to establish joint ventures. There is also a smaller program that helps individuals who want to work in Eastern Europe on a volunteer basis. Program funding might, for example, pay travel expenses and a cost of living supplement for Canadians in a variety of development-related fields.

THE ASSOCIATION OF CANADIAN COMMUNITY COLLEGES places college teachers in Eastern Europe (as well as Latin America and Asia) for short stints, mainly as technical advisors. An association official advises interested teachers to be specific in the kind of assignment you want. "If you have a specific interest and you know of the demand in a particular country and you focus on skills that are relevant and that the people need, your chances of getting a second look are much better."

Other sources that can help place qualified individuals include the CZECH-CANADA CHAMBER OF COMMERCE, and the HUNGARIAN TRADE ORGANIZATION. These associations vary in the degrees to which they are helpful. The names and addresses of such organizations can be obtained from the appropriate embassy.

Russia and the Commonwealth of Independent States (CIS)

Russia is chaotic, difficult, and increasingly dangerous. To work there you will need a spirit of adventure and the ability to take things in stride and not complain when your water is turned off—because it likely will be. You have to be extremely careful to avoid being a target for thieves and hucksters. There is a tremendous amount of business-related crime (extortion is common), and the judicial system is ten paces behind the requirements of the free market business community. As one young Canadian businessperson operating in Russia says, "it isn't a place for quitters."

A partner in a Canadian law firm with an office in Moscow has this to say about danger and the need to be careful when settling in places such as Moscow:

"The lesson we have learned is that if you want to live and work overseas in new markets where there is a major transition going on towards a market economy, and there's a criminal element developing, as there was in the US in the 1920s, then you've got to be really careful not to make yourself too obvious. We have cases of people being robbed, pistol-whipped and shot, not just in Russia but in China and Latin America. The clue is to put to one side your enthusiasm to live like and with the locals. Ninety-nine per cent of the locals will be incredibly generous but that small criminal percentage will learn where you're living and will begin to target your apartment for break and enters, to steal your car, maybe worse. So live and work as much as you can in areas where you don't stand out."

As underlined before, language skills are important in Warsaw, Budapest and Prague, but they are doubly important in Russia. Basic Russian is a minimum requirement for nearly all job seekers. With a good command of the language plus relevant business experience, you can command a high salary, as much as $250,000 a year with a big international company. At the other end of the scale, casual jobs teaching English will bring in about $300 a month (a subsistence wage).

It is very difficult to get organized in Russia, says one Russian-Canadian who travels there often, but once you are organized, "success is guaranteed." You can begin preparation before you leave, by meeting with people who have returned and perusing the Moscow newspapers for classified job ads in English. Recent editions have advertised for all kinds of engineers, as well as chartered accountants, copywriters, lawyers, tax managers, customs officers, property managers, information systems managers, sales people, secretaries, interpreters and translators.

Some experienced hands advise avoiding Moscow, which is saturated with up to 250,000 foreigners, and looking to St. Petersburg, Kiev, Odessa and other large cities.

Although US companies have been the most willing to take the big risks involved in setting up in Russia, there are some notable Canadian adventurers, large and small. MCCAIN, for example, a processed food manufacturer, has operations in Russia. GOWLING, STRATHY AND HENDERSON, an Ottawa-head-quartered law firm, has an office with 12 legal staff in Moscow, including two Canadian lawyers. A Montréal group set up a medical service to treat expatriates and is also serving wealthy Russians. A group of Canadians opened the first GM dealership in Moscow by selling cars designed for the Iraqi market that were sitting in warehouses after the Gulf War. The list goes on.

In addition, there are dozens of young Canadian entrepreneurs who have set out on their own to open photocopy shops, courier businesses, bran muffin kiosks, or dry cleaning outfits. "You name the business and there are young men and women with barely a BA who are doing it with one or two friends," says the Canadian lawyer who represents several of them in Moscow.

When forging business ties, relationships are more important than contracts. You should find a reliable business partner and build a relationship on trust. Your first contacts will probably be made through the Canadian embassy, which is extremely helpful to those seriously trying to start a business in Russia.

PERSONAL STORIES

• A 31-year-old Canadian lawyer and MBA graduate began his sojourn in Russia as a bar bet with a friend on whether *glasnost* and *perestroika* meant anything at all. That bet turned into a proposal to hold a debate in Russia on the topic of collective security vs. liberty, which eventually went ahead on Russian television! He parleyed the experience into a job, bringing 22 MBA students to Russia to offer a very basic business course for arts and science students. The courses were full to overflowing. He urges Canadian graduates to learn basic Russian and go over "with anything, even a contract to teach English. If you get there and you have a pre-arranged contract, you'll be looked after very well." It's not necessary to be young to work in Russia, "just young at heart. If the heat is turned off, you can put on a sweater," he says. "You have to have language skills and you have to be pretty quick, then there is lots of opportunity. I went with the spirit that I'd try to give more than I got and if you do that you'll find Russians generous to a fault."

• A man from Vancouver married to a Russian immigrant went to Russia to flog his family business, which made safety equipment for boats. The Soviet Arctic fleet was very interested in buying equipment but had no hard currency, so he accepted their rubles, which everyone told him he was a fool to do. Then he took the rubles and bought a tanning factory in the Ukraine which is producing world class leathers. He lined up a multi-year contract in Germany that pays him in marks and has already made his money back fifty times over—by ignoring conventional wisdom which says you only deal in hard currency.

• A 22-year-old Canadian student of Croatian descent flew to Split in Croatia in May 1992 to volunteer for the summer. She immediately landed work (at US$80 per month) with the office of the European Community, interpreting meetings between Croatian commanders and UN officials, sometimes crossing the confrontation line and interpreting particularly tense meetings involving ceasefire violations. After a few months, she started interpreting for television stations on location in Sinj, about an hour's drive north of Split, and eventually was hired by the BBC as a "fixer," which paid US$160 per day. In addition to interpreting, she had to find contacts, sniff out news stories, organize checkpoint crossings for the crew, and translate clips for the news. She says it was interesting to see how news is made, and how subjective the process is. "It's a dangerous job and you have to have nerves of steel. There were shells falling and we got shot at, but it's an experience I wouldn't trade. It changed me forever, that's for sure—it changed my perspective as a Canadian and I wish more people could have this experience."

RESOURCES

Russia and Eastern Europe

Eastern and Central Europe Job Bank 🖳
This site proclaims itself as the first Eastern and Central European Internet Job Bank. It is created by a private firm looking to find the best people in the computer and management fields. The job bank is mainly for people who live in this part of Europe, but some postings are open to worldwide competition. [ID:2707]

From Da to Yes: Understanding the East Europeans 📖
1995, *Yale Richmond,* Intercultural Press, 320 pages ➤ Intercultural and Community Development Resources (ICDR), P.O. Box 32108, Millwoods Station, Edmonton, Alberta T6K 4C2; $25; VISA, Amex; (800) 378-3199, fax (403) 462-1925, icdr@compusmart.ab.ca ▪ Essential reading for anyone working in Eastern Europe, with individual chapters on each country and its inhabitants. Visit the distributor's web site at www.compusmart.ab.ca/icdr. [ID:2397]

From Nyet to Da: Understanding the Russians 📖
1996, *Yale Richmond,* Intercultural Press, 219 pages ➤ Intercultural and Community Development Resources (ICDR), P.O. Box 32108, Millwoods Station, Edmonton, Alberta T6K 4C2; $25; VISA, Amex; (800) 378-3199, fax (403) 462-1925, icdr@compusmart.ab.ca ▪ A crosscultural guide that distinguishes between Russia's political structure and culture, connects geography with attitudes and behaviour, and details the state and social system. Discusses how to respond to the extremes and contradictions in Russian character. Valuable section on negotiating business deals and other arrangements. Visit the distributor's web site at www.compusmart.ab.ca/icdr. [ID:1036]

Jobs in Russia and the Newly Independent States 📖
1994, *Moira Forbes,* 235 pages ➤ Impact Publications, 9104 North Manassas Drive, Manassas Park, VA 20111-2366, USA; US$15.95; credit cards; (703) 361-7300, fax (703) 335-9486 ▪ Identifies numerous opportunities in Russia and the newly independent states, from business and government jobs to volunteer opportunities. Summarizes recent developments in each country, describes opportunities, and includes addresses of employers. Visit www.impactpublications.com, the distributor's web site. [ID:1470]

Mind Your Manners: Managing Business Cultures in Europe 📖
1996, *John Mole,* Nicholas Brealy Publishing, 240 pages ➤ Intercultural and Community Development Resources (ICDR), P.O. Box 32108, Millwoods Station, Edmonton, Alberta T6K 4C2; $26; VISA, Amex; (800) 378-3199, fax (403) 462-1925, icdr@compusmart.ab.ca ▪ Major new edition of the best-selling practical guide for managers in the new Europe. Expanded to cover the three new members of the European Union, Austria, Finland, Sweden, and a new section on Russia. Visit the distributor's web site at www.compusmart.ab.ca/icdr. [ID:2380]

Now Hiring! Jobs in Eastern Europe 📖
1996, *Clarke Canfield,* 320 pages ➤ Impact Publications, 9104 North Manassas Drive, Manassas Park, VA 20111-2366, USA; $14.95; credit cards; (703) 361-7300, fax (703) 335-9486 ▪ An insider's guide to working and living in the Czech Republic, Hungary, Poland, and Slovakia. Provides information on teaching English as well as other employment opportunities. Includes a list of language schools that hire native speakers. Visit www.impactpublications.com, the distributor's web site. [ID:1756]

Russian and Eastern European Institute Employment Opportunities 💻
www.indiana.edu/~reeiweb/indemp.html ▪ Created by Indiana University, this site is useful for people interested in working in Russia and Eastern Europe. It is particularly good for those knowledgeable in language, history, or cultures of this region. [ID:2772]

The Middle East
STILL GUSHING

The Middle East has been a hot job market for 50 years and will continue to be a hot spot for the next 50 years, or until the region runs out of oil. Most jobs in this region are in the Gulf Oil States, with strong demand for skilled labour ranging from doctors and nurses to oil rig workers and telecommunications engineers. To be sure, nowadays job applications from the West outstrip the number of jobs available—but it remains a good place to look for work. An advantage is that many agencies in the Oil States hire westerners directly: a telecommunications engineer can apply directly to SAUDI TELEPHONE for a job.

Here is what the Middle East marketing vice president with a large Canadian service company has to say:

> *"The Middle East is an exceptionally good market to aim at because it has the financial resources combined with a lack of skills and a recognition that the West has the skills it needs. It has the mindset—in the Emirates, Kuwait and Saudi—that 'we have the funds to buy technological slaves. We don't need to learn how to do this because the country has enough money to buy what it needs.' So they maintain their dependency on Western technologists. Asia is the opposite: they ask for help but it's restricted and boxed: 'We'll hire you to do this specific job but then you're gone.'"*

This section will focus mainly on job opportunities in the rich Persian Gulf states. The Gulf countries include Bahrain, Kuwait, Oman, Qatar, Saudi Arabia, the United Arab Emirates and Yemen. Other Middle Eastern countries are Egypt, Israel, Turkey, Syria, Jordan, Iraq, Iran and Lebanon. Egypt is the recipient of generous amounts of US funding (and thus job opportunities), and Israel is a popular stop for travellers who want to experience kibbutz life. Yemen, which doesn't border on the Gulf waters, is one of the 10 poorest countries in the world, and is not in the same class as the other Gulf states in terms of jobs and salaries. Turkey, on the other hand, is a member of NATO and, as noted in the discussion of Western Europe, is considering membership in the EU.

The Middle East represents a not insignificant market for Canadian companies. In 1993, Canadian exports to the region totalled $1.6 billion and imports reached $1.2 billion. Direct Canadian investment exceeded $400 million in 1992. A recent federal government brochure points to attractive opportunities for Canadian companies in selected Middle Eastern markets, including some short-term trade deals due to the Middle East peace process and market realignments from the Gulf War.

Membership in the Ottawa-based CANADA ARAB BUSINESS COUNCIL, totals some 80 Canadian businesses that are either working in the Arab world or have an interest in doing so. The members cover a range of industries, including banking, machinery, telecommunications, paper, autos, medical management, and consulting engineering.

The Persian Gulf

In the Persian Gulf, there is demand for people who can fill professional, managerial, supervisory and highly-skilled technical positions. The professions include nurses, doctors, teachers, all kinds of engineers, computer specialists, geologists and oil project managers. While salaries for beginning teachers and nurses are no higher, or possibly lower, than what they could earn in Canada, the salaries are not taxed, which makes a huge difference to the bottom line. Holidays are generous and many people are provided with free housing. Tax-free salaries for pilots, engineers, and other skilled technical personnel are in the $80,000 to $120,000 range.

What's more—there *are* jobs. For example, a young Canadian who specialized in the computer design of highways won a couple of small contracts in Canada after graduation, but was basically out of work for three or four years because no one was building new highways. After sending out more than 300 résumés, mostly in Canada, he was offered a contract in Qatar with a North American firm, where he is now earning $80,000 tax-free. Although he is not enamoured of life in the Gulf, "he likes it a lot better than sitting around Ottawa unemployed," says a close friend.

Unskilled or semi-skilled workers, however, face tough competition from migrants from India, Pakistan, and Yemen who are willing to work for very low salaries.

When applying directly for jobs in the Gulf, résumés should include certain information that might be considered illegal for employers to request in

North America: sex, nationality, marital status, age and number of dependents. Jews who want to work in the Gulf will have to lie about their religion. Women will face restrictions that are more severe than those facing men, and may not be considered for traditionally "male" technical jobs, such as engineering. It is the usual practice to sign the job contract with a Gulf government once you've arrived, not before.

The Oil States vary considerably in terms of lifestyle and restrictions that Western job seekers will encounter. Bahrain and the Emirates are freer, permitting Christian church services and the sale of alcohol. Saudi Arabia has lots of Western services and luxuries and pays the highest salaries, but it also has the most "don'ts." These include no alcohol (though it is available illegally), no driving by women, and no dating (but unmarried men and women get around it by using a married couple as "chaperons"). Women must dress conservatively and cover themselves with an "abaya" in public. When people are caught breaking the laws, as happened to some Canadian nurses caught coming out of a party where alcohol had been served, the punishment can include a jail sentence and deportations. An old Middle Eastern hand says, "You should know what you're doing and make the best of it. Don't try to beat the system. It certainly is a different world, and you can enjoy it if you come to recognize it for what it is."

Israel

Israel has long been a popular destination for Canadians, Americans, Europeans and Australians who want to spend time on a kibbutz, working for several weeks in the fruit orchards or at another communal job. You will earn room and board and a little pocket money and learn a bit more about the Israeli way of life. It used to be that you could arrive at the airport in Tel Aviv and sign up for a kibbutz on the spot, but in recent years there have been more applicants than spaces, so it pays to book ahead of time.

A unique cultural experience for the physically fit is to work as a volunteer on archaeological "digs" in Israel. See the Canadian student guidebook, *A World of Difference,* for more information.

RESOURCES

The Middle East

Border Crossings: American Interactions with Israelis 📖
1995, *Lucy Shahar, David Kurz,* Intercultural Press, 202 pages ➤ Intercultural and Community Development Resources (ICDR), P.O. Box 32108, Millwoods Station, Edmonton, Alberta T6K 4C2; $24; VISA, Amex; (800) 378-3199, fax (403) 462-1925, icdr@compusmart.ab.ca ▪ The first systematic analysis of American-Israeli cultural differences in commercial, bureaucratic, professional and social settings. Visit the distributor's web site at www.compusmart.ab.ca/icdr. [ID:2396]

How to Live and Work in Saudi Arabia 📖
1997, *Rosalie Rayburn, Kate Bush,* 160 pages ➤ How To Books Ltd., 3 Newtec Place, Magdalen Road, Oxford, OX4 1RE, UK; £12.99; credit cards; (44) (1752) 202-301, fax (44) (1865) 202-331 ▪ Information for those planning long-term stays. More useful for those on overseas assignment than for those looking for a job. [ID:1468]

How to Live and Work in The Gulf 📖
1994, *Hamid Atiyyah,* 128 pages ➤ How To Books Ltd., 3 Newtec Place, Magdalen Road, Oxford, OX4 1RE, UK; £9.99; credit cards; (44) (1752) 202-301, fax (44) (1865) 202-331 ▪ Expert information for expatriates and their families. Practical overview of Arab values, customs, lifestyle and working environment, country by country. Includes information on passports, customs regulations, labour laws, education, and more. [ID:2440]

Job Serve 💻
www.jobserve.com ▪ This site offers job listings for those in the information technology field. Most listings are for people wanting to work in the UK, but a few other countries, such as Singapore and Saudi Arabia, are also listed. Not only do you have access to recent job notices, but you can also subscribe to a mailing list. [ID:2750]

Living and Working in Israel 📖
1996, *Ahron Bregman,* 160 pages ➤ How To Books Ltd., 3 Newtec Place, Magdalen Road, Oxford, OX4 1RE, UK; £10.99; credit cards; (44) (1752) 202-301, fax (44) (1865) 202-331 ▪ Practical information on working or travelling in Israel. [ID:2441]

SASIS INC 💻
www.sasis.com, sasis@cncnet.com ▪ Web site for SASIS Inc., a company which specializes in recruiting western personnel for contract positions in the Middle East, Africa and South America. Also has some general international postings. [ID:2520]

Understanding Arabs: A Guide for Westerners 📖
1997, *Margaret Kleffner Nydell,* 192 pages ➤ Intercultural and Community Development Resources (ICDR), P.O. Box 32108, Millwoods Station, Edmonton, Alberta T6K 4C2; $25; VISA, Amex; (800) 378-3199, fax (403) 462-1925, icdr@compusmart.ab.ca ▪ For Westerners who want to better understand how Arabs think and what motivates them. Sheds light on the aspects of culture which most critically affect crosscultural relationships. Visit www.compusmart.ab.ca/icdr, the distributor's web site at. [ID:1037]

Asia Pacific
FOR THE HIGHLY EDUCATED, YOUNG OR MOBILE ADVENTURER

Although crystal ball gazing lies beyond the scope of this book, it is easy to believe that the coming decades belong to the Asia Pacific region. Even with the economic correction and sharp decline of some Asian currencies in late 1997, economic activity is expected to thrive into the new millennium. Countries that were developing nations a decade ago are now tigers of growth. China, with 1.2 billion people, has lifted many trade and investment restrictions, as has Vietnam. Places such as Hong Kong, Singapore and, of course, Japan, support a standard of living comparable to that of many European countries.

Thanks to an expanding basic infrastructure, business also continues to evolve in countries like South Korea, Taiwan, and the Philippines. In Thailand, a huge freeway system in Bangkok as well as two oil refineries are under way. The world's tallest office building was recently completed in Kuala Lumpur, Malaysia. A frequent business traveller to Southeast Asia says he is reminded of what Canadian cities were like in the 1950s, with construction on every corner.

The term Asia Pacific commonly includes the following 12 countries: China (including Hong Kong), Australia, New Zealand, Singapore, Indonesia, Japan, Taiwan, Thailand, Malaysia, Vietnam, the Philippines, and South Korea. It is a huge, populous and varied region.

The region's markets, which will have a projected 60 per cent of the world's population, 50 per cent of global production and 40 per cent of total consumption by the year 2000, are of vital interest to Canada. In 1993, exports to the region totalled $16.3 billion and imports were $23.2 billion, with most of these flows concentrated in British Columbia. Canadian-owned assets, or direct investment in the region, currently stand at about $10 billion. Meanwhile, there are more new immigrants arriving from Asia than from any other continent, making Vancouver the second-largest Chinese-speaking city on the continent, after San Francisco.

For Canadians with experience in finance, banking, engineering, mining, geology, and computers, there are good work opportunities in the Asia Pacific region. Similarly, young entrepreneurs (particularly MBA graduates) have enjoyed considerable success in selected markets. For those who speak Mandarin, Cantonese or another Asian language, the chances of finding good jobs are even better. Canadian and American firms doing business in Asia advertise regularly in the *Globe and Mail* and Vancouver newspapers. Some companies even recruit and hold interviews in Vancouver.

There are two standard strategies for the professional seeking overseas work in the area. One is to apply from outside the region. If successful, you're likely to get a better job package than if you apply from inside the country, and your working papers will be taken care of. A Canadian management consultant working in Malaysia cautions that many good jobs in finance are recruited internationally, usually through London, which is where he was based when he received the offer.

Canadian graduates armed with little more than a business degree have been moving to Hong Kong and Singapore to find work, and have met with some success. A Toronto lawyer with foreign experience advises more experienced professionals to visit the country of their choice before actually moving there:

"Spend your own money to go there and make some local contacts. It's not just a case of faxing CVs from Toronto. You have to pound the pavement a bit, get a sense of meeting people and not just at the embassy, to get a better picture of where the opportunities are. If you spend that $5,000 and two or three weeks in your destination of choice, it's amazing what you can accomplish. It's geometric: what you learned in Day One is 10 times more in Day Two and 100 times more in Day Three. You've got to get over there. The rewards are surprising and extensive and not necessarily what you think they'll be."

Casual work can be found teaching English, especially in Japan, Taiwan, China, Thailand and Indonesia. At the time of writing, South Korea was reputed to be a particularly good market for well-paid English-teaching jobs.

China

Teaching English is in great demand in Beijing and elsewhere in China. A Vancouver student who spent 10 months learning Chinese at a Beijing university says he tutored a couple of students, but practically had to be rude as he turned others away because he didn't have the time. Other young westerners he met earned money editing and translating from "Chinglish" to English.

For those with an entrepreneurial bent, buying artifacts and silk for sale in North America, Japan and Europe is a popular route. Would-be traders should check out their home market for pricing and demand. (Sizes can be a problem—even large Chinese sizes are small by Canadian standards.) One couple brought clothing designs from Europe to have made into clothes in China and then sold the results in Japan for a killing. "In Canada there are obvious channels to get things done, whereas in China it is a case of who you know," says the student. "Once you have good connections, they will always help you."

For professionals, China is not the best destination to seek a well-paid job. The president of a California database company that matches trades and professionals with overseas jobs says, "China is a revolving door. China wants all the technology and investment it can get without having to commit itself to a lot of employment of foreigners. It has never been the large employment market many companies thought it would be, but we do have people working there on highways, airports, and oil-related projects." A Canadian who has worked in China on development projects concurs: "China is always on the lookout for people who are willing to come and work for next to nothing."

The ASSOCIATION OF COMMUNITY COLLEGES places college teachers for stints in China, with demand strongest for individuals with management and business administration skills.

Hong Kong

Hong Kong returned to Chinese rule in 1997.

Work opportunities for westerners are still comparatively good. Partly because of the strong interest in emigration, there remains a high demand for English teachers. Foreign investment is still flowing into the country, taking advantage of its low tax rates and favourable disposition toward foreign companies. Its main industries are in the light manufacturing sector, especially textiles, electronics and plastics, and machinery, with most production destined for export. Tourism also occupies an important place in the economy.

In recent years, with poor job prospects at home, quite a few Canadians, fresh out of business schools, have moved to Hong Kong with their MBAs and a few thousand dollars, and within a few months have found jobs. (See Personal Stories below.) *The South China Morning Post*, especially the Saturday edition, is the newspaper to check for job ads.

Japan

Japan, with one of the world's strongest economies and highest standards of living, is an important trading partner for Canada. More than half of our trade with the Asia Pacific region is conducted there. Canadian companies currently have investments worth $3 billion in the country.

Teaching English has long been the traditional avenue for westerners wanting to work in Japan, partly because such positions pay well and also because few other jobs have been open to foreigners. But this is changing for several reasons. First, the high cost of living in Japan means that salaries for English teachers offered in some neighbouring countries, such as South Korea, are increasingly competitive. Second, the poor economic climate in western countries has made competition for such jobs more intense. And, in small but growing numbers, westerners are being hired for jobs that don't involve teaching—mostly working for foreign companies but increasingly with Japanese companies. A CARLETON UNIVERSITY graduate who speaks fair Japanese works full-time for a building materials company, processing orders and dealing with foreign customers.

The English-language *Japan Times,* especially the Monday edition, is a good source for those interested in English-teaching jobs. The JAPANESE EXCHANGE AND TEACHING PROGRAM annually hires about 400 Canadians who have university degrees and are 35 years old or under to teach English in the school system for one year. (Please see Chapter 29, Teaching Abroad.)

Australia and New Zealand

With chronic high unemployment in the 1990s, New Zealand and Australia are difficult places for professionals and backpackers alike to find work. In Australia, a temporary residence visa is available to someone with a firm job offer from an Australian employer who can prove that no Australian can do the job. If you have unique or very advanced skills in computer-related industries, you may be able to swing it. There is also a working holiday visa available for people 18 to 30 years of age, to be used "once in a lifetime". The visa allows young people to travel and see the country, and get jobs lasting not more than three months with one employer, harvesting fruit, waiting on tables, typing or the like.

New Zealand offers a similar working holiday scheme but temporary work visas are even more difficult to come by than in Australia. In both countries, one-year job exchanges are available with people in your profession who can switch jobs, homes, cars and everything else with you and your family. Used frequently by teachers, this system has also been tried by journalists and film producers, and can be a wonderful way to experience the country.

PERSONAL STORIES

• With zero job opportunities at home, a 29-year-old Canadian with an MBA from CONCORDIA UNIVERSITY moved to Hong Kong with some money, a suit and a résumé. Within a month he had a job. He lived in a hotel for the first month, sent out dozens of résumés and knocked on dozens of doors, acting far more aggressively than he would in Canada. He soon got his first job with an industrial company. About a year later, with fluency in French, a North American business background, a bit of business experience and a smattering of Cantonese, he was hired by a French company trying to break into Asia. He now has the lofty title of Director of Operations for the PanPacific branch. He travels frequently to Europe and is earning good money, but he finds the lifestyle lonely and has to put up with things he wouldn't accept in Canada: for example, cramped living quarters. He rents a small apartment for $3,600 a month, and sublets two of the three rooms (one of the rooms is 2 by 3 metres). A friend says, "I thought he was a little crazy going there but he has done really well. Like anywhere else, you have to make your own opportunities and he is really good at it. He's created his own chances in a very competitive, fast-paced market. You have to have a really good business sense and be willing to make deals."

- A Vancouver man in his mid-30s had a small company that made a unique airproof product used as a sheath over decaying pylons to repair docks underwater. The business in Vancouver employed five or six people, but wasn't doing terribly well, so he went to Australia to try to sell the product, with no success. On his way home, he stopped in Manila for a short holiday, asked some questions, and learned the Philippine government had just received US$500 million from the ASIAN DEVELOPMENT BANK to refurbish their docks over 10 years. He had found a buyer! A Canadian who spent time with him there says, "He has 150 divers working for him and you can't imagine how well he is living in Manila. A big house, parties—a young millionaire. All he has to do is the paperwork and some diving when he feels like it. He is one happy camper, let me tell you."

- An editor for *The Ottawa Citizen* with dreams of moving to Australia was able to live out his dream—at least for one year. He switched jobs, houses and cars with a copy editor on the *West Australian* and moved to Perth with his two children and journalist wife for a year. (She enjoyed her time learning to surf with a moms and tots group called Moms on Boards.) They loved their time in Australia and would have emigrated if they could, but because of massive layoffs in the newspaper industry they were unable to find permanent work.

- An American woman who taught business English in Taiwan was asked to give a seminar on table settings for some Chinese women who had to accompany their husbands on frequent business trips to Europe or North America: they knew not to spit the crab shells on the table, but needed help with which fork, spoon or glass to use at the proper moment. Figuring there would be 10 to 15 participants for a half-day seminar, she set the fee at US$150 each. A couple of weeks before the scheduled seminar, she was invited to have a look at the room where it would take place: she was shown the ballroom of a downtown hotel. Realizing more people had signed up than she'd bargained for, the teacher revised her plans. She had a large table set up on a stage that people could walk around, and used overheads with diagrams of the different utensils so that everyone could see. In the end, some 625 women showed up and even in the ballroom it was standing room only. It was the most lucrative transaction of her life: more than US$90,000 for four hours' work!

RESOURCES
Asia Pacific

The Asia Pacific region has the largest number of resources. For resources focusing exclusively on teaching in the Asia Pacific region, or for more cross-cultural information, see the Resources section in Chapter 29, Teaching Abroad.

Asia for Women on Business 📖
1995, *Tracey Wilen, Patricia Wilen,* Stone Bridge Press, 256 pages ➤ Weatherhill, 41 Monroe Turnpike, Trumbull, CT 06611, USA; US$15; credit cards; (800) 437-7840, fax (800) 557-5601, weath1212@aol.com ▪ This practical handbook bolsters the visiting woman's authority and effectiveness in the "Four Tigers": Hong Kong, Taiwan, Singapore and South Korea. Visit the distributor's web site at www.weatherhill.com. [ID:2407]

Asia-Net 🖥
www.asia-net.com ▪ Appropriate for people who can juggle more than one (or even two) languages. This is a job resource site for people who are fluent in English, Japanese, Chinese, or Korean and are also professionals in technical areas. [ID:2755]

Asian Development Bank Business Opportunities 📖 🖥
Monthly ➤ Central Operations Services Office, Asian Development Bank, P.O. Box 789, Manilla Central Post Office, 0980 Manila, Philippines; free; (632) 632-4444, fax (632) 636-4444, erosales@mail.asiandevbank.org ▪ Provides advance information on goods and service requirements of projects under consideration by the Asian Development Bank. The Internet edition is available at www.asiandevbank.org. Visit this web site and look under "Business Opportunities." [ID:2608]

Behind the Japanese Bow: An In-Depth Guide to
Understanding and Predicting Japanese Behaviour 📖
1993, *Boye Lafayette de Mente,* NTC Contemporary Publishing Co., 142 pages ➤ Intercultural and Community Development Resources (ICDR), P.O. Box 32108, Millwoods Station, Edmonton, Alberta T6K 4C2; $20; VISA, Amex; (800) 378-3199, fax (403) 462-1925, icdr@compusmart.ab.ca ▪ Explains Japanese behaviour and reveals the existence of a comprehensive set of cultural molds (kata) that control the character and behaviour of the Japanese in business. Visit the distributor's web site at www.compusmart.ab.ca/icdr. [ID:1392]

The Business of Korean Culture 📖
1995, *Richard Saccone,* 200 pages ➤ Weatherhill, 41 Monroe Turnpike, Trumbull, CT 06611, USA; US$14.95; credit cards; (800) 437-7840, fax (800) 557-5601, weath1212@aol.com ▪ Living in Korea, dealing with cultural differences, and developing relationships. Visit the distributor's web site at www.weatherhill.com. [ID:2409]

CanAsian Businesswomen's Network
CanAsian Businesswomen's Network, c/o Asia Pacific Foundation of Canada, Suite 666, 999 Canada Place, Vancouver, B.C. V6C 3E1; (604) 684-5986, fax (604) 681-1370, cabninfo@apfc.apfnet.org ▪ The CanAsian Businesswomen's Network assists companies led by women to increase their trade between Canada and Southeast Asia. In Canada, firms must be ready for import or export, Canadian-owned, and have a woman in a key executive or decision-making position. The network provides resources, contacts, business briefings, crosscultural readiness information, workshops and special events to members and associates. Visit the Asia Pacific Foundation web site, at www.apfnet.org, for more information. [ID:2614]

CareerChina 🖥
www.globalvillager.com/villager/CC.html ▪ Posts job opportunities in China, Taiwan, and Hong Kong. [ID:2516]

China Books & Periodicals Inc. (Catalogue) ▢
Semiannual ➤ China Books & Periodicals Inc., 2929 - 24th Street, San Francisco, CA 94110, USA; free; credit cards; (415) 282-2994, fax (415) 282-0994 ■ Probably the single best source for China-related job-search books, from an independent company specializing in books and periodicals from and about China. Visit the distributor's web site at www.chinabooks.com. [ID:1112]

China Bound: A Guide to Academic Life and Work in the PRC ▢
1994, *L. Reed, K. Turner-Gottschang* ➤ National Academy Press, 2101 Constitution Ave. N.W, Washington, DC 20418, USA; US$14.95; credit cards; (800) 624-6242, fax (202) 334-2451 ■ Chock-full of valuable inside information on life in China. Based on the experiences of Americans who have recently studied, conducted research, or taught in the People's Republic of China, it covers a broad spectrum of topics, from customs, regulations, taxation, and medical care to hotel life and getting your laundry done. Visit the distributor's web site at www.nap.edu. [ID:1209]

A Common Core: Thais and Americans ▢
1989, *John Paul Fieg, Elizabeth Mortlock,* Intercultural Press, 120 pages ➤ Intercultural and Community Development Resources (ICDR), P.O. Box 32108, Millwoods Station, Edmonton, Alberta T6K 4C2; $18; VISA, Amex; (800) 378-3199, fax (403) 462-1925, icdr@compusmart.ab.ca ■ Emphasizes both the commonalities and the differences between Thais and Americans, by examining attitudes towards individualism, self-reliance, saving face, competition, group harmony, and the expression of negative emotion. Visit www.compusmart.ab.ca/icdr, the distributor's web site. [ID:1024]

Considering Filipinos ▢
1990, *Theodore Gochenour,* Intercultural Press, 120 pages ➤ Intercultural and Community Development Resources (ICDR), P.O. Box 32108, Millwoods Station, Edmonton, Alberta T6K 4C2; $22; VISA, Amex; (800) 378-3199, fax (403) 462-1925, icdr@compusmart.ab.ca ■ Describes the emotional and historic ties between the US and the Philippines. The Filipino peoples' sense of community is compared with American individualism, and includes practical suggestions for bridging the difference. With case studies to help readers test their grasp of American-Filipino interaction. Visit the distributor's web site at www.compusmart.ab.ca/icdr. [ID:1383]

DailyJob ▢
www.dailyjob.com ■ Lists job postings for Hong Kong and China. Information on the site is updated daily. Look under "Education" for teaching opportunities. [ID:2415]

Doing Business in Asia's Booming "China Triangle":
People's Republic of China, Taiwan, Hong Kong ▢
1994, *Christopher Engholm,* Prentice Hall Canada, 392 pages ➤ Intercultural and Community Development Resources (ICDR), P.O. Box 32108, Millwoods Station, Edmonton, Alberta T6K 4C2; $35; VISA, Amex; (800) 378-3199, fax (403) 462-1925, icdr@compusmart.ab.ca ■ A complete guide to selling to and investing in the booming region of Greater China. Case histories of companies reaping profits in this region and dozens of business-tested strategies and proven techniques for successfully investing and manufacturing in the China Triangle. Visit the distributor's web site at www.compusmart.ab.ca/icdr. [ID:2382]

Doing Business in Asia: The Complete Guide ▢
1995, *Sanjyot P. Dunung,* Lexington, 264 pages ➤ Intercultural and Community Development Resources (ICDR), P.O. Box 32108, Millwoods Station, Edmonton, Alberta T6K 4C2; $35; VISA, Amex; (800) 378-3199, fax (403) 462-1925, icdr@compusmart.ab.ca ■ A concise, comprehensive handbook for doing business in 20 Asian countries, including India, South Korea, Pakistan, Indonesia and Malaysia. Visit the distributor's web site at www.compusmart.ab.ca/icdr. [ID:2385]

Doing Business with Japanese Men: A Woman's Handbook ▢
1993, *Christalyn Brannen, Tracey Wilen,* Stone Bridge Press, 176 pages ➤ Weatherhill, 41 Monroe Turnpike, Trumbull, CT 06611, USA; US$9.95; credit cards; (800) 437-7840, fax (800) 557-5601, weath1212@aol.com ■ The only book aimed at Western businesswomen meeting Japanese clients and confronting Japan's tradition of male dominance. Uses real-life anecdotes to help women

establish their authority and work effectively with Japanese men. Visit the distributor's web site at www.weatherhill.com. [ID:1405]

Employment Opportunities for Australia ⌨
http://employment.com.au/index.html ▪ This is a job site listing opportunities "down under." The site is searchable by companies, consultants, and government positions. Also contains an international database of job listings. [ID:2770]

Encountering the Chinese: a Guide for Americans ▥
1991, *Hu Wenzhong, Cornelius L. Grove,* Intercultural Press, 224 pages ➤ Intercultural and Community Development Resources (ICDR), P.O. Box 32108, Millwoods Station, Edmonton, Alberta T6K 4C2; $25; VISA, Amex; (800) 378-3199, fax (403) 462-1925, icdr@compusmart.ab.ca ▪ American and Chinese authors pool their experience to analyze China's complex culture. Identifies the cultural factors that lead to embarrassing faux pas and misunderstandings. A guide to more rewarding relationships with Chinese people everywhere. Visit the distributor's web site at www.compusmart.ab.ca/icdr. [ID:1362]

A Fair Go for All: Australian and American Interactions ▥
1991, *George W. Renwick,* Intercultural Press, 96 pages ➤ Intercultural and Community Development Resources (ICDR), P.O. Box 32108, Millwoods Station, Edmonton, Alberta T6K 4C2; $17; VISA, Amex; (800) 378-3199, fax (403) 462-1925, icdr@compusmart.ab.ca ▪ Explores similarities and reveals points of potential conflict between Australians and Americans. Cultural trainers examine a variety of issues, and offer guidelines for managing interpersonal relations more effectively. Visit the distributor's web site at www.compusmart.ab.ca/icdr. [ID:1317]

Finding a Job in New Zealand ▥
1996, *Joy Muirhead,* 128 pages ➤ How To Books Ltd., 3 Newtec Place, Magdalen Road, Oxford, OX4 1RE, UK; £9.99; credit cards; (44) (1752) 202-301, fax (44) (1865) 202-331 ▪ A unique source on finding work in New Zealand's growing economy. [ID:2437]

Going to Japan on Business:
Protocol, Stategies & Language for the Corporate Traveler ▥
1997, *Christalyn Brannen,* 176 pages ➤ Stone Bridge Press, P.O. Box 8202, Berkeley, CA 94707, USA; US$11.95; VISA, MC; (800) 947-7271, fax (510) 524-8711, sbp@stonebridge.com ▪ Quick-reference tips for first time and seasoned travellers. Includes information on preparing for your trip, getting around, making introductions, conducting business meetings, socializing, sounding good in Japanese, and much more. Visit the publisher's web site, www.stonebridge.com. [ID:2466]

How to Live and Work Series—Pacific Rim ▥
How To Books Ltd., approx. 150 pages each ➤ Capricorn Business Services, Inc., 28 Clear Lake Ave., West Hill, Ontario M1C 4L6; approx. $25 each; credit cards; (416) 282-3331, fax (416) 282-0015 ▪ This series will help you prepare for working and living in the Pacific Rim. Provides information on visas, housing, schools, customs and language, looking for work, and more. Individual books available for Australia, New Zealand, Hong Kong, China, and Japan. [ID:2500]

Jobs in Japan: The Complete Guide to
Living and Working in the Land of Rising Opportunity ▥
1993, *John Wharton,* Global Press, 268 pages ➤ Capricorn Business Services, Inc., 28 Clear Lake Ave., West Hill, Ontario M1C 4L6; $19.95; credit cards; (416) 282-3331, fax (416) 282-0015 ▪ Explains how English speakers with little experience can help meet Japan's constant demand for English teachers. Details on over 400 English schools and other useful organizations, plus advice on other jobs open to foreigners, negotiating with employers, obtaining visas and coping with the culture. [ID:1429]

Living in China: A Guide to Teaching and Studying in China including Taiwan ▥
1997, *R. Weiner, M. Murphy, A. Li,* 283 pages ➤ China Books & Periodicals Inc., 2929 - 24th Street, San Francisco, CA 94110, USA; US$19.95; credit cards; (415) 282-2994, fax (415) 282-0994 ▪ Crosscultural guide with advice for teacher or tourist, student or businessperson. Complete listings of Chinese colleges and universities, in both the Peoples' Republic of China and Taiwan,

which accept foreign teachers or students. The authors are amusingly frank about surviving, working and even dating in China. Visit the distributor's web site, www.chinabooks.com. [ID:1111]

Now Hiring! Jobs in Asia 📖

1996, *Clarke Canfield, Jennifer DuBois, Steve Gutman,* 217 pages ➤ Impact Publications, 9104 North Manassas Drive, Manassas Park, VA 20111-2366, USA; US$17.95; credit cards; (703) 361-7300, fax (703) 335-9486 ▪ This book provides current, detailed information on teaching English in Japan, Korea, and Taiwan. Identifies hundreds of schools. Includes information on visas, expenses, budget airfare and accommodations. Visit www.impactpublications.com, the distributor's web site. [ID:1755]

Overseas Employment 🖥

www.run-ti.com/employment/world/world.html ▪ This is a small but excellent series of links to job banks and employment services in several countries. The site is focused on the Asia Pacific region but there are also links to Europe and several worldwide resources. [ID:2552]

Pacific Rim Profiles 📖

1997, 12 pages each ➤ Asia Pacific Foundation, Suite 666, 999 Canada Place, Vancouver, B.C. V6C 3E1; $9.50 each or $99.50 for set; VISA, MC; (604) 684-5986, fax (604) 681-1370 ▪ A series of booklets on 14 Pacific Rim countries plus APEC. A teaching resource for senior high school and college levels. Includes historical background, government and economy, international trade profiles, information on student life, current affairs, crosscultural information and more. Visit the distributor's web site at www.apfc.ca. [ID:2404]

The Rice Paper Ceiling 📖

1994, *Rochelle Kopp,* 256 pages ➤ Weatherhill, 41 Monroe Turnpike, Trumbull, CT 06611, USA; US$25; credit cards; (800) 437-7840, fax (800) 557-5601, weath1212@aol.com ▪ Explains what the American employee of a Japanese company can do to advance his or her career prospects. Visit the distributor's web site at www.weatherhill.com. [ID:2406]

The Rising Sun on Main Street: Working with the Japanese 📖

1992, *Alison Lanier,* 267 pages ➤ International Information Associates, Inc., P.O. Box 773, Morrisville, PA 19067-0773, USA; US$12.95; VISA, MC; (215) 493-9214, fax (215) 493-9421 ▪ Offers advice for understanding and dealing with the Japanese and Japan's changing world role. [ID:1193]

Stone Bridge Catalogue 📖 🖥

Stone Bridge Press, P.O. Box 8202, Berkeley, CA 94707, USA; free; VISA, MC; (800) 947-7271, fax (510) 524-8711, sbp@stonebridge.com ▪ This catalogue lists books and software about Japan, including a number of CD-ROMs for learning Japanese. You can also browse or order online, at www.stonebridge.com. [ID:2411]

The Taiwan Business Primer 📖

1991, 296 pages ➤ Asia Pacific Foundation, Suite 666, 999 Canada Place, Vancouver, B.C. V6C 3E1; $20; VISA, MC; (604) 684-5986, fax (604) 681-1370 ▪ A quick reference tool on Taiwanese business practices, local customs, business relationships, and political, social and economic trends. Profiles major industries and professions, and lists addresses of useful contacts. Visit www.apfc.ca. [ID:1305]

Understanding and Working with the Japanese Business World 📖

1992, *Hiroki Kato, Joan Kato* ➤ Prentice Hall Canada, 539 Collier MacMillan Drive, Cambridge, Ontario N1R 5W9; $28.95; credit cards; (800) 567-3800, fax (800) 563-9196 ▪ A guide to overcoming the business-related differences that exist between the United States and Japan. The authors explain the Japanese mind and show how to master Japanese protocol. Visit the publisher's web site at www.phcanada.com. [ID:1354]

Unlocking Japan's Distribution System in the '90s: The Complete Exporter's Guide 📖

1994, *James Keenan,* 399 pages ➤ Asia Pacific Foundation, Suite 666, 999 Canada Place, Vancouver, B.C. V6C 3E1; $39.95; VISA, MC; (604) 684-5986, fax (604) 681-1370 ▪ A book based on the premise that exporters seeking to succeed in the Asia Pacific market must know how to select and motivate their intermediaries—distributors, trading firms and agents. Includes contact information for over 450 trade associations, credit investigation firms, government trade offices, and more. Visit www.apfc.ca. [ID:1663]

Unlocking the Japanese Business Mind 📖

1995, *Gregory Tenhover,* 300 pages ➤ Weatherhill, 41 Monroe Turnpike, Trumbull, CT 06611, USA; US$17.95; credit cards; (800) 437-7840, fax (800) 557-5601, weath1212@aol.com ▪ An in-depth analysis of the complex cultural dynamics of doing business in Japan. Visit the distributor's web site at www.weatherhill.com. [ID:2408]

When Business East Meets Business West:
The Guide to Practice and Protocol in the Pacific Rim 📖

1991, *Christopher Engholm,* 368 pages ➤ John Wiley & Sons, 22 Worchester Drive, Rexdale, Ontario M9W 1L1; $14.95; credit cards; (800) 567-4797, fax (800) 565-6802 ▪ The Pacific Basin has emerged as the biggest new frontier for American business and being able to understand the Orient is no longer a choice, but a requirement for American managers and entrepreneurs. The book addresses business situations and contexts: buying and selling, bargaining, resolving conflict, Asian corporate culture, and more. Visit the distributor's web site at www.wiley.com/products/worldwide/canada. [ID:1002]

With Respect to the Japanese: A Guide for Americans 📖

1984, *John C. Condon,* Intercultural Press, 110 pages ➤ Intercultural and Community Development Resources (ICDR), P.O. Box 32108, Millwoods Station, Edmonton, Alberta T6K 4C2; $18; VISA, Amex; (800) 378-3199, fax (403) 462-1925, icdr@compusmart.ab.ca ▪ Handbook for Americans who deal with the Japanese in a business or educational setting. Visit the distributor's web site at www.compusmart.ab.ca/icdr. [ID:1038]

Working in Asia: A Fact-Filled Guide to Working Opportunities 📖

1996, *Nicki Grihault,* In Print Publishing, 488 pages ➤ Weatherhill, 41 Monroe Turnpike, Trumbull, CT 06611, USA; $16.95; credit cards; (800) 437-7840, fax (800) 557-5601, weath1212@aol.com ▪ Provides addresses of employers, embassies and recruitment agencies; details on obtaining visas and accommodation, and employment possibilities, from tour guiding in Nepal to nannying in Singapore. Explains the advantages and disadvantages of working in each country, doesn't glamorize the experience. Visit the distributor's web site at www.weatherhill.com. [ID:1810]

The Yin and Yang of American Values 📖

1998, *Eun Y. Kim,* Kodansha International, 208 pages ➤ Fitzhenry and Whiteside Ltd., 195 Allstate Parkway, Markham, Ontario L3R 4T8; $31; VISA, MC; (800) 387-9776, fax (800) 260-9777, godwit@fitzhenry.ca ▪ A critique of American values from an Asian perspective. Insight into American behaviour and how Americans are perceived by the rest of the world, particularly Asia. Visit the distributor's web site at www.fitzhenry.ca. [ID:2429]

Chapter 28

Jobs in International Development

The term *international development* commonly refers to aid programs directed towards countries in the South. ("The South" is the new term replacing "Developing Countries" and "Third World.") As Canada is a very active donor, many Canadians work overseas in the field of international development. (An estimated 5,000 Canadians work overseas on CIDA-funded projects; 1,600 Canadians are permanent employees of UN organizations. Countless others work as consultants, volunteers, and business suppliers to CIDA, the UN, and numerous other aid agencies in the world.) There is a wide variety of employment possibilities involving the administration and implementation of these programs by international bodies, the federal government, NGOs and private firms.

TYPES OF OVERSEAS POSTINGS

International positions are not always permanent overseas jobs. The following explains some of the many types of postings.

The Consulting Visit

Government departments, international bodies and consulting firms often hire independent, highly-qualified consultants. The visit is usually a few weeks in duration, with hotel accommodation, and may include a tour of several countries in one region. The international visit (often called a mission in government circles) is usually a fact-finding evaluation visit.

The Business Visit

These are mostly in-house, temporary transfers by business or large UN agencies. Postings are usually up to six months in duration and generally involve training, application of a special skill, or temporarily assuming a position waiting to be filled permanently. Personal effects are not moved overseas. Housing arrangements are usually temporary, in a hotel or guesthouse.

The International Posting

These are long-term positions lasting from two to three years. Personal effects and family accompany the employee. The one- or two-year renewable contract is also often applied. The objectives may be: to fill a job for which the applicant is highly qualified, to provide international training for the employee which will benefit head office upon his or her return, for a specific project for which the employee's skills are required.

Long-term Volunteer Placement with an NGO

The normal length of time for volunteer placements with NGOs is two years followed by one-year renewal contracts. The average age of volunteers is between 30 and 35 years. Volunteers must have specialized skills and experience. They generally work with local government agencies or local grassroots organizations. Salaries are basic, enough to provide a comfortable lifestyle by local standards and allow you some local, regional travel but which leave you with little savings at the conclusion of your posting.

Cooperant Placements with an NGO

These positions are becoming increasingly common within large NGOs. They are different than volunteer positions in that salaries are usually equivalent to the low-end salary scale for your field in Canada. This allows you to accumulate moderate savings during a two-year placement, or to purchase a car locally, for example. Technical specialization and previous work experience are usually a prerequisite.

ADMINISTRATIVE JOBS IN INTERNATIONAL DEVELOPMENT

The following short job descriptions cover many of the standard administrative jobs available in development organizations. Regardless of your position overseas, most international jobs require that you also perform some or all of the following tasks: training local nationals, supervising personnel, working with local officials, general office administration, and budget management. Employees are also expected to be knowledgeable about project management.

In-Country Program Coordinator

As the country representative of your agency overseas (program director), you are responsible for a number of projects. You are somewhere between an entrepreneur and a diplomat. You must, above all else, be versatile and able to work effectively in the face of stress. You alone will manage an office in which your duties will include writing reports to the Canadian head office, accounting, financial budgeting, administration of local staff, filing, and logistics work.

Country representatives normally fall into two categories: those primarily concerned with supervising Canadian volunteers, and those supervising projects funded by your organization and administered by local organizations. Volunteer administrators must deal mostly with the personnel administration of their volunteers. Project supervision requires, on the other hand, a good understanding of local customs and the ability to negotiate solutions with local officials. The biggest headaches associated with these jobs are communicating effectively with the Canadian head office, coupled with managing a wide range of endeavours in your region under usually difficult economic and social conditions. A major plus is that you are your own boss and are able to influence in-country policies and programs. This will enable you to see direct results from your efforts.

Project Director

As the on-site coordinator of a development project, you are often isolated from the capital region of the country. You may have a number of Canadian employees to supervise. You are responsible for overseeing all aspects of a particular project. As you are involved directly with implementing a program, you must be adept at problem-solving. This suggests a need for well-developed interpersonal skills to solve problems and maintain motivation. You must also be able to resolve the conflict between outside supervision of your program (from visiting consultants or administrators from head office) and the realities faced by on-site workers. Given the difficulties of implementing new programs, there is often a high risk of failure in such jobs. As a hands-on coordinator, you have to exercise the full breadth of leadership.

Diplomatic Staff

Aid programs are increasingly being supervised by Canadian diplomatic staff, many of whom are closely linked with the CANADIAN INTERNATIONAL DEVELOPMENT AGENCY (CIDA). Most overseas UN personnel have the status of diplomats and many of their positions are related to the administration of international development programs. Diplomatic staff don't usually work directly on development projects. Rather, they monitor programs or negotiate with the implementing agencies or operational partners such as the local government, a private firm or an NGO. Thus, diplomats are more involved with monitoring, writing policy, or processing paper than doing hands-on work. Their skills are usually in writing and negotiating in a highly protocol-oriented environment. Thus, career paths tend to be more hierarchical and promotions come after longer periods of time.

Junior Professional Officer (JPO)

These UNITED NATIONS posts are open to Canadians under 30 with a master's degree. The Canadian government sponsors these positions through various UN agencies so that young Canadians can acquire overseas experience with the UN. Jobs usually consist of monitoring UN-sponsored projects. Tasks include reviewing project proposals to ensure that they fit certain criteria, helping to push the proposals though the UN bureaucracy, and evaluating projects. These are desk jobs, involving some travel to project sites. They are certainly not hands-on positions. The major frustration mentioned by former JPOs is learning to work in the large, formal, slow-moving, impersonal UN system where you see few concrete results from your efforts. Positive aspects of this work are learning to work with "the system," seeing the international development scene in its widest perspective, learning writing skills, acquiring diplomatic skills, and meeting a variety of experienced leaders in the field of international development. Excellent experience for beginners! (For information on how to apply see Chapter 17, International Internships and Chapter 36, United Nations.)

Overseas Volunteer

There are hundreds of volunteer positions available in almost every field imaginable. Contracts are usually for a two-year period and require a special skill or trade. As a volunteer, you will usually live and work at the local grassroots level. Salaries and housing are modest, but usually adequate. While you won't be able to join the local polo club or eat in five-star hotels, you will have enough money to live well and travel within the country by local transportation. Volunteering is one of the best ways to acquire experience in your field and is often a prerequisite for a career in international development. With this experience, you will have the credibility and expertise to make further inroads into your field. (Note that there is an increasing trend in the NGO community to create cooperant positions, where pay scales lie somewhere between a volunteer position and a standard overseas salaried position. Inquire about this category when approaching NGOs.)

Community Development Worker

As the teaching of certain skills is a major objective in development work, having good group communication techniques is important for overseas development jobs. Community development work involves dealing with local groups to forge links, facilitate, train, maintain continuity, motivate and help promote change. Most large development projects employ a full-time community development officer, while many smaller projects employ only one person, whose main job responsibility is community development work. You should have a lot of experience in organizing local committees at the grassroots level and be adept at maintaining motivation in the face of frustration.

Office Manager, Accountant

Most overseas projects, especially country-wide programs, have an office in the capital which requires an office manager and an accountant or controller. These posts are most often available from private sector firms having contracts with CIDA. As in similar Canadian operations, you need to have the versatility normally associated with working in a small firm. Micro-computer skills are becoming especially important in the management of overseas operations.

Logistician

In this job, you are the person responsible for transportation, warehousing, travel arrangements, communications, building maintenance, local purchases and vehicle maintenance. Above all, you are an organizer. Depending on the size of the program, you may specialize in emergency food stock warehousing for the INTERNATIONAL RED CROSS, or perhaps supervising the transportation of equipment which is imported or locally purchased for a development project. You should be streetwise for this type of job, have inside knowledge about where to purchase local products, acquire a visa quickly, obtain special forms from the local government, or deal with merchants and local staff. The difficulty with this job is the stress of being on the frontline, having to complete concrete tasks in an atmosphere where unforeseeable obstacles dominate. The great thing about this work is that you deal directly with the local population at all levels. It's very hands-on and includes non-bureaucratic problem-solving.

Support Staff

These jobs include everybody from the secretary, the telephone or communications expert and the security guard, to the assistant administrator. While most overseas employers hire local people for this work, security reasons dictate that key diplomatic posts be held by Canadians. (For more information see Chapter 34, Careers in Government.)

Project or Program Officer (in Canada)

Most staff in Canadian NGOs and many in CIDA are program officers. In this position, you provide the link between the field operations (overseas operations) and the Canadian administration. Your job is primarily to monitor the overseas program (usually specific to one country or one region) and support overseas personnel. As a good organizer or administrator, you must be proficient in writing, interviewing and financial administration. The job usually involves travel once a year to the program country. The position can be frustrating as it is bureaucratic, but it is often a stepping-stone to an overseas position. Emphasis is on learning the Canadian component of development administration.

OTHER FIELDS OF INTERNATIONAL DEVELOPMENT

Here is a sample of job areas recently advertised:

Agriculture: Agronomist, land use officer, extension coordinators, credit officer, marketing officer, vocational agriculture teachers, veterinarian, livestock extension officer, range management officers

Community Development: Development officers, home economists, small business consultants, management of cooperatives, specific women's programs for each of these areas

Trades: Teachers of carpentry, blacksmithing, boat building, masonry, mechanics

Health: Doctors, nurses, public health specialists, nutritionists

Economist: Rural development planners, health, environment, finance, small business, industry, transportation, tourism

Public Administration: Human resource development, project management, institution-building, logistics, procurement, planning, accounting systems

Education: Sciences, mathematics, literacy, teacher training

Engineering: Irrigation, water, forestry, environment, agriculture, mining, transportation

Fisheries: Marketing, processing, management, boat design, fish farming

RESOURCES

For related resources consult the Resources for the section on the CANADIAN INTERNATIONAL DEVELOPMENT AGENCY (CIDA) in Chapter 34, Careers in Government; Chapter 35, Nongovernmental Organizations; Chapter 36, United Nations; Chapter 37, Environmental & Agricultural Research Centres; and Chapter 38, International Organizations.

For resources describing the all important crosscultural aspects of international development, consult the Resources in the following chapters: for general crosscultural skills see Chapter 1, The Effective Overseas Employee; for the more practical aspects of living overseas see Chapter 3, Living Overseas and Chapter 12, Crosscultural Travel; for material which is helpful to all, but focuses on crosscultural business skills, see Chapter 7, The Canadian Identity in the International Workplace; and for country-specific advice on social and business customs see Chapter 27, Jobs by Regions of the World.

Canadian Association of International Development Consultants (CAIDC)
Canadian Association of International Development Consultants (CAIDC), 116 Promenade du Portage, Hull, Québec J8X 2K1; (819) 771-9367, fax (819) 771-7953 ■ The Canadian Association of International Development Consultants (CAIDC) is a national association that gives voice to the concerns and interests of international development consultants. Member benefits include: a newsletter reporting consulting opportunities, new governmental policies, emerging trends in international development, and how to access relevant information, sources, and sites; the CAIDC listserv, an e-mail distribution system used by members to communicate with each other; the continuously expanding CAIDC web site; access to the CAIDC database which contains detailed information on over 450 member consultants; a listing in the CAIDC Member Directory; access to the CAIDC Search Service, an indexed listing of contract opportunities available with CIDA, all levels of Canadian government, public sector organizations, publicly funded entities, and several international establishments; professional development and valuable networking opportunities through social, educational, and professional events provide a forum for the exchange of professional expertise; liaison, consultation, and advocacy with key organizations including CIDA, DFAIT, the Alliance of Manufacturers and Exporters of Canada, the Canadian Co-operative Association, the Association of Canadian Community Colleges, and Consulting and Audit Canada. Visit their web site at www.caidc.ca. [ID:2617]

Canadian World Federalist Newsletter 📖
3/year ➤ World Federalists of Canada, 145 Spruce Street, Ottawa, Ontario K1R 6P1; $8; VISA, MC; (613) 232-0647, fax (613) 563-0017, wfcnat@web.net ■ Provides information on the World Federalists of Canada and discusses issues in world federalism. Also covers developments within the

United Nations and international law. For more information, visit the publisher's web site at www.web.net/~wfcnat/WFC.html. [ID:1599]

Care Canada 🖳
www.care.ca ▪ This site not only gives detailed job information on Care Canada, but also on overseas work in general. In its Human Resources sub-directory, there is a wealth of information: questions to ask yourself, important characteristics for overseas work, and questions candidates should prepare for in an interview. A definite must for anyone interested in NGO work overseas! [ID:2449]

Career Opportunities for American Planners in International Development 📖
1994, *Charles Boyce, Ralph Gakenheimer*, 86 pages ➤ International Division, American Planning Association, c/o The Institute of Public Administration, 55 West 44th Street, New York, NY 10016, USA; $10; credit cards; (212) 730-5480 ext. 340 or 330, fax (212) 768-9071 ▪ Aimed at the American reader, this book provides a wealth of information on educational requirements and how to get started. Planners with varying backgrounds provide their insights on opportunities with international development agencies, the US government, consulting firms and nongovernment organizations. Publishers of a monthly newsletter called *Interplan*. [ID:1638]

Cross-Cultural Effectiveness 📖
1990, *Daniel Kealey*, 68 pages ➤ Public Inquiries, Canadian International Development Agency, 200 Promenade du Portage, Hull, Québec K1A 0G4; free; (800) 230-6349, fax (819) 953-6088, info@acdi-cida.gc.ca ▪ Report of a three-year study involving 1,400 people engaged in Canadian development programs in 16 countries. Aimed at measuring the effectiveness of technical advisors in trans-ferring much-needed skills. Well written, in English and French. [ID:1101]

Development Business 📖 🖳
24 per year ➤ United Nations Publications, 1 United Nations Plaza, Room DC1-570, New York, NY 10017, USA; US$495/year; credit cards; (212) 963-1516, fax (212) 963-1381 ▪ *Development Business* is the primary source for information on goods, works, and services required for projects financed by all of the Development Banks and the UN system. A one-year subscription includes 12 World Bank and 12 Inter-American Development Bank Monthly Operational Summaries and 4 African Development Bank Quarterly Operational Summaries. Also available online, as Scan-a-Bid. There are charges for connect time and retrieval fees. For sign-up information see the web site www.krinfo.com and click on the Sales icon in the left-hand frame. [ID:1303]

Directory of Non-Governmental Organizations
(NGOs) Active in Sustainable Development 📖
1997, 768 pages ➤ Organization of Economic Cooperation and Development (OECD), Suite 700, 2001 L Street N.W., Washington, DC 20036, USA; US$138; credit cards; (202) 785-6323, fax (202) 785-0350 ▪ This updated and revised directory is a comprehensive source of information on 3,900 NGOs in 26 countries in Europe. Contains NGO profiles, indexes of their activities in developing countries and Europe. Visit the publisher's web site at www.oecdwash.org. [ID:1220]

The Executive Contact List: US Private and Voluntary
Organizations Registered with the Agency for International Development 📖
Semiannual, 192 pages ➤ Bureau for Humanitarian Assistance and Response, US Agency for International Development, 1300 Pennsylvannia Avenue N.W., Washington, DC 20523, USA; free; (202) 712-4810, fax (202) 216-3237 ▪ Lists names of executive contacts for US organizations registered with the US Agency for International Development. [ID:1263]

Health, Population and Reproductive Health Resources 🖳
www.jhpiego.jhu.edu/RELATED/RELATED.HTM#Health ▪ Johns Hopkins University has compiled a list of links to organizations involved in this area of development. [ID:2453]

MERX 🖳
MERX at CEBRA INC., 2 Watts Ave., Charlottetown, P.E.I. C1E 1B0; (800) 964-6379, fax (888) 235-5800 ▪ A national electronic tendering service. MERX is like the classifieds for contracts with most federal government departments, some provincial and territorial ministries, and some municipalities. Register or access the system by phone, fax, mail or on the web. You can also

access MERX using Datapac (a dial-in service via modem). Supplier registration costs $8.95/month. Prices for document requests and other services vary. Visit them at www.merx.cebra.com. [ID:2645]

The Oxfam Handbook of Development and Relief 📖
1995, OXFAM UK, 1200 pages ➤ Fernwood Books Ltd., P.O. Box 9409, Stn. A, Halifax, N.S. B3K 5S3; $39; VISA; (902) 422-3302, fax (902) 422-3179 ■ This three-volume set is a valuable reference tool for development practitioners, planners, students, and teachers of development. [ID:2479]

PACT Publications Catalogue 📖
3/year ➤ PACT Media Services, 777 United Nations Plaza, New York, NY 10017, USA; free; (212) 697-6222, fax (212) 692-9748, books@pactpub.org ■ Excellent catalogue offering training materials, communications and multimedia information for use by international development professionals. Intended as a forum for the very best development materials from around the world. Highly recommended. Visit the distributor's web site at www.pactpub.com. [ID:1228]

Resources for Development and Relief: 1996 Oxfam Catalogue 📖
1996, Oxfam Canada, 39 pages ➤ Fernwood Books Ltd., P.O. Box 9409, Stn. A, Halifax, N.S. B3K 5S3; free; VISA; (902) 422-3302, fax (902) 422-3179 ■ This excellent catalogue includes books, journals, videos, research papers and training manuals on a wide variety of topics, including: Trade, Aid and Debt, Understanding Global Issues, Health, Gender, Agriculture and Environment, Conflict and Development, and more. [ID:2428]

Service Contracts and Lines of Credit 📖
Semiannual, *External Business Relations, Corporate Management Branch,* 66 pages ➤ Public Inquiries, Canadian International Development Agency, 200 Promenade du Portage, Hull, Québec K1A 0G4; free; (800) 230-6349, fax (819) 953-6088, info@acdi-cida.gc.ca ■ Lists firms and consultants who currently have contracts with CIDA. Lists contracts according to size, project title, supplier and approximate dollar value. A must for Canadian international job seekers. [ID:1103]

Signposts: Looking for Work in International Development 📖
1995 ➤ Communications Branch, Canadian International Development Agency (CIDA), Communications Branch, 200 Promenade du Portage, Hull, Québec K1A 0G4; free; (613) 997-5006, fax (613) 953-6087 ■ This Canadian reference booklet on international development gives a brief description of the types of work involved, their main characteristics and requirements, and the initial steps in applying for them. It lists and provides brief summaries of the major Canadian employers and volunteer agencies. [ID:1100]

Supplyline 📖 💻
Quarterly, *Maureen Johnson* ➤ CODE International, 321 Chapel Street, Ottawa, Ontario K1N 7Z2; free; (613) 232-7101, fax (613) 235-2506 ■ A bilingual four-page flyer on CODE International's activities, aimed at consultants and companies with interests in procuring supplies for education and other basic needs overseas, and in project management for development. Available on the web at www.codeinc.com. [ID:1115]

Third World Resource Directory: A Guide to Organizations and Publications 📖
1994-95, *Thomas P. Fenton, Mary J. Heffron* ➤ Novalis, 2nd Floor, 49 Front Street E., Toronto, Ontario M5E 1B3; $92.95; credit cards; (800) 387-7164 ext. 24, fax (416) 363-9409 ■ This 800-page resource guide is one of the most comprehensive for current and hard-to-find print, audio-visual, and organizational resources related to Africa, Asia and the Pacific, Latin America and the Caribbean, and the Middle East. Covers a range of issues. Well-indexed. [ID:1221]

Virtual Library on International Development 💻
w3.acdi-cida.gc.ca/virtual.nsf ■ Published by the Canadian International Development Agency (CIDA), this site is an excellent collection of links to international development resources on the Internet. Organized by theme, organization, region and country, report and publication. A constantly-updated new links section. [ID:2450]

Chapter 29

Teaching Abroad

Whether you're a seasoned professional teacher or someone just finishing university studies, you've probably imagined yourself in a far-off land where the pace of life is slower, more relaxed, and where fresh discoveries await you at every turn: new foods, new smells, and friendly people. These are more than dreams and fantasies for some: they are reality for thousands of Canadians who teach abroad.

Teaching remains one of the *biggest* areas of overseas employment for Canadians. Teachers of English are in especially high demand, with an estimated one billion people worldwide wanting to learn English.

The range of opportunities abroad for teachers and school administrators runs the gamut, from private English language schools, to international and American schools, NGO-sponsored positions, universities, technical institutions, multinational firms, professional organizations, and teaching private lessons for a few weeks or months while travelling. Assignments range from a couple of months to three years or more. And while positions often require formal teaching qualifications, many do not—especially in the English language field where one can find employment in virtually any country in which English is not the first language.

Indeed, there are few careers more portable than teaching. There are opportunities in every corner of the world, from Prague to Paris, Istanbul to Bangkok, and from Chicago to Sao Paulo. The field is wide open and waiting for you.

WHY TEACH ABROAD?

Educators are in the enviable position of being able to use work for travel-learning experiences. Going abroad may be a way to enhance your career or get into the education field, a chance to see a part of the world which has always appealed to you, have an adventure, make new friends, rejuvenate a career that has gone stale, do some humanitarian work, or simply earn an honest living.

On a professional level, teachers who work overseas almost always find new enthusiasm and a fresh outlook on their subject area and their careers. A successful experience in another culture also results in greater confidence in your own teaching ability. And of course, many overseas postings present the opportunity to learn another language.

You can use teaching as a stepping-stone to other international careers. Once you have learned another language, the ins-and-outs of the local culture, and made some valuable contacts, you have cleared some of the biggest obstacles to finding international work. You are, in effect, an insider!

FACING MYTHS AND REALITIES

While the overwhelming majority of educators find their stints overseas immeasurably rewarding, most have experienced some degree of surprise, frustration and disappointment.

For example, it is a mistake to expect that personal and professional difficulties will disappear with a change of scenery. A foreign career should not be used to run away from problems or undesirable situations. In most instances, depression, marital discord or romantic disillusionment, boredom or burnout are intensified by unfamiliar surroundings.

Professionally, an educator who is unhappy with her or his job at home will usually find similar or even greater frustrations abroad. As one teacher returning from Zambia said, "The realities of an eight-to-three schedule and the daily regimen of lesson plans, student discipline, hall duty and the rest are much the same, whether the school is in Lusaka or Vancouver."

As for getting rich teaching abroad, this is more myth than reality. While most teachers report their standard of living as equivalent to or higher than what they had been accustomed to at home, the expenses of travelling and sightseeing eat up any surplus. Many are surprised at the cost of automobiles, gasoline, housing, food and so on. In short, seeking a teaching job in order to "come home with a bundle" is usually a misguided notion.

You can avoid some of the pitfalls of teaching overseas if you heed some words of caution from experienced overseas teachers and administrators. We strongly recommend you speak to at least two such teachers before you leave.

WHAT ARE THE QUALITIES OF AN EXPERIENCED INTERNATIONAL TEACHER?

Making the final decision takes courage and enthusiasm. For some, moving abroad can be tremendously disruptive. Experienced international teachers, on the other hand, think nothing of giving up their possessions, renting out their home for a year or two, and freeing themselves of the worries of retirement and savings. They have a realistic understanding of loneliness and homesickness. Overseas teachers see themselves as free spirits, able to pick up and move themselves, and in many cases, their families, to each new posting with enthusiasm, anticipation, and curiosity.

International teachers see themselves as patient, observant, and curious about human relations. They are sensitive to individual differences and needs. International teachers set aside professional commitments to their field in Canada, and continue their professional interests overseas. They understand the crosscultural classroom environment. They understand second language acquisition, and see the need for flexibility in their roles as teachers. They are more concerned with fitting in than introducing new teaching methods. They work hard at teaching, are not unnerved by unfamiliar surroundings, and can deal with low task accomplishment, frustration, and failure. For them, the point of teaching abroad is the human experience.

WHAT RETURNING TEACHERS SAY

The following quotes will assist you in answering the question "am I the sort of teacher who could live and work overseas?"

Generally, people who are independent, healthy and flexible, with a degree of interest in the foreign culture into which they will be immersed, whatever their motivations, return home singing the praises of their experience abroad. As one teacher returning from Japan said, "Teaching abroad made me realize there is a world outside Canada. I gained the concept of internationalism. I saw first-hand the interaction of world politics and economics. Plus, I was able to travel during holiday periods, meet people of other nationalities, and, all in all, gain a broader perspective."

After you make that first step and get your initial overseas teaching job, you may become "addicted," as one educator from Calgary says: "Teaching in a new culture is like entering a new life; around each corner is an entirely different experience. I have taught in Thailand, Iran and now Austria, and it just keeps getting better."

This is not to imply that you'll have only positive experiences. As a teacher from Sarnia, Ontario put it after returning from a CUSO posting in Papua New Guinea: "You really have to throw your old teaching methods out the window. The school I taught at had no lab facilities, no audiovisual equipment, one text for every three students. Basically, I had a chalkboard and chalk. It was tough for the first few months."

Good advice is offered by a Québec teacher recently returned from Turkey: "Go into the overseas assignment with a completely open mind, with tolerance, and with curiosity, and wherever you go it will be a rewarding experience. Be willing to learn and be patient with yourself."

A Toronto teacher, after a posting in an international school in Egypt, cautions against the tendency to confine yourself to the "known," the expatriate "ghetto," in your overseas community: "Beware of participating in the bitch sessions, complaining about how the local shopping, customs, transportation and so on aren't up to Canadian standards. It's a way of short-changing yourself in your overseas experience."

You may find more room for creativity, greater freedom to experiment, in your new teaching situation. A Vancouver professor recalls her experience at the University of Indonesia: "I was given more responsibility, independence, and authority and had to attend fewer meaningless meetings than back home. I could even create my own teaching assignment—what classes I'd teach and what materials I'd use."

On the subject of teaching materials, returning teachers at all levels, and in all types of schools, advise not to go to your new job empty-handed (unless you've been assured of their availability). Says one Saskatchewan teacher after returning from Swaziland: "Any teaching aid that you find indispensable at home you should bring—reference books, dictionaries, language books, paper, blank ditto sheets, pens, tapes, carbon paper, a small portable typewriter. You name it."

Finally, some encouragement for the inexperienced, unqualified traveller cum teacher. An Ottawa woman returning from an extensive trip that included a six-month stint teaching English in Greece says: "I ended up in a small Peloponnesian town with no experience, no teaching qualifications, no degree and no knowledge of Greek, and I had the most memorable experience of my life."

WHO CAN TEACH OVERSEAS?

A large and well-defined market exists for educators of all types—teachers, school administrators, librarians, counsellors. While anyone with a university degree can generally find work, especially teaching English, the best candidates are those with teacher certification and two years' experience. For administrative, library, and counselling positions, advanced degrees (minimum MA) are usually required.

Since most formal teaching jobs are on a contract basis (usually two to three years in length) there is always a substantial staff turnover. Language schools have even shorter contracts (usually one year or less) and higher rates of staff turnover.

Because of the isolation and difficulty in adapting to new cultures, there is often a preference for singles and teaching couples without dependents. Couples with one non-teacher member may find the job search difficult. Competition is fierce in European schools, but there are opportunities for recent graduates in the South.

WHAT TYPES OF TEACHING POSITIONS ARE OUT THERE?

Teaching as a Volunteer in the South

Several NGOs recruit teachers at all levels for postings in the South. Contracts are usually for two or three years and remuneration varies from subsistence to professional levels. Some NGOs accept only those with teacher training and relevant experience, while others require only a university degree. Most positions are in the local education systems rather than with private schools. School facilities are often sparse. Your housing will vary from comfortable to very basic. You will often be the only volunteer around, and your friends will be from the local population. A WUSC volunteer describes teaching in rural villages of Bhutan in this way: "Each morning started with cooking bread on an open fire. I rarely could afford meat, but the sheer pleasure of getting to know local Bhutanese families made it all worthwhile."

Teaching at an International School in the South

International schools exist to serve the needs of expatriates—diplomats, missionaries, aid workers, military personnel, and international business-people. A network of French and English international schools operates worldwide and offers curriculums comparable to "those back home." These schools are usually certified by an agency in the US or Europe and are sponsored locally by parent associations, an international company, or a government body. Contracts for these jobs usually range from two to three years.

As a teacher in an international school, you and your family will be based in a large city, usually the capital. The school will usually be very well equipped, and will follow a well-developed standard international curriculum. Housing will be comfortable, you will enjoy the company of many other expatriate teachers and the parents of the children you teach, (usually diplomatic staff, employees of large multinationals, and sometimes, local elites). You may, however be somewhat removed from the local population.

The privately-funded and -operated network of international schools is spread over some 90 countries. Salaries and benefits vary depending on the size of the school, the location, and the cost of living in the community. Many corporations employing US, Canadian, British, Belgian, or French citizens pay the tuition for dependent children attending these international or American-sponsored schools. There are two umbrella organizations for English international schools, the EUROPEAN COUNCIL OF INTERNATIONAL SCHOOLS and the INTERNATIONAL SCHOOLS SERVICES who offer placement services, hold job fairs, and publish directories. The French system works under the ALLIANCE FRANÇAISE. (For more details see Resources section at the end of this chapter.)

Other Private Schools in the South

A number of other independent boarding schools exist overseas for English-speaking students. These schools have been established by private citizens of the host country, citizens of the United States, Britain or Canada residing in the community, religious organizations, or other special interest groups. Information about these independent international schools can be found in a number of directories, for example the *ISS Directory of Overseas Schools* and *Peterson's Annual Guide to Independent Secondary Schools*. (For more details see the Resources section at the end of this chapter.)

Teaching in an Industrialized Country

Private language schools, and international schools systems exist in Western countries. As these are industrialized countries, competition is fierce. Jobs usually pay enough to offer a middle class existence. You would have a traditional employee-employer relationship. It is therefore unlikely you would socialize with the parents of your students, and you would be responsible for your own housing and travel.

Private Tutoring as a Business Overseas

Are you following a spouse to a foreign land or have you rented an apartment in Madrid for six months? Do you have experience teaching music, English, French, computers, accounting? While it is generally illegal to set up your own business, small private tutoring contracts, especially amongst the expatriate community, are a good possibility and can help finance an extended stay abroad. The people you market yourself to can be embassy staff, employees of multinationals or local businesspeople.

Teacher Exchanges

Teachers and administrators can gain first-hand experience of another country and its culture by working in a foreign education system. Canadian and foreign teachers exchange classroom responsibilities and, in some cases, houses, apartments, and even cars.

If a local school board is involved, the foreign teacher must be approved before the exchange can take place. For more information on teacher exchange programs, contact your local federation office or your school board.

Application forms and additional information can be obtained from the following agencies.

NATIONAL

Canadian Education Association

252 Bloor Street W., 8-200, Toronto, Ontario M5S 1V5; (416) 924-7721, fax (416) 924-3188, acea@hookup.net, www.acea.ca

PROVINCIAL

BRITISH COLUMBIA:
Teacher Exchange Program

Ken MacCulloch, 2870 Seaview Rd., Victoria, B.C. V8L 1L1; (250) 472-1106, fax (250) 472-1107

ALBERTA:
National and International Education Branch

Alberta Education, Devonian Building, 11160 Jasper Ave., Edmonton, Alberta T5K 0L2; (403) 427-2035, fax (403) 422-3014, http://ednet.edc.gov.ab.ca/nie

SASKATCHEWAN:
Teacher Services Unit

Saskatchewan Education, 1500 - 4th Ave., Regina, Sask. S4P 3V7; (306) 787-6085, fax (306) 787-0035, www.gov.sk.ca

MANITOBA:
Department of Education and Training

P.O. Box 700, Russell, Man. R0J 1W0; (204) 773-2998, fax (204) 773-2411, www.gov.mb.ca

ONTARIO:
Canadian Education Exchange Foundation

250 Bayview Drive, Barrie, Ontario L4N 4Y8; (705) 739-7596, fax (705) 739-7764, www.ceef.ca

QUÉBEC:

Has no exchange program.

NEW BRUNSWICK:
Director of Professional Development

Department of Education, P.O. Box 6000, Fredericton, N.B. E3B 5H1; (506) 453-2157, fax (506)453-3325, www.gov.nb.ca/education/index.htm

NOVA SCOTIA:
Director Registrar – Teacher Certification

Department of Education, P.O. Box 578, Halifax, N.S. B3J 2S9; (902) 424-6620, fax (902) 424-3814, www.gov.ns.ca

PRINCE EDWARD ISLAND:
Office of the Registrar

Department of Education, P.O. Box 2000, Charlottetown, P.E.I. C1A 7N8; (902) 368-4651, fax (902)368-4663, www.gov.pe.ca/edu

NEWFOUNDLAND:
Director of School Services and Professional Development

Department of Education, P.O. Box 8700, St. John's, Newfoundland A1B 4J6; (709) 729-2997, fax (709) 729-5896, www.gov.nf.ca

University Teaching in the South

If you have a master's degree, a spirit of adventure, and initiative, you can often arrange your own job teaching at a university in, for example, China. Many people find work simply by writing a year ahead of time to a few far-flung universities and offering their services. The salary is usually not great but you can live comfortably and gain an incredible experience. If you have a PhD from a recognized Western university and have teaching experience, formal positions are advertised in professional journals, or in newspapers such as the *Chronicle of Higher Education,* the *New York Times,* the *Times Education Supplement,* and the *Globe and Mail* (see Resources section at the end of this chapter). Large libraries will have many useful directories, such as *Commonwealth Universities Yearbook, International Handbook of Universities* and *World Guide to Universities.* Local embassies are also worth contacting.

DIFFERENT STRATEGIES FOR DIFFERENT LEVELS OF EXPERIENCE

Depending on your level of experience (defined as a mix of teaching experience and international experience), a variety of opportunities are open to you. Beginners often teach in Southern countries where living conditions are spartan and salaries low. A senior teacher with good international credentials can land a job in Rome teaching at an international school for diplomats and international executives. University teaching is available to all, from Southern countries accepting an MA and no experience, to industrialized countries where senior credentials are required.

Recent Graduates, No Teaching or International Experience

Unless you want to teach English (see next section) you will have a difficult time finding work using the traditional method of résumé and covering letter, unless you have some specialized, sought-after skills or outstanding achievements (for example, a degree in agricultural sciences or medicine). Your best bet is to take six months off and travel the world. Visit schools, language-learning centres, and try to find a volunteer or short-term paid position.

Experienced Teachers with No International Teaching Experience

You must demonstrate that you are familiar with and can excel in a multicultural environment. Have you travelled extensively and lived with local peoples? Have you participated in multiracial issues and activities here in Canada? Have you demonstrated true "excellence" in teaching? Can you put all the above together in a résumé which demonstrates to international employers that you and your family will thrive in another culture? Are you prepared to teach overseas for a number of years in a row?

Two or More Years Overseas Teaching Experience

Hopefully you have taken every opportunity during your first international job to demonstrate leadership, initiative, commitment, and your love of the crosscultural teaching experience. You should also have glowing letters of reference from two or three officials. You are now ready to apply to almost any international school. You can participate in international recruitment fairs and respond to international job postings.

THE HIRING PROCESS

Obviously, perseverance and patience play a role in your search. Don't be easily discouraged. Experienced educators know that the international teaching market is a fragmented one. This can mean long or short lead times, where both luck and a planned, systematic approach play a part in landing a teaching position.

How Long Will it Take?

The search for the right job can take a full year. If you're aiming for a job for the coming September, you should begin an active search twelve or fourteen months in advance. This said, you should be aware that many teachers and administrators find jobs in a matter of weeks, often near the time for departure. Last-minute cancellations by other teachers are frequent. So keep up those contacts even close to the start of the school year.

What Time of Year Should I Start?

To time your job search properly, call embassies to find out when the school year begins in their countries. Most international schools approximate the Canadian timetable (August to June). Some exceptions include the public schools of southern African countries, where the school year begins in February and ends in November; two big breaks happen during December-January, and June-July. And in the Philippines, the public system begins in June and goes until March.

Who Makes the Hiring Decisions?

When making initial contact with a school overseas, it is important to know who makes the hiring decisions. Many international schools hire professional recruiters, but final decisions usually rest with principals, directors, superintendents. Always call ahead, as the title of headperson varies among school systems.

The First Step: Focus Your Job Search

The first rule before starting to look is to *focus* your job search. You should be clear about the exact kind of job you want and what part of the world you want to work in. Narrow your research to two or three countries. First, your choice should be based on where you are most likely to get a job; second, on personal contacts who can refer you to a school; and third, make sure your job experience and qualifications are appropriate to the positions you're applying for.

Where to Research

Locating appropriate materials about the particular country may involve trips to a library or bookstore (See the books listed in the Resources section at the end of this chapter). Send inquiry letters to a number of overseas schools. Contact foreign embassies, where you can also often get a list of private schools. Visit university placement offices or university international centres. Countries which send many of their own students to Canadian universities are generally receptive to Canadian teachers. Hong Kong, Indonesia and Malaysia are good prospects.

Personal Contacts and Networks

You may already be lucky enough to know someone in your community who has worked in the region you are interested in, and who can offer first-hand advice. If you haven't spoken to someone who has lived and taught overseas in circumstances similar to those you seek, you should. What you want is to impress potential employers with your strong understanding of the overseas working and living environment. A network of contacts can also be extremely useful for providing inside information on employment possibilities.

For example, contact with a teacher who has worked at a particular school in Singapore could result in a job there for you. It is a well-known fact that overseas administrators are cautious about who they hire, and are likely to favour someone they are familiar with. If you state the name of a personal contact in a letter of introduction or application, you immediately set your letter apart from the dozens of others the school receives.

Here are a few suggestions to get you started in your networking. Make inquiries in your local school district concerning colleagues with international experience. Telephone or visit an international school in Canada or overseas. Attend speeches or conferences related to global education.

Direct Inquiries

Only a small percentage of schools advertise in the foreign press. The vast majority depend on local advertisements, personal contacts and direct approaches. The best source of addresses is usually local directories. Go to the embassy or consulate of the country you are considering to consult telephone books. If you know someone who has taught English abroad and recommends a particular school, send a letter of inquiry there. A speculative job search is more realistic with EFL jobs than with most other areas of overseas employment.

Advertisements

Many jobs in international education are advertised in specialized magazines or newspaper supplements. Two of the very best are *The Times Educational Supplement* and *The International Educator. The TESOL Bulletin* is also worth checking. You'll sometimes find overseas teaching jobs advertised in the *Globe and Mail*, the *New York Times*, and the *Manchester Guardian* on Tuesdays. The latter two British newspapers carry a large number of English teaching ads, especially between March and July for jobs starting in September. A word of caution: do not be discouraged if most ads insist on formal TEFL qualifications: in practice they are not always essential. (See Resources section at the end of this chapter.)

Recruiting Fairs and Agencies

Job fairs should rate at the top of your "must do" list if you are serious about finding a full-time overseas teaching job. Job fairs bring together teachers and recruiters from overseas schools. Most are held in February, with some in June and September. Pre-registration is usually a must and some fairs even have a pre-acceptance criteria. You will certainly have a golden opportunity to collect information, make comparisons, talk to other teachers and administrators looking for overseas jobs, and perhaps meet your future employer. Job fairs often provide that "extra shove" to move you into first gear in your job search. So don't hesitate to spend a few dollars to travel to one. (Please see Profiles of Recruiting Fairs and Agencies at the end of this chapter.)

While Living Abroad

Many teachers have obtained satisfying employment overseas without a preliminary job search in Canada. Spouses of international employees often find employment after settling into a community. If you expect to be in such a position, plan ahead by taking academic and professional credentials, copies of good assessments from previous jobs, your résumé and letters of recommendation. Once abroad survey the education scene and make your move!

While Travelling Abroad

If you're planning extensive travel or are travelling as a tourist for a few weeks, you may want to try visiting a school and arranging an interview.

A recently returned traveller reports finding a good job, on the spot, teaching math in a secondary school in Botswana. He was away six months longer than he expected, but avoided a Canadian winter, and incidentally, is now enthusiastically planning his next teaching venture overseas. Another successful and organized teacher credits getting a good teaching job in Turkey to a covering letter he sent prior to vacationing there. He got an interview, checked out the school and the city, and returned six months later to teach full-time for two years.

The British School System

As Canadians tend to be unfamiliar with the widely-used British school system for classroom levels, we thought it would be helpful to provide a broad description of it. Our examples are taken from southern African countries.

The all-important leaving exams discussed in the third column below are national examinations covering subjects from all previous years up to that level of schooling. Year-end marks are not important; advancement is based solely on the results of your comprehensive leaving exam. O-level and A-Level standard exams are not only developed in Britain by the COSC (Cambridge Overseas Secondary Certificate) but are marked there as well.

THE BRITISH SCHOOL SYSTEM		
LEVEL	CANADIAN EQUIVALENT	LEAVING EXAMS
Primary School	Kindergarten to Grade 7, generally equivalent to our Elementary	Primary School leaving examination
Form 1 to Form 3	First three years of High School, Grades 8 to 10	Junior Certificate Examination (the JC)
Form 4 and 5 (O-Level)	Grades 11 to 12 to complete high school	Eligible to go on to "local" university but not universities abroad
A-Level	Grade 13	Offered in a select few schools; eligible for universities abroad

THE COVERING LETTER

You should send an initial letter of inquiry requesting application instructions, stating your general qualifications, and why you are interested in their school. Offer to send a more detailed package describing your credentials. To demonstrate your teaching abilities you may even want to offer to send them a teaching session on videotape (assuming you have one).

Your covering letter should contain three essential elements in addition to the regular advice given in Chapter 25, Covering Letters. First, explain why you are a good teacher; second, stress your commitment to extracurricular activities; and third, show that you understand and enjoy the challenges of the crosscultural teaching environment.

Always send a follow-up letter after you've received a refusal letter. If you are turned down for a position after a seemingly successful interview, do not hesitate to write and offer your services on a standby basis. International recruitment is precarious. Recruits don't always show up, or they become unavailable for numerous reasons. Let recruiters know you can leave on short notice.

Don't forget to add CANADA to your address, and state clearly in your letter and at the top of your résumé that you are a Canadian citizen. Having a fax number as part of your return address is crucial for an international job search. Faxing is used more than the mail during the international teacher recruitment process. Large print permits easy faxing. Use a minimum of 10 or 11 point font size for your correspondence and résumés.

THE RÉSUMÉ FOR TEACHING OVERSEAS

The following are a few pointers specific to teachers and not covered in Chapter 24, International Résumés.

- International résumés for teachers are longer than Canadian ones. Being so far away, you want to make sure all your information is clear.

- Résumés for teachers tend to follow the traditional chronological format. You can still de-emphasize dates in your job description by stating *what* you did first, then indicating the date. Format of job description begins as; job title, school, year. Example, "Head of Social Studies Department, St. Patrick High School, September 1992 to March 1993." Always include the month to avoid confusion. Because school years are different, employers may assume you worked only one year, not two.

- Be careful with terms such as "Separate School Board" which is confusing unless you live in Canada. Use Catholic School Board instead. Simplify institution names where possible. Use Toronto School Board instead of Toronto Public School Board. Do not use Carleton Roman Catholic Separate School Board, but Carleton Catholic School Board.

- Provide exact description of courses taught, not just subject headings. Instead of Grade 13 Geography or History, use Geography—World Issues, or History—Africa.

- Stay away from jargon. For example, in your covering letter, don't say "I taught development studies"; rather, explain what development studies means. "I taught an innovative program called development studies, which is a combination of African and international history, geography, politics and economics."

- If you have little experience, put your major student teaching experience under "Teaching Experience." However, don't try to pass off your student teaching as professional experience. Call your four-month student teaching job a "Queens University Internship," for example.

- Include a section entitled "Professional Activities" in your résumé, to cover extracurricular activities. If you have little experience and are a recent graduate, list your high school and university extracurricular activities. If you are currently a teacher, list your participation in all student activities outside the classroom. International schools expect you to devote a lot of your free time to student activities. The balance is important. Emphasize a blend of sports, international programs, music, and academic pursuits. Underline events you organized to demonstrate initiative and leadership. If you are weak in extracurricular areas you can add, toward the end of your résumé, a section called "Interests and Abilities" and "Volunteer Work."

- Don't put your Social Insurance Number in any résumé.

- Because of great distances and short time frames in the recruitment process, some of our advice on references is different for teachers than for other international work. Put names of references directly on the résumé (do not use the traditional "references available upon request"). Always include full mailing address and *both* a telephone and fax number for each reference. You may even include your letters of reference, along with copies of your degrees, teaching certificates and even transcripts.

THE INTERVIEW

Many international schools attend recruiting fairs to save on recruitment and interview costs. It is not unheard of, however, for a school to request that you come there for an interview, at your own expense. Fortunately, phone interviews are much more common. Standard questions for teachers may include the following.

Questions about the crosscultural teaching environment:
- What qualities do you have that would make you a good teacher in a crosscultural environment?
- Have you ever taught students whose mother tongue is not English?
- What is important when you first start teaching in a classroom where the cultural norms are different from yours?

General questions:
- What are the qualities of a good teacher?
- How do you view the role of the principal?
- What do you have to say about your current principal?

Questions about living overseas:
- Why do you want to teach overseas?
- What do you know about our country?
- Tell me about your previous travel experience.
- What do you think will be most difficult about moving here?

Your questions to employers which demonstrate knowledge of the overseas teaching environment:
- How is this school's environment different from a typical Canadian school? Inquire about teaching methods and discipline.
- Does the school's curriculum take into account reintegration of children into the US or Canadian systems? Ask which agency certifies the school program?
- About the students: How are they selected? Who generally pays the children's tuition: parents, sponsoring agency or scholarship? Are the students children of diplomats, foreign businesspersons, local elites, local population, high achievers?

THE CONTRACT

Try not to be carried away by the euphoria and, in some cases, anxiety that follows a successful job search. Remember that working conditions are *everything*, so investigate the following: class size, available equipment, makeup of student body, number of teaching periods per day, support staff. Salaries, method of payment and contracts are additionally important. Be prepared for last-minute arrangements.

Working Conditions

You should be clear about how many classes and periods are involved, as well as how many students you'll face in each class. It's important, though, not to appear overly "fussy," as you are supposedly a flexible person, open to new experiences. Nevertheless, you should have some idea before signing a contract of such items as: access to photocopying equipment and teaching aids, such as film projectors, television sets/VCRs, overhead projectors and even availability of chalk. Knowing in advance exactly when holidays are and for how long is also useful.

Contracts

All but the most informal of teaching arrangements involve signing a contract. It should spell out clearly the length of the agreement, your salary and method of payment, your duties and benefits. If housing is to be provided by the employer, or if you're to be allotted a housing allowance, the contract should stipulate exact responsibilities of each party for maintenance, services and utilities. In addition, return travel expenses, charges for shipment of belongings, provision for interim lodging, life insurance and health insurance (including provisions for sick pay) should be covered. If you are bringing your family, the cost of your children's schooling is also normally included. The list of special benefits varies with the post. While you may not have much bargaining power, you can judge the seriousness of the school by the contract proposed to you.

GETTING READY

The period between signing the contract with a foreign school and the first day of work can be both exhilarating and exhausting. Sharing the news of your upcoming adventure with family, friends and colleagues, securing all your required documents, completing travel arrangements and organizing personal affairs will involve much time and effort. Most of you will have begun learning about your host country during your job search, but no teacher/administrator who has worked abroad has expressed regret about spending too much time learning the language (if applicable), history and culture of a new country. Many, however, have lamented their ignorance in these areas upon arrival overseas.

Learning the Language

Even if you don't need to know the local language in the classroom, your ability to communicate with locals will increase your enjoyment of your overseas experience many times over (see Chapter 5, Learning a Foreign Language). Daily tasks such as shopping will be easier and more enjoyable, as will chance meetings or social encounters with neighbours. If you have time before your departure, consider taking a conversation course at a local institution. Or try a self-study program using books and tapes.

Don't Burn your Bridges

Among the multitude of pre-departure tasks, take time to develop a clear picture of what awaits you upon your return to Canada in one, two or three years' time. If you have arranged a leave-of-absence with an employer, make sure the terms are specified. You don't want to return home and find the superintendent who "promised" you your old job back has moved to Whitehorse. One teacher who has regularly faced insecurity between international contracts recommends, "Keep your options open. Before returning from overseas, I had already registered for a course, so when I walked off the plane, 'Bang,' I was in school. This helped me get over re-entry shock quickly. Always think about what you'll do if you don't get another overseas assignment immediately. Always have a Plan B. Fill in time with volunteer work or take an extra course."

Finally, while it is important to take care of such things as pension plans, income tax, work visas, insurance, international drivers licences and so on, don't be discouraged by the seemingly endless list. You will get through it. This "preparation period" can be extremely fulfilling and exciting. Enjoy the anticipation!

WORDS OF WISDOM FOR WHEN YOU ARRIVE

The following are comments from teachers who have worked in Africa. Their advice should help you get off to a good start in your new job.

"To have a truly full experience, you must be 'captured' by the culture."

"Stand back and listen for at least the first month and even up to one year. As a new teacher, you are usually very welcome. They are happy to have you. In the initial excitement, a new teacher will have lots of ideas, and will be eager to present them, but... You should take the time to see if your ideas are appropriate. You must get to know your students first. Find out what their needs are, how they learn best, what works for them."

"Going slowly when you first arrive and being culturally sensitive does not imply relaxing your academic standards. Show that you are there for a good reason."

"Get used to cultural practices that you cannot change, even when they go against the grain. I had a hard time accepting that students were beaten. My advice is to get used to it, but don't accept it."

"Don't get caught up in heavy school politics. Avoid taking sides. There are cultural aspects that you don't yet understand. Try to stay neutral."

"Reduce your expectations. Go with the changes as they happen. If they tell you to teach something you didn't expect, do it. As an outsider, you may not understand their rationale."

"Get as involved as possible in school activities, to show that you are an active participant, you want to share the load, and you want to learn from them."

"In a rural or small community, get to know the parents of your students. I found it was so easy to visit them, you didn't even have to announce your visit. Getting to know the parents really helped me become accepted."

"It is normal for students to visit teachers at home. This can be very enriching. Students like to see pictures of your family...they want to know you. In this way, you can teach outside the classroom. With all the discussion about the world, your house becomes a sort of external office."

"Students often helped me with my household chores. This was a normal thing. At first I felt I was taking advantage of them, but when my conscience made me give a pen as payment, I was berated by the other profs. They said this was the students' role... It is also quite normal to support a student. You don't have to do it, but quite often you do help out a needy student. The actual cost is low, but your help is invaluable to them."

TEACHING ENGLISH OVERSEAS

It is accurate to say that you can get a job teaching English in any country in the world in which English is not the first language. The field is wide open, both for experienced English teachers (who, granted, will obtain the best paying jobs) and for the world traveller who can take advantage of one of the best ways of financing a sojourn abroad. In many countries English is taught from elementary school to the university level, and in large companies, private language schools, and private homes.

For many reasons, English has become the world's dominant language in the late twentieth century. It is the official or joint-official language in 80 countries. The newly-liberated countries of Eastern Europe turned to English after they rejected Russian. Countries as far-flung as China, Japan and Namibia have made knowledge of English one of the focal points in their education systems. English is the international language of trade, science and air traffic control. Thus, English-speakers possess a much sought-after commodity: literally hundreds of millions of people are out there waiting to talk to them. And simply *talking* is what teaching English as a Foreign Language (EFL) is all about!

The General Market

It is almost impossible to think of anywhere in the world that is closed to English teachers. The market is wide open: instructing local students, hotel clerks, foreign embassy staff, foreign students coming to Canada, entrepreneurs, businesspeople, scientists, researchers, academics, and émigres worldwide. Currently, the *big markets* are Eastern Europe, Turkey, Korea, Taiwan, Hong Kong, Thailand, Indonesia, China, and Japan.

In Western European countries, you will encounter strict work visa laws. Nonetheless, there remains a high demand in Spain, Portugal and Greece, and many language schools continue to hire unqualified teachers. There are also opportunities for live-in private tutoring of children. And Turkey has an exceptionally high demand for qualified teachers.

In Eastern Europe, Hungary, Poland, and Czechoslovakia are currently the most active in recruiting teachers, but this region suffers from acute accommodation shortages and low salaries. ESL-trained teachers are preferred, but untrained English-speakers are used at high schools when necessary.

Hong Kong, Korea, Taiwan, and Thailand offer the greatest opportunities for teachers without official certification. There is also a consistent demand for highly-qualified teachers in China and Japan.

And in Latin America, it is relatively easy to find work in private schools in Mexico, Costa Rica, Chile, Peru, and Venezuela.

Who Can Teach?

There are more qualified EFL teachers out there than ever before. Many positions require qualified and experienced teachers. However, anyone who can speak English fluently and has a positive attitude has a chance of landing a job. That said, it is unwise to assume that fluency in English will make you an adequate EFL teacher. Most, if not all, English teachers have at least one university degree. And if you're serious about teaching English abroad, you should consider taking at least a short training program. (See the sub-section below, Training to Become an English Teacher.)

There are many fine teachers, however, who have carved solid niches for themselves, having learned to teach through practice rather than formal training. In some cases, for example, a strong background in business can serve you better than any diploma for landing a job teaching business English.

A postgraduate TESL Certificate, an MEd or a BEd with ESL specialization are generally required for positions with overseas universities, international schools or multinational corporations. For smaller private language schools and private tutoring, requirements are less stringent and vary widely.

How Much does it Pay?

Everyone has heard of or met someone teaching English in Japan tax-free for a salary of upwards of US$30,000 a year, with free board. Those jobs do exist in Japan (and increasingly in Korea), but generally the take-home pay is substantially less. People who work in Japan often complain about the cost of living, the cultural isolation and even, surprisingly, the geographic isolation of living in remote villages. Generally, TESL doesn't pay as well as a regular teaching job in an international school. English teaching contracts are more numerous and easier to find, but terms tend to be shorter and less generous.

Qualities of a Good English Teacher

Above all, an ability to be creative will take you a long way. EFL teachers, perhaps more than other teachers going abroad, have to be performers, able to draw out students who are as insecure and shy as any of us would be learning a foreign language. And of course, you must enjoy teaching! Experienced teachers tell us it is not love of the subject matter that carries them through the school year, but a strong interest in their students.

Training to Become an English Teacher

Without academic certification in one of the following areas, your chances of landing a job, especially a well-paid job, are reduced.

Some basic definitions for TEFL, TESL and TEAL

TEFL: pronounced TEFEL, is Teaching English as a Foreign Language. In countries where English is not the language of the indigenous culture.

TESL: is Teaching English as a Second Language. Usually used where English is an official working language, i.e. teaching English to immigrants in Canada.

TEAL: Teaching English as an Additional Language, i.e. teaching English to speakers of more than one other language. Usually taught in multicultural societies.

Canadian Universities with Teaching ESL Programs

University of Alberta	University of Ottawa
University of British Columbia	University of Toronto
University of Calgary	University of Victoria
Carleton University	York University
Concordia University	International House (Halifax)

International House in Halifax offers the R.S.A. (Royal Society of Arts) Certificate in TEFL. While the Certificate is not recognized as a teaching qualification in Canada, it is recognized as such overseas.

Other Ways to Gain English Teaching Experience in Canada

Another way of compensating for a lack of formal EFL training is to volunteer as a tutor for local immigrants. Placing advertisements in local newspapers can also lead to paid tutorials or language exchange sessions. Assisting classroom teachers with these newcomers is another good possibility. Contact schools in your community. You will likely be welcomed with open arms!

Become a Teacher to Land Another Type of Job

If you want to work in international finance, or become a computer programmer, try contacting people in your field while travelling and offering your services as an English teacher specialized in their exact field. The contacts you make will help you better understand the international aspects of your field of work and perhaps lead to a job.

Teaching Materials to Take

If you know where you'll be teaching, find out in advance what facilities the school has. After gathering all the useful materials at your disposal, visit the English-teaching section of a large bookstore, or perhaps a university bookstore. The following are materials recommended by experienced English teachers: a picture dictionary, tapes for listening and role-playing, blank tapes and a cassette recorder, a games and activities book, a map of Canada, a grammar exercise book, carbon paper and a collection of photos of your home environment. (These will be of great interest to your students, for whom Canada is as exotic as far-flung Asian or African countries may be for you.) If possible, ship bulkier items ahead. Remember: anything that encourages students to *talk* is invaluable!

A LAST WORD

Teaching abroad can be one of the most rewarding overseas experiences. Few professions or careers are so portable and offer such tremendous possibilities for immersion in foreign cultures, close relationships far from home, and travel to places where no tourists go.

RESOURCES

Teaching Abroad

Teaching abroad is still one of the biggest areas of overseas employment for Canadians. Entry-level English-language teaching positions are especially easy to come by. For all entry-level job seekers, these positions are important for building your International IQ and pole vaulting you into other international careers.

Consult related resources in Chapter 5, Learning a Foreign Language; Chapter 10, Short-term Programs Overseas; Chapter 14, Study Abroad; Chapter 15, Awards & Grants; Chapter 16, International Studies in Canada & Abroad; the Resources for the section on Language Careers in Chapter 22, Resources for the International Job Search; and Chapter 27, Jobs by Regions of the World.

The Internet TESL Journal (For Teachers of English as a Second Language) ▣
www.aitech.ac.jp/~iteslj ▪ This journal is a monthly web magazine comprised of selected submissions written by ELS/EFL teachers. The topics include lesson plans, handouts, articles, and research of immediate practical use. [ID:2790]

Asia Fact Unlimited ▣
http://asiafacts.kingston.net ▪ Recruitment information, publications and online resources for those interested in teaching in Asia. [ID:2615]

Association of Canadian Teachers In Japan ▣
www.tesl.ca/japan ▪ This organization is open to Candian educators interested in teaching in Japan. ACTJ can supply members with information on finding work in Japan and on professional development opportunities. [ID:2734]

Awards for University Teachers and Research Workers 📖
Biennial, Association of Commonwealth Universities, 364 pages ➤ UBC Press, University of British Columbia, 6344 Memorial Rd., Vancouver, B.C. V6T 1Z2; $49.95; VISA, MC; (604) 822-3259, fax (800) 668-0821, orders@ubcpress.ubc.ca ▪ Contains 730 award schemes, primarily within the Commonwealth. Includes information on some non-university institutions, organizations providing appointments, services, and consultancy opportunities, and organizations providing other forms of assistance. [ID:1566]

China Bound: A Guide to Academic Life and Work in the PRC 📖
1994, *L. Reed, K. Turner-Gottschang* ➤ National Academy Press, 2101 Constitution Ave. N.W, Washington, DC 20418, USA; US$14.95; credit cards; (800) 624-6242, fax (202) 334-2451 ▪ Chock-full of valuable inside information on life in China. Based on the experiences of Americans who have recently studied, conducted research, or taught in the People's Republic of China, it covers a broad spectrum of topics, from customs, regulations, taxation, and medical care to hotel life and getting your laundry done. Visit the distributor's web site at www.nap.edu. [ID:1209]

DailyJob 🖥
www.dailyjob.com ▪ Lists job postings for Hong Kong and China. Information on the site is updated daily. Look under "Education" for teaching opportunities. [ID:2415]

Developing Intercultural Awareness: A Cross-Cultural Training Handbook 📖
1994, *L. Robert Kohls, John M. Knight,* Intercultural Press, 158 pages ➤ Intercultural and Community Development Resources (ICDR), P.O. Box 32108, Millwoods Station, Edmonton, Alberta T6K 4C2; $24; VISA, Amex; (800) 378-3199, fax (403) 462-1925, icdr@compusmart.ab.ca ▪ This book features outline designs of one- and two-day cultural awareness workshops, and training materials that include simulation games, case studies, and exercises on values and ice-breaking. Designed for intercultural educators and trainers, and useful to anyone wishing to expand his or her general training or teaching repertoire. Visit the distributor's web site at www.compusmart.ab.ca/icdr. [ID:1380]

Ed-U-Link Services Online Recruiting Fair 🖥
www.edulink.com/#fair, info@edulink.com ▪ An Internet job fair for educators, with online listings of positions available overseas. [ID:2519]

ESL Job Links 🖥
www.pacificnet.net/~sperling/joblinks.html ▪ Primarily oriented to those seeking international work as English teachers, this site has a number of links to general overseas recruiting agencies and job opportunities. This site is impressive in its scope, offering links to countries throughout the world. There are also several links to American-based job centres which offer career counselling and résumé assistance services. This is a very good site, with opportunities for all job seekers, not just those interested in teaching overseas. [ID:2547]

The ESLoop 🖥
www.linguistic-funland.com/esloop ▪ The ESLoop is a collection of sites for English Language Teaching. Each site is linked to the next, so that no matter your point of departure, you will make your way around all the sites. [ID:2792]

Fact Sheets 📖 🖥
Annual, US Department of State ➤ Office of Overseas Schools (A/OS), Overseas Schools Advisory Council, SA-29, Room 245, US Department of State, Washington, DC 20522-2902, USA; free; (703) 875-7800, fax (703) 875-7979, overseas.schools@dos.us_state.gov ▪ Excellent descriptions of American-sponsored elementary and secondary schools overseas, including enrolment, facilities, and finances. Useful for educational job seekers or prospective users of the schools. Fact sheets distributed by country. Also available free on the web at
www.state.gov/www/about_state/schools/. [ID:1225]

Guide to Living, Studying, and Working
in the People's Republic of China and Hong Kong ⌨
Annual, *Jane Parker, Janet Rodgers* ➤ Yale-China Association, 442 Temple Street, Box 208223, New Haven, CT 06520, USA; US$5; cheque or money order; (203) 432-0880, fax (203) 432-7246, ycassoc@minerva.cis.yale.edu ■ Contains information on language programs, tuition, travel, living conditions and up-to-date information on procedures for obtaining teaching positions and other jobs. [ID:1274]

How to Teach Abroad ⌨
1996, *Roger Jones*, 192 pages ➤ How To Books Ltd., 3 Newtec Place, Magdalen Road, Oxford, OX4 1RE, UK; £8.99; credit cards; (44) (1752) 202-301, fax (44) (1865) 202-331 ■ A wealth of information on where and how to apply, work permits, accommodation, transport of luggage, provision for children, training courses, health, and more. [ID:1680]

The International Educator ⌨
5/year ➤ International Educator's Institute, P.O. Box 513, Cummaquid, MA 02637, USA; US$25; credit cards; (508) 362-1414, fax (508) 362-1411 ■ Excellent educational newspaper containing articles of interest to educators teaching or intending to teach abroad. Large listing of job vacancies worldwide. Special "Jobs-Only" supplement in June. Highly recommended. [ID:1190]

The ISS Directory of Overseas Schools ⌨
1997, International Schools Service, 533 pages ➤ Impact Publications, 9104 North Manassas Drive, Manassas Park, VA 20111-2366, USA; US$34.95; credit cards; (703) 361-7300, fax (703) 335-9486 ■ The guide educators, corporate officials, expatriate families, and teachers seeking employment abroad rely on for accurate and up-to-date information on American-style elementary and secondary schools overseas. Visit distributor's web site, www.impactpublications.com. [ID:1167]

Jobs in Japan: The Complete Guide to
Living and Working in the Land of Rising Opportunity ⌨
1993, *John Wharton*, Global Press, 268 pages ➤ Capricorn Business Services, Inc., 28 Clear Lake Ave., West Hill, Ontario M1C 4L6; $19.95; credit cards; (416) 282-3331, fax (416) 282-0015 ■ Explains how English speakers with little experience can help meet Japan's constant demand for English teachers. Details on over 400 English schools and other useful organizations, plus advice on other jobs open to foreigners, negotiating with employers, obtaining visas and coping with the culture. [ID:1429]

Living in China: A Guide to Teaching and Studying in China including Taiwan ⌨
1997, *R. Weiner, M. Murphy, A. Li*, 283 pages ➤ China Books & Periodicals Inc., 2929 - 24th Street, San Francisco, CA 94110, USA; US$19.95; credit cards; (415) 282-2994, fax (415) 282-0994 ■ Crosscultural guide with advice for teacher or tourist, student or businessperson. Complete listings of Chinese colleges and universities, in both the Peoples' Republic of China and Taiwan, which accept foreign teachers or students. The authors are amusingly frank about surviving, working and even dating in China. Visit distributor's web site at www.chinabooks.com. [ID:1111]

Make a Mil-Yen: Teaching English in Japan ⌨
1994, *Don Best*, Stone Bridge Press, 176 pages ➤ Weatherhill, 41 Monroe Turnpike, Trumbull, CT 06611, USA; US$14.95; credit cards; (800) 437-7840, fax (800) 557-5601, weath1212@aol.com ■ Up-to-date information on everything from preparation and the job search, to settling in. Visit the distributor's web site at www.weatherhill.com. [ID:1528]

Making it in Japan ⌨
1994, *Mark Gauthier*, Vacation Work ➤ Capricorn Business Services, Inc., 28 Clear Lake Ave., West Hill, Ontario M1C 4L6; $21.95; credit cards; (416) 282-3331, fax (416) 282-0015 ■ A British publication, this handbook covers every aspect of living and working in Japan. Advice for Westerners includes where to get free Japanese lessons, finding teaching jobs that require no experience, and the 75 things you should never do in Japan. [ID:1592]

Monarch ESL Catalogue 📖
Annual ➤ Monarch Books of Canada Ltd., 5000 Dufferin Street, Downsview, Ontario M3H 5T5; free; VISA, MC; (416) 663-8231, fax (416) 736-1702 ▪ A catalogue of educational titles listed under such headings as Grammar, TOEFL Preparation, Basic Text, Conversation and Phonics. This is a useful planning tool for teachers before planning to go overseas. [ID:1578]

Now Hiring! Jobs in Eastern Europe 📖
1996, *Clarke Canfield,* 320 pages ➤ Impact Publications, 9104 North Manassas Drive, Manassas Park, VA 20111-2366, USA; $14.95; credit cards; (703) 361-7300, fax (703) 335-9486 ▪ An insider's guide to working and living in the Czech Republic, Hungary, Poland, and Slovakia. Provides information on teaching English as well as other employment opportunities. Includes a list of language schools that hire native speakers. Visit the distributor's web site at www.impactpublications.com. [ID:1756]

O-Hayo Sensei 💻
www.ohayosensei.com ▪ This site stems from the twice-monthly publication, O-Hayo Sensei, the most comprehensive compilation of teaching positions in Japan. Information about accommodation, application procedures, benefits, contact names, qualifications, and salaries. [ID:2739]

**Overseas American-Sponsored Elementary and
Secondary Schools Assisted by the US Department of State** 📖 💻
Annual, US Department of State ➤ Office of Overseas Schools (A/OS), Overseas Schools Advisory Council, SA-29, Room 245, US Department of State, Washington, DC 20522-2902, USA; free; (703) 875-7800, fax (703) 875-7979, overseas.schools@dos.us_state.gov ▪ Each entry gives the name and title of the school's chief administrator, address, grade levels taught and enrolment figures. Also available in its entirety on the web at www.state.gov/www/about_state/schools/. [ID:1224]

Overseas Work for Teachers 💻
www.state.gov/www/about_state/schools/ ▪ Maintained by the Overseas Schools Advisory Council; posts international vacancies for elementary and secondary school teachers. [ID:2478]

Schools Abroad of Interest to Americans 📖
1998, 590 pages ➤ Porter Sargent Publishers Inc., Suite 1400, 11 Beacon Street, Boston, MA 02108, USA; US$48; cheques; (617) 523-1670, fax (617) 523-1021 ▪ List of 800 elementary and secondary schools in 130 countries, of interest to young Americans and others seeking pre-college programs abroad. [ID:1233]

Teaching English—Japan: Finding Work, Teaching, and Living in Japan 📖
1996, *Jerry O'Sullivan,* 227 pages ➤ NTC Contemporary Publishing Co., 4255 West Touhy Ave., Lincolnwood, IL 60646, USA; US$14.95; credit cards; (800) 323-4900, fax (800) 998-3103 ▪ User-friendly resource with information on how to find teaching jobs, arrange visas and accommodation, as well as providing model lesson plans for school, private, and business classes. [ID:1807]

Teaching English Abroad 📖
1994, *Susan Griffith,* 368 pages ➤ Peterson's Guides, P.O. Box 2123, Princeton, NJ 08543-2123, USA; US$16.95; cheque or money order; (800) 338-3282, fax (609) 243-9150 ▪ Guide to opportunities for both trained and untrained teachers in the booming field of teaching English as a Foreign Language. Describes over 20 countries where EFL is a major industry. Includes a directory of language schools which hire English teachers. Visit the publisher's web site at www.petersons.com. [ID:1306]

The Teaching Overseas Information Handbook 📖
Annual, *Robert Barlas,* 40 pages ➤ Search Associates, c/o Bob Barlas, RR 5, Belleville, Ontario K8N 4Z5; $12.50; (613) 967-4902, fax (613) 967-8981, rbarlas@connect.reach.net ▪ Written especially for Canadian teachers interested in furthering their careers overseas, either on a short- or long-term basis. This excellent handbook deals with the myriad questions to be asked before such a venture, including how to search for teaching positions overseas. Also gives contact information. An affiliated service is Search Associates, which recruits and places qualified

teachers in international schools throughout the world. Visit the distributor's web site at www.search-associates.com. [ID:1132]

TESOL Online (Teachers of English to Speakers of Other Languages 💻
www.tesol.edu ▪ TESOL's online service provides a worldwide link for those involved in teaching English to speakers of other languages. Areas covered include: professional preparation, programs, services, and products. [ID:2791]

Times Educational Supplement 📖
Weekly, Times of London ➤ Gordon & Gotch, Unit 11, 110 Jardin Drive, Toronto, Ontario L4K 4R4; $5 per issue or $278/year; VISA; (800) 438-5005, fax (905) 669-3654; Available at international newsstands ▪ Excellent resource published every Friday. Includes listings of hundreds of international teaching positions. [ID:1706]

Transcending Stereotypes: Discovering Japanese Culture and Education 📖
1991, *Barbara Finkelstein, Joseph Tobin, Anne Imamura,* Intercultural Press, 224 pages ➤ Intercultural and Community Development Resources (ICDR), P.O. Box 32108, Millwoods Station, Edmonton, Alberta T6K 4C2; $42; VISA, Amex; (800) 378-3199, fax (403) 462-1925, icdr@compusmart.ab.ca ▪ A collection of articles by Japanese and American scholars which confronts the stereotypes of the Japanese by delving into the instructional practices, cultural patterns, and early childhood environment that form the basis of the Japanese educational system. Visit the distributor's web site at www.compusmart.ab.ca/icdr. [ID:1689]

Teacher Recruitment Agencies

The recruiting business is not regulated in Canada and the quality of service can vary. On a positive note, there does not seem to be a lot of scamming in this industry. Some teachers have been disappointed with the conditions and service received when abroad. (It's a fact of life that when overseas, not everything is going to go smoothly.) Since there are so many recruiting agencies to choose from, check out references, ask to speak to former recruits, study their advertising material and documentation, and check out their web site. The size of the firm is not always an indicator of the level of service; satisfaction from former recruits is.

AEON Corporation
AEON Corporation, Suite 1000, 230 Park Ave., New York, NY 10169, USA; (212) 808-3080, fax (212) 599-0340 ▪ The AEON Corporation owns and operates more than 230 English conversation schools throughout Japan. Ongoing recruitment is carried out by AEON's three North American offices. Applicants must have a university degree. Teaching experience is preferred but not required. To apply, submit a résumé to the recruiting office nearest you and an essay stating why you want to live and work in Japan. The AEON Corporation's web site, www.aeonet.com, contains further information for potential applicants. [ID:2625]

Association of American Schools in South America (AASSA)
Association of American Schools in South America (AASSA), Suite 210, 14750 N.W. 77th Court, Miami Lakes, FL 33016, USA; (305) 821-0345, fax (305) 821-4244, aassa@gate.net ▪ AASSA recruits teachers for 40 private American/International schools located throughout South America. In most cases, applicants must be certified teachers and have at least two years' experience teaching K-12. The annual recruiting fair takes place in Florida in December. Candidates may request applications for the fair by phone, fax or e-mail. Fees to attend the recruiting fair are set at US$125, there is a US$300 placement fee if contracted (placement fees are sometimes reimbursed by the schools). Job listings are also posted on AASSA's web site, www.aassa.com. [ID:2626]

English Teachers Overseas (ETO)
English Teachers Overseas (ETO), 202-1450 Burnaby Street, Vancouver, B.C. V6G 1W7; (604) 689-3677, fax (604) 682-2905, eto@direct.ca ▪ English Teachers Overseas (ETO) is a Canadian organization which recruits for the Japanese market. ETO represents a variety of schools, serving children, teens, adults, and corporate clients. We recruit for companies which provide only good working and living conditions with competitive salaries. Candidates must have at least a bachelor's degree. Those with ESL or teaching qualifications or ESL teaching experience will receive priority placements. ETO recruits on an ongoing basis throughout the year. Applicants should forward a comprehensive résumé package including a picture. A refundable $100 security deposit is required if the candidate's résumé is sent overseas. [ID:2627]

European Council of International Schools
European Council of International Schools, 21B Lavant Street, Petersfield, Hampshire GU32 3EL, UK; (44) (1730) 268244, fax (44) (1730) 267914, ecis@ecis.org ▪ The European Council of International Schools, a US nonprofit corporation based in the UK, acts as a placement service for English-speaking teachers and administrators. ECIS works with over 450 international schools in Europe, the Middle East, Asia, the Americas and Africa, and provides information on hundreds of primary and secondary school vacancies annually. It conducts annual recruitment fairs in London (UK) in January and May ,and in Vancouver in February. Their web site advertises both teaching and senior administrative jobs online. Visit www.ecis.org. [ID:2628]

Friends of World Teaching
Friends of World Teaching, P.O. Box 1049, San Diego, CA 92112-1049, USA; (619) 224-2365, fax (619) 224-5363, fowt@wordnet.att.net ▪ Friends of World Teaching is affiliated with more than 1,000 English-language schools and colleges in 100 countries worldwide. The organization offers teaching and administrative opportunities to American and Canadian educators. Positions exist in most subject areas and at most levels, from kindergarten to university, and are filled throughout the year. Qualifications are similar to those in Canada but foreign language knowledge is usually not required. Salaries vary from country to country, but are in most cases adequate for overseas living. Their web site at www.fowt.com offers information on their services. [ID:2620]

Goal Recruiting
Goal Recruiting, 307 Glebemount Ave., Toronto, Ontario M4C 3V3; (416) 696-2344, fax (416) 423-0195, apply@goalasia.com ▪ Goal Recruiting is a Toronto based company that recruits university graduates from English-speaking countries to teach conversational English in South Korea. The firm represents over 300 schools and offers placements year round. Applicants must have a university degree and must be flexible and adventurous. Teaching experience or an education degree is useful but not necessary. Goal Recruiting charges no fees for its services. Canadian applicants are responsible for the costs of a Korean visa and certified copies of their degrees (approximately $65). Americans pay only for their visa (approximately US$20). Transportation to, accommodation within, and often a return flight from, Korea are paid for by the contracting schools. The firm maintains an excellent web site, www.goalasia.com, that tells you how to apply, and provides general information on Korea and tips on improving your application. [ID:2629]

Hess Language School of Taiwan
Hess Language School of Taiwan, North American Operations, 4 Horicon Ave., Glens Falls, NY 12801, USA; (518) 793-6183, fax (518) 793-6183, dhess@capital.net ▪ With over 70 branches, Hess Language School is Taiwan's largest English school for children. The school recruits native English-speakers to teach in a tested and effective after-school language learning program. To apply, you must have a bachelor's degree, hold a valid passport from an English speaking country, and be prepared to make a one-year commitment to the school. Teaching experience with children is preferred but not required. Recruiting is on-going with four starting dates each year. Information for applicants, including an application form, can be found on the Hess Language School web site, www.hess.com.tw. [ID:2630]

Interact Nova Group Canada 📖
Interact Nova Group Canada, Suite 700, 1881 Yonge Street, Toronto, Ontario M4S 3C4; (416) 481-6000, fax (416) 481-1362, novacan@globalserve.net ▪ This agency operates the largest private

English conversation school with 270 locations throughout the islands of Japan. They recruit university graduates from a variety of disciplines (any major considered but ideally English or Education). Teaching or tutoring experience is preferred. Japanese language ability is not necessary. No application deadline. [ID:2684]

International Educators Co-operative Inc.
International Educators Co-operative Inc., 212 Alcott Road, East Falmouth, MA 02536, USA; (508) 540-8173, fax (508) 540-8173 ■ International Educators Co-operative Inc. recruits certified teachers from both Canada and the United States. Their focus is upon jobs in Mexico, Central America, the Caribbean, South America and Spain. The firm hold an annual "Overseas Teacher Recruitment Fair" each year in Houston Texas. Applicants with experience are preferred, but the firm is also successful in placing recent graduates. There is a US$150 fee to register for the recruiting fair, and spaces are limited. There is a US$75 fee to register with the agency. [ID:2631]

International Schools Services (ISS)
International Schools Services (ISS), P.O. Box 5910, Princeton, NJ 08543, USA; (609) 452-0990, fax (609) 452-2690, edustaffing@iss.edu ■ International Schools Services (ISS) is a private, nonprofit organization which provides services to overseas American and international schools in the areas of recruitment, curricular and administrative guidance, school management and consulting services, purchasing services and publications. They publish The ISS Directory of Overseas Schools, an annotated directory of all international schools with American students. The Educational Staffing program of ISS has placed K-12 teachers and administrators in overseas schools since 1955. Most candidates obtain their overseas positions by attending the organization's International Recruitment Centres (IRCs) where ISS candidates have the opportunity to interview with overseas school heads seeking new staff. You must be an active ISS candidate to attend an IRC. Applicants must have a BA and two years of current relevant experience. ISS maintains a web site, www.iss.edu, that contains advice for teachers considering an international career, a list of current opportunities and information on how to apply to ISS, and the dates of their three annual IRCs. [ID:2632]

K.I.S. Recruiters
K.I.S. Recruiters, Suite 102, 557 Marlee Ave., North York, Ontario M6B 3J6; free; (416) 783-4339, fax (416) 783-7348, kis@interlog.com ■ K.I.S. recruits native English-speakers to teach in private language institutes, children's schools, and universities in South Korea, and in private language institutes and firms in Japan. A bachelor's degree is required for placements in private language institutes. A master's degree is required to teach at the university level. Preferred but not required: BEd, BA in English, TEFL (or equivalent) certification, related teaching experience. Applicants should be open-minded and prepared for the challenges of working overseas. See the K.I.S. web site, www.interlog.com/~kis, for information on the agency and advice about working and living in South Korea and Japan. [ID:2633]

Michigan State University
Career Services and Placement, Michigan State University, 113 Student Services Building, East Lansing, MI 48824-1113, USA; (517) 355-9510 ext. 134, fax (517) 353-2597, Scheetz@pilot.msu.edu ■ Career Services and Placement at Michigan State University assists certified teachers to find placements in American and US Department of Defence schools throughout the world. Overseas experience is preferred but not required. The language of instruction is English. The annual Overseas Teacher Recruitment Fair is open to all qualified teachers. A registration fee applies (US$75 in 1998). Those who cannot attend the fair can have their résumés included in the résumé book provided to employers attending the fair (US$25 in 1998). Details are available on the Career Services and Placement web site, www.msu.edu/csp. [ID:2634]

Overseas Placement Services for Educators
Overseas Placement Services for Educators, University of Northern Iowa, Cedar Falls, IA 50614-0390, USA; (319) 273-2083, fax (319) 273-6998, overseas.placement@uni.edu ■ Overseas Placement Services for Educators is a top-notch placement service which holds an annual overseas recruiting fair for teachers and administrators. It attracts representatives from over 100 schools around the world, it provides excellent fact sheets on schools, and periodically sends newsletters to registrants. A recruitment fair for overseas schools is held every February. A

registration fee of US$140 for single educators, and US$260 for teaching couples is applicable. Candidates must have a teacher's certification from the US or Canada, and preferably a minimum of two years' teaching experience. Their web site, www.uni.edu/placemnt/student/internat.html, outlines a variety of services offered at the University and provides valuable links to a number of international resources. [ID:2635]

Queen's Teachers' Overseas Recruiting Fair
Queen's Teachers' Overseas Recruiting Fair, Placement Office, Faculty of Education, Queen's University, Kingston, Ontario K7L 3N6; (613) 545-6222, fax (613) 545-6691, placemnt@educ.queensu.ca ▪ The Queen's Teachers' Overseas Recruiting Fair (TORF) is the original recruiting fair for teachers in Canada. It is held annually at Queen's University, usually in February. Registration is limited to about 275 teachers. Registration materials are available in September. Teacher certification and a minimum of two years of full-time teaching experience are required. The fair typically attracts approximately 40 schools from 30 countries. Certified teachers, with or without experience, can also register with the year-round International Teacher Placement Service (ITPS). There is a $100 fee to register for and attend the TORF, while the ITPS charges a $100 fee only if the applicant is placed in a school. For more detailed information on their recruiting services, visit http://educ.queensu.ca/admin_and_services/placement/, their web site. [ID:2636]

Search Associates
Search Associates, c/o Bob Barlas, RR 5, Belleville, Ontario K8N 4Z5; (613) 967-4902, fax (613) 967-8981, rbarlas@connect.reach.net ▪ Search Associates places qualified teachers and administrators in international schools all over the world through a year-round placement service and a series of recruitment fairs held in various North American cities. Interested teachers should apply early in the academic year prior to the one in which they plan to go overseas. A three-year registration with Search Associates costs US$100, and a further placement fee of US$300 is payable upon signing an overseas contract. Search Associates maintains an excellent web site, listing more detailed information on services, registration, and living overseas. Visit www.search-associates.com. [ID:2637]

T.E.L. Opportunities (Teach the English Language)
T.E.L. Opportunities (Teach the English Language), 1049 Craigdarroch Road, Victoria, B.C. V8S 2A5; (250) 370-2291, fax (250) 370-2291, telop@kudosnet.com ▪ T.E.L. Opportunities helps Canadians and Americans locate university, junior college and private language institute teaching positions in South Korea. Applicants must have a four-year bachelor's degree, be native speakers of English and have no dependants. They should also be flexible, tolerant and ready to undertake the "working overseas" challenge. Positions are available year-round. Applicants should contact T.E.L. or visit their web site, www.kudosnet.com/telop, for further information. [ID:2638]

TESOL Placement Service
TESOL Placement Service, Suite 300, 1600 Cameron Street, Alexandria, VA 22314-2705, USA; (703) 836-0774, fax (703) 836-7864, tesol@tesol.edu ▪ TESOL Placement Services is the place to go to find a job worldwide: Asia, Central America, the Middle East, North America and Europe. The monthly Placement Bulletin lists position openings for ESL/EFL teachers and administrators. The Résumé Search Service maintains a list of résumés for recruiters requesting searches – many of these job openings are never advertised. This services is free to those who subscribe to the Placement Bulletin. The Employment Clearinghouse is an annual job fair where recruiters from around the world post hundreds of job announcements, and interview on-site. The job openings listed with TESOL are for qualified professionals with certification, an MA or a PhD in TESOL. Visit the web site, www.tesol.edu, for more information or for valuable advice on becoming a TESOL professional. The site also lists a number of useful resources. [ID:2639]

Chapter 30

Freelancing Abroad

This chapter is written for spouses or partners of overseas employees, or for those going abroad with enough financial security and enough spunk to try and make it on their own. Freelancer, consultant, independent businessperson are all words for people who earn money working for themselves rather than working for a company or organization.

Working independently abroad has a lot going for it. If you are interested in part-time work or want to travel as well as work, your time is your own. You can often avoid the need for a work permit or skirt labour laws that restrict job opportunities for foreigners. You can work out of your home and you get a wonderful sense of accomplishment when you find work for yourself.

Self-employment is often the ideal solution for the spouse of a wife or husband who has the "real" job abroad. That's partly because self-employment, at least to start, is unlikely to bring in enough money to support one, never mind two or more people. It can also be frustrating and lonely if you're not used to working alone. And it takes a lot of motivation. You have to sell yourself everyday, not just until you land a job.

That said, this section will give tips on which skills are best suited to self-employment, what it takes to work for yourself overseas, and how to go about finding contracts.

WHAT CAN YOU DO ABROAD?

Certain skills and professions lend themselves to self-employment overseas more easily than others. The following are samples of the wide variety of skills that have been turned into paid work abroad:

- writing, researching, journalism, editing (most of the examples in this chapter are drawn from these highly portable freelance careers)

595

- public relations work
- teaching English and other languages
- teaching music, yoga, aerobics, art, flower arranging and other crafts
- translation
- selling things that you make, such as stained glass, paintings, quilts. Also, teaching any of these arts and crafts
- selling personal services such as picture framing, catering, facials
- selling services aimed at expatriates, including investment advice, résumé writing or tax planning
- buying artifacts to sell in Canada
- computer services and skills
- counselling and therapy

PERSONAL STORIES

Successful international freelancers have many common traits. The following personal stories demonstrate how they have prevailed over the natural shyness of marketing themselves. They also show how persistent, curious, entrepreneurial, flexible and adaptable a self-employed person must be.

- An experienced journalist who moved to The Hague with her husband found it took longer than she had expected to get started. But after a year and a half she had a wide variety of work: writing articles for an English-language trade magazine; selling reports to BBC and CBC radio; selling stories to Canadian and British magazines and newspapers; and writing and editing for two international development agencies based in the Netherlands. Some of the work she might have disdained at home. "I don't think I would have considered writing for a trade publication in Canada. But you have to start somewhere and it often leads to something more interesting."

- Among the expatriate spouses she met in The Hague over a two-year period, more than a dozen of them made work for themselves. One was an ornithologist who taught bird-watching once a week, and in the afternoons did bookkeeping for an English-language editing company owned by a neighbour. Another signed up for a museum guide course at the local art museum, and later led English-speaking women's clubs to art museums around Holland. Yet another was an accomplished picture framer who took a course in restoring antiques and old furniture. She opened her own antique shop when she moved back to Calgary.

- An American friend with energy to spare shows how someone with the right attitude can do almost anything. On a previous posting to Taiwan, she had taught business English to local business people. Through one of her contracts, she met someone who wanted to buy heavy equipment in Europe. She ended up travelling to Europe and closing the deal on his behalf. This time, with her husband based in The Hague, she again taught business English but also studied Russian on the side. With her Russian tutor, a refugee doctor, she compiled a list of medical doctors and professors in the former Soviet Union, which they then rented to pharmaceutical firms in the US.

BEFORE YOU GET THERE

Before you leave home, update your résumé—perhaps bring a few versions highlighting different skills. Also bring letters of recommendation, especially if you've worked for well-known companies or institutions, and take along samples of your work where possible.

If you belong to a professional association, check for the names of companies based in the country you're headed for that use people in your field.

If you think you might need some equipment to get started—for example a computer or a tape recorder—think seriously about buying it in Canada. For one thing, it's always more difficult to find where to buy the right tools in a foreign country. And, as one reporter said to another who was wondering whether to buy a broadcast quality tape recorder before moving to Europe, "well, if you don't have it, you certainly won't do radio reporting."

It's helpful to talk to people who have been where you are going and get names of possible contacts. But keep in mind that some people you meet may not have had a positive experience trying to set up work for themselves. They could be more discouraging than helpful. A Canadian journalist who had lived in The Hague told another writer headed for the same city not to even think of working as a writer, and that the Dutch language was so difficult she'd have to write down every phone number she was given because she'd never find them in the phone book. The advice proved to be totally wrong on both counts.

Self-employment may be one of the few kinds of "jobs" where you're better off waiting until you get overseas to really get cracking. Especially if you're going along as a "spouse of," you're best not to commit yourself to anything beforehand. You don't know where you'll be living, how much time it will take to set up your family and household, and the pressures that you will face on arrival.

GETTING STARTED AND GETTING MOTIVATED

Looking for work always demands motivation, and making a job for yourself overseas takes all that you've got.

Many people who move overseas with a working spouse go with the best intentions, and then face depression and inertia almost as soon as they touch ground. This is normal. To be pulled up from your roots, without a job or career to tag next to your name, can be a tremendous blow to your self-esteem. Sometimes you have to wait for the worst to pass before getting started in your job search.

In many countries, just going out to do the shopping takes a huge amount of energy and initiative. You're not alone if you feel this way, so make sure you pat yourself on the back when you accomplish what seem like minor feats: opening a bank account, buying food for dinner, taking the bus downtown.

But everyone is different. One writer who has lived in India and the Sudan as the wife of a development worker says, "Inertia sets in after a few months in a developing country so it's better to make use of the get-up-and-go that you bring from Canada while you still have it."

One way to help yourself acclimatize is to study the local language. Don't expect to be able to converse after three months of twice-a-week classes, but you should know enough to perform your daily tasks with more confidence. This will also boost your self-esteem.

It is especially important to act professionally. Set up an office for yourself in your new apartment or house, even if it's just a desk and telephone in the corner of your living room. Making cold calls is hard for everyone, but if you set yourself a certain amount of time each week or a certain number of calls, you'll feel like you're getting somewhere.

WHERE TO MAKE CONTACTS?

The ability to make and develop contacts differentiates those who find freelance work from those who do not.

When her husband was posted to Sudan, a freelance writer brought CVs, work samples and letters of reference from editors. "When I got there I just started knocking on doors." She heard that the Canadian chargé d'affaires to Cairo would be coming through Khartoum and that he always stayed at the Hilton Hotel. She telephoned him and arranged to meet him for tea. The official confided that the CANADIAN INTERNATIONAL DEVELOPMENT AGENCY (CIDA) was about to update its briefing report on the Sudan. Instead of flying someone in from Ottawa, she got the contract.

For the less brave, taking a volunteer job or becoming active in a social club for new arrivals will give you the confidence you need to look for paid contracts. And, for artisans and other people with items to sell, meeting other expatriates is the easiest way to get started. You can't fake enthusiasm, motivation or an outgoing personality—but you can make the most of what you have.

Get out and meet people, as many as you can. The writer who quickly nabbed the CIDA contract in the Sudan also made a job for herself in India by talking to the right people. She says it's not enough to talk to one person in an organization who can hand out contracts—talk to as many as you can. "That way, when they meet each other your name may come up. And, while one might not have wanted to rock the boat, working together they might find something for you."

"Be systematic," advises another experienced freelancer. Be creative in thinking up possibilities and use your common sense to hunt down information. One contact often leads to another. The Canadian (or foreign) community abroad is tightly-knit and contracts or jobs for English-speakers are often awarded to competent friends or acquaintances because it's quicker than advertising.

If you're based in a city large enough to have clubs and associations geared to foreigners, these may offer you the best opportunity to advertise your services by word-of-mouth or through their newsletters. English-language schools offering evening courses for adults frequently need instructors. Women's groups can be hotbeds for people selling services or courses and a good way to get your name known, even if you don't think of yourself as someone who would normally join such a group. The Canadian consulate or embassy may be a good source of information about English-language associations which might otherwise take you months to track down.

Canadian embassies usually have a list of Canadian companies operating in the country. The commercial attaché may be loathe to hand it out if you just state you're looking for work, but the lists are not secret. Often there will be a chamber of commerce devoted to trade between Canada and the country you're in and it may be more helpful.

Do not neglect to contact the foreign missions and firms from the United States, Britain and other Western countries. Your familiarity with Western culture and your specialized skills will impress employers and individuals seeking consultants' services.

BE CLEAR IN YOUR JOB OBJECTIVE

One important point to remember in freelance work is to clearly state to potential employers that you are looking for contract work. Use phrases in your covering letter or at the top of your resume such as: seeking freelance assignments, short-term consultancy, contract work, editing and writing services, temporary secretarial help, consultant, etc. If your level of availability is a factor, mention your restrictions. Example: available three days per week, mornings, between August and September.

Your first reaction to this advice may be to say that it is too limiting and could discourage employers from offering you a "full-time" job. To the contrary, most employers find that it is a lot easier and less threatening to hire consultants and short-term workers. If a full-time job appears, the employer could well take the initiative to offer you an alternative work contract. But all in all, your chances of landing short-term work or selling your services on an assignment basis are much improved when you clearly state this objective.

HOW MUCH CAN YOU EARN AS A SELF-EMPLOYED PROFESSIONAL?

Your income from self-employment will depend on a number of factors: where you are based, how valuable your skills are, how much time you devote to the job, and a certain amount of luck.

A Canadian in southern Africa lost his job as a development worker while overseas. However, the cost of living was so reasonable that he was able to earn enough money on a freelance basis to be able to afford to keep his four-bedroom house with a swimming pool and two servants.

When finding contracts or freelance work is difficult, trade is often an exciting option, especially in developing countries. Two Canadian students learning Chinese in Beijing plan to finance their next year's schooling at a Canadian university by buying silk scarves and pyjamas for next-to-nothing in China to sell in Vancouver on their return. An art dealer from Washington who moved to Dubai with her oil industry boyfriend made a lucrative business buying Moghul miniature paintings, which she later sold through US galleries.

A Canadian journalist who moved to Amsterdam got enough contracts writing business stories and profiles for trade publications, both Dutch and Canadian, that his income almost equalled his wife's salaried wage within a year. Two Canadian journalists based in Ottawa set up a syndicated feature service specializing in the banking industry. They travel all over the world and earn very good incomes. One of them, who has freelanced for 10 years, has written for more than 100 publications in that time, and in some years has travelled outside Canada for more than 250 days. "The key is to invest in long distance phone calls because the nature of news is that what everyone knows in one place is news somewhere else. You can sell anything Canadian in Hong Kong easier than in Canada—and vice versa. If you travel around, you become an expert on Asia in Europe and on Europe in Asia."

Some people, including many journalists, can earn enough through free-lance work to support a family. But for many, if not most people who are self-employed abroad, the work is enough to pay for some travel or supplement an already generous salary earned by the working spouse.

The Canadian journalist based in the Hague says that her work rarely took more than half her time. "And luckily we weren't dependent on my income." On the other hand, some of the new experience she gained through writing a book for an international agency broadened her CV and gained her another contract with the WORLD BANK on her return to Canada.

TAXES AND LABOUR LAWS

Many countries have strict rules prohibiting the hiring of foreigners for jobs that locals can do. But often they do allow foreigners to start their own businesses or work for themselves. It is in your interest to check the labour and tax laws before you get serious, preferably by seeing a lawyer who can do it for you anonymously. If you are still a Canadian resident for tax purposes, you'll be paying taxes to the Canadian government; if you're a non-resident of Canada, you may be liable for income taxes in the country you're living in. Some countries have wealth taxes (a percentage of your worldwide income) and it is better to check into the tax rules beforehand to ensure that it makes financial sense for you to work. In many countries, like Canada, a very low income won't be taxable, and you may not have to file.

A LAST WORD

One last word to those who are contemplating giving up a rewarding professional job in Canada for the exotic unknown of living abroad to accompany your working spouse. When you first arrive, the experience of being unable to define yourself through your job or profession may be ego-deflating and depressing. But once you have overcome that hurdle through gainful self-employment as a freelancer or (if no work is forthcoming) learning to define yourself differently, then you probably won't feel that fear so strongly again. Chances are you will be stronger and more optimistic. Freelancing can be a very liberating experience.

RESOURCES

There are limited resources available in this area of interest. This short list of books does not do justice to all the professional freelancing opportunities and strategies available abroad, but it's a start.

Adult Education Resources 🖳
www. teleeducation.nb.ca/distanceed/adult ▪ This site will help you take courses online. You will find a list of web sites related to general adult education, distance education, literacy, women's education, training, human resource development, and online teaching. [ID:2732]

Culture Shock!: Successful Living Abroad, A Wife's Guide 📖
1992, *Robin Pascoe,* Graphic Arts Center Publishing Co. ➤ Raincoast Books, 8680 Cambie Street, Vancouver, B.C. V6P 6M9; $17.50; VISA, MC; (800) 663-5714, fax (800) 565-3770 ▪ Written by a Canadian, the book is easy to read, and provides useful advice for the wife going overseas for the first time, especially if her husband is with Foreign Affairs or an international agency. Chapters on maids, entertaining and home leave may be off-putting, but after you've lived in her shoes, they may seem pertinent. Has a useful chapter on getting a job or freelancing overseas. [ID:1307]

How to Find Temporary Work Abroad 📖
1994, *Nick Vandome,* 176 pages ➤ How To Books Ltd., 3 Newtec Place, Magdalen Road, Oxford, OX4 1RE, UK; £8.99; credit cards; (44) (1752) 202-301, fax (44) (1865) 202-331 ▪ A practical book explaining where to find the opportunities suited to your particular interests, how to apply and be selected, how to manage money, passports, permits, insurance and accommodation, and how to get the most out of your experience overseas. [ID:1678]

Work Your Way Around The World 📖
Annual ➤ Peterson's Guides, P.O. Box 2123, Princeton, NJ 08543-2123, USA; US$17.95; cheque or money order; (800) 338-3282, fax (609) 243-9150 ▪ An excellent resource describing numerous ways the enterprising traveller can find work anywhere in the world, travel free by working for passage, and survive when money runs out. Appropriate for the non-career-minded, the book lists jobs by country, describing everything from orange picking to sheep shearing, with direct quotes from people who have actually done the jobs. Well-written and inspiring. Visit the publisher's web site at www.petersons.com. [ID:1154]

The World on a String: How to become a Freelance Foreign Correspondent 📖
1997, *Al Goodman, John Pollack,* Harry Holt and Company Inc., 198 pages ➤ Fitzhenry and Whiteside Ltd., 195 Allstate Parkway, Markham, Ontario L3R 4T8; $17.95; VISA, MC; (800) 387-9776, fax (800) 260-9777, godwit@fitzhenry.ca ▪ Colorful anecdotes and practical advice from successful stringers around the world highlight the trials and triumphs of freelancing abroad. This is a step-by-step manual which describes how to choose a region to work in, select the right equipment, establish vital editorial contacts at home and abroad, make ends meet while filing stories to various media, prepare for the risks of reporting from war zones, and work effectively with distant editors. Visit the distributor's web site at www.fitzhenry.ca. [ID:2711]

Chapter 31

Job Hunting When You Return to Canada

So you and your family have just returned from a four-year posting in Islamabad, Pakistan. You arrive in Calgary after a two-month vacation in South Asia. The kids are about to start school, you're unpacking your belongings after four years in storage. Now it dawns on you that you face the Canadian job search process. What a daunting task! Where do you begin?

This chapter will advise "returnees" (those recently returned from long-term overseas assignments) on how to conduct their non-international job search. The focus will be on adjusting to the Canadian job scene after a long stint abroad. Re-entry concerns, the new international skills you acquired, how to search for a job with Canadian employers who have no international experience will be discussed.

RE-ENTRY ADJUSTMENTS

You are probably finding re-entry to Canada more difficult than you expected. (For more on this topic see Chapter 8, Re-Entry.) On a personal level, you find Canadian social life booooring! No one is interested in world events. Talk revolves around the weather or gossip about in-laws. Social conversations seem trivial. You miss the blend of international friends you had. Everyone here seems to conduct their friendships by phone. No one drops by for a good face-to-face conversation, or a cup of tea. You even have to do your own dishes and laundry!

The worst part—let's face it, it's the most common re-entry problem—is that no one will take an active interest in your overseas experience. Not even your parents or your brothers or sisters are interested. They have perhaps looked at your slide show and asked a few polite questions at the time, but nothing more. You are bursting with stories, ideas, new insights, and they have

603

closed the book on the last four years of your life. They are all very happy to see you and to have you safely at home, but no one seems interested in your adventures or the incredible changes you have undergone.

Before losing your sense of purpose and becoming totally discouraged about finding a job and starting your new life in Canada, stop and consider some important aspects of your overseas experience.

RETURNING HOME, A STRONGER YOU

Success in an international career often rests more on your personality than on your technical skills. Now that you are home, it is worthwhile to reflect on the strengths and new, non-technical skills you acquired overseas. Once you've done this, your Canadian job search will not seem so frightening.

Most people return from their trips abroad feeling empowered. You have probably learned to deal with enormous ambiguities. You feel able to meet almost any challenge. You have experienced the bizarre, dangerous situations, intense heat, floods, disease. You have even survived daily shopping in Southern markets! All of these challenges have strengthened you.

You have probably developed a better understanding of yourself. Most expatriates experience a sense of freedom living overseas, where you are free of the normal Canadian cultural and societal restraints. As a foreigner, you can do a pirouette in the street and no one will bother you. As a manager or stay-home spouse, you have had the freedom to hire and fire at will and to manage your affairs to your liking, without outside pressure. This freedom has allowed you to clarify your individual boundaries of behaviour. Thus you have pushed your limits and come to know yourself better. You have learned to behave according to your own ethics, not those enforced by convention or peer pressure. This understanding is empowering and you know you can face new situations on the strength of your own judgement.

THE IMPORTANCE OF UNDERSTANDING YOUR SKILLS

Throughout this book we stress the importance of having a firm understanding of your skills during the job search. Knowing your strengths and weaknesses, and being able to steer discussions with potential employers onto topics which demonstrate your suitability, are crucial parts of any job search. Unless you are good at talking about what you do well, why you do it well, and how you can bring knowledge from past work experience to benefit your new employer, you will have difficulty finding a good job in this competitive market.

It is now time to look at some practical factors affecting your job search as a returnee from overseas. We will start with the most difficult.

WHY CANADIAN EMPLOYERS
AVOID INTERNATIONAL EMPLOYEES

Canadian employers with little or no international experience may have misconceptions about job seekers returning from postings abroad. While not all employers believe the following myths about returnees, you may want to keep them in mind. While not all employers believe the following myths about returnees, you may want to keep them in mind.

EMPLOYERS' ASSUMPTIONS:

* **Returnees have emotional re-adjustment problems**. Because of the hardships they've encountered, expatriates have undergone personality changes and traumas. Their re-adjustment to Canada will be difficult and will adversely affect their work.

* **Returnees are not used to Canadian business customs**. Having adapted to a very different culture (they may even have "gone native"), returnees have lost sight of standard Canadian business practices. They lack finesse. They no longer fit the Canadian corporate mould.

* **Returnees are too exotic**. They have adopted alternative lifestyles and can't be team players. They are excessively individualistic and independent. Their differences are threatening.

* **Returnees are flighty**. They don't really want permanent jobs or long-term responsibilities. They will soon be off travelling again.

* **Returnees have health problems**. They may have strange tropical diseases. They may be contagious. They will require a lot of sick leave.

YOUR SOLUTIONS:

* **Do not overstate or dwell on your re-entry adjustment problems**. Stress positive aspects of your overseas experience and return to Canada.

* **Do not say that you plan to return overseas**.

* **State that you are happy to be back in Canada**. Canada is your home. You are anxious to join your peers in the work world.

* **Demonstrate your business acumen**. Draw attention to your good work habits, adaptability to new technologies, willingness to be a team player, understanding of Canadian leadership style. Avoid wearing souvenir clothing or jewellery. Dress in smart, businesslike clothing. Focus on fitting in. Downplay your independence. You have already made this clear through your willingness to travel outside your own culture.

* **Show your attachment to Canadian society**. Mention your enthusiasm for something Canadian, such as the CBC, a particular university, hockey.

* **Mention the clean bill of health** you received for your recent physical.

HOW TO EXPLAIN YOUR INTERNATIONAL EXPERIENCE TO CANADIAN EMPLOYERS

You are already aware that, with the exception of others who have lived abroad, very few people are interested or able to understand your international work experiences. You must therefore be cautious when discussing them with Canadian employers. Here are a few tips to help you down this delicate path.

- **Be professional in describing your overseas work responsibilities.** You are probably fairly animated about the challenges you faced when overseas. Practice rewording your description of job responsibilities in a more businesslike manner. Be formal. Be articulate.

- **Use the language of your future work.** You will have to give up the expatriate jargon which may have become second nature to you. In the following chart, the left-hand column features words that are unfamiliar, and therefore intimidating, to Canadian employers. The right-hand column shows equivalent terminology better-suited to the Canadian work environment.

- **Speak in terms familiar to Canadians.** Use titles to describe your overseas customers, not foreign names which are difficult to pronounce. Avoid detailed geographical descriptions. State what government departments you worked with; simplify the name of the department or use the Canadian equivalent.

EXAMPLES OF INTERNATIONAL TERMS AND THEIR CANADIAN EQUIVALENTS

AVOID International Terms	USE Canadian Terms
Mission/Field Missions	Business Trip
Field Staff, Field Offices	Regional Staff, Regional Office
Cooperant/Volunteer/Expert	Employee/Consultant
Counterpart/Homologue/Local Staff	Staff (avoid making reference to the distinction between local and expatriate or international staff)
Delegate	Outside Company Representative
Culture Shock	Adjustment
Crosscultural Adaptability	Able to Deal with Change
Cultural Sensitivity	Interpersonal Skills
Crosscultural Communication	Effective Listening Skills
Diplomacy	Political Astuteness
Protocol	Politeness/Tact

- **Speak of your successes, your accomplishments.** Do not discuss insurmountable challenges, or why you did not succeed at something. Canadian employers with no international experience will be unable to judge the context and could form erroneous judgements on your capabilities.

- **Use concrete and measurable examples of your work.** How many employees? Size of budget? The number of warehouses, number of trucks, number of hectares? Describe the project's strategic and long-term work plans, management objectives.

- **Avoid shocking stories.** Do not go into the bizarre tales from hell. The harder the posting, the more cautious you should be talking about the difficulties you encountered.

- **Play down your love for adventure,** your need for change.

INTERNATIONAL SKILLS YOU SHOULD EMPHASIZE TO CANADIAN EMPLOYERS

As a returnee from abroad, you have brought back important skills which are readily transferable to Canadian contexts. Despite some of the negative expectations mentioned at the beginning of the chapter, you can demonstrate to Canadian employers that internationally-experienced job candidates are more savvy, sophisticated, in tune with office politics, with customers, and with the world at large. It is to your advantage to emphasize the intuitive side of your international awareness to Canadian employers. Below is a list of "Canadianized" skills usually attributed to internationally-experienced personnel.

Interpersonal Skills

- Open-mindedness, sensitivity, tact
- Listening and observing skills
- Ability to deal with stress
- Sense of humour
- Awareness of office politics, protocol
- Loyalty and tenacity

Professional Work Skills

- Ability to take on challenging work
- Independence, self-discipline
- Training experience
- Flexibility, resourcefulness
- Ability to deal with change and the unexpected
- Persistence
- Writing and report writing

SKILLS ON WHICH YOU MAY HAVE FALLEN BEHIND

Having adapted yourself to your overseas position, you may find that you need to work at those skills that were neglected, and adjust others to Canadian standards. The following incomplete list should help get you started.

Skills Related to Administration

- Canadian business protocol, business practices
- Leadership, managing and motivating colleagues and subordinates
- Self-reliance, typing and photocopying your own work, making your own coffee, driving your own car

Skills Related to Technology

- **Computers:** Basic understanding of DOS, Windows and Networks. A minimum level of proficiency usually includes strong knowledge of a word processing program, and familiarity with e-mail, spreadsheets, and databases.

- **Telecommunications:** Telephone systems, call waiting, call answer, call return, last call return, call display, calling cards, 800, 888, 900 and even 700 numbers. Answering machines, e-mail, the Internet, fax and fax modems, and automated banking.

A LAST WORD

No matter what your career objectives are upon returning to Canada, the task of finding a place for yourself will be scary. Jobs are out there, however, and internationally-experienced personnel are respected. As your first step, I strongly recommend you make the major effort of developing a detailed skills inventory, using Canadian terminology. It is empowering to see how good your professional self looks on paper. The second step is to go out and, in a focused manner, research the job you want. Remember, job hunting can be exciting!

PART FIVE

International Career Contacts

32. The Private Sector 611
33. Services for International
      Businesses & Entrepreneurs 693
34. Careers in Government 713
35. Nongovernmental Organizations 763
36. United Nations 835
37. Environmental &
      Agricultural Research Centres 857
38. International Organizations 867
39. Canadian Diplomats Abroad 887
40. Foreign Diplomats in Canada 903

Chapter 32

The Private Sector

The private sector is easily the largest employer in the international arena. It is also a sector where prospects for continued job growth are excellent. This chapter profiles over 250 Canadian firms with international activities, providing up-to-date contact information and appraisals of size, areas of expertise, and preferred backgrounds. Whenever relevant to job hunters, a brief note on a profiled company's web site is also included.

Along with the Canadian government's endorsement of a wide array of bilateral, regional, and multilateral trade agreements, the last decade has witnessed a widespread liberalization of international trade and investment (with some opposition to these agreements by people who claim a variety of adverse effects). These changes have been reflected, on a global scale, by an increasing number of corporations developing or expanding international operations through export, partnering, or other forms of strategic alliance. Many Canadian firms have been at the forefront of this transformation.

In contrast to government agencies and international organizations, which are primarily involved in defining problems and funding projects, private firms are typically the implementing agents at the local level. For practical, hands-on individuals interested in the day-to-day operational aspects of international work, the private sector can provide a challenging and varied overseas career.

SIZE OF FIRMS

The firms profiled in this chapter range from small consulting operations to large multinational corporations with several thousand staff. Companies are classified according to the size of their international operations: SMALL firms have international budgets of less than $500,000/year; MID-SIZED firms between $500,000 and $2,000,000; and LARGE firms over $2,000,000/year.

SECTORS

A concerted effort has been made to accurately reflect those sectors in which Canadian firms are globally competitive, such as mining, telecommunications, software, engineering and construction, human resources, petrochemicals, financial services, environmental services, and transportation. In addition, a significant number of consulting firms are profiled. Consulting companies are typically recipients of contracts tendered by the CANADIAN INTERNATIONAL DEVELOPMENT AGENCY (CIDA) and some of the larger UN agencies and international organizations. With only a few exceptions, generally professional organizations with Canadian partners, all of the companies listed meet the criteria of majority Canadian ownership.

QUALIFICATIONS

Private sector employers typically recruit candidates with very high skill levels, and look for a unique combination of technical business acumen and international know-how. You will be assessed on the basis of education, language skills, overseas experience, and previous work experience. There are, of course, important exceptions noted in the profiles below.

Most firms require a master's or professional undergraduate degree with functional expertise. A generalist is often perceived to be less useful than someone with a professional designation or specialty in international finance, strategic planning, marketing, or a specific sector.

Competence in languages other than English and French is an asset. While specifications will vary depending on the location of a firm's overseas contracts, Spanish currently seems in highest demand. Alongside foreign language proficiency, area expertise is actively recruited.

Less tangible skills are also evaluated: previous overseas experience, effective crosscultural communication, adaptability and openness to change, and sensitivity to and respect for, overseas cultures. An executive from a large consulting firm put it this way:

> *"We are interested if, on top of your education and technical expertise, you consider yourself an adaptable individual who is open to learning and new situations, and tolerant of ambiguity..."*

HOW TO BEGIN

Overseas vacancies in the private sector are rarely advertised. Instead, they tend to be filled from within the organization or from a pool of registered experts. Most firms maintain an active data bank for résumés, so don't get discouraged if prospective employers tell you that your application has been placed on file. The nature of international contracting is uncertain, and a sojourn on file is not necessarily the end of the line.

Some companies are understandably reluctant to send new recruits overseas immediately. A recurring theme in the profiles below is that many companies prefer to fill their international positions from within. Depending on your profession, then, you should be prepared to spend some time with a firm in Canada in order to position yourself for an eventual overseas posting. This is commonly the case in, for example, the banking industry; the up-side is that, once you've made that leap, the overseas opportunities can be extensive. Some firms actively encourage employees to groom themselves for work abroad, and even offer foreign internships to nurture their staff's global vision.

Note that many firms with international operations prefer to work with local businesses, and let such overseas partners make all hiring decisions there rather than in Canada. There is, thus, a considerable amount of international contract work available that cannot be accessed simply by contacting the head office of Canadian firms with significant overseas activities. Sometimes, you'll have to contact the local partners of Canadian firms, or even actually be in their country. As a rule, Canadian companies that never hire for foreign positions within Canada are not included in these profiles; an exception is made when the Canadian head office can help you learn about such contracts.

Prior to applying or making direct contact with an organization, some preliminary research is required. Make sure you thoroughly understand a company's organizational objectives and international activities. Not only does this make it easier to determine which firms are compatible with your objectives, but it also indicates to the firm the seriousness of the application. This can be accomplished by soliciting annual reports and corporate brochures, keeping abreast of relevant issues by reviewing business magazines and newsletters, reading company and industry web sites and newsgroups on the Internet, and making telephone enquiries.

RESOURCES

There are a wide variety of directories, how-to manuals, crosscultural effectiveness books and so forth that can assist you in embarking upon a successful career in the private sector. For more information please see the Resources sections in Chapter 1, The Effective Overseas Employee; Chapter 7, The Canadian Identity in the International Workplace; Chapter 21, The Internet Job Search; Chapter 27, Jobs by Regions of the World; and Chapter 33, Services for International Businesses and Entrepreneurs.

Profiles of Private Firms

The following list profiles 256 Canada-based employers with significant overseas activities. As much as possible, we've tried to let companies speak for themselves. Note that some subsidiaries are listed in addition to their parent company if they have their own separate hiring process. You will want to visit the web site of any company you intend to contact to find the most current contact information and learn more about the company's current operations and job opportunities.

A.D.I. Group Inc.

Suite 300, 1133 Regent Street, Fredericton,
N.B. E3B 3Z2; (506) 452-9000, fax (506) 459-3954, adigroup@adi.ca, www.adi.ca

MID-SIZED PROFESSIONAL EXCHANGE: Construction, Consulting, Engineering, Environment, Project Management, Technical Assistance, Water Resources

The A.D.I. Group Inc. is an employee-owned multidisciplinary group of companies organized into separate operations for each technology or service. The companies provide engineering, consulting, project management, and construction services worldwide.

A.D.I. employs over 200 highly-skilled professionals and has operations throughout the Americas, Europe, India, and Korea. Offices are located throughout Canada and there is a US office in New Hampshire. Overseas operations are focused on the environmental sector, with projects ranging from environmental management to the engineering of water supply and treatment systems to complete wastewater treatment systems on a turnkey basis. The firm currently has 10 staff with international responsibilities.

Prospective applicants should have a degree in environmental science or engineering coupled with overseas experience in consulting or construction. Fluency in another language, Spanish in particular, is an asset. Internships are infrequent. The web site offers information on the companies within the A.D.I. Group but does not offer any specific advice to job seekers. [ID:5646]

Acres International Limited (AIL)

P.O. Box 1001, 4342 Queen Street, Niagara Falls, Ontario L2E 6W1;
(905) 374-5200, fax (905) 374-1157, postmaster@niagarafalls.acres.com, www.acres.com

LARGE ENGINEERING FIRM: Consulting, Economics, Engineering, Environment, Project Management, Teaching, Water Resources

Acres International Limited (AIL) provides consulting engineering services for all phases of the project cycle, from preliminary studies, through engineering design, construction supervision, and start-up operations. The company is active in power generation and transmission, ports and airports, irrigation and water resources development, industrial, environmental, and waste management projects. The firm also has expertise in resource development planning, environmental management, and institutional strengthening.

AIL has a staff of 50 working abroad, and 200 in Canada with international responsibilities. Activities are concentrated in developing countries in Asia, anglophone Africa, the Middle East, and Latin America.

Applicants with professional engineer status (civil, mechanical, electrical) as well as economists and environmental scientists will be considered. Previous experience on engineering projects in developing countries is an asset. The firm maintains a data bank for résumés. The web site includes an employment opportunities section which lists specific openings with the firm, including overseas positions. [ID:5648]

Adamac Management Group Inc.

Suite 403, 265 North Front Street, Sarnia, Ontario N7T 7X1; (519) 332-3930, fax (519) 332-7010

MID-SIZED GENERAL CONSULTING FIRM: Accounting, Administration, Advocacy, Business Development, Community Development, Economics, Energy Resources, Engineering, Environment, Human Resources, International Trade, Logistics, Petrochemicals, Project Management, Technical Assistance

The Adamac Management Group Inc. is a mid-sized consulting firm specializing in process and technology development for the chemical, petrochemical, and energy sectors. The company is involved in international trade services, including customs consulting and logistics management, commodity procurement through Canadian international aid programs, corporate expansions and international market development, and human resource services.

Adamac's personnel are independent associates of the corporation rather than salaried staff. Currently, there are 10 salaried associates in Canada and an additional 35 based overseas.

Prospective applicants should have experience in international marketing, engineering, project development, and management. [ID:5649]

AGRA Earth & Environmental Limited

221 - 18th Street S.E., Calgary, Alberta T2E 6J5;
(403) 248-4331, fax (403) 248-2188, agraenv@connect.ab.ca, www.agraee.com

LARGE ENVIRONMENTAL FIRM: Agriculture, Business Development, Community Development, Computer Systems, Construction, Consulting, Development Assistance, Development Education, Economics, Energy Resources, Engineering, Environment, Fisheries, Forestry, Gender and Development, Human Resources, Human Rights, Petrochemicals, Project Management, Technical Assistance, Water Resources

AGRA Earth & Environmental Limited (AEE) is a Canadian based environmental sciences, geotechnical, and materials services company. AEE offers professional engineering, scientific and contracting services to industry, investors, financial institutions, and governments in all international markets. The company is a wholly-owned subsidiary of Calgary-based AGRA Industries Limited, a diversified Canadian public stock company with annual revenues of about $700 million from engineering, construction, environmental services, waste management, and recycling.

AEE has over 40 years of experience, staff of over 1,400 worldwide, and operates in over 55 offices. In addition, they have access to over 100 AGRA offices around the world.

AEE has traditionally carried out the majority of its work in western and northern Canada. Starting in 1984, the company began to market skills outside Canada and has developed consulting assignments in over 40 countries.

AEE employs full-time professionals in engineering, hydrogeology, occupational hygiene, agrology, biology, forestry, and geology as well as other experts in wildlife, fisheries, heritage resources, socio-economic planning and occupational hygiene, and safety, to offer an integrated approach to development project planning. The company uses state-of-the-art techniques and resources including satellite and air photo interpretation, geographic information systems (GIS), computerized literature searches, modern statistical methods, detailed protocols for sample collection and analysis, and computerized word processing and graphics systems.

Recruiters for international projects look for academic qualifications, cultural background, languages, etc. The firm offers internships and maintains a data bank of résumés. AEE also maintains a detailed web site that posts employment opportunities and offers advice for those seeking to join their team. [ID:5651]

AGRA Monenco

Suite 100, 2010 Winston Park Drive,
Oakville, Ontario L6H 6A3; (905) 829-5400, fax (905) 829-5401, www.agra.com

LARGE ENGINEERING FIRM: Accounting, Administration, Business/Banking/Trade, Business Development, Computer Systems, Engineering, Human Resources, Media/Communications, Project Management

AGRA Monenco is an international engineering, procurement and construction management company and a leader in technologies related to infrastructure, power, process industries, and systems. AGRA Monenco provides its clients with integrated project solutions, offering a complete range of professional engineering, project development and financing, systems, project execution, operation, and maintenance services.

The company has four primary business groups: Infrastructure, including highways, roads, rail, ports, airports, and bridges; Power, including hydroelectric, thermal, cogeneration, and nuclear projects as well as transmission, distribution, control, and telecommunications; Process, including oil and gas processing, pipelines, petrochemicals, pharmaceutical, mining and industrial industries; and Systems, including systems integration, project management, radio spectrum management, geographic information systems, and data conversion.

AGRA Monenco is a wholly-owned subsidiary of AGRA Inc., an international engineering, construction, environment, and technology corporation. Its headquarters are in Calgary. AGRA employs about 5,000 people and operates 155 offices in 22 countries. The firm is active internationally, in such places as Latin America, Asia Pacific region, India, the Middle East, and Africa.

Candidates from all backgrounds are considered for employment. The firm maintains a data bank for résumés and offers co-op programs for summer students. The firm is in the process of constructing a web site. [ID:6837]

AGRA Monenco Inc.
900 Monenco Place, 801 - 6th Ave. S.W., Calgary, Alberta T2P 3W3;
(403) 298-4170, fax (403) 298-4125, monencoagra@cal.cybersurf.net, www.agra.ca

LARGE ENGINEERING FIRM: Engineering, Management Training, Project Management, Technical Assistance

The AGRA Engineering, Procurement, and Construction Management Group is a major international engineering company providing innovative solutions to the development and use of global resources in a manner which balances society's needs with capital and conservation requirements. The firm has expertise in the generation, transmission, and distribution of power, petrochemical processing, mining and processing minerals and metals, and construction and management of transportation systems and infrastructures.

There are a total of 16 companies within the AGRA Engineering Group with international offices in Argentina, India, Indonesia, Iran, Malaysia, Nigeria, Singapore, China, the US, and Venezuela. [ID:5652]

AGRA ShawMont Limited
P.O. Box 9600, Bally Rou Place, 280 Torbay Road,
St. John's, Nfld. A1A 3C1; (709) 754-0250, fax (709) 739-6823

MID-SIZED ENERGY CONSULTING FIRM: Adult Training, Consulting, Development Education, Energy Resources, Engineering, Project Management, Water Resources

AGRA ShawMont Limited is an industrial energy conservation consulting firm that performs energy audits, retrofit demonstration projects, training programs, promotion and communications programs, and develops long-range energy conservation plans.

The company is currently working in the textile and beverage industries in southern Africa, in Angola, Zambia, Zimbabwe, Botswana, Malawi, Mozambique, Tanzania, Lesotho, and Swaziland.

AGRA ShawMont has eight overseas employees and a total staff of 96. The firm is not actively seeking applicants, although it maintains a data bank for résumés. [ID:5859]

Agriteam Canada Consulting Ltd.
International Division, Suite 890, 10201 Southport Road S.W.,
Calgary, Alberta T2W 4X9; (403) 253-5298, fax (403) 253-5140, agriteam@compuserve.com

LARGE GENERAL CONSULTING FIRM: Agriculture, Community Development, Consulting, Development Assistance, Development Education, Economics, Energy Resources, Environment, Exchange Programs, Gender and Development, Human Resources, Intercultural Briefings, Micro-Enterprises, Project Management, Technical Assistance, Telecommunications, Water Resources

Agriteam Canada Consulting Ltd. is a Canadian consulting company specializing in international development. The company provides a full range of services to governments, businesses, and financial institutions in many regions of the developing world. Agriteam is involved in all phases of the project cycle, including project preparation, appraisal, implementation, monitoring, and evaluation. While much of Agriteam's work has been in agriculture and agro-industry, rural development, natural resources management, and environmental protection, the company also has expertise in community-level infrastructure, public health, and public administration.

Established in 1987, Agriteam has implemented more than 90 development projects in 24 different countries throughout Asia, Africa, South and Central America, the Caribbean, Eastern Europe, and the former Soviet Union. Agriteam is currently the executing agency for a portfolio of projects worth approximately $40 million in China, Mongolia, Sri Lanka, Thailand, India, and Bangladesh and also manages smaller projects in South and Central America. Agriteam has an overseas staff of 14 and 19 Canadian-based corporate staff. Its head office is in Calgary, with a satellite office in Hull and project offices in Beijing, Dhaka, Jakarta, Colombo, New Delhi, and Ulan Bator. The company is also represented in Manila, Philippines.

Agriteam recruits candidates with graduate degrees that relate to agriculture, development, human resources development, health or water resources. Previous overseas experience is preferred. Canadian citizenship is an asset, as is multiple language capability. Agriteam maintains a data bank for résumés. [ID:5654]

Agrodev Canada, Division of Stanley Consulting Group Ltd.
Suite 600, 222 Somerset Street W., Ottawa, Ontario K2P 2G3;
(613) 234-1781, fax (613) 563-9621, agrodev.ott@stantech.com, www.stantech.com

MID-SIZED AGRICULTURAL CONSULTING FIRM: Agriculture, Business Development, Community Development, Consulting, Development Assistance, Economics, Environment, Fisheries, Forestry, Gender and Development, Project Management, Technical Assistance, Water Resources

A natural resource management and rural development firm, Agrodev Canada provides professional consulting services in the areas of agriculture, aquaculture, fisheries, environmental planning and protection, women in development, and human resource development. It provides overall project management using a multidisciplinary approach.

Agrodev has offices in Ottawa (operational head office), Edmonton (corporate head office), Vancouver, Islamabad and Amman. The firm has 25 staff with international responsibilities who work abroad or in Canada.

Agrodev Canada requires candidates who have the following qualifications: master's degree or PhD in a related field, a minimum of ten years professional experience in a related field, and overseas experience on international development projects, preferably working with international development agencies or banks. The firm maintains a data bank for résumés.

Information on Agrodev Canada appears on the Stanley Technology Group web site, which offers a section on career opportunities. [ID:5656]

Alcan Aluminium Limited
1188 Sherbrooke Street W., Montréal, Québec H3A 3G2;
(514) 848-8000, fax (514) 848-8115, jean-claude_savoie@alcan.ca

LARGE METALS FIRM: Business Development, Computer Systems, Energy Resources, Engineering, Environment, Exchange Programs, Human Rights, International Trade, Media/Communications, Medical Health, Project Management, Telecommunications

Alcan Aluminium Limited is the parent company of a multinational industrial group engaged in all aspects of the aluminium business. With sales in over 30 countries, Alcan is one of the most internationally recognized metals firms in the world. Through subsidiaries and related companies around the world, the activities of the Alcan Group include bauxite mining, alumina refining, smelting, manufacturing, power generation, sales, and recycling. Over 35,000 people are employed directly by the company, predominantly in Canada, but also in the US, Latin America, Europe, and the Asia Pacific region. [ID:5658]

Alpine Environmental Ltd.

Suite 101, 3740E-11A Street N.E., Calgary, Alberta T2E 6M6;
(403) 291-1081, fax (403) 291-1190, msmith@alpine-env.com, www.alpine-env.com

SMALL ENVIRONMENTAL FIRM: Consulting, Environment, Project Management, Teaching

Alpine Environmental Ltd. is a well-established environmental company dedicated to providing services in water, soil, and waste management. The company has completed projects for major corporations, utility companies, municipalities, financial institutions, and private investors. It has begun to pursue international joint ventures in Southeast Asia and is committed to establishing a long-term business presence in the international market.

Alpine employs 50 full-time and 50 part-time staff in the fields of geology, engineering, chemistry and geochemistry, biology, toxicology, agrology, and geomorphology. Many of their staff are fluent in foreign languages.

The company maintains a web site with a number of useful links and interesting information on the firm's services. [ID:5660]

AmCan Minerals Ltd.

Suite 250, 36 Toronto Street, Toronto, Ontario M5C 2C5;
(416) 214-6296, fax (416) 214-6299, kimberlite@amcan.com, www.amcan.com

MID-SIZED MINING FIRM: Mining

AmCan Minerals Ltd. is a Canadian mining company listed on the Vancouver Stock Exchange. It focuses exclusively on diamond and gold properties in Sierra Leone, West Africa. Currently, the company is preparing for diamond production from several locations. [ID:6997]

Americas Trading Corporation (ATC)

1201 Esso Tower, Scotia Place, 10060 Jasper Ave.,
Edmonton, Alberta T5J 3R8; (403) 414-1335, fax (403) 414-1336

MID-SIZED GENERAL CONSULTING FIRM: Business Development, Consulting, International Trade, Logistics

Americas Trading Corporation (ATC) is a mid-sized firm specializing in assisting Canadian and Mexican firms expand their operations into one another's markets. ATC identifies potential partners, suppliers, customers, and other relationships; it then assists with market assessment, procurement negotiations, financial issues, and ongoing monitoring of subsequent operations performance.

Industries in which ATC has experience include construction, real estate development, educational services, telecommunications, mining, plastics, and the establishment of manufacturing facilities. Some activities have been undertaken in other Latin American jurisdictions as well. [ID:5663]

Analytical Service Laboratories Ltd. (ASL)

1988 Triumph Street, Vancouver, B.C. V5L 1K5;
(604) 253-4188, fax (604) 253-6700, info@asl-labs.bc.ca, www.asl-labs.bc.ca

MID-SIZED ENVIRONMENTAL FIRM: Business Development, Consulting, Environment, Project Management, Technical Assistance

Analytical Service Laboratories Ltd. (ASL) is a full-service environmental testing, research, and consulting laboratory. Internationally, the firm offers a broad range of services including laboratory design and management, regulation reviews, equipment acquisition, training, data management, and protocol development.

ASL has 95 salaried staff in Canada with international projects being organized from their Vancouver headquarters. ASL also operates environmental laboratories in Indonesia and Chile. Future international activities are expected in South America, Southeast Asia, Vietnam, and China.

Prospective applicants should have environmental laboratory experience, coupled with an understanding of the language and culture of the above-mentioned countries. ASL maintains a data bank for résumés and offers summer internships for degreed chemists. [ID:5664]

Apotex Inc.
150 Signet Drive, Weston, Ontario M9L 1T9; (416) 749-9300, fax (416) 749-2646

LARGE PHARMACEUTICAL FIRM: Medical Health

Apotex Inc. is the largest Canadian-owned diversified pharmaceutical company, with exports and international offices in a variety of regions including Africa, the Middle East, Eastern Europe, Asia, and the South Pacific.

The Apotex group of companies currently has 2,300 employees in Canada, 25 of whom are in the export department, and approximately 1,000 employees overseas engaged in the research, production, and marketing of pharmaceutical products. [ID:5666]

The ARA Consulting Group Inc.
Suite 405, 121 Bloor Street E.,
Toronto, Ontario M4W 3M5; (416) 969-6568, fax (416) 922-5380, sigsworth@aragroup.ca

LARGE HUMAN RESOURCES FIRM: Business/Banking/Trade, Consulting, Development Education, Economics, Environment, Human Resources, Human Rights, International Trade, Medical Health, Project Management, Tourism

The ARA Consulting Group Inc. is a management consulting firm active internationally in implementing long-term technical assistance. ARA's practice covers sectors of public administration and finance, tertiary education and adult training, health, social services, and enterprise development. Services include the strengthening and/or reform of capacity in: policy formulation, strategic and operational planning, organizational design, management systems, human resource development and management training institutions, program and curriculum design and delivery, training, coordination of fellowship programs, personnel planning, workforce adjustment, job grading and compensation, personnel systems, financial institutions' restructuring, financial management, and divestiture.

The firm operates in Canada, anglophone Africa, South and Southeast Asia, and the Caribbean. ARA has up to 15 Canadians working abroad. Twelve partners in Canada lead the international practice.

The firm recruits candidates with postgraduate degrees and a minimum of 10 years of related experience, preferably some in the geographic region where they will be placed. ARA maintains a data bank for résumés. [ID:5668]

Arborescence Communications Inc.
Suite 201, 204, du St-Sacrement, Montréal, Québec H2Y 1W8;
(514) 845-3736, fax (514) 499-3629, info@arborescence.com, www.arborescence.com

SMALL COMMUNICATIONS FIRM: Accounting, Administration, Adult Training, Business Development, Community Development, Computer Systems, Consulting, Development Assistance, Development Education, Media/Communications, Medical Health, Project Management, Technical Assistance, Telecommunications

Arborescence Communications Inc. is a mid-sized multisectoral communications firm specializing in program communications for health and nutrition, and the promotion and operation of wireless telecommunications infrastructures in developing countries. The firm also specializes in the social applications of new information technologies.

The Arborescence web site is under construction at the time of printing. [ID:5669]

Ariel Resources
Suite 1135, 1188 West Georgia Street,
Vancouver, B.C. V6E 4A2; (604) 682-2201, fax (604) 682-0318, ariel@istar.ca, www.ariel-au.com

LARGE MINING FIRM: Engineering, Exploration and Development, Mining, Project Management

Ariel Resources is a large gold and metals mining firm. The company is the largest gold producer in Costa Rica, where it operates three underground gold mines and has recently begun mining its first open-pit reserve site.

Candidates should have education and expertise in mining, milling, and environmental preservation. New overseas positions are open to mining engineers and geologists. [ID:6966]

Associated Engineering International Ltd. (AEIL)
International Division, Suite 1400, 910 - 7th Ave. S.W.,
Calgary, Alberta T2P 3N8; (403) 262-4500, fax (403) 269-7640

LARGE WATER RESOURCES FIRM: Consulting, Engineering, Water Resources

Associated Engineering International Ltd. (AEIL) provides consulting engineering services for water and sanitation in developing countries. The company deals primarily with urban and rural potable water supply and is also involved in integrated rural development projects. The majority of projects have been undertaken in East and West Africa and Southeast Asia. Small staff teams in international operations are supported by personnel in offices across Canada.

Candidates should have at least 10 to 15 years relevant experience with appropriate technical qualifications. Most openings are in the water sector. AEIL maintains a data bank for résumés. [ID:5672]

Baker & McKenzie
P.O. Box 874, BCE Place, Suite 2100, 181 Bay Street,
Toronto, Ontario M5J 2T3; (416) 863-1221, fax (416) 863-6275, www.bakerinfo.com

LARGE LAW FIRM: Advocacy

Baker & McKenzie is the world's pre-eminent international law firm. Established in 1949, the firm provides a full range of business-oriented legal services and employs more than 2,000 lawyers in over 50 offices in 33 countries which comprise an unequalled multinational network that offers clients something no other law firm can match: resources and expertise in every area of business law in virtually every important financial and commercial centre in the world.

The Toronto office of Baker & McKenzie is uniquely positioned as a gateway to the dynamic markets of Europe, Asia Pacific, and the Americas. The firm's lawyers provide legal solutions to Canadian corporations with business interests overseas, as well as to domestic and foreign companies with Canadian operations and projects. Clients include established major multinational corporations, small and medium-sized companies, and individuals.

Prospective applicants should have a relevant professional designation, along with experience and/or expertise in their jurisdiction of interest.

The firm maintains an excellent web site that contains information on international operations, publications and career opportunities. [ID:5674]

Ballard Power Systems Inc.
9000 Glenlyon Parkway, Burnaby, B.C. V5J 5J9;
(604) 454-0900, fax (604) 412-4700, careers@ballard.com, www.ballard.com

SMALL ENGINEERING FIRM: Accounting, Administration, Business Development, Computer Systems, Engineering, Human Rights, Project Management, Technical Assistance

Ballard Power Systems Inc. is a world leader in the development of proton exchange membrane fuel cell power systems. At the heart of its products is the Ballard Fuel Cell, which converts hydrogen and oxygen into electricity without producing any harmful emissions. Ballard is working with leading international companies including Daimler-Benz, General Motors, Ford, Chrysler, Nissan, Hitachi, Honda, Volkswagen, Volvo, and GPU International to develop zero-emission engines for vehicles and clean stationary power plants. Ballard Power Systems Inc. has a location in Poway, California, USA.

The Ballard web site has a strong careers section. It lists the major responsibilities and requirements for open positions and provides instructions on how to apply. International experience is not typically required. [ID:7018]

Bank of Montréal
105 Saint-Jacques Street, 3rd fl., Montréal, Québec; (514) 877-1101, fax (514) 877-1805, www.bmo.com

LARGE FINANCIAL SERVICES FIRM: Business/Banking/Trade, Computer Systems, Economics

Bank of Montréal, Canada's first bank, is a highly diversified financial services institution that ranks as one of the 10 largest banks in North America with assets of $203 billion. The bank's group of companies include Nesbitt Burns, one of Canada's largest full service investment firms; the Chicago-based Harris Bank, a major US mid-western financial institution; and mbanx, the first North American virtual banking unit. Bank of Montréal has an equity position in and an alliance with Grupo Financiero Bancomer, the leading Mexican financial institution.

The bank is also represented in other global locations such as Brazil, the UK, Ireland, Australia, Japan, Korea, Hong Kong, Taiwan, Singapore, and China where it operates two full-service commercial branches. [ID:7097]

The Bank of Nova Scotia
Scotia Plaza, 44 King Street W., Toronto, Ontario M5H 1H1;
(416) 866-6161, fax (416) 866-3750, email@Scotiabank.ca, www.scotiabank.ca

LARGE FINANCIAL SERVICES FIRM: Accounting, Administration, Business/Banking/Trade

The Bank of Nova Scotia is a major Canadian chartered bank with over 34,000 employees in more than 50 countries on five continents.

The Bank of Nova Scotia's International Banking division provides worldwide retail, commercial, and trade finance services and continues to expand its global coverage, building on the potential of markets in the Caribbean, Asia, Europe, the Middle East, and Latin America. It has recently opened new branches and made new acquisitions in the Caribbean, Greece, Costa Rica, Thailand, Vietnam, and elsewhere in Latin America and Asia.

The bank maintains a web site that provides detailed descriptions and contact information on their international activities. [ID:6981]

Barrick Gold Corp.
Royal Bank Plaza, South Tower, Suite 2700, 200 Bay Street, PO Box 119,
Toronto, Ontario M5J 2J3; (800) 720-7415, fax (416) 861-2492, www.barrick.com

LARGE MINING FIRM: Exploration and Development, Metals, Mining

Barrick Gold Corp. is a large international gold company with mine operations and exploration teams in Chile, Peru, Argentina and Indonesia as well as the US and Canada. In addition to its mining and exploration staff, the company employs full-time staff in each country of operation and at each operating site to oversee and implement its environmental and occupational health and safety policies and programs. [ID:5661]

BDO Dunwoody
Royal Bank Plaza, South Tower, 200 Bay Street, P.O. Box 32,
Toronto, Ontario M5J 2J8; (416) 865-0111, fax (416) 367-3912, info@national.bdo.ca, www.bdo.ca

LARGE FINANCIAL SERVICES FIRM: Accounting, Computer Systems, Consulting, Human Resources, Project Management

BDO Dunwoody, Chartered Accountants and Consultants is a Canadian partnership specializing in accounting, auditing, taxation, financing, personal financial planning, and business consulting. The firm has a staff of approximately 1,500 in over 70 offices throughout Canada. Internationally, BDO Binder serves over 80 countries, with a staff in excess of 15,000.

Prospective applicants should have an accounting designation and related work experience. BDO maintains a data bank for résumés and an interesting web site that provides direct access to information on the firm's international offices and activities. [ID:5678]

Bell Canada International Inc. (BCI)
1000, de la Gauchetiere ouest, Montréal, Québec H3B 4Y8;
(514) 392-2444, fax (514) 392-2292, jsenecal@bci.ca, www.bci.ca

LARGE TELECOMMUNICATIONS FIRM: Accounting, Business Development, Construction, Engineering, Human Resources, Logistics, Project Management, Telecommunications

Bell Canada International (BCI), a wholly-owned subsidiary of Bell Canada Enterprises Inc. (BCE), Canada's largest telecommunications group, is the primary vehicle of BCE for investment in network operations outside Canada. Interests extend to broadband cablephone and mobile wireless companies located in the UK, US, Brazil, China, India, Taiwan, and Japan. Approximately 50 personnel work in the Montréal head office. Assignments overseas are in a variety of management capacities.

Applicants should have expertise in the following areas; languages (Spanish, Portuguese and Mandarin), telecommunications, software and hardware design, network engineering, and microwave engineering. Applications for positions in marketing and customer relations are also considered. BCI maintains a data bank for résumés. [ID:5679]

Bema Gold Corp.
Three Bentall Centre, Suite 3113, 595 Burrard Street, P.O. Box 49113,
Vancouver, B.C. V7X 1G4; (800) 316-8855, fax (604) 681-6209, info@bema.com, www.bema.com

LARGE MINING FIRM: Exploration and Development, Gold and Metals Production, Mining

Bema Gold Corp. is an intermediate mining company involved in the exploration, development, and production of gold. The company, together with its joint venture partner, Amax Gold, has a gold production facility at its Refugio mine in Chile. In collaboration with other mining companies, Bema conducts exploration and development activities in Chile, Argentina, and Venezuela. The bulk of Bema's overseas employees are locally hired. Canadian applicants should have a background in geology or mine-related engineering. [ID:6998]

Bennett Environmental Inc.
2nd Floor, 1130 West Pender Street, Vancouver, B.C. V6E 4A4;
(604) 681-8828, fax (604) 681-6825, info@bennettenvironmental.com, www.bennettenvironmental.com

SMALL ENVIRONMENTAL CONSULTING FIRM: Energy Resources, Engineering, Environment

Bennett Environmental Inc. has been in the environmental business for over 25 years. The firm's recent focus has been the development and marketing of thermal oxidizer technology for remediating soils heavily contaminated with hydrocarbons, and for incinerating wastes. The firm also specializes in sales and joint ventures related to incinerators and waste processing.

In the past, exporting efforts were focused on the US. More recently, Bennett's focus has shifted towards Asia and Eastern Europe. Incineration projects are currently being negotiated in Taiwan, South Korea, and Slovakia. The company currently has six salaried staff with international responsibilities. Prospective applicants should have an engineering degree and experience in Computer Aided Design (CAD). Knowledge of incineration would be an asset. [ID:5680]

BFC Civil

3660 Midland Ave., Scarborough, Ontario M1V 4V3;
(416) 754-8691, fax (416) 754-8692, corp@bfc.ca, www.bfc.ca

LARGE CONSTRUCTION FIRM: Construction, Engineering, Project Management

Established in 1948, BFC Civil is the largest publicly-held, most diversified construction company in Canada. Through its subsidiaries and affiliated companies, the firm provides quality services in civil, pipeline, building, utilities, nuclear, and industrial construction, as well as engineering, procurement, and construction management expertise to the petroleum and petrochemicals industries.

BFC Civil and its subsidiaries have worked in over 30 countries over the past three decades. Current overseas construction projects include hydroelectric developments in India and Colombia and airports in Hungary.

The firm currently has 350 salaried staff in Canada and an additional 90 posted overseas. Prospective applicants should have an education in engineering or cost accounting, on-site construction experience, and fluency in a language other than English or French (Spanish preferred). BFC Civil maintains a data bank for résumés and the firm also maintains a web site that provides information on the firm and its activities. Job openings are posted at this site. [ID:5675]

Biomira Inc.

Human Resources, 2011 - 94th Street, Edmonton Research Park,
Edmonton, Alberta T6N 1H1; (403) 450-3761, fax (403) 463-0871, www.biomira.com

LARGE BIOTECHNOLOGY FIRM: Accounting, Administration, Business Development,
Computer Systems, Engineering, Human Resources, International Trade,
Media/Communications, Medical Health, Project Management

Biomira Inc. is a fully-integrated biotechnology company whose operations centre around the development of diagnostic and therapeutic products for applications in the field of cancer treatment. Clinical trials of several products are ongoing in the US, the UK, Germany, and Canada. Current business development activities focus on securing licensing and partnership agreements in the US, Western Europe, and Asia.

Prospective applicants should have a solid educational background in pharmacology, immunology, toxicology, chemistry, biochemistry, microbiology, or in a related discipline. Previous professional international experience is an asset. Biomira maintains a data bank for résumés. The firm considers applications for internships throughout the year, with the majority of positions opening in the summer.

Biomira maintains a web site that contains general information on the firm, copies of its annual reports, and some job-related information. [ID:5681]

Biothermica International Inc.

3333, boul. Cavendish, Bureau 440, Montréal, Québec H4B 2M5;
(514) 488-3881, fax (514) 488-3125, biotherm@total.net, www.biothermica.com

LARGE ENVIRONMENTAL CONSULTING FIRM: Consulting, Energy Resources, Engineering,
Environment, Technical Assistance

Biothermica International Inc. is a technology company specializing in the environment and engineering. It uses thermal processes to solve environmental problems. Its team of 18 engineers, scientists, and technicians search for and develop practical solutions to the problems associated with air pollution and the production of energy from waste and landfill gas. Biothermica's services focus on four areas: thermal oxidation of air pollutants in process fumes, particle control from high-temperature gases, energy-oriented biomass valorization, and solid waste and landfill gas management and valorization. Biomass energy conversion is one of its main research activities.

Outside Canada, the firm has done projects in France, Tunisia, Morocco, Chile, and French Guyanna. Seasonal internship positions are offered to students in Québec. [ID:7218]

Boileau & Associates Inc.
Suite 201, 420, boul. Maloney est,
Gatineau, Québec J8P 1E7; (819) 663-9294, fax (819) 663-0084, www.stantech.com

SMALL ENGINEERING CONSULTING FIRM: Development Assistance, Engineering, Project Management

Boileau & Associates Inc. is an engineering consulting firm engaged in international development. It currently supervises a roads construction contract in Trinidad and Tobago and was recently involved in a large water distribution rehabilitation and expansion project in Nicaragua. The firm has also had projects in Mali, Malawi, Columbia, Jamaica, Haiti, Rwanda, Morocco, Sudan, Madagascar, Bangladesh and the Czech Republic.

Boileau & Associates Inc. has three engineers working overseas and nine in Canada with international responsibilities. The firm is comprised mainly of engineers with strong technical and project management experience. Personnel currently conduct international business in English, French, Spanish, and Czech. Boileau and Associates Inc. maintains a data bank for résumés.

Basic information about the firm's activities is available at the Stantech web site. Career opportunities are also posted at this site, as is information on related companies. [ID:5682]

Bombardier Inc.
800 René Lévesque Blvd. W.,
Montréal, Québec H3B 1Y8; (514) 861-9481, fax (514) 861-7053, www.bombardier.com

LARGE TRANSPORTATION MANUFACTURING FIRM: Administration, Aerospace Technology, Business Development, Engineering, Human Resources, Project Management

Bombardier Inc. is a Canadian corporation engaged in design, development, manufacturing, and marketing activities in the field of transportation equipment, aerospace, motorized consumer products, financial services, and services related to its products and core competencies.

The Montréal-based corporation operates plants in Canada, the US, Mexico, Austria, Belgium, Finland, France, Germany, and the UK, employing 41,000 people. Bombardier's revenues for its last fiscal year totalled $8 billion; more than 85 per cent of its revenue is generated in markets outside Canada.

Bombardier maintains a web site that provides basic information on its products and services. [ID:5683]

Bovar Inc.
P.O. Box 6620, Stn. D, Calgary, Alberta T2P 3R3;
(403) 235-8300, fax (403) 248-3306, bovarinc@bovar.com, www.bovar.com

LARGE ENVIRONMENTAL FIRM: Business Development

BOVAR Inc. is one of Canada's leading environmental and waste management companies. A fully integrated firm, BOVAR provides consulting and technical services, manufactures gas monitoring instrumentation and control equipment, and is an owner/operator of waste management facilities.

In 1996, BOVAR purchased Spectrum Diagnostix Inc. and its tunable diode laser technology-based process and environmental monitoring instrumentation. The company was merged with BOVAR Western Research. BOVAR also purchased the Government of Alberta's 40 per cent interest in the Alberta Special Waste Management System. BOVAR now owns 100 per cent of the system and operates the Swan Hills Treatment Centre.

The firm has worldwide contracts and extensive international operations, with overseas offices in the US, Germany, China, and Malaysia.

Bovar maintains a beautiful web site that contains information on its activities as well as recent news and a number of environmentally-oriented links. [ID:5684]

Breakwater Resources Ltd.
Suite 2000, 95 Wellington Street W., Toronto, Ontario M5J 2N7;
(416) 363-4798, fax (416) 363-1315, investorinfo@breakwater.ca, www.breakwater.ca

LARGE MINING FIRM: Accounting, Administration, Engineering, Exploration and Development, Metals, Mining

Breakwater Resources Ltd. is engaged in the acquisition, exporation, development, and mining of both base and precious metal properties in North, Central, and South America, and North Africa. In addition to its Canadian mines in New Brunswick and Baffin Island, the company owns and operates El Mochito Mine, an underground zinc/lead/silver mine in Honduras; El Toqui Mine, a zinc/gold mine in Chile; and the Bougrine mine, a zinc/lead mine in Tunisia expected to begin production in early 1998. The company has a marketing office in Bridgetown, Barbados.

Although this expanding firm has a large number of overseas employees (three-quarters of its approximately 2000 staff), the majority are locally hired. Candidates for overseas positions should be seasoned professionals, generally mining or metallurgical engineers and geologists. The company maintains a data bank for résumés. [ID:6972]

Breton, Banville & Associates (BBA)
Suite 200, 325, boul. Raymond-Dupuis, Mont-Sainte-Hilaire,
Québec J3H 5H6; (514) 464-2118, fax (514) 464-0901, bba@bbasenc.com, www.bbasenc.com

MID-SIZED ENGINEERING FIRM: Consulting, Engineering, Technical Assistance

Breton, Banville & Associates (BBA) provides electrical engineering services in power systems, electro-technology, control and automation, and instrumentation. Their services include project planning, preliminary and basic engineering, detail engineering, inspection and expediting, construction supervision, training, commissioning and testing, and project management.

BBA has worked on electrical energy projects in Cameroon, Colombia, Ivory Coast, Ghana, Guinea, Jamaica, Haiti, Mali, Peru, Senegal, and Tunisia. The company has 80 employees (40 engineers). Many employees have extensive international experience.

The firm is looking for engineers and senior technicians who specialize in electrical power systems. Breton, Banville and Associates maintains a data bank for résumés. [ID:5685]

Bridgehead Inc.
Unit 99, 880 Wellington Street, Ottawa, Ontario K1R 6K7;
(613) 567-1455, fax (613) 567-1468, bridgehd@oxfam.ca, www.web.net/oxfamgft

MID-SIZED IMPORT/EXPORT FIRM: Accounting, Administration, Advocacy, Business Development, Community Development, Gender and Development, Human Resources, Human Rights, International Trade, Micro-Enterprises, Project Management, Technical Assistance

Bridgehead Inc. provides marginalized communities of artisans and farmers around the world with a multifaceted marketing system for their crafts and food produce. This enables its producer partners to earn a fair return for their work, thus helping to improve their economic and social conditions.

Bridgehead also works to advance public awareness of ethical business practice as a powerful development tool by linking producers directly with consumers. Finally, Bridgehead supports the activities of its sister organization, Oxfam, both promotionally and programmatically.

Candidates should have a background in business (direct mail, wholesale, retail), some development experience and a commitment to social and economic justice.

Bridgehead maintains a beautifully-designed web site that provides information on stores and services. [ID:5686]

Britannia Gold Corp.
Suite 1440, 1066 West Hastings St.,
Vancouver, BC V6E 3X1; (604) 687-6690, fax (604) 688-0426, www.britannia-gold.com

LARGE MINING FIRM: Engineering, Exploration and Development, Metals, Project Management

Britannia Gold Corp. is a mineral exploration and mine development company with branch offices in Lima, Peru, and La Paz, Mexico. The company's most active gold exploration projects are in Peru, where it has eight properties. In addition, Britannia Gold Corp. has six exploration sites in Mexico. [ID:6986]

British Columbia Hydro International Limited (BCHIL)
6911 South Point Drive, Burnaby, B.C. V3N 4X8;
(604) 528-1600, fax (604) 528-3007, bchil@bchydro.bc.ca, http://ewu.bchydro.bc.ca

LARGE ENERGY RESOURCES FIRM: Administration, Business Development, Computer Systems, Consulting, Energy Resources, Engineering, Project Management, Technical Assistance, Water Resources

British Columbia Hydro International Limited (BCHIL) is a wholly-owned subsidiary of B.C. Hydro, and is engaged in a full range of utility operations and institutional development consulting work worldwide. BCHIL has undertaken a wide variety of international consulting projects in conjunction with private sector Canadian consultants. The company has been active for a number of years providing engineering and electrical utility consulting services and sophisticated electronic and fibre optic monitoring equipment for clients in many countries.

Through BCHIL, the technical expertise of B.C. Hydro's engineers, technicians and support staff (a total of 5,000) in all facets of electric system engineering and operation is available to international clients.

BCHIL has worked on electrical energy projects in Brazil, Venezuela, Canada, China, India, Egypt, and Jordan.

The firm generally hires from within B.C. Hydro and established consultant staff. BCHIL maintains a web site that provides basic information about their products, services, and organization. [ID:5905]

Cambior Inc.
Bureau 850, 800, boul. René-Lévesque,
Montréal, Québec H3B 1X9; (514) 878-3166, fax (514) 878-3324, info@cambior.com, www.cambior.com

LARGE MINING FIRM: Exploration and Development, Gold and Metals Production, Mining, Project Management

Cambior Inc. is a major, diversified gold producer with operations, development projects, and exploration activities in Guyana, French Guyana, Suriname, Peru, Argentina, and North America. It has also been active in Mexico and Chili. The company's existing projects are aimed at increasing gold reserves while maintaining a moderate diversification in base metals, primarily copper and zinc.

Cambior Inc.'s development efforts are centered on four specific regions: Northwestern Québec, the Western US, Mexico, the Guyana Shield, and the Andes. [ID:6999]

Cameco Corp.
Human Resources Dept., 2121-11th Street W.,
Saskatoon, Sask. S7M 1J3; (306) 956-6200, fax (306) 956-6201, www.cameco.com

LARGE MINING FIRM: Accounting, Administration, Business/Banking/Trade, Business Development, Community Development, Computer Systems, Energy Resources, Engineering, Environment, Exploration and Development, Human Resources, Media/Communications, Mining

Cameco, with its head office in Saskatoon, is the world's largest publicly traded uranium company and a growing gold producer. Its uranium products are used to generate electricity in nuclear power plants around the world. Cameco obtains uranium from operations in Wyoming and Nebraska. It has gold mining operations in Saskatchewan and Kyrgyzstan and exploration sites in North and South America, Australia, and Central Asia. Cameco hires a wide range of staff beyond mining specialists. [ID:7001]

Canac International Inc.
Suite 500, 1100 University St., Montréal, Québec H3B 3A5;
(800) 588-4387, fax (514) 399-8298, pubmail@mail.canac.com, www.canac.com

LARGE TRANSPORTATION CONSULTING FIRM: Consulting, Engineering, Logistics, Transportation

Canac International Inc. is a major consulting engineering firm involved in the following areas: large project development, joint venturing, turnkey projects, operation and construction management, planning and implementation, design and engineering, personnel training, materials procurement and inspection, and the provision of new and used railway supplies. The firm specializes in railroad productivity improvement, privatization initiatives, intermodal systems, advanced technology applications, and all related aspects of railway operations.

The number of staff working abroad fluctuates according the number and importance of contracts. To date, the company's 300 railway specialists have completed 800 projects in 60 countries. Recruiters look for candidates with degrees or equivalent expertise in transportation, engineering, management, information systems, telecommunications, and related disciplines. Applicants with overseas experience are preferred. Canac International Inc. maintains a data bank for résumés. [ID:5688]

Canada Trust
Human Resources, 3rd Floor, 161 Bay Street,
Toronto, Ontario M5J 2T2; (416) 361-8000, fax (416) 361-4633, www.canadatrust.com

LARGE FINANCIAL SERVICES FIRM: Accounting, Administration, Business/Banking/Trade, Business Development, Computer Systems, Customer Services, International Trade

A major Canadian financial institution, Canada Trust provides financial, trust, mutual fund, investment managment, and advisory services. The Canada Trust family of companies includes the Canada Trust Company, CT Investment Management Group Inc., CT Securities International Inc., and many others. It is exploring the possibility of establishing a US franchise based on a "virtual bank." It is heavily involved in global stock markets, notably in the US, UK, Japan, France, Germany, and Hong Kong.

Only a very small proportion of positions involve overseas work; most international-oriented positions are concentrated in Toronto and London, Ontario. Overseas positions are, as a rule, filled within the organization and are positions in the strategic business or support units. Positions typically require a background in fields such as investment management, information technology, marketing, finance, or law.

The Canada Trust web site features a comprehensive employment section explaining how to apply (including online) and what careers and current opportunities are available. It offers co-op and summer student programs. Applicants are encouraged to contact the human resources department at their nearest Canada Trust office or branch. [ID:6679]

Canadian Fishery Consultants Limited (CFCL)

1312 Queen Street, Halifax, N.S. B3J 2H5;
(902) 422-4698, fax (902) 422-8147, canfish@fox.nstn.ca, http://fox.nstn.ca/~canfish

MID-SIZED GENERAL CONSULTING FIRM: Business Development, Computer Systems, Construction, Consulting, Development Assistance, Economics, Engineering, Environment, Fisheries, Gender and Development, International Trade, Project Management, Technical Assistance

Canadian Fishery Consultants Limited (CFCL) is an international consulting firm specializing in fisheries development, aquaculture development, and ports operation. Its staff have worked in over 70 countries worldwide, mostly in Asia, Africa, and the Caribbean.

CFCL has eight staff members working out of Halifax. Recruitment of additional professionals is on a project-by-project basis for short-term assignments.

CFCL recruits specialists in all aspects of the fishing and aquaculture industries. Specialists in the warm water species have been needed in the past. Expertise in fishing, fishing gear, fishing vessel design and construction, economics, biology, engineering, maintenance, environmental assessment, and marketing are occasionally needed. Internships are considered during any season for individuals interested in fisheries and aquaculture. CFCL maintains a data bank for résumés. [ID:5691]

Canadian Fracmaster Ltd.

Suite 1700, 355 - 4th Avenue S.W., Calgary, Alberta T2P 0J1;
(403) 262-2222, fax (403) 265-4967, corp@fracmaster.com, www.fracmaster.com

LARGE PETROLEUM INDUSTRY FIRM: Accounting, Administration, Business/Banking/Trade, Business Development, Computer Systems, Engineering, Environment, Human Rights, International Trade, Logistics, Technical Assistance

Canadian Fracmaster Ltd. is an international oil and gas well service and oil production company which specializes in pumping services. It is one of Canada's largest suppliers of cementing, acidizing, fracturing, and coiled tubing products, services and technologies, including industrial and pipeline services. Fracmaster researches, develops and fabricates products, services, and specialized equipment for use in the worldwide petroleum industry.

Through alliances with three of Russia's largest oil companies, Fracmaster participates in four operating joint enterprises in Russia. The company is endeavouring to expand and diversify its operations in Russia and to expand its international markets to include the Middle East, Southeast Asia, China, and Latin America.

Applicants should typically be experienced field hands, engineers, or geologists with experience in the petroleum industry. [ID:7029]

Canadian Imperial Bank of Commerce (CIBC)

Human Resources Division, Commerce Court Postal Station,
Toronto, Ontario M5L 1A2; (416) 980-2211, fax (416) 784-6799, www.cibc.com

LARGE FINANCIAL SERVICES FIRM: Business/Banking/Trade

Canadian Imperial Bank of Commerce (CIBC), one of the largest banks in North America, is a highly diversified, full-service financial institution operating on a global basis. Operations around the world are carried out through two strategic business units. CIBC's Personal and Commercial Bank provides a full range of products and services to over six million individual customers, 300,000 small businesses, and 10,000 commercial customers across Canada, the West Indies, and private banking centres around the world. CIBC Wood Gundy, CIBC's corporate and investment banking business creates innovative credit and capital market solutions for its clients through offices in 21 countries. CIBC employs 41,000 people worldwide.

Recruiters consider candidates from a wide variety of backgrounds depending on the position sought. The bank maintains a data bank for résumés.

CIBC also maintains a web site that offers a number of online banking services and provides information on the bank's global activities. [ID:5692]

Canadian International Project Managers Ltd. (CIPM)
1100, boul. René Lévesque ouest,
Montréal, Québec H3B 4P3; (514) 876-1150, fax (514) 876-9273, www.snc-lavalin.com

LARGE ENGINEERING FIRM: Engineering, Power Generation, Transmission and Distribution, Water Resources

Canadian International Project Managers (CIPM) is a permanent joint venture company, legally registered in Canada and founded in 1972 by three leading Canadian engineering project management firms. CIPM has international experience and expertise in water resources and hydroelectric developments. As a result of mergers and acquisitions of its original owner, CIPM is now a joint venture with equal participation of SNC-Lavalin Inc. and Acres International Limited. CIPM has a permanent joint venture with BC Hydro International Ltd. and Hydro-Québec to work on water resources and hydroelectric projects in China.

CIPM joint ventures provide professional services in hydroelectric and water resource development and associated substation and transmission lines. Services include studies and investigations, design and specifications, project management, procurement and quality assurance, testing and commissioning, operation and maintenance, and transfer of know-how. Several overseas contracts have been completed in the People's Republic of China.

Applicants should possess skills to suit the various assignments in each sector and are generally required to have at least 15 years of work experience in water resources and hydroelectric projects in Canada and overseas. CIPM's staff are seconded from its partner companies as required. [ID:5693]

Canadian International Water and Energy Consultants (CIWEC)
Projects Administrator, P.O. Box 1001, Niagara Falls,
Ontario L2E 6W1; (905) 374-5200 ext. 5312, fax (905) 374-1157, nf@acres.com, www.acres.com

LARGE WATER RESOURCES FIRM: Accounting, Administration, Computer Systems, Consulting, Development Assistance, Development Education, Economics, Energy Resources, Engineering, Environment, Fisheries, Forestry, Gender and Development, Human Resources, Project Management, Technical Assistance, Water Resources

Canadian International Water and Energy Consultants (CIWEC) is a joint venture of Acres International Limited and SNC-Shawinigan Inc. CIWEC currently provides consulting services for water and energy resources development projects in Nepal.

CIWEC draws on over 1,000 professional and technical staff from both companies, as required. The firm currently has 19 staff working on long- and short-term assignments in Nepal.

Candidates should have a master's-level university degree in engineering, economics or environmental studies and at least five years experience on engineering or development planning projects in Asia (preferably Nepal). Candidates must also be willing to travel frequently. The firm maintains a data bank for résumés. [ID:5694]

Canadian Marconi Company (CMC)
600 Dr. Frederik Philips Blvd.,
Saint-Laurent, Québec H4M 2S9; (514) 748-3000, fax (514) 748-3184, www.mtl.marconi.ca

LARGE HIGH TECHNOLOGY FIRM: Aerospace Technology, Business Development, Engineering, Human Resources, Project Management, Telecommunications

Canadian Marconi Company (CMC) designs, manufactures, tests and markets sophisticated avionics, communications and radar systems for commercial and military applications. Over 70 per cent of its products are exported for sale in more than 100 countries.

A network of CMC sales and service agents and representatives help support Canadian Marconi Company's activities worldwide. Recruits should have degrees in electronic engineering and experience in international marketing. CMC has established partnerships with various universities in Ontario and Québec that accept student interns.

CMC maintains an excellent web site that contains information on the company and posts job opportunities and descriptions online. [ID:5695]

Canadian Ocean Resource Association (CORA) Inc.

Suite 901, TD Place, 140 Water Street,
St. John's, Nfld. A1C 6H8; (709) 753-1015, fax (709) 753-1016, pdobbin@nfld.com

MID-SIZED ENVIRONMENTAL CONSULTING FIRM: Accounting, Administration, Aerospace Technology, Business/Banking/Trade, Business Development, Development Assistance, Economics, Environment, Fisheries, Gender and Development, Human Resources, Micro-Enterprises, Project Management, Tourism

Canadian Ocean Resources Association (CORA) Inc. is currently operating in 20 countries throughout the South Pacific and Asia. Projects are based upon nearshore and offshore ocean resources and on development in education and the private sector.

The firm employs seven full-time staff in Canada and an additional two overseas. Applicants should have a university degree and experience in private sector development issues. CORA maintains a data bank for résumés. [ID:6472]

Canadian Petroleum International Resources Ltd.

International Human Resources Department, 635 - 8th Ave. S.W.,
Calgary, Alberta T2P 2C9; (403) 234-6700, fax (403) 234-6863, www.cadnoxy.com

LARGE PETROLEUM EXPLORATION FIRM: Energy Resources, Engineering, Oil and Gas Exploration

Canadian Petroleum International Resources Ltd., a wholly-owned subsidiary of their parent, Canadian Occidental Petroleum Ltd., is a global oil and natural gas exploration and production corporation with operations in Canada, the US, Latin America, Yemen, Indonesia, Vietnam, the North Sea, and North Africa.

Those individuals working overseas with Canadian Petroleum International Resources are primarily oil industry professionals with international experience in engineering, geology, geophysics, drilling, and production. The firm has 112 salaried staff overseas. An additional 500 based in Canada work in their international division.

Prospective applicants must have at least a bachelor's degree in science (engineering or geoscience), international experience, and preferably language skills relevant to the countries listed above. The firm maintains a data bank for résumés. [ID:5696]

Canadians Resident Abroad Inc. (CRA)

305 Lakeshore Road E., Oakville, Ontario L6J 1J3;
(905) 842-0080, fax (905) 842-9814, cra@inforamp.net, www.cdnsresabroad.com

SMALL FINANCIAL SERVICES FIRM: Personal Taxation/Financial Planning, Publishing

Canadians Resident Abroad Inc. (CRA) publishes UPDATE, a periodic newsletter covering taxation and financial topics of interest to Canadians living outside Canada and the US.

CRA is sponsored by its affiliate, Canadian Investment Consultants (888) Inc., which offers financial planning services to expatriate Canadians. CRA maintains a web site containing information on the firm's services and activities. [ID:5697]

Canarc Resource Corp.

Suite 800, 850 West Hastings St.,
Vancouver, B.C. V6C 1E1; (604) 685-9700, fax (604) 685-9744, www.mcomm.com/canarc

LARGE MINING FIRM: Exploration and Development, Mining

Canarc Resource Corp. is a Canadian-based international gold exploration and mining company with significant operations in Costa Rica and Suriname. In 1993, it launched an international expansion program focusing on the Guyana Shield area, acquiring properties in Venezuela and Guyana. As of 1997, it also had projects in Mexico, Senegal, and Indonesia.

Canarc's overall focus is likely to remain in developing properties in British Columbia.
[ID:6973]

Canedcom International Ltd.
Suite 230, 55 Nugget Ave., Scarborough,
Ontario M1S 3L1; (416) 292-2080, fax (416) 292-7544, canadcom@worldnet.att.net

MID-SIZED HUMAN RESOURCES FIRM: Business Development, Consulting, Development
Education, Human Resources, Project Management, Teaching, Technical Assistance

Canedcom International is a mid-sized consulting firm specializing in education,
technical assistance, human resource development, and management consulting to clients in
international markets. The organization has been in operation since 1979, and has successfully completed assignments in 32 countries worldwide.

Applicants usually require a master's degree and extensive overseas experience in a
field related to the company's operations. Canedcom maintains a web site that posts job
openings online and provides detailed information about the firm's scope and activities.
[ID:5699]

Canora Asia Inc.
Suite 901, 1155 University Street, Montréal, Québec H3B 3A7; (514) 393-9110, fax (514) 393-1511

LARGE ENVIRONMENTAL CONSULTING FIRM: Engineering, Environment, Waste Water
Management

Canora Asia is an incorporated network of 28 small and medium-sized Canadian firms
which provide environmental engineering and equipment services in Southeast Asia. Canora
undertakes large, vertically-integrated projects in large urban centres and industrial zones.

With over 3,000 employees in its member companies, Canora draws on their diverse
backgrounds in the service, manufacturing, and construction sectors. It helps its members
identify opportunities and reduce the risks and costs of doing business in Asia. It has an
office in Jakarta, Indonesia and is currently involved in several large projects in that country,
including the JIEP Waste Water Treatment Project in Jakarta. [ID:6561]

CFC International Inc. (CFCI)
P.O. Box 1086, Suite 800, 300, Leo-Parizeau, Montréal, Québec
H2W 2P4; (514) 286-8212, fax (514) 286-1500, cfc@groupecfc.qc.ca, www.groupecfc.qc.ca

LARGE HUMAN RESOURCES FIRM: Development Education, Human Resources, Project
Management, Technical Assistance

CFC International Inc. (CFCI) is a consulting firm that provides human resource
management consulting. The firm carries out strategic planning, organization, operation, and
appraisal of international projects, and specializes in project management, staff training,
instructor training, technical training, technological transfer and management development.
CFCI is a subsidiary of Group CFC, a leading Canadian firm in human resource management.

The firm has 100 Canadian-based employees, some of whom have international responsibilities. Recruiters look for senior consultants with technical skills and expertise in
management and human resources. Past international experience is required for international assignments. CFC International Inc. maintains a data bank for résumés. [ID:5701]

Chauvco Resources Ltd.
Suite 2900, 255 - 5th Avenue S.W., Calgary, Alberta T2P 3G6;
(800) 805-4536, fax (403) 269-9497, hr@chauvco.com, www.chauvco.com

LARGE PETROCHEMICALS FIRM: Energy Resources, Oil and Gas Exploration

Chauvco Resources is a large oil and gas exploration and production company with
operations in Canada, Argentina, and Gabon. The company is actively pursuing new
international opportunities for development and exploration in North and West Africa and
the Middle East, with three specific projects in those regions soon to be announced.

In 1996, Chauvco had 181 employees, including 59 field staff. Chauvco Resources Ltd. recently announced the merging of its Canadian and Argentine operations with Dallas-based Pioneer Natural Resources Co. Chauvco Resources International Ltd. will independently run other Chauvco overseas operations.

Candidates should have experience and expertise in an area relevant to the firm's operations and a high level of international exposure, versatility, and understanding of the cultural barriers of overseas location and language. Staff include experienced management professionals as well as technical and support staff in exploration, land, production, drilling, engineering, marketing, finance, information systems, and administration. Chauvco maintains a file for résumés for relevant areas of expertise in specific locations. Its web site includes a regularly-updated career opportunities section. [ID:5702]

Cinram International Inc.
2255 Markham Road, Scarborough,
Ontario M1B 2W3; (416) 298-8190, fax (416) 298-9307, www.cinram.com

LARGE HIGH TECHNOLOGY FIRM: Computer Systems, Engineering, Manufacturing

Cinram is an expanding player in the disk and tape duplication industry with major production and sales activities outside of Canada. One of the world's largest providers of both blank and pre-recorded media to a wide range of clients, it is involved in both video and music duplication. The US operations design and build manufacturing systems for the optical disc industry. The California operations provide a full range of services for DVD authoring and multiplexing for major motion picture clients. European operations duplicate pre-recorded tapes. Cinram owns 50% of a compact discs and video tape manufacturer in Mexico.

In addition to its Canadian operations, Cinram has offices and subsidiaries throughout the US as well as multiple locations in France, Spain, the UK, and one in Mexico servicing all of Latin America. Recent acquisitions, including a unit in the Netherlands, have more than doubled its number of plants to 13 in North America and Europe. [ID:7223]

Cognos Inc.
3755 Riverside Drive, P.O. Box 9707, Stn. T, Ottawa,
Ontario K1G 4K9; (613) 738-1440, fax (613) 738-0002, jobs@cognos.com, www.cognos.com

LARGE HIGH TECHNOLOGY FIRM: Computer Systems, Consulting, Engineering, Technical Assistance

An international corporation, Cognos is the world's leading supplier of business intelligence software. Cognos develops software which enables users to extract vital information from corporate data. Cognos offers comprehensive support plans to its customers, providing technical support around the world, around the clock. Its products are sold through its direct sales force as well as a network of 800 resellers and distributors.

With more than 1300 employees worldwide, Cognos has more than 32 offices in 12 countries: Australia, Belgium, France, Germany, Hong Kong, Italy, Japan, the Netherlands, Singapore, Sweden, the UK, and US. US headquarters are in Burlington, Massachusetts.

Its web site includes a careers section which gives detailed information on job opportunities in the US and Canada as well as instructions for applying in Canada, the US, and UK. Cognos's US division is mainly a sales and marketing organization, thus requiring people with experience in sales, marketing, support, and administration. Current available positions include help desk technicians and training specialists; to apply, e-mail usjobs@cognos.com. The growing UK division typically requires software and marketing specialists as well as account managers and support; to apply, e-mail résumés to sarah.naylor@cognos.com or write to Cognos Ltd., Westerley Point, Market Street, Bracknell, Berkshire, RG12 1QB, or fax 013-44-869022. [ID:6963]

Collavino Inc.
1600 Moro Drive, Windsor, Ontario N9A 6J3; (519) 966-0506, fax (519) 966-8872

LARGE CONSTRUCTION FIRM: Accounting, Construction, Engineering, Logistics

Collavino Inc. is a general construction firm that has completed buildings and heavy civil projects throughout the world. Some projects include electrical transmission lines in Kenya, a water supply project in Cameroon, a Jeep plant for AMC in Egypt, a sewage project in United Arab Emirates, an irrigation system in the Republic of Yemen, a high school in Nigeria, and several related projects in Sri Lanka.

Collavino Inc. has 25 salaried staff overseas and six staff in Canada. The firm is interested in candidates who are engineers, project managers, accountants, or foremen (steel, carpentry, mechanics). [ID:5707]

Cominco Ltd.
200 Burrard Street, Suite 500, Vancouver, B.C. V6C 3L7;
(604) 682-0611, fax (604) 685-3019, public.relations@cominco.com, www.cominco.com

LARGE MINING FIRM: Gold and Metals Production, Mining

Cominco is a leading international exploration and mining company specializing in gold and copper. It is Canada's oldest continually-operating mining company and is also involved in smelting and refining. With over 5800 employees worldwide, the firm has extensive overseas operations. These include mines in Alaska, Chile, Turkey, and Mexico; refining in Oregon and Peru; exploration sites in Mexico, Bolivia, and Turkey; and sales offices in Singapore and Japan.

Seeking to rejuvenate its workforce, Cominco is actively recruiting candidates under 35, especially graduates in geology and metallurgical, chemical, and mechanical engineering. It offers university scholarships at all levels. After gaining experience in Canada, employees can go overseas. [ID:5708]

Compass Business Strategies, Inc.
Suite 3-408 North Service Road, Oakville, Ontario L6H 5R2;
(905) 339-1898, fax (905) 339-1896, compass@globalserve.net, www.compassbusiness.com

MID-SIZED MANAGEMENT CONSULTING FIRM: Business Development, Consulting, Exchange Programs, Intercultural Briefings, International Trade

Compass Business Strategies develops and implements business strategies, including market assessments, market entry strategies, and business development activities. It manages the Horizons Plus International Internship Program on behalf of Industry Canada. The program pays interns a working allowance and operates year round to all parts of the world, providing practical skills development and mentoring.

Compass has 15 staff based in Canada, eight overseas. It seeks applicants with a background in business development, business strategy skills, appropriate academic skills, languages, diverse ethnic or country of origin backgrounds. It maintains a data bank of résumés. The web site lists Horizons Plus position openings. [ID:6753]

Consultaction Nadeau International Inc.
625, ave. Notre-Dame, Saint-Lambert,
Québec J4P 2K8; (514) 923-4140, fax (514) 923-8682, manatco@sympatico.ca

MID-SIZED GENERAL CONSULTING FIRM: Agriculture, Business/Banking/Trade, Business Development, Consulting, International Trade, Project Management, Technical Assistance

Consultaction Nadeau International Inc. is a mid-sized consulting firm specializing in the agro-industrial sector. The firm provides financial and nonfinancial export development, market research, product adaptation, quality control, technology transfer, and export promotion services.

Recent overseas projects include the rehabilitation of agro-processing factories, quality control improvement, and export development in a number of countries in South America and Southeast Asia. The firm has six salaried staff overseas, and six Canadian staff.

Prospective applicants should have a master's degree, expertise and experience in project management, agro-industry, marketing, finance, and production in developing countries. Knowledge of French, English, Spanish, and Portuguese is an asset. Consultaction Nadeau International Inc. maintains a data bank for résumés. [ID:5710]

Consultants Canarail Inc.
Bureau 1050, 1140, boul. Maisonneuve ouest,
Montréal, Québec H3A 1M8; (514) 985-0930, fax (514) 985-0929, inbox@canarail.com

LARGE TRANSPORTATION CONSULTING FIRM: Computer Systems, Consulting, Economics, Engineering, Project Management, Railways, Technical Assistance, Transportation

CANARAIL CONSULTANTS INC. (CANARAIL) is a consulting firm specializing in railway transportation. The company was formed in 1990 by a group of engineers and specialists who acquired their professional experience with major Canadian railways and railway consulting organizations. CANARAIL has, over the years, completed over 120 consulting assignments throughout the world. CANARAIL prides itself on providing expertise on the latest railway technology and being able to effect the technology transfer efficiently and effectively.

Four core areas, which respond to the targeted markets, are currently defining CANARAIL's business focus. Project-specific teams are being built around these core groups: an economic group which targets railway privatization, concessioning projects and project financing; the engineering group comprised of the track and civil engineering division; the mechanical and industrial engineering group which undertakes rolling stock and facility design and maintenance projects, including performance based maintenance contracts, and the communications engineering group.

Current CANARAIL staff includes 32 full-time employees in Canada and 25 employees overseas. In addition, contractual employees are hired according to various project needs, for short or long-term contracts.

CANARAIL continually searches for qualified professionals with solid experience in transportation, railway technical activities, engineering, transport planning, financial analysis, economics, computer systems, and telecommunications. The firm seeks consultants who are adaptable to change, have good listening skills and are sensitive to other cultures. CANARAIL maintains a résumé data bank of potential consultants. The company's web site is currently under construction. [ID:5711]

Consulting Resource Group International Inc. (CRG)
Suite 203, 2760 Trethewey Street, Abbotsford, B.C. V2T 3R1;
(604) 852-0566, fax (604) 850-3003, crgi@crgleader.com, www.crgleader.com

MID-SIZED GENERAL CONSULTING FIRM: Business Development, Community Development, Consulting, Human Resources, Leadership Assessment, Organization Development, Personal Development, Publishing

Consulting Resource Group International Inc. (CRG) has produced over 30 learning systems and assessments that have been used in over 30,000 organizations worldwide. The firm specializes in assessments, custom designed development programs, seminars, training, conference speeches and facilitation in a variety of organizational and personal fields.

The firm has completed overseas contracts in nine countries around the world, including the US, Japan, Australia, New Zealand, Sweden, the Netherlands, Hungary, and the UK, and has served both public- and private-sector clients.

Prospective applicants should be professional independent leaders in a defined region in one or more of the fields of consulting, training development, sales, marketing, personnel, education, career planning, or counselling; have a network of other professional contacts or intend to develop such a network; and have the required sales, marketing, and financial capabilities to develop and support at least 10 associates.

CRG has a web site which provides information on distance learning. [ID:5712]

Coopers & Lybrand
Human Resources, 145 King Street W., Toronto, Ontario M5H 1V8;
(416) 869-1130, fax (416) 941-8417, TOR.Human.Resources@ca.coopers.com, www.ca.coopers.com

LARGE FINANCIAL SERVICES FIRM: Accounting, Business Development, Consulting, Project Management

Strategic business advisors, Coopers & Lybrand is one of Canada's largest professional service firms with some 2,400 partners and staff. It plans to merge with Price Waterhouse in 1998. More than just Chartered Accountants, the group is a multidisciplinary partnership offering a wide range of business and consulting services to individuals, industry, and governments. Staff include management consultants, tax advisors, information technology and telecommunications specialists, actuaries, insurance investigators, engineers, and more.

Coopers & Lybrand believes in exposing its people to as many global markets as possible. To help develop their international experience, qualified CA's are offered overseas exchange programs to countries like the UK, the Netherlands, Australia, Italy, Chile, and China. It also has an International Summer School Program and, for undergraduate business students, an International Careers Program. As a result, Coopers & Lybrand hires from within for international positions whenever possible.

Their web site offers a wealth of information for job seekers, from students to senior executives. [ID:6833]

Corel Corporation
The Corel Building, 1600 Carling Ave.,
Ottawa, Ontario K1Z 8R7; (613) 728-3733, fax (613) 761-9176, hr@corel.com, www.corel.com

LARGE HIGH TECHNOLOGY FIRM: Advanced Technology, Human Resources,
Media/Communications, Quality Assurance, Research and Development, Software Development

Corel Corporation is an internationally recognized developer and marketer of productivity applications, graphics, and multimedia software. The company ships its products in over 17 languages through distributors in 70 countries and has international offices in Orem, Utah, and Dublin, Ireland. It plans 6 new regional sales offices in the US, including one in Miami to service Latin America.

Suitable candidates hold Bachelor of Science, Computer Science, or Computer Engineering degrees as well as Master of Science and doctorates. Product management, technical writing, and quality assurance staff generally hold degrees in relevant disciplines and tend to be innovators in their field or seasoned high-tech professionals.

Corel lists numerous employment opportunities on its web site. Applications for US positions should be directed to the Utah offices, e-mail: hr-US@corel.com, quoting the position number of the specific job being applied for. [ID:6958]

Corporation for International Settlements (CIS)
Suite 500, 357 Bay Street, Toronto, Ontario M5H 2T7; (416) 363-2874, fax (416) 368-8740, cis@istar.ca

MID-SIZED FINANCIAL SERVICES FIRM: Business/Banking/Trade, Business Development,
Consulting, International Trade

The Corporation for International Settlements (CIS) is a mid-sized consulting firm specializing in international trade, project finance, risk management, foreign debt recovery, and overseas asset management in developing countries. Prospective employees should have some experience in trade or project management, but need not have overseas experience. CIS does consider internships, but not on a regular basis. [ID:5713]

Cott Corporation
Human Resources, 207 Queen's Quay W., Suite 800,
Toronto, Ontario M5J 1A7; (416) 203-3898, fax (416) 203-3914, www.cott.com

LARGE FOOD PROCESSING FIRM: Manufacturing

Cott is a worldwide supplier of beverages. It produces and distributes a wide variety of private label soft drinks for over 120 corporate clients in over 20 countries. It is expanding its line of juices, bottled water, and iced teas. It has primary subsidiaries in the US, UK, and Australia and has additional production facilities in Norway. It plans further expansion in the US.

The majority of Cott's 1930 worldwide employees, including 930 in Canada, are directly involved in local production. Cott employs co-op students in Canada. Jobs with an overseas component are management positions. [ID:7216]

Courey International (Commerce) Inc.
4107 Cousens, Saint-Laurent, Québec H4S 1V6;
(514) 956-9711, fax (514) 956-0599, quick@coureycan.com, www.quickstyle.com.

SMALL GENERAL CONSULTING FIRM: Business Development, Consulting, Development Assistance, Project Management, Telecommunications

Courey International (Commerce) Inc. is a major export trading company with expertise in procurement and supply logistics. It is a procurement advisor, agent, and monitor for the Canadian International Development Agency (CIDA).

The firm currently has projects in the Caribbean, Central and South America, and Ghana. There are six overseas staff members and five staff in Canada.

Suitable candidates should have a university degree and be able to write reports clearly and effectively. All candidates will receive on-the-job training. [ID:5714]

Cowater International Inc.
Suite 400, 411 Roosevelt Ave., Ottawa, Ontario K2A 3X9;
(613) 722-6434, fax (613) 722-5893, cowater@compuserve.com

LARGE GENERAL CONSULTING FIRM: Accounting, Adult Training, Business/Banking/Trade, Business Development, Community Development, Computer Systems, Consulting, Development Assistance, Development Education, Economics, Engineering, Environment, Gender and Development, Human Resources, Micro-Enterprises, Project Management, Technical Assistance, Waste Water Management, Water Supply

Cowater International Inc. is a multidisciplinary consulting company that carries out international development in six principal sectors: water supply, sanitation and environment, enterprise development, accountability, social development and information management. The company's mission is to provide high-quality consulting services which support social and economic development of self-reliance and sustainability through participatory development.

Cowater undertakes projects in developing countries. The firm has 14 overseas professional staff and 15 Canadian-based professional staff. Individuals are often hired for short-term contracts.

Most candidates require a master's degree and substantial experience. The following skills will be given priority: information systems and computing, institution capacity building, water, sanitation related engineering, project management, social and community development, forestry, finance, economics, business, and accounting. Candidates should have a minimum of two years overseas experience in development and the ability to speak English, French or Spanish. Cowater International occasionally accepts interns if the needs of the company can be matched with an applicant. [ID:5715]

CRC SIMA

405, St-Dizier, Montréal, Québec H2Y 2Y1;
(514) 651-2800, fax (514) 651-1681, sogema@crc.sogema.com

MID-SIZED HUMAN RESOURCES FIRM: Development Assistance, Environment, Geomatics, Logistics, Project Management

CRC SIMA is a subsidiary of CRC SOGEMA Inc. It is the continuation of SIMA géographes-conseils ltée created in 1979. The firm specializes in the management of geographic information. It has been most active in the fields of regional and international development, strategic planning, natural resources management, environmental evaluation, capacity-building in environment, and program management in Canada and abroad. CRC SIMA is involved with public and private sector institutions and organizations whose mandates deal with geographic information management.

CRC SIMA has completed most of its mandates in Africa, but is also active in Central America and Asia. The firm maintains a data bank for résumés. [ID:5861]

CRC SOGEMA Inc.

Bureau 454, Tour Est, 1111 St-Charles ouest,
Longueuil, Québec J4K 5G4; (514) 651-2800, fax (514) 651-1681

LARGE MANAGEMENT CONSULTING FIRM: Administration, Adult Training, Business Development, Community Development, Computer Systems, Consulting, Environment, Human Resources, Micro-Enterprises, Project Management, Telecommunications

CRC SOGEMA Inc. is a management consulting firm with expertise in: technical assistance; institutional support and reinforcement; organizational development; information system development and implementation; public enterprise; small and medium-sized enterprises; human resources development and training; project management and evaluation.

CRC SOGEMA has a strong relationships with more than 15 countries in Africa and expertise in the Caribbean and Central America. The firm has more than 75 permanent consultants and employees working abroad, and 40 managers and administrative staff in Canada with international responsibilities.

Candidates should have a master's degree in business, accounting or economics. They should have work experience in government agencies or ministries, or small-scale enterprises, and knowledge of structural adjustment programs in developing countries. CRC SOGEMA Inc. maintains a database for résumés. [ID:5717]

Cumming Cockburn Limited

Suite 300, 65 Allstate Parkway, Markham, Ontario L3R 9X1;
(905) 475-4222, fax (905) 475-5051, engineering@ccl-toronto.com, www.cumming-cockburn.com

MID-SIZED ENGINEERING FIRM: Business/Banking/Trade, Construction, Energy Resources, Engineering, Environment, Project Management, Water Resources

Cumming Cockburn Ltd. provides overseas professional engineering services in such fields as transportation, marine structures, community planning, small hydro, and the environment. Typical projects include small hydro projects in Zimbabwe, the Philippines, and Costa Rica; a bridge in Kenya, an aircraft maintenance complex in Antigua, a cruise ship berth in Dominica, feeder roads and jetties in St. Vincent, storage reservoir rehabilitation in Trinidad, a stormwater management master plan in Barbados, and a marina in Florida.

The firm has five staff working abroad and 130 staff in Canada. It has two offices in Florida which can be emailed at: ccl@icanect.net. The company recruits professional personnel with language skills, flexibility, and personality. It maintains a data bank for résumés. Job listings are posted on their web site. [ID:5718]

Dayton Mining Corporation

P.O. Box 49186, Suite 2453, Three Bentall Centre, 595 Burrard Street, Vancouver, B.C.
V7X 1K8; (604) 662-8383, fax (604) 684-1329, dmining@dayton-mining.com, www.dayton-mining.com

LARGE MINING FIRM: Mining

Dayton Mining Corporation is a Canada-based international mining company engaged in the exploration and development of precious metals properties in North and South America. The company's primary asset is the Andacollo Gold mine located in central Chile. The company is also actively evaluating several other properties worldwide.

Dayton Mining maintains a web site that contains information on its operations, financial situation and corporate structure. Current news releases are also posted online. [ID:5720]

Delcan International Corporation

Human Resource Department, 133 Wynford Drive, North York,
Ontario M3C 1K1; (416) 391-7550, fax (416) 441-4131, info@delcan.com, www.interlog.com/~delcan

LARGE ENGINEERING FIRM: Engineering, Environment, Project Management, Technical Assistance

Delcan International Corporation provides consulting engineering services in transportation, municipal engineering, systems engineering, urban planning, structural engineering, infrastructure rehabilitation and maintenance management. Services provided also include feasibility studies, design, planning, contract administration, construction supervision, project management, and technical assistance.

Delcan has undertaken projects in Europe, Africa, Asia, Latin America and the Caribbean. Their offices are located in most major cities across Canada and in the US, Mexico, Ethiopia, Hong Kong, Malawi, Taiwan, Venezuela, Barbados, and Turkey. Delcan has 30 overseas staff and 14 Canadian staff who have international responsibilities.

Candidates require a bachelor's degree in engineering, economics, or management and at least five years of experience in their area of expertise. International work experience is an asset, and in some cases, is absolutely necessary. Knowledge of French, Spanish, or another language is an asset, especially the local language in the area of work. Demonstrated ability to adapt to local conditions and work with local people is also an asset. Delcan International maintains a data bank for résumés. [ID:5721]

Dessau International Ltd/Ltée

1200, boul. St-Martin ouest, Laval, Québec H7S 2E4;
(514) 384-5660, fax (514) 668-8232, dessau@dessau.com, www.dessau.com

LARGE ENGINEERING FIRM: Business Development, Construction, Consulting, Development Assistance, Economics, Engineering, Environment, Fisheries, Gender and Development, Power Generation, Transmission and Distribution, Project Management, Quality Assurance, Technical Assistance, Urban Development, Waste Water Management, Water Supply

Dessau International Ltd/Ltée is a multidisciplinary consulting firm specializing in transportation, power, environment, urban development, buildings and structures, geotechnical studies, metallurgy, materials testing, quality assurance, and telecommunications.

Dessau International has a staff of 50 who work overseas and 100 in Canada with international responsibilities. The firm is supported technically by Group Dessau, the third-largest consulting firm in Québec, with a staff of some 500 people.

For the most part, the firm hires engineers with past overseas experience. Other useful qualifications include specific expertise in areas such as environmental planning, urban planning, economics, computers/systems and a good knowledge of French, English, and Spanish. The firm maintains a data bank for résumés.

Dessau also maintains a web site that posts new job openings on the "What's New" web page. [ID:5725]

DiamondWorks Ltd.
9th Floor, Waterfront Centre, 200 Burrard St.,
Vancouver, B.C. V6C 3L6; (604) 669-8871, fax (604) 682-2060, www.diamondworks.com

LARGE MINING FIRM: Adult Training, Community Development, Exploration and Development,
Gold and Metals Production, Project Management, Sustainable Development

DiamondWorks Ltd., the successor to Carson Gold, is a Canada-based diamond production and exploration company with mineral properties in Canada, Africa, China and South America. Internationally, the company is completing feasibility studies and test-mining in Sierra Leone and has commenced commercial diamond production, bulk-sampling, drilling, and test-mining operations at sites in Angola as well as an airborne magnetic survey of one of its diamond properties. The company has launched a gold exploration program in Yunnan Province, China. It also has offices in the UK, South Africa, and Venezuela. [ID:7062]

Dillon Consulting
100 Sheppard Ave. E., Suite 300, Toronto, Ontario M2N 6N5;
(416) 229-4646, fax (416) 229-4692, toronto@dillon.ca, www.porterdillon.com/dillon.html

LARGE GENERAL CONSULTING FIRM: Architecture and Planning, Community Development,
Construction, Consulting, Development Assistance, Economics, Engineering, Environment,
Fisheries, Forestry, Gender and Development, Human Resources, Intercultural Briefings, Project
Management, Technical Assistance, Tourism, Water Resources

Dillon Consulting works internationally in environmental sciences and engineering, environmental assessment, urban development, and transportation planning and engineering. The firm is active in water resources and conservation, sanitation, infrastructure rehabilitation, waste management, natural systems, resource management, hydrogeology, urban and regional planning, recreation and tourism development, highway and bridge planning and design, and public transit studies.

Dillon has international activities in the US, the Caribbean, China, Indonesia, Thailand, and the Philippines. The firm has 500 staff members with skills in over 30 distinct disciplines, including professional engineers, architects, planners, economists, hydrologists, and physical and social scientists.

Candidates should have an accredited degree and technical experience in environmental engineering, planning, infrastructure or transportation; prior experience working overseas, crosscultural sensitivity, and good communication skills. Foreign language capability is an asset. Dillon maintains a data bank for résumés. [ID:5795]

DMR Group Inc.
Human Resources Division, Suite 2300, 1200 McGill College Ave.,
Montréal, Québec H3B 4G7; (514) 877-3301, fax (514) 866-0423, www.dmr.com

LARGE INFORMATION SYSTEMS FIRM: Computer Systems

DMR Group Inc. is a leading international provider of information technology services to business and public enterprises. The company's services include information technology planning, enterprise architecture, knowledge transfer, outsourcing, systems development, and systems integration.

DMR employs over 2,000 professionals in Canada and an additional 4,000 in the US and overseas. Prospective applicants must have a relevant educational background and at least five years of experience. DMR maintains an extensive web site that provides information on the firm and its activities and posts international job opportunities online. [ID:5731]

DPA Group (International) Inc.
1801 Hollis Street, Suite 1030,
Halifax, N.S. B3J 3N4; (902) 422-9601, fax (902) 429-9791, dpa@aragroup.ca

LARGE GENERAL CONSULTING FIRM: Consulting, Economics, Environment, Project
Management, Social Policy, Technical Assistance

The DPA Group (International) is an affiliate of the ARA Consulting Group, a
management consulting firm active internationally in implementing long-term technical
assistance. The DPA Group provides services for institutional strengthening in integrated
environmental and resource economics analysis and economic and social impact assessment, policy formulation and organizational design for resource management systems,
integrated community and rural development, and (eco)tourism master planning.

Applicants should have postgraduate degrees and some experience in their field.
Familiarity with the country or region where a candidate will be posted is expected. [ID:5732]

E.T. Jackson & Associates Ltd.
Suite 100, 858 Bank Street, Ottawa, Ontario K1S 3W3;
(613) 230-5221, fax (613) 230-0639, etjack@fox.nstn.ca, http://fox.nstn.ca/~etjack

MID-SIZED MANAGEMENT CONSULTING FIRM: Accounting, Administration, Adult Training,
Advocacy, Agriculture, Business/Banking/Trade, Business Development, Community
Development, Consulting, Development Assistance, Economics, Exchange Programs,
Fundraising, Gender and Development, Human Resources, Human Rights, Humanitarian Relief,
Micro-Enterprises, Project Management, Technical Assistance, Volunteer

E.T. Jackson & Associates Ltd. is a management consulting firm specializing in project
management, evaluation and planning, public policy, and human resource development. The
company operates offices in Bangladesh and Ghana, where projects in rural development,
basic human needs, micro-credit, governance, economic policyy and management training
are managed. The firm also mobilizes some 20 short-term consulancies per year to evallate
bilateral and nongovernmental projeecs in AAia, Africa, theeAmericas, and Central and
Eastern Europe. Firm associates are bbsed in Bangkok,,Islamab d, Gabarone, Bridgetown
and Kampala.

Candidates should have postgraduate degrees and overseas experience in any of a
number of sectors. The firm will also consider arranging internships with universities and
colleges. The firm is currently interested in individuals with skills in business management,
banking and finance, private philanthropy, public administration, economics, politics, labour
markets, basic education, community water supply, ad primaay healthcare. Experience in
South and SoutheasttAsia, West and outhernnAfrica, Latin AAerica, the Caribbean, and
Centrrl and Eastern Europe is desirable. E.T. Jackson & Assoccates maintains a data bank
for résumés and a web site which contains information about the company's activities.
[ID:5733]

Econolynx International
Suite 202, 1900 Merivale Road, Nepean,
Ontario K2G 4N4; (613) 723-8698, fax (613) 723-7333, khay@ccs.carleton.ca

SMALL GENERAL CONSULTING FIRM: Accounting, Agriculture, Business Development,
Consulting, Economics, Environment, Fisheries, Forestry, Gender and Development, Human
Rights, International Trade, Project Management, Telecommunications, Water Resources

Econolynx International is a mid-sized economic consulting firm specializing in international trade, investment, and project and program evaluation. Current overseas work
includes projects in Sub-Saharan Africa, South America, Poland, China, Bangladesh, and
Vietnam.

Fact-finding missions are sent abroad to support analysis and local consultants are
hired on a sub-contract basis as needs arise. Applicants should have development experience
and/or a degree in economics. Language skills are an asset. Econolynx maintains a data
bank for résumés. [ID:5736]

Econotec Inc. Consultants

5185, boul. St-Laurent, Montréal, Québec H2T 1R9;
(514) 274-0106, fax (514) 272-4480, bergeron@econotec.qc.ca, www.econotec.qc.ca

MID-SIZED GENERAL CONSULTING FIRM: Consulting, Economics, Energy Resources, Gender and Development

Econotec Inc. Consultants is a mid-sized consulting firm specializing in development planning and economics, program and project monitoring and evaluation, and institutional development. Sectors of experience include macro-economic policy, energy, industrial development, state-owned enterprises, and agriculture. [ID:5737]

EdperBrascan

Suite 4400, P.O. Box 762, BCE Place, 181 Bay Street,
Toronto, Ontario M5J 2T3; (416) 363-9491, fax (416) 865-1288

LARGE INVESTMENT MANAGEMENT FIRM: Business/Banking/Trade, Energy Resources, Forestry, Metals, Mining

EdperBrascan is a diversified company with natural resources, power generation, real estate, and financial services operations. Its mining and metallurgy, power generation, and real estate operations have expanded in recent years. Its merchant banking services provide financial and management services to affiliates, other corporations, and individual clients in North America and internationally. [ID:5764]

ELI Eco Logic International Inc.

143 Dennis Street, Rockwood, Ontario N0B 2K0;
(800) 596-9591, fax (519) 856-9235, info@eco-logic-intl.com, www.eco-logic-intl.com

LARGE ENVIRONMENTAL CONSULTING FIRM: Environment, Technical Assistance

ELI Eco Logic International specializes in environmental restoration, including landfill remediation. It has several major foreign contracts, including one with the US Army for a Chemical Warfare Agent Clean-Up Program and in Japan for PCB destruction technology. Outside Canada, ELI has major offices in Kwinana, Western Australia, and Ann Arbor, Michigan. It employs over 100 environmental professionals. [ID:7191]

Ellis-Don Construction

2045 Oxford Street E., London, Ontario N5V 2Z9; (519) 455-6770, fax (519) 455-2944

LARGE CONSTRUCTION FIRM: Construction, Engineering, Project Management

Ellis-Don Construction is a large, integrated firm specializing in general contracting, project management, design, and construction. The firm has extensive overseas operations, is currently involved in projects in Malaysia, Mexico, and Lithuania, and is pursuing opportunities in China.

Ellis-Don has international offices in the US, Europe, and the Caribbean. [ID:5741]

Environmental Technologies International Inc.

Unit 12, 286 Attwell Drive, Rexdale, Ontario M9W 5B2; (416) 674-0573, fax (416) 674-1765

MID-SIZED ENVIRONMENTAL FIRM: Business Development, Consulting, Engineering, Environment

Environmental Technologies International Inc. (ETI) supplies technology, equipment and services in the fields of environmental protection and pollution control both in Canada and overseas. Its international operations focus on the design and supply of water and wastewater treatment systems and controls.

ETI has 10 employees in Canada with international responsibilities, and no permanent overseas staff. [ID:5743]

Ernst & Young (Canada) Actuaries & Consultants Inc.
1, Place Vile Marie, Suite 2400, Montréal, Québec H3B 3M9;
(514) 392-7810, fax (514) 878-1043, yves.guerard@ca.eyi.com, www.eycan.com

LARGE MANAGEMENT CONSULTING FIRM: Accounting, Business/Banking/Trade,
Consulting, Human Resources, International Trade, Project Management, Technical Assistance

Affiliated with the Ernst & Young family of businesses, Ernst & Young (Canada)
Actuaries & Consultants Inc. is a Montréal-based business consulting service. It has seven
staff overseas in addition to five staff in Canada. It specializes in financial services, social
security systems, health, utilities, and re-engineering. Current projects are in Indonesia,
India, China, and Latin America.

Ernst & Young (Canada) seeks people with backgrounds in accounting, finance, project
management, human resources, and international trade. Candidates should be familiar with
the region in which their project would be based. A data bank for résumés is kept. Only in
special cases are applications for internship positions considered. [ID:6564]

Ernst & Young Canada
P.O. Box 251, 222 Bay Street, Ernst & Young Tower, Toronto-Dominion Centre,
Toronto, Ontario M5K 1J7; (416) 943-2496, fax (416) 864-1174, info@ca.eyi.com, www.eycan.com

LARGE MANAGEMENT CONSULTING FIRM: Accounting, Administration,
Business/Banking/Trade, Business Development, Consulting, International Trade, Logistics,
Project Management, Technical Assistance

Ernst & Young Canada is a member firm of Ernst & Young International, one of the
leading professional service organizations helping companies strategize business opportunities around the globe. Ernst & Young Canada considers its own international operations
to be limited, but can assist people in seeking positions with fellow Ernst & Young firms
overseas.

Ernst & Young focuses on serving key transnational industries and important local
industries, including automotive, consumer products, energy, finance, insurance, transportation, manufacturing, and high technology. Using integrated industry knowledge, it offers
management consulting, accounting and auditing services, and corporate advisory services.

Ernst & Young International has 72,000 employees, including 10,500 consultants, in
over 100 countries and over 660 locations. Experiencing dynamic growth, Ernst & Young
has many openings for seasoned professionals, recent graduates, and interns alike. A wide
variety of professions are sought by Ernst & Young, but a background in business management or accounting are commonly required. Positions are in such fields as real estate
services, tax services, information systems, actuarial services, healthcare consulting, management consulting, and mergers and acquisitions.

Its web site provides general information on Ernst & Young, detailed information on
how to apply for positions, and has detailed listings for openings in Australia, Belgium,
Bermuda, Brazil, South Africa, Sweden, the UK, and Zimbabwe. The link to its US web site
provides extensive information on job openings. [ID:7181]

ESSA Technologies Ltd.
International Office, 3rd Floor, 1765 West 8th Ave.,
Vancouver, B.C. V6J 5C6; (604) 733-2996, fax (604) 733-4657, info@essa.com, www.essa.com

MID-SIZED ENVIRONMENTAL CONSULTING FIRM: Accounting, Administration, Adult
Training, Business Development, Community Development, Computer Systems, Consulting,
Development Education, Energy Resources, Environment, Fisheries, Forestry, Project
Management, Technical Assistance, Water Resources

ESSA Technologies Ltd. provides clients with consulting services, innovative software
and proven technologies to help them achieve creative and profitable solutions to
environmental and natural resource problems. The company blends three elements: leading-
edge scientific expertise, advanced tools for systems analysis, and innovative communication

techniques to address global problems such as acid rain, climatic change, and resource management.

ESSA has completed more than 900 projects in Canada, the US, Southeast Asia, and several other countries worldwide. From three offices in Canada and one in Southeast Asia, ESSA's capacities are reinforced by strategic working relationships with other carefully chosen consulting corporations and NGOs in Europe, the Asia Pacific region, and North America. Its professional staff of about 35 all have degrees in ecology or other natural sciences, business or engineering.

ESSA's excellent web site provides a broad range of information about the company and posts current job openings. [ID:5744]

EVS Consultants
195 Pemberton Ave., North Vancouver, B.C. V7P 2R4;
(604) 986-4331, fax (604) 662-8548, evs_consultants@mindlink.bc.ca

MID-SIZED ENVIRONMENTAL CONSULTING FIRM: Consulting, Environment, Fisheries, Forestry, Petrochemicals, Project Management, Technical Assistance, Water Resources

EVS Consultants is a mid-sized consulting firm specializing in marine science. Areas of expertise include environmental impact and risk assessment, toxicology, coastal zone management, and training.

Since 1986, the company has been involved in projects in 10 Asian countries: Brunei, Indonesia, Malaysia, the Philippines, Singapore, Thailand, Cambodia, Vietnam, Hong Kong, and China. Staff are currently involved in a seven-year project in Southeast Asia to provide technical assistance, particularly technology transfer and training, in marine science. The firm has a total staff of 102, of which two work overseas and an additional 11 work in Canada and have primarily international responsibilities.

Prospective applicants should have an MSc or PhD with practical multidisciplinary or specific experience in the environmental industry (particularly consulting). The firm also looks for candidates with technical backgrounds, along with proven business development and project management skills. EVS maintains a data bank for résumés. [ID:5734]

Experco Ltée.
Bureau 205, 5400, boul. des Galeries, Québec, Québec G2K 2B4;
(418) 623-0598, fax (418) 623-1636, expdrv@experco.ca, http://experco.ca

MID-SIZED GENERAL CONSULTING FIRM: Agriculture, Consulting, Energy Resources, Engineering, Environment, Technical Assistance

Experco Ltée. is a mid-sized general consulting firm specializing in agro-ecology, natural resource management, environmental protection, construction, urban infrastructure and transportation, telecommunications, and project management.

The firm currently employs over 300 people and is engaged in a variety of international projects. In addition to projects in Tunisia, Rwanda, Cameroon, Côte d'Ivoire, Mali, Burkina Faso, Senegal, Mexico, Columbia, Pakistan, and Vietnam, the firm has offices in Mexico City, Ho Chi Minh City, Kigali, and Bogota.

The firm maintains a web site that provides general information on the company and its range of activities. [ID:5747]

Falconbridge Ltd.
Suite 1200, 95 Wellington Street, Toronto, Ontario M5J 2V4;
(416) 956-5700, fax (416) 956-5757, corpcomm@falconbridge.com, www.falconbridge.com

LARGE MINING FIRM: Metals, Mining

Falconbridge is one of the world's largest fully integrated and diversified base metals mining companies. Founded in 1928, Falconbridge now employs 6600 people in over 10 countries. The firm is the western world's second largest producer of primary nickel products and a significant producer of cobalt and copper.

Falconbridge has operations in Canada, Norway, and the Dominican Republic; development projects in northern Québec and Chile; exploration offices in Canada, the Dominican Republic, and southern Africa; and sales and marketing offices in the US, Belgium, Russia, and Japan.

Falconbridge's web site provides basic information on the firm's activities. [ID:5748]

Finning International Inc.
555 Great Northern Way, Vancouver, B.C. V5T 1E2;
(604) 872-4444, fax (604) 872-2994, jobline@finning.ca, gsmith@finning.co.uk, www.finning.ca

LARGE CONSTRUCTION FIRM: Construction, Manufacturing, Merchandising

Finning International Inc. is a Canadian-based international corporation which sells, finances, and provides customer services for Caterpillar and complementary equipment. Finning is one of the largest dealers in the world for products distributed by Caterpillar Inc. It also buys and sells used equipment domestically and worldwide.

With 4200 employees worldwide, the company has operations in Western Canada, the UK, Poland, and Chile. The Canadian web site lists positions open in Canada and provides a link to the UK site which lists international positions. Typical positions require various levels of experience in mechanics, service field dispatching, and sales. [ID:7012]

First Dynasty Mines Ltd.
Waterfront Centre, 9th Floor, 200 Burrard Street,
Vancouver, B.C. V6C 3L6; (604) 685-8382, fax (604) 682-2060, www.firstdynasty.com

LARGE MINING FIRM: Exploration and Development, Metals, Mineral Resources, Mining

First Dynasty Mines Ltd. is a Canadian mining company based in Singapore. It is constructing a gold plant in Armenia and conducting feasibility studies on expanding two additional gold mines. The company also explores for gold in Myanmar and Indonesia. [ID:6990]

Fishery Products International (FPI)
P.O. Box 550, St. John's, Nfld. A1C 5L1; (709) 570-0000, fax (709) 570-0479, www.fpil.com

LARGE CUSTOMER SERVICES FIRM: Fisheries

Fishery Products International (FPI) is a global seafood enterprise with US sales offices in Danvers, Massachusetts; Seattle, Washington; and European sales offices in Reading, England and Cuxhaven, Germany. The company also has an extensive brokerage and distribution network throughout North America and Europe and a seafood sourcing network throughout North America, Southeast Asia, South America, and Europe.

Fishery Products International employs 2,600 people around the world. [ID:7057]

Fondation Paul Gérin-Lajoie/Paul Gérin-Lajoie Foundation
449, rue Ste-Hélène, 2e étage, Montréal, Québec H2Y 2K9;
(514) 288-3888, fax (514) 288-4880, fpgl@odyssee.net, www.odyssee.net/~fpgl/index.html

LARGE GENERAL CONSULTING FIRM: Development Assistance, Teaching

The Paul Gérin-Lajoie Foundation works on cooperation projects in the field of education in developing countries. It has 12 staff based in Canada and 44 overseas. Applicants should have experience in international cooperation and in education. The foundation maintains a data bank for résumés. [ID:6544]

Four Seasons Hotels Inc.
Human Resources, 1165 Leslie Street,
Don Mills, Ontario M3C 2K8; (416) 449-1750, fax (416) 441-4341, www.fshr.com

LARGE CUSTOMER SERVICES FIRM: Customer Services, Marketing, Tourism

Four Seasons Hotels Inc. operates the world's largest network of five-star hotels and resorts. The company currently owns 38 properties within major business centres and key leisure destinations in 16 countries, with another 14 under construction or development. It has 13 worldwide sales offices. Four Seasons has properties across North America as well as in Asia-South Pacific, Berlin, Istanbul, London, and Milan.

Four Seasons Hotels has approximately 21,000 employees. Positions with overseas potential are typically in management and require a university degree with an emphasis on business or hotel administration and some direct experience. [ID:7027]

Fulcrum Technologies Inc.
785 Carling Ave., Ottawa, Ontario K1S 5H4;
(613) 238-1761, fax (613) 238-7695, info@fulcrum.com, www.fulcrum.com

LARGE HIGH TECHNOLOGY FIRM: Computer Systems, Technical Assistance

Fulcrum Technologies Inc. develops and markets information retrieval and knowledge management software products around the world. The company employs 200 people in its offices in Canada, the US, Japan, France, Germany, Italy, the UK, and Australia. Among its clients and partners are the Bibliothèque nationale de France, the Australian government, Deutsche Telekom, Italia Online, Fujitsu Limited, AMEC Process and Energy in the UK, and SmithKline Beecham and Charles Schwab in the US.

Fulcrum posts career opportunities on their web site. [ID:7016]

Geac Computer Corporation Ltd.
Suite 300, 11 Allstate Parkway, Markham, Ontario L3R 9T8;
(905) 475-0525, fax (905) 475-3847, info@geac.com, www.geac.com

LARGE HIGH TECHNOLOGY FIRM: Computer Systems, Customer Services, Information Technologies, Manufacturing, Marketing, Project Management, Research and Development, Software Development

Geac Computer Corporation Ltd. delivers and supports total computer solutions, including complete mission-critical client/server applications to various cross-industry and vertical markets worldwide. The company's markets include libraries, financial services, hotels, construction management, property management, newspapers, cross-industry accounting, restaurants, manufacturing and distribution, and public safety.

Geac Computer Corporation Ltd. employs approximately 3,000 people in its principal offices in Canada, the US, the UK, France, the Netherlands, Belgium, Australia, New Zealand, Brazil, Hong Kong, Malaysia, Singapore, and Spain. [ID:7013]

General Woods and Veneers Consultants International Limited
1220, boul. Marie-Victorien,
Longueuil, Québec J4G 2H9; (514) 674-4957, fax (514) 674-3523, www.gwv.com

LARGE FORESTRY CONSULTING FIRM: Consulting, Forestry, Technical Assistance

General Woods and Veneers Consultants International Limited is a forestry consulting firm that provides nursery and reforestation development, logging and wood processing, marketing and forest product development, feasibility studies, forestry programs, wood industry technical evaluations, and financial studies.

The firm operates in North America, South America, Asia, Africa, and Europe and has both overseas and Canadian-based staff who work on international projects.

Candidates should have an engineering degree in forestry with expertise in forest development programs, wood processing, wood product marketing, silviculture and reforestation. Consultants should have overseas experience. The firm maintains a data bank for résumés. [ID:5752]

Geophysics GPR International Inc.

2545, rue DeLorimier, Longueuil, Québec J4K 3P7;
(514) 679-2400, fax (514) 521-4128, gprmtl@citnet.net, www.geophysicsgpr.com

MID-SIZED EARTH SCIENCES FIRM: Energy Resources, Engineering, Geophysics, Water Resources

Geophysics GPR International Inc. is an earth sciences consulting firm. Areas of specialization include technology transfer, training programs in geology and geophysics, seismic surveys such as reflection and refraction, ocean floor surveys, environmental impact studies and aeromagnetic surveys.

Geophysics GPR International has completed over 100 contracts in 37 countries. Currently, the firm holds contracts in India, Pakistan, Sudan, Tunisia, Zimbabwe, Botswana, Chile, and Guatemala. An estimated 10 employees work overseas. Another 45 working in Canada have international responsibilities.

Candidates should have educational qualifications and work experience in geology or geophysics and international experience. The company maintains a data bank for résumés.

Geophysics GPR's web site provides a wide range of useful information on past and current activities as well as business opportunities and a company newsletter. [ID:5753]

Global Alliance for Infrastructure Advancement Corp. (GAIA)

116 Promenade du Portage,
Hull, Québec J8X 2K1; (819) 778-0945, fax (819) 778-2143, wharton@ngl.com

MID-SIZED INFORMATION SERVICES FIRM: Business Development, Community Development, Consulting, Development Assistance, Development Education, Gender and Development

Global Alliance for Infrastructure Advancement (GAIA) Corporation specializes in the communications and information technology sectors, international development and business planning, and human resources training and education. GAIA supports the planning and implementation of information infrastructure throughout the world. The company is currently focused on developing opportunities for Canadian communications and information technology companies in Canada and Vietnam.

GAIA presently has three overseas employees and three Canadian employees with international responsibilities.

Candidates require one or more degrees or professional designations. They should possess a background in long-term, multiphased international projects and a proven track record in related knowledge-based sectors. The company offers year-round, long-term internships in Vietnam and junior consultancy placements for candidates with backgrounds in international information technology projects. GAIA maintains a data bank for résumés. [ID:6477]

Golden Knight Resources Inc.

Suite 1180, 999 West Hastings Street, Vancouver, B.C. V6C 2W2;
(604) 689-3846, fax (604) 689-3847, invest@golden-knight.com, www.golden-knight.com

LARGE MINING FIRM: Exploration and Development, Mining

Incorporated in 1981, Golden Knight Resources Inc. is a large mining company with a considerable portfolio of advanced gold exploration projects in West Africa. New gold production is scheduled to begin in 1998. It has regional offices in Ghana and Burkina Faso [ID:6965]

Golder Associates
2180 Meadowvale Blvd., Mississauga, Ontario L5N 5S3;
(905) 567-4444, fax (905) 567-6561, gac@golder.com, www.golder.com

LARGE ENGINEERING CONSULTING FIRM: Consulting, Energy Resources, Engineering, Environment, Fisheries, Forestry, Petrochemicals, Project Management, Water Resources

Golder Associates is an international group of consulting engineering companies specializing in geotechnical engineering, environmental management, environmental restoration, environmental and socio-economic assessments, surface and underground mining geotechnics, surface and groundwater management, waste management, project management, and quality assurance. The firm has completed assignments in over 140 countries in the environmental, ground water, waste management, industrial, mining, energy, transportation, and civil engineering sectors.

Currently, Golder Associates has 1900 employees in more than 80 offices worldwide. Offices are located in Canada, the US, Europe, Asia, Australia, and South America. The company has approximately 800 staff in Canada. All professionals may be called on for international projects.

Three quarters of the staff have an advanced degree in engineering or science. Preferred candidates have a relevant postgraduate degree plus five to 10 years experience in geotechnical engineering, hydrogeology, or a related scientific field. Golder Associates occassionally considers applications for internships. Except for senior level appointments, overseas experience is not essential. The firm maintains a data bank for résumés. [ID:5754]

Graybridge International Consulting Ltd.
76 Hôtel-de-Ville, Hull, Québec J8X 2E2;
(819) 776-2262, fax (819) 776-6491, success@graybridge.ca, www.graybridge.ca

MID-SIZED HUMAN RESOURCES FIRM: Adult Training, Consulting, Intercultural Briefings, Management Consulting

Graybridge International Consulting Inc. provides specialized services in international education, training and management. In-house trainers and a worldwide network of associates deliver training and cross-cultural effectiveness programs to public and private sector personnel working on international projects.

Graybridge currently has twelve full-time staff based in Canada. Applicants should have international work experience and possess language abilities, crosscultural sensitivity, knowledge of international development and be both flexible and autonomous. The firm maintains a data bank for résumés, particularly for Canadians who have lived and worked overseas. [ID:6616]

Greenstone Resources Ltd.
Suite 910, 26 Wellington Street E., Toronto, Ontario M5E 1S2;
(416) 862-7300, fax (416) 862-7604, tony@greenstone.ca, www.greenstone.ca

LARGE MINING FIRM: Environment, Exploration and Development, Metals, Mineral Resources, Mining

Greenstone Resources Ltd. is a gold mining company involved in gold and minerals exploration, development, and production. The company's focus is on production and building reserves in Central America. It also implements environmental and social programs within all project development activities. Greenstone Resources Ltd. has regional offices in Nicaragua, Honduras, Panama, and Miami, Florida. [ID:7019]

Groupe AFH International Inc./The AFH Group International Inc.

Bureau 410, 3333, boul. Cavendish, Montréal, Québec H4B 2M5;
(514) 484-9973, fax (514) 484-5298, hydrosukt1@p1.aofnet.org, www.hydrosult.com

LARGE GENERAL CONSULTING FIRM: Consulting, Water Resources

The AFH Group International Inc., a wholly owned subsidiary of Hydrosult Inc., is a large consulting firm specializing in the water resources sector. It provides integrated services in agriculture, forestry, and hydrology in projects addressing integrated rural development. A typical past overseas contract involved the policy, planning, and administration of water projects in Indonesia. [ID:5755]

Groupe Conseil Saguenay

159, Côte Salaberry,
Chicoutimi, Québec G7H 4K2; (418) 549-6471, fax (418) 549-3268, grinfret@gcs.qc.ca

LARGE ENGINEERING CONSULTING FIRM: Energy Resources, Engineering, Roads, Water Resources

Groupe Conseil Saguenay is a consulting engineering firm specializing in water, energy, sanitation, roads, and port and harbour planning and design. Activities include institutional strengthening of organizations and personnel, design of new organizational structures, development of consumer relations, establishment of an operation and maintenance control centre for equipment and material procurement and shipping, and design of new buildings.

The firm has four staff members working overseas on the Island of Dominica and five in Canada who have international responsibilities. The firm recruits municipal engineers with water and sanitation expertise and one year of work experience. The company maintains a data bank for résumés. [ID:5757]

Gulf Canada Resources Limited

401 - 9th Ave. S.W., Calgary, Alberta T2P 3C5; (403) 233-4000, fax (403) 233-5520, www.gulf.ca

LARGE PETROCHEMICALS FIRM: Accounting, Administration, Computer Systems, Energy Resources, Engineering, Project Management

Gulf Canada Resources Limited is a large petrochemical firm specializing in the exploration for, and production of, oil and natural gas. The firm currently has international operations in Indonesia, the North Sea and Australia. Further exploration is underway in Algeria, Yemen, Romania, Côte d'Ivoire and the US.

The firm employs 20 salaried staff based in Canada and an additional 100 overseas (this figure includes Gulf Indonesia Resources Ltd., Australian Gas Liquids and Gulf Australia Resources Ltd., wholly-owned subsidiaries of Gulf Canada Resources Ltd.).

Prospective applicants should have professional designations and significant experience in engineering, geology, geophysics or finance and administration. Gulf Canada Resources Limited maintains a data bank for résumés. Gulf Canada maintains a web site that provides basic information on its programs and services. [ID:5760]

H.A. Simons Ltd.

Suite 1400, 401 West Georgia Street, Vancouver, B.C. V6B 2J6;
(604) 664-4315, fax (604) 664-4804, intjobs@hasimons.com, www.hasimons.com

LARGE ENGINEERING FIRM: Engineering, Environment, Project Management

H.A. Simons Ltd. is a consulting engineering firm that provides service to the forestry, mining and metals, water resources, energy, transportation, and food and beverage sectors.

The firm has over 100 employees based overseas and 1,600 staff in Canada who work on international projects. Currently, the firm is active in South America, South Africa, Australia, New Zealand, Indonesia, Asia, and Europe.

Candidates should have experience working in foreign countries and knowledge of project management, finance, and marketing. Language skills for countries of interest are an asset. The firm maintains a data bank for résumés.

H.A. Simons has a web site that provides detailed information on the firm's activities. Career opportunities are posted online and you may respond to job openings by e-mail. [ID:5761]

Hatch Associates Ltd.

Manager, Human Resources, 2800 Speakman Drive,
Mississauga, Ontario L5K 2R7; (905) 855-7600, fax (905) 855-8270, hr@hatch.ca, www.hatch.ca

LARGE ENGINEERING FIRM: Construction, Consulting, Energy Resources, Engineering, Environment, Metals, Mineral Handling, Transportation

Hatch Associates is a major employee-owned, multidisciplinary engineering group with a focus on iron, steel, non-ferrous minerals and metals, and transportation. Its services include civil, mechanical, electrical, and process-control engineering; project and construction management; transportation and tunnelling; and consulting services for management, lenders, and investors. With offices in the US, UK, South Africa, Poland, and Czech Republic, Hatch has carried out projects in more than 80 countries. It has over 1000 salaried staff.

Applicants should have a relevant professional designation and expertise in one or more engineering disciplines related to the firm's areas of expertise as well as several years of experience. Their web site provides information on career opportunities. Hatch also participates in university co-op programs and urges engineering, metallurgy, computer technology, and MBA students to submit their résumés at the Hatch web site. [ID:5763]

Helen Ziegler and Associates Inc. (HZA)

Suite 2403, 180 Dundas Street W., Toronto, Ontario M5G 1Z8;
(800) 387-4616, fax (416) 977-6128, hza@medhunters.com, www.hziegler.com

MID-SIZED HUMAN RESOURCES FIRM: Health/Medical, Human Resources, Technical Assistance

In business since 1981, Helen Ziegler & Associates (HZA) recruits healthcare staff for international locations, specifically Saudi Arabia and Beijing, China. HZA's focus is on "hard-to-get" positions in all clinical and technical areas such as MDs, management staff, nurses, medical imaging staff, respiratory therapists etc., although all healthcare professionals are recruited. Since 1981 HZA has placed almost 4,000 healthcare professionals overseas. A data bank for résumés is maintained.

HZA also offers an interesting web site that focuses on its relations with Saudi Arabia and identified international contacts in the Middle East and China. [ID:5765]

Hickling Corporation

6th Floor, 350 Sparks Street, Ottawa, Ontario K1R 7S8;
(613) 237-2220, fax (613) 237-7347, hickling@hickling.ca, http://fox.nstn.ca/~hickling

MID-SIZED GENERAL CONSULTING FIRM: Business Development, Consulting, Development Assistance, Development Education, Gender and Development, Human Resources, Institution Building, International Trade, Micro-Enterprises, Teaching

Hickling Corporation's International Division provides management consulting services in the fields of human resources development, education, training, institutional development, enterprise development, gender, and micro-credit. The firm works on projects funded by CIDA, the World Bank, the Asian Development Bank, and the Inter-American Development Bank.

With its associate and affiliated companies, Hickling Corporation has about 60-65 employees, including those regularly working overseas on short and long-term assignments. Currently, the company is undertaking assignments in Indonesia, Nepal, Vietnam, China, Barbados, and Papua New Guinea and maintains overseas offices in Manila and Jakarta.

Consultants should have a minimum of five years experience and a master's degree. Work experience in developing countries is a prerequisite. Knowledge of multilateral donors is an asset. The firm maintains a database for résumés. [ID:5766]

HN Telecom Inc.
1160 Douglas Road, Burnaby, B.C. V5C 4Z6;
(604) 294-3401, fax (604) 299-6712, dave.redick@hntelecom.com, www.hntelecom.com

MID-SIZED TELECOMMUNICATIONS FIRM: Computer Systems, Telecommunications

HN Telecom Inc. provides telecommunications engineering consulting services world-wide. Candidates should have a degree in electrical or electronics engineering and at least 10 years of experience in telecommunications. HN Telecom's web site offers information on the company's mandate and services and provides several useful links to other telecom-munication firms. [ID:5767]

Hongkong Bank of Canada
Suite 300, 885 Georgia Street W., Vancouver, B.C. V6C 3E9;
(604) 685-1000, fax (604) 641-1849, info@hkbc.com, www.hkbc.com

LARGE FINANCIAL SERVICES FIRM: Business/Banking/Trade, Business Development, International Trade

The Hongkong Bank of Canada is a leading Canadian financial institution providing domestic banking and international financial services to a wide array of private and corporate clients. It is Canada's seventh largest bank and the largest foreign bank in Canada. Its 117 branches and 3,500 staff across Canada provide outstanding service to small and mid-sized businesses. It also has two branches in the western US.

It is a principal member of the HSBC Group, one of the world's largest banking and financial services organizations. Although the Hongkong Bank of Canada does provide services specifically for clients outside Canada, it has no permanent staff abroad and any international positions are filled internally. Instead, overseas needs are met by the HSBC Group's international network of 5,500 offices in 79 countries and territories.

For overseas positions, see the career section of the HSBC Group's own web site: www.hsbcgroup.com. It provides a sample of international executive vacancies and graduate career opportunities. The annual recruitment campaign is also posted there. Recent available positions have included information technology specialists and human resource develop-ment consultants. Although many openings do not require experience in banking, graduate career candidates should have a background in invesment and international banking. [ID:5768]

Hummingbird Communications Ltd.
1 Sparks Avenue,
North York, Ontario M2H 2W1; (416) 496-2200, fax (416) 496-2207, www.hummingbird.com

LARGE TELECOMMUNICATIONS FIRM: Advanced Technology, Computer Systems, Information Technologies, Manufacturing, Marketing, Media/Communications, Project Management, Research and Development, Software Development

Hummingbird Communications Ltd. is a rapidly expanding software company speciali-zing in communications technology. The company has local offices in the US, the UK, Switzerland, Germany, France, and Australia. Hummingbird Communications Ltd. generally seeks candidates with degrees in software engineering, systems engineering and analysis, and programming. The company lists career opportunities on its web site. [ID:7014]

Husky Oil International Corp.

International Canada Frontier Department, P.O. Box 6525, Stn. D, 707 - 8th Ave. S.W., Calgary, Alberta
T2P 3G7; (403) 298-6111, fax (403) 298-6378, recruitment@husky-oil.com, www.husky-oil.com

LARGE PETROCHEMICALS FIRM: Energy Resources

Husky Oil International Corp. is a large firm specializing in the exploration for and production of oil and natural gas. The firm has international operations in Libya and Indonesia
and anticipates an increase in overseas assignments with new contracts. The firm currently
has three overseas staff and 17 Canadian-based staff who work on international projects.

Husky Oil International recruits geologists, geophysicists, petroleum engineers, and
oilfield operation personnel with five to 10 years experience. The web site features a detailed
careers section which lists openings in a wide variety of professions, mainly based in
Canada. Most positions are filled in-house and the company maintains a data bank for
résumés. [ID:5770]

Hydro-Québec International (HQI)

23ième étage, 800, de Maisonneuve boul. est,
Montréal, Québec H2L 4L8; (514) 985-4200, fax (514) 985-3076, postmaster@hqi.qc.ca, www.hqi.qc.ca

LARGE ENGINEERING FIRM: Construction, Energy Resources, Engineering, Power Generation,
Transmission and Distribution, Project Management

Hydro-Québec International (HQI) is a consulting engineering corporation that specializes in planning, design, construction and management of electrical power systems. HQI is a
subsidiary of a provincially-owned public utility with major energy, engineering and management contracts in 40 countries abroad.

HQI draws on the resources of three major organizations: its parent company, Hydro-
Québec; the James Bay Energy Power Corporation; and the Institut de recherche d'Hydro-
Québec (IREQ), an internationally-renowned electrical testing and research centre.

Hydro-Québec International has contracts in Africa, Eastern Europe, the Middle East,
Asia and the Caribbean. It has 75 staff members overseas; 35 in Canada have international
responsibilities.

HQI uses the services of engineers, accountants, economists, and MBAs specializing in
hydroelectric projects, high voltage transmission, financial planning and administration. The
firm generally employs people from Hydro-Québec. HQI maintains a data bank for internal
résumés only. HQI's web site provides a variety of information on the firm's activities and
services. [ID:5929]

IMAX Corporation

2525 Speakman Dr., Mississauga, Ontario L5K 1B1; (905) 403-6500, fax (905) 403-6450, www.imax.com

LARGE HIGH TECHNOLOGY FIRM: Camera and Projector Design, Film Distribution, Film
Production and Post Productions, Manufacturing, Media/Communications, Project Management,
Research and Development

IMAX Corporation is involved in a wide variety of out-of-home entertainment business
activities including the design, leasing, marketing, maintenance, and operation of IMAX
theatre systems; film development, production, post-production, and distribution of large-
format films; camera and projector design and manufacturing as well as ongoing research
and development.

IMAX Corporation has offices in New York, Los Angeles, Europe, Singapore, Japan,
and three subsidiaries in the US. [ID:6824]

IMP Group International Ltd.

Suite 400, 2651 Dutch Village Road, Halifax, N.S. B3L 4T1;
(902) 453-2400, fax (902) 453-6931, impaero@impgroup.com, www.impgroup.com/impaero

LARGE ENGINEERING FIRM: Accounting, Administration, Business Development, Human Resources, Project Management

IMP Group International Ltd. is a large, diversified aerospace company. The firm has entered into a joint venture with Aeroflot to construct capital projects in Russia. The projects include a hotel and conference centre. Other projects may be initiated in the future. Currently the firm employs almost 3,000 people. Offices are maintained throughout Canada and in the US, England, and Russia.

Prospective applicants must have international work experience at the international level in the hospitality industry. Knowledge of Russian or Slavic languages is not a requirement. IMP Group Inc. maintains a data bank for résumés. Their web site provides basic information on the company's activities. It is anticipated that job openings will be posted online in the future. [ID:5771]

Inco Limited

Suite 1500, 145 King Street W., Toronto, Ontario M5H 4B7;
(416) 361-7511, fax (416) 361-7781, inco@toronto.incoltd.com, www.incoltd.com

LARGE MINING FIRM: Metals, Mining

Inco Limited is the world's largest producer of nickel, supplying about one quarter of the total world demand. In addition, Inco is an important producer of copper, precious metals and cobalt. Inco's primary markets are in the US, Europe and Asia.

Inco has over 13,000 employees in 22 countries around the world. The firm has offices in Canada, the US, England, Wales, Japan, Hong Kong, France, Indonesia, Belgium, and Brazil. Inco hires personnel for all aspects of geological exploration, mining and metals production as well as for marketing and financial positions. Overseas staff are often, but not exclusively, hired locally.

The firm maintains an attractive web site that contains a wide variety of information on mining and on the company's activities. [ID:5772]

Indochina Goldfields Ltd.

Suite 900, 200 Burrard St.,
Vancouver, B.C. V6C 3L6; (604) 688-5755, fax (604) 682-2060, www.goldfields.com

LARGE MINING FIRM: Community Development, Exploration and Development, Gold and Metals Production, Mining, Project Management, Training and Technology Transfer

Indochina Goldfields Ltd. is a Canadian registered, Singapore-based mining and exploration company active in Indonesia, Burma (Myanmar), Korea, Kazakstan, Vietnam, and Fiji as well as corporate offices in Singapore and Vancouver. The company is in the process of building a major mining force in Southeast Asia through the discovery, acquisition, and development of world class copper and gold deposits.

The company's management, technical, and exploration teams are internationally drawn and have experience in project development and financing, contract negotiation, feasibility evaluation, and mineral resource exploration. Indochina Goldfields Ltd. also employs field assistants and contract geologists to support exploration and reconnaissance activities. [ID:6991]

Intelcan Technosystems Inc.

69 Auriga Drive, Nepean, Ontario K2E 7Z2;
(613) 228-1150, fax (613) 228-1149, markwhit@compuserve.com, www.intelcan.com

MID-SIZED TELECOMMUNICATIONS FIRM: Computer Systems, Engineering

Intelcan Technosystems Inc. is a diversified firm involved in the sale and implementation of multidisciplinary projects in telecommunications, solar power, civil aviation, information technology, transportation, and machinery. The company's activities include feasibility studies, design engineering, technical assistance, equipment procurement and supply, system integration, on-site and in-factory training, and ongoing operations and maintenance.

For more than 20 years, Intelcan has been active in over 60 countries. The firm currently has staff posted overseas, and an additional 40 in Canada have international responsibilities.

Candidates should have an educational background in electrical engineering or computer science, or experience as a telecommunications technician. Overseas experience and language skills are assets. Intelcan considers applications for internships, particularly in the fields of engineering and computer science. The firm maintains a data bank for résumés and a web site containing a variety of information about the company's products and services. [ID:5773]

Intercan Development Company Ltd.
Suite 900, 275 Slater Street,
Ottawa, Ontario K1P 5H9; (613) 238-6827, fax (613) 828-1373, sherifm@storm.ca

MID-SIZED BUSINESS AND MANAGEMENT COMPANY: Adult Training, Business Development, Computer Systems, Consulting, Development Assistance, Economics, Engineering, Environment, Fisheries, Human Resources, International Trade, Media/Communications, Medical Health, Micro-Enterprises, Project Management, Technical Assistance, Telecommunications, Tourism, Water Resources

Intercan Development Company Ltd. is a mid-sized firm specializing in technology transfer, international business development, management consulting, international trade, feasibility studies, and project management. The firm focuses primarily on the Middle East, Europe, and North America. Intercan Development Company Ltd. is currently developing a web site. [ID:5776]

Intercultural Systems / Systèmes interculturels (ISSI)
P.O. Box 588, Stn. B, Ottawa, Ontario K1P 5P7;
(613) 238-6169, fax (613) 238-5274, feedback@WorkingOverseas.com, www.WorkingOverseas.com

SMALL GENERAL CONSULTING FIRM: Intercultural Briefings, Publishing

Intercultural Systems / Systèmes interculturels (ISSI) is the publisher of *The Canadian Guide to Working and Living Overseas*. The firm's activities revolve around researching, writing, and marketing the guide. The author, Jean-Marc Hachey, conducts seminars and workshops on topics related to the guide, such as international employment strategies, international résumés, interviews, skills for succeeding overseas, and job hunting when you return to Canada. Clients include the Canadian International Development Agency (CIDA), the Department of Foreign Affairs and International Trade (DFAIT), professional associations, and university departments.

ISSI also operates under the name ISSI Consulting and is involved in training and consulting in project management and database design.

ISSI hires entry-level research staff for six-month terms to update *The Canadian Guide to Working and Living Overseas*. Research staff generally have a master's degree in international affairs or an MA with work, volunteer, or study experience overseas. They also possess solid writing skills, organizational abilities, and are comfortable using computers and the Internet. Bilingualism is an asset. In 1998, ISSI is recruiting research staff who have knowledge of the United States, its culture, politics, and geography and have recent extensive (more than two years) experience living in the US.

ISSI maintains a data bank for résumés and offers internship positions. ISSI's web site contains information on the book, *The Canadian Guide to Working and Living Overseas* as well as advice on international job hunting. [ID:5778]

Intermap Technologies
Human Resources, Suite 900, 645 - 7th Ave. S.W.,
Calgary, Alberta T2P 4G8; (403) 266-0900, fax (403) 265-0499, jobs@intermap.ca, www.intermap.ca

LARGE INFORMATION SYSTEMS FIRM: Consulting, Geomatics, Project Management, Software
Development

Intermap Technologies is a multinational company specializing in geomatics. The firm
provides consulting, software development, data capture and compilation, data interpretation
and analysis, and project management services.

Intermap is a multidisciplinary organization involved in all aspects of mapping. The firm
compiles spatial data sets using data acquired from satellite-borne and airborne sensors,
aerial photography and ground survey. The company provides various spatial information
solutions to a wide range of private and public sector clients.

Intermap has its headquarters in Calgary, Alberta and has worked in over 40 countries
worldwide. The firm maintains production facilities in Calgary, Alberta; Nepean, Ontario; and
Denver, Colorado.

Intermap employs some 150 professional scientists, engineers, photogrammetrists,
geologists and technicians around the world, with more than 15 per cent of the staff involved
in ongoing research and development.

Applicants should have an educational background in geology, geophysics, forestry,
computers, photogrammetry, remote sensing, or GIS. Language skills in French, Spanish,
Russian, and Arabic are an asset. Intermap technologies maintains a data bank of résumés.
Their excellent web site posts all job openings as well as information on who to contact and
what qualifications are expected. [ID:5775]

International Briefing Associates, Inc. (IBA)
116, Promenade du Portage, Hull, Québec J8X 2K1; (819) 776-9985, fax (819) 776-9776

SMALL HUMAN RESOURCES FIRM: Adult Training, Advocacy, Business Development,
Community Development, Consulting, Development Assistance, Development Education,
Exchange Programs, Human Resources, Intercultural Briefings, International Trade, Project
Management, Teaching, Technical Assistance

International Briefing Associates Inc. (IBA) provides training services for North
Americans going overseas and for people from other cultures coming to Canada. The firm
designs and delivers a variety of workshops to improve the intercultural business skills of
personnel sent overseas. Other services include research, training, transfer of technology,
conference management, monitoring, and evaluating international projects.

International Briefing Associates works in developing countries, especially in the Asian
countries of Indonesia, Malaysia, the Philippines, India, China, and Nepal. The firm has eight
Canadian-based employees.

Candidates should have international development, multicultural or race relations
training expertise, and a wide range of experience, especially with people of other cultures.
Candidates should also possess academic qualifications in cultural anthropology, crosscultural psychology, community development or international development. IBA considers
internship placements for a wide variety of skills and positions. [ID:5779]

International Petroleum Corporation (IPC)
Suite 1320, 885 West Georgia Street,
Vancouver, B.C. V6C 3E8; (604) 689-7842, fax (604) 689-4250, sandyk@namdo.com

LARGE PETROCHEMICALS FIRM: Energy Resources, Exploration and Development,
Petrochemicals

The International Petroleum Corporation (IPC) is a large, diversified petrochemicals
firm specializing in the acquisition, exploration, and production of hydrocarbons, primarily in
the Middle East and surrounding areas with particular emphasis on the Arabian Gulf region.

Through its subsidiaries, IPC currently holds 17 concessions in 11 countries with its primary operations in the UK, Libya, Sudan, Eritrea, Oman, Thailand, Malaysia, and Papua New Guinea. IPC's technical centre is located in the United Arab Emirates. [ID:5780]

International Rail Consultants
1190 Hornby Street, Vancouver, B.C. V6Z 2H6;
(604) 684-4233, fax (604) 688-5913, irc@sandwell.com, www.sandwell.com

LARGE RAILWAY TRANSPORTATION FIRM: Construction, Consulting, Development Assistance, Economics, Engineering, Logistics, Project Management, Technical Assistance

International Rail Consultants is a joint venture of BC Rail and Sandwell Inc. The firm provides comprehensive railway consulting services, from planning and engineering to commissioning both domestically and with overseas operations in China, Asia, South America, and Africa. The firm's expertise includes railway plant design and maintenance, telecommunications, capacity and network analysis, computer services, economic and feasibility analysis, training programs, railway management information systems, railway electrification, railway operations and train control, costing and tariff analysis, rolling stock procurement, rebuilding and maintenance, commercialization and privatization, and general management.

There are 10 overseas employees and 10 Canadian-based employees with international responsibilities. The firm is active in Indonesia, Thailand, China, Mozambique, Tanzania, Kenya, Bangladesh, Columbia, Venezuela and Australia.

Recruits have technical expertise, relevant experience, and are usually drawn from personnel at BC Rail and Sandwell Inc. Candidates must have a sound command of English, good communication skills, and a willingness to work as part of a team. The firm maintains a data bank for résumés. [ID:5781]

International Road Dynamics Inc. (IRD)
Suite 702, 43rd Street E., Saskatoon, Sask. S7K 3T9;
(306) 653-6600, fax (306) 242-5599, info@ird.ca, www.ird.ca

LARGE TRANSPORTATION MANUFACTURING FIRM: Accounting, Administration, Business Development, Computer Systems, Engineering, Human Resources, Project Management, Technical Assistance

International Road Dynamics Inc. (IRD) designs, manufactures, and markets integrated traffic monitoring and weight enforcement systems that enable corporations and transportation agencies to design, build, expand, monitor, enforce, and manage vehicular traffic systems and infrastructures.

Currently, IRD has over 175 employees located in Canada and the US. It also has a UK division and recently won a major contract in Brazil. Travel throughout the world can be extensive. Candidates could include marketing specialists and systems engineers with computer science, electronic or transportation engineering degrees, diplomas, or technical courses. IRD maintains a data bank for résumés.

IRD considers applications for internship positions. [ID:5782]

IPL Energy International Inc.
Suite 2900, 421 - 7th Avenue S.W.,
Calgary, Alberta T2P 2V7; (403) 231-3900, fax (403) 231-3920, www.iplenergy.com

LARGE ENERGY RESOURCES FIRM: Energy Resources, Logistics, Oil and Gas Distribution, Petrochemicals, Training and Technology Transfer

IPL Energy International Inc. participates in foreign projects that utilize technical and operating expertise in liquids transportation and natural gas distribution. One of the company's major operations is the Cusiana crude oil pipeline project in Colombia. Additional opportunities are being pursued in Latin America and the Asia-Pacific region and the company has opened a development office in Caracas, Venezuela.

IPL Energy International's Technology and Consulting Services unit presently offers pipeline operation technologies and training, supervisory control and data acquisition, computer systems, and technical support services contracts in Malaysia, Brazil, South Korea, and Mexico. [ID:7031]

ISG Technologies Inc.
Human Resources, 6509 Airport Road, Mississauga, Ontario L4V 1S7;
(905) 672-2100, fax (905) 672-2307, webmaster@isgtec.com, www.isgtec.com

LARGE MEDICAL IMAGING SOFTWARE FIRM: Accounting, Administration, Advanced Technology, Computer Systems, Engineering, Information Technologies, Management Training, Manufacturing

ISG Technologies Inc. is a world leader in the design, manufacture, and marketing of visual data processing technology for the medical imaging industry. ISG provides software to companies selling products and services in the medical imaging and informatics industry. ISG's software is currently embedded in three sectors of the industry: image production (CT scanners, MRI, nuclear medicine imaging, digital X-ray etc.); image review and diagnosis (picture archive and communication systems and hospital information systems); and image-guided surgery. ISG's products and services include: software platforms that accelerate the development of all medical imaging software applications; image-guided surgery systems that enable less intrusive surgery; radiology application software used to view, analyze and diagnose imaging information; contract engineering, involving software development of scanner operator consoles that large medical imaging companies outsource to ISG; and service and technical support, application support, clinical development, marketing support and after-sales service. The company was the recipient of the 1991 Canada Export Award.

ISG is a publicly-traded company, with over 230 employees worldwide. Applicants should have a background in software development, medical imaging, programming in C, C++, UNIX, X/Motif and Windows NT. ISG maintains a data bank for résumés. While internships are not common, the firm will make provisions for exceptional applicants.

ISG maintains an informative web site that posts full-time permanent positions under "Career Opportunities." [ID:5783]

JetForm Corporation
Human Resources, 560 Rochester Street, Ottawa, Ontario K1S 5K2;
(613) 230-3676, fax (613) 594-2944, hr@jetform.com, www.jetform.com

LARGE HIGH TECHNOLOGY FIRM: Accounting, Computer Systems, Logistics

JetForm is the world's leading provider of software and support for electronic forms and forms-routing workflow automation. With 550 employees worldwide, it has offices throughout the US, as well as in Sweden, France, Germany, the UK, Singapore, China, New Zealand, and Australia. In particular, its Australian operations are expanding.

JetForm seeks applicants not only with a background in computer science and engineering, but also in business and accounting. It offers co-op programs for students in all these fields. Its web site has a detailed careers section which includes a listing of current openings and information on its co-op program. All résumés are reviewed and kept on file for six months. [ID:7205]

John van Nostrand Associates Limited Architects & Planners (JVA)
Suite 850, 10 Saint Mary Street,
Toronto, Ontario M4Y 2W8; (416) 921-4377, fax (416) 921-0784, nostrand@inforamp.net

MID-SIZED ARCHITECTURE AND PLANNING FIRM: Architecture and Planning, Community Development, Consulting, Project Management, Technical Assistance, Water Resources

John van Nostrand Associates Limited Architects and Planners (JVA) works internationally as an architecture and planning consultant group. The firm provides project and construction management, urban planning and development, squatter upgrading, sites-and-services, housing and institutional design, water engineering and sanitation.

JVA works in southern and eastern Africa and in China. The firm has five overseas employees and eight employees in Canada with international responsibilities. Candidates should have an architecture or planning degree, previous overseas experience or travel, and language capability. [ID:5784]

KAP Resources Ltd.
Suite 1305, 1090 West Georgia Street,
Vancouver, B.C. V6E 3V7; (604) 669-7995, fax (604) 684-3499, admin@kap.com, www.kap.com

LARGE MINING FIRM: Energy Resources, Mineral Handling, Mining

KAP Resources Ltd. is primarily involved in the exploration for and development of nitrite-rich mineral resources. These minerals are then used in the production of fertilizer products and in other industrial applications. The firm is also a major producer of iodine, which has a variety of medical and industrial uses.

KAP Resources has large-scale mining operations in northern Chile. The firm is also adding to its holdings and infrastructure through the construction of nitrate and iodine plants. The firm soon expects to become the world's third largest producer of sodium nitrate.

The firm's web site contains information on its mining and processing operations and posts news releases online. [ID:5786]

Kinross Gold Corp.
57th Floor, Scotia Plaza, 40 King Street W.,
Toronto, Ontario M5H 3Y2; (416) 365-5123, fax (416) 363-6622, info@kinross.com, www.kinross.com

LARGE MINING FIRM: Exploration and Development, Gold and Metals Production, Mining

Kinross Gold Corp. is a large mining company involved in the exploration, development, and production of gold and silver. The company has production facilities in Canada, the US, and Zimbabwe; and exploration and development operations in Canada, the US, El Salvador, and Zimbabwe. The company is also in the process of financing a gold project for development on the Kamchatka Peninsula of the Russian Far East.

In 1996, Kinross Gold Corp. had 1,840 employees worldwide. [ID:6962]

Kleinfeldt Consultants Limited
Suite 100, 2400 Meadowpine Place,
Mississauga, Ontario M5N 6S2; (905) 542-1600, fax (905) 542-9210, admin@kcl.ca, www.kcl.ca

SMALL ENGINEERING FIRM: Engineering, Environment, Project Management

Kleinfeldt Consultants Limited provides consulting services in construction, civil engineering, building science, project management, and construction economics.

The majority of KCL's work is in Canada, although it has staff focused purely on Latin America. The firm's consultants work overseas in the UK, Mexico, and the Caribbean. Kleinfeldt Consultants Limited maintains a data bank for résumés. The web site provides e-mail addresses for job seekers to contact specific managers. [ID:5788]

Klohn-Crippen Consultants Ltd.
600 - 510 Burrard Street, Vancouver, B.C. V6C 3A8;
(604) 273-0311, fax (604) 279-4300, admin@rmd.klohn.com, www.klohn.com

LARGE ENGINEERING FIRM: Engineering, Project Management, Transportation, Water Resources

Klohn-Crippen Consultants is a transportation and water resource consulting engineering firm which offers services in master planning, feasibility studies, design and construction supervision, project management, procurement and financing.

The firm is active in Indonesia, Mexico, Thailand, and Vietnam. There are 50 overseas staff members and 200 Canadian-based staff with international responsibilities.

Candidates should have a minimum of two years overseas experience and a transportation and water resource background. The ability to speak other languages is an advantage but not essential. Candidates should be able to adapt to a crosscultural setting and have a flexible attitude. The firm maintains a data bank for résumés. [ID:5789]

KPMG

Suite 1000, 45 O'Connor Street, Ottawa, Ontario K1P 1A4;
(613) 560-0011, fax (613) 560-2896, www.kpmg.ca

LARGE FINANCIAL SERVICES FIRM: Accounting, Administration, Management Consulting

KPMG carries out a broad range of business, finance, tax, and accounting work for the Canadian International Development Agency (CIDA), especially in Africa. The firm also does forensic accounting work for CIDA throughout the world. It has 20 staff members overseas, and hundreds in Canada with international responsibilities. KPMG is the world's largest professional services organization, with offices in 140 countries. The firm serves many international clients in Canada.

Candidates must be chartered accountants, multilingual, have international experience, and be interested in forensic accounting. KPMG maintains a data bank for résumés. From KPMG's excellent web site you may download or request the firm's employment information disk, which provides information on career opportunities and pathways. [ID:5791]

Kyrgoil Corp.

Roslyn Building, Suite 500, 400 - 5th Avenue S.W., Calgary, Alberta T2P 0L6;
(403) 215-2400, fax (403) 215-2404, kyrgoil@cadivision.com, www.kyrgoil.com

MID-SIZED ENERGY RESOURCES FIRM: Energy Resources, Engineering, Exploration and Development, Petrochemicals, Project Management, Training and Technology Transfer

Kyrgoil Corp. is a resource company with a mandate to explore, develop, produce, refine, and market crude oil and natural gas in the Kyrgyz Republic. Using western expertise and technology, Kyrgoil Corp. and the Kyrgyz Republic are working toward energy self-sufficiency and the development of the country's hydrocarbon reserves. [ID:6995]

Lane Environment Ltd.

1663 Oxford Street, Halifax, N.S. B3H 3Z5; (902) 423-8197, fax (902) 429-8089, lane@cs.dal.ca

SMALL ENVIRONMENTAL CONSULTING FIRM: Consulting, Development Assistance, Development Education, Environment, Sustainable Development, Water Resources

Lane Environment Ltd. is a consulting firm specializing in environmental and water resource management and sustainable development planning. Recent overseas projects include an innovative biotechnology project for water pollution abatement in Egypt, expert advice for the Bangladesh Flood Action Plan, and special consultant services for environmental management and sustainability planning in Cuba.

The company has pioneered methodologies in cumulative effects assessment, environmental impact assessments, ecological risk analysis, and sustainability evaluation criteria. [ID:5792]

Lithos Corporation

1695 Laval blvd, suite 410, Laval, Québec H7S 2M2;
(514) 667-0098, fax (514) 667-0099, info@lithos.qc.ca, www.lithos.qc.ca

LARGE MINING FIRM: Exploration and Development, Gold and Metals Production, Metals Distribution, Mining

Lithos Corporation is a young, Canadian mining company with gold mines in Québec and West Africa. It owns a 50 per cent interest in a highly economic alluvial deposit in Guinea. The company intends to begin exploration and development operations in the Ivory Coast, Mali, and Burkina Faso. Lithos is forming strategic alliances with companies in South America, Japan, and the US for the production and sale of lithium metal. [ID:6996]

M.L. Cass Petroleum Corp.
Suite 620, 140 - 4th Avenue S.W., Calgary, Alberta T2P 3N3; (403) 269-5191, fax (403) 269-5375

MID-SIZED PETROLEUM EXPLORATION FIRM: Oil and Gas Exploration

M.L. Cass Petroleum Corporation is a junior oil and gas producer involved in the exploration and development of oil and natural gas in Canada and internationally. The company's strategy is to evaluate and participate in eight exploratory concessions in Australia and Pakistan, with drilling expected to commence in 1997. [ID:6992]

M.T. Ellis & Associates Ltd.
678 Southmore Drive W., Ottawa, Ontario K1V 7A1;
(613) 523-5113, fax (613) 523-8507, mtellis.consultant@sympatico.ca

MID-SIZED HUMAN RESOURCES FIRM: Adult Training, Air Transportation, Community Development, Development Education, Energy Resources, Environment, Human Resources, Information Technologies, Management Training, Micro-Enterprises, Project Management, Railways, Teaching, Water Resources

M.T. Ellis & Associates Ltd., is a human resource and organizational development consulting organization that provides education and training services to a number of sectors, including agriculture, education, energy, environment, small business, transportation, water supply, and sanitation. The firm operates in Africa, Asia, Central and North America, Europe and the Middle East, and currently employs five salaried staff overseas; an additional five stationed in Canada have international responsibilities. Short-term contractual assignments account for an additional five person-years per calendar year.

Prospective applicants should have, as a minimum, a bachelor's degree, five years of overseas working experience in developing countries, and educational and/or training experience in one or more sectors of the firm's portfolio. Analytical, organizational and language (Spanish and Eastern European) skills are an asset, as are the abilities to work as part of a team, and communicate effectively. The company maintains a data bank of résumés. [ID:5796]

MacDonald, Dettwiler and Associates Ltd.
13800 Commerce Parkway, Richmond, B.C. V6V 2J3;
(604) 278-3411, fax (604) 278-2117, jobs@mda.ca, www.mda.ca

LARGE HIGH TECHNOLOGY FIRM: Computer Systems, Software Development, Systems Engineering

MacDonald Dettwiler is one of Canada's largest export-oriented systems engineering and software companies. Our advanced system solutions merge state of the art software technology with real-world expertise in satellite and airborne remote sensing, image mapping, spatial data information, transportation management systems, space programs, and defence applications.

MDA employees work in an ISO 9001-certified environment to create solutions for customers in over 20 countries. MDA has about 20 salaried staff overseas, owns a subsidiary company with a staff of 75 in the UK, and employs about 650 engineering, technical and support staff in offices located in Richmond, B.C., Ottawa, and Halifax.

Prospective applicants must be highly motivated and possess relevant educational background and experience in one or more of the following fields: remote sensing, software engineering, systems engineering or specific software development. New technologies and applications are under constant development, enhancing and changing the way information is acquired, assessed, and used.

MDA considers work term assignments for co-op students and interns in image analysis and classification, dimensional visualization, algorithm development, and PC/NT based applications using Java, C++ and Borland. The firm also maintains a data bank for résumés.

MDA's excellent web site contains a wide variety of useful information about the company, its products, services, and activities. Employment opportunities are also posted online. [ID:5797]

Macleod Dixon

Suite 3700, 400 - 3rd Ave. S.W., Calgary, Alberta T2P 4H2;
(403) 267-8222, fax (403) 264-5973, calgary@macleoddixon.com, www.macleoddixon.com

MID-SIZED LAW FIRM: International Trade, Law

Macleod Dixon is one of western Canada's largest law firms whose practice has continually evolved to reflect the interests of its clients. The firm provides legal services and advice to Canadian and international clients engaged in the energy, mining, financial, trade, technology, and service sectors within Canada, the Commonwealth of Independent States, Mongolia, South America, and many other countries. The firm has offices in Calgary, Toronto, Moscow, Almaty, Kazakstan, and Caracas, Venezuela.

Prospective applicants must have a relevant professional designation with a specialty in international trade, languages, and excellent crosscultural and interpersonal skills. Macleod Dixon maintains a data bank for résumés. [ID:5798]

Malkam Consultants Ltd.

Suite 201, 1673 Carling Ave., Ottawa, Ontario K2A 1C4;
(613) 761-7440, fax (613) 761-7481, malkam@malkam.com, www.malkam.com

MID-SIZED HUMAN RESOURCES FIRM: Adult Training, Consulting, Intercultural Briefings, Teaching

Malkam Consultants is a mid-sized intercultural consulting firm that provides training designed to strengthen skills in the global marketplace. The firm offers training in two key areas—crosscultural awareness and language and communication skills to government and private-sector companies.

Malkam also provides intercultural briefings for Canadian companies operating internationally. Services are tailored to organizational needs and include: pre-departure briefings, on-arrival orientation, re-entry briefings, cultural awareness training, and seminars on crosscultural team building. Training is provided anywhere in the world it is required.

Candidates for language training positions must have teaching experience and native-like fluency in the language being taught. Candidates for intercultural briefings must have experience in the design and delivery of training programs and strong, current knowledge of the culture of the countries for which they are briefing. Malkam Consultants maintains a data bank for résumés.

Their web site posts job openings online and provides a variety of information about the company and its services. [ID:5799]

Manitoba Hydro

Export Services Department, P.O. Box 815, 820 Taylor Ave., Winnipeg, Manitoba
R3C 2P4; (204) 474-3013, fax (204) 475-7745, brstamant@hydro.mb.ca, www.hydro.mb.ca

MID-SIZED ENERGY RESOURCES FIRM: Accounting, Construction, Consulting, Engineering, Environment, Human Resources, Project Management, Technical Assistance, Telecommunications, Water Resources

Manitoba Hydro is a provincial corporation offering electrical power utility consulting and training services internationally. It has provided training to nationals in HVDC operation, maintenance, system planning, corporate planning, construction management, hydraulic generating station operations and maintenance, distribution operations and maintenance, utility interconnection agreements, etc. Manitoba Hydro has worked on a variety of international contracts including projects in China, Honduras, Zimbabwe, Egypt, and Jamaica. It has several overseas employees and various personnel working on short-term contracts in Canada and abroad.

Candidates should be engineers or senior financial or accounting staff with strong track records in their professional vocation. The company maintains an internal data bank for résumés. Manitoba Hydro has an entertaining web site that provides a wealth of information on the industry in general and the company in particular. [ID:5935]

Maple Leaf Foods International
Human Resources, 3080 Yonge Street, Suite 2000, Toronto, Ontario
M4N 3N1; (416) 480-8900, fax (416) 480-8950, info@mlfi.com, www.mlfi.com

LARGE AGRICULTURAL FIRM: Accounting, Administration, Agriculture, Business/Banking/Trade, Computer Systems, Economics, Engineering, Human Resources, International Trade, Logistics

Maple Leaf Foods International is one of the world's largest international traders and niche marketers of food and agricultural products. A member of the Maple Leaf family of companies, it develops new food products for the international market with the help of its global network of partners, including producers, processors, and retailers. One notable overseas success is its Commodities Business Group, which, among other things, has recently established alliances in China. [ID:7025]

Marshall Macklin Monaghan Limited
International Division, 80 Commerce Valley Drive E., Thornhill, Ontario
L3T 7N4; (905) 882-1100, fax (905) 882-0055, mmm@mmm.ca, www.mmm.ca

MID-SIZED ENGINEERING CONSULTING FIRM: Accounting, Administration, Business Development, Computer Systems, Engineering, Environment, Project Management, Technical Assistance, Water Resources

Marshall Macklin Monaghan Limited is a large consulting engineering firm with multidisciplinary expertise. The company has carried out assignments in the Caribbean, Africa, the Middle East, Asia, Central America, Latin America, Eastern Europe, and Turkey.

Prospective applicants should have relevant educational backgrounds and experience in the fields of civil, mechanical, electrical and structural engineering, urban design, or landscape architecture. Marshall Macklin Monaghan Limited maintains a data bank for résumés.

The firm provides a comprehensive web site that documents domestic and international experience, lists corporate services and information, and posts job openings online. [ID:5800]

Martec Recycling Corporation
P.O. Box 1011, 1490 - 885 West Georgia Street, Vancouver, B.C.
V6C 3E8; (604) 687-7088, fax (604) 687-7016, info@martec.ca, www.martec.ca

LARGE ENVIRONMENTAL FIRM: Manufacturing

Martec Recycling Corporation designs and supplies hot-in-place asphalt recycling equipment. Martec's parent company, Japan's Marubeni Corporation, is active in over 85 countries. Martec itself maintains offices in Canada and Belgium. The firm is not currently accepting job applications. Martec maintains a basic web site that provides information on the firm and its activities. [ID:5671]

MDS Inc.
100 International Blvd.,
Etobicoke, Ontario M9W 6J6; (416) 675-7661, fax (416) 213-4220, www.mdsintl.com

LARGE BIOTECHNOLOGY FIRM: Health/Medical, Laboratory Automation Systems, Laboratory Services, Medical Diagnostics, Pharmaceuticals

MDS Inc. is a health and life sciences company whose products and services are used in the prevention, diagnosis, and management of disease. The company's international activities are expanding, particularly in China where it has entered into a joint venture to provide drug research and development services. Its Pharmaceutical Services Division operates in Canada, Germany, China, Taiwan, the US, and the UK. MDS Nordion, based in Kanata,

Ontario, has growing radio-chemical and radio-pharmaceutical manufacturing operations in Europe. Approximately 20 per cent of MDS Inc.'s employees work in the US, Europe, and Asia. [ID:6982]

MedHunters
Suite 2403, 180 Dundas Street W., Toronto, Ontario M5G 1Z8;
(800) 664-0278, fax (416) 977-6128, jobs@medhunters.com, www.medhunters.com

MID-SIZED HUMAN RESOURCES FIRM: Human Resources, Medical Health

MedHunters (MH) is the sister-company of Helen Ziegler & Associates, Inc., a leading international healthcare recruitment agency. MH was founded in 1996 to provide worldwide recruitment services on the Internet for healthcare employers and professionals. MH is at the forefront of internet healthcare recruitment and has developed unique and advanced job-matching technology. MH has established links with many hospitals and employers in the USA, England, New Zealand, Singapore, and other international locations.

MedHunters maintains a web site which offers an electronic résumé data bank and international medical news. [ID:6709]

Mega Engineering Ltd.
International Division, 625 - 4th Ave. S.W., Calgary, Alberta T2P 0K2;
(403) 263-0894, fax (403) 263-6628, rrussell@cadvision.com

MID-SIZED PETROLEUM CONSULTING FIRM: Engineering, Management, Oilfield Services

Mega Engineering Ltd. provides engineering and management services for oil and gas drilling and production operations. The firm has completed overseas contracts in South America, North Africa, the Middle East, and South Asia. Mega has four overseas staff and six in Canada with international responsibilities.

Candidates should have a BSc in engineering, extensive experience in oil and gas operations, and be open to working under unusual conditions in foreign cultures. Mega Engineering maintains a data bank for résumés. [ID:5801]

Met-Chem Canada Inc. (MET-CHEM)
Suite 401, 425, boul. de Maisonneuve ouest.,
Montréal, Québec H3A 3G5; (514) 288-5211, fax (514) 288-7937, www.met-chem.com

LARGE ENGINEERING CONSULTING FIRM: Accounting, Administration, Business Development, Computer Systems, Construction, Engineering, Environment, Human Resources, Logistics, Project Management, Technical Assistance

Met-Chem Canada Inc. (MET-CHEM) provides a wide range of engineering and consulting services to the mining, metallurgical, and steel-making industries around the world. These services include conceptual and feasibility studies, basic and detailed design, project and construction management, environmental services, computer systems, procurement, start-up and commissioning, maintenance, and operations management.

The firm also offers consulting and technical services to operating mines and plants for operations improvements, plant organization and staffing, market studies and economic evaluations, implementation of management control systems, production scheduling, maintenance management, operator and management training, and long-term operations assistance. MET-CHEM is currently providing engineering and technical assistance to clients in Australia, Brazil, China, Guinea, Guyana, India, Malawi, Mexico, Sierra Leone, Turkey, Thailand, the US, and Venezuela.

The firm offers co-op placements for students majoring in various engineering disciplines. Met-Chem also maintains an excellent web site that provides general information on the firm's activities, lists past and ongoing projects by country, and posts job opportunities online. [ID:5802]

Minefinders Corporation Ltd.
Suite 904 - 675 West Hastings Street,
Vancouver, B.C. V6B 1N2; (604) 687-6263, fax (604) 688-0378, www.minefinders.com

LARGE MINING FIRM: Exploration and Development, Gold and Metals Production, Mining

Run by geologists, Minefinders is a Vancouver-based precious metals exploration and development company which has controlling interest in 16 properties in Mexico, the US, and Canada. Its main project is drilling for gold and silver in Chihuahua, Mexico. It also has projects in the state of Sonora, Mexico as well as in Nevada and Arizona in the US.

When it requires additional staff or consultants, Minefinders exclusively seeks geologists. Their web page is primarily directed towards investors, but does provide information on upcoming projects. [ID:7103]

Miramar Mining Corp.
311 West First St., North Vancouver, B.C. V7M 1B5;
(800) 663-8780, fax (604) 980-0731, www.miramarmining.com

LARGE MINING FIRM: Exploration and Development, Gold and Metals Production, Mining, Sustainable Development

Miramar Mining Corp. is a Canadian gold mining company that is actively pursuing international markets. Primarily through its control of Northern Orion Explorations Ltd., the company is involved in the exploration and development of base and precious metals in Latin America, namely Cuba and Argentina. The company provides resources, personnel, and training in the implementation of its environmental policies. Miramar Mining Corp. has offices in Vancouver, Yellowknife, and Virginia City, Nevada. [ID:6977]

Mitel Corporation
Human Resources, 350 Legget Drive,
Kanata, Ontario K2K 1X3; (613) 592-2122, fax (613) 592-4784, www.mitel.com

LARGE TELECOMMUNICATIONS FIRM: Engineering, Marketing, Telecommunications

Mitel Corporation designs, manufactures, and markets systems, subsystems, and microelectronic components for sale to world markets in the telephony, computer telephony integration (CTI) and communications industries. The company's products include voice communications systems; networked voice and data systems and CTI applications; client/server telecom products; public switching systems; network enhancement and access products; custom silicon wafers, integrated and hybrid circuits, and optoelectronic devices. Mitel's leadership strategy focuses on advancing people-to-people communications in an open, distributed, and standards-based environment.

Mitel's major international centres outside Canada are in Hong Kong, Sweden, Wales, and the US. It also has a joint venture in China. In 1997, Mitel acquired Gandalf Technologies Inc., thus expanding its international presence. The web site includes current openings listed by country. [ID:5803]

Moore Corporation Limited
P.O. Box 78, First Canadian Place,
Toronto, Ontario M5X 1G5; (416) 364-2600, fax (416) 364-1667, www.moore.com

LARGE INFORMATION SYSTEMS FIRM: Accounting, Administration,
Business/Banking/Trade, Computer Systems, Human Resources

Moore Corporation Limited is a leading global partner in helping companies communicate through print and digital technologies. As a leading supplier of document-formatted information, print outsourcing, and databased marketing, Moore designs, manufactures, and delivers business communications products, services, and solutions to customers. Founded in 1882, Moore has approximately 20,000 employees and over 100 manufacturing facilities serving customers in 47 countries. Sales in 1996 were US$2.5 billion. [ID:5805]

N.D. Lea International Ltd. (NDLI)

6th Floor, 1455 West Georgia Street, Vancouver, B.C. V6G 2T3;
(604) 654-1945, fax (604) 654-1551, lea_int@istar.ca, www.lea.inter.net

MID-SIZED ENGINEERING FIRM: Computer Systems, Consulting, Engineering, Environment, Gender and Development, Human Resources, Project Management, Technical Assistance

N.D. Lea International Ltd. (NDLI) offers a broad range of international consulting services, focusing primarily on the transportation sector: highways, bridges, airports, railways, transit, public transport, ports, and multi-modal transport systems. It also engages in technical and economic feasibility studies, institutional strengthening, training, and advisory services. NDLI has completed projects in more than 40 countries and currently has overseas offices in Indonesia, Nepal, India, Thailand, China, Trinidad, Mozambique, and Albania. The firm has 50 staff members who work overseas, and an additional 100 in Canada.

Candidates should possess at minimum a bachelor's degree, and preferably a master's degree, and have expertise in highway or airport maintenance, rehabilitation planning, design, and supervision, technology transfer, training, or computer systems. Prior overseas experience and knowledge of Spanish, Portuguese or an Asian language is an asset. N.D. Lea International maintains a résumé and skills inventory data bank.

The firm maintains a very good web site that posts job opportunities and provides a variety of useful information about the company's projects. There are also a number of links to similar organizations. [ID:5806]

National Bank of Canada/Banque Nationale du Canada

International Division, 5th Floor, 600, de la Gauchetiere W., Montréal, Québec H3B 4L3;
(514) 394-6400, fax (514) 394-8276, telnat@bnc.ca, www.nbc.ca (English) or www.bnc.ca (French)

MID-SIZED FINANCIAL SERVICES FIRM: Business/Banking/Trade, Business Development

The National Bank of Canada is Canada's sixth largest chartered bank, with assets valued at approximately $50 billion and over 12,000 employees. With headquarters in Montréal, the bank maintains offices and provides services in each of the Canadian provinces. It offers an extensive range of financial services to individuals, commercial enterprises, financial institutions and governments in Canada and abroad.

Through its international division, the bank offers importers and exporters services to support and enhance cross-border activities. Such services include foreign exchange operations, traveller's cheques, drafts and money orders, funds transfer, foreign currency accounts, collections, precious metals, import/export financing, letters of credit and letters of guarantee. The international division has more than 100 employees working in New York, London, Paris, Nassau, Hong Kong, Tokyo, Taipei, Seoul, Singapore, and Shanghai

Candidates must have an MBA in finance and economics and speak English and French. Credit experience is preferred. The bank maintains a data bank for résumés. Their web site provides information about online banking services and corporate structure. [ID:5807]

Nawitka Resource Consultants Ltd.

International Division, 840 Cormorant Street,
Victoria, B.C. V8W 1R1; (250) 384-5133, fax (250) 384-1841, www.cfbc.bc.ca/Nawitka.html

SMALL FORESTRY CONSULTING FIRM: Consulting, Development Assistance, Economics, Environment, Forestry

Founded in 1974, Nawitka is a small firm of senior forest-sector analysts. It offers services in applied research and development studies, policy studies and institutional reform, economics, resource management, conservation, and (with associates) geographic information systems (GIS) services. The firm has conducted planning, research, monitoring, and evaluation studies on forestry sector projects in over 40 countries and is on the international forestry advisors roster for the Canadian International Development Agency (CIDA) and other international agencies.

Nawitka has two staff working overseas and four in Canada who have international responsibilities. The firm seeks long-term associations with experienced consultants and also offers short-term internships, depending on current work in Canada or abroad. Candidates should have postgraduate degrees in forest economics, biometrics and economics on microcomputers, and experience in the field. French or Spanish and overseas experience are desirable. The firm maintains a data bank for résumés. [ID:5808]

Nelson Gold Corp.

Suite 404, 347 Bay Street, Toronto, Ontario M5H 2R7;
(416) 777-1167, fax (416) 777-1871, info@nelsongold.com, www.nelsongold.com

LARGE MINING FIRM: Metals

Nelson Gold is a Toronto-based mining company with interests in Central Asia. It is exploring sites in Tajikstan, Kyrgyzstan, Russia, the CIS, Africa, and Mali. Its main focus has been the start-up production of a gold mine in Kyrgyzstan. It also has offices in the UK, Kazakstan, and Uzbekistan. [ID:6988]

Newbridge Networks Corp.

600 March Road, P.O. Box 13600,
Ottawa, Ontario K2K 2E6; (613) 591-3600, fax (613) 599-3615, www.newbridge.com

LARGE TELECOMMUNICATIONS FIRM: Computer Systems, Consulting

Newbridge Networks Corp. is a large telecommunications firm specializing in the development of computer communications equipment. It provides multimedia communication solutions to organizations around the world. It is a global leader in the design, manufacture, marketing, and support of software-driven advanced digital networks for wide area and LAN applications.

With 6,400 employees worldwide, the company has extensive international operations. Present in over 100 countries, it has research and development, sales, support, and manufacturing facilities throughout Canada, the US, Latin America, Europe, the Middle East, Africa, Asia, and Australia.

Thirty per cent of Newbridge's workforce works on research and development. The career section of its web site provides detailed instructions for applying for positions as well as frequently updated worldwide job listings. Positions generally require a background in electrical engineering or software; overseas experience is not required, but fluency in local language(s) is. Management positions require experience in a high technology environment. Résumés are accepted as general applications and are kept for six months. Résumés can be faxed to 703-471-7080 for the US, 613-599-3688 for Asia, 613-599-3615 for Latin America, and +44 (0) 1633-413680 for Europe, Africa, and the Middle East. [ID:5809]

Noranda Inc.

P.O. Box 755, Suite 4100, BCE Place, 181 Bay Street, Toronto, Ontario M5J 2T3;
(416) 982-7111, fax (416) 982-7423, request@noranda.com, www.noranda.com

LARGE NATURAL RESOURCES FIRM: Accounting, Administration, Advocacy, Business
Development, Computer Systems, Development Education, Energy Resources, Engineering,
Environment, Forestry, Human Resources, International Trade, Media/Communications, Mining,
Oil and Gas Exploration, Project Management

Noranda Inc. is a diversified natural resources company that operates in three areas: forest products, mining and metals, and oil and gas. In the mining and metals division, the company's mining, smelting, refining, and recycling group produces a significant share of the world's zinc, nickel, copper, gold, silver, aluminium, lead, wire rope, cobalt, and sulphuric acid.

Noranda's Mining and Metals group operates 22 mines, 13 metallurgical plants and 12 fabricating facilities in Canada, the US, the Dominican Republic, Chile, and Norway. The company's forest products division operates several mills in Canada, the US, and the UK. Noranda's oil and gas sector is comprised of two companies that explore for, develop, and produce natural gas liquids and crude oil in Canada, the US, Argentina, Venezuela, Guatemala, and Australia. Noranda employs more than 33,000 people at operations and sales offices around the world.

The company maintains a web site that provides detailed information on its activities. Information concerning job opportunities and contact information can be obtained by accessing the "We Listen" web page on their site. [ID:5810]

Norcen Energy Resources Ltd.
International Division, P.O. Box 2595, Station M,
Calgary, Alberta T2P 4V4; (403) 231-0111, fax (403) 231-0302

LARGE ENERGY RESOURCES FIRM: Energy Resources, Oil and Gas Exploration

Norcen Energy Resources Ltd. is a large, integrated firm specializing in the exploration and production of oil and natural gas. The company currently has producing operations in Western Canada, the Gulf of Mexico of the US, Venezuela, and Argentina. [ID:5811]

Norenco Associated Ltd.
671 Kenwood Road W., Vancouver, B.C. V7S 1S7; (604) 925-0570, fax (604) 925-0571

SMALL ENGINEERING CONSULTING FIRM: Engineering Management

Norenco Associated Ltd. offers professional services for civil engineering and transportation projects. Areas of expertise include: feasibility studies; project planning; engineering management; project management; quality assurance; computer technology. Training and technology transfer are main components of the firm's international projects. Norenco provides consulting services for a wide range of projects in Canada and internationally in Africa, Asia and Latin America. [ID:5812]

Nortel (Northern Telecom)
8200 Dixie Road, Suite 100,
Brampton, Ontario L6T 5P6; (905) 863-0000, fax (905) 863-8505, www.nortel.com

LARGE TELECOMMUNICATIONS FIRM: Engineering, Marketing, Research and Development, Telecommunications

Nortel (Northern Telecom) is a leading global manufacturer of telecommunications equipment, providing products and services to public and private institutions, utilities, cable television companies, Internet providers, and local, long-distance, cellular mobile, and PCS communications companies. It works with customers in more than 150 countries to design, build, and integrate their communication products and advanced digital networks.

Nortel's technology, research, and development organization has made it a world leader in the design of advanced telecommunications systems. Nortel's research capabilities around the world include a network of research and development facilities, affiliated joint ventures, and collaborations fostering innovative product development and advanced design research in 16 countries.

Nortel has revenues in excess of US$12.8 billion and has approximately 70,000 employees. Recent overseas projects have included building a network infrastructure in Colombia, supplying fixed wireless equipment to Mexico, and investing in a large-scale research and development, manufacturing, sales and service organization in China. It has major subsidiaries in the US, Europe, and Asia. [ID:5813]

Northern Orion Explorations Ltd.
311 West First St., North Vancouver, B.C. V7M 1B5; (604) 980-0573,
fax (604) 980-0731, norion@miramarmining.com, www.miramarmining.com/orion/orion.html

LARGE MINING FIRM: Exploration and Development, Gold and Metals Production, Mining, Sustainable Development

Northern Orion Explorations Ltd. is a premier mineral and exploration development company with international operations in Latin America ranging from the pre-feasibility stage to mine construction. The company has begun construction in Cuba of a new producing mine and has planned a strategic program of airborne geophysics, geochemical sampling, and trenching. In Argentina, the company has interests in over 30 exploration projects. Northern Orion Explorations Ltd. conducts environmental assessments in the prefeasibility and feasibility studies at its advanced stage projects.

Northern Orion Explorations Ltd. has exploration offices in Buenos Aires, Mendoza, and Havana. [ID:6976]

Northwest Hydraulic Consultants (NHC)
Manager, International Operations, 2 - 40 Gostick Place, North Vancouver, B.C.
V7M 3G2; (604) 980-6011, fax (604) 980-9264, okun@nhc-van.com, www.eskimo.com/~nhc

LARGE WATER RESOURCES FIRM: Consulting, Development Assistance, Engineering, Environment, Project Management, Technical Assistance, Water Resources

Northwest Hydraulic Consultants (NHC) specializes in water resource development and management. The firm's technical experience includes basin resource planning, management of water resources, irrigation, drainage and flood control, agricultural planning and analysis, watershed management, hydrology, hydraulics and river engineering, design of hydraulic structures, hydrometric assessment, technology and knowledge transfer, and project management.

NHC has acquired experience through more than 1,700 projects in Canada, the US, Asia, Africa, and Latin America. The firm has eight employees who work overseas and 10 in Canada who have international responsibilities.

Candidates must have a postgraduate degree and domestic experience in their field of specialization, or a BSc, experience in developing countries, and high technical competence. The firm gives preference to people who have volunteered for overseas assignments and possess strong technical and interpersonal skills. NHC maintains a data bank for résumés. They accept interns throughout the year, depending upon project opportunities and suitability of the candidates. The firm maintains a web site that provides information on its services and activities. [ID:5815]

NOVA Gas International Ltd. (NGI)
645-7th Ave. S.W., Calgary, Alberta T2P 4G8; (403) 290-6000, fax (403) 290-6300, www.nova.ca

LARGE ENERGY RESOURCES FIRM: Energy Resources, Oil and Gas Distribution, Project Management

NOVA Gas International Ltd. is a wholly-owned subsidiary of NOVA Corporation. The firm develops equity investments in natural gas ventures worldwide and provides pipeline and related project management, design engineering, and operating expertise. NGI has undertaken projects in several regions, including Asia Pacific, Latin America, the Middle East, North America, and Europe.

NOVA Gas International Ltd. currently employs 247 salaried staff in Canada and overseas. Prospective applicants should have relevant education and experience, a willingness to relocate, and appropriate language/crosscultural skills. [ID:6546]

Novaport Vaughan International Consultants Ltd.
P.O. Box 3662, Halifax, N.S. B3J 3K6;
(902) 429-9632, fax (902) 422-0950, johnjay@netcom.ca, www.mgnet.ca/novaport.html

SMALL TRANSPORTATION CONSULTING FIRM: Consulting, Engineering, Environment, Project Management

Novaport Vaughan International Consultants Ltd., incorporated in 1992, is a merger of Novaport Limited and Vaughan Engineering Associates' international practice. The firm undertakes all aspects of port and transportation consulting including site selection, feasibility studies, environmental assessments, design, construction and project management, institutional strengthening, and training.

Novaport Vaughan has completed contracts in 10 countries in the Caribbean, and has also undertaken projects in Pakistan and Saudi Arabia. In addition to local contractors, the company has worked under the World Bank, the Canadian International Development Agency (CIDA), the Caribbean Development Bank and other international organizations. The firm has approximately 100 employees in Canada with international responsibilities, and one salaried staff member overseas.

Candidates should have degrees in civil engineering, and marine design or construction experience. The firm considers engineering internships during the summer months. Novaport Vaughan maintains a data bank for résumés. Their web site provides information on their activities and on a number of international contracts and activities. [ID:5817]

O & T Agdevco Ltd.
Suite 101, 320 Gardner Park Road, Regina, Sask.
S4V 1R9; (306) 721-8077, fax (306) 721-6140, otagdevco@cabler.cableregina.com

MID-SIZED AGRICULTURAL CONSULTING FIRM: Agriculture, International Trade, Project Management

O & T Agdevco Ltd. provides consulting and management services to both institutional and commercial agricultural clients. These services include project identification, design and development, operational and business management, procurement, and training.

Current overseas projects include large scale integrated poultry and commercial dairy production, mechanized crop production, small holder business development, and institutional support programs. The firm has 22 overseas employees and four Canadian employees with international responsibilities.

Candidates should be graduates in agricultural, environmental, or related disciplines and/or have appropriate experience related to international development projects or agribusiness management. O & T Agdevco maintains a data bank for résumés. [ID:5818]

Ocelot Energy Inc.
Suite 3000, West Tower, Petro-Canada Centre, 150-6th Ave. S.W.,
Calgary, Alberta T2P 3Y7; (403) 299-5700, fax (403) 299-5691, ocelot@ocelot.ca, www.ocelot.ca

LARGE ENERGY RESOURCES FIRM: Energy Resources

Ocelot Energy Inc. is an independent, financially solid, publicly traded company focused on identification and development of projects which create long-term value and provide substantial sustainable earnings for shareholders. Ocelot is engaged primarily in the exploration, production and marketing of oil and natural gas and has properties and development projects in North America and overseas. To date, the firm has advanced a Tanzanian gas development project, committed to three oil projects in Gabon, and established a London office to co-ordinate Ocelot's international prospecting.

Ocelot employs 10 people at offices in Dar Es Salaam, Libreville, and London. In addition, many of the 66 head office employees in Calgary have international responsibilities. The firm considers internships throughout the year; honorariums are based upon the candidate's experience and the position filled. The firm maintains a data bank for résumés. [ID:5819]

Ontario Hydro International Inc. (OHII)
Ontario Hydro International, Suite A14, 700 University Ave., Toronto, Ontario
M5G 1X6; (416) 506-4700, fax (416) 506-4684, tomlinson.j@hydro.on.ca, www.hydro.on.ca

MID-SIZED ENERGY RESOURCES FIRM: Energy Resources, Engineering, Environment, Project Management, Technical Assistance

Ontario Hydro International Inc. (OHII) markets the services of Ontario Hydro worldwide. Its international services reflect the full range of Ontario Hydro's experience and expertise and have been developed, applied, and refined in the daily operations of Ontario Hydro. OHII has been providing products, consulting, training, engineering, and construction services in all aspects of electric power to utilities around the world for over 35 years.

Having already served customers in more than 50 countries worldwide, OHII continues to pursue opportunities in international power plant development and operations. In addition, OHII offers integrated environmental services for all phases of electrical generation, transmission and operation, from planning to design and construction, through to commissioning, operation, and decommissioning. Ontario Hydro International also has recognized expertise in energy management.

OHII maintains a web site that outlines corporate structure and activities. [ID:5947]

Opim Consultants Inc.
355 Power Road, Edmunston, N.B. E3V 3V7;
(506) 739-7378, fax (506) 735-5729, opim@nbnet.nb.ca, www.terra-tech.nb.ca

MID-SIZED GENERAL CONSULTING FIRM: Forestry, Human Resources, Pulp and Paper, Technical Assistance

Opim Consultants Inc. provides forest industry services in management, operations, technology, training, and procurement. The firm has undertaken contracts in Guyana, Zaire, Zimbabwe, Congo, Gabon, Côte d'Ivoire, Cameroon, Malaysia, Indonesia, the Philippines, Thailand, India and Singapore, and currently has two salaried staff overseas and seven in Canada who have international responsibilities.

Prospective applicants should have an engineering background with management, procurement, and training experience. Bilingualism and international experience are assets. Opim Consultants maintains a data bank for résumés.

Opim also maintains a comprehensive web site that provides detailed information on its activities as well as biographies of employees. [ID:5820]

P.A. Conseils International (Canada) Inc.
Suite 800, 1 Westmount Square,
Montréal, Québec H3Z 2P9; (514) 932-8050, fax (514) 932-8960, conseil@cam.org

LARGE GENERAL CONSULTING FIRM: Accounting, Administration, Adult Training, Agriculture, Business/Banking/Trade, Business Development, Computer Systems, Consulting, Development Assistance, Development Education, Economics, Human Resources, Medical Health, Micro-Enterprises, Project Management, Technical Assistance

P.A. Conseils International (Canada) Inc. provides consulting services in data processing, economics, management, training and education, planning, accounting and financial diagnostics. The firm has 10 employees overseas and four in Canada with international responsibilities.

Candidates should have a PhD or master's degree combined with pertinent experience. P.A. Conseils International maintains a data bank for résumés. The firm anticipates having a web site in the near future. [ID:5821]

The Partners Film Company Limited
53 Ontario Street, Toronto, Ontario M5A 2V1; (416) 869-3500, fax (416) 869-3365, pfcl@inforamp.net

MID-SIZED COMMUNICATIONS FIRM: Film Production and Post Productions, Media/Communications

The Partners Film Company Limited is a large firm specializing in commercial production. The firm currently has an affiliate in Mexico City and several others in the US. Typically, key Canadian personnel are required for production in different parts of the world in conjunction with local and foreign freelance crews.

The firm offers entry level positions for freelance production assistants. Applicants should have some knowledge of film production. [ID:5822]

Pasteur Mérieux Connaught Canada
Human Resources Division, 1755 Steeles Ave. W.,
North York, Ontario M2R 3T4; (416) 667-2701, fax (416) 667-0313, www.pmc-vacc.com

LARGE BIOTECHNOLOGY FIRM: Medical Health, Research and Development

Pasteur Mérieux Connaught (Rhône-Poulenc Group) is the world's largest vaccine manufacturer. Pasteur Mérieux Connaught Canada is Canada's leading vaccine supplier and the nation's largest fully-integrated biotechnology research company. The firm contributes to the improvement of human health by creating superior immunological products for the prevention and treatment of infectious diseases and cancers.

The firm offers a stimulating work environment and a generous benefits package. As a multidisciplinary company, job openings may arise in any number of sectors.

The firm's excellent web site contains everything from health tips for travellers to career opportunities. [ID:5709]

Petro-Canada
P.O. Box 2844, Calgary, Alberta T2P 3E3; (403) 296-8000,
fax (403) 296-3030, investor@petro-canada.ca, www.petro-canada.ca

LARGE PETROCHEMICALS FIRM: Energy Resources, Marketing, Oil and Gas Exploration, Petrochemicals, Research and Development, Transportation

Petro-Canada is a major Canadian oil and gas company and a leader in the Canadian petroleum industry. Petro-Canada explores for, develops, produces, and markets crude oil, natural gas, and natural gas liquids. In addition, the company transports, refines, distributes, and markets petroleum products and related goods and services.

Petro-Canada operates an oil development and exploration project in Algeria and owns a working interest in two oil fields in the Norwegian sector of the North Sea. The company expects to continue exploration and development activities in these regions in the coming years. [ID:6967]

Phair-Sutherland Consulting
Suite 301, 350 Oxford Street W., London, Ontario
N6J 1T3; (519) 472-2029, fax (519) 472-0470, psconsulting@compuserve.com

MID-SIZED INFORMATION SERVICES FIRM: Consulting, Telecommunications

Phair-Sutherland Consulting is a mid-sized consulting firm specializing in strategic planning, new product and new market development strategies and management consulting for the telecommunications industry. The firm has extensive international experience and is currently active in Mexico, Colombia, Ecuador, Canada, and the US. [ID:5823]

Photosur Géomat International Inc. (PGI)
Bureau 300, 5160, boul. Decarie, Montréal, Québec H3X 2H9;
(514) 369-5000, fax (514) 369-5059, pgi@photosur.com, www.photosur.com

LARGE EARTH SCIENCES FIRM: Adult Training, Aerospace Technology, Computer Systems, Consulting, Development Assistance, Energy Resources, Environment, Fisheries, Forestry, Logistics, Photo Mapping, Project Management, Technical Assistance, Water Resources

Photosur Géomat International Inc. (PGI) is a subsidiary of the SSiG Group whose shareholders include SNC-Lavalin, BCE Capital, Technology Horizons, and Bergecap. It uses geomatic services to conduct feasibility studies and to build and install turnkey projects. It also provides information management services, cadastre and facilities management, system design and implementation, data capture, and technology transfer.

PGI provides services in geographic information systems (GIS), mapping, remote sensing, land management consulting, natural resources management, and the design and maintenance of public and private infrastructures. It designs, develops, installs, and runs GIS systems. It also provides specialized training. Its clients include all levels of governments, public utilities, businesses and international development agencies.

PGI has international projects in Latin America, West Africa, and Eastern Europe. It has 100 employees who work both overseas and in Canada with international responsibilities.

Candidates should have a bachelor's or master's degree related to natural resources, computer sciences, or environmental sciences such as forestry, soil, water, and air. They should also possess some background in the use of remote sensing, GIS, digital mapping, and other advanced computer techniques. The company maintains a data bank for résumés.
[ID:5824]

Piteau Associates
Suite 215, 260 West Esplanade, North Vancouver, B.C.
V7M 3G7; (604) 986-8551, fax (604) 985-7286, astewart@piteau.com

MID-SIZED GENERAL CONSULTING FIRM: Consulting, Engineering, Hydrographic Surveys, Mining

Piteau Associates is a mid-sized consulting company specializing in domestic and overseas geotechnical engineering, groundwater surveys, mining projects, and infrastructural projects. Currently, some employees travel overseas for brief projects, but there are no overseas postings. Only experienced engineers are sent on overseas projects. [ID:5825]

Placer Dome Inc.
P.O. Box 49330, Bentall Postal Station, 1600 - 1055 Dunsmuir Street, Vancouver, B.C.
V7X 1P1; (604) 682-7082, fax (604) 682-7092, goldpanner@placerdome.com, www.placerdome.com

LARGE MINING FIRM: Accounting, Administration, Business Development, Community Development, Computer Systems, Construction, Development Assistance, Economics, Engineering, Environment, Human Resources, Human Rights, Media/Communications, Project Management, Sustainable Development

Placer Dome is a global mining company whose primary concern is the exploration for, and extraction of, gold. In addition to interests in four mines in Canada, the firm has international operations in the US, Australia, Chile and Papua New Guinea. Placer Dome maintains corporate international offices in Santiago and Sydney.

The firm also maintains a web site that posts job opportunities online and provides general information about the company's activities. [ID:5826]

PLAN:NET 2000 Limited
201- 1225A Kensington Road N.W., Calgary, Alberta T2N 3P8;
(403) 270-0217, fax (403) 270-8672, plannet@cadvision.com, www.cadvision.com/plannet

MID-SIZED MANAGEMENT CONSULTING FIRM: Community Development, Consulting, Development Assistance, Development Education, Environment, Gender and Development, Micro-Enterprises, Project Management, Technical Assistance, Water Resources

PLAN:NET 2000 Limited provides planning, management, monitoring, and evaluation services to governments, institutions, nongovernmental organizations, and corporations on a wide range of policy, program, and project activities.

PLAN:NET has demonstrated expertise in the following areas: program evaluation, results-based management, community development and planning, program planning, social and environmental impact assessment, and the design and implementation of university-level planning programs.

A small core of staff is reinforced by a current roster of 30 professionals. They have a wide range of national and international experience. PLAN:NET 2000 personnel have provided services in Nepal, China, Sri Lanka, India, Bangladesh, Thailand, Malaysia, Indonesia, Korea, Philippines, Taiwan, Kenya, Tanzania, Ethiopia, Ghana, Senegal, Egypt, Honduras, El Salvador, Bolivia, Nicaragua, Chile, Venezuela, Brazil, Colombia, Guyana, Bahamas, Barbados, St. Lucia, St. Vincent, Jamaica, Trinidad, and Canada. No personnel are permanently stationed overseas; staff are typically sent abroad on short-term assignments.

PLAN:NET maintains a web site that offers information on its programs and services.
[ID:5727]

Policy Research International Inc. (PRI)

6 Beechwood Ave., Ottawa, Ontario K1L 8B4;
(613) 746-2554, fax (613) 744-4899, arath@pri.on.ca, www.pri.on.ca

SMALL GENERAL CONSULTING FIRM: Consulting, Development Education, Economics,
Energy Resources, Environment, Human Resources, Project Management, Technical Assistance

Policy Research International Inc. (PRI) is a small consulting firm specializing in research, strategy, policy and program design, and evaluation needs for international development projects. The firm has expertise in the areas of economics, environment, science and technology, energy, education, and health policy. For large projects, PRI relies on strategic partnerships with associates in Europe, the US, Mexico, India, Kenya, and Canada.

All senior consultants with PRI have postgraduate degrees and over 20 years of working experience in the areas of economics, policy analysis, business and strategic planning, organizational development, trade, and technology and are competent in a number of languages other than English. Similar profiles are sought for junior consultants; naturally less experience is expected. PRI considers applications for internships in the fields of computer applications, research, and communications. PRI maintains a web site and a data bank for résumés. [ID:5828]

Potash & Phosphate Institute of Canada (PPIC)

Suite 704, CN Tower, Midtown Plaza,
Saskatoon, Sask. S7K 1J5; (306) 652-3535, fax (306) 664-8941, ldoell@ppi-far.com

MID-SIZED AGRICULTURAL INSTITUTE: Agriculture

The Potash & Phosphate Institute of Canada (PPIC) administers an active international agronomic research and education program which emphasizes the importance of balanced fertilization in sustainable crop production systems. PPIC's Saskatoon headquarters links programs in more than 20 countries through offices and consultancies in Bangladesh, Brazil, Canada, China, Ecuador, Hong Kong, Pakistan, India, Mexico, Japan, Singapore, and the US

The institute has 15 professional employees overseas and four Canadian-based employees with international responsibilities. Candidates must possess postgraduate training, preferably a PhD in agronomy, soil fertility or plant nutrition. Demonstrated interest in international agriculture development and related experience is a prerequisite for employment. [ID:5829]

Precision Drilling Corp.

Suite 700, 112 - 4 Avenue S.W., Calgary, Alberta T2P 0H3;
(403) 264-4882, fax (403) 266-1480, info@precision.com, www.precisiondrilling.com

LARGE CUSTOMER SERVICES FIRM: Drilling Services, Industrial Services, Oilfield Services

Precision Drilling Corp. provides comprehensive services to the oil and gas exploration and production sector throughout western Canada and internationally. The company operates drilling programs for heavy oil in Venezuela, Oman, and Azerbaijan and has an agreement with a Chinese company for the exclusive distribution of mud pumps throughout North America. [ID:7054]

Premdor Inc.

1600 Britania Road E., Mississauga, Ontario L4W 1J2; (905) 670-6500, fax (905) 670-6520

LARGE MANUFACTURING FIRM: Building Supplies, Manufacturing, Merchandising

Premdor Inc. is among the largest manufacturers and merchandisers of doors in the world. The company manufactures, merchandises, and sells its products to large distributors, jobbers, home-centre chains, and wholesale and retail building supply dealers worldwide.

Premdor Inc. has 4,250 employees in over 40 locations across five countries. The company's manufacturing facilities in Mexico, France, the UK, the US, and Canada provide exports to North and South America and western and eastern Europe.

Premdor Inc. is presently concentrating on developing export markets in the Asia Pacific region and has added sales representation in Russia, the Czech Republic, Israel, and Turkey. [ID:6983]

Proctor & Redfern International Limited
45 Green Belt Drive, Don Mills, Ontario M3C 3K3;
(416) 445-3600, fax (416) 445-5276, fcmoir@pandr.com or rtoledo@pandr.com

SMALL GENERAL CONSULTING FIRM: Construction, Consulting, Economics, Engineering, Environment, Gender and Development, Geophysics, Information Technologies, Water Resources

Established in 1912 Proctor & Redfern International Ltd. is one of Canada's oldest consulting engineering firms. The firm is wholly-owned by its employees and consists of approximately 325 staff, of whom some 175 are professional. Proctor & Redfern International Ltd. operates from seven regional offices in Canada and two international offices, one in Managua, Nicaragua and one in Quito, Ecuador. As part of their corporate strategy to prepare Proctor & Redfern for the next century, international efforts have been focused on Latin America and the Caribbean. The firm offers consulting services in the following areas: water supply and distribution, water treatment technology, wastewater treatment, sewerage conveyance and disposal systems, marine outfalls, water pollution control, environmental audits, assessments, incinerators, liquids, waste, PCB treatment, disposal, project management, hazardous waste recycling, information technology services, and computer systems/software design.

Currently, Proctor & Redfern International Ltd., is operating in Canada, Bermuda, the Bahamas, Latin America, and the Caribbean. [ID:5833]

Project Services International
102, Promenade du Portage, Hull, Québec J8X 2K1; (819) 771-8521, fax (819) 776-9973

MID-SIZED GENERAL CONSULTING FIRM: Consulting, Logistics, Project Management

Project Services International is a mid-sized consulting firm specializing in project design, planning, and evaluation. The firm currently has eight salaried staff in Canada and two overseas in Thailand and Barbados. Prospective applicants should have education and experience in economics, business, sciences, or engineering. Project Services International maintains a data bank for résumés. [ID:5834]

PWA Corporation
Suite 2800, 700 - 2nd Street S.W.,
Calgary, Alberta T2P 2W2; (403) 294-2000, fax (403) 294-6115, www.cdnair.ca

LARGE TRANSPORTATION SERVICES FIRM: Air Transportation, Tourism

Canadian Airlines is a broadly-held Canadian holding company whose investments are primarily in the airline industry. Canadian Airlines has assembled a network of global partners, and with these partners offers air service to over 300 North American destinations, and more than 500 international destinations. PWA is also involved in the leisure tour business. The firm currently has 16,000 employees stationed in Canada and overseas.

PWA maintains a web site that offers information on flight schedules, frequent flyer programs and career opportunities. [ID:5835]

QuébecTél International
Développement des marchés internationaux, 6, rue Jules-A-Brillant, Rimouski, Québec
G5L 7E4; (418) 722-5500, fax (418) 722-2034, psamsom@quebectel.qc.ca, www.quebectel.qc.ca

MID-SIZED TELECOMMUNICATIONS FIRM: Business Development, Consulting, Human Resources, International Trade, Project Management, Telecommunications

QuébecTel is a large telecommunications firm with six primary fields of expertise: technology/telecommunications, human resources management, finance/accounting, marketing, data processing, and logistics.

QuébecTel has developed technological expertise, particularly in the field of telecommunications technology, of considerable value to foreign countries. While its international operations are currently small, the firm has completed a number of projects in West Africa and Latin America.

Overseas staff placements vary and are on a contractual basis. Prospective applicants should have a background in telecommunications and knowledge of French, English and Spanish. QuébecTel considers applications for internships throughout the year, in a number of fields including finance, project management, market development, and international sales. QuébecTel's web site offers a variety of information, in French, on the company's services. [ID:5836]

RADARSAT International
Human Resources, 3851 Shell Road, Suite 200,
Richmond, B.C. V6X 2W2; (604) 231-4916, fax (604) 231-4999, info@rsi.ca, www.rsi.ca

LARGE ENVIRONMENTAL FIRM: Aerial Surveys, Aerospace Technology, Computer Systems, Engineering

RADARSAT International Inc., a private Canadian company, was established in 1989 to market, process, and distribute satellite data gathered by RADARSAT. RADARSAT is an advanced earth observation satellite project developed in Canada to monitor environmental change and to support resource sustainability. Led by the Canadian Space Agency and supported by strong industry, provincial governments, and international partnerships, the RADARSAT program upholds Canada's tradition of global leadership in the development of remote sensing technology.

Overseas projects have included a land-use monitoring study in Costa Rica, an agricultural landscape monitoring study in China, a natural resource management project in Brazil, and a landcover mapping project in Africa. [ID:5838]

Ranger Oil Limited
Personnel Manager, Suite 1600, 321 - 6th Ave. S.W., Calgary, Alberta
T2P 3H3; (403) 232-5200, fax (403) 263-0090, InRel@calgary.ranger-oil.com, www.ranger-oil.com

LARGE PETROCHEMICALS FIRM: Energy Resources, Oil and Gas Exploration, Petrochemicals

Ranger Oil Limited is a large petrochemicals firm involved in the exploration for and production of oil and natural gas. Currently, the firm has international operations in Canada, the UK for the North Sea, Angola, Namibia, Ecuador, Peru, and the US along the Gulf of Mexico.

The firm has 100 salaried staff based in Canada and an additional 80 posted overseas. Prospective applicants should have a relevant professional designation and some overseas experience. Overseas staff are typically recruited locally, but some international opportunities do exist. Ranger Oil maintains a web site that provides information on the firm's international activities on a country-by-country basis. [ID:5840]

Rayrock Yellowknife Resources Inc.
Suite 500, 30 Soudan Ave., Toronto, Ontario
M4S 1V6; (416) 489-0022, fax (416) 489-0096, mkangas@total.net

LARGE MINING FIRM: Accounting, Administration, Computer Systems, Construction, Engineering, Environment, Human Resources, Mining, Project Management

Rayrock Yellowknife Resources Inc. is a large mining firm involved in the exploration for, and extraction of, minerals. The company currently has overseas operations in the US, Chile and Panama. Candidates should have an educational background in mining and/or engineering and several years of overseas experience. Knowledge of Spanish is an asset.

The firm expects to open a web site in the near future. [ID:5841]

Reid and Associates (1994) Ltd.
Engineering Department, P.O. Box 910, Barrie, Ontario
L4M 4Y6; (705) 728-0141, fax (705) 728-0788, reid@bconnex.net

SMALL ENGINEERING FIRM: Consulting, Engineering

Reid and Associates is a consulting engineering firm specializing in municipal infrastructure engineering. The firm's international experience includes technical monitoring of the Canadian International Development Agency's (CIDA) Jamaican Bridges Development Program; progress monitoring of road, marine facilities, sewage, and water systems for the United Nations Development Programs in Bhutan and Nepal; and preparation of technical and financial proposals for projects in the Caribbean, Suriname, and Guyana.

Candidates require overseas work experience, expertise and education in civil engineering (bridges, roads and services) and marine engineering. Language skills in English, French, and Czech are an asset. The company maintains a data bank for résumés. [ID:5842]

Reid Crowther International Ltd.
Suite 300, 340 Midpark Way S.E., Calgary, Alberta T2X 1P1;
(403) 254-3301, fax (403) 254-3333, rcpl-cal_ddany@reid-crowther.com, www.reid-crowther.com

LARGE ENGINEERING FIRM: Accounting, Administration, Business Development, Consulting, Engineering, Environment, Project Management, Technical Assistance, Water Resources

Reid Crowther International Ltd. is an international consulting engineering firm specializing in the following areas: water supply and water treatment; sewage collection, treatment, and disposal; urban commuter rail transit systems; transportation and traffic planning; environmental issues study and resolution; and hazardous waste management.

The company is currently active in Africa, Europe, Latin America and the Caribbean, and China, where it specializes in biological nutrient removal and all aspects of advanced wastewater treatment. The company has 140 staff members working overseas and an additional 500 in Canada. The firm recruits staff with relevant work experience and specific areas of expertise. Reid Crowther maintains a data bank for résumés. Applications for internships will also be considered throughout the year on an individual basis depending upon the applicant's qualifications and the needs of the company.

Reid Crowther maintains an excellent and comprehensive web site that lists job openings online and provides detailed information about the firm's domestic and international activities. [ID:5843]

Resource Futures International (RFI)
Suite 406, 1 Nicholas Street, Ottawa, Ontario
K1N 7B7; (613) 241-1001, fax (613) 241-4758, rfi@dragon.achilles.net

MID-SIZED ENVIRONMENTAL CONSULTING FIRM: Consulting, Environment, International Trade, Technical Assistance, Water Resources

Resource Futures International is a mid-sized, Canadian-owned firm specializing in capacity building for environment and sustainable development. Areas of expertise include: public policy and administration, environmental law, environmental science, environmental economics, environmental indicators and information, international relations, international trade and development policies, communications, training and workshop preparation, facilitation and conflict resolution, and project management. International projects have included: audits of environmental assessments in the transportation sectors in Iran and China, strengthening the environmental assessment procedures and capabilities in Cambodia, and providing environmental and socio-economic advice to engineering and development project teams in Thailand and India. RFI has also enhanced the policy development capacity of the Pakistani government to implement their National Conservation Strategy and the Egyptian government in using environmental information to support policy development. In Canada, RFI has worked with the Canadian International Development Agency (CIDA) to integrate environmental considerations into their programs and policies.

RFI has five employees in Ottawa with international responsibilities and one consultant based in an associate office in Phnom Penh, Cambodia. Prospective applicants should have relevant educational background in environmental policy or capacity development and some prior work experience. Resource Futures International maintains a data bank for résumés.

The firm hopes to open a web site in early 1998. [ID:5844]

Rio Algom Ltd.
Suite 2400, 120 Adelaide Street W.,
Toronto, Ontario M5H 1W5; (416) 367-4000, fax (416) 365-6870, corpcomm@rioalgo.com

MID-SIZED MINING FIRM: Metals Distribution, Mining

Rio Algom Ltd. is a large, diversified mining company specializing in the exploration for, and production of, uranium, copper, molybdenum and coal. The firm is also a major metals distributor in Canada and the US. Overseas mining operations are concentrated in Latin America, Chile, Argentina, and Peru. [ID:5845]

RMC Resources Management Consultants Ltd.
55 Ormskirk Ave., Toronto, Ontario M6S 4V6; (416) 762-8166, fax (416) 762-1963, rmc@inforamp.net

MID-SIZED MANAGEMENT CONSULTING FIRM: Accounting, Human Resources,
Management Consulting, Management Information Systems, Management Training, Project
Management, Technical Assistance

RMC Resources Management Consultants Ltd. is a clinic of independent consultants whose professional corporations work through RMC on behalf of clients. Established in 1967, RMC provides management consulting services to clients in Canada and throughout the world in these areas of expertise: health, social services and education, facility planning, equipment planning and commissioning, corporate planning, productivity improvement, computing and information systems, and human resources development. Consulting services include: project management, procurement, health information services, health reform including institutional strengthening, needs assessment, feasibility studies, strategic options and planning, resource allocation, location analysis, facility evaluations and planning, master planning, policy development, work program development, management training and education, and health promotion.

Owners and managers are the firm's principals; other full-time professionals are associates. RMC also has established affiliations with consulting associates who represent a variety of management disciplines. Recent projects have been in Eastern Europe and the Baltics.

The ideal international consultant possesses relevant higher education, extensive experience in both consulting and management positions, speaks fluently two or more languages including English, and is culturally aware and sensitive. Preferred languages are English, French, Spanish, German, Polish, Ukrainian, and Russian. RMC maintains a data bank for résumés. RMC is developing a web site. [ID:5837]

Roche Ltée., Groupe-Conseil/Roche Ltd. Consulting Group
3075 Chemin des Quatre-Bourgeois, Sainte-Foy, Québec
G1W 4Y4; (418) 654-9600, fax (418) 654-9699, marketing@roche.ca, www.roche.ca

LARGE GENERAL CONSULTING FIRM: Agriculture, Architecture and Planning, Community
Development, Construction, Consulting, Development Assistance, Energy Resources,
Engineering, Environment, Fisheries, Forestry, Geomatics, Mining, Project Management,
Technical Assistance, Water Resources

One of Canada's premier engineering and consulting firms, the Roche Group provides a variety of international services. These include integrated natural resource management, environmental engineering and technologies, ecosystems and environmental assessments, energy, health, information systems and geomatics, infrastructure engineering, industrial development, and public finances and property assessments. Roche builds partnerships overseas with local companies by using techniques adapted to local conditions.

With over 700 employees, Roche has completed numerous projects in more than 40 African, Asian, and Latin American countries. Projects include the award-winning Beira Lake restoration study in Sri Lanka, fisheries monitoring, control, and surveillance in Malaysia, a natural resource management project in Thailand, establishing a tree nursery in China, a land management pilot project in Russia, rehabilitating hospital infrastructures in Côte d'Ivoire, rural development in Guinea, studying mine development in Morocco, forest management in St.Lucia, and ocean management in the Caribbean.

Roche prefers to promote internally for international positions, but it does hire seasoned professionals. Applicants must have previous international experience and should have a background in environmental studies or natural resource management, or technical expertise in, for example, geographic information systems (GIS). The firm maintains a data bank for résumés. [ID:7098]

Rousseau, Sauvé, Warren Inc.
Suite 600, 500, boul. René-Lévesque ouest, Montréal, Québec
H2Z 1W7; (514) 878-2621, fax (514) 397-0085, rsw@rswinc.com

MID-SIZED ENGINEERING CONSULTING FIRM: Consulting, Energy Resources, Engineering, Environment, Project Management, Water Resources

Rousseau, Sauvé, Warren Inc. is a consulting firm that specializes in hydroelectric development and power transmission systems. Several members of the firm also sit on international consulting boards and fill positions in worldwide technical societies.

The company has completed contracts in the US, Argentina, Brazil, Venezuela, Mali, Cameroon, Egypt, Korea, Pakistan, and India and is currently active in Venezuela, India, China, Pakistan, Mexico, Costa Rica, and Honduras.

Candidates must have either an engineering degree or a technical or administrative certificate as well as expertise in hydropower or transmission systems. The company also looks for overseas experience, good health, and an interest in working abroad. The company currently has 25 salaried staff with international responsibilities and maintains a data bank for résumés. [ID:5846]

Roy Consultants Group
Director, International Affairs,
P.O. Box 584, 548 King Ave., Bathurst, N.B. E2A 1P7;
(506) 546-4484, fax (506) 548-2207, roygroup@nbnet.nb.ca, www.grouperoy.com

MID-SIZED GENERAL CONSULTING FIRM: Adult Training, Consulting, Engineering, Environment, Forestry, Water Resources

Roy Consultants Group is a multidisciplinary engineering firm offering services in environmental sciences, water resources, energy, industry, buildings, agriculture, geomatics, and surveying. The firm has international expertise in the areas of land management, water supply, soil conservation, irrigation, water treatment, solid waste, and energy and has completed overseas projects in West and Central Africa, Nicaragua, the Caribbean, and Hong Kong.

The firm is currently seeking to develop and implement new technologies for specific situations for African clients. Applicants with international experience and education in the environmental sciences and geomatics are encouraged to apply. Roy Consultants Group maintains a data bank for résumés. Their web site contains basic information on the group's activities and areas of specialization. [ID:5847]

Royal Bank of Canada
Employment Resource Centre, 970 Lawrence Ave., Suite 110,
Toronto, Ontario M6A 3B6; (416) 256-0088, fax (416) 256-0169, emp@rb-erc.com, www.royalbank.com

LARGE FINANCIAL SERVICES FIRM: Administration, Adult Training, Business/Banking/Trade, Computer Systems, Customer Services, Human Resources, International Trade, Project Management

Royal Bank Financial Group is Canada's leader in financial services, offering products and services to over 10 million consumer and business customers in 35 countries. In Canada, they have leading market shares in residential mortgages, consumer loans, personal deposits, and Canadian business loans. They also maintain successful business in money management, mutual funds, discount brokerage, insurance, and own the largest and most profitable full-service investment dealer, RBC Dominion Securities. The Royal Bank provides its international business customers with treasury services, corporate and investment banking, trade finance, and correspondent banking. Their global private banking operation is the largest and most profitable among Canadian financial institutions.

The Royal Bank's delivery network includes nearly 1,600 branches, more than 4,200 automated banking machines, over 500 self-serve account updaters, and some 50,000 point of sale terminals. Over 1.3 million clients utilize Royal Direct telephone and PC/Internet home banking and the bank has recently piloted Mondex, the electronic cash card. Royal Bank Financial Group employs over 55,000 people, 3,400 outside of Canada.

Recruiters look for graduate and undergraduate degrees, specific areas of expertise, relevant work experience, and special qualifications such as language skills. Valued competencies include teamwork, communication, information seeking, and achievement motivation. The bank offers a number of internship opportunities in fields such as systems and technology and personal banking. Internships are also provided via "Career Edge", at www.careeredge.org. Résumés are maintained on a database for a period of six months.

Royal Bank Financial Group maintains an excellent web site which posts job opportunities in the "News and Community" section. [ID:5848]

S.L.I. Consultants
International Division, 1190 Hornby Street, Vancouver, B.C.
V6Z 2H6; (604) 684-9311, fax (604) 688-5913, irc@sandwell.com, www.sandwell.com

LARGE TRANSPORTATION CONSULTING FIRM: Adult Training, Air Transportation, Construction, Consulting, Economics, Engineering, Forestry, Logistics, Marine Engineering, Project Management, Railways, Roads, Technical Assistance

S.L.I. Consultants is a joint venture of Sandwell Inc., N.D. Lea International, and International Rail Consultants. It provides technical assistance to the Southern Africa Transport and Communications Commission (SATCC), funded by the Canadian Transport Technical Services Group. The SATCC coordinates regional transport efforts in 12 African countries. The joint-venture project team provides technical assistance for railways and rail transport, ports and water transport, roads and road transport, and civil aviation. The provision of ongoing technical assistance over a 11 year period includes undertaking project preparation studies, training, and conducting seminars which will promote regional operational coordination within all transport sectors. Other recent projects include Dar es Salaam Port Development Study in Tanzania.

There are 300 overseas staff and 600 staff in Canada who have international components in their jobs. Candidates should have experience in consulting or transportation and experience in training others. Degrees in transportation, engineering, or economics are desirable but not mandatory. The company maintains a data bank for résumés. [ID:5849]

Samson Belair/Deloitte & Touche
Suite 3000, 1 Place Ville Marie, Montréal, Québec
H3B 4T9; (514) 393-7115, fax (514) 393-7140, www.deloitte.ca

LARGE FINANCIAL SERVICES FIRM: Business/Banking/Trade, Consulting

Samson Belair/Deloitte & Touche is the Québec practice of the accounting firm Deloitte & Touche. The firm provides a full spectrum of audit, tax, and consulting services.

Many partners and professionals work on projects with an international dimension. There is also an exchange program within the firm for young Canadian professionals and young professionals abroad. Deloitte Touche Tohmatsu International provides service in more than 100 countries around the world. They are represented in the Asia Pacific, North America, Europe (including several Eastern-European countries), and the world's major financial and trading regions. The firm maintains a data bank for résumés.

Deloitte & Touche maintains an excellent web site that contains a wide variety of information on the firm's scope and activities. Career opportunities are posted at the Canadian site, and there is a direct link to Deloitte Touche Tohmatsu International. [ID:5851]

Sandwell Inc.
1190 Hornby Street, Vancouver, B.C. V6Z 2H6;
(604) 684-9311, fax (604) 688-5913, info@sandwell.com, www.sandwell.com

LARGE ENGINEERING CONSULTING FIRM: Construction, Consulting, Engineering, Environment, Forestry, Marine Engineering, Mineral Handling, Project Management, Pulp and Paper

Sandwell Inc. is a comprehensive engineering consulting firm involved in the areas of forestry, pulp and paper, material handling and transportation. The firm also undertakes planning and feasibility studies, market studies, technical audits and reviews, and construction progress reviews. Other services include project management, design and detail engineering, procurement, contract management, construction management, start-up and operational assistance, and training and environmental studies.

Sandwell requires varied staff levels overseas and in Canada depending on the project and the skills required for its execution. The company has completed over 14,000 projects in more than 75 countries.

Applicants require engineering and science degrees and experience related to the sectors in which the company works. Recruiters also look for candidates who show sensitivity to other cultures, have previous overseas experience, well-developed inter-personal skills, and a flexible and willing attitude. The company maintains a data bank for résumés.

Sandwell's excellent and creative web site contains information about job openings and allows applicants to submit their résumés electronically. There is also a wide variety of information about the company's activities and the industry in general. [ID:5852]

Saskatchewan Institute of Applied Science and Technology (SIAST)
International Services Division, P.O. Box 556, Regina, Sask.
S4P 3A3; (306) 787-0113, fax (306) 787-4840, International@siast.sk.ca, www.siast.sk.ca

SMALL HUMAN RESOURCES FIRM: Agriculture, Computer Systems, Environment, Gender and Development, Intercultural Briefings

The International Services Division of the Saskatchewan Institute for Applied Science and Technology (SIAST) promotes development awareness within the broader institution. Abroad, SIAST implements projects of various types in Africa, the Caribbean, South Asia, Southeast Asia, and China.

Applicants must have strong crosscultural sensitivity and flexibility along with strong academic and professional credentials in particular fields of work. Currently, there are three staff in Canada with international responsibilities; overseas staff are hired on a project-by-project basis. SIAST maintains a data bank for résumés.

SAIST maintains a web site that is oriented towards the institute's academic programs and activities. [ID:5854]

SaskTel International
3rd Floor, 2121 Saskatchewan Drive, Regina, Sask.
S4P 3Y2; (306) 777-4523, fax (306) 359-7475, www.sasktel.com

LARGE TELECOMMUNICATIONS FIRM: Computer Systems, Construction, Consulting, Engineering, Project Management, Technical Assistance, Telecommunications

SaskTel International was created to globally market SaskTel's technological expertise to clients. The organization assists clients throughout the world to improve and expand their unique telecommunication system requirements in a functional and economically viable manner. SaskTel is a provincial Crown corporation with 3,900 employees and assets of approximately $1.2 billion.

Recent overseas projects have been completed in Europe, the Philippines, China, and Tanzania in the fields of rural microwave and switching systems and integrated microwave radio systems. SaskTel International currently employs 17 staff in Canada while the number of overseas staff varies according to contracts.

Prospective applicants should have a background in engineering and high technology. Some marketing experience is also desirable. SaskTel maintains a data bank for résumés.

SaskTel International maintains a presence on the SaskTel web site that provides information on its international activities and contracts. [ID:5961]

The Seagram Company Ltd.
Human Resources, 1430 Peel Street, Montréal, Québec H3A 1S9;
(800) 387-9260, fax (514) 987-5201, Career_Opportunities@Seagram.com, www.seagram.com

LARGE FOOD PROCESSING FIRM: Film Distribution, Film Production and Post Productions, Marketing

A world-leader in distilled spirits and wines, Seagram is a multinational organization founded in Canada which has had major international operations since 1933 when it first expanded production into the US. It now has a diverse range of interests around the world far beyond its original base in distilling; it acquired Tropicana Products, Inc. in 1988 and acquired control of Universal Studios, Inc. in 1995.

As a result of its strong US presence, corporate headquarters in New York City now handle hiring for international positions. With over 16,000 employees worldwide, Seagram also has major operations in Europe as well as throughout the Americas, Africa, and Asia.

Overseas positions typically require a background in senior-level management. Their web site includes a careers' section which gives detailed information on specific openings in the US. Multilingualism is a highly valued asset at Seagram. [ID:7215]

The Semex Alliance
130 Stone Road W., Guelph, Ontario N1G 3Z2;
(519) 821-5060, fax (519) 821-7225, choong@semex.com, www.semex.com

LARGE AGRICULTURAL CONSULTING FIRM: Agriculture, Business Development, Development Assistance, International Trade, Project Management, Technical Assistance

The Semex Alliance is an agricultural consulting firm that implements bilateral dairy cattle production, management, and breeding projects overseas, especially in developing countries.

At the International Livestock Management School the company provides hands-on training in management and breeding as well as in dairy and beef cattle production. Semex markets about $40 million worth of frozen bovine semen, live cattle, and embryos to about 60 countries worldwide. The company has 35 Canadian employees who have international responsibilities.

Recruits should have academic training in animal health, breeding and management, hands on farm experience, and at least five years work experience.

The Semex Alliance maintains an extensive web site that provides a wide variety of information about the company's activities and the general state of livestock genetics. There is also information on training and a number of industry-related links. [ID:5857]

Shaw Industries Ltd.
25 Bethridge Road, Rexdale, Ontario M9W 1M7; (416) 743-7111, fax (416) 743-7199

LARGE ENERGY RESOURCES FIRM: Energy Resources, Engineering, Oilfield Services, Technical Assistance

Shaw Industries Ltd. provides products and services to energy related industries. The company is organized into three business units: pipeline and tubular products, resource products, and electrical products. Its activities are carried out through various divisions and subsidiaries operating from plants located in Canada, the US, Mexico, the UK, and Australia. In addition to these temporary installations, project-specific plants are installed anywhere in the world as circumstances demand. [ID:5858]

SHL Systemhouse
Suite 501, 50 O'Connor Street, Ottawa, Ontario K1P 6L2;
(613) 236-1428, fax (613) 236-2043, www.systemhouse.mci.com

LARGE HIGH TECHNOLOGY FIRM: Adult Training, Computer Systems, Consulting, Technical Assistance

SHL Systemhouse, MCI's global information technology company, is the industry's only single-source provider of convergence products and services that address businesses' total networking, communications, consulting, and overall information technology needs. With 120 offices and approximately 7000 professionals world-wide, Systemhouse is preparing major corporate, mid-sized, and public sector clients in North and South America, Europe, and Asia with enterprise solutions for the new millenium.

Candidates should posses a relevant educational background when applying for available positions. Additionally, applicants must be results-oriented team players who also demonstrate leadership skills.

SHL maintains a comprehensive web site that includes job openings, advice for job seekers, and information on how to build and submit an online résumé. [ID:5860]

Simons Reid Collins
Suite 400, 111 Dunsmuir Street, Vancouver, B.C. V6B 5W3;
(604) 664-3134, fax (604) 664-5433, src@hasimons.com, www.hasimons.com/src

MID-SIZED FORESTRY CONSULTING FIRM: Business Development, Consulting, Development Assistance, Environment, Forestry, Project Management, Technical Assistance

Simons Reid Collins, a division of H.A. Simons Ltd., is a forest resource consulting firm with long-established affiliations in many countries around the world. The company provides consulting services to the forestry sector and forest-related resource fields. Services include feasibility assessment, measurement and management of forest resources for social and industrial development, agroforestry, environmental management, geographic information systems (GIS), technology transfer, human resource development, and equipment procurement. In conjunction with both the private and public sectors, the company has completed international projects in Asia, Latin America, Pakistan, Indonesia, southern Africa, the Caribbean, and Central and South America.

Applicants selected for short-term overseas positions must have specialized areas of expertise. Candidates are also assessed on past work experience, especially of a similar nature in similar regions of the world. Language skills are an asset. Most positions have specific academic or professional requirements but experience, the ability to communicate, and adaptability to local conditions are more important in all but the most specialized disciplines. Simons Reid Collins maintains a data bank for résumés.

The company also maintains a web site that posts job openings including descriptions and response instructions. [ID:5862]

SNC-Lavalin Agriculture Inc.

11th Floor, 485 McGill Street, Montréal, Québec H2Y 2H4;
(514) 393-1000, fax (514) 281-1471, agriculture@snc-lavalin.com, www.snc-lavalin.com

LARGE GENERAL CONSULTING FIRM: Agriculture, Development Assistance, Development Education, Engineering, Environment, Fisheries, Forestry, Gender and Development, Human Resources, Humanitarian Relief, Project Management, Technical Assistance, Water Resources

SNC-Lavalin Agriculture Inc. undertakes agricultural projects in the international marketplace with a commitment to worldwide sustainable agricultural development. This committment is expressed in the provision of a comprehensive range of quality professional services. The division's expertise encompasses all areas of agricultural development from water resources development and primary production, to secondary agro-industrial food processing.

Specific areas of expertise include: project management, irrigation and drainage design, participatory irrigation and drainage management, tropical agronomy, water resources engineering and planning, regional planning and integrated rural development, geographic and management information services, procurement, livestock husbandry, agricultural economics, environmental impact assessments, human resources development, technology transfer, agriculture extension, socio-economic assessments, development support communications, women in development, institutional strengthening, and agro-industrial and agro-food processing.

SNC-LAVALIN maintains a web site that provides information on the company and its international activities. [ID:5698]

SNC-Lavalin Group

1100 René-Lévesque Blvd. W.,
Montréal, Québec H3B 4P3; (514) 393-1000, fax (514) 954-0267, www.snc-lavalin.com

LARGE ENGINEERING FIRM: Agriculture, Business Development, Construction, Consulting, Development Assistance, Energy Resources, Engineering, Environment, Petrochemicals, Project Management, Technical Assistance, Telecommunications, Water Resources

SNC-Lavalin Group is a Canadian-based company of international scope principally operating in engineering through its subsidiary, SNC-Lavalin, the largest engineering firm in Canada and one of the largest in the world. It has carried out thousands of projects in North, Central, and South America, Africa, Asia, and Europe. Among many others, new projects are located in Saudi Arabia, Mozambique, and Ukraine.

SNC-Lavalin provides engineering, construction, procurement, and project management services in the power, industrial, general engineering, environment, and transport sectors. The company has broadened its services beyond its traditional engineering base to offer total solutions for clients' project needs, regardless of industry or location. It is well-established in sectors such as power transportation, telecommunications, aerospace, infrastructure, and the environment. The group also operates a number of manufacturing facilities.

Having offices around the world, the company employs approximately 4,900 people in Canada and 1,500 overseas. Applicants should have a strong engineering background and international experience. The company maintains a data bank for résumés and has engineering internship positions throughout the year. [ID:5863]

Sofeg Inc.

Bureau 600, 500, boul. René-Lévesque,
Montréal, Québec H2Z 1W7; (514) 878-2621, fax (514) 397-0085, rsw@rswinc.com

MID-SIZED GENERAL CONSULTING FIRM: Consulting, Development Assistance, Management, Social Policy, Technical Assistance

Sofeg Inc. is a general consulting firm specializing in social infrastructure, planning, and management. Current overseas contracts include a micro-development project in

Burkina Faso and subcontracting work in Cameroon. The firm is also involved in projects in Guinea and Algeria. [ID:5865]

Soprin ADS
Bureau 500, 1441, boul. René Lévesque,
Montréal, Québec H3G 1T7; (514) 875-1441, fax (514) 875-2666, www.soprin.com

LARGE ENGINEERING CONSULTING FIRM: Construction, Energy Resources, Environment, Gender and Development, Geomatics, Information Technologies, Logistics, Mining, Public Health and Family Planning, Telecommunications, Translation

Soprin ADS est une des plus grandes firmes de génie-conseil au Québec, ayant des origines remontant à plus de 40 ans. Elle compte près de 500 employés répartis dans ses bureaux en Amérique du Nord, en Afrique et en Amérique latine. Leur mandat est de se faire reconnaître mondialement pour son génie créatif dans les domaines de l'efficacité énergétique et de l'environnement. La compétence de son équipe et la maîtrise des langues telles le français, l'anglais, l'arabe et l'espagnol permettent de répondre plus efficacement aux besoins des clients qu'il s'agisse d'organismes publics, para-publics ou privés. Soprin ADS a mis sur pied des bureaux aux États-Unis, au Cameroun, au Maroc, au Costa Rica ainsi que créé de solides partenariats en Asie, en Afrique et en Amérique latine. [ID:6462]

SR Telecom
8150 Trans-Canada Highway, Saint-Laurent,
Québec H4S 1M5; (514) 335-1210, fax (514) 334-7783, www.srtelecom.com

LARGE TELECOMMUNICATIONS FIRM: Accounting, Administration, Business Development, Engineering, International Trade, Logistics, Telecommunications

SR Telecom is a large telecommunications firm specializing in the development, design, manufacture, sale, installation, supervision, and project management of point-to-multipoint TDMA microwave wireless telecommunications systems. The firm has completed overseas contracts in all regions of the world.

Currently, the firm has approximately 800 salaried staff in Canada and an additional 120 overseas. Prospective applicants should have a telecommunications background (sales or technical fields), some overseas experience, and a demonstrated ability to work in different cultures.

SR Telecom's web site posts career opportunities and provides general information on the firm and its activities. [ID:5866]

Stanley Industrial Consultants Ltd.
Suite 200, 1122 - 4th Ave. S.W., Calgary, Alberta T2R 1M1;
(403) 269-9933, fax (403) 269-1527, industrial.calg@stantech.com, www.stantech.com

LARGE ENGINEERING FIRM: Consulting, Energy Resources, Engineering, Marketing

Stanley Industrial Consultants Ltd., which includes the RTM Energy Division, is a consulting engineering firm that works in the oil, gas, and light industrial process industries. The firm carries out international studies in natural gas and gas liquids marketing, de-bottlenecking and energy use analysis of oil and gas plants, heavy oil refining, and product market analysis.

Stanley has 25 overseas employees and 40 in Canada who have international responsibilities. Candidates should have an undergraduate engineering degree and extensive oil, gas, and energy experience. Stanley maintains an excellent web site with detailed job postings and information about the company and its activities. [ID:5868]

Stanley International Group Inc.

10160 - 112 Street, Edmonton, Alberta T5K 2L6; (403) 917-7000,
fax (403) 917-7330, international.edm@stantech.com, www.stantech.com

Formerly Stanley Associates Engineering

Stanley International Group Inc., a member company of Stanley Technology Group Inc., is a multidisciplinary engineering consulting firm that operates throughout the world. The company provides services in the following areas: water resource development; water supply; wastewater collection, treatment, disposal, and reuse; transportation services including road, rail, and airport engineering; solid waste management; environmental engineering; and urban and rural planning and development.

The firm has 15 overseas employees and 25 Canada-based employees who work exclusively on international activities. There are over 1,500 staff (engineers, technicians, economists, planners, landscape architects, sociologists, and other professionals of the Stanley Technology Group) who can be deployed on international assignments. Stanley has worked in conjunction with the United Nations Development Program (UNDP), World Health Organization (WHO), International Bank for Reconstruction and Development (IBRD), Asian Development Bank (ADB), Inter-American Development Bank (IADB), African Development Bank (AfDB), and the Canadian International Development Agency (CIDA), and has established a reputation for successful completion of assigned international projects in Africa, Asia, the Caribbean, and the South Pacific.

Candidates should have degrees in municipal engineering, water engineering, transportation engineering, water resources or environmental engineering and sciences. Recruiters prefer candidates with relevant experience in developing countries. The firm maintains a data bank for résumés. [ID:5869]

Stellar Metals Inc.

Suite 700, 1285 West Pender Street, Vancouver, B.C.
V6E 4B1; (800) 498-8828, fax (604) 685-2345, info@stellarmetals.com, www.stellarmetals.com

LARGE MINING FIRM: Exploration and Development, Mineral Resources

Stellar Metals Inc. is a junior resource company engaged in the acquisition, exploration, development, and subsequent production of mining properties. The company is undertaking extensive exploration at its three large nickel properties in the Philippines. It expects to be mining and exporting nickel ore from one of these properties beginning in 1997-1998.

Stellar Metals Inc. has an international office in Manila. [ID:6994]

Stothert Management Ltd. (SMI)

14th Floor, 609 Granville Street, Vancouver, B.C.
V7Y 1G5; (604) 681-8165, fax (604) 687-3589, rharmer@stothert.com, www.stothert.com

LARGE ENGINEERING FIRM: Chemicals, Consulting, Engineering, Environment, Forestry, Management, Mining, Power Generation, Transmission and Distribution, Project Management, Pulp and Paper, Transportation

Stothert Management Ltd. (SMI) provides management, engineering, forestry, and environmental consulting services to manufacturing and processing industries. The firm's industrial experience includes forestry, wood products, pulp and paper, chemical processing, oil refining, power production and transmission, transportation, mining and aquaculture. Its functional experience includes feasibility studies, design, detailed engineering, marketing, operations management, training, financial analysis, socio-economic impact assessments, environmental impact assessments, inspections and evaluations, and operational and strategic planning.

Stothert has carried out assignments in over 50 countries for the past 40 years. Current overseas projects are located in Nigeria, Tanzania, Bangladesh, Thailand, Malaysia, and Vietnam. Canadian domestic and international staff number between 100 and 300 depending on project requirements. Consultants are hired on a project-by-project basis; term contracts last from months to years. Staffing requirements change rapidly.

The firm recruits candidates with varied academic backgrounds ranging from high school to PhDs. All recruits must be highly accomplished in their field. Most staff are professional engineers, foresters, and managers. The firm also looks for previous overseas experience and language capability. Stothert Management maintains a data bank for résumés.

Stothert's comprehensive web site provides information about the firm and the various sectors in which it is active. [ID:5872]

Sustainable Resource Development (SRD)
Suite 605, 222 Somerset Street W., Ottawa, Ontario K2P 2G3;
(613) 234-6234, fax (613) 563-9621, agrodev.ott@stantech.com, www.stantech.com

MID-SIZED ENVIRONMENTAL CONSULTING FIRM: Adult Training, Consulting, Development Education, Environment, Project Management

Within the context of sustainable social and economic development, Sustainable Research Development (SRD) specializes in the application of Canadian and international expertise to multi-faceted challenges of environmental and natural resource planning and management. SRD specializes in assisting countries in the South to strengthen their capabilities to deal with environmental protection and management, sustainable development, and management of their natural resources.

Recent projects include environmental planning and assessment in Palestine, institutional strengthening for environmental impact assessment in Nepal, environmental training in Pakistan, and environmental management training courses in Taiwan.

SRD requires candidates who have master's degrees or PhDs in related fields, a minimum of ten years professional experience in a related field, and overseas experience on international development projects, preferably working with international development agencies or banks. The firm maintains a data bank for résumés.

The web site, that of the Stanley Consulting Group, offers a number of interesting services including a section on career opportunities. [ID:6455]

Sylvitec Inc.
3083, Chemin des Quatre-Bourgeois, Ste-Foy, Québec G1W 2K6; (418) 845-3737, fax (418) 845-3838

LARGE FORESTRY CONSULTING FIRM: Development Assistance, Environment, Forestry

Sylvitec Inc. is a large forestry consulting company. Formerly Blais, McNeil & Associates, its international projects have included a forest protection project and rural forestry support in Senegal, administrative support of forestry in Zaire, communal reforestation support in Zaire, and sawmill implementation (turnkey project) in Norilsk, Russia.

The company has 10 people employed overseas and six people employed on these projects in Québec City. Sylvitec Inc. recruits people with technical experience or administration capacity who easily adapt to international postings. Qualified foresters, forest engineers, agronomists, forestry technicians, and sawmill designers are mostly needed. [ID:5875]

Syndel Laboratories Ltd.
9211 Shaughnessy Street,
Vancouver, B.C. V6P 6R5; (604) 321-7131, fax (604) 321-3900, info@syndel.com

MID-SIZED PHARMACEUTICAL FIRM: Consulting, Environment, Marketing, Medical Health, Project Management

Syndel Laboratories Ltd. sells veterinary pharmaceuticals overseas and selects, develops, and supports pharmaceutical distributors and agents around the world. The firm carries out some short-term, international, technical contract work, including environmental impact assessments and project management in water basin projects, such as marine aquaria and aquaculture sites.

Syndel has four staff members with primary international responsibilities. Candidates should possess a combination of appropriate education (minimum BSc), technical expertise, overseas experience, and language and intercultural skills. Syndel Laboratories maintains a data bank for résumés. [ID:5876]

Sypher-Mueller International Inc.

International Division, Suite 500,
220 Laurier Ave. W., Ottawa, Ontario K1P 5Z9; (613) 236-4318, fax (613) 236-4850, sypher@magi.com

MID-SIZED TRANSPORTATION CONSULTING FIRM: Consulting, Management Consulting, Transportation

Sypher-Mueller International Inc. provides global aviation and airport management consulting and sets up environmental emissions standards and alternative transportation fuels in North America, Japan, and Europe.

The firm employs three people overseas and 12 in Canada. Candidates require engineering or commerce degrees, experience in airport and aviation management, transportation energy and fuels, transportation economics, and transportation management. [ID:5877]

Talisman Energy Inc.

Suite 2400, 855 - 2nd Street S.W., Calgary, Alberta T2P 4J9;
(403) 237-1234, fax (403) 237-1902, tlm@talisman-energy.com, www.talisman-energy.com

LARGE PETROCHEMICALS FIRM: Petrochemicals

Talisman Energy Inc. is an independent, Canadian-based, international upstream oil and gas company whose main business activities include exploration, development, production, and marketing of crude oil, natural gas, and natural gas liquids. The company's main production comes from Canada, the North Sea, and Indonesia. Talisman is active in a number of high-potential international exploration areas, including Algeria, Trinidad, and Peru. Talisman Energy maintains a web site that provides information about the firm and its international activities. [ID:5879]

Technology Training Associates (TTA)

6th Floor, 1455 West Georgia Street, Vancouver, B.C.
V6G 2T3; (604) 688-3535, fax (604) 688-7037, lea@bc.sympatico.ca

MID-SIZED TRANSPORTATION CONSULTING FIRM: Adult Training, Consulting, Economics, Environment, Project Management, Technical Assistance

Technology Training Associates (TTA) is a mid-sized consulting firm specializing in the provision of human resource development services to international clients in the transportation sector. It is a corporation established between N.D. Lea International, an internationally established consulting company, and the British Columbia Institute of Technology. TTA has relevant expertise in the areas of transportation planning and economics, road and bridge design and maintenance, construction supervision, road transport management and operations, airport planning, aircraft maintenance, intermodal facilities, and port operations. The firm has completed projects in Africa, Asia, and the Caribbean.

The firm seeks candidates with experience and a relevant educational background in transportation and/or training. TTA maintains a data bank for résumés. [ID:5878]

Teck Corporation

Suite 600, 200 Burrard Street, Vancouver, B.C.
V6C 3L9; (604) 687-1117, fax (604) 687-6100, info@teck.com, www.teck.com

LARGE MINING FIRM: Gold and Metals Production

Teck Corporation is a large, diversified firm involved in the exploration for, and extraction of, minerals. The company presently produces gold, copper, zinc, lead, silver, niobium, and metallurgical coal with varying interests in nine mines located across Canada. Teck has a copper mine in Chile and a gold mine in Australia. It has exploration offices in the

US, Mexico, Brazil, Chile, and Peru and a representative office in Singapore. It also has significant activities in Southeast and Central Asia.

Teck had 3,343 employees in 1996, mainly working on Canadian mining projects. Its web site offers infomation on current projects. [ID:5880]

TECSULT

85 Ste-Catherine Street W., Montréal, Québec H2X 3P4;
(514) 287-8500, fax (514) 287-8643, techsult@techsult.com, www.techsult.com

LARGE ENGINEERING FIRM: Accounting, Administration, Adult Training, Agriculture, Arms Control, Business/Banking/Trade, Business Development, Community Development, Construction, Consulting, Development Assistance, Development Education, Economics, Energy Resources, Engineering, Environment, Forestry, Gender and Development, Human Resources, Petrochemicals, Project Management, Water Resources

TECSULT is a consulting engineering firm that provides services in hydroelectric developments and water resources, thermal and nuclear energy, transmission and distribution, industrial plants, municipal engineering, agricultural development, and economic and financial studies. It has performed management consulting and human resource development work, geotechnics, data processing, land and project management.

TECSULT operates in about 60 countries in South and Central America, Africa, Southeast Asia, and North America. The firm has 75 employees working overseas and 200 employees in Canada who have international responsibilities.

TECSULT's French language web site contains a variety of useful information on the company's activities and posts job openings online. [ID:5881]

TECSULT Environment Inc.

4700, boul. Wilfrid Hamel, Québec, Québec G1P 2J9;
(418) 871-7488, fax (418) 871-5868, mlcaron@tecsult.com, www.tecsult.com

LARGE ENVIRONMENTAL FIRM: Adult Training, Consulting, Development Education, Economics, Energy Resources, Engineering, Environment, Forestry, Human Resources, Media/Communications, Project Management, Technical Assistance, Water Resources

TECSULT Environment Inc. is an environmental consulting firm that carries out studies in the fields of environmental impact assessments and audits, forestry, phytoecology, biodiversity, waste and waste water management, communications, education, risk assessment, site remediation, database conception and treatment, rural land planning, and conservation of natural resources.

TECSULT Environment Inc. is the environmental arm of TECSULT, a large Montréal-based engineering firm with 1000 employees and a very active overseas division. The company has recently completed projects in West Africa, South America, the Caribbean, and Central America on environmental and forestry management consultation, land classification and cartography, and industrial waste management.

Candidates should be specialists with a master's degree and international experience in forestry, engineering, biology, pedology, geomorphology, or environmental management. The firm maintains a data bank for résumés. [ID:5758]

Tecsult Foresterie Inc.

Division internationale, 4700, boul. Wilfrid-Hamel, Québec, Québec
G1P 2J9; (418) 871-2412, fax (418) 871-5868, ptitec@tecsult.com, www.tecsult.com

LARGE FORESTRY FIRM: Forestry

Tecsult Foresterie Inc. est une société d'ingénierie forestière qui se spécialise, entre autres, en inventaire forestier, en sylviculture, en agro-foresterie, en études environnementales et en géomatique forestière. Cette entreprise contracte ses projets par l'entremise de l'ACDI et d'autres bailleurs de fonds internationaux.

Des mandats importants sont en cours en Inde, en Indonésie, au Cameroun, au Congo, au Gabon, en Côte d'Ivoire, en Colombie, au Vénézuéla, au Honduras, en Éthiopie et en République Centrafricaine. Tecsult Foresterie Inc. compte 123 employés, dont 25 à l'étranger.

Les candidats recherchés doivent avoir un diplôme correspondant au poste et une expérience acquise dans le pays concerné, sinon, dans la région géographique du projet. Leur site web en français comprend des renseignements sur la companie et ses activités. [ID:5830]

Teleglobe
1000 rue de la Gauchetière W., Montréal, Québec H3B 4X5;
(514) 868-7272, fax (514) 868-7234, jobs@teleglobe.com, www.teleglobe.com

LARGE TELECOMMUNICATIONS FIRM: Accounting, Administration, Business Development, Engineering, Human Resources, Telecommunications

Teleglobe is a global North American-based overseas carrier whose capabilities can be accessed in virtually all countries. Teleglobe develops and provides intercontinental telecommunications services. Based in Montréal, Teleglobe Canada Inc. is Canada's overseas telecommunications carrier. Over the past 45 years Teleglobe Canada has built up one of the world's most extensive telecommunications networks, including satellite links and interests in some 100 sub-marine cables. The firm is a member of INTELSAT and INMARSAT, two international organizations that own multi-satellite systems.

Through Teleglobe International Corporation, based in Washington, D.C., Teleglobe serves the US and Europe via facilities in the US, UK, and Germany. It also has offices in Hong Kong, Israel, Singapore, Australia, and Austria and has operations around the world. It regularly has openings in countries around the globe, typically involving sales or management work, or occasionally technical positions in areas such as software engineering or network planning. The web site includes international job listings. Interested canditates can apply by e-mail, or fax résumés to (703) 610-6354. [ID:5883]

Telesat Canada
1601 Telesat Court, Gloucester, Ontario K1B 5P4;
(613) 748-0123, fax (613) 748-8712, info@telesat.ca, www.telesat.ca

MID-SIZED TELECOMMUNICATIONS FIRM: Advanced Technology, Business Development, Consulting, Engineering, Technical Assistance

Telesat Canada provides consulting services and customer support in all areas of satellite communications, including feasibility studies, business plan analysis, system design and definition, RFP preparation and evaluation, contract negotiation, procurement monitoring, and in-orbit testing and operations. In addition to space consulting, Telesat also provides services related to all aspects of satellite ground station requirements.

Telesat has provided services to more than 20 countries worldwide and has 450 salaried staff in Canada and 10 posted overseas. Prospective applicants should have business or engineering degrees with a minimum of 10 years international experience in the field of satellite communications. The firm maintains a data bank for résumés. [ID:5884]

Telus
10020 - 100th Street, Edmonton, Alberta T5J 0N5;
(403) 498-7300, fax (403) 493-6565, hr@telus.com, www.telus.com

MID-SIZED TELECOMMUNICATIONS FIRM: Telecommunications

Telus is Canada's third largest telecommunications and information management company. With six subsidiaries, one of which is overseas, the firm provides voice, data, and visual communications services, information, and advertising to both domestic and international clients.

The majority of its 9,000 employees are based in Alberta, but there is some overseas work, primarily establishing telecommunication systems in developing countries. Prospective applicants should have relevant educational background and work experience in the telecommunications sector. Telus maintains a data bank for résumés. [ID:5885]

Terra Surveys Limited
2060 Walkley Road, Ottawa, Ontario K1G 3P5; (613) 731-9571,
fax (613) 731-0453, terra@Ottawa.TerraSurveys.com, www.terrasurveys.com

LARGE EARTH SCIENCES FIRM: Aerial Surveys, Hydrographic Surveys, Photo Mapping, Project Management

Terra Surveys Limited is one of Canada's largest resource mapping and development organizations. The firm focuses on surveying, mapping, and engineering services in rural and urban development, agriculture, forestry and hydrology, transportation, distribution, and communication. Terra also has expertise in topographic mapping, aerial photography, GIS Applications, Digital Orthophoto, and control surveys. Terra's Hydrographic Division provides a complete surface and airborne surveying service in all types of water including offshore, coastal, inland, and Arctic. Terra's abilities to collect and compile hydrographic data can be used for charting, drill site investigations, port and harbor development and maintenance, pipe and transmission line crossings, water inventory, marine park development, and environmental assessments.

There are three employees currently working overseas and 50 employees in Canada working on international projects, primarily in the Middle East and Asia Pacific regions.

It is an asset, but not essential, for candidates to have international work experience or experience in a remote area of Canada. Applicants must have experience in a specific field to qualify for international positions. Particular project language skills may be important. Terra maintains a data bank for résumés. [ID:5886]

Teshmont Consultants Inc.
1190 Waverly Street, Winnipeg, Manitoba R3T 0P4;
(204) 284-8100, fax (204) 475-4601, teshmont@teshmont.mb.ca, www.stantech.com

MID-SIZED ENGINEERING CONSULTING FIRM: Engineering, Power Generation, Transmission and Distribution, Project Management, Technical Assistance

Teshmont Consultants Inc. is affiliated with the Stanley Technology Group family of engineering companies. Teshmont has established itself as a world leader in high voltage transmission projects. It specializes in direct current high voltage transmission and sub-station design and maintenance systems. It has project offices around the globe. Positions typically require a background in engineering or project management, but international experience is not required. Teshmont maintains a data bank of résumés. [ID:6549]

Toronto Dominion Bank
TD Tower, Toronto, Ontario M5K 1A2;
(416) 982-8222, fax (416) 944-6955, tdinfo@tdbank.ca, www.tdbank.ca

LARGE FINANCIAL SERVICES FIRM: Architecture and Planning, Business/Banking/Trade

In terms of total assets, the Toronto-Dominion Bank ranks as the fifth largest Canadian bank and serves individuals, businesses, financial institutions, and governments through a network of approximately 925 branches and offices across Canada. Internationally, the bank offers a broad range of credit, non-credit, and financial advisory services to businesses, multinational corporations, governments, and correspondent banks through offices in the US, London, Tokyo, Hong Kong, Singapore, and through a subsidiary bank in Australia. Worldwide, the bank employs over 27,000 people.

The bank maintains an excellent web site that provides a variety of online banking services and posts current job opportunities. [ID:5888]

Townsend Trade Strategies Inc. (TTS)
859 Rozel Crescent, Ottawa, Ontario K2A 1H8;
(613) 725-9338, fax (613) 798-0866, jtownsen@magnacom.com

SMALL GENERAL CONSULTING FIRM: Business Development, Consulting, International Trade, Marketing

Townsend Trade Strategies Inc. (TTS) is a Canadian-based consulting company started in 1989 to respond to the growing demand of Canadian corporations for advice and guidelines on developing international business opportunities in Latin America. TTS investigates the niche for a product or service in the market, develops background information on the most important competitors in the market, and then works with its clients to evolve and implement a market entry strategy. The firm's team of professionals travel extensively in the region and are familiar with the markets of Mexico, Guatemala, Panama, Trinidad, Barbados, Guyana, Venezuela, Colombia, and Chile. TTS also has an office in Mexico City.

Prospective applicants should have a bachelor's degree, fluency in English and Spanish, and experience in market research and business development in Latin America. Townsend Trade Strategies maintains a data bank for résumés. [ID:5890]

TransCanada PipeLines Limited
Human Resources Department, P.O. Box 1000, Stn.M, Calgary, Alberta
T2P 4K5; (403) 267-6100, fax (403) 267-2483, tcpl_recruiting@tcpl.ca, www.transcanada.com

LARGE ENERGY RESOURCES FIRM: Energy Resources, Management, Marketing, Oil and Gas Distribution

TransCanada PipeLines transmits, markets, and processes energy for customers around the world. It is also involved in energy management. Its pipeline system brings natural gas and crude oil from western Canada to North America's major energy markets. Now expanding globally, it evaluates and invests in energy-related development opportunities around the world. In addition to its operations in Canada and the US, it has offices in Tanzania.

Employees are encouraged to gain varied experience within the firm. Positions draw on a variety of professions, ranging from management and commerce to engineering and information technology. Most openings are based in the Calgary head office, but there is a growing international component.

The TransCanada web site includes a recruitment section with a link to another web site which lists TransCanada openings along with available positions with other western Canadian companies. Interested applicants may also call (403) 267-4884 for an updated list of current openings. [ID:7033]

Triton Mining Corp.
Suite 1620, 1140 West Pender Street,
Vancouver, B.C. V6E 4G1; (604) 689-9554, fax (604) 688-3639, www.triton-mining.com

LARGE MINING FIRM: Drilling Services, Exploration and Development, Gold and Metals Production, Management Training, Project Management, Training and Technology Transfer

Triton Mining Corp. is an international gold producing company active in the acquisition, exploration, and development of gold properties in Central and South America. The company has operations in Nicaragua and Argentina where it conducts exploration and mine/mill development programs utilizing new technology, capital injection, and improved management. [ID:7017]

UMA Group Ltd.
Suite 1700, 1066 West Hastings St., Vancouver, B.C.
V6E 3X2; (604) 689-3431, fax (604) 685-1035, www.umagroup.com

LARGE ENVIRONMENTAL FIRM: Architecture and Planning, Community Development, Construction, Consulting, Development Assistance, Engineering, Environment, Forestry, Geomatics, International Trade, Project Management, Transportation, Water Resources

UMA Group Ltd. is a consulting engineering firm with projects worldwide. Recent international projects include: feasibility studies and detailed design of water supply and sewage systems in Ukraine and St. Kitts & Nevis; land registration systems in Ukraine, Moldova and Armenia; environmental regulation and pollution assessment studies in Trinidad and Venezuela; heritage conservation in the USA, Barbados and Puerto Rico; agricultural drainage and urban mapping in India; water management in the Aral Sea Basin; industrial engineering in Mexico and oil extraction facilities in Australia. Candidates should have appropriate academic training, appropriate experience for a specific project, and a record of completed assignments in developing countries. The firm maintains a data bank for résumés. [ID:5891]

Unigec Experts-Conseils
1846, rue Outarde, Chicoutimi, Québec G7K 1H1;
(418) 545-8333, fax (418) 696-1951, www.stas-unigec.com

LARGE ENGINEERING FIRM: Consulting, Economics, Energy Resources, Engineering, Environment, Transportation

Unigec Experts-Conseils is a consulting company of engineers, planners, technologists, and designers that provides services in the energy, communication, and transport sectors. Consultants prepare engineering and economic planning for resource development, energy system management and analysis, engineering design, energy conservation, and environmental studies. Unigec also has informal associations with individuals and organizations that offer complementary, specialized services in agriculture, training, and social development.

The firm has about 10 overseas employees and 50 Canadian employees with international responsibilities. Candidates should have a Bachelor of Science degree and experience in the construction or engineering fields and should preferably speak both English and French. The firm maintains a data bank for résumés. [ID:5892]

Universalia Management Group Ltd.
Personnel Department, Suite 310, 5252 de Maisonneuve Street W.,
Montréal, Québec H4A 3S5; (514) 485-3565, fax (514) 485-3210, univers@umg.ca

MID-SIZED HUMAN RESOURCES FIRM: Adult Training, Human Resources, Management, Research

Universalia Management Group Ltd. is a human resources consulting firm specializing in evaluation, planning, training, research and management in such areas as business, community and economic development, education, social services and transport. The firm has completed projects in 50 countries in Africa, Asia and the Americas. It has 18 Canadian-based employees with international responsibilities. Candidates must be university-educated and have experience in education, administration, and international development. [ID:5893]

Urgel Delisle & Associates (UDA)
International Division, C.P. 60, 426, Chemin des Patriotes, Saint-Charles-sur-Richelieu,
Québec J0H 2G0; (514) 584-2207, fax (514) 584-2523, udelisle@urgel.interax.net, www.udainc.com

MID-SIZED FORESTRY CONSULTING FIRM: Agriculture, Consulting, Development Assistance, Engineering, Environment, Forestry, Water Resources

Urgel Delisle and Associates (UDA) provides technical expertise in agriculture, forestry, water management, and the environment in developing countries. In international development, its work includes training in biomass management, soil and water conservation engineering, crop protection, establishing experimental farms, technology transfer, and feasibility studies for product marketing. It also works in such fields as urban forestry, quarry management, and environmental impact assessment.

UDA has done projects in Russia, Hungary, Ukraine, Pakistan, Uruguay, Peru, Costa Rica, Haiti, Nigeria, Rwanda, Egypt, Morocco, Sudan, Algeria, Germany, Belgium, France, Holland, and Switzerland. A small Canadian staff work in St.-Charles-sur-Richelieu, Québec and travel overseas on two- to four-week technical assistance and evaluation assignments.

Candidates should hold master's or bachelor degrees in agricultural engineering and have good management skills and overseas experience. [ID:5894]

Vaughan International Consultants
1801 Hollis Street, Suite 1600, P.O. Box 2045, Stn.M, Halifax, N.S.
B3J 2Z1; (902) 425-3980, fax (902) 423-7593, vaughan@mgnet.ca, www.mgnet.ca

LARGE ENGINEERING CONSULTING FIRM: Engineering, Environment, Project Management

Vaughan International Consultants is a Halifax-based multidiscipline engineering, environmental, and project management company. A subsidiary of Vaughan Engineering Associates Ltd., it represents the international practice of the companies in the MacDonnell Group, a global technology and consulting solutions group providing expert services in engineering, geomatics, environmental, computer graphics, and management consulting.

Vaughan has completed over 6,000 projects for clients in government and industry. Current projects include environmental management and consulting in India, Indonesia, and Brunei; past projects have been in Egypt, Pakistan, and Jamaica. With annual projects worth over $8 million, Vaughan employs over 100 professionals and technical staff, including engineers, scientists, planners, CG and GIS specialists, and management consultants. [ID:7102]

Wardrop Engineering Inc.
International Division, Suite 400, 386 Broadway Street, Winnipeg, Manitoba
R3C 4M8; (204) 956-0980, fax (204) 957-5389, winnipeg@wardrop.com, www.wardrop.com

LARGE ENGINEERING FIRM: Aerospace Technology, Business Development, Community Development, Computer Systems, Consulting, Development Assistance, Development Education, Engineering, Environment, Gender and Development, Logistics, Project Management, Technical Assistance, Water Resources

Wardrop Engineering Inc. is a multidisciplinary engineering firm providing service in the traditional fields of public health engineering, hydrotechnical, geotechnical, civil, mechanical, electrical, structural, and process engineering as well as in nuclear safety, computer modelling, robotics, aerospace, information technology, and computer and software systems design. It has approximately 200 staff in Canada and abroad. The International Division accounts for more than 20 per cent of Wardrop's business and has completed projects in Burkina Faso, Cameroon, Eritrea, Ghana, India, Iran, Côte d'Ivoire, Kenya, Mali, Mexico, Niger, Nigeria, Pakistan, Peru, Philippines, Senegal, Sri Lanka, and Uganda.

Job requirements are occasionally posted on the web site. Internship positions are solicited by Wardrop as required. [ID:5895]

Westcoast Energy International Inc.
Park Place, Suite 3400, 666 Burrard Street, Vancouver, B.C.
V6C 3M8; (604) 488-8000, fax (604) 488-8099, www.WestcoastEnergy.com

LARGE PETROCHEMICALS FIRM: Energy Resources, Oil and Gas Distribution

Westcoast Energy Inc. is one of the largest corporations in the North American natural gas industry which specializes in the processing and transport of natural gas. The company's interests include natural gas gathering and processing, transmission, storage, distribution, energy services, power generation, and international energy ventures.

Through its subsidiary, Westcoast Energy International Inc, it is actively pursuing energy related projects in the Asia-Pacific region and Latin America. It has major operations in Indonesia and Australia and is part of a consortium in Mexico that will build and operate the world's largest nitrogen production complex. [ID:5897]

Chapter 33

Services for International Businesses & Entrepreneurs

Imagine that you have identified an international business opportunity in Mexico. Or perhaps a senior manager from Malaysia has contacted you for product details and prices. What next? This chapter will assist you in getting a handle on the numerous export services available to help you or your business "go international."

To successfully engage in international trade, you need timely and accurate information on market accessibility, sales potential, the regulatory environment, currencies and terms of payment, distribution channels, and so on. Canadian businesses and entrepreneurs interested in penetrating export markets will find an extensive array of support and incentive programs designed to encourage and facilitate this interest.

Support is available in many forms—from private consultants and associations with specialized knowledge of a particular market or sector to broad-based government programs. This chapter does not offer ready-made strategies. Rather, it provides information on how to make use of many available export services and programs and reach the most knowledgeable and experienced sources. An extensive list of resources for the international entrepreneur, in print and on the web, is provided in the Resources section. The Profiles section contains 70 descriptions of services for international businesses provided by the federal government and private trade associations and listings of provincial government contacts and foreign trade councils in Canada.

WHY GO INTERNATIONAL?

Businesspeople and individuals with international career objectives often overlook opportunities in international trade. Yet with the recent proliferation

693

of regional and global trade agreements, opportunities in this realm are exceptional. Exports already account for 38 per cent of gross domestic product (GDP), or one in eight Canadian jobs, and have grown at an annualized rate of about 12 per cent in recent years, easily outpacing the domestic economy. Each $1 billion in new exports translates into an estimated 7,500 new jobs.

Many Canadian entrepreneurs and companies have still not taken full advantage of emerging global opportunities. While large firms can devote significant resources to researching and developing export markets, many small and medium-sized enterprises cannot. Less than 10 per cent of Canadian businesses are directly involved in exporting, while just 100 large companies account for more than 60 per cent of Canada's exports.

The high cost of doing business internationally calls for clear priorities, sound and well-executed business development strategies, flexibility to meet changing circumstances, and astute management of financial and human resources. It also calls for crosscultural knowledge, as learning how to conduct business with people from a variety of cultures is an important asset for becoming a successful international entrepreneur.

KEYS TO SUCCESS

What does it take to succeed in an international business venture? While exporting is open to operations of all sizes, it is not a quick fix for financially troubled individuals or companies. Nor is it recommended for the halfhearted. Like most interesting endeavours, international business holds risks as well as rewards. Success requires serious, long-term commitment, thorough research and careful planning.

In any commercial venture there are a number of vital factors to consider including the strength of your idea, market accessibility, capital requirements and so forth. However, a key determinant of your international success will be your willingness and ability to make use of the host of services offered by federal, provincial, and private organizations. These organizations will help you expand your overseas trade prospects and embark upon an exciting international opportunity.

GETTING STARTED

There is no shortage of resources and services available to assist you in making your business international. In fact, it may be difficult to choose just where to begin. In this section you will find some recommended points of entry. (For contact information on the organizations mentioned below, see the Profiles section of this chapter.)

The best way to begin is to contact the DEPARTMENT OF FOREIGN AFFAIRS AND INTERNATIONAL TRADE (DFAIT) Inquiries Service. The Inquiries Service acts as a gateway to a myriad of other services and resources. Inquiries Service staff can refer you to a variety of specialized services tailored to your needs. Typically, the first referral will be to the INTERNATIONAL TRADE CENTRE nearest you. These centres are the delivery points in Canada's regions for the trade-development programs and services of DFAIT. Services include basic export counselling and market opportunity information.

Another excellent starting point is the CANADIAN CHAMBER OF COMMERCE. As the largest and most representative business group in Canada, the Chamber manages a variety of networks designed to help small- and medium-sized enterprises find domestic and international partners and to provide customized trade and investment services.

Fellow exporters can also be an excellent source of first-hand information. Each has successfully developed strategies and techniques for conducting business overseas and most are willing to share their experience with first-time exporters in areas in which they are not in direct competition.

Few entrepreneurs or small enterprises have the financial resources to take on the additional risks of initiating an international venture. With this in mind, individuals are advised to contact the EXPORT DEVELOPMENT CORPORATION or the BUSINESS DEVELOPMENT BANK OF CANADA. Both institutions provide innovative financing and risk management services.

In recent years, there has been an explosion of business services and resources available on the Internet. Almost all of the services profiled in this chapter now have some presence on the web. Some major government services, such as INDUSTRY CANADA's Strategies, are primarily Internet-based. Keep in mind that most services on the Internet are still in a period of growth and development, and that web sites may look very different only a few months after an initial visit. Also, new services are going online everyday. Check in often with key sites to see what's new and check out links to new services and resources.

Look in both the Resources and the Profiles sections that follow for web sites and online publications that may help you get started.

RESOURCES

Occupational and crosscultural knowledge are needed to succeed in international business. These resources will help you with the occupational and business-research side of international business. For more related resources see the section on Job Search Directories in Chapter 22, Resources on the International Job Search.

For resources describing the all important crosscultural aspects of international business, consult the Resources sections in the following chapters: for general crosscultural skills see Chapter 1, The Effective Overseas Employee; for the more practical aspects of living overseas see Chapter 3, Living Overseas and Chapter 12, Crosscultural Travel; for material which focuses on crosscultural business skills see Chapter 7, The Canadian Identity in the International Workplace; and for country-specific advice on social and business customs see Chapter 27, Jobs by Regions of the World.

Access North America 📖 🖥️
Monthly ➤ InfoCentre, Department of Foreign Affairs and International Trade (DFAIT), 125 Sussex Dr., Ottawa, Ontario K1A 0G2; (800) 267-8376, fax (613) 996-9709 ▪ A monthly newsletter of the Access North America Program. Provides news about government activities, visas, and programs and publications under the North American Free Trade Agreement (NAFTA). Published as a supplement to the "CanadExport Newsletter." Also available on their web site under the heading "Trade" at www.dfait-maeci.gc.ca. [ID:1636]

Asian Development Bank Business Opportunities 📖 💻
Monthly ➤ Central Operations Services Office, Asian Development Bank, P.O. Box 789, Manilla Central Post Office, 0980 Manila, Philippines; free; (632) 632-4444, fax (632) 636-4444, erosales@mail.asiandevbank.org ▪ Provides advance information on goods and service requirements of projects under consideration by the Asian Development Bank. Internet edition is available at www.asiandevbank.org. Visit this web site and look under "Business Opportunities." [ID:2608]

Building an Import/Export Business 📖
1997, *Kenneth Weiss*, 488 pages ➤ John Wiley & Sons, 22 Worchester Drive, Rexdale, Ontario M9W 1L1; $18.95; credit cards; (800) 567-4797, fax (800) 565-6802 ▪ Step-by-step guide for those involved in, or just starting, an international trade business. Covers locating foreign suppliers, target markets, regulatory agencies, preparing business plans, sample supply agreements, international shipping and trade contacts, and a variety of other topics related to international trade. Visit the distributor's web site at www.wiley.com/products/worldwide/canada. [ID:1004]

Business Opportunities Sourcing System (BOSS) 📖
Annual, Industry Canada , Tyrell Press ➤ Tyrell Press Ltd., 2714 Fenton Road, Gloucester, Ontario K1G 3N3; $78.75; credit cards; (613) 822-0740, fax (613) 822-1089 ▪ The BOSS database is a set of directories, compiled by Industry Canada, of manufacturers (products and companies), trading houses, consulting engineers, architects, geometrics, computer services, customs brokers, management consultants, agrologists, and construction companies. For easy reference companies are listed by name and product or service. Contact names, titles, phone and fax numbers are also provided. [ID:1508]

Canada and the New Global Economy 📖
1994, *Ingrid A. Bryan*, 360 pages ➤ John Wiley & Sons, 22 Worchester Drive, Rexdale, Ontario M9W 1L1; $32.95; credit cards; (800) 567-4797, fax (800) 565-6802 ▪ This book synthesises and clarifies materials published on the Canadian economy into an accessible summary of key economic issues. Designed for the "non-specialist" who wants a solid understanding of the changing economic world of the 1990s. Visit www.wiley.com/products/worldwide/canada, the distributor's web site. [ID:1782]

Canada Business Service Centres 💻
www.cbsc.org ▪ Designed to serve Canadian business people, the CBSC internet site contains searchable collections of information on federal and provincial government services, programs and regulations. The site also allows the user to contact Business Information Officers by e-mail. This is an excellent site for those interested in government. (See their profile in Chapter 33, Services for International Businesses & Entrepreneurs.) [ID:2517]

CanadExport 📖 💻
Biweekly ➤ InfoCentre, Department of Foreign Affairs and International Trade (DFAIT), 125 Sussex Dr., Ottawa, Ontario K1A 0G2; free; (800) 267-8376, fax (613) 996-9709 ▪ Foreign Affairs' primary publication for keeping the Canadian business community and exporters informed about key trade matters. A biweekly newsletter, it provides timely information on business opportunities, trade fairs and other related matters. See the online version at www.dfait-maeci.gc.ca/english/news/newsletr/canex. [ID:1495]

Canadian Corporate News 💻
www.cdn-news.com ▪ A full-text database of news releases issued by over 1,000 Canadian companies and indexed by company name, stock symbol, industry, and keywords. [ID:2725]

Canadian Exporter's Guide to the Internet 💻
http://strategis.ic.gc.ca/SSG/bi18106e.html ▪ Useful internet links for Canadian exporters. Updated regularly. [ID:2649]

Canadian Index 📖
Monthly, *Lucy Lemieux* ➤ Micromedia Ltd., 20 Victoria Street, Toronto, Ontario M5C 2N8; $100/ issue; VISA, MC; (800) 387-2689, fax (416) 362-6161; Available in large libraries ▪ The Canadian Business and Current Affairs (CBCA) database includes this index on CD-ROM. Topics include

management, administrative studies, economics and history. Combines three former publications: Canadian Business Index, Canadian News Index, Canadian Magazine Index. [ID:1556]

Canadian Representatives Abroad 📖 💻
Annual, Department of Foreign Affairs and International Trade (DFAIT), 142 pages ➤ Canada Government PublishingOttawa, Ontario K1A 0S9; $17.95; VISA, MC; (819) 956-4800, fax (819) 994-1498, publishing@ccg-gcc.ca ▪ A bilingual directory of Canadian diplomatic and consular missions. Available on the web at the DFAIT site, under "Embassies and Missions" at www.dfait-maeci.gc.ca/english/missions. [ID:1089]

Corpus Almanac and Canadian Sourcebook 📖
Annual ➤ Southam Information and Technology Group, 1450 Don Mills Rd., Don Mills, Ontario M3B 2X7; $179; credit cards; (800) 668-2374, fax (416) 442-2219; Available in large libraries ▪ Contains a broad range of information on Canadian business and government, including associations, societies, industry and trade, government and finance. [ID:1512]

Crossborder Tax and Transactions 💻
www.crossborder.com ▪ An informative site for people doing business or investing internationally, specifically between Canada and the US. The site is maintained by an international tax lawyer and provides updated Canadian and US trade laws. [ID:2757]

Directory for Trade Commissioners 📖
1997 ➤ InfoCentre, Department of Foreign Affairs and International Trade (DFAIT), 125 Sussex Dr., Ottawa, Ontario K1A 0G2; (800) 267-8376, fax (613) 996-9709 ▪ A booklet designed for exporters examining foreign market representation options, and for companies that have received an unsolicited proposal from a potential agent or distributor and require guidance in the assessment process. [ID:1589]

Directory of the Canadian Trade Commissioner Service Abroad 📖 💻
Canada Government Publishing, Ottawa, Ontario K1A 0S9; free; VISA, MC; (819) 956-4800, fax (819) 994-1498, publishing@ccg-gcc.ca ▪ Address and contact information for over 125 Canadian trade missions abroad. Includes some tips and information for exporters. Also available online at www.infoexport.gc.ca. [ID:2535]

Do's and Taboos of International Trade: A Small Business Primer 📖
1994, *Roger E. Axtell,* 336 pages ➤ John Wiley & Sons, 22 Worchester Drive, Rexdale, Ontario M9W 1L1; $17.95; credit cards; (800) 567-4797, fax (800) 565-6802 ▪ A useful guide that shows small businesses how to increase sales by tapping into the international market. This book looks at how and where to get started, dealing with language barriers, habits and customs of other nationalities, financing and pricing per export, and much more. Visit the distributor's web site at www.wiley.com/products/worldwide/canada. [ID:1005]

**Exporting from Canada: A Practical Guide to Finding
and Developing Export Markets for Your Product or Service** 📖
1994, *Anne Curran, Gerhard Kautz,* 136 pages ➤ Self-Counsel Press, 1481 Charlotte Road, North Vancouver, B.C. V7J 1H1; $19.95; VISA, MC; (604) 986-3366, fax (604) 986-3947, sales@self-counsel.com ▪ Publication with information on export assessment, market studies, establishing contacts, contracts, shipping, financing, exporting to the US & Mexico. Viisit the distributor's web site at www.self-counsel.com. [ID:1570]

ExportSource 💻
http://exportsource.gc.ca ▪ Team Canada's online service for Canadian businesses seeking export information. Contains export guides, market information, contacts and resources for Canadian exporters. [ID:2618]

Fischer Report 📖
Bimonthly ➤ George E. Fischer & Associates, Inc., P.O. Box 9348, Newport Beach, CA 92658, USA; US$400 first year, $US300 renewal; VISA, MC; (714) 759-3374, fax (714) 760-1792 ▪ Excellent source of information on contracts awarded in the field of international business. [ID:1149]

Government Assistance Programs & Subsidies (GAPS) 📖

Annual, Canada Pack ➤ Renouf Publishing Co. Ltd., Unit 1, 5369 Canotek Road, Ottawa, Ontario K1J 9J3; $240; credit cards; (613) 745-2665, fax (613) 745-7660 ▪ Available at libraries. This easy-to-use directory lists federal and provincial grants available across Canada, benefits of the grants, who is eligible, contact names and how to apply. [ID:1349]

Guide to Export Services 📖

1997, 26 pages ➤ InfoCentre, Department of Foreign Affairs and International Trade (DFAIT), 125 Sussex Dr., Ottawa, Ontario K1A 0G2; free; (800) 267-8376, fax (613) 996-9709 ▪ InfoCentre, the public information office of DFAIT, has over 2,000 publications on the subject of international trade. A variety of country-specific booklets containing detailed economic overviews, tips on doing business, customs, and foreign exchange regulations are available. [ID:1497]

Hoover's Directory of World Business 📖

1996, *Gary Hoover, Alta Campbell, Alan Chai,* 421 pages ➤ Impact Publications, 9104 North Manassas Drive, Manassas Park, VA 20111-2366, USA; US$27.95; credit cards; (703) 361-7300, fax (703) 335-9486 ▪ This directory provides detailed information on major international businesses, including statistics, corporate profiles, and contact information. Identifies the world's top 10 companies. Visit the distributor's web site at www.impactpublications.com. [ID:1762]

How to Be An Importer and Pay for Your World Travel 📖

1993, *Mary Green, Stanley Gilmar,* 160 pages ➤ Ten Speed Press, P.O. Box 7123, Berkeley, CA 94707, USA; US$11.95; credit cards; (510) 845-8414, fax (510) 559-1629, order@tenspeed.com ▪ This book covers all the major aspects of importing, including what to buy, developing markets, working in a foreign culture, and customs procedures and clearances. New, completely revised edition of a classic. [ID:1459]

How to Form and Manage Successful Business Alliances 📖

1992 ➤ Prospectus Publications, Suite 900, Barrister House, 180 Elgin Street, Ottawa, Ontario K2P 2K3; $29.95; VISA, MC; (613) 231-2727, fax (613) 237-7666 ▪ This book discusses the steps to a successful business alliance, from finding the right partner to negotiating and managing a successful agreement. Visit the distributor's web site at www.prospectus.com. [ID:1626]

IDB Projects 📖 🖥

10/year, Inter-American Development Bank ➤ John Hopkins University Press (JHUP), P.O. Box 19966, Baltimore, MD 21211, USA; US$150/year; VISA, MC; (800) 548-1784, fax (410) 516-6968, jlorder@jhunix.hcf.jhu.edu ▪ Advertises business opportunities arising from projects financed by the Inter-American Development Bank. Visit the IDB web site at www.iadb.org and enter the "Business Opportunities" menu. Also visit www.press.jhu.edu/press/journals, the distributor's web site. [ID:2609]

IESCOnet-International Trade with Mexico 🖥

www.iesconet.com ▪ The main purpose of this site is to encourage trade with Mexico. The site describes services related to export-import businesses. It also includes information on immigration issues and currency exchange. [ID:2759]

IFInet 🖥

www.dfait-maeci.gc.ca/ifinet ▪ Provides Canadian exporters with information on projects financed by international financial institutions. Site includes business guides and hotlinks. Register to receive a password. [ID:2648]

Importing: A Practical Guide to an Exciting and Rewarding Business 📖

1995, *Anne Curran, Glen Mullett,* 208 pages ➤ Self-Counsel Press, 1481 Charlotte Road, North Vancouver, B.C. V7J 1H1; $24.95; VISA, MC; (604) 986-3366, fax (604) 986-3947, sales@self-counsel.com ▪ Guide to understanding Canada Customs' rules and regulations. Practical advice on every aspect of importing: filling out forms, dealing with customs brokers, NAFTA, finding suppliers, restricted goods. Visit the distributor's address at www.self-counsel.com. [ID:1572]

InfoExport 🖥

www.infoexport.gc.ca ▪ Provides links to a number of important sources of information for Canadian exporters. [ID:2534]

The International Business Dictionary and Reference 📖

1991, *Lewis Presner,* 504 pages ➤ John Wiley & Sons, 22 Worchester Drive, Rexdale, Ontario M9W 1L1; $69.95; credit cards; (800) 567-4797, fax (800) 565-6802 ▪ Uses an integrative approach stressing the cross- and interdisciplinary dynamics of international business. Visit the distributor's web site at www.wiley.com/products/worldwide/canada. [ID:1009]

International Dimensions of Human Resource Management 📖

1993, *Peter Dowling, Randall Schuler,* Wadsworth ➤ Nelson Canada, 1120 Birchmount Road, Scarborough, Ontario M1K 5G4; $38.95; credit cards; (800) 268-2222, fax (800) 430-4445 ▪ Focuses on managing human resources in the international environment. Examines recruitment and selection of international employees, performance appraisal, training and development and international labour relations. A new edition will be published in 1998. [ID:1183]

The International Directory of Importers 📖

1998 ➤ International Directory of Importers, 1741 Kekamek NW, Poulsbo, Washington 98730, USA; Price varies from US$225 to $450; credit cards; (800) 818-0140, fax (360) 697-4696 ▪ Extensive directory with 150,000 listings of worldwide importers. Designed for use by exporters, manufacturers, and trading firms, this nine-volume set covers Europe, the Middle East, North America, South and Central America, Asia Pacific, and Africa. Firms are listed alphabetically under commodity headings. Area directories sell at different prices ranging from $225 to $450. [ID:1188]

International Trade Tips 💻

www.iceonline.com/home/panthony/tips.htm ▪ This site is maintained by a private firm specializing in trade between Canada and other countries. They offer tips on various topics such as payment methods, sales contracts and other vital information to run your globally-minded business. [ID:2760]

Multiculturalism Means Business: a Directory of Business Contacts 📖

1993, 88 pages ➤ Department of Canadian Heritage, Multiculturalism and Citizenship Canada, 15 Eddy Street, Hull, Québec K1A 0M5; free; (819) 953-0628 ▪ Designed to promote networking, this directory reflects the ethnocultural diversity of Canada. Extensive listings of bilateral business councils and ethnocultural directories are very useful for establishing contacts. Also in French. [ID:1310]

Open Network Trade Resources Access (onTrac) 💻

www.ontrac.yorku.ca ▪ This Canadian site provides a variety of business information for small and medium enterprises. You can make business contacts and find trade leads. You can even find specific information such as ethnocultural business associations located in Canada. [ID:2761]

So You Want To Export? 📖

1995 ➤ InfoCentre, Department of Foreign Affairs and International Trade (DFAIT), 125 Sussex Dr., Ottawa, Ontario K1A 0G2; free; (800) 267-8376, fax (613) 996-9709 ▪ This booklet examines vital factors to consider prior to any venture into new markets. It takes you through each step of your decision-making process, from analyzing your product or service to dealing with a trade commissioner. [ID:1498]

StatsCan Online 💻

www.statcan.ca; $40 registration plus $25 subscription; ▪ Statistics Canada's premier online service for fast and reliable access to Canadian trade commodity data. Subscribers can access StatsCan Online from anywhere in Canada, 24 hours a day, with no long distance charges. Subscription includes software and 1-800 Help Line. [ID:2613]

Strategis 💻

http://strategis.ic.gc.ca ▪ Industry Canada's powerful Internet-based information service for Canadian business people. Up-to-date information on international business opportunities, trade and investment is available at this site, along with information for small businesses. [ID:2518]

Supplyline 📖 💻

Quarterly, *Maureen Johnson* ➤ CODE International, 321 Chapel Street, Ottawa, Ontario K1N 7Z2; free; (613) 232-7101, fax (613) 235-2506 ▪ A bilingual four-page flyer on CODE International's activities, aimed at consultants and companies with interests in procuring supplies for education and other basic needs overseas, and in project management for development. Available on the web at www.codeinc.com. [ID:1115]

Ten Steps for Export Success 📖 💻
1997 ➤ InfoCentre, Department of Foreign Affairs and International Trade (DFAIT), 125 Sussex Dr., Ottawa, Ontario K1A 0G2; free; (800) 267-8376, fax (613) 996-9709 ▪ A publication which fosters small business export activity by providing information on such aspects as evaluating your export potential, selecting and researching foreign target markets, choosing an entry strategy, determining your price, and implementing your export plan. Available on the Web at www.infoexport.gc.ca. [ID:1590]

US Government National trade Data Bank 💻
www.stat-usa.gov/BEN/databases.html ▪ The US government's comprehensive international trade and export promotion database includes international market research reports, export opportunities, indexes of foreign and domestic companies, how-to market guides, and reports on demographic, political, and socio-economic conditions for hundreds of countries. [ID:2616]

Western Economic Diversification 💻
www.wd.gc.ca ▪ WD's goal is to help western Canadian small and medium-sized businesses grow and create jobs. This web site offers information on business planning, accessing capital, export and trade development, selling to government markets, and government programs and services for small and medium-sized businesses. [ID:2727]

World Trade Organization 💻
www.wto.org ▪ Primary internet site for the World Trade Organization. Provides information on international trade policy, research reports and other trade-related resources. [ID:2610]

WorldClass 💻
http://web.idirect.com/~tiger ▪ The WorldClass supersite links you to over 650 of the world's best business sites in over 80 countries. From here you can obtain news of current business trends or research a potential employer. The site also offers an excellent opportunity to connect with important people in your field. [ID:2584]

Profiles of International Business Services

The profiles which follow focus on federal government incentives and activities in the area of international trade and investment (13 profiles), as well as services offered by private trade associations and private firms (10 profiles). Many of the federal government services are specially designed to assist small- and medium-sized businesses moving into the international arena. Such programs are usually provided free of charge, or on a cost-sharing basis. Privately funded industry and trade associations provide a forum to promote the export interests of member firms and offer a wide array of informational services, such as seminars and business publications.

16 provincial government business and trade contacts are also listed in this section. Full profiles on many of these can be found in Chapter 34, Careers in Government. Finally, there is a listing of 31 foreign trade councils, both bilateral councils promoting Canadian trade and investment with one country and regional organizations with a broader mandate.

FEDERAL GOVERNMENT SERVICES

Agriculture and Agri-Food Canada (AAFC)

Market & Industry Services Branch, 10th Floor, 930 Carling Ave.,
Ottawa, Ontario K1A 3O5; (613) 759-1000, fax (613) 759-7503, www.agr.ca

AAFC's international mandate includes participating in the negotiation of multilateral, regional and bilateral trade agreements, ensuring that such agreements are effectively implemented by our international partners and that market access gains achieved through these agreements are realized. This mandate is complemented by the identification of worldwide export opportunities and the furnishing of timely advice and information on trade policies and practices affecting agri-food trade. In an effort to take full advantage of emerging trade opportunities in the agri-food sectors, the government is placing additional agri-food trade and marketing specialists in priority markets abroad. Specialists have already been placed in Japan, South Korea, Singapore, Taiwan, Dubai, and Mexico.

AAFC's web site provides a wealth of information for potential exporters under the Agri-Food Trade Network menu. Overseas market analysis, advice for exporters, a discussion of foreign regulations and an extensive list of domestic and international trade contacts make this site a must visit for anyone contemplating an export venture in the agribusiness sector. [ID:5591]

Atlantic Canada Opportunities Agency

Head Office, P.O. Box 6051, Blue Cross Centre, 644 Main Street,
Moncton, N.B. E1C 9J8; (800) 561-7862, fax (506) 851-7403, www.acoa.ca

The Atlantic Canada Opportunities Agency (ACOA) is a federally funded organization created to help improve the economic diversity and health of the Maritimes. The agency works with various federal and provincial government departments as well as the private sector to encourage and facilitate the emergence of new businesses in Atlantic Canada. The agency is also active in promoting the capabilities of Atlantic businesses on a national and international scale.

ACOA's head office is in Moncton and there are regional offices located in Fredericton, Halifax, Sydney (Enterprise Cape Breton Corporation—see listing below), Charlottetown and St. John's. The agency maintains an interesting web site with information on its activities and profiles of a number of successful companies in the Atlantic region. There are also links to several related sites. [ID:6736]

Business Development Bank of Canada

Suite 400, BDC Building, 5 Place Ville Marie, Montréal, Québec H3B 5E7;
(888) 463-6232, fax (514) 283-2872, bus_service_center@bdc.x400.gc.ca, www.bdc.ca

The Business Development Bank of Canada (BDC) is Canada's small business bank. It plays a leadership role in delivering financial and management services, with a particular focus on the emerging and exporting sectors of the economy.

BDC's financial services include working capital loans, such as Working Capital for Growth. Management services include a wide range of business counselling, management support and mentoring services for new and expanding businesses, exporters, women, young entrepreneurs and Aboriginal entrepreneurs. BDC also offers a New Exporters program (NEXPRO). BDC maintains an excellent web site that provides information on the bank's services and advice for those considering starting or expanding a business. [ID:5580]

Canada Business Service Centres

Offices throughout Canada, info@cbsc.ic.gc.ca, http://cbsc.org

Canada Business Service Centres (CBSCs) provide Canadian business people with a wide range of information on government services, programs and regulations. The centres reduce the complexity of dealing with various levels of government.

Each CSBC offers a variety of products and services to help clients obtain quick, accurate and comprehensive business information. The CBSBs minimize telephone run-around, inadequate or incorrect information, and duplication of government services. This enables clients to make well-informed business decisions in an increasingly global economy.

Services are available in person at each CBSC and also via toll-free telecentres for each province and territory. Toll-free fax-on-demand service and services on the Web are also available. Visit a provincial CBSC site as your first stopping point. [ID:6737]

Alberta: The Business Link, Suite 100, 10237 - 104 Street, Edmonton, Alberta T5J 1B1; (403) 422-7722 or (800) 272-9675, fax (403) 422-0055, Buslink@cbsc.ic.gc.ca

B.C.: 601 West Cordova Street, Vancouver, B.C. V6B 1G1; (604) 775-5525 or (800) 667-2272, fax (604) 775-5520, howe.linda@cbsc.ic.gc.ca

Manitoba: P.O.Box 2609, 8th Floor, 330 Portage Ave., Winnipeg, Manitoba R3C 4B3; (204) 984-2272 or (800) 665-2019, fax (204) 983-3852, manitoba@cbsc.ic.gc.ca

New Brunswick: 570 Queen Street, Fredericton, N.B. E3B 6Z6; (506) 444-6140 or (800) 668-1010, fax (506) 444-6172, cbscnb@cbsc.ic.gc.ca

Newfoundland: P.O. Box 8687, 90 O'Leary Ave., St. John's, Nfld. A1B 3T1; (709) 772-6022 or (800) 668-1010, fax (709) 772-6090, St.Johns@cbsc.ic.gc.ca

Nova Scotia: 1575 Brunswick Street, Halifax, N.S. B3J 2G1; (902) 426-8604 or (800) 668-1010, fax (902) 426-6530, halifax@cbsc.ic.gc.ca

Ontario: Ontario Business Call Centre, 230 Richmond Street West, 9th Floor, Toronto, Ontario, M5V 3E5; (416) 954-4636 or (800) 567-2345, fax (416) 954-8597, cobcc@cbsc.ic.gc.ca

P.E.I.: P.O. Box 40, 75 Fitzroy Street, Charlottetown, P.E.I. C1A 7K2; (902) 368-0771 or (800) 668-1010, fax (902) 566-7377, pei@cbsc.ic.gc.ca

Québec: Info entrepreneurs, Suite 12500, Plaza Level, 5 Place Ville Marie, Montréal, Québec H3B 4Y2; (514) 496-4636 or (800) 322-4636; fax (514) 496-5934, Info-entrepreneurs@bfdrq-fordq.gc.ca

Saskatchewan: 122 - 3rd Ave. N., Saskatoon, Sask. S7K 2H6; (306) 956-2323 or (800) 667-4374; fax (306) 956-2328, saskatooncsbsc@cbsc.ic.gc.ca

N.W.T.: P.O. Box 1320, 8th Floor, Scotia Centre, Yellowknife, N.W.T. X1A 2L9; (403) 873-7958 or (800) 661-059, yel@cbsc.ic.gc.ca

Yukon: 201-208 Main Street, Whitehorse, Yukon Y1A 2A9; (403) 633-6257 or (800) 661-0543, perry.debbie@cbsc.ic.gc.ca

Canadian Commercial Corporation (CCC)

11th Floor, 50 O'Connor Street, Ottawa, Ontario K1A 0S6; (613) 995-0560, fax (613) 995-2121, info@ccc.ca, www.ccc.ca

Canadian Commercial Corporation (CCC), a federal Crown corporation, offers exporters a wide range of services designed to help them negotiate sales to foreign governments and international agencies. In such transactions, CCC assumes the role of prime contractor and assists the Canadian supplier through all phases leading to the conclusion of a transaction.

CCC's participation, on behalf of the Canadian government, normally guarantees performance of the contract. This enhances the supplier's credibility while increasing the customer's confidence. Exporters using the services of CCC benefit from the authority, technical expertise, and support of the Canadian government in their foreign export ventures.

For further information, ask for the CCC Infokit at the number shown above or visit the CCC's creative web site called the "Virtual Trade Plaza." This site provides information on programs, recent developments, staffing and offers a number of useful links to other trade organizations. [ID:5579]

Canadian Foreign Service Institute

Centre for Intercultural Learning (CIL), 15 Bisson Street, Hull, Québec J8Y 5M2; (800) 852-9211, fax (819) 997-5409, monique.marion@bisson01.x400.gc.ca, www.dfait-maeci.gc.ca

The Centre for Intercultural Learning (CIL) assists Canadian professionals from NGOs, universities, private industry, and government to develop crosscultural competencies essential for their success. The centre takes a comprehensive approach when preparing professionals for their international activity, identifying the clients' requirements and developing learning solutions that enable them to effectively engage in their activities.

Pre-departure briefing sessions for short- and long-term assignments are held regularly. In addition, the CIL provides project-related programs, country anthologies, in-country programming, on-arrival orientations, and intercultural training. [ID:6617]

Canadian International Development Agency (CIDA)

Industrial Cooperation Program (INC), Canadian Partnership Branch, 200 Promenade du Portage, Hull, Québec K1J 0G7; (819) 997-5006, fax (819) 953-6088, http://w3.acdi-cida.gc.ca

CIDA's Industrial Co-operation Program (INC) helps Canadian firms seeking opportunities for investment, joint ventures and transfers of proven technology in Asia, Latin America, the Caribbean, Africa, and the Middle East. The program offers financial incentives to Canadian firms to develop long-term arrangements for business cooperation and to undertake project definition studies in developing countries. To be eligible for funding assistance, proposals must clearly demonstrate social, economic and industrial benefits to both the host country and Canada. For an information kit, contact CIDA's Enquiries and Public Service Unit, (819) 997-5006. CIDA's web site also has information on INC. [ID:5592]

Export and Import Controls Bureau (EPD)

Department of Foreign Affairs and International Trade (DFAIT), 125 Sussex Drive, Ottawa, Ontario K1A 0G2; (613) 996-2387, fax (613) 996-9933, www.dfait-maeci.gc.ca

Canada has established export and import controls on a number of products in order to support domestic policies and international commitments and agreements. Export controls impose restrictions on goods that may be sold or sent from Canada to other countries, while import controls set out restrictions on goods that may be brought into Canada.

DFAIT experts can provide advice on relevant restrictions, permits, and quotas that may apply to the product of interest and any other documentation required. [ID:5589]

Export Development Corporation (EDC)

151 O'Connor Street, Ottawa, Ontario K1A 1K3; (888) 332-3320, fax (613) 862-1267, export@edc4.edc.ca, www.edc.ca

The Export Development Corporation (EDC) is a financial services corporation dedicated to helping Canadian businesses compete in world markets. EDC provides a wide range of financial and risk management services, including export credit insurance, financing to foreign buyers of Canadian goods, and services and guarantees. Supported by a network of centres of expertise that provide in-depth knowledge, research, analysis, and skills, the corporation delivers its products and services through eight sector-based customer teams plus a cross-sector team dedicated to serving smaller exporters.

EDC is a Crown corporation owned by the Government of Canada. It is financially self-sustaining, operates on commercial principles, charges fees and premiums for its products and interest on its loans. It does not provide grants or subsidies.

EDC export insurance services include short-term and medium-term credit insurance, bid/performance related insurance and guarantees, surety bond support, equipment (political risk) insurance, and foreign investment insurance. EDC insurance policies protect exporters against various losses due to commercial and political risks. Examples include buyer insolvency, default on payments, repudiation of goods, contract termination, foreign exchange conversion or transfer difficulties, war, revolution, or insurrection preventing payment, cancellation of government import or export permits, wrongful calls on bid/performance letters of guarantee, and inability to repatriate capital or equipment due to political problems.

EDC financing products enable Canadian exporters to provide their customers with flexible medium- or long-term financing. Such services include lines of credit with foreign banks or agencies worldwide, protocols, note purchase arrangements, direct buyer loans, long-term preshipment financing, leveraged lease financing, and project risk financing packages.

EDC offices are located in Vancouver, Edmonton, Calgary, Winnipeg, London, Toronto, Montréal, Moncton, and Halifax. EDC maintains an excellent web site that contains information on its services and posts job opportunities online. [ID:5578]

Export Orientation/Training Programs (NEBS, NEXOS)
Export and Investment Programs Division,
Department of Foreign Affairs and International Trade (DFAIT),
125 Sussex Drive, Ottawa, Ontario K1A 0G2; (613) 944-0018, fax (613) 995-5773, www.dfait-maeci.gc.ca

The Department of Foreign Affairs and International Trade offers two training programs to help small and medium-sized Canadian companies expand into selected export markets. The New Exporters to Border States (NEBS) program is for Canadian companies that have not previously exported but are "export-ready." Participants are invited to a Canadian trade office across the US border for a one- or two-day course on the entire process of exporting. For more information, contact the International Trade Centre nearest you or the United States Trade and Investment Development Division of DFAIT.

The New Exporters to Overseas (NEXOS) program extends the NEBS concept to help exporters new to Western Europe learn the essentials of doing business there. Each NEXOS mission focuses on a specific sector in a specific country and includes a visit to a major sectoral trade fair. For more information contact the Western Europe Trade, Investment and Technology Division of DFAIT. [ID:5581]

Federal Office of Regional Development - Québec (FORD-Q)
Montréal, Québec; (514) 283-6412, fax (514) 283-3302, www.bfdrq-fordq.gc.ca

Le Bureau fédéral de développement régional (Québec) aide les PME à devenir davantage compétitive sur la scène économique internationale. Le Bureau donne aux PME accès à de l'information et des services conseils, de l'aide pour l'animation économique ainsi qu'à un soutien financier complémentaire. Les trois volets d'intervention sont l'aide à l'innovation et à la recherche et le développement, l'aide au développement des marchés et à l'exportation et l'aide à l'entrepreneurship et au développemement du climat des affaires. Le Bureau fédéral de développement régional (Québec) a des bureaux à travers la province. [ID:7035]

Federal Economic Development Initiative in Northern Ontario (FedNor)
302 Queen Street E., Sault Ste. Marie, Ontario P6A 1Z1;
(800) 461-6021, fax (705) 942-5434, fednor@ic.gc.ca, http://fednor.ic.gc.ca

FedNor is the federal government agency responsible for promoting economic growth, diversification, and job creation throughout the Northern Ontario region. FedNor has several projects: a Not-For-Profit Fund, a Business Planning Initiative, the Northern Ontario Economic Development Fund, a Tourism Fund, and a pre-commercial fund. FedNor aids communities and small- to medium-sized enterprises to manage local economic development. It uses partnerships and financing to make scarce federal resources effective, to improve local access to investment capital, skills training, information, and new technology. It also has offices in Thunder Bay and Sudbury. [ID:7036]

Geographic Trade Divisions
Department of Foreign Affairs and International Trade (DFAIT), 125 Sussex Drive,
Ottawa, Ontario K1A 0G2; (800) 267-8376, fax (613) 996-9709, www.dfait-maeci.gc.ca

The Department of Foreign Affairs and International Trade has five geographic branches: Africa and Middle East, Asia Pacific, Europe, Latin America and Caribbean, and the US. Within these branches, geographic trade divisions provide advice and information about doing business in a particular country or region of the world. Trade officers for individual countries can identify promising export markets, help companies prepare for visits to potential markets, arrange participation in trade fairs, and involve exporters in visits to

Canada by foreign buyers. Interested persons should contact DFAIT's Inquiries Service for referrals. [ID:5577]

Department of Foreign Affairs and International Trade (DFAIT): Inquiries Service

Department of Foreign Affairs and International Trade (DFAIT), 125 Sussex Drive, Ottawa, Ontario K1A 0G2; (800) 267-8376, fax (613) 996-9709, sxcii.extott@extott09.x400.gc.ca, www.dfait-maeci.gc.ca

The Inquiries Service is DFAIT's public information resource centre. It provides information, advice and referrals. Staff can advise clients on DFAIT trade programs, services and publications.

The Inquiries Service maintains two interactive fax-on-demand systems which provide immediate access to Departmental publications. FaxLink Domestic stores a wide variety of trade and foreign policy related documents and is accessible within Canada only. Dial (613) 944-4500 from the handset of your fax machine. FaxLink International is available worldwide. Dial (613) 944-6500 from the handset of your fax machine. Inquiries Service publications are also available at the DFAIT web site. (For information on their international internships see the Canadian Government International Internships profile in Chapter 17, International Internships.) [ID:5573]

International Trade Centres (ITC)

Trade Development Operations (TDO), Department of Foreign Affairs and International Trade (DFAIT), 125 Sussex Drive, Ottawa, Ontario K1A 0G2; (800) 267-8376, fax (613) 996-9709, exportsource.gc.ca

There are currently 11 International Trade Centres (ITCs) located in major cities across Canada. These centres are the delivery point in Canada's regions for the trade development programs and services of DFAIT, offering a full-range of trade services including: basic export counselling, market opportunity information, guidance in the development of foreign marketing plans, information on technology transfer and joint venture opportunities, recruitment of participants for trade fairs and missions abroad, and arrangement of trade-related conferences and seminars. Each centre is linked to the DFAIT's computerized information network (WIN Exports, profiled below). [ID:5574]

ST. JOHN'S: Industry Canada, Cabot Place, 10th Floor, Phase II, Barter's Hill; P.O. Box 8950, St. John's, Nfld. A1B 3R9; (709) 772-5511, fax (709) 772-5093

CHARLOTTETOWN: Industry Canada, 75 Fitzroy Street; P.O. Box 1115, Charlottetown, P.E.I. C1A 7M8; (902) 566-7443, fax (902) 566-7450

HALIFAX: Industry Canada, 1800 Argyle Street, Fifth Floor, World Trade & Convention Centre; P.O. Box 940, Station M, Halifax, N.S. B3J 2V9; (902) 426-7540, fax (902) 426-5218

MONCTON: Industry Canada, Unit 103, 1045 Main Street, Moncton, N.B. E1C 1H1; (506) 851-6452, fax (506) 851-6429

MONTRÉAL: Industry Canada, 7th Floor, 5 Place Ville-Marie, Montréal, Québec H3B 2G2; (514) 283-6328, fax (514) 283-8794

TORONTO: Industry Canada, 4th Floor, Dominion Public Building, 1 Front Street W., Toronto, Ontario M5J 1A4; (416) 973-5053, fax (416) 973-8161

WINNIPEG: Industry Canada, 400 St.Mary Ave., 4th Floor; P.O. Box 981, Winnipeg, Manitoba R3C 2V2; (204) 983-5851, fax (204) 983-3182

SASKATOON: Industry Canada, 7th Floor, Princeton Tower, 123 - 2nd Ave. S., Saskatoon, Sask. S7K 7E6; (306) 975-5315, fax (306) 975-5334

REGINA: Industry Canada, 7th Floor, Princeton Tower, 123-2nd Ave.S.; P.O. Box 3750, Regina, Sask. S4P 3N8; (306) 975-5314, fax (306) 975-5334

EDMONTON (and the NWT): Industry Canada, Suite 540, Canada Place, 9700 Jasper Ave., Edmonton, Alberta T5J 4C3; (403) 495-2944 fax (403) 495-4507

CALGARY: Industry Canada, Suite 400, 639 - 5th Ave. S.W., Calgary, Alberta T2M 0M9; (403) 292-4575, fax (403) 292-4578

VANCOUVER (and the Yukon Territory): Industry Canada, Suite 2000, 300 West Georgia Street, Vancouver, B.C. V6B 6E1; (604) 666-0434, fax (604) 666-0954

Program for Export Market Development (PEMD)
Contact the nearest International Trade Centre; (800) 267-8376, fax (613) 996-9709,
sxci.enqserv@extott09.x400.gc.ca, www.dfait-maeci.gc.ca/english/trade/handbook/menu.htm

Jointly administered by DFAIT and Industry Canada, the Program for Export Market Development (PEMD) is the federal government's primary export promotion program, supporting a variety of activities designed to assist Canadian companies to expand into international markets. The objective of PEMD is to increase export sales of Canadian goods and services by sharing the costs of activities that companies normally could or would not undertake alone, thereby reducing risks involved in entering a foreign market.

PEMD will share up to 50 per cent of eligible expenses, financed as a repayable contribution rather than a grant. Funded activities include: market development strategies; assistance to new-to-exporting companies; capital projects bidding and trade association activities. The principal element, Market Development Strategies (MDS), provides assistance on the basis of a company's market-targeted, multi-activity, one- to two-year international marketing plan. The PEMD web site includes links to a variety of other useful programs, including other DFAIT trade initiatives and private industry trade associations. [ID:5575]

Renaissance Eastern Europe
Central and Eastern Europe (CEE) Branch,
Canadian International Development Agency, 200 Promenade du Portage, Hull, Québec
K1A 0G4; (819) 997-5456, fax (819) 953-6088, info@acdi-cida.gc.ca, http://w3.acdi-cida.gc.ca

The Renaissance Eastern Europe (REE) program is the commercial component of Canada's technical assistance program for the Central and Eastern Europe region. It is managed by the CEE Branch of the Canadian International Development Agency. The objective of the REE Program is to assist Canadian companies in positioning themselves in the emerging markets of Central and Eastern Europe and the former Soviet Union. Although REE is not a trade promotion program, it cost-shares certain business expenses and is complementary to the Program for Export Market Development of the Department of Foreign Affairs and International Trade.

Funding is available to Canadian companies for two types of projects in the region: feasibility studies leading to the formation of joint ventures or subsidiaries, or structured cooperation agreements with local firms and/or direct investment; and training programs related to the above. For further information on eligibility, refer to the CEE Branch page on the CIDA Internet site, or contact CIDA at the numbers above. [ID:5586]

Strategis
1st Floor, East Tower, 235 Queen Street, Ottawa, Ontario K1A 0H5;
(800) 328-6189, fax (613) 954-1894, hotline.service@ic.gc.ca, http://strategis.ic.gc.ca

Strategis is Industry Canada's powerful online business information source. Information formerly on the BOSS system has been moved over to Strategis. Visit Strategis for information on international business opportunities, trade and investment.

The Canadian Company Capabilities database, used globally to find Canadian supply sources, investment partners, agents and joint venture projects, is part of Strategis. Registration is free. Go to http://strategis.ic.gc.ca/cdncc to register your company, or call the tollfree help line. [ID:6952]

The Standards Council of Canada
Suite 1200, 45 O'Connor Street, Ottawa, Ontario K1P 6N7;
(613) 238-3222, fax (613) 995-4564, info@scc.ca, www.scc.ca

The Standards Council of Canada (SCC) is a Crown corporation with the mandate to promote effective voluntary standardization in Canada. The Council maintains strategic alliances with a number of international standards organizations in order to ensure that Canadian standards remain compatible with those on the world stage. The Council also works to develop mutual recognition of national standards between Canada and its key trading partners. The Council sells copies of foreign and international standards, which can be ordered toll-free at (888) 782-6327.

The SCC maintains a web site that contains information on its mandate and activities and links to a number of transnational and foreign standards regulation bodies. This is a rich source of standards-related information. [ID:5590]

Trade Commissioner Service

Overseas Operations, Department of Foreign Affairs and International Trade (DFAIT),
125 Sussex Drive, Ottawa, Ontario K1A 0G2; (613) 996-0245, fax (613) 996-1225, www.infoexport.gc.ca

Trade Commissioners have been serving the Canadian business community throughout the world for over 100 years. Through the Department of Foreign Affairs and International Trade (DFAIT), Trade Commissioners work to promote and enhance Canadian business interests in the global marketplace. From posts in more than 125 cities worldwide, Trade Commissioners support and complement the efforts of export- and market-ready companies (whether they are large firms or small and medium sized enterprises) in achieving tangible and significant results in international markets.

Before contacting a Trade Commissioner abroad, you should develop your international market entry strategy and get in touch with one of the 12 International Trade Centres (ITCs) located in Canada (for contact information, see the profile included in this section). Trade Commissioners at the ITCs provide assistance to Canadian companies that are finalizing their export plans. They can identify key foreign markets and help you refine your market strategy. Visit DFAIT's InfoExport web site for more information. [ID:5576]

Trade Facilitation Office Canada (TFOC)

Suite 500, 56 Sparks Street, Ottawa, Ontario K1P 5A9;
(800) 267-9674, fax (613) 233-7860, tfoc@ottawa.net, www.tfoc.ca

Trade Facilitation Office Canada (TFOC), a not-for-profit organization funded by the Canadian International Development Agency, helps exporters from developing countries to find markets in Canada. The office fosters contact between exporters in the developing world and Canadian importers and maintains a data bank of importers, exporters, and their products.

TFOC services available to Canadian importers include access to information on the TFOC data bank of 2,000 exporters from client countries, access to incoming missions of exporters, and opportunities to participate in outgoing missions of Canadian importers to client countries. Importers can register with TFOC by phone or through the TFOC web site. [ID:5587]

Western Economic Diversification (WD)

1200-1055 Dunsmuir Street, Bentall Tower 4, Box 49276,
Bentall Postal Station, Vancouver, B.C. V7X 1L3; (888) 338-9378, fax (604) 666-2353, www.wd.gc.ca

Western Economic Diversification (WD) was established in 1987 to encourage the development of nontraditional business in the western provinces of Manitoba, Saskatchewan, Alberta, and British Columbia, with offices in Edmonton, Saskatoon, Winnipeg, and Vancouver. WD utilizes partnerships with both the government and private sector to provide financial, management, and planning assistance to emerging companies.

The Western Business Service Network offers comprehensive information on government programs and regulations as well as business counselling from over 100 offices throughout western Canada. WD also offers information on exporting and marketing products overseas. WD maintains a comprehensive web site that offers information on its services, a number of useful links, and contact information for regional offices. [ID:6738]

WIN Exports

Export Development Division (TCE), Department of Foreign Affairs and International Trade (DFAIT), 125 Sussex Drive, Ottawa, Ontario K1A 0G2; (800) 551-4946, fax (800) 667-3802, www.dfait-maeci.gc.ca

The World Information Network for Exports–WIN Exports–is DFAIT's computerized system used by 1,200 trade staff around the world. It currently lists over 26,000 Canadian exporting firms and their capabilities, including their products and services available for export, foreign markets/countries that the firm is considering or currently active in, and company contacts responsible for export activities. Over 100,000 requests for export information from foreign buyers are received annually.

DFAIT trade development officers use WIN Exports to identify Canadian suppliers able to respond to sales opportunities, make appropriate contacts on behalf of Canadian companies, and report back with advice to help them make informed decisions. To apply for WIN registration, contact the International Trade Centre nearest you. (See the International Trade Centres (ITC) listings included in this chapter.) [ID:5584]

PROVINCIAL GOVERNMENT SERVICES

Below is a listing of provincial and territorial government offices involved in export promotion. (For detailed profiles see Chapter 34, Careers in Government.)

Alberta Economic Development

4th Floor, Commerce Place, 10155 - 102 Street, Edmonton, Alberta T5J 4L6; (403) 422-6236, fax (403) 422-9127, imsa@censsw.gov.ab.ca, www.edt.gov.ab.ca [ID:5595]

British Columbia Centre
Trade and Investment Office

Suite 730, 999 Canada Place, Vancouver, B.C. V6C 3E1; (604) 844-1900, fax (604) 660-2457, jburnes@eivic.ei.gov.bc.ca, www.ei.gov.bc.ca [ID:5596]

Enterprise Cape Breton Corporation

4th Floor, Commerce Tower, 15 Dorchester Street, Sydney, N.S. B1P 6T7; (800) 705-3926, fax (902) 564-3825, info@ecbc.ca, www.ecbc.ca [ID:6318]

Manitoba Trade and
Investment Corporation

Suite 410, 155 Carlton Street, Winnipeg, Manitoba R3C 3H8; (800) 529-9981, fax (204) 957-1793, mbtrade@itt.gov.mb.ca, www.gov.mb.ca/itt/trade [ID:5597]

New Brunswick Department of
Economic Development and Tourism

P.O. Box 6000, Centennial Building, Fredericton, N.B. E3B 5H1; (506) 453-3984, fax (506) 453-5428, wwwedt@gov.nb.ca, http://inter.gov.nb.ca/edt [ID:5598]

Newfoundland and Labrador Department
of Industry, Trade and Technology

P.O. Box 8700, St. John's, Nfld. A1B 4J6; (709) 729-5600, fax (709) 729-5936, info@ditt.gov.nf.ca, http://success.nfld.net [ID:5599]

Newfoundland Department of
Development and Rural Renewal

P.O. Box 8700, St. John's, Nfld. A1B 4J6; (709) 729-7000, fax (709) 729-7244, INFO@GOV.NF.CA, www.gov.nf.ca [ID:6316]

Northwest Territories
Department of Resources,
Wildlife and Economic Development

P.O. Box 1320, 6th Floor, Scotia Centre, Yellowknife, N.W.T. X1A 2L9; (403) 873-7115, fax (403) 873-0563, www.rwed.gov.nt.ca [ID:5600]

Nova Scotia Economic
Development and Tourism

Investment and Trade, P.O. Box 519, World Trade and Convention Centre, 1800 Argyle Street, Halifax, N.S. B3J 2R7; (902) 424-6650, fax (902) 424-5739, iat@gov.ns.ca, www.gov.ns.ca/ecor [ID:5601]

Ontario International Trade Corporation

5th Floor, Hearst Block, 900 Bay Street, Toronto, Ontario M7A 2E1; (416) 325-6665, fax (416) 325-6653, www.gov.on.ca [ID:5602]

Ontario Ministry of Economic
Development, Trade and Tourism

Exporter Development, 5th Floor, Hearst Block, 900 Bay Street, Toronto, Ontario M7A 2E1; (416) 325-6665, fax (416) 325-6653, www.gov.on.ca [ID:5603]

P.E.I.-Enterprise
Prince Edward Island

P.O. Box 910, Charlottetown, P.E.I. C1A 7L9; (902) 368-6300, fax (902) 368-6301, invest@gov.pe.ca, www.gov.pe.ca [ID:5604]

Québec: Ministère de l'industrie,
du commerce, de la science
et de la technologie (MICST)

710 Place d'Youville, Québec, Québec G1R 4Y4; (418) 691-5950, fax (418) 644-0118, info@micst.gouv.qc.ca, www.micst.gouv.qc.ca [ID:6319]

Saskatchewan Trade
and Export Partnership

P.O. Box 1787, Regina, Sask. S4P 3C6; (306) 787-9210, fax (306) 787-6666, www.sasktrade.sk.ca [ID:5606]

Yukon Department
of Economic Development

P.O. Box 2703, Suite 400, 211 Main Street, Whitehorse, Yukon Y1A 2C6; (403) 667-3014, fax (403) 667-
8601, www.gov.yk.ca [ID:5607]

CANADIAN TRADE ASSOCIATIONS

Alliance of Manufacturers & Exporters Canada

4th Floor, 75 International Blvd., Toronto, Ontario M9W 6L9;
(416) 798-8000, fax (416) 798-8050, national@the-alliance.com, www.the-alliance.org

The Alliance of Manufacturers & Exporters Canada was formed in 1996 when the Canadian Exporters' Association merged with the Canadian Manufacturers' Association. The Alliance seeks to improve the overall competitiveness of Canadian industry and its export opportunities. It does this by lobbying the federal government on issues of concern to its members, providing timely information on trade and manufacturing related matters, providing opportunities for professional training and promoting the development and utilization of new technologies. The Alliance has an extensive information network and provides services to members through a wide variety of publications and electronic services. The Alliance also maintains a web site that contains much of its information online. [ID:6314]

Canadian Chamber of Commerce

Suite 501, Delta Office Tower, 350 Sparks Street,
Ottawa, Ontario K1R 7S8; (613) 238-4000, fax (613) 238-7643, info@chamber.ca, www.chamber.ca

The Canadian Chamber of Commerce provides a wide array of services to businesses interested in international trade and investment, and in developing or expanding overseas operations. International connections are maintained through trade missions and a network of worldwide Chambers of Commerce. International trade information is available through seminars, networking ventures, cooperation with other business groups and the Internet. The Chamber also serves the business community by providing analyses of national and international political developments which may affect trade. Furthermore, the Chamber advocates to government bodies on a policy framework that supports Canadian business in the international arena.

The Chamber is the only authorized issuer of Carnets in Canada. A Carnet is a simple customs document for businesspeople working and travelling internationally. In simple terms, it is a passport for goods enabling the holder to make customs arrangements in advance and enter foreign countries with fewer delays. The Chamber's web site provides information on services, programs, seminars and other business-related topics. [ID:5611]

Canadian Council for International Business (CCIB)

Delta Office Tower, Suite 501, 350 Sparks Street,
Ottawa, Ontario K1R 7S8; (613) 230-5462, fax (613) 230-7087, hecnar@ccib.org, www.chamber.ca

The Canadian Council for International Business (CCIB) is a not-for-profit business association concerned with global policy developments affecting Canadian business. As the Canadian secretariat to the International Chamber of Commerce (ICC) and the Business and Industry Advisory Committee (BIAC) of the OECD, the CCIB provides Canadian business input into the development of global business policy. As a business policy advocate, the CCIB represents business views to the Canadian government, and through ICC and BIAC to international institutions such as the World Trade Organization and the United Nations.

The CCIB is also the exclusive Canadian distributor of a range of International Chamber of Commerce (ICC) publications—a premier source of information about trade rules, standard terms, and model contracts developed by the ICC such as the widely-used

ICC INCOTERMS. These practical guides explain in detail how trade and financial mechanisms work, and alert users to potential pitfalls. [ID:5613]

Canadian Importers Association Inc.
Suite 700, 210 Dundas Street W., Toronto, Ontario M5G 2E8;
(416) 595-5333, fax (416) 595-8226, info@importers.ca, www.importers.ca

The Canadian Importers' Association is a nonprofit, private sector trade association representing the interests of Canadian importers. The Association offers members three primary services. First, it represents the interests of Canadian importers to various federal departments. Second, it offers consultation to members on issues of international trade. And third, it provides detailed information on the latest developments in trade law and practice. The association is also affiliated with a number of other trade-related organizations. [ID:5615]

Canadian International Freight Forwarders' Association (CIFFA)
P.O. Box 929, Streetsville, Ontario L5M 2C5;
(905) 567-4633, fax (905) 542-2716, admin@ciffa.com, www.ciffa.com

The Canadian International Freight Forwarders' Association (CIFFA) provides a membership directory useful to businesses involved in overseas activities. Members adhere to professional standard trading conditions and participate in the CIFFA education system to ensure the professional quality of their staff. CIFFA also encourages Parliament to enact legislation which improves the conditions of international trade and the freight industry.

CIFFA's web site contains basic information on its activities and an online version of the association's newsletter. [ID:5616]

Canadian Society of Customs Brokers
111 York Street, Ottawa, Ontario K1N 5T4;
(613) 562-3543, fax (613) 562-3548, cscb@cscb.ca, www.cscb.ca

The Canadian Society of Customs Brokers (CSCB) undertakes two primary tasks for its members. One, it provides timely information on a variety of technical and business issues. Two, it represents members' interests to government departments and agencies, primarily Revenue Canada. Customs brokers clear incoming imports, collect duties owed to the government and prepare customs documentation for Canadian exports. Currently, brokers clear more than 80 per cent of all shipments into Canada. The CSBC provides a range of educational services and courses which are required by Revenue Canada before an individual may be considered a "Qualified Person" entitled to work as a customs broker.

The CSCB's web site contains information on the society and its efforts and provides helpful links to international trade organizations and the International Federation of Customs Brokers Association. [ID:5617]

Commercial Bank Services
All of the large chartered banks have international trade divisions offering a wide array of services to exporters. These services include letters of credit, performance guarantees, trade promotion, and informational services. General guides on export financing are also available. Banks also typically maintain up-to-date information on international markets and analyze credit worthiness of potential foreign purchasers in order to minimize client risk. (For contact information and profiles on commercial banks see Chapter 33, The Private Sector.) [ID:5618]

International Chamber of Commerce
38, Cours Alberta 1er, Paris75008, FRANCE;
(33) (1) 49 53 28 28, fax (33) (1) 49-53-2942, www.iccwbo.org

The International Chamber of Commerce (ICC) represents members from over 130 countries and 7000 member organizations. Through the International Bureau of Chambers of Commerce the ICC helps to encourage international trade and investment. The International

Court of Arbitration, the ICC's principle service to the business community, ensures that such trade occurs in a fair manner governed by international standards. The ICC also offers commercial crime services to help combat global fraud and piracy. Finally, the ICC coordinates a number of international conferences each year to encourage information exchange between member nations. The ICC maintains a web site that provides information on its services and a number of useful links. [ID:6739]

Québec Association of Export Trading Houses
Suite 201, 666 Sherbrooke Street W., Montréal, Québec H3A 1E7;
(800) 465-9615, fax (514) 848-9986, amceq@amceq.org, www.amceq.org

The Québec Association of Export Trading Houses (AMCEQ) was established in 1985 to promote the interests of trading houses and develop this sector. Members include not only trading houses but also internationally-oriented manufacturers. Trading houses account for over 50 per cent of non-US exports and can offer exporters a variety of assistance in trade-related matters. AMCEQ publishes a directory of Québec Trading Houses and offers information on a number of other similar issues. AMCEQ maintains a web site with information on its services and activities. [ID:6741]

FOREIGN TRADE COUNCILS

The foreign trade councils in the following list promote trade and investment between Canada and specific countries or groups of countries. They provide a wide range of trade-related services to enhance collaboration among member nations, such as close liaison with key government and private sector contacts and partnering facilitation. Several of these associations produce newsletters profiling opportunities and recent developments affecting Canadian business interests, and organize conferences and seminars. A small annual membership fee is usually required.

A number of foreign embassies in Canada also have Trade Development Branches or Commercial Services Branches which can provide useful information and contacts. (For more information see Chapter 40, Foreign Diplomats in Canada.)

ASEAN-Canada Business Council
Suite 501, Delta Office Tower, 350 Sparks Street, Ottawa, Ontario K1R 7S8; (613) 238-4000, fax (613) 238-7643, info@chamber.ca [ID:5622]

Asia Pacific Foundation
of Canada (APFC)
Suite 666, 999 Canada Place, Vancouver, B.C.   V6C 3E1; (604) 684-5986, fax (604) 681-1370, www.apfc.org [ID:5623]

Brazil-Canada Chamber of Commerce
Suite 300, 360 Bay Street, Toronto, Ontario M5H 2V6; (416) 364-3555, fax (416) 364-3453, bccc@ibm.net, web site forthcoming [ID:5624]

British Trade & Investment Office
British Consulate General, Suite 2800, 777 Bay Street, Toronto, Ontario M5G 2G2; (416) 593-1290, fax (416) 593-1229, remote-printer.Commercial_Enquiries@ 9.2.2.1.3.9.5.6.1.4.1.tpc.int, (e-mail sent to fax) www.uk-canada-trade.org [ID:6873]

Canada-Arab Business Council
Suite 501, Delta Office Tower, 350 Sparks Street, Ottawa, Ontario K1R 7S8; (613) 238-4000, fax (613) 238-7643, info@chamber.ca [ID:5626]

Canada-China Business Council
Suite 802, 110 Yonge Street, Toronto, Ontario M5C 1T4; (416) 954-3800, fax (416) 954-3806, ccbc@istar.ca, www.ccbc.com [ID:5625]

Canada-India Business Council
P.O. Box 818, Heritage Building, BCE Place, 181 Bay Street, Toronto, Ontario M5J 2T3; (416) 868-6415, fax (416) 868-0189, admin.c-ibc@sympatico.ca, www.canada-indiabusiness.ca [ID:5627]

Canada-Indonesia Business Council
P.O. Box 110, 260 Adelaide Street E., Toronto, Ontario M5A 1N1; (416) 366-8490, fax (416) 947-1534 [ID:5628]

Canada-Japan Trade Council
Suite 903, 75 Albert Street, Ottawa, Ontario K1P 5E7; (613) 233-4047, fax (613) 233-2256, cjtc@magi.com, www.magi.com/~cjtc [ID:5629]

Canada-Korea
Business Council (CKBC)
Suite 501, Delta Office Tower, 350 Sparks Street, Ottawa, Ontario K1R 7S8; (613) 238-4000, fax (613) 238-7643, info@chamber.ca, www.chamber.ca [ID:5630]

Canada-Pakistan Business Council

Suite 2103, 2 Forest Laneway, North York, Ontario M2N 5X7; (416) 590-0929, fax (416) 590-0945 [ID:7053]

Canada-Singapore Business Association

07-00 RELC Building, 30 Orange Grove Road, 258352, SINGAPORE; (65) 738-9232, fax (65) 738-9227, csba@cyberway.com.sg, www.csba.org.sg [ID:6872]

Canada-Taiwan Business Association

Suite 501, Delta Office Tower, 350 Sparks Street, Ottawa, Ontario K1R 7S8; (613) 238-4000, fax (613) 238-7643, info@chamber.ca, www.chamber.ca [ID:5631]

Canada-Taiwan Trade Association

Suite 95, 910 Mainland Street, Vancouver, B.C. V6B 1A9; (604) 682-2848, fax (604) 662-3754, jchi@direct.ca, www.jurock.com/ctta/ [ID:6677]

Canada-Ukraine Chamber of Commerce

Unit 609, 302 The East Mall, Etobicoke, Ontario M9B 6E2; (416) 234-5334, fax (416) 234-5351, shym@msn.com, www.ukrainetrade.com [ID:6593]

Canadian Council for the Americas

Suite 300, 360 Bay Street, Toronto, Ontario M5H 2V6; (416) 367-4313, fax (416) 367-5460, cca@ibm.net, www.ccacanada.com [ID:5632]

Canadian-German Chamber of Industry and Commerce

Suite 1410, 480 University Ave., Toronto, Ontario M5G 1V2; (416) 598-3355, fax (416) 598-1840 [ID:5633]

Conseil d'Affaires et de Culture Québec-Bulgarie

2735, McWillis, Suite 1, Ville de St-Laurent, Québec H4R 1M5; (514) 334-4713, fax (514) 334-4714, cacqb@accent.net, www.accent.net/cacqb/cacqb.htm [ID:6927]

Enterprise Malaysia Canada

Suite 1202, 90 Burnhamthorpe Road W., Mississauga, Ontario L5B 3C3; (905) 279-6966, fax (905) 279-0137 [ID:5635]

Enterprise Thailand Canada

Suite 700, 1111 West Hastings, Vancouver, B.C. V6E 2J3; (604) 661-5706, fax (604) 661-5770 [ID:5636]

French Chamber of Commerce in Canada

360 St. Francois Xavier Street, Montréal, Québec H2Y 2S8; (514) 281-1246, fax (514) 289-9594 [ID:5637]

Hong Kong-Canada Business Association

National Office, 1010, de la Gauchetiere W., Montréal, Québec H3B 2N2; (514) 875-5426, fax (514) 866-0247 [ID:5638]

Hungarian-Canadian Chamber of Commerce

P.O. 256, Toronto Dominion Centrre, Toronto, Ontario M5K 1J5; (416) 865-9110, fax (416) 865-9117, hccccent@ica.net [ID:5639]

Italian Chamber of Commerce

Suite 306, 901 Lawrence Ave. W., Toronto, Ontario M6A 1C3; (416) 789-7169, fax (416) 789-7160, mail@italchamber-tor.on.ca, www.italchamber-tor.on.ca [ID:5640]

Japan External Trade Organization (JETRO)

Suite 1600, 181 University Ave., Toronto, Ontario M5H 3M7; (416) 861-0000, fax (416) 861-9666, inquiry@toronto.jetro.org, www.toronto.jetro.org [ID:7039]

Korea Trade Centre

Suite 1710, 505 Burrard Street, Vancouver, B.C. V7X 1M6; (604) 683-1820, fax (604) 687-6249, www.kotra.or.kr [ID:5641]

Norwegian-Canadian Chamber of Commerce

Suite 909, South Tower, 175 Bloor Street E., Toronto, Ontario M4W 3R8; (416) 920-0434, fax (416) 920-5982, cathrin@ntc-can.com, www.ntc-can.com [ID:6881]

Scandinavian Canadian Chamber of Commerce

Suite 822, 602 West Hastings Street, Vancouver, B.C. V6B 1P2; (604) 669-4428, fax (604) 669-4420, web site forthcoming [ID:5643]

Swedish Trade Office (Canada) Inc.

Suite 1504, 2 Bloor Street West, Toronto, Ontario M4W 3E2; (416) 922-8152, fax (416) 929-8639, www.swedentrade.com [ID:7050]

Swiss Chamber of Commerce

Suite 700, 1130 West Pender Street, Vancouver, B.C. V6E 4A4; (604) 688-7947, fax (604) 688-7943 [ID:5644]

Chapter 34

Careers in Government

The range of international job opportunities in the government sector is broad. From a career commitment to the Canadian Foreign Service to a youth internship program overseas, there are many avenues to explore. While government downsizing and cutbacks have reduced the number of permanent jobs available, Canada's ongoing international activities mean some positions will always exist, particularly in the federal public service. The sections on the PUBLIC SERVICE COMMISSION (PSC), THE DEPARTMENT OF FOREIGN AFFAIRS AND INTERNATIONAL TRADE (DFAIT), and the CANADIAN INTERNATIONAL DEVELOPMENT AGENCY (CIDA), below, describe some of these opportunities and how to apply for them. But don't forget—full-time, permanent positions are not the only jobs to look for—short-term employment and consulting are alternative routes into the government sector.

While the majority of international opportunities are with the federal government, provincial governments also have some ongoing international activities, especially in the fields of trade promotion and tourism. (For addresses and descriptions of provincial-level international programs see the Profiles section in this chapter.) Even large municipalities sometimes have a few international positions related to specific projects and activities. Application procedures and opportunities will be different for each jurisdiction: investigate each independently. Finally, some Crown corporations, such as the CANADIAN BROADCASTING CORPORATION (CBC) and the EXPORT DEVELOPMENT CORPORATION (EDC), have significant international activities. (For details, see the Profiles section in this chapter.)

RESOURCES

For more government resources, see the other Resources sections in this chapter (Foreign Affairs, CIDA) and the Resources for Chapter 33, Services for International Businesses & Entrepreneurs.

Canada Business Service Centres 🖥

www.cbsc.org ▪ Designed to serve Canadian business people, the CBSC internet site contains searchable collections of information on federal and provincial government services, programs and regulations. The site also allows the user to contact Business Information Officers by e-mail. This is an excellent site for those interested in government. (See their profile in Chapter 33, Services for International Businesses & Entrepreneurs.) [ID:2517]

Export Development Corporation 🖥

www.edc.ca ▪ The Export Development Corporation assists Canadians wishing to do business with foreign countries. Services include risk assessment, export insurance, and financial management assistance. [ID:2606]

Government Assistance Programs & Subsidies (GAPS) 📖

Annual, Canada Pack ➤ Renouf Publishing Co. Ltd., Unit 1, 5369 Canotek Road, Ottawa, Ontario K1J 9J3; $240; credit cards; (613) 745-2665, fax (613) 745-7660 ▪ Available at libraries. This easy-to-use directory lists federal and provincial grants available across Canada, benefits of the grants, who is eligible, contact names and how to apply. [ID:1349]

Government Electronic Directory Services 🖥

http://canada.gc.ca/search/direct500 ▪ Contact information, including e-mail addresses, phone numbers and mailing addresses for over 170,000 federal public servants throughout Canada. [ID:2489]

Government of Canada Primary Internet Site 🖥

http://canada.gc.ca/main_e.html ▪ The government at your fingertips. This site provides access to all federal departments and programs as well as links to provincial governments and several international organizations. [ID:2605]

Government of Canada Telephone Directory: National Capital Region 📖

1996, Supply and Services Canada ➤ Renouf Publishing Co. Ltd., Unit 1, 5369 Canotek Road, Ottawa, Ontario K1J 9J3; $29.95; credit cards; (613) 745-2665, fax (613) 745-7660 ▪ Updated frequently, this directory is an indispensable tool for individuals who make frequent contact with Canadian government departments. [ID:1242]

MERX 🖥

MERX at CEBRA INC., 2 Watts Ave., Charlottetown, P.E.I. C1E 1B0; (800) 964-6379, fax (888) 235-5800 ▪ A national electronic tendering service. MERX is like the classifieds for contracts with most federal government departments, some provincial and territorial ministries, and some municipalities. Register or access the system by phone, fax, mail or on the web. You can also access MERX using Datapac (a dial-in service via modem). Supplier registration costs $8.95/month. Prices for document requests and other services vary. Visit them at www.merx.cebra.com. [ID:2645]

Department of National Defence (DND) 🖥

www.dnd.ca ▪ From information on the latest UN peacekeeping operations to recruiting guidelines, this is the gateway to Canada's military. It also provides a statement of defence policy and information on financial management assistance. [ID:2566]

Reference Canada 📖

Reference Canada, 47 Clarence Street, 3rd Floor, Ottawa, Ontario K1A 0S5; (800) 667-3355 ext. except MB and QC, fax (613) 941-5383, refcda@hookup.net ▪ The federal government's bilingual telephone referral and basic information service. Available nationwide, this toll-free service helps the public find answers to questions about federal programs and activities. The service improves accessibility to federal contacts, helps the public track down information with a minimum number of calls, and greatly reduces misdirected inquiries. In Manitoba and Québec, Reference Canada has a joint program with the province. Manitoba residents should call the Citizens' Inquiry Service at (800) 282-8060. In Québec, interested individuals should call (800) 363-1363 or contact the Communication-Québec office in their area. These numbers are listed on the web site http://canada.gc.ca/programs/refcda/refcda_e.html. [ID:2660]

The Public Service Commission (PSC)

West Tower, L'Esplanade Laurier,
300 Laurier Street W., Ottawa, Ontario, K1A 0M7 www.psc-cfp.gc.ca/jobs.htm

Check the government listings (blue pages) in your phone book for the PSC office nearest you, or visit the PSC web site for a full list of offices across the country.

The PUBLIC SERVICE COMMISSION OF CANADA (PSC) is the parliamentary agency responsible for the appointment of qualified individuals to, and within, the federal public service, and for the delivery of public service training and development programs. The PSC functions to ensure that the people of Canada are served by a highly professional public service that is both non-partisan and representative of Canadian society.

Federal government employees work in a wide assortment of disciplines worldwide. Canada's international activities extend into many government departments, agencies and Crown corporations. Diplomats in capital cities around the world, development specialists in Africa, Asia, and Latin America, and immigration authorities working throughout the world—all are federal public servants.

You will find opportunities for international government employment in many fields, but your chances of working in the international sphere are greatest in the areas of development, diplomacy and trade promotion. The profiles provided later in this chapter list several federal government organizations with international divisions.

TYPES OF FEDERAL GOVERNMENT EMPLOYMENT

Competitions for federal government positions are classified as either open or closed. Only employees already working for the public service are eligible to apply for *closed competition* vacancies. If you are not a public servant already, you can apply only for *open competition* vacancies.

Due to government downsizing, permanent positions with the public service are now few and far between. Another option for the job seeker however, is a term position: a position filled on a temporary basis, and lasting anywhere from a few months to several years. Term employees may participate in both open and closed competitions for other positions in the public service.

There are also short-term contract and casual positions available with the federal government. Individual departments fill these positions directly. Employees in this category are not eligible for closed competitions.

CRITERIA AND PROCEDURES FOR EMPLOYMENT

Most federal public service jobs require you to apply to the PSC. The PSC maintains few résumé inventories and only where a significant demand for particular skill sets is anticipated. Most positions are advertised. You can find out about job openings by visiting www.psc-cfp.gc.ca/jobs.htm, the PSC's web site, or by visiting the PSC's newsgroup for job postings (can.jobs.gov), or by calling the PSC information line for your area, listed under "Public Service Commission of Canada" in the blue pages of your phone book. If you call the information line, have a pen and paper ready to take notes and be prepared to navigate a complicated set of menus. Job applications are available on the Internet or from the PSC office nearest you. When applying for advertised jobs, make sure that your résumé corresponds to the basic requirements of the position. Competition is stiff, and only those who meet the basic requirements will be considered.

Through its employment equity program, the federal government actively recruits people with disabilities, members of visible minority groups, aboriginal peoples and women in non-traditional occupations.

Routes to international work with the federal government vary according to your age and level of experience. The MANAGEMENT TRAINEE PROGRAM (MTP), aimed at recent master's degree graduates, has appointed 420 participants to officer-level positions in the public service since 1991. MTP trainees are placed with many different departments, including those with international activities, but if you are accepted into this program you may have little choice about your place. (At the time of writing, this program was under review.)

If you are a young professional person with an international background, you should contact a department's international division directly. Be prepared to accept a term position as very few entry-level positions are permanent. If you accept another position in a department and hope to transfer to the international section later on, you could be in for a long wait.

If you are a mid-career professional with little international experience, it is unrealistic to assume you will be hired directly into an international position. However, accepting a position related to international affairs may provide you with a bridge to a subsequent international position.

Seasoned professionals with international experience should apply directly to the departments that most interest them. Departments normally look for highly-qualified people with international experience, especially those from business or from another international agency or organization. If you are applying for a position as a public service executive, you should contact the PSC's EXECUTIVE PROGRAMS BRANCH.

For information on international consulting opportunities with the federal government, see the profile on CONSULTING AND AUDIT CANADA in this chapter.

POST-SECONDARY RECRUITMENT (PSR)

The PSC's POST-SECONDARY RECRUITMENT CAMPAIGN (PSR) seeks graduating and recently-graduated students of universities, CEGEPs, technical institutes, and, in some cases, community colleges. Positions are available for a wide variety of specializations. In 1997 the PSR campaign placed graduates with degrees in economics, social sciences, computer science, mathematics and engineering with various federal departments. Recruiting starts at the beginning of September each year. PSC career information and application brochures are available through campus placement offices, online at www.psc-cfp.gc.ca/jobs.htm, or from the PSC office nearest you.

Foreign service officers, placed with the DEPARTMENT OF FOREIGN AFFAIRS AND INTERNATIONAL TRADE (DFAIT), and development officers, placed with the CANADIAN INTERNATIONAL DEVELOPMENT AGENCY (CIDA), are hired through the PSR Campaign. Candidates are required to write examinations held each year in October (for more information on the application process see the sections on DFAIT and CIDA in this chapter). Provided they are recent graduates, people who are already in the workforce are also eligible to write these exams.

STUDENT EMPLOYMENT IN AN INTERNATIONAL DIVISION

The federal public service is Canada's single largest employer of students in co-op programs. On average, students from over 100 institutions across Canada carry out more than 5,000 work terms with the government each year. For information on co-op programs, contact high school or university career centres in your area.

Federal Student Work Experience Program (FSWEP)

The FEDERAL STUDENT WORK EXPERIENCE PROGRAM (FSWEP) offers full-time high school, CEGEP, college, technical institute and university students the opportunity to apply for student jobs with the federal government. There are a limited number of overseas assignments available under FSWEP (see the profile on VETERANS AFFAIRS CANADA, in Chapter 10, Short-term Programs Overseas). Also, FSWEP students may be placed with a federal government department or agency involved in international activities, such as the DEPARTMENT OF FOREIGN AFFAIRS AND INTERNATIONAL TRADE (DFAIT) or the CANADIAN INTERNATIONAL DEVELOPMENT AGENCY (CIDA).

Students interested in these opportunities should consult the FSWEP application package, available each year in mid-September. To receive one, call the federal government's toll-free Youth Info Line (1-800-935-5555) or try one of the following locations: your student career office at school or on campus, your local Human Resources Centre, or the Public Service Commission office nearest you (check the blue pages of your phone book). Or visit the PSC web site at www.psc-cfp.gc.ca/jobs.htm.

SPECIFIC PROGRAMS OF THE PSC

The INTERNATIONAL PROGRAMS DIRECTORATE of the PSC, working with the DEPARTMENT OF FOREIGN AFFAIRS AND INTERNATIONAL TRADE (DFAIT), monitors middle- and senior-level positions within the secretariats of the international organizations to which Canada belongs. The PSC coordinates the nomination of highly qualified Canadian candidates for vacancies deemed of interest to and attainable by Canada. Each year 40 to 50 Canadians compete successfully for secretariat positions in international organizations. Candidates should have university degrees and a minimum of five years' experience in their fields, preferably in international organizations. The PSC maintains an inventory of potential candidates, drawn from all areas of Canadian society. Visit their web site for more information. (For contact information, see PUBLIC SERVICE COMMISSION—INTERNATIONAL PROGRAMS DIRECTORATE in the Profiles section of this chapter.)

INTERCHANGE CANADA facilitates partnerships between Canada's private sector and various levels of government, building bridges that will last long after exchange assignments have ended. Over the last 20 years, INTERCHANGE CANADA has arranged exchanges for close to 3,000 people, promoting linkages between the federal public service and some 650 organizations in the private sector, nonprofit organizations, academic institutions and provincial governments. By taking assignments in a new sector, employees develop themselves personally and professionally and their organizations benefit from their new skills, and insights. INTERCHANGE CANADA has been specifically targeted by Canada's science and technology community as a vehicle to enhance career development and employee mobility. Within the government sector, the federal and provincial governments are currently working on a plan to increase inter-jurisdictional mobility, which would make exchanges more feasible.

In the realm of training, the PSC is involved in language instruction and orientation services; professional, technical, policy, middle management and supervisory training; and the design of courses and consultations for federal government departments.

A LAST WORD ON THE PUBLIC SERVICE COMMISSION

Opportunities for government sector employment, especially permanent positions in the federal public service, are very limited. If you are interested in working with the government, it is best to pursue a dual strategy—look for permanent jobs with the PSC while tracking down opportunities for short-term work or consulting with specific departments or agencies. In the longer term, this situation is likely to change. As the federal budget is brought under control, the government is faced with the challenge of rejuvenating an aging civil service and restoring public programming.

For youth, opportunities are already opening up. The PSC is recruiting recent graduates of MA programs for entry-level positions in several government departments. Student employment is available through the FEDERAL STUDENT WORK EXPERIENCE PROGRAM (FSWEP). Most significant, however, are the large numbers of youth internship positions, including internationally-oriented internships, now being offered under the federal government's youth employment strategy (see the profile listed under CANADIAN GOVERNMENT INTERNATIONAL INTERNSHIPS in Chapter 17, Interna-tional Internships). At the time of writing, Ottawa had just announced an additional $90 million for a three-year program to create 1,000 public service internships. If you are a young person interested in government work, this is a good time to apply.

Department of Foreign Affairs and International Trade (DFAIT)

Lester B. Pearson Bldg. 125 Sussex Drive, Ottawa,
Ontario, K1A 0G2; (800) 944-4000; Fax: (613) 995-1405 www.dfait-maeci.gc.ca

A career in the Canadian Foreign Service is a way of life. Typically, it involves extensive overseas travel, stimulating assignments and diverse international experiences. The DEPARTMENT OF FOREIGN AFFAIRS AND INTERNATIONAL TRADE (DFAIT) seeks highly qualified, creative people with strong analytical and communication skills to fill a variety of international positions. Employees keep the Canadian government apprised of the international situation and represent Canada's diplomatic, trade and human interests abroad.

As a member of the Foreign Service, you can expect to spend roughly one-half to two-thirds of your career working and living outside Canada. The remainder of your time will be spent in Ottawa. This ongoing job rotation means officers and their families must be comfortable with frequent and dramatic change. With this challenge, DFAIT offers interesting and meaningful careers in the international arena.

At the time of writing, DFAIT has 1,594 rotational officers, with 701 posted abroad. There are also 440 rotational support staff (clerks, communicators, data production staff, couriers and secretaries), with 192 posted abroad.

TYPES OF EMPLOYMENT WITH DFAIT

Applicants to DFAIT can choose between two principal career paths. The first, and most common, leads to a career as a Foreign Service Officer (FSO), the second leads to employment as support staff. To become an FSO, you must be a Canadian citizen and meet specific academic requirements. Candidates need not be bilingual, but those who aren't must agree to undertake language training in the second official language. You must also be willing to accept assignments anywhere in the world, be healthy, and qualify for a top security clearance.

As an FSO, you will be assigned to one of the following career streams: the Trade Commissioner Service, Political and Economic Affairs, or the International Region Branch of CITIZENSHIP AND IMMIGRATION CANADA (CIC). Assignment to a stream is usually permanent, and comes about as a result of the selection process. It is determined by the department's needs and the interview team's report. This report takes into account a candidate's aptitude, interview performance, and expressed stream preference.

FSO candidates normally compete for approximately 50 jobs during each recruitment campaign. Competition is understandably tough, given the thousands of applications. Recruitment is done through the PUBLIC SERVICE COMMISSION's (PSC) Post-secondary Recruitment Campaign (see the PSC section earlier in this chapter). Applicants must register with the PSC and write the Foreign Service Exam, held every year in late October.

The selection priorities can vary from year to year. The fall 1997 selection criteria for FSO positions called for candidates with master's degrees or PhDs in any field; law degrees if called to the Bar; or two bachelor's degrees, provided one was in business administration, commerce, economics or law. Those with bachelor's degrees in other disciplines were only permitted to take the exam if they had significant international experience in business or possessed an acceptable level of language proficiency in Mandarin, Japanese, Korean, Arabic or Russian.

These criteria reflect the high level of competition for FSO positions. For information on the Foreign Service Recruitment campaign contact:

Recruitment Section SPSS
Department of Foreign Affairs and International Trade (DFAIT),
125 Sussex Drive, Ottawa, Ontario K1A 0G2; (613) 992-5241 Fax: (613) 944-0439

Management and Consular Affairs also offers opportunities for rotational foreign service careers. Management and Consular Affairs officers are responsible for managing human and material resources and providing consular services to Canadians in difficulty. Candidates for this stream must be Canadian citizens with university degrees in business administration, public or general administration, commerce or accounting. A separate application process exists for this stream. For information, call the PUBLIC SERVICE COMMISSION (PSC) at the number listed in the blue pages of your phone book, or visit their web site at www.psc-cfp.gc.ca/jobs.htm.

In addition to employment as a Foreign Service Officer, the department also has overseas positions for secretaries, clerks, and technical personnel. Support personnel are hired either through the PUBLIC SERVICE COMMISSION or directly through Foreign Affairs. You should note that foreign posts often hire locally to fill jobs that do not require a Foreign Service Officer (there are over 4,000 locally-filled positions with DFAIT missions at the time of writing). For those of you who are interested in working in a specific country, you may find it useful to contact the embassy or consulate directly to inquire about possible support positions. For further information on support staff positions contact:

Recruitment Section SPV
Department of Foreign Affairs and International Trade (DFAIT)
125 Sussex Drive, Ottawa, Ontario K1A 0G2; (613) 992-1849 Fax: (613) 944-0439

LIFE IN THE FOREIGN SERVICE

Foreign Service personnel are a special breed. They spend their careers moving from one culture to another, and one continent to another as a matter of course. Typically, FSOs are posted overseas on rotations of two to four years. After this period, they either return to Ottawa or are assigned to another foreign post.

Before your first overseas assignment, you will undergo on-the-job training in Ottawa. The first year of an FSO's appointment to the Public Service is spent on probation. During the training phase, FSOs must become proficient in both of Canada's official languages. Preparation also includes practical assignments, some courses, and any necessary foreign language training prior to posting. Depending upon your career specialty, your training program may take anywhere from one to four years. When first posted, entry-level officers work as third-level secretaries and/or vice-consuls.

The most sought-after posts are those in Washington and London, where you will find many top diplomats, lots of activity and a more firmly entrenched hierarchy. It is, however, in the smaller missions that new FSOs can take on greater responsibilities and be involved in a wider variety of activities than they would at larger, more specialized posts. While in Ottawa, FSOs often take up responsibilities as desk officers for particular countries or groups of countries, or in one of the functional branches dealing with trade policy, cultural liaison, management, or other functions.

Salary and benefits within the Foreign Service are comparable to those of other Government of Canada employees. However, once assigned to a post, you will receive, in addition to your usual salary, a premium for serving abroad, a cost of living or hardship allowance where applicable, and supplemental vacation leave with payment of some travel costs. The government also subsidizes education costs for children of FSOs. Most dependants abroad attend British, American or French schools if the standard of education in the country of posting is significantly different from Canada's.

Life with the Foreign Service does have its drawbacks. One problem faced by most Foreign Service employees is the strain of rotating job postings on family life and relationships. For married employees, this means their families must continually adjust to new locations. Spouses often postpone career opportunities, accept limited local employment, or don't work at all. Single people in the Foreign Service may face other problems, such as loneliness and a perceived lack of a social support network. Despite these difficulties, however, many people find the Foreign Service an interesting and exciting employer.

An excellent source of information on life in the Foreign Service is the PROFESSIONAL ASSOCIATION OF FOREIGN SERVICE OFFICERS (PAFSO). In their publication, *Bout de Papier*, members recount overseas experiences, discuss issues of importance to FSOs, and provide valuable insights into FSOs' work and lifestyle. More information is available online at the Foreign Affairs web site. (See also the Resource section of this chapter.)

THE FOREIGN SERVICE RECRUITMENT CAMPAIGN

Joining the Foreign Service entails a four-part process that includes the following steps: the application, the examination, the screening phase, and the selection phase.

The Application Process

Prior to taking the Foreign Service exams, you must complete the PUBLIC SERVICE COMMISSION'S Post-secondary Recruitment Application. The code "FS" indicates your career choice. These forms can be obtained from the PSC, any university campus placement office, or Canadian diplomatic posts abroad. Submit this form, along with copies of your university transcripts, to the nearest PSC office or Canadian diplomatic post abroad, by the deadline, which usually falls in early October, several weeks before the annual test date. You should enclose a résumé with your application. Tailor it to emphasize important personal background information, such as foreign language ability and crosscultural experience. Candidates should also make sure they meet the specified academic requirements.

In 1997, for the first time, candidates were able to apply online. You can visit the PSC web site (www.psc-cfp.gc.ca/jobs.htm) or the DFAIT web site (www.dfait-maeci.gc.ca) for more information.

The Foreign Service Exam

Since 1928, the Foreign Service Exam has been the sole route to obtaining an entry-level position as a Canadian Foreign Service Officer. Today, DFAIT uses an updated Foreign Service Exam along with two other tests administered by the PSC. These exams are held in succession on the same date, and take between 55 minutes and 2½ hours each to write. The exams can be written on university campuses across Canada, in certain government offices, or at Canadian diplomatic missions abroad.

The first exam is the *General Competency Test - Level 2* (GCT2). Used to select individuals for positions throughout the federal government, the GCT2 consists of 90 multiple-choice questions. These questions assess vocabulary, mathematical skills and logic, as well as memory and conceptual abilities. In the 1996 competition, the passing number of correct answers for this exam was 78.

The second exam is the *Written Communication Test* (WCT). The applicant is given an article of approximately 2,000 words, and asked to summarize it in 450 words. The summary is scored on the basis of grammar, spelling, punctuation and style, as well as content. Although there is no official "pass" mark, candidates must do well to advance to the next stage of the selection process.

The third and final exam is the *Foreign Service Knowledge Test*, the successor to the original Foreign Service Exam. This test measures general knowledge of Canada, its people and culture, as well as specific knowledge of the issues and policies related to the international order. It is composed of 75 multiple-choice questions. You can prepare for the test by becoming well-informed about Canada's domestic and international political and economic relations, immigration and trade, and by keeping up to date on all areas of current affairs. The passing grade for this exam in 1996 was 38 correct responses.

To get past this stage of the campaign, you must score in the top 15 to 20 per cent of the people taking the exams. The PSC informs candidates of their test results and forwards the names and applications of top candidates to DFAIT and CITIZENSHIP AND IMMIGRATION CANADA (CIC).

The Screening Phase

During the screening phase, the applications received from the PSC are reviewed, taking into account merit and employment equity objectives, and a few hundred are selected to participate in interviews and a group simulation exercise. The interviews are generally held in February. They take place across Canada and in selected Canadian missions abroad; the candidate assumes responsibility for any costs incurred in attending the interview.

On the morning of the specified day, candidates have a 45-minute personal interview with a four-person interview team. The interviewers will ask a range of questions to assess how you handle yourself in different situations and roles. Some of the characteristics they are looking for are the ability to analyze and evaluate situations, oral communication skill, and the ability to plan, organize and control projects. They also want someone with strong interpersonal skills, who displays leadership and teamwork ability, exercises good judgement, has personal integrity, and is creative, flexible, and adaptable. In addition, an FSO must also possess concern for the public good.

In the afternoon, candidates participate in a three-hour group simulation exercise administered by the interviewers. Each candidate is given a project proposal and asked to present the proposal to the group, which must then arrive at a consensus on the merits of the different project proposals. The purpose of the exercise is to strike a balance between promoting a project and facilitating a group decision. Candidates are thereby expected to demonstrate those abilities and characteristics required of an FSO representing Canada abroad.

The Selection Phase

The Personnel Branch of DFAIT evaluates all information from the application, examination, interview and references, and retains approximately one-quarter of those interviewed as final candidates. The candidate's score on the Foreign Service Exam and the interview report are the main items used in establishing the list of final candidates. Other aspects of a candidate's background, such as a demonstrated interest and experience in foreign cultures or "fluency" in a particular discipline, may emerge in the interview process. Knowledge of other languages is taken into consideration in the selection process and candidates on the "short list" after interviews will have their abilities assessed in an oral test.

If you are a final candidate and decide to accept the stream for which you've been chosen, you will be asked to take a medical examination and to provide detailed personal background information to finalize your security clearance. This security clearance is a complex process that normally takes several months to complete. If you pass this last hurdle, you become a successful FSO candidate and are placed on a list of similar candidates.

CONSULTING WITH FOREIGN AFFAIRS

Various divisions at DFAIT's central offices in Ottawa hire short-term employees or contractors to work on special projects or to fill staff positions on a temporary basis. Many of these temporary positions are "advertised" only by word-of-mouth. If you want to hear about them, you will have to do some networking. One contract employee at DFAIT gives this advice:

"Send a résumé to an official working in an area that interests you, then follow up with a phone call to let your contact know you are still interested and available. If you are a graduate student, plan to do some research at DFAIT. This is an excellent way to make contacts. While you might not speak directly to those with the authority to hire, others you do meet may be helpful.

"Divisions needing to fill positions on short notice often contact graduate schools with international programs, such as Carleton University's Norman Paterson School of International Affairs (NPSIA), to find candidates. DFAIT is packed with NPSIA students and graduates doing contract work."

STUDENT OPPORTUNITIES WITH FOREIGN AFFAIRS

As a student, you may be trying to get your foot in the door at Foreign Affairs. Besides consulting opportunities, the department has two main avenues open to students.

The most common way for a student to find work with the federal government is through the FEDERAL STUDENT WORK EXPERIENCE PROGRAM (FSWEP). This initiative, managed by the PUBLIC SERVICE COMMISSION (PSC), provides full-time high school, CEGEP, college and university students with the chance to apply for non co-op student jobs throughout the federal government. The FSWEP relies upon a computerized national inventory of students who have applied to the program. There is no deadline for applying, but students are encouraged to complete the process as early as possible. Students should be aware that being chosen for a FSWEP position is rather like winning a lottery—names of students who fit the desired parameters (level of education, demonstrated interests) are forwarded at random to the department. The final selection is at the discretion of the department. DFAIT generally hires between 20 and 25 students each summer, mostly for clerical jobs. For more information on FSWEP, see the profile on the PUBLIC SERVICE COMMISSION (PSC) in this chapter.

The other avenue for students interested in working at DFAIT is the CO-OPERATIVE PROGRAM, which is open only to students enrolled in cooperative programs at universities or colleges. Foreign Affairs is one of many federal departments that takes on students for their co-op semesters. Work is Ottawa-based and lasts for a four-month period. DFAIT places from 60 to 75 students per year, and most are second- or third-year students with backgrounds in economics or political science (although there are a few from other disciplines as well, especially computer science). Students work on projects similar to those of entry-level FSOs. If you are interested in finding out which universities or colleges offer co-op programs, refer to *Choices That Count: Co-op Education in the Public Service of Canada* (see the Resources section, Chapter 16, International Studies in Canada & Abroad), or contact your school's career placement office.

Students should also be aware of the YOUTH INTERNATIONAL INTERNSHIP PROGRAM, sponsored by DFAIT. The program is targeted at young people (generally under 30) across Canada who have postsecondary education but are having difficulty making the transition to the workplace. Internships are given in partnership with private sector and nongovernmental organizations in various fields related to trade, global issues, culture and values. The objective of the program is to provide youth with career-related international work experiences that also further the objective of Canada's foreign policy. In 1997-98, 439 participants are expected, with another 401 anticipated in 1998-99. For more information, visit the DFAIT web site and select "Canadian Youth" from the "Culture" menu. You can apply for internships online at the *National Graduate Register* (http://ngr.schoolnet.ca). (See also the profile listed under Canadian Government International Internships in Chapter 17, International Internships.)

A LAST WORD ON THE FOREIGN SERVICE

All in all, the DEPARTMENT OF FOREIGN AFFAIRS offers exciting opportunities for experienced professionals as well as students wanting to build career experience. Those who become FSOs or support staff can expect a lifetime of travel, with postings in such diverse places as Tallinn and Osaka. For students, a summer of employment at DFAIT's headquarters in Ottawa will provide you with valuable experience within the federal government, allow you to establish important contacts, and help increase your International IQ Keep in mind, however, that placements are limited, competition is stiff, and only those with the best qualifications are taken on.

RESOURCES

For related resources, consult the Resources for Chapter 33, Services for International Businesses & Entrepreneurs; Chapter 39, Canadian Diplomats Abroad; and Chapter 40, Foreign Diplomats in Canada.

Bout de papier 📖
Quarterly ➤ Professional Association of Foreign Service Officers, 600-45 Rideau Street, Ottawa, Ontario K1N 5W8; $16 for 1 year, $30 for 2; cheque or money order; (613) 241-1391, fax (613) 241-5911 ▪ A must-read for all those interested in Canadian diplomacy and foreign service. Each issue features guest columnists, tales and photos from far and wide, special interviews, book reviews, and media coverage of Canadian diplomacy. Delves into major policy issues and provides first-hand accounts of life in diplomatic postings abroad. [ID:1291]

Canada and the Developing World: Key Issues in Canada's Foreign Policy 📖
1994, 56 pages ➤ North-South Institute, Suite 200, 55 Murray Street, Ottawa, Ontario K1N 5M3; $12; VISA, MC; (613) 241-3535, fax (613) 241-7435, nsi@nsi-ins.ca ▪ This booklet represents the North-South Institute's contribution to the public review of Canada's foreign policy. It takes the position that Canada's aid program, limited as it is, needs radical restructuring to help reduce poverty and promote human development. Visit distributor's web site at www.nsi-ins.ca. [ID:1659]

CanadExport 📖 🖥️
Biweekly ➤ InfoCentre, Department of Foreign Affairs and International Trade (DFAIT), 125 Sussex Dr., Ottawa, Ontario K1A 0G2; free; (800) 267-8376, fax (613) 996-9709 ▪ Foreign Affairs' primary publication for keeping the Canadian business community and exporters informed about key trade matters. A biweekly newsletter, it provides timely information on business opportunities, trade fairs and other related matters. For more information, see the online version at www.dfait-maeci.gc.ca/english/news/newsletr/canex. [ID:1495]

Canadian Representatives Abroad 📖 🖥️
Annual, Department of Foreign Affairs and International Trade (DFAIT), 142 pages ➤ Canada Government Publishing, Ottawa, Ontario K1A 0S9; $17.95; VISA, MC; (819) 956-4800, fax (819) 994-1498, publishing@ccg-gcc.ca ▪ A bilingual directory of Canadian diplomatic and consular missions. Available on the web at the DFAIT site, under "Embassies and Missions" at www.dfait-maeci.gc.ca/english/missions. [ID:1089]

Diplomat & International Canada 📖
Bimonthly, *Bhupinder Liddar* ➤ Raddil Communications, P.O. Box 1173, Station B, Ottawa, Ontario K1P 5R2; (613) 789-6890, fax (613) 789-6889, diplomat@sympatico.ca ▪ A news journal for Canada's international community focusing on diplomatic news in Ottawa. [ID:1237]

Diplomatic, Consular, and Other Representatives in Canada 📖
Annual, Department of Foreign Affairs and International Trade (DFAIT), 151 pages ➤ Canada Government PublishingOttawa, Ontario K1A 0S9; $19.95; VISA, MC; (819) 956-4800, fax (819) 994-1498, publishing@ccg-gcc.ca ▪ A bilingual directory of diplomatic missions in Ottawa and consular and other missions throughout Canada, including names and titles of staff. Visit the publisher's web site at http://publications.pwgsc.gc.ca. [ID:1088]

Directory for Trade Commissioners 📖
1997 ➤ InfoCentre, Department of Foreign Affairs and International Trade (DFAIT), 125 Sussex Dr., Ottawa, Ontario K1A 0G2; (800) 267-8376, fax (613) 996-9709 ▪ A booklet designed for exporters examining foreign market representation options, and for companies that have received an unsolicited proposal from a potential agent or distributor and require guidance in the assessment process. [ID:1589]

Foreign Service 📖
1993, *John Neale,* 240 pages ➤ Captus Press Inc., c/o York University Campus, 4700 Keele Street, North York, Ontario M3J 1P3; $14.95; VISA; (416) 736-5537, fax (416) 736-5793 ▪ The author's personal account of experiences as a foreign service officer in Algeria, Iran, Ecuador, Mexico and New York. Exposes the difficulties in representing Canada's interests abroad, and offers a critique of how Canada manages its foreign missions. Visit distributor's web site, www.captus.com. [ID:1343]

Mindsets: The Role of Culture and Perception in International Relations 📖
1988, *Glen Fisher,* Intercultural Press, 200 pages ➤ Intercultural and Community Development Resources (ICDR), P.O. Box 32108, Millwoods Station, Edmonton, Alberta T6K 4C2; $23; VISA, Amex; (800) 378-3199, fax (403) 462-1925, icdr@compusmart.ab.ca ▪ Examines the impact of cultural "programming" on international affairs, how a society's reasoning affects their assumptions and values. Such "mindsets" represent a collective world view that governs how decisions are made. They influence international relations, how development assistance is implemented, and business conducted. For more information, visit the distributor's web site at www.compusmart.ab.ca/icdr. [ID:1327]

No Fixed Address 📖
1993, *Hansel Fraser* ➤ University of Toronto Press, 5201 Dufferin Street, North York, Ontario M3H 5T8; $24.95; VISA, MC; (800) 565-9523, fax (416) 667-7832, utpbooks@utpress.utoronto.ca ▪ Details a Foreign Service officer's job, including life in the foreign service, lessons in foreign service living, the selection process, and organization of the Foreign Affairs headquarters. Visit the distributor's web site at www.utpress.utoronto.ca. [ID:1344]

A Rich Broth: Memoirs of a Canadian Diplomat 📖
1993, *David Chalmer Reese,* 231 pages ➤ Carleton University Press, 1400 CTTC, Carleton University, 1125 Colonel By Drive, Ottawa, Ontario K1S 5B6; $13.95; VISA, MC; (613) 520-3740, fax (613) 520-2893 ▪ A witty autobiography based on a 38-year career in the Canadian foreign service. Visit the publisher's web site at www.carleton.ca/cupress. [ID:1342]

Understanding Arabs: A Guide for Westerners 📖
1997, *Margaret Kleffner Nydell,* 192 pages ➤ Intercultural and Community Development Resources (ICDR), P.O. Box 32108, Millwoods Station, Edmonton, Alberta T6K 4C2; $25; VISA, Amex; (800) 378-3199, fax (403) 462-1925, icdr@compusmart.ab.ca ▪ For Westerners who want to better understand how Arabs think and what motivates them. Sheds light on the aspects of culture which most critically affect crosscultural relationships. For more information, visit the distributor's web site at www.compusmart.ab.ca/icdr. [ID:1037]

This Week in Trade and Foreign Policy 📖
Weekly ➤ InfoCentre, Department of Foreign Affairs and International Trade (DFAIT), 125 Sussex Dr., Ottawa, Ontario K1A 0G2; free; (800) 267-8376, fax (613) 996-9709 ▪ Weekly updates of Canadian foreign policy developments and ministerial statements. A good source of detailed information on specific situations and events. [ID:1645]

Canadian International Development Agency (CIDA)

5th Floor, Place du Centre, 200 Promenade du Portage, Hull, Québec K1A 0G4;
(800) 230-6349, (819) 997-5006; Fax: (819) 953-6088; http://w3.acdi-cida.gc.ca

International assistance is a subject close to the hearts of many Canadians. With peacekeeping, development assistance reflects Canada's concern for global justice and peace.

Canada has been an active participant in international development since the federal government delivered its first food aid shipments to countries in Asia, Africa, and the Caribbean more than 40 years ago. In 1968, the Canadian International Development Agency (CIDA) was created to provide assistance to the poorest countries and people of the world. The 1995 foreign policy statement, *Canada in the World*, renewed the mandate for Canada's Official Development Assistance (ODA) Program, stating that:

> *"The purpose of Canada's ODA is to support sustainable development in developing countries, in order to reduce poverty and to contribute to a more secure, equitable and prosperous world."*

CIDA is by far the most influential agent of Canada's ODA Program. In 1995-96, CIDA received about 80 per cent of Canada's $2.1 billion ODA budget. Three federal departments—Finance, Foreign Affairs and International Trade, and Public Works and Government Service Canada—along with the INTERNATIONAL DEVELOPMENT RESEARCH CENTRE (IDRC) and the INTERNATIONAL CENTRE FOR HUMAN RIGHTS AND DEMOCRATIC DEVELOPMENT (ICHRDD) handle the remainder. CIDA now supports projects in more than 100 countries.

CIDA PROGRAMS AND STRUCTURE

Over the last five years Canada has taken a new approach to development assistance, consistent with the mandate set out in *Canada in the World*. The aid program, implemented by CIDA, focuses on the poorest countries of the world, with Africa receiving the greatest share of assistance. CIDA concentrates on the following six priorities: Basic Human Needs; Women in Development; Infrastructure Services; Human Rights, Democracy and Good Governance; Private Sector Development; and the Environment.

This section provides a brief synopsis of CIDA's programs and structure, with the aim of helping international job hunters focus their job search efforts. CIDA has a staff of 1,190, with about 80 staff members posted abroad. However, jobs within CIDA are not the only opportunities related to Canadian development assistance. Currently, there are over 36,000 Canadians employed directly or indirectly by Canada's aid program. Over 2,000 private firms, 200 nongovernmental organizations (NGOs), 110 educational institutions, 40 federal, provincial and municipal government departments, and 60 professional associations are involved in Canada's development assistance program.

The majority of opportunities to work with CIDA are with organizations or initiatives involved in one of the following four program areas.

Geographic Programs (formerly called Bilateral Programs) are bilateral arrangements between Canada and a number of recipient countries. Under the direction of CIDA, and upon the advice of the target country, Canadian businesses, NGOs, and institutions deliver a variety of aid packages. This is the largest of the four program areas, with more than 500 Canadian employees at the time of writing.

Multilateral Programs represent Canada's membership in a number of development-related international organizations. From the UN to La Francophonie, these organizations direct the efforts of Canada and other states to provide coordinated development assistance on a global scale. Currently, this program area accounts for 55 positions at CIDA.

Partnership Programs assist and provide funding for firms in the private sector as well as NGOs, institutions, government departments, and professional associations involved in delivering development assistance. CIDA's *Industrial Co-operation Program* helps Canada's private sector forge links with businesses in developing countries to promote sustainable economic development. Partnership Programs currently account for over 140 positions at CIDA.

Finally, the *Program of Co-operation with Central and Eastern Europe and the former Soviet Union* is dedicated to helping countries of the former Soviet bloc develop democratic institutions and market-driven economies. It transfers knowledge, skills, and technology through partnerships between Canadian organizations, universities, and businesses and their counterparts in the recipient country. Funding for this program is in addition to, and separate from, the ODA budget. The *Renaissance Eastern Europe Program (REE)* helps Canadian businesses position themselves in the emerging markets of the region (see the description of REE under Business Opportunities with CIDA, below). Individuals interested in working in specific countries can contact CIDA Public Enquiries, at (819) 997-5006 in the National Capital Region and

(800) 230-6349 from other parts of Canada, for a list of organizations participating in the program. The Central and Eastern Europe program currently accounts for 85 staff positions at CIDA.

There may be other employment opportunities available through CIDA's corporate branches. The branches of Policy (81 staff members), Corporate Services (291 staff members), and Communications (38 staff members) are gradually being rejuvenated and opportunities exist for dedicated individuals who wish to take part in the formulation process of Canada's aid policy.

WHAT IS IT LIKE TO WORK AT CIDA?

Individuals are interested in working at CIDA for a variety of reasons. Many are motivated by a personal commitment to international development. Others view a stint at CIDA as a stepping stone in a career with the public service. Still others value the satisfaction and prestige associated with managing the "big money" that tends to go with CIDA programming work. What is clear is that CIDA, owing to the diversity of its programs and the agencies and institutions with which it interacts, offers its employees an extremely wide and varied field of opportunity. Furthermore, CIDA offers the excitement of international work and travel without the personal and family upheaval that accompanies long-term overseas postings (although a limited number of these are available).

Many of the people who came to CIDA from CUSO and other NGOs during the 1980s are now at middle and senior levels in the organization. They are as likely to view themselves as career public servants as development workers, so if grassroots development work is what you are looking for, CIDA is probably not your best choice. The largest part of the agency's work is in the areas of contract management, grants and contributions to organizations, institutions, companies, international agencies, and the bureaucratic processes associated with them. Insiders advise that your individual success within CIDA often depends on your acceptance of the bureaucratic process and your ability to make the system work for you. There are very limited opportunities for "hands-on" development work: if you want to get your hands dirty, you may be better off pursuing a career with an NGO or private sector firm supported by CIDA or contracted as an executing agency.

These are changing times for CIDA. As the employee population ages, CIDA is attempting to rejuvenate itself with fresh ideas and new people. While federal government hiring restrictions have somewhat limited these aspirations, there are still opportunities for dedicated individuals interested in assisting with Canada's development agenda.

Nevertheless, CIDA has faced some challenges over the past couple of years, and will likely continue to do so. Efforts to balance the federal budget have resulted in numerous changes in Canada's approach to development assistance. In particular, recent developments have affected the level of ODA resources, the linkages between trade and aid, and the process of tying aid and the criteria for targeting aid.

TYPES OF CIDA EMPLOYMENT

About 1,190 staff members work for CIDA in Canada and overseas. Most employees are based at CIDA headquarters in Hull, Québec; however, 80 employees live and work in the field, delivering Canada's development assistance program in Africa, Asia, the Americas, and Central and Eastern Europe. Employees assigned overseas normally have five years experience with CIDA in program planning and project management, and possess a broad knowledge of bilateral, multilateral, and partnership policies and procedures. There are few, if any, entry-level overseas positions.

If you want to work with CIDA, there are several routes you can take, depending on your skills, experience, and career path. These are explored in the sections below.

CONSULTING WITH CIDA

Finance and Contracting Management Division, CIDA
Corporate Management Branch; (819) 997-7778 or (819) 997-1317 Fax: (819) 994-5395

CIDA's contracting process was recently changed to become more open and transparent. Competition to provide services is now open to both the private and nonprofit sectors. The agency recently introduced its "Unsolicited Proposal Mechanism," which allows organizations to submit original, unsolicited proposals related to development issues. These proposals are assessed on their own merit, not in competition with other proposals. They must conform to country or regional frameworks. To keep partners informed, CIDA may periodically use the MERX system, a national electronic tendering service (see the Resources section at the end of this chapter), and the CIDA web site to indicate the programming priorities and countries of concentration. In addition to this approach, the Agency also awards approximately 1,500 service contracts per year at a total value of about $200 million. The majority of these contracts are associated with CIDA's geographic programs. Proposals are evaluated on such things as technical merit, the organization's experience, its personnel and methodology, and on financial competitiveness. CIDA contracts individuals and organizations for a variety of services, including pre-feasibility and feasibility studies; project identification, management, and monitoring; project and program evaluation; project implementation and execution; and all levels of management support.

Consultants' services are required in the technical, professional, scientific, and managerial fields. While priorities may change according to country program frameworks, the main consulting sectors include human resource development, education and training, environment, health and nutrition, institutional development, agriculture, energy, and population. Assignments can vary in length. Consultants may travel overseas as part of their assignments.

Contracts over $100,000: Each year CIDA awards 50 to 60 contracts over $100,000 totalling approximately $180 million. The agency does not maintain a registry of consultants, but uses the MERX system. (For more information, see the Resources section at the end of this chapter.)

Through MERX, consultants, job hunters and small, specialized organizations can find out when larger organizations have requested bid documents or expressed interest in projects, and contact them directly. By selecting the "International" menu when you log on to the system, you can identify opportunities and find the names of organizations that have requested bid documents. You can then offer your services to these organizations even before the CIDA contract is negotiated.

Contracts valued at less than $100,000: Each year CIDA awards over 1,000 contracts with values under $100,000. There are several mechanisms for awarding these contracts. "Standing Offer" arrangements, for example, provide the Agency with quick access to consulting services. Standing Offer arrangements are advertised on the MERX system. Information is also available under "Doing Business with CIDA" on the CIDA web site (see the Resources section at the end of this chapter). Standing Offers are awarded on the basis of "best value" (technical merit and cost). CIDA also uses the government-wide Standing Offers administered by PUBLIC WORKS AND GOVERNMENT SERVICES CANADA (PWGSC) and maintains special arrangements with two divisions of PWGSC: CONSULTING AND AUDIT CANADA (CAC) and PUBLIC RELATIONS AND PRINT CONTRACT SERVICES. To register for the PWGSC database roster, call the Public Works office nearest you (check the blue pages in your phone book).

CIDA may advertise its needs for contracts under $100,000 through MERX. In some cases, the Agency may also award a contract to a sole supplier and advertise it on MERX in the form of an "Advance Contract Award Notice."

Finally, CIDA sometimes uses a "Non-competitive Selection Process" to meet operational requirements in a cost-effective way. A contract may be awarded to a consultant without competition or based on a review of the qualifications of a limited number of competitors. Such contracts are generally smaller in dollar value than those discussed above and pertain to services not available through existing Standing Offer arrangements.

CIDA uses another important mechanism to award contracts—*networking*. Since the Agency no longer maintains a central registry for consultants, networking with individual CIDA officers is doubly important, for junior as well as senior consultants. Do some homework before you start contacting people directly. Learn about the organization, its mandate, and where potential opportunities lie. CIDA's web site is a valuable source of information.

Your networking efforts should not be limited to CIDA alone—there may be opportunities within the larger organizations involved in international development work. The publication *Service Contracts and Lines of Credit*, available through CIDA's Communications Branch or online at http://w3.acdi-cida.gc.ca, provides a list of current bilateral service contracts and contribution agreements by sector, country, and project. The MERX system may also be helpful for identifying organizations with active international interests. (For details on both of the above, and other useful resources, see the Resources section at the end of this chapter.)

OTHER CONSULTING WITH CIDA

Consulting and Audit Canada (CAC),
International Services Directorate
112 Kent Street, Ottawa, Ontario K1A 0S5;
(613) 996-0188; fax: (613) 995-9203; http://w3.pwgsc.gc.ca/cac

Although it is not part of CIDA, CONSULTING AND AUDIT CANADA (CAC) can be a source of employment with CIDA for both junior and senior professionals. The International Services Directorate of CAC provides management consulting and audit services to international development projects funded by CIDA and the DEPARTMENT OF FOREIGN AFFAIRS AND INTERNATIONAL TRADE (DFAIT).

Services are provided in the following areas: country program reviews; program design; implementation and review; corporate, strategic, and operational planning; project management; economic studies; structural adjustment; accounting systems; operational reviews; decentralization; contracting; joint ventures; policy analysis and development; and women in development. In 1996/97 the International Services Directorate carried out 360 assignments, involving 6,070 days of consulting services.

International Services maintains a permanent pool of over 500 private-sector consultants who have passed a competitive screening process. New consultants are added regularly. Candidates should have a bachelor's degree and preferably a masters or PhD in any field related to development as well as consulting experience in international development. Applications are sent to everyone who requests them. (For more information, see CONSULTING AND AUDIT CANADA in the Profiles section of this chapter.)

PROFESSIONAL NETWORKING ASSOCIATION

Canadian Association of
International Development Consultants (CAIDC)
116 Promenade du Portage, Hull, Québec J8X 2K1;
(819) 771-9367; fax: (819) 771-7953; www.caidc.ca

THE CANADIAN ASSOCIATION OF INTERNATIONAL DEVELOPMENT CONSULTANTS (CAIDC) is a national organization that represents the interests and concerns of international development consultants. The association offers members a forum for the exchange of professional expertise; it also organizes seminars and publishes a quarterly newsletter. (See CAIDC's listing in the Resources section, below.)

BUSINESS OPPORTUNITIES AT CIDA

Industrial Cooperation Program (INC), CIDA
Canadian Partnership Branch, 200 Promenade du Portage, Hull, Québec K1A 0G4;
(819) 953-5444 or (800) 230-6349; fax: (819) 953-5024

CIDA's Industrial Cooperation Program (INC) assists Canadian firms seeking opportunities for investment, joint ventures, and transfers of proven technologies in Asia, Latin America, the Caribbean, Africa, and the Middle East. The program offers financial incentives to Canadian firms to develop long-term agreements for business cooperation and to undertake project definition studies. To be eligible for INC funding assistance, proposals must clearly demonstrate social, economic, and industrial benefits to both the host country and Canada. The host country benefits from new technology, job opportunities, business expansion, and savings in foreign exchange; Canada benefits by supplying equipment, components, and services.

Renaissance Eastern Europe Program (REE), CIDA
Central and Eastern Europe Branch, 200 Promenade du Portage, Hull, Québec K1A 0G4; (819) 997-5006 or (800) 230-6349; fax: (819) 953-6088

CIDA's Renaissance Eastern Europe Program (REE) supports the development of joint ventures and trade, and investment opportunities in the markets of Central and Eastern Europe and the former Soviet Union. Projects are undertaken on a cost-sharing basis with Canadian commercial partners. Eligible projects include feasibility studies to evaluate joint ventures or other investment opportunities, and training programs for local partners. Other initiatives include support for bilateral business councils and business information programs, seminars, and trade fairs. Since it began in 1990, the REE program has committed nearly $17.5 million to some 380 projects. The major sectors of activity have been oil and gas, construction, machinery, and technology. (See the profile on REE in Chapter 33, Services for International Businesses & Entrepreneurs).

CIDA COOPERANTS
Contracting Management Division, CIDA
Corporate Management Branch, 200 Promenade du Portage, Hull, Québec K1A 0G4; (819) 994-7923; fax: (819) 994-5395

CIDA hires well-qualified Canadians to be "cooperants" for a variety of activities in projects overseas. Cooperants are considered self-employed workers, generally responsible to the host government or host country institutions. Cooperants must have Canadian citizenship or landed immigrant status and extensive professional experience in their fields. Cooperant assignments normally run for two years.

Cooperants receive a fee based on the amount they would be paid for similar work in Canada. These fees are taxable; CIDA also pays certain benefits, such as an overseas allowance, pension contributions, housing and school benefits, and return airfare for the candidate and approved family members.

PERMANENT OR TERM POSITIONS AT CIDA
Personnel and Administration Branch, CIDA
200 Promenade du Portage, Hull, Québec K1A 0G4; (819) 997-6383; fax: (819) 953-6212

Public Service Commission (PSC)
Offices across the country: check the blue pages in your phone book.
www.psc-cfp.gc.ca/jobs.htm

Despite ongoing government downsizing, permanent and term positions are opening up at CIDA. As a large number of CIDA's senior employees approach retirement age, the agency is in a dedicated process of rejuvenation and annual competitions are now held for entry-level positions. CIDA has begun a five-year program to recruit recent master's degree graduates from outside the agency to be trained as development officers. The first group of 20 were recruited in 1996. Applications must be submitted to the PUBLIC SERVICE COMMISSION (PSC) Post-Secondary Recruitment Campaign. Request an application package from your nearest PSC office or apply online at www.psc-cfp.gc.ca/jobs.htm, the PSC web site. Applicants must register to write an exam, held annually in October. The top candidates selected by the PSC are interviewed by CIDA. The process is lengthy—it extends right into the following summer—so be prepared for a long wait.

Term employees are hired for a fixed period, usually from three months to two years. One of the benefits of a term position is that it allows you to apply to "closed" government competitions for which only federal public servants can apply. To be considered by CIDA for a term position you must be registered with the PSC. In most cases, because of the equal access clause, CIDA staff cannot directly request your résumé from the PSC. Therefore, your best bet when registering with the PSC is to draw attention to your international expertise. By doing this, the PSC is more likely to forward your résumé to CIDA if a term position opens in your field. You can also register directly with the CIDA personnel office. They maintain an internal database for applicants; however, because of hiring constraints, it is seldom used.

In applying for any position at CIDA, you should be aware of the five key competencies identified in the agency's new *Human Resources Strategy (1997-2000)*. They are:

- Leadership and empowerment (team-building, listening skills, integrity and accountability, problem solving)

- Rigorous thinking/knowledge development (information seeking, conceptual and analytical thinking)

- Positive interaction (communication skills, influence, relationship-building, client service orientation)

- Focus on results (initiative, quality orientation, achievement, drive)

- Valuing diversity, both abroad and in the workplace

CIDA'S STRATEGY FOR YOUTH

CIDA Public Inquiries
200 Promenade du Portage, Hull, Québec K1A 0G4;
(800) 230-6439 or (819) 997-5006, fax: (819) 953-6088

Federal Government Youth Info Line
(800) 935-5555; www.youth.gc.ca

Our World Too is a CIDA initiative designed to promote and facilitate the involvement of youth in international cooperation. To create an environment where youth can gain actual work experience in this area, the agency plans a number of measures to encourage the involvement of youth in the private and nonprofit sectors. CIDA itself plans to make greater use of the many cooperative, work-study, contracting, and summer employment programs available through educational institutions.

The recently launched CIDA INTERNATIONAL YOUTH INTERNSHIP PROGRAM offers six- to 12-month internships (a portion of which includes work outside Canada) for recent university or college graduates between the ages of 19 and 30. Interns may work with a private firm, public institution, or NGO that carries out international development activities in partnership with CIDA. Partner organizations submit their internship proposals directly to CIDA. The program is expected to run until 1999. A list of organizations approved for internship is available on CIDA's web site. For information, contact CIDA Public Inquiries or call the federal government's toll-free youth information line at 1-800-935-5555.

CIDA hires summer students through the Federal Student Work Experience Program (FSWEP). (For more information, see the section on the PUBLIC SERVICE COMMISSION in this chapter.)

CIDA SERVICES

CIDA offers a number of resources and services to the public. CIDA PUBLIC INQUIRIES can be reached toll-free at (800) 230-6349 or (819) 997-5006 in the National Capital area. They will answer any questions about the Agency and Canada's international development assistance program. There is also a TDD/TTY service for the hearing and speech impaired: (819) 953-5023. Documents published by CIDA are available to the public free of charge; the departmental library is open to the public. The INTERNATIONAL DEVELOPMENT PHOTO LIBRARY contains over 80,000 images related to international development. Photo editing/research services are available to the public for a nominal fee. The Virtual Library on International Development can be found on CIDA's web site at http://w3.acdi-cida.gc.ca/virtual.nsf/. It contains links to other international development resources on the Internet.

CIDA's Development Information Program works in partnership with nongovernmental organizations and public awareness firms to inform Canadians about international development issues. The range of activities is wide: support for television and radio broadcasting; publishing initiatives, including the placement of inserts in major Canadian magazines and newspapers; exhibitions; initiatives to inform youth about development; interactive computer products, including utilization of "new media" and the Internet; building media awareness; public awareness campaigns; and other works. Calls for proposals go out at least once a year.

(For more information on all of these services, consult the Resources section, below.)

A LAST WORD ON CIDA

There are very few direct employment opportunities with CIDA at this time. Unless you have recently completed a master's degree, which would make you eligible for the Post-Secondary Recruitment Campaign administered by the PUBLIC SERVICE COMMISSION, or you are a young graduate eligible for the International Youth Internship Program, your efforts are best concentrated on seeking indirect CIDA employment with implementing agents such as private firms and NGOs or as a junior or senior consultant.

It is possible that more opportunities will open up with CIDA over the next several years. The process of rejuvenating the agency has only just begun and the public service seems poised for a change. What is certain is that both the task of international development and the Canadian commitment to this task remain.

RESOURCES

For related resources consult the Resources for Chapter 13, Global Education; Chapter 28, Jobs in International Development; Chapter 35, Nongovernmental Organizations; Chapter 36, United Nations; Chapter 37, Environmental & Agricultural Research Centres; Chapter 38, International Organizations.

Aid as a Peacemaker: Canadian Development Assistance and Third World Conflict 📖
1994, *Robert Miller,* 224 pages ➤ Carleton University Press, 1400 CTTC, Carleton University, 1125 Colonel By Drive, Ottawa, Ontario K1S 5B6 ; $15.95; VISA, MC; (613) 520-3740, fax (613) 520-2893 ▪ Case studies on Canadian aid highlight the problems of development and conflict and discuss whether aid can be used as an instrument of peace in these circumstances. Visit the publisher's web site at www.carleton.ca/cupress. [ID:1662]

Canadian Association of International Development Consultants (CAIDC)
Canadian Association of International Development Consultants (CAIDC), 116 Promenade du Portage, Hull, Québec J8X 2K1 ; (819) 771-9367, fax (819) 771-7953 ▪ The Canadian Association of International Development Consultants (CAIDC) is a national association that gives voice to the concerns and interests of international development consultants. Member benefits include: a newsletter reporting consulting opportunities, new governmental policies, emerging trends in international development, and how to access relevant information, sources, and sites; the CAIDC listserv, an e-mail distribution system used by members to communicate with each other; the continuously expanding CAIDC web site; access to the CAIDC database which contains detailed information on over 450 member consultants; a listing in the CAIDC Member Directory; access to the CAIDC Search Service, an indexed listing of contract opportunities available with CIDA, all levels of Canadian government, public sector organizations, publicly funded entities, and several international establishments; professional development and valuable networking opportunities through social, educational, and professional events provide a forum for the exchange of professional expertise; liaison, consultation, and advocacy with key organizations including CIDA, DFAIT, the Alliance of Manufacturers and Exporters of Canada, the Canadian Co-operative Association, the Association of Canadian Community Colleges, and Consulting and Audit Canada. Visit their web site at www.caidc.ca. [ID:2617]

Canadian International Development Assistance Policies: An Appraisal 📖
1994, *Cranford Pratt,* McGill-Queen's University Press, 378 pages ➤ University of Toronto Press, 5201 Dufferin Street, North York, Ontario M3H 5T8 ; $22.95; VISA, MC; (800) 565-9523, fax (416) 667-7832, utpbooks@utpress.utoronto.ca ▪ A collection of essays providing contemporary, independent analyses of the major components of the Canadian aid program, the issues which have challenged CIDA, and the many and conflicting pressures that have influenced the agency. Visit the distributor's web site at www.utpress.utoronto.ca. [ID:1661]

Centre for Intercultural Learning
Canadian Foreign Service Institute, 15 Bisson Street, Hull, Québec J8Y 5M2 ; (800) 852-9211, fax (819) 997-5409, monique.marion@bisson01.x400.gc.ca ▪ The Centre for Intercultural Learning assists Canadian professionals from NGOs, universities, private industry, and government to develop the crosscultural competencies essential for their success overseas. Services and products include pre-departure and project-related programs, on-arrival orientations, in-country

programming, re-entry programs, country anthologies, and intercultural training. Their web site is under construction. [ID:2642]

CIDA Public Inquiries 📖
Public Inquiries, Canadian International Development Agency, 200 Promenade du Portage, Hull, Québec K1A 0G4 ; (800) 230-6349, fax (819) 953-6088, info@acdi-cida.gc.ca ▪ Staff will answer any questions about the agency or Canada's international development assistance program as well as provide you with appropriate contacts elsewhere in the organization. [ID:2641]

CIDA Publications 📖
Communications Branch, Canadian International Development Agency (CIDA), Communications Branch, 200 Promenade du Portage, Hull, Québec K1A 0G4 ; free; (613) 997-5006, fax (613) 953-6087 ▪ Documents published by CIDA cover a wide range of topics: Canadian development assistance, environment, women in development, business and development, geographic regions, and resources for children and educators. They are available free of charge. CIDA also has a library that is open to the public. While there is no publications catalogue, CIDA does produce a list of publications. Visit the CIDA web site at http://w3.acdi-cida.gc.ca. [ID:2640]

CIDA: Development Information Program 📖
Communications Branch, Canadian International Development Agency (CIDA), Communications Branch, 200 Promenade du Portage, Hull, Québec K1A 0G4 ; (613) 997-5006, fax (613) 953-6087 ▪ Established by CIDA to encourage public understanding of international development issues, the program works in partnership with NGOs and firms that specialize in public awareness. Program activities include: support for television and radio broadcasting; publishing initiatives; exhibitions; initiatives to inform youth about development; interactive computer products, including use of "new media" and the Internet; building media awareness; public awareness campaigns; and publishing. Calls for proposals, specifying desired themes and program priorities, go out at least once a year. [ID:2643]

CIDA: International Development Photo Library (IDPL) 📖
Communications Branch, Canadian International Development Agency (CIDA), Communications Branch, 200 Promenade du Portage, Hull, Québec K1A 0G4 ; (613) 997-5006, fax (613) 953-6087 ▪ IDPL is a resource of over 80,000 slides depicting life in the South, international development, and Canada's role in it. Staff will provide photo editing/research services to the public for a nominal fee. Requests take five to 10 working days to complete. [ID:2644]

Cross-Cultural Effectiveness 📖
1990, *Daniel Kealey,* 68 pages ➤ Public Inquiries, Canadian International Development Agency, 200 Promenade du Portage, Hull, Québec K1A 0G4 ; free; (800) 230-6349, fax (819) 953-6088, info@acdi-cida.gc.ca ▪ Report of three-year study involving 1,400 people engaged in Canadian development programs in 16 countries. Aimed at measuring the effectiveness of technical advisors in transferring much-needed skills. Well written, in English and French. [ID:1101]

Development Business 📖 💻
24 per year ➤ United Nations Publications, 1 United Nations Plaza, Room DC1-570, New York, NY 10017, USA; US$495/year; credit cards; (212) 963-1516, fax (212) 963-1381 ▪ *Development Business* is the primary source for information on goods, works, and services required for projects financed by all of the Development Banks and the UN system. A one-year subscription includes 12 World Bank and 12 Inter-American Development Bank Monthly Operational Summaries and 4 African Development Bank Quarterly Operational Summaries. It is also available online as "Scan-a-Bid." There are charges for connect time and retrieval fees. For sign-up information see the site www.krinfo.com; click on the Sales icon in the left hand frame. [ID:1303]

MERX 💻
MERX at CEBRA INC., 2 Watts Ave., Charlottetown, P.E.I. C1E 1B0 ; (800) 964-6379, fax (888) 235-5800 ▪ A national electronic tendering service. MERX is like the classifieds for contracts with most federal government departments, some provincial and territorial ministries, and some municipalities. Register or access the system by phone, fax, mail, or on the web. You can also access MERX using Datapac (a dial-in service via modem). Supplier registration costs

$8.95/month. Prices for document requests and other services vary. Visit them at www.merx.cebra.com. [ID:2645]

Service Contracts and Lines of Credit 📖
Semiannual, *External Business Relations, Corporate Management Branch,* 66 pages ➤ Public Inquiries, Canadian International Development Agency, 200 Promenade du Portage, Hull, Québec K1A 0G4 ; free; (800) 230-6349, fax (819) 953-6088, info@acdi-cida.gc.ca ▪ A listing of firms and consultants who currently have contracts with CIDA. Lists contracts according to size, project title, supplier, and approximate dollar value. A must for Canadian international job seekers. [ID:1103]

Signposts: Looking for Work in International Development 📖
1995 ➤ Communications Branch, Canadian International Development Agency (CIDA), Communications Branch, 200 Promenade du Portage, Hull, Québec K1A 0G4 ; free; (613) 997-5006, fax (613) 953-6087 ▪ This Canadian reference booklet on international development gives a brief description of the types of work involved, their main characteristics and requirements, and the initial steps in applying for them. It lists and provides brief summaries of the major Canadian employers and volunteer agencies. [ID:1100]

Virtual Library on International Development 🖥
w3.acdi-cida.gc.ca/virtual.nsf ▪ Published by the Canadian International Development Agency (CIDA), this site is an excellent collection of links to international development resources on the Internet. Organized by theme, organization, region and country, report and publication. This site has a constantly-updated new links section. [ID:2450]

Your Guide to Working With CIDA 📖 🖥
1997 ➤ Communications Branch, Canadian International Development Agency (CIDA), Communications Branch, 200 Promenade du Portage, Hull, Québec K1A 0G4 ; free; (613) 997-5006, fax (613) 953-6087 ▪ This very useful guide outlines employment opportunities both within and outside CIDA. Information on how to bid for consulting contracts and potential areas of employment is provided, as is a detailed discussion of CIDA's mandate and activities. This publication can be found on the CIDA web site at http://w3.acdi-cida.gc.ca. [ID:2646]

Profiles of Government Organizations

There are 66 profiles included in this chapter. They cover a range of international opportunities in the government sector. Thirty-one profiles deal with federal government departments and agencies, 18 with international activities carried out by provincial governments, and 10 with Crown corporations. There are also 7 profiles dealing with government-funded institutes and research councils with international activities. This list is extensive but not exhaustive.

Agriculture and Agri-Food Canada
International Market Service Division, Room 1009,
Market and Industry Services Branch, Sir John Carling Bldg.,
930 Carling Ave., Ottawa, Ontario K1A 0C5; (613) 759-1000, fax (613) 759-7499, http://atn-riae.agr.ca

FEDERAL GOVERNMENT: Administration, Agriculture

The International Markets Bureau (IMB) is a primary instrument of Agriculture and Agri-Food Canada and the Market and Industry Services Branch (MISB), providing support to industry efforts to increase agri-food exports. IMB works in partnership with the Regional

Offices and Directorates of MISB, other branches, other federal departments, provincial governments, and with the Canadian agriculture and agri-food sector to secure and increase Canada's share of the world agri-food trade. The bureau influences domestic and foreign policy, programs and financial decisions on behalf of its clients.

IMB consists of four divisions: Grain and Oilseeds, International Agriculture Development, International Market Services and Trade Evaluation and Analysis. These divisions focus their activities on facilitating export sales of grain and oilseeds and their products; influencing policies which contribute to an internationally competitive grains and oilseeds sector; taking an advocacy role within the federal government and with foreign governments for industry; supporting Canada's agri-food industry in creating longer-term trade opportunities and partnerships in developing markets; identifying international trade opportunities; providing advice, assistance and program support to industry to increase Canadian agri-food exports; managing Canada's relationship with the Food and Agriculture Organization (FAO) in Rome; coordinating the Agri-Food Trade Service; coordinating investment activities; analyzing global trade patterns and factors that affect trade, including foreign competition and market information and analysis.

Applications to the department can be made through the Public Service Commission. The department also accepts interns on a case-by-case basis.

The department maintains a web site that provides information on programs and services as well as basic information on the department. [ID:5899]

Alberta Department of Education
National and International Education, 7th Floor, East Tower, 11160 Jasper Ave., Edmonton, Alberta T5K 0L2; (403) 427-2035, fax (403) 422-3014, aturnbull@edc.gov.ab.ca, http://ednet.edc.gov.ab.ca/nie

PROVINCIAL GOVERNMENT: Education, Exchange Programs, Intercultural Briefings

The Alberta Department of Education's international activities may be divided into four principal areas: student exchanges, teacher exchanges, school twinnings, and the marketing of educational services.

There are four salaried staff in the department with international responsibilities. Prospective applicants should be certified teachers with fluency in foreign languages and some international experience. The department accepts qualified interns, with teaching certificates and second languages skills, throughout the year.

The department maintains a web site which provides information on Alberta's various international exchange programs. [ID:5900]

Alberta Economic Development
4th Floor, Commerce Place, 10155 - 102 Street, Edmonton, Alberta T5J 4L6; (403) 422-6236, fax (403) 422-9127, imsa@censsw.gov.ab.ca, www.edt.gov.ab.ca

PROVINCIAL GOVERNMENT: Business Development, International Trade

Alberta Economic Development works with the Alberta and federal governments to promote the export of Alberta goods and services to world markets. It is also actively involved in the development of strategic partnerships between Alberta and international businesses.

Alberta Economic Development has almost 160 Canadian-based staff, 25 of whom have extensive international experience. There are 10 overseas staff located in offices in Japan, China and Hong Kong.

Candidates should have a Bachelor of Commerce degree or a strong technical background. Marketing experience, language skills, crosscultural sensitivity, global awareness, computer skills, and interpersonal skills are all desired qualities. Alberta Economic Development maintains a data bank for résumés.

The department maintains an interesting web site that offers economic information about Alberta, lists available programs and services, and provides other trade-related information. [ID:5901]

Alberta: Wild Rose Foundation

International Development Program, Suite 2007, Toronto Dominion Tower,
Edmonton Centre, Edmonton, Alberta T5J 2Y8; (403) 422-9305, fax (403) 427-4155, www.gov.ab.ca/~wrf

SMALL PROVINCIAL GOVERNMENT: Business Development, Development Assistance,
Development Education, Gender and Development, Human Resources, Human Rights

The Wild Rose Foundation, an Alberta government lottery funded foundation, serves to enhance and encourage Alberta's humanitarian presence in international development through the International Development Granting Program. This initiative provides financial assistance to improve the health, social, and economic conditions in eligible developing countries. This assistance is provided in cooperation with registered and recognized NGOs, and promotes a spirit of volunteerism and respect for the culture, environment, dignity, and independence of the beneficiaries. The categories of projects for which financial assistance is available are primary healthcare, vocational training, small business development and food production. The foundation also administers the International Volunteer Exchange Program, which overseas exchanges between Alberta and Hokkaido, Japan.

Information on the Wild Rose Foundation, including its mandate and scope of activities, can be found on the Government of Alberta's web site documenting its mandate and scope of activities. [ID:5965]

Atomic Energy of Canada Limited (AECL)

2251 Speakman Drive, Mississauga, Ontario L5K 1B2; (905) 823-9060, fax (905) 823-8006, www.aecl.ca

CROWN CORPORATION: Accounting, Administration, Business/Banking/Trade, Business
Development, Computer Systems, Engineering, Environment, Human Resources,
Media/Communications, Project Management

Atomic Energy of Canada Limited (AECL) is a federal Crown corporation which provides Canadians with nuclear energy. AECL sells CANDU power reactors and MAPLE research reactors. Since 1952, AECL has been the force behind Canada's leading position in nuclear power development.

There are 21 CANDU reactors currently in operation in Canada, providing approximately 20 per cent of the nation's energy. Another four reactors operate overseas, one each in Argentina and Romania, and two in South Korea. Four CANDU reactors are currently under construction: two in China and another two in South Korea. AECL's technology is internationally regarded as among the world's safest and most efficient.

Although the CANDU power system is AECL's best-known product, the company has a wide range of research and development activities. AECL provides nuclear engineering services to Canadian utilities and overseas customers and is regarded as a world leader in nuclear waste management research. AECL also markets a wide range of products and services to customers at home and abroad in both nuclear and non-nuclear industries.

AECL's Chalk River Laboratories, located about 200 kms north of Ottawa, has world-class expertise in physics, metallurgy, chemistry, biology and engineering. The site also provides most of the world's supply of medical isotopes, used for diagnosing and treating cancer and other illnesses.

AECL employs over 3,500 people and has offices in Montréal, Ottawa, Mississauga, Chalk River (Ontario) and Pinawa (Manitoba). Internationally, AECL has offices in Seoul, Beijing, Bucharest, Ankara, Jakarta, Moscow, Buenos Aires, Cairo and Zoetermeer, the Netherlands.

AECL offers co-op placements through a number of Canadian universities. It maintains a web site providing detailed information on the firm's products and services including technical data on the nuclear industry and information on the corporation's mandate and activities. [ID:5902]

Bank of Canada
Information Office, 234 Wellington Street, Ottawa, Ontario K1A 0G9;
(613) 782-8021, fax (613) 782-8655, paffairs@bank-banque-canada.ca, www.bank-banque-canada.ca

FEDERAL GOVERNMENT: Business/Banking/Trade

The Bank of Canada's overseas activities are conducted primarily through its International Department. The International Department has three main responsibilities. First, it produces timely analysis of current and prospective developments in foreign countries. Second, it provides analysis and policy advice on issues addressed by international financial institutions such as the International Monetary Fund. Third, it undertakes studies on topics related to international financial markets and economic activity in foreign countries. The International Department employs 31 people located at the bank's head office in Ottawa.

The Bank of Canada also conducts exchange market liaison and analysis. This is carried out by the Financial Markets Department based in Ottawa, Montréal and Toronto. This department employees 106 people.

For recent publications and press releases, current market rates, and other information about the bank's activities and Canada's financial sector, visit their web site. [ID:5903]

British Columbia Centre for International Education (BCCIE)
Suite 950, 409 Granville Street, Vancouver, B.C. V6C 1T2;
(604) 895-5070, fax (604) 895-5079, bccie@bccie.bc.ca, www.bccie.bc.ca/~bccie

PROVINCIAL GOVERNMENT: Consulting, International Education

The British Columbia Centre for International Education (BCCIE) supports the development and coordination of British Columbia's public postsecondary international education activities and strengthens the international expertise and understanding among students, scholars and staff in the B.C. public postsecondary education system.

The organization is funded by the B.C. Ministry of Education, Skills and Training and has the following goals: to increase the internationalization of the B.C. postsecondary school system; to increase international project opportunities for member institutions; to increase the international expertise among faculty, staff, and students at B.C.'s postsecondary institutions; and to promote the capabilities of the postsecondary system internationally.

The centre maintains a web site providing general information on the services and programs offered. [ID:5904]

British Columbia Ministry of Forests
Economics and Trade Branch, 2nd Floor, 610 Johnson Street, Victoria, B.C. V8W 3E7;
(250) 387-8610, fax (250) 387-5050, lois.mcnabb@gems8.gov.bc.ca, www.for.gov.bc.ca

PROVINCIAL GOVERNMENT: Economics, Forestry, International Trade

The British Columbia Ministry of Forests manages the province's trade in forestry products, with an annual value of $15 billion. Work centres on trade issues such as tariffs, log export restraints, and regulatory policies.

The ministry currently has ten salaried staff in Canada with international responsibilities. There are no staff stationed overseas. It also networks with overseas agents and the Department of Foreign Affairs and International Trade.

Prospective applicants should have a postgraduate degree in business, trade policy or economics, and/or comparable field experience. Those with experience in forest-related issues are preferred.

The Ministry maintains an extensive web site that contains information on the forestry sector as well as on the ministry's mandate and activities. [ID:5907]

British Columbia Trade and Investment Office (BCTIO)

Suite 730, 999 Canada Place, Vancouver, B.C. V6C 3E1;
(604) 844-1900, fax (604) 660-2457, jburnes@eivic.ei.gov.bc.ca, www.ei.gov.bc.ca

PROVINCIAL GOVERNMENT: Business/Banking/Trade, Business Development, International
Trade, Project Management

The British Columbia Trade and Investment Office (BCTIO), which provides one-stop
access for both investors and exporters, focuses on pursuing investment opportunities,
fostering industry development and enhancing the export of B.C.'s goods and services.

The office is part of the Ministry of Employment and Investment, B.C.'s lead ministry
for economic development and job creation. BCTIO assists investors and exporters in a
number of ways, including informing investment and export proponents of potential joint
ventures, identifying key private sector projects, providing information on government
policies, establishing contacts between clients, and developing sectoral trade opportunities.

BCTIO staff are action-oriented, highly-focused professionals with extensive experience at senior levels in both the private and public sectors. Their expertise includes: international business development, international government relations, project development and
management, commercial and investment banking, trade and public policy analysis. Staff in
BCTIO's overseas offices ensure B.C.'s strong presence in established and emerging
markets, especially in the Asia Pacific region. BCTIO does not anticipate any employment
opportunities for the foreseeable future.

BCTIO maintains a web site that provides information on its services and activities.
[ID:5909]

Canada Mortgage and Housing Corporation (CMHC)

International Relations Division, 700 Montréal Road, Ottawa, Ontario K1A 0P7;
(613) 748-2817, fax (613) 748-2302, ird@cmhc-schl.gc.ca, www.cmhc-schl.gc.ca

CROWN CORPORATION: Housing/Human Settlements, International Trade, Urban
Development

Canada Mortgage and Housing Corporation (CMHC) represents Canada internationally on housing and urban environment issues in various multilateral forums. CMHC partici-
pates in the Organization for Economic Cooperation and Development (OECD) Group on
Urban Affairs, the United Nations Commission on Human Settlements (HABITAT), and the
United Nations Economic Commission for Europe's Committee on Human Settlements. The
Corporation is also playing a lead role in the development of an export strategy for Canada's
housing industry and specific research is underway to ascertain the export readiness of
Canada's housing industry. CMHC is involved in information exchanges on housing and
urban matters with other similar international organizations.

Candidates applying to the International Relations Division at CMHC should have backgrounds in housing policy, housing finance, urban and regional planning, and Canadian
social policy. Employees are expected to represent Canada at various international multilateral governmental forums and at conferences and meetings.

Visit CMHC's web site for more information. [ID:5910]

Canada Post Corporation (CPC)

International Business Division, Suite E0420, 2701 Riverside Drive,
Ottawa, Ontario K1A 0B1; (613) 734-9787, fax (613) 734-9793, www.mailposte.ca

CROWN CORPORATION: Consulting, International Trade, Technical Assistance

Canada Post's International Business Division manages the corporation's international
postal business activity. As well, it supports global postal initiatives to improve the viability of
the network through focused programs and initiatives.

International Business, which employees 25 people, looks for university-educated
candidates who can solve problems. They should be able to deal effectively with a variety of
assignments and environments. A proven professional track record is needed but prime

assets are innovative thinking and adaptability. Its office employs 25 people. In addition, Canada Post Corporation has created a fully-owned subsidiary called Canada Post Systems Management Limited to provide postal consulting services on a commercial basis. It has been successful in transferring Canadian-based technology and management expertise as well as that of its teaming partners to all corners of the world.

Canada Post maintains an interesting and comprehensive web site that provides information on everything from its corporate structure to stamp collecting. [ID:5911]

Canadian Broadcasting Corporation (CBC)

International Relations, P.O. Box 3220, Stn. C,
Ottawa, Ontario K1Y 1E4; (613) 724-5710, fax (613) 724-5699, roreilly@ottawa.cbc.ca, www.cbc.ca

CROWN CORPORATION: Accounting, Administration, Business/Banking/Trade, Business Development, Computer Systems, Consulting, Engineering, Human Resources, Media/Communications, Project Management, Telecommunications

The Canadian Broadcasting Corporation (CBC) is a publicly-owned corporation created in 1936 to provide a national broadcasting service to Canada. The corporation is active on several fronts in the international arena: radio and television programming abroad; program sales to other countries, international program festivals and competitions; and foreign office headquarters.

The International Relations section is responsible for international program and staff exchanges, festivals and competitions, as well as for international training, and arranging agendas for foreign visitors. It is a member or associate member of several international broadcasting unions and maintains relations with other world broadcasting unions. Radio Canada International provides CBC broadcasts overseas (see separate profile). In cooperation with international and Canadian agencies such as the Canadian International Development Agency (CIDA), and UNESCO, CBC has sent personnel to aid foreign broadcasting organizations and provides corporate points of contact for foreign broadcasters and international associations.

The CBC maintains foreign offices in London, Paris, Washington D.C., and at the UN headquarters in New York. CBC News has staff correspondents based in the same locations and in Moscow, Beijing, Jerusalem, Berlin, Vienna, Johannesburg, Mexico City, New Delhi, and Hong King. Candidates must have 10 years of experience in a relevant field.

While the CBC does not currently offer internship positions, they would like to do so when the fiscal climate improves. CBC maintains an interesting web site that contains a wide variety of information on the corporation's activities and programming. [ID:5912]

Canadian Commercial Corporation (CCC)

Overseas Division, 11th Floor, 50 O'Connor Street,
Ottawa, Ontario K1A 0S6; (613) 996-0034, fax (613) 995-2121, info@ccc.ca, www.ccc.ca

CROWN CORPORATION: Business/Banking/Trade, Business Development, International Trade

The Canadian Commercial Corporation (CCC) helps Canadian companies sell their goods and services abroad, acting as the prime contractor on behalf of suppliers seeking to export to foreign governments and agencies. In transactions, CCC provides Canadian companies with the backing of their own government, thereby enhancing suppliers' credibility and competitiveness, and reassuring foreign customers that they will receive quality goods and services in accordance with contract terms.

The CCC is divided into four major divisions to assist with foreign trade: the Operations Division, Major Projects Division, Business Development Division and External Relations Division. The CCC provides information to Canadian exporters on a variety of issues such as negotiation of contract terms; price structure; risk management; methods of payment; financial instruments; peculiarities in foreign laws and regulations.

CCC assists companies from almost every industrial sector, the largest being aerospace. Over 60 per cent of CCC's suppliers are small or medium-sized enterprises and over 70 per cent of contracts are valued at below $100,000. Customers include federal, state, provincial and municipal governments throughout the world as well as private sector buyers and international organizations. The US market is responsible for over 75 per cent of CCC's business, with the largest customers being NASA and the Department of Defense.

Candidates should have a university degree in economics or business or an equivalent amount of experience in international contracting.

The CCC maintains a web site called the "Virtual Trade Plaza" that provides information on corporate programs, recent developments, staffing, and offers a number of useful links to other trade organizations. [ID:5913]

Canadian Commission for UNESCO
P.O. Box 1047, 7th Floor, 350 Albert Street, Ottawa, Ontario K1P 5V8; (613) 566-4325,
fax (613) 566-4405, unesco@comcdn@canadacouncil.ca, www.canadacouncil.ca/unesco/unesco.htm

FEDERAL GOVERNMENT: Community Development, Development Assistance, Development Education, Gender and Development, Human Rights, Intercultural Briefings, International Education, Media/Communications, Social Sciences

The Canadian Commission for UNESCO advises the Government of Canada on its relations with the United Nations Educational, Scientific and Cultural Organization (UNESCO). The Commission fosters cooperation between Canadian organizations and UNESCO and coordinates UNESCO program activities in Canada. The commission, created in 1957 as a division of the Canada Council, is one of 178 National Commissions for UNESCO around the world.

The commission's membership of 180 represents a cross-section of Canadian society. Members include federal government departments and agencies, intergovernmental bodies, nongovernmental organizations, professional associations, institutions and individuals. It has a 19-member executive committee and consultative bodies for the following sectors: education, the natural sciences, culture, communication, information, informatics, the social and human sciences, and the status of women. The secretariat of the Canadian Commission for UNESCO numbers 9. Its budget for 1997-98 is $815,000. UNESCO programs of special relevance to Canadians include: ethics, education and literacy, environmental education, human rights, world heritage, oceanography, status of the artist, bioethics, pluralism and cities.

The commission considers applications for internships through the Canada Council, which can be reached at the above address.

The commission also maintains a web site that offers a brief explanation of its mandate and provides a number of useful links to other UN-related sites. [ID:5914]

Canadian Foreign Service Institute
Centre for Intercultural Learning (CIL), 15 Bisson Street,
Hull, Québec J8Y 5M2; (800) 852-9211, fax (819) 997-5409, www.dfait-maeci.gc.ca/intranet/training.htm

INSTITUTE/RESEARCH COUNCIL: Intercultural Briefings

The Centre for Intercultural Learning (CIL) assists Canadian professionals from NGOs, universities, private industry, and government to develop the crosscultural competencies essential for their success. The centre takes a comprehensive approach when preparing professionals for their international activity, identifying the clients' requirements and developing learning solutions that enable them to effectively engage in their activities.

Pre-departure briefing sessions for short- and long-term assignments are held regularly. In addition, the CIL provides project-related programs, country anthologies, in-country programming, on-arrival orientations, and intercultural training. [ID:7064]

Canadian Heritage
International Relations, 13-G-27, 13th Floor, 25 Eddy Street,
Hull, Québec K1A 0M5; (819) 997-2730, fax (819) 997-2553, www.pch.gc.ca

FEDERAL GOVERNMENT: Advocacy, Consulting, International Trade

Canadian Heritage's International Relations Division is the focal point for the extensive international activities undertaken by the various components of the department. In some areas of endeavour, the division itself undertakes activities; in others, it provides advice and assistance to the rest of the department on their international work. Information on developments in other countries as well as in many international organizations is collected and analyzed by the division, for use in developing domestic policies and programs.

The division's international activities cover the full range of departmental responsibility, including: Canada's participation in international expositions (world fairs) which have been registered with the Bureau International des Expositions (BIE) in Paris; national parks and historic sites, events and organizations; marketing and promotion of Canada's cultural industries; international cooperation in film and television co-productions; broadcasting and publishing policies; human rights and multicultural issues; amateur sports events such as the Olympics and les Jeux de la Francophonie; cooperation in the museums field; and participation in United Nations Educational, Scientific & Cultural Organization (UNESCO), Council of Europe, La Francophonie and several others.

Approximately 15 staff at Canadian Heritage have international responsibilities. Prospective candidates ideally have a bachelor's degree in the humanities, public administration or international studies, employment experience in related fields, and good language and communications skills. While Canadian Heritage maintains a data bank for résumés, hiring is currently limited by government restraint policies. Canadian Heritage's International Relations Division considers applications for summer interns specializing in international relations.

Canadian Heritage maintains an interesting web site with an abundance of information about Canada, Canadian symbols and history. (For information on their international internships see the Canadian Government International Internships profile in Chapter 17, International Internships.) [ID:5915]

Canadian International Development Agency (CIDA)
Communications Branch, 5th Floor, Place du Centre, 200 Promenade du Portage,
Hull, Québec K1A 0G4; (819) 997-5006, fax (819) 953-6088, http://w3.acdi-cida.gc.ca

See the detailed profile at the beginning of this chapter. (For information on their international internships see the Canadian Government International Internships profile in Chapter 17, International Internships.) [ID:6676]

Canadian International Grains Institute (CIGI)
Suite 1000, 303 Main Street, Winnipeg, Manitoba R3C 3G7;
(204) 983-5344, fax (204) 983-2642, tremere@cigi.mb.ca, www.cigi.mb.ca

INSTITUTE/RESEARCH COUNCIL: Agriculture, Job Training, Marketing

Canadian International Grains Institute (CIGI) is an instructional organization offering courses in grain handling, marketing and technology. The institute's activities are funded 40 per cent by The Canadian Wheat Board and 60 per cent by the Grain Marketing Bureau of Agriculture Canada. International programs form the core of CIGI's activities, bringing together representatives from as many as 20 countries at a time. The institute has 28 staff members based in Winnipeg. It has no positions overseas. [ID:5916]

Canadian International Trade Tribunal (CITT)

333 Laurier Ave. W., Ottawa, Ontario K1A 0G7;
(613) 993-3595, fax (613) 990-2439, secretary@citt.gc.ca, www.citt.gc.ca

FEDERAL GOVERNMENT: Economics, International Trade, Law

The Canadian International Trade Tribunal (CITT) is an independent, quasi-judicial body which reports to Parliament through the Minister of Finance. Its activities include all of the former inquiry and appeal functions of the Tariff Board, the Canadian Import Tribunal, and the Textile and Clothing Board.

In addition to its legal responsibilities, CITT personnel undertake economic and financial analyses of firms, industries and other parties involved in tribunal inquiries.

CITT maintains a web site detailing with its mandate and activities. [ID:5917]

Canadian Security Intelligence Service (CSIS)

Headquarters, P.O. Box 9732, Stn. T, Ottawa, Ontario
K1G 4G4; (613) 231-0100, fax (613) 231-0612, www.csis-scrs.gc.ca

FEDERAL GOVERNMENT: Intelligence

Canadian Security Intelligence Service (CSIS) investigates, analyzes, and reports to the government on information or intelligence activities that constitute threats to the security of Canada. It is a defensive, domestic intelligence service that offers only very limited opportunities for employment overseas.

When overseas, CSIS personnel conduct liaison with various police, security and intelligence organizations and assists Citizenship and Immigration Canada (CIC) in screening, on security grounds, prospective immigrants and travellers. CSIS employees abroad do not perform covert or offensive operations of any kind with respect to foreign intelligence.

The service has offices in most major cities across Canada and some offices overseas, of which only London, Paris and Washington have, for personnel security reasons, been publicly acknowledged. CSIS has an estimated workforce of 2,030 people, although the number of overseas personnel is not available.

Recruits to the intelligence officer stream must be mature, tolerant, and understanding of political systems, particularly the Canadian parliamentary system. Candidates must also have sound judgement and emotional stability. Applicants must also be Canadian citizens who possess undergraduate university degrees and valid driver's licenses. The service has a policy of career employment and is an equal opportunity employer. Due to security constraints, internships are rare at CSIS.

The service maintains an excellent web site that provides a wealth of information on the agency's mandate and operations. [ID:5918]

Canadian Space Agency (CSA)

6767 route d'Aeroport, Saint-Hubert, Québec J3Y 8Y9;
(514) 926-4800, fax (514) 926-4352, info@www.space.gc.ca, www.space.gc.ca

The Canadian Space Agency's (CSA) mandate is to promote the peaceful use and development of space for the social and economic benefit of Canadians. International cooperation is central to all major CSA space programs.

Internationally, the CSA is primarily involved with the design, production and operation of the Mobile Serving System (MSS), Canada's contribution to the International Space Station, a joint venture among the US, Canada, the European Space Agency, Japan and Russia. The station will provide a permanently manned space base in low Earth orbit which will allow for continued scientific research in a microgravity environment.

The CSA is also responsible for the RADARSAT remote sensing satellite, the Canadian Astronaut Program, the David Florida Laboratory, the Space Science Program, and the Space Technology Program. [ID:5919]

Canadian Transportation Agency

Les Terrasses de la Chaudiere, 15 Eddy Street, Hull, Québec K1A 0N9;
(819) 953-5074, fax (819) 953-5562, gavin.currie@cta-otc.gc.ca, www.cta-otc.gc.ca

FEDERAL GOVERNMENT: Air Transportation, Marine, Railways, Transportation

The Canadian Transportation Agency is responsible for administering the licensing system for Canadian and foreign air carriers with domestic and international operations relevant to Canada. It also administers and participates in negotiating international air agreements, including the regulation of international air tariffs. Currently, there are 40 salaried staff in Canada with international responsibilities.

The agency maintains a web site that describes its mandate and activities and provides information on transportation regulations, agency decisions and orders and transportation of travellers with disabilities. Several publications and news releases are also provided online.
[ID:5940]

Citizenship and Immigration Canada

International Region, 16th Floor, Jean Edmonds Tower S., 365 Laurier Ave. W.,
Ottawa, Ontario K1A 1L1; (613) 996-8436, fax (613) 996-8048, http://cicnet.ingenia.com

FEDERAL GOVERNMENT: Immigration, Social Policy

The International Region at Citizenship and Immigration Canada is responsible for delivering Canada's immigration program abroad and for contributing to Canada's migration, refugee, and social policies.

International Region Foreign Service Officers have a university degree and a good knowledge of Canada's immigration policy and procedures and of supporting legislation which impacts on the overseas delivery of the immigration program. They also have good knowledge of Canadian history, the political environment, social conditions, and working and living conditions affecting immigration issues. They typically also have expertise in one or more of the following areas: politics, economics, trade, finance, public affairs, development assistance etc.

Recruitment is typically achieved through the postsecondary foreign service campaigns conducted by the Public Service Commission (PSC). There are currently 170 salaried Canadian staff overseas and an additional 85 based in Canada with international responsibilities. Employment inquiries should be directed to the PSC. [ID:5920]

Consulting and Audit Canada (CAC)

International Services Directorate, 112 Kent Street, Ottawa, Ontario K1A 0S5;
(613) 996-1577, fax (613) 995-9203, lynne.deachman@cac.gc.ca, http://w3.pwgsc.gc.ca/cac

FEDERAL GOVERNMENT: Accounting, Administration, Adult Training, Business/Banking/Trade, Community Development, Consulting, Development Assistance, Development Education, Economics, Environment, Exchange Programs, Gender and Development, Human Resources, Human Rights, Humanitarian Relief, Intercultural Briefings, International Trade, Logistics, Project Management, Technical Assistance, Telecommunications, Tourism, Water Resources

Canadian public service standards are recognized for their excellence worldwide. As a Canadian government agency, CAC has earned a solid reputation in the international community for providing high quality consulting and audit services in more than 40 countries. The CAC's client roster includes United Nations agencies, the Canadian International Development Agency (CIDA), the Department of Foreign Affairs and International Trade (DFAIT) and the World Bank.

Their assignments in the international arena are as varied as their clients. They include planning for complete public service reform, establishing public sector consulting services, enhancing government audit capacity and evaluating a wide variety of development projects.

International Services Directorate maintains a pool of private sector consultants, with new candidates added regularly through a competitive screening process. Candidates should have a bachelor's degree and preferably a master's or PhD in any field related to develop-ment activities, as well as consulting experience in the field of international development. Applications are available on request. [ID:5921]

Elections Canada
International Services, 257 Slater Street,
Ottawa, Ontario K1A 0M6; (800) 267-7360, fax (613) 990-2173, www.elections.ca

FEDERAL GOVERNMENT: Election Monitoring, Institution Building, Technical Assistance

The International Services Directorate of Elections Canada is involved principally with electoral support and democratic development. This entails constitutional and legislative guidance, election procedures assessments, assistance and technical advice to electoral bodies, voter education, and the monitoring of elections themselves.

Prospective applicants preferably have election-related experience, and must be willing to participate on a voluntary basis, unless the mission is a lengthy one requiring particular technical expertise. Elections Canada maintains a data bank for résumés and an interesting web site that contains information on Canada's political environment and provides links to a number of related sites. [ID:5922]

Environment Canada (EC)
International Affairs Branch, Policy and Communications, 22nd Floor, Les Terrasses de la Chaudiere,
10 Wellington Street, Hull, Québec K1A 0H3; (613) 997-2800, fax (613) 953-2225, www.ec.gc.ca

FEDERAL GOVERNMENT: Economics, Environment, Policy Dialogue

Environment Canada's International Affairs Branch provides strategic and policy advice and support for international environmental issues and fosters policy innovation in the area of economy-environment integration. This branch is responsible for the Green Corps, a group that works to market the department's expertise internationally.

Environment Canada also manages the Canadian Wildlife Service (CWS). The CWS conducts research on wildlife problems of national and international significance and cooperates with foreign countries, especially on issues surrounding endangered species and migratory birds.

Applications to the International Affairs Branch and the Canadian Wildlife Service must be made through the Public Service Commission. Candidates should have a background in the sciences, particularly geography.

Environment Canada maintains an interesting web site offering a wealth of information on environmental issues. (For information on their international internships see the Cana-dian Government International Internships profile in Chapter 17, International Internships.) [ID:5924]

Export Development Corporation (EDC)
151 O'Connor Street, Ottawa, Ontario K1A 1K3;
(613) 598-2500, fax (613) 237-2690, export@edc4.edc.ca, www.edc.ca

CROWN CORPORATION: Accounting, Administration, Business/Banking/Trade, Business
Development, Economics, Engineering, Human Resources, International Trade,
Media/Communications

The Export Development Corporation (EDC) helps Canadian exporters compete in world markets by providing a wide range of financial and risk management services. EDC is a financially self-sustaining Crown corporation that operates on commercial principles, charging fees and premiums for its products and interest on its loans. It does not provide grants or subsidies.

EDC has more than 650 employees, all located within Canada. The corporate head office is in Ottawa, with regional offices in Vancouver, Edmonton, Calgary, Winnipeg, Lon-don, Toronto, Montréal, Moncton and Halifax.

Most professional employees have degrees in business, finance, economics or marketing. They can choose to work in a variety of areas in EDC's head office or in regional offices as business development managers. Financial service managers on EDC's business teams and regional managers in its International Markets Division often represent EDC in Canada and abroad. They provide financial and risk management advice to exporters and deal with other lending institutions, development banks and foreign governments. Other areas of employment include economics, political and risk assessment, project financing and equity groups, treasury operations, corporate finance and government relations, corporate and public affairs, communications, marketing, legal services, information services, administration and human resources.

EDC maintains an excellent web site that provides specific information on employment opportunities as well as general information on the corporation's programs and services. [ID:5925]

Department of Finance Canada
19th Floor, East Tower, 140 O'Connor Street,
Ottawa, Ontario K1A 0G5; (613) 992-1573, fax (613) 992-0938, www.fin.gc.ca

---

FEDERAL GOVERNMENT: Business/Banking/Trade, Economics, Policy Dialogue

The Department of Finance Canada (FC) is the central agency of the federal government responsible for analysis and advice on the economic and financial affairs of Canada. It is concerned with all aspects of the performance of the Canadian economy, following the development of external factors that bear on domestic economic performance, and examining the economic actions taken by other levels of government.

FC oversees four programs in the areas of public debt, fiscal arrangements, external affairs, and services to government. These programs are: Financial and Economic Policies, Public Debt, Fiscal Transfer Payments, and Special Programs. Eight major branches administer these programs: Economic and Fiscal Policy, Tax Policy, Federal-Provincial Relations and Social Policy, Financial Sector Policy, International Trade and Finance, Economic Development and Corporate Finance Branch/Privatization, Law Branch, Consultations and Communications, and Corporate Services.

Several branches deal with international issues, although the International Trade and Finance Branch has the lead responsibility. The Tax Policy Branch's Business Income Tax Division oversees a variety of international taxation and market analysis issues; the Financial Sector Policy Branch coordinates activities related to financial markets and analysis; and the International Branch participates actively in the development of Canada's policies on international trade and investment, and conducts analyses relating directly to those areas.

The department recruits candidates with graduate degrees and strong academic backgrounds in economics, business administration, or related disciplines. The International Branch expects further concentration on international trade, international finance, and international economic relations. Recruitment at the entry level is normally conducted through the department's university recruitment program. Candidates are also referred by the Public Service Commission.

FC has foreign postings in G-7 countries and in select international economic institutions such as the International Monetary Fund (IMF), the World Bank, and the Organization for Economic Co-operation and Development (OECD). Organizations such as the GATT/WTO and the United Nations, in turn, recruit individuals from all areas of the department, depending on their needs at the time.

FC maintains a comprehensive web site that includes a departmental overview and a wide variety of publications, press releases, and speeches online. [ID:5926]

Department of Fisheries and Oceans (DFO)
International Directorate, 13th Floor, 200 Kent Street, Ottawa, Ontario
K1A 0E6; (613) 993-1852, fax (613) 993-5995, info@www.ncr.dfo.gc.ca, www.dfo-mpo.gc.ca

FEDERAL GOVERNMENT: Fisheries, International Law/International Agreements, International Trade

The Department of Fisheries and Oceans (DFO) International Directorate in Canada negotiates international agreements affecting bilateral and multilateral fishery relations with other countries. The directorate then administers these agreements, formulates and represents Canadian fisheries trade positions, represents Canadian international discussions on fisheries trade issues, and participates in eight bilateral and multilateral scientific and conservation fisheries commissions.

The directorate currently has 14 officers with international responsibilities. The department also coordinates, in cooperation with Western Economic Diversification, the International Trade Personnel Program, which matches recent graduates with businesses seeking to expand their international operations. Prospective applicants should have graduated from a recognized university with an acceptable degree in social science, commerce, or law, and be proficient in both official languages. Other requirements include experience in policy development; negotiation of bilateral and multilateral fisheries and trade agreements; and drafting and analysis of intergovernmental communications. There are occasional opportunities for consulting in specialized areas of research.

The department maintains a web site that contains recent publications and general information on aquaculture and departmental programs. [ID:5927]

Department of Foreign Affairs and International Trade (DFAIT)
Lester B. Pearson Bldg., 125 Sussex Drive,
Ottawa, Ontario K1A 0G2; (613) 996-3386, fax (613) 995-1405, www.dfait-maeci.gc.ca/

See the detailed profile at the beginning of this chapter. (For information on their international internships see the Canadian Government International Internships profile in Chapter 17, International Internships.) [ID:6675]

Health Canada
International Affairs Directorate (IAD), Room 829B, 8th Floor, Brooke Claxton Bldg., Tunney's Pasture, Postal Locator 0908A, Ottawa, Ontario K1A 0K9; (613) 957-7298, fax (613) 952-7417, www.hwc.ca

FEDERAL GOVERNMENT: International Law/International Agreements, International Trade, Medical Health

Health Canada's International Affairs Directorate (IAD) is responsible for Canada's relationship with international health organizations and for bilateral relations in the health field. It also works closely with nongovernmental and professional organizations with international interests and activities in the health policy field.

Individuals working for IAD have experience with international health issues, backgrounds in health policy, medicine, international affairs and trade, and a broad knowledge of Canadian health policy.

IAD is involved in promoting Canadian exports of healthcare products and services, assisting Canadian firms in exporting, and attracting foreign investors to Canada. IAD works in close collaboration with Foreign Affairs and International Trade Canada and Industry Canada, and is an active participant in the Sectoral Advisory Group on International Trade (SAGIT) on medical and healthcare products and services and is a member of the health industry's National Sector Team (NST) and its sub-committees. On occasion, IAD will also be in a position to recommend Canadian consultants to international organizations and agencies, such as the World Health Organization (WHO). IAD has 14 salaried staff in Canada.

Health Canada's web site provides information on the department's activities and has useful links to international health-related sites. [ID:5928]

Human Resources Development Canada (HRDC)

International Affairs Branch, 7th Floor, 360 Laurier Ave. W.,
Ottawa, Ontario K1A 0J9; (613) 941-4239, fax (613) 941-4576, Int.Affairs@spg.org, www.hrdc-drhc.gc.ca

FEDERAL GOVERNMENT: Human Resources

Human Resources Development Canada (HRDC) works with a wide range of inter-national organizations. These include the United Nations and its agencies, the Council of Europe, the Asia-Pacific Economic Cooperation (APEC), and the International Labour Organization (ILO). HRDC also markets its extensive expertise in human resources development to other countries and international organizations.

International Affairs Branch, with 15 staff members, coordinates all international activities within HRDC and provides strategic advice to the department. Staff members must have experience dealing with foreign delegations, a background in policy or economics, and a good knowledge of the federal government.

For information on how to apply for federal government positions, contact the Public Service Commission. (For information on their international internships see the Canadian Government International Internships profile in Chapter 17, International Internships.)
[ID:6968]

Industry Canada

International Business Branch, 5th Floor, 235 Queen Street E., Ottawa, Ontario
K1A 0H5; (613) 954-3506, fax (613) 957-4454, publications@ic.gc.ca, www.ic.gc.ca

FEDERAL GOVERNMENT: Business/Banking/Trade, Business Development, Environment,
International Trade

Industry Canada's International Business Branch is involved in developing international trade and investment policies within Industry Canada. Industry Canada employs approxi-mately 4,500 people, including 32 in the International Business Branch. All personnel are Canadian-based and travel abroad, although some are seconded to Foreign Affairs or other international companies and organizations.

The work of the International Business Branch requires experience in international marketing, trade negotiations, investment policies and technology issues. This branch is also responsible for developing Internet-based data on international business. There are occa-sional consulting opportunities in these fields as well.

Industry Canada maintains an extensive web site (http://strategis.ic.gc.ca) that provides information on the department, as well as offering advice to those interested in international trade and investment. (For information on their international internships see the Canadian Government International Internships profile in Chapter 17, International Internships.) [ID:5930]

International Centre for Human Rights and Democratic Development (ICHRDD)

Suite 100, 63 de Bresoles Street, Montréal, Québec H2Y 1V7;
(514) 283-6073, fax (514) 283-3792, ichrdd@web.net, www.ichrdd.ca

INSTITUTE/RESEARCH COUNCIL: Advocacy, Development Assistance, Gender and
Development, Human Rights, Media/Communications

The International Centre for Human Rights and Democratic Development (ICHRDD) provides support for projects emanating primarily from nongovernmental organizations in developing countries. The organization has 23 employees, of whom 10 travel regularly.

Applicants should have a university degree in social sciences, knowledge of human rights issues and international human rights protection mechanisms and organizations. Knowledge of, and experience with, nongovernmental organizations, computer literacy and, in some cases, languages other than English and French, are also required. Internship positions are occasionally offered. The ICHRDD has no overseas postings.

The centre maintains an interesting web site that provides information on their mandate and activities and offers access to a number of online publications. [ID:5931]

International Development Research Centre (IDRC)
P.O. Box 8500, Ottawa, Ontario K1G 3H9; (613) 236-6163, fax (613) 238-7230, info@idrc.ca, www.idrc.ca

INSTITUTE/RESEARCH COUNCIL: Accounting, Administration, Agriculture, Business/Banking/Trade, Business Development, Community Development, Computer Systems, Development Assistance, Development Education, Economics, Environment, Fisheries, Forestry, Fundraising, Gender and Development, Human Resources, International Trade, Media/Communications, Micro-Enterprises, Water Resources

The International Development Research Centre (IDRC) funds scientific research in Africa, Asia, Latin America, and the Caribbean to help communities in the developing world find solutions to social, economic, and environmental problems. IDRC-supported projects are designed to alleviate poverty, maximize the use of local resources, and strengthen human and institutional capacity. IDRC research efforts are directed towards the following themes: Food Security, Biodiversity Conservation, Sustainable Employment, Equity in Natural Resource Use, Strategies and Policies for Healthy Societies, and Information and Communication. In its 27 years of existence, IDRC has funded over 6,000 projects throughout the world.

IDRC receives an annual federal grant and is governed by an international autonomous board of 21 governors. The centre is a public corporation rather than an agent of the Canadian government, and its employees are not public servants.

IDRC has 357 full-time employees of whom 266 work in Ottawa and 91 work in regional offices in Uruguay, Senegal, Kenya, Egypt, South Africa, Singapore, and India.

Program staff evaluate project proposals according to their scientific merit and feasibility, so these positions must be filled by highly qualified individuals. While IDRC works mainly with researchers in Third World institutions, projects are sometimes done in collaboration with Canadian scientists. Canadians involved in IDRC projects work in equal partnership with researchers in developing countries. IDRC offers a number of internship positions. (For information on internships see Chapter 17, International Internships.)

IDRC maintains a useful web site that contains information on past and present research projects, access to online publications, and a number of other resources relating to development issues. [ID:5932]

Department of Justice Canada
External Liaison Unit, Room 209, 239 Wellington Street, Ottawa, Ontario K1A 0H8;
(613) 952-8346, fax (613) 941-4165, lamirande.manon@justice.x400.gc.ca, http://canada.justice.gc.ca

FEDERAL GOVERNMENT: Development Assistance, Development Education, Gender and Development, Human Rights, International Law/International Agreements, International Trade, Technical Assistance

The Department of Justice is responsible for the legal affairs of the federal government and for ensuring that federal acts and regulations are effectively administered and are both fair and responsive to Canadian needs. It also serves as legal advisor to the Governor General, represents the Crown in litigation, and provides legal counsel to federal departments and agencies.

The department represents Canada at legal meetings in several international forums, including the United Nations Commission on International Trade Law (UNCITRAL), the Hague Conference on Private International Law, the International Institute for the Unification of Private Law (Unidroit), the International Civil Aviation Organization (ICAO), the Organization of American States (OAS), and the Council of Europe.

The department is involved in legal technical assistance with a number of countries, including the Czech Republic, Slovakia, Ukraine, Haiti, and South Africa. Currently, two Justice officials are posted abroad and the department contributes to the salary of another federal official posted at the Canadian Embassy to the European Union in Brussels. The department also runs the Visiting Professional Interchange Program which facilitates placement of qualified staff in unique law-related employment situations both within and outside Canada.

There are some opportunities for students, including articling students, with the Department of Justice. For details on these, the Visiting Interchange Program, and general recruitment visit their web site. [ID:5933]

Manitoba Trade & Investment Corporation (Manitoba Trade)
Suite 410, 155 Carlton Street, Winnipeg, Manitoba R3C 3H8;
(204) 945-2466, fax (204) 957-1793, mbtrade@itt.gov.mb.ca, www.gov.mb.ca/itt/trade

PROVINCIAL GOVERNMENT: Business Development, International Trade

Manitoba Trade is the lead international business agency of the Manitoba government. The corporation assists Manitoba enterprises to increase their exports and promotes trade and investment opportunities in the province to foreign companies and investors. The Corporation coordinates its activities with agencies and organizations of other governments, in Canada and abroad.

Manitoba Trade currently has 23 staff members based in Canada and seven agents overseas. Applicants should have a business background. Desired qualifications and experience for candidates include: a degree in business and/or international trade, overseas business experience, crosscultural skills, and language capabilities. [ID:6878]

Medical Research Council of Canada (MRC)
Tower B, 5th Floor, Jeanne Mance Bldg., 1600 Scott Street, Ottawa, Ontario
K1A 0W9; (613) 941-2672, fax (613) 954-1800, mrcinfocrm@hpb.hwc.ca, http://wwwmrc.hwc.ca

INSTITUTE/RESEARCH COUNCIL: Exchange Programs, Medical Health, Research

The Medical Research Council of Canada (MRC) is a federal agency which promotes, assists, and undertakes basic applied and clinical research in the health sciences. MRC also advises the federal Minister of Health on health research issues.

The council's international programs include travel grants for researchers, sponsorship for visiting professors and scientists, and exchange programs with Argentina, Brazil, China, France, Italy and the UK. For more information on these programs, please see the Grants and Awards Guide posted on the MRC web site. (Also see the profiles in Chapter 15, Awards and Grants.) MRC staff are recruited through the Public Service Commission. [ID:5936]

Department of National Defence (DND)
Recruiting, Canadian Forces Recruiting Services Headquarters,
Building 0-110, P.O. Box 1000 Stn Main, Canadian Forces Base Borden,
Borden, Ontario L0M 1C0; (800) 856-8488, fax (613) 992-2272, www.recruiting.dnd.ca

FEDERAL GOVERNMENT: Peacekeeping and Defence

The Canadian Forces have four areas of international activity. These areas are: peacekeeping and contingency operations for collective security agencies such as the UN; service in inter-country units, such as at NATO Headquarters in Brussels or NORAD Headquarters in Colorado; exchange postings to foreign units, military schools, and academic institutions as students or faculty; and employment in Military Attaché and Embassy staff positions.

Members of the Canadian Forces are not hired specifically for overseas employment. Depending on requirements and your military occupation, you may have several opportunities to serve overseas. Presently, there are approximately 30 Officer Military Occupations and 110 Non-Commissioned Member Occupations. Most of these can serve overseas in their trade area or in a general service capacity. There are also approximately 60,000 Regular Force personnel, 2,900 based overseas. Service in the Primary Reserves is the closest the Canadian Forces has to an internship program. Applications for recruitment will soon be made available through the Department of Defence's web site. [ID:6857]

Department of National Defence (DND)

Headquarters, 101 Colonel By Drive,
Ottawa, Ontario K1A 0K2; (613) 992-3210, fax (613) 992-2073, www.dnd.ca

FEDERAL GOVERNMENT: Teaching

The Department of National Defence (DND) operates elementary education programs in Brunssum, the Netherlands and Casteau, Belgium for dependent children of Canadian service persons. There are approximately 250 Canadian children being educated by 18 Canadian teachers. The teachers serve initially on a two-year "Loan of Service" agreement between themselves, their sponsoring board of education and DND. After the initial two years, two one-year extensions are possible. This arrangement has the advantage of protecting the teachers' superannuation and staff rights, as staff remain under contract to their Canadian school boards for the duration of their term overseas.

Teachers and principals assigned to the two overseas locations are selected based upon their academic qualifications, background, experience and their ability to live in and adapt to a small Canadian community. Second language skills are preferred. DND solicits applications from school boards across Canada whenever the candidate database is insufficient to meet the needs of the system. Teachers must have a minimum of five years teaching experience to be considered. [ID:5938]

National Film Board of Canada (NFB)

International Program, P.O. Box 6100, Station Centre Ville,
Montréal, Québec H3C 3H5; (514) 283-9447, fax (514) 496-1895, www.nfb.ca

CROWN CORPORATION: Marketing

The National Film Board of Canada (NFB) promotes and markets NFB films and videos internationally. The International Division consists of offices in Montréal, New York, London and Paris which are staffed by two officers and one to two support staff each.

These offices arrange commercial distribution of NFB titles with private distributors, direct sales of prints and videos, and sales of television and theatrical rights. The NFB is currently in a period of downsizing and does not expect any job openings in the foreseeable future. The NFB maintains an interesting web site that contains information on the NFB as well as a number of current productions. [ID:5939]

Natural Resources Canada (NRCan)

International Energy Relations Division, 580 Booth Street, Ottawa, Ontario
K1A 0E4; (613) 996-2993, fax (613) 995-5576, ihelpdes@nrcan.gc.ca, www.nrcan.gc.ca

FEDERAL GOVERNMENT: International Trade

Natural Resources Canada (NRCan) has several units responsible for managing relations with other nations and international organizations. These units ensure that the government's energy and mineral policies, programs, and activities are understood internationally, that senior officials in the department are kept informed of pertinent international events and commitments, that Canada's trade interests are protected and supported, and that NRCan's international responsibilities are discharged appropriately and consistently with overall Canadian foreign policy objectives.

Staff in these units number around 20 and are all Ottawa-based. Other staff, particularly in the scientific areas, also have ongoing contacts with counterparts overseas, with whom they may pursue collaborative research or technological exchanges.

Staff in international sections are generally public servants with a university degree and experience in international relations or economics. There are very few international consulting opportunities at NRCan. [ID:5941]

New Brunswick Department of Economic Development and Tourism
Trade and Investment, P.O. Box 6000, Centennial Building, Fredericton, N.B.
E3B 5H1; (506) 453-2876, fax (506) 453-3783, nbtradeinv@gov.nb.ca, www.gov.nb.ca/nbfirst

PROVINCIAL GOVERNMENT: Information Technologies, International Trade

The New Brunswick Department of Economic Development and Tourism attracts investment and technology to New Brunswick through key overseas contacts, joint ventures, and trade. The focus is on manufacturing, value-added processing, and high-technology companies in the software, information, and environmental sectors. Efforts are concentrated on North America, Europe, and Asia Pacific.

The department is currently looking for information technology specialists. Fluency in a second language is an asset. The department currently employs one staff member overseas, and eight with international responsibilities in Canada.

The department's web site contains information on the provincial economy and investing in New Brunswick. A related web site, http://itjobnet.gov.nb.ca, provides information on information technology job openings in the province. [ID:5942]

New Brunswick Department of Intergovernmental and Aboriginal Affairs
Co-operation Division, P.O. Box 6000, Fredericton, N.B. E3B 5H1;
(506) 453-2976, fax (506) 453-2995, NBInter@gov.nb.ca, www.gov.nb.ca

PROVINCIAL GOVERNMENT: Policy Dialogue

The mission of New Brunswick's Department of Intergovernmental and Aboriginal Affairs is to develop strategies and policies on intergovernmental cooperation with a view to maximizing possible economic and social benefits and to promoting and developing New Brunswick through cooperation at the provincial, national and international levels.

The Intergovernmental Co-operation Division gives priority to La Francophonie as a forum for promoting New Brunswick at the international level. The province has been an official member of La Francophonie since 1977, when it became a participating government. As such, it acts autonomously in the sectors it considers most important, such as education, technical and vocational training and new technologies.

The department occasionally offers employment on a contractual basis. As a rule, applicants must be bilingual. Information on the department is available through the Government of New Brunswick's internet site. Annual reports, news releases and links to La Francophonie are among the information offered. [ID:6557]

Newfoundland and Labrador Department of Industry, Trade and Technology (ITT)
P.O. Box 8700, St. John's, Nfld. A1B 4J6;
(709) 729-5600, fax (709) 729-5936, info@ditt.gov.nf.ca, http://success.nfld.net

PROVINCIAL GOVERNMENT: Business Development, International Trade

The Newfoundland and Labrador Department of Industry, Trade and Technology (ITT) actively forges links between Newfoundland and the international community. The department's mandate is to maximize industrial benefits from large scale projects such as the Voisey's Bay project and from the oil and gas industry (Hibernia, Terra Nova, Whiterose etc.) It is also responsible for enhancing export development and attracting investment.

Departmental staff are divided along sectoral and geographic bases. They provide business and marketing advice and information to local firms looking to export internationally. ITT marketing and investment personnel are also the first point of contact for international firms seeking to invest in, or form joint ventures with, Newfoundland and its business community.

Most of the marketing and investment staff are educated in the fields of business (BComm, MBA) or economics. Specialized divisions also employ experts in engineering and sciences. Investment officers can be contacted at (800) 563-2299 for business information on the province. ITT maintains a web site that provides information on the department's programs and activities. [ID:5943]

Newfoundland Department of Tourism, Culture, and Recreation
Tourism Development Division, P.O. Box 8700, St. John's, Nfld. A1B 4J6;
(709) 729-2831, fax (709) 729-0057, info@tourism.gov.nf.ca, www.gov.nf.ca/tourism

PROVINCIAL GOVERNMENT: Media/Communications, Tourism

The Newfoundland Department of Tourism, Culture, and Recreation's Tourism Development Division works in cooperation with Canadian embassies and the Atlantic Canada Tourism Partners in the area of trade development. Prospective applicants should have knowledge of French and German, and an education in travel or commerce. Paid summer internships relating to visitor services and public relations are typically available. The department maintains a data bank for résumés. [ID:5944]

Nova Scotia Economic Development and Tourism
Investment and Trade, P.O. Box 519, World Trade and Convention Centre, 1800 Argyle Street,
Halifax, N.S. B3J 2R7; (902) 424-6650, fax (902) 424-5739, iat@gov.ns.ca, www.gov.ns.ca/ecor

PROVINCIAL GOVERNMENT: Business Development, International Trade

The mission of the Nova Scotia Economic Development and Tourism is to work with people and communities to build the province's economy. Its objectives are to create and sustain a strong and positive development climate; increase local, national, and international investment in Nova Scotia; develop and strengthen trade relationships with existing and new trading partners; increase exports from the province; develop and market strategic sectors; and advance Nova Scotia as a strategic international centre of excellence for technology innovation.

The department has two divisions directly involved in international activities. The Investment and Trade Division assists Nova Scotia companies in selling products and services domestically and internationally, through trade promotion shows, missions, and research. It also promotes the province as a location for new business investment. The Nova Scotia Marketing Agency promotes Nova Scotia as a tourist destination for international travellers and as a convention location.

The department considers applications from student interns interested in business and trade development. Check their web site for information on various activities, press releases, job opportunities in Nova Scotia and other information. [ID:5946]

Ontario International Trade Corporation (OITC)
Capital Projects Division, 7th Floor, 56 Wellesley Street W., Toronto, Ontario M7A 2E4;
(416) 314-8200, fax (416) 314-8222, www.gov.on.ca/MBS/english/programs/EDT0440.html

PROVINCIAL GOVERNMENT: Business/Banking/Trade, Consulting, International Trade

The Capital Projects Division of the Ontario International Trade Corporation (OITC), formerly known as the Ontario International Corporation (OIC), has a broad mandate to increase the export of Ontario goods and services through export education and by assisting Ontario's professional services and capital projects sector in obtaining contracts for international projects. Clients of the Capital Projects Division include consulting engineers, project planners and developers, contractors, and a consortia of service companies and capital goods manufacturers.

The OITC is a Crown corporation which reports to the Ontario Minister of Economic Development and Trade. It is governed by a board of private sector representatives with extensive knowledge of Ontario business and international trade. The Capital Projects Division is responsible for the international marketing of public sector expertise and supports the development of Ontario-based consortia to bid on international capital projects. Area directors travel to world regions four times a year in search of projects on behalf of Ontario companies. These areas include Asia Pacific, Southeast Asia, the Far East, Central America and the Caribbean, South America, Africa, the Middle East, East and West Europe, and the US.

The division looks for candidates with international experience, experience in the professional services sector, knowledge of the cultures and languages of the regions, marketing skills, and familiarity with international finance. [ID:5948]

Ontario Ministry of Citizenship, Culture Recreation
Arts and Cultural Industries Unit, Culture Division, 2nd Floor, 77 Bloor Street W., Toronto, Ontario M7A 2R9; (416) 314-7645, fax (416) 314-7091, matsonm@mczcr.gov.on.ca, www.mczcr.gov.on.ca

PROVINCIAL GOVERNMENT: Culture

The Ontario Ministry of Citizenship, Culture and Recreation has limited services available to assist with international cultural activities. Through the Cultural Programs Branch, the ministry's objective is to assist in opening new markets for Ontario's artists and their work. The Visiting Programmers/Journalists program provides per diem assistance to visiting programmers or journalists to be introduced to the works of Ontario artists. Staff may also assist in the development of itineraries for visiting programmers. The ministry maintains an interesting web site that contains information about its mandate and activities. [ID:5949]

Ontario Ministry of Education and Training
Policy Branch, National and International Liaison Unit,
Ontario Ministry of Education and Training, 15th Floor, Mowat Block,
900 Bay Street, Toronto, Ontario M7A 1L2; (416) 314-3869, fax (416) 325-2664, www.edu.gov.on.ca

PROVINCIAL GOVERNMENT: Intercultural Briefings, International Education

The National and International Liaison Unit coordinates and enhances communication between the Ontario Ministry of Education and Training and other national and international organizations. The unit works on strengthening the ministry's association with other jurisdictions and supporting meetings between senior officials and the Minister of Education and foreign visitors. [ID:5950]

Ontario: ORTECH
Manager, Human Resources, Sheridan Science and Technology Park, 2395 Speakman Drive, Mississauga, Ontario L5K 1B3; (905) 822-4111, fax (905) 823-1446, www.info.ortech.on.ca

CROWN CORPORATION: Advanced Technology, Research, Technical Assistance

ORTECH is a provincially sponsored corporation that offers, on a fee basis, a variety of services to the private sector. These services include the delivery of technical assistance and expertise, and involvement in research and development in a variety of sectors.

The corporation currently supports a staff of 300 who are engaged in research in a number of fields including automotive technology, pharmaceuticals, and computer simulations. ORTECH maintains a data bank for résumés. As the corporation moves into privatization, job opportunities are currently limited. [ID:5952]

Enterprise Prince Edward Island
P.O. Box 910, Charlottetown, P.E.I. C1A 7L9;
(902) 368-6300, fax (902) 368-6301, invest@gov.pe.ca, www.gov.pe.ca

PROVINCIAL GOVERNMENT: Adult Training, Agriculture, Community Development, Computer Systems, Development Assistance, Energy Resources, Environment, Fisheries, Forestry, Human Resources, International Trade, Micro-Enterprises, Telecommunications, Tourism, Water Resources

Enterprise Prince Edward Island is a provincial Crown corporation working directly and in conjunction with the federal government to assist exporters with market investigation, market research, product promotion, and incoming and outgoing missions. Specific divisions work to attract investment in a number of sectors including aerospace and food, manufacturing, information and communications technology and marketing and communications. The Trade Development Centre also assists PEI businesses to act internationally.

Enterprise PEI can be reached via the PEI government Internet site. Press releases concerning new economic development initiatives and employment opportunities are posted at this site, as well as detailed information about the corporation's mandate and activities. [ID:5923]

Public Service Commission
21st Floor, West Tower, L'Esplanade Laurier, 300 Laurier Ave., W.,
Ottawa, Ontario K1A 0M7; (613) 996-8436, fax (613) 954-7541, www.psc-cfp.gc.ca/jobs.htm

See the detailed profile at the beginning of this chapter. [ID:6674]

Public Service Commission, International Programs Directorate (PSC-IPD)
21st Floor, West Tower, L'Esplanade Laurier,
300 Laurier Ave. W., Ottawa, Ontario K1A 0M7; (613) 992-5902,
fax (613) 943-0771, debbie.wright@ms.psc-cfp.w400.gc.ca, www.psc-fp.gc.ca/intpgm/epbhome.htm

FEDERAL GOVERNMENT: Human Resources

The Public Service Commission (PSC), in conjunction with the Department of Foreign Affairs and International Trade, monitors middle- and senior-level positions within the secretariats of international organizations to which Canada belongs. PSC coordinates the nomination of Canadian candidates for vacancies deemed of interest to and attainable by Canada. Every year, between 40 and 50 Canadians compete successfully for secretariat positions in international organizations. Candidates should have a university degree and a minimum of five years' experience in their field, preferably with an international organization. (For more information see Chapter 36, United Nations and Chapter 38, International Organizations.)

The International Programs Directorate maintains a very useful web site that offers information on the availability of employment with international organizations of which Canada is a member state. [ID:5953]

Public Works and Government Services Canada: Canadian Government Publishing (CGP)
International Division, 4th Floor, 350 Alberta Street, Ottawa, Ontario
K1A 0S5; (613) 990-5863, fax (613) 956-5539, http://publications.pwgsc.gc.ca

FEDERAL GOVERNMENT: Marketing, Publishing

Canadian Government Publishing (CGP) is the official publisher for the Government of Canada. Every year they coordinate the publishing, distribution, and marketing of the many new titles that are produced or sponsored by departments, agencies, or scientific and social research organizations within Canada's federal government. The publications are available in either French or English, or in bilingual format.

CGP selects distribution outlets for the marketing and sales of priced federal government publications (electronic or print format) outside Canada. They coordinate CGP's participation in international events such as trade shows, book fairs, conferences, and professional associations. They also coordinate the promotion and publicity of government publications to the international market.

CGP maintains a web site that allows you to browse government publications by title or subject and offers instructions on how to order these publications. [ID:5954]

Québec : Ministère de l'Agriculture, des Pêcheries et de l'Alimentation (MAPAQ)

Direction des relations intergouvernementales, Ministère de l'Agriculture, des Pêcheries et de l'Alimentation, 200, chemin Ste-Foy, Québec, Québec G1R 4X6; (418) 643-2460, fax (418) 646-6564, info@agr.gouv.qc.ca, www.riq.gouv.qc.ca/mapaq/

PROVINCIAL GOVERNMENT: Agriculture, Fisheries, International Trade, Training and Technology Transfer

La Direction du développement des marchés est responsable du soutien des exportations des produits alimentaires québécois. Elle emploie 16 agents dont 5 à l'étranger pour réaliser ce mandat. Une formation d'agent de développement commercial est requise pour occuper ce type de poste. Le MAPAQ ne maintient pas de répertoire des candidats et n'engage pas de stagiaires. Les instituts de technologie agroalimentaire qui dépendent du MAPAQ organisent pour des étrangers des stages de formation dans le domaine de l'agroalimentaire. [ID:6862]

Québec : Ministère des Relations internationales (MRI)

525, boul. René-Lévesque est, Québec, Québec G1R 5R9; (418) 649-2300, fax (418) 649-2304, communications@mri.gouv.qc.ca, www.mri.gouv.qc.ca

PROVINCIAL GOVERNMENT: Administration, Commerce, Culture, Economics, International Trade, Law, Management, Science and Technology, Tourism

Le mandat du Ministère des Relations internationales (MRI) est de planifier, organiser et diriger l'action du Gouvernement à l'étranger ainsi que de coordonner les activités, au Québec, des ministères et des organismes en matière d'affaires internationales. Il est en outre chargé, en collaboration avec les ministères et organismes concernés, de la mise en oeuvre de la politique d'affaires internationales du Gouvernement. Cette politique a pour but de favoriser le rayonnement et le développement du Québec sur les plans commercial, économique, politique, social et culturel.

Le MRI emploie 538 personnes, dont 213 oeuvrent à l'étranger. Le ministère peut faire appel à des ressources extérieures pour analyser ou résoudre certaines situations qui requièrent une expertise professionnelle spécialisée. Les personnes désireuses de postuler au MRI devront posséder une formation générale en affaires internationales avec des compétences particulières, selon le domaine visé, en économie, commerce, droit, promotion culturelle et touristique, science et technologie, administration et gestion. [ID:5937]

Radio Canada International - Canadian Broadcasting Corporation (RCI CBC)

International Programming, 1055, boul. René Lévesque E., Montréal, Québec H2L 4S5; (514) 597-7500, fax (514) 284-9550, rci@montreal.src.ca, www.rcinet.ca

CROWN CORPORATION: Information Technologies, Telecommunications

Radio Canada International (RCI) is the external short-wave radio service of the CBC which transmits radio programming abroad. It provides international audiences with programs reflecting Canadian life, and culture, national interests and policies, and the spectrum of Canadian viewpoints on national and international affairs. The service broadcasts news, information, and entertainment programs from the English and French domestic networks. Programs are in English, French, Russian, Ukrainian, Spanish, Standard Chinese (Mandarin), and Arabic.

Broadcasts are aimed at Europe, Asia, Latin America, the Caribbean, the Middle East, Africa, and the US. RCI has approximately 120 staff members, all of whom are based in Canada, with the majority working in programming.

Minimum requirements for journalists and announcer-producers include a university degree, five years of relevant experience, fluency in English and French, and in the appropriate third language for those working in foreign-language sections, and knowledge of

Canadian and international affairs. Opportunities arise, from time to time, for freelance journalists, analysts, and commentators. Freelancers are commissioned in Canada.

RCI has a very interesting web site that offers real-time audio news in several languages as well as a wealth of information on the organization's activities. [ID:5955]

Reference Canada

47 Clarence Street, 3rd Floor,
Ottawa, Ontario K1A 0S5; (800) 667-3355, fax (613) 941-5383,
refcda@hookup.net, http://canada.gc.ca/programs/refcda/refcda_e.html

Reference Canada is the federal government's bilingual telephone referral and basic information service. Available nationwide, this toll-free service helps the public find answers to questions about federal programs and activities. The service improves accessibility to federal contacts, helps the public track down information with a minimum number of calls, and greatly reduces misdirected inquiries.

In Manitoba and Québec, Reference Canada has a joint program with the province. Manitoba residents should call the Citizens' Inquiry Service at (800) 282-8060. In Québec, interested individuals should contact the Communication-Québec office in their area, or call (800) 363-1363. [ID:7173]

Revenue Canada

International Relations Coordination Office, Albion Tower,
25 Nicholas Street, Ottawa, Ontario K1A 0L5; (613) 957-9775, fax (613) 941-6618, www.rc.gc.ca

FEDERAL GOVERNMENT: Business/Banking/Trade, International Trade

Revenue Canada is mandated to collect revenues; to administer tax laws both for the federal government and on behalf of some provinces and territories; to administer trade policies and legislation; provide border services; and to make certain social and economic payments to individuals and corporations.

Revenue Canada has primary responsibility for administering certain laws pertaining to revenue collection, such as the Income Tax Act and the Customs Act. As well, Revenue Canada helps to administer several other pieces of legislation while working in close cooperation with other federal government departments and provincial and territorial governments. This spirit of cooperation extends to the customs and revenue agencies of other countries thereby providing jobs and stimulating economic growth by facilitating trade and investment. Revenue Canada's administration of international customs and tax agreements benefits legitimate international commerce.

Revenue Canada's international activities are managed by its International Relations Coordination Office in Ottawa. The department also has representatives at the Canadian embassies in Brussels (European Union) and Tokyo. Applications for employment must be made through the Public Service Commission.

The department maintains a web site that provides information on its mandate and activities and presents a number of online publications. [ID:5956]

Royal Canadian Mint (RCM)

Corporate Communications, 320 Sussex Drive,
Ottawa, Ontario K1A 0G8; (613) 993-3500, fax (613) 991-2628, www.rcmint.ca

FEDERAL GOVERNMENT: Business/Banking/Trade, Marketing

Royal Canadian Mint (RCM) produces and exports the following goods around the world: foreign coinage, Canadian bullion coins, Canadian numismatic coins. The mint also offers gold refining services. Products are marketed and sold by the marketing group, located in Ottawa and sales staff are assigned geographic areas of responsibility. Foreign coinage contracts are usually with foreign governments. Bullion and numismatic coins are sold to selected local distributors/banks. Refinery contracts are typically with mining interests or foreign contracts.

Royal Canadian Mint has 535 salaried staff based in Canada. Most sales staff require previous experience in international sales. University-level education is an asset as is education or experience in related fields such as metallurgy, engineering, banking, or investment. [ID:5957]

Royal Canadian Mounted Police (RCMP)
Public Information Branch, Room 316, 1200 Vanier Parkway,
Ottawa, Ontario K1A 0R2; (613) 993-1085, fax (613) 993-5894, www.rcmp-grc.gc.ca

FEDERAL GOVERNMENT: Policing

The Royal Canadian Mounted Police maintains 31 members in 22 overseas posts. RCMP members serve as attachés to the Canadian Embassy and assist foreign national police services in the exchange of investigative or police-related information. Each officer is responsible for liaising with several countries in the general geographical location of the embassy.

Liaison officers must be peace officers of the RCMP and have policing experience. A prerequisite for liaison work is an investigative background in drug enforcement or economic crime. The ability to communicate in more than one language is an asset.

The RCMP maintains a web site that offers information on the force and provides recruiting information for interested parties. [ID:5958]

Saskatchewan Institute of Applied Science and Technology (SIAST)
International Services Division, P.O. Box 556, Albert South Centre,
Regina, Sask. S4P 3A3; (306) 787-0113, fax (306) 787-4840, international@siast.sk.ca, www.siast.sk.ca

INSTITUTE/RESEARCH COUNCIL: Intercultural Briefings, Technical Assistance

In Canada, the International Services Division of the Saskatchewan Institute of Applied Science and Technology (SIAST) promotes development awareness within the broader institution. Abroad, SIAST implements projects in Africa, the Caribbean, South Asia, Southeast Asia, and China.

Applicants must have strong crosscultural sensitivity and flexibility, along with strong academic and professional credentials in their particular fields. Currently, there are three staff in Canada with international responsibilities. Overseas staff are hired on a project-by-project basis. SIAST maintains a data bank for résumés and a web site that provides information on the various programs offered at each of its four campuses. [ID:5960]

Social Sciences and Humanities Research Council of Canada (SSHRC)
P.O. Box 1610, Constitution Square, 350 Albert Street,
Ottawa, Ontario K1P 6G4; (613) 992-0691, fax (613) 992-1787, z-info@sshrc.ca, www.sshrc.ca

INSTITUTE/RESEARCH COUNCIL: Research, Social Sciences

The Social Sciences and Humanities Research Council (SSHRC) promotes and assists university-based research and scholarship in the social sciences and humanities. SSHRC supports international research activities through all of its programs, but particularly through: Aid to Occasional Research Conferences and International Congresses in Canada, which provides assistance to Canadian researchers organizing conferences in Canada or periodic congresses of major international scholarly associations; Aid to Research and Transfer Journals, which, among other types of support, offers special initiative grants to help Canadian scholarly journals publish special joint international editions with recognized journals from other countries; International Summer Institutes, to support Canadian universities in convening summer institutes attended by researchers from around the world; Doctoral and Postdoctoral Fellowships, which may be used to assist PhD students or postdoctoral fellows studying at foreign universities (Canadian citizens only).

The council's programs of support for Canadian research and international relations are administered by officers in SSHRC's three program divisions: Fellowships and Institutional Grants, Research and Communication Grants, and Strategic Programs and Joint Initiatives.

The Policy, Planning, and International Relations Division is responsible for managing and promoting international relations as a community outreach and policy development activity.

The small number of staff members working in these divisions are all based at SSHRC's offices in Ottawa. Officers must have an honours bachelor's degree in the humanities or social sciences and knowledge of the university research environment. They must also be familiar with the work of other granting agencies active at the national or international level.

SSHRC maintains an extensive and creative web site that provides information on research opportunities, grant applications, statistics, and SSHRC's mandate. [ID:5962]

Statistics Canada (SC)
International and Professional Relations Division, 25th Floor, R.H. Coats Bldg., Tunney's Pasture, Ottawa, Ontario K1A 0T6; (613) 951-8917, fax (613) 951-1231, prigly@statcan.ca, www.statcan.ca

FEDERAL GOVERNMENT: Accounting, Administration, Computer Systems, Economics, Social Sciences, Statistics

Statistics Canada (SC) participates in a wide range of international statistical activities with the objective of improving the Canadian statistical system through bilateral and multilateral consultation. Based on specific agreements and with the intent of developing international standards and classifications, SC participates in cooperative programs which aim to improve the availability of internationally comparable statistics. In support of Canada's foreign policy objectives and through the provision of technical assistance, SC researches statistical policies, methods, and approaches in foreign countries in an attempt to improve foreign statistical systems. These goals also encompass maximizing the cooperation of international organizations for the purpose of improving the efficiency and cost-effectiveness of their statistical work.

SC represents Canada on the United Nations Statistical Commission and at statistical meetings called by bodies such as the various regional commissions of the United Nations, the Organization for Economic Co-operation and Development (OECD), the European Union, and the Commonwealth Secretariat. At the bilateral level, close contacts are maintained with a number of countries, such as Australia, France, the Netherlands, Sweden, the UK, and the US.

SC maintains a web site that contains interesting information on several topics, including Canadian population and economy. [ID:5963]

Telefilm Canada (TFC)
14th Floor, National Bank of Canada Tower, 600 de la Gauchetière Street W., Montréal, Québec H38 4L8; (514) 283-6363, fax (514) 283-8212, www.telefilm.gc.ca

CROWN CORPORATION: Marketing, Media/Communications

Telefilm Canada is a Crown corporation which provides private companies with funds and resources to help develop Canada's film, television, and video industry. The corporation markets and promotes Canadian film, television, and video abroad and coordinates Canada's participation in international festivals. Telefilm Canada also manages co-production agreements for film or television programs between Canada and 44 foreign countries, from Algeria to Yugoslavia. Telefilm Canada has its head office in Montréal and offices in Toronto, Vancouver, Halifax and Paris.

Telefilm Canada maintains an excellent web site that provides detailed information on its international affairs, co-productions, markets and a catalogue of projects it has helped finance. [ID:5964]

Chapter 35

Nongovernmental Organizations

Thousands of groups based in the North operate worldwide on a nonprofit basis in the public interest. These groups are known as *nongovernmental organizations* or NGOs. In the field of international development, they are usually volunteer agencies, working in partnership with like-minded groups in the South for social justice and the eradication of poverty. Unions, professional associations, co-operatives, and research departments of universities and colleges also operate as NGOs.

Canada is known throughout the world as having one of the most extensive government-supported NGO sectors and similar grassroots organizations now operate in Europe, the US and Australia. Working for Canadian or foreign NGOs is possible, especially if you have language or other skills that may be in short supply.

Of the approximately 300 registered NGOs working in international development in Canada, 181 of the most active are listed in this chapter.

BRIEF HISTORY OF NGOs

Long before any official Canadian government involvement in foreign aid programs, Canadian volunteer agencies were at work in the South. While missionary groups were active before the turn of the century, the first Canadian government aid program, the Colombo Plan, wasn't launched until the post-World War II era of the early 1950s.

In 1968 the federal CANADIAN INTERNATIONAL DEVELOPMENT AGENCY (CIDA) was established. Within CIDA, a Nongovernmental Organizations (NGO) division was set up with a mandate to promote Canadian participation in development activities, provide government assistance to nations through

763

nongovernmental channels, and tap the expertise and resources of nongovernmental sectors for development purposes.

In the 1990s, CIDA's NGO division encourages and facilitates the participation of Canadians in international development by co-financing projects and programs of autonomous Canadian NGOs which are compatible with Canadian foreign and development policies. It also supports the efforts of people in the South, particularly the least privileged, to meet their basic human needs and to improve their quality of life through sustainable development, a development process which supports the use of local resources.

As aid agencies, NGOs have traditionally been regarded as an effective alternative to government aid programs, mainly because they are exempt from some of the constraints involved in government-to-government (bilateral) aid. NGOs are generally better able to work at the grassroots level and are flexible in the type of work they engage in. Many work in partnership with Southern-based NGOs or local people's movements and it is also common to find NGOs with well-defined political agendas that consider sensitive issues such as human rights or social action.

WHO FUNDS NGOs?

The NGO community has grown, with increasing public support and government funding. NGOs receive much of their funding through government channels. It now administers some 20 per cent of Canada's Official Development Assistance (ODA) to developing countries. However, the strength of NGOs depends greatly on financial donations from individuals and private businesses. Not only do these donations contribute substantially to the programming capacity of NGOs, but they also indicate to government that the Canadian public values the goals and activities of NGOs. We strongly recommend that you become a regular donor or volunteer with an NGO. Making a regular contribution to a large organization such as CARE CANADA, GREENPEACE CANADA or OXFAM, or a smaller group like WATERCAN or INTER PARES, will go a long way! Your support is needed.

CIDA's contribution to NGOs has remained fairly constant since the late 1980s. In 1996-97 CIDA supported approximately 250 NGOs through various thematic and regional programs. CIDA's NGO division respects the independence, integrity and personality of NGOs, and seldom provides more than a part of the funds necessary for a project or program. Generally, CIDA supplements funds raised by the NGOs through a matching grant system. Project/program planning, implementation and management, and liaison with countries in the South are the responsibility of the NGO.

NGO WORK OVERSEAS

NGOs have historically been linked in the public mind with emergency aid. Less attention has been given to the principal work of NGOs, of long-term development and advocacy on behalf of Southern NGOs and people's movements. NGOs strive to head off famine and environmental disintegration by promoting health, education, food self-sufficiency and other basic needs. They have become effective innovators in the field of development and have demonstrated an edge over government in effectiveness due to their closeness to the people and their community-based approach.

The current wisdom among NGOs is to respond to requests for assistance from like-minded groups in the South rather than initiate projects. Community-based, or so-called grassroots activities, refer to projects that are initiated indigenously, embraced and directed by the people themselves. More and more, NGOs are listening to what people in the South have to say about their own development. They act increasingly as advocates on behalf of their Southern partners, often placing broad causes such as disarmament, social justice, gender issues and environmental sustainability on their agendas. As such, they have come to be known as global goodwill ambassadors.

NGO workers typically receive the lowest salaries in the international field, although these days development workers seem to have adopted the formal attire and customs of the business world. While NGOs remain committed to working in the front line of development, you may be hard put to find the sandals and backpacks of the past.

APPLYING FOR A JOB

Given the limited resources available to most NGOs, it is important for them to be as efficient and effective as possible in their activities. For this reason, most people who are employed in NGOs are highly-skilled, motivated individuals. Finding a job within the NGO community is very challenging, but certainly not impossible. The following tips will assist you in your job search strategy.

If you are a graduate in international studies, be conservative in your expectations of finding work in the areas of development policy or planning economic models. The work of development is 80 per cent administration, no matter where you work, and no matter what sector of international development you work in. Most overseas NGO employees must be able to write a project work plan, formulate budgets, understand basic accounting systems, and write out personnel policies.

Consider the other special skills required for grassroots development: advocacy, community relations, public speaking, community-building and negotiating skills, organizing, organizing, and more organizing. It helps to be a proficient writer and speaker. It's also helpful to be fluent in two languages and willing to learn others throughout your career.

Be sensitive, creative and persistent when approaching NGOs. You can obtain information on job opportunities among member organizations of coordinating bodies such as the CANADIAN COUNCIL FOR INTERNATIONAL CO-OPERATION (CCIC) or its provincial Councils in British Columbia, Saskatchewan, Manitoba, Ontario and the Atlantic region. Other provincial councils are the DEVELOPMENT EDUCATION CO-ORDINATING COUNCIL OF ALBERTA (DECCA), and ASSOCIATION QUÉBÉCOISE DES ORGANISMES DE COOPÉRATION INTERNATIONALE (AQOCI). Other leads can be found in the job binders or boards in the reception areas of OXFAM, CUSO and MATCH. Check them out when you're in Ottawa! The above organizations are listed in the NGO profiles that follow. Global Education Centres are also excellent sources of information about overseas jobs. (See Chapter 13, Global Education Centres.)

JOBS OVERSEAS

Many development groups are shifting away from overseas program support toward fundraising and advocacy work on behalf of an increasing number of partner NGOs in the South. Even for jobs in Canada, many of the NGOs listed here demand previous experience overseas. Consider first supporting yourself through volunteering or internships overseas. (See Chapter 10, Short-term Programs Overseas and Chapter 17, International Internships.)

Many opportunities abroad still remain, but stringent hiring requirements reflect the increasing tendency of developing countries to train and hire indigenous development workers. Four major Canadian NGOs send highly skilled volunteers or cooperants to developing countries; they are CUSO, WUSC, CECI and OXFAM-QUÉBEC. Note that while the working language of these organizations is either English or French, all four organizations work in both French- and English-speaking developing countries. The average volunteer is approximately 37 years old and has accumulated technical or professional experience in Canada. Assignments usually last two years.

NGO staff tend to integrate more with the local population than employees of the UN, CIDA or industry, a compensatory consequence of their lower salaries and general commitment to grassroots development. Take time to get to know your hosts and absorb the popular culture—in itself a rewarding experience! Learn their needs and aim for mutual confidence and co-operation. Bring a sense of humour, patience and tolerance. Before you go, ask yourself: Can you maintain a grip on your own needs and limitations? Do you open up easily to others? Are you naturally relaxed, positive and non-judgemental? Can you sustain this manner in hot, sticky climates while barraged by unfamiliar sights, sounds, smells and customs?

VOLUNTEERING IN CANADA

A sure-fire way of finding work is to demonstrate volunteer leadership in almost any international or crosscultural organization. Many people get hired by NGOs following extensive volunteer work with them. Get active with local committees of the CANADIAN CATHOLIC ORGANIZATION FOR DEVELOPMENT AND PEACE, CANADIAN CROSSROADS INTERNATIONAL, UNICEF, etc. Confirm your commitment to yourself—don't do it just to pad your résumé. Most NGO workers have a long history of volunteering in the international community.

Investigate local activities such as benefits and awareness-raising events. Volunteer to billet Southern visitors. Join or initiate NGO advocacy campaigns if you want to directly influence economic and social progress in the South. Get involved in NGO community outreach programs which form the foundation of public support. NGOs have pioneered many new approaches—including global education centres, Canada-South twinning programs between communities, and organizational partnerships and networks.

WORDS OF ADVICE

NGOs have some key suggestions regarding appropriate attitude and experience for those contemplating working in the challenging field of overseas grassroots development. Much of the advice given by NGOs is related to the attitude an individual must possess to adapt well to a new culture. The first step is to ask yourself why you want a career working in the South— then learn as much as you can about the part of the world which interests you. It is important to go with an open mind. No amount of professional training will prepare you for the different life you will live. Be willing to adjust to whatever the circumstances require, and don't expect others to adjust to you. The old cliché, "When in Rome, do as the Romans do," certainly rings true for Canadians working overseas. Living and working in the ways of your host country expands your understanding and lets you grow by leaps and bounds.

Other advice given by NGOs is linked to the underlying philosophy and goal of their activities. Most NGOs work towards a more just and equitable global community, and place importance on human dignity and self-determination of the communities in which they work. So as a Canadian working overseas, you must direct your first efforts to learning from the poor and the marginalized. Never assume that more sophisticated technology will improve the lifestyles of those you seek to help. Let indigenous people teach you their ways and inform you of their own needs—do not teach them your way and attribute needs to them that are not their own. In other words, don't bring a superior Western attitude, but be willing to learn and share ideas and expertise. Development work is a process by which local people increase control over the decisions that affect their lives. Active involvement and full participation of the local people—men and women—is crucial to the success of any development activity.

Working on a project overseas requires a great deal of flexibility. Don't expect to have all the necessary tools, equipment and materials that would be readily available in your home country. Instead, you must adapt easily to the environment and to the help that is available there. Set realistic goals and expectations of what can be accomplished during your one- or two-year posting. It is virtually impossible to make radical changes in the short term. Be certain of your commitment before taking on a position. The scope of responsibilities involved, and the limited financial and other resources of most international development NGOs mean that they cannot afford drop-outs.

Most importantly, have a sense of humour! You most probably will need it.

YOUR EXPERIENCE

Ask most staff members of an NGO how to establish a career in international development, and you will learn first that competition in this field is fierce; however, there are a variety of ways that individuals can beat the competition and gain valuable experience.

First, to start a career in international development it is often necessary to have work experience in a developing country. This prerequisite is often attainable only through a volunteer experience which requires a sacrifice in terms of financial compensation. However, the other rewards more than make up for this short-term sacrifice.

If you are unable to go overseas as a volunteer, one way to gain international development exposure is to get involved in development-related activities in Canada, even as a volunteer. The activity can be focused on international or domestic development issues. Be knowledgeable and skilful in your particular area of endeavour. It is also important to demonstrate your ability and interest in broadening your horizons, both personally and professionally. Increasingly, agencies are looking for people who already have some understanding of development issues or development-related experience prior to their placements overseas.

In terms of formal academic qualifications, some say it is valuable to have a university degree that has a practical application overseas, such as administration, nursing, medicine, teaching or engineering. You might work as a volunteer overseas for a period of time. If you still want to work in the area of international development, then pursue a master's degree in this or a related field.

Whatever your particular strategy, remember—persistence pays!

RESOURCES

The following resources will be useful for anyone interested in NGO involvement in the international sphere. Included are directories of American, Canadian, and international NGOs as well as a number of periodicals and books providing information on current Canadian NGO activities and job openings. Another chapter with related resources and advice is Chapter 28, Jobs in International Development.

For those interested in NGOs, you will also want to learn about global education in Chapter 13, Global Education Centres. You may also appreciate the section on Personal Stories Overseas in Chapter 4, What Canadians Overseas Say, and, of course, it is strongly recommended you read about crosscultural communication skills and study the Resources sections in Chapter 1, The Effective Overseas Employee; Chapter 3, Living Overseas; and Chapter 7, The Canadian Identity in the International Workplace.

Associations Canada 1997/98 ▢
Annual, Canadian Almanac and Directory ➤ Renouf Publishing Co. Ltd., Unit 1, 5369 Canotek Road, Ottawa, Ontario K1J 9J3; $249.50; credit cards; (613) 745-2665, fax (613) 745-7660 ▪ An alphabetical listing of over 18,000 Canadian organizations and 1,000 international groups covering industry, commercial and professional associations, registered charities, special interest and common interest organizations. Indexed by subject, geographic location, and budget size. Includes contact name, conferences, publications, acronym, and mailing list availability. Available in libraries. [ID:1348]

Au Courrant ▢ ▢
10/year ➤ Canadian Council for International Cooperation, Suite 300, 1 Nicholas Street, Ottawa, Ontario K1N 7B7; $30/year; VISA; (613) 241-7007, fax (613) 241-5302, ccicpubs@web.net ▪ Bilingual newsletter on development issues, resources and events affecting the Canadian NGO community. Also lists NGO job openings. Available on the Web (with a two-month delay) at www.web.net/ccic-ccci. [ID:1094]

The Best Résumés for $75,000+ Executive Jobs ▢
1992, *William Montag,* 256 pages ➤ John Wiley & Sons, 22 Worchester Drive, Rexdale, Ontario M9W 1L1; $14.95; credit cards; (800) 567-4797, fax (800) 565-6802 ▪ A unique résumé workbook aimed exclusively at executives making $75,000 or more. This book will greatly benefit and assist in the critical job search and self-marketing process. Features over 75 proven achievement-

oriented and market-tested résumés, along with cover letters. Visit the distributor's web site at www.wiley.com/products/worldwide/canada. [ID:1000]

Bridges of Hope? Canadian Voluntary Agencies and the Third World 📖
1988, *Tim Brodhead,* 172 pages ➤ North-South Institute, Suite 200, 55 Murray Street, Ottawa, Ontario K1N 5M3; $14; VISA, MC; (613) 241-3535, fax (613) 241-7435, nsi@nsi-ins.ca ▪ Excellent book summarizing a two-year study of Canadian NGOs. Assesses NGO effectiveness, strengths and weaknesses, and provides recommendations. Visit the publisher's web site at www.nsi-ins.ca. [ID:1219]

Canadian International Development Agency (CIDA) 🖳
http://w3.acdi-cida.gc.ca ▪ This comprehensive site provides information on almost every aspect of CIDA's operations. Official publications, contracting information and profiles of existing programs are all offered at this site. A number of useful links connect to other development agencies and like-minded organizations. [ID:2462]

Canadian World Federalist Newsletter 📖
3/year ➤ World Federalists of Canada, 145 Spruce Street, Ottawa, Ontario K1R 6P1; $8; VISA, MC; (613) 232-0647, fax (613) 563-0017, wfcnat@web.net ▪ Provides information on the World Federalists of Canada and discusses issues in world federalism. Also covers developments within the United Nations and international law. Visit the publisher's web site at www.web.net/~wfcnat/WFC.html. [ID:1599]

Care Canada 🖳
www.care.ca ▪ This site not only gives detailed job information on Care Canada, but also on overseas work in general. In its Human Resources sub-directory, there is a wealth of information: questions to ask yourself, important characteristics for overseas work, and questions candidates should prepare for in an interview. A definite must for anyone interested in NGO work overseas! [ID:2449]

Career Opportunities for American Planners in International Development 📖
1994, *Charles Boyce, Ralph Gakenheimer,* 86 pages ➤ International Division, American Planning Association, c/o The Institute of Public Administration, 55 West 44th Street, New York, NY 10016, USA; $10; credit cards; (212) 730-5480 ext. 340 or 330, fax (212) 768-9071 ▪ Aimed at the American reader, this book provides a wealth of information on educational requirements and how to get started. Planners with varying backgrounds provide their insights on opportunities with international development agencies, the US government, consulting firms and nongovernment organizations. Publishers of a monthly newsletter called "Interplan." [ID:1638]

Charity Village 🖳
www.charityvillage.com/cvhome.html ▪ A visually appealing and well-organized site, it can take you on a voyage through an imaginary village of Canadian charity and not-for-profit organizations. Ideal for the socially conscientious, the site provides information for fundraisers, volunteers, the media, and not-for-profit managers. This is also a good place to look for jobs in this field. [ID:2752]

Directory of Non-Governmental
Organizations (NGOs) Active in Sustainable Development 📖
1997, 768 pages ➤ Organization of Economic Cooperation and Development (OECD), Suite 700, 2001 L Street N.W., Washington, DC 20036, USA; US$138; credit cards; (202) 785-6323, fax (202) 785-0350 ▪ This updated and revised directory is a comprehensive source of information on 3,900 NGOs in 26 countries in Europe. Contains NGO profiles, indexes of their activities in developing countries and Europe. Visit the publisher's web site at www.oecdwash.org. [ID:1220]

The Directory of Work & Study in Developing Countries 📖
1997, *David Leppard,* Vacation Work ➤ Capricorn Business Services, Inc., 28 Clear Lake Ave., West Hill, Ontario M1C 4L6; $23.95; credit cards; (416) 282-3331, fax (416) 282-0015 ▪ British reference guide to short- and long-term work, volunteer and educational opportunities in the developing world. Listings in each of the three sections are organized by region. [ID:1158]

The Executive Contact List: US Private and Voluntary Organizations Registered with the Agency for International Development 📖
Semiannual, 192 pages ➤ Bureau for Humanitarian Assistance and Response, US Agency for International Development, 1300 Pennsylvannia Avenue N.W., Washington, DC 20523, USA; free; (202) 712-4810, fax (202) 216-3237 ■ Lists names of executive contacts for US organizations registered with the US Agency for International Development. [ID:1263]

Focus 📖
Quarterly ➤ Canadian Executive Service Organization (CESO), Suite 400, 175 Bloor Street E., Toronto, Ontario M4W 3R8; free; (416) 961-2376, fax (416) 961-1096 ■ This newsletter features articles about the organization's worldwide activities. CESO is a nongovernmental voluntary agency that sends Canadians with professional, technical and managerial skills to be volunteer consultants to business organizations in Canadian aboriginal communities and in developing countries. [ID:1095]

InterAction: American Council for Voluntary International Action 🖥
InterAction: American Council for Voluntary International Action, Suite 801, 1717 Massachusetts Ave. N.W., Washington, DC, 20036, USA; (202) 667-8227, fax (202) 667-8236 ■ This is a coalition of over 150 American NGOs involved in a broad spectrum of activities such as development projects and advocacy work. To find out more about them, you can subscribe to their newsletter, *Monday Developments,* or purchase their publication, *InterAction Member Profiles.* A visit to their web site www.interaction.org will also prove to be useful as it provides links to their member organizations. [ID:2783]

Jobs and Careers with Nonprofit Organizations 📖
1997, *Caryl Krannich, Ronald Krannich,* 230 pages ➤ Impact Publications, 9104 North Manassas Drive, Manassas Park, VA 20111-2366, USA; US$15.95; credit cards; (703) 361-7300, fax (703) 335-9486 ■ Exposing numerous myths and identifying major trends, this new book provides information on over 300 domestic and international nonprofit organizations: arts, entertainment, child welfare, civil liberties, consumer advocacy, economic development, education, environment, food, housing, health care and more. Rich with insights, tips, sample résumés and letters, contact information and resources. Visit distributor's web site at www.impactpublications.com. [ID:1751]

Managing the Nonprofit Organization 📖
1995, 500 pages ➤ Sequus International, 381 Churchill Drive, Winnipeg, Manitoba R3L 1W1; $150; cheque or money order; (204) 992-2410, fax (204) 478-5390, btrump@infobahn.mb.ca ■ This excellent Canadian manual is the latest in a series of updates and revisions originating from a pilot training program started in the 1970's. Aimed at leaders and managers in the international development field. Based on classroom experience with thousands of managers from the nonprofit sector. [ID:1299]

Multi-sector Directory of BC Global Organizations and Resources 📖 🖥
1998, *BCCIC,* 152 pages ➤ BC Council for International Cooperation (BCCIC), 930 Mason Street, Vancouver, B.C. V8T 1A2, Canada; $15; no credit cards; (250) 360-1405, fax (250) 360-2295 ■ Created by a nongovernmental organization, this directory contains over 140 listings of global organizations, information on resources concerning international issues, and global education. Visit the publisher's web site at www.bccic.bc.ca/bccicweb/. [ID:2795]

NGLS Handbook
1997, 306 pages ➤ United Nations Non-Governmental Liaison Service (UN/NGLS), Room FF 346, United Nations, New York, NY 10017, USA; no charge; (212) 963-3125, fax (212) 963-8712 ■ This annual book is designed by the UN's Non-Governmental Liaison Service to provide information about UN agencies, programs, and funds working for economic and social development. [ID:2700]

PACT Publications Catalogue 📖
3/year ➤ PACT Media Services, 777 United Nations Plaza, New York, NY 10017, USA; free; (212) 697-6222, fax (212) 692-9748, books@pactpub.org ■ Excellent catalogue offering training materials, communications and multimedia information for use by international development

professionals. This catalogue is intended as a forum for the very best development materials from around the world. Highly recommended. Visit distributor's web site, www.pactpub.com. [ID:1228]

Third World Resource Directory: A Guide to Organizations and Publications 📖
1994-95, *Thomas P. Fenton, Mary J. Heffron* ➤ Novalis, 2nd Floor, 49 Front Street E., Toronto, Ontario M5E 1B3; $92.95; credit cards; (800) 387-7164 ext. 24, fax (416) 363-9409 ▪ This 800-page resource guide is one of the most comprehensive for current and hard-to-find print, audio-visual, and organizational resources related to Africa, Asia and the Pacific, Latin America and the Caribbean, and the Middle East. Covers a range of issues. Well-indexed. [ID:1221]

The World Bank and Cooperation with NGOs 📖
1992, *Ann Thomson,* 30 pages ➤ CODE, 321 Chapel Street, Ottawa, Ontario K1N 7Z2; $14; VISA; (613) 232-3569, fax (613) 232-7435, codehq@codecan.com ▪ This booklet offers a general introduction to the World Bank and the mechanisms for NGO involvement in World Bank projects. Good for anyone wishing to make contact with the World Bank. [ID:1114]

Profiles of Nongovernmental Organizations

Of the approximately 300 registered NGOs working in international development in Canada, 181 of the most active are listed in this chapter. The number of NGOs in their primary fields of activity are: Community Development 11, Community Health 7, Co-ordinating Body 17, Development Assistance 50, Development Education 7, Environmental Action 8, Exchange 4, Evangelical 10, International Advocacy 16, International Research 6, Media Development 2, Medical Assistance 6, Organizational Training 5, Relief And Development Agency 14, Special Needs 10, and Volunteer 7.

The greatest concentration of NGOs is in Ottawa, with clusters in Montréal and Toronto, which reflects the organizations' continuing dependence on federal government funding. But even a very remote community can harbour a branch or committee. Fifty-two of the NGOs have their headquarters in Ottawa, with 32 in Toronto, and 19 in Montreal. Provincially, the NGOs are broken down as follows, Alberta 5, British Columbia 12, Manitoba 11, Nova Scotia 1, Ontario 116, Québec 35. Many NGOs have regional offices or have local volunteer committees even in the smallest communities.

Adventist Development and Relief Agency Canada (ADRA CANADA)
1148 King Street E., Oshawa, Ontario L1H 1H8; (905) 433-8004, fax (905) 723-1903, adra@web.net

MID-SIZED RELIEF AND DEVELOPMENT AGENCY: Adult Training, Agriculture, Community Development, Development Assistance, Gender and Development, Humanitarian Relief, Medical Health, Project Management, Water Resources

Adventist Development and Relief Agency Canada (ADRA CANADA) is the development and relief agency of the Seventh-day Adventist Church. ADRA works with communities and NGOs in developing countries to promote self-reliance and provide people with basic needs and skills. ADRA emphasizes projects in education, primary healthcare, income generation, and other integrated community development projects. ADRA works in over 100 countries; ADRA Canada supports projects in about 70 of these countries at any given time.

ADRA Canada has nine staff in Canada and about 20 volunteers overseas but, at present, no longer recruits volunteers. Most ADRA staff have spent some time working overseas and all have several years experience in international development. Most staff hold a university degree. ADRA maintains a data bank for résumés. [ID:5966]

Africa Evangelical Fellowship (AEF)
51 Cambridge Street, Cambridge, Ontario N1R 3R8;
(519) 622-7818, fax (519) 622-7129, 102653.410@compuserve.com

MID-SIZED EVANGELICAL GROUP: Humanitarian Relief, Medical Health, Micro-Enterprises, Religious, Teaching

Africa Evangelical Fellowship (AEF) is an interdenominational, international, Christian mission organization involved in evangelism, the establishment of churches, leadership training, medical, educational, literacy and agricultural work.

It operates in the following countries in Africa and the Indian Ocean: South Africa, Botswana, Namibia, Angola, Zimbabwe, Zambia, Swaziland, Malawi, Mozambique, Tanzania, Madagascar, Mauritius, and Reunion.

Sixty-two Canadian missionaries currently serve in Africa and eight staff work in Canada. AEF also sends a number of people on short-term missions (two to 12 months).

Applicants must have academic training equivalent to Canadian requirements for similar jobs. Some work experience in Canada is also required, as well as at least one year of Bible and theological education, and the ability to raise one's own support. [ID:5967]

Africa Inland Mission International (Canada) (AIM)
1641 Victoria Park Ave., Scarborough, Ontario M1R 1P8;
(416) 751-6077, fax (416) 751-3467, aim@aimint.org, www.goshen.net/aim-ca

LARGE EVANGELICAL GROUP: Accounting, Administration, Adult Training, Agriculture, Community Development, Consulting, Development Assistance, Medical Health, Project Management, Religious, Teaching

Africa Inland Mission (Canada) (AIM) is an interdenominational foreign mission organization. AIM's primary goal is to establish and develop maturing churches through the evangelization of unreached people and the effective preparation of church leaders.

AIM has missions in over 15 Central and East African countries including Chad, Sudan and Mozambique, as well as on Indian Ocean islands such as the Seychelles. Types of ministries include medicine, evangelism, public health, church-planting, bible school, avionics, agriculture, water development, veterinary medicine, community development, and missionary children's education. Missions are also established in three urban centres in the US, including prison ministries and evangelism in local black churches. AIM supports over 700 active missionaries.

AIM examines an applicant's Christian character, academic achievements, emotional stability, and ability to work with others. Successful applicants complete a thorough application and orientation procedure, then seek funds for their travel and monthly expenses. AIM offers some internship positions in various African countries for periods ranging from two months to two years. AIM posts job openings on their web site. [ID:5968]

African Medical and Research Foundation (AMREF)
59 Front Street E., Toronto, Ontario M5E 1B3;
(416) 601-6981, fax (416) 601-6984, amref@web.net, www.amref.org

MID-SIZED COMMUNITY HEALTH GROUP: Administration, Adult Training, Community Development, Development Assistance, Development Education, Environment, Fundraising, Humanitarian Relief, Medical Health

The African Medical and Research Foundation's (AMREF) aim is to identify health needs in East Africa and develop, implement, and evaluate methods and programs to meet those needs through service, training, and research. AMREF Canada runs a variety of innovative projects which emphasize appropriate, low-cost healthcare for people in rural areas.

In Canada, AMREF Canada maintains three staff to provide fundraising and program support for programs administered from its headquarters in Nairobi. It maintains 600 paid staff overseas, but does not recruit staff in Canada for overseas work. All such applications are processed by the Nairobi office. AMREF also does not recruit volunteers for overseas placement, but volunteers are always welcome in the Toronto office. For staff in Canada, knowledge of healthcare in East Africa, fundraising skills, general administrative skills, and development education are required. [ID:5969]

AFS Interculture Canada (AFS)
Suite 505, 1231 St. Catherine Street W., Montréal, Québec H3G 1P5;
(514) 288-3282, fax (514) 843-9119, info-canada@afs.org, www.afscanada.org

LARGE EXCHANGE GROUP: Agriculture, Architecture and Planning, Business/Banking/Trade, Community Development, Development Assistance, Development Education, Engineering, Environment, Exchange Programs, Fisheries, Forestry, Gender and Development, Human Rights, Humanitarian Relief, International Trade, Media/Communications, Medical Health, Teaching, Technical Assistance, Telecommunications, Tourism, Volunteer, Water Resources

AFS Interculture Canada (AFS) is a volunteer-driven educational organization that promotes global education, entrepreneurship and community involvement through international school-based and work-based (internship) programs for young people and adults. It is a member of the international AFS network and Canada's leading international exchange organization.

AFS offers three types of international work programs: (1) vocational programs in Europe focused on trade, for those between 18 and 20 years of age; (2) internship programs in Asia, Latin America and Africa for unemployed university graduates aged 20 to 29; and (3) volunteer work programs in Latin America which focus on environmental projects, for young adult with previous experience in developing countries.

The AFS network has over 100,000 volunteers, a staff of 460, and 54 offices in five countries. The Canadian office, located in Montréal, has a staff of 15. Visit the AFS web site for job postings and internship opportunities. (For more information on AFS see Chapter 10, Short-term Programs Overseas and Chapter 11, Hosting Programs.) [ID:5971]

Aga Khan Foundation Canada (AKFC)
Suite 1820, 350 Albert Street, Constitution Square,
Ottawa, Ontario K1R 1A4; (613) 237-2532, fax (613) 567-2532

LARGE DEVELOPMENT ASSISTANCE GROUP: Most Job Categories

Aga Khan Foundation Canada (AKFC) is a nonprofit, international development agency supporting projects in Africa and Asia. These projects benefit all people, regardless of race, religion and political persuasion. Areas of focus include preventative healthcare, environmental protection, rural income generation, early childhood education and women's development.

Projects are enhanced by the North-South links within the worldwide Aga Khan Development Network. Local expertise in developing countries ensures projects are wisely chosen and effectively implemented. The foundation collaborates with the Canadian International Development Agency (CIDA) and many other private development agencies.

AKFC also runs the Fellowship in International Development Management Program, an intensive training and structured field experience. The program is offered to outstanding young Canadians committed to pursuing careers in international development. The program consists of a four-week management training course in Canada, followed by an eight-month work-study placement with a respected Asian, nongovernmental organization. (For more information on AKFC see Chapter 10, Short-term Programs Overseas and Chapter 38, International Organizations.) [ID:5972]

Aide médicale internationale à l'enfance (L'AMIE)
100 - 4e ave., C.P. 282, La-Pocatière, Québec G0R 1Z0;
(418) 856-4082, fax (418) 856-4082, amie@mercure.net

SMALL COMMUNITY HEALTH GROUP: Humanitarian Relief, International Education, Literacy, Volunteer

L'Aide médicale internationale à l'enfance (L'AMIE) est une organisation de bénévoles qui soutient et collabore au travail de communautés ou d'ONG. L'AMIE accueille des réfugiés, forme des groupes d'accompagnement pour un soutien moral, matériel et technique, tout en sensibilisant le public aux besoins et aux réalités du tiers-monde, tout particulièrement des enfants. Grâce à un service d'écolage et de parrainage, elle permet l'alphabétisation des enfants et un soutien aux familles, tout en développant des projets d'éducation et de santé. Toute l'action de l'organisation se fait dans le plus grand respect des cultures traditionnelles. [ID:5973]

Alternatives
Bureau 440, 3680, rue Jeanne-Mance, Montréal, Québec H2X 2K5;
(800) 982-6646, fax (514) 982-6122, alternatives@alternatives.ca, www.alternatives.ca

LARGE COMMUNITY DEVELOPMENT GROUP: Development Assistance, Environment, Gender and Development, Human Rights, Policy Dialogue

Alternatives is not a "charity" in the traditional sense of the term. It provides training and financial assistance to hundreds of popular organizations in such areas as policy formulation and research, planning, education, gender equity, environmental protection, service delivery, conflict resolution, mobilization, communication, and evaluation. Alternatives also helps set up networks and coalitions and South-South and North-South encounters in order to foster direct exchanges and the developments of common solutions and actions.

Several specialized committees advise the board on activities and publications related to young people, women, immigration, and other themes. Alternatives operates in Canada, Africa, Asia, the Middle East, South America, and Eastern Europe [ID:6721]

Amnistie internationale (section canadienne francophone)
6250, boul. Monk, Montréal, Québec H4E 3H7;
(514) 766-9766, fax (514) 766-2088, aimtl@cam.org, www.amnistie.qc.ca

MID-SIZED INTERNATIONAL ADVOCACY GROUP: Advocacy, Human Rights

Amnistie internationale est une organisation qui lutte pour le respect des droits de la personne. Elle intervient dans tous les pays et ne dépend d'aucune subvention gouvernementale. Amnistie internationale contribue à la libération des prisonniers d'opinion, à l'amélioration des conditions de détention et à l'obtention de procès justes et rapides, à l'aide de lettres ou de télégrammes. La section canadienne francophone compte plus de 20000 membres actifs. Les moyens de pression comme les lettres et les télégrammes sont rédigés par des bénévoles au Canada. L'organisation n'envoie donc aucune personne à l'étranger.

La section francophone canadienne d'Amnistie internationale n'est pas à la recherche de personnel. Toutefois, les candidats peuvent faire parvenir leur C.V. au bureau du personnel. L'organisme accueille des stagiaires (non rémunérés), particulièrement ceux avec une formation en politique internationale, communications ou informatique.

Le site web d'Amnistie internationale, à l'intention des bénévoles, propose des actions d'envoi de lettre et informe de la situation des droits de la personne dans le monde. [ID:5975]

Asia Pacific Foundation of Canada (APFC)
Suite 666, 999 Canada Place, Vancouver, B.C. V6C 3E1;
(604) 684-5986, fax (604) 681-1370, info@apfc.apfnet.org, www.apfc.ca

SMALL INTERNATIONAL ADVOCACY GROUP: Business Development, Intercultural Briefings,
Media/Communications, Micro-Enterprises

The Asia Pacific Foundation of Canada (APFC) is a national nonprofit organization
established in 1984. Its mandate is to develop networks and business skills and disseminate
information to make Canadians better informed and more successful in the Asia Pacific.

APFC runs programs and provides consulting services in the areas of education,
crosscultural communication, research, and media. It also houses the APEC Study Centre
and is the Canadian Secretariat for the Pacific Basin Economic Cooperation Council.

A subsidiary of APFC, the GLOBE Foundation, organizes a series of international
conference and trade shows on business and the environment. APFC has its headquarters in
Vancouver, with regional offices in Regina, Winnipeg, Toronto, and Montréal. In partnership
with the Government of Canada, APFC operates a network of offices in Asia for the purpose
of marketing Canadian educational services. It has education offices in Seoul, Taipei,
Bangkok, Jakarta, Kuala Lumpur, Singapore, Hong Kong, New Delhi, and Mexico City. (For
more information on APFC see Chapter 15, Awards and Grants.) [ID:5976]

Association of Canadian Community Colleges (ACCC)
International Services Bureau, Suite 200, 1223 Michael Street N.,
Ottawa, Ontario K1J 7T2; (613) 746-2222, fax (613) 746-6721, postmaster@accc.ca, www.accc.ca

LARGE COORDINATING BODY: Accounting, Administration, Adult Training, Agriculture,
Architecture and Planning, Business Development, Computer Systems, Consulting, Development
Assistance, Development Education, Energy Resources, Environment, Gender and Development,
Human Resources, Media/Communications, Micro-Enterprises, Project Management, Teaching,
Technical Assistance, Telecommunications, Water Resources

The International Services Bureau of the Association of Canadian Community Colleges
(ACCC) specializes in the overseas transfer of technical, vocational and professional skills
and the export of educational consultancy and management services. ACCC arranges these
transfers through client contracts, cooperative projects, international linkages and technical
assistance financed through CIDA and the IFIs.

The ACCC secretariat, located in Ottawa, operates with 55 full-time staff. Field offices
are located in Bangladesh, Egypt, Hungary, India, Indonesia, Jordan, Jamaica, Nicaragua,
Pakistan, Poland, Tunisia, and Zambia. As a membership association, ACCC has access to
30,000 college instructors and administrators, and the capability to identify college/institute
strengths, areas of optimum contribution to human resource development, the target groups
they are best able to serve and the best models of project implementation.

ACCC's international experience includes over 250 projects in 65 countries. Community college instructors/professionals are hired for international contract work based on their
business, industry and trade experience. ACCC maintains a data bank for résumés. Visit the
ACCC web site for job postings. [ID:5977]

Association of Universities and Colleges of Canada (AUCC)

International Relations, Suite 600, 350 Albert Street,
Ottawa, Ontario K1R 1B1; (613) 563-1236, fax (613) 563-9745, jgoldsto@aucc.ca, www.aucc.ca

MID-SIZED COORDINATING BODY: Accounting, Administration, Adult Training, Advocacy, Aerospace Technology, Agriculture, Architecture and Planning, Business Development, Community Development, Computer Systems, Construction, Consulting, Development Assistance, Development Education, Economics, Energy Resources, Engineering, Environment, Exchange Programs, Fisheries, Forestry, Gender and Development, Human Resources, Human Rights, Humanitarian Relief, Intercultural Briefings, International Trade, Logistics, Media/Communications, Medical Health, Micro-Enterprises, Project Management, Teaching, Technical Assistance, Telecommunications, Water Resources

The Association of Universities and Colleges of Canada (AUCC) is the voice of Canada's 89 universities and degree-granting colleges on the national and international scene.

AUCC has approximately 20 Canadian-based staff involved in international relations. The organization represents Canadian universities at international meetings and at meetings with foreign government officials, education leaders, development organizations and members of the diplomatic community. AUCC offers information about Canada's university system, promotes scientific, scholarly and technical exchanges between Canadian universities and international universities and administers programs linking Canadian and foreign universities.

AUCC maintains data banks on Canadian university involvement in international development projects, and on international exchange agreements between Canadian and foreign universities for students and faculty and for the purpose of research collaboration. AUCC publishes newsletters and reports on the increasingly important role of Canadian universities in international affairs. AUCC organizes workshops and international conferences and administers programs that link Canadian universities with institutions in both the South and the North. AUCC also administers graduate and undergraduate scholarships and exchange programs offered by Canadian and foreign governments, Canadian corporations and other agencies.

Qualifications for work with AUCC include a master's degree in international relations, and five to ten years' experience in international development or international affairs. Proficiency in French and English is also an asset. Visit the AUCC web site for information on university development and exchange programs and job openings at member universities. (For more information on AUCC see Chapter 15, Awards & Grants.) [ID:5979]

Association québécoise des organismes de coopération internationale (AQOCI)

1er étage, Bureau 510, rue Ste-Catherine est, Montréal, Québec
H2X 1K9; (514) 871-1086, fax (514) 871-9866, aqociadm@aqoci.qc.ca, www.aqoci.qc.ca

MID-SIZED COORDINATING BODY: Development Education, Exchange Programs, Policy Dialogue

L'AQOCI est une association québécoise regroupant 39 organismes (ONG) de coopération et d'éducation à la solidarité internationale. Elle favorise la concertation de ses membres autour d'activités visant à favoriser la sensibilisation et l'engagement de la population québecoise en faveur de développement solidaire. Elle représente aussi les vues et les politiques de ses membres auprès des gouvernements et autres partenaires sociaux. De plus, l'AQOCI gère un fonds provenant du ministère des Relations internationales du Québec et destiné aux ONG membres pour le programme Québec sans frontières. Ce programme offre à des Québécois et Québécoises âgés de 18 à 30 ans de participer à des stages dans les pays d'Afrique, d'Amérique latine et des Caraibes. [ID:5981]

British Columbia Council for International Co-operation
930 Mason Street, Victoria, B.C. V8T 1A2;
(250) 360-1405, fax (250) 360-2295, bccic@web.net, http://bccic.bc.ca/bccicweb/

MID-SIZED COORDINATING BODY: Accounting, Administration, Advocacy, Development
Education, Volunteer

The British Columbia Council for International Co-operation (BCCIC) is a coordinating
body of 35 international development organizations that include: church organizations,
regional offices of Canadian international development agencies, development education
centres, and other nonprofit B.C.-based development organizations. BCCIC provides a forum
for action on global development at the provincial level, and brings a B.C. perspective to
national policy discussions through its participation in committees, working groups and
coalitions.

BCCIC supports the work of member agencies, shares information and communication
about global issues, organizes professional development and skills training for members,
coordinates and represents members' interests to governments and others, and establishes
support for international development in communities not currently part of established
networks. It also publishes guides related to gender and development, the environment and
development, and directories of development education materials for NGOs. Job and volunteer openings at member organizations are often posted on the BCCIC web site. [ID:5984]

Brace Research Institute
P.O. Box 900, McDonald College, McGill University, Ste-Anne-de-Bellevue,
Québec H9X 3V9; (514) 398-7833, fax (514) 398-7767, ae12@musica.mcgill.ca, www.mcgill.ca

MID-SIZED INTERNATIONAL RESEARCH GROUP: Adult Training, Consulting, Development
Education, Energy Resources, Engineering, Environment, Water Resources

The Brace Research Institute conducts research and development into appropriate
water and renewable energy technology for the rural poor in developing countries, in collaboration with associates in Canada and overseas. It specializes in developing methods for
desalination of sea or brackish water for use by local populations, irrigation, etc.

The institute organizes short-term training sessions for visitors from developing areas.
It provides assistance to similar groups, primarily in Africa, Asia, and Latin America. About
10 staff are employed in Canada, and generally one or two volunteers work overseas.

Applicants should be bilingual, possess an engineering or technical degree and be
interested in the development of arid and rural zones. The institute maintains a data bank for
résumés. [ID:5983]

Calmeadow
International Operations, Suite 600, 365 Bay Street,
Toronto, Ontario M5H 2V1; (416) 362-9670, fax (416) 362-0769, calmead@inforamp.net

MID-SIZED DEVELOPMENT ASSISTANCE GROUP: Business/Banking/Trade, Micro-
Enterprises

Calmeadow supports the development of strong, sustainable, micro-credit delivery
organizations in developing countries which are locally incorporated and managed. It offers a
wide range of technical advisory services and currently works with partner organizations in
Africa, Asia, and Latin America.

Calmeadow has five international department staff based in Canada and one in
Washington. It seeks people with a business degree, knowledge of micro-enterprise development, or familiarity with the banking sector. Ability to travel a minimum of one-third of the
year, as well as fluency in Spanish or French is required. [ID:5987]

Canada China Child Health Foundation (CCCHF)
Suite 113, 999 Beach Ave., Vancouver, B.C. V6E 4M2; (604) 682-6064, fax (604) 682-6012

MID-SIZED COMMUNITY HEALTH GROUP: Exchange Programs, Gender and Development, Humanitarian Relief, Medical Health, Teaching, Youth and Development

Canada China Child Health Foundation's (CCCHF) primary goal is to improve the health of Canadian and Chinese children and enhance child health globally. CCCHF engages in a wide variety of health-related activities in all regions of Canada and China. These include: coordinating exchanges between Canadian and Chinese health professionals and government personnel in the health sector; creating teaching hospital and university linked programs; shipping medical supplies and equipment to Chinese institutions; and conducting collaborative research and needs assessments. CCCHF works primarily in the areas of maternal and child health, paediatric dental health, education and training, and disaster relief. The "Child Friendly Centre" a major project, has recently been initiated to improve healthcare for children and mothers in rural areas throughout China.

CCCHF currently has three staff members in Canada and about 12 overseas. The number of volunteers overseas varies according to the type and size of projects underway. CCCHF maintains a data bank for résumés. [ID:5989]

Canada World Youth (CWY)
3rd Floor, 2330 Notre Dame Street W., Montréal, Québec H3J 1N4;
(514) 931-3526, fax (514) 939-2621, cwy-jcm@cwy-jcm.org, www.cwy-jcm.org

LARGE EXCHANGE GROUP: Community Development, Development Education, Exchange Programs, Fundraising, Intercultural Briefings, Project Management, Volunteer

Canada World Youth (CWY) is a national, nonprofit organization that promotes international cooperation and understanding through coordinating international exchanges and non-formal education experiences for youth since 1971. CWY offers five different programs.

The Youth Exchange Programs are CWY's longest running programs for youth between the ages of 17 and 20. They are six- to seven-month exchanges, in which participants spend half their time living and working as volunteers in a host community in Canada, and the other half in Africa, Asia, Latin America or the Caribbean. The Central and Eastern Europe Programs follow a similar structure, and are adapted to the realities of these regions.

The Work Partner Programs provide youth from 18 to 29 years of age with an opportunity to participate in international cooperation and development through volunteer work placements overseas, in partnership with host-country organizations. Although it does not have a Canadian phase, the volunteers undertake public awareness activities before and after their programs.

The Customized Programs meet the needs of specific clientele or partners or are designed around a specific theme. They respect the underlying philosophy of CWY's educational programming while customizing the structure, components and form to fit the specific project.

The Joint Initiatives Programs are responsive in nature. CWY assists other organizations to carry out their programs by offering them the service or expertise they need.

CWY also offers a wide range of professional and consultative services, including intercultural training, leadership training, international transportation, pre-departure and re-entry briefings, Spanish immersion courses, development education, etc.

CWY seeks professionally-oriented field staff to implement program objectives by working with young people in host communities and supervising its exchanges. Qualifications for these positions require a college or university degree, bilingualism, experience in a developing country or cross cultural context. Experience in budget planning and project coordination, supervision and personnel evaluation are also assets. CWY maintains a data bank for résumés. (For information on CWY exchange programs see Chapter 10, Short-Term Programs Overseas.) [ID:5990]

Canadian Auto Workers' Social Justice Fund (CAW-SJF)

205 Placer Court, North York, Ontario M2H 3H9; (416) 495-6544, fax (416) 495-6554, cawint@caw.ca

MID-SIZED DEVELOPMENT ASSISTANCE GROUP: Gender and Development, Trade Unions

The Canadian Auto Workers' Social Justice Fund (CAW-SJF) is a nongovernmental organization working to strengthen trade unions and improve labour conditions in Canada, South Africa, the Middle East, Asia, and Central America. Its overseas development projects are developed in conjunction with other NGOs and focus on refugees and displaced persons, trade union support, human rights, civics, and gender issues. In Canada, CAW-SJF engages in anti-poverty activities through its support of food banks, women's organizations, and First Nations' organizations.

CAW-SJF currently has two staff in Canada. [ID:5991]

Canadian Baptist International Ministries

Volunteer Division, 7185 Millcreek Drive,
Mississauga, Ontario L5N 5R4; (905) 821-3533, fax (905) 826-3441

Canadian Baptist Ministries (CBM) carries out an overseas mission program for the four regional Baptist Conventions in Canada. It encourages the establishment of indigenous church groups and works with them in their development and outreach programs.

CBM concentrates its efforts in Europe, Asia, South America and Asia in the areas of water, food production, community health, medical services and forestry.

Candidates must be members of a Canadian Baptist Ministries church, be flexible and adaptable to working in a different culture, and give a satisfactory statement of personal Christian beliefs. Ideally, medical doctors specialize in a certain area and registered nurses have training in community health. Teachers generally must have provincial certification and a university degree. All applicants, except those for short-term service (under two years), must have at least one year of biblical studies. Regular positions overseas last four years.

Canadian Baptist Volunteers, an organization sponsored by Canadian Baptist Ministries, offers the opportunity for individuals to broaden their international experience. (For more information see Chapter 10, Short-term Programs Overseas.) [ID:5992]

Canadian Bureau for International Education (CBIE)

Suite 1100, 220 Laurier Ave. W.,
Ottawa, Ontario K1P 5Z9; (613) 237-4820, fax (613) 237-1073, info@cbie.ca, www.cbie.ca

LARGE COORDINATING BODY: Advocacy, Community Development, Development Assistance, Development Education, Exchange Programs, Human Resources, Intercultural Briefings, International Trade, Media/Communications, Membership Relations, Project Management, Technical Assistance

The Canadian Bureau for International Education (CBIE) is comprised of educational institutions and individuals working together to promote international education, international development and crosscultural understanding. Its focus is on international students: those from other countries studying in Canada and Canadians studying in other countries. It offers a wide variety of services and publications to members, international students and the Canadian public.

CBIE administers education and training programs on behalf of Canadian and foreign agencies, as well as some awards programs. CBIE administers the Celanese Canada Internationalist Fellowships, the Nortel Globalization Challenge Program, and the Canadian International Development Agency (CIDA) Awards Programs for Canadians. (CIDA awards are open to master's students and professionals wishing to undertake research or work in a developing country for a maximum period of 12 months. Application deadlines vary and details can be found in the Awards and Grants section of this book.)

CBIE employs 30 staff in Canada. Staff manage projects, counsel students, research, write, edit and manage publications, promote programs and services, develop new programs and consult membership. CBIE sometimes hires consultants for research projects or to provide training.

For staff positions, CBIE prefers candidates with developing country experience and graduate degrees in relevant fields. Bilingualism (English-French) is either required or considered an asset for virtually all positions. Other languages are an asset, as is work experience in an educational institution. CBIE also offers internships from January to May and May to August. [ID:5993]

Canadian Catholic Organization for Development and Peace (CCODP)
5633 Sherbrooke Street E., Montréal, Québec H1N 1A3;
(514) 257-8711, fax (514) 257-8497, info@devp.org, www.devp.org

LARGE DEVELOPMENT ASSISTANCE GROUP: Accounting, Administration, Advocacy, Computer Systems, Development Education, Fundraising, Media/Communications, Project Management, Technical Assistance

The Canadian Catholic Organization for Development and Peace (CCODP) is a non-governmental organization founded in 1967 by Canada's Catholic Bishops. It promotes programs that foster sustainable development and the formation of North-South partnerships. Along with its efforts to develop an information network of Northern and Southern NGOs, CCODP attempts to actively involve partners in decision-making and implementation of projects and programs. It also aims to transform attitudes, behaviours and social structures that hinder the necessary conditions for the development and solidarity of all people. It does this by developing a responsible political consciousness among individuals and groups capable of assessing, and lobbying where necessary, the Canadian government's position towards the South. CCODP also has an annual fundraising campaign across Canada.

CCODP has 60 staff in Canada. It looks for people with experience in advocacy, pertinent work experience both in Canada and the South, and sufficient knowledge of the Catholic Church and its commitments in the field of international development. Bilingualism (in addition to speaking and writing the languages required in certain developing countries) is also required.

CCODP keeps suitable résumés on file for six months. Visit the CCODP web site for job openings and internship positions. [ID:5994]

Canadian Centre on Minority Affairs Inc.
Suite 110, 869 Yonge Street, Toronto, Ontario M4W 2H2;
(416) 966-1226, fax (416) 966-1182, ccma@interlog.com, www.interlog.com/~ccma

MID-SIZED DEVELOPMENT ASSISTANCE GROUP: Development Assistance, Education, Exchange Programs, Policy Dialogue, Youth and Development

The Canadian Centre on Minority Affairs is a nongovernmental organization dedicated to improving the social and economic conditions of Caribbean Canadians in Canada. It functions as a public policy forum; provides training in community economic development; facilitates research and manages a Youth Internship program between Canada and the Eastern Caribbean. CCMA partners in the Caribbean include the Grenada Save the Children Development Agency (GRENSAVE), the Dominica Association of Industry and Commerce, the St. Vincent and the Grenadines Chamber of Commerce, the Antigua and Barbuda Chamber of Commerce, the St. Lucia Chamber of Commerce and the government of St. Kitts.

The CCMA promotes partnership between Canada and the Eastern Caribbean through its International Cooperation Program. The ICP aims to establish a human resources and basic needs development fund to assist rural youth, raise public awareness regarding business development, improve communications between Canadian and Caribbean educational institutions, NGOs and business groups, and formulate strategies to improve Canada's development policies toward the Eastern Caribbean. [ID:6683]

Canadian Co-operative Association (CCA)

Suite 400, 275 Bank Street, Ottawa, Ontario K2P 2L6;
(613) 238-6711, fax (613) 567-0658, support@coopcca.com, www.coopcca.com

LARGE DEVELOPMENT ASSISTANCE GROUP: Accounting, Administration, Agriculture, Business/Banking/Trade, Business Development, Community Development, Development Assistance, Development Education, Exchange Programs, Fundraising, International Trade, Logistics, Micro-Enterprises, Project Management, Technical Assistance, Volunteer

The Canadian Co-operative Association (CCA) brings anglophone cooperatives and credit unions together to support and promote a distinct cooperative alternative, embracing both social and economic objectives. Through CCA, these organizations speak with a unified voice and act in concert to strengthen the cooperative system in Canada and abroad.

CCA employs 30 salaried staff, overseas and in Canada, who are involved in international development work. The International Development Department assists in the development of cooperatives in the South, raises awareness among CCA members and the public of the roles of cooperatives in international development, and fosters cooperation between Canada and the South.

CCA seeks flexible university graduates with direct experience overseas or with a cooperative/credit union, and who are sensitive to other cultures. CCA maintains a data bank for résumés. [ID:5995]

Canadian Coalition for the Rights of Children (CCRC)

Suite 339, 180 Argyle Street, Ottawa, Ontario K2P 1B7;
(613) 788-5085, fax (613) 788-5106, ccrc@web.net, www.cfc-efc.ca/ccrc

SMALL INTERNATIONAL ADVOCACY GROUP: Human Rights

The Canadian Coalition for the Rights of Children (CCRC) monitors and promotes Canada's implementation of the United Nations Convention on the Rights of the Child. CCRC undertakes a variety of activities primarily in Canada but also abroad.

CCRC has one employee based in Canada and maintains a data bank for résumés. CCRC has received funding for internships, which are provided to those with degrees in social science, education, international relations or related fields and who demonstrated an interest in human rights. [ID:6684]

Canadian Council for International Co-operation (CCIC)

3rd Floor, 1 Nicholas Street, Ottawa, Ontario K1N 7B7;
(613) 241-7007, fax (613) 241-5302, ccic@web.net, www.web.net.ccic-ccci

LARGE COORDINATING BODY: Advocacy, Economics, Environment, Gender and Development, Human Rights, Media/Communications

The Canadian Council for International Co-operation (CCIC) advocates for Canadian policies and programs which will reduce global poverty and promote sustainable human development. It also seeks to strengthen the role of the voluntary sector in development cooperation.

CCIC is a coalition of Canadian organizations who seek to change the course of human development in ways that favour social and economic equity, democratic participation, environmental integrity, and respect for human rights. Established in 1968, the Council conducts research, disseminates information, and creates learning opportunities for its members. CCIC coordinates their collective efforts to shape new models for world development, press for national and international policies that serve the global public interest, and strives to build a social movement for global citizenship in Canada.

The Council consists of more than 100 Canadian nonprofit organizations working in Canada and overseas; they include religious and secular development groups, professional associations, and labour unions. They work with NGOs, cooperatives and citizens' groups in the South to enable people in Africa, Asia and Latin America to meet basic needs for food, shelter, education, health, and sanitation. Many conduct research and campaign with their Southern partners for fair trade, global security, children's rights, biodiversity, or forgiveness of multi-lateral debt. Some members work exclusively in Canada, designing education materials for use in classrooms and resource centres. Others use their overseas program experience as a springboard for public awareness campaigning in Canada. [ID:5996]

Canadian Council of Churches (CCC)
40 St. Clair Ave. E., Toronto, Ontario M4T 1M9;
(416) 921-7759, fax (416) 921-7478, ccchurch@web.net, www.web.net/~ccchurch

---

SMALL COORDINATING BODY: Accounting, Administration, Human Rights, Religious

In Canada, the Canadian Council of Churches (CCC) coordinates response by some churches to requests from ecumenical partners overseas for short-term emergency relief and, occasionally, long-term development assistance.

The CCC assists in some aspects of church efforts to influence government policy on international issues such as Official Development Assistance (ODA) and human rights, and engages in some public education concerning these policies. The CCC occasionally sponsors exchange programs or exposure tours.

The CCC employs six staff in Canada. See the CCC web site for job openings. [ID:5997]

Canadian Crossroads International /
Carrefour Canadien International (CCI)
31 Madison Ave., Toronto, Ontario M5R 2S2;
(416) 967-0801, fax (416) 967-9078, cci@web.net, www.crossroads-carrefour.ca

---

LARGE EXCHANGE GROUP: Community Development, Development Education, Exchange Programs, Gender and Development, Intercultural Briefings, Volunteer

Canadian Crossroads International (CCI) fosters global understanding by placing Canadian volunteers in the developing world, bringing volunteers from developing nations to Canada, and sponsoring community education programs. Each year, more than 260 volunteers in 22 countries and 60 Canadian communities work in placements in health, education, agriculture and community development.

In Canada, Crossroads has 25 full- and part-time staff who work closely with 200 national volunteer leaders to deliver the organization's program. Overseas there are fifty volunteer leaders.

CCI looks for applicants with experience working with volunteers, facilitation and administrative skills. No special degrees are needed. Application deadlines for individual programs is August 1 and October 15 for group programs. Their web site is currently under construction. (For more information on CCI see Chapter 10, Short-term Programs Overseas and Chapter 11, Hosting Programs.) [ID:5998]

Canadian Environmental Network (CEN)
National Director, Suite 300, 945 Wellington Street,
Ottawa, Ontario K1Y 2X5; (613) 728-9810, fax (613) 728-2963, cen@web.net

---

MID-SIZED COORDINATING BODY: Environment

The Canadian Environmental Network (CEN) is comprised of networks of environmental organizations and First Nations people's groups. CEN's mission is to facilitate and advance the work of its member groups to protect the Earth and promote ecologically sound ways of life. CEN has seven staff in Canada, and does not provide overseas placements or postings. [ID:6000]

Canadian Executive Service Organization (CESO)

Suite 400, South Tower, 175 Bloor Street E., Toronto, Ontario M4W 3R8;
(416) 961-2376, fax (416) 961-1096, toronto@ceso-saco.com, www.ceso-saco.com

LARGE VOLUNTEER GROUP: Most Job Categories

Canadian Executive Service Organization (CESO) sends Canadians with professional, technical or managerial skills to work as Volunteer Advisers (VAs) with businesses and organizations in Canadian aboriginal communities, developing countries and the new market economies of Central and Eastern Europe. One of its initiatives is its Women in Development strategy, designed to bring qualified women to CESO as VAs, and to identify more projects, both overseas and in Canada, that will directly benefit women.

CESO maintains 55 salaried staff in Canada, and recruits hundreds of VAs every year to work in Canada and overseas. Volunteers completed over 800 overseas projects in 1996, with an average duration of two months. Most VAs are retired or semi-retired and have the time and the willingness to share their expertise without pay. The average age of a volunteer is 62 years.

CESO encourages multilateral agencies, regional development banks, international NGOs and other funded, international agencies, to use its VAs to train and advise clients who are as yet unable to afford the full cost of international consultants. CESO also posts difficult-to-fill positions on its web site. [ID:6026]

Canadian Feed the Children Inc. (CFTC)

174 Bartley Drive, Toronto, Ontario M4A 1E1;
(416) 757-1220, fax (416) 757-3318, Canadian_Feed_the_Children@compuserve.com

LARGE RELIEF AND DEVELOPMENT AGENCY: Accounting, Administration, Computer Systems, Fundraising, Humanitarian Relief, Project Management, Volunteer

Canadian Feed the Children Inc. (CFTC) is a non-sectarian international relief and development agency which focuses on reducing hunger, poverty and suffering of children in Canada and overseas, and is affiliated with Feed the Children International. In cooperation with CIDA, CFTC supports community and micro-enterprise development programs and capacity building programs in Ethiopia, Haiti, Uganda, Russia and Eastern Europe. Relief efforts consist primarily of procuring and shipping commodities overseas where they are distributed by FTC field officers or other partner agencies to those in need. In 1996, CFTC distributed over $15 million in commodities throughout the world.

CFTC has 20 people on staff at the head office in Toronto. Overseas staff are nationals of the countries in which they work. CFTC maintains a data bank for résumés. [ID:6001]

Canadian Food for the Hungry

Personnel Director, Suite 5, 2580 Cedar Park,
Abbotsford, B.C. V2T 3S5; (604) 853-4262, fax (604) 853-4332, info@cfh.ca, www.cfh.ca

LARGE RELIEF AND DEVELOPMENT AGENCY: Accounting, Administration, Advocacy, Agriculture, Community Development, Development Assistance, Development Education, Forestry, Humanitarian Relief, Medical Health, Micro-Enterprises, Project Management, Volunteer, Water Resources

Canadian Food for the Hungry is a relief and development organization with long-range development programs in 20 developing countries. Its programs focus on agricultural training, community development, micro-enterprise, child survival, reforestation, wells/irrigation, primary healthcare, education and literacy, and emergency relief. All programs emphasize the organization's Christian motivation.

Food for the Hungry has 11 staff based in Canada and five overseas employees who work with over 1,000 staff members of their partner agency, Food for the Hungry International. Applicants should have a biblically-based Christian worldview and possess education or work experience in food production, land reclamation, agro-forestry, primary healthcare, relief and development or health-related fields. Business or management experience is useful, but not necessary. Canadian Food for the Hungry maintains a data bank for résumés. Visit the Food for the Hungry's web site for job openings. [ID:6002]

Canadian Foodgrains Bank Association Inc. (CFGB)
P.O. Box 767, Suite 400, 280 Smith Street, Winnipeg, Manitoba R3C 2L4;
(204) 944-1993, fax (204) 943-2597, cfgb@foodgrainsbank.ca, www.foodgrainsbank.ca

MID-SIZED RELIEF AND DEVELOPMENT AGENCY: Accounting, Consulting, Development Assistance, Humanitarian Relief, Project Management, Relief and Development

Canadian Foodgrains Bank Association Inc. (CFGB) provides donated foodgrains to people in developing countries in emergency situations and in food-for-work and other development projects. The Foodgrains Bank is comprised of 13 church denominations.

The CFGB has 16 salaried staff in Canada and one overseas. It seeks workers with expertise in the areas of Third World relief, development, and hunger situations. The association maintains a data bank for résumés. [ID:6003]

Canadian Foundation for the Americas (FOCAL)
55 Murray Street, Ottawa, Ontario K1N 5M3;
(613) 562-0005, fax (613) 562-2525, focal@focal.ca, www.focal.ca

MID-SIZED INTERNATIONAL RESEARCH GROUP: Development Education, Economics, Social Sciences

Canadian Foundation for the Americas (FOCAL) promotes political, academic, business and cultural cooperation between Canada, Latin America, and the Caribbean. Its mandate is to become a national clearinghouse for ideas and activities linking Canada with the regions it serves. FOCAL also promotes public awareness of Latin American and Caribbean issues through its media fellowship program, in which journalists are sent to Latin America for two-month study periods. In addition, it operates an MBA internship program with Canadian missions overseas. Canadian Foundation for the Americas currently has 10 staff in Canada and none overseas. Job openings are posted on FOCAL'S web site. [ID:6004]

Canadian Friends of Burma
Suite 206, 145 Spruce Street,
Ottawa, Ontario K1R 6P1; (613) 237-8056, fax (613) 563-0017, cfob@web.net, www.web.net/~cfob

SMALL INTERNATIONAL ADVOCACY GROUP: Advocacy, Fundraising, Human Rights, Humanitarian Relief, Media/Communications, Refugee Services

Canadian Friends of Burma works within a global movement to establish democracy and human rights in Burma. It is active in government relations, media, public advocacy, public education and humanitarian assistance.

Canadian Friends of Burma has one staff member in Canada. The group does not promote employment in Canada or overseas, but is interested in volunteers and can act as a resource for people interested in volunteering overseas. Occasionally, it offers contracts and internships in the areas of public advocacy and human rights. [ID:6959]

Canadian Friends Service Committee (CFSC)
Suite 208, 145 Spruce Street, Ottawa, Ontario K1R 6P1;
(613) 231-6894, fax (613) 233-9028, ottcfsc@web.net, www.web.net/~cfsc/

SMALL COMMUNITY DEVELOPMENT GROUP: Agriculture, Religious, Water Resources

Canadian Friends Service Committee (CFSC) is a committee of the Religious Society of Friends, Quakers in Canada. CFSC works with NGOs in Mexico, Central America, Thailand, Vietnam, Cambodia, and Zimbabwe, many of which are involved in organic farming and wells and sanitation. Where possible, relationships with NGOs are made in partnership with the Quakers' Friends organizations or at monthly meetings.

CFSC has one staff based in Canada and none overseas. [ID:6005]

Canadian Higher Education Group (CHEG)
6th Floor, 350 Sparks Street,
Ottawa, Ontario L1R 7S8; (613) 237-2220, fax (613) 237-7347, hickling@hickling.ca

MID-SIZED COORDINATING BODY: Administration, Consulting, Human Resources, Institution Building, International Education, Project Management

Canadian Higher Education Group (CHEG) consists of a partnership of six organizations: Carleton University, University of Guelph, Hickling Corporation, McMaster University, University of Waterloo and University of Western Ontario. CHEG deals with international higher education projects worldwide, and their activities include institutional strengthening, human resource development and education planning for ministries of education.

Qualified applicants have international higher education experience. CHEG maintains a data bank for résumés. [ID:6404]

Canadian Home Economics Association (CHEA)
Partnership Program Manager, Suite 307, 151 Slater Street, Ottawa, Ontario
K1P 5H3; (613) 238-8817, fax (613) 238-8972, cheappm@web.net, www.zu.com/beta/chea/

MID-SIZED DEVELOPMENT ASSISTANCE GROUP: Adult Training, Business Development, Child Care, Community Development, Curriculum Development, Development Education, Environment, Gender and Development, Human Rights, Micro-Enterprises, Nutrition, Project Management, Teaching

The International Development Program of the Canadian Home Economics Association (CHEA) assists local and provincial professional home economics associations in Canada to work on joint projects with similar associations in developing countries. CHEA's development education program informs and sensitizes CHEA's own membership, the general public, and home economics students.

CHEA has partner associations in Africa, the Caribbean, Asia, and Brazil. Areas of expertise include home economics curricula, textbook and educational materials development, village-level food technology development and adoption, childcare worker training, association strengthening, small business training, vocational education support, community development and consumer education, and continuing education.

CHEA has 2.5 staff (in full-time equivalents) in Canada. Participants in CHEA programs must be professional home economists and be eligible for membership in the Canadian Home Economics Association. In order to participate in an international development project they must join a local or provincial home economics association that works with an overseas partner association, or they must want to form a partnership. CHEA maintains a data bank for résumés. [ID:6006]

Canadian Human Rights Foundation
Executive Director, Suite 307, 1425 René Lévesque Blvd. W., Montréal, Québec
H3G 1T7; (514) 954-0382, fax (514) 954-0659, chrf@vir.com, www.web.net/chrf-fcdp

MID-SIZED INTERNATIONAL ADVOCACY GROUP: Human Rights, International Education

The Canadian Human Rights Foundation is involved in human rights education and training in Asia, Africa, East-Central Europe and the Former Soviet Union. Thematic regional training programs which the foundation is associated with include Refugee Rights in the Former Soviet Union, Moscow Rights for Migrant Workers in Asia, Human Rights Education in Africa and Women's Rights.

The Canadian Human Rights Foundation employs 11 staff in Canada, all of whom have extensive international experience. The foundation maintains a data bank for résumés and considers internship positions from those who have funding. [ID:6407]

Canadian Institute of Cultural Affairs (ICA Canada)

579 Kingston Road, Toronto, Ontario M4E 1R3;
(416) 691-2316, fax (416) 691-2491, icacan@web.net, www.web.net/~icacan and www.icaworld.org.icai

SMALL ORGANIZATIONAL TRAINING GROUP: Business Development, Community Development

The Canadian Institute of Cultural Affairs (ICA Canada) is a unique facilitation, training and research organization. It provides participatory skills to thousands of people across Canada which enables them to effectively change their communities. ICA Canada is on the leading edge of change and consistently delivers quality programs to hundreds of committees and organizations.

ICA Canada has sister organizations in 32 nations. Some of these organizations accept volunteers on a six- or 12-month basis. All requests should be directed to the national office in question. For additional information, visit www. icaworld.org.icai, ICA's international web site. [ID:6008]

Canadian Jesuits International (CJI)

P.O. Box 31029, Guelph, Ontario N1H 8K1; (519) 821-3100, fax (519) 821-3060

MID-SIZED EVANGELICAL GROUP: Advocacy, Development Assistance, Development Education, Religious, Volunteer

Canadian Jesuits International (CJI)) is committed to the service of faith and the promotion of justice among poor and marginalized groups in the global community. It supports efforts to build a local base for the community and religious development capacities of partners with whom it works. CJI fosters a holistic approach to human development which responds to today's spiritual values; honours the transformative power of respect for elders, women and children and increases solidarity and support for indigenous peoples' struggles and demands. CJI promotes dialogue and understanding among world religions and ethnic groups and supports educational advocacy. CJM currently works with Jesuit and other partners in Canada, India, Nepal, Bhutan, Zambia, Jamaica, and Russia.

CJI has three staff in Canada and approximately 30 Canadian Jesuits overseas. Those interested in volunteer work overseas are usually directed to the Jesuit International Volunteers office, P.O. Box 25478, Washington, DC, 20007. Tel: (202) 944-1594, fax: (202) 687-5082. [ID:6009]

Canadian Labour Congress (CLC)

International Department, 2841 Riverside Drive,
Ottawa, Ontario K1V 8X7; (613) 521-3400, fax (613) 521-8949, nstooley@clc-ctc.ca, www.clc-ctc.ca

LARGE COORDINATING BODY: Adult Training, Advocacy, Community Development, Computer Systems, Development Assistance, Development Education, Exchange Programs, Gender and Development, Human Rights, Humanitarian Relief, Project Management, Technical Assistance

Canadian Labour Congress (CLC) strives to build international trade union solidarity through technical, material, humanitarian and financial assistance overseas, and through projects sponsored by Third World union organizations. CLC staff assist project partners in the field where CLC International Development Projects take place. CLC international staff manage projects in Africa, the Americas, the Caribbean, Central and Eastern Europe, Asia, and Haiti. [ID:6010]

Canadian Lutheran World Relief (CLWR)
1080 Kingsbury Ave., Winnipeg, Manitoba R2P 1W5;
(204) 694-5602, fax (204) 694-5460, clwr@mbnet.mb.ca, www.mbnet.mb.ca/~clwr

LARGE RELIEF AND DEVELOPMENT AGENCY: Administration, Agriculture, Community
Development, Consulting, Development Assistance, Development Education, Environment,
Gender and Development, Human Resources, Humanitarian Relief, Medical Health, Project
Management, Technical Assistance, Water Resources

Canadian Lutheran World Relief (CLWR) provides overseas relief and development service on behalf of the Evangelical Lutheran Church in Canada and Lutheran Church - Canada.
CLWR supports projects in Africa, Asia, the Middle East and Latin America. It also provides
disaster relief and enables sponsorships for refugee resettlement in Canada. Twelve staff
work in Canada. [ID:6011]

Canadian National Institute for the Blind (CNIB)
Government Relations & International Liaison, 320 McLeod Street, Ottawa, Ontario
K2P 1T4; (613) 563-4021, fax (613) 232-9070, nat-government@east.cnib.ca, www.cnib.ca

The Canadian National Institute for the Blind (CNIB) participates in the area of
blindness rehabilitation. Through its activities with the World Blind Union (WBU), it has
initiated improvements in the field and developed a strong international community for
information sharing and resource development.

Although CNIB is active internationally, it does not initiate or financially support international programs or projects due to financial and human resource limitations. However,
with the assistance of the Canadian International Development Agency (CIDA) and such
organizations as the Caribbean Council for the Blind, Sight Savers, Perkins School for the
Blind, and the World Blind Union, CNIB does act as a major advisor and developer of certain
projects.

At CNIB, two of the 1,500 staff work on international projects. CNIB is not in a position
to hire personnel for international activities at this time. [ID:6013]

Canadian Organization for Development through Education (CODE)
Development Department, 321 Chapel Street, Ottawa, Ontario K1N 7Z2;
(613) 232-3569, fax (613) 232-7435, codehq@codecan.com, www.web.net/~code

LARGE DEVELOPMENT ASSISTANCE GROUP: Accounting, Administration, Development
Assistance, Development Education, Fundraising, Media/Communications, Project Management,
Volunteer

Formed in 1959, the Canadian Organization for Development through Education
(CODE) is a nonprofit NGO which supports a sustainable literate environment in developing
countries. It provides support by supplying funding and other resources for publishing.
Priority is given to publishing projects which promote children's literature, primary-level
reference material, and newspapers and magazines aimed at adult learners.

CODE supports activities in Africa and the Caribbean and concentrates on remote
regions with high illiteracy rates. Programming is directed to primary-level students and
adult learners. CODE also carries out development education programs in Canada about the
need to support literacy and education in the developing world.

The organization has 15 employees in Canada. [ID:6014]

Canadian Physicians for Aid and Relief (CPAR)

Suite 202, 111 Queen Street E., Toronto, Ontario M5C 1S2;
(416) 369-0865, fax (416) 369-0294, codehq@codecan.com, www.web.net/~code

LARGE RELIEF AND DEVELOPMENT AGENCY: Accounting, Administration, Computer Systems, Construction, Development Assistance, Development Education, Engineering, Environment, Forestry, Gender and Development, Humanitarian Relief, Medical Health, Water Resources

Canadian Physicians for Aid and Relief (CPAR) initiates long-term integrated rural development projects focusing on primary healthcare and the environment (Agroforestry). CPAR also responds to emergencies, such as famine, on short notice.

CPAR is currently in Ethiopia, Malawi, and Uganda. CPAR minimizes expatriate involvement and maximizes local involvement to ensure that local people are adequately trained to sustain the program once expatriates withdraw.

Two Canadian staff are now working with about 200 local staff. The Canadian office is responsible for support and administration, fundraising, and public relations. Successful applicants will have hands-on experience or skills in agroforestry, health, engineering, management or administration. Experience living and working in the developing world is an asset. CPAR looks for innovative, self-directed, and resourceful people willing to commit to a minimum of two years overseas. All expatriate staff, excluding senior management positions, are expected to undertake voluntary work for CPAR in Canada following a position overseas. CPAR maintains a data bank for résumés. [ID:6016]

Canadian Public Health Association (CPHA)

International Programs, Suite 400, 1565 Carling Ave.,
Ottawa, Ontario K1Z 8R1; (613) 725-3769, fax (613) 725-9826, info@cpha.ca, www.cpha.ca

LARGE COMMUNITY HEALTH GROUP: Advocacy, Community Development, Development Education, Gender and Development, Medical Health, Project Management

The Canadian Public Health Association (CPHA) is a national, nonprofit organization of professionals and non-professionals committed to improving and maintaining personal and community health in Canada and around the world. CPHA's aims to be a special national resource that advocates for the improvement and maintenance of personal and community health according to the public health principles of disease prevention, health promotion, and a healthy public policy.

Through its International Programs, and with the support of the Canadian International Development Agency (CIDA) and the Department of Foreign Affairs, CPHA cooperates with public health and similar organizations in Africa, Asia, the Caribbean, Latin America, the Middle East, and Eastern and Central Europe. Its projects extend and strengthen primary healthcare. In addition, CPHA provides an opportunity for Canadian community health workers to learn innovative approaches to primary healthcare in developing countries, and to assist in an exchange of information and mutual support between Canadians and their southern counterparts. CPHA also manages the Family Health Project, the Caribbean HIV/AIDS Project and the Southern Africa AIDS Training Program.

CPHA's International Programs have ten staff in Canada and two overseas. CPHA maintains a data bank for résumés. [ID:6017]

Canadian Red Cross Society (CRCS)

1800 Alta Vista Drive, Ottawa, Ontario K1G 4J5;
(613) 739-3000, fax (613) 731-1411, cancross@redcross.ca, www.redcross.ca

LARGE RELIEF AND DEVELOPMENT AGENCY: Accounting, Administration, Advocacy, Agriculture, Community Development, Development Assistance, Development Education, Humanitarian Relief, Logistics, Media/Communications, Medical Health, Technical Assistance, Volunteer, Water Resources

The Canadian Red Cross Society (CRCS) is a branch of the International Red Cross and Red Crescent Movement. Along with over 170 other national societies, the agency focuses on improving the situations of the world's most vulnerable. The mission of the Canadian Red Cross is to help people deal with situations that threaten their survival and safety, their security and well being, and their human dignity. CRCS is committed to upholding and advocating the principles of humanity, impartiality, neutrality, independence, voluntary service, unity and universality. Canadian operations include international relief and development assistance, a domestic tracing and family reunion service, and educational and international humanitarian law dissemination activities.

The CRCS recruits and trains specialized personnel for overseas assignments with the International Committee of the Red Cross (ICRC) and the International Federation of Red Cross and Red Crescent Societies in its international relief operations. Assignments, organized in response to natural disasters and conflict, are six to 12 months in length. Overseas positions include: working with displaced persons and unaccompanied children, working in places of detention, or in finance and administration, telecommunications, water and sanitation, medical/health, disaster preparedness, relief administration, and information dissemination. Individuals recruited for these assignments have five years work experience in their fields.

People are recruited both from within the CRCS and on a contract basis. Applicants are recruited through Regional and Zonal Offices, and must first participate in the Basic Training Course for Overseas Personnel. The CRCS also manages a large domestic emergency response program and encourages potential international staff to become actively involved as volunteers at the local level. Applicants should contact one of the following regional offices: Western Zone, 815 - 8th Ave. S.W., Calgary, Alberta, T2P 3P2, Tel: (403) 205-3448, Fax: (403) 205-3463; Ontario Zone, 5700 Cancross Court, Mississauga, Ontario, L5R 3E9, Tel: (905) 890-1000, Fax: (905) 890-1008; Zone du Québec, 6, place du Commerce, Ile-des-Souers, Verdun, Québec, H3E 1P4, Tel: (514) 362-2929, Fax: (514) 362-9991; Atlantic Zone, P.O. Box 39, 405 University Ave., Saint John, N.B., E2L 3X3, Tel: (506) 648-5000, Fax: (506) 648-5095. General information about employment opportunities is available on the CRCS web site. [ID:6018]

Canadian Resource Bank for Democracy and Human Rights (CANADEM)

1 Nicholas Suite 1102, Ottawa, Ontario K1N 7B7;
(613) 789-3328, fax (613) 789-6125, canadem@ibm.net, www.web.net/~canadem

CANADEM was set up to create and manage a resource bank of Canadians with skills in areas such as human rights, peace building or democracy, to serve as a civilian standby mechanism for the UN and other international agencies conducting field operations. [ID:7233]

Canadian Rotary Committee for International Development (CRCID)

Suite 101, 49 Emma Street, Guelph, Ontario N1E 6X1; (519) 763-6311, fax (519) 837-0729

MID-SIZED COMMUNITY DEVELOPMENT GROUP: Agriculture, Business Development, Community Development, Development Education, Gender and Development, Human Resources, Medical Health, Micro-Enterprises, Teaching, Technical Assistance, Volunteer, Water Resources

The Canadian Rotary Committee for International Development (CRCID) supports community development through project development, assessment, funding and management. It also monitors and evaluates existing projects, and has a development education program. CRCID has three staff in Canada and many volunteers overseas, however, limited opportunities exist for Canadians seeking employment. [ID:6019]

Canadian Society for International Health (CSIH)

Suite 1105, 1 Nicholas Street, Ottawa, Ontario K1N 7B7;
(613) 241-5785, fax (613) 241-3845, csih@fox.nstn.ca, www.csih.org

MID-SIZED COMMUNITY HEALTH GROUP: Medical Health

The Canadian Society for International Health (CSIH) is committed to promoting international health and development. CSIH links individuals and organizations from all health sectors and all health and related professions. Through the mobilization of Canadian resources, CSIH advocates and facilitates research, education and service activities in international health. Its 900 members include physicians, nurses, managers, therapists, nutritionists, social and laboratory scientists, and other professionals in fields related to international health. CSIH's activities include the annual Canadian Conference on International Health, the dissemination of travel health information to Canadians, and the publication of the newsletter *Synergy*.

CSIH also manages a variety of program overseas. Building Capacity for Health Reform in Bolivia is a technical cooperation project aimed at supporting health reform there. The Partners in Health Program is a technical cooperation project which aims to contribute, within the context of Ukraine's initiative, to the sustainable improvement of the health status of the Ukrainian population. The new International Health Youth Internship Program addresses recent graduates and students about to graduate who are planning a career in health or a health-related field.

CSIH is also the technical representative of the Pan American Health Organization. It currently employs 15 staff in Canada. CSIH operates the International Health Human Resources Registry, a listing of Canadian professionals with expertise in international health which is accessed by international development organizations and professionals seeking colleagues. It also maintains a data bank for résumés. (For more information on CSIH see Chapter 10, Short-Term Programs Overseas.) [ID:6020]

Canadian Teachers' Federation (CTF)

International Programs, 110 Argyle Ave., Ottawa, Ontario
K2P 1B4; (613) 232-1505, fax (613) 232-1886, info@ctf-fce.ca, www.ctf-fce.ca

LARGE ORGANIZATIONAL TRAINING GROUP: Development Assistance, Teaching, Volunteer

Canadian Teachers' Federation (CTF) is a national organization of 13 provincial and territorial teacher associations with a membership of approximately 250,000 teachers. As a principal aim is to strengthen teacher unions, CTF operates the International Development Assistance Program to give professional assistance to fellow teachers and their organizations in developing countries. Types of assistance range from teacher training, to leadership training, to organizational skills development, and to secretariat support.

In-service training programs of three to 16 weeks are held during July and August and any time from September to June. Requirements for direct participation include five years of Canadian teaching experience. Teachers must apply through their provincial or territorial teacher organizations or, in Ontario, through their OTF affiliates. Deadline for applications is mid-November. [ID:6021]

Canadian UNICEF Committee (UNICEF Canada)

443 Mount Pleasant Road, Toronto, Ontario M4S 2L8;
(416) 482-4444, fax (416) 482-8035, secretary@unicef.ca, www.unicef.ca

---

LARGE DEVELOPMENT ASSISTANCE GROUP: Adult Training, Community Development, Development Assistance, Gender and Development, Humanitarian Relief, Medical Health, Project Management, Technical Assistance, Water Resources

The Canadian UNICEF Committee (UNICEF Canada) raises funds in Canada for United Nations Children's Fund's projects in developing countries. These include community-based projects in protective nutrition, primary healthcare and basic education of mothers and children. UNICEF Canada also educates Canadians on development issues.

UNICEF employs three staff in Canada to manage and monitor Canadian contributions to international programs. Like other National Committees for UNICEF, the group establishes working relationships with NGOs in industrialized and developing countries in order to fulfil UNICEF's mandate to protect the lives of children and promote their development. Overseas recruitment for UNICEF is conducted by UNICEF headquarters in New York. Applicants must have past work experience in developing countries and different areas of expertise. UNICEF Canada occasionally recruits consultants with specialized areas of expertise. It keeps résumés suitable to these requirements on file. UNICEF Canada is also involved in the Junior Professional Officer (JPO) program. (For more information on JPO see Chapter 17, International Internships.) [ID:6022]

CARE Canada

Unit 300, Phase 3, 6 Antares Drive, Ottawa, Ontario K1G 4X6;
(800) 267-5232, fax (613) 226-5777, hr@care.ca, www.care.ca

LARGE DEVELOPMENT ASSISTANCE GROUP: Accounting, Administration, Agriculture, Business/Banking/Trade, Business Development, Community Development, Computer Systems, Construction, Consulting, Engineering, Environment, Fisheries, Forestry, Fundraising, Gender and Development, Human Resources, Human Rights, Humanitarian Relief, Logistics, Media/Communications, Medical Health, Micro-Enterprises, Project Management, Water Resources

CARE Canada implements development projects throughout the world in water supply and sanitation, agroforestry and natural resources, income generation, emergency assistance, and small economic activities. Its major programs are agriculture, forestry, public health, water supply, construction, emergency response, and project management. In each program there are many specialized areas for which CARE seeks applicants with appropriate education and experience.

CARE applicants require a university degree or equivalent in a relevant field of study; a minimum of two years overseas development experience in a Third World country, preferably with a development organization similar to CARE; experience in one or more areas such as public health, agriculture, forestry, water supply, construction, project management, engineering, apiculture; the ability to live and work with different cultures and to take on extensive and difficult field travel in remote and extreme climatic areas; and speaking ability in English plus other languages, preferably French or Spanish. Other specific requirements are established for each overseas assignment.

CARE maintains a data bank for résumés and accepts a small number of interns each year, namely from the International Development Studies Program at the University of Toronto. CARE Canada has an excellent web site which gives job applicants specific information on "Important Characteristics of Overseas Work," "Questions All Candidates Should Prepare For," and "CARE Recruits Staff Experienced in... ," which lists sectors encompassed by CARE's programs. Job openings are also posted. (For more information on CARE International see Chapter 38, International Organizations.) [ID:6023]

Carrefour de solidarité internationale (CSI)
555, rue Short, Sherbrooke, Québec J1H 2E6; (819) 566-8595, fax (819) 566-8076, csi-sher@login.net

SMALL DEVELOPMENT ASSISTANCE GROUP: Adult Training, Agriculture, Community Development, Development Assistance, Development Education, Environment, Exchange Programs, Gender and Development, Human Resources, Human Rights, Logistics, Media/Communications, Project Management, Teaching, Technical Assistance, Volunteer, Water Resources

Le Carrefour de solidarité internationale (CSI) est une ONG régionale qui, dans sa programmation régulière, développe des liens de partenariat avec des organismes au Mali, en République Dominicaine, à Haiti, au Nicaragua, et au Pérou. Sa programmation intégrée comprend trois volets: soutien de projets de développement, stages d'échanges et communications sociales.

Carrefour de solidarité internationale a un personnel de 7 employés au Canada. Le CSI considère les demandes de stages dans les domaines de l'organisation communautaire, la santé, l'agriculture et le développement durable et maintient une banque de données des c.v. de ses ex-stagiaires. [ID:7009]

Carrefour tiers-monde (CTM)
1er étage, 454, rue Caron, Québec, Québec
G1K 8K8; (418) 647-5853, fax (418) 647-5719, ctm@mediom.qc.ca

SMALL DEVELOPMENT EDUCATION GROUP: Adult Training, Agriculture, Business/Banking/Trade, Community Development, Development Assistance, Development Education, Environment, Exchange Programs, Gender and Development, Human Resources, Human Rights, Humanitarian Relief, Media/Communications, Project Management, Teaching, Technical Assistance, Telecommunications, Volunteer

Carrefour tiers-monde est une organisation non gouvernementale vouée à l'éducation du public à la solidarité internationale dans la région de Québec. Ses objectifs sont de sensibiliser la population aux situations vécues par les peuples du tiers-monde; offrir des occasions de formation sur les différents aspects du développement; servir de lieu de rencontres et de ressources pour les groupes et les individus intéressés aux questions de développement international. Par ailleurs elle organise aussi, par exemple, des conférences publiques, des sessions de formation et des campagnes d'actions de solidarité internationale. Elle possède son propre centre de documentation. [ID:5089]

CAUSE Canada
Overseas Program Director, P.O. Box 8100, Canmore, Alberta T1W 2T8;
(403) 678-3332, fax (403) 678-8869, causecan@telusplanet.net, www.cause.ca

MID-SIZED DEVELOPMENT ASSISTANCE GROUP: Agriculture, Community Development, Construction, Development Education, Environment, Forestry, Fundraising, Gender and Development, Humanitarian Relief, Medical Health, Micro-Enterprises, Water Resources

CAUSE Canada is committed to supporting sustainable development projects in geographical regions underrepresented by the international aid community. Assistance is focused in West Africa and Central America, especially Guatemala, Honduras, Sierra Leone, Liberia, Mali and Côte d'Ivoire. Development priorities include primary healthcare, water and sanitation, reforestation, gender-specific development and micro-enterprise projects.

CAUSE Canada employs four staff in Canada and seven overseas. CAUSE seeks individuals with university degrees in business management, health-related disciplines and accounting. Previous overseas experience and fluency in Spanish or French is a must. Individuals must also be able to work in a team environment with flexibility and initiative. CAUSE Canada maintains a data bank for résumés and offers six to 12-month internships with no honorariums. Current areas of focus for internships are computer literacy, accounting, and agriculture. [ID:6942]

Centre canadien d'étude et de coopération internationale (CECI)
Recruitment Director, 180 St. Catherine Street E.,
Montréal, Québec H2X 1K9; (514) 875-9911, fax (514) 875-6469, info@ceci.ca, www.ceci.ca/ceci/

LARGE DEVELOPMENT ASSISTANCE GROUP: Accounting, Administration, Adult Training, Agriculture, Architecture and Planning, Business Development, Community Development, Computer Systems, Development Assistance, Economics, Engineering, Environment, Exchange Programs, Fisheries, Forestry, Gender and Development, Human Rights, Humanitarian Relief, Media/Communications, Medical Health, Micro-Enterprises, Project Management, Technical Assistance, Volunteer, Water Resources

The Canadian Centre for International Studies and Cooperation (CECI) promotes sustainable development through the fulfilment of four objectives: 1) to fully involve Canadians in international development as cooperants, preparing them to be effective development agents overseas and in Canada; 2) to provide support to developing country partners in their efforts to cope with their biophysical, socioeconomic and cultural environment 3) to take part in the ongoing exchange of ideas on international cooperation, and 4) to educate the Canadian public towards building equitable relations with developing countries.

CECI meets these objectives mainly through operations in three areas: the Volunteers Program, the Development Studies and Projects Program, and youth programs.

Since its inception over 30 years ago, CECI has developed expertise in several sectors and has put emphasis on four key areas: grassroots development, human resources, organizational development, and gender and development. Types of support to developing country partners includes assistance in the planning of projects and programs, joint research for funding sources and negotiation of funding agreements, implementation and/or co-management of projects, assigning cooperants (volunteers or other professionals), and liaising between similar organizations in Canada and the South.

CECI currently has 50 staff based in Canada, 75 paid staff and 200 volunteers overseas. Desired education and background varies. CECI maintains a data bank for résumés and posts job openings on their web site. CECI also offers internships though youth programs, involving two to six months work in developing countries. [ID:6025]

Centre de coopération internationale en santé et développement inc.
Pavillon de l'Est, 2180, chemin Ste-Foy,
Québec, Québec G1K 7P4; (418) 656-5525, fax (418) 656-2627, ccisd@ccisd.org, www.ccisd.org

LARGE DEVELOPMENT ASSISTANCE GROUP: Community Development, Development Assistance, Development Education, Health/Medical, Project Management

Le Centre de coopération internationale en santé et développement inc. (CCISD inc.) est maintenant un organisme à but non lucratif dont la principale mission est de favoriser la formation de partenariats avec d'autres institutions, organismes ou entreprises, domaine où il a acquis une expérience unique. Sur le terrain, le CCISD inc. privilégie la participation des clientèles locales (ministères, agents de santé, communauté) à la définition et à l'exécution des projets dans une perspective de développement durable. Ses projets s'inscrivent dans les grandes problématiques de santé internationale : réforme des systèmes de santé, décentralisation, autofinancement des services, promotion de la santé des femmes, santé de la reproduction dont la lutte contre le sida intégrée aux services de santé de base et formations adaptées aux besoins. [ID:5312]

Centre for International Statistics at the Canadian Council on Social Development (CCSD)

441 MacLaren Street, 4th Floor, Ottawa, Ontario K2P 2H3;
(613) 236-8977, fax (613) 236-2750, council@ccsd.ca, www.ccsd.ca

SMALL INFORMATION SERVICES FIRM: Advocacy, Economics, Gender and Development

The Canadian Council on Social Development (CCSD) maintains the Centre for International Statistics to complement its own research. Six researchers, none with international responsibilities, compile international statistics for comparison with Canadian statistics. The centre occasionally hires researchers for specific projects, always Canada-based, but does not specifically seek job candidates with international experience. The CCSD maintains a data bank for résumés. [ID:6801]

Change for Children Association (CFCA)

10545 - 92 Street, Edmonton, Alberta T5H 1VI; (403) 448-1505, fax (403) 448-1507, cfca@web.net

MID-SIZED COMMUNITY DEVELOPMENT GROUP: Community Development, Development Assistance, Development Education, Project Management

Change for Children Association (CFCA) primarily undertakes grassroots projects in Latin America and the Caribbean. Indigenous cooperants determine project sectors, priorities, and costs. They also administer and implement projects. In Canada, CFCA has an extensive development education program that educates Canadians on such issues as social justice, international cooperation and the root causes of poverty.

CFCA has two staff: one in charge of project management and financial administration of the organization, another responsible for the development education program. CFCA has numerous volunteers in Canada and hundreds of indigenous volunteers overseas. Canadians wishing to visit CFCA's overseas projects must do so at their own expense and initiative.

For employment in Canada, CFCA requires a strong commitment to the ideals of development assistance and social justice. Depending on the position, applicants should have strong administrative skills or a meaningful background in international development combined with an ability to articulate the concepts of development and social justice. CFCA maintains a data bank for résumés. [ID:6027]

Christian Blind Mission International (CBMI)

P.O. Box 800, Stouffville, Ontario L4A 7Z9; (905) 640-6464,
fax (905) 640-4332, cbmican@compuserve.com, http://cbmi-can.org

LARGE SPECIAL NEEDS GROUP: Administration, Adult Training, Community Development, Humanitarian Relief, Logistics, Medical Health, Project Management, Teaching, Technical Assistance

Christian Blind Mission International (CBMI) assists blind and physically challenged people in developing countries, operates blindness prevention programs, runs schools for blind and deaf students, and organizes rehabilitation workshops. The objective is to train nationals to continue assistance without foreign help. CBMI employs 154 paid staff overseas and 34 in Canada. CBMI also employs over 10,000 skilled nationals.

Applicants should have work experience corresponding to CBMI's mandate in a specific country, usually in teaching. But as a medical mission, CBMI also requires physiotherapists, agriculturalists, special education teachers for blind and deaf students, ophthalmologists and ophthalmic-trained nurses. CBMI maintains a data bank for résumés. Applicants should be willing to work in a Christian environment. Although no formal internship program exists, internships have occasionally been organized for medical students and others working with people with disabilities. [ID:6028]

Christian Children's Fund of Canada (CCFC)
1027 McNicoll Ave., Scarborough, Ontario M1W 3X2; (416) 495-1174, fax (416) 495-9395, ccfc@web.net

LARGE DEVELOPMENT ASSISTANCE GROUP: Accounting, Administration, Adult Training, Agriculture, Business Development, Community Development, Computer Systems, Development Assistance, Development Education, Environment, Exchange Programs, Fisheries, Forestry, Fundraising, Gender and Development, Human Resources, Human Rights, Humanitarian Relief, Micro-Enterprises, Project Management, Teaching, Technical Assistance, Volunteer, Water Resources

Christian Children's Fund of Canada (CCFC) provides financial and technical assistance to several hundred childcare and community development projects in 20 developing countries. Programs begin by trying to meet the basic needs of children: adequate food, water, housing, clothing, education and healthcare. Additional programs provide basic development services such as potable water, irrigation, housing projects, and sanitation. In selected projects, CCFC cooperates with the community in developing programs for income generation, food production, education, and institutional strengthening to achieve self-sufficiency.

CCFC has 45 staff in Canada. All overseas work is done in partnership with indigenous church or community agencies in an effort to strengthen their organizations and encourage participation in programs affecting the lives of themselves and their children. CCFC seeks workers with skills in education, healthcare, agriculture, sanitation, engineering related to irrigation and water projects, small business management, and basic construction. Multilingualism and strong planning and administrative skills are also assets.

International Skills in Service (ISIS), a program of CCFC, looks for skilled volunteers for short- and long-term placements. Candidates must be self-directed, work well under very limited supervision, and be able to find solutions to the inevitable problems that occur in a development project. Applicants must commit to an egalitarian relationship with partners in developing countries. CCFC maintains a data bank for résumés and considers internship appications on an individual basis. [ID:6029]

Christian Reformed World Relief Committee of Canada (CRWRC)
P.O. Box 5070, 3475 Mainway, Burlington, Ontario L7R 3Y8;
(905) 336-2920, fax (905) 336-8344, knight@crcnet.mhs.compuserve.com, www.crcna.org

LARGE DEVELOPMENT ASSISTANCE GROUP: Adult Training, Agriculture, Business Development, Community Development, Development Education, Fisheries, Micro-Enterprises, Project Management, Religious, Teaching, Water Resources

The Christian Reformed World Relief Committee of Canada (CRWRC) promotes community development in the South. It assists local groups to identify their own and others' basic needs, and to respond appropriately and compassionately to those needs.

CRWRC has eight employees in Canada. There are 61 salaried staff and six volunteers overseas. Staff and volunteers come from both Canada and the US (through CRWRC USA). They work in 25 countries in Asia, Africa, and Latin America, and provide management consulting in agriculture, health, literacy, income generation, sanitation, and diaconal development.

CRWRC hires a variety of skilled, mission-minded Christians. Most have training or comparable experience in agriculture, health, social work, literacy, management, or community development. Most have college degrees, and many have advanced degrees. CRWRC maintains a data bank for résumés. [ID:6030]

CLUB 2/3

Suite 1, 1671 Henri-Bourassa Blvd. E., Montréal, Québec
H2C 1J4; (514) 382-7922, fax (514) 382-3474, www.mlink.net/~2tiers

LARGE DEVELOPMENT EDUCATION GROUP: Administration, Development Education,
Education, Global Communication, Youth and Development

CLUB 2/3 uses development projects as a basis for global education and the promotion of intercultural understanding among Canadian youth, primarily high school students. Projects are multi-sectoral and are generally executed in the following core areas: Burkina Faso, Cameroon, Chad, Senegal, El Salvador, Brazil, Bolivia, Peru, Haiti, Nepal, China, and the Philippines. Canadian high school students and youth overseas are directly engaged in projects involving such activities as the preparation of kits for youth overseas or the sale of Southern products in Canada. One example of a project recently initiated by CLUB 2/3 is an international contest requiring the construction of toys from recycled materials.

CLUB 2/3 has one staff person overseas and 20 in Canada. Depending on the position available, CLUB 2/3 looks for people with administrative skills, international experience, knowledge of the NGO community, or a background in education. The group maintains a data bank for résumés. [ID:6031]

Coady International Institute

St. Francis Xavier University, P.O. Box 5000, Antigonish, N.S. B2G 2W5;
(902) 867-3960, fax (902) 867-3907, ogladkik@stfx.ca, www.stfx.ca/institutes/coady

LARGE ORGANIZATIONAL TRAINING GROUP: Adult Training, Advocacy, Community
Development, Development Education, Environment, Gender and Development, Human Rights,
Media/Communications, Micro-Enterprises, Project Management

The Coady International Institute is committed to the growth of a more just, humane, inclusive, participatory, and sustainable society. It promotes this by providing training, consultancies, participatory evaluation, and technical assistance to organizations working with disadvantaged communities in the South. Areas of expertise include people-based development, adult education, micro-enterprise development and gender and development. The training is offered in Canada at Antigonish, and in Southern countries in cooperation with and the request of groups and institutions. The institute also engages in development education, mainly in Atlantic Canada.

The institute has 10 full-time teaching staff. It looks for candidates at the MA and PhD levels with expertise in adult education, community development, cooperatives and credit unions, program planning, implementation, and evaluation. International experience in people-based development is preferred.

The COADY Institute keeps résumés on file for two years. Youth internships are funded separately. Qualifications, duration and honorariums vary and depend upon the program offering funding. Potential applicants should check the web site for announcements regarding openings and new intern opportunities. [ID:6032]

CoDevelopment Canada (CoDev)

Executive Director, Suite 205, 2929 Commercial Drive,
Vancouver, B.C. V5N 4C8; (604) 708-1495, fax (604) 708-1497, codev@web.net

MID-SIZED DEVELOPMENT EDUCATION GROUP: Advocacy, Community Development,
Development Assistance, Development Education, Environment, Fundraising, Gender and
Development, Human Rights, Intercultural Briefings, Teaching

CoDevelopment Canada (CoDev) is a nonprofit agency founded in 1985 to promote alliances between people in Canada and the developing world. CoDev has channelled extensive support to educators in Latin American, providing training in women's leadership and guidance in the development of educational policy. CoDev has similarly supported health and legal education for women in unions and local communities and education for the disabled. Other initiatives include international exchanges and resources for schools.

CoDev has three staff based in Canada. [ID:6410]

Collaboration santé internationale (CSI)
1001, de la Canardière, Québec, Québec G1J 5G5;
(418) 522-6065, fax (418) 522-5530, csi@quebectel.com

MID-SIZED MEDICAL ASSISTANCE GROUP: Health/Medical, Medical Health, Volunteer

L'organisation CSI oeuvre dans le domaine de la santé en approvisionnant en médicaments et en équipements médicaux les missionnaires canadiens basés outre-mer et dont la communauté a un établissement au Québec. Toute personne désirant s'impliquer dans l'organisation devra être un professionnel de la santé, un pharmacien ou un infirmier. La CSI ne considère que des candidats bénévoles. [ID:6033]

Compassion Canada
International Division, P.O. Box 5591, London, Ontario
N6A 5G8; (519) 668-0224, fax (519) 685-1107, www.web.net/compassion

LARGE RELIEF AND DEVELOPMENT AGENCY: Agriculture, Media/Communications, Religious, Teaching, Volunteer

Compassion Canada is a Christian child development organization with programs in 20 developing countries. These countries include Kenya, Ethiopia, Uganda, Mexico, and Guatemala. The agency focuses on community development projects such as micro-enterprise, agroforestry, healthcare, literacy, water, and agriculture.

Compassion Canada has 20 staff located in Canada and one serving in Africa. [ID:6034]

Cooperation Canada Mozambique (COCAMO)
Suite 307, 323 Chapel Street, Ottawa, Ontario K1N 7Z2;
(613) 233-4033, fax (613) 233-7266, cocamo@magma.ca, www.cocamo.com

SMALL COORDINATING BODY: Administration, Agriculture, Civil Society, Community Development, Development Education, Logistics, Medical Health

Cooperation Canada Mozambique (COCAMO) is a coalition of 15 Canadian NGOs operating a long-term development program in Nampula, Mozambique. The coalition supports local NGOS working in education, water, agriculture, small industries, health, and development education in Mozambique and Canada. COCAMO employs three staff in Canada and Mozambique. [ID:6036]

Council of Canadians with Disabilities (CCD)
Suite 926, 294 Portage Ave., Winnipeg, Manitoba R3C 0B9;
(204) 947-0303, fax (204) 942-4625, ccd@pcs.mb.ca, www.pcs.mb.ca/ccd

SMALL INTERNATIONAL ADVOCACY GROUP: Micro-Enterprises

The Council of Canadians with Disabilities (CCD) is the national voice of people with disabilities. It has a small international program whose primary focus is to provide development education to NGOs and the disabled community about the needs and concerns of disabled people in developing countries. Physically disabled consultants work with NGOs with related goals in the Caribbean and Central America to build solidarity between those with similar experiences of oppression and marginalization.

CCD has seven salaried staff based in Canada. [ID:6037]

Cultural Survival

Suite 304, 200 Isabella Street, Ottawa, Ontario K1S 1V7;
(613) 237-5361, fax (613) 237-1547, csc@web.net, www.cscanada.org/~csc

SMALL DEVELOPMENT ASSISTANCE GROUP: Administration, Advocacy, Community Development, Development Assistance, Development Education, Environment, Exchange Programs, Forestry, Fundraising, Gender and Development, Human Resources, Human Rights, Intercultural Briefings, Media/Communications, Project Management, Teaching, Technical Assistance, Volunteer

Cultural Survival's mandate is to support indigenous people's struggles for self-determination including supporting the pursuit of sustainable economies, gender equity, rights to cultural and environmental integrity, rights to land, resources, intellectual property, and genetic property.

Cultural Survival has seven employees in Canada and between three and 10 employees overseas. Employees have a strong interest and knowledge of issues facing indigenous people's worldwide. They also have specific knowledge for specific projects in the areas of humanitarianism, publishing, forests, traditional agriculture, sustainable development, and tourism. Cultural Survival maintains a data bank for résumés and also considers summer interns who have relevant expertise. Honorariums for these internships are dependent on the program. [ID:7056]

CUSO

Suite 400, 2255 Carling Ave., Ottawa, Ontario K2B 1A6;
(613) 829-7445, fax (613) 829-7996, cuso.secretariat@cuso.ca, www.cuso.org

LARGE VOLUNTEER GROUP: Administration, Adult Training, Advocacy, Agriculture, Business Development, Community Development, Consulting, Development Assistance, Development Education, Environment, Fisheries, Forestry, Fundraising, Gender and Development, Intercultural Briefings, Medical Health, Micro-Enterprises, Project Management, Volunteer, Water Resources

CUSO is a Canadian organization which supports alliances for global justice. CUSO works with people striving for freedom, self-determination, gender and racial equality, and cultural survival. CUSO achieves its goals by sharing information, human and material resources, and by promoting policies for developing global sustainability.

CUSO has three main areas of activity: it recruits skilled Canadians to work on two-year postings in developing countries; it funds locally-controlled, sustainable projects that are sensitive to the environment and to women's issues; and it raises public awareness in Canada of international development issues and the causes of global economic imbalances.

CUSO employs about 70 staff in Ottawa and about 65 overseas. Most have some experience in international development.

CUSO also has about 230 volunteers at any one time (known within CUSO as cooperants because of their cooperative role with Southern partners), working on two-year contracts in developing countries. They include health workers, tradespeople, engineers, fisheries advisors, forestry specialists, agriculturalists, teachers and community development workers. All are experienced in their fields and have academic qualifications or trade papers. In some cases (forestry and fisheries, for example), many years of on-the-job experience is sufficient. Cooperants are generally paid a local wage adequate to cover overseas living costs and provided with a benefits package. For staff positions in Canada and overseas, apply to the Human Resources Department of the Ottawa Office. For cooperant postings, apply to a local CUSO office or to the Cooperant Programming Unit of the Ottawa office. [ID:6038]

Developing Countries Farm Radio Network (DCFRN)

Box 12, Suite 227B, 40 Dundas Street W., Toronto, Ontario M5G 2C2;
(416) 593-7279, fax (416) 593-3752, dcfrn@web.net, www.web.net/~dcfrn/

MID-SIZED MEDIA DEVELOPMENT GROUP: Administration, Agriculture, Fundraising,
Media/Communications, Volunteer

The Developing Countries Farm Radio Network (DCFRN) researches and produces
radio scripts on simple, practical methods of farming, health, and nutrition relevant to rural
families in developing countries. It has partnerships with the Farm Information Network in
Zimbabwe for East and Southern Africa as well as with InfoReach in South Africa. DCFRN
sends scripts to professional rural communicators who pass on this information to local
farmers. DCFRN participants include radio broadcasters, extension agents, community
development workers and teachers. DCFRN has 1,500 participants in 121 countries, and
estimates that the supplied information reaches over 1.5 million farm families each month by
radio alone. Scripts are published in English, French, and Spanish.

DCFRN has six full-time staff equivalents in Canada and none overseas. It looks for
people working in the South with degrees in communications, journalism, or agriculture who
can use DCFRN material to help improve the quality of life for families. Participants in the
network must communicate with large numbers of farmers and agree to provide information
for future packages. DCFRN maintains a data bank for résumés. [ID:6039]

Développement International Desjardins (DID)

150, ave. des Commandeurs, Lévis, Québec G6V 6P8;
(418) 835-2400, fax (418) 833-0742, info@did.qc.ca, www.did.qc.ca

LARGE DEVELOPMENT ASSISTANCE GROUP: Business/Banking/Trade, Micro-Enterprises,
Project Management

DID est une corporation sans but lucratif rattachée au Mouvement des caisses
Desjardins du Québec et partenaire de l'Agence canadienne de développement international
(ACDI) Depuis près de 30 ans, DID réalise des projects dans plus de 25 pays d'Afrique,
d'Amérique latine, des Antilles, d'Asie, d'Europe Centrale et de l'Est. DID appuie plus de 50
partenaires institutionnels à renforcer la capacité d'agir des populations moins nanties en
favorisant l'accessibilité aux services financiers.

L'encadrement et la supervision des activités de la DID requièrent un appui institutionnel permanent et une infrastructure professionnelle et administrative dont les ressources
professionnelles, au nombre de 44, sont regroupées autour du siège social à Lévis. Trente
coopérants assurent l'encadrement et la supervision des activités outre-mer. Le conseiller
sur le terrain ou le consultant ponctuel doit au minimum avoir obtenu un diplôme universitaire de premier cycle en administration, en économie, en finance ou l'équivalent. Il doit
avoir cumulé au moins cinq ans d'expérience dans le domaine financier, de préférence au
sein du Mouvement Desjardins, et avoir une excellente connaissance de la gestion du crédit
et de la mobilisation de l'épargne pratiquée dans les caisses. Il doit également maîtriser les
principes de base des coopératives, s'exprimer dans deux, voire trois langues, et avoir une
excellente maîtrise du français et une bonne connaissance de l'anglais et\ou de l'espagnol.
Une description des profils demandés sera publiée sur leur site Web. [ID:6123]

Disabled Peoples International (DPI)

Suite 101, 7 Evergreen Street, Winnipeg, Manitoba R3L 2T3;
(204) 287-8010, fax (204) 453-1367, dpi@dpi.org, www.dpi.org

MID-SIZED SPECIAL NEEDS GROUP: Administration, Adult Training, Advocacy, Development
Assistance, Fundraising, Gender and Development, Human Rights

Disabled Peoples International (DPI) was founded in 1980 as a unique cross-disability
self-help coalition of disabled persons from around the world. DPI has a decentralized structure comprised of elected regional representatives from Latin America, Africa, Asia Pacific,

North America, the Caribbean, and Europe. It is based on principles of full participation and equal opportunity for disabled persons. DPI works closely with the UN to ensure that disabled peoples' needs are recognized and responded to by national and international bodies. The overall goal of DPI's self-help development program is to enhance the resources and skills of disabled persons. Specific priorities of the program are defined and addressed regionally or nationally. One of the program's main activities has been the organization of training seminars, through which participants gain the leadership qualities and marketable skills they require to take a more active role in their communities. DPI members have also initiated a variety of income-generating projects, among them a textile factory in Botswana, a technical-aids factory in Nicaragua, and a network of agricultural cooperatives in Zimbabwe.

DPI has a small staff. Canadian regional offices are in charge of their own hiring. DPI occasionally offers internships of less than one year if sponsorships are available. [ID:6041]

Earthkeeping
Executive Director, Suite 205, 10711 - 107th Ave., Edmonton, Alberta
T5H 0W6; (403) 428-6981, fax (403) 428-1581, earthkpg@web.net, www.web.net/~earthkpg/

SMALL ENVIRONMENTAL ACTION GROUP: Agriculture, Community Development, Environment, Media/Communications, Religious, Volunteer, Water Resources

Earthkeeping is a nonprofit NGO which focuses on the links, both locally and globally, between people and the earth. Earthkeeping promotes food security. It advocates environmentally sound agricultural practices for sustainable agriculture and self-sufficient communities and supports lifestyle choices that consider the impact of people on the environment.

Earthkeeping consists of 200 city and farm families throughout Alberta. They have no overseas placements, but on occasion offer study tours. Visit the Earthkeeping web site for volunteer opportunities. (For more information on Earthkeeping see Chapter 10, Short-term Programs Overseas.) [ID:6799]

Emmanuel International of Canada
P.O. Box 4050, Stouffville, Ontario L4A 8B6;
(905) 640-2111, fax (905) 640-2186, info@e-i.org, www.e-i.org

MID-SIZED EVANGELICAL GROUP: Accounting, Administration, Adult Training, Agriculture, Community Development, Forestry, Humanitarian Relief, Logistics, Medical Health, Micro-Enterprises, Project Management, Religious, Water Resources

Emmanuel International of Canada is an interdenominational, evangelical Christian relief, rehabilitation and community development agency which works through local churches to meet both spiritual and physical needs. Emmanuel seeks to give responsibility back to local church bodies by fostering partnerships between churches in Canada and churches in the South. Emmanuel currently works in Haiti, Brazil, Sudan, Tanzania, Malawi, Uganda and the Philippines. Overseas staff work under the authority of a national church in projects on primary health, water, sanitation, agricultural assistance, reforestation, income generation, cottage industry, evangelism and discipleship.

Emmanuel International of Canada is the head office for Emmanuel Relief and Rehabilitation International, an international organization with five offices worldwide. The Canadian office currently has seven staff in Canada, and 12 staff and 10 volunteers serving overseas. Applicants must be over 18 years of age and agree with Emmanuel's Statement of Faith. Emmanuel accepts mature, ministering Christians, active in, and recommended by, their local church. International experience is an asset, as is training/experience in specific project areas. Emmanuel International maintains a data bank for résumés. [ID:6043]

Evangelical Medical Aid Society (EMAS)
P.O. Box 160, Warkworth, Ontario K0K 3K0; (705) 924-2323,
fax (705) 924-3384, cmdsemas@oncomdis.on.ca, www.cmdsemas.ca

MID-SIZED EVANGELICAL GROUP: Adult Training, Human Resources, Medical Health

The Evangelical Medical Aid Society (EMAS) coordinates and organizes teaching teams of physicians, dentists, and paramedical personnel. It currently has projects in Angola, China, Cuba, Romania, and Vietnam. EMAS packs and ships medical and dental supplies for overseas needs and arranges and sponsors doctors and surgeons to go overseas. It also provides administrative instruction and support for overseas church-related health centres as well as specialized teaching and introduction of new equipment and techniques in overseas healthcare settings.

EMAS supports variable numbers of short-term overseas volunteers and has two salaried staff members in Canada. Continuing Medical Education seminars are offered for national physicians. Applicants require medical, dental or nursing degrees, medical or hospital administrative expertise, or other medically-related training. EMAS maintains a data bank for résumés. [ID:6045]

Federation of Canadian Municipalities (FCM)
International Office, 3rd Floor, 24 Clarence Street, Ottawa, Ontario
K1N 5P3; (613) 241-8484, fax (613) 241-7117, international@fcm.ca, www.fcm.ca

LARGE COMMUNITY DEVELOPMENT GROUP: Accounting, Administration, Consulting,
Development Assistance, Media/Communications, Project Management

The Federation of Canadian Municipalities (FCM) is a national organization representing the interests of local governments across Canada. Consistent with the overall mission of FCM, its International Office serves municipal governments internationally, promotes their power of action, fosters their economic opportunities, and directs local energies in pursuit of sustainable development. Through this office an extensive international program of municipal partnerships is administered which includes urban professional exchanges and training in local government through its Partnerships, Municipal Initiatives Support Fund, and Training and Research Programs. The International Office manages a large number of municipal partnerships in Africa and a major training program for municipal officials in China. It has recently expanded its focus to include municipal exchange programs and training activities in South Africa and the Czech Republic.

FCM employs 15 staff in Canada and none overseas. Generally, applicants require a university degree and work experience related to urban studies and international development. Second languages or other specialized skills and expertise are viewed as assets. FCM maintains a data bank for résumés. [ID:6046]

Fondation CRUDEM
2240, rue Fullum, Montréal, Québec H2K 3N9; (514) 527-4082, fax (514) 527-4082, j.j.legris@total.net

MID-SIZED DEVELOPMENT ASSISTANCE GROUP: Adult Training, Business Development,
Development Assistance, Gender and Development, International Education, Medical Health

La Fondation CRUDEM oeuvre dans les secteurs de l'éducation, de la santé et du développement du secteur privé. Dans l'ensemble de sa programmation, la Fondation priorise également la participation des femmes au développement et à la prise en charge de leur milieu. Bien que la Fondation ait oeuvré dans près de 17 pays différents, elle concentre maintenant son appui en Haïti et au Mali, où elle fonctionne sur une base de programmes triennaux. Les activités appuyées dans d'autres pays le sont dans une moindre mesure, c'est-à-dire à partir de fonds de projets.

Les bureaux permanents de la Fondation CRUDEM sont situés à Montréal où deux employés à temps pleins assurent la coordination de l'ensemble des activités avec les membres et partenaires outre-mer. Sur le terrain, la Fondation CRUDEM bénéficie de deux représentants, au Mali et en Haïti. La Fondation dispose également d'un bureau au Mali où l'on peut retrouver toute la documentation sur les programmes entrepris au pays. Aucun coopérant n'est engagé pour l'extérieur. [ID:6047]

Forum for International Trade Training
4th Floor, 30 Metcalfe Street, Ottawa, Ontario
K1P 5L4; (800) 561-3488, fax (613) 230-6808, corp@fitt.ca, www.fitt.ca

MID-SIZED ORGANIZATIONAL TRAINING GROUP: Business,Banking and Trade, Intercultural Briefings, International Trade

The Forum for International Trade Training (FITT) combines the resources and leadership of the federal government and private sector organizations to provide practical international business training. FITT offers trade know-how in two distinct and complementary programs. The FITTskills program is a series of eight individual courses focusing on the mechanics of international business in the core areas of entrepreneurship, marketing, trade finance, logistics, market entry, research, trade law, and international management. CustomFITT, the organization's other program, provides detailed courses in international knowledge and skills, tailored to the specific needs of businesses. Turning international business opportunities into profitable successes is emphasized.

FITT programs are delivered at more than 20 colleges and universities nation-wide. For more information call toll-free at (800) 561-3488 (230-3553 in Ottawa). FITT's web site provides information on its mandate and services and has a number of useful links to trade-related sites. [ID:7051]

Foster Parents Plan of Canada
Suite 1001, 95 St. Clair Ave. W., Toronto, Ontario
M4V 3B5; (416) 920-1654, fax (416) 920-9942, n-cno@plan-geis.com

LARGE DEVELOPMENT ASSISTANCE GROUP: Adult Training, Agriculture, Business Development, Community Development, Consulting, Development Assistance, Development Education, Medical Health, Micro-Enterprises, Technical Assistance

Plan International Canada (PLAN) recruits and maintains links with Canadian sponsors of international foster children. This involves easing communications between the sponsors here with their foster children overseas, and maintaining clerical services, public relations and marketing activities. Plan operates in 40 countries throughout the Africa, Asia, Latin America and the Caribbean.

The Canadian office has approximately 60 employees and many departments including Donor Services, Controls, Marketing, Public Relations and Creative Services. There are positions at all levels in each area. Field directors require a degree in International Development. Please sent requests for overseas employment to our international address: PLAN International, International Headquarters, Chobham Way, Woking, Surrey, UK, GU21 1JG. (For information on PLAN International see Chapter 37, International Organizations.) [ID:6412]

Fraternité Vietnam
1040, rue Jean-Dumetz, Sainte-Foy, Québec G1W 4K5; (418) 659-2845, fax (418) 659-2845

MID-SIZED DEVELOPMENT ASSISTANCE GROUP: Accounting, Adult Training, Community Development, Development Assistance, Forestry, Fundraising, Gender and Development, Teaching, Volunteer

Fraternité Vietnam supporte des oeuvres dans les domaines suivants : éducation et formation de métiers, développement social et économique, crédits pour petites et moyennes entreprises (PME), élimination de la pauvreté, promotion féminine, et enfants en difficulté au Vietnam. Cet organisme à but non lucratif est l'intermédiaire entre les donateurs et les organisations partenaires au Vietnam mettant les projets en oeuvre. Fraternité Vietnam n'a pas d'employés mais fonctionne à partir de travail bénévole. [ID:6726]

Friends of the Earth (FoE)

Suite 306, 47 Clarence Street, Ottawa, Ontario K1N 9L1;
(613) 241-0085, fax (613) 241-7998, foe@intranet.ca, www.intranet.ca/~foe

MID-SIZED INTERNATIONAL ADVOCACY GROUP: Advocacy, Environment, Fundraising

Friends of the Earth (FoE) is a local, national, and international voice for the environment. It works with and motivates others to promote sustainable communities and a sustainable global environment through research, education and advocacy. Its primary campaign areas include ozone depletion, mining, toxication, and sustainable societes. As a member of FoE International's network of 57 environmental NGOs (ENGOs), FoE's leadership, expertise and credibility is widely recognized. It is an active participant in national forums, the National Atmospheric Protection Team, and also consults in international forums such as the United Nations Environment Program and the Montréal Protocol.

FoE has five staff, numerous volunteers and over 8,000 members in Canada. FOE does not have overseas programs for employees or volunteers. [ID:6050]

Frontiers Foundation Inc.

Suite 203, 2615 Danforth Ave., Toronto, Ontario M4C 1L6;
(416) 690-3930, fax (416) 690-3934, www.amtak.com/frontiers

LARGE DEVELOPMENT ASSISTANCE GROUP: Community Development, Volunteer

Frontiers Foundation Inc. is a voluntary service organization that works in partnership with requesting rural, low-income communities across Northern Canada. The foundation works with these groups (and with occasional projects in Bolivia and Haiti) for the purpose of community advancement.

The foundation's headquarters are in Toronto, with regional offices located in Surrey, British Columbia, and Kenora and Mattawa, Ontario. Staff work primarily in volunteer recruitment, administration, and follow-up programs. Volunteers must be at least 18 years old to work on housing construction and recreation projects which last a minimum of 12 weeks. Skills in carpentry, plumbing and electrical work are preferred. Volunteers will be provided with accommodation, food, and transportation within Canada. A limited number of volunteer tutors are also needed for Arctic educational placements that entail a commitment of at least five months. If you are willing to become part of an international team, have the spirit of adventure, and are able to endure trying conditions, Frontiers Foundation is looking for you! [ID:6051]

Gems of Hope

Executive Director, Suite 1105, 8 King Street E., Toronto, Ontario M5C 1B5;
(416) 362-4367, fax (416) 362-4170, gems@web.net, www.argun.com/gemsofhope

MID-SIZED COMMUNITY DEVELOPMENT GROUP: Accounting, Administration, Community Development, Development Assistance, Development Education, Fundraising, Gender and Development, Micro-Enterprises, Project Management

Gems of Hope's mission work with local partners promotes the self-sufficiency of families and communities in the neediest areas of the developing world by supporting community development initiatives in health, local enterprise, and basic education. Gems of Hope currently has projects in Bolivia, Brazil, Haiti, and India.

Gems of Hope has three full-time staff in Canada and does not place people overseas, preferring to work with local people and organizations with the countries in which they are involved. Gems of Hope is always looking for volunteers to assist with fundraising and event planning. [ID:6053]

Global Vision

13 Berthier Street, Cantley, Québec J8V 2V5;
(819) 827-2838, fax (819) 827-2571, gvamy@ican.ca., www.globalvision.ca

SMALL EXCHANGE GROUP: International Trade

Global Vision is active in Canada and internationally. The program organizes projects to give international work experience to Canada's youth. Global Vision targets youth aged 15-25 through four programs: Junior Team Canada, training centres, Junior Team Canada Trade Missions, and Youth International Internships. Global Vision is active in the following markets: Chile, China, Europe, Japan, Korea, Singapore, Malaysia, Thailand, Mexico, Taiwan, and the southern US.

Global Vision has four employees in Canada. Employees have experience and knowledge of different economies, cultures, and languages as well as strong people skills and the ability to take on more than one project at a time. Global Vision maintains a data bank for résumés and considers interns in the areas of languages, international trade, business and economics. [ID:6682]

Greenpeace Canada

6th Floor, 185 Spadina Ave., Toronto, Ontario M5T 2C6;
(416) 597-8408, fax (416) 597-8422, www.greenpeacecanada.org

LARGE ENVIRONMENTAL ACTION GROUP: Accounting, Administration, Advocacy, Environment, Fundraising, Media/Communications

Greenpeace was established in 1971 and has evolved into a global organization with offices in over 30 countries. Greenpeace campaigns throughout the world on today's most pressing environmental issues and is known for its nonviolent direct action. Greenpeace Canada's national office is located in Toronto and has four departments: Campaigns, Development, Finance, and the Executive Director's Office. Canadian campaign offices are located at the national office in Toronto and the regional offices in Vancouver and Montréal. The Development department coordinates all fundraising and public education activities while the Finance department tracks and accounts for all income and expenditures of the organization. The Executive Director is the Canadian liaison to Greenpeace International and other Greenpeace offices around the world; this office also includes office management and human resources staff. Contact the national office to find out about job and volunteer opportunities across the country. (For information on Greenpeace International see Chapter 38, International Organizations.) [ID:6951]

The Group of 78

Suite 206, 145 Spruce Street, Ottawa, Ontario
K1R 6P1; (613) 230-0860, fax (613) 563-0017, group78@web.net

SMALL INTERNATIONAL ADVOCACY GROUP: Accounting, Administration, Arms Control, Business/Banking/Trade, Development Assistance, Editing, Fundraising, Gender and Development, Human Rights, Humanitarian Relief, International Trade, Religious, Research, Translation, Writing

The Group of 78 is an informal association of Canadians who promote global priorities for peace and disarmament, equitable development for all, and a strong and revitalized United Nations system. The Group's work includes organizing conferences to address needed changes in foreign policy, lunches with invited speakers, and producing publications on conference findings and special issues.

The Group of 78 has one paid staff member in Canada. [ID:6054]

Habitat for Humanity Canada Inc.
40 Albert Street, Waterloo, Ontario N2L 3S2;
(519) 885-4565, fax (519) 885-5225, hfhc@sentex.net, www.sentex.net/~hfhc

LARGE VOLUNTEER GROUP: Accounting, Administration, Adult Training, Architecture and
Planning, Business Development, Community Development, Computer Systems, Construction,
Consulting, Engineering, Environment, Exchange Programs, Fundraising, Human Resources,
Media/Communications, Project Management, Religious, Teaching, Water Resources

Habitat for Humanity Canada is a nonprofit, nongovernmental, ecumenical Christian
organization that works in partnership with the economically disadvantaged to help them
become homeowners. The Canadian organization operates in conjunction with Habitat for
Humanity International Inc.

Internationally, Habitat for Humanity Canada is active in over 50 countries. Volunteers
work as International Partners on long-term projects in development and construction. A
three-year commitment is required.

Volunteers work on a stipend basis and are paid their living costs. They must have an
attitude of service, of partnering with local people, and have both education and work
experience that relates to community development and home construction. Visit the Habitat
for Humanity Canada web site for volunteer information. [ID:6056]

Help the Aged
Unit 12, 99 - 5th Avenue, Ottawa, Ontario K1S 5K4;
(613) 232-0727, fax (613) 232-7625, helpage@cyberus.ca, www.cyberus.ca/~helpage/

MID-SIZED SPECIAL NEEDS GROUP: Administration, Fundraising, Project Management,
Technical Assistance

Help the Aged provides assistance to destitute elderly people in Canada and 12 developing countries. Volunteer project managers are occasionally required to coordinate special
grant programs overseas or to monitor our Adopt-a-Gran Sponsorship Program.

The organization has five staff in Canada, and works through caring organizations such
as the Salvation Army and St. Vincent de Paul. Volunteers throughout Canada are needed to
assist with the creation of Help the Aged chapters and groups. Help the Aged has a low staff
turnover, but normally looks for individuals with past work experience in the country in
which a specific grant program is offered. [ID:6057]

HOPE International Development Agency
214 - 6th Street, New Westminster, B.C. V3L 3A2;
(604) 525-5481, fax (604) 525-3471, hope@web.apc.net, www.idirect.ca/~hope

LARGE DEVELOPMENT ASSISTANCE GROUP: Accounting, Administration, Agriculture,
Community Development, Construction, Consulting, Development Assistance, Development
Education, Engineering, Environment, Forestry, Fundraising, Gender and Development, Human
Resources, Humanitarian Relief, Medical Health, Micro-Enterprises, Project Management,
Teaching, Technical Assistance, Volunteer, Water Resources

HOPE International Development Agency aims to increase self-sufficiency among the
people of developing countries through its focus on water resources and agricultural
development. Deep wells, shallow wells, spring capping, and forestry are key sectors in
which HOPE has expertise. HOPE's programming takes place in Africa, South Asia, Southeast Asia, and the Americas.

The agency has 10 staff in Canada, two staff overseas and five volunteers overseas. A
group of 15 to 20 people spend five months in part-time preparation in Canada, then up to
four months during the summer in a developing country working at the community level.
HOPE also offers a development education program for Canadians interested in overseas
development.

Qualifications include a university or technical college degree or diploma, five years
experience, a strong level of commitment to the poor, and technical transfer training skills.

Crosscultural experience is also desired. HOPE maintains a data bank for résumés and offers unpaid project management internships for a period up to one year. (For more information see HOPE's profile in Chapter 10, Short-Term Programs Overseas.) [ID:6058]

Horizons of Friendship (HOF)
P.O. Box 402, 50 Covert Street,
Cobourg, Ontario K9A 4L1; (905) 372-5483, fax (905) 372-7095, horizons@web.net

MID-SIZED DEVELOPMENT ASSISTANCE GROUP: Administration, Agriculture, Community Development, Gender and Development, Medical Health, Volunteer

Horizons of Friendship (HOF) supports community development and advocacy in Mesoamerica—the part of the hemisphere which includes Costa Rica, El Salvador, Guatemala, Honduras, Nicaragua, Panama, and Mexico. HOF incorporates gender into its joint community development projects which support health, low-cost housing, agriculture, irrigation, training of women, and indigenous communities. In keeping with HOF's efforts to strengthen local organizations and institutions in the fight against poverty, all projects work through local partners. Horizons of Friendship has no overseas positions. [ID:6059]

Human Concern International (HCI)
877 Shefford Road, Gloucester, Ontario K1J 8H9;
(613) 742-5948, fax (613) 742-7733, hei@istar.ca, http://home.istar.ca/~hci

MID-SIZED RELIEF AND DEVELOPMENT AGENCY: Agriculture, Community Development, Fundraising, Human Resources, Humanitarian Relief, Medical Health, Trades, Water Resources

Human Concern International (HCI) runs various programs in relief, development and restoration, rehabilitation and reconstruction projects aimed at self-reliance and human dignity. HCI initiates projects to help refugees and displaced people help themselves. It fully utilizes the local labour force in these projects.

The organization has 55 staff and five volunteers overseas and four staff in Canada. HCI seeks volunteer workers with degrees from recognized universities and experience dealing with refugees, displaced people and disaster victims in developing countries. Applicants must also have extensive experience in international development work, mainly in the areas of health, agriculture, and water resource projects. Sensitivity to, and full understanding of, local cultures and traditions is very important. HCI maintains a data bank for résumés. [ID:6060]

Infant Feeding Action Coalition Canada (INFACT)
10 Trinity Square, Toronto, Ontario M5G 1B1;
(416) 595-9819, fax (416) 591-9355, infact@ftn.net, www.infactcanada.ca

SMALL SPECIAL NEEDS GROUP: Infant and Youth Child Health, Maternal and Infant Nutrition

Infant Feeding Action Coalition Canada (INFACT) participates in the International Baby Food Action Network (IBFAN) and supports breastfeeding promotion and protection projects in Nicaragua and Africa. Those interested in applying to INFACT should possess a health education background, have experience in primary healthcare, and/or have worked internationally. INFACT maintains a data bank for résumés and sometimes considers internships. [ID:6061]

Institut de développement nord-sud
C.P. 1929, bureau 700, 140, 4e ave. est, La-Pocatière, Québec
G0R 1Z0; (418) 856-4327, fax (418) 856-4330, IDNS@globetrotter.net

MID-SIZED DEVELOPMENT ASSISTANCE GROUP: Adult Training, Agriculture, Consulting, Development Education, Environment, Gender and Development, Human Resources, International Education, Micro-Enterprises, Technical Assistance

L'IDNS est un organisme dont les domaines d'expertise sont: l'agriculture, la formation des élus municipaux et l'appui à la décentralisation, la réalisation et la gestion de projets à caractère environnemental (aménagement des ordures ménagères et création d'emplois). Il joue un rôle important dans la sensibilisation au développement international auprès de la population québécoise. L'IDNS poursuit des activités au Maghreb, en Haïti et en Amérique Centrale. De plus, des publications reliées au développement sont disponibles. [ID:6062]

Institute of Peace and Conflict Studies
Conrad Grebel College, University of Waterloo, Waterloo, Ontario N2L 3G6;
(519) 885-0220, fax (519) 885-0014, ipacs2@watserv1.uwaterloo.ca, www.uwaterloo.ca

SMALL INTERNATIONAL RESEARCH GROUP: Advocacy, Development Education, Exchange Programs, Research

The Institute of Peace and Conflict Studies, located within Conrad Grebel College, is involved in citizen diplomacy at the levels of research, public education and advocacy. Housed in an academic institution, it bridges the gap between academic research and the more practical work of NGOs. One of its key programs is Project Ploughshares, which undertakes research and policy development in support of Canadian Peace and Security Measures and developing political advocacy campaigns in support of those policies. The institute also supports a network of community groups across Canada that undertake peace education and participates in national campaigns. The World Order and Regional Conflict (WORC) Program—Horn of Africa, is jointly sponsored by Project Ploughshares and the Institute to monitor regional conflict and arms flow in the region.

The institute offers internships, many of which are overseas, for a period of four months. It also has a specific Internship Program which annually sends a dozen students of peace and conflict studies overseas (See Chapter 14, Study Abroad). [ID:6064]

Inter-Pares
58 Arthur Street, Ottawa, Ontario K1R 7B9; (613) 563-4801, fax (613) 594-4704

MID-SIZED INTERNATIONAL ADVOCACY GROUP: Community Development

Inter-Pares builds relationships with existing Southern groups by offering support to their locally-determined, community-based programs, their efforts to challenge the structural obstacles to self- determination, and their alternative development approaches. Inter-Pares learns from and attempts to enlighten Canadians about efforts by Southern groups, particularly through global justice advocacy at national and international levels. It currently works in Africa, Asia, Central America, and the Caribbean. Inter-Pares also links Canadian social and economic justice issues and social action at home with social change in developing countries. Inter-Pares currently has 11 staff based in Canada. [ID:6065]

Interagency Coalition on AIDS and Development (ICAD)
180 Argyle Ave., Ottawa, Ontario K2P 1B7; (613) 788-5107, fax (613) 788-5052, icad@web.net

SMALL INTERNATIONAL ADVOCACY GROUP: Development Education, Medical Health

The Interagency Coalition on AIDS and Development (ICAD) develops and promotes positions on HIV/AIDS issues, and advocates for appropriate responses to these issues among major stakeholders such as the Canadian government, NGOs, multilateral agencies, the Canadian public and the media. An important component of ICAD's work is researching the capacities, activities and attitudes of Canadian NGOs regarding AIDS prevention, support and care in the South. ICAD informs NGOs of the impact of AIDS in developing countries through its organization of workshops and conferences, the production of a bilingual newsletter, and maintenance of a comprehensive resource centre.

ICAD has one staff member in Canada. [ID:6066]

Intercultural Institute of Montréal (IIM)

4917 St. Urbain Street, Montréal, Québec H2T 2W1;
(514) 288-7229, fax (514) 844-6800, andre_giguere@lcmm.qc.ca

MID-SIZED INTERNATIONAL RESEARCH GROUP: Advocacy, Community Development, Consulting, Culture, Development Education, Environment, Human Rights, Intercultural Briefings, Religious

The Intercultural Institute of Montréal (IIM) promotes cultural pluralism, intercultural relations, and social change. It provides training programs and crosscultural studies in Canada through intercultural forums, workshops, training programs, symposia, and research on intercultural issues. The centre employs 10 staff in Canada. The IIM publishes *Interculture*, an international journal for intercultural and transdisciplinary research. [ID:6068]

International Association for Transformation (IAT)

P.O. Box 30090, Saanich Centre, Victoria, B.C. V8X 5E1; (250) 382-8113, fax (250) 382-8113

SMALL DEVELOPMENT ASSISTANCE GROUP: Agriculture, Development Education, Education, Gender and Development, Health/Medical

The International Association for Transformation (IAT) helps impoverished people in developing countries transform their living conditions. IAT's efforts are centred on community-based, small-scale, self-help programs in education, agriculture, reforestation, and healthcare.

IAT programs support initiatives by individuals and groups in the Philippines to improve their own communities and with an increasing focus on women's initiatives. The association also promotes awareness in Canada through development education programs. IAT's all-volunteer support staff in Canada work with one Canadian and 11 Filipino staff overseas. [ID:6070]

International Child Care (Canada) Inc. (ICC)

Suite 113, 2476 Argentia Road, Mississauga, Ontario L5N 6M1;
(905) 821-6318, fax (905) 821-6319, icc.canada@sympatico.ca, www.intlchildcare.org

MID-SIZED COMMUNITY HEALTH GROUP: Accounting, Business/Banking/Trade, Computer Systems, Media/Communications

International Child Care (Canada) Inc. (ICC) carries out community health and education programs in Haiti and the Dominican Republic. ICC undertakes programs for tuberculosis control, community health promotion, health for children, training for holistic health, and community-based rehabilitation. One of Haiti's leading health development agencies, ICC works in partnership with the Pan-American Health Organization, the World Health Organization (WHO) and the Canadian International Development Agency (CIDA). A Christian health development agency, ICC looks for dedicated Christian men and women willing to live in Haiti or the Dominican Republic. Candidates must also be willing to learn French/Creole and/or Spanish. Expertise in accounting, writing, and preparing project proposals is an asset. ICC maintains a résumé data bank. [ID:6071]

International Christian Aid Canada (ICA Canada)

P.O. Box 5090, 4401 Harvester Road, Burlington, Ontario L7R 4G5; (905) 632-5703, fax (905) 632-5176

LARGE RELIEF AND DEVELOPMENT AGENCY: Administration, Humanitarian Relief, Medical Health, Micro-Enterprises, Water Resources

International Christian Aid Canada (ICA Canada) conducts relief and development work in East Africa, Southeast Asia and Central America contributing in the areas of water supply, agriculture, medicine, education, and emergency relief.

There are approximately 300 salaried staff overseas, supported by eight staff in Canada. ICA Canada requires a minimum of two years previous experience in relief and development work, preferably in Asia, Africa or Latin America. Résumés are kept for three to six months. [ID:6072]

International Council for Adult Education (ICAE)
Suite 500, 720 Bathurst Street, Toronto, Ontario M5S 2R4;
(416) 588-1211, fax (416) 588-5725, icae@web.net, www.web.net/icae

MID-SIZED COORDINATING BODY: Development Education, Fundraising, Gender and Development, Human Rights, Media/Communications, Volunteer

The International Council for Adult Education (ICAE) is a nonprofit, nongovernmental federation of approximately 100 autonomous regional and national associations. Each member association is self-sufficient, generating its own funds and managing its own projects. ICAE works in several key education areas: literacy, environmental education, gender and education, and peace and human rights. It engages in a variety of activities, including creating a worldwide forum for the exchange of ideas, collaborating on projects with other organizations, strengthening NGO administrative structures, and providing information sources to NGOs and other interested parties, including a quarterly journal and newsletter.

In Canada, ICAE has a secretariat and volunteer international and regional coordinators for its programs and networks. It does not send people overseas or offer overseas placements, but it can provide contacts for those wishing to work or live abroad. Internship applications are considered on an individual basis. [ID:6073]

International Council on Social Welfare
General Secretariat, Suite 3200, 380 St. Antoine Street W., Montréal, Québec
H2Y 3X7; (514) 287-3280, fax (514) 987-1567, iscwintl@web.net, www.icsw.org/socdev/

SMALL ORGANIZATIONAL TRAINING GROUP: Human Rights

The International Council on Social Welfare (ICSW) is a nongovernmental global organization which represents a wide range of national and international member organizations that seek to advance social welfare, social justice and social development.

The Council currently has four staff based in Canada. ICSW considers internships year-round for those with expertise in social development and social and economic rights. A small monthly honorarium may be provided for these positions. [ID:6074]

International Development and Refugee Foundation (IDRF)
2201 Warden Ave., Scarborough, Ontario M1T 1V5;
(416) 497-0818, fax (416) 497-0686, idrf@web.net, www.web.net/idrf

MID-SIZED DEVELOPMENT ASSISTANCE GROUP: Agriculture, Community Development, Construction, Development Assistance, Development Education, Gender and Development, Human Resources, Humanitarian Relief, Medical Health

The International Development and Refugee Foundation (IDRF) undertakes community development activities in the areas of health, education, skills training, income generation, and sanitation. It also provides humanitarian assistance and relief in cases of war and natural disasters. IDRF primarily works in South Asia, the Horn of Africa, the Middle East, and Eastern Europe. It currently has two staff in Canada and no staff or volunteers overseas. IDRF maintains a data bank for résumés. [ID:6075]

International Development Education Resource Association (IDERA)
Suite 400, 1037 West Broadway, Vancouver, B.C. V6H 1E3;
(604) 732-1496, fax (604) 738-8400, idera@web.net, www.vcn.ba.ca./idera

SMALL DEVELOPMENT EDUCATION GROUP: Development Education,
Media/Communications

International Development Education Resource Association (IDERA) is a nonprofit educational society that provides film and video resources to educational institutions, film festivals, repertory cinemas, libraries and broadcasters. Whether they are tales from around the world or educational documentaries, IDERA's films and videos reveal perspectives not often included in the mainstream media.

IDERA assists filmmakers in their struggles to be heard in their own countries and internationally where film production and distribution is controlled by foreign interests or government media services. IDERA believes that people in developing countries must be able to represent their own cultures and histories on their own terms if they are to gain control of their social and economic destinies.

As a part of its overseas programs, IDERA assists independent film producers from Latin America, Africa and Asia to gain access to the North American market, by distributing their films in Canada and by arranging professional exchanges and workshops.

IDERA welcomes volunteers to its community programming activities, and offers film and media-related internships through which Canadians can gain valuable experience at home or overseas. IDERA offers internships which, along with volunteer openings, are posted on the WorldWorks page of the IDERA web site. [ID:6076]

International Federation of L'Arche
6644 boul. Monk, Montréal, Québec H4E 3J1; (514) 761-7307, fax (514) 761-0823, www.larchecanada.org

MID-SIZED SPECIAL NEEDS GROUP: Humanitarian Relief, Volunteer

L'Arche is an international federation of communities in which people with developmental disability and their assistants live, work, pray and share their lives together. There are over 100 L'Arche communities in 22 countries. The organization operates in India, Haiti, Honduras, Australia, Dominican Republic, Mexico, Brazil and throughout Africa and Europe. Only volunteers are sent overseas.

The most important requirement is the desire to share daily life with people with a mental challenge. Applicants must be mature, responsible, and have lived at least 12 months with L'Arche Canada before going overseas. Rather than a job or a career, L'Arche is a way of life based on the Gospel, where faithful relationships, forgiveness and celebration reveals God's personal presence and love. [ID:5978]

International Institute for Sustainable Development
6th Floor, 161 Portage Ave. E., Winnipeg, Manitoba
R3B 0Y4; (204) 958-7700, fax (204) 958-7710, info@iisd.ca, http://iisd.ca

SMALL ENVIRONMENTAL ACTION GROUP: Accounting, Administration, Agriculture, Business Development, Community Development, Development Assistance, Development Education, Economics, Energy Resources, Environment, Fisheries, Forestry, Fundraising, International Trade, Media/Communications

The mission of the International Institute for Sustainable Development (IISD) is to promote sustainable development in decision-making, both in Canada and internationally. IISD contributes new knowledge and concepts, analyzes policies, identifies and disseminates information about best practices, demonstrates how to measure progress, and builds partnerships to amplify these messages. IISD is involved in the following program areas: business strategies, trade and sustainable development, community adaptation and sustainable livelihoods, measurements and indicators, common security, and information and communication.

IISD has 50 employees in Canada and 10 overseas. Employees have knowledge of sustainable development policies and considerable international experience. IISD maintains a data bank for résumés. Job postings can be found on the IISD web site. [ID:6403]

International Society of Bangladesh (ISB)
P.O. Box 113, Pointe-Claire, Québec H9R 4A5; (514) 630-7765, fax (514) 426-9497

SMALL INTERNATIONAL RESEARCH GROUP: Development Education, Research, Volunteer

The International Society of Bangladesh (ISB) is a voluntary research organization whose mission is to identify medium- to long-term social and economic problems in Bangladesh, and to provide an international forum on possible solutions to these problems. To this end, ISB sponsors and supports national and international study, research and seminars which promote public awareness of these issues. ISB has three staff and 60 volunteers in Canada, and 20 volunteers overseas. [ID:6080]

Jamaican Self-Help Organization
P.O. Box 1992, Unit C, 227 George Street,
Peterborough, Ontario K9J 7X7; (705) 743-1671, fax (705) 743-4020

MID-SIZED COMMUNITY DEVELOPMENT GROUP: Development Assistance, Development Education

Jamaican Self-Help forms partnerships with disadvantaged groups in Jamaica. Its goal is to improve services in health, education, skills training, housing and community development, and to bring Canadians to a deeper understanding of North-South issues such as poverty, debt, cultural integrity and global interdependence.

Jamaican Self-Help is currently involved in 10 projects with its partner organization in Jamaica, Jamaican Self-Help Partners. It has two part-time staff and 100 volunteers in Canada. [ID:6081]

Jeunesse du monde (JDM)
920, rue Richelieu, Québec, Québec G1R 1L2; (418) 694-1222,
fax (418) 694-1227, jeune@jeunessedumonde.qc.ca, www.jeunessedumonde.qc.ca

SMALL DEVELOPMENT EDUCATION GROUP: Development Assistance, Development Education, Human Rights, Youth and Development

Jeunesse du monde est une organisation sans but lucratif. Ses objectifs comprennent l'éducation et la formation des jeunes de 13 à 25 ans à la solidarité internationale, au développement et à l'entraide communautaire. Pour ce faire, elle intervient dans les milieux scolaires canadiens, dans les milieux religieux et culturels et reste présente en Afrique, en Asie et en Amérique latine. Pour l'information sur différents pays, visiter leur site web. [ID:6083]

Manitoba Council for International Co-operation (MCIC)
Suite 202, 583 Ellice Ave., Winnipeg, Manitoba R3B 1Z7;
(204) 786-2106, fax (204) 956-0031, mcic@web.net, www.escape.ca/~mcic

MID-SIZED COORDINATING BODY: Administration, Advocacy, Community Development, Development Assistance, Development Education, Fundraising, Humanitarian Relief

The Manitoba Council for International Co-operation (MCIC) is an umbrella organization which supports the international development efforts of a number of Manitoban NGOs. It coordinates information and resources among its members and promotes public awareness of development issues in Manitoba by holding workshops, sponsoring speakers, and distributing literature.

MCIC administers the Manitoba Government Matching Grant Program. MCIC employs two permanent staff in Canada. While it does not arrange overseas employment, it does act as an information resource for those interested in becoming involved in any of its member agencies, which operate throughout the developing world.

For its office staff, MCIC seeks team players with good interpersonal, oral, writing and word processing skills, as well as experience in international development. [ID:6085]

MAP-Canada
356 Sherbrooke Street E., Montréal, Québec H2X 1E6; (514) 843-7875, fax (514) 843-3061

MID-SIZED MEDICAL ASSISTANCE GROUP: Medical Health

MAP-Canada provides medical assistance and funding to health centres and community development projects in Lebanon, Jordan and Palestine. Through its office in Jerusalem, MAP-Canada works closely with its local partners, which identify projects defined by the local population in the areas of health, education, gender and development, the environment, agriculture and fisheries. It also provides technical assistance and humanitarian assistance and relief where necessary. In Canada, MAP-Canada publishes a quarterly newsletter and regularly sponsors lectures, film and video screenings, theatrical performances and other cultural events.

MAP-Canada's staff consists of two full-time employees and several volunteers in Canada, and one staff member based in Jerusalem. Work is primarily in the areas of fundraising, documentation, lobbying and public relations. Staff are usually university-educated, with some experience in project development and management. MAP-Canada also hires experts on a contract basis. [ID:6086]

Marquis Project
Executive Director, 711 Rosser Ave., Brandon, Manitoba
R7A 0K8; (204) 727-5675, fax (204) 727-5683, marquis@docker.com

SMALL DEVELOPMENT ASSISTANCE GROUP: Accounting, Administration, Adult Training, Agriculture, Arms Control, Community Development, Computer Systems, Consulting, Development Assistance, Development Education, Environment, Exchange Programs, Forestry, Fundraising, Gender and Development, Human Resources, Human Rights, Intercultural Briefings, Media/Communications, Medical Health, Micro-Enterprises, Project Management, Tourism, Water Resources

The Marquis Project is a non-profit, charitable organization which tries to educate Canadians on international development issues. Marquis is active in partnerships with NGOs in Central America and East Africa/Horn of Africa. The Marquis' work supports the emancipation of women and children and concentrates on environmental concerns, including organic production and reforestation. The group is also active in development education with schools and youth and operates a "Worldly Goods" craftshop as part of its educational and fundraising work.

The Marquis Project has four staff based in Canada. The project currently has a CIDA-funded intern and welcomes other inquiries and proposals. (For more information on the Marquis Project see Chapter 13, Global Education Centres.) [ID:6415]

MATCH International Centre
Suite 1102, 200 Elgin Street, Ottawa, Ontario
K2P 1L5; (613) 238-1312, fax (613) 238-6867, matchint@web.net

MID-SIZED COMMUNITY DEVELOPMENT GROUP: Accounting, Administration, Gender and Development

MATCH International Centre supports women through overseas project funding and education in Canada. MATCH and its sister organizations in the South are committed to a feminist vision of development: the eradication of all forms of injustice, in particular, the exploitation and marginalization of women. Current programs: Violence against Women, Words of Women, Women and Sustainable Human Development, Women's Organizing and

MATCH's Resource Clearing House. Programs focus on Africa, Asia, Latin America, and the Caribbean.

MATCH employs 10 staff in Canada. It does not send people overseas and has no overseas offices. Candidates must have educational and work experience relevant to MATCH's job positions. Candidates must also be active in the feminist movement. MATCH is an affirmative action employer. [ID:6087]

Médecins Sans Frontières / Doctors Without Borders (MFS)

Recruitment Manager, Suite 5B, 355 Adelaide Street,
Toronto, Ontario M5V 1S2; (416) 586-9820, fax (416) 586-9821, msfcan@passport.ca, www.msf.org

LARGE MEDICAL ASSISTANCE GROUP: Advocacy, Construction, Engineering, Humanitarian Relief, Logistics, Medical Health, Volunteer, Water Resources

Médecins Sans Frontières / Doctors Without Borders (MSF) is an international emergency medical relief organization that works with populations affected by war, political instability, epidemics and natural disasters. It provides care regardless of race, religion, or political affiliation. MSF Canada focuses on the recruitment of field personnel, fundraising and education. Over 300 Canadians have worked with MSF, most in refugee or displaced persons camps. MSF operates projects in over 70 countries, with about 2,500 expatriate volunteers departing each year. A large proportion of the volunteers' responsibilities includes supervision and training of local staff. MSF provides a volunteer contract that covers travel, food, accommodation, full insurance, and a monthly stipend. Initial contracts range from nine to 12 months.

MSF sends a wide variety of health professionals, but is in greatest need of medical doctors. Physicians with experience in small surgery, obstetrics, public health, tropical medicine, and training of personnel are desirable. Specialists and nurses with at least two years of practical experience in Canada are also in demand. In some cases, "paramedical" personnel such as lab technicians, nutritionists or physiotherapists are required. MSF also uses four types of non-medical personnel: technical logisticians, general logisticians, financial controllers, and a limited number of country managers. Generally country managers must have prior MSF experience, but persons with strong experience in management of development or relief projects should apply.

All applicants should have travel experience, and preferably work experience, in developing countries. They should be flexible, energetic and able to work in a team setting. Interest in and sensitivity to other cultures as well as the ability to speak and write in English is essential. Applicants who can function in French, Spanish or Portuguese have a much better chance of placement. Visit their web site for more information. [ID:6088]

Mennonite Brethren Missions/Services (MBM/S)

Suite 2, 169 Riverton Ave., Winnipeg, Manitoba R2L 2E5;
(204) 669-6575, fax (204) 654-1865, http://mobynet.com~mbms

MID-SIZED EVANGELICAL GROUP: Community Development, Religious

Mennonite Brethren Missions/Services (MBM/S) sends missionaries to communities all over the world, including Latin America, Asia, Africa, and Europe, primarily to engage in church-planting and community development activities. MBM/S currently works in 22 countries. MBM/S has four full- and one part-time Canadian staff who coordinate the Missions' international services. Visit their web site for job postings and missionary and service-related opportunities. [ID:6089]

Mennonite Central Committee, Canada (MCC Canada)
Personnel Services, 134 Plaza Drive, Winnipeg, Manitoba R3T 5K9;
(204) 261-6381, fax (204) 269-9875, prs@mennonitecc.ca, www.mennonitecc.ca

---

LARGE RELIEF AND DEVELOPMENT AGENCY: Adult Training, Agriculture, Community
Development, Development Assistance, Development Education, Environment, Exchange
Programs, Humanitarian Relief, Religious, Teaching, Technical Assistance, Volunteer

The Mennonite Central Committee (MCC) is the relief and development agency of the
Mennonite and Brethren in Christ Churches in Canada. MCC works in Africa, Europe, the
Middle East, Asia, and Latin America in the areas of development, emergency relief, social
concerns, peace, and justice.

MCC is involved in a broad range of projects in agriculture, education, economic and
technical development, health, and social services. It has over 900 volunteers, of which about
400 are based overseas on three-year assignments in over 50 countries. MCC covers travel
costs and provides a subsistence allowance.

MCC overseas assignments generally require a university or college degree. Candidates must be active members of a Christian church and show commitment to a lifestyle of
non-violence and peacemaking. The MCC web site posts specialized and urgent openings
and also gives information about volunteering with MCC. [ID:6090]

Mennonite Economic Development Associates (MEDA)
Suite 302, 280 Smith Street, Winnipeg, Manitoba R3C 1K2;
(204) 944-1995, fax (204) 942-4001, 102556@Compuserve.com, www.meda.org

---

LARGE DEVELOPMENT ASSISTANCE GROUP: Adult Training, Agriculture,
Business/Banking/Trade, Economics, Human Resources, Micro-Enterprises, Project
Management, Technical Assistance

Mennonite Economic Development Associates (MEDA) promotes economic growth
with equity for the benefit of, and in partnership with, disadvantaged groups in developing
countries. MEDA operates in Latin America, the Caribbean, and East Africa.

MEDA has one volunteer and eight North American staff overseas (where it employs
150 nationals), and 31 staff in North America. Areas of expertise are small business development projects and rural business development programs. Candidates must have overseas
experience, appropriate language ability, related university degrees, management experience, and commitment to the Christian faith. MEDA maintains a data bank for résumés.
Although it does not have its own internship program, MEDA will consider collaborating
with other organizations in placing interns. Visit their web site for job postings. [ID:6091]

Mission Aviation Fellowship Canada (MAF Canada)
P.O. Box 368, Guelph, Ontario N1H 6K5;
(519) 821-3914, fax (519) 823-1650, pgoodwin@maf.org, www.mafc.org

---

LARGE RELIEF AND DEVELOPMENT AGENCY: Accounting, Administration, Adult Training,
Air Transportation, Community Development, Computer Systems, Construction, Development
Assistance, Development Education, Humanitarian Relief, Media/Communications, Religious,
Teaching, Technical Assistance, Telecommunications

Mission Aviation Fellowship of Canada (MAF Canada) is part of a worldwide aviation
association supporting Christian outreach and humanitarian assistance in over 30 developing
countries. MAF Canada serves the transportation and radio communication needs of close to
400 different overseas agencies by providing air support for hospitals, schools, water
projects, agricultural improvement projects, medical clinics, and church outreach. Much of
MAF Canada's work is medical, and has helped save thousands of lives. Most flying is to
remote and inhospitable parts of the world, using tiny, primitive airstrips with minimal or no
navigational or radio aids.

MAF Canada currently has 40 staff overseas and employs 10 in Canada. It seeks
workers with a Christian commitment. Pilots must have commercial and instrument ratings,

with a minimum of 500 hours of flying time, and aircraft mechanics must possess an AME or A & P, and have at least two years of experience. MAF Canada maintains a data bank for résumés and offers aircraft mechanical apprenticeships. [ID:6092]

The North-South Institute (NSI)
Suite 200, 55 Murray Street, Ottawa, Ontario K1N 5M3;
(613) 241-3535, fax (613) 241-7435, nsi@nsi-ins.ca, www.nsi-ins.ca

LARGE INTERNATIONAL RESEARCH GROUP: Accounting, Business/Banking/Trade, Civil Society, Conflict Prevention, Corporate Ethics, Economics, Gender and Development, Human Rights, International Trade, Media/Communications, Micro-Enterprises, Project Management, Resource Centre Management, States and Markets, Statistics

The North-South Institute (NSI) is an independent, nonprofit and nonpartisan organization that conducts policy-relevant research on relations and cooperation between industrialized and developing countries. Its main areas of research are international finance, trade, states and markets, civil society, conflict prevention, gender and development, and social equity. The NSI works to stimulate other groups and individuals in Canada to collaborate on research into important issues and to exchange views and information.

The institute employs 20 staff in Canada. Research staff have graduate degrees or work experience in the above areas of research. Researchers do hire interns and honorariums vary. The NSI maintains a data bank for résumés and job openings are posted on the NSI web site. [ID:6093]

OMF International
Director of Public Ministries, 5759 Coopers Ave., Mississauga, Ontario
L4Z 1R9; (905) 568-9971, fax (905) 568-9974, gdykema@omf.ca, www.omf.ca

LARGE EVANGELICAL GROUP: Administration, Adult Training, Community Development, Human Resources, Medical Health, Religious, Teaching, Volunteer

OMF International is committed to a crosscultural ministry of evangelism and church-planting in 18 nations of East Asia along the Pacific Rim, ranging from Japan to Indonesia. It provides professional services, usually at the university level, in community development and medical assistance. OMF International is comprised of over 1,000 members. Of the approximately 120 Canadian members, about one-fifth of them help to recruit, screen, enable people to serve in Asia, and give administrative support.

OMF qualifications cover areas of university, college and Bible training, and experience in churches or para-church organizations. All members must be in agreement with the doctrine of the fellowship. OMF International operates a short-term volunteer program for university students. Members may benefit from an academic in-service training program. Approximately 90 Canadian staff and 20 volunteers work overseas. A minimum of four years of college is generally required; some professional services require a doctorate. Formal theological education should be part of an applicant's educational background as well as evidence of the practice of Biblical principles. OMF maintains a data bank for résumés. Visit the OMF web site for more information. [ID:6094]

Ontario Council for International Cooperation (OCIC)
Suite 612, 590 Jarvis Street, Toronto, Ontario M4Y 2J4;
(416) 972-6303, fax (416) 972-6996, ocic@web.net, www.web.net/~ocic

SMALL COORDINATING BODY: Administration, Advocacy, Development Education, Environment, Fundraising, Media/Communications, Volunteer

The Ontario Council for International Cooperation (OCIC) is an umbrella group of 70 Ontario NGOs who work in international development and global education. The Council assists its members through information exchanges on members' activities; skills development workshops for members; and networking with special interest groups and communities in Ontario. OCIC has two full-time staff. OCIC is not directly involved in overseas or local placements, but has an ongoing job board and resource centre for public use. [ID:6095]

Operation Eyesight Universal (OEU)
4 Parkdale Crescent N.W., Calgary, Alberta T2N 3T8;
(403) 283-6323, fax (403) 270-1899, oevca@cadvision.com

LARGE MEDICAL ASSISTANCE GROUP: Accounting, Administration, Community Development, Consulting, Development Education, Fundraising, Gender and Development, Media/Communications, Medical Health, Project Management, Volunteer

Operation Eyesight Universal (OEU) finances over 40 sight restoration and blindness prevention programs in 10 developing countries, which include medical training, health and nutrition education. Its annual objective is to treat one million affected people and restore sight to 100,000 eyes blinded by cataracts. OEU partners perform more than 20,000 other eye operations each year, most of which are preventative. OEU has projects in India, Nepal, Bangladesh, Pakistan, Sri Lanka, Kenya, Malawi, Zambia, Chile, and Peru. It works as a partner with indigenous groups of eye care specialists, who staff their hospitals and outreach programs with nationals only. In November 1990, OEU marked its millionth sight restoring operation. In Canada, OEU engages in development education, fundraising and an eyeglass recycling program.

Canadian staff travel overseas only to monitor programs. Staff generally have a college or university education, with experience in fundraising, public relations or accounting. OEU maintains a data bank for résumés. [ID:6096]

Organization for Co-operation in Overseas Development (OCOD)
Suite 307, 1 Wesley Ave., Winnipeg, Manitoba R3C 4C6;
(204) 946-0600, fax (204) 956-5939, ocod@ocod.mb.ca, www.mbnet.mb.ca/~ocod

MID-SIZED VOLUNTEER GROUP: Teaching, Technical Assistance

The Organization for Co-operation in Overseas Development (OCOD) is a nonprofit volunteer-sending organization based in Winnipeg with a regional office in Castries, St. Lucia, West Indies. OCOD has a nine-person board, and membership is open to educators from across Canada. Members must be committed to offering their services, on a volunteer basis, to develop and upgrade educational expertise in the Eastern Caribbean. OCOD selects from its membership qualified individuals to deliver programs in the Caribbean as requested by host countries. Please write to OCOD for a membership application. As a member you will receive OCOD's monthly development bulletin which advertises positions as they come up.

Placements in the Caribbean vary from two weeks to three-months. OCOD also has a Youth Volunteer Program open to any graduate of a post-secondary institution who is between the ages of 18 and 30. As youth volunteer positions become open, they are posted on the OCOD web site. [ID:6097]

ORT CANADA
Suite 604, 3101 Bathurst Street, Toronto, Ontario M6A 2A6;
(416) 787-0339, fax (416) 787-9420, ortcan@pathcom.com, www.ortorg/ortnet.htm

MID-SIZED DEVELOPMENT ASSISTANCE GROUP: Accounting, Administration, Business/Banking/Trade, Development Education, Fundraising, Human Resources, Project Management, Teaching, Volunteer

ORT CANADA (Organization for Educational Resources and Technological Training) was incorporated in 1942 and is the largest nongovernmental training organization in the world. ORT assists disadvantaged individuals and communities towards becoming self-sufficient by educating and training them in skills that will provide them with sustainable employment. CIDA has supported initiatives by ORT in developing countries. ORT has four full-time staff. [ID:6015]

OXFAM-Canada

Suite 300, 294 Albert Street, Ottawa, Ontario K1P 6E6;
(613) 237-5236, fax (613) 237-0524, enquire@oxfam.ca, www.oxfam.ca

LARGE RELIEF AND DEVELOPMENT AGENCY: Accounting, Administration, Advocacy, Community Development, Development Education, Fundraising, Gender and Development, Human Resources, Humanitarian Relief, Media/Communications, Project Management

OXFAM-Canada supports grassroots, community-based development activities of popular organizations in Southern Africa, the Horn of Africa, the Caribbean, Central America, the Andean region of South America, and Canada. Its programs focus on institutional capacity building, promoting environmentally sustainable development, and issues of gender and development. Its contacts with community-based organizations also provide an effective mechanism for responding to emergency needs in times of war and natural disaster. In Canada the organization supports groups involved in community development and undertakes fundraising, development education, and advocacy work in support of its domestic and overseas programs.

OXFAM-Canada has 45 staff in Canada and two overseas positions filled on a permanent basis. It is not involved in the short- or medium-term placement of staff or volunteers overseas; however, it does promote exchanges between community development groups overseas and in Canada, providing opportunities for Canadian volunteers to participate in activities such as election monitoring.

Candidates must have extensive knowledge and experience in the region of concentration, proven program development and administrative skills, the ability to direct one's own work with minimal supervision, and demonstrated commitment (through paid or volunteer work) to international development issues. It works in cooperation with nine other organizations that share the OXFAM name around the world. Each works independently and administers its own employment program, maintaining large overseas staffs. OXFAM-Canada maintains a data bank for résumés and has limited internships when funding is available. [ID:6098]

OXFAM-Québec

Bureau 200, 2330, rue Notre-Dame ouest, Montréal, Québec
H3J 2Y2; (514) 937-1614, fax (514) 937-9452, oxfamocs@web.net, www.oxfam.ca

LARGE VOLUNTEER GROUP: Community Development, Environment, Gender and Development, Human Rights, Humanitarian Relief, Micro-Enterprises, Social Justice and Development, Sustainable Development

OXFAM-Québec, membre de la grande famille OXFAM INTERNATIONAL, est une importante organisation non gouvernementale, non partisane et non confessionnelle de coopération et de solidarité internationale. La mission d'OXFAM-QUÉBEC est «d'appuyer les populations défavorisées des pays en développement qui luttent pour leur survie, pour leur progrès, pour la justice sociale et pour le respect des droits humains; de mobiliser la population du Québec et faciliter l'expression de sa solidarité pour un monde plus équitable.»

Dans une perspective de développement durable, OXFAM-QUÉBEC oeuvre dans les domaines du renforcement institutionnel, des activités économiques des femmes, de la micro-entreprise et du microcrédit, de l'environnement (eau, reboisement), de l'autosuffisance et de la sécurité alimentaires, de la santé, du développement communautaire et de la formation en développement. Dans une perspective d'action humanitaire, OXFAM-QUÉBEC intervient dans l'aide humanitaire d'urgence, la reconstruction et la réhabilitation.

OXFAM-QUÉBEC a un effectif de 35 employés au Canada et 120 coopérants-volontaires outre-mer. Pour son programme de coopération volontaire et pour satisfaire les besoins exprimés par ses partenaires, OXFAM-QUÉBEC requiert les services de personnes ayant une formation universitaire, une expérience pertinente, de la flexibilité et une bonne capacité d'analyse et d'adaptation. [ID:6099]

Partners in Rural Development (PARTNERS)
Deputy Director, 323 Chapel Street, Ottawa, Ontario
K1N 7Z2; (613) 237-0180, fax (613) 237-5969, info@partners.ca

LARGE DEVELOPMENT ASSISTANCE GROUP: Accounting, Administration, Adult Training, Advocacy, Agriculture, Community Development, Development Assistance, Development Education, Fundraising, Gender and Development, Human Rights, Micro-Enterprises, Project Management, Technical Assistance

Partners in Rural Development (PARTNERS) is an international voluntary organization that addresses poverty at the village level in developing countries. In partnership with southern NGOs, PARTNERS supports self-help projects, strengthens the capacity of community organizations, promotes policies that alleviate poverty, and raises public understanding of development issues. In doing so, the partnership increases the access of the rural poor to lands, water, energy, technology, and training. These productive resources enable poor communities to attain food security and sustainable livelihoods.

PARTNERS currently employs ten staff in Canada and nine overseas. It seeks individuals who have technical and management expertise, leadership skills and the ability to relate to the social and cultural milieu of the countries where PARTNERS implements programs. [ID:6424]

Partnership Africa Canada (PAC)
Suite 1200, 1 Nicholas Street, Ottawa, Ontario
K1N 7B7; (613) 562-8242, fax (613) 562-8334, pac@web.net

MID-SIZED DEVELOPMENT ASSISTANCE GROUP: Agriculture, Policy Dialogue

Partnership Africa Canada (PAC) is an NGO coalition which focuses on policy work. Over 100 Canadian and African NGOs work to promote joint action and research in Canada and Africa on major development issues such as popular participation, democratization, debt and aid programs. It is not a funding agency. PAC has three staff in Canada, all with extensive NGO experience in Canada and/or Africa. [ID:6100]

PATH Canada
Executive Director, Suite 1105, 1 Nicolas Street, Ottawa, Ontario K1N 7B7;
(613) 241-3927, fax (613) 241-7988, path@synapse.net, www.synapse.net/~path/

MID-SIZED COMMUNITY HEALTH GROUP: Community Development, Consulting, Medical Health, Technical Assistance, Volunteer

PATH Canada is a nonprofit NGO whose goal is to improve health in developing countries, particularly the health of women and children. They have four main sectors of activity: malnutrition, malaria control, tobacco control and HIV/AIDS control. They work with local partners to design and implement projects which bridge the gap between user and provider of primary health services. [ID:6425]

Peacefund Canada
Suite 206, 145 Spruce Street,
Ottawa, Ontario K1R 6P1; (613) 230-0860, fax (613) 563-0017, pfcan@web.net

SMALL DEVELOPMENT EDUCATION GROUP: Administration, Advocacy, Development Education, Fundraising, Human Rights, Media/Communications, Project Management, Volunteer

Peacefund Canada is an independent fundraising and granting organization with three key objectives: to help individuals and groups in Canada and around the world work for a just and sustainable peace through adult education; to initiate and fund projects that increase public support for disarmament, equitable development and reduction of global tensions; and to use and support existing networks engaged in peace education. Peacefund gives priority to educational activities which seek to inform, educate, and mobilize public opinion about peace, equitable development and global security.

Peacefund has three staff based in Canada and occasionally sponsors overseas volunteers. Staff generally have experience in conflict resolution, adult education, non-violence training, international politics or development, or human rights. [ID:6101]

Plenty Canada
Cooperant Department, RR 3, Lanark, Ontario K0G 1K0;
(613) 278-2215, fax (613) 278-2416, plentycanada@perth.igs.net

MID-SIZED DEVELOPMENT ASSISTANCE GROUP: Administration, Agriculture, Development Assistance, Health/Medical, Social Justice and Development, Sustainable Development

Plenty Canada promotes self-sufficiency and human dignity in developing countries. It responds to locally-identified needs for technically-oriented programs that support sustainable development. It works among indigenous peoples in Guatemala and Nicaragua and with The Six Nations of the Grand River in Brantford, Ontario. Other projects are located in El Salvador, Sri Lanka, the Transkei in South Africa, Botswana and Lesotho.

Plenty Canada has 4 employees in Canada, but overseas positions are filled by its local partners. It hires persons with civil engineering or agricultural degrees. It also looks for workers with administrative experience and a background in international studies or rural planning and development. It will occasionally train people with a background in nutrition or small business as soy-food processors. Plenty maintains a data bank for résumés. [ID:6104]

Presbyterian Church in Canada (PCC)
International Ministries, 50 Wynford Drive, North York,
Ontario M3C 1J7; (800) 619-7301, fax (416) 441-2825, pcc@web.net, www.presbyterian.ca

LARGE DEVELOPMENT ASSISTANCE GROUP: Community Development, Education, Exchange Programs, Humanitarian Relief, Religious

Presbyterian Church in Canada (PCC) responds to requests for personnel and project support from international partners who are established national churches, councils of churches, and development organizations. The Presbyterian Church also conducts education programs in Canada, and international visitor and exchange programs to and from Canada, both at the youth and adult level.

Internationally, the PCC is active through Presbyterian World Service & Development (PWS&D), which has recently done emergency relief work in North Korea, Rwanda and Zaire (where it coordinates the Canadian Foodgrains Bank). PWS&D's development partners in Africa and Asia continue to implement community-based development programs, notably in India. It also has an overseas exposure grant program which sends youth to the South.

The Church requires commitment to the faith, goals, and style of the PCC. Overseas partners usually specify qualifications, but normally they request postsecondary degrees or diplomas as well as work experience. Youth and young adult programs are usually organized by someone who has earned the confidence and cooperation of PCC staff. [ID:6105]

Probe International
225 Brunswick Ave., Toronto, Ontario M5S 2M6; (416) 964-9223,
fax (416) 964-8239, ProbeInternational@nextcity.com, www.nextcity.com/ProbeInternational

SMALL INTERNATIONAL ADVOCACY GROUP: Administration, Advocacy, Business/Banking/Trade, Energy Resources, Environment, Water Resources

Probe International is an independent environmental advocacy organization concerned with the environmental effects of Canada's aid and trade activities in developing countries. Working closely with environmentalists from Western and developing countries, Probe monitors the Canadian International Development Agency (CIDA), the Export Development Corporation (EDC), and such international agencies as the World Bank and Regional Development Banks.

Probe helped create a worldwide information network of citizens' groups to expose environmental wrongdoing in developing countries. Special emphasis is now given to the impact of hydro-electric dams, mining projects, forced resettlement, and the projects and policies of financing agencies. [ID:6107]

Pueblito Canada
Suite 304, 720 Spadina Ave., Toronto,
Ontario M5S 2T9; (416) 963-8846, fax (416) 963-8853, pueblito@web.net

MID-SIZED DEVELOPMENT ASSISTANCE GROUP: Community Development, International Education, Volunteer

Pueblito Canada supports the efforts of Latin American community groups that organize around children issues such as daycare, health, and education. The groups which Pueblito works with generally have a direct role in preventing child abandonment.

Pueblito Canada is also committed to increasing awareness in Canada about the causes and effects of child abandonment and poverty in Latin America. It produces "Under the Tree," a global education development kit for elementary schools and families.

Staff and volunteer positions are based in Canada. Pueblito Canada has a number of volunteer committees that carry out awareness programs and fundraising activities. [ID:6109]

RESULTS Canada
President, 503-49th Ave S.W., Calgary, Alberta T2S 1G4;
(403) 287-7212, fax (403) 287-7212, littlec@cadvision.com, www.ualberta.ca/~ckunzle/results/

LARGE INTERNATIONAL ADVOCACY GROUP: Humanitarian Relief, Micro-Enterprises, People's Organizations, Policy Dialogue

RESULTS Canada (Responsibility for Ending Starvation Utilizing Legislation, Trimtabs and Support) is a nonpartisan and nondenominational network of concerned citizens. RESULTS encourages the public to lobby their elected representatives to create the political will to end world hunger. It is primarily dedicated to reforming Canada's foreign aid policy. RESULTS has sister organizations in the US, UK, Germany, Japan, Australia, and Mexico with whom it lobbies international financial institutions such as the World Bank and International Monetary Fund. Its specific goals are universal access to clean water, primary healthcare, basic education, and adequate nutrition. The Microcredit Summit held in Washington, DC, in February 1997 was a project of RESULTS Educational Fund USA. It launched a global campaign to reach 100 million of the world's poorest families (especially women) with access to credit, by the year 2005. [ID:6426]

Rooftops Canada Foundation
Suite 207, 2 Berkeley Street, Toronto, Ontario
M5A 2W3; (416) 366-1445, fax (416) 366-3876, rooftops@web.net

MID-SIZED DEVELOPMENT ASSISTANCE GROUP: Housing/Human Settlements

Rooftops Canada Foundation is the international program of cooperative and social housing organizations in Canada. It provides technical assistance to cooperative and community-based shelter organizations in the South, builds networks between Canadian and overseas housing organizations, and educates Canadians about shelter issues in developing countries. The foundation has experience with African regional projects, and currently works in Kenya, Zimbabwe, South Africa, Uganda, Tanzania, and Senegal. It also works in the Philippines, India, and Cuba.

Rooftops sends about eight consultants overseas each year. Three staff work in Canada. Consultants require extensive experience in cooperative and/or social housing, including financing, land and housing development, administration and training. Generally, consultants come from the co-op social housing sector in Canada. Working languages are English, French, Spanish, and Portuguese. The foundation maintains a data bank for résumés. [ID:6110]

Rural Advancement Foundation International (RAFI)
Executive Director, Suite 504, 71 Bank Street, Ottawa, Ontario
K1P 5N2; (613) 567-6880, fax (613) 567-6884, rafican@web.net, www.rafi.ca

SMALL ENVIRONMENTAL ACTION GROUP: Fundraising

Rural Advancement Foundation International (RAFI) is dedicated to the conservation and improvement of sustainable agricultural biodiversity, and to the development of socially responsible technologies that are useful to rural societies. RAFI focuses on international policy work in the areas of biotechnology, biodiversity, biopolicy and biopiracy. RAFI does not send staff or volunteers overseas. [ID:6428]

SalvAide
Suite 411, 219 Argyle Ave., Ottawa, Ontario
K2P 2H4; (613) 233-6215, fax (613) 233-7375, salvaide@web.net

MID-SIZED COMMUNITY DEVELOPMENT GROUP: Administration, Advocacy, Community Development, Development Education, Exchange Programs, Fundraising, Human Rights, Project Management

SalvAide supports economic development and organizational strengthening programs in rural communities in El Salvador. There, the group works in partnership with Salvadorean NGOs and popular organizations. In Canada, SalvAide engages in policy, information and educational work to inform decision-makers and the Canadian people about issues affecting development in El Salvador.

SalvAide has one full-time and two part-time staff in Canada and one full-time staff overseas. SalvAide's personnel have a variety of professional qualifications and a demonstrated commitment to build social and economic justice and democracy with the people of El Salvador. To work in El Salvador, the ability to communicate in Spanish is essential. [ID:6111]

Salvation Army Overseas Development Department
Suite 1705, 130 Albert Street,
Ottawa, Ontario K1P 5G4; (613) 234-3372, fax (613) 234-0713, ejolly@web.net

LARGE DEVELOPMENT ASSISTANCE GROUP: Administration, Adult Training, Agriculture, Business/Banking/Trade, Community Development, Construction, Consulting, Development Assistance, Development Education, Environment, Exchange Programs, Fundraising, Gender and Development, Human Resources, Humanitarian Relief, Media/Communications, Medical Health, Project Management, Religious, Teaching, Technical Assistance, Volunteer, Water Resources

The Salvation Army in Canada has been part of an international religious movement since 1865. The Army carries out evangelical and humanitarian work in 100 countries and 136 languages. Both in Canada and overseas, it provides healthcare services, housing for single mothers and the elderly, food, shelter and clothing for disadvantaged groups, counselling and rehabilitation centres, day care and education services.

The Ottawa office is part of an international network of overseas partners. It currently has six staff based in Canada. Several volunteers work overseas but come under the jurisdiction of their respective territories. Employees should possess some understanding of the international aspect of the Salvation Army. Overseas experience in developing countries is a definite advantage. The current staff have experience in public relations, fundraising, government relations, community development experience in India and Africa, and administrative, technical, and tour experience in 30 countries. [ID:6112]

Saskatchewan Council for International Co-operation (SCIC)
2138 McIntyre Street, Regina, Sask. S4P 2R7; (306) 757-4669, fax (306) 757-3226, scic@web.net

SMALL COORDINATING BODY: Housing/Human Settlements

The Saskatchewan Council for International Co-operation (SCIC) is a coalition of over 30 Saskatchewan-based international development NGOs. SCIC supports its members' international programs and communicates with governments on concerns between Saskatchewan, Canada, and the South.

The Council administers both the Saskatchewan government's Matching Grants in International Aid Programs and its Emergency Aid Program for emergency relief projects. It also manages a Small Projects Fund for short-term development education projects and promotes public education on international issues. Six staff members and approximately 200 volunteers work for SCIC. SCIC manages the "Global Connections" database which matches Saskatchewan residents with international expertise to local businesses and institutions seeking such expertise. [ID:6113]

Save A Family Plan, St. Peter's Seminary (SAFP)
Executive Director, P.O. Box 3622, London, Ontario N6A 4L4;
(519) 672-1115, fax (519) 672-6379, safpinfo@safp.org, www.safp.org

LARGE DEVELOPMENT ASSISTANCE GROUP: Agriculture, Community Development, Job Training, Medical Health, People's Organizations, Water Resources

Save A Family Plan (SAFP) of St. Peter's Seminary works primarily in India and Haiti to alleviate hunger and homelessness, and to enable the poor to become self-supporting. SAFP assists families and communities through various development projects, including healthcare, housing, irrigation, agriculture, and job-oriented training programs.

SAFP employs five full-time staff: an executive director, an office administrator and three administrative assistants. It also employs regional coordinators in 57 centres throughout India. The paid staff there are supplemented by thousands of volunteers in India (seminarians and community volunteers) who assist with clerical work. In Canada and the US, seminarians and many community volunteers also assist the program.

SAFP welcomes North American volunteers who can assist with its work here; it can also make arrangements for North American supporters to visit SAFP operations in India. Visit the SAFP web site for details. [ID:6114]

Save the Children—Canada
Suite 300, 4141 Yonge Street, Toronto, Ontario M2P 2A8;
(416) 221-5501, fax (416) 221-8214, sccan@savethechildren.ca, www.savethechildren.ca

LARGE DEVELOPMENT ASSISTANCE GROUP: Accounting, Administration, Advocacy, Community Development, Development Assistance, Fundraising, Human Rights, Humanitarian Relief, Project Management, Volunteer

Save the Children—Canada is guided by volunteers dedicated to meeting the objectives of the United Nations Convention on the Rights of the Child. Through community development and advocacy initiatives in partnership with local communities in Canada and overseas, Save the Children—Canada assists, enables and empowers communities to improve the quality of life for children. Save the Children works primarily in the areas of healthcare, education, agriculture, institutional development, and human resource development in Bolivia, Peru, Nicaragua, Jamaica, Haiti, Kenya, Burkina Faso, India, and Mali.

Save the Children's international projects are implemented by nine overseas offices; 20 staff work in Canada. Applicants must have a university degree, overseas development experience, management experience and English, French and Spanish language fluency for certain positions. The agency maintains a data bank for résumés and occasionally offers internship positions for which honorariums are negotiated. Visit the Save the Children web site for job postings and information on volunteering. [ID:6115]

Scarboro Foreign Mission Society (SFMS)
Lay Mission Office, 2685 Kingston Road, Scarborough, Ontario M1M 1M4;
(416) 261-7135 ext. 165, fax (416) 261-0820, lmo@web.net, www.web.net/~sfms

SMALL COMMUNITY DEVELOPMENT GROUP: Administration, Adult Training, Community
Development, Development Education, Engineering, Human Rights, Medical Health, Religious,
Teaching, Technical Assistance, Volunteer, Water Resources

Scarboro Missions is a Roman Catholic missionary organization consisting of 70 priests
and 14 lay people. The Lay Mission Office coordinates the training and placing of lay
missioners who serve for three years in overseas settings. The skills of lay missioners are
matched to the needs of the receiving community and include teaching, healthcare, pastoral
work, community building, maintenance work and social work.

Current placement countries include Brazil, Guyana, Malawi and China. Applicants
must be motivated by faith and a desire to serve and to learn, and have post secondary
education and/or applicable work experience. Lay missioners have their basic expenses
covered and receive a small stipend. [ID:6117]

Secours aux lépreux - Leprosy Relief (Canada)
Bureau 125, 1275, rue Hodge, Montréal, Québec H4N 3H4;
(514) 744-3199, fax (514) 744-9095, secours-lepreux@msn.com

MID-SIZED MEDICAL ASSISTANCE GROUP: Fundraising, Medical Health

Secours aux lépreux - Leprosy Relief (Canada) is a nonprofit organisation whose sole
purpose is to assist leprosy victims through medical and social actions and through support
of scientific research. The organization acts as an intermediary between donors and the
world's millions of lepers. Secours aux lépreux - Leprosy Relief does not offer overseas
employment opportunities. [ID:6118]

Seva Service Society
Suite 200, 2678 West Broadway, Vancouver, B.C. V6K 2G3;
(604) 733-4284, fax (604) 733-4292, sevacan@axionet.com, www.eyewear.com/excel/seva/seva.html

MID-SIZED DEVELOPMENT ASSISTANCE GROUP: Administration, Business Development,
Computer Systems, Consulting, Development Assistance, Development Education, Fundraising,
Human Resources, Media/Communications, Medical Health, Micro-Enterprises, Project
Management, Teaching, Technical Assistance

Seva Service Society supports development programs in national and international
communities. Seva's principal activities abroad focus on: the prevention and reversal of
blindness in Nepal, Tibet, and India and sustainable community development in the
highlands of Guatemala. Seva's emphasis is on building self-sustaining programs with
committed local partners. The society focuses on local empowerment in the belief that the
best help leads towards self-reliance. [ID:6947]

Sierra Club of Canada
Suite 412, 1 Nicholas Street, Ottawa, Ontario K1N 7B7;
(613) 241-4611, fax (613) 241-2292, sierra@web.net, www.sierraclub.ca/

LARGE ENVIRONMENTAL ACTION GROUP: Arms Control, Development Education,
Environment, Forestry, Fundraising, Human Resources, Media/Communications

Since 1969, the Sierra Club has been working in Canada on matters of public policy and
environmental awareness. They have local chapters and working groups in every region of
the country. The national office, located in Ottawa, organizes and supports several campaigns at national and international levels, including biodiversity, climate change, forestry
and wilderness protection, nuclear phaseout, multilateral lending reform, trade, the environment, pesticide awareness, and shrimp aquaculture awareness. There are also regional

chapters in British Columbia, the Prairies, and Eastern Canada. For more information, visit the Sierra Club of Canada web site. [ID:7075]

SIM Canada
10 Huntingdale Blvd., Scarborough, Ontario M1W 2S5;
(416) 497-2424, fax (416) 497-2444, postmaster@sim.ca, www.sim.org

LARGE EVANGELICAL GROUP: Agriculture, Community Development, Environment, Forestry, Humanitarian Relief, Medical Health, Religious, Water Resources

SIM Canada is a national office of SIM International, a privately supported, independent mission agency involved in activities overseas such as church ministries, education, translation, health, relief, and development. SIM International is currently active in 17 countries in Africa, eight countries in Asia, and six countries in South America. SIM works in direct partnership with national churches and community groups. Community development activities include: community healthcare, literacy, skills training, agriculture, crop research, reforestation, environmental conservation, water development, and natural disaster relief.

SIM Canada employs 140 staff overseas, including 35 staff in Canada and 20 staff in Canadian ministries. Actual qualifications will vary with the requirements set by the host country. SIM looks for individuals with good interpersonal skills who are able to spend time developing genuine relationships with local people. [ID:6119]

Sir Edmund Hillary Foundation
Lower Main HQB, 222 Jarvis Street, Toronto, Ontario M58 2B8; (416) 941-3315, fax (416) 941-2321

SMALL MEDICAL ASSISTANCE GROUP: Education, Medical Health

The Sir Edmund Hillary Foundation runs programs in the Solu Khumbu area of Nepal in health, conservation, and education. The Foundation funds a hospital and 13 health centres and is involved in building schools and in reforestation projects. The foundation has no permanent staff, but it sends two Canadian volunteer medical doctors (usually a couple) to Nepal every two years. [ID:6120]

Society of Partnership (SOPAR Inc.)
1 des Erables Road, Gatineau, Québec J8V 1C1;
(819) 243-3616, fax (819) 243-6280, sopar@magmacom.com

MID-SIZED DEVELOPMENT ASSISTANCE GROUP: Adult Training, Agriculture, Community Development, Fundraising, Gender and Development, Humanitarian Relief, Micro-Enterprises, Water Resources

Society of Partnership (SOPAR) works through partner NGOs in India to alleviate poverty and promote self-sufficiency. It supports community development, primarily in the state of Andhra Pradesh. SOPAR's main areas of expertise include women's credit cooperatives and micro enterprises, and the construction of water bore wells and water tanks.

Sopar has one staff in Canada and one staff overseas. Their experiences range from project and program management to administration and fundraising. [ID:6124]

SOCODEVI
(Société de coopération pour le développement international)
Bureau 2300, 1245, chemin Ste-Foy, Québec, Québec
G1S 4P2; (418) 683-7225, fax (418) 683-5229, administration@socodevi.org

LARGE DEVELOPMENT ASSISTANCE GROUP: Accounting, Administration, Agriculture, Business Development, Consulting, Development Assistance, Development Education, Forestry, Gender and Development, Insurance, Media/Communications, Micro-Enterprises, Project Management, Technical Assistance

Formée d'institutions coopératives et mutualistes, SOCODEVI a pour mission de contribuer à l'avancement de pays en développement par la promotion et le renforcement de la formule coopérative ou de toute formule apparentée en favorisant l'engagement de ses institutions membres dans ses programmes.

SOCODEVI intervient particulièrement dans les secteurs de l'agro-alimentaire, les assurances et services financiers, la foresterie, la production industrielle, les services funéraires et autres. Elle détient des mandats en Bolivie, au Pérou, en Équateur, au Salvador, au Guatemala, en Haïti, au Togo, en Côte-d'Ivoire, au Bénin et au Sénégal.

Pour assurer la maîtrise d'oeuvre de ses projets, SOCODEVI compte sur une équipe de professionnels qualifiés dont une vingtaine à son siège social et une quinzaine basés outremer. De plus, la mobilisation d'experts-conseils est rendue possible par ses institutions membres afin d'apporter des appuis d'appoint spécialisés dans des secteurs précis.

Les candidats recherchés par SOCODEVI doivent posséder une formation et une expérience de travail reliées au domaine de l'emploi. Ils doivent avoir acquis une certaine connaissance du monde coopératif et des pays en développement tout en ayant un niveau de compétence démontrée en gestion de projets. SOCODEVI utilise, entre autres, un répertoire de candidatures pour combler les postes disponibles, et recrute occasionnellement des stagiaires. [ID:6122]

Solidarité Canada Sahel (SCS)
Suite 510, 1030 Cherrier St.,
Montréal, Québec H2L 1H9; (514) 522-6077, fax (514) 522-2370, scsmtl@web.net

MID-SIZED COORDINATING BODY: Administration, Development Education

The objective of Solidarité Canada Sahel's main program is to support the strengthening of civil society in Burkina Faso, Mali, and Niger. SCS has several Canadian personnel, some of whom work on overseas programs but are not based overseas. Overseas programs consist of bolstering institutional capacities within the movement of NGOs and associations in the Sahel and increasing collaboration among NGOs on regional, national, and international levels. SCS specifically focusses on helping to implement the United Nations Convention to Combat Desertificiation. [ID:6125]

SOS Children's Villages Canada
National Director, Suite 1203, 130 Albert Street, Ottawa, Ontario K1P 5G4;
(613) 232-3309, fax (613) 232-6764, sos@web.net, www.web.net/~sos/index.htm

LARGE SPECIAL NEEDS GROUP: Children's Rights, Fundraising

SOS Children's Villages Canada is a member of the SOS-Kinderdorf International network of organizations which has member groups in over a 100 countries around the globe. Its purpose is to help orphaned and abandoned children regardless of their ethnic roots, nationality, and religion, by giving them a family, a permanent home, and a sound basis for an independent life. SOS Canada was founded in 1969 as a fundraising arm of the SOS international network to support overseas programs; it has since grown to coordinate and oversee programs within Canada while maitaining its commitment to international programs. [ID:6417]

South Asia Partnership Canada (SAP)
Suite 200, 1 Nicholas Street, Ottawa, Ontario K1N 7B7;
(613) 241-1333, fax (613) 241-1129, sap@web.net, www.web.net/~sap

LARGE COORDINATING BODY: Advocacy, Development Assistance, Gender and Development, Human Rights, Intercultural Briefings, Media/Communications, Policy Dialogue

South Asia Partnership Canada (SAP) is a coalition of Canadian and South Asian organizations which supports the long term development of socially and economically disadvantaged people in South Asia. It brings together a broad network of Canadian organizations involved in sustainable development in South Asia, including NGOs, solidarity groups, South Asian-Canadian organizations, the social justice community, women's groups, academic organizations, research institutes, consulting firms, and businesses. SAP Canada also manages the Sri Lanka Canada Development Fund and the Pakistan NGO Support Program.

SAP Canada is a member of South Asian Partnership International, based in Colombo, Sri Lanka. SAP Canada works through counterpart SAP organizations in Bangladesh, India, Nepal, Pakistan and Sri Lanka. These national SAPs identify, select and monitor projects partnered with Canadian development agencies and covering a wide spectrum of community development activities.

SAP employs eight people in Canada, and occasionally hires consultants for specific projects. The Asian SAP organizations employ local program staff. For staff and contractual positions in Canada, SAP looks for candidates with a blend of formal training and relevant experience. SAP maintains a data bank for résumés. Visit the SAP web page for job openings and volunteer information. [ID:6126]

South Pacific Peoples Foundation of Canada (SPPF)

1921 Fermwood Road, Victoria, B.C. V8T 2Y6;
(250) 381-4131, fax (250) 388-5258, sppf@sppf.org, www.sppf.org

SMALL INTERNATIONAL ADVOCACY GROUP: Advocacy, Development Education, Environment, Gender and Development, Intercultural Briefings

The South Pacific Peoples Foundation of Canada (SPPF) is primarily a development education and advocacy group, but it also supports a few overseas projects in the Pacific Islands. These projects involve support to local groups, not placement of Canadian personnel. Projects have generally been women's programs, education and training, environment, and health. SPPF publishes a quarterly magazine on Pacific issues, organizes annual conferences, and has an extensive resource centre.

SPPF has three staff. Previous experience in international education, advocacy and/or development is essential. Pacific Islands experience is an asset. SPPF does not recruit and place staff overseas, nor does it usually hire given its small and stable staff. SPPF does provide, for a charge, orientation briefings and resources for people who will be working and living in the Pacific Islands. [ID:6127]

Steelworkers Humanity Fund

Suite 700, 234 Eglinton Ave. E., Toronto, Ontario M4P 1K7;
(416) 487-1571, fax (416) 487-1473, shf@web.net, www.uswa.ca/steelworkers

MID-SIZED DEVELOPMENT ASSISTANCE GROUP: Advocacy, Food Security, Labour, Medical Health

The Steelworkers Humanity Fund raises aid and supports community development in the South and in Canada. It lends financial support to development initiatives, primarily in the areas of food security, primary healthcare, potable water, income generation, and social communications. In Canada, it carries out development education activities through week-long labour courses and "mini" courses related to its areas of focus. Steelworkers Humanity Fund has three staff based in Canada. [ID:6128]

Street Kids International

Production Manager, Suite 1000, 10th Floor, 398 Adelaide Street W., Toronto, Ontario
M5V 1S7; (416) 504-8994, fax (416) 504-8977, ski@streetkids.org, www.streetkids.org/~ski

MID-SIZED SPECIAL NEEDS GROUP: Administration, Adult Training, Children's Rights, Development Education, Fundraising, Media/Communications, Micro-Enterprises, Project Management, Technical Assistance

Street Kids International promotes independence and self-respect among street children around the world. Street Kids works with child-serving agencies to develop micro-businesses, and non-formal education and training programs that advance the talents, dreams, rights, and needs of street and working children.

Street Kids International has eight staff based in Canada, and employs consultants for overseas work. Specific language and education requirements vary according to position. They prefer candidates with overseas experience and a demonstrated participatory (child-centred) approach. Street Kids look for candidates with superb written and oral communications skills, who are highly organized, efficient self-starters and who collaborate well. Energetic candidates who have an easy-going manner and sense of humour are welcome. Street Kids maintains a data bank for résumés. Internship applications are considered on an individual basis. Look for job openings and volunteer positions on their web site. [ID:6405]

Ten Days for Global Justice
Suite 401, 77 Charles Street W., Toronto, Ontario M5S 1K5;
(416) 922-0591, fax (416) 922-1419, tendays@web.net, www.web.net/~tendays

MID-SIZED DEVELOPMENT EDUCATION GROUP: Development Education, International Education, Religious

Ten Days for Global Justice is a coalition of over 200 inter-church and community-based ecumenical groups that work toward global justice. It is sponsored by the Presbyterian Church in Canada, the Evangelical Lutheran Church in Canada, the United Church of Canada, the Canadian Catholic Organization for Development and Peace, and the Anglican Church of Canada. Through education and action, Ten Days challenges dehumanizing and destructive forces, promoting alternative models of society that put people and creation first.

Ten Days' mandate is three-fold: 1) increase efforts in developing educational strategies to engage local congregation and parishes in its programs, 2) facilitate closer collaboration and networking with other groups in Canada and in the South who share its vision, and 3) develop initiatives to engage youth in education and action on global justice issues. [ID:6948]

Terre des hommes Canada inc. (TDH Canada)
Bureau 5, 2520, rue Lionel-Groulx, Montréal, Québec
H3J 1J8; (514) 937-3325, fax (514) 933-7125, tdhcan@org, www.tdh.ca

SMALL SPECIAL NEEDS GROUP: Children's Rights

Terre des hommes est établie au Québec depuis 1967. Son objectif est de donner une assistance aux enfants qui en ont besoin dans le monde, et notamment en intervenant dans des processus d'adoption, plus particulièrement dans des pays tels que le Salvador ou Honduras. [ID:6130]

Terre sans frontières (TSF)
Regroupement de PRODEVA Tiers-Monde et Avions
Sans Frontières, Bureau 23, 399, rue des Conseillers, La Prairie, Québec
J5R 4H6; (514) 659-7717, fax (514) 659-2276, tsf@odyssee.net, www.odyssee.net/~tsf/

LARGE DEVELOPMENT ASSISTANCE GROUP: Community Development, Development Assistance, Development Education, Gender and Development, International Education, Media/Communications, Medical Health, Project Management, Technical Assistance, Training and Technology Transfer, Transportation, Volunteer, Water Resources

Les secteurs d'intervention de Terre sans frontières (TSF) s'articulent autour des besoins de base des populations via des activités de microréalisations, d'appui institutionnel et de projets d'assistance technique dans les domaines suivants: éducation et formation, adduction d'eau et assainissement, agriculture, appui à l'entrepreneurship, communication et transport (grâce à deux avions en opération dans le nord-est du Congo (RDC).

TSF compte une vingtaine d'employés permanents et 400 bénévoles, dont un certain nombre sur le terrain. TSF s'intéresse à des candidats ayant une Maîtrise en gestion de projets ou de l'expertise dans l'un de ses domaines d'intervention, et une facilité d'adaptation à des milieux différents. Le bilinguisme est un atout. TSF maintient un dossier de c.v., mais n'accepte pas de stagiaires, ni n'envoie de coopérants. [ID:6108]

Turtle Island Earth Stewards Society (TIES)
Executive Director, P.O. Box 3308, Salmon Arm, B.C. V1E 4S1;
(250) 832-3993, fax (250) 832-9942, ties@jetstream.net, www.landtrust.org/turtleisland

SMALL ENVIRONMENTAL ACTION GROUP: Community Development, Development
Education, Ecoforestry, Environment, Forestry, Fundraising, Land Stewardship, Permaculture,
Volunteer

Turtle Island Earth Stewards Society (TIES) concentrates on land and resource-related
issues. TIES assists in creating community land trusts for the protection and management of
environmentally-sensitive areas of private property. TIES also promotes private conservancy,
land stewardship ethics and natural resource management. As well, it facilitates multi-party
roundtable discussions on watershed and bioregional land use planning which implement
cross-sector processes.

TIES has three full-time staff based in Canada and draws on a list of in-house
consultants as needed. TIES maintains a data bank for résumés. [ID:6418]

L'Union pour le développement durable
C.P. 38022, 1411, chemin Ste-Foy, Québec, Québec G1S 4W8;
(418) 682-5949, fax (418) 682-3797, udd_usd@mlink.net, www.mlink.net/~udd_usd/index.html

MID-SIZED ENVIRONMENTAL ACTION GROUP: Environment, Sustainable Development

L'Union pour le développement durable (UDD) est une ONG canadienne qui regroupe
essentiellement des écologistes et des scientifiques et qui est reconnue pour sa capacité à
favoriser la concertation dans le domaine de la gestion durable des ressources. À l'étranger,
l'UDD gère, pour le compte de l'Agence canadienne de développement international (ACDI),
le projet APEC (Appui à la protection de l'environnement au Cameroun), qui a pour but
principal de renforcer les organisations non gouvernementales environnementales (ONG)
camerounaises. [ID:6553]

The United Church of Canada,
Division of World Outreach (UCC, DWO)
3250 Bloor Street West, Etobicoke, Ontario M8X 2Y4;
(416) 231-5931, fax (416) 232-6008, uccdwo@uccan.org, www.uccan.org

LARGE DEVELOPMENT ASSISTANCE GROUP: Accounting, Administration, Adult Training,
Advocacy, Community Development, Construction, Development Assistance, Development
Education, Environment, Gender and Development, Human Rights, Medical Health, Micro-
Enterprises, Project Management, Teaching, Technical Assistance, Volunteer

The United Church of Canada, Division of World Outreach (UCC, DWO) sends staff
overseas in response to specific requests by overseas partners in Africa, the Caribbean,
Central and South America, East and South Asia, and the Pacific Islands.

UCC, DWO presently has 40 staff and 6 volunteers overseas. Regular appointments are
for a minimum of three years; special English as a Second Language assignments are two
years; volunteer service ranges from three months to two years.

The United Church sends pastors, physicians, nurses, teachers, agriculturalists, engineers, and community development animation workers overseas. Eligible candidates have
relevant training and experience. UCC requires a Christian commitment, including active
involvement in the life and work of the Christian community. Previous crosscultural experience is an asset, as is previous work with marginalized people. [ID:6131]

United Nations Association in Canada (UNA Canada)
Suite 900, 130 Slater Street, Ottawa, Ontario K1P 6E2;
(613) 232-5751, fax (613) 563-2455, unac@magi.com, www.unac.org

MID-SIZED INTERNATIONAL ADVOCACY GROUP: Environment, Human Rights,
Peacekeeping and Defence

The United Nations Association in Canada (UNA Canada) is a national organization of
Canadians interested in the United Nations. UNA's national office and over 20 branches
work to educate the Canadian public about the UN, to promote awareness of its activities,
and to encourage public and official support for the multilateral organization. UNA Canada's
main areas of programming include distribution of materials from and about the UN,
coordination of services and conferences, media briefings, interaction with government, and
publications. The association has no overseas activities.

Twelve staff work in the national office and several branches also have staff. All offices
use volunteer assistance. Employees must have an interest in international affairs and applicants with related degrees or past experience are welcome. Degree of expertise required
depends on the position. Bilingualism is an asset, and often obligatory and computer knowledge is required. UNA Canada maintains a data bank for résumés and considers internship
applicants year-round, in the areas of peacekeeping, sustainable development and human
rights. The UNA Canada web site does not provide job notices for UNA offices. However, the
site contains job vacancies for the UN and other useful information. (For more information
see Chapter 36, United Nations.) [ID:6132]

USC Canada
Suite 705, 56 Sparks Street, Ottawa, Ontario K1P 5B1;
(613) 234-6827, fax (613) 234-6842, uscanada@web.net, www.usc-canada.org

LARGE DEVELOPMENT ASSISTANCE GROUP: Adult Training, Agriculture, Business
Development, Community Development, Development Education, Environment, Gender and
Development, Micro-Enterprises

USC Canada (also known as the Unitarian Service Committee of Canada) works to help
the poor of developing countries meet basic needs and improve their standard of living, and
to promote human development and self-reliance. USC also provides emergency relief to
areas of extreme need, in countries where it has programs. It supports projects in Mali,
Ethiopia, Lesotho, South Africa, Nepal, Bangladesh, and Indonesia.

The organization works in a variety of fields including education, health, income
earning and employment creation, agriculture, rehabilitation, community development, and
reforestation.

The USC operates a national volunteer program in Canada, and has provincial offices in
Ontario and British Columbia that focus on volunteers and development education. Its overseas programs have 29 staff and hundreds of indigenous volunteers. [ID:6134]

Vidéographe Inc.
4550 Garnier Street, Montréal, Québec H2J 3S7; (514) 521-2116, fax (514) 521-1676, signalv@cam.org

MID-SIZED MEDIA DEVELOPMENT GROUP: Community Development, Human Resources,
Media/Communications

Vidéographe Inc. is Canada's first independent video production centre. The centre
produces and distributes independent videos, and supports the development of artists and
producers. Vidéographe has experience producing videos in Africa and in South America.
Members of Vidéographe have also conducted video training sessions with some South
American groups. Vidéographe has six paid staff in Canada. [ID:6136]

Volunteer Service Overseas Canada (VSO Canada)
Suite 806, 151 Slater Street, Ottawa, Ontario K1P 5H3;
(613) 234-1364, fax (613) 234-1444, clare@vsocan.com, www.magi.com/~vsocan

MID-SIZED VOLUNTEER GROUP: Agriculture, Business Development, Community Development, Computer Systems, Development Education, Energy Resources, Engineering, Environment, Fisheries, Forestry, Fundraising, Intercultural Briefings, Media/Communications, Medical Health, Teaching, Trades, Volunteer, Water Resources

VSO Canada, a registered charity, is the Canadian partner of VSO, the world's largest independent volunteer-sending agency, with volunteers serving in 60 countries worldwide. The international headquarters is located in London, England. VSO is a development agency working exclusively with volunteers because it believes that individuals can make a real difference in the lives of others, through practical action, person-to-person.

VSO Canada has seven full-time staff and one part-time staff based in Ottawa and approximately 110 volunteers are currently serving overseas. This covers a small percentage of VSO's international staff, which includes 38 field offices and over 1800 volunteers from North America and Europe. VSO Canada recruits from several professional groups, including health professionals, teachers, business advisors, technical and natural resource professionals. Applicants must be qualified in their fields. Some postings require previous work experience.

All inquiries and applicant information are maintained on a central database. A visit to VSO's web site will also provide applicants with helpful information. [ID:6137]

Volunteers in Mission
The Anglican Church of Canada, 600 Jarvis Street,
Toronto, Ontario M4Y 2J6; (416) 924-9192, fax (416) 924-3483)

SMALL EVANGELICAL GROUP: Administration, Community Development, Forestry, Fundraising, Medical Health, Religious, Water Resources

The Volunteers in Mission Program of the Anglican Church of Canada provides opportunities for qualified Canadians to serve overseas or in Canada, usually for two years, in response to specific requests. Volunteers are required to raise the funds necessary to cover the costs of such things as return airfare, medical insurance and a modest living allowance. Host organizations provide housing.

Sixteen to 20 volunteers are overseas at any given time. Volunteers generally fill requests for teachers at the primary, secondary and postsecondary levels, teachers of English as a Second Language, physicians, other health personnel, agriculturalists, pastors, theological educators, and translators. Requests come from the regions of Africa, Asia and the Pacific, and Latin America and the Caribbean and from such countries as Brazil, China, Tanzania, and the Solomon Islands. [ID:6138]

WaterCan
323 Chapel Street, Ottawa, Ontario K1N 7Z2; (613) 230-5182, fax (613) 237-5969, www.watercan.com

MID-SIZED DEVELOPMENT ASSISTANCE GROUP: Development Assistance, Fundraising, Water Resources

WaterCan provides funds for clean water and sanitation projects in developing countries. Fund raising efforts consist of inserting a WaterCan leaflet describing the need for clean water and sanitation around the world into the water bills of Canadian homes. Funds raised support clean water and sanitation projects. WaterCan receives a matching grant from the Canadian International Development Agency (CIDA).

WaterCan has four staff in Ottawa whose work is overseen by a board of directors. In addition to the paid staff, a group of senior volunteers provide assistance in fundraising, project evaluation, and training. WaterCan regularly looks for volunteers to participate in evaluating projects submitted for funding, in fundraising activities, and in managing its overall activities. [ID:6139]

Western Canada Wilderness Committee

Executive Director, 20 Water Street, Vancouver, B.C. V6B 1A4;
(604) 683-8220, fax (604) 683-8229, wc2wild@direct.ca, www.web.net/wcwild/welcome.html

MID-SIZED ENVIRONMENTAL ACTION GROUP: Environment, Forestry,
Media/Communications, Research

Western Canada Wilderness Committee is involved in trail building, educational products, and newsletters on temperate rainforests in Canada and Chile. It also has a BETR (Bear, Elephant, Tiger, and Rhinoceros) program which seeks to ban the hunting and trade of endangered species. Western Canada Wilderness Committee has 12 staff based in Canada and three overseas. Successful applicants have a background in forestry and biology and have undertaken relevant language training. [ID:6420]

World Accord (WA)

145 Columbia Street W., Waterloo, Ontario N2L 3L2;
(519) 747-2215, fax (519) 747-2644, aaccord@web.net, www.web.net/~aaccord

MID-SIZED DEVELOPMENT ASSISTANCE GROUP: Adult Training, Agriculture, Community
Development, Development Assistance, Development Education, Environment, Forestry, Gender
and Development, Human Resources, Micro-Enterprises, Water Resources

World Accord (WA) works in partnership with local indigenous community organizations and NGOs in Asia and Latin America on a range of development activities, with local institutional capacity-building central to all its activities. WA supports micro-enterprise and cooperative development; environmental agriculture; agroforestry; rice production, milling, storage and marketing; women's rights and development; health; and education. It works primarily in the Philippines, Nepal, Sri Lanka, India, Honduras, and Guatemala.

WA has four staff based in Canada. Staff generally have experience in international development and are dedicated to eliminating world poverty and inequality. Development education is a critical part of the work done in Canada. Accounting, administrative, communications, and desktop publishing skills are also required. [ID:6140]

World Federalists of Canada (WFC)

Suite 207, 145 Spruce Street, Ottawa, Ontario K1R 6P1;
(613) 232-0647, fax (613) 563-0017, wfcnat@web.net, www.web.net/~wfcnat.wfc.html.

SMALL INTERNATIONAL ADVOCACY GROUP: Administration, Advocacy, Editing, Fundraising,
Volunteer, Writing

World Federalists of Canada (WFC) is a national organization which promotes global awareness and political support for world institutions of law and governance. There are eight branches across Canada. WFC is one of 22 national members of the World Federalist Movement (WFM), an accredited NGO at the United Nations.

Two staff, an executive director and an administrator, are based in Ottawa. In general, all staff have university degrees in political science or the social sciences and an extensive history of participation in volunteer organizations. Bilingualism is an asset. [ID:6141]

World Literacy of Canada (WLC)

2nd Floor, 59 Front Street E., Toronto, Ontario M5E 1B3;
(416) 863-6262, fax (416) 601-6984, worldlit@web.net, www.nald.ca/wlc.htm

SMALL DEVELOPMENT ASSISTANCE GROUP: Adult Training, Community Development,
Development Education, Gender and Development, Literacy, Social Justice and Development,
Teaching

World Literacy of Canada (WLC) promotes international development and social justice in South Asia through the funding of community-based programs that emphasize adult literacy and nonformal education. WLC supports literacy programs which integrate health, housing, vocational training, and credit and savings programs in a holistic approach to community development. Particular attention is given to the needs of disadvantaged women. In Canada, WLC promotes public awareness and understanding of literacy and international development issues through their own projects and in cooperation with other agencies.

For their overseas projects, WLC stands by its commitment to employ local people who have the necessary expertise to work on their own projects. At present, WLC has six full-time staff in India. Local languages, cultural knowledge, and gender equity are fundamental to considerations for staffing overseas. WLC currently employs two full-time staff in Canada. Although staff turnover is minimal, it maintains a data bank for résumés. [ID:6143]

World Relief Canada (WRC)
Overseas Personnel Coordinator, International Ministries Dept.,
Suite 310, 600 Alden Road, Markham, Ontario L3R 0E7; (905) 415-8181, fax (905) 415-0287

MID-SIZED RELIEF AND DEVELOPMENT AGENCY: Accounting, Administration, Agriculture, Business/Banking/Trade, Business Development, Community Development, Development Assistance, Development Education, Fundraising, Gender and Development, Humanitarian Relief, Medical Health, Micro-Enterprises, Project Management, Teaching, Water Resources

World Relief Canada (WRC) is the disaster relief, development assistance, and refugee service arm of the Evangelical Fellowship of Canada. WRC works with national partners in agriculture, reforestation, health, income generation, water development, training, and relief.

WRC works exclusively through its overseas partners and no longer sends personnel overseas. [ID:6144]

World University Service of Canada (WUSC)
P.O. Box 3000, Stn. C, Ottawa, Ontario K1Y 4M8;
(613) 798-7477, fax (613) 798-0990, wusc@wusc.ca, www.wusc.ca

LARGE VOLUNTEER GROUP: Adult Training, Business Development, Community Development, Computer Systems, Development Assistance, Development Education, Economics, Environment, Exchange Programs, Forestry, Gender and Development, Human Resources, Logistics, Media/Communications, Micro-Enterprises, Project Management, Teaching, Technical Assistance, Telecommunications, Volunteer

World University Service of Canada (WUSC) recruits Canadian development workers and technical experts for technical assistance and community development programs in 11 developing countries. WUSC also implements development education programs through its network of members and local committees on college and university campuses across Canada.

WUSC has approximately 60 staff at its secretariat office in Ottawa. It has field offices in 11 countries abroad. The organization has approximately 100 volunteers overseas, and supports approximately 30 refugee students each year and well over 100 international trainees in Canada under WUSC-administered scholarship and training programs. WUSC also implements development assistance projects in Africa, Latin America, the Middle East, and Southeast Asia.

WUSC is the Canadian cooperating agency for the United Nations Volunteers Programme (UNV), handling the recruitment process for Canadians and landed immigrants on behalf of the UNV office in Bonn. UNV offers mid-career professionals the opportunity to volunteer overseas in a humanitarian effort. Currently, over 2,000 people from more than 100 countries volunteer as specialists and field workers. Visit the UNV web site at www.unv.org.

As one of the largest NGOS in Canada, WUSC has local committees (LCs) in universities and colleges across the country. It works with many indigenous NGOs in its program countries and actively encourages linkages between academic institutions in Canada and those overseas. Some of the fields in which WUSC offers internships are environmental management, small enterprise development, information, technology, education and training, community development, and institutional strengthening. WUSC also posts both long-term and short-term overseas positions on its web site. (For more information see Chapter 10, Short-term Programs Overseas.) [ID:6145]

YMCA Canada, International Office (YMCA)
Room 309, 180 Argyle Avenue, Ottawa, Ontario K2P 1B7; (613) 233-5647, fax (613) 233-3096

LARGE DEVELOPMENT ASSISTANCE GROUP: Administration, Development Assistance, Development Education, Project Management

The YMCA in Canada is dedicated to the growth of all persons in spirit, mind and body, and to a sense of responsibility for each other and the global community. YMCA Canada supports international education and overseas project activities of local YMCAs and YMCA-YWCAs.

The Canadian YMCA involves about 500,000 people a year in its international education activities. Primary targets are YMCA members and participants who have not had previous involvement in international issues. Many local associations conduct programs in schools, and in the broader community with other NGOs. National themes for education work include refugees, environment, peace and women in development.

Canadian YMCAs and YMCA-YWCAs contribute to international development in over 50 countries around the world through a model of local Y-to-Y partnerships. Overseas projects are generally implemented by indigenous YMCA staff and volunteers, and support a wide variety of sectors: education, health, agriculture, community development, leadership training, refugees and rehabilitation. There are two International Program staff in the YMCA Canada office and about 35 staff across the country in local associations who have some responsibility for international education or overseas projects. A very limited number of opportunities exist to go overseas as part of a Partnership Exchange or on short-term work placements. Programs are organized between a local Canadian Y and an overseas partner. Selection and orientation of individuals for overseas opportunities is done by the local association. Candidates should have previous volunteer involvement with the YMCA, YMCA-YWCA or other community services, and commit themselves to sharing their experience with YMCA staff, volunteers and the community upon their return. [ID:6146]

Young Women's Christian Association of Canada (YWCA)
5th Floor, 590 Jarvis Street, Toronto, Ontario M4Y 2J4;
(416) 962-8881, fax (416) 962-8084, national@ywcacanada.ca, www.ywcacanada.ca

SMALL COMMUNITY DEVELOPMENT GROUP: Development Assistance, Development Education, Gender and Development, Project Management

YWCA - Canada has four paid staff across Canada and about 100 volunteers. It does not place volunteers overseas; however, an individual may write directly to its overseas affiliates seeking a placement. It may provide some assistance to interested individuals seeking volunteer work overseas. YWCA - Canada maintains a data bank for résumés. [ID:6147]

Youth Action Network
Suite 410, 67 Richmond Street W., Toronto, Ontario M5H 1Z5; (800) 718-5465, fax (416) 368-8354

SMALL INTERNATIONAL ADVOCACY GROUP: Community Development, Development Education, Exchange Programs

Youth Action Network is a fully independent nonprofit organization committed to bettering our world. This means confronting such issues as human rights, world peace, the environment and international development. Youth Action Network believes in the ability of youth to effect constructive change. The group understands the need for a stronger youth voice and for greater youth participation in local and global communities. The Network publishes the Youth Action Forum which is distributed across Canada. Youth Action Network also maintains a Resource Action Centre and sponsors Youthweek. [ID:6148]

Youth Challenge International (YCI)

11 Soho Street, Toronto, Ontario M5T 1Z6;
(416) 971-9846, fax (416) 971-6863, info@yci.org, www.yci.org

MID-SIZED SPECIAL NEEDS GROUP: Accounting, Community Development, Construction, Development Assistance, Engineering, Environment, Exchange Programs, Logistics, Medical Health, Volunteer

Youth Challenge International (YCI) allows volunteers aged 18 to 25 an opportunity to combine community service and scientific research in adventurous, three-month cooperative projects in developing regions. YCI works with scientific institutes, universities, government agencies and local self-help groups in an effort to mitigate social problems in the South. Activities include construction, medical projects and environmental conservation work. Projects are organized and led by youth leaders, specialists, and educators in liaison with scientific consultants and researchers.

YCI employs six staff in Canada and three overseas,. It has about 70 volunteers per project and approximately 25 international volunteers who serve as board of directors, country liaisons or coordinators. The majority of field staff are volunteers, but YCI also recruits a small number of full-time project managers annually for international projects. Volunteer field staff lead youth groups on field development projects. In 1996 YCI sought 200 volunteers for projects in Guyana and Costa Rica.

All staff must be at least 25 years old, have first aid training, be able to swim 500 metres, have a thorough grounding in outdoor leadership, and have international development or conservation experience. YCI needs specialists in medicine, nursing, engineering, and construction. Project managers should be competent with logistics, accounting, reporting, and staff evaluation. Candidates must show reliability, resourcefulness, enthusiasm, high compatibility, and dedication to promoting the interests and well-being of participants. YCI requires a three-month volunteer commitment from qualified individuals in youth-leadership positions. YCI maintains a data bank for résumés. [ID:6149]

Chapter 36

United Nations

The United Nations was created in 1945 with high hopes for the role that it would play. It was to be an international adjudicator, which would provide a fair and impartial forum for sovereign nations to resolve inter-state conflict through peaceful dialogue. The preamble to the Charter of the United Nations outlines the organization's idealistic mandate: "to save succeeding generations from the scourge of war," "to reaffirm faith in fundamental human rights," "to encourage adherence to international law," and to "promote social progress and better standards of life."

Unfortunately, the dream contrasts sharply with the reality. The UN has faced extensive criticism over its lack of binding authority in global issues. Although many nations have high regard for the UN, others are deeply suspicious. Questions have also been raised about the relevancy of the UN in the new age of globalization and changing geopolitical interests.

It is in this context of increasing criticism that reform of the UN is now taking place. The UN has stated that this process of modification of its structure is being undertaken to narrow the gap between its aspirations and achievements. The process has involved assessing the UN's major strengths and weaknesses, and planning for changes in required areas.

Despite its problems, the UN still stands as one of the only bodies which can address international interests, and obtain participation from most of its members. For example, 1998 marks the 50th anniversary celebration of one of the UN's greatest accomplishments, the Universal Declaration of Human Rights.

This chapter is divided into three parts. First, the purposes and structure of the UN and its related agencies are examined. Second, the chapter looks at employment opportunities and recruitment procedures. And third, 54 UN organizations and related bodies are profiled.

STRUCTURE AND PURPOSES

In a nutshell, the UN system is a framework for international cooperation. There are 185 states represented in the GENERAL ASSEMBLY. The UN charter outlines its principal objectives: to maintain international peace and security; to resolve international economic, political, social, and cultural disputes; and to promote human rights and fundamental freedoms.

The biennial budget for 1996-97 is approximately US$2.6 billion. This figure belies the actual extent of UN expenditures, as it does not include voluntary contributions lying outside the regular UN budget that finance the activities of some of the major players in the UN system, such as the UNITED NATIONS DEVELOPMENT PROGRAM (UNDP), WORLD FOOD PROGRAM (WFP), UNITED NATIONS HIGH COMMISSIONER FOR REFUGEES (UNHCR), and the UNITED NATIONS CHILDREN'S FUND (UNICEF).

The UN system is comprised of the Secretariat and 25 other organizations such as: councils, authorities, funds, programs, and specialized agencies. This figure does not include any subsidiary machinery, such as committees that convene occasionally or at irregular intervals. Its basic structure has five principal organs. Each is briefly described below.

The GENERAL ASSEMBLY is the UN's main deliberative organ, composed of representatives of all member states, each of which has one vote. All UN bodies report to the Assembly, which votes on their recommendations and budget proposals. Decisions on important questions of security, admission of new members, and budgetary matters require a two-thirds majority; others are resolved by simple majority or consensus.

The SECURITY COUNCIL has primary responsibility for the maintenance of international peace and security. The Council's functions generally fall under two headings: pacific settlement of disputes; and action with respect to threats to the peace, breaches of the peace, and acts of aggression. The Council has 15 members, five of whom are permanent: China, France, the Russian Federation, the United Kingdom, and the United States. The remaining 10 are elected by the General Assembly for two-year terms. Canada last served in this capacity in 1989-90.

The ECONOMIC AND SOCIAL COUNCIL (ECOSOC) coordinates the economic and social work of the UN and the specialized agencies and institutions known as the "United Nations family" of organizations. Bodies under this umbrella promote higher standards of living, economic and social progress, solutions to international economic, social, health and related problems, international cultural and educational cooperation, and universal respect for and observance of human rights and fundamental freedoms.

The INTERNATIONAL COURT OF JUSTICE is the principal judicial organ of the UN. The Court resolves disputes submitted by member states, applying international conventions, international custom, the general principles of law recognized by nations, and judicial precedents. It also gives advisory opinions to the Assembly and the Council on legal questions.

The UN SECRETARIAT is comprised of an international staff working at headquarters in New York and in the field, assuming responsibility for the day-to-day operations of the UN and servicing its affiliated organs. By itself, it employs more than 14,800 individuals from over 160 countries.

RECRUITMENT

With about 53,333 employees, the UN and its affiliated organizations are a vast source of potential international employment. There are currently about 1,700 Canadians in the secretariats of international organizations. A much larger number of Canadians work as consultants with implementing agencies (private firms or organizations who have contracts with the UN). There is no doubt that if you're seeking an international career close to the action, the UN offers a unique vantage point.

The system has been under severe fiscal constraints in recent years, primarily because many member countries have been negligent in paying their dues. In fact, Canada's near perfect track-record in this regard is the exception rather than the rule. In practical terms, this has meant little or no growth in staffing.

Professional positions constitute a little over one third of UN staff and are subject to fierce international competition and the steel-trap quota system that filters candidates by nationality. In filling vacancies, the UN and other international organizations maintain a proportionate balance (with respect to regular budget contributions) among member states, with a view to enabling as many as possible to have national representation on the professional staffs. An additional consideration is improving the gender balance, particularly in the areas of science, economics, management, and other areas where female representation has been unsatisfactory.

While it is impossible to provide a comprehensive listing of the types of professional positions for which the international organizations recruit, the major categories are: administration, agriculture, development, economics, education, engineering, environment, information systems, law, international affairs, public affairs, public health, and social welfare.

QUALIFICATIONS

The UN values, in particular, MAs and PhDs in economics, economic development, area studies, administration, agriculture, and communications. Candidates ideally have international experience in more than one of these areas, which enables them to take an integrated and interdisciplinary approach. Other desirable areas of expertise include energy and natural resources, statistics, planning, and environment.

Proficiency in languages, particularly English, French and Spanish, is highly regarded by recruiters and is required for some positions. Applicants with fluency in Arabic and Eastern European languages have also been evaluated favourably in recent years.

UN salaries have not increased for a number of years and serious cuts have had their impact. Salaries range from about US$30,000 for entry-level positions to over US$100,000 for director positions.

ENTRY LEVEL PROGRAMS

Most people we know who are now working at entry-level positions for the UN, started their career by taking advantage of volunteering opportunities open to Canadians with the UN. Many of these volunteer positions actually have a decent salary. Also worth pointing out are the international internship programs offered by the federal government, which have created many windows for gaining internship positions with the UN. For information on these international internships see the Canadian Government International Internships profile in Chapter 17, International Internships.

Junior Professional Officer Program (JPO)
Human Resources Division, Personnel and Administration Branch,
Canadian International Development Agency (CIDA),
200 Promenade du Portage, Hull (Québec) K1A 0G4;
(800) 230-6349; fax: (819) 953-6088

The Junior Professional Officer Program (JPO) is administered under the auspices of the United Nations. Its primary objectives are to provide experience in managing a development program, support the UN through JPO services, place Canadians in the UN, and use knowledge gained from assignments. General duties of a JPO include the administration and coordination of projects and liaison between local authorities, regional offices, and headquarters.

Through the CANADIAN INTERNATIONAL DEVELOPMENT AGENCY (CIDA), Canada sponsors several JPOs annually in the following UN agencies: UNITED NATIONS DEVELOPMENT PROGRAM (UNDP), UNITED NATIONS INTERNATIONAL CHILDREN'S FUND (UNICEF), UNITED NATIONS HIGH COMMISSIONER FOR REFUGEES (UNHCR), and the WORLD FOOD PROGRAM (WFP).

Candidates should be under the age of 30 and possess a completed master's degree in a relevant discipline. Knowledge of a third language is an asset and prior work experience (paid or voluntary) is becoming increasingly important as placements become more competitive.

Information about the JPO program and application forms are available on CIDA's web site.

United Nations Volunteers (UNV)
Postfach 260111, Bonn, Germany; (49) (228) 815-2000,
fax (49) (228) 815-2001; enquiry@unv.org, www.unv.org

The United Nations Volunteers (UNV) program, a multilateral volunteer-sending organization, has become one of the foremost suppliers of experienced professionals for governments of developing countries and for the UN system agencies which assist them. They work under five different "windows": technical cooperation; facilitation of the developmental (including environmental) initiatives of local communities; humanitarian relief and rehabilitation; peace-building, including democratization; and fostering entrepreneurship in the public and private sectors.

UNV specialists comprise some 115 professional categories under 11 broad headings: Administration, Agriculture, Communication and Transport, Education, Engineering, Technicians, Skilled Trades, Health, Human

Settlement/Construction, Natural Science, and Social Science. Currently, over 2,000 specialists are serving in 125 countries worldwide. The UNV program is administered in Canada by WORLD UNIVERSITY SERVICE OF CANADA (WUSC). (For more information, see WUSC's profile in Chapter 35, Nongovernmental Organizations.)

United Nations Association in Canada (UNA-Canada)
National Office, 130 Slater Street, Suite 900, Ottawa, Ontario K1P 6E2;
(613) 232-5751, fax (613) 563-2455; unac@magi.com, www.unac.org

The United Nations Association in Canada (UNA Canada) is a national organization of Canadians interested in the United Nations. UNA's national office and over 20 branches work to educate the Canadian public about the UN, to promote awareness of its activities, and to encourage public and official support for the multilateral organization. UNA Canada's main areas of programming include distribution of materials from and about the UN, coordination of services and conferences, media briefings, interaction with government, and publications. The association has no overseas activities.

Twelve staff work in the national office and several branches also have staff. All offices use volunteer assistance. Employees must have an interest in international affairs and applicants with related degrees or past experience are welcome. Degree of expertise required depends on the position. Bilingualism is an asset, and often obligatory and computer knowledge is required. UNA Canada maintains a data bank for résumés and considers internship applicants year-round, in the areas of peacekeeping, sustainable development and human rights. The UNA Canada web site does not provide job notices for UNA offices. However, the site contains job vacancies for the U.N. and other useful information.

INTERNSHIPS AND AWARDS

The United Nations and its affiliates offer a number of paid and unpaid internships as well as academic awards. (For more detailed information see Chapter 17, International Internships and Chapter 15, Awards & Grants.)

PROFESSIONAL OPPORTUNITIES

The Canadian government is committed to ensuring that the representation of Canadians in the secretariats of international organizations fairly reflects our level of contribution. Canada's 1994 contribution amounted to 3.10 per cent of the total, eighth-highest in the world.

International Programs Directorate (IPD)
Public Service Commission of Canada, 300 Laurier Ave. W.,
Ottawa, Ontario K1A 0M7; (613) 943-0771, fax: (613) 992-5902

The Public Service Commission (PSC), in conjunction with the Department of Foreign Affairs and International Trade, monitors middle and senior level positions within the secretariats of international organizations to which Canada belongs. The PSC coordinates the nomination of Canadian candidates for vacancies deemed to be of interest to and attainable by Canada.

Between 40 and 50 Canadians annually compete successfully for secretariat positions in international organizations. Candidates should have a university degree and a minimum of five years experience in their field, preferably with an international organization.

The International Programs Directorate maintains a very useful web site that offers information on the availability of employment with international organizations of which Canada is a member state.

Peacekeeping/Relief

The UN is hiring increasing numbers in the areas of peacekeeping, election monitoring, logistics and emergency relief in trouble spots throughout the world, and recruits selectively for operational and technical posts. These positions are usually short in duration and require extensive unaccompanied travel. Applicants are expected to have experience in difficult foreign postings and possess a unique blend of initiative, judgement, and humanitarian sensitivity.

There are many routes to take when you are searching for work in peacekeeping or relief. With persistence, these are often the easiest fields to break into as working conditions are often difficult. Contact the UN or international agency directly.

In Canada, the INTERNATIONAL PROGRAMS DIRECTORATE OF THE PUBLIC SERVICE COMMISSION sometimes works closely with WORLD UNIVERSITY SERVICES CANADA (WUSC), CARE CANADA, and various other NGOs in identifying candidates for these missions. See the profiles section in this chapter for more information.

Consulting

There are a variety of consulting opportunities for individuals and firms within the UN system. The UN organizations which use consulting services are: the ASIAN DEVELOPMENT BANK, FOOD AND AGRICULTURE ORGANIZATION (FAO), INTERNATIONAL CIVIL AVIATION ORGANIZATION (ICAO), INTERNATIONAL LABOUR ORGANIZATION (ILO), INTERNATIONAL TELECOMMUNICATIONS UNION (ITU), UNITED NATIONS HIGH COMMISSIONER FOR REFUGEES (UNHCR), UNITED NATIONS OFFICE FOR PROJECT SERVICES (UNOPS), UNITED NATIONS PROCUREMENT DIVISION (UN/PD), UNITED NATIONS DEVELOPMENT PROGRAM (UNDP), UNITED NATIONS INDUSTRIAL DEVELOPMENT ORGANIZATION (UNIDO), UNITED NATIONS EDUCATIONAL, SCIENTIFIC AND CULTURAL ORGANIZATION (UNESCO), the WORLD BANK, and WORLD HEALTH ORGANIZATION (WHO).

Information regarding business opportunities with UN organizations can be found in the *Procurement Update* which is produced by the Inter-Agency Procurement Services Office (IAPSO). It lists procurement notices, contract awards, project endorsements, and vacancy notices. The *Procurement Update* is only available through IAPSO's web site, www.iapso.org/pu/pu.html, or by e-mail at procurement.update@undp.org.

Technical Assistance

The Technical Assistance Recruitment and Administration Service, Program Support Division, Room DC-1-1208, United Nations, New York, NY 10017 USA; (212) 963-6418, fax: (212) 963-1272

The United Nations technical cooperation programs are administered by the UNITED NATIONS DEVELOPMENT PROGRAM (UNDP). An estimated 7,500 people work throughout the UN system as technical assistance experts in areas such as, energy, water resources, minerals, public infrastructure, social and community development, demography and statistics. Junior candidates are rarely selected; applicants should have high professional standing and previous international experience.

Translation/Interpretation

Translators and interpreters are hired by the UN based on the results of competitive examinations. General requirements include a university degree, relevant experience, and a thorough knowledge of at least three official UN languages. Candidates should contact the UN RECRUITMENT OFFICE in New York at (212) 963-1234 or communicate directly with the organization in which they are interested.

UN Public Inquiries

(212) 963-4475, fax: (212) 963-0071; www.un.org

The Public Enquiries telephone number at UN Headquarters is staffed by operators who can answer questions and provide more specific contact information.

RESOURCES

The list of books below is presented with a view to assisting you in embarking on an international career with the United Nations or related agencies.

For further resources consult the Resources for Chapter 37, Environmental & Agricultural Research Centres; Chapter 38, International Organizations; and Chapter 17, International Internships.

The World Bank Group 🖳
www.worldbank.org ▪ Provides information on the World Bank Group and its constituent members. News releases, country and regional summaries, and a public information centre are all useful features of this site. Employment opportunities with the World Bank are posted here too. [ID:2574]

Asian Development Bank Business Opportunities 📖 🖳
Monthly ➤ Central Operations Services Office, Asian Development Bank, P.O. Box 789, Manilla Central Post Office, 0980 Manila, Philippines; free; (632) 632-4444, fax (632) 636-4444, erosales@mail.asiandevbank.org ▪ Provides advance information on goods and service requirements of projects under consideration by the Asian Development Bank. Internet edition is available at www.asiandevbank.org. Visit this site, look under "Business Opportunities." [ID:2608]

Basic Facts About the United Nations 📖
1993, United Nations Publications ➤ Information Office, United Nations Association in Canada, Suite 900, 130 Slater Street, Ottawa, Ontario K1P 6E2; $11.25; VISA, MC; (613) 232-5751, fax (613)

563-2455 ▪ This compact, inexpensive book provides a general introduction to the role and functions of the United Nations and its related agencies, highlighting and outlining the main objectives and achievements of the organization. Updated regularly. [ID:1258]

Development Business 📖 🖥
24 per year ➤ United Nations Publications, 1 United Nations Plaza, Room DC1-570, New York, NY 10017, USA; US$495/year; credit cards; (212) 963-1516, fax (212) 963-1381 ▪ *Development Business* is the primary source for information on goods, works, and services required for projects financed by all of the Development Banks and the UN system. A one-year subscription includes 12 World Bank and 12 Inter-American Development Bank Monthly Operational Summaries and 4 African Development Bank Quarterly Operational Summaries. Also available online as Scan-a-Bid. There are charges for connect time and retrieval fees. For sign-up information see the web site www.krinfo.com and click on the Sales icon in the left hand frame. [ID:1303]

IDB Projects 📖 🖥
10/year, Inter-American Development Bank ➤ John Hopkins University Press (JHUP), P.O. Box 19966, Baltimore, MD 21211, USA; US$150/year; VISA, MC; (800) 548-1784, fax (410) 516-6968, jlorder@jhunix.hcf.jhu.edu ▪ Advertises business opportunities arising from projects financed by the Inter-American Development Bank. Visit the IDB web site at www.iadb.org and enter the "Business Opportunities" menu. Visit www.press.jhu.edu/press/journals, the distributor's web site. [ID:2609]

IFInet 🖥
www.dfait-maeci.gc.ca/ifinet ▪ Provides Canadian exporters with information on projects financed by international financial institutions. Site includes business guides and hotlinks. Register to receive a password. [ID:2648]

International Directory for Youth Internships 📖
1993, *M. Culligan, C. Morehouse,* 58 pages ➤ Council on International and Public Affairs, Apex Press, Suite 3C, 777 United Nations Plaza, New York, NY 10017, USA; $7.50; VISA, MC; (914) 271-6500, fax (914) 271-2039 ▪ Booklet includes list of about 40 intern positions related to the UN secretariat and other international programs sponsored by nongovernmental organizations. All academic levels are represented, but many positions require graduate or postgraduate status. [ID:1071]

Internships & Careers in International Affairs 📖
1992, *James Muldoon* ➤ Model UN & Youth Dept., United Nations Association of the USA, 801 Second Ave., New York, NY 10017-4706, USA; US$10; cheque or money order; (212) 697-3232, fax (212) 682-9185, unhq@unausa.org ▪ Aimed at postsecondary students wishing to pursue careers in international affairs. Booklet concentrates on three areas: the US government, the United Nations, and nongovernmental organizations. Visit distributor's web site, www.unausa.org. [ID:1040]

NGLS Handbook
1997, 306 pages ➤ United Nations Non-Governmental Liaison Service (UN/NGLS), Room FF 346, United Nations, New York, NY 10017, USA; no charge; (212) 963-3125, fax (212) 963-8712 ▪ This annual book is designed by the UN's Non-Governmental Liaison Service to provide information about UN agencies, programs, and funds working for economic and social development. [ID:2700]

United Nations Handbook 📖
Annual, *Ministry of External Relations & Trade* ➤ New Zealand High Commission, Suite 727, 99 Bank Street, Ottawa, Ontario K1P 6G3; $37; money order; (613) 238-5991, fax (613) 238-5707 ▪ Contains up-to-date lists of all the organizations of the United Nations, including aims, committee structure, and legal basis. Legalistic reading but very comprehensive. [ID:1213]

United Nations System 🖥
www.un.org ▪ The United Nation's home page, this site provides links to all UN organizations. There is also news on UN-related matters, a search engine for member organizations, and links to a number of useful non-UN international organizations. [ID:2572]

United Nations Volunteers ⌨
www.unv.org ▪ This program offers mid-career professionals the opportunity to volunteer overseas in a humanitarian effort. Currently, over 2,000 people from more than 100 countries are volunteering in developing countries as specialists and field workers. This site can help start you on the way to becoming a volunteer for the United Nations. [ID:2482]

The World Bank and Cooperation with NGOs 📖
1992, *Ann Thomson,* 30 pages ➤ CODE, 321 Chapel Street, Ottawa, Ontario K1N 7Z2; $14; VISA; (613) 232-3569, fax (613) 232-7435, codehq@codecan.com ▪ This booklet offers a general introduction to the World Bank and the mechanisms for NGO involvement in World Bank projects. Good for anyone wishing to make contact with the World Bank. [ID:1114]

World Trade Organization ⌨
www.wto.org ▪ Primary internet site for the World Trade Organization. Provides information on international trade policy, research reports and other trade-related resources. [ID:2610]

Profiles of UN Agencies

The 55 UN organizations profiled in this chapter are working on diverse issues affecting our global community. While this sampling has focused on the largest and most well known organizations, an effort was also made to include new agencies, which are focusing on contemporary issues.

The organizations were categorized under nine headings as follows: six were listed under the Economic and Social Council; two were under the General Assembly; one is the International Court of Justice; 11 are Related UN Programs; four are Regional Development Banks; one is the Security Council; 17 are specialized agencies of the UN; six are part of the World Bank Group; and six are other UN bodies.

These organizations are located across the world, but the majority have their headquarters in western nations. There were 29 located in Europe, 14 in North America, four in Africa, one in South America, three in Asia, two in the Caribbean, and two in the Middle East.

This list is only meant to serve as a broad introduction to UN organizations. For more detailed information visit the web sites for the organizations listed. The UN homepage (www.un.org) is also a very good resource and has links to other web sites.

African Development Bank
Personnel Office, 01B.P.-1387, Abidjan 01, COTE D'IVOIRE; (225) 204-444, fax (225) 217-471

REGIONAL DEVELOPMENT BANK ▪ The mandate of the African Development Bank is to contribute to the economic development and social progress of its members. There are currently 77 member states, comprising 53 African and 24 non-African states, including Canada.

The ADB employs approximately 950 staff. Job postings are advertised in major newspapers and magazines, and consultants can register their résumés by faxing them to (225) 217-471. [ID:6150]

Asian Development Bank (ADB)
Human Resources Division (Professional Staff Section),
P.O. Box 789, 6 ADB Ave., Mandaluyong, 0401 Metro Manila, 0980 Manila,
PHILIPPINES; (63) (2) 711-3851, fax (63) (2) 636-4444, www.asiandevbank.org

REGIONAL DEVELOPMENT BANK ▪ The Asian Development Bank makes loans for the economic and social advancement of developing member countries; provides technical assistance for the preparation and execution of development projects, programs and advisory services; and promotes investment of private and public capital for development projects. There are currently 56 member countries, comprising 40 regional and 16 non-regional members.

The ADB web site contains hiring and employment information. [ID:6151]

Caribbean Development Bank (CDB)
P.O. Box 408, Wildey, St. Michael, BARBADOS; (246) 431-1600, fax (246) 426-1600

REGIONAL DEVELOPMENT BANK ▪ The purpose of the Caribbean Development Bank (CDB) is to contribute to harmonious economic growth and development of member countries in the Caribbean, and to promote economic cooperation and integration among them, with particular concern for the less-developed member countries of the region. Membership is open to states and territories in the region and to non-regional states which are members of the UN, or its specialized agencies, and currently comprises 40 regional and 16 non-regional members. [ID:6152]

Committee on the Peaceful Uses of Outer Space (COPUOS)
Office for Outer Space Affairs, Vienna International Centre,
Wagramerstrasse 5, A-1400 Vienna, AUSTRIA; (43) (1) 21345-4950,
fax (43) (1) 21345-5830, OOSA@unov.un.or.at, www.un.or.at/OOSA_Kiosk/index.html

GENERAL ASSEMBLY ▪ The tasks of the Committee on the Peaceful Uses of Outer Space (COPOUS) are to review the scope of international cooperation in peaceful uses of outer space, to devise programs in this field to be carried out under UN auspices, to research and disseminate information, and to study legal problems arising from the exploration of outer space. [ID:6153]

Consultative Group on International Agricultural Research (CGIAR)
1818 H Street N.W., Washington, DC, 20433, USA;
(202) 473-8951, fax (202) 473-8110, cgiar@cgnet.com, www.cgiar.org

WORLD BANK GROUP ▪ The Consultative Group on International Agricultural Research (CGIAR), an associated organization within the World Bank Group, aims to harness modern science to the sustainable development of agriculture in poor countries. CGIAR and its Technical Advisory Committee provide 16 autonomous international centres with a funding system, scientific advice, a programming and review process, and financial and management advice. (For information on these centres see Chapter 37, Environmental & Agricultural Research Centres.)

Job offers are posted at their web site. [ID:6154]

Economic and Social Commission for Asia and the Pacific (ESCAP)
Office 1508A, United Nations Building, Rajadamnern Ave., Bangkok10200, THAILAND;
(66) (2) 288-12341, fax (66) (2) 282-1000, yoo.unescap@un.org, www.un.org/Depts/escap/

ECOSOC ▪ The Economic and Social Commission for Asia and the Pacific (ESCAP) assists in the development of Asia and the Pacific, with a view to raising the level of economic activity and standard of living in that region. ESCAP's new intergovernmental bodies comprise three thematic committees on regional economic cooperation, the environment and sustainable development, and poverty alleviation through economic growth and social development; two other committees, on statistics and transport and communications; and two special bodies on least-developed and landlocked, and Pacific island developing countries. Major research areas include agriculture and rural development, environment, development planning, statistics, industrial development, science and technology, human settlements, natural resources and energy, population, social development, international trade and transportation and communications. (For ESCAP internship information see Chapter 17, International Internships.) [ID:6155]

Economic and Social Commission for Western Asia (ESCWA)

P.O. Box 927115, Plaza Hotel, Amman, JORDAN; (962) (6) 669 4351, fax (962) (6) 669 4981

ECOSOC ▪ The Economic and Social Commission for Western Asia (ESCWA) assists in the economic and social development of that region and strives to strengthen economic relations among member countries and with other parts of the world. Principal areas of work include development planning, agriculture, natural resources, human settlements, transportation, communications and tourism, social development and population, statistics, technical cooperation, and the environment. [ID:6156]

Economic Commission for Africa (ECA)

Personnel Section, P.O. Box 3001, Africa Hall,
Addis Ababa, ETHIOPIA; (251) (1) 51-72-00, fax (251) (1) 51-44-16

ECOSOC ▪ The Economic Commission for Africa's (ECA) mandate is to initiate and participate in measures to facilitate the economic development of Africa, including its social aspects. It also acts to maintain and strengthen economic relations among the countries and territories of Africa and with other countries of the world. Major research areas include socio-economic research and planning, food and agriculture, industry, human settlements, trade, development finance, natural resources, transport, communications, tourism, public administration, social developmen, and population. [ID:6157]

Economic Commission for Europe (ECE)

Secretariat Recruitment Section, Office 370,
Palais des Nations, 8 - 14 Avenue de la Paix, 1211 Geneva 10, SWITZERLAND;
(41) (22) 917-2727, fax (41) (22) 917-4444, info.ece@unece.org, www.unece.org/Welcome.html

ECOSOC ▪ The Economic Commission for Europe (ECE) works to generate and improve economic relations among member states and with other countries and to strengthen intergovernmental cooperation and coordination, particularly in the areas of environment, transport, statistics, trade facilitation and economic analysis. Subsidiary themes include agriculture, timber, human settlements, chemicals, steel, engineering, energy, and science and technology. Particular emphasis is currently on activities to assist transitional economies in Central and Eastern Europe. (For ECE internship information see Chapter 17, International Internships.) [ID:6158]

Economic Commission for Latin America and the Caribbean (ECLAC)

P.O. Box 179-D, Avenida Vitacura 3030,
Santiago, CHILE; (56) (2) 210-2000, fax (56) (2) 208-0252, www.eclac.cl

ECOSOC ▪ The Economic Commission for Latin America and the Caribbean (ECLAC) promotes the economic and social development of member countries, and seeks to maintain and expand economic relations among member countries, and with other countries of the world. ECLAC also provides governments and other regional intergovernmental organizations with timely statistical information. Major themes include economic development, social development and humanitarian affairs, international trade, transnational corporations, food and agriculture, science and technology, population, human settlements, natural resources, energy, environment, transport, and statistics.

ECLAC employs 565 full-time staff and maintains a data bank for résumés. Its application procedures are the same as those for the United Nations Secretariat and can be found at the web site www.un.org/Depts/OHRM. (For ECLAC internship information see Chapter 17, International Internships.) [ID:6159]

Food and Agriculture Organization (FAO)
Information Materials Production Branch, Information Division,
Viale delle Terme di Caracalla, Rome, ITALY; (39) (6) 52251, fax (39) (6) 5225-3152, www.fao.org

SPECIALIZED AGENCY ▪ The Food and Agriculture Organization's (FAO) mandate is to raise the levels of nutrition and standards of living, secure improvements in the production and distribution of all food and agricultural products, and better the conditions of rural populations worldwide, thereby contributing toward an expanded global economy and ensuring humanity's freedom from hunger.

FAO currently employs 400 full-time professional and support staff worldwide. This includes 73 Canadians. Check out employment opportunities at their web site. [ID:6160]

Inter-American Development Bank (IADB)
1300 New York Ave. N.W.,
Washington, DC, 20577, USA; (202) 623-1000, fax (202) 623-3096, www.iadb.org

REGIONAL DEVELOPMENT BANK ▪ The purpose of the Inter-American Development Bank (IADB), the largest regional multilateral development institution, is to help accelerate economic and social development in the Americas. Its principal functions are: to utilize its own capital as well as funds raised by it in financial markets and other available resources, (these funds to be used for financing development in borrowing member countries); to supplement private investment when private capital is not available on reasonable terms and conditions; and to provide technical assistance for the preparation, financing and implementation of development plans and projects. At present, there are 46 member countries, comprised of 25 Latin American countries, the US, Canada and 19 non-regional states.

Vacancies are posted at their web site, along with information for consultants and private sector briefings. You can also submit your résumé electronically to their human resources department. (For IADB internship information see Chapter 17, International Internships.) [ID:6163]

International Atomic Energy Agency (IAEA)
Division of Personnel, P.O. Box 100, Wagramerstrasse 5, A-1400 Vienna, AUSTRIA;
(43) (1) 20600, fax (43) (1) 20607, iaeo@iaea1.iaea.or.at, www.iaea.or.at/worldatom

SPECIALIZED AGENCY ▪ The International Atomic Energy Agency (IAEA) aims to accelerate and enlarge the contribution of atomic energy to peace, health and prosperity throughout the world, and is charged with ensuring that assistance provided by it is not used to further any military purpose. The agency performs research on atomic energy for peaceful purposes; acts as an intermediary in supply of materials, services, equipment and facilities; fosters the exchange of scientific and technical information and of scientists and experts; administers safeguards against the misuse of aid provided through IAEA; and establishes safety standards.

The IAEA employs approximately 2,000 staff from over 80 countries (including Canada). Staff have expertise in a variety of scientific, technical, managerial, and professional disciplines. Most work at headquarters in Vienna, while some are posted in Toronto, Tokyo, New York, Geneva, Siebersdorf, and Monaco. Detailed information about employment opportunities can be obtained by writing to the Recruitment Unit, Division of Personnel, IAEA, P.O. Box 100, A-1400 Vienna, Austria. Also check their web site for job postings, application procedures, and to download an application form. (For IAEA internship information see Chapter 17, International Internships.) [ID:6164]

International Bank for Reconstruction and Development (IBRD)
Personnel Office, 1818 H Street N.W., Washington, DC, 20433,
USA; (202) 477-1234, fax (202) 477-6391, www.worldbank.org/

WORLD BANK GROUP ▪ The International Bank for Reconstruction and Development (IBRD) (also known as the World Bank) lends funds to carry out projects or to finance economic and institutional reform programs in less-developed member countries. The bank is also attempting to increase the proportion of funding allocated to directly assist the poorest people in these countries. IBRD is one of three member organizations comprising the World Bank Group. (For World Bank internship information see Chapter 17, International Internships.) [ID:6165]

International Centre for Settlement of Investment Disputes (ICSID)
1818 H Street N.W., Washington, DC, 20433, USA;
(202) 458-1534, fax (202) 522-2615, www.worldbank.org/

WORLD BANK GROUP ▪ The International Centre for Settlement of Investment Disputes (ICSID) provides facilities for settling disputes between governments and foreign investors through arbitration and conciliation. ICSID is an organization of the World Bank Group. As of June, 1997, 127 countries had ratified the 1965 convention establishing ICSID. [ID:6166]

International Civil Aviation Organization (ICAO)
Personnel Office, 999 University Street, Montréal, Québec,
H3C 5H7, CANADA; (514) 954-8219, fax (514) 954-6077, icaohq@icao.org, www.cam.org/~icao

SPECIALIZED AGENCY ▪ The International Civil Aviation Organization (ICAO) develops the principles and techniques of international air navigation, and fosters the planning and development of international air transport with a view to ensuring the safe and orderly growth of international civil aviation throughout the world.

ICAO employs approximately 400 professional and support staff. For recruitment information, e-mail them at recruitment@icao.org. Vacancy notices are posted on their web site. [ID:6167]

International Court of Justice (ICJ)
Peace Palace, The Hague, NETHERLANDS; (31) (70) 302-2323, fax (31) (70) 364-9928

INTERNATIONAL COURT OF JUSTICE ▪ The International Court of Justice (ICJ) is the principal judicial organ of the UN. Its primary function is to decide, in accordance with international law, such cases as are submitted to it by member states. In addition to making determinations concerning contesting states, ICJ also advises the Assembly and the Security Council on any legal questions that arise. [ID:6168]

International Development Association (IDA)
Recruitment Division Personnel, 1818 H Street N. W.,
Washington, DC, 20433, USA; (202) 477-1234, fax (202) 477-6391, www.worldbank.org/

WORLD BANK GROUP ▪ The International Development Association (IDA), part of the World Bank Group, promotes economic development by providing finance to the less-developed areas of the world on much more concessionary terms than those of conventional loans. It is designed especially to finance projects or reform programs in countries unable to service loans from the International Bank for Reconstruction and Development. [ID:6169]

International Finance Corporation (IFC)
Higher Level Recruitment, The World Bank/IFC/MIGA, 1818 H Street N.W.,
Washington, DC, 20433, USA; (202) 473 7896, fax (202) 477-6391, www.worldbank.org/

WORLD BANK GROUP ▪ The International Finance Corporation (IFC), part of the World Bank Group, invests in productive private or governmental enterprises, without government guarantee of repayment in cases where sufficient private capital is not available on reasonable terms. It also serves as a clearinghouse to bring together investment opportunities, private capital, both foreign and domestic, and experienced management. Its special purpose is to promote the growth of the private sector and to assist private enterprises in its developing country members, where such enterprises can advance economic development. (For World Bank internship information see Chapter 17, International Internships.) [ID:6170]

International Fund for Agricultural Development (IFAD)
Via del Serafico 107, 00142 Rome, ITALY; (39) (6) 54591,
fax (39) (6) 504-3463, ifad@ifad.org, www.unicc.org/ifad/home.html

SPECIALIZED AGENCY ▪ The International Fund for Agricultural Development (IFAD) aims to mobilize additional financial resources from donors for programs to improve food production systems, and strengthen related policies and institutions, especially among the . poorest people in least-developed countries.

IFAD's Personnel Division maintains a roster of consultants. (For IFAD internship information see Chapter 17, International Internships.) [ID:6171]

International Labour Organization (ILO)
Technical Co-operation Personnel Branch, 4 route des Morillons, 1211 Geneva 22,
SWITZERLAND; (41) (22) 799-6111, fax (41) (22) 798-8685, relconf@ilo.org, www.ilo.org/

SPECIALIZED AGENCY ▪ The International Labour Organization (ILO) seeks to improve working and living conditions through the adoption of international labour conventions and recommendations which set minimum standards for wages, hours of work, conditions of employment, and social security. ILO also conducts research and technical cooperation activities, including vocational training and management development.

ILO employs approximately 39 Canadian professional and support staff. Check "What's New" at their web site for job postings. (For ILO internship information see Chapter 17, International Internships.) [ID:6172]

International Maritime Organization (IMO)
Personnel Section, 4 Albert Embankment, London SE1 7SR, UK;
(44) (171) 735-7611, fax (44) (171) 587-3210, info@imo.org, www.imo.org

SPECIALIZED AGENCY ▪ The International Maritime Organization (IMO) facilitates cooperation among governments on technical matters affecting international shipping, in order to achieve the highest practicable standards of maritime safety and efficiency in navigation. IMO is also responsible for protecting the marine environment by preventing pollution of the sea by ships and other craft. [ID:6173]

International Monetary Fund (IMF)
Recruitment Division, 700 - 19th Street N.W., Washington, DC,
20431, USA; (202) 623-7000, fax (202) 623-4661, recruit@imf.org, www.imf.org

SPECIALIZED AGENCY ▪ The International Monetary Fund (IMF) promotes international monetary cooperation, facilitates the expansion and balanced growth of international trade, promotes exchange rate stability and assists in the establishment of a multilateral system of payments and the elimination of foreign exchange restrictions. The IMF also assists members, through the temporary provision of financial resources, to correct maladjustments in their balance of payments.

Recruitment activities center on the Economist Program (a two-year program for entry into the IMF's economist staff), mid-career economist positions and support-level positions. Openings in these areas are not advertised: for information on these jobs and how to apply, see their web site. (For IMF internship information see Chapter 17, International Internships.) [ID:6174]

International Telecommunication Union (ITU)
Personnel Office, Palais des Nations, CH 1211 Geneva 20,
SWITZERLAND; (41) (22) 730-5111, fax (41) (22) 733-7256, itumail@itu.int, www.itu.int

SPECIALIZED AGENCY ▪ The International Telecommunication Union's (ITU) promotes international cooperation among its members, and facilitates the improvement and availability of telecommunications services and technical assistance to developing countries.

ITU employs approximately 700 individuals, representing 72 nationalities, at its headquarters and in the field. Short-term vacancies are usually filled locally, while long-term professional jobs are advertised in the mainstream press. ITU's web site also posts vacancies and an application form that can be downloaded. [ID:6176]

International Trade Centre UNCTAD/ WTO (ITC)
Selection and Recruitment Section, 54-56 rue de Montbrillant, Geneva,
SWITZERLAND; (41) (22) 730-0111, fax (41) (22) 733 4439, itcreg@intracen.org, www.unicc.org/itc

SPECIALIZED AGENCY ▪ The International Trade Centre UNCTAD/GATT (ITC) works with developing countries to set up effective national trade promotion programs for expanding their exports and improving their import operations. ITC also provides trade publications and training to government and private-sector officials.

ITC employs approximately 10 Canadian professional and support staff. Vacancies are posted on their web site under "ITC News." [ID:6177]

Joint United Nations Programme on HIV/AIDS (UNAIDS)
20 Avenue Appia, CH - 1211, Geneva, 27, SWITZERLAND; , unaids@unaids.org, www.unaids.org

RELATED UN PROGRAM ▪ The Joint United Nations Programme on HIV/AIDS, functions as the main advocate for global action on HIV/AIDS. UNAIDS seeks to lead, strengthen and support an international response aimed at preventing the transmission of HIV, providing care and support, reducing the vulnerability of individuals and communities to HIV/AIDS, and alleviating the impact of the epidemic. UNAIDS medium-term objectives include: fostering a greater national response to HIV/AIDS, particularly in the developing world; promoting strong commitments by governments to HIV/aids; and strengthening and coordinating UN action on HIV/AIDS at the global and national levels. [ID:7105]

Multilateral Investment Guarantee Agency (MIGA)
1818 H Street N.W., Washington, DC, 20433, USA; (202) 473-6163, fax (202) 522-2630, www.miga.org

WORLD BANK GROUP ▪ The Multilateral Investment Guarantee Agency (MIGA), member of the World Bank Group, encourages the flow of direct foreign investment to its developing member countries for economic development. Its primary means of facilitating investment is through provision of investment guarantees against the risks of currency transfer, expropriation, and war and civil disturbance (political risks). It also provides technical assistance to host governments to enhance their ability to attract foreign direct investment. (For World Bank internship information see Chapter 17, International Internships.) [ID:6179]

UN Office For Project Services (UNOPS)
Information Section, 14th fllor, 220 East 42nd Street,
New York, NY, 10017, USA; (212) 906-6500, fax (212) 906-6501, www.unops.org

RELATED UN PROGRAM ▪ The United Nations Office for Project Services provides high-quality, timely and cost effective development services for the successful implementation of projects undertaken by United Nations Member States. [ID:7212]

United Nations Centre for Human Settlements (Habitat)
P.O. Box 30030, UN Office at Nairobi, Nairobi,
KENYA; (254) (2) 621-234, fax (254) (2) 624-266, www.undp.org/un/habitat/

ECOSOC ▪ The United Nations Centre for Human Settlements (Habitat) provides a focal point for human settlements action, and the coordination of activities within the UN system related principally to housing, building, and planning. (For Habitat internship information see Chapter 17, International Internships.) [ID:6182]

United Nations Children's Fund (UNICEF)
Development Section, Division of Personnel (H-5F), UNICEF House,
3 United Nations Plaza, New York, NY, 10017, USA; (212) 326-7000, fax (212) 888-7465, www.unicef.org/

RELATED UN PROGRAM ▪ The United Nations Children's Fund (UNICEF) was established to provide emergency assistance to children in war-ravaged countries. Its permanent mandate is to assist in the development of permanent children's health and welfare services, particularly to developing countries.

UNICEF employs approximately 65 Canadian professional and support staff. (For UNICEF internship information see Chapter 17, International Internships.) [ID:6183]

United Nations Commission on International Trade Law (UNCITRAL)
P.O. Box 500, Vienna International Centre, Wagramerstrasse 5, A-1400 Vienna,
AUSTRIA; (43) (1) 21345-4060, fax (43) (1) 21345-5813, uncitral@unov.un.or.at, www.un.or.at.uncitral

GENERAL ASSEMBLY ▪ The United Nations Commission on International Trade Law (UNCITRAL) was established to promote, in collaboration with UNCTAD, the progressive harmonization and unification of international trade law. There are currently 36 member countries. (For UNCITRAL internship information see Chapter 17, International Internships.) [ID:6184]

United Nations Conference on Trade and Development (UNCTAD)
Palais des Nations, 8-14 ave. de la Paix, 1211 Geneva 10, SWITZERLAND;
(41) (22) 907-1234, fax (41) (22) 917-0057, webmaster@unctad.org, www.unicc.org/unctad

RELATED UN PROGRAM ▪ The United Nations Conference on Trade and Development (UNCTAD) is the principal organ of the General Assembly in the fields of trade and development. It is also the focal point for the integrated treatment of development and interrelated issues in key areas, including trade, commodities, finance, investment, services, and technology. UNCTAD has five principal functions: to promote international trade, particularly between countries at different levels of development; to formulate and implement principles and policies on international trade and related problems of development; to review and facilitate the coordination of activities of other institutions within the UN system in this field; to initiate action for the negotiation and adoption of multilateral legal instruments in the field of trade; and to act as a centre for the harmonization of trade and related development policies of governments and regional economic groups.

UNCTAD employs approximately 400 people. Since the UNCTAD secretariat is part of the United Nations Secretariat, vacancy notices for professional posts usually go through the United Nations—check the UN web site in New York. Recruitment for general service posts—secretaries, clerks, typists—are done directly in Geneva. [ID:6185]

United Nations Development Programme (UNDP)
Division of Personnel, 1 United Nations Plaza, New York, NY, 10017,
USA; (212) 906-5000, fax (212) 826-2057, hq@undp.org, www.undp.org/

RELATED UN PROGRAM ▪ The United Nations Development Programme's (UNDP) objective is to assist developing countries to accelerate their economic and social development by providing systematic and sustained assistance geared to the development objectives of the concerned states. UNDP is the principal administrative and coordinating body providing technical assistance through the UN system.

UNDP employs approximately 90 Canadian professional and support staff. Their web site gives information for consultants under the section "UNDP Consultancies and Technical Assistance Information." [ID:6187]

United Nations Educational, Scientific and Cultural Organization (UNESCO)
Office of Public Information, 7 place de Fontenoy, 75352 Paris 07-SP, FRANCE;
(33) (1) 4568-1000, fax (33) (1) 4567-1690, i.surname@unesco.org, www.unesco.org

SPECIALIZED AGENCY ▪ The United Nations Educational, Scientific and Cultural Organization (UNESCO) works to contribute to peace and security by promoting collaboration among nations in the areas of education, science, and culture. Through their work, UNESCO aims to further universal respect for justice, for the rule of law, and for the fundamental human rights and freedoms affirmed by the global community.

UNESCO currently employs approximately 30 Canadian professional and support staff. Junior program and administrative posts (generally for people under 30) require a university degree, two to three years of related professional experience, French and English. Higher grade posts require an MA and several years of relevant experience in responsible positions. There are also positions available for translators and interpreters, teacher trainers who work in developing countries, and general support staff. (For UNESCO internship information see Chapter 17, International Internships.) [ID:6188]

United Nations Environment Programme (UNEP)
Recruitment Unit, P.O. Box 30552, Nairobi, KENYA;
(254) (2) 621234, fax (254) (2) 226886, unepinfo@unep.org, www.unep.org

RELATED UN PROGRAM ▪ The United Nations Environment Programme (UNEP) comprises three entities: a Governing Council, a Secretariat, and a voluntary Environment Fund. UNEP's chief functions are to promote international cooperation in the environment field and recommend policies to this end, and, to provide general policy guidance for the direction and coordination of environmental programs within the UN system. The Environment Fund finances such programs as regional and global environmental monitoring, assessment and data-collecting systems; environmental research; informational exchange, and the dissemination of research information to develop forms of economic growth compatible with sound environmental management. (For UNEP internship information see Chapter 17, International Internships.) [ID:6189]

United Nations High Commissioner for Refugees (UNHCR)
Career Development and Recruitment Section, C.P. 2500, CH - 1211, Geneva, 2, Depot,
SWITZERLAND; (41) (22) 739-8111, fax (41) (22) 731-9546, webmaster@unhcr.ch, www.unhcr.ch/

RELATED UN PROGRAM ▪ The United Nations High Commissioner for Refugees' (UNHCR) mandate is to provide international protection and material assistance to refugees and to search for permanent solutions to their ongoing plight. In seeking such solutions, UNHCR attempts to help those wishing to go home to do so, and attempts to assist them in reintegrating into their home communities. Where this is deemed not feasible, it works to help refugees in countries of asylum or, failing that, to resettle them in other countries.

UNHCR employs approximately 31 Canadian professional and support staff. [ID:6190]

United Nations Industrial Development Organization (UNIDO)
P.O. Box 300, Vienna International Centre, Wagramerstrasse 5, A-1400 Vienna,
AUSTRIA; (43) (1) 211-310, fax (43) (1) 232-156, org_web@www.UNIDO.org, www.UNIDO.org

SPECIALIZED AGENCY ▪ The United Nations Industrial Development Organization (UNIDO) is dedicated to promoting susutainable idustrial development in countries with developing and transitional economies. It has developed five fundamental developmental objectives as a framework for its future programs: industrial and technical growth and competitiveness; human resource development; equitable development through industrialization; environmentally sustainable industrial development; and international cooperation in industrial investment and technology.

Vacancy notices are posted on their web site in the section "About UNIDO." (For UNIDO internship information see Chapter 17, International Internships.) [ID:6191]

United Nations Institute for Disarmament Research (UNIDIR)
Palais des Nations, 8 - 14 Avenue de la Paix, CH - 1211 Geneva 10,
SWITZERLAND; (41) (22) 917-4292, fax (41) (22) 917-0176, unidir@ties.itu.ch

OTHER UN BODY ▪ The United Nations Institute for Disarmament Research (UNIDIR) undertakes independent research on disarmament and security-related issues. The organization provides the international community with data on problems relating to international security, the arms race and disarmament in all fields, with a view to facilitating progress, through negotiations, toward greater security for all states and toward the economic and social development of all peoples. [ID:6192]

United Nations Institute for Training and Research (UNITAR)
Palais des Nations, 8 - 14 Avenue de la Paix, CH -1211 Geneva 10,
SWITZERLAND; (41) (22) 798-5850, fax (41) (22) 733-1383, unitar@unep.ch, www.rio.net/unitar

OTHER UN BODY ▪ The United Nations Institute for Training and Research (UNITAR) prepares training materials and conducts research on a variety of subjects surrounding the UN system. Currently, the institute provides training in the areas of multilateral diplomacy, and economic and social development. In this latter area, the 1994 programs included various aspects of environmental management training, debt and financial management, and disaster management training. In recent years, programs have addressed the training needs of diplomats in the specific areas of multilateral negotiations, conflict resolution and preventative diplomacy, the work of the General Assembly, the use of United Nations information, and the development of international law. [ID:6193]

United Nations International Drug Control Programme (UNDCP)
P.O. Box 500, Vienna International Centre, Wagramerstrasse 5, A-1400 Vienna, AUSTRIA;
(43) (1) 21345-4251, fax (43) (1) 21345-5866, undcphq@undcp.un.or.at, http://undcp.org/index.html

RELATED UN PROGRAM ▪ The United Nations Fund for Drug Abuse Control Programme (UNDCP) coordinates all UN drug control activities and serves as the focal point for concerted international action for drug abuse control. The program, established in 1990, integrates the structures and functions of the former Division of Narcotic Drugs of the Secretariat, the secretariat of the International Narcotics Control Board, and the UN Fund for Drug Abuse. [ID:6194]

United Nations International Research and Training Institute for the Advancement of Women (INSTRAW)
P.O. Box 21747, Santo Domingo, DOMINICAN REPUBLIC;
(809) 685-2111, fax (809) 685-2117, instraw.hq@codetel.net.do, www.un.org/instraw

OTHER UN BODY ▪ The objective of the United Nations International Research and Training Institute for the Advancement of Women (INSTRAW) is to stimulate and assist—through research, training, and the collection and dissemination of information—the advancement of women and their integration in the development process, both as participants and beneficiaries.

INSTRAW employs nine professional, eight technical, and 14 support staff, and maintains a consultants roster. Application procedures and vacancies are advertised on the UN web site: www.un.org. [ID:6175]

United Nations Interregional Crime and Justice Research Institute (UNICRI)

Via Giulia 52, 00186 Rome, ITALY;
(39) (6) 687-7437, fax (39) (6) 689-2638, unicri@unicrit.it, www.unicri.it

OTHER UN BODY ▪ The objective of the United Nations Interregional Crime and Justice Research Institute (UNICRI) is to contribute, through research, training, field activities and the collection, exchange and dissemination of information, to the formulation of improved policies in the field of crime protection and control. Due regard is paid to the integration of such policies within broader policies for socio-economic change and development, and the protection of human rights.

UNICRI's small staff of 22 are recruited through the UN Secretariat. [ID:6195]

United Nations Peacekeeping Forces

Field Administrator, Logistics Division, UN Peacekeeping Operations,
UN Headquarters, New York, NY, 10017, USA; (212) 963-8079, fax (212) 963-9222, www.un.org/peace/

SECURITY COUNCIL ▪ The United Nations Peacekeeping Forces have two regularly-funded operations and, at the time of publication, were involved in 14 peacekeeping operations worldwide. As of March 1994, 71,000 military and civilian police personnel were deployed, at an annual cost of over US$3.2 billion. Canada participates in 10 of these operations: UN Truce Supervision Organization (UNTSO); UN Disengagement Observer Force (UNDOF); UN Interim Force in Lebanon (UNIFIL); UN Military Observer Group in India and Pakistan (UNMOGIP); UN Force in Cyprus (UNFICYP); UN Angola Verification Mission (UNAVEM II); UN Iraq-Kuwait Observation Mission (UNIKOM); UN Mission for the Referendum in Western Sahara (MINURSO); UN Observer Mission in El Salvador (ONUSAL); UN Protection Force - Former Yugoslavia (UNPROFOR); UN Observer Mission Uganda - Rwanda (UNOMUR); UN Operations in Somalia (UNOSOM II); UN Operation in Mozambique (ONUMOZ); UN Observer Mission in Georgia (UNOMIG); UN Assistance Mission for Rwanda (UNAMIR); UN Observer Mission in Liberia (UNOMIL); UN Aouzou Strip Observer Group (UNASOG); and UN Mission in Haiti (UNMIH).

A large non-military staff supports these operations, and vacancies occasionally arise. Interested applicants should apply to the above address, stating which operation they are interested in and in what capacity. Requisite qualifications vary depending on the position sought. [ID:6196]

United Nations Population Fund (UNFPA)

Personnel Office, 220 East, 42nd Street, New York, NY, 10017,
USA; (212) 297-5000, fax (212) 370-0201, HQ@unfpa.org, www.unfpa.org

RELATED UN PROGRAM ▪ The United Nations Population Fund (UNFPA) is the world's largest source of population assistance in developing countries. UNFPA assists developing countries, countries in transition, and other countries, at their request, to improve reproductive healthcare and to promote sustainable development. Reproductive healthcare includes family planning, sexual health, information and counselling, and medical services, all on the basis of individual choice. The fund also provides data on population and its effects on human rights, quality of life, economic development, and the environment. UNFPA is guided by, and promotes, the principals of the Programme of Action of the International Conference on Population and Development (1994).

UNIDO employs approximately 900 staff, two-thirds of whom work in the field. The other one third work in Geneva. Forty-eight per cent of UNIDO's professional staff are women, one of the highest percentages in the UN. Their web site posts job openings, an area now under construction will provide advice to job seekers. Online application forms can be filled out and submitted electronically. UNIDO maintains a roster of potential candidates and a consultant registry. (For UNFPA internship information see Chapter 17, International Internships.) [ID:6197]

United Nations Relief and Works Agency for Palestine Refugees in the Near East (UNRWA)

P.O. Box 371, UNRWA Headquarters (Gaza), Gaza City,
WEST BANK AND GAZA STRIP; (972) (7) 677-7700, fax (972) (7) 677-7555

OTHER UN BODY ▪ The UN Relief and Works Agency for Palestine Refugees in the Near East (UNRWA) carries out relief and works programs for Palestinian refugees in collaboration with local governments. UNRWA's three principal areas of activity are education, health services, and relief and social services. At the end of 1993, the UNRWA was providing essential services to 3.7 million refugees residing in Lebanon, Syria, Jordan, the West Bank, and the Gaza Strip.

The UNRWA currently employs more than 20,000 local staff and about 160 international staff – of which 10 are Canadian. [ID:6198]

United Nations Research Institute for Social Development (UNRISD)

Palais des Nations, 1211 Geneva 10, 16 ave. Jean-Trembley, 1209 Geneva,
SWITZERLAND; (41) (22) 798-8400, fax (41) (22) 740-0791, info@unrisd.org, www.unic.org/unirsd

RELATED UN PROGRAM ▪ The United Nations Research Institute for Social Development (UNRISD) undertakes multidisciplinary research on the social dimensions of contemporary problems affecting development. Its work is premised on the conviction that for effective development policies to be formulated, an understanding of the social and political context is crucial. Current research themes include: Rebuilding War-torn Societies; Gender and Development; Culture and Development; Community Perspectives on Urban Governance; Information Technologies and Social Development; Business Responsibility for Sustainable Development; Public Sector reform and Crisis-Ridden States; Land Reform in Developing Countries; and Mass Tourism in Developing Countries. (For UNRISD internship information see Chapter 17, International Internships.) [ID:6199]

United Nations University (UNU)

53-70, Jingumae 5-chome, Shibuya-ku, Tokyo 150, JAPAN;
(81) (3) 3499-2811, fax (81) (3) 3499-2828, mbox@hq.unu.edu, www.unu.edu

OTHER UN BODY ▪ The United Nations University (UNU) is a system of decentralized academic institutions integrated into the world university community. UNU is devoted to action-oriented research on the global problems of human survival, development, and welfare, and to postgraduate training of young scholars and research workers. Current program activities are focused on four areas: peace and governance, development; environment and science and technology.

UNU employs approximately 80 full-time staff recruited from universities, research institutions, international organizations, often on secondment for fixed terms. A wide variety of nationalities and cultures are represented. [ID:6200]

Universal Postal Union (UPU)

C.P. 3000, Weltpoststrasse 4, Berne 15, SWITZERLAND;
(41) (31) 350-3111, fax (41) (31) 350-3110, ib.info@ib.upu.org, http://ibis.ib.upu.org

SPECIALIZED AGENCY ▪ The Universal Postal Union's (UPU) objective is to organize and improve global postal services and to promote international collaboration and technical assistance in postal matters among member countries. In this way, countries which have adopted the convention constitute a single postal territory.

The UBU employs 151 full-time staff. In general, the UPU hires staff from the postal administrations of member countries. [ID:6202]

World Bank

See the International Bank for Reconstruction and Development (IBRD) profile in this chapter.

World Food Programme (WFP)

Recruitment and Staffing Branch, Office of Personnel and Administrative Services, 426 Via Cristoforo Colombo, Roma 00145, ITALY; (39) (6) 522-821, fax (39) (6) 5960 - 2111, www.wfp.org/

RELATED UN PROGRAM ▪ The World Food Programme (WFP) was established as the food aid organization of the UN system, providing services primarily to low-income, food-deficit countries. It also assists in the implementation of economic and social development projects, and strives to meet the relief needs of victims of natural and other disasters.

WFP currently employs approximately 35 Canadian professional and support staff. Check their web site under "Vacancies" for job postings. (For WFP internship information see Chapter 17, International Internships.) [ID:6205]

World Health Organization (WHO)

Personnel, 20 ave. Appia, 1211 Geneva 27, SWITZERLAND;
(41) (22) 791-2111, fax (41) (22) 791-0746, posstmaster@who.ch, www.who.ch/

SPECIALIZED AGENCY ▪ The World Health Organization's (WHO) stated objective is the attainment by all peoples of the highest possible level of health. Its principal strategy is based on the primary healthcare approach, involving eight elements: education concerning prevailing health problems; proper food supply and nutrition; safe water and sanitation; maternal and child health, including family planning; immunization against major infectious diseases; prevention and control of local diseases; appropriate treatment of common diseases and injuries; and the provision of essential drugs.

WHO currently employs approximately 45 Canadian professional and support staff. Vacancies are advertised on their web site. (For WHO internship information see Chapter 17, International Internships.) [ID:6206]

World Intellectual Property Organization (WIPO)

Personnel Section, 34 chemin des Colombettes, 1211 Geneva 20,
SWITZERLAND; (41) (22) 338-9111, fax (41) (22) 733-5428, personnel.mail@wipo.int, www.wipo.int

SPECIALIZED AGENCY ▪ The World Intellectual Property Organization (WIPO) was established to promote the protection of intellectual property throughout the world through cooperation among states, and to ensure administrative cooperation among the unions established to afford protection in the field of intellectual property. Intellectual property comprises two main branches: industrial property including inventions, trademarks, industrial designs and appellations of origin; and copyright in literary, musical, artistic, photographic and audiovisual work. The International Bureau of WIPO has 325 permanent staff members.

WIPO vacancies are advertised at the International Civil Service Commission home page: www.un.org/Depts/icsc/vab/index.htm [ID:6207]

World Meteorological Organization (WMO)

Personnel Division, Case postale no. 2300, 41 ave. Giuseppe Motta, 1211 Geneva 2,
SWITZERLAND; (41) (22) 730-8111, fax (41) (22) 734-2326, ipa@www.wmo.ch, www.wmo.ch/

SPECIALIZED AGENCY ▪ The World Meteorological Organization (WMO) aims to facilitate worldwide cooperation in the establishment of international networks of stations for making meteorological, hydrological and other geophysical observations, and to provide related services. The organization also promotes the rapid exchange and standardization of meteorological information, and furthers the application of meteorology to aviation, shipping, water problems, agriculture and other human activities.

The WMO employs 246 full-time staff. WMO maintains a consultants registry for assignments in the field. [ID:6208]

World Tourism Organization (WTO)

Personnel Office, Capitan Haya 42, E-28020 Madrid, SPAIN;
(34) (1) 567 8100, fax (34) (1) 571-3733, omt@world-tourism.org, www.world-tourism.org

SPECIALIZED AGENCY ▪ The World Tourism Organization (WTO) aims to promote and develop tourism with a view to contributing to economic development, international understanding, peace, prosperity and universal respect for, and observance of, fundamental human rights and freedoms for all peoples. WTO's work focuses on five fields: International Technical Cooperation/Cooperation for Development, Education and Training, Quality of Tourism and Services, Environment and Planning, Statistics and Market Research. [ID:6209]

World Trade Organisation (WTO)

154 rue de Lausanne, Centre William Rappard, 1211 Geneva 21,
SWITZERLAND; (41) (22) 739-5111, fax (41) (22) 731-4206, enquiries@wto.org, www.wto.org

SPECIALIZED AGENCY ▪ The WTO administers multilateral trade agreements, the objectives of which are to reduce existing trade barriers and to expand international trade and economic development. Trade in goods, services, intellectual property and investment, trade and environment questions, and trade in agricultural goods are some of the issues the secretariat deals with. It also administers a dispute settlement mechanism for trade conflicts.

The WTO recruits applicants with graduate degrees in economics, international relations, or law, with an emphasis on trade issues. At least five years experience with a national government or international organization dealing with trade policy and trade relations is also highly desirable. Some entry-level positions exist for which relevant work experience is not a prerequisite, but a relevant academic background is particularly important in these cases. You will be expected to work in two of three languages: French, English and Spanish. The WTO's comprehensive web site includes recruitment information and an application form to download. [ID:6161]

Chapter 37

Environmental & Agricultural Research Centres

In recent decades, the world's ecosystems have come to be viewed as interconnected parts of a vast biological whole. Recognition of the cumulative and damaging effect of human activities on that global system (such as growing food for over five billion people season after season, year after year) is also mounting.

So it's not surprising that agricultural research, a field formerly dominated by plant breeders rather narrowly defined, today embraces scientific work in many other areas of environmental stewardship. These areas include fisheries, forestry, and watershed management. Research also embraces the social and economic aspects of food, fuel, and fibre production (for example, the role of women, the effects of government policy, and the need for better information and training).

"Agricultural" research, then, has expanded and become a multidisciplinary enterprise. There is currently a stable, if not growing, global need for related expertise in areas of economics, environmental science, communications, anthropology, remote sensing, computer applications, and training, as well as the more traditional core disciplines of plant physiology, genetics, soil science, and entomology.

OPPORTUNITIES IN THE SOUTH

Agriculture typically accounts for the lion's share of gross domestic product (GDP) and employs a large proportion of the working population in most regions of the South. This contrasts with countries like Canada where agriculture is capital-intensive, employs very few people, and accounts for a relatively small share of the GDP in comparison with manufacturing and services. While Canadians may not think of agriculture and agricultural research as a major domestic employer of professionals, there are numerous opportunities at the international level.

The total number of scientists working at the national level worldwide is estimated at 130,000. At this level, priority for research jobs is, of course, given to the citizens of the country in question, although some countries, especially in Africa, still rely on foreign scientific expertise.

But in addition to these national scientists, there are several thousand researchers and other supporting professionals working in more than two dozen international agricultural research centres around the world. It is in this second layer of agricultural research that Canadians are more likely to qualify for professional postings.

THE CONSULTATIVE GROUP ON INTERNATIONAL AGRICULTURAL RESEARCH (CGIAR)

Several of these research centres are grouped under a funding umbrella called the CONSULTATIVE GROUP ON INTERNATIONAL AGRICULTURAL RESEARCH (CGIAR). CGIAR aims to harness modern science to the sustainable development of agriculture in poor countries. Its mission statement, revised in 1990, gives a clear picture of its perceived role:

"Through international research and research related activities, and in partnership with national research systems, to contribute to sustainable improvements in the productivity of agriculture, forestry, and fisheries, in developing countries in ways that enhance nutrition and well being, especially of low income people."

The WORLD BANK and about 40 other donors, of which Canada is one, currently support 16 affiliated international agricultural research centres which, in close cooperation with national research facilities, develop more resource-efficient technologies for food production while protecting and improving the natural resource base. Members meet twice a year to coordinate their financial support and guide the scientific research and related work of the centres. Although in recent years there has been a reduction in staff at sites in Asia, there are still approximately 1,500 internationally recruited senior scientists, among a total staff of approximately 12,000, most of whom are locals, employed as laboratory technicians, research assistants and farm workers.

Some of the CGIAR centres concentrate on specific crops. The INTERNATIONAL RICE RESEARCH INSTITUTE, in the Philippines, and the INTERNATIONAL MAIZE AND WHEAT IMPROVEMENT CENTRE, in Mexico, are two such examples. Both organizations were instrumental in launching the Green Revolution of the late 1960s and 1970s and averting massive famine, especially in Asia. Other centres have non-biological or non-research programs such as conducting studies on food policy questions, helping countries in the South organize and manage their research better, or coordinating the collection and storage of seeds.

In addition to the 16 centres that comprise the CGIAR system, there are more than half a dozen other international research organizations around the world with similar mandates but which lack formal standing. The ASIAN

VEGETABLE RESEARCH AND DEVELOPMENT CENTRE is one such example. Some of these "cousin" organizations also receive funding from the CGIAR members' donor budget.

TYPES OF POSITIONS AVAILABLE

In most international agricultural research centres, there are two types of positions: internationally recruited and locally recruited. The former are generally professional scientific posts, while the latter are support positions in which detailed knowledge of the host country is critical. In most, but not all cases, local recruitment means hiring nationals of the host country rather than foreigners such as Canadians.

Internationally recruited positions in the CGIAR centres, of the kind Canadians are eligible for, are generally offered as contracts of fixed duration, usually between one and three years. But because contracts are often routinely renewed, these positions amount to permanent jobs.

Many of the international posts at the CGIAR centres are research positions demanding advanced training in the natural and social sciences, usually at the PhD level. Substantial work experience is normally a prerequisite as well. But the centres, especially those operating as semi-sufficient "scientific islands" in developing countries, also need skilled professionals to provide support services—for example, institutional management, computer science, library science, public relations, scientific editing, and translation. Apart from the purely scientific or technical skills demanded by these positions, ability in a second language (often French or Spanish) is usually an important asset.

For those with little or no professional experience in this field, take a look at internships offered through government ministries such as the DEPARTMENT OF FOREIGN AFFAIRS AND INTERNATIONAL TRADE, (DFAIT) or ENVIRONMENT CANADA. For more information see Chapter 17, International Internships.

RECRUITING PROCEDURES

Many of the centres advertise their internationally recruited positions in widely circulated publications such as *The Economist*, the *International Herald Tribune*, and *New Scientist*. Another important employment resource would be the web sites for these organizations. Of course, there is also a great deal of recruitment going on within the CGIAR system itself, with job announcements routinely circulated among all the sister centres by regular or electronic mail. Many of the web sites for these organizations also post job openings.

Although there is currently no official mechanism for transfers among CGIAR centres, there is nonetheless an ongoing game of "musical chairs." CGIAR staff often have an edge over qualified outsiders because of their international experience. International competition for jobs, which is tough at the best of times, is often made more difficult by the sizable pool of qualified "insiders" looking for greener pastures.

WHAT TO EXPECT FROM CGIAR EMPLOYMENT

Each of the international centres has an agreement with the host country in which its headquarters are situated. Among other things, these agreements specify the income tax status of employees, which, in most instances, is favourable. In the case of internationally recruited staff, salaries are denominated in US dollars. In addition, a cost-of-living allowance adjustment is often paid to insulate employees from drops in the value of the dollar against the local currency.

Other standard benefits enjoyed by employees of CGIAR include housing and child education subsidies; medical and life insurance packages; medical evacuation for travelling staff in cases of emergency; a home leave subsidy (usually return air tickets for the employee and dependents to her or his home country); six weeks paid vacation; and a pension plan fully funded by the employing centre.

While benefits packages may seem overly generous, there are good reasons for offering them, especially in rural areas. Clearly, incentives are needed to get highly qualified professionals, often accompanied by a spouse and children, to move away from friends and family to the Tropics or other remote regions of the South. The host country may be less comfortable than prospective employees are used to. It may also present more of a threat to personal health because of the presence of endemic diseases such as malaria and schistosomiasis, especially in the rural agricultural areas.

OTHER CONSIDERATIONS

In most cases, the campuses and living compounds of the CGIAR research centres are well serviced by amenities such as piped water and electricity. However, personal security remains a constant worry for many employees when they are off the work site. Colombia, Nigeria, Peru, the Philippines and Sri Lanka, each of which hosts a CGIAR centre, are all countries in which political or criminal violence has been a serious threat at various times since the CGIAR system was set up more than two decades ago. For example, in October 1994, the head of the communications department of the international research centre located in Colombia, was kidnapped by armed rebels in the Cauca Valley. The rebels released him 11 months later, after obtaining a ransom from his family.

The message here is that you owe it to yourself and your family to seriously address questions of personal health and security before accepting a post in an international agricultural research centre, especially in a Southern country. You must be satisfied that the increased risk, if there is one, is worth it. Bear in mind that the vast majority of foreign staff at such international centres live without incident. Being prudent and taking standard preventative measures will go a long way towards minimizing threats to personal health and security.

Profiles of Environmental & Agricultural Research Centres

The following list of 23 environmental and agricultural research centres includes the largest and most widely recognized global institutions in this field. Of these, 16 receive their funding directly from THE CONSULTATIVE GROUP ON INTERNATIONAL AGRICULTURAL RESEARCH (CGIAR), while the other seven are either partly funded by CGIAR, or independent from it. This list was compiled with the assistance of experts who offered very helpful advice. Most of these centres are located overseas, with eight located in the Asia Pacific region, one in the Middle East, two in South America, six in Africa, three in Europe, and four in North America. (For related information see the Resources sections of the following chapters: Chapter 36, United Nations; Chapter 38, International Organizations; and Chapter 17, International Internships.)

ASEAN Institute of Forest Management
Forestry Department Headquarters, Jalan Sultan Salahuddin, 50660 Kuala Lumpur, MALAYSIA; (60) (3) 294-3477, fax (60) (3) 294-3499, info@)aifm.po.my, www.jaring.my/aifm/

The focus of the ASEAN Institute of Forest Management (AIFM) is the support of research and development in tropical forest management. AIFM promotes the transfer and application of appropriate technologies, such as remote sensing and computer applications. The institute was officially inaugurated with the signing of the Memorandum of Understanding (MOU) between ASEAN and Canada.

IAFM has an operating budget of approximately $15 million. Visit the host web site, www.jaring.my, for extensive information on research centres and industry in Malaysia. [ID:6210]

CAB INTERNATIONAL (CABI)
Wallingford OXON 10 8DE, UK; (44) (1491) 832111, fax (44) (1491) 830508, cabi@cabi.org, www.cabi.org

CAB INTERNATIONAL (CABI) provides information and scientific development services to researchers and other professional workers in the areas of agricultural and related applied science fields. CABI services include the identification of pests and diseases, biological control and research and publishing.

CABI's staff consists of 230 scientists, 80 other professionals, and approximately 150 support staff. Vacancies are posted on their web site. Scientific vacancies are also advertised in the *New Scientist*, while non-scientific posts appear in the *Oxford Times*. Résumés are kept on file for six months. [ID:6239]

Centre for International Forestry Research (CIFOR)
P.O. Box 6596, JKPWB, Jakarta 10065, INDONESIA; (62) (251) 622-622, fax (62) (251) 622-100, cifor@cgnet.com, www.cgiar.org/cifor

The Centre for International Forestry Research (CIFOR) supports and conducts research on all aspects of the forestry sector, such as technology transfer, trade and sustainable forest management practices. CIFOR also publishes and disseminates research in this field. The web site for CIFOR provides links to other forestry related sites on the Internet. [ID:6211]

Centro Internacionale de Agricultura Tropical (CIAT)

6713 Apartado Aéreo, Recta Cali-Palmira, Km 17, Cali, COLOMBIA;
(57) (2) 445-0000, fax (57) (2) 445-0073, ciat@cgnet.com, www.ciat.cgiar.org

The mandate of the Centro Internacional de Agricultura Tropical (CIAT) is the alleviation of hunger and poverty in tropical developing countries. They pursue this objective by the development of scientific and technological advances that will lead to sustainable increases in agricultural output, while preserving the natural resource base.

The web site for CIAT lists information about job openings and provides links to related sites on the internet. [ID:7170]

Inter-American Institute for Co-operation on Agriculture (IICA)

Suite 320, 1775 "K" Street, N.W., Washington, DC, 20006,
USA; (202) 458-3767, fax (202) 458-6335, iica@ac.cr, www.iica.ac.cr

The Inter-American Institute for Co-operation on Agriculture (IICA) promotes and supports the efforts of member states to achieve agricultural development and advance rural well-being. The institute promotes the strengthening of national education, research and rural development institutions; formulates plans, programs and activities in accordance with the needs of member governments; and maintains consultative relations with related entities, such as the Organization of American States (OAS).

The IICA currently employs 250 professionals and a large support staff. Employment opportunities are advertised through the ministries of agriculture and foreign affairs of the member countries. A data bank for résumés and consultancy registry is maintained at IICA's Human Resources Division in Costa Rica. Contact them at P.O. Box 55, 2200 Coronado, Costa Rica, Central America. [ID:6212]

International Board for Soil Research and Management (IBSRAM)

P.O. Box 9-109, Bangkhen, Bangkok10900, THAILAND; (66) (2) 579-7590,
fax (66) (2) 561-1230, oibsram@montri.ku.ac.th, www.uia.org/uiademo/org/f0299f.htm

The International Board for Soil Research and Management (IBSRAM) promotes and assists research in sustainable improved soil management technologies. IBSRAM's objective is to remove soil constraints to food and agricultural production in developing countries. They produce a number of publications.

IBSRAM currently has a staff of 22. International positions are advertised in *The Economist*. [ID:6213]

International Center for Living Aquatic Resources Management (ICLARM)

MC P.O. Box 2631, Makati City 0718Metro Manila, PHILIPPINES;
(63) (2) 818-0466, fax (63) (2) 816-3183, ICLARM@cgnet.com, www.cgiar.org/iclarm

The International Center for Living Aquatic Resources Management (ICLARM) conducts research on fish production, management, and utilization to assist the world in meeting nutritional and economic needs. They work to improve the efficiency of fisheries through research, education and training, and strive to upgrade the social, economic, and nutritional status of the poor in developing countries by improving small-scale fisheries.

ICLARM has a staff of 200. Job openings are advertised on their web site, with information on qualifications for application. Openings are also advertised in *The Economist*. [ID:6214]

International Center of Insect Physiology and Ecology (ICIPE)

P.O. Box 30772, Nairobi, KENYA; (254) (2) 802-501, fax (254) (2) 803-360, icipe@cgnet.com

The International Centre of Insect Physiology and Ecology (ICIPE) is a forum for the development and exchange of research and/or training projects, such as pest management.

The centre also investigates major livestock diseases and insect carriers of human diseases in the tropics. ICIPE has an international staff of approximately 540. [ID:6215]

International Centre for
Agricultural Research in The Dry Areas (ICARDA)
P.O. Box 5466, Aleppo, SYRIA; (963) (21) 213-433,
fax (963) (21) 225-105, icarda@cgnet.com, www.cgiar.org/icarda

The International Centre for Agricultural Research in Dry Areas (ICARDA) works to increase agricultural productivity, especially in the low rainfall areas of West Asia and North Africa, thereby to increase the availability of food in these areas and improve the economic and social well-being of their populations.

The ICARDA employs 500 people full-time, with an international staff of 96. They maintain a data bank for résumés. International positions are advertised in *The Economist*. The web site lists helpful research networks and employment opportunities. [ID:6216]

International Centre for Research in Agroforestry (ICRAF)
P.O. Box 30677, ICRAF House, United Nations Ave., Nairobi, KENYA;
(254) (2) 521-450, fax (254) (2) 521-001, icraf@cgnet.com, www.cgiar.org/icraf

The International Centre for Research in Agroforestry (ICRAF) initiates and supports research leading to sustainable and productive land use in developing countries. The ICRAF's approach integrates the environmental, technological, social, and economic components of tree management in land-use systems.

ICRAF has a staff of 53 international professionals, 48 national professionals, 204 support workers and 76 seconded staff. Their web site posts job openings, with details of application procedures. [ID:6217]

International Commission on Irrigation and Drainage (ICID)
48 Nyaya Marg, Chanakyapuri, New Delhi 110 021, INDIA;
(91) (11) 301-6837, fax (91) (11) 301-5962, icid@sirnetd.ernet.in, www.hrwallingford.co.uk

The International Commission on Irrigation and Drainage (ICID) promotes the development and application of scientific and technical expertise in agriculture, economics, ecology, and social science to the management of water and land resources for irrigation, drainage, flood control, and river training. ICID has approximately 30 staff members. ICID's web site provides further information and links to related organizations. [ID:6218]

International Crops Research Institute
for the Semi-Arid Tropics (ICRISAT)
PatancheruAndhra Pradesh 502-324, INDIA;
(91) (40) 596-161, fax (91) (40) 241-239, www.cgiar.org/icrisat

The International Crops Research Institute for the Semi-Arid Tropics (ICRISAT) focuses on crop improvement and cropping systems. The institute's research covers sorghum, millet, chickpea, pigeonpea and groundnut.

ICRISAT's web site has information on training and links to other sites. [ID:6219]

International Food Policy Research Institute (IFPRI)
1200-17 Street N.W., Washington, DC, 20036-3006, USA;
(202) 862-5600, fax (202) 467-4439, ifpri@cgnet.com, www.cgiar.org/ifpri

The International Food Policy Research Institute (IFPRI) focuses on strategies to meet world food needs, with research covering all aspects of policy analysis. The institute is active in the publication and dissemination of relevant materials. The IFPRI has over 80 researchers on staff.

Information about job openings at IFPRI is contained on their web site. [ID:6220]

International Institute of Tropical Agriculture (IITA)

PMB 5230, Oyo Road, Ibadan, NIGERIA;
(234) (22) 241-2626, fax (234) (22) 241-2221, iita@cgnet.com, www.cgiar.org/iita

The International Institute of Tropical Agriculture (IITA) works to improve tropical food crops such as cassava, cowpeas, maize, plantain, soybeans, and yams. IITA develops sustainable agricultural systems to replace slash-and-burn cultivation methods in humid and sub-humid tropical regions. The institute has an international staff of approximately 1,100.

The web site for IITA has information about job opportunities and partnership contracts. [ID:6221]

International Irrigation Management Institute (IIMI)

P.O. Box 2075, Colombo, SRI LANKA; (94) (1) 867-404,
fax (94) (1) 566-854, iimi@cgnet.com, www.cgiar.org/iimi

The International Irrigation Management Institute (IIMI) conducts research on irrigation and drainage in the South. Their research goal is the improvement of agricultural productivity and lessening of fluctuations in crop yields. There are more than 40 researchers on staff at IIMI. Current job openings are posted on its web site. [ID:6222]

International Livestock Research Institute (ILRI)

P.O. Box 30709, Nairobi, KENYA; (254) (2) 630743,
fax (254) (2) 631499, ILRI-Kenya@cgnet.com, www.cgiar.org/ilri

The International Livestock Research Institute (ILRI) seeks to increase livestock productivity without depleting the resources on which farming depends. Its mission is to contribute to the welfare of developing countries through research that improves sustainable livestock production. The ILRI conducts research in Asia, North Africa, Latin America, the Caribbean, and sub-Saharan Africa. While its main headquarters are in Nairobi, Kenya, responsibilities are shared with the site in Addis Ababa, Ethiopia.

ILRI employs 110 internationally recruited scientific and administrative staff. Supervisory and support staff, numbering 769, are recruited from Kenya and Ethiopia. Job postings are available on their web site. [ID:7172]

International Maize and Wheat Improvement Centre (CIMMYT)

Apdo Postal 6-641, Lisboa 27-Col Juarez, 06600 Mexico, D.F., MEXICO;
(52) (5) 726-9091, fax (52) (5) 726-7558, cimmyt@cimmyt.mx, www.cimmyt.mx

The International Maize and Wheat Improvement Center (CIMMYT) is an internationally funded, nonprofit scientific research and training organization. The centre works with agricultural research institutions worldwide to improve the productivity and sustainability of maize and wheat systems in developing countries. Research programs focus on natural resource management, applied biotechnology, and economics.

The centre has a staff of 250, representing a range of disciplines within the biological and social sciences. Job openings and information about partnersips with CIMMYT are listed on their web site. [ID:6225]

International Plant Genetic Resources Institute (IPGRI)

Via del Sette Chiese 142, I-00145 Rome, ITALY;
(39) (6) 518-921, fax (39) (6) 575-0309, ipgri@cgnet.com, www.cgiar.org/ipgri

The International Plant Genetic Resources Institute (IPGRI) promotes the collection, documentation, evaluation, conservation, and utilization of genetic resources of important species, especially in those areas where the spread of new varieties may put traditional varieties in danger of extinction. The IPGRI supports strategic research and training in genetic resources work. The institute has a worldwide staff of over 30 professionals.

The IPGRI web site provides information about job openings and fellowships. [ID:6227]

International Potato Centre (IPC)
Apartado 1558, Lima 12, PERU; (51) (1) 349-6017,
fax (51) (1) 349-5638, cip@cgnet.com, www.cgiar.org/cip/org

The International Potato Centre (IPC) supports and conducts research on improving potato crop yields, particularly in the South. The IPC considers the potato and other Andean root and tuber crops to be underexploited resources for agricultural development and hunger relief in developing countries. CIP works to enhance the cultivation, yield, processing and consumption of potatoes. The IPC publishes and disseminates relevant findings. The IPC's web site lists job openings, information, and contains links to related sites. [ID:6228]

International Rice Research Institute (IRRI)
P.O. Box 933, 1099 Manila, PHILIPPINES; (63) (2) 845-0563,
fax (63) (2) 845-0600, postmaster@irri.cgnet.com, www.cgiar.org/irri

The International Rice Research Institute (IRRI) conducts research on all aspects of rice production, focusing on national production in the South. The institute is active in the publication and dissemination of information materials. IRRI employs 1,400 scientific and support staff, 93 per cent of whom are Filipino. More than 100 senior scientists are recruited internationally, with the majority being posted in Manila. Staff are also posted in Cambodia, India, Indonesia, Japan, Lao PDR, Madagascar, Burma (Myanmar), Nigeria, and Thailand. [ID:6229]

International Service for National Agricultural Research (ISNAR)
P.O. Box 93375, 2509 AJ, The Hague, NETHERLANDS;
(31) (70) 349 6100, fax (31) (70) 381 9677, isnar@cgnet.com, www.cgiar.org/isnar

The International Service for National Agricultural Research (ISNAR) helps developing countries make improvements in the performance of their agricultural research systems and organizations. It promotes appropriate agricultural research policies, helps to develop sustainable research institutions, and improve research management. ISNAR's research related services are intended to benefit producers and consumers in developing countries and to safeguard the natural environment.

ISNAR employs a staff of 100, of whom 43 are recruited internationally. Vacancies are listed on their web site under "General Information," along with application information. Professional vacancies are also advertised in *The Economist* and *Le Monde*. ISNAR maintains a consultant registry and a data bank for résumés. [ID:6230]

West Africa Rice Development Association (WARDA)
01 BP 2551, Bouaké 1, COTE D'IVOIRE;
(225) 634-514, fax (225) 634-714, warda@cgnet.com, www.cgiar/warda

The West Africa Rice Development Association (WARDA) works to support and strengthen the growing West African capability in the science, technology, and socio-economics of rice production. WARDA's objective is to sustain and improve the livelihood of smallholder farm families, increase opportunities for rural employment and contribute to increased food security in the region. The Association has a staff of 177. [ID:6232]

Winrock International Institute for Agricultural Development (WI)
Director, Human Resource Management, International Division, 38 Winrock Drive, Morrilton,
AR, 72110-9537, USA; (501) 727-5435, fax (501) 727-5473, information@winrock, www.winrock.org

The Winrock International Institute for Agricultural Development (WI) is a global leader in promoting sustainable agricultural development and environmental programs that stimulate economic growth without threatening natural resources. WI's activities include technical assistance, human resource development, policy and institutional improvement.

Winrock currently has 192 full-time staff members. Their consultant registry is known as Winrock International's Professional Register. Contact their office to request an information package, including the register application form, or visit their web site for more information and job postings. [ID:6286]

Chapter 38

International Organizations

Opportunities for Canadians in international organizations are numerous and, in many instances, remain under-subscribed. No matter what type of overseas career you aspire to, experience working with an international organization is extremely valuable.

The 68 organizations profiled in this chapter are bodies which operate outside the UNITED NATIONS system. They are international in scope, membership and interest. Most were created to tackle specific international problems in a unified way, or to look after the common interests of member countries.

TYPES OF INTERNATIONAL ORGANIZATIONS

The organizations are divided into four primary categories: International NGOs; Multilateral (political and financial) Institutions; International Professional Associations; and International "Think Tanks" (research centres). For information on other international organizations see Chapter 37, Environmental & Agricultural Research Centres.

International NGOs

International NGOs typically work in the areas of poverty alleviation, environment concerns, and social justice. While some NGOs are involved in lobbying and advocacy efforts, others compile and analyze data, and offer policy solutions. In general, these organizations have a number of overseas or field staff. Examples of international NGOs profiled below include HUMAN RIGHTS WATCH, and CONSERVATION INTERNATIONAL.

Multilateral Institutions

Multilateral political and financial institutions tend to be regionally focused, addressing intergovernmental concerns in a consensual manner or looking after the common interests of member countries. They tend to be involved in issues of international economics and collective security. Examples of such institutions are the COMMONWEALTH SECRETARIAT and the ORGANIZATION OF AMERICAN STATES.

International Professional Associations

The fourth category is International Professional Associations and includes federations of national organizations operating at the international level. These associations provide a forum for the assimilation of ideas, interests and concerns particular to specific industries, professions, or groups. Examples include the INTERNATIONAL CONFEDERATION OF FREE TRADE UNIONS, and the INTERNATIONAL BAR ASSOCIATION.

International "Think Tanks"

International research centres, or "think tanks" as they are sometimes called, formulate and communicate ideas on issues of public interest. These international organizations seek to educate or influence citizens, academics, and/or decision-makers, thereby affecting both the substance and direction of public policy. Some of these organizations are nonpartisan, publishing and disseminating objective educational materials, while others promote a political or ideological cause. In general, these types of organizations have few permanent overseas staff, although employment often involves travel. Examples profiled include the OVERSEAS DEVELOPMENT INSTITUTE (ODI), and The INTERNATIONAL UNION OF PUBLIC TRANSPORT (IUPT).

JOB HUNTING TIPS

There are a variety of employment alternatives with international organizations: permanent professional, administrative, short-term consultancy, and so forth. Most non-clerical positions require previous international experience and a specific area of expertise. There is also a marked tendency for these organizations to look for generalists who can approach issues from an interdisciplinary perspective. Because recruitment procedures vary among organizations, it is essential to familiarize yourself with the hiring system of each prior to applying.

In general, the larger international organizations recruit in a manner not unlike that of the UNITED NATIONS. Funding is furnished by member countries that jealously guard their right to contribute qualified personnel on a proportionate basis. Hence, hiring tends to be based on a mixture of nationality and professional qualifications according to a formal or informal quota system.

Finding work with smaller organizations is often much less formal. They tend to be less bureaucratic and more receptive to intrepid applicants. The rate of staff turnover is also favourable. Many of these organizations also offer internships, which are an excellent way to compensate for lack of experience (see Chapter 17, International Internships). Don't be afraid to apply directly to overseas organizations with which Canada has no formal affiliation. Our reputation abroad is sound. Canadians are actively recruited on the basis of language skills, international exposure, and perceived neutrality.

Another important route through which positions in international organizations can be obtained is through the PUBLIC SERVICE COMMISSION'S International Programs Directorate. For a full description see their profile in Chapter 34, Careers in Government.

RESOURCES

The resources below are presented with a view to assisting you in broader, more extensive searches. While this chapter profiles many of the largest and most respected agencies, there are more than 20,000 international organizations worldwide.

For related references consult the resources for Chapter 36, United Nations; Chapter 37, Environmental & Agricultural Research Centres; and Chapter 17, International Internships.

The World Bank Group ⌨
www.worldbank.org ▪ Provides information on the World Bank Group and its constituent members. News releases, country and regional summaries, and a public information centre are all useful features of this site. Employment opportunities with the World Bank are posted here too. [ID:2574]

Careers in International Affairs 📖
1997, *Linda Powers,* Georgetown University ➤ Scholarly Book Services, 77 Mowat Avenue, Suite 403, Toronto, Ontario M6K 3E3, Canada; $27.95; VISA, MC; (800) 847-9736, fax (800) 220-9895 ▪ One of the best sources of information on international careers. Contains background, addresses and telephone numbers for 378 international organizations, including public, government, commercial banking, business, consulting, research, nonprofit and educational organizations. [ID:1150]

Encyclopedia of Associations: International Organizations 1997 📖
1997, *Linda Irvin,* 3,300 pages, 2 vols. ➤ Gale Research Inc., 835 Penobscot Bldg., 645 Griswold Street, Detroit, MI 48226-4094, USA; US$550; credit cards; (800) 877-4253 ext. 1330, fax (800) 414-5043; Available in large libraries ▪ Directory provides descriptions of 19,400 multinational for-profit and international nonprofit organizations around the world. Indexed by geographic region, name, and key word. Visit the distributor's web site at www.gale.com. [ID:1148]

The European Union ⌨
www.chemie.fu-berlin.de/adressen/eu.html ▪ This site provides extensive information on the Union, its programs, and member states. [ID:2569]

International Agencies and Programs ⌨
www.lrc.state.ky.us/other/internat/bmiller.htm ▪ Maintained by the state government of Kentucky, this site provides links to various international organizations as well as information on international law, culture, and foreign languages. Offers a link to the CIA World Factbook, which provides basic information on almost every country in the world. [ID:2563]

International Marine Mammal Association Inc. (IMMA) ⌨
www.imma.org ▪ IMMA is a not-for-profit organization, founded in New Brunswick, Canada in 1974. This web site contains information on several conservation issues, briefings, and educational materials as well as the full text of selected technical reports. [ID:2723]

La recherche d'un emploi dans les organisations internationales 📖
1994, *Louis Sabourin,* 143 pages ➤ Éditions Vermette Inc., 6255, Hutchison, Montréal, Québec
H2V 4C7, Canada; $14.95; VISA, MC; (514) 278-3025, fax (514) 278-3030 ■ Un guide qui présente
un tableau d'ensemble des principaux organismes internationaux, qui indique leurs adresses
complètes et qui propose des suggestions quant à la meilleure façon de se préparer pour obtenir
un emploi. [ID:1587]

Vacancies in International Organizations 💻
www3.itu.ch/MISSIONS ■ This Italian site provides links to the personnel departments of several
international organizations. The focus is on supra-national organizations rather than NGOs. Links
range from the Asian Development Bank to the World Trade Organization, and to other specialized organizations. [ID:2573]

World Wildlife Fund-Canada 💻
www.wwfcanada.org ■ The WWF was established to conserve wildlife and wild places. This web
site provides information on the programs and the activities of WWF Canada. [ID:2724]

Yahoo's List of International Organizations 💻
www.yahoo.com/Government/International_Organizations ■ Yahoo provides hypertext links to
241 international organizations from this site. [ID:2575]

Yearbook of International Organizations 📖
Annual, *Union of International Associations (Geneva)* ➤ Bowker-Saur, 121 Chanlon Road, New
Providence, NJ 07974, USA; US$1170; credit cards; (800) 521-8110, fax (908) 665-6688; Available
in large libraries ■ Exhaustive, comprehensive listings of 32,000 international organizations by
subject, region and organization type, and includes descriptions and contact information. Visit
www.reedref.com. [ID:1198]

Profiles of
International Organizations

The following list of 68 international organizations is only a small sampling of
the several thousand that exist. We strived for a balanced representation of the
different types of international organizations operating on a global level. We
did a number of things to narrow our list and make it more relevant: we
consulted with experts from a wide array of institutions for their suggestions;
we generally included the largest international organizations; and we included
organizations having some form of Canadian representation.

The profiles are divided into four broad categories. There are 22 Multi-
lateral Institutions, 26 International NGO's, eleven International Professional
Institutions; and nine International "Think Tanks." As well, we cross-
referenced all the profiles with 10 job categories. There are ten for Business,
Banking and Trade; four for the Commonwealth; eleven for the Environment;
three for La Francophonie; three for Global Communication; four for Law and
Good Governance; three for Public Health and Family Planning; eight for
Peace and Security; 17 for Social Justice and Development; and five for Science
and Technology.

The majority of the organizations are based in Europe or North America,
but are international in their activities and membership. Most have inter-

nationally affiliated offices. The remaining organizations are located in Africa and the Asia Pacific region.

This chapter provides you with a preliminary list, but we suggest that you visit the web sites for the organizations you are interested in. Where relevant, the office of the Canadian affiliation to the international organizations listed has been included.

African Economic Research Consortium (AERC)
P.O. Box 47543, Nairobi, KENYA; (254) (2) 228057,
fax (254) (2) 721318, aerc@elci.gn.apc.org, www.tomco.net/~edinp/africa/aerc.htm

INTERNATIONAL THINK TANK: Business/Banking/Trade

The African Economic Research Consortium (AERC) aims to strengthen local capacity for conducting independent, rigorous enquiry into problems pertinent to the management of economies in Sub-Saharan Africa. AERC also organizes seminars and workshops and is active as a publisher and disseminator of information. AERC's web site offers details on its structure and membership. [ID:6233]

Aga Khan Foundation (AKF)
PO Box 2369, CH-1211 Geneva 2, SWITZERLAND; (41) (22) 909 7200, fax (41) (22) 909 7291

INTERNATIONAL NGO: Social Justice and Development

The objective of the Aga Khan Foundation (AKF) is to promote social development through philanthropic activities in the developing world. AKF supports programs in the fields of health, education, rural development, human resource development, communications, and institutional development.

The AKF has 140 staff worldwide, with branch offices and independent affiliates in 12 countries and territories. Most staff members are nationals of the country they work in. A web site is currently being developed. (For information about AKF's Canadian office see Chapter 35, Nongovernmental Organizations.) [ID:6234]

L'Agence de coopération culturelle et technique (ACCT)
13, Quai André-Citroën, Paris75015, FRANCE;
(33) (1) 44 37 33 00, fax (33) (1) 45 79 14 18, www.francophonie.org

MULTILATERAL INSTITUTION: La Francophonie

L'Agence de la Francophonie assure le secrétariat de toutes les instances de la Francophonie, opère le Sommet de la Francophonie et est au service de la coopération multilatérale entre les gouvernements francophones. [ID:7114]

Amnesty International (AI)
1118 - 22 Street N.W., Washington, DC20037, USA;
(202) 775-5161, fax (202) 775-5992, aiusamaro@igc.apc.org, www.amnesty.org

INTERNATIONAL NGO: Law and Good Governance

Amnesty International (AI) campaigns to free all prisoners of conscience—people detained anywhere because of their beliefs, ethnic origin, sex, colour, or language—who have neither used nor advocated violence. AI seeks to ensure fair and prompt trials for political prisoners and to end extra-judicial executions, disappearances, and other abuses.

AI currently has nearly 300 paid staff and is supported by an extensive network of volunteers. Amnesty's web site provides useful links to related organizations. Amnesty offices in Canada are located in Ottawa and Montréal. (For information on Amnesty Canada see Chapter 35, Nongovernmental Organizations and Chapter 17, International Internships.) [ID:6236]

Association for the Advancement of Policy, Research and Development in the Third World (AAPRDTW)

P.O. Box 70257, Washington, DC, 20024-0257, USA; (202) 723-7010, fax (202) 723-7010

INTERNATIONAL THINK TANK: Social Justice and Development

The Association for the Advancement of Policy, Research and Development in the Third World (AAPRDTW) promotes science, technology, and development through the generation and exchange of practical solutions to problems facing governments in developing countries. AAPRDTW currently has approximately 20 staff. Its membership comprises individuals and organizations in 58 countries and territories. [ID:6237]

L'AUPELF-UREF opérateur francophone

C.P. 400, succursale Côte des Neiges, Montréal, Québec,
H3S 2S7, CANADA; (514) 343-6630, fax (514) 343-2107, refer@refer.qc.ca, www.aupelf-uref.org

INTERNATIONAL PROFESSIONAL ASSOCIATION: La Francophonie

L'Association des universités partiellement ou entièrement de langue française opère les Sommets francophones pour l'enseignement supérieur et la recherche et est active dans les domaines culturels et politiques, faisant, entre autres, la promotion des identités culturelles. [ID:7112]

Bank for International Settlements (BIS)

Centralbahnplatz 2, CH-4002 Basel, SWITZERLAND;
(41) (61) 280-8080, fax (41) (61) 280-9100, webmaster@bis.org, www.bis.org

MULTILATERAL INSTITUTION: Business/Banking/Trade

The chief function of the Bank for International Settlement (BIS) is to promote and facilitate cooperation between central banks. The BIS provides additional facilities for international financial operations and acts as a trustee or agent in financial settlements under agreements with the parties concerned. The BIS has approximately 470 staff. Its Canadian affiliate is the Bank of Canada. [ID:6238]

CARE International

Boulevard du Régent 58/10, B-1000 Brussels, BELGIUM;
(32) (2) 502-4333, fax (32) (2) 502-8202, careeci2@ibm.net, www.care.org

INTERNATIONAL NGO: Social Justice and Development

CARE International assists people to achieve long-term positive change in their social and economic conditions by promoting the development and use of indigenous resources and providing relief and rehabilitation support in emergencies and disasters.

CARE International works in nearly all areas of development and has approximately 500 overseas international staff. Vacancies are posted on their web site, under CARE USA Jobs' Newsletter. CARE's web site also provides links to related organizations. (For information on CARE Canada see Chapter 34, Nongovernmental Organizations.) [ID:6240]

Commonwealth Fund for Technical Co-operation (CFTC)

Marlborough House, Pall Mall, LondonSW1Y 5HX, UK;
(44) (171) 839-3411, fax (44) (171) 930-0827, cftc@commonwealth.int, www.tcol.co.uk/comorg/cftc.htm

MULTILATERAL INSTITUTION: Commonwealth

The Commonwealth Fund for Technical Co-operation (CFTC) differs from traditional development agencies by functioning as a system of mutual assistance. CFTC supplies experts at the request of member governments, helps countries build their expertise, finances consultancy studies, and provides specialist advice to governments on legal, economic, fiscal, and financial matters. CFTC also provides its members with computer systems for debt management. CFTC employs 300 people. [ID:6241]

Commonwealth Human Ecology Council (CHEC)
57/58 Stanhope Gardens, LondonSW7 5RF, UK;
(44) (171) 373-6761, fax (44) (171) 244-7470, chec@unl.ac.uk, www.tcol.co.uk/comorg

MULTILATERAL INSTITUTION: Commonwealth

The Commonwealth Human Ecology Council (CHEC) both initiates and acts as a clearinghouse of new ideas in human ecology. CHEC acts as a catalyst to promote inter-action between government and nongovernmental agencies, organizes educational activities, sponsors conferences and workshops, and assists in local community projects. CHEC's web site provides useful links to related organizations. [ID:6242]

Commonwealth of Learning (COL)
Suite 600, 1285 West Broadway, Vancouver, B.C.,
V6H 3X8, CANADA; (604) 775-8200, fax (604) 775-8210, info@col.org, www.col.org

MULTILATERAL INSTITUTION: Commonwealth

The Commonwealth of Learning (COL) is the only Commonwealth intergovernmental organization located outside of Britain. COL works to create and widen access to education, improve its quality, and utilize distance learning techniques and the associated communi-cation technologies required to meet the needs of member countries. COL has a total of 35 employees in Canada and overseas. COL's web site has job postings (look under employ-ment opportunities) and links to related sites. [ID:7184]

Commonwealth Secretariat (ComSec)
Marlborough House, Pall Mall, London SW1Y 5HX, UK; (44) (171) 839-3411,
fax (44) (171) 930-6128, info@commonwealth.int, www.the commonwealth.org/secret

MULTILATERAL INSTITUTION: Commonwealth

The Commonwealth Secretariat (ComSec) facilitates consultation and cooperation among member countries and collects and disseminates information useful to them. ComSec is essentially a bridge between races and religions, and between rich and poor. ComSec provides a forum where members are able to address their common problems and work together for a more just global society. ComSec currently has 400 staff from over 30 coun-tries. The web site for Comsec provides useful resource links to related agencies. [ID:6243]

Conservation International (CI)
Suite 2000, 2501"M" Street, N.W., Washington, DC, 20037, USA;
(202) 429-5660, fax (202) 887-5188, newmember@conservation.org, www.conservation.org

INTERNATIONAL NGO: Environment

Conservation International's (CI) aim is to encourage and support charitable, scientific, and educational programs and objectives and to conserve ecosystems and biological diver-sity that support life on earth. CI supports local capacity building and empowerment. CI currently has approximately 350 staff. Jobs and internship positions are advertised on the "Employment and Internships" page of their web site, with relevant information on appli-cation procedures. [ID:6244]

Development Innovations and Networks
BP 13457, Niamey, NIGER; (227) 723-111, fax (227) 723-108, ired@intnet.ne

INTERNATIONAL NGO: Social Justice and Development

Development Innovations and Networks discovers and/or instigates initiatives which contribute to endogenous, self-reliant development at the local, regional, and national levels. The organization also supports and creates networks facilitating communication and joint action between local development initiatives, in particular South-South and North-South exchanges. Development Innovations and Networks currently has 25 staff, a membership of 225 individuals, and approximately 1000 partners in 59 countries. They maintain a data bank for résumés and a consultant registry. [ID:6246]

Earthwatch

P.O Box 9104, 680 Mt. Auburn Street, Watertown, MA, 02272, USA;
(800) 776-0188, fax (617) 926-8532, info@earthwatch.org, www.earthwatch.org

INTERNATIONAL NGO: Science and Technology

Earthwatch is an international, nonprofit organization which supports scientific field research worldwide. Earthwatch volunteers and scientists work together conducting research in seven areas: world oceans, world forests, biodiversity, cultural diversity, learning from the past, monitoring global change, and world health.

Since its founding in 1972, Earthwatch has mobilized over 50,000 volunteers to work on more than 2,083 projects in 118 countries. Interested applicants can check Earthwatch's web site for current job postings. (For more information see Earthwatch's profile in Chapter 10, Short-term Programs Overseas.) [ID:7179]

Environmental Defense Fund (EDF)

257 Park Avenue South, New York, NY, 10010, USA; ·
(212) 505-2100, fax (212) 505-2375, susanh@edf.org, www.edf.org/index.html

INTERNATIONAL NGO: Environment

The Environmental Defense Fund (EDF) provides effective environmental solutions to problems of pollution and natural resource degradation that are also attentive to economic constraints. The EDF is staffed by 163 scientists, economists, attorneys, and other professionals. Information about jobs and internships with EDF is available on their web site. [ID:6248]

European Space Agency

8 - 10 rue Mario Nikis, 75738, Paris CEDEX 15, FRANCE;
(33) (1) 53-69-76-54, esaweb@esrin.esa.it, www.esrin.esa.it

MULTILATERAL INSTITUTION: Science and Technology

The European Space Agency (ESA) was established to exclusively promote peaceful purposes and cooperation among European states in their pursuit of space research, technology, and space applications. ESA does have non-European members, such as Canada, whose representatives participate in ESA programs and sit on the ESA Council. The ESA web site has links to other organizations as well as contact addresses, publications, and a search mechanism. [ID:7178]

Family Health International (FHI)

P.O. Box 13950, Research Triangle Park,
Durham, NC, 27709, USA; (919) 544-7040, fax (919) 544-7261, www.fhi.org

INTERNATIONAL NGO: Public Health and Family Planning

Family Health International (FHI) seeks to improve reproductive health worldwide. FHI conducts clinical trials on new and improved methods of fertility control; conducts studies of contraceptive safety, reproductive health, and maternal mortality and morbidity; disseminates results of studies; and transfers the technology of contraceptive research and analysis. Under the purview of FHI, the AIDS Control and Prevention Project (AIDSCAP) is designed to support the local capacity of developing countries to prevent and control HIV.

FHI has approximately 300 staff. Job openings are posted on their web site which also contains related internet resources and search engines. (For FHI internship information see Chapter 17, International Internships.) [ID:6249]

Greenpeace International

Keizersgracht 176, Amsterdam1016DW,
NETHERLANDS; (31) (20) 523-6222, fax (31) (20) 523-6000, www.greenpeace.org

INTERNATIONAL NGO: Environment

Greenpeace has offices in 34 countries. The people who work in these offices do a wide variety of jobs from environmental campaigning to general office duties. Greenpeace offers a vast range of overseas positions in a broad range of occupations.

Greenpeace posts job openings on their web site. Greenpeace also offers internship positions which vary from country to country. Interested applicants should apply directly to the Greenpeace office in the country they want to work in. (For information on Greenpeace Canada see Chapter 35, Nongovernmental Organizations.) [ID:7101]

Human Rights Internet (HRI)

8 York Street, Suite 302, Ottawa, Ontario,
K1N 5S6, CANADA; (613) 789-7407, fax (613) 789-7414, hri@hri.ca, www.hri.ca

INTERNATIONAL NGO: Law and Good Governance

Human Rights Internet (HRI) is a global leader in the exchange of information within the international human rights community. It promotes human rights education, research, sharing of information, and solidification of ties with those who share its commitment to the International Bill of Human Rights. It publishes the *HRI Reporter*, which systematically abstracts and indexes thousands of publications received by HRI. HRI networks with over 5000 organizations and individuals around the world. Their web site contains information on publications, internships, and jobs. [ID:7183]

Human Rights Watch

485 - 5th Ave., New York, NY, 10017- 6104, USA;
(212) 972-8400, fax (212) 972-0905, hrwnyc@hrw.org, www.hrw.org

INTERNATIONAL NGO: Law and Good Governance

Human Rights Watch reports on worldwide human rights' practices. It documents cases of imprisonment, censorship, disappearance, and other abuses of internationally recognized human rights with a view to pressing governments to cease abusive practices. Each year the organization conducts over 100 investigative missions to gather current information. Human Rights Watch is staffed by over 30 country specialists. (For Human Rights Watch internship information see Chapter 17, International Internships.) [ID:6250]

L'Institut de l'Énergie des pays ayant en commun l'usage du français (IEPF)

56, rue Saint-Pierre, 3e étage, Québec, Québec,
G1K 4K1, CANADA; (418) 692-5727, fax (418) 692-5644, iepf@iepf.org, www.iepf.org

MULTILATERAL INSTITUTION: La Francophonie

L'Institut de l'Énergie des pays ayant en commun l'usage du français (IEPF) a pour mission de contribuer au renforcement des capacités nationales et au développement des partenariats dans le secteur de l'énergie ainsi que dans le domaine de l'environnement. [ID:7113]

Inter-Parliamentary Union (IPU)

CP 438, 1211 Geneva 19, SWITZERLAND;
(41) (22) 919-4150, fax (41) (22) 733-3141, postbox@mail.ipu.org, www.ipu.org/english/whatipu.htm

MULTILATERAL INSTITUTION: Law and Good Governance

The work of the Inter-Parliamentary Union (IPU) falls into three fields: action for peace and cooperation, human rights of parliamentarians, and strengthening of parliamentary institutions. IPU's main areas of activity are: representative democracy, international peace and security, sustainable development, human rights and humanitarian law, women's issues and education, science and culture. The IPU has a staff of 30 internationally-recruited individuals. [ID:6251]

International Air Transport Association (IATA)
2000 Peel Street, Montréal, Québec,
H3A 2R4, CANADA; (514) 844-6311, fax (514) 844-5286, www.iata.org

INTERNATIONAL PROFESSIONAL ASSOCIATION: Global Communication

The International Air Transport Association (IATA) promotes safe, regular, and economical air transport, fosters air commerce, and studies problems in the field. The IATA organizes collaboration among air transport enterprises engaged in international air or transport service. The IATA has three principal roles: trade association, industry coordination, and industry services. The association employs approximately 450 staff. The IATA web site lists jobs and contains links to related sites. [ID:6252]

International Bar Association (IBA)
271 Regent Street, Hanover Square, London
W1R 7PA, UK; (44) (171) 629-1206, fax (44) (171) 409-0456,
alexphillips@int-bar.org, http://lexsun.law.uts.edu.au/~john/iba.html

INTERNATIONAL PROFESSIONAL ASSOCIATION: Law and Good Governance

The International Bar Association (IBA) maintains permanent relations and exchanges between bar associations and law societies throughout the world, advances the science of jurisprudence, and promotes the administration of justice under law among peoples of the world. The IBA has national or local associations in 104 countries and territories. It currently employs 43 full-time staff and hires part-time assistants as required. The IBA web site provides useful links to related organizations. [ID:6253]

International Campaign to Ban Landmines (ICBL)
2001 "S" Street N.W., Suite 740, Washington, DC, 20009, USA;
(202) 483-9222, fax (202) 483-9312, banmines@sover.net, www.vvaf.org/landmine.htm

INTERNATIONAL NGO: Peace and Security

The International Campaign to Ban Landmines (ICBL) is a steering committee which coordinates 11 organizations working together for a worldwide ban on antipersonnel landmines. This committee brings together over 1,000 groups from 55 countries from fields as diverse as human rights advocacy and medical development.

The ICBL web site contains contact information on these 11 organizations, a resource list, and landmine library. The ICBL's Canadian affiliate is Mines Action Canada, which is located in Ottawa and can be reached at (613)234-6755. [ID:7187]

International Chamber of Commerce
38 Cours Albert 1er, F-75008 Paris, FRANCE;
(33) (1) 4953-2828, fax (33) (1) 4953-2942, webmaster@icaiccwbo.org, www.iccwbo.org

INTERNATIONAL PROFESSIONAL ASSOCIATION: Business/Banking/Trade

The International Chamber of Commerce (ICC) represents all the economic factors of international business, including commerce, industry, transportation, and finance. ICC ascertains and expresses the considered judgement of its worldwide membership and promotes global trade and investment based on free and fair competition. The ICC currently has 93 staff at its headquarters. To further your job research, a look at ICC's web site is helpful as it provides links to other organizations. [ID:6254]

International Co-operative Alliance (ICA)

Route des Morillons 15, Grand Saconnex, 1218 Geneva,
SWITZERLAND; (41) (22) 929-8888, fax (41) (22) 798-4122, ica@coop.org, www.coop.org/

INTERNATIONAL PROFESSIONAL ASSOCIATION: Social Justice and Development

The International Co-operative Alliance (ICA) is a channel for the exchange of information and experience among national cooperative organizations. The ICA also represents the cooperative movement at the international level. The ICA undertakes research on subjects relevant to cooperatives and manages technical assistance programs for cooperatives in developing countries. The Alliance has 11 staff at its headquarters and an additional 50 in regional offices. If further information on cooperatives is needed, ICA's web site provides links to related organizations. [ID:6255]

International Committee of the Red Cross (ICRC)

Public Information Division, 19 avenue de la Paix CH 1202, Geneva, SWITZERLAND;
(41) (22) 734-6001, fax (41) (22) 733-2057, webmaster.gva@icrc.org, www.icrc.ch/unicc/icrcnews.nsf

INTERNATIONAL NGO: Social Justice and Development

The mandate of the International Committee of the Red Cross (ICRC) is to provide assistance to the victims of war and internal violence and to promote compliance with international humanitarian law. It is a broad-based organization which currently employs 7,022 local employees: 673 staff at its headquarters and 1,109 expatriates in the field. The ICRC's web site employs a search mechanism and its Human Resources page offers job information. (For information on the Canadian Red Cross Society see Chapter 35, Nongovernmental Organizations.) [ID:7194]

International Confederation of Free Trade Unions (ICFTU)

International Trade Union House, boul. Emile Jacqmain 155, B-1210
Brussels, BELGIUM; (32) (2) 224-0211, fax (32) (2) 218-8415, www.icftu.org

INTERNATIONAL PROFESSIONAL ASSOCIATION: Business/Banking/Trade

The International Confederation of Free Trade Unions (ICFTU) maintains and develops international organizations at worldwide and regional levels. It is composed of free and democratic trade unions. Independent of any external domination, it is pledged to the tasks of promoting the interests of working people throughout the world and enhancing respect for labour. ICTFU promotes measures to guarantee full employment, abolish forced labour practices, limit the power of monopolies, shorten working hours, and win for workers their say in the formation and application of economic and social policies. ICTFU has 90 international staff at its headquarters. Their web site contains information about their youth program and provides links to related sites. The ICFTU's Canadian affiliate is the Canadian Labour Congress(CLC), which is located in Ottawa and can be reached at (613) 521-3400. [ID:6256]

International Council for Adult Education (ICAE)

720 Bathurst Street, Suite 500, Toronto, Ontario, M5S 2R4, CANADA;
(416) 588-1211, fax (416) 588-5725, icae@web.net, http://www.web.net/icae

INTERNATIONAL NGO: Social Justice and Development

The objective of the International Council for Adult Education (ICAE) is to strengthen the adult education movement and its ability to act on critical global issues. These goals are promoted by creating an international forum for the exchange of ideas, collaborating on projects with other organizations, and strengthening nongovernmental adult education structures. The ICAE has 106 regional and national member associations in 85 countries. ICAE's web site has information on publications, links to other organizations, and a search mechanism. (For information on ICAE's Canadian office see Chapter 35, Nongovernmental Organizations.) [ID:6257]

International Criminal Police Organization (OIPC-INTERPOL)
BP 6041, F-69411 Lyon CEDEX 06, FRANCE;
(33) 7244-7000, fax (33) 7244-7163, www.interpol-pr.com

MULTILATERAL INSTITUTION: Peace and Security

Within the limits of laws existing in different countries, the International Criminal Police Organization (INTERPOL) promotes the widest possible mutual assistance among all criminal police authorities. The organization is forbidden to undertake any intervention or activities of a political, military, religious, or racial character. INTERPOL currently employs 326 staff. Positions are advertised in the major newspapers of France and the UK. Candidates must be university graduates and trilingual in French, English, and either Spanish or Arabic. The web site for OIPC-INTERPOL contains links to related organizations. [ID:6258]

International Energy Agency (IEA)
2 rue de la Federation, 75739 Paris CEDEX 15, FRANCE;
(33) (1) 40 57 65 54, fax (33) (1) 40 57 65 59, info@iea.org, www.iea.org

MULTILATERAL INSTITUTION: Environment

The International Energy Agency (IEA) fosters cooperation among member countries of the Organization for Economic Co-operation and Development (OECD). IEA's mandate to ensure and increase energy security is achieved through the promotion of diversification of energy supplies, cleaner, more efficient use of energy, and energy conservation. In order to promote wise management of world energy resources, IEA cooperates with oil-producing and oil-consuming countries in facilitating a stable international energy trade. The IEA has 140 full-time staff. Vacancies are posted on their web site under "What's New." [ID:6260]

International Federation of Red Cross and Red Crescent Societies
P.O. Box 372, CH-1211, Geneva 19, SWITZERLAND;
(41) (22) 730-4222, fax (41) (22) 733-0395, secretariat@ifrc.org, www.ifrc.org

INTERNATIONAL NGO: Social Justice and Development

The International Federation of Red Cross and Red Crescent Societies seeks to prevent and alleviate human suffering by coordinating international relief and encouraging development support.

The International Federation employs approximately 650 people: 250 at the secretariat in Geneva and 400 more in 65 delegations around the world. Visit their web site for more information, online publications, and job vacancies. (For information on the Canadian Red Cross Society see Chapter 35, Nongovernmental Organizations.) [ID:6261]

International Fellowship of Reconciliation (IFOR)
Spoorstraat 38, 1815 BK Alkmaar,
NETHERLANDS; office@ifor.ccmail.compuserve.com, www.gn.apc.org/ifor

INTERNATIONAL NGO: Peace and Security

The International Fellowship of Reconciliation (IFOR) is a spirtually-based movement. Its work is organized into five programs: disarmament and peacebuilding, interreligious cooperation, nonviolence education and training, women peacemakers, and youth empowerment and children's rights. The IFOR has branches, groups, and affiliates in over 40 countries on all continents. The web site for IFOR provides useful information about publications and contact addresses for its affiliates. [ID:7193]

International Institute for Applied Systems Analysis (IIASA)

A-2361, Laxenburg, AUSTRIA; (43) 2236-807-0, fax (43) 2236-71313, inf@iiasa.ac.at, www.iiasa.ac.at

INTERNATIONAL THINK TANK: Science and Technology

The International Institute for Applied Systems Analysis (IIASA) is a centre for innovative scientific research on environmental, economic, technological, and social issues. It provides a forum for international, interdisciplinary collaboration and for networking with scientists around the world. IIASA's web site contains information about publications, employment opportunities, and also has a search device. [ID:7182]

International Maritime Satellite Organization (INMARSAT)

99 City Road, LondonEC1Y 1AX, UK;
(44) (171) 728-1000, fax (44) (171) 728-1044, webmaster@inmarsat.org, www.inmarsat.org

INTERNATIONAL PROFESSIONAL ASSOCIATION: Global Communication

The International Maritime Satellite Organization (INMARSAT) was set up in 1979 to provide worldwide mobile satellite communications for the maritime community. Today it has a staff of 500 and 81 member countries. It is the only provider of global mobile satellite communications for commercial, emergency, and safety applications on land, at sea, and in the air. Job vacancies and the INMARSAT magazine are posted on their web site. [ID:7189]

The International Organization for Migration (IOM)

CP 71, 17 route des Morillons, CH-1211 Geneva 19,
SWITZERLAND; (41) (22) 717-9111, fax (41) (22) 798-6150, telex@geneva.iom.ch, www.iom.ch

MULTILATERAL INSTITUTION: Social Justice and Development

The International Organization for Migration (IOM) organizes and supervises the processing and movement of refugees, displaced persons, and other persons in need of international migration services. IOM promotes the economic, educational, and social advancement of developing countries by facilitating the transfer of technological expertise through migration. Through the organization of seminars and research projects, IOM provides a forum in which migration issues can be addressed. IOM has 1439 international staff; 150 are stationed at the head office while the rest are located in field offices. Positions are advertised through international organizations, missions of member states, and sometimes in *The Economist*. [ID:6264]

International Organization for Standardization (ISO)

1 rue de Varembe, C.P. 56, CH-1211, Geneva 201, SWITZERLAND;
(41) (22) 749 01 11, fax (41) (22) 733 34 30, iso9000@isocs.iso.ch, www.iso.ch

INTERNATIONAL PROFESSIONAL ASSOCIATION: Science and Technology

The International Organization for Standardization is a wordwide federation of national standards bodies from approximately 100 countries. Its goal is to faciliate trade, exchange, and technology transfer through international standardization. The Canadian affiliate to ISO is the Standards Council of Canada, which is located in Ottawa and can be reached at (613) 238-3222, or by e-mail at info@scc.ca. [ID:7177]

International Planned Parenthood Federation (IPPF)

Regent's College, Inner Circle, Regent's Park, LondonNW1 4NS, UK;
(44) (171) 487-7900, fax (44) (171) 487-7950, info@ippf.org, www.ippf.org

INTERNATIONAL NGO: Public Health and Family Planning

The International Planned Parenthood Federation (IPPF) promotes family planning services worldwide. IPPF assists family planning associations to offer contraceptive services, set and maintain high clinical standards, and train personnel. The Federation assists in the preparation of education programs on the personal, health, social, and economic benefits of family planning and works to develop public support for sustainable population, environment, and development policies.

IPPF currently has 120 staff at its international office. Its Canadian office, the Planned Parenthood Federation of Canada, is located in Ottawa and can be reached at (613) 241-4474, or by e-mail at ppfed@web.net. The IPPF web site has links to related web sites. [ID:6265]

International Rescue Committee (IRC)
12th Floor, 122 East 42nd Street, New York, NY, 10168 - 1289, USA;
(212) 551-3000, fax (212) 551-3180, denise@intrescom.org, www.intrescom.org

INTERNATIONAL NGO: Social Justice and Development

The International Rescue Committee (IRC) assists refugees and internally displaced individuals through its education and training programs in the fields of public health and sanitation. The committee is also comprised of personnel specializing in logistics, program management, accounting, and civil engineering. IRC has 15 offices in the US and 20 overseas offices in Africa, Asia, and Central Europe. Visit IRC's web site for more information on employment opportunities and overseas programs. [ID:6266]

International Social Security Association (ISSA)
C.P. 1, CH-1211 Geneva 22, SWITZERLAND;
(41) (22) 799-6617, fax (41) (22) 799-8509, issa@ilo.org, www.aiss.org

INTERNATIONAL THINK TANK: Social Justice and Development

The International Social Security Association (ISSA) provides a forum for the exchange of information, experience, and mutual technical support; ISSA organizes technical meetings, round tables, and seminars on questions relating to the development of social security. ISSA has a staff of 47. Vacancies are advertised in international newspapers and applications should be sent to the ISSA General Secretariat in Geneva. Their web site provides useful links to other organizations. [ID:6267]

International Telecommunications Satellite Organization (INTELSAT)
3400 International Drive N.W., Washington, DC, 20008-3098, USA;
(202) 944-6800, fax (202) 944-7898, webmaster@intelsat.int, www.intelsat.int

INTERNATIONAL PROFESSIONAL ASSOCIATION: Global Communication

The International Telecommunications Satellite Organization (INTELSAT) owns and operates the world's most extensive global communications satellite system, providing voice/data and video services to more than 135 countries via satellite. INTELSAT employs approximately 600 staff. Visit their web site for information on jobs and internships. (For INTELSAT internship information see Chapter 17, International Interships.) [ID:6268]

International Tropical Timber Organization (ITTO)
5th Floor, Pacifico-Yokohama IOC, 1-1-1 Minato-Mirai,
Nishi-ku, Yokohama 220, JAPAN; (81) (45) 233-1110, fax (81) (45) 233-1111, www.itto.or.jp

MULTILATERAL INSTITUTION: Environment

The International Tropical Timber Organization (ITTO) provides a framework for cooperation and consultation between tropical timber producing and consuming members on all aspects of the tropical timber economy. ITTO promotes the expansion and diversification of international trade in tropical timber, taking into account the relation between a long-term increase in consumption and continuity of supplies with measures aimed at sustainable utilization rates and conservation. ITTO currently employs a staff of 25. Vacancies are posted on ITTO's web site. [ID:6270]

International Union Association of Public Transport (UITP)
Ave. de l'Uruguay 19, B-1000 Brussels, BELGIUM;
(32) (2) 673-6100, fax (32) (2) 660-1072, administration@uitp.com, www.uitp.com

INTERNATIONAL THINK TANK: Environment

The International Union of Public Transport (UITP) studies all problems connected with urban and regional public transport and overall mobility. UITP promotes the development of public transport from technical, economic, and social aspects. UITP provides members with contacts, research results, and published studies. They currently have a staff of 40. [ID:6272]

International Wildlife Coalition (IWC)
P.O. Box 461, Port Credit Postal Association, Mississauga, Ontario,
L5G 4M1, CANADA; (905) 765-6341, fax (905) 765-6435, adncstr@muskok.com, www.iwc.org

INTERNATIONAL NGO: Environment

The International Wildlife Coalition (IWC) conducts and supports rescue, rehabilitation, and protection projects around the world. IWC initiates public education programs, legal actions, and scientific research in the struggle to save wildlife. They monitor the abuse of conventions of animal protection and support projects to save endangered species. [ID:6274]

North America Commission for Environmental Cooperation (CEC)
393 St. Jacques West, Room 200, Montréal, Québec,
H2Y 1N9, CANADA; (514) 350-4357, fax (514) 350-4314, NAFEC@ccemtl.org, www.cec.org

MULTILATERAL INSTITUTION: Environment

The North American Commission for Economic Cooperation (CEC) strives to foster the conservation, protection, and enhancement of the North American environment in the context of increasing economic, trade, and social links between Canada, Mexico, and the US. CEC's web site provides information on job openings (look under "Contracts"), listings of resources, and publications. [ID:7175]

North Atlantic Treaty Organization (NATO)
B-1110 Brussels, BELGIUM; (32) (2) 728-4111, fax (32) (2) 728-4579, www.nato.int

MULTILATERAL INSTITUTION: Peace and Security

The primary objective of the North Atlantic Treaty Organization (NATO) is to establish and maintain the collective security of its 16 member countries in accordance with the principles of the United Nations Charter. NATO has recently taken on additional tasks, including promoting stability and security throughout Europe, and providing support to the UN in its crisis management and peacekeeping initiatives.

Approximately 3,750 people are employed at the headquarters in Brussels: 250 are members of national delegations, 1,180 are international civilian staff, and 420 are international military staff. In addition to general information, NATO's web site lists job vacancies and publications. [ID:6275]

Organization for Economic Co-operation and Development (OECD)
2 rue Andre-Pascal, F-75775 Paris CEDEX 16, FRANCE;
(33) (1) 4524-8200, fax (33) (1) 4524-8500, www.oecd.org

MULTILATERAL INSTITUTION: Business/Banking/Trade

The Organization for Economic Co-operation and Development (OECD) is concerned with all aspects of economic and social policy. The organization promotes policies to achieve the highest sustainable economic growth and employment and to raise the standard of living among member countries while maintaining financial stability and the development of the world economy.

OECD's primary fields of policy and research cover a broad spectrum, including economic policy, energy, nuclear energy, development cooperation, international trade, financial and fiscal affairs, food, agriculture and fisheries, environment, industrial science and technology, education, employment, labour and social affairs, and road research.

Currently, OECD has approximately 1,800 staff. Recruiters look for outstanding educational qualifications and several years of relevant experience. See the "Jobs and Recruitment" area on their web site for full job descriptions. OECD maintains a consultant registry. [ID:6276]

Organization for Security and Co-operation in Europe (OSCE)
Karntnerring 5-7, 4th Floor, 1010, Vienna, AUSTRIA;
(43) (1) 51-436-150, fax (43) (1) 51-436-99, webmaster@osceprag.cz, www.osceprag.cz

MULTILATERAL INSTITUTION: Peace and Security

The membership of the Organization for Security and Co-operation in Europe (OSCE) is drawn from Vancouver to Vladivostok. The OSCE takes a comprehensive view of security and is involved in a wide range of security-related issues such as arms control and preventative diplomacy. There are approximately 125 staff within the OSCE secretariat. OSCE has a user friendly web site where job postings (look under "Vacancy Notices") and contact addresses for its affliates can be found. [ID:7188]

Organization of American States (OAS)
Department of Human Resources, 1889 "F" Street, N.W.,
Washington, DC, 20006, USA; (202) 458-3000, fax (202) 458-3967, info@oas.org, www.oas.org

MULTILATERAL INSTITUTION: Peace and Security

The Organization of American States (OAS) is a regional body comprised of 32 member countries in the Americas whose objectives include strengthening peace and security; promoting and consolidating representative democracy, human rights, and trade; ensuring the pacific settlement of disputes among members; and promoting economic, social, and cultural development. Currently, the OAS has 600 staff at its headquarters and in regional offices in member countries. Visit their web site to see program information, job vacancies, and internship information. [ID:6277]

Overseas Development Institute (ODI)
Portland House, Stag Place, LondonSW1E 5DP, UK;
(44) (171) 393-1600, fax (44) (171) 393-1699, odi@odi.org.uk, www.oneworld.org/odi

INTERNATIONAL THINK TANK: Business/Banking/Trade

The Overseas Development Institute (ODI) promotes research in and public awareness of the economic relationship between developing and industrialized nations. ODI conducts research on trade and aid policy; operates an agricultural administration unit to coordinate contact between practitioners, managers, and academics working in agriculture; and administers a relief and disaster policy program. ODI has a staff of 40. For information about ODI's fellowship program for postgraduate economists, check their web site. [ID:6278]

Pacific Economic Cooperation Council (PECC)
4 Nassim Road, 258372, SINGAPORE;
(65) 737-9823, fax (65) 737-9824, peccsec@pacific.net.sg, www.pecc.net

MULTILATERAL INSTITUTION: Business/Banking/Trade

The Pacific Economic Cooperation Council (PECC) promotes regional economic cooperation in the Pacific Basin. PECC conducts policy research in the areas of agriculture, fisheries, human resource development, science and technology, transportation, telecommunications, tourism, minerals, energy, and trade policy. For information on the Canadian secretariat, contact the Canadian National Committee for Pacific Economic Cooperation (CANCPEC) at (604) 684-5986. PECC's web site provides links to related sites. [ID:6279]

Pan African Institute for Development (PAID)
B.P. 4056, Douala, CAMEROON; (23) (7) 421061, fax (23) (7) 424335

INTERNATIONAL THINK TANK: Social Justice and Development

The Pan-African Institute for Development (PAID) works to further the economic, social, and cultural development of African countries. PAID promotes integrated and participatory development, provides training for rural development officers, conducts research, and provides support to local self-help projects. PAID has a staff of 66 professionals, 150 support staff, and a network of consultants hired on a part-time basis. [ID:6280]

Pan American Health Organization (PAHO)
525 - 23rd Street N.W., Washington, DC, 20037, USA;
(202) 974-3000, fax (202) 974-3663, webmaster@paho.org, www.paho.org

MULTILATERAL INSTITUTION: Public Health and Family Planning

The Pan-American Health Organization (PAHO) assists its member governments in the development and improvement of national and local public health services. To this end PAHO provides services to consultants, grants fellowships, organizes seminars and training courses, coordinates activities of neighbouring countries having common public health programs, and collects and disseminates health information and statistics. PAHO currently has 1500 international staff. PAHO's web site lists job vacancies and provides links to other sites. [ID:6281]

Peace Brigades International (PBI)
5 Caledonia Road, LondonN1 9DX, UK;
(44) (171) 713-0392, fax (44) (171) 837- 2290, pbiio@gn.apc.org, www.igc.apc.org

INTERNATIONAL NGO: Peace and Security

The Peace Brigades International (PBI) explores and implements nonviolent approaches to peacekeeping and supports basic human rights. Their role includes activities such as providing protective international accompaniment for individuals or organizations threatened by political violence or who are otherwise at risk. More information about this grassroots organization can be found at their web site. It also contains worldwide addresses for PBI's branches and outlines projects they are currently working on. [ID:7186]

Peace Bureau International (PBI)
41 rue de Zurich, CH-1201, Geneva, SWITZERLAND;
(41) (22) 731-6429, fax (41) (22) 738-9419, www.itu.ch/ipb

INTERNATIONAL NGO: Peace and Security

The International Peace Bureau is one of the world's oldest and most comprehensive international peace networks. It encompasses 19 international and 141 national/local members in over 40 countries (including seven affiliated branches in Canada). PBI brings together various groups working for peace, such as women, youth, labour, religious, political, and professional bodies. The web site for PBI is a useful resource as it lists publications and has links to other sites. [ID:7192]

PLAN International
Chobham House, Christchurch Way, Woking, Surrey, GU21 1JG, UK;
(44) (1483) 755-755, fax (44) (1483) 733-262, hodgesc@plan.geis.com

INTERNATIONAL NGO: Social Justice and Development

PLAN International is a humanitarian, child-focused development organization with no religious, political, or governmental affiliations. It strives to achieve lasting improvements in the quality of life of underprivileged children in the developing world. PLAN works in Africa, Asia, South and Central America, and the Caribbean. It has a worldwide staff of 4,200. [ID:6282]

Population Council
1 Dag Hammarskjöld Plaza, New York, NY, 10017, USA;
(212) 339-0500, fax (212) 755-6052, pubinfo@popcouncil.org, www.popcouncil.org

INTERNATIONAL THINK TANK: Social Justice and Development

The Population Council undertakes social and health science programs relevant to developing countries and conducts biomedical research to develop and improve contraceptive technology. The council also provides advice and technical assistance to governments, international agencies, and nongovernmental organizations. It also disseminates information on population issues through publications, conferences, seminars, and workshops. The Population Council has 350 staff. Their web site lists jobs, fellowships, and links to related organizations. [ID:6283]

Sierra Club, International Program
2nd Floor, 85 Second Street, San Francisco, CA, 94105-3441, USA;
(415) 977-5500, fax (415) 977-5799, information@sierraclub.org, www.sierraclub.org

INTERNATIONAL NGO: Environment

The Sierra Club's International Program aims to protect wild places, to promote the responsible treatment of the earth's ecosystems and use of its resources, and to protect and restore the quality of natural and human environments. The International Program currently has 250 staff. (For information on the Sierra Club of Canada see Chapter 35, Nongovernmental Organizations.) [ID:6284]

World Association of Industrial and Technical Research Organizations (WAITRO)
P.O. Box 141, DK-2630, Taastrup, DENMARK;
(45) 43504350, fax (45) 43507050, waitro@dti.dk, http://waitro.dti.dk/

INTERNATIONAL THINK TANK: Science and Technology

The World Association of Industrial and Technical Research Organizations (WAITRO) was created to provide an international voice for technological research and development. WAITRO is a global clearinghouse for technological information and an agency for promoting cooperation between member research establishments. WAITRO represents 121 members in 70 countries. Its staff is comprised of several thousand highly qualified research and development personnel who have grassroots contact with domestic industry and policy making bodies. [ID:7180]

World Association of Small and Medium Enterprises (WASME)
27 Nehru Place, New Delhi110019, INDIA;
(91) (11) 641-1417, fax (91) (11) 641-4058, CDA.WASME@GEMS.VSNL.net.in

INTERNATIONAL PROFESSIONAL ASSOCIATION: Business/Banking/Trade

The World Association of Small and Medium Enterprises (WASME) advises on policy, strategy, and support systems for the promotion of small and medium enterprises in 107 member countries. WASME organizes seminars and conferences, providing a forum for discussions of enterprise-related hardships and expectations in national, regional, and international contexts. WASME currently has 42 international staff. They maintain a data bank for résumés and a consultant registry. [ID:6287]

World Confederation of Labour (WCL)
Rue de Trèves 33, B-1040 Brussels, BELGIUM;
(32) (2) 285 4700, fax (32) (2) 230-8722, info@cmt-wcl.org, www.cmt-wcl.org

INTERNATIONAL PROFESSIONAL ASSOCIATION: Social Justice and Development

The World Confederation of Labour (WCL) promotes the establishment, development, and consolidation of a trade union movement at national, regional, and world levels. The WCL provides trade union representation to international institutions, organizes seminars and leader training in Africa, Asia, and Latin America, and provides technical assistance to confederations in developing countries. WCL has 25 staff. The web site for WCL can help in job research as it provides links to related organizations. [ID:6288]

World Conservation Union (IUCN)
28 rue Mauverney, CH 1196, Gland, SWITZERLAND;
(41) (22) 999-0001, fax (41) (22) 999-0002, mail@hq.iucn.org, www.iucn.org

MULTILATERAL INSTITUTION: Environment

The World Conservation Union (IUCN) is one of the world's most established conservation organizations. It brings together 74 governments, 105 government agencies, and more than 700 nongovernmental organizations to form a global network of 895 institutions. The IUCN membership is made up of over 8,000 technical, scientific, and policy experts as well as leaders in the field of conservation and the sustainable use of renewable natural resources.

IUCN has over 820 staff members in more than 40 regional and country offices. Further information on the regional offices (including 24 affiliates in Canada) and job postings can be found on IUCN's web site. The World Conservation Union of Canada is located in Montréal and can be reached at (514) 287-9704, or by fax at (514) 287-9057. [ID:7174]

World Customs Organization
Rue de l'Industrie 26-38, B-1040 Brussels, BELGIUM;
(32) (2) 508-4211, fax (32) (2) 508-4240, www.unicc.org/unece/trade/facil/cccstr.htm

MULTILATERAL INSTITUTION: Business/Banking/Trade

The World Customs Organization promotes the harmonization of customs procedures and facilitates cooperation among customs administrators by encouraging the widest application of relevant rules of the General Agreement on Trade and Tariffs (GATT). It is active in developing improved control and enforcement measures and in improving the management of customs administrations worldwide. The council currently employs 116 international staff. [ID:6245]

World Economic Forum
53 chemin des Hauts - Crêts, 1223 Cologny, Geneva, SWITZERLAND;
(41) (22) 869-1212, fax (41) (22) 786-2744, contact@weforum.org, www.weforum.org

INTERNATIONAL NGO: Business/Banking/Trade

The World Economic Forum integrates leaders from business, government, and academia into partnerships to address key political, economic, and social issues facing the global community. The web site for the World Economic Forum provides a guide to help your search and posts career opportunities. [ID:7169]

World Vision International

800 West Chestnut Avenue, Monrovia, CA, 91016-3198, USA;

(626) 303-8811, fax (626) 301-7786, worvis@wvi.org, www.wvi.org

INTERNATIONAL NGO: Social Justice and Development

World Vision International is a nondenominational Christian humanitarian agency dedicated to spiritually and physically ministering to people. Its activities include tranformational development, emergency relief, public awareness, and the promotion of justice. World Vision International employs more than 3,500 individuals, primarily in field offices.

The web site for World Vision International provides you with information about job openings and links to other web sites. (For information on World Vision Canada see Chapter 20, Short-term Programs Overseas.) [ID:6290]

World Wide Fund for Nature (WWF)

WWF International, Ave. du Mont-Blanc, CH-1196 Gland, SWITZERLAND;

(41) (22) 364-9111, fax (41) (22) 364-3239, infobo@Ian.wwf.ch, www.panda.org

INTERNATIONAL NGO: Environment

The World Wide Fund for Nature (WWF) seeks to conserve natural, ecological processes by preserving genetic, species, and ecosystem diversity. The WWF works to ensure the sustainable use of renewable resources, promotes actions to reduce pollution and wasteful exploitation and consumption of resources, and creates public awareness of threats to the natural environment.

Since its inception WWF has invested over $330 million in more than 10,000 projects in 130 countries. WWF currently has 160 staff at their headquarters and additional positions in the field. Their web site has helpful information about job postings. The Canadian office of WWF is in Toronto at (416) 489-8800, or e-mail pdover@wwfcanada.org. [ID:6291]

Chapter 39

Canadian Diplomats Abroad

Every day, the employees of the DEPARTMENT OF FOREIGN AFFAIRS AND INTERNATIONAL TRADE (DFAIT) strive to bring Canada to the world and the world to Canada. Their activities fall under a host of categories, yet all are managing Canada's political, economic, and cultural relations in the international sphere.

This chapter gives an overview of DFAIT's main activities and provides details on the locations of Canadian embassies, High Commissions, Consulates, and other offices abroad. All forms of diplomatic representation have been listed, except for honourary positions, which are usually voluntary. In countries where there are no Canadian embassy or High Commission, we have included Offices to Canadian Embassies if they performed basic consular functions, such as the issuance of visas.

DFAIT's visibility and public presence as well as their domestic and international profile is enhanced through the posting of diplomats abroad. DFAIT has two types of overseas missions: bilateral missions, which are accredited to specific countries and organized by function, and multilateral missions, which serve Canadian interests with respect to specific international organizations such as the UNITED NATIONS (UN) and the NORTH ATLANTIC TREATY ORGANIZATION (NATO). Private citizens travelling, studying or living abroad are more likely to encounter the bilateral missions in the form of Canadian Embassies, High Commissions and Consulates. For Canadian travellers, these offices can be an oasis of familiar territory in unfamiliar places.

SERVICES TO INDIVIDUALS

Providing a wide range of services to Canadians abroad is one of the primary activities of DFAIT's overseas missions. Their staff have consummate skill in providing help in cases of accident or other emergencies, and providing practical and expert advice when Canadians run into difficulty. Every year, Canadian consular services help over two million Canadians sort out problems, acquire practical and often vital information, and obtain support when needed.

SERVICES TO CANADIAN BUSINESSES

Helping Canadian businesses promote and sell their goods and services in foreign markets is another major function of Canadian missions abroad. The ability of missions to sell goods and services abroad, attract job-creating investment, and develop and acquire the best technology is key to sustaining Canada's high standard of living.

Every year, trade commissioners strive to expand Canada's share of export markets. Trade commissioners help Canadian exporters by organizing export fairs, missions and other major projects, identifying market opportunities, acting as corporate liaison, and reporting on appropriate sources of foreign investment and new technology. The trade activities of DFAIT change with shifts in markets.

FOREIGN AID

Through official development assistance, the DEPARTMENT OF FOREIGN AFFAIRS AND INTERNATIONAL TRADE (DFAIT) and the CANADIAN INTERNATIONAL DEVELOPMENT AGENCY (CIDA) implement Canada's aid programs abroad. In addition to providing humanitarian assistance, Canadian missions overseas work toward the economic, technical, educational, and social advancement of southern countries. A related function is to ensure that Canadian development policies are consistent with Canada's political and economic interests, and conversely, to report on the development plans of host countries, identify potential aid projects and negotiate aid protocols.

COMMUNICATIONS AND CULTURE

The COMMUNICATION AND CULTURE branch of DFAIT fosters a positive and informed image of Canada among significant foreign groups, such as business-people, investors and journalists. At home, this branch enhances Canadians' understanding of Canada's role in world affairs by providing information about specific foreign policy and trade issues. COMMUNICATION AND CULTURE also awards grants in the area of international cultural relations.

OTHER FUNCTIONS

There are a host of related activities in which Canadian missions abroad are involved. Examples of such activities include working with representatives of other countries to develop international laws and regulations, managing administrative, personnel, financial and material programs, and managing immigration programs.

An important function of Canadian representatives abroad is to organize official visits to Canada by foreign heads of state, heads of government, and ministers as well as arranging overseas visits by the Governor General, Prime Minister, and other Canadian ministers.

Canadian missions abroad are also active in promoting Canada as a vacation destination. Their tourism-related activities include advertising and marketing, public relations, mounting exhibits, and organizing educational tours.

CANADIAN DIPLOMATIC TERMINOLOGY

A word about the terminology used to describe Canadian representations abroad. *Mission* is the generic term for a Canadian government office abroad. A mission may be a large operation with as many as 100 Canadians and other locally engaged staff, or a one-person *Satellite Office*.

A mission in a foreign capital is called an *Embassy*, unless the other country is a member of the Commonwealth in which case it is called a *High Commission*.

Where there is an office in a city other than the capital of a country, for example New York in the United States or Osaka in Japan, it is called a *Consulate*. If it is relatively large, delivers several programs, or has satellite offices, it is called a *Consulate General*.

A *Liaison Office* functions for a special purpose, such as co-ordination of Canadian military operations.

A Canadian government *Trade* (or *Aid*) *Office* has a single assigned function and is usually a satellite of a larger mission.

A *Permanent Mission* is the Canadian representation at the UNITED NATIONS or one of its agencies, or other multilateral bodies.

Embassies and High Commissions are classified according to the number of Canadians they employ. They are considered *small* if between one and 10 employees, *mid-sized* if between 11 and 24 employees, and *large* if there are 25 or more employees. Similarly, Consulates and Consulates General are classified as *small* if between one and four employees, *mid-sized* if between five and nine employees, and *large* if there are 10 or more employees.

A LAST WORD

Diplomats abroad wear many hats and have a host of official responsibilities. However, the great majority of Canadians who encounter diplomats are tourists or businesspeople. If you're a tourist, it's likely your encounter with Canadian embassy officials will take place when you're in some sort of trouble. For Canadian businessmen and women, one of the most significant roles the department plays is helping Canadian businesses expand their exports. Promoting foreign investment and the flow of foreign technology into Canada is all in a day's work for diplomats.

RESOURCES

For related resources consult the Resources section on Foreign Affairs in Chapter 34, Careers in Government and the resources in Chapter 40, Foreign Diplomats in Canada.

Bottin International du Québec 📖
Annuelle, *Denis Turcotte* ➤ Québec dans le monde, C.P. 8503, Ste-Foy, Québec G1V 4N5; $27,95; chèque ou mandat poste; (418) 659-5540, fax (418) 659-4143 ▪ Le bottin prend en compte un millier d'intervenants internationaux québécois ou partenaires étrangers du Québec. Il énumère leur adresse postale, leur numéro de téléphone, leurs secteurs d'activités, et le pays ou les régions d'intervention. [ID:1597]

Canadian Passport Office 💻
www.dfait-maeci.gc.ca/passport/passport.htm ▪ Provides useful information needed for both novice to seasoned travellers. There are details on how to obtain a passport, office locations, and what to do in case of a lost or stolen passport. [ID:2746]

Canadian Representatives Abroad 📖 💻
Annual, Department of Foreign Affairs and International Trade (DFAIT), 142 pages ➤ Canada Government PublishingOttawa, Ontario K1A 0S9; $17.95; VISA, MC; (819) 956-4800, fax (819) 994-1498, publishing@ccg-gcc.ca ▪ A bilingual directory of Canadian diplomatic and consular missions. Available on the web at the DFAIT site, under "Embassies and Missions" at www.dfait-maeci.gc.ca/english/missions. [ID:1089]

The Diplomatic Handbook 📖
1993, *R. G. Feltham* ➤ Addison Wesley Longman Publishers, P.O. Box 580, Don Mills, Ontario M3C 2T8; $37.95; credit cards; (800) 387-8028, fax (800) 465-0536 ▪ Comprehensive, concise guide for those involved in managing international relations. Lots of practical advice. [ID:1643]

Directory for Trade Commissioners 📖
1997 ➤ InfoCentre, Department of Foreign Affairs and International Trade (DFAIT), 125 Sussex Dr., Ottawa, Ontario K1A 0G2; (800) 267-8376, fax (613) 996-9709 ▪ A booklet designed for exporters examining foreign market representation options, and for companies that have received an unsolicited proposal from a potential agent or distributor and require guidance in the assessment process. [ID:1589]

Directory of the Canadian Trade Commissioner Service Abroad 📖 💻
Canada Government Publishing, Ottawa, Ontario K1A 0S9; free; VISA, MC; (819) 956-4800, fax (819) 994-1498, publishing@ccg-gcc.ca ▪ Address and contact information for over 125 Canadian trade missions abroad. Includes some tips and information for exporters. Also available online at www.infoexport.gc.ca. [ID:2535]

Department of Foreign Affairs and International Trade (DFAIT) 💻
www.dfait-maeci.gc.ca/ ▪ This excellent homepage for DFAIT provides a vast amount of information on the international system, from travel advisories to international trade. It has links to DFAIT departments, services, country profiles, foreign embassies and missions in Canada, and Canadian government activities abroad. [ID:2565]

Canadian Diplomatic Missions Abroad

This chapter profiles 149 Canadian overseas missions in 113 countries. For the remaining 82 countries, Canadian missions operate through neighbouring countries or U.S embassies. Canadian representation abroad includes 72 embassies, 21 High Commissions, 31 consulates, 10 Offices of Canadian Embassies, 13 permanent missions to international organizations, and two trade offices.

Canadian representation overseas consists of missions (whether they be a single embassy or a series of consulates) in the following regions: 22 in Africa, 19 in Asia-Pacific, 37 in Europe, five in the Caribbean, 17 in Latin America, nine in the Middle East, and four in North America.

For more information, visit the web sites listed. Othersources of up-to-date information are DFAIT's general inquiry line 1-800-267-8376 and web site (www.dfait-maeci.gc.ca).

(To find out more about some of the international organizations listed, see Chapter 38, International Organizations and Chapter 36, United Nations. For further information on specific countries, see the section Country Information on the Internet, in Chapter 21, The Internet Job Search, and Chapter 40, Foreign Diplomats in Canada.)

ALBANIA (Republic of Albania)

Contact the Canadian Embassy in Budapest, Hungary.

ALGERIA
(People's Democratic Republic of Algeria)

EMBASSY IN ALGIERS (mid-sized): 27 bis, rue de Freres Benhafid, Hydra, ALGERIA. Postal Address: P.O. Box 48, Alger-Gare, 16000, Alger, ALGERIA; (213) (2) 69 16 11, fax (213) (2) 69 39 20

ANDORRA (Principality of Andorra)

Contact the Canadian Embassy in Madrid, Spain.

ANGOLA (People's Republic of Angola)

Contact the Canadian High Commission in Harare, Zimbabwe.

ANTIGUA AND BARBUDA

Contact the Canadian High Commission in Bridgetown, Barbados.

ARGENTINA (Argentine Republic)

EMBASSY IN BUENOS AIRES (mid-sized): 2828 Tagle, 1425 Buenos Aires, ARGENTINA. Postal Address: Casilla de Correo 1598, Buenos Aires, ARGENTINA; (54) (1) 805-3032, fax (54) (1) 806-1209

ARMENIA (Republic of Armenia)

Contact the Canadian Embassy in Moscow, Russia.

AUSTRALIA
(Commonwealth of Australia)

Area of jurisdiction includes the Solomon Islands and Vanuatu.

HIGH COMMISSION IN CANBERRA (mid-sized): Commonwealth Ave., Canberra ACT 2600, AUSTRALIA; (61) (2) 6273-3844, fax (61) (2) 6273-3285

CONSULATE GENERAL IN SYDNEY (small): Level 5, Quay West Building, 111 Harrington Street, N.S.W. 2000, Sydney, AUSTRALIA; (61) (2) 9364-3000, fax (61) (2) 9364-3098

AUSTRIA (Republic of Austria)

EMBASSY IN VIENNA (mid-sized): Laurenzerberg 2, A-1010 Vienna, AUSTRIA; (43) (1) 531 38 3000, fax (43) (1) 531 38 3321

AZERBAIJAN (Republic of Azerbaijan)

Contact the Canadian Embassy in Ankara, Turkey.

BAHAMAS
(Commonwealth of the Bahamas)

Contact the Canadian High Commission in Kingston, Jamaica.

BAHRAIN (State of Bahrain)

Contact the Canadian Embassy in Saudi Arabia.

BANGLADESH
(People's Republic of Bangladesh)

HIGH COMMISSION IN DHAKA (small): House CWN 16/A, Road 48, Gulshan, Dhaka, BANGLA-DESH. Postal Address: G.P.O. Box 569, Dhaka, BANGLADESH; (880) (2) 88 70 91, fax (880) (2) 88 30 43

BARBADOS

Area of jurisdiction includes the territories of Antigua and Barbuda, British Virgin Islands, Dominica, Anguilla, Montserrat, St. Maarten, Grenada, Guadeloupe, Martinique, Saint Kitts and Nevis, Saint Lucia and Saint Vincent and the Grenadines.

HIGH COMMISSION IN BRIDGETOWN (mid-sized): Bishop's Court Hill, St. Michael, BARBADOS. Postal Address: P.O. Box 404 Bridgetown, BARBADOS; (809) 429-3550, fax (809) 429-3780

BELARUS (Republic of Belarus)

Contact the Canadian Embassy in Moscow, Russia.

BELGIUM (Kingdom of Belgium)

Area of jurisdiction includes Luxembourg.

EMBASSY IN BRUSSELS (mid-sized): 2 ave. de Tervuren, 1040 Brussels, BELGIUM; (32) (2) 741-0611, fax (32) (2) 741-0619

BELIZE

Contact the Canadian High Commission in Kingston, Jamaica.

BENIN (Republic of Benin)

Contact the Canadian High Commission in Abidjan, Côte D'Ivoire.

BERMUDA

Contact the Canadian Consulate General in New York.

BHUTAN (Kingdom of Bhutan)

Contact the Canadian High Commission in New Delhi, India.

BOLIVIA (Republic of Bolivia)

The affairs of the Canadian Embassy in Bolivia are managed by the Canadian Embassy in Peru. There is one development officer in La Paz, Bolivia.

OFFICE OF CANADIAN COOPERATION IN LA PAZ (small):Avenida 20 de Octubre 2475, Plaza Avaroa Sapochia, La Paz, BOLIVIA. Postal Address: Casilla Postal 13032, La Paz, BOLIVIA; (591) (2) 432-838, fax (591) (2) 430-250

BOSNIA AND HERZEGOVINA (Republic of Bosnia and Herzegovina)

EMBASSY IN SARAJEVO (small): Logavina 7, 71 000 Sarajevo, BOSNIA AND HERZEGOVINA; (387) (71) 447- 900, fax (387) (71) 447-901

BOTSWANA (Republic of Botswana)

Contact the Canadian High Commission in Harare, Zimbabwe.

BRAZIL (Federative Republic of Brazil)

EMBASSY IN BRASILIA (mid-sized): Setor de Exmbaixadas Sul, Avenida das Naçoes, Quadra 803, lote 16, 70410-900 Brasilia, D.F., BRAZIL. Postal Address: Caixa Postal 00961, 70359-900 Brasilia D.F., BRAZIL; (55) (61) 321-2171, fax (55) (61) 321-4529

CONSULATE GENERAL IN SAO PAULO (large): Edificio Top Centre, Avenida Paulista 854, 5th Floor, 01310-913 Sao Paulo, BRAZIL. Postal Address: Caixa Postal 62693, 01214-970 Sao Paulo, BRAZIL; (55) (11) 287-2122, fax (55) (11) 251-5057

BRITAIN (United Kingdom of Great Britain and Northern Ireland)

HIGH COMMISSION IN LONDON (large): Macdonald House, 1 Grosvenor Square, London W1X 0AB, England, UNITED KINGDOM; (44) 1 (71) 258-6600, fax (44) 1 (71) 258-6333

BRUNEI DARUSSALAM (Negara Brunei Darussalam)

HIGH COMMISSION IN BANDAR SERI BEGAWAN (mid sized): Britannia House, Suite 51, Jalan Cator, Bandar Seri Begawan, BRUNEI DARUSSALAM; (673) (2) 22 00 43, fax (673) (2) 22 00 40

BULGARIA (Republic of Bulgaria)

Contact the Canadian Embassy in Bucharest, Romania.

BURKINA FASO

EMBASSY IN OUAGADOUGOU (small): Street Agostino Neto, Ouagadougou, BURKINA FASO. Postal Address: P.O. Box 548, Ouagadougou 01 Province du Kadiogo, BURKINA FASO; (226) 31 18 94, fax (226) 31 19 00

BURMA (Union of Myanmar)

Contact the Canadian Embassy in Bangkok, Thailand.

BURUNDI (Republic of Burundi)

Contact the Canadian High Commission in Nairobi, Kenya.

CAMBODIA (Kingdom of Cambodia)

EMBASSY IN PHNOM PENH (small): Villa 9,Senei Vinnavaut Oum Sangkat Chaktamouk, Khand Daun Penh, Phnom Penh, CAMBODIA; (855) (23) 426 000, fax (855) (23) 211 389

CAMEROON (Republic of Cameroon)

Area of jurisdiction includes the Central African Republic and Chad.

EMBASSY IN YAOUNDÉ (small): Immeuble Stamatiades, Place de l'Hôtel de Ville, Yaoundé, CAMEROON. Postal Address: P.O. Box 572 Yaoundé, CAMEROON; (237) 22 19 36, fax (237) 22 10 90

CAPE VERDE (Republic of Cape Verde)

Contact the Canadian Embassy in Dakar, Sénégal.

CENTRAL AFRICAN REPUBLIC

Contact the Canadian Embassy in Yaoundé, Cameroon.

CHAD (Republic of Chad)

Contact the Canadian Embassy in Yaoundé, Cameroon.

CHILE (Republic of Chile)

EMBASSY IN SANTIAGO (small): Nueva Tajamar 481, 12th Floor, Santiago, CHILE. Postal Address: Casilla 139,Correo 10, Santiago, CHILE; (56) (2) 362-9660, fax (56) (2) 362-9665

CHINA (People's Republic of China)

Area of jurisdiction includes Mongolia.

EMBASSY IN BEIJING (large): 19 Dong Zhi Men Wai Street, Chao Yang District, Beijing, PEOPLE'S REPUBLIC OF CHINA, 100600; (86) (10) 6532-3536, fax (86) (10) 6532-4311

CONSULATE GENERAL IN SHANGHAI (small): American International Centre at Shanghai Centre, West Tower, Suite 604, 1376 Nanjing Xi Lu, Shanghai, 200040, PEOPLE'S REPUBLIC OF CHINA,; (86) (21) 6279-8400, fax (86) (21) 6279-8401

CONSULATE IN GUANGZHOU (small): China Hotel, Office Tower, Suite 1563-4 Liu Hua Lu, Guangzhou, PEOPLE'S REPUBLIC OF CHINA, 510015; (86) (20) 8666-0569, fax (86) (20) 8667-2401

CONSULATE IN HONG KONG SPECIAL ADMINISTRATIVE REGION (large): 11-14th Floors, One Exchange Square, 8 Connaught Place, PEOPLE'S REPUBLIC OF CHINA; (852) 2810-4321, fax (852) 2810-6736

COLOMBIA (Republic of Colombia)

EMBASSY IN BOGOTA (mid-sized): Calle 76, No. 11-52, Bogota, COLOMBIA. Postal Address: Apartado Aereo 53531, Bogota 2, COLOMBIA; (57) (1) 313-1355, fax (57) (1) 313-3071

COMOROS (Islamic Federal Republic of the Comoros)

Contact the Canadian High Commission in Dar–e–Salaam, Tanzania.

CONGO (People's Republic of the Congo)

Contact the Embassy of the United States in Kinshasa, Democratic Republic of the Congo.

CONGO(Democratic Republic of the Congo, formerly Zaire)

Area of jurisdiction includes The People's Republic of the Congo.

CANADIAN OFFICE IN KINSHASA C/O THE EMBASSY OF THE UNITED STATES (small): 310 avenue des Aviateurs, Kinshasa, CONGO; (243) (12) 21 532, fax (243) (88) 43 805

COSTA RICA (Republic of Costa Rica)

Area of jurisdiction includes Nicaragua.

EMBASSY IN SAN JOSÉ (mid-sized): Oficentro Ejectuivo La Sabana–detras de la Contraloria, Sabana Sur, San José, COSTA RICA; (506) 296-4149, fax (506) 296-4270

CÔTE D'IVOIRE (Republic of Côte D'Ivoire)

EMBASSY IN ABIDJAN (mid-sized): Immeuble Trade Centre, 23 Nogues Ave., Le Plateau, Abidjan, CÔTE D'IVOIRE. Postal Address: P.O. Box 4104, Abidjan 01, CÔTE D'IVOIRE; (225) 21 20 09, fax (225) 21 77 28

CROATIA (Republic of Croatia)

EMBASSY IN ZAGREB (small): Hotel Esplanade, Mihanovieva 1, 10000 Zagreb, CROATIA; (385) (1) 457-7885, fax (385) (1) 457-7913

CUBA (Republic of Cuba)

EMBASSY IN HAVANA (small): Calle 30, No. 518 Esquina a7a, Miramar, Havana, CUBA; (53) (7) 24 25 16, fax (53) (7) 24 20 44

CYPRUS (Republic of Cyprus)

Contact the Canadian Embassy in Tel Aviv, Israel.

CZECH REPUBLIC

Area of jurisdiction includes Slovakia.

EMBASSY IN PRAGUE (mid-sized): Mickiewiczova 6, 125 33 Prague 6, CZECH REPUBLIC; (420) (2) 431-1108, fax (420) (2) 431-0294, www.dfait-maeci.gc.ca/~prague

DENMARK (Kingdom of Denmark)

EMBASSY IN COPENHAGEN (small): Kr. Bernikowsgade 1, 1105 Copenhagen K, DENMARK; (45) (33) 12 22 99, fax (45) (33) 14 05 85

DJIBOUTI (Republic of Djibouti)

Contact the Canadian Embassy in Addis Ababa, Ethiopia.

DOMINICA (Commonwealth of Dominica)

Contact the Canadian High Commission in Bridgetown, Barbados.

DOMINICAN REPUBLIC

The Office of the Canadian Embassy in Santo Domingo can perform basic consular functions. If further assistance is required contact the Canadian Embassy in Caracas, Venezuela.

OFFICE OF THE CANADIAN EMBASSY IN SANTO DOMINGO (small): Maximo Gomez 30, Santo Domingo, DOMINICAN REPUBLIC. Postal Address: P.O. Box 2054, Santo Domingo 1 DOMINICAN REPUBLIC; (809) 689-0002, fax (809) 682-2691

ECUADOR (Republic of Ecuador)

EMBASSY IN QUITO (small): Avenida 6 de Diciembre 2816 y James Orton, Edificio Josueth Gonzales, 4th floor, Quito, EQUADOR; (593) (2) 564 795, fax (593) (2) 503 108; canada1@uio.satnet.net

EGYPT (Arab Republic of Egypt)

EMBASSY IN CAIRO (mid-sized): Arab International Bank Building 5 Midan El Saraya el Kobra, Garden City, Cairo, EGYPT. Postal Address: P.O. Box 1667, Cairo, EGYPT; (20) (2) 354-3110, fax (20) (2) 356-3548

EL SALVADOR (Republic of El Salvador)

The Office of the Canadian Embassy in San Salvador can perform basic consular functions. If further assistance is required contact the Canadian Embassy in San Salvador, El Salvador.

OFFICE OF THE CANADIAN EMBASSY IN SAN SALVADOR (small): AvenidaLas Palmas no.111, Colonia San Benito, San Salvador, EL SALVADOR; (503) (2) 794-655, fax (503) (2) 790-765

EQUITORIAL GUINEA (Republic of Equatorial Guinea)

Contact the Canadian Embassy in Libreville, Gabon.

ERITREA (State of Eritrea)

Contact the Canadian Embassy in Addis Ababa, Ethiopia.

ESTONIA (Republic of Estonia)

The Office of the Canadian Embassy in Tallinn can perform basic consular functions. If further assistance is required contact the Canadian Embassy in Riga, Latvia.

OFFICE OF THE CANADIAN EMBASSY IN TALLINN (small): Toomkooli 13, 2nd floor, 0100 Tallinn, ESTONIA; (372) 631-3570, fax (372) 631-3573

ETHIOPIA

Area of jurisdiction includes Sudan, Eritrea and Djibouti.

EMBASSY IN ADDIS ABABA (small): Old Airport Area, Higher 23, Kebele 12, House No. 122, Addis Ababa, ETHIOPIA. Postal Address: P.O. Box 1130, Addis Ababa, ETHIOPIA; (251) (1) 71 30 22, fax (251) (1) 71 30 33

FIJI (Republic of Fiji)

Contact the Canadian High Commission in Wellington, New Zealand.

FINLAND (Republic of Finland)

EMBASSY IN HELSINKI (small): P.Esplanadi 25B, 00100 Helsinki, FINLAND. Postal Address: P.O. Box 779, 00101 Helsinki, FINLAND; (358) (9) 17 11 41, fax (358) (9) 60 10 60

FRANCE (French Republic)

Area of jurisdiction includes Monaco.

EMBASSY IN PARIS (large): 35-37 avenue Montaigne, 75008 Paris, FRANCE; (33) (1) 44 43 29 00, fax (33) (1) 44 43 29 99; www.dfait-maeci.gc.ca/~paris

GABON (Gabonese Republic)

Area of jurisdiction includes Sao Tome and Principe, and Equatorial Guinea.

EMBASSY IN LIBREVILLE (small): Postal Address: P.O. Box 4037 Libreville, GABON; (241) 74 34 64, fax (241) 74 34 66

GAMBIA (Republic of the Gambia)

Contact the Canadian Embassy in Dakar, Sénégal.

GEORGIA (Republic of Georgia)

Contact the Canadian Embassy in Ankara, Turkey.

GERMANY (Federal Republic of Germany)

EMBASSY IN BONN (large): Friedrich-Wilhelm-Strasse 18, 53113 Bonn, GERMANY; (49) (228) 9680, fax (49) (228) 968-3904, www.dfait-maeci.gc.ca/~bonn

CONSULATE GENERAL IN BERLIN (small): Friedrichstrasse 95, 10117 Berlin, GERMANY; (49) (30) 261-1161, fax (49) (30) 262-9206

CONSULATE IN DÜSSELDORF (small): Prinz-Georg-Strasse 126, 40479 Düsseldorf, GERMANY; (49) (211) 17 21 70, fax (49) (211) 35 91 65

CONSULATE IN HAMBURG (small): ABC Strasse 45, 20534 Hamburg, GERMANY; (49) (40) 355-56290, fax (49) (40) 355-56294

CONSULATE GENERAL IN MUNICH (small): Tal 29, 80331 Munich, GERMANY; (49) (89) 219 9570, fax (49) (89) 219-95757

GHANA (Republic of Ghana)

Area of jurisdiction includes Liberia, Sierra Leone, and Togo.

HIGH COMMISSION IN ACCRA (mid-sized): 42 Independence Ave., Accra, GHANA. Postal Address: P.O. Box 1639, Accra, GHANA; (233) (21) 77 37 91, fax (233) (21) 77 37 92

GREECE (Hellenic Republic)

EMBASSY IN ATHENS (mid-sized): 4 I Gennadiou Street, Athens 115 21, ATHENS; (30) (1) 725-4011, fax (30) (1) 725-3629

GRENADA

Contact the Canadian High Commission in Bridgetown, Barbados.

GUATEMALA (Republic of Guatemala)

EMBASSY IN GUATEMALA CITY (mid-sized): 13 calle 8-44, Zona 10, Guatemala City, GUATEMALA. Postal Address: P.O. Box 400, GUATEMALA, C.A.; (502) 333 6104 , fax (502) 333 6161

GUINEA (Republic of Guinea)

EMBASSY IN CONAKRY (small): Postal Address: P.O. Box 99 Conakry, GUINEA; (224) 41 23 95, fax (224) 41 42 36

GUINEA-BISSAU (Republic of Guinea-Bissau)

Contact the Canadian Embassy in Dakar, Sénégal.

GUYANA (Co-operative Republic of Guyana)

Area of jurisdiction includes Suriname.

HIGH COMMISSION IN GEORGETOWN (small): High and Young Streets, Georgetown, GUYANA. Postal Address: P.O. Box 10880, Georgetown, GUYANA; (592) (2) 72081, fax (592) (2) 58380

HAITI (Republic of Haiti)

Area of jurisdiction includes Martinique, Guadeloupe, French Guyana, Saba, St. Eustatius, St. Martin, and the Dominican Republic.

EMBASSY IN PORT-AU-PRINCE (mid-sized): edifice Banque Nova Scotia, route de Delmas, Port-au-Prince, HAITI. Postal Address: C.P. 826 Port-au-Prince, HAITI; (509) 23-2358, fax (509) 23-8720

HOLY SEE (VATICAN)

EMBASSY IN ROME (small): Via della Conciliazione 4/D, 00193 Rome, ITALY; (39) (6) 6830-7316, fax (39) (6) 6880-6283

HONDURAS (Republic of Honduras)

The Office of the Canadian Embassy in Tegucigalpa can perform basic consular functions. For further assistance contact the Canadian Embassy in San Jose, Costa Rica.

OFFICE OF THE CANADIAN EMBASSY IN TEGUCIGALPA (small): Edificio Comercial Los Castanos, 60 Piso, Boulevard Morazan, Tegucigalpa, HONDURAS. Postal Address: Apartado Postal 351-1007 Centro Colon, San José, COSTA RICA; (504) 31-4551, fax (504) 31-5793

HUNGARY (Republic of Hungary)

Area of jurisdiction includes Albania.

EMBASSY IN BUDAPEST (mid-sized): Budakeszi ut.32, 1121 Budapest, HUNGARY; (36) (1) 275-1200, fax (36) (1) 275-1210

ICELAND (Republic of Iceland)

Contact the Canadian Embassy in Oslo, Norway.

INDIA (Republic of India)

Area of jurisdiction includes Bhutan and Nepal.

HIGH COMMISSION IN NEW DELHI (large): 7/8 Shantipath, Chanakyapuri, New Delhi, 110021, INDIA. Postal Address: P.O. Box 5207, Chanakyapuri, New Delhi, 110021, INDIA; (91) (11) 687-6500, fax (91) (11) 687-6579

CONSULATE IN MUMBAI (small): 41/42 Maker Chamber VI, Jamnalal Bajaj Marg, Nariman Point, Bombay 400021, INDIA; (91) (22) 287-6027, fax (91) (22) 287-5514

TRADE OFFICE IN BANGALORE (small): 103 Prestige Meridien 1, 29 M.G. Road, Bangalore, Karnataka 560001, INDIA; (91) (80) 559-9418, fax (91) (80) 559-9424

INDONESIA (Republic of Indonesia)

EMBASSY IN JAKARTA (mid-sized): 5th Floor, WISMA Metropolitan, Jalan Jendral Sudirman, Jakarta, 12920, INDONESIA. Postal Address: P.O. Box 8324, JKS.MP, Jakarta 12084, INDONESIA; (62) (21) 525-0709, fax (62) (21) 571-2251

IRAN (Islamic Republic of Iran)

EMBASSY IN TEHRAN (mid-sized): 57 Shahid Sarfaraz , Ostad Motahari Ave.,15868, Tehran, IRAN. Postal Address: P.O. Box 11365-4647, Tehran, IRAN; (98) (21) 873-2623, fax (98) (21) 873-3202

IRAQ (Republic of Iraq)

There are no permanent representatives in Iraq. Assistance should be sought at the Canadian Embassy in Amman, Jordan.

IRELAND

EMBASSY IN DUBLIN (small): 65 St. Stephen's Green, Dublin 2, IRELAND; (353) (1) 478-1988, fax (353) (1) 478-1285

ISRAEL (State of Israel)

Area of jurisdiction includes Cyprus.

EMBASSY IN TEL AVIV (mid-sized): 3 Nirim, Tel Aviv 67060, ISRAEL. Postal Address: P.O. Box 6410, Tel Aviv 63405 ISRAEL; (972) (03) 636-3300, fax (972) (03) 636-3380

ITALY (Italian Republic)

Area of jurisdiction includes Malta and San Marino.

EMBASSY IN ROME (large): Via G.B. de Rossi 27, 00161 Rome, ITALY; (39) (6) 445981, fax (39) (6) 4459 8750, www.canada.it

CONSULATE GENERAL IN MILAN (small): Via Vittor Pisani 19, 20124 Milan, ITALY; (39) (2) 67581, fax (39) (2) 6758-3900

IVORY COAST

See CÔTE D'IVOIRE

JAMAICA

Area of jurisdiction includes the Bahamas and Belize.

HIGH COMMISSION IN KINGSTON (mid-sized): Mutual Security Bank Bldg., 30-36 Knutsford Blvd., Kingston 5, JAMAICA. Postal Address: P.O. Box 1500, Kingston 10, JAMAICA; (809) 926-1500, fax (809) 926-1702

JAPAN

EMBASSY IN TOKYO (large): 3-38 Akasaka 7-chome, Minato-ku, Tokyo 107, JAPAN; (81) (3) 3408-2101, fax (81) (3) 5412-6303,
www.dfait-maeci.gc.ca/ni-ka/menu-e.asp

CONSULATE GENERAL IN OSAKA (small): Daisan Shoho Bldg., 12th Floor, 2-2-3 Nishi-Shinsaibashi, Chuo-Ku, Osaka 542, JAPAN. Postal Address: P.O. Box 150, Osaka, Minami 542-91, JAPAN; (81) (6) 212-4910, fax (81) (6) 212-4914

CONSULATE IN FUKUOKA (small): FT Building, 9F, 4-8-28 Watanabe-Dori, Chuo-Ku, Fukuoka-Shi, Fukuoka Pref. 810, JAPAN ; (81) (92) 752-6055, fax (81) (92) 752-6077

CONSULATE IN NAGOYA (small): Nakato Marunouchi Bldg. 6F, 3-17-6 Marunouchi, Naka-Ku, Nagoya-Shi, Aichi Pref., JAPAN; (81) (52) 972-0450, fax (81) (52) 972-0453

JORDAN (Hashemite Kingdom of Jordan)

EMBASSY IN AMMAN (mid-sized): Pearl of Shmeisani Bldg., Shmeisani, Amman, JORDAN. Postal Address: P.O. Box 815403, Amman, 11180, JORDAN; (962) (6) 66 61 24, fax (962) (6) 68 92 27

KAZAKHSTAN (Republic of Kazakhstan)

Area of jurisdiction includes Kyrgyzstan.

EMBASSY IN ALMATY (mid sized): 34 Vinagradova Street, Almaty, Kazakhstan, (7) (327) 250 11 51, fax (7) (327) 581 14 93

KENYA (Republic of Kenya)

Area of jurisdiction includes Burundi.

HIGH COMMISSION IN NAIROBI (mid-sized): Comcraft House, Hailé Sélassie Ave., Nairobi, KENYA. Postal Address: P.O. Box 30481, Nairobi, KENYA; (254) (2) 21 48 04, fax (254) (2) 22 69 87

KIRIBATI (Republic of Kiribati)

Contact the Canadian High Commission in Wellington, New Zealand.

KOREA (Republic of Korea)

EMBASSY IN SEOUL (mid-sized): Kolon Building, 10th and 11th Floors, 45 Mugyo-Dong, Chung-Ku, Seoul 100-170, KOREA. Postal Address: P.O. Box 6299, Seoul 100-662, KOREA; (82) (2) 753-2605, fax (82) (2) 755-0686

KUWAIT (State of Kuwait)

EMBASSY IN KUWAIT CITY (mid sized): Area 4, Villa 24, Plot 121, Al-Mutawakel, Da' aiyah, Kuwait City, KUWAIT. Postal Address: P.O. Box 25281, Safat 13113, Kuwait City, KUWAIT; (965) 256-3025, fax (965) 256-4167

KYRGYZSTAN (Republic of Kyrgyzstan)

Contact the Canadian Embassy in Almaty, Kazakhstan.

LAOS (Lao People's Democratic Republic)

Contact the Canadian Embassy in Bangkok, Thailand.

LATVIA (Republic of Latvia)

EMBASSY IN RIGA (mid sized): Doma laukums 4, 4th floor, Riga, LATVIA-1977; (371) 783-0141, fax (371) 783-0140

LEBANON (Lebanese Republic)

EMBASSY IN BEIRUT (mid sized): Coolrite Building (seaside), 434 Autostrade, Jal-el-Dib, LEBANON. Postal address: P.O. Box 60163, Jal-el- Dib, LEBANON; (961) (1) 521-163, fax (961) (1) 521-167

LESOTHO (Kingdom of Lesotho)

Contact the Canadian High Commission in Pretoria, South Africa.

LIBERIA (Republic of Liberia)

Contact the Canadian High Commission in Accra, Ghana.

LIBYA (Socialist People's Libyan Arab Jamahiriya)

Contact the Canadian Embassy in Tunis, Tunisia.

LIECHTENSTEIN (Principality of Liechtenstein)

Contact the Canadian Embassy in Berne, Switzerland.

LITHUANIA (Republic of Lithuania)

The Office of the Canadian Embassy in Vilnius can perform basic consular functions. If further assistance is required contact the Canadian Embassy in Riga, Latvia.

OFFICE OF THE CANADIAN EMBASSY IN VILNIUS (small): Gedimino pr. 64, 2001 Vilnius, LITHUANIA; (370) (2) 220 898, fax (370) (2) 220-884

LUXEMBOURG (Grand Duchy of Luxembourg)

Contact the Canadian Embassy in Brussels, Belgium.

MACAO

Contact the Canadian Consulate General in the Hong Kong Special Administrative Region, People's Republic of China.

MACEDONIA (Republic of Macedonia, Former Yugoslav)

EMBASSY IN BELGRADE (small): Kneza Milosa 75, 11000, Belgrade, YUGOSLAVIA; (381) (11) 64 46 66, fax (381) (11) 64 14 80

MADAGASCAR (Democratic Republic of Madagascar)

Contact the Canadian High Commission in Dar-es-Salaam, Tanzania.

MALAWI (Republic of Malawi)

Contact the Canadian High Commission in Lusaka, Zambia.

MALAYSIA

HIGH COMMISSION IN KUALA LUMPUR (mid-sized): Plaza MBF, 7th Floor, 172 Jalan Ampang, 50450 Kuala Lumpur, MALAYSIA. Postal Address: P.O. Box 10990, 50732 Kuala Lumpur, MALAYSIA; (60) (3) 261-2000, fax (60) (3) 261-3428

MALDIVES (Republic of Maldives)

Contact the Canadian High Commission in Colombo, Sri Lanka.

MALI (Republic of Mali)

The Office of the Canadian Embassy in Bamako can perform basic consular functions. If further assistance is required contact the Canadian Embassy in Abidjan, Côte D'Ivoire.

OFFICE OF THE CANADIAN EMBASSY IN BAMAKO (small): Postal Address: P.O. Box 198 Bamako, MALI; (223) 22 22 36, fax (223) 22 42 62

MALTA (Republic of Malta)

Contact the Canadian Embassy in Rome, Italy.

MAURITANIA (Islamic Republic of Mauritania)

Contact the Canadian Embassy in Dakar, Sénégal.

MAURITIUS (Republic of Mauritius)

Contact the Canadian High Commission in Pretoria, South Africa.

MEXICO (United Mexican States)

EMBASSY IN MEXICO CITY (large): Calle Schiller no. 529 (Rincon del Bosque), Colonia Polanco, 11560 Mexico, D.F., MEXICO. Postal Address: Apartado Postal 105-05, 11580 Mexico, D.F., MEXICO; (525) 724 7900, fax (525) 724-7980

CONSULATE IN MONTERREY (small): Edificio Kalos, Piso C-1, Local 108-A, Zaragoza 1300 Sur y Constitucion, 6400 Monterrey, Nuevo Leon, MEXICO; (52) (8) 344-27-53, fax (52) (8) 344-30-48

CONSULATE IN GUADALAJARA (small): Hotel Fiesta Americana, Local 31, Aurelio Aceves 225, Col. Vallarta Poiente, 44100, Guadalajara, Jalisco, MEXICO; (52) (3) 616 56 42, fax (52) (3) 615 86 65

MOLDOVA (Republic of Moldova)

Contact the Canadian Embassy in Bucharest, Romania.

MONACO (Principality of Monaco)

Contact the Canadian Embassy in Paris, France.

MONGOLIA
(Mongolian People's Republic)

Contact the Canadian Embassy in Beijing, China.

MOROCCO (Kingdom of Morocco)

EMBASSY IN RABAT (small): 13 bis, rue Jaafar As-Sadik, Rabat-Agdal, MOROCCO. Postal Address: C.P. 709, Rabat-Agdal, MOROCCO; (212) (7) 67 28 80, fax (212) (7) 67 21 87

MOZAMBIQUE
(Republic of Mozambique)

EMBASSY IN MAPUTO (small): rue Tomas Nduda, 1345 Maputo, MOZAMBIQUE. Postal Address: P.O. Box 1578, Maputo, MOZAMBIQUE; (258) (1) 492-623, fax (258) (1) 492-667

MYANMAR

See BURMA

NAMIBIA (Republic of Namibia)

Contact the Canadian High Commission in Pretoria, South Africa.

NEPAL (Kingdom of Nepal)

The affairs of the Canadian Embassy in Nepal are managed by the Canadian High Commission in New Delhi, India. There is one development officer in Kathmandu, Nepal.

NETHERLANDS
(Kingdom of the Netherlands)

EMBASSY IN THE HAGUE (mid-sized): Sophialaan 7 2514 JP, The Hague, NETHERLANDS; (31) (70) 311-1600, fax (31) (70) 442-3220, www.dfait-maeci.gc.ca/~thehague

NEW ZEALAND

Area of jurisdiction includes Fiji, Kiribati, Tonga and Tuvalu.

HIGH COMMISSION IN WELLINGTON (small): 61 Molesworth St., 3rd Floor, Thorndon, Wellington, NEW ZEALAND. Postal Address: P.O. Box 12-049, Thorndon, Wellington, NEW ZEALAND; (64) (4) 473 9577, fax (64) (4) 471-2082

CONSULATE IN AUCKLAND (small): Level 9, Jetset Centre, 44-48 Emily Place, Auckland, NEW ZEA-LAND. Postal Address: P.O. Box 6186, Wellesley Street, Auckland, NEW ZEALAND; (64) (9) 309-3690, fax (64) (9) 307-3111

NICARAGUA (Republic of Nicaragua)

Contact the Canadian Embassy in San José, Costa Rica.

NIGER (Republic of Niger)

The Office of the Canadian Embassy in Niamey can perform basic consular functions. If further assistance is required, contact the Canadian Embassy in Abidjan, Côte D'Ivoire.

OFFICE OF THE CANADIAN EMBASSY IN NIAMEY (small): Sonara ll Building, ave. du Premier Pont, Niamey, NIGER. Postal Address: P.O. Box 362 Niamey, NIGER; (227) 73 36 86, fax (227) 73 31 01

NIGERIA (Federal Republic of Nigeria)

Contact the Canadian High Commission in Accra, Ghana.

NORWAY (Kingdom of Norway)

EMBASSY IN OSLO (small): Wergelandsveien 7, N-0244, Oslo, NORWAY; (47) 22 99 53 00, fax (47) 22 99 53 01

OMAN (Sultanate of Oman)

Contact the Canadian Embassy in Saudi Arabia.

PAKISTAN (Islamic Republic of Pakistan)

HIGH COMMISSION IN ISLAMABAD (mid-sized): Diplomatic Enclave, Sector G-5, Islamabad, PAKIS-TAN. Postal Address: G.P.O. Box 1042, Islamabad, PAKISTAN; (92) (51) 279100, fax (92) (51) 279110

PANAMA (Republic of Panama)

EMBASSY IN PANAMA CITY (mid sized): Avenida Samuel Lewis, Edificio Banco Central Hispano, 4th floor, Panama City, PANAMA. Postal Address: Apartado 3658, Balboa Ancon, Panama City, PANAMA; (507) 264 9731, fax (507) 263-8083

PAPUA NEW GUINEA
(Independent State of Papua New Guinea)

Contact the Canadian High Commission in Canberra, Australia.

PARAGUAY (Republic of Paraguay)

Contact the Canadian Embassy in Santiago, Chile.

PERU (Republic of Peru)

Area of jurisdiction includes Bolivia.

EMBASSY IN LIMA (mid-sized): Calle Federico Gerdes 130 (antes Libertad), Miraflores, Lima, PERU. Postal Address: Casilla 18-1126, Correo Miraflores, Lima, PERU; (51) (1) 444 4015, fax (51) (1) 242 4050

PHILIPPINES
(Republic of the Philippines)

EMBASSY IN MANILA (mid-sized): Allied Bank Centre, 9th and 11th Floors, 6754 Ayala Ave., Makati, Manila, PHILIPPINES. Postal Address: P.O. Box 2168, Makati Central Post Office, 1261 Makati, Manila, PHILIPPINES; (63) (2) 867-0001, fax (63) (2) 810-8839

POLAND (Republic of Poland)

EMBASSY IN WARSAW (mid-sized): Ulica Matejki 1/5, Warsaw 00-481, POLAND; (48) (22) 629 80 51, fax (48) (22) 629 64 57

PORTUGAL (Portuguese Republic)

EMBASSY IN LISBON (mid-sized): Avenida da Liberdade 144/56, 4th Floor, 1250 Lisbon, PORTUGAL; (351) (1) 347-4892, fax (351) (1) 347-6466

QATAR (State of Qatar)

Contact the Canadian Embassy in Kuwait.

ROMANIA (Republic of Romania)

Area of jurisdiction includes Moldova.

EMBASSY IN BUCHAREST (mid-sized): 36 Nicolae Iorga, 71118, Bucharest, ROMANIA. Postal Address: P.O. Box 117, Post Office No.22, Bucharest, ROMANIA; (40) (1) 222 9845, fax (40) (1) 312 9680.

RUSSIA (Russian Federation)

Area of jurisdiction includes Armenia and Belarus.

EMBASSY IN MOSCOW (large): 23 Starokonyushenny Pereulok, Moscow, 121002, RUSSIA; (7) (095) 956-6666, fax (7) (095) 232-9948

CONSULATE GENERAL IN ST. PETERSBURG (small): 32 Malodetskoselsky Pkt., St. Petersburg, 198013, RUSSIA; (7) (812) 325 84 48, fax (7) (812) 325-83 93

RWANDA (Rwandese Republic)

The Office of the Canadian Embassy in Kigali can perform basic consular functions. If further assistance is required, contact the Canadian High Commission in Nairobi, Kenya.

OFFICE OF THE CANADIAN EMBASSY IN KIGALI (small): Postal Address: rue Akagera, P.O. Box 1177 Kigali, RWANDA; (250) 73210, fax (250) 72719

SAINT KITTS AND NEVIS
(Federation of Saint Kitts and Nevis)

Contact the Canadian High Commission in Barbados.

SAINT LUCIA

Contact the Canadian High Commission in Barbados.

SAINT VINCENT
AND THE GRENADINES

Contact the Canadian High Commission in Barbados.

SAN MARINO (Republic of San Marino)

Contact the Canadian Embassy in Rome, Italy.

SAO TOME AND PRINCIPE (Democratic Republic of Sao Tome and Principe)

Contact the Canadian Embassy in Libreville, Gabon.

SAUDI ARABIA
(Kingdom of Saudi Arabia)

EMBASSY IN RIYADH (mid-sized): Diplomatic Quarter, Riyadh, SAUDI ARABIA. Postal Address: P.O. Box 94321, Riyadh 11693, SAUDI ARABIA; (966) (1) 488-2288, fax (966) (1) 488-1997

SÉNÉGAL (Republic of Sénégal)

Area of jurisdiction includes Cape Verde, Gambia, Guinea Bissau, and Mauritania.

EMBASSY IN DAKAR (mid-sized): 45 ave. de la République, Dakar, SÉNÉGAL. Postal Address: P.O. Box 3373 Dakar, SÉNÉGAL; (221) 23 92 90, fax (221) 23 87 49

SEYCHELLES (Republic of Seychelles)

Contact the Canadian High Commission in Tanzania.

SIERRA LEONE
(Republic of Sierra Leone)

Contact the Canadian High Commission in Accra, Ghana.

SINGAPORE (Republic of Singapore)

HIGH COMMISSION IN SINGAPORE (mid-sized): 80 Anson Road, 14th and 15th Floors, IBM Towers, 079907, SINGAPORE. Postal Address: Robinson Road, P.O. Box 845, 901645, SINGAPORE; (65) 325-3200, fax (65) 325-3297

SLOVAKIA (Slovak Republic)

Contact the Canadian Embassy in Prague, Czech Republic.

SLOVENIA (Republic of Slovenia)

Contact the Canadian Embassy in Budapest, Hungary.

SOLOMON ISLANDS

Contact the Canadian High Commission in Canberra, Australia.

SOMALIA (Somali Democratic Republic)

Contact the Canadian High Commission in Nairobi, Kenya.

SOUTH AFRICA
(Republic of South Africa)

Area of jurisdiction includes Lesotho, Swaziland and Mauritius.

HIGH COMMISSION IN PRETORIA (mid-sized): 1103 Arcadia Street, Hatfield 0083, Pretoria, SOUTH AFRICA. Postal Address: Private Bag X13, Hatfield 0028, Pretoria, SOUTH AFRICA; (27) (12) 422-3000, fax (27) (12) 422-3052, www.canada.co.za

OFFICE OF CANADIAN HIGH COMMISSION IN CAPETOWN (mid-sized): 19th Floor, Reserve Bank Building, 360 St. George's Mall Street, Capetown 8001, SOUTH AFRICA. Postal Address: P.O. Box 683, Capetown 8000, SOUTH AFRICA; (27) (21) 23-5240, fax (27) (21) 23-4893

TRADE SECTION OF THE CANADIAN HIGH COMMISSION IN JOHANNESBURG (small): Cradock Place, 1st Floor, 10 Arnold Street, Rosebank, Johannesburg, SOUTH AFRICA. Postal Address: P.O. Box 1394, Parklands 2121, Johannesburg, SOUTH AFRICA; (27) (11) 442-3130, fax (27) (11) 442-3325

SPAIN (Kingdom of Spain)

EMBASSY IN MADRID (mid-sized): Calle Nunez de Balboa 35-28001, Madrid, SPAIN. Postal Address: Apartado 587, 28080 Madrid, SPAIN; (34) (1) 431-4300, fax (34) (1) 435-7488, www.jrnet.com/canada

SRI LANKA (Democratic Socialist Republic of Sri Lanka)

Area of jurisdiction includes the Maldives.

HIGH COMMISSION IN COLOMBO (small): 6 Gregory's Road, Cinnamon Gardens, Colombo 7, SRI LANKA. Postal Address: P.O. Box 1006, Colombo 7, SRI LANKA; (94) (1) 69 58 41, fax (94) (1) 68 70 49

SUDAN (Republic of The Sudan)

Contact the Canadian Embassy in Addis Ababa, Ethiopia.

SURINAME (Republic of Suriname)

Contact the Canadian High Commission in Georgetown, Guyana.

SWAZILAND (Kingdom of Swaziland)

Contact the Canadian High Commission in Pretoria, South Africa.

SWEDEN (Kingdom of Sweden)

EMBASSY IN STOCKHOLM (small): Tegelbacken 4, Seventh Floor, Stockholm, SWEDEN. Postal Address: P.O. Box 16129, 10323 Stockholm, SWEDEN; (46) (8) 453-3000, fax (46) (8) 24 24 91

SWITZERLAND (Swiss Confederation)

EMBASSY IN BERNE (small): Kirchenfeldstrasse 88, 3005 Berne, SWITZERLAND. Postal Address: P.O. Box 3000, Berne 6, SWITZERLAND; (41) (31) 357 32 00, fax (41) (31) 357 3210

SYRIA (Syrian Arab Republic)

Area of jurisdiction includes Lebanon.

EMBASSY IN DAMASCUS (mid-sized): Lot 12, Mezzeh Autostrade, Damascus, SYRIA. Postal Address: P.O. Box 3394, Damascus, SYRIA; (963) (11) 611 6692, fax (963) (11) 611-4000

TAJIKISTAN (Republic of Tajikistan)

Contact the Canadian Embassy in Almaty, Kazakhstan.

TANZANIA (United Republic of Tanzania)

Area of jurisdiction includes Madagascar, Mauritius, Seychelles, and Comoros.

HIGH COMMISSION IN DAR-ES-SALAAM (small): 38 Mirambo Street/Garden Avenue, Dar-es-Salaam, TANZANIA. Postal Address: P.O. Box 1022, Dar-es-Salaam, TANZANIA; (255) (51) 112-832, fax (255) (51) 112-897

THAILAND (Kingdom of Thailand)

Area of jurisdiction includes Laos and Burma (Myanmar).

EMBASSY IN BANGKOK (mid-sized): Boonmitr Bldg, 11th Floor, 138 Silom Road, Bangkok 10500, THAILAND. Postal Address: P.O. Box 2090, Bangkok 10500, THAILAND; (66) (2) 237-4125, fax (66) (2) 236-6463

TOGO (Togolese Republic)

Contact the Canadian High Commission in Accra, Ghana.

TONGA (Kingdom of Tonga)

Contact the Canadian High Commission in Wellington, New Zealand.

TRINIDAD AND TOBAGO (Republic of Trinidad and Tobago)

HIGH COMMISSION IN PORT OF SPAIN (mid-sized): Huggins Building, 72 South Quay, Port of Spain, TRINIDAD AND TOBAGO. Postal Address: P.O. Box 1246, Port of Spain, TRINIDAD AND TOBAGO; (868) 622 6232, fax (809) 628-2581

TUNISIA (Republic of Tunisia)

Area of jurisdiction includes Libya.

EMBASSY IN TUNIS (small): 3 du Sénégal Street, Place d'Afrique, Tunis, TUNISIA. Postal Address: P.O. Box 31, Belvédère, 1002 Tunis, TUNISIA; (216) (1) 796-577, fax (216) (1) 792-371

TURKEY (Republic of Turkey)

Area of jurisdiction includes Azerbaijan, Georgia and Turkmenistan.

EMBASSY IN ANKARA (mid-sized): Nenehatun Caddesi 75, Gaziosmanpasa 06700, Ankara, TURKEY; (90) (312) 436-1275, fax (90) (312) 446-4437

TURKMENISTAN

Contact the Canadian Embassy in Ankara, Turkey

TUVALU

Contact the Canadian High Commission in Wellington, New Zealand.

UGANDA (Republic of Uganda)

Contact the Canadian High Commission in Nairobi, Kenya.

UKRAINE

EMBASSY IN KIEV (mid-sized): 31 Yaroslaviv Val Street, Kiev, 252034, UKRAINE; (380) (44) 212-2112, fax (380) (44) 212-2339

UNITED ARAB EMIRATES

EMBASSY IN ABU DHABAI (small): Tawan Tower 1, 1ˢᵗ Floor, Suite 00-1 (between Khalifa Street and The Corniche), Abu Dhabi UNITED ARAB EMIRATES. Postal Address: P.O. Box 6970, Abu Dhabi, UNITED ARAB EMIRATES; (971) (2) 263-655, fax (971) (2) 263-424

CONSULATE IN BUR DUBAI (small): Juma Al Majid Building, Suite 708, Khalid Ibn Al Waleed Street, Bur Dubai, UNITED ARAB EMIRATES. Postal Address: P.O. Box 52472, Dubai, UNITED ARAB EMIRATES; (971) (4) 52 17 17, fax (971) (4) 51 77 22

UNITED STATES OF AMERICA

Area of jurisdiction of the Consulate General in New York includes Bermuda.

EMBASSY IN WASHINGTON, DC (large): 501 Pennsylvania Ave. N.W., Washington, DC 20001, USA; (202) 682-1740, fax (202) 682-7726, www.cdembwashdc.org

CONSULATE GENERAL IN ATLANTA (mid-sized): 1175 Peachtree Street N.E., 100 Colony Square, Suite 1700, Atlanta, GA 30361-6205 USA; (404) 532-2000, fax (404) 532-2050

CONSULATE GENERAL IN BOSTON (mid-sized): 3 Copley Place, Suite 400, Boston, MA 02116, USA; (617) 262-3760, fax (617) 262-3415, www.dfait-maeci.gc.ca/~boston

CONSULATE GENERAL IN BUFFALO (mid-sized): 1 Marine Midland Centre, Suite 3000, Buffalo, NY 14203-2884, USA; (716) 858-9500, fax (716) 852-4340, www.canadianconsulatebuf.org

CONSULATE GENERAL IN CHICAGO (small): Two Prudential Plaza, 180 North Stetson Ave., Suite 2400, Chicago, IL 60601, USA; (312) 616-1860, fax (312) 616-1877, www.canadaonlinechicago.net

CONSULATE GENERAL IN DALLAS (small): St. Paul Place, 750 North St. Paul Place Street, Suite 1700, Dallas, TX 75201, USA; (214) 922-9806, fax (214) 992-9815, www.canada-dallas.org

CONSULATE GENERAL IN DETROIT (mid-sized): 600 Renaissance Center Suite 1100, Detroit, MI 48243-1798, USA; (313) 567-2340, fax (313) 567-2164, www.dfait-maeci.gc.ca/~detroit

CONSULATE GENERAL IN LOS ANGELES (mid-sized): 300 South Grand Ave., 10th Floor, Los Angeles, CA 90071, USA; (213) 687-7432, fax (213) 620-8827

CONSULATE GENERAL IN MIAMI (small): 200 South Biscayne Blvd., Suite 1600, Miami, FL 33131, USA; (305) 579-1600, fax (305) 374-6774

CONSULATE GENERAL IN MINNEAPOLIS (small): 701-4th Ave. South, Minneapolis, MN 55415, USA; (612) 332-7486, fax (612) 332-4061

CONSULATE GENERAL IN NEW YORK (large): 1251 Avenue of the Americas, 16th Floor, New York, NY 10020-1175, USA; (212) 596-1600, fax (212) 596-1790, www.canada-ny.org

CONSULATE GENERAL IN SEATTLE (mid-sized): 412 Plaza 600, Sixth and Stewart, Seattle, WA 98101-1286, USA; (206) 443-1777, fax (206) 443-9662, www.canadian.consulate-seattle.org

URUGUAY (Eastern Republic of Uruguay)

EMBASSY IN MONTEVIDEO (small): Edifio Torre Libertad, Plaza Cagangha 1335, off. 1105, 11100 Montevideo URUGUAY; (598) (2) 92 20 30, fax (598) (2) 92 20 29

UZBEKISTAN (Republic of Uzbekistan)

Contact the Canadian Embassy in Moscow, Russia.

VANUATU (Republic of Vanuatu)

Contact the Canadian High Commission in Canberra, Australia.

VENEZUELA (Republic of Venezuela)

EMBASSY IN CARACAS (mid-sized): Edificio Torre Europa, 7th Floor, Avenida Francisco de Miranda, Campo Alegre, Caracas, VENEZUELA. Postal Address: Apartado 62302, Caracas 1060A, VENEZUELA; (58) (2) 951 6166, fax (58) (2) 951 4950

VIETNAM (Socialist Republic of Vietnam)

EMBASSY IN HANOI (small): 31 Hung Vuong Street, Hanoi, VIETNAM; (84) (4) 823-5500, fax (84) (4) 823-5351

CONSULATE IN HO CHI MINH CITY (small): 203 Dong Khoi St., District 1, Suite 102, Ho Chi Minh City, VIETNAM; (84) (8) 824-2000, fax (84) (8) 829-4528

WESTERN SAMOA (Independent State of Western Samoa)

Contact the Canadian High Commission in Wellington, New Zealand.

YEMEN (Republic of Yemen)

Contact the Canadian Embassy in Riyadh, Saudi Arabia.

YUGOSLAVIA (Federal Republic of Yugoslavia)

EMBASSY IN BELGRADE (mid-sized): Kneza Milosa 75, 11000 Belgrade, YUGOSLAVIA; (381) (11) 64 46 66, fax (381) (11) 64 14 80

ZAMBIA (Republic of Zambia)

Area of jurisdiction includes Malawi.

HIGH COMMISSION IN LUSAKA (small): 5199 United Nations Ave., Lusaka, ZAMBIA. Postal Address: P.O. Box 31313, Lusaka, ZAMBIA; (260) (1) 25 08 33, fax (260) (1) 25 41 76

ZIMBABWE (Republic of Zimbabwe)

Area of jurisdiction includes Angola and Botswana.

HIGH COMMISSION IN HARARE [mid-sized]: 45 Baines Avenue, Harare, ZIMBABWE. Postal Address: P.O. Box 1430, Harare, ZIMBABWE; (263) (4) 733 881, fax (263) (4) 732 917

CANADIAN REPRESENTATION IN INTERNATIONAL ORGANIZATIONS

EUROPEAN COMMUNITIES

PERMANENT MISSION IN BRUSSELS (mid-sized): 2 avenue de Tervuren, 1040 Brussels, BELGIUM; (32) (2) 735-9125, fax (32) (2) 735-3383, www.dfait-maeci.gc.ca/eu-mission

NORTH ATLANTIC COUNCIL

PERMANENT MISSION IN BRUSSELS (large): Lèopold III Blvd., 1110 Brussels, BELGIUM; (32) (2) 707-7100, fax (32) (2) 707-7150

ORGANIZATION FOR ECONOMIC CO-OPERATION AND DEVELOPMENT

PERMANENT MISSION IN PARIS (mid sized):15 bis, rue de Franqueville, 75116 Paris, FRANCE; (33) (1) 44 43 20 99, fax (33) (1) 44 43 20 99

ORGANIZATION FOR SECURITY AND CO-OPERATION IN EUROPE

PERMANENT MISSION IN VIENNA (small): Laurenzerberg 2, A-1010 Vienna, AUSTRIA; (43) (1) 531 38 3002, fax (43) (1) 531 38 3903

ORGANIZATION OF AMERICAN STATES

PERMANENT MISSION IN WASHINGTON (small): 501 Pennsylvania Avenue N.W., Washington, DC 20001, USA; (202) 682-1768, fax (202) 682-7624

UNITED NATIONS

PERMANENT MISSION IN NEW YORK (large): One Dag Hammarskjold Plaza, 885 Second Avenue, 14th Floor, New York, NY 10017, USA; (212) 751-5600, fax (212) 486-1295

CONFERENCE ON DISARMAMENT AND THE WORLD TRADE ORGANIZATION

PERMANENT MISSION IN GENEVA (large): 1, rue du Pré-de-la-Bichette, 1202 Geneva, SWITZERLAND; (41) (22) 919-9200, fax (41) (22) 919-9233

INTERNATIONAL CIVIL AVIATION ORGANIZATION

PERMANENT MISSION IN MONTRÉAL (small): 999 University Street, Suite 1535, Montréal, Québec, H3C 5J9, CANADA; (514) 954-5800, fax (514) 954-5809

UNITED NATIONS CENTRE FOR HUMAN SETTLEMENTS (HABITAT)

PERMANENT MISSION IN NAIROBI (small): Comcraft House, Hailé Sélassie Avenue, Nairobi, KENYA. Postal Address: P.O. Box 30481, Nairobi, KENYA; (254) (2) 214-804, fax (254) (2) 216-485

UNITED NATIONS ENVIRONMENT PROGRAM (UNEP)

PERMANENT MISSION IN NAIROBI (small): Comcraft House, Hailé Sélassie Avenue, Nairobi, KENYA. Postal Address: P.O. Box 30481, Nairobi, KENYA; (254) (2) 214-804, fax (254) (2) 216-485

UNITED NATIONS EDUCATIONAL, SCIENTIFIC, AND CULTURAL ORGANIZATION (UNESCO)

PERMANENT MISSION IN PARIS (small): 1 rue Miollis, 75015 Paris, FRANCE; (33) (1) 45 68 35 17, fax (33) (1) 43 06 87 27

THE FOOD AND AGRICULTURAL ORGANIZATION (FAO)

PERMANENT MISSION IN ROME (small): Via Zara 30, 00198 Rome, ITALY; (39) (6) 44598 551, fax (39) (6) 44598 930

INTERNATIONAL ORGANIZATIONS IN VIENNA

PERMANENT MISSION IN VIENNA (small): Laurenzberg 2, A-1010 Vienna, AUSTRIA; (43) (1) 531 38 3001, fax (43) (1) 531 38 3903

Chapter 40

Foreign Diplomats in Canada

This chapter provides a comprehensive listing of foreign missions to Canada. These missions are of several types: Embassies, High Commissions, Consulates, and Commercial or Trade Offices.

For smaller nations, the Canadian mission is often handled through the embassy in Washington or the Permanent Mission to the United Nations in New York. All forms of diplomatic representation are listed, with the exception of honourary positions which are usually voluntary.

As the political, economic, social, and cultural arms of their countries, diplomatic representatives have extensive international responsibilities. These missions offer a number of services to Canadians interested in living, working, or travelling overseas. They provide you with information on the current political and economic climate in their countries, trade and commercial transactions, and also issue visas and work permits.

A WORD ON TERMINOLOGY

Mission is the generic term used to describe foreign offices in Canada. They range in size from having dozens of foreign nationals and local staff to one-person satellite offices.

A foreign mission in Ottawa is called an *Embassy*, unless the country is a member of the Commonwealth. In such instances it is called a *High Commission*. One exception is the European Union where representation is designated a *Commission*.

Where a country has an office in a Canadian city other than Ottawa (for example, Montréal, Toronto, or Vancouver) it is called a *Consulate*.

A *commercial or trade office* is usually a satellite of a larger mission and is responsible for the promotion of international transactions.

HOW MISSIONS ARE CLASSIFIED

Embassies and High Commissions are classified by size according to the number of foreign representatives stationed in each. A SMALL classification is used where there are fewer than 10 employees; MID-SIZED where there are 11 to 24; and LARGE where there are 25 or more.

For Consulates and Commercial or Trade Offices, SMALL connotes fewer than five personnel; MID-SIZED is between five and nine; and LARGE is more than 10.

RESOURCES

For related references consult the Resources in the section on Foreign Affairs in Chapter 34, Careers in Government and Chapter 39, Canadian Diplomats Abroad.

Diplomat & International Canada 📖
Bimonthly, *Bhupinder Liddar* ➤ Raddil Communications, P.O. Box 1173, Station B, Ottawa, Ontario K1P 5R2; (613) 789-6890, fax (613) 789-6889, diplomat@sympatico.ca ▪ A news journal for Canada's international community focusing on diplomatic news in Ottawa. [ID:1237]

Diplomatic, Consular, and Other Representatives in Canada 📖
Annual, Department of Foreign Affairs and International Trade (DFAIT), 151 pages ➤ Canada Government PublishingOttawa, Ontario K1A 0S9; $19.95; VISA, MC; (819) 956-4800, fax (819) 994-1498, publishing@ccg-gcc.ca ▪ A bilingual directory of diplomatic missions in Ottawa and consular and other missions throughout Canada, including names and titles of staff. Visit the publisher's web site at http://publications.pwgsc.gc.ca. [ID:1088]

Department of Foreign Affairs and International Trade (DFAIT) 💻
www.dfait-maeci.gc.ca/ ▪ This excellent homepage for DFAIT provides a vast amount of information on the international system, from travel advisories to international trade. It has links to DFAIT departments, services, country profiles, foreign embassies and missions in Canada, and Canadian government activities abroad. [ID:2565]

Foreign Diplomatic Missions in Canada

This chapter profiles 291 foreign missions: 115 Embassies, 118 Consulates, 36 High Commissions, 21 Commercial or Trade Offices, and one Commission. There are 251 missions in Canada, with the remainder managing their Canadian affairs from offices in New York or Washington, D.C.

Of the 158 countries which maintain offices in Canada (whether a single embassy, high commission, or a series of consulates), 47 are from Africa, 26 are from Asia-Pacific, 12 are from the Caribbean, 37 are from Europe, 20 are from Latin America, 15 are from the Middle East and one is from North America.

If you would like to further your research on a particular country, visit the embassy or consulate web sites listed. For more information and resources see

Chapter 21, The Internet Job Search, under the section Country Information on The Internet.

ALBANIA (Republic of Albania)

EMBASSY TO CANADA C/O THE EMBASSY IN WASHINGTON, DC (small): 1511 K Street, N.W., Suite 1000, Washington, DC 20005, USA; (202) 223-4942, fax (202) 628-7342

ALGERIA
(People's Democratic Republic of Algeria)

EMBASSY IN OTTAWA (small): 435 Daly Ave., Ottawa, Ontario K1N 6H3; (613) 789-8505,-0282, fax (613) 789-1406; ambalgatto@commercialsympatico.ca
CONSULATE IN MONTRÉAL (small): 450 Sherbrooke Street E., Suite 120, H2L 1J8; (514) 289-1710, fax (514) 289-1966

ANDORRA

EMBASSY TO CANADA C/O THE PERMANENT MISSION OF ANDORRA TO THE UNITED NATIONS (small): Two United Nations Plaza, 25th Floor, New York, NY 10017, USA; (212) 750-8064, fax (212) 750-6630

ANTIGUA AND BARBUDA

CONSULATE IN TORONTO (small): 60 St. Clair Ave. E., Suite 304, Toronto, Ontario M4T 1N5; (416) 961-3143, fax (416) 961-7218

ARGENTINA (Argentine Republic)

EMBASSY IN OTTAWA (small): 90 Sparks Street, Suite 910, Ottawa, Ontario K1P 5B4; (613) 236-2351, fax (613) 235-2659
CONSULATE IN MONTRÉAL (small): 2000 Peel Street, Suite 710, Montréal, Québec H3A 2W5; (514) 842-6582, fax (514) 842-5797; www.consargenmtl.com
CONSULATE IN TORONTO (small): One First Canadian Place, 58th Floor, Suite 5840, Toronto, Ontario M5X 1K2; (416) 955-9075, fax (416) 955-0868, consarg@inforamp.net, www.consargtoro.org

ARMENIA (Republic of Armenia)

EMBASSY IN OTTAWA (small): 130 Albert Street, Suite 1006, Ottawa, Ontario, K1P 6L2; (613) 234-3710, fax (613) 234-3444.

AUSTRALIA

HIGH COMMISSION IN OTTAWA (mid-sized): 50 O'Connor Street, Suite 710, Ottawa, Ontario K1P 6L2; (613) 236-0841, fax (613) 236-4376, ahcl.otwa@sympatico.ca, www.aust.emb.nw.dc.us
CONSULATE IN TORONTO (small): 175 Bloor Street E., Suite 314, 3rd Floor, Toronto, Ontario M4W 3R8; (416) 323-1155, fax (416) 323-3910
CONSULATE IN VANCOUVER (small): 999 Canada Place, Suite 602, Vancouver, B.C. V6C 3E1; (604) 684-1177, fax (604) 684-1856

AUSTRIA (Republic of Austria)

EMBASSY IN OTTAWA (small): 445 Wilbrod Street, Ottawa, Ontario K1N 6M7; (613) 789-1444, fax (613) 789-3431
COMMERCIAL OFFICE IN MONTRÉAL (small): 1010 Sherbrooke Street W., Suite 1410, Montréal, Québec H3A 2R7; (514) 849-3708, fax (514) 849-9577
COMMERCIAL OFFICE IN TORONTO (small): 2 Bloor Street E., Suite 3330, Toronto, Ontario M4W 1A8; (416) 967-3348, fax (416) 967-4101
COMMERCIAL OFFICE IN VANCOUVER (small): 200 Granville Street, Suite 1380, Vancouver, B.C. V6C 1S4; (604) 683-5808, fax (604) 662-8528

AZERBAIJAN (Republic of Azerbaijan)

EMBASSY TO CANADA C/O THE EMBASSY IN WASHINGTON, DC (small): 927 - 15th Street N.W., Suite 700, Washington, DC 20005, USA; (202) 842-0001, fax (202) 842-0004

BAHAMAS
(Commonwealth of the Bahamas)

HIGH COMMISSION IN OTTAWA (small): 360 Albert Street, Suite 1020, Ottawa, Ontario K1R 7X7; (613) 232-1724, fax (613) 232-0097

BAHRAIN (State of Bahrain)

EMBASSY TO CANADA C/O THE EMBASSY IN WASHINGTON, DC (small): 3502 International Dr. N.W., Washington, DC 20008, USA; (202) 342-0741, fax (202) 362-2192
CONSULATE IN MONTRÉAL (small): 1869 René Lévesque Blvd. W., Montréal, Québec H3H 1R4; (514) 931-7444, fax (514) 931-5988

BANGLADESH
(People's Republic of Bangladesh)

HIGH COMMISSION IN OTTAWA (small): 275 Bank Street, Suite 302, Ottawa, Ontario K2P 2L6; (613) 236-0138, fax (613) 567-3213

BARBADOS

HIGH COMMISSION IN OTTAWA (small): 130 Albert Street, Suite 600, Ottawa, Ontario K1P 5G4; (613) 236-9517, fax (613) 230-4362
CONSULATE IN NORTH YORK (mid-sized): 5160 Yonge Street, Suite 1800, North York, Ontario M2N 6L9; (416) 512-6565, fax (416) 512-6580

BELGIUM (Kingdom of Belgium)

EMBASSY IN OTTAWA (small): 80 Elgin Street, 4th Floor, Ottawa, Ontario K1P 1B7; (613) 236-7267, fax (613) 236-7882
CONSULATE IN MONTRÉAL (small): 999 de Maissoneuve Blvd. W., Suite 850, Montréal, Québec H3A 3L4; (514) 849-7394, fax (514) 844-3170

CONSULATE IN TORONTO (small): 2 Bloor Street W., Suite 2006, Toronto, Ontario M4W 3E2; (416) 944-1422, fax (416) 944-1421

BELIZE

HIGH COMMISSION TO CANADA C/O THE EMBASSY IN WASHINGTON, DC (small): 2535 Massachusetts Ave. N.W., Washington, DC 20008, USA; (202) 332-9636, fax (202) 332-88

BENIN (Republic of Benin)

EMBASSY IN OTTAWA (small): 58 Glebe Ave., Ottawa, Ontario K1S 2C3; (613) 233-4429, fax (613) 233-8952

BOLIVIA (Republic of Bolivia)

EMBASSY IN OTTAWA (small): 130 Albert Street, Suite 504,Ottawa, Ontario K1P 5G4; (613) 236-5730, fax (613) 236-8237, http://jaguar.pg.cc. md.us

BOTSWANA (Republic of Botswana)

HIGH COMMISSION TO CANADA C/O THE EMBASSY IN WASHINGTON, DC (small): 3400 International Dr. N.W., Suite 7M, Washington, DC 20008, USA; (202) 244-4990, fax (202) 244-4164

BRAZIL (Federative Republic of Brazil)

EMBASSY IN OTTAWA (small): 450 Wilbrod Street, Ottawa, Ontario K1N 6M8; (613) 237-1090, fax (613) 237-6144

CONSULATE IN MONTRÉAL (mid-sized): 2000 Mansfield Street, Suite 1700, Montréal, Québec H3A 3A5; (514) 499-0968, fax (514) 499-3963

CONSULATE IN TORONTO (small): 77 Bloor Street W., Suite 1109, Toronto, Ontario M5B 1M2; (416) 922-2503, fax (416) 922-1832

CONSULATE IN VANCOUVER (small): 1140 Pender Street W., Suite 1300, Vancouver, B.C. V6E 4G1; (604) 687-4589, fax (604) 681-6534

BRITAIN (United Kingdom of Great Britain and Northern Ireland)

HIGH COMMISSION IN OTTAWA (large): 80 Elgin Street, Ottawa, Ontario K1P 5K7; (613) 237-1530, fax (613) 569-1478, af572@freenet.carleton.ca, www.britcoun.org/canada/index.htm

CONSULATE IN MONTRÉAL (small): 1000 ouest rue de la Gauchère Bureau 4200, Montréal, Québec H3B 4W5; (514) 866-5863, fax (514) 866-0202, britcnl@alcor.concordia.ca

CONSULATE IN TORONTO (small): 777 Bay Street, Suite 2800, Toronto, Ontario M5G 2G2; (416) 593-1290, fax (416) 593-1229

CONSULATE IN VANCOUVER (small): 1111 Melville Street, Suite 800, Vancouver, B.C. V6E 3V6; (604) 683-4421, fax (604) 681-0693

BRUNEI DARUSSALAM (Negara Brunei Darussalam)

EMBASSY IN OTTAWA (small): 395 Laurier Ave. E., Ottawa, Ontario K1N 6R4; (613) 234-5656, fax 234-4397

BULGARIA (Republic of Bulgaria)

EMBASSY IN OTTAWA (small): 325 Stewart Street, Ottawa, Ontario K1N 6K5; (613) 789-3215, fax (613) 789-3524

CONSULATE IN TORONTO (small): 65 Overlea Blvd., Suite 406, Toronto, Ontario M4H 1P1; (416) 696-2420, fax (416) 696-8019

BURKINA FASO

EMBASSY IN OTTAWA (small): 48 Range Road, Ottawa, Ontario K1N 8J4; (613) 238-4796, fax (613) 238-3812, burkina.faso@sympatico.ca, www.multiservices.com/burkina

BURMA (Union of Myanmar)

EMBASSY IN OTTAWA (small): 85 Range Road, Suite 902, Ottawa, Ontario K1N 8J6; (613) 232-6434, fax (613) 232-6435

BURUNDI (Republic of Burundi)

EMBASSY TO CANADA C/O THE EMBASSY IN WASHINGTON DC (small): 2232 Wisconsin Ave. N.W., Suite 212, Washington DC, 20007; (202) 342-2574, fax (202) 342-2578, burundiembassy@erols.com

CAMEROON (Republic of Cameroon)

EMBASSY IN OTTAWA (small): 170 Clemow Ave., Ottawa, Ontario K1S 2B4; (613) 236-1522, fax (613) 236-3885

CAPE VERDE (Republic of Cape Verde)

EMBASSY TO CANADA C/O THE EMBASSY IN WASHINGTON, DC (small): 3415 Massachusetts Ave. N.W., Washington, DC 20007, USA; (202) 965-6820, fax (202) 965-1207

CENTRAL AFRICAN REPUBLIC

The Embassy in Washington is temporarily closed.

CHAD (Republic of Chad)

EMBASSY TO CANADA C/O THE EMBASSY IN WASHINGTON, DC (small): 2002 R Street N.W., Washington, DC 20009, USA; (202) 462-4009, fax (202) 265-1937

CHILE (Republic of Chile)

EMBASSY IN OTTAWA (mid-sized): 50 O'Connor St., Suite 1412, Ottawa, Ontario K1P 6L2; (613) 235-9940, fax (613) 235-1176

CONSULATE IN MONTRÉAL (small): 1010 Sherbrooke Street W. Suite 710, Montréal, Québec H3A 2R7; (514) 499-0405, fax (514) 499-8914

CONSULATE IN TORONTO (small): 170 Bloor Street, Suite 800, Toronto, Ontario M5S 1T9; (416) 924-0106, fax (416) 924-2627

CONSULATE IN VANCOUVER (small): 1185 West Georgia, Suite 1250,Vancouver, B.C. V6E 4E6; (604) 681-9162, fax (604) 682-2445

CHINA (People's Republic of China)

EMBASSY IN OTTAWA (large): 515 St. Patrick Street, Ottawa, Ontario K1N 5H3; (613) 789-3434, fax (613) 789-1911; www.chinaembassycanada.org

CONSULATE IN TORONTO (large): 240 St. George Street, Toronto, Ontario M5R 2P4; (416) 964-7260, fax (416) 324-6468

CONSULATE IN VANCOUVER (large): 3380 Granville Street, Vancouver, B.C. V6H 3K3; (604) 734-7492, fax (604) 734-0154

COLOMBIA (Republic of Colombia)

EMBASSY IN OTTAWA (small): 360 Albert Street, Suite 1002, Ottawa, Ontario K1R 7X7; (613) 230-3761, fax (613) 230-4416; embcolot@travel-net.com, www.travel-net.com/~emcolot

CONSULATE IN MONTRÉAL (small): 1010 Sherbrooke Street W., Suite 420, Montréal, Québec H3A 2R7; (514) 849-4852, fax (514) 849-4324

CONSULATE IN TORONTO (small): 1 Dundas St. W., Suite 2108, Toronto, Ontario M5G 1Z3; (416) 977-0098, fax (416) 977-1025; consulado.toronto@sprintcol.sprint.com

COMMERCIAL OFFICE IN TORONTO (small): One First Canadian Place, 58th floor, Suite 5801, Toronto, Ontario M5X 1E2; (416) 363-9225, fax (416) 363-0808

COMOROS ISLANDS (Islamic Federal Republic of Comoros)

EMBASSY TO CANADA C/O THE PERMANENT MISSION OF THE COMOROS ISLANDS TO THE UNITED NATIONS (small): 336 East 45th Street, 2nd Floor, New York, NY 10021, USA; (212) 972-8010, fax (212) 983-4712

CONGO (Republic of Congo)

EMBASSY TO CANADA C/O EMBASSY IN WASHINGTON, DC (small): 4891 Colorado Ave. N.W., Washington, DC 20011, USA; (202) 726-5500, fax (202) 726-1860

CONGO (Democratic Republic of the Congo, formerly Zaire)

EMBASSY IN OTTAWA (small): 18 Range Road, Ottawa, Ontario K1N 8J3; (613) 565-8245, fax (613) 565-8246

COSTA RICA (Republic of Costa Rica)

EMBASSY IN OTTAWA (small): 135 York Street, Suite 208, Ottawa, Ontario K1N 5T4; (613) 562-2855, fax (613) 562-2582, embrica@travel-net.com

CONSULATE IN MONTRÉAL (small): 1425 René Lévesque Blvd. W., Suite 602, Montréal, Québec H3G 1T7; (514) 393-1057, fax (514) 393-1624

CONSULATE IN VANCOUVER (small): 789 West Pender Street, Suite 430, V6C 1H2; (604) 681-2152, fax (604) 688-2152

CÔTE D'IVOIRE (Republic of Côte d'Ivoire)

EMBASSY IN OTTAWA (small): 9 Marlborough Ave., Ottawa, Ontario K1N 8E6; (613) 236-9919, fax (613) 563-8287

CROATIA (Republic of Croatia)

EMBASSY IN OTTAWA (small): 130 Albert Street, Suite 1700, Ottawa, Ontario K1P 5G4; (613) 230-7351, fax (613) 230-7388

CONSULATE IN MISSISSAUGA (small): 918 Dundas Street E., Suite 302, Mississauga, Ontario L4Y 2B8; (905) 277-9051, fax (905) 277-5432

CUBA (Republic of Cuba)

EMBASSY IN OTTAWA (small): 388 Main Street, Ottawa, Ontario K1S 1E3; (613) 563-0141, fax (613) 563-0068, cuba@iosphere_net

CONSULATE IN MONTRÉAL (mid-sized): 1415 Pine Ave. W., Montréal, Québec H3G 1B2; (514) 843-8897, fax (514) 845-1063

CONSULATE IN TORONTO (small): 5353 Dundas Street W., Suite 401, Toronto, Ontario M9B 6H8; (416) 234-8181, fax (416) 234-2754

CYPRUS (Republic of Cyprus)

HIGH COMMISSION TO CANADA C/O THE EMBASSY IN WASHINGTON, DC (small): 2211 R Street N.W., Washington, DC 20008, USA; (202) 462-5772, fax (202) 483-6710

CZECH REPUBLIC

EMBASSY IN OTTAWA (small): 541 Sussex Dr., Ottawa, Ontario K1N 6Z6; (613) 562-3875, fax (613) 562-3878

CONSULATE IN MONTRÉAL (small): 1305 Pine Ave. W., Montréal, Québec H3G 1B2; (514) 849-4495, fax (514) 849-4117. Commercial office: (514) 844-5511, fax (514) 844-1894

DENMARK (Kingdom of Denmark)

EMBASSY IN OTTAWA (small): 47 Clarence St., Suite 450, Ottawa, Ontario K1N 9K1; (613) 562-1811, fax (613) 562-1812

DJIBOUTI (Republic of Djibouti)

EMBASSY TO CANADA C/O THE EMBASSY IN WASHINGTON, DC (small): 1156-15th Street N.W., Suite 515, Washington, DC 20005, USA; (202) 331-0270, fax (202) 331-0302

DOMINICA (Commonwealth of Dominica)

See Eastern Caribbean States (Organization of)

DOMINICAN REPUBLIC

CONSULATE IN MONTRÉAL (small): 1055 St. Mathieu, Central Tower, Suite 241, Montréal, Québec H3H 2S3; (514) 933-9008, fax (514) 933-2070

EASTERN CARIBBEAN STATES (Organization of Eastern Caribbean States)

HIGH COMMISSION IN OTTAWA (small): 112 Kent St., Suite 1610, Place de Ville, Tower B, Ottawa, Ontario K1P 5P2; (613) 236-8952, fax (613) 236-3042

ECUADOR (Republic of Ecuador)

EMBASSY IN OTTAWA (small): 50 O'Connor Street, Suite 1311, Ottawa, Ontario K1P 6L2; (613) 563-8206, fax (613) 235-5776, www.ncf.carleton.ca:12345/freeport/government/embassies/south.am/equador/menu

CONSULATE IN MONTRÉAL (small): 1010 St. Catherine Street W., Suite 440, Montréal, Québec H3B 3R3; (514) 874-4071, fax (514) 874-9078

CONSULATE IN TORONTO (small): 151 Bloor Street W., Suite 470, Toronto, Ontario M5S 1S4; (416) 968-2077, fax (416) 968-3348

EGYPT (Arab Republic of Egypt)

EMBASSY IN OTTAWA (mid-sized): 454 Laurier Ave. E., Ottawa, Ontario K1N 6R3; (613) 234-4931, fax (613) 234-9347

COMMERCIAL OFFICE IN OTTAWA (small): 85 Range Road, Suite 207, Ottawa, Ontario K1N 8J6; (613) 238-6263, fax (613) 238-2578

CONSULATE IN MONTREAL (mid-sized): 1 Place Ville-Marie, Suite 2617, Montréal, Québec H3B 4S3; (514) 866-8455, fax (514) 866-0835

EL SALVADOR (Republic of El Salvador)

EMBASSY IN OTTAWA (small): 209 Kent Street, Ottawa, Ontario K2P 1Z8; (613) 238-2939, fax (613) 230-6940, 103234.607@compuserve.com

CONSULATE IN MONTRÉAL (small): 1080 Beaver Hall Hill, Suite 1604, Montréal, Québec H2Z 1S8; (514) 861-6515, fax (514) 861-6513

CONSULATE IN TORONTO (small): 151 Bloor Street W., Suite 470, Toronto, Ontario M5S 1S4; (416) 968-2077, fax (416) 968-3348

ERITREA (State of Eritrea)

EMBASSY IN OTTAWA (small): 75 Albert Street, Suite 610, Ottawa, Ontario K1P 5E7; (613) 234-3989, fax (613) 234-6213

ESTONIA (Republic of Estonia)

EMBASSY TO CANADA C/O THE EMBASSY IN WASHINGTON, DC (small): 2131 Massachusetts Ave., Washington, DC 20005, USA; (202) 588-0101, fax (202) 588-0108, info@estemb.org

ETHIOPIA

EMBASSY IN OTTAWA (small): 151 Slater Street, Suite 210, Ottawa, Ontario K1P 5H3; (613) 235-6637, fax (613) 235-4638, infoethi@magi.com

COMMISSION OF THE EUROPEAN COMMUNITIES (Delegation of the Commission of the European Communities)

COMMISSION IN OTTAWA (small): 350 Sparks Street, Suite 1110, Ottawa, Ontario K1R 7S8; (613) 238-6464, fax (613) 238-5191

FIJI (Republic of Fiji)

EMBASSY IN NEW YORK (small): 630 Third Ave., 7th floor, New York, NY 10017, USA; (212) 687-4130, fax (212) 687-3963

FINLAND (Republic of Finland)

EMBASSY IN OTTAWA (small): 55 Metcalfe Street, Suite 850, Ottawa, Ontario K1P 6L5; (613) 236-2389, fax (613) 238-1474, www.finemb.com

CONSULATE IN TORONTO (small): 1200 Bay Street, Suite 604, Toronto, Ontario M5R 2A5; (416) 964-0066, fax (416) 964-1524, Commercial Section: (416) 964-7400, fax (416) 964-1524

FRANCE (French Republic)

EMBASSY IN OTTAWA (large): 42 Sussex Dr., Ottawa, Ontario K1M 2C9; (613) 789-1795, fax (613) 789-3484, www.ambafrance.org

CONSULATE IN EDMONTON (small): 10010 - 106th Street, Suite 300, Edmonton, Alberta T5J 3L8; (403) 428-0232, fax (403) 426-1450

CONSULATE IN MONCTON (small): 250 Lutz Street, Moncton, N.B. E1C 8P6; (506) 857-4191, fax (506) 858-8169

CONSULATE IN MONTRÉAL (mid-sized): 1 Place Ville Marie, Suite 2601, Montréal, Québec H3B 4S3; (514) 878-4381, fax (514) 861-4614

COMMERCIAL OFFICE IN MONTRÉAL (small): 1000 de la Gauchetière Street W., 27th floor, Suite 2710, Montréal, Québec H3B 4W5; (514) 878-9851, fax (514) 878-3677

CONSULATE IN QUÉBEC (large): 1110 Laurentides Ave., Québec City, Québec G1S 3C3; (418) 688-0430, fax (418) 688-1263

CONSULATE IN TORONTO (small): 130 Bloor Street W., Suite 400, Toronto, Ontario M5S 1N5; (416) 925-8041, fax (416) 925-3076

COMMERCIAL OFFICE IN TORONTO (mid-sized): 20 Queen Street W., Suite 2004, Toronto, Ontario M5H 3R3; (416) 977-1257, fax (416) 977-7944

CONSULATE IN VANCOUVER (small): 736 Granville Street, Suite 1201, Vancouver, B.C. V6Z 1H9; (604) 681-5875, fax (604) 681-4287

COMMERCIAL OFFICE IN VANCOUVER (small): 750 West Pender Street, Suite 601, Vancouver, B.C. V6C 2T7; (604) 684-1271, fax (604) 684-2359

GABON (Gabonese Republic)

EMBASSY IN OTTAWA (small): 4 Range Road, Ottawa, Ontario K1N 8J5; (613) 232-5301, fax (613) 232-6916

GAMBIA (Republic of the Gambia)

HIGH COMMISSION TO CANADA C/O THE EMBASSY IN WASHINGTON, DC (small): 1155 - 15th Street N.W., Suite 1000, Washington, DC 20005, USA; (202) 785-1399, fax (202) 785-1430

GERMANY
(Federal Republic of Germany)

EMBASSY IN OTTAWA (large): 1 Waverly St., Ottawa, Ontario K2P 0T8; (613) 232-1101, fax (613) 594-9330, 100566.2620@compuserve.com, www.DocuWeb.CA/Germany

CONSULATE IN MONTRÉAL (mid-sized): 1250 René Lévesque Ouest, 43rd floor Montréal, Québec H3B 4W8; (514) 931-2277, fax (514) 931-7239, 106167.425@compuserve.com

CONSULATE IN TORONTO (mid-sized): 77 Admiral Road, Toronto, Ontario M5R 2L4; (416) 925-2813, fax (416) 925-2818, 106167.430@compuserve.com

CONSULATE IN VANCOUVER (mid-sized): 999 Canada Place, Suite 704, Vancouver, B.C. V6C 3E1; (604) 684-8377, fax (604) 684-8334, 106167.431@compuserve.com

GHANA (Republic of Ghana)

HIGH COMMISSION IN OTTAWA (small): 1 Clemow Ave., Ottawa, Ontario K1S 2A9; (613) 236-0871, fax (613) 236-0874

GREECE (Hellenic Republic)

EMBASSY IN OTTAWA (mid-sized): 80 MacLaren Street, Ottawa, Ontario K2P 0K6; (613) 238-6271, fax (613) 238-5676

CONSULATE IN MONTRÉAL (mid-sized): 1170 Place du Frère, 3rd Floor, Suite 300, Montréal, Québec H3B 3C6; (514) 875-2119, fax (514) 875-8781, congrem@citenet.net, www.citenet.net/grconsulate

CONSULATE IN TORONTO (small): 365 Bloor Street E., Suite 1800, Toronto, Ontario M4W 3L4; (416) 515-0133, fax (416) 515-0209

CONSULATE IN VANCOUVER (small): 1200 Burrard Street, Suite 501,Vancouver, B.C. V6Z 2C7; (604) 681-1381, fax (604) 681-6656

GRENADA

See also Eastern Caribbean States (Organization of)

CONSULATE IN TORONTO (small): 439 University Ave., Suite 920, Toronto, Ontario M5G 1Y8; (416) 595-1343, fax (416) 595-8278

GUATEMALA (Republic of Guatemala)

EMBASSY IN OTTAWA (small): 130 Albert Street, Suite 1010, Ottawa, Ontario K1P 5G4; (613) 233-7237, fax (613) 233-0135

CONSULATE IN VANCOUVER (small): 777 Hornby Street, Suite 760, Vancouver, B.C. V6Z 1S4; (604) 688-5209, (604) 688-5210

GUINEA (Republic of Guinea)

EMBASSY IN OTTAWA (small): 483 Wilbrod Street, Ottawa, Ontario K1N 6N1; (613) 789-8444, fax (613) 789-7560

GUINEA-BISSAU
(Republic of Guinea-Bissau)

EMBASSY TO CANADA C/O THE EMBASSY IN WASHINGTON, DC (small): 1511 Kay St. N.W., Suite 519 Washington, DC 20007, USA; (202) 347-3950, fax (202) 347-3954

GUYANA
(Co-operative Republic of Guyana)

HIGH COMMISSION IN OTTAWA (small): 151 Slater Street, Suite 309, Ottawa, Ontario K1P 5H3; (613) 235-7249, fax (613) 235-1447, guyanahcott@travel-net.com

CONSULATE IN WILLOWDALE (small): 505 Consumers Road, Suite 206, Willowdale, Ontario M2J 4V8; (416) 494-6040, fax (416) 494-1530

HAITI (Republic of Haiti)

EMBASSY IN OTTAWA (small): 112 Kent St., Suite 205, Place de Ville, Tower B, Ottawa, Ontario K1P 5P2; (613) 238-1628, fax (613) 238-2986

CONSULATE IN MONTRÉAL (small): 1801 McGill College Ave., 13th floor, Suite 1335, Montréal, Québec H3A 2N4; (514) 499-1919, fax (514) 499-1818

HOLY SEE (VATICAN)

EMBASSY IN OTTAWA (small): 724 Manor Ave., Rockliffe Park, Ottawa, Ontario K1M 0E3; (613) 746-4914, fax (613) 746-4786

HONDURAS (Republic of Honduras)

EMBASSY IN OTTAWA (small): 151 Slater Street, Suite 908, Ottawa, Ontario K1P 5H3; (613) 233-8900, fax (613) 232-0193

HUNGARY (Republic of Hungary)

EMBASSY IN OTTAWA (small): 299 Waverley Street, Ottawa, Ontario K2P 0V9; (613) 230-2717, fax (613) 230-7560, www.DocuWeb.ca/Hungary

CONSULATE IN MONTRÉAL (small): 1200 McGill College Ave., Suite 2040, Montréal, Québec H3B 4G7; (514) 393-3302, fax (514) 393-8226. Commercial section: (514) 393-1555, fax (514) 393-3528

CONSULATE IN TORONTO (small): 121 Bloor Street W., Suite 1115, Toronto, Ontario M4W 3M5; (416) 923-8981, fax (416) 923-2732, Commercial section: (416) 923-3596, fax (416) 923-2097

ICELAND (Republic of Iceland)

EMBASSY TO CANADA C/O THE EMBASSY IN WASHINGTON, DC (small): 1156 - 15th Street N.W., Suite1200 Washington, DC 20005, USA; (202) 265-6653, fax (202) 265-6656

INDIA (Republic of India)

HIGH COMMISSION IN OTTAWA (mid-sized): 10 Springfield Road, Ottawa, Ontario K1M 1C9; (613) 744-3751, fax (613) 744-0913, hicomind@ottawa.net, www.DocuWeb.ca/India

CONSULATE IN TORONTO (mid-sized): 2 Bloor Street W., Suite 500, Toronto, Ontario M4W 3E2;

(416) 960-0751, fax (416) 960-9812, cgindia@pathcom.com

CONSULATE IN VANCOUVER (mid-sized): 325 Howe Street, 2nd Floor, Vancouver, B.C. V6C 1Z7; (604) 662-8811, fax (604) 682-2471, indiaadm@axiotnet.com

INDONESIA (Republic of Indonesia)

EMBASSY IN OTTAWA (mid-sized): 55 Parkdale Ave., Ottawa, Ontario K1Y 1E5; (613) 724-1100 fax (613) 724-1105, kbri@prica.org, www.prica.org

CONSULATE IN TORONTO (mid-sized):129 Jarvis Street, Toronto, Ontario M5C 2H6; (416) 360-4020, fax (416) 360-4295

CONSULATE IN VANCOUVER (small):1455 West Georgia Street, 2nd Floor, Vancouver, B.C. V6G 2T3; (604) 682-8855, fax (604) 662-8396

IRAN (Islamic Republic of Iran)

EMBASSY IN OTTAWA (mid-sized): 245 Metcalfe Street, Ottawa, Ontario K2P 2K2; (613) 235-4726, fax (613) 232-5712, iranemb@www.salamiran.org, www.salamiran.org,

IRAQ (Republic of Iraq)

EMBASSY IN OTTAWA (small): 215 McLeod Street, Ottawa, Ontario K2P 0Z8; (613) 236-9177, fax (613) 567-1101

IRELAND (Republic of Ireland)

EMBASSY IN OTTAWA (small): 130 Albert Street, Suite 1105, Ottawa, Ontario K1P 5G4; (613) 233-6281, fax (613) 233-5835

ISRAEL

EMBASSY IN OTTAWA (small): 50 O'Connor Street, Suite 1005, Ottawa, Ontario K1P 6L2; (613) 567-6450, fax (613) 237-8865, www.DocuWeb.CA/Israel

CONSULATE IN MONTRÉAL (small): 1155 René Lévesque Blvd., Suite 2620, Montréal, Québec H3B 4S5; (514) 393-9372, fax (514) 393-8795

CONSULATE IN TORONTO (mid-sized): 180 Bloor Street W., Suite 700, Toronto, Ontario M5S 2V6; (416) 961-1126, fax (416) 961-7737

ITALY (Italian Republic)

EMBASSY IN OTTAWA (mid-sized): 275 Slater Street, 21st Floor, Ottawa, Ontario K1P 5H9; (613) 232-2401, fax (613) 233-1484, www.trytel.com/~italy

CONSULATE IN MONTRÉAL (small): 3489 Drummond Ave., Montréal, Québec H3G 1X6; (514) 849-8351, fax (514) 499-9471

CONSULATE IN TORONTO (small): 136 Beverley Street, Toronto, Ontario M5T 1Y5; (905) 977-1566, fax (905) 977-1119

CONSULATE IN VANCOUVER (small): 1200 Burrard Street, Suite 705, Vancouver, B.C. V6Z 2C7; (604) 684-7228, fax (604) 688-2147

IVORY COAST

See Côte D'Ivoire

JAMAICA

HIGH COMMISSION IN OTTAWA (small): 275 Slater Street, Suite 800, Ottawa, Ontario K1P 5H9; (613) 233-9311, fax (613) 233-0611

CONSULATE IN TORONTO (small): 214 King Street W., Suite 402, Toronto, Ontario M5H 3S6; (416) 598-3008, fax (416) 598-4928

JAPAN

EMBASSY IN OTTAWA (large): 255 Sussex Drive, Ottawa, Ontario K1N 9E6; (613) 241-8541, fax (613) 241-7415, infocul@embjapan.can.org, www.embjapan.can.org

CONSULATE IN EDMONTON (mid-sized): 2480 Manulife Place, 10180 - 101st Street, Edmonton, Alberta T5J 3S4; (403) 422-3752, fax (403) 424-1635

CONSULATE IN MONTRÉAL (mid-sized): 600 de la Gauchetière Street W., Suite 2120, Montréal, Québec H3B 4L8; (514) 866-3429, fax (514) 395-6000

CONSULATE IN TORONTO (mid-sized): Toronto Dominion Centre, Suite 2702, Toronto, Ontario M5K 1A1; (416) 363-7038, fax (416) 363-6074

CONSULATE IN VANCOUVER (mid-sized): 1177 Hastings Street W., Suite 900, Vancouver, B.C. V6E 2K9; (604) 684-5868, fax (604) 684-6939, japanvcr@istar.ca

JORDAN (Hashemite Kingdom of Jordan)

EMBASSY IN OTTAWA (small): 100 Bronson Ave., Suite 701, Ottawa, Ontario K1R 6G8; (613) 238-8090, fax (613) 232-3341

KENYA (Republic of Kenya)

HIGH COMMISSION IN OTTAWA (mid-sized): 415 Laurier Ave. E., Ottawa, Ontario K1N 6R4; (613) 563-1773, fax (613) 233-6599, www.ncf.carleton.ca:12345/freeport/government/embassies/africa/kenya/menu

KOREA (Republic of Korea)

EMBASSY IN OTTAWA (mid-sized): 150 Bateler Street, 5th Floor, Ottawa, Ontario K1A 5A6; (613) 244-5010, fax (613) 232-0928

CONSULATE IN MONTRÉAL (small): 1002 Sherbrooke Street W., Suite 2500, Montréal, Québec H3A 3L6; (514) 845-3243, fax (514) 845-8517

CONSULATE IN TORONTO (mid-sized): 555 Avenue Road, Toronto, Ontario M4V 2J7; (416) 920-3809, fax (416) 924-7305

CONSULATE IN VANCOUVER (mid-sized): 1066 West Hastings Street, Suite 830, Vancouver, B.C. V6E 3X1; (604) 681-9581, fax (604) 681-4864

KUWAIT (State of Kuwait)

EMBASSY IN OTTAWA (small): 80 Elgin St., 3rd Floor, Ottawa, Ontario K1P 1C6; (613) 780-9999, fax (613) 780-9905, info@embassyofkuwait.com, http://embassyofkuwait.com

KYRGYZSTAN (Republic of Kyrgyzstan)

EMBASSY TO CANADA C/O THE EMBASSY IN WASHINGTON, DC (small): 1511 K Street N.W., Suite 705, Washington, DC 20005, USA; (202) 347-3732, fax (202) 347-3718

LAOS (Lao People's Democratic Republic)

EMBASSY TO CANADA C/O THE EMBASSY IN WASHINGTON, DC (small): 2222 S Street N.W., Washington, DC 20008, USA; (202) 332-6416, fax (202) 332-4923, http://laosembassy.com

LATVIA (Republic of Latvia)

EMBASSY IN OTTAWA (small): 112 Kent Street, Suite 208, Place de Ville, Tower B, Ottawa, Ontario K1P 5P2; (613) 238-6014, fax (613) 238-7044, latvia-embassy@magnaccom.com, www2.magnacom.com/~latemb

LEBANON (Lebanese Republic)

EMBASSY IN OTTAWA (small): 640 Lyon Street, Ottawa, Ontario K1S 3Z5; (613) 236-5825, fax (613) 232-1609, emblebanon@synapse.net, www.synapse.net/~emblebanon

CONSULATE IN MONTRÉAL (small): 40 Côte-Ste-Catherine, Montréal, Québec H2V 2A2; (514) 276-2638, fax (514) 276-0090

LESOTHO (Kingdom of Lesotho)

closed

LIBYA (Socialist People's Libyan Arab Jamahiriya)

EMBASSY TO CANADA C/O THE PERMANENT MISSION OF LIBYA TO THE UNITED NATIONS (small): 309 - 315 East 48th Street, New York, NY 10017, USA; (212) 752-5775, fax (212) 593-4787

LITHUANIA

EMBASSY IN OTTAWA (small): 130 Albert Street, Suite 204, Ottawa, Ontario K1P 5G4; (613) 567-5458, fax (613) 567-5315

LUXEMBOURG (Grand Duchy of Luxembourg)

EMBASSY TO CANADA C/O THE EMBASSY IN WASHINGTON, DC (small): 2200 Massachusetts Ave. N.W., Washington, DC 20008, USA; (202) 265-4171, fax (202) 328-8270, washington.amb@mae.etat.lu

MADAGASCAR (Republic of Madagascar)

EMBASSY IN OTTAWA (small): 649 Blair Rd., Gloucester, Ontario K1J 7M4; (613) 744-7995, fax (613) 744-2530

MALAWI (Republic of Malawi)

HIGH COMMISSION IN OTTAWA (small): 7 Clemow Ave., Ottawa, Ontario K1S 2A9; (613) 236-8931, fax (613) 236-1054

MALAYSIA

HIGH COMMISSION IN OTTAWA (small): 60 Boteler Street, Ottawa, Ontario K1N 8Y7; (613) 241-5182, fax (613) 241-5214

CONSULATE IN TORONTO (mid-sized): 150 York Street, Suite 1110, Toronto, Ontario M5H 3S5; (416) 947-0004, fax (416) 947-0006

CONSULATE IN VANCOUVER (small): 925 West Georgia Street, Suite 1900, Vancouver, B.C. V6C 3L2; (604) 685-9550, fax (604) 685-9520

MALDIVES

PERMANENT MISSION TO THE UNITED NATIONS: 820 Second Ave., Suite 800C, New York, NY 10017, USA; (212) 599-6914, fax (212) 661-6405, mdvun@undp.org, www.undp.org/missions/maldives

MALI (Republic of Mali)

EMBASSY IN OTTAWA (small): 50 Goulbourn Ave., Ottawa, Ontario K1N 8C8; (613) 232-1501, fax (613) 232-7429, www.ambramaliottawa.com

MALTA (Republic of Malta)

HIGH COMMISSION TO CANADA C/O THE EMBASSY IN WASHINGTON, DC (small): 2017 Connecticut Ave. N.W.,Washington, DC 20008, USA; (202) 462-3611, fax (202) 387-5470

MAURITANIA (Islamic Republic of Mauritania)

EMBASSY IN OTTAWA (small): 249 McLeod Street, Ottawa, Ontario K2P 1A1; (613) 237-3283, fax (613) 237-3287

MAURITIUS (Republic of Mauritius)

HIGH COMMISSION TO CANADA C/O THE EMBASSY IN WASHINGTON, DC (small): 4301 Connecticut Ave. N.W., Suite 441, Washington, DC 20008, USA; (202) 244-1491, fax (202) 966-0983, mauritius.embassy@mci1.com

MEXICO (United Mexican States)

EMBASSY IN OTTAWA (large): 45 O'Connor Street, Suite 1500, Ottawa, Ontario K1P 1A4; (613) 233-8988, fax (613) 235-9123, www.DocuWeb.CA/Mexico

CONSULATE IN MONTRÉAL (small): 2000 Mansfield Street, Suite 1015,Montréal, Québec H3A 2Z7; (514) 288-2502, fax (514) 288-8287

COMMERCIAL OFFICE IN MONTRÉAL (small): 1501 McGill College, Suite 1540, Montréal, Québec H5H 2T5; (514) 287-1669, fax (514) 287-1884

CONSULATE IN TORONTO (mid-sized): 199 Bay Street, Suite 4440, Toronto, Ontario M5L 1E9; (416) 368-2875, fax (416) 368-1672

COMMERCIAL OFFICE IN TORONTO (small): Commerce Court W., 66 Wellington Street, Suite 2715, Toronto, Ontario M5K 1A1; (416) 867-9292, fax (416) 867-1847

CONSULATE IN VANCOUVER (small): 1130 West Pender Street, Suite 810, Vancouver, B.C. V6E 4A4; (604) 684-3547, fax (604) 684-2485

COMMERCIAL OFFICE IN VANCOUVER (small): 200 Granville Street, Suite 1365, Vancouver, B.C. V6C 1S4; (604) 682-3648, fax (604) 682-1355

MONGOLIA
(Mongolian People's Republic)

EMBASSY TO CANADA C/O THE EMBASSY IN WASHINGTON, DC (small): 2833 M Street N.W., Washington, DC 20007, USA; (202) 333-7117, fax (202) 298-9227

MONTSERRAT

See Eastern Caribbean States (Organization of)

MOROCCO (Kingdom of Morocco)

EMBASSY IN OTTAWA (mid-sized): 38 Range Road, Ottawa, Ontario K1N 8J4; (613) 236-7391, fax (613) 236-6164

CONSULATE IN MONTRÉAL (small): 1010 Sherbrooke Street W., Suite 1510, Montréal, Québec H3A 2R7; (514) 288-8750, fax (514) 288-4859

MOZAMBIQUE
(Republic of Mozambique)

HIGH COMMISSION TO CANADA C/O THE EMBASSY IN WASHINGTON, DC (small): 1990 M Street N.W., Suite 570, Washington, DC 20036, USA; (202) 293-7146, fax (202) 835-0245

MYANMAR

See BURMA.

NAMIBIA (Republic of Namibia)

HIGH COMMISSION TO CANADA, C/O THE EMBASSY IN WASHINGTON, DC (small): 1605 New Hampshire Ave. N.W., Washington, DC 20009, USA; (202) 986-0540, fax (202) 986-0443

NEPAL (Kingdom of Nepal)

EMBASSY TO CANADA C/O THE EMBASSY IN WASHINGTON, DC (small): 2131 Leroy Place N.W., Washington, DC 20008, USA; (202) 667-4550, fax (202) 667-5534

NETHERLANDS
(Kingdom of the Netherlands)

EMBASSY IN OTTAWA (small): 350 Albert Street, Suite 2020, Ottawa, Ontario K1R 1A4; (613) 237-5030, fax (613) 237-6471, nlgovott@ott.net

CONSULATE IN MONTRÉAL (small): 1002 Sherbrooke Street W., Suite 2201, Montréal, Québec H3A 3L6; (514) 849-4247, fax (514) 849-8260

CONSULATE IN TORONTO (small): 1 Dundas Street W., Suite 2106, Toronto, Ontario M5G 1Z3; (416) 598-2520, fax (416) 598-8064

CONSULATE IN VANCOUVER (small): 475 Howe Street, Suite 821, Vancouver, B.C. V6C 2B3; (604) 684-6448, fax (604) 684-3549

NEW ZEALAND

HIGH COMMISSION IN OTTAWA (small): 99 Bank Street, Suite 727, Ottawa, Ontario K1P 6G3; (613) 238-5991, fax (613) 238-5707, www.nzhcottawa.org

CONSULATE (small): 888 Dunsmuir Street, Suite 1200, Vancouver, B.C. V6C 3K4; (604) 684-7388, fax (604) 684-7333

NICARAGUA (Republic of Nicaragua)

EMBASSY IN OTTAWA (small): 130 Albert Street, Suite 407,Ottawa, Ontario K1P 5G4; (613) 234-9361, fax (613) 238-7666

NIGER (Republic of Niger)

EMBASSY IN OTTAWA (small): 38 Blackburn Ave., Ottawa, Ontario K1N 8A3; (613) 232-4291, fax (613) 230-9808

NIGERIA (Federal Republic of Nigeria)

closed

NORWAY (Kingdom of Norway)

EMBASSY IN OTTAWA (small): 90 Sparks Street, Suite 532,Ottawa, Ontario K1P 5B4; (613) 238-6571, fax (613) 238-2765, nor-emb-ott@intranet.ca

OMAN (Sultanate of Oman)

EMBASSY TO CANADA C/O THE EMBASSY IN WASHINGTON, DC (small): 2342 Massachusetts Ave. N.W., Washington, DC 20008, USA; (202) 387-1980, fax (202) 745-4933

PAKISTAN (Islamic Republic of Pakistan)

HIGH COMMISSION IN OTTAWA (small): 151 Slater Street, Suite 608, Ottawa, Ontario K1P 5H3; (613) 238-7881, fax (613) 238-7296

CONSULATE IN MONTRÉAL (small): 3421 Peel Street, Montréal, Québec H3A 1W7; (514) 845-2297 fax (514) 845-1354, pakistan@globale.net, http://global.globale.net:80/~pakistan

CONSULATE IN WILLOWDALE (small): 4881 Yonge Street, Suite 810, Willowdale, Ontario M2N 5X3; (416) 250-1255, fax (416) 250-1321

PANAMA (Republic of Panama)

EMBASSY IN OTTAWA (small): 130 Albert St. Suite 300, Ottawa, Ontario K1P 5G4; (613) 236-7177, fax (613) 236-5775,pancanem@travel-net.com

CONSULATE IN MONTRÉAL (small): 1425 René Lévesque Blvd. W., Suite 904, Montréal, Québec H3G 1T7; (514) 874-1929, fax (514) 874-1947

CONSULATE IN TORONTO (small): 879 St. Clair Ave. W., Toronto, Ontario M6C 1C4; (416) 651-2350, fax (416) 651-3141

PAPUA NEW GUINEA
(Independent State of Papua New Guinea)

HIGH COMMISSION TO CANADA C/O THE EMBASSY IN WASHINGTON, DC (small): 1615 New Hampshire Ave. N.W., Washington, DC 20009, USA; (202) 745-3680, fax (202) 745-3679

PARAGUAY (Republic of Paraguay)

EMBASSY IN OTTAWA (small): 151 Slater Street, Suite 401, Ottawa, Ontario K1P 5H3; (613) 567-1283, fax (613) 567-1679, embar@magmacom.com, www.magmacom.com/embapar

PERU (Republic of Peru)

EMBASSY IN OTTAWA (small): 130 Albert Street, Suite 1901,Ottawa, Ontario K1P 5G4; (613) 238-1777, fax (613) 232-3062

CONSULATE IN MONTRÉAL (small): 550 Sherbrooke St. W., Suite 376, West Tower, Montréal, Québec H3A 1B9; (514) 844-5123, fax (514) 843-8425

CONSULATE IN TORONTO (small): 10 Saint Mary Street, Suite 301, Toronto, Ontario M4Y 1P9; (416) 963-9696, fax (416) 963-9074

CONSULATE IN VANCOUVER (small): 505 Burrard Street, Suite 1850, Vancouver, B.C. V7X 1M6; (604) 662-8880, fax (604) 662-3564

PHILIPPINES
(Republic of the Philippines)

EMBASSY IN OTTAWA (mid-sized): 130 Albert Street, Suite 606, Ottawa, Ontario K1P 5G4; (613) 233-1121, fax (613) 233-4165

CONSULATE IN TORONTO (small): 151 Bloor Street W., Suite 365, Toronto, Ontario M5S 1S4; (416) 922-7181, fax (416) 922-3638

TRADE OFFICE IN TORONTO (small): 60 Bloor Street W., Suite 409, Toronto, Ontario M4W 3B8; (416) 967-1788, fax (416) 967-6236

CONSULATE IN VANCOUVER (small): 301-308, 470 Granville Street, Vancouver, B.C. V6C 1V5; (604) 685-7645, fax (604) 685-9945

POLAND (Republic of Poland)

EMBASSY IN OTTAWA (small): 443 Daly Ave., Ottawa, Ontario K1N 6H3; (613) 789-0468, fax (613) 789-1218, polamb@hookup.net, www.polanianet.com/eng

CONSULATE IN MONTRÉAL (small): 1500 Pine Ave. W., Montréal, Québec H3G 1B4; (514) 937-9481, fax (514) 937-7272

COMMERCIAL OFFICE IN MONTRÉAL (small): 3501 Musée Ave., Montréal, Québec H3G 2C8; (514) 282-1732, fax (514) 282-1784

CONSULATE IN TORONTO (mid-sized): 2603 Lakeshore Blvd. W., Toronto, Ontario M8V 1G5; (416) 252-5471, fax (416) 252-0509

COMMERCIAL OFFICE IN TORONTO (small): 3300 Bloor Street W., Suite 2860, Centre Tower, Toronto, Ontario M8X 2W8; (416) 252-5471, fax (416) 252-0509

CONSULATE IN VANCOUVER (small): 1177 West Hastings Street, Suite 1600, Vancouver, B.C. V6E 2K3; (604) 688-3530, fax (604) 688-3537

PORTUGAL (Portuguese Republic)

EMBASSY IN OTTAWA (small): 645 Island Park Dr., Ottawa, Ontario K1Y 0B6; (613) 729-0883, fax (613) 729-4236

CONSULATE IN MONTRÉAL (small): 2020 University Street, Suite 1725, Montréal, Québec H3A 2A5; (514) 499-0359, fax (514) 499-0366

COMMERCIAL OFFICE IN MONTRÉAL (small): 500 Sherbrooke Street W., Suite 940, Montréal, Québec H3A 3C6; (514) 282-1264, fax (514) 499-1450

CONSULATE IN TORONTO (small): 121 Richmond Street W., 7th Floor, Toronto, Ontario M5H 2K1; (416) 360-8260, fax (416) 360-0350

COMMERCIAL OFFICE IN TORONTO: 60 Bloor Street W., Suite 1005, Toronto, Ontario M4W 3B8; (416) 921-4925, fax (416) 921-1353

CONSULATE IN VANCOUVER (small): 700 West Pender Street, Suite 904, Vancouver, B.C. V6C 1G8; (604) 688-6514, fax (604) 685-7042

QATAR (State of Qatar)

EMBASSY TO CANADA C/O THE PERMANENT MISSION OF THE STATE OF QATAR TO THE UNITED NATIONS (small): 747 Third Ave., 22nd Floor, New York, NY 10017, USA; (212) 486-9335, fax (212) 758-4952

ROMANIA (Republic of Romania)

EMBASSY IN OTTAWA (small): 655 Rideau Street, Ottawa, Ontario K1N 6A3; (613) 789-5345, fax (613) 789-4365, www.embassy.org/romania/consular/ world.html

RUSSIA (Russian Federation)

EMBASSY IN OTTAWA (large): 285 Charlotte Street, Ottawa, Ontario K1N 8L5; (613) 235-4341, fax (613) 236-6342, www.russia.net/travel/visas.html

TRADE OFFICE IN OTTAWA (small): 95 Wurtemburg Street, Ottawa, Ontario K1N 8Z7; (613) 789-1222, fax (613) 789-2951

CONSULATE IN MONTRÉAL (mid-sized): 3655 Musée Ave., Montréal, Québec H3G 2E1; (514) 843-5901, fax (514) 842-2012

RWANDA (Rwandese Republic)

EMBASSY IN OTTAWA (small): 121 Sherwood Dr., Ottawa, Ontario K1Y 3V1; (613) 722-5835, fax (613) 722-4052

SAINT KITTS AND NEVIS

See Eastern Caribbean States (Organization of)

SAINT LUCIA

See Eastern Caribbean States (Organization of)

SAINT VINCENT
AND THE GRENADINES

CONSULATE IN WILLOWDALE (small): 210 Sheppard Ave. E., Ground Floor, Willowdale, Ontario M2N 3A9; (416) 222-0745, fax (416) 222-3830

SAUDI ARABIA
(Kingdom of Saudi Arabia)

EMBASSY IN OTTAWA (mid-sized): 99 Bank St., Suite 901, Ottawa, Ontario K1P 6B9; (613) 237-4100, fax (613) 237-0567

SÉNÉGAL (Republic of Sénégal)

EMBASSY IN OTTAWA (small): 57 Marlborough Ave., Ottawa, Ontario K1N 8E8; (613) 238-6392, fax (613) 238-2695

SEYCHELLES (Republic of Seychelles)

HIGH COMMISSION TO CANADA C/O THE PERMANENT MISSION OF SEYCHELLES TO THE UNITED NATIONS: 820 Second Ave., Suite 900F, New York, NY 10017, USA; (212) 687-9766, fax (212)922-9177

SIERRA LEONE
(Republic of Sierra Leone)

HIGH COMMISSION TO CANADA C/O THE EMBASSY IN WASHINGTON, DC (small): 1701 - 19th Street N.W., Washington, DC 20009, USA; (202) 939-9261, fax (202) 483-1793

SINGAPORE (Republic of Singapore)

EMBASSY IN WASHINGTON, DC (small): 3501 International Place, N.W., Washington, DC 20008, USA; (202) 537-3100, fax (202) 537-0876

CONSULATE IN VANCOUVER (small): 999 West Hastings, Suite 1305, Vancouver B.C., V62 2W2; (604) 669-5115, fax (604) 669-5153

SLOVAKIA (Slovak Republic)

EMBASSY IN OTTAWA (small): 50 Rideau Terrace, Ottawa, Ontario K1M 2A1; (613) 749-4442, fax (613) 749-4989

SLOVENIA (Republic of Slovenia)

EMBASSY IN OTTAWA (small): 150 Metcalfe Street, Suite 2101, Ottawa, Ontario K2P 1P1; (613) 565-5781, fax (613) 565-5783

SOLOMON ISLANDS

HIGH COMMISSION TO CANADA C/O THE PERMANENT MISSION OF THE SOLOMON ISLANDS TO THE UNITED NATIONS (small): 820 - 2nd Ave., Suite 800B, New York, NY 10017, USA; (212) 599-6192, fax (212) 661-8925

SOUTH AFRICA
(Republic of South Africa)

HIGH COMMISSION IN OTTAWA (small): 15 Sussex Dr., Ottawa, Ontario K1M 1M8; (613) 744-0330, fax (613) 741-1639, safrica@ottawa.net, www.DocuWeb.ca/SouthAfrica

CONSULATE IN MONTRÉAL (small): 1 Place Ville Marie, Suite 2615, Montréal, Québec H3B 4S3; (514) 878-9217, fax (514) 878-4751

CONSULATE IN TORONTO (mid-sized): 2 First Canadian Place, Suite 2300, King and York Streets, Toronto, Ontario M5X 1E3; (416) 364-0314, fax (416) 363-1737

SPAIN (Kingdom of Spain)

EMBASSY IN OTTAWA (small): 74 Stanley Ave., Ottawa, Ontario K1M 1P4; (613) 747-2252, fax (613) 744-1224,consule@DocuWeb.ca, www.DocuWeb.ca/ SpainInCanada

COMMERCIAL OFFICE IN OTTAWA (small): 151 Slater Street, Suite 801,Ottawa, Ontario K1P 5H3; (613) 236-0409, fax (613) 563-2849, 104702.3121@compuserve.com

CONSULATE IN MONTRÉAL (small): 1 Westmount Square, Suite 1456, Wood Ave., Montréal, Québec H3Z 2P9; (514) 935-5235, fax (514) 935-4655, consular@total.net, www.total.net:8080/~consular

COMMERCIAL OFFICE IN MONTRÉAL (small): Place Bonaventure, Mart E, 10 Elgin, P.O. Box 1137, Montréal Québec H5A 1G4; (514) 866-4914, fax (514) 866-6850, 104702.2544@compuserve.com

CONSULATE IN TORONTO (small): 200 Front St. Suite 2401, Toronto, Ontario M4W 1A5; (416) 977-1661, fax (416) 593-4949

COMMERCIAL OFFICE IN TORONTO (small): 55 Bloor Street W., Suite 1204, Toronto, Ontario M4W 1A5; (416) 967-0488, fax (416) 968-9547, buzon.oficial@toronto.ofcomes.mcx.es

SRI LANKA (Democratic
Socialist Republic of Sri Lanka)

HIGH COMMISSION IN OTTAWA (small): 333 Laurier Ave. Suite 1204, Ottawa, Ontario K1P 1C1; (613) 233-8449, fax (613) 238-8448, lanka@magi.com, http://infoweb.magi.com/~lankacom

SUDAN (Republic of The Sudan)

EMBASSY IN OTTAWA (small): 85 Range Road, Suite 507, Ottawa, Ontario K1N 8J6; (613) 235-4000, fax (613) 235-6880

SURINAME (Republic of Suriname)

EMBASSY TO CANADA C/O THE EMBASSY IN WASHINGTON, DC (small): 4301 Connecticut Ave. N.W., Suite 460, Washington, DC 20008, USA; (202) 244-7488, fax (202) 244-5878

SWAZILAND (Kingdom of Swaziland)

HIGH COMMISSION IN OTTAWA (small): 130 Albert Street, Suite 1204,Ottawa, Ontario K1P 5G4; (613) 567-1480, fax (613) 567-1058

SWEDEN (Kingdom of Sweden)

EMBASSY IN OTTAWA (small): 377 Dalhousie Street, Ottawa, Ontario K1N 9N8; (613) 241-8553, fax (613) 241-2277

SWITZERLAND (Swiss Confederation)

EMBASSY IN OTTAWA (small): 5 Marlborough Ave., Ottawa, Ontario K1N 8E6; (613) 235-1837, fax (613) 563-1394

CONSULATE IN MONTRÉAL (small): 1572 Dr. Penfield Ave., Montréal, Québec H3G 1C4; (514) 932-7181, fax (514) 932-9028

CONSULATE IN TORONTO (small): 154 University Ave., Suite 601, Toronto, Ontario M5H 3Y9; (416) 593-5371, fax (416) 593-5083

CONSULATE IN VANCOUVER (small): 999 Canada Place, Suite 790, Vancouver, B.C. V6C 3E1; (604) 684-2231, fax (604) 684-2806

SYRIA (Syrian Arab Republic)

EMBASSY TO CANADA C/O THE EMBASSY IN WASHINGTON, DC (small): 2215 Wyoming Ave. N.W., Washington, DC 20008, USA; (202) 232-6313, fax (202) 234-9546

TANZANIA (United Republic of Tanzania)

HIGH COMMISSION IN OTTAWA (small): 50 Range Road, Ottawa, Ontario K1N 8J4; (613) 232-1500, fax (613) 232-5184

THAILAND (Kingdom of Thailand)

EMBASSY IN OTTAWA (mid-sized): 180 Island Park Dr., Ottawa, Ontario K1Y 0A2; (613) 722-4444, fax (613) 722-6624, tthcotta@cyberus.ca, www.cyberus.ca

COMMERCIAL OFFICE IN OTTAWA (small): 275 Slater Street, Suite 1801, Ottawa, Ontario K1P 5H9; (613) 238-4002, fax (613) 238-6226

TOGO (Republic of Togo)

EMBASSY IN OTTAWA (small): 12 Range Road, Ottawa, Ontario K1N 8J3; (613) 238-5916, fax (613) 235-6425

TRINIDAD AND TOBAGO
(Republic of Trinidad and Tobago)

HIGH COMMISSION IN OTTAWA (small): 75 Albert Street, Suite 508, Ottawa, Ontario K1P 5E7; (613) 232-2418, fax (613) 232-4349; tthcotta@travel-net.com, www.travel-net.com:80/~tthcotta

CONSULATE IN WILLOWDALE (mid-sized): 2005 Sheppard Ave. E., Suite 303, Willowdale, Ontario M2J 5B4; (416) 495-9442, fax (416) 495-6934

TUNISIA (Republic of Tunisia)

EMBASSY IN OTTAWA (small): 515 O'Connor Street, Ottawa, Ontario K1S 3P8; (613) 237-0330, fax (613) 237-7939

CONSULATE IN MONTRÉAL (small): 511 Place d'Armes, Suite 501, Montréal, Québec H2Y 2W7; (514) 844-6909, fax (514) 844-5895

TURKEY (Republic of Turkey)

EMBASSY IN OTTAWA (mid-sized): 197 Wurtemburg St., Ottawa, Ontario K1N 8L9; (613) 789-4044, fax (613) 789-3422

TURKMENISTAN
(Republic of Turkmenistan):

EMBASSY TO CANADA C/O THE EMBASSY IN WASHINGTON, DC: 2207 Massachusetts Ave. N.W., Washington, DC 20008, USA; (202) 588-1500, fax (202) 588-0697

UGANDA (Republic of Uganda)

HIGH COMMISSION IN OTTAWA (small): 231 Cobourg Street, Ottawa, Ontario K1N 8J2; (613) 789-7797, fax (613) 789-8909

UKRAINE

EMBASSY IN OTTAWA (small): 310 Somerset ST. W, Ottawa, Ontario K2P 0J9; (613) 230-2961, fax (613) 230-2400, www3.sympatico.ca/tem~ukraine

CONSULATE IN TORONTO (small): 2120 Bloor Street W., Toronto, Ontario M6S 1M8; (416) 763-3115, fax (416) 763-2323

UNITED ARAB EMIRATES

EMBASSY TO CANADA C/O THE EMBASSY IN WASHINGTON, DC: 1255 26th Street N.W., Suite 700, Washington, DC 20037; (202) 337-7029, fax (202) 955-7999

UNITED STATES OF AMERICA

EMBASSY IN OTTAWA (large): 100 Wellington Street, Ottawa, Ontario K1P 5T1; (613) 238-5335, fax (613) 238-8750

CONSULATE IN CALGARY (small): 615 MacLeod Trail S.E., Calgary, Alberta T2G 4T8; (403) 266-8962, fax (403) 264-6630

CONSULATE IN HALIFAX (small): Cogswell Tower, 2000 Barrington St., Suite 910, Halifax, N.S. B3J 3K1; (902) 429-2480, fax (902) 423-6861

CONSULATE IN MONTRÉAL (large): 455 René Lévesque Blvd. 19th Floor, Montréal, Québec H5B 1G1 (514) 398-9695, fax (514) 398-0973

CONSULATE IN QUÉBEC (small): 2 Place Terrasse Dufferin, Québec, Québec G1R 4T9; (418) 692-2095, fax (418) 692-4640

CONSULATE IN TORONTO (large): 360 University Ave., Toronto, Ontario M5G 1S4; (416) 595-1700, fax (416) 595-0051

CONSULATE IN VANCOUVER (mid-sized): 1095 West Pender Street, Vancouver, B.C. V6E 2M6; (604) 685-4311, fax (604) 685-5285

URUGUAY (Eastern Republic of Uruguay)

EMBASSY IN OTTAWA (small): 130 Albert Street, Suite 1905, Ottawa, Ontario K1P 5G4; (613) 234-2727, fax (613) 233-4670, www.iosphere.net/~uruott/

VENEZUELA (Republic of Venezuela)

EMBASSY IN OTTAWA (small): 32 Range Road, Ottawa, Ontario K1N 8J4; (613) 235-5151, fax (613) 235-3205, embavene@travel-net.com, www.ottawa.net/ ~embavene

CONSULATE IN MONTRÉAL (mid-sized): 2055 Peel Street, Suite 400, Montréal, Québec H3A 1V4; (514) 842-3417, fax (514) 287-7101, venconsul@dsuper.net

CONSULATE IN TORONTO (small): 365 Bloor Street E., Suite 1904, Toronto, Ontario M4W 3L4; (416) 960-6070, fax (416) 960-6077, consuven@tor.hookup.net, www.hookup.net/~consuven

VIETNAM (Socialist Republic of Vietnam)

EMBASSY IN OTTAWA (small): 226 MacClaren Street, Ottawa, Ontario K2P 0L6; (613) 236-0772, fax (613) 236-2704

WESTERN SAMOA
(The Independent State of Samoa)

HIGH COMMISSION TO CANADA C/O THE PERMANENT MISSION OF WESTERN SAMOA TO THE UNITED NATIONS (small): 820 Second Ave., Suite 800, New York, NY 10017, USA; (212) 599-6196, fax (212) 599-0797

YEMEN (Republic of Yemen)

EMBASSY IN OTTAWA (small): 788 Island Park Drive, Ottawa, Ontario K1Y 0C2; (613) 729-6627, fax (613) 729-8915

YUGOSLAVIA
(Federal Republic of Yugoslavia)

EMBASSY IN OTTAWA (small): 17 Blackburn Ave., Ottawa, Ontario K1N 8A2; (613) 233-6289, fax (613) 233-7850

ZAMBIA (Republic of Zambia)

HIGH COMMISSION TO CANADA C/O THE EMBASSY IN WASHINGTON, DC (small): 2419 Massachusetts Ave. N.W., Washington, DC 20008, USA; (202) 265-9717, fax (202) 332-0826

ZIMBABWE (Republic of Zimbabwe)

HIGH COMMISSION IN OTTAWA (small): 332 Somerset Street W., Ottawa, Ontario K2P 0J9; (613) 237-4388, fax (613) 563-8269; zim.highcomm@sympatico.ca, www.DocuWeb.ca/Zimbabwe

Indexes

Bibliographies 919
ID Number Index 933
Cities in Canada with
    International Contacts 941
Countries & Regions of the World 945
Job Categories 953
Organizations 957

How this Book was Researched 970
Contents at a Glance 972

Bibliographies by Subject

58 bibliographies indexed by subject, with some repeated for ease of reference.

Living Overseas

Crosscultural Skills 17
Health Overseas 45
Children & Families Overseas 47
Educating Your Children 49
Moving Abroad 49
Taxes & Investment 51
Personal Stories Overseas 66
Learning a Foreign Language 73
Women Working & Living Overseas 83
Crosscultural Business Skills 102
Re-Entry 125
International Business 695

Acquiring Experience

Short-term Programs Overseas 142
Hosting Programs 166
Crosscultural Travel 177
International IQ Periodicals 186
Book, Film & Video Distributors 187
Global Education 189
Tools for Teachers 193
International Internships 357

Academic Studies

Learning a Foreign Language 72
International IQ Periodicals 186
Study Abroad 207
Awards & Grants 217
International Studies
    in Canada and Abroad 242

The Job Search

General Job Search: All 395
General Job Search: Students 396
Books on the Internet Job Search 415
International Job Hunting
    Services on the Internet 417
Country Information on the Internet 424
International Job Search 429
Employment Agencies 432
Job Search Directories 433

Internet Job Search

New to the Internet? 405
Books About the Internet 406
Search Engines 409
Books on the Internet Job Search 415
Directories on the Web 416
International Job Hunting
    Services on the Internet 417
Country Information on the Internet 424

Country Information

Country Information on the Internet 424
Global Guide Books 515
United States of America 524
Mexico & Latin America 534
Western Europe 540
Russia & Eastern Europe 547
Middle East 550
Asia Pacific 556

International Career Contacts

Women Working & Living Overseas 83
Short-term Programs Overseas 137
International Internships 357
International Job Search 429
Other Careers 437
Health Careers 438
Language Careers 441
Tourism Industry Careers 442
Jobs in International Development 566
Teaching Abroad 587
Teacher Recruitment Agencies 591
Freelancing Abroad 600
International Business 695
Government 714
Foreign Affairs 725
CIDA 736
Nongovernmental Organizations 768
United Nations 841
International Organizations 869
Canadian Diplomats Abroad 890
Foreign Diplomats in Canada 904

Bibliography by Title

There are 682 resources indexed below. Many repeated for ease of reference, for a total of 1338 entries in this book. The resources are made up of publications, web sites, and career services.

175 High Impact Cover Letters 🕮 395
A Canadian Guide to International Adoptions 🕮 48
A Common Core: Thais and Americans 🕮 525, 557
A Fair Go for All: Australian and American Interactions 🕮...525, 558
A Healthy Stay in Canada 🕮 46, 166
A Journey of One's Own: Uncommon Advice for the Independent Woman Traveler 🕮.........48, 84, 179
A Manager's Guide to Globalization: Six Keys to Success in a Changing World 🕮 106
A Rich Broth: Memoirs of a Canadian Diplomat 🕮 67, 727
A World of Options: Guide to International Education
   Exchange, Community Services, and Travel for Persons with Disabilities 🕮 141, 182, 212
A Year Between 🕮 142, 182
Academic Year Abroad 🕮 207
Access North America 🕮 🖳 524, 534, 695
Adams Electronic Job Search Almanac 1997 🕮 416
Adventure of Working Abroad: Hero Tales from the Global Frontier (The) 🕮............................18, 66
Adventures in Good Company 🕮 83, 177
AEON Corporation 591
Africa on Film and Videotape: A Guide to Audio-Visual Resources Available in Canada 🕮 187
After Latin American Studies: A Guide to Graduate Study,
   Fellowships, Internships, and Employment for Latin Americanists 🕮 217, 243, 357, 534
Aid as a Peacemaker: Canadian Development Assistance and Third World Conflict 🕮 736
Airlines of the World 🖳 177
All Hotels on the Web 🖳 177
Alternative Travel Directory 1996 (The) 🕮 177, 207
American Cultural Patterns: A Cross-Cultural Perspective 🕮 18, 524
American Ways: A Guide for Foreigners 🕮 524
Apex Press Catalogue 🕮...187
Argus ClearingHouse (The) 🖳 410
Art of Coming Home (The) 🕮 47, 125
Art of Crossing Cultures (The) 🕮 18
Au Pair & Nanny's Guide to Working Abroad (The) 🕮 137
Awards Almanac (The) 🕮 217
Asia Fact Unlimited 🖳 587
Asia for Women on Business 🕮 83, 556
Asian Development Bank Business Opportunities 🕮 🖳 556, 696, 841
Asia-Net 🖳 418, 556
Association of American Schools in South America (AASSA) 591
Association of Canadian Teachers In Japan 🖳 587
Association of Universities and Colleges of Canada 🖳..217
Associations Canada 1997/98 🕮 433, 768
Au Courrant 🕮 🖳 768
Awards for First Degree Study at Commonwealth Universities 🕮...217

Awards for Postgraduate Study at Commonwealth Universities ⌨ 217
Awards for University Administrators and Librarians ⌨ 217, 437
Awards for University Teachers and Research Workers ⌨ 218, 588
AYUSA International ⌨ 166
Background Notes Series ⌨ 515
Bargaining Across Borders: How to Negotiate Business Successfully Anywhere in the World ⌨ 103
Barnga ⌨ 18, 189
Basic Facts About the United Nations ⌨ 841
Basics and Tools - A Collection of Popular Education Resources and Activities ⌨ 189
Behind the Japanese Bow: An In-Depth Guide to Understanding and Predicting Japanese Behaviour ⌨ 556
Berkeley Guides ⌨ 177
Best Résumés for $75,000+ Executive Jobs (The) ⌨ 768
Big 9: The Most Commonly Used Metasearch Engines (The) ⌨ 410
Big 9: The Most Commonly Used Search Engines (The) ⌨ 410
Bilingual-Jobs.Com ⌨ 441
Blue Book of Canadian Business ⌨ 433
Bon Voyage But... ⌨ 177
Book Passage Catalogues ⌨ 178
Border Crossings: American Interactions with Israelis ⌨ 524, 550
Bottin International du Québec ⌨ 434, 890
Bout de papier ⌨ 725
Bowker Annual Library and Book Trade Almanac ⌨ 437
Breakthrough Series: Self-Guided Language Courses ⌨ 73
Bridges of Hope? Canadian Voluntary Agencies and the Third World ⌨ 769
Building an Import/Export Business ⌨ 696
Business of Korean Culture (The) ⌨ 556
Business Opportunities Sourcing System (BOSS) ⌨ 696
Canada and the Developing World: Key Issues in Canada's Foreign Policy ⌨ 725
Canada and the New Global Economy ⌨ 696
Canada Business Service Centres ⌨ 696, 714
Canada Post (The) ⌨ 540
Canada Post Corporation ⌨ 416
Canada Year Book ⌨ ⌨ 49, 103, 515
Canada's Best Employers for Women ⌨ 83
Canada-Mexico: Partnering for Success ⌨ 535
Canada-US Fulbright Program ⌨ 218
CanadExport ⌨ ⌨ 696, 726
Canadian Association of International Development Consultants (CAIDC) 566, 736
Canadian Association of University Schools of Nursing (CAUSN) 438
Canadian Awards Program ⌨ 218
Canadian Based Information Systems ⌨ 410
Canadian Bureau for International Education ⌨ 207, 243
Canadian Business Advertising Network ⌨ 418
Canadian College Directory (The) ⌨ 243
Canadian Corporate News ⌨ 418, 696
Canadian Development Report 1997-98 ⌨ 189
Canadian Directory to Foundations and Grants ⌨ 218
Canadian Exporter's Guide to the Internet ⌨ 696
Canadian Gophers ⌨ 411
Canadian Human Rights Commission ⌨ 189
Canadian Index ⌨ 696
Canadian International Development Agency (CIDA) ⌨ 424, 769
Canadian International Development Assistance Policies: An Appraisal ⌨ 736
Canadian Key Business Directory ⌨ 434
Canadian Nurses Association ⌨ 438
Canadian Parents for French 73
Canadian Passport Office ⌨ 178, 890
Canadian Red Cross 438
Canadian Representatives Abroad ⌨ ⌨ 424, 697, 726, 890
Canadian Society for International Health (CSIH) 438
Canadian University Distance Education Directory ⌨ 49, 208

Canadian Women's Internet Association ⊑ 405
Canadian World Federalist Newsletter ⊞ 566, 769
Canadian WWW Central Index ⊑ 411
Canadians Resident Abroad ⊞ 51
CanAsian Businesswomen's Network 83, 556
Care Canada ⊑ 567, 769
Career and Job Links ⊑ 418
Career City ⊑ 418, 525
Career Mosaic ⊑ 418
Career Opportunities for American Planners in International Development ⊞ 437, 567, 769
Career Opportunities in Travel and Tourism ⊞ 442
Career Options: The Graduate Recruitment Annual ⊞ 396
Career Path ⊑ 418
Career Resource Center ⊑ 418
Career Web ⊑ 419
CareerChina ⊑ 556
Careers for Foreign Language Aficionados and Other Multilingual Types ⊞ 441
Careers for Travel Buffs ⊞ 442
Careers in International Affairs ⊞ 429, 869
Careers in International Business ⊞ 437
Careers in International Law ⊞ 437
Catapult Employment Centers ⊑ 419
Catapult Sites for General Job Listings by Region ⊑ 419
Centre for Intercultural Learning 18, 103, 126, 736
Change Your Job, Change Your Life: High Impact Strategies for Finding Great Jobs in the '90s ⊞ 395
Charity Village ⊑ 769
Chile: A Partner for the Future ⊞ 535
China Books & Periodicals Inc. (Catalogue) ⊞ 557
China Bound: A Guide to Academic Life and Work in the PRC ⊞ 557, 588
Choices That Count: Co-operative Education in the Public Service of Canada ⊞ ⊑ 243, 357, 397
CIA World Factbook (The) ⊑ 178, 424, 516
CIDA Public Inquiries ⊞ 737
CIDA Publications ⊞ 737
CIDA: Development Information Program ⊞ 737
CIDA: International Development Photo Library (IDPL) ⊞ 187, 737
CNN Interactive ⊑ 424
Commonwealth Universities Yearbook ⊞ 208, 218
Communicating With Customers Around the World:
    A Practical Guide to Effective Cross-Cultural Business Communication ⊞ 103
Communication Between Cultures ⊞ 18
Competitive Frontiers: Women Managers in a Global Economy ⊞ 83, 103
Complete Guide to International Jobs and Careers (The) ⊞ 430
Complete Idiot's Guide to the Internet (The) ⊞ 406
Comportement Organisationnel ⊞ 103
Connexions Online ⊑ 189
Considering Filipinos ⊞ 557
Consultants and Consulting Organizations Directory (The) ⊞ 434
Contact Point ⊑ 395, 419
Corpus Almanac and Canadian Sourcebook ⊞ 434, 697
Country Backgrounders ⊞ 516
Cours de français langue étrangère et stages pour
    professeurs Répertoire des centres de formation en France ⊞ 208
Craighead's International Business Travel and Relocation Guide to 78 Countries: 1996-97 ⊞ 50, 103, 516
Crossborder Tax and Transactions ⊑ 51, 525, 697
Cross-Cultural Adaptability Inventory (The) ⊞ 18
Cross-Cultural Dialogues ⊞ 18, 193
Cross-Cultural Effectiveness ⊞ 104, 567, 737
Crossing Cultures Through Film ⊞ 187
Cultural Dimension of International Business (The) ⊞ 104
Cultural Survival Quarterly ⊞ 190
Cultural Survival ⊞ 190

Culture and the Clinical Encounter: An Intercultural Sensitizer for the Health Professions ⌨ 439
Culture Clash: Managing in a Multicultural World ⌨ 19
Culture Shock! A Parent's Guide ⌨ 19, 48
Culture Shock! Canada ⌨ 19, 104
Culture Shock! Series ⌨ 19, 516
Culture Shock!: Successful Living Abroad, A Wife's Guide ⌨ 48, 84, 601
Culture Shock: All You Need to Know about Studying Overseas ⌨ 208
Cultures and Organizations: Software of the Mind ⌨ 104
Culturgrams: The Nations Around Us ⌨ 19, 104, 516
Current History ⌨ ⌨ 516
Current World Leaders ⌨ ⌨ 424, 516
DailyJob ⌨ 557, 588
Department of Foreign Affairs and International Trade (DFAIT)- Business Directories ⌨ 417
Department of Foreign Affairs and International Trade (DFAIT) ⌨ 178, 425, 890, 904
Department of Foreign Affairs and International Trade (DFAIT)-Directory ⌨ 417
Department of National Defence (DND) ⌨ 421, 714
Developing Global Development Perspectives in Home Economics Education ⌨ 193
Developing Global Organizations: Strategies for Human Resource Professionals ⌨ 104
Developing Ideas ⌨ 190
Developing Intercultural Awareness: A Cross-Cultural Training Handbook ⌨ 19, 193, 588
Development Alternatives:
    Communities of the South in Action—A Teacher's Guide for World Issues Courses ⌨ 193
Development Business ⌨ ⌨ 567, 737, 842
Development Dictionary: A Guide to Knowledge as Power ⌨ 190
Development is... An Introductory Study Kit on Development ⌨ 190
Development: Journal of the Society for International Development ⌨ 190
Diplomat & International Canada ⌨ 726, 904
Diplomatic, Consular, and Other Representatives in Canada ⌨ 434, 726, 904
Diplomatic Handbook (The) ⌨ 890
Directory for Trade Commissioners ⌨ 697, 726, 890
Directory of American Firms Operating in Foreign Countries ⌨ 434, 525
Directory of Associations (The) ⌨ 434
Directory of Canadian Consulting Engineers 1994-95 ⌨ 434
Directory of Canadian Universities ⌨ 243
Directory of EC Information Sources ⌨ 517, 540
Directory of E-mail Discussion Groups ⌨ 411
Directory of Executive Recruiters ⌨ 435
Directory of Foreign Firms Operating in the US ⌨ 435
Directory of International Internships: A World of Opportunities ⌨ 357
Directory of Jobs and Careers Abroad (The) ⌨ 430
Directory of Low Cost Vacations with a Difference ⌨ 178
Directory of Non-Governmental Organizations (NGOs) Active in Sustainable Development ⌨ 769, 567, 435
Directory of Summer Jobs Abroad ⌨ 137
Directory of Summer Jobs in Britain ⌨ 137
Directory of the Canadian Trade Commissioner Service Abroad ⌨ ⌨ 697, 890
Directory of US Based Agencies Involved In International Health Assistance ⌨ 439
Directory of Volunteer Opportunities ⌨ 138
Directory of Work & Study in Developing Countries (The) ⌨ 138, 208, 769
Do What You Are ⌨ 395
Do's and Taboos Around the World for Women in International Business ⌨ 84, 104
Do's and Taboos Around the World ⌨ 19, 517
Do's and Taboos of Hosting International Visitors ⌨ 105, 166
Do's and Taboos of International Trade: A Small Business Primer ⌨ 105, 697
Doing Business in Asia: The Complete Guide ⌨ 557
Doing Business in Asia's Booming "China Triangle":
    People's Republic of China, Taiwan, Hong Kong ⌨ 557
Doing Business Internationally: The Cross-Cultural Challenges Resource Book ⌨ 105
Doing Business Internationally: The Guide to Cross-Cultural Success ⌨ 105
Doing Business Internationally: The Workbook to Cross-Cultural Success ⌨ 105
Doing Business with Japanese Men: A Woman's Handbook ⌨ 84, 557
Doing Voluntary Work Abroad ⌨ 138

Don't Drink the Water: The Complete Traveller's Guide to Staying Healthy in Warm Climates ☐ 46
Dynamics of Successful International Business Negotiations ☐ 105
Eastern and Central Europe Job Bank ☐ 419, 547
Economics Departments, Institutes and Research Centres Around the World ☐ 243
Economist (The) ☐ 186, 430
Ecotonos ☐ 105
Ecotours and Nature Getaways: A Guide to Environmental Vacations Around the World ☐ 178
Ed-U-Link Services Online Recruiting Fair ☐ 588
Effective Communication in Multicultural Health Care Settings ☐ 439
Employment Conditions Abroad Ltd. (ECA) 432
Employment in France for Students ☐ 138, 208, 540
Employment Opportunities for Australia ☐ 419, 558
Employment Resources on the Internet ☐ 397, 419
Encountering the Chinese: a Guide for Americans ☐ 558
Encyclopedia of Associations: International Organizations 1997 ☐ 435, 869
English Teachers Overseas (ETO) 592
Escape from America ☐ 50
ESL Job Links ☐ 419, 588
ESLoop (The) ☐ 419, 588
Euromanagers & Martians: The Business Cultures of Europe's Trading Nations ☐ 540
European Council of International Schools 592
European Union (The) ☐ 869
Europrail International ☐ 178
Evaluating an Overseas Job Opportunity ☐ 430
Exchange Opportunities for Canadians ☐ 138
Exchange Student Survival Kit (The) ☐ 138, 166, 208
Executive Contact List: US Private and Voluntary
   Organizations Registered with the Agency for International Development (The) ☐ 435, 567, 770
Expatriate Group Inc. (The) 51
Exploring the Greek Mosaic: A Guide to Intercultural Communication in Greece ☐ 540
Export Development Corporation ☐ 714
Exporting from Canada: A Practical Guide to Finding and Developing Export Markets for Your Product
   or Service ☐ 697
ExportSource ☐ 697
Fact Sheets ☐ ☐ 49, 588
Far Eastern Economic Review ☐ 186
Federal and Provincial Support to Post-Secondary Education in Canada ☐ 218
Fellowships in International Affairs: A Guide to Opportunities in the United States and Abroad ☐ 218
FGI's Global Relocation Services 50
Fielding's: The World's Most Dangerous Places ☐ ☐ 178
Financial Aid for Research & Creative Activities Abroad: 1996-98 ☐ 218
Financial Post Survey of Predecessor and Defunct Companies ☐ 435
Financial Times ☐ 186
Finding a Job in New Zealand ☐ 558
Finding Work Overseas ☐ 430
First Job: A New Grad's Guide to Launching Your Business Career ☐ 397
Fischer Report ☐ 435, 697
Flying High in Travel: A Complete Guide to Careers in the Travel Industry ☐ 442
Focus ☐ 770
For the Working Artist ☐ 437
Foreign Government Awards Program ☐ 209, 219
Foreign Language Learning Resources ☐ 73
Foreign Service ☐ 726
Four 11 Directory Services ☐ 417
French Fun: The Real Spoken Language of Québec ☐ 73
French or Foe? ☐ 541
Friends of World Teaching 592
From Da to Yes: Understanding the East Europeans ☐ 547
From Nyet to Da: Understanding the Russians ☐ 547
Fundraising for Social Change ☐ 190
Gestures: the Do's and Taboos of Body Language Around the World ☐ 20

Get Ready! Hints for a Healthy Short-Term Assignment Overseas 📖 46
Get the Right Visa: To Work or Do Business in the United States or Mexico Under NAFTA 📖 525, 535
Get Wired, You're Hired 📖 416
Global Change Game 📖 193
Global Directory of Peace Studies Programs 📖 243
Global Winners: 74 Activities for Inside and Outside the Classroom 📖 194
Globalwork: Bridging Distance, Culture and Time 📖 106
Goal Recruiting 592
Going Abroad: The Bathroom Survival Guide 📖 46, 178
Going to Japan on Business: Protocol, Stategies & Language for the Corporate Traveler 📖 558
Golden Opportunities: A Volunteer Guide for Americans Over 50 📖 138, 437, 439
Good Neighbours: Communicating with the Mexicans 📖 535
Gordon Group Home Page (The) 💻 397, 420
Government Assistance Programs & Subsidies (GAPS) 📖 698, 714
Government Electronic Directory Services 💻 714
Government of Canada Primary Internet Site 💻 714
Government of Canada Telephone Directory: National Capital Region 📖 714
Graveyard For Dreamers: One Woman's Odyssey in Africa 📖 20, 66, 84
Graybridge International Consulting Inc. 126
Great Jobs Abroad 📖 430
Great Jobs for Foreign Language Majors 📖 441
Green Teacher Magazine 📖 194
Group Fischer 430, 433
Group of Ten (The) 💻 244
Guide to Business Schools 📖 244
Guide to Careers in World Affairs 📖 430
Guide to Cruise Ship Jobs 📖 442
Guide to Export Services 📖 517, 698
Guide to Internet Job Searching (The) 📖 💻 416
Guide to Living Abroad 📖 50, 517
Guide to Living, Studying, and Working in the People's Republic of China and Hong Kong 📖 209, 589
Handbook of Foreign Student Advising (The) 📖 209
Health Advice for Living Overseas 📖 46
Health Information for Canadian Travellers 📖 46
Health, Population and Reproductive Health Resources 💻 190, 439, 567
Helen Ziegler and Associates 439
Helping Health Workers Learn 📖 440
Hess Language School of Taiwan 592
High Impact Resumes & Letters: How to Communicate Your Qualifications to Employers 📖 395
Hook Up, Get Hired! 📖 416
Hoover's Directory of World Business 📖 435, 698
Hoovers On-Line 💻 420, 436
Host Family Survival Kit: A Guide for American Host Families 📖 138, 166
Hostelling International 📖 179
How to be a More Successful Language Learner 📖 74
How to Be An Importer and Pay for Your World Travel 📖 179, 698
How to Become an Au Pair 📖 138
How to Emigrate 📖 50
How to Find Temporary Work Abroad 📖 601
How to Form and Manage Successful Business Alliances 📖 698
How to Get a Job Abroad 📖 431
How to Get a Job in America 📖 525
How to Get a Job in Europe 📖 541
How to Get a Job in France 📖 541
How to Get a Job in Germany 📖 541
How to Live and Work in Saudi Arabia 📖 550
How to Live and Work in The Gulf 📖 551
How to Live and Work Series—Pacific Rim 📖 558
How to Live and Work Series—Western Europe 📖 541
How to Study Abroad 📖 209
How to Study and Live in Britain 📖 244, 541

How to Teach Abroad ▢ 589
How to Travel Around the World ▢ 179
How We Work for Peace ▢ 190
Human Languages Page ▢ 441
Human Resources International (HRI) 433
I Am Going to France: 1994-1995 ▢ 209
I Should Have Stayed at Home: The Worst Trips of the Great Writers ▢ 66
IDB Projects ▢ ▢ 698, 842
IESCOnet-International Trade with Mexico ▢ 535, 698
IFInet ▢ 698, 842
IISD Products Catalogue ▢ 191
IISDnet ▢ 191
Impact Publications Catalogue ▢ 188
Importing: A Practical Guide to an Exciting and Rewarding Business ▢ 698
Infinite Ink Newsgroup Search ▢ 411
InfoExport ▢ 698
Insight: International Development Film and Video Catalogue ▢ 188
Interact Nova Group Canada ▢ 592
InterAction: American Council for Voluntary International Action ▢ 770
INTERCRISTO, The Christian Career Specialists 433, 437
Intercultural and Community Development Resources (ICDR) Catalogue ▢ 188
Intercultural Communication: A Reader ▢ 20
Intercultural Interviewing: The Key to Effective Hiring in a Multicultural Workforce ▢ 106
Intercultural Marriage: Promises and Pitfalls ▢ 48
Intercultural Press Catalogue ▢ 188
International Agencies and Programs ▢ 425, 869
International Business Case Studies for the Multicultural Marketplace ▢ 106
International Business Dictionary and Reference (The) ▢ 699
International Businesswoman of the 1990s (The) ▢ 84, 106
International Career and Employment Network ▢ 420
International Centre for Research on Women ▢ 84, 191
International Centre, Queen's University ▢ 139, 244
International Development Research Centre (IDRC) ▢ 191
International Dimensions of Human Resource Management ▢ 431, 699
International Dimensions of Organizational Behaviour ▢ 106
International Directory for Youth Internships ▢ 357, 842
International Directory of Canadian Studies ▢ 209
International Directory of Importers (The) ▢ 436, 699
International Directory of Voluntary Work (The) ▢ 139
International Educator (The) ▢ 589
International Educators Co-operative Inc. 593
International Employment Gazette ▢ 431, 433
International Employment Hotline ▢ 431
International Employment Resources ▢ 431
International Employment Resources, On-line ▢ 420, 431
International Federation of Red Cross and Red Crescent Network ▢ 440
International Handbook of Universities ▢ 209
International Human Rights Resources ▢ 191
International Jobs ▢ 431
International Jobs and Expat Career Opportunities ▢ 420
International Jobs Directory: A Guide to Over 1001 Employers (The) ▢ 431
International Journal of Intercultural Relations ▢ 20
International Language Schools ▢ ▢ 74
International Marine Mammal Association Inc. (IMMA) ▢ 869
International Resources Group ▢ 420
International Retail Price Comparisons (Post Indexes) ▢ 50, 517
International Schools Services (ISS) 593
International Telephone Directory ▢ 417
International Trade Tips ▢ 699
International Travel and Health ▢ 46
International Travel Health Guide (The) ▢ 47

International Workcamp Directory ☐ 139
International Youth and Young Workers Exchange Programs ☐ 139, 209, 357
Internet Access Essentials ☐ 406
Internet for Dummies (The) ☐ 406
Internet Job Surfer ☐ 420
Internet Jumpstation ☐ 411
Internet Literacy Consultants ☐ 405
Internet Sleuth (The) ☐ 411
Internet TESL Journal (For Teachers of English as a Second Language) (The) ☐.....................................587
Internships & Careers in International Affairs ☐ 358, 842
Internships 1997: The Hotlist for Job Hunters ☐ 358
Internships in Foreign and Defense Policy: a Complete Guide for Women (& Men) ☐ 84, 139, 358
Internships ☐ 358
Introducing the World:
    A Guide to Developing International and Global Awareness Programs ☐ 194
Invest Yourself: The Catalogue of Volunteer Opportunities ☐ 139
Irish Jobs Page (The) ☐ 420, 541
ISS Directory of Overseas Schools (The) ☐ 49, 589
It's Only Right: A Practical Guide for
    Learning About the Convention on the Rights of the Child ☐ 194
Japanese For Professionals ☐ 73
Job and Career Related Sites ☐ 420
Job Listings ☐ 420
Job Serve ☐...421, 541, 551
Job Track ☐..421
Jobs Abroad: Opportunities Overseas ☐ 139, 438
Jobs and Careers with Nonprofit Organizations ☐ 770
Jobs for People Who Love Travel ☐ 442
Jobs in Japan: The Complete Guide to Living and Working in the Land of Rising Opportunity ☐ 558, 589
Jobs in Paradise ☐ 442
Jobs in Russia and the Newly Independent States ☐ 548
Jobs Worldwide ☐ 432
JobWeb ☐ 421
John December's Internet Guide ☐ 405
K.I.S. Recruiters...593
Kibbutz Volunteer ☐ 140
Kiss, Bow or Shake Hands: How to Do Business in Sixty Countries ☐ 106, 517
Kumarian Press Catalogue ☐...188
La recherche d'un emploi dans les organisations internationales ☐ 432, 870
Language 3 Initiative (The) ☐..74
Language Resource Center, American University ☐...74
Latin America Traveller ☐...179, 425, 535
Latin American Weekly Reports ☐ 535
Le Monde ☐ 186
Learning Across Cultures ☐ 194, 210
Learning Adventures Around the World ☐..210
Let's Go Guides ☐..179
Life on the Internet Resource Lists ☐ 411
Living and Working in America ☐ 525
Living and Working in Israel ☐ 551
Living in China: A Guide to Teaching and Studying in China including Taiwan ☐.................................558, 589
Living in the USA ☐ 526
Lonely Planet Travel Survival Kits ☐ 179
Lonely Planet ☐ 179, 425
Looking for Work Series (The) ☐ 397
Lynne Rienner Catalogue ☐...188
Make a Mil-Yen: Teaching English in Japan ☐ 589
Making it in Japan ☐...589
Management in Two Cultures: Bridging the Gap between US and Mexican Managers ☐.......................526, 535
Managing Cultural Differences ☐ 106
Managing the Nonprofit Organization ☐ 770

Manchester Guardian Weekly 🔲 186
Master Craft 🖳 421, 433
Mastering the Internet 🔲 406
Médecins Sans Frontières/Doctors Without Borders (MSF) 140, 440
MedHunters 🖳 440
MERX 🖳 567, 714, 737
Michigan State University 593
Mind Your Manners: Managing Business Cultures in Europe 🔲 541, 548
Mindsets: The Role of Culture and Perception in International Relations 🔲 107, 726
Monarch ESL Catalogue 🔲 194, 590
Monster Board (The) 🖳 421
Moody's International Manual 🔲 436
Moving Abroad 🔲 50
Moving Your Family Overseas 🔲 48
Multiculturalism Means Business: a Directory of Business Contacts 🔲 436, 699
Multi-sector Directory of BC Global Organizations and Resources 🔲 🖳 191, 770
NACEL International 🖳 166
NAFSA's Guide to Education Abroad for Advisors and Administrators 🔲 210
National Graduate Register 🖳 397, 421
Natural Science and Engineering Research Council of Canada
    (NSERC)–International Relations 🖳 219
NetJobs 🖳 421
New Internationalist (The) 🔲 🖳 191, 194, 244
New York Times 🔲 187
Newbies Anonymous: A Newcomer's Guide to the Internet 🖳 405
NGLS Handbook 770, 842
No Fixed Address 🔲 66, 726
Now Hiring! Jobs in Asia 🔲 559
Now Hiring! Jobs in Eastern Europe 🔲 548, 590
NTC's Grammar Series 🔲 74
O-Hayo Sensei 🖳 590
On a Shoestring Guides 🔲 179
On Being Foreign: Culture Shock in Short Fiction, an International Anthology 🔲 20, 66, 194
ON VILLAGE Yellow Guide 🖳 417
Once Again At Forty 🔲 67, 179
On-Line Job Search Companion (The) 🔲 416
Online Study Abroad Directory 🖳 210, 219
Open Network Trade Resources Access (onTrac) 🖳 699
Opportunities in Foreign Language Careers 🔲 441
OPTIONS (Project Concern International) 440
Outpost: The Traveller's Journal 🔲 67, 180
Overseas American-Sponsored Elementary and
    Secondary Schools Assisted by the US Department of State 🔲 🖳 49, 590
Overseas Employment 🖳 421, 559
Overseas Jobs Express 🖳 140, 422, 432
Overseas Placement Services for Educators 593
Overseas Summer Jobs 🔲 140
Overseas Work for Teachers 🖳 590
Oxfam Country Profiles 🔲 191, 517
Oxfam Handbook of Development and Relief (The) 🔲 191, 568
Oxfam Poverty Report (The) 🔲 191
Pacific Rim Profiles 🔲 195, 559
PACT Publications Catalogue 🔲 568, 770
Passport to Overseas Employment: 100,000 Job Opportunities Abroad 🔲 432
Peace Corps and More: 120 Ways to Work, Study and Travel in the Third World 🔲 140
People Development Ltd. 126
Peterson's Guides 🔲 🖳 210, 244
Polaris Internet Guide 🖳 406
Principal International Businesses: The World Marketing Directory 🔲 436
Purdue International Career Center 🖳 422
Queen's Teachers' Overseas Recruiting Fair 594

Re-Entry Counselling Services 126
Reference Canada ▢ 714
Renouf Catalogue ▢ 188
Report on Business: Canada Company Handbook ▢ 436
Resources for Development and Relief: 1996 Oxfam Catalogue ▢ 192, 568
Resumes that Work: How to Sell Yourself on Paper ▢ 396
Reuters On-Line ▢ 425
Review ▢ ▢ 192
Rice Paper Ceiling (The) ▢ 559
Riding the Waves of Culture: Understanding Diversity in Global Business ▢ 107
Rising Sun on Main Street: Working with the Japanese (The) ▢ 559
Roosters at Two A.M. ▢ 67
Rough Guides ▢ 180
Round-the-World Travel Guide ▢ 180
Russian and Eastern European Institute Employment Opportunities ▢ 422, 548
SASIS INC ▢ 422, 536, 551
Schools Abroad of Interest to Americans ▢ 49, 590
Search Associates 594
Service Contracts and Lines of Credit ▢ 436, 568, 738
Signposts: Looking for Work in International Development ▢ 568, 738
SJM Consulting 126
Smart Interviewer (The) ▢ 396
So You Want To Export? ▢ 699
South Magazine ▢ 187
Spain is Different ▢ 542
Special Career Opportunities for Linguists/Translators/Interpreters ▢ 441
Spending a Year Abroad ▢ 140
Sports Scholarships and College Athletic Programs in the USA ▢ 210, 219
StatsCan Online ▢ 699
Staying Healthy While Living in Canada ▢ 47, 166
Stone Bridge Catalogue ▢ ▢ 559
Strategis ▢ 699
Student Center (The) ▢ 398, 422, 425
Student Travels Magazine ▢ 140, 210
Students Abroad, Strangers At Home: Education for a Global Society ▢ 211
Study Abroad 1997/1998 Council Study Centres ▢ 211, 358
Study Abroad ▢ 211
Study Abroad ▢ 211, 219
Studying Abroad / Learning Abroad ▢ 211
Summer Jobs Britain ▢ 542
Summer Jobs Search ▢ 140
Summer Jobs USA ▢ 141, 526
Supplyline ▢ ▢ 568, 699
Survival Kit for Overseas Living ▢ 20, 107
Swan's How to Pick the Right People Program ▢ 396
Taiwan Business Primer (The) ▢ 559
Teach Yourself Series ▢ 74
Teach Yourself the Internet in 24 Hours ▢ 406
Teaching English Abroad ▢ 590
Teaching English—Japan: Finding Work, Teaching, and Living in Japan ▢ 590
Teaching Overseas Information Handbook (The) ▢ 590
T.E.L. Opportunities (Teach the English Language) 594
Ten Steps for Export Success ▢ ▢ 700
TESOL Online (Teachers of English to Speakers of Other Languages ▢ 422, 591
TESOL Placement Service 594
Third World Guide ▢ 192
Third World Quarterly: Journal of Emerging Areas ▢ 192
Third World Resource Directory: A Guide to Organizations and Publications ▢ 568, 771
Third World Resurgence ▢ 192
This Week in Trade and Foreign Policy ▢ 727
Three Boxes of Life: An Introduction to Life Work Planning (The) ▢ 396

Times Educational Supplement ◫ 591
Tips for Travellers Series ◫ 517
Top Companies to Work for in Canada (The) ◫ 397
Total Physical Response ◲ 74
Tourism Offices Worldwide Directory ◲ 180, 425
Tourism Training Institute..442
Trade Office for the Mexican Embassy ◲ 536
Transcending Stereotypes: Discovering Japanese Culture and Education ◫ 591
Transcultural Leadership: Empowering the Diverse Workforce ◫...107
Transcultural Odysseys: The Evolving Global Consciousness ◫ 20, 126
Transitions Abroad: The Magazine of Overseas Opportunities ◫ 141, 180, 211
Travel Cuts..180
Travel Finder ◲ 180, 411, 425
Travel That Can Change Your Life: How to Create a Transformative Experience ◫ 67, 180
Travel Tips for the 90's ◫..180
Travel with Children ◫...48, 181
Traveler's Medical Alert Series (Mexico and China) ◫...47
Travelers' Self-Care Manual:
   A Self-Help Guide to Emergency Medical Treatment for the Traveler ◫ 47
Traveller's Reading Guide (The) ◫ 181
Travels with a Laptop: Canadian Journalists Head South ◫ 67
TravLang's Foreign Language for Travelers ◲ 74
"Treasures and Pleasures... Best of the Best" Series (The) ◫ 181
Trillium Human Resources Inc..440
Understanding and Working with the Japanese Business World ◫ 559
Understanding Arabs: A Guide for Westerners ◫ 551, 727
Understanding Cultural Differences: Germans, French and Americans ◫...526, 542
United Nations Handbook ◫..842
United Nations System ◲ 842
United Nations Volunteers ◲ 141, 358, 843
United States Postal Service ◲ 417
United States State Department ◲ 425
University Affairs ◫ 244
University of Alberta International Centre ◲ 207
Unlocking Japan's Distribution System in the '90s: The Complete Exporter's Guide ◫ 559
Unlocking the Japanese Business Mind ◫ 560
Update ◫ 211
UPDATE ◫..51
US Government National trade Data Bank ◲ 526, 700
US Immigration Resource for Canadians ◲..526
Vacancies in International Organizations ◲...432, 870
Vacation Study Abroad ◫ 181, 211
Vehicle Exports ◲..51
Virtual Internet Guide ◲...406
Virtual Library on International Development ◲...192, 568, 738
Waiting for Li Ming ◫..67
Wall Street Journal ◫...187
We Europeans ◫ 542
Web Magazine (The) ◫ ◲..181, 406
Web Sites All Countries: Martindale's "The Reference Desk" ◲ 181, 425
Web Sites on Africa and the Middle East ◲ 426
Web Sites on Asia/Pacific ◲ 426
Web Sites on Eastern Europe and the Former Soviet Union ◲ 426
Web Sites on Latin America and the Caribbean ◲ 426
Web Sites on Western Europe ◲ 426
Western Economic Diversification ◲ 700
Westview Press Catalogue ◫ 188
What Colour Is Your Parachute?
   A Practical Manual for Job Hunters and Career Changers (The 1997) ◫..396
What In The World Is Going On?
   A Guide For Canadians Wishing to Work, Volunteer, or Study in Other Countries ◫ 141, 212, 219

When Business East Meets Business West:
The Guide to Practice and Protocol in the Pacific Rim ⌨ 560
When Cultures Collide: Managing Successfully Across Cultures ⌨ 107
Where in the World Are You Going? ⌨ 48
Where There is No Doctor: A Village Health Care Handbook: Revised Edition ⌨ 47, 440
Whole World Guide to Culture Learning (The) ⌨ 21, 181
Whole World Guide to Language Learning (The) ⌨ 74
WhoWhere ⌨ 417
Wiley Publishers and Distributors Catalogue ⌨ 188
With Respect to the Japanese: A Guide for Americans ⌨ 560
Women in Management Worldwide ⌨ 85, 107
Women on the Move: A Christian Perspective on Cross-Cultural Adaptation ⌨ 21, 85
Women's Guide to Overseas Living ⌨ 49, 85
Work Abroad: The Complete Guide to Finding a Job Overseas ⌨ 141, 432
Work Your Way Around The World ⌨ 141, 181, 601
Working Abroad: The Daily Telegraph Guide to Living and Working Overseas ⌨ 51
Working as a Holiday Rep ⌨ 442
Working in Asia: A Fact-Filled Guide to Working Opportunities ⌨ 560
Working in Ski Resorts—Europe & North America ⌨ 442
Working on Cruise Ships ⌨ 442
World 1995/1996: A Third World Guide (The) ⌨ 192
World Bank and Cooperation with NGOs (The) ⌨ 771, 843
World Bank Group (The) ⌨ 841, 869
World Development ⌨ 192
World in Your Kitchen (The) ⌨ 193
World of Learning 1997 ⌨ 212
World of Maps Catalogue ⌨ ⌨ 182
World on a String: How to become a Freelance Foreign Correspondent (The) ⌨ 441, 601
World Press Review ⌨ 187
World Trade Organization ⌨ 700, 843
World Wide Web Employment Office (The) ⌨ 422
World Wildlife Fund-Canada ⌨ 870
WorldClass ⌨ 422, 700
WorldWorks ⌨ 141
Yahoo's List of International Organizations ⌨ 870
Yearbook of International Organizations ⌨ 436, 870
Yin and Tang of American Values (The) ⌨ 21, 526, 560
Your Guide to Canadian Colleges ⌨ 245
Your Guide to Working With CIDA ⌨ ⌨ 738
Your Own Business in Europe ⌨ 542
Youth Link 1997-1998 ⌨ ⌨ 142, 398
Youth Resource Network of Canada's International Job Opportunities Page ⌨ 142, 358, 398, 422
Zen and the Art of the Internet ⌨ 407

ID Number Index

This is an index to the page location of the ID numbers found throughout this book. Every resource listing and organization profile has a randomly generated and unique ID number (for example: [ID:5683] is for BOMBARDIER INC., and [ID:2708] is for the Canadian magazine *Outpost: The Traveller's Journal*). We use these ID numbers on our web site to help you quickly search for any corresponding updated information, such as an address change. You may also want to use the ID number as a quick pointer when doing your job research with this book. (For example, you may note to yourself, "Call these organizations for application procedures: ID:5683 page 624, and ID:6196 page 853.") You may find this quicker than writing the full name of the organization.

We are relying on reader feedback to help us keep the contact and resource information in this book current. If you have any information you want us to share or research, visit us at *www.WorkingOverseas.com*. Please also include the ID number to identify the organization profile or resource when contacting us by phone, e-mail, or via our web site. (See inside front cover for publisher's contact information.) And while visiting our web site, keep an eye out for new and related services. The 1998 third edition will be regularly updated on our site until December of the year 2001.

1000: 769
1001: 19
1002: 560
1004: 696
1005: 105, 697
1007: 442
1009: 699
1011: 105, 166
1014: 397
1015: 396
1016: 396
1021: 19, 517
1022: 396
1023: 211
1024: 525, 557
1025: 18
1027: 524
1029: 209, 219
1031: 535
1032: 74
1034: 21, 85
1035: 542
1036: 547
1037: 551, 727
1038: 560
1039: 442

1040: 358, 842
1041: 194
1043: 358
1044: 139, 438
1045: 188
1046: 139
1048: 395
1049: 395
1050: 430
1051: 432
1055: 541
1057: 435
1062: 436
1063: 397
1066: 431
1067: 208
1071: 357, 842
1075: 217
1076: 435
1079: 208, 218
1083: 178
1085: 19, 104
1085: 516
1087: 437
1088: 434, 726, 904

1089: 424, 697, 726, 890
1090: 141, 212, 219
1091: 218
1094: 768
1095: 770
1100: 568, 738
1101: 104, 567, 737
1103: 436, 568, 738
1105: 188
1107: 45
1110: 190
1111: 559, 589
1112: 557
1114: 771, 843
1115: 568, 700
1117: 190
1118: 217, 243, 357, 534
1120: 441
1132: 591
1137: 177
1143: 431
1144: 49, 104, 516
1146: 212
1147: 434

1148: 435, 869
1149: 435, 697
1150: 430, 869
1152: 139
1153: 430
1154: 141, 181, 601
1155: 137
1158: 138, 208, 769
1159: 46, 441
1161: 187
1162: 244, 541
1166: 396
1167: 48, 589
1168: 181, 211
1169: 207
1177: 20, 107
1180: 84, 106
1182: 107
1183: 431, 699
1184: 425, 516
1186: 209
1188: 436, 699
1190: 589
1193: 559
1198: 437, 870
1199: 50

1204: 434
1205: 141, 182, 212
1207: 137
1208: 436
1209: 557, 588
1211: 74
1212: 191, 194, 244
1213: 842
1217: 142, 182
1218: 19, 104
1219: 769
1220: 435, 567, 769
1221: 568, 771
1224: 48, 590
1225: 48, 588
1228: 568, 771
1229: 191
1230: 442
1231: 178
1232: 430
1233: 48, 590
1236: 437
1237: 726, 904
1239: 211, 219
1242: 714
1244: 218

1245: 84, 139, 358
1247: 140
1248: 20
1249: 187
1251: 396
1253: 141, 180, 211
1254: 45
1256: 515
1258: 842
1263: 435, 567, 770
1267: 49
1268: 138
1269: 139
1272: 434, 525
1274: 209, 589
1275: 431, 433
1284: 47, 181
1285: 46
1286: 180
1288: 517
1291: 725
1293: 46
1299: 770
1303: 567, 737, 842
1305: 559
1306: 590
1307: 47, 84, 601
1309: 19, 47
1310: 436, 699
1313: 517, 540
1314: 138, 166
1315: 526, 542
1316: 526
1317: 525, 558
1320: 47
1321: 47
1322: 48, 85
1324: 138, 166, 208
1327: 107, 726
1329: 209
1332: 20
1335: 18, 524
1337: 104
1340: 178
1341: 66
1342: 66, 727
1343: 726
1344: 65, 726
1347: 138
1348: 433, 768
1349: 698, 714
1350: 105
1351: 526, 535
1354: 559
1357: 105
1358: 106
1359: 18
1361: 535
1362: 558
1363: 45
1365: 243
1366: 48, 208
1380: 19, 193, 588
1381: 18, 193
1382: 19, 516
1383: 557
1385: 20, 66, 195

1388: 104
1391: 106
1392: 556
1397: 188
1398: 194
1399: 20, 181
1405: 84, 558
1417: 137
1418: 138, 208, 540
1419: 442
1425: 357
1429: 558, 589
1431: 140
1432: 49, 517
1436: 439
1446: 441
1448: 138, 437, 439
1451: 180
1454: 218
1457: 441
1458: 437
1459: 179, 698
1468: 550
1470: 548
1472: 432
1477: 441
1478: 179
1480: 179
1484: 179
1486: 177
1487: 83, 177
1490: 181
1495: 696, 726
1496: 434
1497: 517, 698
1498: 699
1503: 188
1504: 45
1507: 434
1508: 696
1509: 436
1511: 435
1512: 434, 697
1518: 397
1521: 187
1528: 589
1538: 217
1543: 210, 244
1552: 211
1556: 697
1563: 45
1565: 217, 437
1566: 218, 588
1570: 697
1571: 525, 535
1572: 698
1573: 50
1578: 194, 590
1579: 103
1580: 106
1584: 65
1585: 193
1586: 192
1587: 432, 870
1589: 697, 726, 890
1590: 700
1591: 141, 526

1592: 589
1593: 210, 219
1597: 434, 890
1598: 103
1599: 567, 769
1605: 210
1609: 193
1611: 194
1614: 194
1616: 193
1619: 84, 103
1621: 85, 107
1623: 245
1624: 46
1626: 698
1631: 106
1634: 218
1635: 186, 430
1636: 524, 534, 695
1638: 437, 567, 769
1639: 179
1640: 209
1642: 209
1643: 890
1645: 727
1648: 192
1649: 190
1650: 186
1651: 190
1652: 187
1653: 187
1654: 186
1655: 186
1656: 186
1657: 192
1658: 66, 179
1659: 725
1660: 66
1661: 736
1662: 736
1663: 560
1665: 432
1666: 243, 357, 397
1668: 217
1670: 526
1671: 431
1672: 541
1673: 525
1674: 541
1676: 139
1677: 49
1678: 601
1679: 209
1680: 589
1682: 138
1683: 140
1686: 516
1687: 194, 210
1689: 591
1690: 18
1691: 542
1692: 107
1695: 106
1699: 45
1701: 46, 167
1702: 45, 166
1704: 180

1706: 591
1708: 192
1709: 535
1710: 83
1711: 182
1712: 188
1713: 188
1714: 188
1715: 189
1751: 770
1752: 442
1753: 442
1754: 442
1755: 559
1756: 548, 590
1758: 177, 207
1761: 437
1762: 435, 698
1774: 181
1781: 73
1782: 696
1784: 398
1787: 47, 84, 179
1788: 430
1795: 17, 65
1796: 416
1797: 142, 398
1798: 416
1799: 416
1801: 395
1804: 358
1807: 590
1810: 560
1814: 395
2372: 107
2375: 46, 126
2376: 107
2377: 103
2378: 105
2379: 105
2380: 541, 548
2381: 104
2382: 557
2383: 106, 517
2384: 19
2385: 557
2386: 540
2389: 440
2390: 439
2391: 439
2392: 47
2395: 540
2396: 525, 550
2397: 547
2399: 18, 189
2400: 106
2401: 190
2404: 195, 559
2405: 140, 210
2406: 559
2407: 83, 556
2408: 560
2409: 556
2411: 559
2412: 190
2413: 189
2414: 166

2415: 557, 588
2416: 73
2417: 74
2418: 74
2419: 395
2420: 166
2422: 433
2423: 207
2424: 219
2425: 142
2426: 84, 105
2428: 568, 192
2429: 21, 526, 560
2430: 74
2432: 139, 244
2433: 430
2435: 442
2436: 442
2437: 558
2440: 551
2441: 551
2443: 542
2444: 179
2445: 395, 419
2446: 20, 126
2447: 211
2449: 567, 769
2450: 192, 568, 738
2451: 84, 191
2452: 191
2453: 190, 439, 567
2454: 190
2455: 430, 433
2456: 439
2457: 433, 438
2459: 431
2460: 440
2462: 769
2466: 558
2468: 66, 180
2469: 438
2472: 244
2473: 207, 243
2474: 50
2475: 541
2477: 217
2478: 590
2479: 191, 568
2480: 192
2481: 192
2482: 141, 358, 843
2483: 191, 517
2484: 536
2485: 418
2486: 418
2487: 418, 525
2488: 418
2489: 714
2490: 441
2491: 419
2492: 418
2493: 243
2494: 244
2495: 218
2497: 210
2498: 542
2499: 140

2500: 558
2501: 541
2502: 191
2503: 191
2504: 190
2505: 139, 210, 358
2506: 420
2512: 397, 420
2513: 397, 419
2514: 421
2515: 140
2516: 556
2517: 696, 714
2518: 699
2519: 588
2520: 422, 536, 551
2521: 142, 358, 398, 422
2522: 406
2523: 406
2524: 406
2525: 406
2526: 406
2527: 181, 407
2528: 407
2529: 431
2530: 420
2532: 435
2533: 66
2534: 698
2535: 697, 890
2536: 420
2537: 421
2538: 421, 433
2539: 421
2540: 421
2541: 140, 422, 432
2542: 398, 422, 425
2543: 422
2544: 418
2545: 419
2546: 419
2547: 419, 588
2548: 420
2549: 420, 431
2550: 420
2551: 420
2552: 421, 559
2553: 422
2554: 439
2555: 49, 517
2556: 189
2557: 192
2558: 141, 432
2560: 74
2561: 74
2562: 540
2563: 425, 869
2564: 74
2565: 178, 425, 890, 904
2566: 421, 714
2567: 189
2568: 191
2569: 869
2570: 440
2571: 140, 440

2572: 842
2573: 432, 870
2574: 841, 869
2575: 870
2577: 73
2578: 177
2579: 410
2580: 178
2580: 424, 516
2581: 420, 436
2582: 179, 425
2583: 180, 411, 425
2584: 422, 700
2587: 410
2588: 411
2589: 411
2590: 411
2592: 417
2594: 411
2596: 411
2597: 411
2598: 411
2603: 417
2605: 714
2606: 714
2607: 74
2608: 556, 696, 841
2609: 698, 842
2610: 700, 843
2611: 398, 421
2612: 74
2613: 699
2614: 83, 556
2615: 587
2616: 526, 700
2617: 566, 736
2618: 697
2620: 592
2621: 416
2622: 20, 65, 84
2623: 440
2624: 440
2625: 591
2626: 591
2627: 592
2628: 592
2629: 592
2630: 592
2631: 593
2632: 593
2633: 593
2634: 593
2635: 594
2636: 594
2637: 594
2638: 594
2639: 594
2640: 737
2641: 737
2642: 18, 103, 126, 737
2643: 737
2644: 187, 737
2645: 568, 714, 738
2646: 738
2647: 433
2648: 698, 842

2649: 696
2650: 425
2651: 416
2652: 410
2657: 405
2659: 405
2660: 715
2661: 424
2662: 425
2663: 426
2664: 426
2666: 426
2667: 426
2668: 426
2670: 405
2671: 406
2672: 406
2673: 405
2678: 243
2679: 45, 178
2680: 193
2681: 211
2682: 211, 358
2683: 210, 219
2684: 593
2685: 438
2686: 438
2687: 424
2694: 416
2695: 417
2696: 417
2697: 417
2698: 417
2699: 417
2700: 770, 842
2705: 188
2706: 188
2707: 419, 547
2708: 66, 180
2709: 442
2710: 244
2711: 441, 601
2712: 126
2713: 126
2714: 73
2715: 126
2717: 208
2719: 49
2723: 869
2724: 870
2725: 418, 696
2727: 700
2731: 243
2732: 601
2733: 218
2734: 587
2735: 441
2736: 180, 425
2737: 180
2739: 590
2745: 177
2746: 178, 890
2747: 178
2750: 421, 541, 551
2752: 769
2755: 418, 556
2756: 420, 541

2757: 50, 525
2757: 697
2759: 535, 698
2760: 699
2761: 699
2762: 178
2765: 50
2767: 526
2768: 181, 425
2769: 179, 425, 535
2770: 419, 558
2772: 422, 548
2774: 49
2775: 48, 103, 516
2776: 126
2778: 49
2779: 535
2783: 770
2784: 410
2790: 587
2791: 422, 591
2792: 419, 588
2793: 187
2794: 516
2795: 191, 770
5000: 143
5001: 143
5003: 143
5004: 143
5005: 144
5006: 144
5007: 144
5008: 145
5009: 145
5015: 145
5017: 146
5018: 146
5019: 147
5020: 147
5021: 147
5024: 148
5025: 148
5026: 148
5027: 149
5028: 149
5029: 149
5030: 150
5031: 150
5032: 150
5035: 150
5037: 151
5038: 156
5039: 152
5040: 152
5041: 152
5042: 153
5043: 153
5044: 214
5045: 153
5046: 359
5047: 154
5048: 154
5049: 156
5050: 155
5051: 155
5053: 155
5054: 156

5057: 157
5058: 157
5059: 157
5061: 157
5062: 158
5064: 158
5065: 158
5066: 158
5067: 159
5069: 159
5070: 160
5071: 160
5072: 161
5074: 161
5075: 167
5076: 167
5077: 168
5078: 168
5079: 169
5081: 170
5083: 169
5084: 170
5086: 195
5087: 195
5088: 195
5089: 792
5092: 196
5094: 196
5095: 196
5097: 196
5100: 196
5101: 196
5102: 197
5103: 197
5105: 197
5109: 197
5115: 199
5117: 198
5119: 199
5122: 199
5123: 199
5124: 199
5125: 200
5127: 213
5134: 232
5135: 224
5140: 228
5142: 225
5144: 223
5146: 225
5147: 224
5149: 232
5150: 226
5151: 227
5152: 227
5154: 225
5157: 235
5158: 229
5159: 222
5160: 223
5161: 230
5162: 228
5163: 231
5164: 226
5165: 228
5166: 229
5167: 235

5168: 232	**5254:** 292	**5329:** 261	**5409:** 338	**5544:** 360
5169: 227	**5255:** 292	**5330:** 262	**5410:** 339	**5547:** 364
5170: 223	**5256:** 293	**5331:** 262	**5411:** 339	**5548:** 364
5171: 231	**5257:** 293	**5332:** 263	**5412:** 339	**5549:** 365
5173: 227	**5258:** 293	**5333:** 263	**5413:** 340	**5550:** 365
5174: 230	**5259:** 294	**5334:** 263	**5415:** 340	**5551:** 366
5175: 231	**5260:** 294	**5335:** 265	**5416:** 340	**5552:** 367
5176: 234	**5261:** 295	**5336:** 266	**5417:** 344	**5554:** 367
5177: 231	**5263:** 295	**5337:** 266	**5418:** 347	**5555:** 367
5178: 224	**5264:** 295	**5339:** 267	**5419:** 347	**5558:** 368
5180: 221	**5265:** 295	**5340:** 281	**5420:** 347	**5560:** 369
5181: 221	**5266:** 296	**5341:** 281	**5421:** 347	**5561:** 369
5182: 225	**5267:** 282	**5342:** 281	**5422:** 347	**5562:** 370
5183: 232	**5268:** 304	**5344:** 282	**5423:** 343	**5563:** 370
5184: 235	**5270:** 312	**5346:** 276	**5424:** 348	**5564:** 370
5185: 232	**5271:** 313	**5347:** 287	**5425:** 341	**5566:** 371
5186: 233	**5272:** 314	**5348:** 288	**5426:** 348	**5567:** 159
5187: 223	**5273:** 314	**5349:** 288	**5427:** 348	**5568:** 371
5189: 222	**5274:** 314	**5350:** 288	**5428:** 342	**5569:** 371
5192: 234	**5275:** 316	**5351:** 288	**5430:** 347	**5570:** 372
5193: 231	**5276:** 320	**5353:** 289	**5431:** 341	**5571:** 372
5195: 234	**5277:** 316	**5354:** 302	**5432:** 348	**5573:** 705
5196: 235	**5278:** 318	**5355:** 302	**5434:** 344	**5574:** 705
5197: 235	**5279:** 318	**5356:** 303	**5435:** 346	**5575:** 706
5198: 234	**5280:** 318	**5357:** 303	**5439:** 342	**5576:** 707
5199: 236	**5281:** 319	**5359:** 305	**5440:** 344	**5577:** 705
5202: 226	**5282:** 319	**5360:** 306	**5441:** 342	**5578:** 704
5206: 230	**5283:** 319	**5361:** 306	**5442:** 349	**5579:** 702
5207: 254	**5284:** 326	**5363:** 315	**5443:** 341	**5580:** 701
5208: 254	**5285:** 327	**5364:** 317	**5444:** 348	**5581:** 704
5210: 264	**5286:** 305	**5365:** 317	**5445:** 348	**5584:** 708
5211: 264	**5287:** 305	**5366:** 322	**5446:** 344	**5586:** 706
5212: 267	**5288:** 306	**5367:** 324	**5447:** 348	**5587:** 707
5213: 268	**5289:** 306	**5368:** 322	**5448:** 348	**5589:** 703
5214: 268	**5290:** 297	**5369:** 323	**5449:** 341	**5590:** 707
5215: 269	**5291:** 296	**5371:** 322	**5452:** 347	**5591:** 701
5216: 270	**5294:** 298	**5372:** 324	**5453:** 348	**5592:** 703
5217: 269	**5295:** 298	**5373:** 322	**5454:** 343	**5595:** 708
5218: 270	**5296:** 298	**5374:** 324	**5455:** 348	**5596:** 708
5219: 271	**5297:** 300	**5375:** 324	**5456:** 342	**5597:** 708
5220: 271	**5298:** 317	**5376:** 325	**5457:** 349	**5598:** 708
5222: 271	**5299:** 279	**5378:** 325	**5458:** 349	**5599:** 708
5223: 272	**5300:** 310	**5379:** 325	**5459:** 342	**5600:** 708
5225: 272	**5302:** 309	**5380:** 328	**5460:** 347	**5601:** 708
5226: 273	**5303:** 279	**5381:** 329	**5461:** 341	**5602:** 708
5227: 272	**5304:** 308	**5382:** 329	**5462:** 342	**5603:** 708
5228: 272	**5305:** 308	**5383:** 330	**5463:** 342	**5604:** 708
5229: 273	**5306:** 307	**5386:** 331	**5464:** 344	**5606:** 708
5231: 316	**5307:** 285	**5387:** 331	**5465:** 344	**5607:** 709
5232: 258	**5308:** 285	**5388:** 331	**5466:** 343	**5611:** 709
5234: 274	**5309:** 285	**5389:** 332	**5467:** 349	**5613:** 710
5235: 275	**5311:** 286	**5390:** 332	**5468:** 347	**5615:** 710
5237: 276	**5312:** 793	**5392:** 332	**5469:** 347	**5616:** 710
5238: 277	**5313:** 286	**5393:** 334	**5470:** 343	**5617:** 710
5239: 277	**5314:** 287	**5394:** 333	**5471:** 349	**5618:** 710
5240: 277	**5316:** 286	**5395:** 333	**5472:** 341	**5622:** 711
5241: 277	**5317:** 267	**5396:** 334	**5473:** 346	**5623:** 711
5243: 278	**5318:** 267	**5397:** 335	**5474:** 344	**5624:** 711
5244: 278	**5319:** 255	**5398:** 335	**5475:** 347	**5625:** 711
5245: 278	**5321:** 256	**5399:** 336	**5476:** 346	**5626:** 711
5247: 290	**5322:** 256	**5400:** 283	**5477:** 346	**5627:** 711
5248: 291	**5323:** 257	**5402:** 333	**5478:** 348	**5628:** 711
5249: 291	**5324:** 257	**5404:** 336	**5479:** 346	**5629:** 711
5250: 290	**5325:** 260	**5405:** 338	**5480:** 348	**5630:** 711
5251: 291	**5326:** 261	**5406:** 337	**5481:** 342	**5631:** 712
5252: 290	**5327:** 261	**5407:** 337	**5491:** 278	**5632:** 712
5253: 292	**5328:** 260	**5408:** 339	**5543:** 359	**5633:** 712

5635: 712	**5734:** 643	**5825:** 671	**5913:** 744	**5991:** 779
5636: 712	**5736:** 640	**5826:** 671	**5914:** 744	**5992:** 779
5637: 712	**5737:** 641	**5828:** 672	**5915:** 745	**5993:** 780
5638: 712	**5741:** 641	**5829:** 672	**5916:** 745	**5994:** 780
5639: 712	**5743:** 641	**5830:** 688	**5917:** 746	**5995:** 781
5640: 712	**5744:** 643	**5833:** 673	**5918:** 746	**5996:** 782
5641: 712	**5747:** 643	**5834:** 673	**5919:** 746	**5997:** 782
5643: 712	**5748:** 644	**5835:** 673	**5920:** 747	**5998:** 782
5644: 712	**5752:** 645	**5836:** 674	**5921:** 748	**6000:** 782
5646: 614	**5753:** 646	**5837:** 676	**5922:** 748	**6001:** 783
5648: 614	**5754:** 647	**5838:** 674	**5923:** 758	**6002:** 784
5649: 615	**5755:** 648	**5840:** 674	**5924:** 748	**6003:** 784
5651: 615	**5757:** 648	**5841:** 674	**5925:** 749	**6004:** 784
5652: 616	**5758:** 687	**5842:** 675	**5926:** 749	**6005:** 785
5654: 617	**5760:** 648	**5843:** 675	**5927:** 750	**6006:** 785
5656: 617	**5761:** 649	**5844:** 676	**5928:** 750	**6008:** 786
5658: 617	**5763:** 649	**5845:** 676	**5929:** 651	**6009:** 786
5660: 618	**5764:** 641	**5846:** 677	**5930:** 751	**6010:** 786
5661: 621	**5765:** 649	**5847:** 677	**5931:** 752	**6011:** 787
5663: 618	**5766:** 650	**5848:** 678	**5932:** 752	**6013:** 787
5664: 619	**5767:** 650	**5849:** 678	**5933:** 753	**6014:** 787
5666: 619	**5768:** 650	**5851:** 679	**5935:** 661	**6015:** 816
5668: 619	**5770:** 651	**5852:** 679	**5936:** 753	**6016:** 788
5669: 619	**5771:** 652	**5854:** 680	**5937:** 759	**6017:** 788
5671: 661	**5772:** 652	**5857:** 681	**5938:** 754	**6018:** 789
5672: 620	**5773:** 653	**5858:** 681	**5939:** 754	**6019:** 790
5674: 620	**5775:** 654	**5859:** 616	**5940:** 747	**6020:** 790
5675: 623	**5776:** 653	**5860:** 681	**5941:** 754	**6021:** 790
5678: 622	**5778:** 653	**5861:** 637	**5942:** 755	**6022:** 791
5679: 622	**5779:** 654	**5862:** 681	**5943:** 756	**6023:** 791
5680: 622	**5780:** 655	**5863:** 682	**5944:** 756	**6025:** 793
5681: 623	**5781:** 655	**5865:** 683	**5946:** 756	**6026:** 783
5682: 624	**5782:** 655	**5866:** 683	**5947:** 669	**6027:** 794
5683: 624	**5783:** 656	**5868:** 683	**5948:** 757	**6028:** 794
5684: 624	**5784:** 657	**5869:** 684	**5949:** 757	**6029:** 795
5685: 625	**5786:** 657	**5872:** 685	**5950:** 757	**6030:** 795
5686: 625	**5788:** 657	**5875:** 685	**5952:** 757	**6031:** 796
5688: 627	**5789:** 658	**5876:** 686	**5953:** 758	**6032:** 796
5691: 628	**5791:** 658	**5877:** 686	**5954:** 758	**6033:** 797
5692: 628	**5792:** 658	**5878:** 686	**5955:** 760	**6034:** 797
5693: 629	**5795:** 639	**5879:** 686	**5956:** 760	**6036:** 797
5694: 629	**5796:** 659	**5880:** 687	**5957:** 761	**6037:** 797
5695: 630	**5797:** 660	**5881:** 687	**5958:** 761	**6038:** 798
5696: 630	**5798:** 660	**5883:** 688	**5960:** 761	**6039:** 799
5697: 630	**5799:** 660	**5884:** 688	**5961:** 680	**6041:** 800
5698: 682	**5800:** 661	**5885:** 689	**5962:** 762	**6043:** 800
5699: 631	**5801:** 662	**5886:** 689	**5963:** 762	**6045:** 801
5701: 631	**5802:** 662	**5888:** 689	**5964:** 762	**6046:** 801
5702: 632	**5803:** 663	**5890:** 690	**5965:** 740	**6047:** 802
5707: 633	**5805:** 663	**5891:** 691	**5966:** 772	**6050:** 803
5708: 633	**5806:** 664	**5892:** 691	**5967:** 772	**6051:** 803
5709: 670	**5807:** 664	**5893:** 691	**5968:** 772	**6053:** 803
5710: 634	**5808:** 665	**5894:** 692	**5969:** 773	**6054:** 804
5711: 634	**5809:** 665	**5895:** 692	**5971:** 773	**6056:** 805
5712: 635	**5810:** 666	**5897:** 692	**5972:** 773	**6057:** 805
5713: 635	**5811:** 666	**5899:** 739	**5973:** 774	**6058:** 806
5714: 636	**5812:** 666	**5900:** 739	**5975:** 774	**6059:** 806
5715: 636	**5813:** 666	**5901:** 739	**5976:** 775	**6060:** 806
5717: 637	**5815:** 667	**5902:** 740	**5977:** 775	**6061:** 806
5718: 637	**5817:** 668	**5903:** 741	**5978:** 810	**6062:** 807
5720: 638	**5818:** 668	**5904:** 741	**5979:** 776	**6063:** 283
5721: 638	**5819:** 668	**5905:** 626	**5981:** 776	**6064:** 807
5725: 638	**5820:** 669	**5907:** 741	**5983:** 777	**6065:** 807
5727: 671	**5821:** 669	**5909:** 742	**5984:** 777	**6066:** 807
5731: 639	**5822:** 669	**5910:** 742	**5987:** 777	**6068:** 808
5732: 640	**5823:** 670	**5911:** 743	**5989:** 778	**6070:** 808
5733: 640	**5824:** 671	**5912:** 743	**5990:** 778	**6071:** 808

6072: 809
6073: 809
6074: 809
6075: 809
6076: 810
6080: 811
6081: 811
6083: 811
6085: 812
6086: 812
6087: 813
6088: 813
6089: 813
6090: 814
6091: 814
6092: 815
6093: 815
6094: 815
6095: 816
6096: 816
6097: 816
6098: 817
6099: 817
6100: 818
6101: 819
6104: 819
6105: 819
6107: 820
6108: 827
6109: 820
6110: 820
6111: 821
6112: 821
6113: 822
6114: 822
6115: 822
6117: 823
6118: 823
6119: 824
6120: 824
6122: 825
6123: 799
6124: 824
6125: 825
6126: 826
6127: 826
6128: 826
6130: 827
6131: 828
6132: 829
6134: 829
6136: 829
6137: 830
6138: 830
6139: 830
6140: 831
6141: 831
6143: 832
6144: 832
6145: 832
6146: 833
6147: 833
6148: 833
6149: 834
6150: 843
6151: 844
6152: 844

6153: 844
6154: 844
6155: 845
6156: 845
6157: 845
6158: 845
6159: 846
6160: 846
6161: 856
6163: 846
6164: 846
6165: 847
6166: 847
6167: 847
6168: 847
6169: 847
6170: 848
6171: 848
6172: 848
6173: 848
6174: 848
6175: 852
6176: 849
6177: 849
6179: 849
6182: 850
6183: 850
6184: 850
6185: 850
6187: 851
6188: 851
6189: 851
6190: 851
6191: 852
6192: 852
6193: 852
6194: 852
6195: 853
6196: 853
6197: 853
6198: 854
6199: 854
6200: 854
6202: 854
6205: 855
6206: 855
6207: 855
6208: 855
6209: 856
6210: 861
6211: 861
6212: 862
6213: 862
6214: 862
6215: 863
6216: 863
6217: 863
6218: 863
6219: 863
6220: 863
6221: 864
6222: 864
6225: 864
6227: 864
6228: 865
6229: 865
6230: 865

6232: 865
6233: 871
6234: 871
6236: 871
6237: 872
6238: 872
6239: 861
6240: 872
6241: 872
6242: 873
6243: 873
6244: 873
6245: 885
6246: 874
6248: 874
6249: 874
6250: 875
6251: 876
6252: 876
6253: 876
6254: 876
6255: 877
6256: 877
6257: 877
6258: 878
6260: 878
6261: 878
6264: 879
6265: 880
6266: 880
6267: 880
6268: 880
6270: 880
6272: 881
6274: 881
6275: 881
6276: 882
6277: 882
6278: 882
6279: 883
6280: 883
6281: 883
6282: 884
6283: 884
6284: 884
6286: 866
6287: 885
6288: 885
6290: 886
6291: 886
6314: 709
6316: 708
6318: 708
6319: 708
6323: 198
6350: 198
6351: 198
6352: 198
6362: 221
6364: 220
6365: 221
6370: 161
6374: 159
6378: 153
6385: 151
6386: 226
6391: 145

6394: 220
6397: 229
6398: 229
6402: 151
6403: 811
6404: 785
6405: 827
6407: 785
6410: 797
6412: 802
6415: 812
6417: 825
6418: 828
6420: 831
6421: 283
6424: 818
6425: 818
6426: 820
6428: 821
6431: 224
6432: 224
6437: 258
6438: 262
6440: 260
6441: 261
6444: 264
6449: 264
6451: 265
6452: 266
6455: 685
6462: 683
6472: 630
6477: 646
6480: 269
6482: 270
6483: 270
6487: 274
6490: 276
6493: 280
6495: 289
6499: 291
6504: 291
6505: 295
6506: 296
6507: 301
6510: 302
6513: 303
6514: 304
6516: 304
6519: 312
6522: 312
6525: 319
6526: 320
6527: 320
6528: 321
6533: 323
6534: 323
6535: 323
6537: 327
6538: 326
6539: 326
6544: 644
6546: 667
6549: 689
6553: 828
6557: 755
6561: 631

6564: 642
6567: 328
6568: 329
6569: 329
6570: 330
6573: 280
6578: 334
6580: 335
6583: 338
6584: 338
6587: 337
6588: 302
6593: 712
6595: 279
6597: 275
6599: 282
6602: 317
6605: 259
6607: 283
6609: 284
6612: 327
6613: 327
6614: 328
6615: 162
6616: 647
6617: 703
6624: 283
6625: 233
6626: 233
6630: 221
6631: 254
6632: 255
6635: 259
6636: 263
6639: 274
6640: 268
6641: 276
6642: 280
6645: 288
6646: 290
6647: 294
6648: 296
6651: 302
6653: 304
6655: 312
6656: 314
6658: 320
6660: 318
6661: 321
6662: 326
6663: 328
6664: 330
6665: 332
6667: 333
6668: 335
6669: 336
6674: 758
6675: 750
6676: 745
6677: 712
6679: 627
6681: 228
6682: 804
6683: 780
6684: 781
6687: 168
6689: 169

6690: 145
6691: 286
6693: 285
6694: 299
6695: 298
6696: 301
6698: 297
6699: 299
6700: 299
6701: 300
6703: 300
6704: 300
6705: 299
6708: 298
6709: 662
6710: 334
6712: 309
6713: 309
6717: 310
6721: 774
6726: 802
6728: 258
6736: 701
6737: 702
6738: 707
6739: 711
6741: 711
6742: 369
6743: 364
6745: 360
6746: 360
6747: 365
6748: 362
6751: 362
6752: 363
6753: 633
6754: 369
6755: 363
6757: 363
6758: 372
6759: 316
6760: 366
6762: 367
6763: 368
6764: 368
6765: 370
6766: 371
6774: 154
6779: 297
6783: 308
6786: 284
6790: 275
6793: 312
6794: 313
6797: 313
6798: 363
6799: 800
6801: 794
6803: 168
6804: 311
6806: 258
6807: 259
6808: 273
6810: 156
6813: 311
6820: 279
6824: 651

6833: 635
6837: 616
6839: 257
6840: 255
6841: 256
6846: 315
6847: 315
6851: 301
6852: 222
6854: 310
6857: 753
6858: 167
6859: 162
6862: 759
6872: 712
6873: 711
6878: 753
6880: 146
6881: 712
6884: 148
6885: 155
6886: 213
6887: 213
6927: 712
6929: 305
6937: 220
6942: 792
6947: 823
6948: 827
6951: 804
6952: 706
6953: 362
6958: 635
6959: 784
6962: 657
6963: 632
6965: 646
6966: 620
6967: 670
6968: 751
6972: 625
6973: 631
6976: 667
6977: 663
6981: 621
6982: 662
6983: 673
6986: 626
6988: 665
6990: 644
6991: 652
6992: 659
6994: 684
6995: 658
6996: 658
6997: 618
6998: 622
6999: 626
7001: 627
7009: 792
7012: 644
7013: 645
7014: 650
7016: 645
7017: 690
7018: 621
7019: 647

7021: 307
7025: 661
7027: 645
7029: 628
7031: 656
7033: 690
7034: 223
7035: 704
7036: 704
7039: 712
7042: 214
7045: 310
7047: 159
7050: 712
7051: 802
7053: 712
7054: 672
7056: 798
7057: 644
7058: 230
7059: 307
7060: 306
7062: 639
7064: 744
7066: 149
7067: 214
7069: 278
7073: 220
7074: 153
7075: 824
7076: 287
7097: 621
7098: 677
7100: 213
7101: 875
7102: 692
7103: 663
7105: 849
7107: 292
7112: 872
7113: 875
7114: 871
7117: 344
7118: 344
7119: 343
7120: 344
7121: 343
7122: 344
7123: 343
7124: 344
7125: 343
7126: 343
7128: 343
7129: 341
7130: 341
7131: 342
7132: 342
7133: 341
7134: 341
7135: 342
7136: 345
7137: 345
7138: 345
7139: 345
7140: 345
7141: 346
7142: 345

7143: 345
7144: 345
7145: 346
7146: 342
7147: 342
7148: 343
7149: 343
7159: 346
7160: 346
7161: 346
7162: 346
7163: 347
7164: 349
7166: 347
7167: 349
7168: 348
7169: 885
7170: 862
7172: 864
7173: 760
7174: 885
7175: 881
7177: 879
7178: 874
7179: 874
7180: 884
7181: 642
7182: 879
7183: 875
7184: 873
7186: 883
7187: 876
7188: 882
7189: 879
7191: 641
7192: 883
7193: 878
7194: 877
7195: 349
7196: 350
7202: 350
7203: 350
7205: 656
7206: 345
7207: 345
7208: 345
7209: 349
7210: 349
7211: 350
7212: 849
7215: 680
7216: 636
7217: 257
7218: 623
7223: 632
7224: 160
7225: 349
7232: 265
7233: 789

Cities in Canada with International Contacts

What follows are the cities and towns in Canada, listed by province and territory, that are mentioned in this book. This offers you a quick way to find out about international activities happening in your part of Canada.

ALBERTA
Calgary: 51, 153, 157, 195, 198, 235, 265, 266, 493, 615, 616, 618, 620, 624, 628, 630, 631, 648, 651, 654, 655, 658, 659, 660, 662, 666, 667, 668, 670, 671, 672, 673, 674, 675, 683, 686, 690, 705, 789, 816, 820, 915
Camrose: 195, 258, 792
Edmonton: 18, 19, 20, 21, 47, 48, 49, 66, 74, 85, 103, 104, 105, 106, 107, 125, 126, 138, 143, 156, 166, 167, 169, 181, 187, 188, 189, 193, 194, 196, 208, 209, 211, 212, 224, 225, 255, 256, 257, 439, 440, 517, 524, 525, 526, 535, 540, 541, 542, 547, 548, 550, 551, 556, 557, 558, 560, 574, 588, 591, 618, 623, 684, 688, 702, 705, 708, 726, 727, 739, 740, 794, 800, 908, 910
Lethbridge: 199, 287, 489
Medicine Hat: 199

BRITISH COLUMBIA
Abbotsford: 634, 783
Burnaby: 214, 259, 318, 319, 620, 626, 650
Chase: 150
Nanaimo: 197
New Westminster: 153, 805
North Vancouver: 48, 245, 267, 525, 535, 643, 663, 666, 667, 671, 697, 698
Prince George: 303, 304
Salmon Arm: 828
Richmond: 659, 674
Vancouver: 19, 48, 83, 84, 104, 126, 161, 179, 181, 187, 191, 195, 197, 208, 217, 218, 220, 221, 259, 260, 261, 262, 263, 268, 283, 284, 318, 437, 442, 493, 516, 556, 559, 588, 592, 601, 618, 620, 622, 630, 633, 638, 639, 642, 644, 646, 648, 650, 652, 654, 655, 657, 661, 663, 664, 666, 671, 678, 679, 681, 684, 685, 686, 690, 691, 692, 702, 705, 707, 708, 711, 712, 741, 742, 770, 775, 778, 796, 810, 823,

831, 873, 905, 906, 907, 908, 909, 910, 911, 912, 913, 915
Victoria: 146, 267, 287, 328, 329, 574, 594, 664, 741, 777, 808, 826

MANITOBA
Brandon: 197, 812
Elgin: 154
Winnipeg: 153, 155, 157, 169, 190, 191, 193, 214, 231, 287, 288, 289, 335, 336, 660, 689, 692, 702, 705, 708, 745, 753, 770, 784, 787, 797, 799, 810, 811, 813, 814, 816

NEW BRUNSWICK
Bathurst: 677
Edmunston: 669
Fredericton: 67, 301, 302, 303, 574, 614, 702, 708, 755
Moncton: 296, 297,701, 705, 908
Sackville: 301, 789
Saint John: 302

NEWFOUNDLAND
St. John's: 199, 296, 616, 629, 644, 702, 705, 708, 755

NOVA SCOTIA
Antigonish: 319, 796
Halifax: 126, 191, 192, 213, 275, 276, 277, 320, 321, 517, 568, 574, 628, 640, 652, 658, 667, 692, 702, 705, 708, 756, 915
Sydney: 267, 708
Wolfville: 254

NORTHWEST TERRITORIES
Yellowknife: 702, 708

ONTARIO
Alfred: 258
Barrie: 574, 675
Borden: 753
Brampton: 666

Burlington: 795, 808
Cambridge: 106, 162, 406, 407, 416, 432, 559, 772
Cobourg: 806
Don Mills: 431, 434, 492, 644, 673, 697, 890
Etobicoke: 282, 661, 712, 828
Gloucester: 688, 696, 806, 911
Guelph: 197, 280, 281, 282, 533, 680, 786, 789, 814
Hamilton: 156, 294, 295
Kanata: 146, 662, 663
Kingston: 151, 154, 311, 312, 313, 314, 316, 594
Lanark: 489, 819
London: 197, 331, 332, 627, 641, 670, 797, 822
Markham: 21, 179, 181, 191, 192, 193, 194, 244, 441, 526, 560, 601, 637, 645, 832
Mississauga: 147, 155, 160, 177, 178, 396, 433, 434, 436, 647, 649, 651, 656, 657, 672, 712, 740, 757, 779, 789, 808, 815, 881, 907
Nepean: 640, 652, 654
Niagara Falls: 85, 107, 614, 629
North Bay: 303
North York: 66, 169, 336, 337, 338, 339, 340, 593, 638, 650, 670, 712, 726, 736, 779, 819, 905
Oakville: 51, 317, 615, 630, 633
Oshawa: 771
Ottawa: 46, 47, 49, 50, 67, 73, 103, 126, 138, 141, 143, 145, 149, 150, 152, 153, 154, 155, 160, 167, 168, 169, 177, 179, 182, 188, 189, 190, 192, 193, 198, 199, 208, 209, 211, 212, 218, 219, 220, 221, 222, 223, 224, 226, 227, 228, 229, 230, 232, 233, 234, 236, 243, 244, 268, 269, 270, 271, 272, 273, 304, 305, 306, 357, 364, 397, 424, 433, 434, 436, 438, 476, 482, 492, 515, 517, 524, 534, 535, 540, 566, 568, 617, 625, 632, 635, 636, 640, 645, 649, 653, 656, 658, 659, 660, 665, 672, 675, 681, 685, 686, 689, 690, 695, 696, 697, 698, 699, 700, 701, 702, 703, 704, 705, 706, 707, 708, 709, 710, 711, 712, 714, 715, 719, 720, 725, 726, 727, 732, 736, 738, 741, 742, 743, 744, 746, 747, 748, 749, 750, 751, 752, 753, 754, 758, 760, 761, 762, 768, 769, 771, 773, 775, 776, 779, 781, 782, 784, 785, 786, 787, 788, 789, 790, 791, 794, 797, 798, 801, 802, 803, 804, 805, 807, 812, 815, 817, 818, 821, 823, 825, 829, 830, 831, 832, 833, 839, 841, 842, 843, 875, 890, 904, 905, 906, 907, 908, 909, 910, 911, 912, 913, 914, 915, 916
Peterborough: 239, 319, 325, 326, 327, 811
Rexdale: 19, 73, 84, 104, 105, 166, 188, 395, 396, 397, 398, 416, 442, 517, 560, 641, 681, 696, 697, 699, 768
Rockwood: 641
Sarnia: 571, 614
Sault Ste. Marie: 704
Scarborough: 51, 74, 106, 138, 167, 210, 244, 324, 396, 431, 433, 437, 439, 623, 631, 632, 699, 772, 795, 809, 823, 824

St. Catharines: 200, 213, 264
Stouffville: 794, 800
Streetsville: 710
Sudbury: 199
Thornhill: 50, 126, 661
Thunder Bay: 196, 275, 283
Toronto: 18, 67, 74, 83, 140, 147, 148, 158, 159, 161, 168, 180, 187, 193, 194, 218, 230, 233, 279, 304, 321, 322, 323, 324, 325, 339, 345, 348, 359, 395, 397, 429, 434, 435, 439, 440, 491, 568, 574, 591, 592, 618, 619, 620, 621, 625, 627, 628, 635, 636, 639, 641, 642, 643, 647, 649, 652, 656, 657, 661, 662, 663, 665, 668, 669, 674, 676, 678, 689, 696, 702, 705, 708, 709, 710, 711, 712, 756, 757, 770, 771, 772, 777, 780, 782, 783, 786, 788, 791, 799, 802, 803, 804, 806, 809, 813, 815, 816, 819, 820, 822, 824, 826, 827, 830, 831, 833, 834, 869, 877, 905, 906, 907, 908, 909, 910, 911, 912, 913, 914, 915
Warkworth: 801
Waterloo: 138, 196, 214, 330, 331, 333, 805, 807, 831
Weston: 619
Willowdale: 148, 406, 909, 912, 913, 915
Windsor: 333, 334, 633
York: 157

PRINCE EDWARD ISLAND
Charlottetown: 158, 196, 306, 307, 567, 574, 702, 705, 708, 714, 737, 757

QUÉBEC
Alma: 196
Cantley: 804
Chicoutimi: 307, 648, 691
Gatineau: 624, 824
Hull: 18, 30, 103, 104, 106, 126, 142, 148, 155, 187, 218, 355, 360, 366, 398, 436, 566, 567, 568, 646, 647, 654, 673, 699, 702, 703, 706, 727, 730, 732, 733, 734, 736, 737, 738, 744, 745, 747, 748
Joliette: 196
La Prairie: 827
La-Pocatière: 774, 806
LaSalle: 258
Laval: 638, 658
Lennoxville: 273
Lévis: 799
Longueuil: 158, 279, 637, 645, 646
Montréal: 142, 143, 144, 146, 149, 151, 156, 167, 168, 213, 225, 227, 232, 259, 273, 274, 275, 277, 278, 289, 290, 291, 292, 293, 294, 297, 298, 299, 300, 301, 308, 309, 310, 432, 617, 619, 622, 623, 624, 626, 627, 629, 631, 634, 637, 639, 641, 642, 644, 648, 651, 662, 664, 669, 670, 677, 679, 680, 682, 683, 687, 688, 691, 701, 702, 704, 705, 711, 712, 751, 754, 759, 762, 773, 774, 776, 778, 780, 785, 793, 796, 801, 808, 809, 810, 812, 817, 823, 825, 827, 829, 847, 870, 872, 876, 881, 901, 905,

906, 907, 908, 909, 910, 911, 912, 913, 914, 915
Mont-Sainte-Hilaire: 625
Pointe-Claire: 811
Québec: 145, 284, 285, 286, 643, 687, 708, 759, 792, 797, 811, 875, 908, 915
Rimouski: 310, 311, 673
Rivière-du-Loup: 315, 316
Ste-Anne-de-Bellevue: 777
Saint-Charles-sur-Richelieu: 691
Sainte-Foy: 279, 434, 676, 802
Sainte-Hyacinthe: 282
Saint-Hubert: 746
Saint-Lambert: 633
Saint-Laurent: 327, 328, 629, 636, 683
Sherbrooke: 149, 195, 258, 317, 792
Ste-Foy: 685, 759, 793, 824, 828, 890
Ville de St-Laurent: 712

SASKATCHEWAN
Regina: 314, 315, 316, 574, 668, 679, 680, 705, 708, 761, 822
Saskatoon: 157, 317, 626, 655, 672, 702, 705

YUKON
Whitehorse: 702, 709

Countries &
Regions of the World

This index offers you a quick way to find any mention of a country or region of the world listed anywhere in the book.

Countries are usually sorted by continent, with a few exceptions based on various considerations: *AFRICA, AMERICAS* (excluding the Caribbean), *ASIA* (including Turkey and the non-African portion of the Middle East), *CARIB-BEAN* (including Guyana, Suriname and Bermuda), *EUROPE* (excluding Turkey), the *FORMER SOVIET UNION,* and the *PACIFIC* (excluding Southeast Asia). Sub-regions are indexed at the top of each regional section, followed by an alphabetical listing of countries. All countries in the world have been indexed, but some non-standard regions may not be indexed.

No attempt has been made to cross-reference sub-regions to specific countries. French names for countries (if not also used in English) are cross-referenced only if mentioned in the book, and are indicated by parentheses.

AFRICA: Regions
Africa (Afrique): 20, 47, 53, 54, 55, 57, 58, 59, 61, 62, 63, 64, 66, 67, 84, 91, 93, 94, 95, 105, 109, 114, 124, 146, 160, 161, (169), 179, 187, 191, (196), 196, 200, 211, 222, 229, 255, 272, 277, 280, 281, (284), (285), 294, 311, (311), 313, (316), 320, 322, 324, 332, 335, 336, 339, 341, 358, 363, 364, 365, 371, 376, 378, 422, 423, 426, 436, 440, 459, 478, 480, 482, 485, 515, 516, 518, 536, 551, 568, 580, 583, 592, 599, 614, (683), (683), 616, 617, 619, 628, 637, 638, 639, 640, 644, 645, 651, 655, 657, 675, 679, 680, 681, 682, (683), 684, 686, 687, 691, 699, 703, 704, 715, 727, 728, 730, 732, 752, 757, 759, 761, 771, 772, 773, 774, (776), 777, 778, 781, 785, 786, 787, 788, 795, 797, 799, (799), 801, 802, 805, 806, 807, 809, 810, (811), 813, 814, 818, 819, 821, 824, 828, 829, 830, 832, 843, 845, 858, 861, 864, 871, 880, 884, 885, 891, (899), 904
Central Africa: 677, 892
East Africa: 95, 101, 772, 773, 808, 812, 814
Horn of Africa: 807, 809, 812, 817
Maghreb: 807
(Méditéranée): (310)
North Africa: 517, 625, 630, 662, 863, 864
Sahel: 825
Southern Africa: 640, 678, 788, 799, 817
Sub-Saharan Africa: 517, 640, 871
West Africa: 9, 20, 36, 38, 56, 66, 71, 80, 84, 87, 91, 100, 147, 447, 476, 618, 620, 631, 646, 658, 671, 674, 687, 792, 865

AFRICA: Countries
Algeria (Algérie): (282), 648, 670, 683, 686, 692, 726, 762, 891, 905
Angola: 616, 639, 674, 772, 801, 853, 891, 900
Benin (Bénin): (316), (825), 892, 906
Botswana: 578, 616, 646, 772, 800, 819, 892, 900, 906
Burkina Faso: 109, 159, 282, 316, 476, 643, 646, 658, 683, 692, 796, 822, 825
Burundi: 316, 892, 896, 906
Cameroon (Cameroun): 69, 282, 315, 625, 633, 643, 669, 677, 683, (683), (688), 692, 796, (828), 892, 906
Cape Verde: 892, 898, 906

Central African Republic (République
Centrafricaine): (688), 892
Chad: 772, 796, 892, 906
Comoros: 893, 899, 907
Congo, Democratic Republic of [formerly
"Zaire"]: 43, 61, 99, 452, 485, 489, 669,
685, 819, 893, 907
Congo, Republic of (République du Congo):
688, (282), 893, 907
Djibouti: 893, 894, 907
Equatorial Guinea: 893, 894
Eritrea: 655, 692, 894, 908
Ethiopia (Éthiopie): 464, 638, 671, (688),
783, 788, 797, 829, 864, 893, 894, 899
Gabon: 631, 668, 669, 688, 893, 898
Gambia: 62, 426, 894, 898, 908
Ghana: 36, 54, 55, 57, 60, 61, 315, 326, 426,
449, 476, 478, 485, 625, 636, 640, 646,
671, 692, 894, 896, 897, 898, 899, 909
Guinea (Guinée): 60, (308), 571, 625, 649,
655, 658, 662, 671, 677, 683, 894, 897,
898, 909, 912
Guinea-Bissau: 894, 909
Kenya: 41, 94, 415, 426, 482, 633, 637, 655,
671, 672, 692, 752, 797, 816, 820, 822,
864, 892, 896, 898, 899, 910
Lesotho: 616, 819, 829, 896, 898, 911
Liberia: 54, 792, 853, 894, 896
Libya: 651, 655, 899
Madagascar: 387, 624, 772, 865, 896, 899,
911
Malawi: 94, 426, 616, 624, 638, 662, 772,
788, 800, 816, 823, 896, 900, 911
Mali: 109, 149, 316, 624, 625, 643, 658, 665,
677, 692, 792, 801, 802, 822, 825, 829,
896, 911
Mauritania: 896, 898, 911
Mauritius: 772, 896, 898, 899, 911
Morocco (Maroc): 89, 103, 623, 624, 677,
(683), 692, 897, 912
Mozambique: 69, 111, 616, 655, 664, 682,
772, 797, 853, 897, 912
Namibia: 161, 400, 584, 674, 772, 897, 912
Niger: 282, 692, 825, 897, 912
Nigeria: 57, 64, 69, 96, 176, 294, 315, 321,
476, 480, 513, 616, 633, 684, 692, 860,
865, 897, 912
Reunion: 772
Rwanda: 13, 178, 624, 643, 692, 819, 853
Sao Tome and Principe: 894, 898
Senegal (Sénégal): 109, (282), 625, 630,
643, 671, 685, 692, 752, 796, 820, (825),
(892), (894), (896), (898), (899), (914)
Seychelles: 772, 898, 899, 914
Sierra Leone: 56, 62, 618, 639, 662, 792, 894,
898, 914
Somalia: 853
South Africa: 112, 147, 158, 159, 274, 426,
639, 642, 648, 649, 752, 772, 779, 799,
801, 819, 820, 829, 896, 897, 898, 899, 914

Sudan: 324, 479, 480, 481, 597, 598, 624,
646, 655, 692, 772, 800, 894, 899, 914
Swaziland: 287, 572, 616, 772, 898, 899, 914
Tanzania: 93, 96, 159, 306, 479, 480, 482,
616, 655, 671, 678, 680, 684, 690, 772,
800, 820, 830, 893, 896, 898, 899, 915
Togo: 69, 476, 825, 894, 915
Tunisia (Tunisie): 274, (282), 426, 623, 625,
643, 646, 775, 896, 899, 915
Uganda: 159, 229, 294, 426, 692, 783, 788,
797, 800, 820, 853, 899, 915
Western Sahara: 853
Zaire: see Congo, Democratic Republic of.
Zambia: 282, 342, 570, 616, 772, 775, 786,
816, 896, 900, 916
Zimbabwe: 30, 31, 38, 53, 61, 116, 159, 274,
282, 349, 486, 616, 637, 642, 646, 657,
660, 669, 772, 784, 799, 800, 820, 891,
892, 900, 916

AMERICAS: Regions
Americas: 143, 144, 272, 277, 281, 304, 320,
321, 363, 592, 614, 618, 620, 640, 680,
691, 712, 730, 784, 786, 805, 846, 882, 900
Central America (Amérique Centrale): 177,
196, 273, 436, 531, 593, 594, 617, 637,
647, 661, 687, 699, 757, 779, 784, 792,
797, 807, (807), 808, 812, 817, 862, 884
Latin America (Amérique latine): 67, 69, 71,
72, 105, 142, 144, 146, 155, 160, (169),
178, 179, 192, (196), 211, 217, 222, 229,
237, 243, 246, 247, (247), 248, 250, 262,
264, 265, 266, 269, 280, 281, 282, 283,
(284), 287, 288, 289, 290, 294, (298),
(299), 302, (311), 313, 318, 319, 322, 324,
325, 328, 330, 333, 335, 336, 337, 339,
352, 357, 358, 364, 369, 371, 378, 425,
427, 440, 489, 509, 511, 514, 516, 527,
528, 529, 530, 531, 532, 533, 534, 535,
543, 545, 568, 585, 614, 616, 617, 618,
621, 628, 630, 632, 635, 638, 640, 642,
655, 657, 661, 663, 665, 666, 667, 671,
673, 674, 675, 676, 677, 681, (683), 690,
692, 703, 704, 715, 732, 752, 759, 771,
773, (776), 777, 778, 781, 784, 787, 788,
794, 795, 796, (799), 799, 802, 809, 810,
(811), 813, 814, 820, 830, 831, 832, 845,
846, 864, 885, 891, 904
North America (Amérique du Nord): 7, 9,
10, 11, 13, 15, 16, 19, 36, 40, 41, 55, 56,
60, 62, 63, 64, 68, 75, 76, 80, 92, 102, 105,
115, 137, 138, 139, 144, 152, 167, 178,
188, 189, 204, 213, 237, 246, 260, 272,
284, 289, 290, 319, 321, 323, 327, 369,
397, 420, 433, 436, 442, 443, 476, 498,
509, 512, 516, 518, 524, 527, 530, 534,
538, 539, 549, 550, 553, 554, 555, 591,
592, 594, 621, 626, 628, 632, 641, 643,
644, 645, 653, 654, 659, 667, 668, 672,

673, 679, (683), 686, 687, 688, 690, 692,
695, 699, 755, 800, 810, 814, 822, 830,
843, 861, 870, 881, 891, 904
South America: 65, 161, 200, 209, 219, 262,
292, 320, 422, 433, 461, 517, 536, 551,
591, 593, 618, 625, 627, 634, 636, 638,
639, 640, 644, 645, 647, 648, 655, 658,
660, 662, 672, 681, 682, 687, 690, 757,
774, 779, 817, 824, 828, 829, 843, 861

AMERICAS: Countries

Argentina: 232, 263, 290, 427, 531, 532, 616,
621, 622, 626, 631, 663, 666, 667, 676,
677, 690, 740, 753
Belize: 50, 145, 388, 895
Bolivia (Bolivie): 427, 531, 633, 671, 790,
796, 803, 822, (825), 892, 897, 906
Brazil (Brésil): 140, 144, 214, 224, 232, 282,
(282), 321, 399, 422, 432, 531, 532, 533,
621, 622, 626, 642, 645, 652, 655, 656,
662, 671, 672, 674, 677, 687, 753, 785,
796, 800, 803, 810, 823, 830, 892, 906
Chile: 69, 282, 294, 313, 315, 316, 427, 531,
532, 535, 585, 618, 621, 622, 623, 625,
633, 635, 638, 644, 646, 657, 665, 671,
674, 676, 686, 690, 804, 816, 831, 892,
897, 906
Colombia (Colombie): 100, 224, 229, 531,
532 , 623, 625, 655, 666, 670, 671, (688),
690, 860, 893, 907
Costa Rica: 50, 144, 159, 161, 316, 427, 482,
531, 585, 620, 621, 630, 637, 674, 677,
683, 692, 806, 834, 862, 893, 895, 897, 907
Ecuador (Équateur): 73, 98, 144, 145, 161,
326, (308), 412, 427, 531, 532, 670, 672,
673, 674, 726, (825), 893, 908
El Salvador: 531, 657, 671, 796, 806, 819,
821, 853, 893, 908
Guatemala: 317, 427, 531, 646, 666, 690,
792, 797, 806, 819, 823, 825, 831, 894, 909
Honduras: 144, 161, 531, 625, 647, 660, 671,
677, 688, 792, 806, 810, 827, 831, 895, 909
Mexico (Mexique): 8, 47, 51, 71, 72, 144,
156, 159, 161, 177, 178, 179, 224, 229,
248, 258, 274, 281, 282, (282), 287, 288,
290, 295, 302, 305, 313, 316, 319, 326,
329, 427, 435, 440, 493, 509, 525, 527,
528, 529, 530, 531, 532, 533, 534, 535,
536, 543, 585, 593, 624, 626, 630, 632,
633, 638, 641, 643, 656, 657, 662, 663,
666, 669, 670, 672, 674, 677, 681, 687,
690, 691, 692, 693, 697, 698, 701, 726,
743, 775, 784, 797, 804, 806, 810, 820,
858, 864, 881, 897, 911
Nicaragua: 149, 316, 531, 624, 647, 671, 673,
677, 690, 775, 792, 800, 806, 819, 822,
893, 897, 912
Panama: 315, 408, 427, 647, 674, 690, 806,
897, 912
Paraguay: 144, 531, 897, 913

Peru (Pérou): 64, (149), (151), 242, 273,
316, 427, 531, 532, 585, 621, 625, 626,
633, 674, 676, 686, 687, 692, (792), 796,
816, 822, (825), 860, 892, 897, 913
Uruguay: 531, 692, 752, 881, 900, 915
USA (États-Unis): 19, 20, 46, 47, 48, 49, 50,
66, 67, 72, 74, 83, 84, 103, 104, 106, 139,
140, 141, 142, 144, 145, 150, (150), 152,
154, 158, 159, 160, 161, 167, 170, 177,
178, 179, 180, 181, 182, 186, 187, 188,
190, 192, 194, 207, 208, 209, 210, 211,
212, 217, 218, 219, 222, 226, 229, 231,
235, 243, (285), (299), 341, 342, 343, 344,
345, 346, 347, 348, 349, 350, 357, 358,
359, 360, 362, 363, 364, 365, 366, 367,
368, 369, 370, 371, 395, 396, 406, 416,
425, 430, 431, 432, 433, 434, 435, 436,
437, 439, 440, 441, 442, 515, 516, 517,
524, 525, 526, 534, 542, 548, 556, 557,
558, 559, 560, 567, 568, 588, 589, 590,
591, 592, 593, 594, 601, 621, 662, (683),
691, 697, 698, 699, 737, 769, 770, 795,
820, 841, 842, 844, 846, 847, 848, 849,
850, 853, 862, 863, 865, 869, 870, 871,
872, 873, 874, 875, 876, 880, 882, 883,
884, 886, 900, 901, 905, 906, 907, 908,
909, 911, 912, 913, 914, 915, 916
Venezuela (Vénézuéla): 162, 177, 287, 302,
427, 531, 533, 585, 616, 622, 626, 630,
638, 639, 655, 660, 662, 666, 671, 672,
677, (688), 690, 691, 893, 900, 915

ASIA: Regions

Asia (Asie): 19, 21, 67, 83, 91, 100, 105, 142,
146, 161, (169), 186, 192, 195, 200, 211,
220, 229, 246, (247), 248, 250, 255, 260,
261, 262, 266, 267, 272, 277, 280, 282,
283, (284), 289, 290, 291, 295, (297), 304,
(310), 312, 313, 315, 318, 320, 321, 324,
325, 328, 329, 331, 334, 335, 336, 338,
339, 341, 349, 355, 358, 363, 364, 368,
378, 382, 387, 408, 417, 420, 421, 423,
426, 431, 436, 440, 459, 482, 509, 511,
513, 514, 516, 526, 539, 543, 545, 548,
551, 552, 554, 555, 556, 557, 559, 560,
568, 587, 592, 594, 600, 614, 616, 617,
619, 620, 621, 622, 623, 628, 629, 630,
631, 637, 638, 640, 643, 645, 647, 648,
651, 652, 655, 659, 661, 662, 665, 666,
667, 673, 679, 680, 681, 682, (683), 684,
686, 689, 691, 699, 703, 704, 711, 715,
727, 730, 732, 742, 752, 755, 757, 759,
771, 773, 774, 775, 777, 778, 779, 781,
785, 786, 787, 788, 795, (799), 799, 802,
807, 809, 810, (811), 813, 814, 815, 819,
824, 825, 830, 831, 843, 844, 845, 858,
861, 863, 864, 871, 880, 884, 885
ASEAN: 220, 861

Asia-Pacific: 247, 274, 311, 328, 329, 422, 655, 692, 751, 891, 904

Central Asia: 627, 665, 687

East Asia: 72, 178, 222, 246, 247, 248, 255, 265, 290, 291, 294, 318, 321, 322, 336, 337, 815

Middle East (Moyen-Orient): 8, 32, 80, 105, 125, 142, 160, (196), 222, 229, 246, 247, 255, 290, 291, 321, 323, 324, 341, 342, 363, 389, 408, 422, 423, 426, 433, 436, 439, 509, 516, 517, 536, 548, 549, 550, 551, 568, 592, 594, 614, 616, 619, 621, 628, 631, 649, 651, 653, 654, 659, 661, 662, 665, 667, 689, 699, 703, 704, 732, 757, 759, 771, 774, 779, 787, 788, 809, 814, 832, 843, 861, 891, 904

(Monde arabe): (297)

Pacific Rim: 195, 246, 261, 267, 268, 283, 319, 394, 558, 559, 560, 815

South Asia: 96, 143, 246, 247, 260, 261, 265, 321, 323, 517, 602, 662, 679, 761, 805, 809, 825, 826, 828, 831

Southeast Asia: 56, 60, 83, 98, 198, 214, 220, 260, 261, 262, 275, 328, 342, 376, 400, 490, 501, 516, 551, 556, 618, 619, 620, 628, 631, 634, 640, 643, 644, 652, 679, 687, 757, 761, 805, 808, 832

ASIA: Countries

Bahrain: 549, 550, 891, 905

Bangladesh: 76, 274, 323, 387, 617, 624, 640, 655, 658, 671, 672, 684, 775, 811, 816, 826, 829, 891, 905

Bhutan: 315, 572, 675, 786, 892, 895

Brunei Darussalam: 892, 906

Burma: 176, 423, 644, 652, 784, 865, 892, 899, 906

Cambodia: 643, 675, 676, 784, 865, 892

China (Chine) [including Tibet]: 47, 67, 95, 97, 99, 110, 161, 181, 209, 214, 227, 232, 262, 263, 274, 275, 281, (282), (285), 292, (297), (298), 306, 315, 318, 322, 328, 329, 337, 339, 400, 412, 417, 426, 439, 516, 517, 534, 545, 551, 552, 553, 556, 557, 558, 575, 584, 585, 588, 589, 599, 616, 617, 618, 621, 622, 624, 626, 628, 629, 635, 639, 640, 641, 642, 643, 649, 654, 655, 656, 657, 660, 661, 662, 663, 664, 666, 671, 672, 674, 675, 677, 679, 680, 739, 740, 753, 761, 778, 796, 801, 804, 823, 830, 836, 892, 893, 896, 897, 906

Cyprus: 853, 893, 895, 907

Egypt: 282, 324, 426, 482, 549, 571, 626, 633, 658, 660, 671, 677, 692, 752, 775, 893, 908

Hong Kong: 13, 83, 158, 181, 186, 209, 224, 287, 313, 338, 387, 394, 413, 417, 426, 509, 532, 534, 551, 552, 553, 554, 556, 557, 558, 577, 584, 585, 588, 589, 600,

621, 627, 632, 638, 643, 645, 652, 663, 664, 672, 677, 688, 689, 712, 739, 775, 896

India: 13, 32, 69, 83, 89, 92, 140, 157, 229, 235, 274, 281, 287, 292, 315, 321, 322, 323, 426, 433, 511, 549, 557, 597, 598, 614, 616, 617, 622, 623, 626, 642, 646, 654, 662, 664, 669, 671, 672, 675, 677, 691, 692, 752, 775, 786, 803, 810, 816, 819, 820, 821, 822, 823, 824, 826, 831, 832, 853, 865, 892, 895, 897, 909

Indonesia [including occupied East Timor]: 62, 65, 69, 181, 262, 294, 329, 400, 408, 446, 481, 552, 557, 572, 577, 584, 616, 618, 621, 630, 631, 639, 642, 643, 644, 648, 649, 651, 652, 654, 655, 657, 664, 669, 671, 681, 686, 692, 775, 815, 829, 865, 895, 910

Iran: 549, 571, 616, 675, 692, 726, 895, 910

Iraq: 549, 895, 910

Israel: 140, 156, 231, 312, 327, 337, 338, 426, 549, 550, 551, 673, 688, 893, 895, 910

Japan (Japon): 71, 84, 103, 106, 119, 144, 147, 153, 154, 155, 162, 205, 212, 213, 220, 227, 229, 230, 231, 233, 256, 264, 267, (285), (297), (298), 313, 317, 322, 328, 329, 333, 337, 339, 341, 342, 343, 348, 394, 409, 426, 511, 551, 552, 553, 554, 557, 558, 559, 560, 571, 584, 585, 587, 589, 590, 591, 593, 621, 622, 627, 632, 633, 634, 641, 644, 645, 651, 652, 658, 661, 672, 686, 701, 712, 739, 740, 746, 804, 815, 820, 865, 889

Jordan: 274, 324, 549, 626, 775, 812, 854, 895, 910

Korea, South (Corée): 83, 264, (297), (298), 319, 321, 322, 393, 408, 551, 552, 554, 556, 557, 584, 585, 592, 593, 594, 614, 621, 622, 652, 656, 671, 677, 701, 712, 740, 804, 896, 910

Korea, North: 264, 319, 322, 393, 652, 671, 819

Kuwait: 548, 549, 896, 898, 910

Laos: 899

Lebanon: 511, 549, 812, 853, 854, 899

Malaysia: 59, 60, 63, 65, 69, 262, 317, 329, 400, 419, 426, 532, 551, 552, 557, 577, 616, 624, 641, 643, 645, 654, 655, 656, 669, 671, 677, 684, 693, 712, 804, 861

Maldives: 294, 896, 899

Mongolia: 617, 660, 892

Myanmar: see Burma

Nepal: 282, 323, 560, 629, 649, 654, 664, 671, 675, 685, 786, 796, 816, 823, 824, 826, 829, 831, 895, 897, 912

Oman: 549, 655, 672, 897, 912

Pakistan: 89, 93, 274, 282, 294, 323, 417, 426, 484, 549, 557, 602, 643, 646, 659, 668, 672, 677, 681, 685, 692, 775, 816, 826, 853, 897, 912

Philippines: 57, 262, 282, 348, 426, 433, 551, 552, 556, 557, 576, 617, 637, 639, 643, 654, 669, 671, 680, 684, 692, 696, 796, 800, 808, 820, 831, 841, 858, 860, 898, 913
Qatar: 549, 898, 913
Saudi Arabia: 76, 80, 421, 439, 541, 549, 550, 551, 649, 668, 682, 891, 897, 898, 900, 914
Singapore: 83, 181, 287, 317, 321, 329, 342, 344, 402, 417, 421, 426, 440, 514, 523, 532, 541, 551, 552, 556, 560, 577, 616, 621, 632, 633, 643, 644, 645, 651, 652, 656, 662, 664, 669, 672, 687, 688, 689, 701, 752, 775, 804, 898, 914
Sri Lanka: 229, 323, 417, 617, 633, 671, 677, 692, 816, 819, 826, 831, 860, 896, 899, 914
Syria: 324, 549, 854
Taiwan: 83, 221, 313, 329, 532, 551, 552, 555, 556, 557, 558, 559, 584, 585, 589, 592, 596, 621, 622, 638, 661, 671, 685, 701, 804
Thailand: 41, 144, 161, 181, 214, 263, 264, 282, 305, 306, 317, 326, 329, 415, 426, 482, 551, 552, 571, 584, 585, 617, 621, 639, 643, 655, 657, 662, 664, 669, 671, 673, 675, 677, 684, 712, 784, 804, 865, 892, 896, 899, 915
Tibet: see China
Turkey: 324, 536, 549, 571, 578, 584, 585, 633, 638, 661, 662, 673, 891, 894, 899, 915
United Arab Emirates: 549, 633, 655
Vietnam (Viêt-nam): (282) (297), (299), (308), 551, 552, 618, 621, 630, 640, 643, 646, 649, 652, 657, 684, 784, 801, 802, 900, 916
Yemen: 161, 282, 306, 549, 630, 633, 648, 900, 916

CARIBBEAN: Regions
Caribbean (Caraibes): 69, 72, 142, 146, 157, 178, 181, 196, 200, 211, 229, 246, 247, 248, 269, 275, 290, 294, 333, 336, 337, 339, 341, 358, 364, 369, 427, 442, 517, 568, 593, 617, 619, 621, 628, 636, 637, 638, 639, 640, 641, 651, 657, 661, 668, 673, 675, 677, 679, 681, 684, 686, 687, 703, 704, 727, 732, 752, 757, 759, 761, 771, (776), 778, 780, 784, 785, 786, 787, 788, 794, 797, 800, 802, 807, 813, 814, 816, 817, 828, 830, 843, 844, 845, 864, 884, 891, 904, 907, 909, 912, 913
West Indies (Antilles): (169), 274, 302, 337, 628, (799), 816

CARIBBEAN: Countries
Antigua and Barbuda: 780, 891
Bahamas: 427, 671, 673, 891, 895, 905
Barbados: 625, 637, 638, 649, 671, 673, 690, 691, 891, 893, 894, 898
Bermuda: 44, 427, 642, 673, 900

Cuba: 275, 394, 427, 658, 663, 667, 801, 820, 893, 907
Dominica: 637, 648, 780, 891, 893, 907
Dominican Republic (République Dominicaine): 144, (308), 427, 489, 644, 665, (792), 808, 810, 894
Grenada: 427, 780, 891
Guyana: 161, 273, 341, 417, 486, 626, 630, 662, 669, 671, 675, 690, 823, 834, 894, 899, 909
Haiti (Haïti): 149, 427, 482, 624, 625, 692, 752, 783, 786, 792, 796, 800, (801), (802), 803, (807), 808, 810, 822, (825), 853, 894, 909
Jamaica: 147, 281, 427, 624, 625, 660, 671, 692, 775, 786, 811, 822, 891, 892
Martinique: 891, 894
Saint Kitts and Nevis: 891, 898
Saint Lucia: 891
Suriname: 626, 630, 675, 894, 899, 914
Trinidad and Tobago: 427, 624, 899, 915

EUROPE: Regions
Europe: 19, 21, 72, 85, 105, 125, 137, 142, 144, 150, 153, 161, 177, 178, 179, 203, 209, 211, 219, 221, 239, 250, 260, 262, 280, 282, 289, 295, 299, 310, 311, 314, 320, 321, 325, 328, 329, 331, 332, 352, 358, 359, 363, 367, 368, 408, 419, 420, 422, 431, 433, 435, 436, 443, 474, 510, 511, 516, 523, 536, 537, 538, 539, 540, 541, 542, 543, 544, 547, 548, 553, 555, 559, 567, 573, 592, 594, 596, 597, 600, 614, 617, 620, 621, 632, 638, 641, 643, 644, 645, 647, 648, 651, 652, 653, 659, 662, 665, 666, 667, 672, 675, 679, 680, 681, 682, 686, 688, 699, 704, 706, 728, 733, 742, 745, 751, 752, 755, 757, 759, 763, 769, 773, 779, 785, 799, 800, 804, 810, 813, 814, 830, 843, 845, 861, 870, 881, 882, 891, 904
Central Europe (Europe Centrale): 347, 367, 419, 547, 788, (799), 880
Eastern Europe: 146, 160, 177, 222, 246, 272, 280, 287, 288, 311, 313, 327, 330, 421, 422, 426, 431, 509, 511, 513, 514, 537, 542, 543, 544, 545, 547, 548, 584, 585, 590, 617, 619, 622, 640, 651, 659, 661, 671, 676, 706, 728, 730, 733, 774, 778, 783, 786, 809, 837, 845
European Community: 188, 517, 536, 540, 547
European Union: 362, 363, 520, 536, 537, 541, 548, 753, 760, 762, 869, 903
(Méditéranée): (310)
North Sea: 630, 648, 670, 674, 686
Scandinavia: 541

Western Europe: 144, 154, 264, 341, 394, 427, 509, 536, 538, 540, 541, 542, 549, 585, 623, 704

EUROPE: Countries
Albania: 664, 891, 895, 905
Andorra: 891
Austria: 427, 536, 541, 548, 571, 624, 688, 846, 891, 905
Belgium (Belgique): 44, (143), (150), 162, (258), 260, 313, 344, 427, 536, 541, 624, 632, 642, 644, 645, 652, 661, 692, 754, 892, 896, 905
Bosnia and Herzegovina: 892
Bulgaria: 426, 892, 906
Croatia: 426, 547, 893, 907
Czech Republic: 426, 536, 542, 543, 544, 548, 590, 624, 649, 673, 752, 801, 898
Denmark: 162, 223, 225, 260, 305, 412, 427, 536, 539, 893, 907
Finland: 119, 144, 162, 225, 226, 229, 313, 349, 427, 536, 541, 548, 624, 894, 908
France: 71, 73, 92, 138, 144, 146, 147, 150, 156, 157, 158, 177, 181, 203, 208, 209, 224, 226, 229, 232, 260, 270, 275, 285, 305, 313, 329, 339, 365, 427, 536, 540, 541, 623, 624, 627, 632, 645, 650, 652, 656, 672, 692, 753, 762, 836, 878, 897
Germany: 73, 143, 144, 146, 147, 152, 155, 157, 177, 222, 224, 229, 234, 260, 264, 305, 313, 317, 319, 326, 427, 536, 541, 547, 623, 624, 627, 632, 644, 645, 650, 656, 661, 688, 692, 820, 838, 894, 909
Greece: 270, 427, 536, 540, 541, 572, 585, 621
Hungary: 536, 542, 543, 544, 548, 585, 590, 623, 634, 692, 775, 891, 895, 898, 909
Iceland: 223, 427, 537, 895, 909
Ireland: 144, 147, 156, 177, 225, 319, 421, 427, 536, 541, 542, 621, 635, 892, 906, 910
Italy (Italie): 73, 177, 181, 226, 229, 232, 270, 287, (298), 322, 339, 427, 536, 541, 632, 635, 645, 753, 896, 898
Liechtenstein: 896
Luxembourg: 362, 427, 536, 541, 892, 896, 911
Macedonia: 896
Malta: 427, 895, 896, 911
Monaco: 846, 894, 897
Netherlands: 69, 146, 147, 157, 162, 229, 260, 262, 305, 313, 319, 344, 345, 427, 514, 536, 539, 541, 596, 632, 634, 635, 645, 740, 754, 762, 897, 912
Norway: 223, 225, 287, 305, 313, 319, 417, 427, 465, 537, 636, 644, 665, 895, 897, 912
Poland (Pologne): 148, 161, 262, (282), 302, (308), 426, 536, 542, 543, 548, 585, 590, 640, 644, 649, 775, 898, 913
Portugal: 427, 536, 541, 585

Romania (Roumanie): (308), 426, 648, 740, 801, 892, 897, 898, 913
San Marino: 895, 898
Slovakia: 426, 548, 590, 622, 752, 893
Slovenia: 417, 426, 536, 542, 898, 914
Spain: 71, 73, 144, 156, 157, 229, 270, 290, 318, 427, 536, 541, 542, 585, 593, 632, 645, 891, 899, 914
Sweden: 152, 223, 225, 260, 275, 302, 305, 313, 339, 427, 536, 541, 548, 632, 634, 642, 656, 663, 762, 899, 914
Switzerland (Suisse): 144, 146, (151), 157, 427, 537, 541, 650, 692, 896
UK: 50, 51, 138, 139, 140, 142, 143, 144, 146, 153, 157, 179, 180, 182, 190, 191, 192, 209, 221, 222, 224, 225, 229, 231, 232, 233, 234, 244, 260, 264, 275, 287, 302, 341, 342, 343, 345, 346, 348, 349, 350, 421, 430, 431, 432, 438, 440, 443, 512, 517, 525, 535, 537, 540, 541, 542, 550, 551, 558, 568, 589, 592, 601, 621, 622, 623, 624, 627, 632, 634, 635, 636, 639, 642, 644, 645, 649, 650, 655, 656, 657, 659, 661, 665, 672, 674, 681, 688, 753, 762, 802, 820, 848, 861, 872, 873, 876, 878, 879, 882, 883, 884

FORMER SOVIET UNION: Region
Central Asia: 627, 665, 687
Former Soviet Union: 314, 327, 367, 426, 431, 516, 542, 543, 596, 617, 706, 728, 733, 785

FORMER SOVIET UNION: Countries
Armenia: 644, 691, 891, 898, 905
Azerbaijan: 672, 891, 899, 905
Belarus: 168, 426, 536, 892, 898
Estonia: 426, 536, 542, 894, 908
Georgia: 620, 648, 650, 654, 657, 661, 664, 686, 705, 853, 894, 899, 906, 910, 911
Kazakhstan: 895, 896, 899
Kyrgyzstan: 399, 627, 665, 895, 896, 911
Latvia: 426, 894, 896, 911
Lithuania: 161, 426, 641, 896
Moldova: 536, 691, 897, 898
Russia (Russie): 115, 203, 213, 276, 280, (284), (285), (298), 302, 422, 426, 509, 517, 539, 541, 543, 545, 546, 547, 548, 628, 644, 652, 665, 673, 677, 685, 692, 746, 783, 786, 891, 892, 900
Tajikistan: 899
Turkmenistan: 899, 915
Ukraine: 317, 426, 536, 543, 547, 682, 691, 692, 752, 790
Uzbekistan: 665, 900

PACIFIC: Regions
Oceania (Océanie): (169), 211, 294, 328, 358
Pacific Islands: 63, 72, 178, 826, 828

South Pacific: 442, 619, 630, 684, 826

PACIFIC: Countries
Australia: 50, 137, 143, 144, 145, 146, 147,
    153, 154, 156, 157, 162, 228, 264, 321,
    328, 419, 420, 421, 426, 431, 541, 552,
    554, 555, 558, 621, 627, 632, 634, 635,
    636, 641, 642, 645, 647, 648, 650, 655,
    656, 659, 662, 665, 666, 671, 681, 686,
    688, 689, 691, 692, 762, 763, 810, 820,
    891, 897, 898, 900
Fiji: 214, 652, 894, 897, 908
Kiribati: 896, 897
New Zealand: 50, 144, 146, 147, 153, 157,
    162, 229, 421, 426, 440, 541, 552, 554,
    558, 634, 645, 648, 656, 662, 842, 894,
    896, 899, 900
Solomon Islands: 63, 830, 891
Tonga: 897, 899
Tuvalu: 897
Vanuatu: 891, 900
Western Samoa: 426, 900

Job Categories

This is an index to the job categories which are listed between the organization's address and its description in the following four chapters: Chapter 32, The Private Sector; Chapter 34, Careers in Government; Chapter 35, Non-governmental Organizations; and Chapter 38, International Organizations. The job categories in each profile indicate the variety of opportunities available with that organization. The 13 other chapters with profile sections are not indexed here because they contain no job categories. However, they too offer a variety of job opportunities. The surest way to find job opportunities in this book is to scan the contents of all profiles.

Accounting, 614, 615, 619, 620, 621, 622, 623, 625, 626, 627, 628, 629, 630, 633, 635, 636, 640, 642, 648, 652, 655, 656, 658, 660, 661, 662, 663, 665, 669, 671, 674, 675, 676, 683, 687, 688, 740, 743, 747, 748, 752, 762, 772, 775, 776, 777, 780, 781, 782, 783, 784, 787, 788, 789, 791, 793, 795, 800, 801, 802, 803, 804, 805, 808, 810, 812, 814, 815, 816, 817, 818, 822, 824, 828, 832, 834

Administration, 614, 615, 619, 620, 621, 623, 624, 625, 626, 627, 628, 629, 630, 637, 640, 642, 648, 652, 655, 656, 658, 661, 662, 663, 665, 669, 671, 674, 675, 678, 683, 687, 688, 738, 740, 743, 747, 748, 752, 759, 762, 772, 775, 776, 777, 780, 781, 782, 783, 785, 787, 788, 789, 791, 793, 794, 795, 796, 797, 798, 799, 800, 801, 803, 804, 805, 806, 808, 810, 811, 812, 814, 815, 816, 817, 818, 819, 821, 822, 823, 824, 825, 826, 828, 830, 831, 832, 833

Adult Training, 616, 619, 636, 637, 639, 640, 642, 647, 653, 654, 659, 660, 669, 670, 677, 678, 681, 685, 686, 687, 691, 747, 757, 771, 772, 775, 776, 777, 785, 786, 791, 792, 793, 794, 795, 796, 798, 799, 800, 801, 802, 805, 806, 812, 814, 815, 818, 821, 823, 824, 826, 828, 829, 831, 832

Advanced Technology, 635, 650, 656, 688, 757

Advocacy, 614, 620, 625, 640, 654, 665, 745, 751, 774, 776, 777, 779, 780, 781, 783, 784, 786, 788, 789, 794, 796, 798, 799, 803, 804, 807, 808, 811, 813, 815, 817, 818, 819, 821, 822, 825, 826, 828, 831

Aerial Surveys, 674, 689

Aerospace Technology, 624, 629, 630, 670, 674, 692, 776

Agriculture, 615, 616, 617, 633, 640, 643, 661, 668, 669, 672, 676, 679, 680, 682, 687, 691, 738, 745, 752, 757, 759, 771, 772, 773, 775, 776, 781, 783, 784, 787, 789, 791, 792, 793, 795, 797, 798, 799, 800, 802, 805, 806, 808, 809, 810, 812, 814, 818, 819, 821, 822, 824, 829, 830, 831, 832

Air Transportation, 659, 673, 678, 747, 814

Architecture and Planning, 639, 656, 676, 689, 691, 773, 775, 776, 793, 805

Arms Control, 687, 804, 812, 823

Building Supplies, 672

Business Development, 614, 615, 617, 618, 619, 620, 622, 623, 624, 625, 626, 627, 628, 629, 630, 631, 633, 634, 635, 636, 637, 638, 640, 641, 642, 646, 649, 650, 652, 653, 654, 655, 661, 662, 664, 665, 669, 671, 673, 675, 680, 681, 682, 683, 687, 688, 690, 692, 739, 740, 742, 743, 748, 751, 752, 753, 755, 756, 775, 776, 781, 785, 786, 789, 791, 793, 795, 798, 801, 802, 805, 810, 823, 824, 829, 830, 832

Business/Banking/Trade, 615, 619, 621, 626, 627, 628, 630, 633, 635, 636, 637, 640, 641, 642, 650, 661, 663, 664, 669, 678, 679, 687, 689, 740, 741, 742, 743, 747, 748, 749, 751, 752, 756, 760, 773, 777, 781, 791, 792, 799, 804, 808, 814, 815, 816, 819, 821, 832, 871, 872, 876, 877, 881, 882, 884, 885

Camera and Projector Design, 651

Chemicals, 684

Children's Rights, 825, 826, 827

Civil Society, 797, 815

Commerce, 759

Commonwealth, 872, 873

Community Development, 614, 615, 616, 617, 619, 625, 626, 634, 636, 637, 639, 640, 642, 646, 652, 654, 656, 659, 671, 676, 687, 691, 692, 744, 747, 752, 757, 771, 772, 773, 776, 778, 779, 781, 782, 783, 785, 786, 787, 788, 789, 791, 792, 793, 794, 795, 796, 797, 798, 800, 802, 803, 805, 806, 807, 808, 809, 810, 811, 812, 813, 814, 815, 816, 817, 818, 819, 820, 821, 822, 823, 824, 827, 828, 829, 830, 831, 832, 833, 834

Computer Systems, 615, 617, 619, 620, 621, 623, 626, 627, 628, 629, 632, 634, 636, 637, 639, 642, 645, 648, 650, 652, 653, 655, 656, 659, 661, 662, 663, 664, 665, 669, 670, 671, 674, 678, 679, 680, 681, 692, 740, 743, 752, 757, 762, 775, 776, 780, 783, 786, 788, 791, 793, 795, 805, 808, 812, 814, 823, 830, 832

Conflict Prevention, 815

Construction, 614, 615, 622, 623, 628, 633, 637, 638, 639, 641, 644, 649, 651, 655, 660, 662, 671, 673, 674, 676, 678, 679, 680, 682, 683, 687, 691, 776, 788, 791, 792, 805, 809, 813, 814, 821, 828, 834

Consulting, 614, 615, 616, 617, 618, 619, 620, 621, 623, 625, 626, 627, 628, 629, 631, 632, 633, 634, 635, 636, 637, 638, 639, 640, 641, 642, 643, 645, 646, 647, 648, 649, 653, 654, 655, 656, 658, 660, 664, 665, 667, 669, 670, 671, 672, 673, 675, 676, 677, 678, 679, 680, 681, 682, 683, 684, 685, 686, 687, 688, 690, 691, 692, 741, 742, 743, 745, 747, 756, 772, 775, 776, 777, 784, 785, 787, 791, 798, 801, 802, 805, 806, 808, 812, 816, 818, 821, 823, 824

Corporate Ethics, 815

Culture, 757, 759, 808

Curriculum Development, 785

Customer Services, 627, 644, 645, 678

Development Assistance, 615, 616, 617, 619, 624, 628, 629, 630, 636, 637, 638, 639, 640, 644, 646, 649, 653, 654, 655, 658, 664, 667, 669, 670, 671, 676, 680, 681, 682, 685, 687, 691, 692, 740, 744, 747, 751, 752, 757, 771, 772, 773, 774, 775, 776, 779, 780, 781, 783, 784, 786, 787, 788, 789, 790, 791, 792, 793, 794, 795, 796, 798, 799, 801, 802, 803, 804, 805, 809, 810, 811, 812, 814, 818, 819, 821, 822, 823, 824, 825, 827, 828, 830, 831, 832, 833, 834

Development Education, 615, 616, 619, 629, 631, 636, 642, 646, 649, 654, 658, 659, 665, 669, 671, 672, 682, 685, 687, 692, 740, 744, 747, 752, 772, 773, 775, 776, 777, 778, 779, 780, 781, 782, 783, 784, 785, 786, 787, 788, 789, 792, 793, 794, 795, 796, 797, 798, 802, 803, 805, 806, 807, 808, 809, 810, 811, 812, 814, 815, 816, 817, 818, 821, 823, 824, 825, 826, 827, 828, 829, 830, 831, 832, 833

Drilling Services, 672, 690

Ecoforestry, 828

Economics, 614, 615, 616, 617, 619, 621, 628, 629, 630, 634, 636, 638, 639, 640, 641, 653, 655, 661, 664, 669, 671, 672, 673, 678, 686, 687, 691, 741, 746, 747, 748, 749, 752, 759, 762, 776, 781, 784, 793, 794, 810, 814, 815, 832

Editing, 804, 831

Education, 739, 780, 796, 808, 819, 824

Election Monitoring, 748

Energy Resources, 614, 615, 616, 617, 622, 623, 626, 629, 630, 631, 637, 641, 642, 643, 646, 647, 648, 649, 651, 654, 655, 657, 658, 659, 665, 666, 667, 668, 670, 672, 674, 676, 677, 681, 682, 683, 687, 690, 691, 692, 757, 775, 776, 777, 810, 819, 830

Engineering, 614, 615, 616, 617, 620, 622, 623, 624, 625, 626, 627, 628, 629, 630, 631, 632, 633, 634, 636, 637, 638, 639, 641, 643, 646, 647, 648, 649, 651, 652, 653, 655, 656, 657, 658, 660, 661, 662, 663, 664, 665, 666, 667, 668, 671, 673, 674, 675, 676, 677, 678, 679, 680, 681, 682, 683, 684, 687, 688, 689, 691, 692, 740, 743, 748, 773, 776, 777, 788, 791, 793, 805, 813, 823, 830, 834

Engineering Management, 666

Environment, 614, 615, 616, 617, 618, 619, 622, 623, 626, 628, 629, 630, 631, 636, 637, 638, 639,

640, 641, 642, 643, 647, 648, 649, 653, 657, 658, 659, 660, 661, 662, 664, 665, 667, 668, 670, 671, 672, 673, 674, 675, 676, 677, 679, 681, 682, 683, 684, 685, 686, 687, 691, 692, 740, 747, 748, 751, 752, 757, 772, 773, 774, 775, 776, 777, 781, 782, 785, 787, 788, 791, 792, 793, 795, 796, 798, 800, 803, 804, 805, 806, 808, 810, 812, 814, 815, 817, 819, 821, 823, 824, 826, 828, 829, 830, 831, 832, 834, 873, 874, 875, 878, 880, 881, 884, 885, 886

Exchange Programs, 616, 617, 633, 640, 654, 739, 747, 753, 773, 776, 778, 779, 780, 781, 782, 786, 792, 793, 795, 798, 805, 807, 812, 814, 819, 821, 832, 833, 834

Exploration and Development, 620, 621, 622, 625, 626, 630, 639, 644, 646, 647, 652, 654, 657, 658, 663, 666, 684, 690

Film Distribution, 651, 680

Film Production and Post Productions, 651, 669, 680

Fisheries, 615, 617, 628, 629, 630, 638, 639, 640, 642, 643, 644, 647, 653, 670, 676, 682, 750, 752, 757, 759, 773, 776, 791, 793, 795, 798, 810, 830

Food Security, 826

Forestry, 615, 617, 629, 639, 640, 641, 642, 643, 645, 647, 664, 665, 669, 670, 676, 677, 678, 679, 681, 682, 684, 685, 687, 691, 741, 752, 757, 773, 776, 783, 788, 791, 792, 793, 795, 798, 800, 802, 805, 810, 812, 823, 824, 828, 830, 831, 832

Fundraising, 640, 752, 772, 778, 780, 781, 783, 784, 787, 791, 792, 795, 796, 798, 799, 802, 803, 804, 805, 806, 809, 810, 811, 812, 815, 816, 817, 818, 821, 822, 823, 824, 825, 826, 828, 830, 831, 832

Gender and Development, 615, 616, 617, 625, 628, 629, 630, 636, 638, 639, 640, 641, 646, 649, 664, 671, 673, 679, 682, 683, 687, 692, 740, 744, 747, 751, 752, 771, 773, 774, 775, 776, 778, 779, 781, 782, 785, 786, 787, 788, 789, 791, 792, 793, 794, 795, 796, 798, 799, 801, 802, 803, 804, 805, 806, 808, 809, 812, 815, 816, 817, 818, 821, 824, 825, 826, 827, 828, 829, 831, 832, 833

Geomatics, 637, 654, 676, 683, 691

Geophysics, 646, 673

Global Communication, 796, 876, 879, 880

Gold and Metals Production, 622, 626, 633, 639, 652, 657, 658, 663, 666, 686, 690

Health/Medical, 649, 661, 793, 797, 808, 819

Housing/Human Settlements, 742, 820, 822

Human Resources, 614, 615, 616, 619, 621, 622, 623, 624, 625, 626, 629, 630, 631, 634, 635, 636, 637, 639, 640, 642, 649, 652, 653, 654, 655, 659, 660, 661, 662, 663, 664, 665, 669, 671, 672, 673, 674, 676, 678, 682, 687, 688, 691, 740, 743, 747, 748, 751, 752, 757, 758, 775, 776, 779, 785, 787, 789, 791, 792, 795, 798, 801, 805, 806, 809, 812, 814, 815, 816, 817, 821, 823, 829, 831, 832

Human Rights, 615, 617, 619, 620, 625, 628, 640, 671, 740, 744, 747, 751, 752, 773, 774, 776, 781, 782, 784, 785, 786, 791, 792, 793, 795, 796, 798, 799, 804, 808, 809, 811, 812, 815, 817, 818, 821, 822, 823, 825, 828, 829

Humanitarian Relief, 640, 682, 747, 771, 772, 773, 774, 776, 778, 783, 784, 786, 787, 788, 789, 791, 792, 793, 794, 795, 800, 804, 805, 806, 808, 809, 810, 811, 813, 814, 817, 819, 820, 821, 822, 824, 832

Hydrographic Surveys, 671, 689

Immigration, 747

Industrial Services, 672

Information Technologies, 645, 650, 656, 659, 673, 683, 755, 759

Institution Building, 649, 748, 785

Insurance, 824
Intelligence, 746
Intercultural Briefings, 616, 633, 639, 647, 653, 654, 660, 679, 739, 744, 747, 757, 761, 775, 776, 778, 779, 782, 796, 798, 802, 808, 812, 825, 826, 830
International Education, 741, 744, 757, 774, 785, 801, 806, 820, 827
International Law/International Agreements, 750, 752
International Trade, 614, 617, 618, 619, 623, 625, 627, 628, 633, 635, 640, 642, 649, 650, 653, 654, 660, 661, 665, 668, 673, 675, 678, 680, 683, 690, 691, 739, 741, 742, 743, 745, 746, 747, 748, 750, 751, 752, 753, 754, 755, 756, 757, 759, 760, 773, 776, 779, 781, 802, 804, 810, 815
Job Training, 745, 822
La Francophonie, 871, 872, 875
Laboratory Automation Systems, 661
Laboratory Services, 661
Labour, 826
Land Stewardship, 828
Law, 660, 746, 759, 871, 875, 876
Law and Good Governance, 871, 875, 876
Leadership Assessment, 634
Literacy, 774, 831
Logistics, 614, 618, 622, 627, 628, 633, 637, 642, 655, 656, 661, 662, 670, 673, 678, 683, 692, 747, 776, 781, 789, 791, 792, 794, 797, 800, 813, 832, 834
Management, 616, 647, 656, 658, 659, 662, 676, 682, 684, 686, 690, 691, 759
Management Consulting, 647, 658, 676, 686
Management Information Systems, 676
Management Training, 616, 656, 659, 676, 690
Manufacturing, 632, 636, 644, 645, 650, 651, 656, 661, 672
Marine, 678, 679, 747
Marine Engineering, 678, 679
Marketing, 644, 645, 650, 663, 666, 670, 680, 683, 685, 690, 745, 754, 758, 760, 762
Maternal and Infant Nutrition, 806
Media/Communications, 615, 617, 619, 623, 626, 635, 650, 651, 653, 665, 669, 671, 687, 740, 743, 744, 748, 751, 752, 756, 762, 773, 775, 776, 779, 780, 781, 784, 787, 789, 791, 792, 793, 796, 797, 798, 799, 800, 801, 804, 805, 808, 809, 810, 812, 814, 815, 816, 817, 818, 821, 823, 824, 825, 826, 827, 829, 830, 831, 832
Medical Diagnostics, 661
Medical Health, 617, 619, 623, 653, 662, 669, 670, 685, 750, 753, 771, 772, 773, 776, 778, 783, 787, 788, 789, 790, 791, 792, 793, 794, 797, 798, 800, 801, 802, 805, 806, 807, 808, 809, 812, 813, 815, 816, 818, 821, 822, 823, 824, 826, 827, 828, 830, 832, 834
Membership Relations, 779
Merchandising, 644, 672
Metals, 621, 625, 626, 641, 643, 644, 647, 649, 652, 658, 665, 676
Metals Distribution, 658, 676
Mineral Handling, 649, 657, 679
Mineral Resources, 644, 647, 684

Mining, 618, 620, 621, 622, 625, 626, 630, 633, 638, 641, 643, 644, 646, 647, 652, 657, 658, 663, 665, 666, 671, 674, 676, 683, 684
Most Job Categories, 773, 783
Nutrition, 785
Oil and Gas Distribution, 655, 667, 690, 692
Oil and Gas Exploration, 630, 631, 659, 665, 666, 670, 674
Oilfield Services, 662, 672, 681
Organization Development, 634
Peace and Security, 876, 878, 881, 882, 883
Peacekeeping and Defence, 753, 829
People's Organizations, 820, 822
Permaculture, 828
Personal Development, 634
Personal Taxation/Financial Planning, 630
Petrochemicals, 614, 615, 643, 647, 654, 655, 658, 670, 674, 682, 686, 687
Pharmaceuticals, 661
Photo Mapping, 670, 689
Policing, 761
Policy Dialogue, 748, 749, 755, 774, 776, 780, 818, 820, 825
Project Management, 614, 615, 616, 617, 618, 619, 620, 621, 622, 623, 624, 625, 626, 628, 629, 630, 631, 633, 634, 635, 636, 637, 638, 639, 640, 641, 642, 643, 645, 647, 648, 650, 651, 652, 653, 654, 655, 656, 657, 658, 659, 660, 661, 662, 664, 665, 667, 668, 669, 670, 671, 672, 673, 674, 675, 676, 677, 678, 679, 680, 681, 682, 684, 685, 686, 687, 689, 690, 691, 692, 740, 742, 743, 747, 771, 772, 775, 776, 778, 779, 780, 781, 783, 784, 785, 786, 787, 788, 791, 792, 793, 794, 795, 796, 798, 799, 800, 801, 803, 805, 812, 814, 815, 816, 817, 818, 821, 822, 823, 824, 826, 827, 828, 832, 833
Public Health and Family Planning, 683, 874, 879, 883
Publishing, 630, 634, 653, 758
Pulp and Paper, 669, 679, 684
Quality Assurance, 635, 638
Railways, 634, 659, 678, 747
Refugee Services, 784
Relief and Development, 784
Religious, 772, 782, 784, 786, 795, 797, 800, 804, 805, 808, 813, 814, 815, 819, 821, 823, 824, 827, 830
Research, 635, 645, 650, 651, 666, 670, 691, 753, 757, 761, 804, 807, 811, 831
Research and Development, 635, 645, 650, 651, 666, 670
Resource Centre Management, 815
Roads, 648, 678
Science and Technology, 759, 874, 879, 884
Social Justice and Development, 817, 819, 831, 871, 872, 873, 877, 878, 879, 880, 883, 884, 885, 886
Social Policy, 640, 682, 747
Social Sciences, 744, 761, 762, 784
Software Development, 635, 645, 650, 654, 659
States and Markets, 815
Statistics, 762, 815
Sustainable Development, 639, 658, 663, 666, 671, 817, 819, 828
Systems Engineering, 659
Teaching, 614, 618, 631, 644, 649, 654, 659, 660, 754, 772, 773, 775, 776, 778, 785, 789, 790, 792, 794, 795, 796, 797, 798, 802, 805, 814, 815, 816, 821, 823, 828, 830, 831, 832
Technical Assistance, 614, 615, 616, 617, 618, 619, 620, 623, 625, 626, 628, 629, 631, 632, 633, 634, 636, 638, 639, 640, 641, 642, 643, 645, 649, 653, 654, 655, 656, 660, 661, 662, 664, 667, 668, 669, 670, 671, 672, 675, 676, 678, 680, 681, 682, 686, 687, 688, 689, 692, 742, 747, 748, 752, 757,

761, 773, 775, 776, 779, 780, 781, 786, 787, 789, 791, 792, 793, 794, 795, 798, 802, 805, 806, 814, 816, 818, 821, 823, 824, 826, 827, 828, 832

Telecommunications, 616, 617, 619, 622, 629, 636, 637, 640, 650, 653, 660, 663, 666, 670, 673, 680, 682, 683, 688, 743, 747, 757, 759, 773, 775, 776, 792, 814, 832

Tourism, 619, 630, 639, 644, 653, 673, 747, 756, 757, 759, 773, 812

Trade Unions, 779

Trades, 806, 830

Training and Technology Transfer, 652, 655, 658, 690, 759, 827

Translation, 683, 804

Transportation, 627, 634, 649, 657, 670, 684, 686, 691, 747, 827

Urban Development, 638, 742

Volunteer, 640, 773, 774, 777, 778, 781, 782, 783, 786, 787, 789, 790, 792, 793, 795, 797, 798, 799, 800, 802, 803, 805, 806, 809, 810, 811, 813, 814, 815, 816, 818, 820, 821, 822, 823, 827, 828, 830, 831, 832, 834

Waste Water Management, 631, 636, 638

Water Resources, 614, 615, 616, 617, 620, 626, 629, 637, 639, 640, 642, 643, 646, 647, 648, 653, 656, 657, 658, 659, 660, 661, 667, 670, 671, 673, 675, 676, 677, 682, 687, 691, 692, 747, 752, 757, 771, 773, 775, 776, 777, 783, 784, 787, 788, 789, 791, 792, 793, 795, 798, 800, 805, 806, 808, 812, 813, 819, 821, 822, 823, 824, 827, 830, 831, 832

Water Supply, 636, 638

Writing, 804, 831

Youth and Development, 778, 780, 796, 811

Organization Index

There are 1868 profiles of organizations listed under 17 separate categories. The two main groups of profiles are found in Part Two: Acquiring International Experience, and Part Five: International Career Contacts.

ORGANIZATIONS BY CHAPTER

Acquiring International Experience
10. Short-term Programs Overseas 142
11. Hosting Programs 167
13. Global Education Centres 195
14. Study Abroad 212
15. Awards & Grants 219
16. International Studies in Canada 245
16. International Studies Abroad 254
17. International Internships 359

International Career Contacts
32. Private Sector 613
33. International Business Services 700
34. Government 738
35. Nongovernmental Organizations 771
36. United Nations 843
37. Environmental & Agricultural
    Research Centres 861
38. International Organizations 870
39. Canadian Diplomats Abroad 890
40. Foreign Diplomats in Canada 904

INDEX TO ORGANIZATIONS

A.D.I. Group Inc. 614
Acadia University 254
Acres International Limited (AIL) 614
Adamac Management Group Inc. 614
Adventist Development and Relief
    Agency Canada (ADRA CANADA) 771
Africa Evangelical Fellowship (AEF) 772
Africa Inland Mission
    International (Canada) (AIM) 772
African Development Bank 843
African Economic
    Research Consortium (AERC) 871
African Medical and
    Research Foundation (AMREF) 772
AFS Interculture Canada (AFS) 142, 167, 773
Aga Khan Foundation (AKF) 871
Aga Khan Foundation Canada (AKFC):
    Fellowship in International
    Development Management 143
Aga Khan Foundation Canada (AKFC) 773
Agence Québec /
    Wallonie-Bruxelles pour la jeunesse 143
AGRA Earth & Environmental Limited 615
AGRA Monenco Inc. 616, 615
AGRA ShawMont Limited 616

Agriculture and
    Agri-Food Canada (AAFC) 701, 738
Agriteam Canada Consulting Ltd. 616
Agrodev Canada, Division of
    Stanley Consulting Group Ltd. 617
Aide médicale
    internationale à l'enfance (L'AMIE) 774
AIESEC - International
    Student Exchange Organization 359
Alberta Department of Education 739
Alberta Economic Development 708, 739
Alberta Education, National
    and International Education Branch 574
Alberta Education: Alberta
    Teacher Exchange Programs 143
Alcan Aluminium Limited 617
Alliance of Manufacturers
    & Exporters Canada 709
Alpine Environmental Ltd. 618
Alternatives 774
AmCan Minerals Ltd. 618
American University 347
Americas Trading Corporation (ATC) 618
Amigos de las Americas 144
Amnesty International (AI) 359, 871

957

Amnistie internationale
(section canadienne francophone) 774
Analytical Service
Laboratories Ltd. (ASL) 618
Antioch College 342
Apotex Inc. 619
ARA Consulting Group Inc. (The) 619
Arborescence Communications Inc. 619
Archaeological
Institute of America (AIA) 144
Ariel Resources 620
Arusha Centre 195
ASEAN Institute of Forest Management 861
ASEAN-Canada Business Council 711
Ashoka Innovators for the Public 360
Asia Pacific
Foundation of Canada (APFC) 220, 711, 775
Asian Development Bank (ADB) 844
Asian Vegetable and Research Centre
(AVRDC) 360
ASSE International
Student Exchange Programs:
ASSE College Abroad Program 144
Associated Engineering
International Ltd. (AEIL) 620
Association for International
Practical Training (AIPT): Career
Development Exchange Program 144
Association for the Advancement of
Policy, Research and Development
in the Third World (AAPRDTW) 872
Association of Canadian
Community Colleges (ACCC) 775
Association of International
Education, Japan (AIEJ) 220
Association of Universities
and Colleges of Canada (AUCC) 220, 221, 776
Association Québec-France 145
Association québécoise des organismes
de coopération internationale (AQOCI) 776
Association to Unite the Democracies 360
Ateneo de Manila University 343
Atlantic Canada Opportunities Agency 701
Atomic Energy
of Canada Limited (AECL) 740
Augustana University College- 258
Australia Working Holiday Program 145
Australian National University 341, 347
AYUSA International 145, 167
Baker & McKenzie 620
Ballard Power Systems Inc. 620
Bank for International Settlements (BIS) 872
Bank of Canada 741
Bank of Montréal 621
Bank of Nova Scotia (The) 621
Barrick Gold Corp. 621
BDO Dunwoody 621
Bell Canada International Inc. (BCI) 622
Bema Gold Corp. 622
BENDAS 168
Bennett Environmental Inc. 622

BFC Civil 623
Bilkent University 347
Biomira Inc. 623
Biothermica International Inc. 623
Bishop's University 258
Boileau & Associates Inc. 624
Bombardier Inc. 624
Bond University 343
Boston University 345
Boston University: Internship Programs 145
Bovar Inc. 624
Bowers International
Homestay Placement Services 168
Brace Research Institute 777
Brandeis University 347
Brazil-Canada Chamber of Commerce 711
Breakwater Resources Ltd. 625
Breton, Banville & Associates (BBA) 625
Bridgehead Inc. 625
Britannia Gold Corp. 626
British Columbia Centre
Trade and Investment Office 708
British Columbia Centre for International
Education (BCCIE) 741
British Columbia Centre
Teacher Exchange Office 146
British Columbia Council
for International Co-operation 777
British Columbia Hydro International
Limited (BCHIL) 626
British Columbia
Institute of Technology- 259
British Columbia Ministry of Forests 741
British Columbia
Teacher Exchange Program 574
British Columbia
Trade and Investment Office (BCTIO) 742
British Trade & Investment Office 711
Brock University 213, 263, 264
Brookings Institution 222
Business Development Bank of Canada 701
CAB International (CABI) 861
Calmeadow 777
Cambior Inc. 626
Cambridge University 222
Cameco Corp. 626
Camosun College- 267
Camrose International Institute (CII) 195
Canac International Inc. 627
Canada Business Service Centres 701
Canada China Child
Health Foundation (CCCHF) 778
Canada Council for the Arts 222, 223
Canada Mortgage and Housing
Corporation (CMHC) 742
Canada Netherlands
Student Exchange Programs 146
Canada Post Corporation (CPC) 742
Canada Student Loan Program 223
Canada Trust 627
Canada World Youth (CWY) 146, 778

Canada-Arab Business Council............................711
Canada-China Business Council.........................711
Canada-India Business Council 711
Canada-Indonesia Business Council 711
Canada-Japan Trade Council 711
Canada-Korea Business Council (CKBC)...........711
Canada-Pakistan Business Council 712
Canada-Singapore Business Association 712
Canada-Taiwan Business Association 712
Canada-Taiwan Trade Association 712
Canada-Ukraine Chamber of Commerce...........712
Canada-US Fulbright Program 223
Canadian Association of International
     Development Consultants (CAIDC) 732
Canadian Association of University
     Teachers of German (CAUTG):
     Student Summer Work Program....................146
Canadian Auto Workers'
     Social Justice Fund (CAW-SJF) 779
Canadian Baptist International Ministries.........779
Canadian Baptist Ministries (CBM):
     Canadian Baptist Volunteers 147
Canadian Broadcasting
     Corporation (CBC)...743
Canadian Bureau for
     International Education (CBIE) 223, 224, 779
Canadian Catholic Organization
     for Development and Peace (CCODP) 780
Canadian Centre on Minority Affairs Inc...........780
Canadian Chamber of Commerce 709
Canadian Coalition for
     the Rights of Children (CCRC) 781
Canadian Commercial
     Corporation (CCC)...............................702, 743
Canadian Commission for UNESCO..................744
Canadian Co-operative
     Association (CCA)..781
Canadian Council for
     International Business (CCIB).........................709
Canadian Council for
     International Co-operation (CCIC) 781
Canadian Council for the Americas....................712
Canadian Council of Churches (CCC) 782
Canadian Crossroads International /
     Carrefour Canadien International
     (CCI) 147, 168, 782
Canadian Education
     Exchange Foundation....................................574
Canadian Education Association 574
Canadian Environmental
     Network (CEN)..782
Canadian Executive
     Service Organization (CESO) 783
Canadian Federation of Students: Student
     Work Abroad Programme (SWAP) 147
Canadian Federation of Students:
     Volunteer Abroad/
     Bénévoles à l'étrange......................................148
Canadian Federation of
     University Women (CFUW)............................224

Canadian Feed the Children Inc. (CFTC) 783
Canadian Fishery
     Consultants Limited (CFCL) 628
Canadian Food for the Hungry.........................783
Canadian Foodgrains
     Bank Association Inc. (CFGB) 784
Canadian Foreign Service Institute............702, 744
Canadian Foundation
     for the Americas (FOCAL) 784
Canadian Foundation
     for World Development (CFWD) 148
Canadian Fracmaster Ltd. 628
Canadian Friends of Burma 784
Canadian Friends
     Service Committee (CFSC) 784
Canadian Government
     International Internships........................148, 360
Canadian Heritage...745
Canadian Higher
     Education Group (CHEG) 785
Canadian Home
     Economics Association (CHEA).....................785
Canadian Human Rights Foundation.................785
Canadian Imperial
     Bank of Commerce (CIBC) 628
Canadian Importers Association Inc. 710
Canadian Institute
     of Cultural Affairs (ICA Canada) 786
Canadian Institute of Ukrainian Studies.....224, 225
Canadian International
     Development Agency (CIDA)..........703, 727, 745
Canadian International Freight
     Forwarders' Association (CIFFA) 710
Canadian International
     Grains Institute (CIGI) 745
Canadian International
     Project Managers Ltd. (CIPM) 629
Canadian International
     Trade Tribunal (CITT) 746
Canadian International Water and Energy
     Consultants (CIWEC) 629
Canadian Jesuits International (CJI) 786
Canadian Labour Congress (CLC) 786
Canadian Lutheran World Relief (CLWR) 787
Canadian Marconi Company (CMC).................629
Canadian National
     Institute for the Blind (CNIB) 787
Canadian Ocean
     Resource Association (CORA) Inc. 630
Canadian Organization for Development
     through Education (CODE) 787
Canadian Petroleum
     International Resources Ltd...........................630
Canadian Physicians for
     Aid and Relief (CPAR)....................................788
Canadian Polish Congress:
     Education and Training
     Programs for Poland (ETPP) 148
Canadian Public
     Health Association (CPHA) 788

Canadian Red Cross Society (CRCS) 789
Canadian Relief Fund for
    Chernobyl Victims in Belarus.........................168
Canadian Resource Bank for Democracy
    and Human Rights (CANADEM) 789
Canadian Rotary Committee for
    International Development (CRCID).............789
Canadian Security
    Intelligence Service (CSIS) 746
Canadian Society for
    International Health (CSIH) 790
Canadian Society for International Health
    (CSIH): International
    Health Exchange Program 149
Canadian Society of Customs Brokers...............710
Canadian Space Agency (CSA)...........................746
Canadian Teachers' Federation (CTF) 790
Canadian Teachers' Federation (CTF):
    Project Overseas 149
Canadian Transportation Agency.......................747
Canadian UNICEF
    Committee (UNICEF Canada) 791
Canadian Women's Club 225
Canadian-German Chamber
    of Industry and Commerce 712
Canadians Resident Abroad Inc. (CRA)............630
Canadian-Scandinavian Foundation 225
Canarc Resource Corp. 630
Canedcom International Ltd. 631
Canora Asia Inc..631
Capilano College...267, 268
CARE Canada...791
CARE International 872
Caribbean Development Bank (CDB) 844
Carleton University......................................268-273
Carrefour Canadien International (CCI) 169
Carrefour de solidarité
    internationale (CSI) 149, 195, 792
Carrefour tiers-monde (CTM) 792
CAUSE Canada..792
CÉGEP André Laurendeau.................................258
CÉGEP de Rivière-du-Loup.........................315, 316
Center for the Study of Conflict........................362
Central European University, Budapest............347
Centre canadien d'étude et de
    coopération internationale (CECI) 793
Centre de coopération internationale
    en santé et développement inc. 793
Centre de solidarité internationale....................196
Centre for Intercultural Learning.......................30
Centre for International Affairs 226
Centre for International Alternatives.................196
Centre for International
    Forestry Research (CIFOR).............................861
Centre for
    International Mobility (CIMO) 226
Centre for International Statistics at
    the Canadian Council on Social
    Development (CCSD) 794
Centro Internacionale de
    Agricultura Tropical (CIAT)............................862

CFC International Inc. (CFCI) 631
Champlain Lennoxville.......................................273
Change for Children Association (CFCA) 794
Chantiers jeunesse..149
Chauvco Resources Ltd......................................631
Children's International
    Summer Villages (CISV)...................... 150, 169
Christian Blind
    Mission International (CBMI) 794
Christian Children's
    Fund of Canada (CCFC) 795
Christian Reformed World Relief
    Committee of Canada (CRWRC)...................795
CIDA Public Inquiries 734
Cinram International Inc. 632
Citizenship and Immigration Canada 747
CLUB 2/3 796
Coady International Institute 796
CoDevelopment Canada (CoDev) 796
Cognos Inc..632
Collaboration santé internationale (CSI)..........797
Collavino Inc...633
Collège Bois-de-Boulogne 259
Collège de technologie agricole d'Alfred 258
Collège Édouard-Montpetit.................................279
Columbia University
    in the City of New York 346
Columbia University 347
Cominco Ltd..633
Comité régional d'éducation pour le
    développement international de
    Lanaudière (CREDIL) 196
Commercial Bank Services.................................710
Committee on the Peaceful
    Uses of Outer Space (COPUOS) 844
Commonwealth Fund for
    Technical Co-operation (CFTC) 872
Commonwealth Human
    Ecology Council (CHEC) 873
Commonwealth of Learning (COL)...................873
Commonwealth Secretariat (ComSec) 873
Compass Business Strategies, Inc. 633
Compassion Canada..797
Concordia University 213, 273-275
Confederation College of
    Applied Arts and Technology 275
Conseil d'affaires et
    de culture Québec-Bulgarie 712
Conservation International (CI) 873
Consultation Nadeau International Inc..............633
Consultants Canarail Inc. 634
Consultative Group on International
    Agricultural Research (CGIAR).....................844
Consulting and Audit Canada (CAC)................747
Consulting and Audit Canada (CAC),
    International Services Directorate.................732
Consulting Resource
    Group International Inc. (CRG).....................634
Contracting Management
    Division, CIDA...733
Cooper Institute 196

Cooperation Canada
Mozambique (COCAMO) 797
Cooperative Housing Foundation (CHF) 362
Coopers & Lybrand 635
Corel Corporation 635
Cornell University 341
Corporation for
International Settlements (CIS) 635
Cott Corporation 636
Council of Canadians
with Disabilities (CCD) 797
Courey International (Commerce) Inc. 636
Cowater International Inc. 636
CRC SIMA 637
CRC SOGEMA Inc. 637
Cultural Homestay International (CHI) 150
Cultural Survival 798
Cumming Cockburn Limited 637
CUSO 798
Dalhousie University 213, 275-277
Dayton Mining Corporation 638
Delcan International Corporation 638
Department of Finance Canada 749
Department of
Fisheries and Oceans (DFO) 750
Department of Foreign Affairs
and International Trade (DFAIT) ... 228, 719, 750
Department of Foreign Affairs
and International Trade (DFAIT):
Canada-Sweden Working
Holiday Program 152
Department of Foreign Affairs
and International Trade (DFAIT):
Inquiries Service 705
Department of Foreign Affairs and
International Trade (DFAIT):
International Youth Exchange 152
Department of Justice Canada 752
Department of National Defence (DND) 753-754
Dessau International Ltd/Ltée 638
Developing Countries
Farm Radio Network (DCFRN) 799
Development Innovations and Networks 873
Développement
International Desjardins (DID) 799
DiamondWorks Ltd. 639
Dillon Consulting 639
Disabled Peoples International (DPI) 799
DMR Group Inc. 639
DPA Group (International) Inc. 640
E.T. Jackson & Associates Ltd. 640
Earthkeeping 800
Earthwatch 150, 874
École des Hautes
Études Commerciales (HEC) 277, 278
École Nationale
d'administration Publique (ENAP)- 279
Econolynx International 640
Economic and Social Commission
for Asia and the Pacific (ESCAP) 844

Economic and Social Commission
for Western Asia (ESCWA) 845
Economic Commission for Africa (ECA) 845
Economic Commission
for Europe (ECE) 845
Economic Commission for Latin America
and the Caribbean (ECLAC) 845
Econotec Inc. Consultants 641
EdperBrascan 641
El Refuerzo 151
Elderhostel Canada 151
Elections Canada 748
ELI Eco Logic International Inc. 641
Ellis-Don Construction 641
Embassy of France 226
Embassy of Italy 226
Embassy of Japan 227
Embassy of the
People's Republic of China 227
Emmanuel International of Canada 800
Enterprise Cape Breton Corporation 708
Enterprise Malaysia Canada 712
Enterprise Prince Edward Island 757
Enterprise Thailand Canada 712
Environment Canada (EC) 748
Environmental Defense Fund (EDF) 874
Environmental
Technologies International Inc. 641
Erasmus University Rotterdam 343, 345
Ernst & Young (Canada)
Actuaries & Consultants Inc. 642
Ernst & Young Canada 642
ESSA Technologies Ltd. 642
European Space Agency 874
European Union (The) 362
Evangelical Medical Aid Society (EMAS) 801
EVS Consultants 643
Experco Ltée. 643
Expérience-Jeunesse International:
Programme d'Échanges de Jeunes
Travailleurs Canada-Suisse 151
Export and Import
Controls Bureau (EPD) 703
Export Development Corporation (EDC) .. 703, 748
Export Orientation/Training Programs
(NEBS, NEXOS) 704
Falconbridge Ltd. 643
Family Health International (FHI) 363, 874
Federal Economic
Development Initiative
in Northern Ontario (FedNor) 704
Federal Government Youth Info Line 734
Federal Office of Regional
Development - Québec (FORD-Q) 704
Federation of
Canadian Municipalities (FCM) 801
Finance and Contracting
Management Division, CIDA 730
Finland Futures Research Centre 349
Finning International Inc. 644

First Dynasty Mines Ltd. 644
Fishery Products International (FPI) 644
Fondation CRUDEM 801
Fondation Desjardins 227
Fondation Paul Gérin-Lajoie/
  Paul Gérin-Lajoie Foundation.............644
Food and Agriculture
  Organization (FAO) 846
Forum for International Trade Training...........802
Foster Parents Plan of Canada.................802
Four Seasons Hotels Inc. 644
Fraternité Vietnam 802
French Chamber
  of Commerce in Canada 712
Friends of the Earth (FoE) 803
Friends of World Teaching 152
Frontiers Foundation Inc. 803
Fulcrum Technologies Inc....................645
Geac Computer Corporation Ltd. 645
Gems of Hope 803
General Woods and Veneers
  Consultants International Limited 645
Geographic Trade Divisions.................704
Geophysics GPR International Inc. 646
George Brown College.......................279
George Washington University 347
Georgetown University 347
German Embassy: The Canada-Germany
  Young Worker's Exchange Program 152
Global Alliance for Infrastructure
  Advancement Corp. (GAIA) 646
Global Awareness Project
  of Northwestern Ontario (GAP) 196
Global Change Game 153
Global Community Centre 196
Global Information Network.................363
Global Village (Nanaimo) International
  Development Education Association 197
Global Vision................................804
Golden Knight Resources Inc...............646
Golder Associates...........................647
Graduate Institute of
  International Studies.......................347
Graybridge International Consulting Ltd. 647
Great Britain Working
  Holidaymaker Scheme.....................153
Greenpeace Canada.........................804
Greenpeace International 875
Greenstone Resources Ltd...................647
Griffith University.....................228, 348
Group of 78 (The) 804
Groupe AFH International Inc./
  The AFH Group International Inc...........648
Groupe Conseil Saguenay...................648
Guelph International
  Resource Centre (GIRC) 197
Gulf Canada Resources Limited 648
H.A. Simons Ltd............................648
Habitat for Humanity Canada Inc............805
Harvard University..........................342
Hatch Associates Ltd........................649

Health Canada..............................750
Hebrew University of Jerusalem (The) 345, 348
Helen Ziegler and Associates Inc. (HZA).........649
Help the Aged 805
Helsinki School of Economics
  and Business Administration..............343
Hickling Corporation 649
HN Telecom Inc.............................650
Hong Kong-Canada Business Association 712
Hongkong Bank of Canada 650
HOPE International
  Development Agency 153, 805
Horizons of Friendship (HOF)...............806
Human Concern International (HCI) 806
Human Resources
  Development Canada (HRDC) 751
Human Rights Internet (HRI) 875
Human Rights Watch..................363, 875
Humber College of
  Applied Arts and Technology 282
Hummingbird Communications Ltd............650
Hungarian-Canadian
  Chamber of Commerce...................712
Husky Oil International Corp.................651
Hydro-Québec International (HQI) 651
IMAX Corporation 651
IMP Group International Ltd. 652
Inco Limited 652
Indochina Goldfields Ltd. 652
Industrial Cooperation
  Program (INC), CIDA....................732
Industry Canada............................751
INet for Women............................364
Infant Feeding Action
  Coalition Canada (INFACT) 806
Institut de développement nord-sud........806
Institut de technologie agro-alimentaire
  de Sainte-Hyacinthe (ITA)- 282
Institut Universitaire des
  Hautes Études Internationales 228
Institute of Peace and Conflict Studies.......807
Institute of Social Studies 341
Intelcan Technosystems Inc..................652
Interagency Coalition on AIDS
  and Development (ICAD) 807
Inter-American
  Development Bank (IADB) 229, 364, 846
Inter-American Institute for
  Co-operation on Agriculture (IICA) 862
Intercan Development Company Ltd..........653
Intercultural Institute of Montréal (IIM)........808
Intercultural Systems /
  Systèmes interculturels (ISSI) 653
Intermap Technologies.......................654
International Agricultural
  Exchange Association 153
International Air
  Transport Association (IATA) 876
International Association for the
  Exchange of Students for Technical

Experience (IAESTE) / Association for
International Practical Training (AIPT) 154

International Association for the
Exchange of Students for Technical
Experience (IAESTE):
International Student Exchange 154

International Association
for Transformation (IAT)................................808

International Association of
Educators For World Peace............................349

International Atomic
Energy Agency (IAEA)...........................364, 846

International Bank for Reconstruction
and Development (IBRD)................................847

International Bar Association (IBA)....................876

International Board for Soil
Research and Management (IBSRAM) 862

International Briefing
Associates, Inc. (IBA) 654

International Campaign
to Ban Landmines (ICBL) 876

International Centre for Agricultural
Research in The Dry Areas (ICARDA) 863

International Centre for
Human Rights and
Democratic Development (ICHRDD) 751

International Center for Living Aquatic
Resources Management (ICLARM) 862

International Centre for
Research in Agroforestry (ICRAF)................863

International Centre for Settlement
of Investment Disputes (ICSID)....................847

International Center of Insect
Physiology and Ecology (ICIPE) 862

International Chamber of Commerce 710, 876

International Child
Care (Canada) Inc. (ICC) 808

International Christian
Aid Canada (ICA Canada)..............................808

International Civil
Aviation Organization (ICAO).......................847

International Commission
on Irrigation and Drainage (ICID)................863

International Committee
of the Red Cross (ICRC)................................877

International Confederation
of Free Trade Unions (ICFTU) 877

International Co-operative Alliance (ICA) 877

International Council
for Adult Education (ICAE)....................809, 877

International Council
for Canadian Studies.......................................229

International Council on Social Welfare.............809

International Court of Justice (ICJ) 847

International Criminal Police
Organization (OIPC-INTERPOL) 878

International Crops Research Institute
for the Semi-Arid Tropics (ICRISAT) ....:863

International Development
and Refugee Foundation (IDRF)....................809

International Development
Association (IDA) 847

International Development Education
Resource Association (IDERA) 197, 810

International Development
Research Centre (IDRC)..........229, 230, 364, 752

International Energy Agency (IEA) 878

International Federation of L'Arche 810

International Federation of
Red Cross and Red Crescent Societies 878

International Fellowship
of Reconciliation (IFOR) 878

International Finance Corporation (IFC) 847

International Food Policy
Research Institute (IFPRI).............................863

International Fund for
Agricultural Development (IFAD)...........365, 848

International Institute for
Applied Systems Analysis (IIASA) 879

International Institute
for Management Development.......................343

International Institute
for Population Sciences....................................341

International Institute
for Sustainable Development.........................810

International Institute of Human Rights............346

International Institute
of Tropical Agriculture (IITA) 864

International Irrigation
Management Institute (IIMI) 864

International Labour Organization (ILO)...365, 848

International Livestock
Research Institute (ILRI) 864

International Maize and Wheat
Improvement Centre (CIMMYT)...................864

International Maritime
Organization (IMO) 848

International Maritime
Satellite Organization (INMARSAT) 879

International Monetary Fund (IMF) 366, 848

International Organization
for Migration (IOM) 879

International Organization
for Standardization (ISO) 879

International Petroleum
Corporation (IPC)...654

International Planned
Parenthood Federation (IPPF) 879

International Plant Genetic
Resources Institute (IPGRI) 864

International Potato Centre (IPC) 865

International Programs
Directorate (IPD) 839

International Rail Consultants...........................655

International Rescue Committee (IRC)............880

International Rice
Research Institute (IRRI) 865

International Road Dynamics Inc. (IRD) 655

International Rural Exchange (IRE).................154

International Service for National
Agricultural Research (ISNAR) 865
International Social
Security Association (ISSA) 880
International Society of
Bangladesh (ISB) 811
International
Telecommunication Union (ITU) 849
International Telecommunications
Satellite Organization (INTELSAT) 366, 880
International Trade Centre
UNCTAD/ WTO (ITC) 849
International Trade Centres (ITC) 705
International Tropical
Timber Organization (ITTO) 880
International Union
Association of Public Transport (UITP) 881
International University of Japan 341-343, 348
International Wildlife Coalition (IWC) 881
Inter-Pares 807
Inter-Parliamentary Union (IPU) 875
IPL Energy International Inc. 655
ISG Technologies Inc. 656
Italian Chamber of Commerce 712
Jamaican Self-Help Organization 811
Japan Exchange and
Teaching Programme (JET) 154
Japan External
Trade Organization (JETRO) 712
Japan Foundation (The) 230
Japan Working Holiday Program 155
Jawaharlal Nehru University 348
JetForm Corporation 656
Jeunesse du monde (JDM) 811
John Simon Guggenheim
Memorial Foundation 231
John van Nostrand Associates Limited
Architects & Planners (JVA) 656
Johns Hopkins University 345, 348
Joint United Nations
Programme on HIV/AIDS (UNAIDS) 849
Junior Professional
Officer Program (JPO) 155, 366, 838
KAP Resources Ltd. 657
Kinross Gold Corp. 657
Kleinfeldt Consultants Limited 657
Klohn-Crippen Consultants Ltd. 657
Kobe University 341-342
Korea Trade Centre 712
KPMG 658
Kyrgoil Corp. 658
L'Agence de coopération
culturelle et technique (ACCT) 871
L'AUPELF-UREF opérateur francophone 872
L'Institut de l'Énergie des pays ayant
en commun l'usage du français (IEPF) 875
L'Union pour le développement durable 828
Lady Davis Fellowship Trust 231
Lakehead University 283
Lancaster University 350
Lane Environment Ltd. 658

Langara College 283-284
Latin America Mission (LAM) 155
Lesley College Graduate School 342
Lester B. Pearson College of the Pacific 287
Limburg Business School 344
Lithos Corporation 658
London Cross Cultural
Learner Centre (LCCLC) 197
London School of Economics
and Political Science 231, 341, 348
M.L. Cass Petroleum Corp. 659
M.T. Ellis & Associates Ltd. 659
MacDonald, Dettwiler
and Associates Ltd. 659
Macleod Dixon 660
Malkam Consultants Ltd. 660
Manitoba Council for
International Co-operation (MCIC) 811
Manitoba Department
of Education and Training 574
Manitoba Education and Training:
Manitoba - Federal Republic of
Germany Student Exchange 155
Manitoba Hydro 660
Manitoba Trade and Investment
Corporation (Manitoba Trade) 708, 753
MAP-Canada 812
Maple Leaf Foods International 661
Marquis Project 197, 812
Marshall Macklin Monaghan Limited 661
Martec Recycling Corporation 661
Massey University 342
MATCH International Centre 812
McEuen Scholarship Foundation Inc. 232
McGill University 232, 289-294
McMaster University 294-295
MDS Inc. 661
Médecins sans frontières /
Doctors Without Borders (MFS) 813
MedHunters 662
Medical Group Missions (Canada) Inc. 156
Medical Research
Council of Canada (MRC) 232, 753
Mega Engineering Ltd. 662
Memorial University 296
Mennonite Brethren
Missions/Services (MBM/S) 813
Mennonite Central
Committee, Canada (MCC Canada) 814
Mennonite Economic
Development Associates (MEDA) 814
Met-Chem Canada Inc. (MET-CHEM) 662
Minefinders Corporation Ltd. 663
Miramar Mining Corp. 663
Mission Aviation Fellowship Canada
(MAF Canada) 814
Mitel Corporation 663
Monterey Institute of International
Studies 348
Montréal Israel Experience Centre 156
Moore Corporation Limited 663

Moscow State Institute
of International Relations...............................344
Moscow State University 342
Mount Allison University 301
Multilateral Investment
Guarantee Agency (MIGA) 849
N.D. Lea International Ltd. (NDLI) 664
NACEL Canada... 156, 169
National University of Singapore......................342
National Bank of Canada/
Banque Nationale du Canada 664
National Film Board of Canada (NFB) 754
National University of Singapore......................344
Natural Resources Canada (NRCan) 754
Natural Sciences and Engineering
Research Council of Canada (NSERC)... 232, 233
Nawitka Resource Consultants Ltd. 664
Nelson Gold Corp. 665
New Brunswick Department of
Economic Development and Tourism 708, 755
New Brunswick Department
of Intergovernmental and
Aboriginal Affairs.......................................755
New Brunswick Dept. of Education,
Director of Professional Development 574
New York University 344
Newbridge Networks Corp................................665
Newfoundland and Labrador Department
of Industry,
Trade and Technology (ITT)................... 708, 755
Newfoundland Department of
Development and Rural Renewal.....................708
Newfoundland Department of Tourism,
Culture, and Recreation...............................756
Newfoundland Dept. of Education,
Director of School Services and
Professional Development.............................574
Nijenrode University,
The Netherlands Business School.................344
Nipissing University..303
Noranda Inc. 665
Norcen Energy Resources Ltd. 666
Norenco Associated Ltd....................................666
Nortel (Northern Telecom)...............................666
North America Commission for
Environmental Cooperation (CEC) 881
North Atlantic
Treaty Organization (NATO) 881
North-South Institute (NSI)..............................815
Northern Orion Explorations Ltd......................666
Northwest Hydraulic Consultants (NHC) 667
Northwest Territories Department
of Resources, Wildlife and
Economic Development................................708
Norwegian-Canadian
Chamber of Commerce 712
NOVA Gas International Ltd. (NGI)..................667
Nova Scotia Dept. of Education, Director
Registrar - Teacher Certification....................574

Nova Scotia Economic
Development and Tourism......................708, 756
Novaport Vaughan
International Consultants Ltd........................ 667
O & T Agdevco Ltd.. 668
Ocelot Energy Inc... 668
Office Franco-Québecois
pour la Jeunesse 156
OMF International... 815
Ontario Council for International
Cooperation (OCIC)..................................... 815
Ontario Foundation
for Educator Exchanges............................... 157
Ontario Hydro International Inc. (OHII) 668
Ontario Institute for
Studies in Education.................................... 304
Ontario International
Trade Corporation (OITC)......................708, 756
Ontario Ministry of
Citizenship, Culture Recreation..................... 757
Ontario Ministry of Economic
Development, Trade and Tourism 708
Ontario Ministry of
Education and Training................................. 757
Ontario: ORTECH 757
Operation Eyesight Universal (OEU) 816
Opim Consultants Inc..................................... 669
OPIRG-Carleton 198
Organization for Co-operation
in Overseas Development (OCOD) 157, 816
Organization for Economic Co-operation
and Development (OECD) 881
Organization for Security and Co-
operation in Europe (OSCE) 882
Organization of American States (OAS)........... 882
ORS Awards Scheme....................................... 233
ORT CANADA.. 816
Overseas Development Institute (ODI) 882
OXFAM-Canada 198, 817
OXFAM-Québec... 817
P.A. Conseils International (Canada) Inc. 669
P.E.I.-Enterprise Prince Edward Island 708
Pacific Economic
Cooperation Council (PECC) 882
Pan African Institute
for Development (PAID) 883
Pan American
Health Organization (PAHO) 883
Partners Film Company Limited (The)............. 669
Partners in Rural Development
(PARTNERS) 818
Partnership Africa Canada (PAC).................... 818
Pasteur Mérieux Connaught Canada 670
PATH Canada... 818
Peace and Environment
Resource Centre... 198
Peace Brigades International (PBI) 883
Peace Bureau International (PBI) 883
Peacefund Canada.. 818

Personnel and
Administration Branch, CIDA 733
Petro-Canada 670
Phair-Sutherland Consulting 670
Photosur Géomat
International Inc. (PGI) 670
Piteau Associates 671
Placer Dome Inc. 671
PLAN International 884
PLAN:NET 2000 Limited 671
Plenty Canada 819
Policy Research International Inc. (PRI) 672
Population Council 884
Population Institute (The) 367
Potash & Phosphate
Institute of Canada (PPIC) 672
Precision Drilling Corp. 672
Premdor Inc. 672
Presbyterian Church in Canada (PCC) 819
Prince Edward Island Dept. of Education,
Office of the Registrar 574
Princeton University 348
Probe International 819
Proctor & Redfern International Limited 673
Program for Export
Market Development (PEMD) 706
Project Services International 673
Public Service Commission (PSC) 733, 758
Public Service Commission, International
Programs
Directorate (PSC-IPD) 758
Public Works and Government Services
Canada: Canadian Government
Publishing (CGP) 758
Pueblito Canada 820
PWA Corporation 673
Quaid-I-Azam University 348
Québec : Ministère de l'Agriculture, des
Pêcheries et de l'Alimentation
(MAPAQ) 759
Québec : Ministère des Relations
internationales (MRI) 759
Québec Association
of Export Trading Houses 711
Québec: Ministère de l'industrie, du
commerce, de la science et de la
technologie (MICST) 708
QuébecTél International 673
Queen's University 311, 312, 313, 314
RADARSAT International 674
Radio Canada International - Canadian
Broadcasting Corporation (RCI CBC) 759
Radio Free Europe /Radio Liberty 367
Ranger Oil Limited 674
Rayrock Yellowknife Resources Inc. 674
Recruitment Section SPSS 720
Recruitment Section SPV 720
Reference Canada 760
Reid and Associates (1994) Ltd. 675
Reid Crowther International Ltd. 675

Renaissance Eastern Europe
Program (REE), CIDA 706, 733
Resource Futures International (RFI) 675
RESULTS Canada 198, 820
Revenue Canada 760
Rhodes Scholarship Secretariat 233
Rio Algom Ltd. 676
RMC Resources
Management Consultants Ltd. 676
Roche Ltée., Groupe-Conseil/
Roche Ltd. Consulting Group 676
Rooftops Canada Foundation 820
Rotary Foundation
Ambassadorial Scholarships 234
Rousseau, Sauvé, Warren Inc. 677
Roy Consultants Group 677
Royal Bank of Canada 678
Royal Canadian Mint (RCM) 760
Royal Canadian Mounted Police (RCMP) 761
Royal Military College of Canada 316
Royal Society of Canada 234
Rural Advancement
Foundation International (RAFI) 821
S.L.I. Consultants 678
Saint Mary's College 344
SalvAide 821
Salvation Army Overseas Development
Department 821
Samson Belair/Deloitte & Touche 679
Sandwell Inc. 679
Saskatchewan Council for
International Co-operation (SCIC) 822
Saskatchewan Education,
Teacher Services Unit 574
Saskatchewan Indian Federated College 316
Saskatchewan Institute of Applied
Science and Technology (SIAST) 679
Saskatchewan Trade
and Export Partnership 708
Saskatoon Board of Education:
German Exchange 157
SaskTel International 680
Save A Family Plan,
St. Peter's Seminary (SAFP) 822
Save the Children—Canada 822
Scandinavian Canadian
Chamber of Commerce 712
Scarboro Foreign
Mission Society (SFMS) 823
Schiller International University 344
School for International Training (SIT) 235, 343
School of International Training 342
Seagram Company Ltd. (The) 680
Secours aux lépreux -
Leprosy Relief (Canada) 823
Semex Alliance (The) 680
SERVAS Canada 169
Seva Service Society 823
Shastri Indo-Canadian Institute 235
Shastri-Indo-Canadian Institute: Shastri
Foundation Summer Programme 157

Shaw Industries Ltd..681
Sheridan College-...317
SHL Systemhouse 681
Sierra Club of Canada 823
Sierra Club, International Program...................884
SIM Canada..824
Simon Fraser University 214, 318, 319
Simons Reid Collins...681
Sir Edmund Hillary Foundation 824
Sir Sandford Fleming College...........................319
SNC-Lavalin Agriculture Inc. 682
SNC-Lavalin Group..682
Social Science Research Council......................235
Social Sciences and Humanities Research
    Council of Canada (SSHRC)...................236, 761
Society of Partnership (SOPAR Inc.) 824
SOCODEVI (Société de coopération pour
    le développement international) 824
Sofeg Inc..682
Solidarité Canada Sahel (SCS)..........................825
Soprin ADS...683
SOS Children's Villages Canada........................825
South Asia Partnership Canada (SAP)..............825
South Pacific Peoples
    Foundation of Canada (SPPF).........................826
SR Telecom 683
St. Francis Xavier University 319
St. John's OXFAM Committee............................199
St. Mary's University...................................320, 321
Standards Council of Canada (The) 706
Stanley Industrial Consultants Ltd. 683
Stanley International Group Inc. 684
Statistics Canada (SC)......................................762
Steelworkers Humanity Fund............................826
Stellar Metals Inc..684
Stockholm School of Economics.......................344
Stothert Management Ltd. (SMI) 684
Strategis 706
Street Kids International....................................826
Sustainable
    Resource Development (SRD) 685
Swedish Institute (The).....................................343
Swedish Trade Office (Canada) Inc. 712
Swiss Chamber of Commerce 712
Sylvitec Inc...685
Syndel Laboratories Ltd. 685
Sypher-Mueller International Inc. 686
Talisman Energy Inc. 686
Technology Training Associates (TTA).............686
Teck Corporation..686
TECSULT..687
TECSULT Environment Inc.................................687
Tecsult Foresterie Inc. 687
Telefilm Canada (TFC) 762
Teleglobe...688
Telesat Canada...688
Telus..688
Ten Days for Global Justice 827
Terra Surveys Limited 689

Terre des hommes
    Canada inc. (TDH Canada) 827
Terre sans frontières (TSF) 827
Teshmont Consultants Inc. 689
Thunderbird, American Graduate School
    of International Management 344
Toronto Dominion Bank..................................... 689
Townsend Trade Strategies Inc. (TTS) 690
Trade Commissioner Service 707
Trade Facilitation Office Canada (TFOC)......... 707
TransCanada PipeLines Limited....................... 690
Trent University....................................325, 326, 327
Triton Mining Corp.. 690
Tufts University... 349
Turtle Island Earth
    Stewards Society (TIES) 828
UMA Group Ltd. 691
Umea University 345
UN Office for Project Services (UNOPS) 849
UN Public Inquiries... 841
Unigec Experts-Conseils................................... 691
Union des producteurs agricoles:
    Agricultural Exchange 158
Unisphere Global Resource Centre................... 199
United Church of Canada, Division
    of World Outreach (UCC, DWO) 828
United Nations Association
    in Canada (UNA Canada).......................829, 839
United Nations Centre for
    Human Settlements (Habitat)................367, 850
United Nations
    Children's Fund (UNICEF) 368 850
United Nations Commission on
    International Trade Law (UNCITRAL) ...368, 850
United Nations Conference on
    Trade and Development (UNCTAD) 850
United Nations
    Development Programme (UNDP) 850
United Nations Economic and Social
    Commission for Asia and the Pacific
    (ESCAP) 368
United Nations Economic Commission
    for Latin America and the Caribbean 369
United Nations Economic Commission
    for Europe (ECE) 368
United Nations Educational, Scientific
    and Cultural Organization (UNESCO) ...369, 851
United Nations Environment Programme
    (UNEP) 851
United Nations Environment Programme
    Regional Office
    for North America (UNEP/RONA) 369
United Nations
    Headquarters Internship Programme 369
United Nations High
    Commissioner for Refugees (UNHCR) 851
United Nations Industrial Development
    Organization (UNIDO) 370, 851
United Nations Institute for Disarmament
    Research (UNIDIR).. 852

United Nations Institute for
Training and Research (UNITAR) 852
United Nations International Drug
Control Programme (UNDCP) 852
United Nations International Research
and Training Institute for the
Advancement of Women (INSTRAW) 852
United Nations Interregional Crime and
Justice Research Institute (UNICRI) 853
United Nations Office at Vienna (UNOV) 370
United Nations Peacekeeping Forces................853
United Nations
Population Fund (UNFPA) 370, 853
United Nations Relief and Works Agency
for Palestine Refugees in the Near East
(UNRWA) 854
United Nations Research Institute for
Social Development (UNRISD)...............370, 854
United Nations University (UNU) 350, 854
United Nations Volunteers (UNV) 838
Universal Postal Union (UPU)...........................854
Universalia Management Group Ltd..................691
Université d'Aix-Marseille III............................343
Université d'Ottawa 304, 305, 306
Université de Moncton................................296, 297
Université de Montréal 297, 298, 299, 300, 301
Université de Sherbrooke 317
Université du Québec à Chicoutimi 307
Université du Québec à Montréal 308, 309, 310
Université du Québec à Rimouski 310, 311
Université Laval 284, 285, 286
University College of Wales, Aberystwyth 349
University College of Cape Breton......................267
University College of Wales 346
University of California at Los Angeles......345, 347
University of California San Diego 347
University of California, Berkeley 346
University of Kent at Canterbury 350
University of Southern California......................349
University of Alberta 212, 255, 256, 257
University of Bradford..349
University of
British Columbia 221, 259, 260, 261, 262, 263
University of Calgary 265, 266
University of Cambridge....................................346
University of Chicago...347
University of Denver 343
University of Durham...345
University of East Anglia....................................341
University of Essex..346
University of Exeter..346
University of Guelph............................280, 281, 282
University of Guyana..341
University of Hawaii 349
University of Leeds...348
University of Lethbridge....................................287
University of Liege..344
University of Liverpool.......................................345
University of London 341, 346
University of Malaya....................................343, 346

University of Manitoba
International Centre for Students..................169
University of Manitoba 214, 231, 287, 288, 289
University of Nairobi..342
University of New Brunswick 301, 302, 303
University of Northern British Columbia ..303, 304
University of Nottingham 346
University of Ottawa 304, 305, 306
University of Oxford 348
University of Pennsylvania 344
University of Prince Edward Island 306, 307
University of Reading 348
University of Regina..............................314, 315
University of San Diego......................................346
University of Saskatchewan 317
University of Strathclyde 343, 345
University of Sussex 342
University of Sydney............................346, 349
University of the Philippines 348
University of Toronto...........321, 322, 323, 324, 325
University of Toronto, Faculty of Law:
International Human Rights
Internship Programme (IHRP) 158
University of Vaasa..345
University of Victoria..............................328, 329
University of Waterloo 214, 330, 331
University of Western Ontario 331, 332
University of Windsor...............................333, 334
University of Winnipeg..........................335, 336
University of Witwatersrand 344
University of Zambia 342
University of Zimbabwe.....................................349
Up With People 158, 170
Urgel Delisle & Associates (UDA) 691
USC Canada 829
Vanier College 327, 328
Vaughan International Consultants 692
Veterans Affairs Canada:
Vimy Tourist Guides Program.......................158
Victoria University of Wellington.......................349
Vidéographe Inc..829
VIEW Foundation (The).....................................159
Village International Sudbury (VIS).................199
Visions in Action 159, 371
Volunteer Service Overseas
Canada (VSO Canada) 830
Volunteers for Peace...159
Volunteers in Mission 830
Wardrop Engineering Inc...................................692
WaterCan 830
Wayne State University......................................350
West Africa Rice
Development Association (WARDA).............865
Westcoast Energy International Inc. 692
Western Canada Wilderness Committee 831
Western Economic Diversification (WD)..........707
Wild Rose Foundation 740
Wilfrid Laurier University 333
WIN Exports 708
Winrock International Institute
for Agricultural Development (WI) 865

Women's International League
for Peace and Freedom (WILPF)....................371
Woodrow Wilson
International Center for Scholars....................349
World Accord (WA)...831
World Association of Industrial and
Technical Research Organizations
(WAITRO)..884
World Association of Small
and Medium Enterprises (WASME)...............884
World Bank...854
World Bank
Young Professionals Program..........................371
World Bank/MIGA
Summer Employment Program.......................371
World Citizens Centre...199
World Confederation of Labour (WCL).............885
World Conservation Union (IUCN)...................885
World Customs Organization.............................885
World Economic Forum.......................................885
World Federalists of Canada (WFC)..................831
World Food Programme (WFP)................372, 855
World Health Organization (WHO)...........372, 855
World Intellectual
Property Organization (WIPO)......................855
World Inter-Action Mondiale (WIAM)..............199
World Language Program....................................159
World Learning..160
World Literacy of Canada (WLC)......................831
World Meteorological
Organization (WMO).....................................855
World Relief Canada (WRC)...............................832
World Tourism Organization (WTO).................856
World Trade Organisation (WTO)......................856
World University Service
of Canada (WUSC)..................................160, 832
World Vision Canada:
Operation Helping Hand.................................160
World Vision International...................................886
World Wide Fund for Nature (WWF)................886
WorldTeach, Inc..161
Worldwise International
Resource Centre..200
WorldWorks..161
YMCA Canada,
International Office (YMCA)..........................833
YMCA International
Camp Counselor Program Abroad.................161
Yokohama National University...........................342
York University....................336, 337, 338, 339, 340
Young Women's Christian
Association of Canada (YWCA).....................833
Youth Action Network...833
Youth Challenge International (YCI).........161, 834
Youth for Understanding Canada......................162
Yukon Department
of Economic Development..............................709

How this Book was Researched

The process of updating the third edition of *The Canadian Guide to Working & Living Overseas* was particularly exciting because of new advances in software and the new and amazing research capabilities of the Internet. There were two updating phases. Phase I, from October 1995 to April 1997, involved computer and systems design. Phase II, from May 1997 to February 1998, was the production stage in which we completed the research, editing, and layout. The first edition had taken five years to complete and the second edition, nine months. The production cycle for the third edition took ten months. Twenty-six staff (nine full-time equivalents) worked together to produce the book. There were 13 researchers, five editors, four writers, three layout persons, and one computer consultant.

The whole process began in September 1995 when we replaced our nine-station Novell network with a more cost-effective and user-friendly peer-to-peer network, a new feature of *Windows 95*. Staff shared eight computers, including six *Pentiums*, each with 32 to 64 RAM to allow multi-tasking. Each computer eventually had an Internet connection, which proved to be a vital research tool. We converted all our systems from *DOS WordPerfect Office* and *WordPerfect 5.1* to *Windows 95* and *Microsoft Office*: *Microsoft Word* and *Microsoft Access*.

Upgrading our systems from a flat-file database (*WordPerfect Notebook*), to a relational database (*Microsoft Access*) was a long (and costly) task. *Microsoft Access* was chosen because of its compatibility with *Microsoft Word*, its versatility, and its programming simplicity. The new systems greatly improved user productivity. All of our reports and merging features are now one-step operations. The design of our database not only allows us to track research leads, but also to directly fax, e-mail, or print organization profiles, labels, file labels, and letters by pressing one button within the database. This eliminated the cumbersome seven-step merge process we had previously used for printing and faxing.

Our next task was to update our all-important procedures manual. At 120 pages, the *ISSI Standards Manual* is indispensable for managing the 17 database types, ensuring consistency, training staff, and organizing our master work plan. The survey process for updating an organization's profile followed a 24-step flowchart, from initial contact to final printing. The process for updating the resources followed a 12-step flowchart.

In January 1997, the first two of four writers began work on the new chapters. The bulk of the research began in May, when three of the thirteen research staff were hired to update organization profiles. To illustrate how technology has so greatly changed, during our last edition, we mailed over 8,000 letters, but this time we did not mail a single one. Rather, we used the internet as the initial step of research and then faxed or e-mailed directly from the computer. Thanks to Sprint's 15 cents a minute and 22 cents to the US, we liberally used the phone for calling and faxing, compiling an astounding 10,205 phone calls in 10 months. All Canadian and US phone numbers and all web site addresses were verified in December 1997.

One editor began work in September 1997, another in October, and the remaining two in mid-December. Layout work began early in October since we had to document and test the more then 100 styles we developed in *Microsoft Word*. To increase efficiency, (we were adding more information, but did not want to go over the 1,000 page mark), new layouts for organization profiles were developed and new fonts were chosen, *Century Old Style* and *Verdana*. Layout required two people working over four months, each devoting the equivalent of ten full weeks of (fun but sometimes stressful) labour.

The final version was formatted with *Microsoft Word 97* and printed on a small but practical 600dpi printer, the *HP LaserJet 6P*. The cover design was completed on a *Power Macintosh 8600* computer using the *Quark Xpress SS 3.32* layout program, and *Adobe Illustrator 5.0* graphic program. The actual printing of the book took three weeks.

The final result is a 1,008 page guide, divided into 40 chapters and documenting 2,550 separate resources and organizations. (And for trivia buffs, the guide contains 448,908 words, 24 per cent more than the second edition.)

For more information on the publisher, Intercultural Systems / Systèmes interculturels (ISSI), please see the ISSI profile in Chapter 32, The Private Sector.

—BON VOYAGE—

CONTENTS AT A GLANCE

THE CANADIAN GUIDE TO WORKING AND LIVING OVERSEAS (Third Edition)

How to Use This Book xxv

PART ONE: Your International IQ
1. The Effective Overseas Employee ....
2. Myths & Realities ....
3. Living Overseas ....
4. What Canadians Overseas Say ....
5. Learning a Foreign Language ....
6. Women Working & Living Overseas ....
7. The Canadian Identity in the International Workplace 8
8. Re-Entry 10

PART TWO: Acquiring International Experience
9. Starting Your International Career 129
10. Short-term Programs Overseas 137
11. Hosting Programs 163
12. Crosscultural Travel 171
13. Global Education Centres 183
14. Study Abroad 201
15. Awards & Grants 215
16. International Studies in Canada & Abroad 237
17. International Internships 351

PART THREE: Finding that International Job
18. Your Career Path 375
19. The Hiring Process 379
20. The Job Search 385
21. The Internet Job Search 399
22. Resources for the International Job Search 429
23. Phone Research Techniques 443
24. International Résumés 455
25. Covering Letters 483
26. Interviewing for an International Job 495

PART FOUR: What Jobs Are Out There?
27. Jobs by Regions of the World 509
28. Jobs in International Development 561
29. Teaching Abroad 569
30. Freelancing Abroad 595
31. Job Hunting When You Return to Canada 603

PART FIVE: International Career Contacts
32. The Private Sector 611
33. Services for International Businesses & Entrepreneurs 693
34. Careers in Government 713
35. Nongovernmental Organizations 763
36. United Nations 835
37. Environmental & Agricultural Research Centres 857
38. International Organizations 867
39. Canadian Diplomats Abroad 887
40. Foreign Diplomats in Canada 903

INDEXES
Bibliographies (919); ID Numbers (933); Cities in Canada with International Contacts (941);
Countries & Regions of the World (945); Job Categories (953); Organizations (957)

PUBLISHER: Intercultural Systems / Systèmes interculturels (ISSI)
DISTRIBUTOR: University of Toronto Press (UTP), (800) 267-0105

—BON VOYAGE—